UNIVERSITY CASEBOOK SERIES

WOMEN AND THE LAW

SECOND EDITION

by

JUDITH G. GREENBERG
Professor of Law, New England School of Law

MARTHA L. MINOW
Professor of Law, Harvard University Law School

DOROTHY E. ROBERTS
Professor of Law, Northwestern University School of Law

NEW YORK, NEW YORK
FOUNDATION PRESS
1998

Library of Congress Cataloging-in-Publication Data
Greenberg, Judith G.
    Women and the law / Judith G. Greenberg, Martha L. Minow,
Dorothy E. Roberts. — 2nd ed.
        p.   cm. — (University casebook series)
    Includes index.
    ISBN 1–56662–608–0 (hc.)
    1. Women—Legal status, laws, etc.—United States—Cases.
I. Minow, Martha, 1954–   . II. Roberts, Dorothy E., 1956–   .
III. Title. IV. Series.
KF478.A7G74   1998
346.7301'34—dc21   98–21337

*TEXT IS PRINTED ON 10% POST
CONSUMER RECYCLED PAPER*

*To Mary Joe
and our families*

J.G.; M.M.; and D.R.

*

*

INTRODUCTION FROM
THE FIRST EDITION

These materials are organized around concrete legal problems of particular and current concern to women. The problems are grouped into three categories: women and work, women and the family, and women and their bodies. Chapter introductions briefly describe the focus and contents of each chapter and also situate the legal issues to be discussed in the context of one or more feminist theories. In addition to conventional legal readings, such as cases, current statutes and legislative proposals, the chapters typically include historical legal materials, psychological and social material about women, and critical commentary by feminist legal scholars. Each of the course sections contains one chapter specifically devoted to feminist theories.

As you will quickly observe, my (editorial and personal) stance toward the study of women and the law is that of a feminist. For me, this means a commitment to two goals: (1) advancing the position of women socially, economically, and in their personal relationships, and (2) undermining the effect of gender on the lives of women and men. (Gender, as it is used here, refers to a shifting but identifiable bundle of beliefs, qualities, and expectations which are linked to individuals because of their genital characteristics.) Although most feminist legal scholars share those general goals, there are lively and significant differences among the analyses and solutions they advocate for legal issues affecting women. You will find, therefore, feminist readings in these materials that represent cultural, liberal, radical, postmodern, lesbian, race-conscious, and socialist perspectives.

The unity of the course lies in the identification and study of themes and issues that cross conventionally segregated doctrinal categories, themes such as formal versus substantive equality, the public/private distinction, and the role of law in constructing female sexuality. The chapters insistently question the role of law in the creation and destruction of social and economic conditions that disadvantage women. The structure and contents of the materials represent an effort to break away from a dichotomized tendency to assume either a practical or a theoretical approach to legal issues affecting women. Thus, although these materials focus on specific doctrinal questions, more exhaustive treatment of subjects such as domestic relations or employment discrimination is left to other courses. Similarly, although the readings include a significant portion of theoretical materials, "feminist jurisprudence" or "feminist theory" is presented more as an array of alternative approaches to doctrinal issues than as a separate body of thought.

MARY JOE FRUG

January, 1991

INTRODUCTION TO THE
SECOND EDITION

Mary Joe Frug was murdered on April 4, 1991 a few yards from our home here in Cambridge. At the time of her death, she had put together — and was in the process of revising — materials for a course in Women and the Law. She was always in the process of revising her materials. Not only were interesting new cases and articles continuing to pour forth but her own ideas about how best to present the subject were constantly being rethought. In 1992, I edited, with the help of a number of our friends, Mary Joe's course materials as they existed at the time of death, and they were published as the first edition of this casebook,. Even at the time, it was clear that, to be consistent with her own ideas about the topic, a revised edition of the book would be necessary.

Happily, here it is. The three editors have done a remarkable job of keeping Mary Joe's vision of the course alive while, simultaneously, making a multitude of changes in the book. I would like to mention three notable aspects of the first edition that have been retained. The first is the division of the course into the topics Women and Work, Women and the Family, and Women and Their Bodies. This organization was Mary Joe's invention, and many people in the field have found it an important way to think about feminist theory and feminist practice. The second is the emphasis on the role of law in fashioning ideas about and the everyday practice of sexuality. In Mary Joe's hands, this emphasis on the constructed nature of sexual difference did not reduce women to the status of being victims; in this version of the casebook as in her own, the joy of being a woman is a constant theme. Finally, both editions include a considerable amount of feminist theory throughout the book. More than that, both stress the debates within feminist theory, so that the richness and variety of feminist thought is allowed to illuminate every topic. And, unlike much work in the field, one aspect of feminist thinking that was important to Mary Joe — postmodern feminist theory — is as present in this book as it was in her version of it.

Still, there are many differences between this edition and the first one. That's why this second edition was written. These differences are not limited simply to the inclusion of the new cases and articles that have appeared since 1992 — although there are plenty of these. Important substantive areas have been added or significantly expanded: Women and the Professions, Sexual Harassment, The Pregnant Body, Domestic Violence, and Education. The editors have written notes for, and have included a problem in, each chapter of the book — something Mary Joe surely would have done if she had been able to publish the first edition herself. Finally, although the original edition paid attention to the problems affecting women of color, this edition gives so much more sustained attention to these issues that it seems to me proper to label this aspect of the book a difference from, rather than a similarity with, her own materials.

I am personally very grateful to Judi, Martha and Dorothy for their considerable work on this edition. I'm sure that teachers and students who use this book will share my gratitude to them. Without their work, Mary Joe's materials on Women and the Law would have become an historical artifact. The editors have kept her work alive. Because Mary Joe's materials on Women and the Law were so important not only to her but to the field itself, this is simultaneously a wonderful act of friendship and of scholarship.

GERALD E. FRUG

July, 1998

EDITORS' PREFACE

This book began as Mary Joe Frug's, and it remains framed and inspired by her work. We would like to thank Jerry Frug for his support and encouragement of our efforts in this second edition. Thanks also to the team of scholars and friends who joined him in producing the first edition: Marie Ashe, Regina Austin, Betsy Bartholet, Ruth Bolden, Kim Crenshaw, Clare Dalton, Nancy Dowd, Niva Elkin, Karen Engle, Martha Field, Judi Greenberg, Jill Hargis, Michele Jones, Susan Keller, David Kennedy, Karl Klare, Marlee Kline, Martha Minow, Liz Schneider, Elizabeth Sponheim, and Lucie White.

For the second edition, we would like to thank Sara Buehler, Laurie Corzett, Monica Gaboriault, Jean Guttman, Meryl Kessler, and Shirley Scott for their work in producing the final manuscript; Michelle Caprini-Slayton, and Sandra Sells for their admirable assistance in the research on Chapter One; Meryl Kessler for her masterful research assistance on Chapter Two; and Lora Bender and Donyelle Gray for invaluable research assistance on Chapter Three.

Citations and footnotes have been omitted from cases and the work of commentators—and concurring and dissenting opinions have been omitted from cases—without specifically noting these omissions. When footnotes are included, they retain the original numbering.

*

ACKNOWLEDGMENTS

Kathryn Abrams, "Gender Discrimination and the Transformation of Workplace Norms," 42 Vand. L. Rev. 1183 (1989), reprinted with the permission of Vanderbilt Law Review.

Kathryn Abrams, "Title VII and the Complex Female Subject," 92 Mich. L. Rev. 2479 (1994), pp. 2481, 2484-95, 2501-11, 2515-17, 2520-24, 2527-35.

Frederique Delacoste and Priscilla Alexander, SEX WORK (Cleis Press 1987), copyright (C) 1987 by Frederique Delacoste and Priscilla Alexander.

Marie Ashe & Naomi Cahn, "Child Abuse: A Problem for Feminist Theory," 2 Tex. J. Women & Law 75 (1993).

Regina Austin, "Black Women, Sisterhood, and the Difference/Deviance Divide," 26 New Eng. L. Rev. 877 (1992). (C) Copyright New England School of Law 1992. All rights reserved. Reprinted by Permission.

Katherine K. Baker, "Once a Rapist? Motivational Evidence and the Relevancy of Rape Law," 110 Harv. L. Rev. 563 (1997). Copyright (C) 1997 by the Harvard Law Review Association.

Margaret A. Baldwin, "Split at the Roots: Prostitution and Feminist Discourse of Law Reform," 5 Yale J. L. & Feminism 47 (1992), pp. 107-110, 116-117. Reprinted by permission of the Yale Journal of Law and Feminism from The Yale Journal of Law and Feminism, Vol. 5, No. 1, pp. 47-120.

Kathleen Barry, FEMALE SEXUAL SLAVERY (New York University Press 1979), copyright (C) 1979 by Kathleen Barry.

Elizabeth Bartholet, FAMILY BONDS (New York: Houghton Mifflin 1993), pp. 24-85).

Katherine Bartlett, "Feminist Perspectives on the Ideological Impact of Legal Education Upon the Profession," 72 N.C. L. Rev. 1259 (1994). Copyright 1994 by the North Carolina Law Review Association. Reprinted with permission.

Louise Bauschard & Mary Kimbrough, VOICES SET FREE: BATTERED WOMEN SPEAK FROM PRISON (1986), copyright (C) 1986 by Women's Self-Help Center, pp. 2-66.

Mary Becker, "Maternal Feelings: Myth, Taboo, and Child Custody," 1 S. Cal. Rev. of Law and Women's Studies 133-24 (1992), reprinted with the permission of the Southern California Review of Law and Women's Studies.

Shannon Bell, READING, WRITING & REWRITING THE PROSTITUTE BODY (1992), copyright (C) 1992 by Shannon Bell.

Johanna Brenner, "Feminist Political Discourses: Radical Versus Liberal Approaches to the Feminization of Poverty and Comparable Worth," 1 Gender and Society 447, 447-51, 455-61 (1987).

Judith Butler, "Passing Queering," in BODIES THAT MATTER: ON THE DISCURSIVE LIMITS OF "SEX" 167 (New York: Routledge 1993). Copyright (C) 1993. From Bodies That Matter by Judith Butler. Reproduced by permission of Routledge, Inc.

Sue-Ellen Case, "Toward a Butch-Femme Aesthetic," in L. Hart, MAKING A SPECTACLE: FEMINIST ESSAYS ON CONTEMPORARY WOMEN'S THEATRE (University of Michigan Press 1989), copyright (C) 1989 by The University of Michigan.

Nancy Chodorow, "Mothering, Male Dominance, and Capitalism," in Z. Eisenstein, CAPITALIST PATRIARCHY AND THE CASE FOR SOCIALIST FEMINISM (New York: Monthly Review Press, 1979), pp. 380-388. Copyright (C) 1979 by Monthly Review Press. Reprinted by permission of Monthly Review Foundation.

Patricia Hill Collins, "Pornography and Black Women's Bodies," in Patricia Hill Collins, BLACK FEMINIST THOUGHT: KNOWLEDGE, CON-SCIOUSNESS, AND THE POLITICS OF EMPOWERMENT 167 (New York: Routledge 1991). Copyright (C) 1990. From BLACK FEMINIST THOUGHT by Patricia Hill Collins. Reproduced by permission of Routledge, Inc.

Kimberle Williams Crenshaw, "Beyond Racism and Misogyny," in WORDS THAT WOUND: CRITICAL RACE THEORY, ASSAULTIVE SPEECH, AND THE FIRST AMENDMENT 111 (Mari J.Matsuda, et al, eds., Boulder, CO: Westview Press 1993). Approximately 22 pages from Words that Wound by Matsuda, et. al. Copyright (C) 1993 by Kimberle Williams Crenshaw. Reprinted by permission of Westview Press.

Kimberle Crenshaw, "Demarginalizing the Intersection of Race and Sex," 1989 U. Chi. Legal Forum 139, pp. 139-152.

Kimberle Crenshaw, THE INTERSECTION OF RAPE AND GENDER IN RAPE LAW (1991).

Kimberle Crenshaw, "Mapping the Margins," 43 Stan. L. Rev. 1241 (1991), p. 1256-62.

Clare Dalton, "An Essay in the Deconstruction of Contract Doctrine," 94 Yale L. J. 997, reprinted by permission of The Yale Law Journal Company and Fred B. Rothman & Company from The Yale Law Journal, Vol. 94, pages 997-1114.

Clare Dalton, "Domestic Violence, Domestic Torts and Divorce," 31 New Eng. L. Rev. 319 (1997), (C) Copyright New England School of Law 1997. All rights reserved. Reprinted by Permission.

Christine Delphy, "Protofeminism and Antifeminism," in T. Moi, FRENCH FEMINIST THOUGHT (1987).

Muriel Dimen, SURVIVING SEXUAL CONTRADICTIONS (Macmillan 1986), pp. 1-12. Copyright (C) 1986 by Muriel Dimen.

Nitya Duclos, "Some Complicating Thoughts on Same-Sex Marriage," 1 Law & Sexuality 31 (1991), pp. 31-61.

Andrea Dworkin, "Against the Male Flood: Censorship, Pornography, and Equality," 8 Harvard Women's L. J. 1 (1985), permission granted by the Harvard Womens's Law Journal, copyright (C) 1985 by the President and Fellows of Harvard College.

Andrea Dworkin, PORNOGRAPHY: MEN POSSESSING WOMEN (Dutton 1981), copyright (C) 1979, 1980, 1981 by Andrea Dworkin. Used by permission of the publisher, Dutton, an imprint of New American Library, a division of Penguin Books USA Inc.

Susan Estrich, "Rape," 95 Yale L. J. 1087 (1986), reprinted by permission of the Yale Law Journal and Fred B. Rothman & Company from The Yale Law Journal, vol. 95, pp. 1087-1184.

Paula L. Ettelbrick, "Since When Is Marriage a Path to Liberation?" Autumn 1989 OUT/LOOK 8-12.

Martha Fineman, THE ILLUSION OF EQUALITY (U. Chicago Press 1991), pp. 40-52. Copyright (C) 1991 by the University of Chicago.

Katherine M. Franke, "What's Wrong with Sexual Harassment," 49 Stan. L. Rev. 691 (1997), pp. 691-93, 698, 702, 705, 710-16, 723-30, 732, 734-40, 744-47, 759-60, 762-63, 772. (C) 1997 by the Board of Trustees of the Leland Stanford Junior University.

Mary Joe Frug, POSTMODERN LEGAL FEMINISM (Routledge, Chatman and Hall 1990), copyright (C) 1990 by Routledge, Chatman and Hall, Inc.

Mary Joe Frug, "Securing Job Equality for Women," 59 B.U. L. Rev. 55, 56-61 (1979). Volume 59:1, Boston University Law Review (1979) 56-61. Reprinted with permission. (C) 1979 Trustees of Boston University. Boston University bears no responsibility for any errors which have occurred in reprinting or editing.

Mary Joe Frug, "Sexual Equality and Sexual Difference," 26 New Eng. L. Rev. 665 (1992).

Evelyn Nakano Glenn, "From Servitude to Service Work," in THE SECOND SIGNS READER 27, 28, 32-34, 45-4, 49, 57-60 (Joeres & Laslett, eds. 1996, U. Chicago Press). (C) Copyright 1996 by The University of Chicago Press. Reprinted with permission.

Linda Gordon, HEROES OF THEIR OWN LIVES: THE POLITICS AND HISTORY OF FAMILY VIOLENCE (1988), copyright (C) 1988 by Linda Gordon. Used by permission of Viking Penguin, a division of Penguin Putnam Inc.

Lani Guinier, "Becoming Gentlemen," 143 U. Pa. L. Rev. 1 (1994), (C) Copyright 1994 by the University of Pennsylvania Law Review, reprinted with permission.

Mona Harrington, WOMEN LAWYERS, pp. 99-103. Copyright (C) 1993 by Mona Harrington. Reprinted by permission of Alfred A. Knopf, Inc.

Angela P. Harris, "Race and Essentialism in Feminist Legal Theory," 42 Stan. L. Rev. 581 (1990). (C) [1990] by the board of Trustees of the Leland Stanford Junior University.

bell hooks, FEMINIST THEORY: FROM MARGIN TO CENTER (South End Press 1984), copyright (C) 1984 by bell hooks.

bell hooks, "Outlaw Culture: Resisting Representations." "Seduced by Violence No More," by bell hooks was originally published in TRANSFORMING A RAPE CULTURE, edited by Emilie Buchwald, Pamela Fletcher, and Martha Roth (Milkweed Editions 1993), copyright (C) 1993 by bell hooks. Reprinted by permission from Milkweed Editions.

bell hooks, "Violence in Intimate Relationships," reprinted from pp. 84-91, bell hooks, TALKING BACK: THINKING FEMINIST/THINKING BLACK 1989), with permission of the publisher, South End Press, 116 Saint Botolph Street, Boston, MA 02115.

Nan D. Hunter, "Marriage, Law, and Gender: A Feminist Inquiry," 1 Law & Sexuality 9 (1991).

Elizabeth Iglesias, "Rape, Race, and Representation: The Power of Discourse, Discourse of Power, and the Reconstruction of Heterosexuality," 49 Vand. L. Rev. 869 (1996). (C) 1996 by the Vanderbilt Law Review. Reprinted with permission.

Lisa C. Ikemoto, "The Infertile, the Too Fertile, and the Dysfertile," 47 Hastings L. J. 1007 (1996). (C) 1996 by University of California, Hastings College of the Law. Reprinted from Hastings Law Journal Vol. 47, No. 4, pp. 1007, by permission.

Herma Hill Kay, "Equality and Difference: A Perspective on No Fault Divorce and Its Aftermath," 56 U. Cinn. L. Rev. 1 (1987), (C) 1997 University of Cincinnati Law Review.

Susan Etta Keller, "Viewing and Doing: Complicating Pornography's Meaning," 81 Geo. L. J. 2195 (1993), copyright (C) 1993 by the Georgetown Law Journal and Georgetown University.

Reprinted with permission from "Uses of the Erotic: The Erotic as Power," in Audre Lourde, Sister Outsider: Essays and Speeches by Audre Lorde. (C) 1984. Published by The Crossing Press: Freedom, CA.

Catharine MacKinnon, FEMINISM UNMODIFIED: DISCOURSES ON LIFE AND LAW (Cambridge, MA: Harvard University Press 1987), reprinted by permission of the publishers from FEMINISM UNMODIFIED by Catharine MacKinnon, Cambridge, Mass.: Harvard University Press, copyright 1987 by the President and Fellows of Harvard College.

Catharine MacKinnon, "Feminism, Marxism, Method, and the State: Toward Feminist Jurisprudence," 8 Signs 635 (1983), copyright (C) by The University of Chicago.

Catharine MacKinnon, "Sex Equality: On Difference and Dominance," from TOWARD A FEMINIST THEORY OF THE STATE (Harv. U. Press 1989).

Martha R. Mahoney, "Legal Images of Battered Women: Redefining the Issue of Separation," 90 Mich. L. Rev. 1 (1991), pp. 1-25, reprinted with the permission of the Michigan Law Review.

Isabel Marcus, Rhonda Copelone, Ruth Hubbard, Barbara Katz Rothman, and Barbara Omolade, "Looking Toward the Future: Feminism and Reproductive Technologies," 37 Buffalo L. Rev. 203 (1988-89).

Lynda Marin, "Mother and Child: The Erotic Bond" from MOTHER JOURNEYS: FEMINISTS WRITE ABOUT MOTHERING, edited by Maureen T. Reddy, Martha Roth, and Amy Sheldon, pp. 9-17, 19-21. Minneapolis: Spinsters Ink, 1994. Available from Spinsters Ink, 32 East 1st Street, Ste.# 330, Duluth, MN 55802. Reprinted by permission.

Mari Matsuda, "Public Response to Racist Speech: Considering the Victim's Story," 87 Mich. L. Rev. 2320 (1989).

Carlin Meyer, "Sex, Sin, and Women's Liberation: Against Porn-Suppression," 72 Texas L. Rev. 1097, copyright (C) 1994 by the Texas Law Review Association.

Martha Minow & Mary Lyndon Shanley, "Revisioning in the Family" in M. Shanley & V. Narayan, eds., RECONSTRUCTING POLITICAL THEORY: FEMINIST PERSPECTIVES (University Park, PA: The Pennsylvania State Univ. Press, 1997), pp. 85-109. Copyright 1997 by The Pennsylvania State University. Reproduced by permission of the publisher.

Martha Minow, "Words and the Door to the Land of Change," 43 Vand. L. Rev. 1665 (1990), pp. 1688-1695, 1699, reprinted with the permission of Vanderbilt Law Review.

"Note: Cheering on Women and Girls in Sports," 110 Harv. L. Rev. 1627 (1997). Copyright (C) 1997 by the Harvard Law Review Association.

Susan Moller Okin, Ch. 7, "Vulnerability by Marriage" from JUSTICE, GENDER, AND THE FAMILY by Susan Moller Okin. Copyright (C) 1989 by Basic Books, Inc. Reprinted by permission of BasicBooks, a division of HarperCollins Publishers, Inc.

Frances E. Olsen, "The Myth of State Intervention in the Family," 18 U. Mich. J. of L. Reform 835, 835-40, 842-46, 849-57, 861-62 (1985).

Frances Olsen, "Statutory Rape: A Feminist Critique of Rights Analysis," 63 Texas L. Rev. 387 (1984), copyright (C) 1984 by the Texas Law Review Association.

Twila L. Perry, "Alimony," 82 Georgetown L.J. 2481 (1994), reprinted with the permission of the publisher, Georgetown University and Georgetown Law Journal, (C) 1994.

Gail Pheterson, A VINDICATION OF THE RIGHTS OF WHORES (The Seal Press 1989), copyright (C) 1989 Gail Pheterson.

Jennifer L. Pierce, GENDER TRIALS (Univ. Cal. Press, Berkeley, 1995), pp. 103-109, 113-15, 117-18, 120-23, 125, 127-28, 130-35, 137-39, 141-42.

Richard Posner, "Conservative Feminism," 1989 U. Chi. L. Forum 191.

Rosemary Pringle, SECRETARIES TALK: SEXUALITY, POWER AND WORK (Verso 1988), pp. 84, 86-92, 95-98. Copyright (C) 1988 Rosemary Pringle.

Margaret Jane Radin, "Market-Inalienability," 100 Harv. L. Rev. 1849 (1987).

Deborah Rhode, "Occupational Inequality," 1988 Duke L. J. 1207, 1207-23, 1225-26, 1228-48 (1988).

Deborah Rhode, SPEAKING OF SEX (Harv. U. Press 1997), pp. 60-65. Reprinted by permission of the publisher from Speaking of Sex by Deborah L. Rhode, Cambridge, Mass.: Harvard University Press, Copyright (C) 1997 by Deborah L. Rhode, by the President and Fellows of Harvard College.

Adrienne Rich, Blood, BREAD AND POETRY: SELECTED PROSE 1979-1985 (New York: W.W. Norton & Company, 1986). Reprinted with the permission of the author and the publisher, W.W. Norton & Company, Inc., copyright (C) 1986 by Adrienne Rich.

David A.J. Richards, "Commercial Sex and the Rights of the Person: A Moral Argument for Decriminalization of Prostitution," 127 U. Pa. L. Rev. 1195 (1979).

Dorothy E. Roberts, "Punishing Drug Addicts Who Have Babies: Women of Color, Equality, and the Right of Privacy," 104 Harv. L. Rev. 1419 (1991), copyright (C) 1991 by The Harvard Law Review Association.

Katie Roiphe, THE MORNING AFTER: SEX, FEAR, AND FEMINISM ON CAMPUS (Little, Brown and Company 1993), copyright (C) 1993 by Katherine Anne Roiphe. Reprinted by permission of Little, Brown and Company.

Loretta Ross, "Raising Our Voices," in M. Fried, FROM ABORTION TO REPRODUCTIVE FREEDOM (South End Press 1990), copyright (C) 1990 Marlene Gerber Fried.

Elena Salzman, "Note: The Quincy District Court Domestic Violence Prevention Program," 74 B.U. L. Rev. 329 (March 1994). Volume 74:2, Boston University Law Review (1994) 329-364. Reprinted with permission. (C) 1994 Trustees of Boston University. Boston University bears no responsibility for any errors which have occurred in reprinting or editing.

Suzanne Sangree, 47 Rutgers L. Rev. 461 (1995), pp. 463-64, 466-67, 535-40, 551-53, 558-61, used with permission of the copyright holder.

Debra Satz, "Markets in Women's Reproductive Labor," 21 Philosophy & Public Affairs 107. Copyright (C) 1992 by Princeton University Press. Reprinted by permission of Princeton University Press. 1992).

Elizabeth Schneider, "Describing and Changing," 9 Women's Rights Law Rptr. 195-222 (1986).

Vicki Schultz, "Reconstructing Sexual Harassment," 107 Yale L.J. 1683 (1998), reprinted by permission of The Yale Law Journal Company and Fred B. Rothman & Company from The Yale Law Journal, Vol. 107, pp. 1685-1687, 1710-1716, 1720-1721, 1748-1749, 1755-1769, 1773-1774, 1789-1796.

Vicki Schultz, "Telling Stories About Women and Work," 103 Harv. L. Rev. 1750 (1990), pp. 1750-1756, 1758-59, 1769-79, 1797-1811, 1815-31, 1841-43. Copyright 1990 by the Harvard Law Review Association.

Joan W. Scott, "Deconstructing Equality Versus Difference," 14 Feminist Studies 33 (1988). This article is reprinted from Feminist Studies, Volume 14, Number 1 (Spring 1988): 33-50, by permission of the publisher, Feminist Studies, Inc., c/o Department of Women's Studies, University of Maryland, College Park, MD 20742.

Reva Siegel, "Reasoning from the Body: A Historical Perspective on Abortion Regulation and Questions of Equal Protection," 44 Stan. L. Rev.

261 (1992), copyright (C) 1992 by the Board of Trustees of Leland Stanford Junior University.

Cass Sunstein, "Pornography and the First Amendment," 1986 Duke L. J. 589 (1986), reprinted by permission of Cass Sunstein and Duke Law Journal.

Cindy Tobisman, "Marriage vs. Domestic Partnership," 12 Berkeley Women's L. J. 112 (1997), pp. 116-117.

Mariana Valverde, SEX, POWER, AND PLEASURE (Women's Press 1987), copyright (C) 1987 Mariana Valverde.

Carole S. Vance, PLEASURE AND DANGER: TOWARD A POLITICS OF SEXUALITY 1 (Carole S. Vance, ed., 2d ed., London: Pandora 1992).

Diana Vellos, "Immigrant Latina Domestic Workers and Sexual Harassment," 5 Am. U. J. Gender & Law 407 (1997), pp. 411-13, 423-28, 432, (C) Copyright 1997, American University Journal of Gender & the Law.

Eugene Volokh, "Freedom of Speech and Workplace Harassment," 39 UCLA L. Rev. 1791 (1992), pp. 1793-94, 1809-15, 1820-23, 1832-33, 1838-40, 1843-45, 1849-59, 1862-63, 1866-67, 871-72. Originally published in 39 UCLA L. Rev. 1791. Copyright 1992, The Regents of the University of California. All Rights Reserved.

Lenore Walker, Battered Women and Learned Helplessness, 2 Victimology 525-532 (1977-78). Reprinted by permission from Victimology: An International Journal, Volume 2, Number 3-4, 1977-78. Copyright (C) 1978 Victimology Inc. All Rights Reserved.

D. Kelly Weisberg, Professional Women and the Professionalization of Motherhood, 6 Hastings Women's L. J. 295, 313-338 (1995). (C) 1995 by University of California, Hastings College of the Law. Reprinted from Hastings Women's Law Journal, Vol. 6, No. 2, by permission.

Lenore Weitzman, Ch. 10, "The Case for Intimate Contracts," pp.227-254. Reprinted with the permission of The Free Press, a Division of Simon & Schuster from THE MARRIAGE CONTRACT: A GUIDE TO LIVING WITH LOVERS AND SPOUSES by Lenore W. Weitzman. Copyright (C) 1981 by Lenore W. Weitzman.

Laurie Wermuth, "Domestic Violence Reforms," 27 Berkeley J. of Sociology, pp. 27-29, 31-33, 36-40 (1982).

Angela West, "Prosecutorial Activism," 15 Harv. Women's L. J. 249 (1992), pp. 249-50, 256-70, (C) Copyright 1992 by the President and Fellows of Harvard College.

Robin West, "The Difference in Women's Hedonic Lives: A Phenomenological Critique of Feminist Legal Theory," 3 Wis. Women's L. J. 81 (1987), reprinted by permission of Robin West and Wisconsin Women's Law Journal.

Joan Williams, "Deconstructing Gender," 87 Mich. L. Rev. 787 (1989).

Lucy Williams, "The Ideology of Division: Behavior Modification Welfare Reform Proposals," 102 Yale L. J. 719 (1992), permission granted by the Yale Law Journal Company, Fred B. Rothman and Company, and Lucy Williams.

Maxine Baca Zinn, "Family, Race and Poverty in the Eighties," 14 Signs 856-874 (1989). Copyright (C) 1989 by The University of Chicago.

*

SUMMARY OF CONTENTS

*

TABLE OF CONTENTS

*

TABLE OF CASES

Principal cases are in bold type. Non-principal cases are in roman type. References are to Pages.

*

TABLE OF AUTHORITIES

References are to Pages.

WOMEN AND THE LAW

*

CHAPTER ONE

WOMEN AND WORK

A. WOMEN AND THE LEGAL PROFESSION

INTRODUCTION

This section focuses on women in the legal profession. As late as 1970, women represented only five percent of the graduates of American law schools. By 1985, this proportion had risen to about a third and over the next decade increased again to 45%. Indeed, by 1994, approximately 20% of all lawyers were women. Despite this, in the mid–1990s, only 11% of the partners in the country's 250 largest firms were women, only 8% of the judges in the federal courts, only 16% of law school faculty, and only 7% of law school deans. Furthermore, men were twice as likely as women with similar credentials and histories to have been made partner. *See* Deborah L. Rhode, *Gender and Professional Roles*, 63 Fordham L. Rev. 39, 58 (1994). These numbers suggest both that the legal profession has been undergoing a process of feminization during the past two decades and that the dramatic increase of women lawyers may not be entirely welcome to the profession. Indeed, the implications of feminization for the profession and for women are by no means fully understood. This section is designed to introduce the two issues of the profession's response to women and of women's effects on the profession.

The readings begin with an excerpt from the report of the Gender Bias Study Commission appointed by the Supreme Judicial Court of Massachusetts. Many of the states have appointed similar commissions to study gender bias in their court systems. The Massachusetts report is one of the more detailed. The commission found that gender bias was pervasive in the judicial system and affected women in a variety of roles, including attorney, judge, litigant, witness, and juror. The small excerpt included here focuses primarily on bias toward attorneys. Much of the conduct described discusses the ways in which women in the judicial system are treated differently from men. The study raises three important questions. First, should we use men as the model against which to measure whether women are being treated fairly? Second, what types of recommendations for systemic change might we make? And, third, does it make sense to use the category "women" or are the experiences of different women, such as white and Black women or middle class and impoverished women, too disparate to allow for generalization?

The second piece is from Jennifer Pierce's book, *Gender Trials*. Whereas the Massachusetts Gender Bias Commission's study asked whether women attorneys should be treated the same as men or differently, this piece focuses on whether women attorneys respond to their role as attorneys in the same way as men do or differently. Pierce is a sociologist, interested in the socialization of women lawyers. She asks whether women attorneys conform to the existing norms of the profession or whether they bring with them a more caring dimension that had previously been absent from the practice of law. Ultimately she argues that women's ideas of what it means to be a woman influence their responses to the structural constraints in which they must work and to the people with whom they work. Pierce's approach allows us to speculate as to what kinds of effects the presence of large numbers of women might have on the practice and structure of the legal profession. It also raises the question of what *does* it mean to be a woman? Is it possible to think about women as a category without being influenced by stereotypes? Pierce's book is based on field-work performed in the legal department of "Bonhomie" corporation, at the National Institute of Trial Advocacy (NITA) and in a large law firm, which she calls Lyman, Lyman and Portia.

The third piece, from Mona Harrington's *Women Lawyers*, focuses on the sensuality of women's bodies and the way this affects women's positions as lawyers. Harrington notes the fundamental role that the mind/body duality plays in Western thought. Professions of the mind, like the law, try to deny or minimize the threat posed by the body. One strategy for doing so is to make bodies invisible behind the judge's robes or buttoned-up business suits. For women, this process of making one's body invisible is more difficult. No matter what we wear or how we do our hair, it's likely to remind others of our bodies. Harrington argues that this very fact—that we as women are embodied—is likely to undercut our authority as lawyers. This approach to women's position in the legal profession is very different from the Massachusetts Gender Bias Commission's or from Jennifer Pierce's. Unlike them, it neither sets men up as a standard, nor does it assume a particular conception of "womanhood." This excerpt from Harrington could be described as more postmodern in that it reads the ways in which the female body is encoded as dangerous to and possibly subverting of the authority of law. It is important for you to keep these different approaches separate in your mind. We will return to them with some regularity throughout the course.

Title VII of the Civil Rights Act of 1964 has been one of the prime weapons in women's search for equality in the legal profession, and in the workplace more generally. *Ezold v. Wolf, Block, Schorr and Solis–Cohen* is included here to allow you to assess for yourself the power and limitations of Title VII. Can it meet the needs of women who want to be treated as men are treated? What about the needs of women who want space to develop uniquely female values and processes? What limitations in Title VII does a postmodern understanding of the meaning of "woman" disclose?

The two final readings in this section are devoted to legal education. It is not surprising to find that many of the issues created by the increased number of women in the profession are also issues in legal education. For example, Lani Guinier's study of the position of women at the University of Pennsylvania Law School finds that women law students hold positions that are low in the hierarchy, both in terms of grades and the awarding of honors. This mirrors the information at the beginning of this essay that women practicing law tend to have the lower paying, non-partner positions in large law firms. Similarly, Guinier's finding that women law students are often demeaned publicly through the use of sexist epithets reflects the petty humiliations that women face within the court system. Guinier's explanation for this differential treatment of women law students is to look to the structure of law school: the emphasis placed on rational discourse, the Socratic method and informal interactions outside of class.

Katharine Bartlett's article, *Feminist Perspectives on the Ideological Impact of Legal Education Upon the Profession,* identifies two feminist theories that can be used to explain women's position in society and applies them specifically to legal education. The first of these, the different voice perspective (elsewhere referred to as cultural feminism), should sound somewhat familiar from the article by Jennifer Pierce. The second, which Bartlett calls the dominance perspective, is usually associated with the work of Catharine MacKinnon.

This section on the legal profession should help you to think about the issues posed at the beginning of this essay. Why are women disproportionately at the bottom of the pile when it comes to their position in the profession? What effects, if any, can the increasing number of women in the profession be expected to have on the profession itself? This section should also introduce you to different ways of thinking about these issues. First, there is a conception of equality that compares women's position to men's. Second, there is the cultural feminist position described by Bartlett and used in a modified form by Pierce, that identifies and celebrates women's traditional strengths. Third, there is MacKinnon's dominance perspective, also described by Bartlett, and, finally, there is the more postmodern approach exemplified by the excerpt from Harrington's work. As Bartlett said, there is no single feminist stance; different feminists have different stances. These different theories about women's position in modern American society will provide you with a set of tools with which to analyze the various problems that we will encounter throughout this course.

Report of the Gender Bias Study of the Supreme Judicial Court

Commonwealth of Massachusetts (1989).

Introduction

Chief Justice Edward F. Hennessey appointed the Gender Bias Study Committee in December of 1986 and gave its members a broad and challenging mandate to determine the extent, nature, and consequences of gender bias in the judiciary and to make remedial recommendations to promote the fair and equal treatment of men and women. . . .

During the committee's first few months, we undertook a process of self-education about gender bias by reading and consulting experts. We formed the following working definition: gender bias exists when decisions made or actions taken are based on preconceived or stereotypical notions about the nature, role, or capacity of men and women. Myths and misconceptions about the economic and social realities of men's and women's lives and about the relative value of their work also underlie gender bias.

As our work continued we found that simplistic notions of fairness and equality were not sufficient. We found that gender bias can arise from a gender insensitivity that overlooks sex as a significant variable in cases where it is indeed significant. Because the social and economic realities of women's and men's lives *are* often different, there are circumstances in which it may be appropriate to include gender as a factor in judicial decision making. For example, in the areas of child support and alimony, to ignore the primary role most women have played in raising their children and the sacrifice of earning potential they have made to be primary caretakers would not be "neutrality," but gender bias against women. A truly nongender-biased approach to gender issues starts out by asking whether the situation of men and women is comparable. Only when it is, is equal treatment appropriate. When it is not comparable, *different* treatment may be necessary to achieve equal results.

Gender bias underlies the differing experiences and perceptions of men and women in similar situations. On a number of occasions, our survey data were analyzed by the sex of the survey respondent. The results of these analyses show that women report a higher incidence of observing or experiencing gender-biased treatment than do men. These results and their frequency lead us to believe that there is a vast difference between men's and women's experiences and also a difference between how they interpret their experiences.

There was one more powerful understanding about gender bias that became clear during our research. Gender bias hurts everyone. In most cases, the primary injury or disadvantage is experienced by women. Women, as a group, receive less favorable decisions, less opportunity to be in positions of power, and less respect in their interactions with the system. Children may be hurt by the bias directed against their mothers, particularly in the area of divorce. But men are also injured by the effects of gender bias. Stereotypes about women often work hand in hand with stereotypes about men. Ending gender bias in the courts is taking a step toward a society where all individuals may choose whatever role is appropriate and feasible for them, not one defined by gender. . . .

Gender Bias in Courthouse Interactions

During the course of any given day in every courthouse in the Commonwealth of Massachusetts, judges, attorneys, litigants, witnesses, jurors, and court employees interact with one another in a variety of ways. The Gender Bias Study Committee (the Committee) found that gender affects the manner in which members of each group are treated—by their peers, as well as by members of the other groups....

In particular, the Committee found that:

    1. Female attorneys are subjected to gender-biased conduct on the part of male attorneys, court employees of both sexes, and some male judges. Such conduct ranges from discriminatory treatment to sexual harassment and is especially pronounced toward minority attorneys.

    2. There still exists a significant under representation of female attorneys in appointments made by the Trial Court and Committee for Public Counsel Services.

    3. Gender bias on the part of male attorneys, court employees, and some judges also adversely affects female litigants and witnesses. Some forms that this treatment takes include: inappropriate terms of address, suggestive comments, unwanted touching, yelling, and verbal harassment.

    4. Attorneys report that they rarely observe judicial intervention to prevent or correct gender-biased conduct....

    5. Gender-biased treatment of female attorneys, litigants, and witnesses undermines credibility and confidence and thereby places unwarranted burdens upon female advocates and witnesses....

Respondents to the attorneys' survey reported that the most frequent forms of gender bias they experience are: being asked if they are attorneys and being addressed in an unprofessional manner. Over two-thirds of the women responding to the survey have been asked by other attorneys if they were an attorney (compared to only 14% of the male respondents), and almost two-thirds of the female respondents have been addressed by their first names or by a term of endearment when they expected to be addressed by surname or title (compared to 16% of the male respondents).

Furthermore, a large number of the female respondents reported having been subjected to inappropriate comments about their personal appearance or comments of a sexual or suggestive nature by other attorneys (as compared to only 2% and 1%, respectively, of the male respondents), and 12% of the women reported that they had been touched in an inappropriate way by another attorney (compared to only 1% of the male respondents).

Attorneys' observations of gender-biased conduct toward others match their personal experiences.... [Forty-two percent] of all respondents have observed other counsel ask female attorneys if they are attorneys when men are not asked; nearly one third have observed female attorneys being addressed by first names or terms of endearment when men were addressed by surnames or titles; 19% have observed counsel berate female but not male attorneys; 22% have observed counsel cut off female but not male attorneys; 38% have observed counsel address female attorneys in a patronizing manner; 31% have observed counsel make demeaning remarks or jokes about women; and 38% have observed counsel make comments about the personal appearance of women but not about men. In no instance were these isolated incidents—rather the respondents reported observing such behavior often or sometimes. . . .

The consistency between the reported experiences of female attorneys and the observations of incidents of gender bias that are reported by both attorneys and judges, both male and female, is significant and inescapably leads to the conclusion that female attorneys are likely to experience gender-biased treatment, including sexual harassment, by fellow counsel. This conclusion is further reinforced by the written and oral comments collected by the Committee, which are replete with graphic examples of the types of misconduct observed by respondents to the surveys.

Volunteers for Day in the Courts (September 29, 1988) were the recipients of many gender-biased comments. For example, one male attorney noted to one of the volunteers, "Women should be kept in the kitchen." Other observers who participated in the project reported surprise at the open hostility to this study which was expressed by some male lawyers who objected to the study or expressed perceptions of unfair advantages accruing to female attorneys. Many men responded by making fun of the survey, joking, or simply being obnoxious and attempting to discourage others from filling out the questionnaire. For example, one male attorney said: "My only complaint is that no one touches me in inappropriate places." One male lawyer stated to an observer: "Women attorneys are effective in direct correlation to the length of their skirts and the size of their busts." Another stated, that "female lawyers are my biggest problem . . . I'm always losing my cases to them." When asked whether that was because they may be better lawyers, this older male lawyer answered: "Yes. Women are wilier—they're more cunning."

These attitudes support the statement of one female attorney who speaks from the vantage point of experience as a former law clerk as well as a practicing attorney:

> [T]he demeanor of male counsel toward female counsel is appalling. No respect amongst comrades is accorded and terms of endearment are used often, especially . . . toward youthful female attorneys. This behavior should be strongly sanctioned by judges who normally observe and do nothing.

Numerous women reported that male attorneys often act as if they can "push around and take advantage of female attorneys." The principal offenders are reported to be older male attorneys who, it is felt, will simply never take female attorneys seriously. As one female attorney reported, it appears that a female trial lawyer is expected to be either a "pushover" or a "bitch."

Examples of the kinds of improper address or comments that female attorneys complain about are the following: "What this young lady doesn't realize;" "Female intuition notwithstanding;" "My young friend;" "Miss, Mrs., or is it Ms.?;" "My attractive sister;" "Counsel may be beautiful, but she is entirely wrong;" and "This room certainly heats up when you walk in the room."

One lawyer reported that during a contested contempt hearing an older male lawyer demanded that his opposing female counsel not interrupt him any further, stating that "women attorneys have a hard time keeping their mouths shut. "Conversely, many female attorneys reported that their male colleagues apparently feel free to interrupt them at will in an attempt to intimidate or overpower them. Research literature shows that men are much more likely to interrupt than women and that when women interrupt, they are perceived as rude and masculine. Among the other tactics reported by female attorneys are the following: several male lawyers beginning a conference without waiting for the female lawyer, something they probably would not have done had the absent attorney been male; comments designed to fluster a female attorney; refusing to discuss settlement with a female attorney; and refusing to shake a female attorney's hand. By these means, male attorneys not only often succeed in throwing their female opponents off balance, but they also clearly convey to them the message that women are unwanted as colleagues and do not belong in the courtroom.

Attorneys are not the only significant source of gender-biased conduct in the judicial system. Respondents to our various surveys observed gender-biased treatment and sexual harassment by court employees toward female attorneys, witnesses, litigants, and other court employees. The principal difference between the gender-biased conduct of attorneys and court employees is the fact that in many instances (according to attorneys' comments on the attorneys' survey) such conduct was perpetrated by female as well as male court employees. A brief review of the research literature shows a tendency on the parts of both men and women to discriminate against women. This is not surprising when one considers that both men and women are reared in the same culture. While such conduct may well be attributable to ignorance or insensitivity, its impact upon judicial proceedings may be considerable.

Respondents to the attorneys' survey reporting on their own experiences noted that court employees are far more likely to ask a woman if she is an attorney than to address the same question to a man (63% of the women, 29% of the men reported this experience); court employees are also more likely to address female attorneys by first names or terms of endearment than they are to use similar forms of address to male attorneys (32% of the women, 12% of the men reported this experience). . . .

Examples of improper behavior by court employees—both male and female—were reported by many of the attorneys who responded to the attorneys' survey or otherwise provided their oral or written observations. In addition to complaining of improper forms of address—ranging from "girlie" to "honey"—and being asked far too often whether they are attorneys, a substantial number of attorneys who testified before or submitted their observations to the Committee specifically referred to patterns of favoritism toward male attorneys shown by court employees, female as well as male. Included in this category are complaints that clerks often call the cases of older white male attorneys first in some sessions of court. When male attorneys are late coming to court, it is ignored; when the late attorney is a woman, she will be made to wait. Finally, female attorneys are reportedly more likely to be asked to show an identification card at a security checkpoint than are male attorneys.

A variation on the themes of improper address and favoritism is total disregard of female attorneys. As one attorney reported, the most common problem she has experienced with court employees is not being spoken to in an inappropriate manner, but rather, not being spoken to at all. At one district court session the clerk who regularly calls the list always identifies all attorneys, both male and female, as "Mr." Even though a female attorney who frequently appears in that court has asked the clerk on numerous occasions to stop calling her Mr. X, he continues to do so.

Generally, the most offensive behavior complained of by female attorneys consists of joking comments and improper touching of female attorneys, litigants, and witnesses. As one attorney commented, male court officers often treat female attorneys as "sex objects" by making sexual remarks about them. For example, one attorney reported that a bailiff speculated in her presence about how she would look in a bikini. According to our sources, comments such as this appear to be common among male court employees. An attorney also observed that male court officers do not reserve their comments for female attorneys, but also speak disrespectfully about female judges. For example, this attorney has heard court employees wonder aloud about how a female judge "looks under the robe" and also refer to a female judge who is considered tough as a "bitch" or a "dyke."
. . .

Ninety-eight percent of the attorneys who responded to the Committee's survey are white (93% of the women and 99% of the men). Two percent of the respondents are black, and less than 1% are Latino/Hispanic, Asian, or "Other." These numbers are a reliable reflection of the general population of attorneys in Massachusetts. Because so few attorneys in the sample are minorities, the survey was sent to an additional sample of minority attorneys. This mailing produced fifty additional responses. Data from these latter survey responses were not included in the figures provided in the foregoing sections of this report but were used by the Committee to assess the extent to which gender bias in the courts may be more pronounced for women of color. In this regard, the Committee conducted a series of analyses of the impact of gender and race on the experiences of minority attorneys from both the original and additional samples.

The Committee has concluded on the basis of this analysis that race has an impact on the frequency of certain behaviors. In particular, minority attorneys, both men and women, are significantly more likely than their white counterparts to be asked if they are attorneys by judges and court employees. Minority women are more likely than any other group of attorneys to be berated by a judge for no apparent reason. Finally, minority female attorneys are more likely than white women (and both groups are more likely than white or minority men) to be subjected to inappropriate sexual comments or touching by court employees.

In addition to the survey, the Committee received written and oral comments from minority attorneys and court employees which reinforce the impression that an additional burden is imposed by the judicial system of the Commonwealth upon women of color. Many black attorneys testified that they and black female litigants are treated worse than their white counterparts across the board. Indeed, one black female attorney stated that she was required to give testimony in one case that she was not related to her black client, a reflection of an unstated assumption that all blacks must somehow be related to one another. One particularly outrageous incident was reported by a black female attorney who has observed that the combination of race and gender is a great disadvantage in dealing with court officers. She described a situation in which a black attorney for the plaintiff was assaulted by a black male defendant. When the attorney asked a court officer to restrain the defendant, the request was denied.

Based upon these observations, the Committee concludes that minority women bear a double burden which cannot be ignored. . . .

The courts of the Commonwealth are responsible each year for a sizeable number of appointments of attorneys to positions that are compensated by the state. These positions range from private counsel in criminal cases to masters and receivers in civil cases and also include conservators, guardians ad litem, investigators, and counsel in civil commitment, care and protection, and abortion cases. While the manner of appointment may differ, the data collected by the Committee reveal that, with the exception of abortion cases, women are under represented across the board, both in the number of appointments and the amount of compensation they receive.
. . .

Ninety-eight percent of the judicial respondents stated that intervention would be appropriate in situations involving gender-biased conduct by male attorneys toward their female opponents. However, only 4% of the attorney respondents reported having observed intervention in situations in which female attorneys were improperly treated, whether by counsel, judges, or court employees. It should be noted that the judges were not asked whether anyone had intervened in cases, only whether they believe that intervention might be appropriate. When intervention occurs, moreover, it may simply compound the problem if the judge is not sensitive to issues of gender bias, as in the situation recounted by one attorney who reported that a male judge, interceding on her behalf after her male opponent had repeatedly interrupted her, stated: "Look counselor, why don't you let the young girl speak?" Other attorneys observed, however, that female judges in probate courts frequently correct male attorneys who behave improperly and that appellate judges are also particularly "attuned" to such situations.

Ninety-seven percent of the judges who responded to the survey also reported that judicial intervention would be appropriate in cases where male attorneys engage in gender-biased conduct toward female litigants and witnesses. Here again, however, only 4% of those who responded to the attorneys' survey reported having observed intervention in situations in which female clients or witnesses were improperly treated, whether by counsel, judges, or court employees.

Some judges have raised the concern that only overt signs of gender bias allow opportunity for intervention. In the adversarial atmosphere of the courtroom, a judge needs to be sensitive to differentiate between subtle manifestations of gender bias and the general tactical hostility that both male and female attorneys sometimes employ.

When asked whether they had ever objected to the gender-biased treatment they had experienced, 41% of the women and one-third of the men who responded to the attorneys' survey answered that they had done so at least once. These responses do not distinguish among the sources of the objectionable conduct (i.e., other attorneys, judges, or court employees), do not identify the nature of the conduct to which objection was made, and do not indicate whether the objections succeeded in correcting the situation or in preventing further misconduct. Nevertheless, they indicate that attorneys who experience gender-biased treatment do not simply accept such conduct as a "given, even if no one else intervenes on their behalf."
. . .

Credibility or the believability, trustworthiness, and persuasiveness of an individual's statements is a crucial attribute for any attorney, litigant, or witness who appears before a judge or jury. As the previous sections of this report have shown, women have a difficult time establishing and maintaining credibility in Massachusetts courts.

The issue of credibility was specifically addressed by the attorneys' survey, which asked all respondents whether and to what extent they had observed that the statements of women in various roles were given less weight than the statements of men in similar roles. It should be noted that in contrast to questions regarding observed or experienced treatment, the survey questions concerning credibility could only inquire about percep-tions that are much harder to assess because there are no objective criteria for measuring the weight accorded to the statements of advocates or witnesses. It is likely, however, that the higher percentage of female attorneys than male attorneys reporting that they have observed women being accorded less credibility reflects the different experiences of male and female attorneys with gender-biased conduct (i.e., women who are treated disrespectfully by male attorneys and judges are likely to perceive that male attorneys and judges accord less credibility to women).

A substantial number of attorneys who responded to the survey stated that they had sometimes or often observed that female attorneys' state-ments appear to be given less weight than those of male attorneys by judges (13%), by counsel (27%), and by court employees (17%). The propor-tion of respondents who have sometimes or often observed that the state-ments of female victims, litigants, or witnesses appear to be given less weight than those of similarly situated men was substantially similar (14% by judges, 20% by counsel, and 14% by court employees). . . .

Given the fact of women's lesser credibility in society, judges need to understand how little it takes to undermine a woman's authority and status in the courtroom. Even apparently trivial matters, such as calling a woman by her first name or using her marital rather than her professional title, do have consequences for her credibility. Moreover, although it may be an unintended slip when a male witness calls his female cross-examiner "honey," this kind of tactic is often used on women with complete deliberateness. . . .

Female attorneys are as effective as their male counterparts in representing their clients, but credibility remains a problem for women in the Massachusetts judicial system. To the extent that gender bias is "an attitude that affects decisions and behaviors," it certainly is likely to influence determinations of credibility until judges and jurors become more aware of their own stereotypical perceptions. . . .

NOTES AND QUESTIONS

1. **Defining Gender Bias.** How does this commission define "gender bias?" Does it work from the assumption that women should be treated the same as men? Differently from men? Are there times when women should be treated the same and other times when they should be treated differently? Should men always be the model?

In thinking about gender bias, it is also important to think about whether it has the same social meaning and should be prohibited when women discriminate against men on the basis of their sex. Consider the following situation. A female attorney, who specializes in family law, wants to devote her expertise to eliminating gender bias in the court system. In order to do this she feels that she must not take any male clients because the women she represents will speak most openly to her if they believe that she is wholeheartedly committed to their cause. She is not anxious for them to have to sit in her waiting room with male clients. One day she rejects a potential male client specifically on the grounds that he is a man. She does so despite the fact that he was a househusband for numerous years while his children were young, and has recently pursued a career as a rather low-paid teacher, while his wife has pursued her career as a doctor. Should this be considered impermissible gender discrimination? What are the connections between sex discrimination and social power? Does a man in this situation become a "woman" in terms of his position in society or does he remain a "man" despite his non-traditional career pattern? *See* Stropnicky v. Nathanson, 19 MDLR 39 (MA 1997)

2. **Gender Bias and Racial Differences.** The commission recognizes that "minority women bear a double burden." Why is this so and what is meant by this? Should white women be a standard against which we compare the treatment faced by Black, Latina, Asian and other women who do not consider themselves, or are not considered, white? Notice that the questions here echo those posed above.

Here, however, there is the additional question of whether it makes sense to think about women as a group. Throughout the Gender Bias Commission's Study, the commission discusses the treatment of "women" as if this were a meaningful classification. Can we talk about women as a group, or should we always be breaking it up to talk about the experiences of Black women, Latina women, Asian women, lesbians, disabled women, etc.? There is much that makes sense about deconstructing the category "women" in this way, but does it make political action on behalf of "women" impossible? If you think gender bias should be analyzed in terms of the experience of particular groups of women, how should we think about the experiences of women who fit into more than one group, e.g., elderly Asian women?

3.   **Potential Remedies.** Do you think the commission's overall attitude is optimistic or pessimistic? At one point the commission indicates that the worst offenders are older male attorneys. Does this imply that the problem will take care of itself as these men slowly retire from active practice?

The 9th Circuit's Gender Bias Report says:

> Some believe that the passage of time is all that is needed to change attitudes towards women, but our data demonstrate that attitudes about gender bias do not depend upon the *age* of the respondent but rather upon the *gender* of the respondent. Men over and under fifty share the attitude that there is relatively little gender bias in the Circuit, while women over and under the age of fifty share the view that gender bias *is* a problem. Moreover, while some social science literature might have predicted that role would be the critical determinant of one's view—that is, that those who are judges would share views, and that those who are lawyers would share somewhat different views,—our data demonstrate that *gender* is key across roles. Women judges and women lawyers report similar perceptions; men judges and men lawyers also have similar perceptions.

The Effects of Gender in the Federal Courts: Final Report of the Ninth Circuit Gender Bias Task Force, 67 S.Cal. L. Rev. 750, 952–53 (1994).

The Massachusetts Gender Bias Study indicates that women also discriminate against women. According to the Massachusetts Study, women staff in the court houses are as likely to discriminate as anyone else. Does this indicate that perhaps the biases may be an integral part of the socialization process either within the profession or society at large?

If you were a member of a gender bias commission, what types of remedies would you recommend? These can range from proposals for educating (or reeducating) participants in the judicial system, to the creation of new provisions in the code of professional ethics, to the passage of new statutes. Do you think judges and opposing male counsel should be encouraged to speak out openly in court when they think they have seen an incident involving gender bias? Or do you think these events should be dealt with more quietly, perhaps in the privacy of the judge's chambers or a nearby coffee shop?

4. **Women's Credibility.** Both the Ninth Circuit Task Force and the Massachusetts Gender Bias Study found women litigants face special problems: their credibility is often questioned and their claims are viewed as trivial or as an unalterable part of life. Do the next two readings help to explain why this may be so?

Jennifer Pierce, Women and Men as Litigators

From J. Pierce, Gender Trials (Berkeley: Univ. of California Press, 1995).

In *The Merchant of Venice,* Portia poses as a male judge in an attempt to bring the plea for mercy into the halls of justice. Rejecting a binary logic of justice in which one party wins and another loses, Portia argues instead for a resolution to a legal dispute in which none of the parties will be harmed. Carol Gilligan refers to Portia's stance as an illustration of morality based on what she calls an "ethic of care." In her early study of moral reasoning, Gilligan finds that women consistently pose moral questions in a "different voice" than men do. In their attempts to resolve moral dilemmas and issues of responsibility, Gilligan's women, like Portia, are concerned with maintaining relationships so that no one will be hurt, whereas men are concerned with abstract notions of universal rights and justice. More recently, in their study of women and men lawyers, Gilligan's colleagues, Dana Jack and Rand Jack, find that despite variations in behavior between women, as a group women are more likely than men to express a caring orientation in the practice of law.

In contrast to the empirical findings of Gilligan et al., sociologist Rosabeth Moss Kanter finds that women lawyers and managers as tokens or the numerical minority in their occupational group feel strong pressures to conform to existing masculine norms within the workplace and as a consequence minimize, rather than emphasize, whatever differences exist between them and the dominant group. Other studies on token women in male-dominated professions and occupations have confirmed Kanter's thesis. These contradictory sets of findings raise the central questions for consideration. Do women trial lawyers conform to male-defined norms of the adversarial role or do they speak in a Portia-like dissatisfaction with the male voice?

I observed that some women litigators practiced an ethic of care in the resolution of legal disputes, others adopted the adversarial model for the courtroom and a more care-oriented approach in the office, and a small minority conformed to the male model. To make sense of these findings, I reject the "either-personality-or-social-structure" construction of the Gilligan–Kanter debate and argue instead that gender shapes the experiences of women in the legal profession at the structural level at the same time that women and men as litigators reproduce gender at the micro-level of interactions and identity. To make this argument, I examine gender differences on the job at three levels of analysis: structural, behavioral, and the level of individual identity. I discuss the gendered structural constraints women (but not men) face in the law firm, such as their location in the internal system of stratification and their experiences within the male culture of the law firm and the corporate world and within the "male clockwork" of the legal profession. Being a litigator is not the same job for women as it is for men. Moreover, the gendered "feeling rules," or informal norms for appropriate emotional labor that women and men face further reinforce these structural constraints. Women, unlike men, encounter a double bind between the role of the "good women" and the emotional requirements of the adversarial role.

In the final section ... I turn to the micro level of interactions and consider the actual differences in emotional labor that women and men perform. Compared to men, women as a group are less likely to embrace the adversarial model in all aspects of their work, instead expressing a caring orientation toward others, either in the resolution of legal conflicts and/or in relations with staff in the office. Here, I introduce ... [the] concept of "doing gender" as the mediating behavioral link between the structural and individual levels of analysis. In my argument, women litigators, as token members of a male-dominated profession, do not passively conform to the norms of the adversarial model. Instead, they actively construct an emotional style that is consistent with their notion of gender-appropriate behavior. Furthermore, their choice of doing gender is informed in some way by their identity and sense of self as relational or feminine. As I will show, even women who most closely adhere to the male model are preoccupied with relational issues. In my dynamic account, gender shapes the structure of the legal profession, thereby setting gendered limits on lawyers' behavior. At the same time, women attorneys negotiate in and around these constraints, reproducing gender in their interactions with others by constructing a more caring practice of lawyering, creating more humane and caring relations with office staff, or simply by expressing their preoccupation with relational issues.

Structural Differences and Boundary Heightening

The first structural difference can be found within the internal system of stratification with law firms. In 1988, the same year I began my fieldwork, only 8 percent of the partners in the nation's 247 largest law firms were women. This contrasts sharply with the percentage of law students nationwide who were women—42 percent that same year. While this figure is reflected in the increasing number of women who were hired in law firms across the country at this time (40 percent), it is not reflected in the total percentage of women lawyers (19 percent) or in the percentage of women who achieve partnership. Journalists argue that the reason so few women are partners is that women, in significant numbers, have only been on the partnership track in the last fifteen years. In such accounts, parity will be achieved when women have been within the profession for a longer period. The fact that so many women are leaving the legal profession for reasons of discrimination, sexual harassment, the improbability of breaking through the "glass ceiling," and incompatible demands between work and family suggests that such media accounts may be overly optimistic.

In this study, at the private firm, less than 9 percent of the partners are women; at Bonhomie Corporation, 10 percent. These differences in status are further reflected in income differentials. Although the private firm started associates at $58,500 in 1989, after two years men on the average made $2,000 more per year than the women did. Similarly, at Bonhomie Corporation, after two years men on the average were making $1,600 more per year than women lawyers. These salary differentials reflect those found in a national survey conducted by the National Association for Law Placement. Thus, structurally, women are unlikely to be located in positions of power within the law firm and likely to make less money than men with comparable experience.

Not only do men predominate in numbers and in their positions of power, but private elite law firms represent in Epstein's words, "the quintessential upper-class male culture." "Nowhere is the 'old boy' network so characteristic of the formal and informal structure as in the 'establishment bar.' " ... [W]omen still have a hard time gaining admission to the old-boy network. One area in which women lawyers continue to face exclusionary practices is informal socializing with male colleagues. In large law firms, such socializing is an important mechanism for obtaining interesting or important cases and information and for garnering trust and political capital with influential partners. Kanter argues that token members of an occupational group are less likely to be included in informal socializing. This is frequently the case for women attorneys in this study, such as Kelly, a thirty-five-year-old associate from Bonhomie Corporation:

> My supervisor is so disengaged [from me]. But there is an underlying unspoken camaraderie between him and the male associates. There is just no way for me to crack through it. They play golf together, go on long bicycle trips together.... I'm never included.

Leslie, a twenty-nine-year old associate, said:

> I dislike the "macho" atmosphere [at informal social events]. I went once, and all the associates were trying to see who could drink the most beer. Maybe they did it because I was there, I don't know, but I never went again.
>
> Another woman said that when she first started working at Bonhomie, she "went out for drinks with the boys" but found the talk always turned to baseball. "I thought 'Oh, no. Here they go again.' "

These examples suggest not only that women are often excluded from all-male informal social groups but that even when they were included they still felt they did not belong. The response of their male colleagues exemplifies what Kanter calls "boundary heightening," that is, the exaggeration of differences by the dominant group between themselves and tokens. Male lawyers exaggerate the differences between women lawyers and themselves by talking about stereotypical male topics such as sports when women are present and by turning social events such as after-hours drinks into competitions. Such behavior serves, consciously or not, to underscore the differences between women and men, thereby constantly reminding the women that they are different and do not fit in.

Another way that male attorneys remind women they are not part of the "male culture" is by deflating women's occupational status. . . . Women are no longer denied jobs as attorneys; however, they are frequently mistaken for secretaries. Many of the women I interviewed expressed anger and annoyance at such incidences. Jeanette, a thirty-two-year old associate said:

> I'd been with the firm for about eight months working with James [a partner] when Jerry [another partner] came up to me and asked me to type something. I looked surprised and said, "I'm an attorney, not a secretary." I actually sat next to this man at a litigation department luncheon [for attorneys] the week before, so I knew he knew me. He laughed and said with a conspiratorial wink, "Oh yeah, but don't all women know how to type." He sauntered down the hall. I was furious.

Several other women attorneys recalled similar experiences. As one commented sardonically, "Men seem to think women are born to type." Such derogatory remarks serve to deflate the status of women, as attorneys. Deflating the occupational status of female attorneys also serves to heighten boundaries between men and women. It reminds women that male lawyers think of them in stereotypical, subservient female roles, and not as competent professionals, suggesting a reluctance to accept women as colleagues or as equals.

Another means of heightening boundaries between male and female attorneys is through sexual harassment. The sexualization of women is perhaps the most blatant way to exaggerate differences between the sexes. Recent studies of the legal profession suggest that sexual harassment is much more common than was once supposed. Many of the women lawyers I interviewed reported incidences of unwanted sexual invitations, attention, and behavior. For example, Gabriella, a twenty-six-year-old associate, was harassed by a male partner at a firm cocktail party who was notorious for such behavior; she slapped him in response.

> Everyone else knew about George, but I was new, I didn't know to avoid him. So, when he tried to grab my breasts, I didn't even think, I just came out swinging . . . it was so humiliating. Then, afterwards . . . the snide remarks, the knowing glances, the comments, "How's your left hook?" It was the second public humiliation. . . .

[T]he comments male attorneys made about Gabriella after the incident with George suggest that not George's behavior but rather Gabriella's reaction—slapping George—was what they considered inappropriate and worthy of derision. Reminding Gabriella of the incident in this way also drew attention to her status as a woman. By treating women lawyers as sex objects, male lawyers simultaneously heighten the boundaries between themselves and women and assert their authority as men in the work-place. . . .

Gendered Feeling Rules

The double standard posed for women by the "quintessential male culture" of the law can also be seen by looking at the divergent "feeling rules" men and women face about appropriate display of emotional labor. . . . Unlike male attorneys, women encounter a double bind in the aggressive component of emotional labor. At NITA [National Institute of Trial Advocacy] and both law firms, women attorneys were criticized for being "too nice to the witnesses," "not forceful enough," "too bashful," and "unaggressive," at the same time that they were admonished for being "too aggressive." Men, on the other hand, were sometimes criticized for being "too aggressive" and not listening carefully to the witness but were more likely to be praised for their ruthlessness. This double bind emerged not only in the aggressive component of gamesmanship, but in its less confrontational—though equally manipulative—form, strategic friendliness. For example, when male attorneys used cajoling and placating strategies to achieve an instrumental end, they received support and encouragement from their colleagues. Women who adopted similar tactics, were accused of using their "feminine wiles" to get their way with the witness or opposing counsel.

Underlying such attitudes is a gendered division of emotional labor, in which men are expected to be aggressive, manipulative, and instrumental, and women are not. Women who display these qualities are regarded as "unladylike," "domineering," "strident," and "shrill." In her classic study on women lawyers, Epstein (1983) suggests such women violate the cultural myth of the "good woman." . . .

The double bind posed by the aggressive component of gamesmanship is evident in a presentation made by a young woman lawyer at the National Institute for Trial Advocacy. Amanda performed a confrontational cross-examination of the witness, badgering him until he began to admit that he wasn't absolutely sure about the date of the incident in question. Amanda, however, had one mannerism that the teacher did not like—her smile. At the end of one of the leading questions, "You don't remember what you did on August 28th, do you, Mr. Jones?" she smiled. In his comments at the end of her presentation, the teacher said that her smile detracted from the seriousness and aggressiveness of the cross-examination. He told her half-seriously and half-jokingly, that if she smiled again, he would hold her in "contempt of court." His advice to Amanda was to "lose the smile and be more forceful."

At the break, Amanda talked at length with me about the teacher's comment. She knew that she smiled a lot, but she didn't know she smiled so much until she saw the video of her presentation. She added that she smiled at the end of one of her particularly aggressive questions because she didn't want to be perceived as a "bitch." Her comment suggests that although she was capable of playing the part—being aggressive—she was still concerned about, or preoccupied with, how other people thought of her.

In the afternoon session, when Amanda went back to class, she did another cross-examination. This time she didn't smile at all, and instead hammered away at the witness with question after question, looking serious and stern. This time, the teacher told her that her cross-examination was "dull, lacking animation and interest." As Amanda herself said afterwards, "I feel like I can't win. If I smile, I'm not aggressive enough. If I'm aggressive and don't smile, I'm boring. What am I supposed to do to be a good trial lawyer?"

This question plagued many of the women lawyers in this study. They found that if they were polite to the witnesses they cross-examined, they were criticized for not being forceful enough. When they became more aggressive, they were admonished for "overplaying it" or "being phoney." ... As one of the NITA's female teachers astutely observed, "Unlike men, women lawyers have to find a balance in the courtroom between being forceful, but not being too shrill." ...

Doing Gender: Variation and Continuity

The male-dominated structure of the legal profession, as well as the gendered nature of "feeling rules," sets the limits for gender-appropriate emotional labor for male and female litigators. Men as a group were more likely to follow the dictates of the adversarial model and to refrain from developing social relationships with support staff. On the other hand, women were less likely to embrace the adversarial model wholeheartedly, instead performing a relational form of emotional labor emphasizing a caring orientation toward others, either in the adjudication of legal disputes or in office working relations. Women and men did not conform precisely to these limits but rather varied in the degree to which they performed gender appropriate emotional labor. Much like the women lawyers in Jack and Jack's study, women's behavior in this study also varied. At Lyman, Lyman and Portia and in the legal department at Bonhomie Corporation, women's emotional labor fell along a continuum ranging from those who sought to reshape the adversarial role to fit their caring orientation (26 percent), those who "split the role" (58 percent), and those who minimized the feminine self by adopting the male model (16 percent). "Men also varied in how closely they adopted the strategies of gamesmanship. Some wholeheartedly embraced the adversarial role (40 percent), others did it but expressed a more distanced relation to it (50 percent), and a small minority rejected the model altogether (10 percent)."

Resisting and Reshaping the Adversarial Role

Women lawyers who attempted to reshape the adversarial role to fit their caring orientation expressed a strong dissatisfaction with the traditional adversarial role. Twenty-six percent of women fell into this category. They paid more than "lip service" to their expressed values by actively seeking to incorporate alternatives to gamesmanship in their daily practice.

Like the feminist lawyers Epstein interviewed, these women were dedicated to social goals rather than making money and valued egalitarian working relationships with colleagues and with support staff....

The following conversation between two lawyers illustrates the feelings expressed by women in the first group:

Tom: Dealing with the aggressive role is purely personal. If people aren't aggressive by nature, they won't be good litigators. If I had to I could persuade any client to do whatever I wanted....

Linda: But isn't that unethical? You have to inform clients of the downside as well.... *[Later, in a private conversation]* Tom's partially correct, you sometimes do have to be aggressive to survive. But the majority of lawyers aren't cutthroat. There are other possible ways to resolve problems.

Linda's suggestion that there are ways to resolve legal disputes other than being aggressive is not a reference to strategic friendliness. She doesn't believe one has to be manipulative to be a good lawyer. In her view: "I often see my relationship to clients as the creation of a personal relationship. Some would say that's unprofessional. But I really think that relationships based on trust don't emerge from manipulation. I treat clients with respect. I provide them with alternatives and urge them to think for themselves." Thus, Linda is concerned about the quality of her relationship with the client as well as the procedure for obtaining a decision. By contrast, Tom is unconcerned with the relationship and is solely interested in pursuing whatever it takes to win.

The difference in these approaches is reminiscent of Carol Gilligan's early findings on gender differences in moral development. In her study, Gilligan finds that men tend to resolve moral dilemmas using a language of rights and responsibilities and an abstract notion of justice. Men identify the legal issue, balance the rights of each party, and declare one the winner. By contrast, women utilize an "ethic of care," considering the needs of all the parties involved as well as their relationships, and attempt to find a solution that will satisfy everyone, rather than selecting a winner and a loser. Thus, Gilligan finds that women are more concerned with how moral dilemmas are resolved.

Many of the women I interviewed expressed concern for how legal disputes were resolved. Margaret, a young associate at the private firm, expressed a Gilliganesque concern about her working relationship with opposing counsel:

I don't give into being aggressive, rude, and snotty to get the best results. You don't have to stand up to opposing counsel by screaming on the phone, for example. You can always hang up.... They can't win by playing hardball all the time. Being a feminine woman and being reasonable, that's how I see myself. Howard, the partner I work for, adopts the adversarial relationship. That's not me. I don't know what happened before in this case I'm working on or why it had accelerated to such an ugly state. I decided to be reasonable. Now opposing counsel calls me and says, "Look Margaret, I don't trust Howard, but I trust you, I think we can work this out."

In this way, Margaret found an alternative to the aggressive and manipulative aspects of gamesmanship. Her particular style emphasizes mutual trust and respect rather than suspicion and combativeness. This style carried over into her working relations with secretaries and paralegals as well.

I think it's really important to develop working relationships out of mutual respect. I've seen too many attorneys treat their secretaries badly—like they're not people, like they don't matter. But they do matter, it does matter. Every time you treat someone like that, you hurt them, and you hurt yourself. It's a process of dehumanization, and it works both ways. . . .

By reshaping the adversarial role to fit their more relational orientation, these women contradict Kanter's findings on female tokens. Rather than conforming to the male model, these women self-consciously reject the binary win-lose structure of adversarial practice and construct alternative forms of practice that value mutual trust and respect in relationships. Their active participation in creating a more caring orientation within the legal profession serves as both a critique of and a challenge to the male-defined adversarial role. Furthermore, their emphasis on "real" relationships undermines one of the major assumptions of gamesmanship, that is, that relations with others are a game in which people are treated as objects. Rather than deny the subjectivity of the other, these women recognize the other as an authentic subject. . . .

Splitting the Roles versus Distancing

In their study on women lawyers, Jack and Jack found that some women lawyers "split" the lawyering role by living up to the demands of the professional role and, at the same time, maintaining their personal caring morality. They accomplished this by splitting their roles at home and at work, adopting an adversarial role at work but embracing a caring ethic at home. In my research, women also split roles, but in a different way. The second group of female lawyers (58 percent of women) assimilated to the masculine norms of gamesmanship in their dealings with opposing counsel and with clients, but their actions and feelings in the office often belied this stance. Some adopted a combative style with opposing counsel but treated staff and colleagues with concern and/or respect. Others utilized gamesmanship but often expressed strong feelings of guilt and dissatisfaction. . . .

Mary exemplifies women who split the roles. She appeared to adhere to the model of the combative litigator, as in an incident typifying her response to communications with opposing counsel: during a heated argument with opposing counsel on the phone, she told him he was "the most patronizing man" she'd ever met in her life. "Who do you think you are to presume that Sam [the other attorney on the case] and I don't know what we're doing?" Mary, who is five-foot-eleven, explained her future strategy for dealing with this lawyer, who was only five feet tall: "From now on, in every meeting with him, I am going to wear three-inch heels, so that I tower over him. And, if he gets in my way, I'll squash him like a bug with the end of my stiletto heel!"

In another context, Mary appeared ambivalent about being so aggressive. She had a reputation among secretaries and paralegals for being difficult to work with. However, what made her behavior different from that of her male counterparts lay in her interactions with subordinates. She usually gave flowers or candy to subordinates before she went into her work frenzy. In fact, one of her paralegals said that she could always tell when Mary was going to be difficult to work with, because she gave her flowers, as if she were apologizing in advance for what she knew would be inappropriate behavior. Furthermore, the day after she had given paralegals and secretaries a difficult time, she thanked them excessively for the work they had done. . . .

Many of the women I interviewed who fell into the second category were aware of the conflict between their personal morality and the adversarial role. . . .

Mary said:

> Sometimes I feel the conflict, sometimes I don't. I'm from the Midwest. People are more down to earth in the Midwest, more concerned about other people. I know it's a stereotype. . . . Anyway, I try to be a Midwesterner. But it doesn't always work. You know, if you really don't like the other side—no problem. But when it's less black and white, I don't know. Once I did a [personal injury case]. The woman [the plaintiff] really got hurt, and it was definitely the company's fault. But she didn't have a good lawyer. I got the company off on a technicality. I didn't sleep nights after that one. [*Sighs.*] And I'd be lying if I said I still didn't feel guilty about it.

By splitting roles between conforming to masculine norms of gamesmanship in relations with opposing counsel and clients and adopting a caring orientation in the office, the behavior of the women in the second category contradicts Kanter's thesis about the behavior of token women. While these women seemingly conform to the masculine norms, thereby making themselves less visible in Kanter's formulation, their behavior toward support staff and colleagues in the office and the expression of their Gilliganesque concern for relationships suggests that they have not fully assimilated the masculine demands of the profession. Their behavior and expressed feelings underscore instead a fundamental conflict between the adversarial role and their personal feelings about the importance of relationships, civility, and fair play. . . .

Talk Like a Lawyer, Think Like a Lawyer, Act Like a Lawyer

The third and smallest group of women lawyers (16 percent) emulated the behavior of aggressive male litigators in the courtroom and in the office.... This particular model of behavior has been encouraged in popular advice books and articles written for career women. For example, in an article in the American Bar Association journal, a female attorney advises women who want to succeed in a "man's world" to establish themselves as committed and competent professionals by doing top quality work, working long hours, and never shirking late hours or weekend projects. In addition, she suggests rejecting any association with the traditional female role:

> Don't go home to cook dinner—or if you do, don't tell anyone. Keep your personal life in the background.... Never make excuses based on the needs of a spouse or children. Dress and talk in a conservative and professional manner.... Dress like a lawyer. Don't chew gum. When called "dear" or flirted with in business meetings or professional situations, respond only with entirely professional business-like statements, so that all communications are placed on and remain on a highly, professional plane. [And finally] Don't think of yourself, or allow anyone to think of you, as anything but a hard driving, capable lawyer.

The women who fell into the third category closely adhered to the male standard for success. Not only did they adopt hardball tactics in the courtroom, but unlike women lawyers who reshaped or split the adversarial role, they maintained "professional working relationships" with their secretaries and paralegals. Kathryn, for example, said, "I'm not friends with my secretary and I don't intend to be. It's simply a working relationship." And another asked rhetorically, "Why should I be friends with her? She's my secretary." ...

I have shown that female attorneys perform a more varied range of emotional labor. Existing theoretical accounts do not adequately explain the variation in the behavior of these women lawyers. While Kanter's proposition that women conform to male norms of the legal profession describes the behavior of women in the third group, it does not account for those who split roles or those who reshaped the adversarial model. Similarly, Gilligan's social psychological theory explains why some women created alternative, caring practices of lawyering, but it does not explain why others did not. How then can we explain the variation in behavior?

To answer this question, the experiences of women attorneys must be theorized as a dynamic relationship between occupational structure, behavior, and identity. Gender is an integral part of this analysis. In my explanation, gender shapes the experiences of women lawyers at the level of occupational structure while legal workers reproduce gender in their interactions with one another. At the structural level, female litigators find themselves a token minority in a male-dominated occupation, encountering a professional socialization and a career track based on a male model of success. They must contend with boundary heightening, and they face contradictory messages about the appropriate display of emotional labor:

when they adopt gamesmanship strategies they are criticized for "unlady-like" and "shrill" behavior, but when they are "nice" or "pleasant," they are judged "not tough enough" to be good lawyers.

The double bind women attorneys invariably experience explains, in part, the variation in their behavior. There are simply no clear-cut "feeling rules" for women lawyers. Nor is there any one form of acceptable emotional labor for them. Whether they closely adhere to the adversarial model or not, they garner criticism, disapproval, and even ostracism. However, assuming that structure determines behavior in a simple one-to-one relationship denies agency to social actors and neglects the continuous and reciprocal relationship between the two levels of analysis. To improve upon this theoretical weakness, I view the masculinized structure of the legal profession as setting limits on female litigators' behavior. Some women attorneys cross over these boundaries, others move within and around them, and still others remain safely inside the lines.

Regardless of which strategy women select, their negotiation within these limits poses a nagging question: How can I be a lawyer and a woman at the same time? Answering this question entails choosing behavior congruent with their notions of gender-appropriate behavior—which is not necessarily the same thing as behaving in traditionally female ways. Socialization in a masculinized profession has provided these women with life experiences as well as an education that provides them an array of choices for "doing gender." Women lawyers who split roles do gender in accordance with professional norms in the courtroom and with their conceptions of feminine behavior in the office. Those who adopt a more relational orientation reshape the adversarial role to be consistent with their notions of how law ought to be practiced and their sense of how women as traditional caregivers should do law. Finally, the women who adopt the role of the professional combatant do gender by accepting the advice for women lawyers that encourages them to establish themselves as competent professionals and to downplay their association with the traditional female role. Ironically, this group of women sought to be lawyers and women by minimizing the feminine side of themselves.

Despite the variation among women lawyers in doing gender, there is also some continuity, notably their recurring concern with relationships. Those who sought to reshape the adversarial role as well as those who split the role expressed a relational orientation. Although it is most strongly expressed by women who actively sought to create alternatives to the adversarial model, it is also expressed by women who emphasize the importance of relationships in the office. Even the women who most closely adhered to the male model of success expressed misgivings and ambivalence about denying the relational part of themselves.

This recurring concern with relationships supports Chodorow's theory of feminine gender-identity. In her formulation, women develop a sense of self as empathic, and nurturant through the early mother-daughter relationship. As a consequence, feminine identity comes to be defined through attachment and relations to others. For some women litigators, this sense of self is expressed in their alternative practice of law, for others in their relationships in the office, and for still others in their continuing preoccupation with relational issues despite their adherence to the male model.

While Chodorow's theory sheds light on this common theme, it does not explain why some women lawyers are more relational than others because it does not theorize the influence of the workplace on personality. However, by integrating her concept of gender-identity within this historically specific occupational context, the continuity and variation in women's behavior can be explained by theorizing a dynamic relationship between occupational structure, behavior, and gender identity. In a dynamic understanding, the male-dominated legal profession poses a double bind for women in the performance of emotional labor, thereby setting gendered limits on their behavior. In response, women lawyers actively construct an emotional style that is consistent with their notion of gender-appropriate behavior and is informed in some way by their sense of self as relational or feminine. Women attorneys negotiate in and around the gendered constraints of the legal profession, reproducing gender in their interactions with others by constructing a more caring practice of lawyering, creating more humane and caring relations with office staff, or simply becoming preoccupied with relational issues. . . .

NOTES AND QUESTIONS

1. **Gilligan and Kanter.** This article starts by describing the work of Carol Gilligan and that of Rosabeth Moss Kanter as if their findings were in opposition to each other. We can defer the question of whether these are really oppositional approaches until we discuss Catharine MacKinnon's work later in this chapter. For the moment, it will be useful simply to explore Gilligan's and Kanter's work in more detail.

Carol Gilligan's pathbreaking 1982 book, *In A Different Voice*, argued that women's moral development was distinct from men's. Whereas morally mature males look to a hierarchical set of principles to settle moral disputes, women refer to the context of the dispute and the strength of the relationships involved. These differences are often illustrated by reference to interviews Gilligan conducted with two 11–year olds, Jake and Amy. Each was asked whether a hypothetical Heinz should steal a drug that he cannot afford to buy, but which his dying wife needs desperately. Jake answers that Heinz should steal the drug because life is worth more than money. Gilligan sees this and others of Jake's responses as a clear resort to a hierarchy of values. Amy responds to the same question by looking for alternatives to theft or death, neither of which strikes her as a good outcome. When asked why Heinz should not steal the drug she says because he might end up in jail, and his wife might have a continuing need for him. Instead, she proposes that the druggist and Heinz discuss the problem, assuming that when the druggist understands the severity of the problem he will give Heinz the drugs and wait for delayed payment. Unlike Jake, Amy focuses on the importance of relationships in searching for a viable solution. She considers both Heinz's relationship with his wife and the possibility of creating a relationship with the druggist. Gilligan describes this as an "ethic of care."

Pierce is not the first person to apply Gilligan's ideas to the process of lawyering. Carrie Menkel–Meadow has argued that the law, a traditionally male profession, might look very different if women's voices had been listened to earlier. Menkel–Meadow hypothesizes that a legal system created by women might rely more heavily on alternative dispute resolution mechanisms as a means of simultaneously avoiding the "winner take all" outcomes of adversarial litigation and of expressing concern for one's opponent. Furthermore, a legal system that embodied women's voices might also be more client oriented, listening more carefully to the client's goals. Finally, she suggests that women's concern for connection might result in an entirely different understanding of fundamental rights, focusing on collective rights instead of individual liberties. *See* Carrie Menkel–Meadow, *Portia In A Different Voice,* 1 Berkeley Women's L.J. 39 (1985). Do you agree with Menkel–Meadow? What light does Pierce's work throw on Menkel–Meadow's musings? Do you think the presence of women in significant numbers will feminize the profession? What would it mean for the profession to be feminized? Would it mean a change in the way lawyers act toward others, a change in legal doctrine, or a change in institutional practices to reduce the conflicts between work and family? Do you think the work of people like Gilligan, Pierce and Menkel–Meadow reinforces traditional stereotypes about women's behavior?

Kanter's work, as Pierce indicates, predicted that women attorneys who were simply tokens in the profession would try to mimic men's conduct as much as possible. This mimicry could range from adopting aggressive litigation stances to dressing in pin-striped suits with little string ties. Do you think Kanter's work remains relevant given the large increases in the number of women in the profession over the past two decades? Or, do you think that the structural barriers to full participation that Pierce describes mean that women will always functionally be tokens in the profession?

More recently, Elizabeth Chambliss has also studied the effects of law firm structure on women's positions within the firms. She concludes that structure does have a significant effect on how well integrated by gender a firm will become. In particular, she identifies geographical diversity (offices in multiple jurisdictions) and relatively short tracks toward partnership as variables that correlate with higher degrees of gender integration. She attributes the latter to women's reluctance to take time off for pregnancy or maternity leaves prior to attaining partnership, while she conjectures that geographical diversity may be important because it encourages recruitment from a number of different law schools or perhaps because it is tied to compliance with anti-discrimination laws. Whatever the reasons, her data reinforce Kanter's emphasis on the structure of law firms. Elizabeth Chambliss, *Organizational Determinants of Law Firm Integration,* 46 Am. U. L. Rev. 669 (1997).

Interestingly, Chambliss finds that the most important variable when looking at racial integration is not the firm's structure, but its social characteristics—in particular, its client base. Here she suggests that different types of practice encourage different forms of racial integration of the firm because the client base is disproportionately composed of people of that racial group. For example, the presence of an administrative practice is positively correlated with the number of Black lawyers in a firm. She speculates that this is because administrative lawyers tend to have governmental agencies as their clients, and that the government has been a major employer of African Americans. Although Chambliss does not say so, this would cause one to expect to find a disproportionately large number of women in firms that do family or domestic relations practices. If this actually is the case, do you think this creates an area of opportunity for women or does it mean that women in the firm are confined to that particular area of practice?

2. **Agency and Victimhood.** Pierce's thesis is that ideas about gender shape the legal profession at two levels: the structural and the interpersonal. The structural includes such problems as finding mentors or being excluded from office social activities. These problems are structural in that they are part of the framework of the profession. They exist independently of the women attorneys. For example, the women have very little control over whether male senior partners choose to mentor them or include them in social activities. Elsewhere, she argues that the timetable for advancement in the legal profession is geared to men, not women. Maternity leave policies may be skimpy or non-existent; the assumption may be that the attorney has a "wife" at home to attend to family-related matters. Perhaps the most significant of the structural difficulties for women is the question of how to act like an attorney and a woman at the same time.

One could argue that the structure of the legal profession constrains women, forcing them to conform to expectations of how women should act. The difficulty with this is that it tends to see women as victims who merely respond to the conditions in which they find themselves, instead of as active participants who create the conditions of their own lives. This theme will reappear repeatedly throughout this course in the form of the question, "Are women victims of conditions beyond their control or are they agents of their own lives?" Those who see women as victims often cite examples from the areas of sexual harassment, rape, and domestic violence. Those who see women as agents are more likely to refer to the powerful role that women have in determining the lives of their families.

Pierce tries to carve out a middle position that argues that women in the legal profession have some agency, but that their actions are in response to the existence of boundaries created by the structure of the profession. She sees the most room for women to control their own lives in the area of interpersonal relations. How much do you think her choice to identify these particular categories is influenced by the stereotypical images of women which we have discussed above? Notice that this question raises difficult issues of Pierce's agency. Is she using structural and interpersonal categories in this way because our ideological structures code them as male and female and because she is a "victim" of this way of thinking, or is she a participant in the creation of the categories and the ideology?

Mona Harrington, Bodies

From M. Harrington, Women Lawyers (NY: Knopf, 1993).

At issue here ... is the conception of reason and its centrality in the law. We have seen that the explicit purpose of law school professors as they reveal the mysteries of "thinking like a lawyer" is to enthrone reason as the basis for legal judgment—to vanquish emotion with discipline, intuition with logic, assumptions with facts, and personal preferences with objectivity. We have also seen that women are under chronic suspicion as dealers in emotion, intuition, unfounded assumptions, and subjective preferences. What does not generally become explicit in Socratic dialogues is the connection of this suspicion to women's bodies, to the identification of women with their bodies.

This is not to say that the long history of Western thought that produced the tradition of Anglo–American law did not raise the issue of the relation of body to mind. Aristotle worked out in great detail the theory that separated ... public and private, virtue and necessity, mind and body—and the capacities and functions of men and women. The necessity of caring for the physical needs of bodies—raising and preparing food, building shelters, disposing of waste, making and cleaning clothes, giving birth, tending children, nursing the sick, burying the dead—were lower functions carried out in the *oikos,* the household, by slaves and women. Contemplation of what is right and good and the making of rules for the community were higher functions carried out in ... the public space ... by men. And the separation of the two, the functions of the body and the functions of the mind, was necessary to liberate the capacity for reason from the dulling effect, the distractions and confusions, of physical work and needs.

This concept of the body as a threat to the mind, and in Judeo Christian thought as a threat to purity of spirit, rooted itself deeply in Western culture and lived on into modern times. Throughout the ages, men charged with the functions of highest reason have undergone special disciplines to curb the unruly body, to keep its appetites and desires from undermining the careful operations of reason. One mark of this effort is the ritual clothing adopted by the thinking professions in past centuries and continued, at least ceremonially, today. Its main feature is some form of body-enveloping, desexualizing fullness or asceticism. Think of academics' robes, priests' robes, judges' robes, and scientists' long white coats. The standard business suit, with its straight lines and sober colors, covering a shirt buttoned to the neck and held firmly closed with a tie, performs the same function. The body of the wearer is negated or under control. The mind is free to follow the dictates of reason alone.

But the body-subduing, mind-releasing traditions of the reasoning professions do not apply to women in the same way they do to men. The problem—again, going back to Aristotle—is the ancient association of women with bodies. The social assignment of women to the realm of necessity, the physical care of bodily needs, reflected strongly held assumptions about the nature of women themselves. Women *are* their bodies. Women cannot separate mind and body to achieve the same heights of reason that men can—or that elite men can. Women are buffeted by hormones, by their menstrual cycles, by pregnancy, by menopause. They are sensual by nature, animal-like, unpredictable. . . .

[T]he insignia of sexuality still give rise to tension. Hair, for example. . . . [A] woman [attorney] . . . [reported that her] male partners asked her to warn a younger female associate about the inappropriateness of her waist-length hair. Not only was the hair itself too powerful a symbol of carnality to be contained within an ethic of rationality, but the very subject of hair was too hot for the men to handle, and the tension surrounding mind/body issues too confusing for the older woman to sort out with clarity. She ended up doing nothing and feeling guilty about it.

African–American women have particular problems desexualizing their hair because tight curly black hair has an extravagance to it that cannot be concealed unless it is clipped short, close to the head—and then it appears to be tough, defiant. One black woman who joined a big firm right out of law school says that the partner she worked for always criticized her short hair. "It signified rebellion to him. It was unfeminine. It was black, it was stark, instead of being demure and feminine, as he perceived it." And she startled clients, too. "I would walk in and I'd be the only woman, the only young person, black, with short hair. All of these older, silver-haired men. They'd look, and you could see the look of surprise and shock on their faces when I'd walk into the room." And yet long hair, in a bushy Afro, would no doubt have startled them even more. She did not stay long at the firm and eventually left the law entirely for the business side of the entertainment industry—an environment, if anything, tougher and more competitive than the law, but culturally freer.

More recently, an issue for black women in professional roles has been whether or not to wear their hair in beaded braids—a style that is neat and controlled but still bespeaks a lushness, a lavishness, an exoticism, that celebrates both blackness and female sexuality rather than underplaying them. Paulette Caldwell, professor of law at New York University, has said that it took her several years after being tenured before she felt free enough to braid her hair—and that on the way to tenure she so tortured her hair to keep it subdued that she ended up with bald spots.

I heard another hair story from a young white associate who had just received her annual review and been told that she played with her hair too much. When I met her, her hair was shoulder-length, hanging unrestrained from a side part so that it fell forward across her face as she moved her head. And as it fell, she twiddled and twisted it back, continually. She had also been told that some people thought that her clothing was too feminine, that it gave the impression to colleagues and clients who did not know her personally that she was not serious. The dress I saw was enveloping—it was high-necked, long-sleeved, and full-skirted—but the silhouette was soft and loose. Its contours did not contain the body in the straight lines that suits impose. Like her soft, slipping hair, her body's curves, draped in pliable fabric, were not under control. Therefore, the signal being sent was, body, not mind; sensual, not serious.

The issues raised by the female body in traditionally male spaces have a particular pointedness for women judges. Women engaged in any kind of lawyering must operate through the strictures of reasoned analysis, but judges are under an especially demanding charge. They are supposed to subdue in themselves any personal attitudes toward the parties before them, any biases or preferences, which is one reason that they cloak their individuality, symbolically, in voluminous robes. But again, the identity of a woman, and the suspicion that attaches to that identity, is hard to obliterate. One interviewee, a federal district court judge, muses on the issue, not reaching clear conclusions, just trying to locate what she feels is an oddity in her role:

> "I think there's a whole sexuality issue that nobody ever talks about. I think that when you become a judge—and I don't think this is true of men—that you just get neutered, and it takes a long time to even figure out that that's what's happening and then a longer time to come to terms with it. And I don't know what answer there is for it. I'm not sure there is one. You have to become a sexless figure because I think the judges who retain a strong sense of their own sexuality, at least one or two on my bench, women, are subject to a great deal of criticism, none of which, of course, is in those terms, none of it. It's about 'Oh, her hair is too'—I don't know, whatever—'and her earrings are too long, and her skirts are too tight,' but I think it is a very complex, difficult issue how you wear your sexuality when you become a judge."

But the issue of appropriate covering for the female body in court extends beyond judges, as a minor incident recalled by one interviewee suggests. A partner in a small civil rights firm, where casual dress was more the rule than in the corporate world, she got an unexpected call one morning to go to court right away. "I happened to be dressed appropriately," she recalls, "not in jeans, as I sometimes am when I expect to spend the day in the library. And I was all set to go when a young associate—male—said to me, 'Hadn't you better button your blouse?' It was out of the blue! My blouse wasn't unbuttoned unusually low. And this was not a conservative guy. But he thought one more button was necessary for court. I started wondering if my authority was being undermined by one button."

. . .

NOTES AND QUESTIONS

Women's Bodies. Harrington says, "Women *are* their bodies." What does she mean by this? In what way does this statement have a meaning that is different from what it would mean to say that men are their bodies? Can women hide their bodies? What social meanings does Harrington identify with women's bodies? Are these meanings different for the black women she discusses than for the white women?

Do you agree that women's bodies are a source of discrimination against women? If this is the case, what kinds of remedies make sense? Are these different than the remedies that you would propose if you thought that the problems were based in different treatment of women and men or that women's strengths were undervalued by the legal system and society in general?

Focusing on women's bodies and the unexpected meanings that attach to these bodies is a common postmodern move. Postmodernists see women's bodies as semiotic, or, in Mary Joe Frug's words, "constituted by a system of signs that we produce and interpret." *See* Mary Joe Frug, *A Postmodern Legal Manifesto (An Unfinished Draft)*, 105 Harv. L. Rev. 1045 (1992).

Paulette Caldwell's article, referred to in the excerpt by Harrington, is *A Hair Piece*, 1991 Duke L.J. 365 (1991).

Ezold v. Wolf, Block, Schorr and Solis–Cohen

United States Court of Appeals, Third Circuit, 1992.
983 F.2d 509.

WILLIAM D. HUTCHINSON, J.

Wolf, Block, Schorr and Solis–Cohen (Wolf) appeals from a judgment of the United States District Court for the Eastern District of Pennsylvania granting relief in favor of Nancy O'Mara Ezold (Ezold) on her claim that Wolf intentionally discriminated against her on the basis of her sex in violation of Title VII ... when it decided not to admit her to the firm's partnership effective February 1, 1989. At trial Wolf contended that it denied Ezold admission to the partnership because her skills in the category of legal analysis did not meet the firm's standards. The district court disagreed and found that this articulated reason was a pretext contrived to mask sex discrimination....

This case raises important issues that cut across the spectrum of discrimination law. It is also the first in which allegations of discrimination arising from a law firm partnership admission decision require appellate review after trial. Accordingly, we have given it our closest attention and, after an exhaustive examination of the record and analysis of the applicable law, have concluded that the district court made two related errors whose combined effect require us to reverse the judgment in favor of Ezold. The district court first impermissibly substituted its own subjective judgment for that of Wolf in determining that Ezold met the firm's partnership standards. Then, with its view improperly influenced by its own judgment of what Wolf should have done, it failed to see that the evidence could not support a finding that Wolf's decision to deny Ezold admission to the partnership was based upon a sexually discriminatory motive rather than the firm's assessment of her legal qualifications.... We will therefore reverse and remand for entry of judgment in favor of Wolf....

Ezold's performance was reviewed regularly throughout her tenure pursuant to Wolf's evaluation process, which operates as follows: The Associates Committee, consisting of ten partners representing each of the firm's departments, first reviews the performance of all the firm's associates and makes recommendations to the firm's five-member Executive Committee as to which associates should be admitted to the partnership. The Executive Committee then reviews the partnership recommendations of the Associates Committee and makes its own recommendations to the full partnership. The firm's voting partners consider only those persons whom the Executive Committee recommends for admission to the partnership....

The firm's partners are asked to submit written evaluations on standardized forms. ...Ten criteria of legal performance are listed on the forms in the following order: legal analysis, legal writing and drafting, research skills, formal speech, informal speech, judgment, creativity, negotiating and advocacy, promptness and efficiency. Ten personal characteristics are also listed: reliability, taking and managing responsibility, flexibility, growth potential, attitude, client relationship, client servicing and development, ability under pressure, ability to work independently, and dedication....

Given the number of reviewing partners, the evaluations often contain a wide range of divergent views....

The firm's partners evaluated Ezold twice a year as an associate and once a year as a senior associate from October 1983 until the Associates Committee determined that it would not recommend her for partnership in September 1988. The district court found that "[i]n the period up to and including 1988, Ms. Ezold received strongly positive evaluations from almost all of the partners for whom she had done any substantial work." ... Ezold's overall score in legal skills in ... 1988 ... was a "G" for good. It was noted that "overall" that year she received "stronger grades in intellectual skills than last time."

Evaluations in Ezold's file not mentioned by the district court show that concerns over Ezold's legal analytical ability arose early during her tenure at the firm. In an evaluation covering the period from November 1984 through April 1985, Arbittier [a partner] wrote:

> I have discussed legal issues with Nancy in connection with [two cases]. I found her analysis to be rather superficial and unfocused. I am beginning to doubt that she has sufficient legal analytical ability to make it with the firm.... She makes a good impression. with people, has common sense, and can handle routine matters well. However these traits will take you just so far in our firm. I think that due to the nature of our practice Nancy's future here is limited....

Although several partners saw improvement in Ezold's work, negative comments about her analytical ability continued up until, and through, her 1988 senior associate evaluation, the year she was considered for partnership. . . .

In 1988, ninety-one partners submitted evaluations of Ezold. Thirty-two, a little more than one-third, made recommendations with varying degrees of confidence, for Ezold's admission to partnership. Seven of those partners recommended that Ezold be made a partner "with enthusiasm," fourteen "with favor," six with "mixed emotions," four with "negative feelings," and one with "mixed emotions/negative feelings." Three of the four partners who voted for partnership with negative feelings were members of Ezold's department. After reviewing Ezold's evaluations and conducting interviews, the Associates Committee voted 9–1 not to recommend Ezold for . . . partnership.

In a discussion initiated by Davis, the Associates Committee also debated modifying the partnership standard as a matter of general policy or specially in Ezold's case because of her other positive attributes. Davis believed:

> although [Ezold] was not up to par on her legal analytical ability, . . . deficiencies in a particular area, even though it was a traditional area where we required a certain superior level, could be overlooked or relaxed to where there were sufficiently compensating skills in other areas, because I felt as chairman that in staffing a case, I could put together the right skills, and we had enough business where we could fit everybody in usefully and productively. . . .

The other Committee members ultimately rejected this suggestion. . . .

Out of a total of eight candidates in Ezold's class, five male associates and one female associate were recommended for regular partnership. One male associate, Associate X, was not recommended for . . . partnership. . . .

The 5–member Executive Committee voted unanimously not to recommend Ezold's admission as a . . . partner. . . .

Ezold claims Wolf intentionally discriminated against her because of her sex. Intentional discrimination in employment cases falls within one of two categories: "pretext" cases and "mixed-motives" cases. . . . In pretext cases, the familiar McDonnell Douglas/Burdine analysis applies. In a mixed motives case the McDonnell Douglas/Burdine analysis does not apply, and the plaintiff has the burden of showing by evidence tied to a discriminatory animus that an illegitimate factor had a "motivating" or "substantial" role . . . Ezold proceeded only under the McDonnell Douglas/Burdine framework. . . .

Therefore, before considering Wolf's contentions, we think it wise to revisit the alternating burdens of proof in a Title VII discrimination case under the now familiar process set forth in McDonnell Douglas Corp. v. Green, 411 U.S. 792 (1973) and Texas Dep't of Community Affairs v. Burdine, 450 U.S. 248 . . . Ezold relied on this particular method of circumstantial proof of discrimination at trial. The plaintiff must first establish by a preponderance of the evidence a prima facie case of discrimination.... The plaintiff can establish a prima facie case by showing that she is a member of a protected class; that she was qualified for and rejected for the position; and that non-members of the protected class were treated more favorably. After the plaintiff has established a prima facie case, the burden shifts to the defendant to produce evidence of a legitimate, nondiscriminatory reason for the employee's rejection. If the defendant's evidence creates a genuine issue of fact, the presumption of discrimination drops from the case. Then, the plaintiff, since she retains the ultimate burden of persuasion, must prove, by a preponderance of the evidence, that the defendant's proffered reasons were a pretext for discrimination.

The parties do not dispute the district court's conclusion of law that Ezold demonstrated a prima facie case ...

Wolf's articulated nondiscriminatory reason for denying Ezold's admission to the partnership was that she did not possess sufficient legal analytical skills to handle the responsibilities of partner in the firm's complex litigation practice. Ezold attempted to prove that Wolf's proffered explanation was "unworthy of credence" by showing she was at least equal to, if not more qualified than, similarly situated males promoted to partnership. She also contended that her past treatment at the firm showed Wolf's decision was based on a discriminatory motive rather than the legitimate reason of deficiency in legal analytical ability that the firm had articulated.

From this overview of the law, we turn to the specifics of the district court's analysis, its findings and the parties' contentions concerning them. The district court ... concluded:

> Ms. Ezold has established that the defendant's purported reasons for its conduct are pretextual. The defendant promoted to partnership men having evaluations substantially the same or inferior to the plaintiff's, and indeed promoted male associates who the defendant claimed had precisely the lack of analytical or writing ability upon which Wolf, Block purportedly based its decision concerning the plaintiff. The defendant is not entitled to apply its standards in a more "severe" fashion to female associates.... Such differential treatment establishes that the defendant's reasons were a pretext for discrimination....

The district court's resolution of the ultimate issue whether Wolf's reason for denying Ezold's admission to the partnership was a pretext is a finding of fact subject to the clearly erroneous standard ... We may reverse the district court on this finding of fact only if the evidence is insufficient to permit a rational factfinder to infer that Wolf's assertion that Ezold was wanting in legal analytic ability was a mask for unlawful sex discrimination....

In considering a challenge to the sufficiency of the evidence, we must determine based on our own "comprehensive review of the entire record" whether Ezold has satisfied her ultimate burden of proving intentional sex discrimination.

Wolf's articulated reason for refusing to offer Ezold a partnership was its belief, based on a subtle and subjective consensus among the partners, that she did not possess sufficient legal analytic ability to handle complex litigation. Wolf never contended that Ezold was not a good courtroom lawyer, dedicated to her practice, and good with clients. Instead, many partners felt, because of the level of her legal analytical ability, that she could not handle partnership responsibilities in the firm's complex litigation practice. Absent evidence to show that legal analytic ability was not a necessary precondition for partnership at Wolf, the district court's opinion about Ezold's comparative strengths in the other categories on the evaluation form is immaterial.

The record does not show that anyone was taken into the partnership without serious consideration of their strength in the category of legal analytic ability. The evaluations specifically asked each partner whether he or she would feel comfortable turning over to the partnership candidate "to handle on his/her own a significant matter for one of my clients." Several of the partners' responses to this question on Ezold's evaluations show clear concern about the depth of her legal analytical capabilities. This same question, reflecting a requirement that an applicant exhibit analytical abilities sufficient to meet Wolf's perception of the firm's standard, was considered throughout the firm's evaluations of the male associates with whom Ezold was competing. Ezold herself acknowledged at trial that because of the nature of Wolf's litigation practice, its litigators devote much more time to legal analysis than in-court trial work.

Wolf reserves for itself the power to decide, by consensus, whether an associate possesses sufficient analytical ability to handle complex matters independently after becoming a partner. It is Wolf's prerogative to utilize such a standard.... "[B]arring discrimination, a company has the right to make business judgments on employee status, particularly when the decision involves subjective factors deemed essential to certain positions." We stated again that "[a] plaintiff has the burden of casting doubt on an employer's articulated reasons for an employment decision. Without some evidence to cast this doubt, this Court will not interfere in an otherwise valid management decision."

The partnership evaluation process at Wolf, though formalized, is based on judgment, like most decisions in human institutions.... The differing evaluations the partners first submit to the Associates Committee are often based on hearsay or reputation. No precise theorem or specific objective criterion is employed. We have cautioned courts on several occasions to avoid unnecessary intrusion into subjective promotion decisions in the analogous context of academic tenure. While such decisions are not insulated from judicial review for unlawful discrimination, it is clear that courts must be vigilant not to intrude into that determination, and should not substitute their judgment for that of the college with respect to the qualifications of faculty members for promotion and tenure. Determinations about such matters as teaching ability, research scholarship, and professional stature are subjective, and unless they can be shown to have been used as the mechanism to obscure discrimination, they must be left for evaluation by the professionals.... These cautions against "unwarranted invasion or intrusion" into matters involving professional judgments about an employee's qualifications for promotion within a profession inform the remainder of our analysis.

In Ezold's case, the district court correctly recognized the legal premise that should have governed its result: Title VII prohibits only "discrimination." Therefore, "consideration of the practices of the [firm] toward the plaintiff must be evaluated in light of its practices toward the allegedly more favored group, in this case males."

The district court, however, failed to apply this legal premise to the evidence before it. It disagreed not only with Wolf's assessment of Ezold's ability to meet Wolf's standards, but also with Wolf's partnership standards themselves. For example, it found:

> In the magnitude of its complexity, a case may have a senior partner, a younger partner, and an associate(s) assigned to a case. Accordingly, requiring the plaintiff to have the ability to handle on her own any complex litigation within the firm before she was eligible to be a partner was a pretext.

The district court disagreed with Wolf's decision not to overlook Ezold's deficiency in legal analysis because of her other skills and attributes, but the court is not a member of Wolf's Associates Committee or Executive Committee. Its belief that Wolf's high standard of analytical ability was unwise in light of the staffing of senior partners on complex cases does not make Wolf's standard a pretext for discrimination.

The evaluations that the district court did rely upon in making its finding of pretext praised Ezold for skills other than legal analysis, such as client relations and ability in court, that Wolf never disputed she possessed. Where an employer produces evidence that the plaintiff was not promoted because of its view that the plaintiff lacked a particular qualification the employer deemed essential to the position sought, a district court should focus on the qualification the employer found lacking in determining whether non-members of the protected class were treated more favorably. Without such a limitation, district courts would be routinely called upon to act as members of an employer's promotion board or committee. It would subjectively consider and weigh all the factors the employer uses in reaching a decision on promotion and then make its own decision without the intimate knowledge of the history of the employer and its standards that the firm's decisionmakers use in judging the degree to which a candidate exhibits a particular qualification that the employer has decided is of significance or primary importance in its promotion process. Pretext is not established by virtue of the fact that an employee has received some favorable comments in some categories or has, in the past, received some good evaluations. It was not for the district court to determine that Ezold's skills in areas other than legal analysis made her sufficiently qualified for admission to the partnership. . . .

Were the factors Wolf considered in deciding which associates should be admitted to the partnership objective, as opposed to subjective, the conflicts in various partners' views about Ezold's legal analytical ability that this record shows might amount to no more than a conflict in the evidence that the district court as factfinder had full power to resolve. The principles governing valid comparisons between members of a protected minority and those fortunate enough to be part of a favored majority reveal an obvious difficulty plaintiffs must face in an unlawful discrimination case involving promotions that are dependent on an employer's balanced evaluation of various subjective criteria. This difficulty is the lack of an objective qualification or factor that a plaintiff can use as a yardstick to compare herself with similarly situated employees. . . .

Thus, Wolf also argues the district court ignored significant evidence by focusing only on the positive evaluations in Ezold's files and turning a blind eye to the many negative criticisms concerning her analytic ability. Wolf's attack in this respect is even more serious in its consequence than its attack on the court's use of comparisons between Ezold and the successful male candidates in categories other than legal analytic ability. The court's improper comparison of Ezold and the successful males in categories other than legal analytic ability would merely require a remand for appropriate comparison. If, however, Ezold is unable to show that she compared favorably in the category of legal analytic ability with at least one of the successful male candidates, she will have failed to show that Wolf did not pass her over for the legitimate reason it asserted. If she fails in that respect, she loses the benefit of the inference of unlawful discrimination that arises when the employer's legitimate articulated reason is shown not to be the real reason for the employer's discriminatory action. Absent that inference, Ezold cannot prevail on her McDonnell Douglas/Burdine theory unless she has produced direct evidence independently sufficient to show discriminatory animus . . .

Always having in mind that the issue before us is whether the firm passed over Ezold because she is a woman, we begin our specific comparative analysis . . . [I]n 1988, eight partners viewed A's admission to the partnership "with enthusiasm," one "with enthusiasm/favor," thirty-two "with favor," six "with mixed emotions," one "with negative feelings" and the rest had no opinion. Davis was the only partner in the firm to vote for A's admission to the partnership with a negative view. He gave A the same grade as Ezold, however, in the category of legal analysis. In 1988, seven partners viewed Ezold's admission "with enthusiasm," fourteen "with favor," six "with mixed emotions," four "with negative feelings" and one "with mixed emotions/negative feelings." A's analytical skills, while criticized by various partners, were never as consistently questioned as Ezold's. The criticisms of A, found among the comments of the partners evaluating Ezold and A, do not support a finding that Wolf's legitimate non-discriminatory reason for refusing a partnership position to Ezold was incredible.

In a comparison of subjective factors such as legal ability, it must be obvious or manifest that the subjective standard was unequally applied before a court can find pretext. Unequal application of the criterion of legal ability is not manifest between Ezold and Associate A on this record. It does not contain evidence sufficient to show that Ezold was held up to a higher standard than Associate A because she was a woman.

Ezold's ability in legal analysis suffers even more in the partners' eyes when compared with the individual evaluations of the other successful male candidates. All of the other males that Wolf accepted for partnership in 1988 received many scores of distinguished in the category of legal analysis, and none of them ever received a grade of marginal in this category during his final evaluation period prior to admission to the partnership....

Finally, we note that three of the four partners who expressed "negative feelings" towards Ezold's candidacy were members of her own department, while none of the eight male associates was viewed with "negative feelings" by more than one member of their department.

The district court's finding that Wolf applied its partnership standards in a more "severe" fashion to female associates is clearly erroneous. The comparative evidence of more favorable treatment for male employees contained in this record does not support that finding. Our review of the entire evaluation files of the eight male associates discloses that, unlike Ezold, whose staunchest supporters persistently expressed doubts about her ability to meet the firm's criterion of legal analysis, Associates A to H faced no comparable degree of criticism about their legal analytical skills. The snippets of comments critical of these male associates culled from dozens of evaluation forms do not show that Wolf's articulated reason for declining to recommend Ezold for partnership was "obviously weak or implausible" or that the standards were "manifestly unequally applied."

Despite Wolf's request, the district court failed to make findings concerning other male associates who, like Ezold, were passed over for partnership. The evidence concerning their evaluations adds support to our conclusion that the district court's finding that Wolf's asserted legitimate reason for denying Ezold a partnership position was a sham cannot be supported on a theory of discriminatory application.

Male Associates 1 and 2, who were comparable to Ezold in the category of legal analysis, were also rejected for regular partnership. Again, we recognize that the district court, as factfinder, "can accept some parts of a party's evidence and reject others." But when the evidence sheds light on whether the employer treated similarly situated males and females alike, it should not be ignored....

If the district court had employed the appropriate comparative analysis by focusing on whether Wolf's articulated reason of legal analysis was a pretext, it should have reached a different result. Our review of the whole record leaves us with a "definite and firm conviction that a mistake has been committed" by the district court in its comparative analysis. The record does not show that Wolf applied its partnership admission standards unequally to male and female associates, nor that diminished ability in the area of legal analysis was an improper reason for denying admission. We sympathize with Ezold's situation and the long hours and efforts she put toward her partnership goal. On the record before us, however, we cannot affirm the district court's finding that Wolf's asserted reason for denying Ezold's admission to the partnership was unworthy of credence based on her theory that its standard of legal analytic ability was applied to her in an unlawfully discriminatory manner.

Because the evaluation files contain insufficient evidence to show that Ezold was evaluated more severely than the male associates, Ezold has not shown that Wolf's proffered reason for failing to promote her was "unworthy of credence." We therefore hold that the district court's ultimate finding of pretext cannot be sustained on this basis. . . .

We have reviewed the evidence carefully and hold that it is insufficient to show pretext. Despite Ezold's disagreement with the firm's evaluations of her abilities, and her perception that she was treated unfairly, there is no evidence of sex discrimination here. The district court's finding that Wolf's legitimate non-discriminatory reason was incredible because Ezold was evaluated more severely than male associates because of her gender, as well as its finding that Wolf's requirement that she possess analytical skills sufficient to handle complex litigation was a pretext for discrimination, are clearly erroneous and find no support in the evidence. . . .

Accordingly, we will reverse the judgment of the district court in favor of Ezold and remand for entry of judgment in favor of Wolf.

NOTES AND QUESTIONS

1. **Title VII, Summarized briefly.** Title VII, 42 U.S.C. 2000e *et seq.*, prohibits an employer from making decisions in regard to hiring, discharging or terms and conditions of employment on the basis of the individual's or employee's sex (or race, color, religion or national origin.) The statute was enacted in 1964 primarily to deal with problems of employment discrimination on the basis of race. The prohibition as to discrimination on the basis of sex was added to the bill by its opponents in hopes that it would show how ridiculous the whole idea was, and torpedo its passage altogether. Fortunately, it didn't.

As the law under Title VII has developed, there are two different theories under which a case may be litigated: disparate treatment or disparate impact. Disparate impact cases derive from Griggs v. Duke Power Co., 401 U.S. 424, 91 S.Ct. 849, 28 L.Ed.2d 158 (1971), in which the Supreme Court held that facially neutral policies (like a requirement that assembly line job applicants possess a high school diploma) were illegal under Title VII if they had a significantly greater impact on members of a protected class than on others, unless the employer could show that they were justified by a "business necessity." Disparate impact cases usually involve policies that affect a large number of members of a protected class. As a result, they are often proved through statistical analysis.

Cases involving individualized claims of discrimination, such as Nancy Ezold's, usually proceed according to the disparate treatment theory. A woman who bases her Title VII suit on the disparate treatment theory argues that, because of her sex, she was treated differently than a man would have been treated in the same situation. In McDonnell Douglas Corp. v. Green, 411 U.S. 792, 93 S.Ct. 1817, 36 L.Ed.2d 668 (1973), the Supreme Court made clear that in order to prove a disparate treatment case, a plaintiff must demonstrate that the employer's discrimination was intentional. This can be done in one of three ways. First, an employee can demonstrate through direct or circumstantial evidence that something the employer did or said shows intent to discriminate. An example of this would be if the employer said to the employee, "I'm firing you because you're a woman and I can't stand having women around." Today, however, employers are rarely so open about their motives. If the employer has given some other reason as the basis for the employment decision, but the employee believes that the decision was nonetheless based on her sex, she may argue her case as one of "mixed motives" or "pretext." In a mixed motives case, the employee has the burden of showing through evidence tied to intent that an illegitimate factor, e.g. sex, was a motivating factor in the challenged decision. Mixed motive cases do not deny that there may also have been legitimate reasons for the employment decision. Mixed motive cases are very common because employees are rarely perfect.

Ezold was litigated as a pretext case, not as a mixed motive case. In a pretext case, the plaintiff asserts that the reason given by the employer for the decision was not the true reason; instead, the true reason was the employee's sex. This theory of proof is based on the assumption that if the employer offered a rationale for the decision that is not the real basis for its action, then it must be covering up intentional discrimination. Do you agree with this assumption? Pretext cases involve a complicated process of shifting and reshifting the burden of proof. Initially, the plaintiff must simply establish a prima facie case of discrimination by showing that she is a member of a protected class, was qualified for the position and rejected for it, and that others who are not members of her protected class were treated more favorably. Once she has done this, the burden of producing evidence shifts to the defendant to show that there was a legitimate, nondiscriminatory reason for the employment decision. If the defendant succeeds in doing this, then the plaintiff can meet her burden of persuasion by showing that the defendant's articulated reason was a pretext for discrimination. This last step is the most difficult since proving a prima facie case is relatively easy, and since the defendant can usually offer at least one seemingly reasonable justification for the decision.

2. **Stereotyping, Law, and the Limits of Title VII.** Various commentators have identified legal doctrines with characteristics that are stereotypically associated with men and other doctrines with characteristics that are stereotypically associated with women. For example, Kenneth Karst has argued that our conception of constitutional rights and freedoms focuses on making individuals autonomous and independent from others. In contrast, he argues, that if rights were defined with a woman's sensibility and

concern for connections to others, they might be entirely different. *See* Kenneth L. Karst, *Woman's Constitution* 1984 Duke L.J. 447. *See also* Mary Joe Frug, *Rescuing Impossibility Doctrine: A Postmodern Feminist Analysis of Contract Law*, 140 *U. Pa. L. Rev.* 120 (1992). Frances Olsen notes that men are often viewed as rational, objective, abstract and principled, while women are identified with emotionality, subjectivity, contextualization and personalization. Given this dichotomous structure, law fits on the male side since it too is supposed to be rational, objective, abstract and principled. *See* Frances Olsen, *The Sex of Law, in* David Kairys, ed., *The Politics of Law* (1990). This way of thinking about men and women, although not necessarily derived from Gilligan's work, is consistent with it.

In *Gender Trials*, Jennifer Pierce argued that women's behavior is often viewed through the lens of stereotypes. For example, women who fight hard in court and are competitive, are frequently seen as unladylike. If Olsen is correct, and law is identified with the male characteristics of rationality and objectivity, then not only are women unlikely to be seen as behaving properly when they litigate, but the mere fact that a lawyer is a woman is likely to make partners (perhaps female as well as male) skeptical about a woman's ability to analyze legal questions. This is because legal analysis involves a set of skills normally identified with men, including objectivity and rationality. Since ability to conduct legal analysis is usually an important criterion for promotion to partner, the connection between women and irrationality may help explain the disproportionately low number of women partners in large firms nationwide.

Does this analysis also help you to understand the *Ezold* case? If it is harder to imagine a woman being good at legal analysis, does that make it likely Nancy Ezold was reviewed from a different perspective than her male colleagues? The Court recognized that the decision as to whether a particular associate had analytic skills was a subjective decision. It refused to interfere with business decisions, "*particularly* when the decision involves subjective factors deemed essential to certain positions." (Italics added). Do you agree with this stance?

The District Court had held that the Wolf firm violated Title VII. Among its findings were the conclusions that Nancy Ezold had received strongly positive evaluations from all the partners for whom she had done substantial amounts of work and that Wolf would assign a senior partner and others to complex cases. This meant that there was no reason to require an associate to be able to handle the case alone prior to advancement to partner. The Third Circuit claimed that in looking to evaluations done by partners for whom Ezold had done a lot of work and in asserting that an associate need not be able to manage complex litigation single-handedly, the District Court was establishing its own standards separate from Wolf's. Given the discussion above of the connection between stereotypes of women and specific traits, do you think the trial court should review the employer's standards? Does this interfere unacceptably with the employer's ability to run its business?

For further discussion of this topic, *see* S. Elizabeth Foster, Comment, *The Glass Ceiling in the Legal Profession*, 42 UCLA L. REV. 1631 (1995).

3.   **Title VII and the Intent Requirement.** A disparate treatment case under Title VII requires a showing of intent. In pretext cases, like *Ezold*, that intent is inferred from the fact that the employer gave a false reason for the employment decision. The assumption is that the employer would have had no incentive for giving a false reason if it hadn't been discriminating intentionally. As the Court said in Duffy v. Wheeling Pittsburgh Steel Corp., 738 F.2d 1393 (3d Cir. 1984), "[A] showing that a proffered justification is pretextual is itself equivalent to a finding that the employer intentionally discriminated." But why should this be?

If the discussion in Note 2 above of the way stereotypes influence the thought process is correct, an employer's original decision might easily have been based on discriminatory premises and yet the discrimination may not have been intentional. Linda Krieger has argued we must categorize and stereotype in order to make sense of the world. Decisions based on these cognitive frameworks may involve discrimination, but not necessarily intentional discrimination. Charles Lawrence III, in a classic article, made the point that much discrimination derives from unconscious motivations. If Krieger and Lawrence are correct, does it make sense to assume that a finding of pretext necessarily indicates intentional discrimination? Wouldn't it be equally possible that the employer submitted the pretextual explanation because it was unable to analyze and understand the real reason for its decision?

This discussion of the unconscious or cognitive bases of stereotypes also raises the question of whether we should require proof of intent at all in cases under Title VII. The statute does not use the word "intent." Is the plaintiff injured in a different way if the discrimination is intentional than if it is inadvertent? Or is it that the statute is aimed only at punishing those who have acted wrongfully and intent is a necessary component of the idea of wrongfulness?

For further discussion of this topic, *see* Linda Krieger, *The Content of our Categories*, 47 Stan. L. Rev. 1161 (1995); David Oppenheimer, *Negligent Discrimination*, 141 U. Pa. L. Rev. 899 (1993); Barbara Flagg, *Fashioning a Title VII Remedy for Transparently White Subjective Decisionmaking*, 104 Yale L. J. 2009 (1995); Charles Lawrence III, *The Id, The Ego and Equal Protection*, 47 Stan. L Rev. 317 (1987).

Katherine T. Bartlett, Feminist Perspectives on the Ideological Impact of Legal Education Upon the Profession

72 N.C. L. Rev. 1259 (1994).

It is no longer appropriate to speak of "the" feminist position on a particular issue. Feminists are those who think critically about the role gender plays in existing social, political, and legal arrangements and who are committed to changes, of one sort or another, in these arrangements. Because there are different ways to criticize and to improve how gender matters in our culture, there are different feminist points of view. Feminists disagree about matters as basic as what constitutes equality. Some favor formal equality, which compels the elimination of all types of gender-based distinctions and practices, even those intended to help women. Others defend substantive equality approaches that use affirmative, sometimes gender-specific, measures to remove the disadvantages of women's biological and culturally created differences. These approaches can lead to quite different results with respect to such issues as school sports teams, accommodations to pregnancy in the workplace, and the division of marital property, but in their self-conscious orientation toward ending the effects of gender disadvantage, both approaches meet my definition of feminist.

I will discuss, then, not "the" feminist perspective on the ideological impact of legal education upon the profession, but different feminist perspectives. My focus is on two feminist perspectives that are less familiar than the equality approaches to which I just referred: (1) the "different voice" perspective and (2) the dominance, or nonsubordination, perspective....

The primary commitment of different voice theory is to identify those characteristics and values of women that are different and undervalued in this society and to promote affirmatively, or revalue, those characteristics. Unlike equality theory, which attempts to eliminate gender-based disadvantage in a world that presupposes existing values and norms, different voice theory questions existing values and norms and contends that women have priorities that are not only different from, but superior to, the "male" values currently rewarded in society. It questions, for example, the qualities of individualism and privacy upon which our economic system—which values individual effort, merit, and reward—is based. It also questions the individual rights orientation of our legal system, which leaves individuals alone to care for themselves and their families. These values, according to different voice theory, reflect male values and a male version of reality, in contrast to female priorities that favor connections, community, and responsibility for others. This theory supports the view that society as a whole would be improved if women's values were more highly prized.

Dominance, or nonsubordination, theory approaches women's differences from another direction altogether. It posits that feminists' primary concern should not be women's differences but the imbalance of power between men and women; women are harmed not because they are different from men but because they are subordinated to them. It is this subordination, rather than different treatment per se, that dominance theorists strive to eliminate.

Dominance theory's focus on women's subordination has broadened into a critique of some of the most basic principles of the liberal state. It asserts that the very principles which are supposed to guarantee objectivity, neutrality, and justice under the law in fact reflect male interests and help to maintain male dominance. The equality principle upon which feminists have sought equal rights with men is one example. Because this principle only extends to women's equal treatment to men, women are disadvantaged as to all arrangements and settings designed primarily with men in mind. Thus, even if women are given the same access to the same workplace as men, they are not identically affected by such workplace features as the "standard" forty-hour work week, tools and machines requiring employees with "male" strength and size, and workplace safety standards that treat accommodations to hazards that males face as neutral and those necessary to protect women as special.

Privacy is another principle that, in its purported neutrality (the law does not single out some individuals for more or less privacy than others) enables men to dominate women. Dominance theory emphasizes that because men have more social, economic, political, and physical power than women, protecting privacy means leaving women subject to what men do to them in private—which, according to Professor MacKinnon, is decidedly non-neutral from the point of view of women. . . .

The two perspectives I have described offer a number of insights about legal education. After describing these insights, I will attempt to explain their implications for reform. . . .

Different voice theory helps to identify a number of features of legal education that might be labeled "male," and less desirable than the female values to which they might be contrasted. First, legal education idealizes individual performance, competitiveness, and autonomy rather than group process, cooperation, and collective learning. Students are called on to perform in class; they compete with one another to excel; and their grades, made competitive by grading curves, are usually based on an individual's performance on one, single exam. Students receive few, if any, external rewards for performances in joint problem-solving exercises or for treating their adversaries with dignity and respect. Together, these aspects of legal education may reinforce what is damaging and dehumanizing in the law and in the public sphere more generally: excessive competitiveness and cutthroat individualism.

In addition to reinforcing competitiveness and individualism, legal education rewards the ability to take any side and argue any point of view. . . . By the same token, legal education does not encourage any genuine empathy for, or understanding of, either side of the case. What results is the kind of zeal that blinds rather than enlightens. Students are taught to attach themselves to their client's cause with great enthusiasm, without the kind of genuine understanding of either client or adversary that might guide the parties to resolve disputes with the least amount of damage.

Complementing the stress in legal education on competition and zealous advocacy is the emphasis on adversarial appellate cases. This emphasis serves to define the lawyering process primarily in terms of the pre-formed "case" and undervalues the complex interactions through which lawyers and clients work together to define and resolve problems. Similarly, treating cases litigated through the appellate level as the primary texts of legal education contributes to the devaluation of alternative, non-adversarial methods of dispute resolution. These alternatives have been promoted by feminists who have spoken explicitly from "a different voice," arguing that legal education has focused too much on face-to-face, adversarial combat and too little on avoiding conflict.

The emphasis on appellate cases also reinforces abstract reasoning processes over factually rich contextual ones. From the different voice perspective, more attention should be given to contextual reasoning, through which a rule's exceptions and qualifications might be discovered. This in turn would loosen up the predetermined scripts from which abstract legal principles are derived. Contextual reasoning also helps to soften the entrenched dichotomies between reason and emotion, objectivity and subjectivity, and mind and body—dichotomies that alienate law students and distort and impoverish the quality of legal thought and learning. . . .

Dominance theory provides a basis for attack on legal education that both builds on and departs sharply from the insights of different voice theory. It agrees that conventional legal reasoning methodologies are too abstract and limiting. The implications of this critique for dominance theorists, however, are not the same as those drawn by different voice theorists. According to different voice theorists, legal reasoning is improved by greater contextualization, which enhances the possibilities for compassion and innovative decisionmaking. Dominance theorists view the issue in more substantive (or "political") terms. From the dominance perspective, the problem with abstract legal decisionmaking is not the loss of opportunities for richer contextualized dispute resolution per se, but the fact that the particular, concrete abstractions produced within the current legal regime represent and maintain male dominance. These abstractions are not undesirable because they are abstractions, but because, in this current social order, they are derived from male scripts that impose male-serving standards of what is reasonable, consensual, and objective.

Dominance theory's critique of objectivity and neutrality provides another line of analysis that might be aimed at legal education. Law schools teach what they understand the law to be—rational, objective, and neutral. If this understanding is flawed or, worse, a cover for particular interests the law in fact represents, law schools themselves might be said to be complicit in the law's imposition of male dominance and female subordination.

Dominance theory also provides a basis for an attack on the organization and contents of the traditional law school curriculum. This curriculum feeds male dominance by maintaining a hierarchy between a core set of courses in business and finance—affecting mostly men—and a set of more optional, "fringe" courses such as family law, employment discrimination, and even legal ethics—in which women are more likely to be interested. Note that this is a point about power, not values. While different voice theory might be concerned about cultural norms—i.e., how a heavily business-dominated, litigation-centered curriculum reinforces competition and individualism over cooperation and group responsibility—dominance theory is concerned with how the structure of a curriculum might itself become a means by which male dominance is obscured and perpetuated. The marginalization of women in law school textbooks and in the topics covered in law school courses is, likewise, seen as a different issue for each group of theorists. Different voice theorists worry about the primacy of the dominant but inferior "male" values; dominance theorists focus on how the appearance or disappearance of women in legal texts is a means of male control and female subordination.

Dominance theory also provides some insight into the climate issues associated with legal education. Abundant evidence exists that women are disadvantaged by law school pedagogies. A questionnaire administered to law students at the University of California at Berkeley in March 1988, for example, found that men are almost twice as likely to ask questions in class, volunteer in class, and ask questions of their professors after class. These results were duplicated in studies at Stanford and Yale law schools. In the Berkeley study, women students reported lower levels of self-esteem and a steeper decline in confidence since coming to law school than that experienced by men. And although the women studied entered law school with LSAT scores and grades not significantly lower than those of men, the men examined received a significantly larger proportion of the highest grades. Finally, fifty-one percent of women students, as compared to twenty percent of male students, reported pressure to set aside their own values in order to think like a lawyer. Similar gender differences have been identified among practicing attorneys.

What explains these findings? Different voice theory emphasizes the gap between women's sharing, community-focused values and the competitive atmosphere and abstract "male" values prevalent in legal education. It provides a perspective on how legal education may alienate women by reflecting values not their own. Dominance theory moves beyond this explanation to the structural advantages these differences give to men. It underlines how the features of legal education outlined above allocate rewards based on rules that disadvantage women and reinforce male dominance.

Studies of higher education lend some support to this more conspiratorial analysis. A study commissioned by the Association of American University Women, for example, documents a host of behaviors by professors that suppress women's self-esteem and thereby weaken their performance levels. Professors make eye contact with men more often than with women, so that individual male students are more likely to feel recognized and encouraged to participate in class. Professors use tones and postures with male students that communicate interest, which are not similarly employed with female students (for example, leaning forward when men speak while adopting a patronizing tone and inattentive posture, e.g., looking at the clock, when talking to women). Professors are also more likely to call on men than women; call men by name; credit comments to male students; probe a male student's response to a question for a fuller answer requiring a higher level of critical thinking; wait longer for a man to answer before going on to another student; interrupt female students; give a longer and more complete answer to male students; and write stronger recommendation letters for male students....

Despite their divergences, each of the above perspectives offers a useful vantage point for thinking about the gender implications of legal education. Taken separately, they highlight specific aspects of legal education and suggest how legal education might support ideologies that make gender matter. Taken together, they demonstrate how difficult the problem of improving these gender implications will be. I will conclude by noting three specific difficulties in contemplating a feminist reform agenda for legal education.

The first difficulty is that changes in legal education that seek to promote "women's values" tend to reinforce women's identification with qualities, such as cooperativeness and caring for others, that have been used historically to keep women subordinate to men. This is Professor MacKinnon's complaint with different voice theory: To the extent the glorification of women's values reinforces those qualities that have historically made women different—members of the support cast rather than leaders and initiators—women risk falling deeper into the age-old trap upon which the system of male dominance depends. To avoid this trap, the revaluation of traditionally female values must proceed by breaking the link between these values and the gender of those who hold them.

The second difficulty is that special attention to women's interests, as defined under either different voice or dominance theory, tends to reinforce the idea that women are different from the (male) norm. This phenomenon, known as the "difference dilemma," is illustrated through such "special" women's activities and accommodations as women's law student organizations, attention to women in the admissions process, women's law journals, special awards for women, and representation by women on particular committees and boards. Each of these women-centered activities or practices parallels a similar phenomenon in the legal profession itself. Under strict equality-based approaches, or at least an equal treatment approach, these measures are, on balance, undesirable, in that they reinforce difference and stigmatization based on gender. If one accepts the critique that legal education is based on "male values," however—as different voice theorists would contend—or preserves male dominance—as dominance theorists would insist—one could argue that the law and law schools are already organized to accommodate men's interests. Thus, some reordering appears to be justified—not to favor women, but to neutralize the male bias and interests.

Finally, there is the problem of how law schools can best prepare students for the world they are to enter, which is still a very male world. It might be said that the more that is done in legal education either to reflect women's values better or to protect women from male dominance, the less prepared women will be for the male world of legal practice that awaits them. Pursuing this line of thought, it is bad enough that women have to face this bias and the burdens of their imagined, as well as their genuine, differences. It would be unfortunate, indeed, if in attempting to correct a systemic problem in which men and their values predominate, law schools further undermined women's capacities to compete in a male world....

If there is an answer to this difficult problem, it is unlikely that either law schools or law firms can find it on their own. Law firms cannot be expected to resocialize new attorneys whose training reinforces the kind of "male" ideologies feminist theory has identified, nor can law schools make a dent in the gendered ideologies of legal practice if the practice remains determinedly "male." ... [We need] opportunit[ies] for the kind of mutual exchange about the relation between gender and the law—as learned both in law schools and in law practice—on which the successful, and necessarily incremental, reshaping of gendered ideologies depends.

NOTES AND QUESTIONS

1. **Dominance Theory and Catharine MacKinnon.** Katharine Bartlett, in this excerpt, describes yet another perspective on the position of women in society. As she indicates, the dominance approach, developed by Catharine MacKinnon and Andrea Dworkin, focuses on power disparities between men and women. According to dominance theory, men's power in society allows them to structure society in ways that are likely to meet their needs and desires. In particular, sexual relations are organized so as to satisfy men's needs; women are sexual objects. Since women grow up in a society that views them as sexual objects, this feels "natural." It is therefore hard to see, and even hard to believe. The patterns of male dominance that MacKinnon and Dworkin initially identified in discussing rape, sexual harassment and pornography, also function in the market and other institutional structures. MacKinnon and Dworkin have elaborated on their understanding of gender relations in a series of books and articles. For those interested in reading more, good places to begin are, Catharine MacKinnon, *Feminism Unmodified* (1989) and Andrea Dworkin, *Life and Death* (1997), and the articles excerpted elsewhere in this book.

Thinking about how one theory looks through the prism of another allows us to return to the question asked and deferred following the Pierce excerpt: Are Kantor's and Gilligan's understandings of women's behavior in opposition to one another? Would MacKinnon and Dworkin see them as similar in that they use men as the yard-stick and in that neither focuses on power relations?

Bartlett's article elaborates the distinctions between dominance theory and the cultural feminist emphasis on women's different voice. Notice how much more political dominance theory is than the cultural feminist position. Do you think that it is useful to think about legal education from the perspective of dominance theory as Bartlett does? What aspects of this critique ring true to you? Are there also some points about which you are skeptical?

2. **Dominance Theory, Equality Theory, and Different Voice Theory.** At the end of the excerpt, Bartlett describes three "difficulties" for a feminist reform agenda of legal education. Notice that these difficulties arise when one uses one theory to critique the description of an issue that has been seen through the prism of another. Thus, whereas a reformist who approached legal education from the perspective of the different voice theory might favor strengthening the "women's culture" of law school by encouraging more cooperative projects and emphasis on emotion and context, a dominance theorist might caution that this just recreates for women the old trap of being identified with all the "softer" (read: weaker) values. As Bartlett's first "difficulty" notes, if we create more room for the womanly virtues, women will become more like the stereotype of women and instead of breaking free of subjugation, they will be increasingly traditional and easy to dominate. What do you think of this critique of cultural feminism? As you might imagine, it will resurface repeatedly throughout this book.

Bartlett's third "difficulty" for feminist reform of legal education relates to this first one. If we work to restructure legal education so as to adopt more of the "female" values, will we leave women (and men who participate in these activities and courses) in a position in which they are less able to succeed in the profession at large? An "equality feminist" might argue that this would be the case. By emphasizing the ways in which women are different from men and by creating a woman-friendly path through law school, we make it less likely that women will be able to compete equally with men outside of law school.

This, Bartlett notes, in her discussion of the second difficulty for reform of legal education is what is known as the "difference dilemma." Continued emphasis on women's difference, via either the difference or dominance theories, reinforces these differences and the stigma attached to difference. The "difference dilemma," was first identified by Martha Minow:

> The stigma of difference may be recreated both by ignoring and by focusing on it . . . [R]efusing to acknowledge . . . differences may make them continue to matter in a world constructed with some groups, but not others, in mind. The problems of inequality can be exacerbated both by treating members of minority groups the same as members of the majority and by treating the two groups differently. . . .

> I suggest that the dilemma of difference is not an accidental problem in this society. The dilemma of difference grows from the ways in which this society assigns individuals to categories and, on that basis, determines whom to include in and whom to exclude from political, social, and economic activities. Because the activities are designed, in turn, with only the included participants in mind, the excluded seem not to fit because of something in their own nature. . . .

Difference, after all, is a comparative term. It implies a reference: different from whom? I am no more different from you than you are from me.... But the point of comparison is often unstated. Women are compared with the unstated norm of men, "minority" races with whites.... If we identify the unstated points of comparison necessary to the idea of difference, we will then examine the relationships between people who have and people who lack the power to assign the label of difference.... Then difference will no longer seem empirically discoverable, consisting of traits inherent in the "different person." Instead, perceptions of difference can become clues to broader problems of social policy and human responsibility.

Martha Minow, *Making All The Difference* 20–23 (1990)

Minow's discussion of the difference dilemma recognizes the problems inherent in focusing on difference, but it also emphasizes the socially constructed nature of differences. What we see as differences are always differences in relation to a norm that society has decreed to be the norm. This society, with this norm, is constructed. If we begin to ask for whom and why, then we return to the types of problems with which MacKinnon, Dworkin and dominance theory are concerned.

Lani Guinier, et al., Becoming Gentlemen: Women's Experiences at One Ivy League Law School

143 U. Pa. L. Rev. 1 (1994).

... In this Article we describe preliminary research by and about women law students at the University of Pennsylvania Law School—a typical, if elite, law school.... Our database draws from students enrolled at the Law School between 1987 and 1992, and includes academic performance data from 981 students, self-reported survey data from 366 students, written narratives from 104 students, and group-level interview data of approximately eighty female and male students. From these data we conclude that the law school experience of women in the aggregate differs markedly from that of their male peers....

Although men and women enter with virtually equal statistics, men receive, on average, significantly better grades by the end of year one. Further, they maintain this advantage through graduation. ...In terms of rank and GPA, first and second-year men are 1.6 times more likely to be in the top fiftieth percentile of the class than are women. Third-year men are 1.5 times more likely to be in the top fiftieth percentile.

If we rely upon an even more stringent measure—the top 10% of the class—we find that in the first year men are almost three times more likely than women to reach the top 10%; in the second and third years, men are two times more likely to do so.

As a consequence of these disproportionately low class ranks, women law students are underrepresented in the Law School's prestigious positions and extracurricular activities. Over the three years of our study—from 1990 to 1992—women were underrepresented in the Order of the Coif, the graduation awards given by the faculty, the Law Review membership and board, and the moot court competitions and board. . . .

The 1990 . . . Survey tracks the academic performance differential between male and female law students to reveal attitudinal and experiential differences by gender. Female law students are significantly more likely than male law students to report that they "never" or "only occasionally" ask questions or volunteer answers in class. Women, more than men, report that men ask more questions, volunteer more often, enjoy greater peer tolerance of their remarks, receive more attention from faculty during classes, get called on more frequently, and receive more post-class "follow up" than women. . . .

Across years, male students appear to be far more comfortable speaking with faculty of either gender than female students. When asked, "How comfortable are you in interactions occurring outside of class with professors of the same or opposite sex?" 60% of the men, compared to 40% of the women, reported that they felt "very comfortable." Men, in group interviews, confirmed their substantially greater degree of comfort with faculty. In contrast, many women indicated their inability either to approach faculty or, once engaged in conversation, to sustain a useful interaction. Several women in follow-up interviews expressed frustration at what they perceived to be aloofness on the part of the faculty.

The rates of participation reported by women as first-year students and as third-year students differ only to the extent that they reflect a transition from women never asking questions to asking questions infrequently. Women's level of satisfaction with this relatively stable rate of nonparticipation, however, increased over time. To the question, "Are you comfortable with your level of voluntary participation in class?" we see dramatic gender differences for year one (28% of the women responded "yes" versus 68% of the men). By year three, however, 64% of the women respond that they are now comfortable with their essentially unchanged level of participation, as do 72% of the men.

In sum, women and men report significantly different assessments of their own classroom performance and perceptions of gender bias in the classroom. Also interesting, however, are the highly significant differences between the responses of the first-year women and all other categories of students. First-year female students, more than all other groups, report that men are called on more often than women and receive more time and more follow-up in class, that the sex of students affects class experience, and that sexist comments are permitted under the informal "house rules" of the Law School. The concerns expressed by first-year women with male dominance in the classroom and failure to use gender-neutral language, as well as their perception that sexist comments are permitted, are not identified as problems by third-year female respondents. After three years at the Law School, either women seem to tolerate displays of what they, as first-year students, interpreted as offensive incidents of sexism, or, in fact, the frequency of such incidents diminishes. . . .

. . . [A]lmost all the women we interviewed described their first-year experience as a radical, painful, or repressive experience, one that they will never forget (or remember). Several women reported their voices were "stolen" from them in the first year. Some of these women who felt alienated did very well academically, yet they did not recognize their former selves, which they perceived as submerged in the pursuit of succeeding as a "social male." One woman who articulated this dynamic felt silenced by what she termed "a group of frat boys who call you a man-hating lesbian, or feminist—as though those are bad—if you are too outspoken." Other women reported suffering from hissing, public humiliation, and gossip, simply for speaking aloud in class. They expressed profound alienation from the Law School, the educational process, and, most disturbing, themselves, or who they used to be. . . .

Other women seek support from each other. Several women described a pact they had made during their first year to follow up on the comments of any woman who spoke in order to minimize their experience of isolation. For them, supporting other women became a crucial precondition to the learning process, indicating how far they had to go even to begin to learn in this environment. This informal attempt at support and solidarity may have helped to combat some of the alienation that these women felt, but it was a temporary solution that addressed a symptom and not the cause of their alienation.

Furthermore, we are inclined to see this "gendered effect" as implicating the institutional design of the law school experience, rather than personal qualities of individual female or male students. The pedagogical structure of the first year large classes, often constrained by limits on student participation, fierce competition, a mandatory grading curve, and few women faculty, produces alienation and a gender-stratified hierarchy. . . .

Several women who described Socratic-style questioning as intimidating stated matter-of-factly that they could not learn in an intimidating environment. One admitted that she even had a principle of law named after her, which she was called upon weekly to restate. In the large classroom atmosphere, she would repeat the principle by rote without ever truly comprehending its significance. Two years later, she reported that at the time she did not understand the principle, nor could she now explain to her listeners what it meant. A few men also reported discomfort with the Socratic style, although they seemed less permanently disabled by it.

With remarkable consistency, students indicate that law school taught them to be "less emotional," "more objective," and to "put away . . . passions." For some, this ability to suppress feelings [is] considered an enormous accomplishment; for others, it is considered a defeat. Second only to the skills of "objectivity," students report that over time they have learned to stop caring about others and have become more conservative. Some men indicate they have grown more aggressive and abrasive over their three years in law school; some women see themselves as more "humble" and "nitpicking." One woman concluded her interview by saying, "Here [at the Law School], it's okay to be intolerant." . . .

Many men attempt to "explain away" the gender and institutional aspects of the data. These men, who include students and faculty, often resort to alternative explanations, all of which identify a source unrelated to the Law School for the differences we found. For example, they proffered age, undergraduate major, and even participation in varsity sports in college as possible explanations for the differential between women's and men's performances as measured by grades in law school. We found no statistically significant difference between women and men in these categories. Women and men at Penn Law School are roughly the same age and have majored in similar fields as undergraduates. The point, however, is not whether these alternative explanations are worth pursuing. The point is that many men immediately gravitate toward hypotheses that locate the problem outside of gender and outside of the Law School. . . .

From our data, we conclude that the University of Pennsylvania Law School is a hostile learning environment for a disproportionate number of its female students. Our data document that the women at this law school graduate with weaker academic credentials than do the men. The disparate quality of their accumulated credentials interacts with higher levels of alienation and lower self-esteem for many women, even those who do well academically. . . .

[W]e propose three hypotheses to link and possibly explain our findings. In our view, each of these claims deserves further study as part of a serious reevaluation of the formal and informal organization of law school education. . . .

"Becoming gentlemen" appears to exact an academic cost for many women. Women's enfeebled participation within the formal structure of legal education occurs simultaneously with their less successful performance on the anonymously-graded examinations from which law school grades are derived. In other words, low levels of class participation in the formal, structured pedagogy correlate with weak performance on the formal, structured evaluation system. . . .

Many students, especially many women, have simply not been socialized to thrive in the type of ritualized combat that comprises much of the legal educational method. The theory of legal education assumes that learning is induced by self-teaching and that a certain level of stress or anxiety is a necessary precondition to initiate the learning process. But many women claim that neither their initiative nor their problem-solving ability is engaged in an intimidating learning environment. The performance aspect of a large Socratic classroom disables some women from performing up to their potential. Socratic teaching, if designed to intimidate, adds more women to this category. If no comparably significant formal learning experiences, other than large classroom Socratic teaching, are provided, first-year women in particular are most likely to be affected. These phenomena also adversely affect some men. Indeed, elite law schools, such as the University of Pennsylvania, may prepare their top male students "to become law professors but fail to prepare the rest of their students to become practicing lawyers."

From the reactions of their professors and the responses to their performance in all areas of the institution, some female students learn that they cannot thrive within the law school environment. For example, the perception is widespread that within the classroom, white men, more than women of all colors, are encouraged and allowed to speak more often, for longer periods of time, and with greater positive feedback from the professor and peers. When women fail to receive the same level of positive response from faculty, many experience a blow to their self-esteem. Our data suggest that some women internalize the absence of positive feedback, even when the professor's aloofness reaches across gender lines. As a result, some women come to believe that they have nothing worthwhile to contribute, becoming further alienated from the Law School and the process of legal education. Often, these women refuse to engage in discussion and opt for a strong stance of silence. In other words, some women are disengaged from law school because they find its adversarial nature, its focus on argumentation, and its emphasis on abstract as opposed to contextual reasoning to be unappealing and disengaging.

It is important to recognize that peer relations reinforce women's silence via "hazing" imposed on women by white males. Students describe hazing as taking the form of "laughing at what I said" or "lesbian-baiting." Apparently, merely being called a "feminist" is sometimes considered sufficiently insulting to silence women who try to challenge prevailing interpretations of legal texts. . . .

For those whose reaction is not to "fight back," their first contact with the law school environment is one of failure. If they have accepted the norms of the institution, these students come to believe that their place within the hierarchy should be toward the bottom. We believe that this element of socialization to one's "place" in the hierarchy helps to ensure the success of male students at the expense of women. The student culture itself reinforces the low status of many women who fear they cannot measure up because they are just not as good at "playing the game" as their male peers. For these women, the moment they speak out to challenge what they perceive as sexist assumptions or offensive language, they diminish the level at which they are taken seriously. To retain status they must feign indifference and, as one woman reported, feel complimented when rewarded by male peers for being "such a guy." In other words, women cannot discuss issues of concern to "women" without feeling stigmatized and diminished. . . .

Second, we posit that in addition to feeling alienated from the manifest structure of the educational environment, many women are, in fact, excluded from the latent learning structure. Whereas our first hypothesis is that alienation, class participation, and academic performance are interrelated variables within the formal learning environment, our second hypothesis looks at the way women function within the Law School's informal learning structure.

We argue that at least some of the learning in law school takes place outside the classroom.... [O]ur data suggest that women law students are less comfortable, in the aggregate, than men within the Law School's informal structure. Female students are less likely than their male peers to interact with faculty outside of class. Whereas male students report that they are comfortable approaching faculty of either gender, female students apparently require friendliness "cues" before they seek out faculty after class. In addition, many female students believe male professors favor male students. These women also complain that the hazing by their male peers both inside and outside of class forces them to retreat to all-women support groups or to form pacts with other women in order to support women participants in class....

Similarly, we found that the predominantly male faculty bestows a disproportionate number of graduation awards upon male students. This may reflect the first-year academic performance differential that is sustained over the next two years in law school. Alternatively, it may reflect the fact that women also suffer when subjective criteria, such as "best student in X" or "most promising student in Y," govern. Or, it may reflect the fact that male professors are more likely to mentor male students....

The informal barriers we describe may be so "imbedded in our ways of interacting with each other as men and women" that they are invisible to many students and faculty. They may reflect the unconscious imposition of male norms on ways of learning or mentoring that have a gender-based effect. Alternatively, these women may simply be excluded from informal settings in which people who are perceived to be different are invisible or made to feel unwelcome....

Our claim is that the proportional scarcity of "elite women" sets up a dynamic of virtual tokenism, in which the more numerically significant women students are nevertheless treated as, or self-identify as, "tokens." This dynamic exists in both the manifest and latent structure of the Law School, as well as in both the actual treatment of female students and their perception of their treatment by male students and faculty. As with true tokens, the dynamic of virtual tokenism reinforces limitations on the opportunity for success of women law students. Also similar to true tokens, many female students at the Law School enter the institution with identical credentials and then differentiate significantly from their male peers in terms of academic achievement, voluntary class participation, and interaction with faculty. Moreover, even if they are treated no differently than male students, many female students experience the institutional norms in a way that adversely affects their performance. Some women may simply need more encouragement to do well or to approach faculty in a male-dominated school where "merit" is arguably still measured by attributes associated with maleness. Or, these women may need mentors more than men to counterbalance the impersonality of the large Socratic classroom....

This is not an argument for more women role models. We argue that women students need faculty and student mentors, meaning teachers, guides, or more accomplished peers who share their knowledge or experience within the context of an interpersonal relationship. We posit, based on our data, that a disproportionately male faculty and student body—for whatever reason—fail to function in informal settings with female students to the same degree as with male students. . . .

There is also a third hypothesis that others have urged us to consider. The third explanation of women's different law school experience is that women are simply different. There is a tension in the difference hypothesis. On the one hand, women entering law school are different from men in many ways, including their initial interest in public interest law, their expressions of alienation from and nonparticipation in the formal educational pedagogy, and their self-reported needs for more friendliness cues for informal faculty interaction. On the other hand, it is important to remember that, using standard predictors of academic success, women entering law school are fundamentally the same as men entering law school (as a group). We interpret this tension to mean that "difference" as a disadvantage is created at law school over time.

According to the difference hypothesis, women's difference makes them less equipped for law school. The way things are done in law school (the Socratic method, issue-spotting exams, large classrooms, unpatrolled and informal networks) devalues and distorts those characteristics traditionally associated with women such as empathy, relational logic, and nonaggressive behavior. In this understanding, law school unintentionally uses a male-oriented baseline to measure male/female differences.

Although aspects of the third explanation permeate the other two hypotheses, this third explanation invariably conceals a troublesome assumption—that it is women, not law school, who must change. Because of this assumption, the third explanation invites the response that, despite identical entry level credentials, the wrong women are being admitted to law school. In other words, many women simply should not be trained as lawyers.

Despite the predictable response, we do not take a position in this paper on the immutable gender differences theory. In our view, it does not matter why women function "differently" in law school. Our research is limited to identifying the experience of hierarchy and of exclusion masked as difference, and to theorizing about ways that legal education creates or enhances "difference" and converts it into a disadvantage. Even if important pre-institutional gender differences exist, the source of those differences is not the point. Even if we assume that women who enter law school are actually less prepared to be good lawyers—a difference hard to imagine given identical entry credentials—the institution's pedagogy, hierarchy, and male-dominated faculty exacerbate that difference.

Most of this paper is about a group of women at the Law School who cannot or do not want to "become gentlemen." It is important to recognize, however, that even within this group of females, "women" is not a monolithic category. We have sought to identify the fact that some women who are alienated nevertheless do well academically; these women successfully function in the hierarchy and norms of the Law School. Accordingly, we identify two distinct "groups" of women. The first group of women fails academically as well as personally. The second group of women succeeds academically. These are women who do "become gentlemen." Within this category of successful women, there is also a subset who do well but feel alienated. This subset of women resents the sacrifices of self that law school requires them to make. These women perceive that law school is a "game." These women learn the rules in order to play the game, but they are acutely aware of the price they are paying. These women are those who have been described in some of our secondary literature as "bicultural" or "bilingual." They can act both as "women" and as "gentlemen" and they are acutely aware of the difference. . . .

From the three tentative conclusions drawn from our data, we derive two related propositions. First, the institution's examination and educational structure has a disparate psychological and academic impact on an identifiable class of its graduates. . . . Second, analogous to the principles behind disparate impact employment discrimination cases and consistent with the institution's professional and pedagogic responsibilities, the institution should seriously reexamine its teaching and examination methodology. . . .

We believe that our research raises the second-generation diversity issue. If the first generation of women was challenged to demonstrate the need for access into existing, previously all-male institutions, the current (second) generation is challenged to demonstrate that mere access, especially in comparatively low status positions, is inadequate. As now designed, law school fails to equalize the experience and outcomes for all law students across gender. . . .

NOTES AND QUESTIONS

1. **Silence and Women Law Students.** Lani Guinier's study reconfirms what feminists have long known: female law students participate less frequently in law school classes than their male peers. This raises the question of why? One might answer this question from an equality perspective, a cultural feminist perspective, or a dominance perspective. Can you articulate each of these answers? Which perspective does Guinier adopt? What do you see as the strengths of each answer? The weaknesses? Given the information in this reading and the previous one by Katharine Bartlett, do you think legal education should be altered, and if so how? What is the theoretical perspective from which you are working?

2. **Gentlemen Law Students and Race.** In an earlier article, Guinier explained her emphasis on the term "gentlemen." In 1974, as a law student, she, a Black woman, had a white male professor who addressed the entire class, men and women, as "gentlemen."

Every morning, at ten minutes after the hour, he would enter the classroom and greet the upturned faces "Good morning *gentlemen*." He explained this ritual the first day. He had been teaching for many years; he was a creature of habit. He readily acknowledged the presence of the few "ladies" by then in attendance, but admonished those of us born into that other gender not to feel excluded by his greeting. We, too, in his mind, were simply *gentlemen*. . . . It took many intervening years for me to gain the confidence to question directly this term that symbolically stripped me of my race, my gender and my voice.

Guinier notes in a footnote that in law school she resisted becoming a "gentleman" through her silence. Lani Guinier, *Of Gentlemen and Role Models*, 6 Berkeley Women's L. J. 93 (1990).

In the article excerpted in this book, Guinier identifies large classes which limit student participation and generate fierce competition among students, and legal analysis's objective, dispassionate style, as alienating for women. This draws on cultural feminist images of women as non-competitive, interactive, and emotional. Is this image of women equally applicable to all women, or is it an image of the white, bourgeois woman? What images do we have of African American women, Latina women, or Asian women? What about poor women? How does race affect these? What about older women? Lesbian women? Guinier is an African American woman. Do you think the effect of being called a gentleman would be the same or different for her as for a white woman?

B. FEMINIST LEGAL THEORY I

INTRODUCTION

The materials in the preceding section introduced four separate stances toward the relationship between women and law. Cultural feminism, exemplified in that section by the discussion of the work of Carol Gilligan, is an approach that seeks to improve the position of women in the profession through legal and social strategies which validate women's differences from men. Liberal (or equality) feminism, is characterized by the belief that providing women legal rights against discrimination represents the extent to which undesirable social and economic conditions affecting women can be eliminated by legal change. This stance implicitly underlies employment discrimination legislation. Both Rosabeth Moss Kanter's work and the Massachusetts Gender Bias Study frequently articulate a liberal feminist position.

A significant difference between these perspectives is that liberal feminists tend not to take a position on whether there are intractable or desirable differences between women and men. Instead, they concentrate their efforts in challenging the oppression of women on securing legal change. In contrast, cultural feminists seek to validate sex differences; they are less firmly committed to the public/private distinction in their efforts to transform the condition of women. The public/private distinction refers to the contested notion that there is a sharp separation between private and public life. The role of law, according to this view, is to regulate public life in socially desirable and just ways, and to protect and patrol private life against public invasion (no police surveillance of the bedroom; no unwanted aggressions against one's property or person; etc.) Although feminists of other stripes vigorously contest the limited role of law associated with the public/private distinction, liberal feminists are characterized by their support of this concept.

In addition to the liberal and cultural feminist positions represented by Kanter, Gilligan, and the Massachusetts Gender Bias Commission, the previous section introduced Catharine MacKinnon and Andrea Dworkin's dominance theory, and, through Mona Harrington's work, postmodernism. MacKinnon is not interested in the debates as to sameness or difference. Rather, she and Dworkin focus on the mechanisms through which women are subordinated to men. The public/private distinction is one of these. Postmodernists, too, focus on subordination, but primarily on the role that discourse and signs (systems of communication) play in creating dominance. The law is just such a system of communication.

The readings in this section are meant to continue this discussion of different feminist stances toward the relationship between women and the law. The readings revolve around two separate issues. The first is the sameness/difference debate; the second is whether women share some essential characteristic or experience. Sameness feminists (a.k.a. liberal feminists) focus on a definition of equality that emphasizes the ways in which men and women are, or can be, similar. Difference feminists, like cultural feminists, emphasize the differences between men and women, sometimes celebrating these differences. Difference feminists are legal feminists. Therefore, unlike cultural feminists in general, they focus more on legal problems than on broad social or psychological questions.

We have used the case of Equal Employment Opportunity Commission v. Sears, Roebuck & Company as a means of focusing the discussion about different legal approaches to women's problems. The Equal Employment Opportunity Commission sued Sears for sex discrimination in the hiring of commission sales people. In its defense, Sears claimed that fewer women held commission sales positions than other sales positions because women were not interested in the commission sales positions, despite the fact that they were more lucrative. On its behalf, Sears called Rosalind Rosenberg, a feminist historian, who testified that the demands of commission selling made it unattractive to women. For this reason, she stated that women did not apply for the jobs in as large numbers as men. The E.E.O.C. called Alice Kessler–Harris, another feminist historian, as its expert witness. She testified that women can take on men's jobs and that some have done so successfully in the past.

The readings in this section start with the *Sears* case, and are followed by comments on it and on the sameness and difference approaches by four feminists: Joan Williams, Joan Scott, Mary Joe Frug, and Catharine Mac-

Kinnon. It is our hope that after reading these materials, you will have some thoughts about whether sameness or difference approaches are useful, at least in employment discrimination settings. Similarly, we hope you will give some thought to how dominance theory and postmodernism might be applied.

One of the characteristics of postmodern feminism is its claim that women do not share a common identity. This position conflicts with the claims of cultural and liberal feminists, who charge that by exposing differences among and within women postmodernists threaten the political coalition women need to obtain changes in their lives. It also conflicts with dominance feminists, who begin their analysis from the proposition that all women are oppressed by men on account of their sex. We have included in this section excerpts from an article by Angela Harris in which she criticizes MacKinnon and other feminists for taking an essentialist position on women's experience—that is, for claiming that there is an essence or core to what it means to be a woman that is the same for all women. The question of whether all women share something, even their oppression as women, is an essential inquiry when thinking about the condition of women.

Despite the focus in this section on distinctions among feminist theories, it would be a mistake to discuss the multiple meanings of feminism as if there were rigid distinctions in the approaches. Feminist scholars are as uncomfortable with orthodoxy as most people, and their common commitment to the advancement of women has encouraged them to suppress rather than to emphasize the differences among their perspectives. Nevertheless, we hope these readings will enable you to consider how different forms of feminism might yield different kinds of solutions to some of the unsatisfactory conditions women currently experience.

Equal Employment Opportunity Commission v. Sears, Roebuck & Company

United States Court of Appeals, Seventh Circuit, 1988.
839 F.2d 302.

HARLINGTON WOOD, JR., CIRCUIT JUDGE.

These appeals are the outgrowth of protracted litigation stemming from an EEOC commissioner's charge filed against Sears, Roebuck & Company (Sears) . . . alleging several claims of nationwide discrimination against women (and minorities, but those claims were later withdrawn) in employment practices. . . .

II. DISPARATE TREATMENT—HIRING AND PROMOTIONS

The EEOC argues that the district court erred in determining that it did not show a pattern or practice of discrimination by Sears against women in hiring and promotions into commission sales positions. . . .

The nature of the evidence presented by each party in this case was significantly different.... Sears did not respond with like regression analyses based on employment application and payroll records. Instead, most of Sears' evidence was directed at undermining two assumptions Sears claimed were faulty and fatal to the validity of the EEOC's statistical analysis—the assumptions of equal interests and qualifications of applicants for commission sales positions....

Hiring

The district judge found a plethora of problems in the statistical analyses that the EEOC had offered to support the claim that Sears discriminated against women in hiring into commission sales positions from 1973 to 1980. Before addressing the EEOC's specific challenges to the district court's criticisms of its statistical evidence, it is helpful to discuss three key findings made by the district court, which we believe are not clearly erroneous. Those findings are that during the period at issue in this case (1973–1980): (1) commission selling was significantly different from noncommission selling at Sears; (2) women were not as interested in commission selling as were men; and (3) women were not as qualified for commission selling as were men.

The finding that colors the district court's entire treatment of the EEOC's hiring as well as its promotion claims is that selling on commission at Sears is a very different job from "regular," or noncommission selling at Sears. We cannot say that finding is clearly erroneous. The court's description of commission and noncommission selling at Sears indicates that the two forms of selling differed in the type of merchandise sold, the risk involved, which was reflected in the manner of compensation, and the technical knowledge, expertise, and motivation involved. The district court describes the differences at length, thus we need only mention major differences. As the district court found, commission selling at Sears usually involved selling "big ticket" items, which are high-cost merchandise such as major appliances, furnaces, roofing, and sewing machines. Merchandise sold on a noncommission basis understandably was generally low-cost and included apparel, paint, and cosmetics. Commission selling involved some risk, especially before 1977. During that period commission salespersons generally received a commission ranging from 6% to 9% percent plus a "draw" each week. The draw usually did not exceed 70% of average or estimated earnings, but was subject to reduction if the employee's commission did not equal the amount of the draw. There was always a risk that the employee could lose some of the draw if the commissions did not equal the amount of the draw. After 1977, commission salespersons no longer faced deficits. In what the court noted was an effort "to reduce the financial risk of selling on commission in an effort to attract more women to commission sales," Sears paid commission salespersons a nominal salary plus a 3% commission. Noncommission salespersons were paid on a straight hourly rate, and full-time salespersons received 1% commission on all sales until January 1979 when the practice was discontinued. The district court found that commission selling often required salespersons to be available after the normal working hours of 8:00 a.m. to 5:00 p.m., sometimes required that they sell in people's homes, might require a license depending on the products sold, and required qualities usually not as necessary in regular selling, including a high degree of technical knowledge, expertise, and motivation. . . .

Regarding the question of differing interests in general among men and women in commission selling, we have already briefly reviewed the types of evidence presented by Sears to the district court on this issue. We need only highlight some significant findings of the court in support of our determination that the court's finding was not clearly erroneous. The court found that "[t]he most credible and convincing evidence offered at trial regarding women's interest in commission sales at Sears was the detailed, uncontradicted testimony of numerous men and women who were Sears store managers, personnel managers and other officials, regarding their efforts to recruit women into commission sales." These witnesses testified to their only limited success in affirmative action efforts to persuade women to sell on commission, and testified that women were generally more interested in product lines like clothing, jewelry, and cosmetics that were usually sold on a noncommission basis, than they were in product lines involving commission selling like automotives, roofing, and furnaces. The contrary applied to men. Women were also less interested in outside sales which often required night calls on customers than were men, with the exception of selling custom draperies.

Various reasons for women's lack of interest in commission selling included a fear or dislike of what they perceived as cut-throat competition, and increased pressure and risk associated with commission sales. Noncommission selling, on the other hand, was associated with more social contact and friendship, less pressure and less risk. This evidence was confirmed by a study of national surveys and polls from the mid–1930's through 1983 regarding the changing status of women in American society, from which a Sears' expert made conclusions regarding women's interest in commission selling; morale surveys of Sears employees, which the court found "demonstrate[ ] that noncommission saleswomen were generally happier with their present jobs at Sears, and were much less likely than their male counterparts to be interested in other positions, such as commission sales;" a job interest survey taken at Sears in 1976; a survey taken in 1982 of commission and noncommission salespeople at Sears regarding their attitudes, interests, and the personal beliefs and lifestyles of the employees, which the court concluded showed that noncommission salesmen were "far more interested" in commission sales than were noncommission saleswomen, and national labor force data. . . .

If it is argued that there was no interest in commission selling only because there were no opportunities, which disputes Sears' argument that there was instead an actual lack of interest in the existing opportunities, we are faced with the problem of which comes first, interest or opportunity, a chicken-egg problem. This is again an area where EEOC might have called a representative group of disappointed witnesses who preferred commission selling, but were rebuffed. It did not.

In short, we hold that the district court did not clearly err in finding that women were not as interested in commission sales positions as were men....

RICHARD CUDAHY, CIRCUIT JUDGE, concurring in part and dissenting in part:

It is extremely difficult to distinguish superficial blemishes from structural defects in this oversized and confusing case. Although its efforts are impressive and, in many respects, commendable, the majority has been only partially successful. Its opinion properly identifies some important shortcomings in the EEOC's case; but it overstates the significance of others and seems to overlook entirely certain equally serious flaws in Sears' argument. Thus, it is true that the ... EEOC as much as gave the case away by failing to produce any flesh and blood victims of discrimination. Regression statistics by themselves only demonstrate correlations between variables; to move from correlation to causation, there must be some independent theory about the causal relationships of the variables. In this case, much of the dispute centers on whether crucial independent variables have been omitted or misspecified. Therefore, the parties' causal theories, substantiated most convincingly through first-hand accounts, take on particular importance. Hence, the EEOC's failure to present first-hand evidence makes Sears' lopsided victory far easier to understand. I would reiterate, however, that key elements in Sears' case have escaped critical examination.

Perhaps the most questionable aspect of the majority opinion is its acceptance of women's alleged low interest and qualifications for commission selling as a complete explanation for the huge statistical disparities favoring men. The adoption by the district court and by the majority of Sears' analysis of these arguments strikes me as extremely uncritical. Sears has indeed presented varied evidence that these gender-based differences exist, both in our society as a whole and in its particular labor pool. But it remains a virtually insuperable task to overcome the weight of the statistical evidence marshalled by the EEOC or the skepticism that courts ought to show toward defenses to Title VII actions that rely on unquantifiable traits ascribed to protected groups.

I start with the expectation that commission salespeople generally see themselves as the elite of the sales force. They make more money than noncommission sales people and obtain their positions through a more selective hiring process. As a consequence, they enjoy greater prestige. They are people with confidence in their ability to captivate customers and move merchandise. I would expect them to look with condescension, if not contempt, upon retail clerks working as order-takers for a straight wage. I do not therefore quarrel with the majority's proposition that retail order-taking is a "different" task from commission selling. But I would expect that the jobs are most often seen in a vertical alignment with commission selling on top. Whether or not the perspective that gives rise to this hierarchical ranking is commendable, it is certainly pervasive. I think my view differs from that of the majority, who seem to believe that the tasks are perceived as coequally and, not as occupying distinct tiers in a vertical pecking order.

These perspectives are important because the majority's more benign view tends to minimize the significance of Sears' contentions that women lack the interest and qualifications to sell on commission. Women, as described by Sears, the district court and the majority, exhibit the very same stereotypical qualities for which they have been assigned low-status positions throughout history. The majority states that

> [the] reasons for women's lack of interest in commission selling included a fear or dislike of what they perceived as cut-throat competition, increased pressure and risk associated with commission sales. Noncommission selling, on the other hand, was associated with more social contact and friendship, less pressure and less risk.

The district court found

> that noncommission saleswomen were generally happier with their present jobs at Sears, and were much less likely than their male counterparts to be interested in other positions, such as commission sales. . . .

These conclusions, it seems to me, are of a piece with the proposition that women are by nature happier cooking, doing the laundry and chauffeuring the children to softball games than arguing appeals or selling stocks. The stereotype of women as less greedy and daring than men is one that the sex discrimination laws were intended to address. It is disturbing that this sort of thinking is accepted so uncritically by the district court and by the majority. Perhaps they have forgotten that women have been hugely successful in such fields as residential real estate, door-to-door sales and other direct outside merchandising. There are abundant indications that women lack neither the desire to compete strenuously for financial gain nor the capacity to take risks.

Sears, the district court and the majority hang much of their refutation of the EEOC's hiring and promotion claims on the putative difference between men's and women's interest in undertaking commission sales. Huge statistical disparities in participation in various commission selling jobs are ascribed to differences in "interest." Yet there is scarcely any recognition of the employer's role in shaping the "interests" of applicants. Even the majority is willing to concede that lack of opportunity may drive lack of interest, but dismisses the matter as a "chicken-egg" problem. I concede that the government's case would be stronger if it had produced even a handful of women willing to testify that Sears had frustrated their childhood dreams of becoming commission sellers of roofing, sewing machines or air conditioners. However, even absent flesh and blood victims, I find the willingness of the district court and the majority to accept the interest defense uncritically, and without recognition of its close parallel to

the stereotypes that Title VII seeks to eradicate, perplexing and unacceptable. . . .

Joan C. Williams, Deconstructing Gender

87 Mich. L. Rev. 797 (1989).

... I start out, as have many others, from the deep split among
American feminists between "sameness" and "difference." The driving
force behind the mid-twentieth-century resurgence of American feminism
was an insistence on the fundamental similarity of men and women and,
hence, their essential equality. . . .

Mid-century feminism, now often referred to somewhat derisively as
assimilationism, focused on providing opportunities to women in realms
traditionally preserved for men. In the 1980s two phenomena have shifted
feminists' attention from assimilationists' focus on how individual women
are *like* men to a focus on gender *differences*, on how women as a group
differ from men as a group. The first is the feminization of poverty. . . . The
second phenomenon that plays a central role in the current feminist
imagination is that of career women "choosing" to abandon or subordinate
their careers so they can spend time with their small children. These
phenomena highlight the fact that deep-seated social differences continue
to encourage men and women to make quite different choices with respect
to work and family. Thus, "sameness" scholars are increasingly confronted
by the existence of gender differences.

Do these challenges to assimilationism prove that we should stop
trying to kid ourselves and admit the "real" differences between men and
women, as the popular press drums into us day after day, and as the
"feminism of difference" appears to confirm? Do such phenomena mean
that feminists' traditional focus on gender-neutrality is a bankrupt ideal? I
will argue no on both counts, taking an approach quite different from that
ordinarily taken by feminists on the sameness side of the spectrum.
"Sameness" feminists usually have responded to the feminists of difference
by reiterating their basic insight that individual men and women can be
very similar. While true, this is not an adequate response to the basic
insight of "difference" feminists: that gender exists, that men and women
differ as groups. In this article, I try to speak to feminists of difference on
their own terms. While I take gender seriously, I disagree with the
description of gender provided by difference feminists. . . .

The most influential source for the feminism of difference is Carol
Gilligan's book, in which Gilligan argues that women speak "in a different
voice." Women are portrayed as nurturers, defined by their relationships
and focused on contextual thinking; men are depicted as abstract thinkers,
defined by individual achievement. We should listen to women's "voice,"
argue Gilligan and her followers, because women's culture offers the basis
for a transformation of our society, a transformation based on the womanly
values of responsibility, connection, selflessness, and caring, rather than on
separation, autonomy, and hierarchy. . . .

A close analysis of the traits Gilligan attributes to women suggests that she and other scholars who share her view of women offer domesticity with a difference. These "relational feminists," as they have been aptly called, reclaim the compliments of Victorian gender ideology while rejecting its insults. Thus, relational feminists agree with the Victorians that women are more nurturing than men ("focused on relationships"), less tied to the questionable virtues of capitalism, and ultimately more moral than men. But they disagree with the Victorians' view that women are also more passive than men, less competent, more timid and naturally demure. . . .

Relational feminists' interest in "the feminine" stems from its transformative potential. Relational feminists find enshrined in domesticity "female" values that, they believe, will enable women to achieve equality not by buying into the male world on male terms, but by transforming the world in women's image. . . .

Relational feminism is better understood as a critique of possessive individualism than as a description of what men and women are actually like. Gilligan herself acknowledges this when she refuses to associate her "voices" with males and females. Yet Gilligan appears not to heed her own warnings on this point, for in the remainder of her book she invariably associates men with one voice and women with the other, and often makes sweeping statements about the way men and women "are." Gilligan's inconsistent signals about whether she is talking about women or "the feminine" have left relational feminism with the potential to be used as a weapon against women. As evidence of this, I next turn to the *Sears* case, a clear example of the perils of modern domesticity. . . .

In *EEOC v. Sears, Roebuck & Co.*, Sears argued successfully that women were underrepresented in its relatively high-paying commission sales positions not because Sears had discriminated against them, but because women lacked "interest" in commission sales. Sears used the language of relational feminism to support its core argument that women's focus on relationships at home and at work makes them choose to sacrifice worldly advancement in favor of a supportive work environment and limited hours that accommodate their devotion to family. An unmistakable undertone is Sears' subtle intimation that women's sacrifice is limited, since their "different voice" makes the fast track unappealing. Women's "ethic of care" enables them to rise above the fray, so they are not truly hurt when they are excluded from high-powered, competitive jobs in commission sales.

The brilliance of Sears' lawyers lies in their success in enshrining gender stereotypes at the core of Title VII. *Sears* provides a dramatic illustration of the power of relational feminism to provide a respectable academic language in which to dignify traditional stereotypes. The case holds the potential to transform Title VII law in a way that pits gender discrimination plaintiffs against stereotypes in a battle the stereotypes are designed to win, for in effect *Sears* establishes a legal assumption that all women fit gender stereotypes and imposes on plaintiffs a burden to disprove that assumption as part of their prima facie case. . . .

The usual focus of a Title VII class action lawsuit is on statistics comparing the proportion of women in a given job category with the proportion of women in the relevant labor market. Statistics are direct proof that a facially neutral hiring policy has a disparate impact on a group protected under Title VII. . . . In contrast to courts prior to *Sears*, both the trial and appellate *Sears* courts required the EEOC to prove not only statistical disparities but also men's and women's "equal interest." Under *Sears*, therefore, a class of gender discrimination plaintiffs cannot prove their prima facie case simply by proving a disparity between the proportion of women in the relevant labor market and the proportion of women in the jobs at issue. Instead they have the additional burden of establishing what percentage of women in the otherwise relevant labor market was truly "interested" in the jobs at issue.

Sears based its argument, first, upon testimony of managers, one of whom made the now famous claim that women did not want commission sales jobs because such salesmen were required to work outside the store and women do not like to go out "when it's snowing or raining or whatever." The managers' testimony was bolstered by a sociologist who testified about a survey of Sears employees, by a writer on women's issues, and by historian Rosalind Rosenberg, who cited Gilligan and other relational feminists to support her assertion that the EEOC's "assumption that women and men have identical interests and aspirations regarding work is incorrect. Historically, men and women have had different interests, goals and aspirations regarding work."

To support this statement, Rosenberg offered portraits of men and women that closely echoed Gilligan's. Women she depicted as "humane and nurturing," focused on relationships, and averse to capitalist virtues such as competition. Again echoing Gilligan, she painted men as competitive and motivated by self-interest: possessive individualists *par excellence*.

Sears proceeded to use against women the gender stereotypes rehabilitated by relational feminism. The implication of Sears' successful use of domesticity's insults is that relational feminists delude themselves if they think they can rehabilitate domesticity's compliments without its insults. To relational feminists, the key point of domesticity may be women's higher morality; to Sears managers it was that women are weak and dependent, delicate and passive.

A closer look at the trial transcript dramatizes the power of these stereotypes once unleashed, for it shows how Sears systematically used stereotypes to override information about the desires and the aspirations of actual women. The most obvious example of this occurs in the testimony of Joan Haworth, Sears' major statistical witness, who argued that even female applicants who appeared to be interested in commission sales, in fact, were not interested. When the EEOC challenged this statement, Haworth chose three applications that indicated background and experience in commission sales and explained how she knew none was truly interested. The EEOC located two of the three women Haworth discussed, both of whom testified they had in fact been seeking jobs in commission sales. The trial judge glossed over this rebuttal in his opinion. . . .

Sears' doctrinal innovation clashes at a fundamental level with the thrust of Title VII. *Sears* allows information about *gender*, about women *as a group*, to be used to establish a legal presumption about individual plaintiffs consolidated into a class. This is inappropriate because Title VII is designed to protect women who do not fit gender stereotypes, who want to work as physicists, or in auto sales. Title VII's underlying goal is to protect women who want nontraditional work. Establishing a legal presumption that every class of female plaintiffs conforms to gender stereotypes frustrates this goal.

Sears is thus a dramatic reversal of existing Title VII law and should be overruled. From a theoretical standpoint, *Sears* shows the power of gender stereotypes to overshadow evidence about actual women. *Sears* also shows how relational feminism's critique of possessive individualism serves to marginalize both women and the critique itself. . . . [D]omesticity's critique does not compel its followers to confront capitalist practice and to change it. Instead, an abiding tenet of domesticity is that women's aversion to capitalist virtues makes them "choose" home and family. This is an argument that encourages women to "choose" economic marginalization and celebrate that choice as a badge of virtue. . . . [D]omesticity [thus becomes] . . . an ideology designed to enlist women in their own oppression. . . .

One can see how domesticity's compliments add up to its critique: women reject crass competition; they favor a friendly, cooperative, working environment over mere material advancement; they value their commitments to family over career success. Sears' argument demonstrates how domesticity's critique of possessive individualism rests on a claim that women are psychologically unsuited to the economic mainstream. All Sears did was pick this up and use it to argue that women are psychologically unsuited to work in commission sales. . . .

Western wage labor is premised on an ideal worker with no child care responsibilities. In this system men and women workers are allocated very different roles. Men are raised to believe they have the right and the responsibility to perform as ideal workers. Husbands as a group therefore do far less child care, and earn far more, than their wives. Women are raised with complementary assumptions. They generally feel that they are entitled to the pleasure of spending time with their children while they are small. Moreover, even upon their return to work, the near-universal tendency is to assume that women's work commitment must be defined to accommodate continuing child-care responsibilities.

This gender system results in the impoverishment of women, since it leads mothers systematically to "choose" against performing as ideal workers in order to ensure that their children receive high-quality care. . . .

Decoded, the current talk about women's priorities is a translation into new language of domesticity's old argument that women's values lead them to make different choices. The persistence of this classic argument makes it imperative for feminists to analyze why the argument has abiding persuasiveness. The approach most useful to an analysis of women's "choice" is Antonio Gramsci's concept of cultural hegemony. Gramsci painted a complex picture of how the dominant culture rules with the consent of the governed by shaping a "hegemony" of values, norms, perceptions, and beliefs that "helps mark the boundaries of permissible discourse, discourages the clarification of social alternatives, and makes it difficult for the dispossessed to locate the source of their unease, let alone remedy it." . . .

Feminists need to arm women to resist the argument that women's economic marginalization is the product of their own choice. Challenging this argument should be easy, since, in fact, in our deeply gendered system men and women face very different choices indeed. Whereas women, in order to be ideal workers, have to choose not to fulfill their "family responsibilities," men do not. The question women ask themselves is this: Should I make professional sacrifices for the good of my children? In order for the wife's "choice" to be equivalent to her husband's, she would first have to be in a position to ask herself whether or not she would choose to be an ideal worker if her husband would choose to stay home with the children. Second, she would have to pose the question in a context where powerful social norms told her she was peculiarly suited to raising children. When we speak of women's "choices" to subordinate their careers, we are so blinded by gender prescriptions that we can forget that the husband's decision to be an ideal worker rests upon the assumption that his wife will choose not to be in order to allow him that privilege. This is true whether the wife eschews a career altogether or whether (in the modern pattern) she merely subordinates her career to child-care responsibilities. The point is that the husband is doing neither. Women know that if *they* do not sacrifice *no one will*, whereas men assume that if *they* do not, *women* will.

Thus women do not enjoy the same choices as men. But the underlying point is a deeper one: that society is structured so that everyone, regardless of sex, is limited to two unacceptable choices—men's traditional life patterns or economic marginality. Under the current structure of wage labor, people are limited to being ideal workers, which leaves them with inadequate time to devote to parenting, and being primary parents condemned to relative poverty (if they are single parents) or economic vulnerability (if they are currently married to an ideal worker). Wage labor does not have to be structured in this way. . . .

What we need, then, is a rule that avoids the traditional correlation between gender and sex, a rule that is *sex*-but not *gender*-neutral. The traditional goal, properly understood, is really one of *sex*-neutrality, or, more descriptively, one of deinstitutionalizing gender. It entails a systematic refusal to institutionalize gender in any form. This approach mandates not an enforced blindness to gender, but rather a refusal to reinforce the traditional assumption that adherence to gender roles flows "naturally" from biological sex. Reinforcing that assumption reinforces the grip of the gender system as a whole. . . .

How can this be done? Certainly the hardest task in the process of deconstructing gender is to begin the long and arduous process of seeing through the descriptions of men and women offered by domesticity. Feminists need to explain exactly how the traditional descriptions of men and women are false. This is a job for social scientists, for a new Carol Gilligan in reverse, who can focus the massive literature on sex stereotyping in a way that dramatizes that Gilligan is talking about metaphors, not actual people. . . .

The kernel of truth in Gilligan's "voices," then, is that Gilligan provides a description of gender differences related to men's and women's different roles with respect to wage labor and child care under the current gender regime. Yet we see these true gender differences through glasses framed by an ideology that distorts our vision. To break free of traditional gender ideology, we need at the simplest level to see how men nurture people and relationships and how women are competitive and powerful. This is a task in which we as feminists will meet considerable resistance, both from inside and outside the feminist movement. . . .

Joan W. Scott, Deconstructing Equality–Versus–Difference: Or, the Uses of Poststructuralist Theory for Feminism

14 Feminist Stud. 33 (1988).

. . . In the past few years, "equality-versus-difference" has been used as a shorthand to characterize conflicting feminist positions and political strategies. Those who argue that sexual difference ought to be an irrelevant consideration in schools, employment, the courts, and the legislature are put in the equality category. Those who insist that appeals on behalf of women ought to be made in terms of the needs, interests, and characteristics common to women as a group are placed in the difference category. . . . Most recently, the debate about equality and difference has been used to analyze the Sears case, the sex discrimination suit against the retailing giant by the Equal Employment Opportunities Commission (EEOC) in 1979, in which historians Alice Kessler–Harris and Rosalind Rosenberg testified on opposite sides. . . .

A close look at the evidence in the Sears case suggests that equality-versus-difference may not accurately depict the opposing sides in the Sears case. During testimony, most of the arguments against equality and for difference were, in fact, made by the Sears lawyers or by Rosalind Rosenberg. They constructed an opponent against whom they asserted that women and men differed, that "fundamental differences"—the result of culture or long-standing patterns of socialization—led to women's presumed lack of interest in commission sales jobs. In order to make their own claim that sexual difference and not discrimination could explain the hiring patterns of Sears, the Sears defense attributed to [the] EEOC an assumption that no one had made in those terms—that women and men had identical interests. . . .

In the end, the most nuanced arguments of Kessler–Harris were rejected as contradictory or inapplicable, and the judge decided in Sears's favor, repeating the defense argument that an assumption of equal interest was "unfounded" because of the differences between women and men. Not only was [the] EEOCs position rejected, but the hiring policies of Sears were implicitly endorsed. According to the judge, because difference was real and fundamental, it could explain statistical variations in Sears's hiring. Discrimination was redefined as simply the recognition of "natural difference (however culturally or historically produced).... Difference was substituted for inequality, the appropriate antithesis of equality, becoming inequality explanation and legitimation." The judge's decision illustrates a process literary scholar Naomi Schor has described in another context: it "essentializes difference and naturalizes social inequity." ...

When equality and difference are paired dichotomously, they structure an impossible choice. If one opts for equality, one is forced to accept the notion that difference is antithetical to it. If one opts for difference, one admits that equality is unattainable.... Feminists cannot give up "difference"; it has been our most creative analytic tool. We cannot give up equality, at least as long as we want to speak to the principles and values of our political system. But it makes no sense for the feminist movement to let its arguments be forced into preexisting categories and its political disputes to be characterized by a dichotomy we did not invent. How then do we recognize and use notions of sexual difference and yet make arguments for equality? The only response is a double one: the unmasking of the power relationship constructed by posing equality as the antithesis of difference and the refusal of its consequent dichotomous construction of political choices.

Equality-versus-difference cannot structure choices for feminist politics; the oppositional pairing misrepresents the relationship of both terms. Equality, in the political theory of rights that lies behind the claims of excluded groups for justice, means the ignoring of differences between individuals for a particular purpose or in a particular context.... This presumes a social agreement to consider obviously different people as equivalent (not identical) for a stated purpose. In this usage, the opposite of equality is inequality or inequivalence, the noncommensurability of individuals or groups in certain circumstances, for certain purposes. Thus, for purposes of democratic citizenship, the measure of equivalence has been, at different times, independence or ownership of property or race or sex. The political notion of equality thus includes, indeed depends on, an acknowledgment of the existence of difference. Demands for equality have rested on implicit and usually unrecognized arguments from difference; if individuals or groups were identical or the same there would be no need to ask for equality. Equality might well be defined as deliberate indifference to specified differences.

The antithesis of difference in most usages is sameness or identity. But even here the contrast and the context must be specified. There is nothing self-evident or transcendent about difference, even if the fact of difference—sexual difference, for example—seems apparent to the naked eye. The questions always ought to be: What qualities or aspects are being compared? What is the nature of the comparison? How is the meaning of difference being constructed? Yet in the Sears testimony and in some debates among feminists (sexual) difference is assumed to be an immutable fact, its meaning inherent in the categories female and male. The lawyers for Sears put it this way: "The reasonableness of the EEOC's a priori assumptions of male/female sameness with respect to preferences, interests, and qualifications is ... the crux of the issue." The point of the EEOC challenge, however, was never sameness but the irrelevance of categorical differences.

The opposition men/women, as Rosenberg employed it, asserted the incomparability of the sexes, and although history and socialization were the explanatory factors, these resonated with categorical distinctions inferred from the facts of bodily difference. When the opposition men/women is invoked, as it was in the Sears case, it refers a specific issue (the small statistical discrepancy between women and men hired for commission sales jobs) back to a general principle (the "fundamental" differences between women and men). The differences within each group that might apply to this particular situation—the fact, for example, that some women might choose "aggressive" or "risk-taking" jobs or that some women might prefer high-to-low paying positions—were excluded by definition in the antithesis between the groups. The irony is, of course, that the statistical case required only a small percentage of women's behaviors to be explained. Yet the historical testimony argued categorically about "women." It thus became impossible to argue (as EEOC and Kessler–Harris tried to) that within the female category, women typically exhibit and participate in all sorts of "male" behaviors, that socialization is a complex process that does not yield uniform choices. To make the argument would have required a direct attack on categorical thinking about gender. For the generalized opposition male/female serves to obscure the differences among women in behavior, character, desire, subjectivity, sexuality, gender identification, and historical experience. In the light of Rosenberg's insistence on the primacy of sexual difference, Kessler–Harris's insistence on the specificity (and historically variable aspect) of women's actions could be dismissed as an unreasonable and trivial claim.

The alternative to the binary construction of sexual difference is not sameness, identity, or androgyny. By subsuming women into a general "human" identity, we lose the specificity of female diversity and women's experiences; we are back, in other words, to the days when "Man's" story was supposed to be everyone's story, when women were "hidden from history," when the feminine served as the negative counterpoint, the "Other," for the construction of positive masculine identity. It is not sameness or identity between women and men that we want to claim but a more complicated historically variable diversity than is permitted by the opposition male/female, a diversity that is also differently expressed for different purposes in different contexts. In effect, the duality this opposition creates draws one line of difference, invests it with biological explanations, and then treats each side of the opposition as a unitary phenomenon. Everything in each category (male/female) is assumed to be the same; hence, differences within either category are suppressed. In contrast, our goal is to see not only differences between the sexes but also the way these work to repress differences within gender groups. The sameness constructed on each side of the binary opposition hides the multiple play of differences and maintains their irrelevance and invisibility.

Placing equality and difference in antithetical relationship has, then, a double effect. It denies the way in which difference has long figured in political notions of equality and it suggests that sameness is the only ground on which equality can be claimed. It thus puts feminists in an impossible position, for as long as we argue within the terms of a discourse set up by this opposition we grant the current conservative premise that because women cannot be identical to men in all respects, we cannot expect to be equal to them. The only alternative, it seems to me, is to refuse to oppose equality to difference and insist continually on differences as the condition of individual and collective identities, differences as the constant challenge to the fixing of those identities, history as the repeated illustration of the play of differences, differences as the very meaning of equality itself.

Alice Kessler–Harris's experience in the Sears case shows, however, that the assertion of differences in the face of gender categories is not a sufficient strategy. What is required in addition is an analysis of fixed gender categories as normative statements that organize cultural understandings of sexual difference. This means that we must open to scrutiny the terms women and men as they are used to define one another in particular contexts. . . .

If we relativize the categories woman and man, it means, of course, that we must also recognize the contingent and specific nature of our political claims. Political strategies then will rest on analyses of the utility of certain arguments in certain discursive contexts, without, however, invoking absolute qualities for women or men. There are moments when it makes sense for mothers to demand consideration for their social role, and contexts within which motherhood is irrelevant to women's behavior; but to maintain that womanhood is motherhood is to obscure the differences that make choice possible. There are moments when it makes sense to demand a reevaluation of the status of what has been socially constructed as women's work . . . and contexts within which it makes much more sense to prepare women for entry into "non-traditional" jobs. But to maintain that femininity predisposes women to certain (nurturing) jobs or (collaborative) styles of work is to naturalize complex economic and social processes and, once again, to obscure the differences that have characterized women's occupational histories. An insistence on differences undercuts the tendency to absolutist, and in the case of sexual difference, essentialist categories. It does not deny the existence of gender difference, but it does suggest that its meanings are always relative to particular constructions in specified contexts. In contrast, absolutist categorizations of difference end up always enforcing normative rules....

In histories of feminism and in feminist political strategies there needs to be at once attention to the operations of difference and an insistence on differences, but not a simple substitution of multiple for binary difference for it is not a happy pluralism we ought to invoke. The resolution of the "difference dilemma" comes neither from ignoring nor embracing difference as it is normatively constituted. Instead, it seems to me that the critical feminist position must always involve two moves. The first is the systematic criticism of the operations of categorical difference, the exposure of the kinds of exclusions and inclusions the hierarchies it constructs, and a refusal of their ultimate "truth." A refusal however, not in the name of an equality that implies sameness or identity, but rather (and this is the second move) in the name of an equality that rests on differences— differences that confound, disrupt, and render ambiguous the meaning of any fixed binary opposition. To do anything else is to buy into the political argument that sameness is a requirement for equality, an untenable position for feminists (and historians) who know that power is constructed on and so must be challenged from the ground of difference.

Mary Joe Frug, Sexual Equality and Sexual Difference in American Law

26 New Eng. L. Rev. 665 (1992).

The problem of the relationship between sexual difference and equality is illustrated for me by a story told by a woman about her reactions to watching a male friend shop for a suit. Although the man chose a suit which was too short in the arms, too long in the legs, and too tight in the pants, he looked at his reflection in the mirror and said with cheerful confidence, "This looks great. Send for the tailor." The woman reported realizing that if she had been in his position she would have looked at herself in the mirror and said, "This looks terrible. My arms are too long, my legs are too short and my rear is too fat."

Feminist legal scholars over the past fifteen years have generated a body of law review articles on the problem of sexual difference and equality which might be read to suggest several strategies for explaining and re-dressing the sad disparity between the reactions of these two people in their suits. For some feminists, the lesson of the story would be that clothing stores should be transformed, so that women could find power outfits as easily as men, so that we would routinely have tailors standing ready to deal with the divergences between our garments and our bodies. For other feminists, the lesson of the story would be that women somehow must learn to feel more comfortable with our actual appearances, that we should give up our desire to conform to the fantasies men have invented for feminine attractiveness. Still other feminists might challenge such conclusions, arguing that integrating men's clothing stores and validating women's bodies are likely to constitute strategies which themselves recreate and perpetuate the problem of the relationship between sexual difference and equality. For these feminists, whom I designate the postmoderns, equality must come to mean something other than a choice between treating people the same or treating them differently. Since that choice has consistently functioned either to require that women conform to a male standard of conduct or accept inferior treatment as a condition of acknowledging the differences between women and men, the postmoderns maintain that we should try to combat our oppression by avoiding the sameness/difference choice. The tough problem, of course, is how to do that.

The issue of what constitutes equality for women and how they can achieve it is the heart of the feminist legal project. It is implicated by any quest women undertake to combat their subordinate circumstances through legal change. Indeed, although it usually goes unrecognized or unacknowledged, the problem of the relationship between sexual difference and equality is also involved in any efforts lawmakers undertake to structure a just society.

I am going to ... describe four approaches that Feminist Legal Scholars have taken to the problem of the relationship between sexual difference and equality.... I divide the Feminist Legal Scholarship that has been produced since the seventies into four groups of articles, groups which I label Equality Doctrine, Equality Theory, Feminist Theory, and Feminist Doctrine. These categories roughly, but not inevitably, coincide with historical divisions. I believe each category of scholarship I will describe has had and retains significant value for women's efforts to fight their oppression. I claim that the postmodern form of Feminist Legal Scholarship—the version I designate Feminist Doctrine—currently offers the most promise to women and their cause....

Equality Doctrine

Equality Doctrine articles were principally written during the seventies, when the campaign for the Equal Rights Amendment was a spirited and ongoing issue, and sex-based legal classifications restricting women from participation in public life were much more prevalent than they are today.... Equality Doctrinalists analyzed how the position of women could be improved by using and extending civil rights statutes or the Constitution in their behalf.... A dominant doctrinal issue in this period was the scope of the developing equality standard.... Believing that legislatures could treat women differently than men only if women were understood to be differently situated, those working to advance women assumed a sex-blind posture regarding sex differences. Equality Doctrinalists argued either that there were no differences between women and men, or that sexual differences should be considered legally irrelevant. Attempting to make women and men appear similarly situated in a context of social and economic inequality required equality advocates to assume contorted and unconvincing sex-blind postures.... In the end, ... [b]eing sex-blind with your fingers crossed turned out not to work....

Equality Theory

Equality Theorists attempted to account for the doctrinal failures of discrimination law by exploring the origins, the conflicts or the unstated assumptions underlying conventional interpretations of the equality standard.... Equality Theorists claimed that conventional equality has not been calibrated on a neutral principle but has been constructed pursuant to a male perspective. This insight liberated Equality Theorists from the inhibitions of the sex-blind posture that Equality Doctrinalists thought they must assume; it permitted them to argue that equality for women should not be predicated on a requirement that women demonstrate their similarities to men. It permitted Equality Theorists to confront and debate the issues of which sex differences should matter and how much difference should be tolerated in the interpretation of equality....

In addition to disputing the neutrality of the equality principle, Equality Theorists also questioned the merit of conventional equality. They questioned whether male privileges and responsibilities were socially valuable and desirable.... Equality Theorists introduced the possibility of gender pride to jurists. They argued that women's needs were noble, significant and worthy concerns which the equality principle should embrace with dignity rather than tolerate with condescension or ignore.

The shortcomings of Equality Theory and the problems entailed by choosing sameness or difference were illustrated forcefully and publicly by the debate among feminists during the 1986–87 term of the U.S. Supreme Court. In arguments, articles, and briefs connected to the *California Federal Savings & Loan Ass'n v. Guerra (Cal. Fed.)* case, some feminists argued that since women must be like men in order to have equal status in the workplace they should not seek to obtain childbirth benefits. Other feminists argued that since women have unique reproductive characteristics and responsibilities, equality doctrine should afford them special treatment, in the form of childbirth benefits, even if those benefits might reduce their public stature by flagging women's unique needs. The problem with the arguments about women in the *Cal.Fed.* case was not that one argument was true and the other false. Rather, both arguments were simultaneously true: women can be like men in the workplace, but they can also undergo reproductive experiences which can make them different. *Cal.Fed.* demonstrates the way in which the claim that women are either the same as men or they are different forces decisionmakers into risky choices. Either women get benefits or they don't, depending in large part on what a decisionmaker decides women are *really* like....

Feminist Theory

I designate the third group of Feminist Legal Scholarship articles the Feminist Theory category. Often inspired by feminist theory in disciplines other than law, these articles move beyond arguments relating to the extension of legal doctrine or critiques relating to the equality guarantee. Their subject is the more general question of how legal doctrine works in conjunction with other systemic factors to keep women oppressed....

Catharine MacKinnon, a principal author of the Minneapolis antipornography ordinance and the architect of current sexual harassment law, is a particularly trenchant and significant Feminist Theorist. Under her influence, articles in the Feminist Theory category of Feminist Legal Scholarship have identified a politics of gender which infests and contaminates not only conventional equality doctrine but other law as well. MacKinnon argues that focusing on the difference between women and men as a way to obtain equality for women is a doomed enterprise in a society in which power is distributed unequally between the sexes. Indeed, this form of legal analysis perpetuates male oppression of women. . . .

The critique of sexual difference and the shift to a focus on power—the politics of gender, as I am calling these ideas—has had significant implications for the agenda of feminists working in law. . . . In addition to the politics of gender, Feminist Theorists have also questioned the epistemology of gender. That is, in addition to analyzing the allocation of power between the sexes, Feminist Theorists have also written about the meaning of gender; they have addressed the issue of how actual difference is constructed and perpetuated by complex social practices, including law. I find the feminist theoretical critique of the epistemology of gender particularly useful in evaluating . . . assumptions about sexual difference. . . . [One] assumption . . . is that sexual difference can be defined by reference to two separately defined bundles of "feminine" and "masculine" characteristics. Because these bundles are generally understood to contain a predictable or essential group of traits which are relatively intractable, this attitude toward sexual difference is referred to as "essentialist." Although an essentialist stance toward sexual difference unites a number of scholars writing in several different genres of Feminist Legal Scholarship, there are distinctions among them regarding the value of femininity and the degree to which sexual differences may be modified by changes in the law. I refer to these distinctions by the categories of negative and cultural feminisms.

Negative Feminism

The group of feminists I designate as negative feminists believe that women are defined as what men are not, as in: "(unlike men) women are not active, not rational and not aggressive." Negative feminists acknowledge the degraded character which this negative definition casts on our sexual identity, but they believe that sexual difference is a consequence of the superior social and economic power of men over women. Under this etiology of sexual differences, women are what the pornography industry implies: we are holes. Zeros. Ciphers. Because our identity has been wholly constructed by men, we cannot know what a true feminine identity might be. Nevertheless, negative feminists actively oppose the negative sexual identity that has been imposed on women. They seek to change the social order so that women can be whole. Like men. This aspiration is somewhat problematical, because if women are either not-men or what-they-make-us we cannot know what form our self-actualization might take in the absence of male control.

Cultural Feminism

Like negative feminists, cultural feminists also describe sexual difference in oppositional terms. Women are what men are not. But in contrast to negative feminists, cultural feminists appeal to more positive, stereotypically female terms in their description of women's characteristics. Their position about sexual difference is that although men often mistakenly describe women pejoratively by comparing them unfavorably with themselves, the qualities commonly linked with our sex—qualities such as passivity and emotionality—are noble characteristics. These qualities make us nurturing, attentive, and selfless—traits which should be affirmed, rather than denigrated. Cultural feminists believe that women have a unique, feminine identity which men have prevented them from fully developing. They seek, therefore, to challenge the social constraints which devalue and suppress femininity.

Both negative and cultural feminisms have powerful evangelical potential as political organizing themes, although I believe the anger and pessimism connected with negative feminism produces a more positive political residue than the form of sentimental boosterism that often accompanies cultural feminism. Both feminisms, however, represent stances toward the construction of sexual difference which can pose harmful consequences for our common cause. Both attitudes confuse the commonality of women with a universal woman, and both define the content of sexual difference in polarized, dichotomous terms which imply an essentialist gendered selfhood. . . .

Feminist Doctrine

Scholars writing in this category of Feminist Legal Scholarship explicitly acknowledge differences among women. Rather than adopting a static or fixed definition of femininity, they define sexual difference by the relationships or context in which sexual difference is asserted. This stance toward sexual difference leads them to explore concrete, specific legal rules or doctrines that are of interest to particular groups of women; it also leads them to analyze the complex social practices in which laws are taught and used. The significance of shifting points of view and the commitment to an anti-essentialist depiction of human nature within this scholarship are the characteristics that make me link Feminist Doctrine with postmodern scholarship.

Feminist Doctrinalists do not depend on a single doctinal standard. Rather, these scholars seek equality for women through law by questioning, re-contextualizing, and attempting to unsettle existing laws in a wide range of areas. Because, unlike Feminist Theorists, they avoid the dichotomous imagery associated with cultural and negative feminisms by invoking diverse, multiplicitous images of women in their work, I believe that Feminist Doctrinalists offer constructive promise for breaking through the doctrinal impasse of traditional sexual equality doctrine.

In order to indicate more concretely the character of Feminist Doctrine, let me now turn . . . [to] an illustration of this genre. . . .

Feminist Doctrine, or Post Modern Feminism [The Sears Case] ...

In 1973 the Equal Employment Opportunity Commission (EEOC) brought charges of sex discrimination against Sears, Roebuck and Co., the "largest retailer of general merchandise" and the largest civilian employer of women in the United States. After 11 years of investigation and a ten month trial before a U.S. federal district judge in Chicago, the charges against Sears were dismissed.... My reason for discussing this complex litigation is the EEOC's claim that Sears discriminated against women by failing to hire and promote proportionate numbers of women in commission sales positions. The EEOC based this claim on statistics which showed that although two-thirds of the applicants and promotion candidates for commission sales positions were women, women constituted only one-fourth of those actually hired or promoted....

Sears explained the low number of women in commission sales by introducing evidence which described commission sales work and which set forth the personality traits the company considered commission sales workers needed in order to be effective. Specifically, Sears described commission sales work as: 1) sale of "big ticket" items, such as major appliances, roofing, air conditioning, and sewing machines; 2) work which was compensated by commission or a combination of commission and flat sum; 3) work which, despite the "risk" inherent in compensation by commission, is more highly paid than straight saleswork; 4) work which could take personnel away from the stores and which could, therefore, feel more isolated and require more independent than straight saleswork; and 5) work which sometimes required technical knowledge. Sears officials testified that effective commission sales workers should be 1) aggressive, 2) outgoing and good with people, 3) highly motivated, 4) already informed about their products, and 5) "leaders."

Having described commission sales work and commission sales workers' ideal personality traits, Sears then continued its explanation for the disproportionately low number of women in commission sales by introducing testimony which described commonalities among women in relationship to their work. Sears called upon feminist historian Rosalind Rosenberg for evidence drawn from social history that women have subordinated their paid labor activities to their domestic responsibilities. In rebuttal, the EEOC called upon feminist historian Alice Kessler–Harris to testify that women have successfully undertaken "non-traditional" paid labor on the unusual occasions when employers allowed them to do so. Relying on these historical claims, the witnesses then reached opposite conclusions on whether Sears should be considered responsible for the low number of women in commission sales.

... [I]n reaching their conclusions both feminist historians masculinized the traits needed to work in commission sales. That is, they interpreted Sears' description of the ideal commission sales worker by reference to a particular masculine stereotype.... Sears's witness Dr. Rosalind Rosenberg ... testified that because women as a group tended to subordinate their careers to the needs of their families, they were less likely than men to choose commission sales work. She described women as "feminine," "nurturant," and "selfless;" "relationship-centered" rather than "work-centered;" and "less competitive than men." She asserted that employers should not be blamed for these traits, although she also indicated that women themselves were not responsible for their attitudes toward work. She argued, rather, that women have been "trained," "exhorted" and "socialized" to be the way they are.

EEOC's witness, Alice Kessler–Harris, disputed Rosenberg's position that women "have" different interests which lead them to "choose" other jobs over commission saleswork. She claimed that women's qualifications for and attitudes toward work depend on the "framework of available opportunity." "What appear to be women's choices and what are character-ized as women's interests are, in fact, heavily influenced by the opportuni-ties for work made available to them ..." Having argued that women and men can adapt their personalities to their circumstances, Kessler–Harris then recounted many examples of women successfully undertaking tradi-tional men's work—she mentioned welders, crane operators, and typeset-ters, as well as insurance and real estate workers and others. Unfortunate-ly, although she asserted that "ideas about women's traditional roles are neither deeply rooted in women's psyche nor do they form a barrier that inhibits women's work force participation," she did not acknowledge how few women had undertaken the "men's" jobs she described, and she did not dispute Rosenberg's essentialist depiction of domestic women....

Both of the witnesses' claims about the history of working women are undoubtedly true. Women have been disproportionately underrepresented in wage labor, just as Rosenberg suggested, and women have been able to undertake "masculine" work, just as Kessler–Harris testified. The problem with their testimony lies in the dichotomized image of femininity and masculinity which they conveyed in their interpretations of this history.... [B]oth scholars based their judgments on an implicit comparison of the composite woman each had described with a particular male stereotype. That is, Rosenberg's conclusion that Sears should not be held responsible for the low number of women in commission sales was based on her assumption that women are too feminine for that kind of work. In contrast, Kessler–Harris's conclusion that Sears had been discriminating against women was based on her assumption that women could be masculine enough if they were given the chance. Underlying both judgments, I think, is an unnecessarily masculinized image of a successful commission sales worker.

Recall that Sears' personnel testified that effective, competitive sales personnel were "aggressive," "outgoing," "highly motivated," and "lead-ers." The stereotypical masculine image commonly associated with these traits in our gender culture is the image of a back-slapping, joke-telling, arm-twisting, used-car salesman, a man who may have played high school football or been a Marine, an individual accustomed to winning confronta-tions under challenging conditions. This image is also suggested within the opinions by the repeated use of the word "risk" in the descriptions of commission sales work. Commission sales work is considered risky because compensation is predicated on however many sales an employee makes. But since commission sales workers undisputedly made significantly more money at Sears than salaried employees, the "risk" inherent in commission sales work was not actually a danger that employees would be uncompensated or discharged, but an uncertainty regarding the amount of money they would earn. By using the word "risk," the parties invoked a particular masculine stereotype: Rambo precariously but triumphantly selling washing machine after washing machine despite the vicious advertising techniques and desperate sales tactics launched against him by the bad guys, the competitors.

If one envisions the battling male warrior as a model for the ideal commission sales worker, then one can understand why Rosenberg's claim that women are unsuited for commission sales because they are nurturing, selfless, and relation-centered may have sounded persuasive to the court, whereas Kessler–Harris's claim that women could do commission sales if they were permitted to undoubtedly sounded unappealing. Why would we want to encourage women to become like that sort of man?

Although the warrior image of the commission sales worker may have captivated the participants in the *Sears* case, I doubt the commission sales force at Sears actually conformed to such a stereotype. It seems evident to me—avoiding, to the extent I can, exactly that sort of sales person when I buy my washing machines—that no company would or should want its commission sales workers to act in the stereotypical way we think Marines or linebackers act. Moreover, I believe that female sales workers are quite capable of exhibiting the traits Sears claimed that commission sales workers need in order to be effective. Trying to sneak past department store cosmetic counters, for example, without spending twenty-five dollars I don't want to spend, reminds me that women who work in those locales could easily be described as "aggressive," "outgoing," and quite informed about their business.

Other "women's" work also entails the traits Sears ascribed to effective commission sales workers. Think, for example, of a nurse who can coax a depressed patient to eat, of a teacher who can induce a shy child to speak up, of a social worker who can convince a reluctant client to participate in community services. Each of these traditional women's jobs requires individuals to be "aggressive," "outgoing," "highly motivated," and "leaders" in relation to their work. Indeed, if the historians had interpreted the risk individuals must tolerate in commission sales as uncertainty, then they would have been able to link that problem in commission sales with a situation many women have commonly confronted in order to be successful in the psychological aspects of their domestic responsibilities. They might have argued, in other words, that *because* of women's domestic responsibilities they are more likely rather than less likely to be able to adapt to the confused, conflicting or changing *responses* of sales customers. Thus, Rosenberg and Kessler–Harris might have concluded that the qualities commonly associated with traditional women's work are similar to those required for commission sales. Instead, Rosenberg assumed that women's "feminine" qualities disable them from effectively selling on commission, while Kessler–Harris based her claim that women are able to do commission sales on the men's work women have sometimes done, rather than the women's work they have mostly done. Both historians therefore undersold women in the interpretations they offered on the meaning of women's history in the work force. . . .

My critique of the *Sears* case is partial at best. In a longer piece I would want to move beyond my criticism of the feminist historians and try to elaborate an alternative solution to the doctrinal problem in the case. Despite its partiality, however, I propose that my *Sears* discussion is an example of Feminist Doctrine, or postmodern feminism, because of its focus on a particular doctrinal issue rather than a more generalized and abstract examination of women in relation to law; because of its reliance on contested interpretation as a significant legal strategy; and because of its claim that sexual difference is a complex, ever-shifting social practice rather than two rigidly circumscribed and essentialist bundles of traits. By challenging dualistic attitudes toward sexual difference, attitudes such as those Rosenberg and Kessler–Harris exhibited in their testimony, postmodern feminists seek to extend their political goals for women through law beyond the single, amalgamated image of women which other forms of Feminist Legal Scholarship have tended to invoke. By deliberately invoking differences among women—differences such as race, class, sexual preference, and age, as well as the conflicting work histories I have alluded to above—postmodern feminism constitutes, in my view, the most promising strategy available to Feminist Legal Scholars for breaking away from the constraints which the sameness/difference paradigm has imposed on women's equality.

NOTES AND QUESTIONS

1. *E.E.O.C. v. Sears.* This is a significantly edited version of an extremely long and complicated case. The excerpt here focuses on the question of whether women are the same as or different than men in their desires for commission sales positions. The full opinion spends much ink on the use of statistics to prove a case under Title VII.

Did the Seventh Circuit adopt a sameness approach or a difference approach? Joan Williams criticizes the Court in *Sears* for establishing a presumption that women conform to stereotypes about them. Do you think the Court did this, and if you do, in what way is this inimical to the goals of Title VII? Why do you think the Court emphasized the absence of witnesses? The E.E.O.C. did not call any specific applicants to testify to the fact that they preferred commission sales over non-commission. Why was the absence of such witnesses so important to the Seventh Circuit?

2. **Differences about Difference?** Williams, Scott and Frug all discuss feminists' claims that women are different from men and that these differences are important and should be taken into account. Early in her

essay, Williams says forthrightly that she disagrees with the difference feminists' description of gender. What specifically is her criticism? Ultimately, she argues that we need to recognize the ways that men nurture and that women are competitive. Kessler–Harris argues that some women have been extremely successful in fields traditionally associated with men such as operating cranes or welding. This is an argument that some (exceptional?) women can succeed at men's jobs. Judge Cudahy, in dissent, notes that women are highly successful in fields like residential real estate and door-to-door sales. Are these also fields traditionally associated with men? Or is he using examples of jobs that are less gender-associated as a way of making his point that men and women can have the same traits? Are Williams, Kessler–Harris and Judge Cudahy "sameness" feminists, arguing that some men are just like some women, and some women are just like some men?

Frug is also critical of Difference Feminists whom she categorizes as both Equality Theorists and Cultural Feminists, depending on whether they work specifically with the law or more generally. She has slightly different criticisms of each of these approaches. She is skeptical of equality theorists because of the unpredictability of whether a judge will perceive women's differences to require the same treatment as men or treatment different from that afforded to men. On the other hand, she is critical of cultural feminism because of its enervating political effects and its essentializing of "woman."

Of the three commentators presented here, only Scott embraces difference which she calls "our most creative analytic tool." However, she embraces it without rejecting equality as a standard. What she rejects is a dichotomous system in which one can only have sameness or difference. Instead, she calls for a theory that employs them both. Scott's strategy is to deconstruct the idea of equality to show the way in which it is dependent on a recognition of differences. If we didn't recognize differences in the subjects being compared, we would have identity, and would not need to discuss equality. Equality and sameness are not synonymous; equality and difference are not oppositions. Her critique of the Court's opinion in *Sears* depends on a recognition of this. To say men are different from women is not necessarily to say anything about equality.

Scott makes a second extremely important point: the opposing of male and female obscures the differences among men and among women. The result of this is that Kessler–Harris's insistence on detail looks trivial in comparison to Rosenberg's sweeping generalizations. Frug's work takes up the challenge of deconstructing gender stereotypes. In looking at women who are nurses, social workers and cosmetic salespeople, she focuses exactly on the ways that they can be competitive, highly-motivated and aggressive. Is Frug doing the work that Williams called for in asking feminists to see how women are competitive, or is Frug's work different? Keep in mind that unlike Kessler–Harris, Frug is describing women in occupations that are traditionally thought of as women's jobs.

Scott's and Frug's analyses are openly postmodern. Can you identify the ways in which they differ from Williams's and the majority and dissenting opinions in *Sears*? Frug argues that Kessler-Harris's claim that some women can work like men in "men's jobs" does little to break down stereotyped gender categories. Do you agree? Are postmodern approaches more useful in destroying gender constraints? Do Frug's examples of "male" traits in women in traditionally female jobs argue for the multiplicitous self described by Kessler–Harris? After all, don't we assume that women in these jobs also have a nurturing side to their personalities? On the other hand, are Frug's and Scott's postmodern approaches dangerous in that, as MacKinnon argues, by destroying categories they destroy our ability to think about the exercise of power toward particular groups?

3. **Litigation Strategy.** Could Frug's approach serve as a blueprint for a litigation strategy in future Title VII cases? Would evidence of cosmetics salespeople's personal traits be admissible in a suit claiming gender discrimination in the hiring of commission salespeople? If it were, specifically what kind of evidence would you introduce?

Catharine MacKinnon, Sex Equality: On Difference and Dominance

From C. MacKinnon, Toward a Feminist Theory of the State (Cambridge: Harvard University Press, 1989).

...Inequality because of sex defines and situates women as women. If the sexes were equal, women would not be sexually subjected. Sexual force would be exceptional, consent to sex could be commonly real, and sexually violated women would be believed. If the sexes were equal, women would not be economically subjected, their desperation and marginality cultivated, their enforced dependency exploited sexually or economically. Women would have speech, privacy, authority, respect, and more resources than they have now. Rape and pornography would be recognized as violations, and abortion would be both rare and actually guaranteed.

In the United States, it is acknowledged that the state is capitalist; it is not acknowledged that it is male. The law of sex equality, constitutional by interpretation and statutory by joke, erupts through this fissure, exposing the sex equality that the state purports to guarantee. If gender hierarchy and sexuality are reciprocally constituting—gender hierarchy providing the eroticism of sexuality and sexuality providing an enforcement mechanism for male dominance over women—a male state would predictably not make acts of sexual dominance actionable as gender inequality. Equality would be kept as far away from sexuality as possible. In fact, sexual force is not conventionally recognized to raise issues of sex inequality, either against those who commit the acts or against the state that condones them. Sexuality is regulated largely by criminal law, occasionally by tort law, neither on grounds of equality. Reproductive control, similarly, has been adjudicated primarily as an issue of privacy. It is as if a vacuum boundary demarcates sexual issues on the one hand from the law of equality on the other. Law, structurally, adopts the male point of view: sexuality concerns nature not social arbitrariness, interpersonal relations not social distributions of power, the sex difference not sex discrimination.

Sex discrimination law, with mainstream moral theory, sees equality and gender as issues of sameness and difference. According to this approach, which has dominated politics, law, and social perception, equality is an equivalence not a distinction, and gender is a distinction not an equivalence. The legal mandate of equal treatment—both a systemic norm and a specific legal doctrine becomes a matter of treating likes alike and unlikes unlike, while the sexes are socially defined as such by their mutual unlikeness. That is, gender is socially constructed as difference epistemologically, and sex discrimination law bounds gender equality by difference doctrinally. Socially, one tells a woman from a man by their difference from each other, but a woman is legally recognized to be discriminated against on the basis of sex only when she can first be said to be the same as a man. A built-in tension thus exists between this concept of equality, which presupposes sameness, and this concept of sex, which presupposes difference. Difference defines the state's approach to sex equality epistemologically and doctrinally. Sex equality becomes a contradiction in terms, something of an oxymoron. The deepest issues of sex inequality, in which the sexes are most constructed as socially different, are either excluded at the threshold or precluded from coverage once in. In this way, difference is inscribed on society as the meaning of gender and written into law as the limit on sex discrimination....

Equality is comparative in sex discrimination law. Sex in law is compared with sex in life, and women are compared with men. Relevant empirical similarity to men is the basis for the claim to equal treatment for women. For differential treatment to be discriminatory, the sexes must first be "similarly situated" by legislation, qualifications, circumstance, or physical endowment. This standard applies to sex the broader legal norm of neutrality, the law's version of objectivity. To test for gender neutrality, reverse the sexes and compare. To see if a woman was discriminated against on the basis of sex, ask whether a similarly situated man would be or was so treated. Relevant difference supports different treatment, no matter how categorical, disadvantageous, or cumulative. Accurate reflections of situated disparities are thus rendered either noncomparable or rational, therefore differences not inequalities for legal purposes. In this view, normative equality derives from and refers to empirical equivalence. Situated differences produce differentiated outcomes without necessarily involving discrimination....

From women's point of view, gender is more an inequality of power than a differentiation that is accurate or inaccurate. To women, sex is a social status based on who is permitted to do what to whom; only derivatively is it a difference. For example, one woman reflected on her gender: "I wish I had been born a doormat, or a man." Being a doormat is definitely different from being a man. Differences between the sexes do descriptively exist. But the fact that these are a woman's realistic options, and that they are so limiting, calls into question the perspective that considers this distinction a "difference." Men are not called different because they are neither doormats nor women, but a woman is not socially permitted to be a woman and neither doormat nor man.

From this perspective, considering gender a matter of sameness and difference covers up the reality of gender as a system of social hierarchy, as an inequality. The differences attributed to sex become lines that inequality draws, not any kind of basis for it. Social and political inequality begins indifferent to sameness and difference. Differences are inequality's post hoc excuse, its conclusory artifact, its outcome presented as its origin, its sentimentalization, its damage that is pointed to as the justification for doing the damage after the damage has been done, the distinctions that perception is socially organized to notice because inequality gives them consequences for social power. Gender might not even code as difference, might not mean distinction epistemologically, were it not for its conse-quences for social power.... Difference is the velvet glove on the iron fist of domination. The problem then is not that differences are not valued; the problem is that they are defined by power. This is as true when difference is affirmed as when it is denied, when its substance is applauded or disparaged, when women are punished or protected in its name.

Doctrinally speaking, two alternative paths to sex equality for women exist within the mainstream approach to sex discrimination, paths that follow the lines of the sameness/difference tension. The leading one is: be the same as men. This path is termed "gender neutrality" doctrinally and the single standard philosophically.... Legally articulated as conforming normative standards to existing reality, as law reflecting life, the strongest doctrinal expression of sameness would prohibit taking gender into account in any way, with exceptions for "real differences." This is so far the leading rule that the words "equal to" are code for, or/and equivalent to, the words "the same as"—with the referent for both unspecified.

To women who want equality yet find themselves "different," the doctrine provides an alternative route: be different from men. This equal recognition of difference is termed the special benefit rule or special protection rule legally, the double standard philosophically. It is in rather bad odor, reminiscent of women's exclusion from the public sphere and of protective labor laws. Like pregnancy, which always brings it up, it is something of a doctrinal embarrassment. Considered an exception to true equality and not really a rule of law at all, it is the one place where the law of sex discrimination admits it is recognizing something substantive.... Situated differences can produce different treatment—indulgences *or* depri-vations. This equality law is agnostic as to which.

The philosophy underlying the sameness/difference approach applies liberalism to women. Sex is a natural difference, a division, a distinction, beneath which lies a stratum of human commonality, sameness. The moral thrust of the sameness branch of the doctrine conforms normative rules to empirical reality by granting women access to what men have: to the extent women are no different from men, women deserve what men have. The differences branch, which is generally regarded as patronizing and unprincipled but necessary to avoid absurdity, exists to value or compensate women for what they are or have become distinctively as women—by which is meant, unlike men, or to leave women as "different" as equality law finds them.

Most scholarship on sex discrimination law concerns which of these paths to sex equality is preferable in the long run or more appropriate to any particular issue, as if they were all there is. As a prior matter, however, creating issues of sex equality as issues of sameness and difference is to take a particular approach. This approach is here termed the sameness/difference approach because it is obsessed with the sex difference. Its main theme is: "we're the same, we're the same, we're the same." Its counterpoint theme (in a higher register) goes: "but we're different, but we're different, but we're different." Its story is: on the first day, difference was; on the second day, a division was created upon it; on the third day, occasional dominance arose. Division may be rational or irrational. Dominance either seems or is justified or unjustified. Difference *is*.

Concealed is the substantive way in which man has become the measure of all things. Under the sameness rubric, women are measured according to correspondence with man, their equality judged by proximity to his measure. Under the difference rubric, women are measured according to their lack of correspondence from man, their womanhood judged by their distance from his measure. Gender neutrality is the male standard. The special protection rule is the female standard. Masculinity or maleness is the referent for both. Approaching sex discrimination in this way, as if sex questions were difference questions and equality questions were sameness questions, merely provides two ways for the law to hold women to a male standard and to call that sex equality....

Consider imposed differences: what to do about the fact that most women are segregated into low-paying jobs where there are no men? Arguing that the structure of the marketplace will be subverted if comparable worth is put into effect (an interesting comment on the radical potential of a reform with much in common with wages for housework proposals), difference doctrine says that because there is no man to set a standard from which women's treatment is a deviation, there is no sex discrimination, only a sex difference. Never mind that there is no man to compare with because no man would do that job if he had a choice, and because he is a man, he does, so he does not. Straightforward cases of sex discrimination run aground on the same rock. For example, in *Sears* v. *EEOC*, the Equal Employment Opportunities Commission argued that massive statistical disparities between women and men in some categories of better-paying jobs showed sex discrimination by Sears. One expert, Alice Kessler Harris, assuming women's sameness with men in the name of feminism, supported them, saying that whenever women were permitted to be exceptions, they were. Defendant Sears argued that women were different from men, did not necessarily want the same things men want, such as better-paying jobs. Another expert, Rosalind Rosenberg, arguing women's differences from men in the name of feminism, supported them. Given that the women in the data overwhelmingly divided on gender lines, and that neither the doctrinal assumptions nor the sex inequality of the job definitions was challenged, not to mention the social sexism that constructs what people "want," the argument on women's differences won, and women lost....

This law takes the same approach to the social reality of sex inequality that the ideology of sex inequality takes to social life, and considers itself legitimate because the two correspond. For this reason, sex equality law is always being undermined by the problem it is trying to solve. It cannot recognize, for instance, that men do not have to be the same as anyone to be entitled to most benefits. It cannot recognize that every quality that distinguishes men from women is already affirmatively compensated in society's organization and values, so that it implicitly defines the standards it neutrally applies. Men's physiology defines most sports, their health needs largely define insurance coverage, their socially designed biographies define workplace expectations and successful career patterns, their perspectives and concerns define quality in scholarship, their experiences and obsessions define merit, their military service defines citizenship, their presence defines family, their inability to get along with each other—their wars and rulerships—defines history, their image defines god, and their genitals define sex. These are the standards that are presented as gender neutral. For each of men's differences from women, what amounts to an affirmative action plan is in effect, otherwise known as the male-dominant structure and values of American society. But whenever women are found different from men and insist on not having it held against them, every time a difference is used to keep women second class and equality law is brought in as redress, the doctrine has a paradigm trauma.

Clearly, there are many differences between women and men. Systematically elevating one-half of a population and denigrating the other half would not likely produce a population in which everyone is the same. What sex equality law fails to notice is that men's differences from women are equal to women's differences from men. Yet the sexes are not equally situated in society with respect to their relative differences. Hierarchy of power produces real as well as fantasied differences, differences that are also inequalities. The differences are equal. The inequalities, rather obviously, are not....

Sex discrimination law requires that women either be gender objects or emulate maleness to qualify as subject. These criteria interestingly parallel the two-pronged "passionlessness" that Nancy Cott identifies as women's side of the bargain under which women were historically allowed access to this form of institutional equality at all. "Passionlessness"—sexual acted-uponness as female gender definition—was the price of women's admission to Victorian moral equality. Passionless women merit equal protection (equal treatment, separate version female) or qualified permission to be second-class men (equal treatment, version male). Passionateness would merely break the rule, disentitling the women to moral equality but leaving passionlessness standing as the rule for women. Nonpassionless women—

perhaps self-acting, self-defined, self-respecting, not sexually defined, and resisting sex inequality from that position—simply do not exist in these terms. If gender status is sexually based, sexual equality would be real equality. In this light, this form of sexual objectification as the price for equality looks like inequality as the price for equality, and the bourgeois bargain—the terms on which women as a gender were admitted to abstract personhood and individuality in the first place is revealed to have had a sexual price. . . .

Objectivity assumes that equally competent observers similarly situated see, or at least report seeing, the same thing. Feminism radically questions whether the sexes are ever, under current conditions, similarly situated even when they inhabit the same conditions. (It questions some standards for competence as well.) The line between subjective and objective perception which is supposed to divide the idiosyncratic, nonreplicable, religious, partial, and unverifiable—the unscientific—from the real presumes the existence of a single object reality and its noncontingence upon angle of perception. But if women's condition exists, there are (at least) two *object* realms of social meaning. Women's point of view is no more subjective than men's if women inhabit a sex-discriminatory object reality.

In this analysis, social circumstances, to which gender is central, produce distinctive interests, hence perceptions, hence meanings, hence definitions of rationality. This observation neither reduces gender to thinking differently, rightness to relative subjectivity, nor principle to whose ox is gored. It does challenge the view that neutrality, specifically gender neutrality as an expression of objectivity, is adequate to the nonneutral objectified social reality women experience. If differentiation were the problem, gender neutrality would make sense as an approach to it. Since hierarchy is the problem, it is not only inadequate, it is perverse. In questioning the principledness of neutral principles, this analysis suggests that current law to rectify sex inequality is premised upon, and promotes, its continued existence.

The analytical point of departure and return of sex discrimination law is thus the liberal one of gender differences, understood rationally or irrationally to create gender inequalities. The feminist issue, by contrast, is gender hierarchy, which not only produces inequalities but shapes the social meaning, hence legal relevance, of the sex difference. To the extent that the biology of one sex is a social disadvantage, while the biology of the other is not, or is a social advantage, the sexes are equally different but not equally powerful. . . . The relevant issue is the social meaning of the sexuality and gender of women and men, not their sexuality or gender "itself"—if such a distinction can be made. To limit efforts to end gender inequality at the point where biology or sexuality is encountered, termed differences, without realizing that these exist in law or society only in terms of their specifically sexist social meanings, amounts to conceding that gender inequality may be challenged so long as the central epistemological pillars of gender as a system of power are permitted to remain standing.

So long as this is the way these issues are framed, women's demands for sex equality will appear to be demands to have it both ways: the same when women are the same as men, different when different. But this is the way men have it: equal and different too. The same as women when they are the same and want to be, and different from women when they are different or want to be, which usually they do. Equal and different too would be parity. But under male supremacy, while being told women get it both ways—the specialness of the pedestal and an even chance at the race, the ability to be a woman and a person, too—few women get much benefit of either. The sameness route ignores the fact that the indices or injuries of sex or sexism often ensure that simply being a woman may mean seldom being in a position sufficiently similar to a man's to have unequal treatment attributed to sex bias. The difference route incorporates and reflects rather than alters the substance of women's inferior status, presenting a protection racket as equal protection of the laws. In this way, the legal forms available for arguing the injuries of sex inequality obscure the gender of this equality's reference point while effectively precluding complaint for women's sex-specific grievances.

When sameness is the standard for equality, a critique of gender hierarchy looks like a request for special protection in disguise. In fact, it envisions a change that would make a simple equal chance possible for the first time. To define the reality of gender as difference and the warrant of equality as sameness not only guarantees that sex equality will never be achieved; it is wrong on both counts. Sex in nature is not a bipolarity, it is a continuum; society makes it into a bipolarity. Once this is done, to require that one be the same as those who set the standard—those from whom one is already socially defined as different—simply means that sex equality is conceptually designed in law never to be achieved. Those who most need equal treatment will be the *least* similar, socially, to those whose situation sets the standard against which their entitlement to equal treatment is measured. The deepest problems of sex inequality do not find women "similarly situated" to men. Practices of inequality need not be intentionally discriminatory. The status quo need only be reflected unchanged. As a strategy for maintaining social power, descriptively speaking, first structure social reality unequally, and then require that entitlement to alter it be grounded on a lack of distinction in situation; first structure perception so that different equals inferior, and then require that discrimination be activated by evil minds who *know* that they are treating equals as less, in a society in which, epistemologically speaking, most bigots will be sincere.

The mainstream law of equality assumes that society is already fundamentally equal. It gives women legally no more than they already have socially, and little it cannot also give men. Actually doing anything for women under sex equality law is thus stigmatized as special protection or affirmative action rather than simply recognized as nondiscrimination or equality for the first time. So long as sex equality is limited by sex difference—whether valued or negated, staked out as a ground for feminism or occupied as the terrain of misogyny—women will be born, degraded, and die. Protection will be a dirty word and equality will be a special privilege.

NOTES AND QUESTIONS

1. **Thinking about MacKinnon's work.** Do you agree with MacKinnon that arguing that women are the same as men, and therefore should be treated as men, or arguing that women are different, and therefore should be treated differently, is not a promising strategy? One of MacKinnon's central insights is the recognition that men are always the model, whether we are arguing that women should be treated the same as men or differently. Does this strike you as appropriate? If this is the case, are men always "equal?"

MacKinnon argues that what we have previously simply identified as differences should instead be identified as instances of subordination of women to men. She calls her own position, with its emphasis on power and hierarchy, the "dominance approach." Women's reality, according to Mac-Kinnon, is very real and quite different from men's. If this is the case, how can we retain any conception of objectivity? Most feminists would accept much of MacKinnon's argument, but if we do, will we have to reevaluate many fundamental principles of the law, including the idea of objectivity?

2. **Sameness and Difference.** The controversy over whether women should be considered as being the same as men or different from them raged throughout the 1970s and 1980s, and continues today. It structures the Supreme Court cases that appear in the next section. The early focus was on pregnancy. While issues relating to the treatment of pregnancy linger, many other current debates, such as those over child custody or welfare reform, can be seen as efforts by women to hold on to equality ("special benefits") that has been created to protect our special role as child nurturers, while the attacks on these rights have often been articulated in terms of treating men and women equally.

The equal treatment position was cogently argued by Wendy Williams in the early 1980s. Focusing on whether women should be entitled to leaves and benefits when they are pregnant, she argued that they should not. Instead, she favored treating pregnancy as any other disability was treated. "The reality," she noted, meant "that conceptualizing pregnancy as a special case permits unfavorable as well as favorable treatment of pregnancy." Certainly, U.S. history is rife with examples of special treatment (e.g., wage and hour laws) that were justified as benefitting women and ended up harming them. She also worried that better treatment of pregnancy would focus attention on "the unfairness of protecting one class of worker and not others," and that allowing the state to "claim an interest in women's special procreational capacity" might ultimately endanger women's reproductive freedom. Williams's position can be summarized as "Be careful what you wish for." Wendy W. Williams, *The Equality Crisis: Some Reflections On Culture, Courts, and Feminism*, 7 Women's Rts. L. Rep. 175 (1982).

Many feminists did, however, support the position that women should receive special treatment in areas in which they differ from men. The goal of those who endorsed special treatment was not so much to create a form of formal equality as to make gender differences costless so that women are able to engage in lifestyles and activities that are what might otherwise have been considered either male or female, without penalty. Special treatment approaches to women's differences raise the question as to which differences should be recognized and afforded such special treatment. Some legal feminists argued that special treatment should be available only for those biological differences that distinguish all (or at least most) women from men. Sylvia A. Law, *Rethinking Sex and the Constitution*, 132 U. Pa. L. Rev. 955 (1984). The prime example of such differences are those that revolve around the reproductive system. Others believed that special treatment should encompass culturally-based differences as well as biological ones. Christine A. Littleton, *Reconstructing Sexual Equality,* 75 Calif. L. Rev. 1279 (1987). Which of these positions do you believe is the stronger one?

Does it make sense to try to distinguish biological differences between men and women from cultural ones? Surely, if the distinctions are viable, pregnancy would be classified as a biological difference. But what flows from this? For example, if the debate is over hospital insurance, we might once have thought that a week of in-patient care was essential for the woman who had just delivered. Now, it turns out that some women can feasibly be released within 24 hours of delivery. Others can safely be delivered at home. Should we think of required delivery care as based in biology or culture?

With this admittedly very brief introduction to the equal treatment/special treatment debate, what do you think about MacKinnon's criticisms of the two positions? She claims that they are two sides of the same argument. How do you think she justifies this position? Do you agree? She also claims that they reinforce traditional stereotypical nineteenth century ideals about women. Finally, she enters the debate over whether the focus should be only on biological differences. MacKinnon says, "The relevant issue is the social meaning of the sexuality and gender of women and men, not their sexuality or gender 'itself'—if such a distinction can be made." Does she think such a distinction can be made? Do you?

3. **Deconstructing Gender.** One's gender is often differentiated from one's sex on the grounds that gender involves the culturally constructed norms identified with male or female, whereas sex refers to biological characteristics. Of course, these differentiations depend on the ability to distinguish biology from culture.

Christine Littleton, in *Reconstructing Sexual Equality,* uses the term "social male" to describe women who conform to male norms of behavior and therefore are treated as equal to men. It is important to recognize the possibility that people who are biologically categorized as women might nonetheless be social males in Littleton's terms. Littleton does not see the possibility of social males as a way out of the sameness/difference bind.

Instead, she sees it as a way in which society forces women to be either social women (different) or social males (the same).

Postmodern feminist Judith Butler finds the possibility of reconstructing gender ideas in the ways people act out their gender roles. In her book, *Gender Trouble*, she argues that female impersonators

> give[] us a clue to the way in which the relationship between primary identification—that is, the original meanings accorded to gender—and subsequent gender experience might be reframed. The performance of drag plays upon the distinction between the anatomy of the performer and gender that is being performed. But we are actually in the presence of three contingent dimensions of significant corporeality: anatomical sex, gender identity, and gender performance. If the anatomy of the performer is already distinct from the gender of the performer, and both of those are distinct from the gender of the performance, then the performance suggests a dissonance not only between sex and performance, but sex and gender, and gender and performance. As much as drag creates a unified picture of "woman" (what its critics often oppose), it also reveals the distinctness of those aspects of gendered experience which are falsely naturalized as a unity through the regulatory fiction of heterosexual coherence. *In imitating gender, drag implicitly reveals the imitative structure of gender itself—as well as its contingency....*
>
> The notion of gender parody defended here does not assume that there is an original which such parodic identities imitate.... [G]ender parody reveals that the original identity after which gender fashions itself is an imitation without an origin. To be more precise, it is a production which, in effect—that is, in its effect— postures as an imitation. This perpetual displacement constitutes a fluidity of identities that suggests an openness to resignification and recontextualization; parodic proliferation deprives hegemonic culture and its critics of the claim to naturalized or essentialist gender identities.

J. Butler, Gender Trouble 137-38.

Do you agree with Butler that reenactments of gender stereotypes are bound to differ from some imagined norm, and in that difference to recreate norms? Or do you agree with Littleton that enforcing gender norms simply strengthens and rigidifies them? Is there a difference between the law's declaration of norms and individuals' efforts to embody them?

Angela P. Harris, Race and Essentialism in Feminist Legal Theory

42 Stan. L. Rev. 581 (1990).

... In this article, I discuss some of the writings of feminist legal theorists.... I argue that [their] work, though powerful and brilliant in many ways, relies on what I call gender essentialism—the notion that a unitary, "essential" women's experience can be isolated and described independently of race, class, sexual orientation, and other realities of experience. The result of this tendency toward gender essentialism, I argue, is not only that some voices are silenced in order to privilege others (for this is an inevitable result of categorization, which is necessary both for human communication and political movement), but that the voices that are silenced turn out to be the same voices silenced by the mainstream legal voice . . . the voices of black women.

This result troubles me for two reasons. First, the obvious one: As a black woman, in my opinion the experience of black women is too often ignored both in feminist theory and in legal theory, and gender essentialism in feminist legal theory does nothing to address this problem. A second and less obvious reason for my criticism of gender essentialism is that, in my view, contemporary legal theory needs less abstraction and not simply a different sort of abstraction. To be fully subversive, the methodology of feminist legal theory should challenge not only law's content but its tendency to privilege the abstract and unitary voice, and this gender essentialism also fails to do . . . .

Essentialism in feminist theory has two characteristics that ensure that black women's voices will be ignored. First, in the pursuit of the essential feminine, woman [is] leached of all color and irrelevant social circumstance, issues of race are bracketed as belonging to a separate and distinct discourse—a process which leaves black women's selves fragmented beyond recognition. Second, feminist essentialists find that in removing issues of "race" they have actually only managed to remove black women—meaning that white women now stand as the epitome of Woman. . . . [A] consequence of feminist essentialism is that the racism that was acknowledged only in brackets quietly emerges in the feminist theory itself—both a cause and an effect of creating "Woman" from white woman. . . .

I call . . . [the following] the "nuance theory" approach to the problem of essentialism: by being sensitive to the notion that different women have different experiences, generalizations can be offered about "all women" while qualifying statements, often in footnotes, supplement the general account with the subtle nuances of experience that "different" women add to the mix. Nuance theory thus assumes the commonality of all women—differences are a matter of "context" or "magnitude"; that is, nuance.

The problem with nuance theory is that by defining black women as "different," white women quietly become the norm, or pure, essential woman. Just as . . . [some] would argue that being female is more than a "context" or a "magnitude" of human experience, being black is more than a context or magnitude of all (white) women's experience. . . .

In this society, it is only white people who have the luxury of "having no color"; only white people have been able to imagine that sexism and racism are separate experiences. Far more for black women than for white women, the experience of self is precisely that of being unable to disentangle the web of race and gender—of being enmeshed always in multiple, often contradictory, discourses of sexuality and color. The challenge to black women has been the need to weave the fragments, our many selves, into an integral, though always changing and shifting, whole: a self that is neither "female" nor "black," but both-and.... [I]nsistence that every self is deeply and primarily gendered, then, with its corollary that gender is more important to personal identity than race, is finally another example of white solipsism.... [S]uggest[ions] that gender is more deeply embedded in self than race, ... privilege[] the experience of white people over all others, and thus serve[] to reproduce relations of domination in the larger culture....

In this part of the article, I want to talk about what black women can bring to feminist theory to help us move beyond essentialism and toward multiple consciousness as feminist and jurisprudential method. In my view, there are at least three major contributions that black women have to offer post-essentialist feminist theory: the recognition of a self that is multiplicitous, not unitary; the recognition that differences are always relational rather than inherent; and the recognition that wholeness and commonality are acts of will and creativity, rather than passive discovery.

The Abandonment of Innocence

Black women experience not a single inner self (much less one that is essentially gendered), but many selves. This sense of a multiplicitous self is not unique to black women, but black women have expressed this sense in ways that are striking, poignant, and potentially useful to feminist theory....

This experience of multiplicity is also a sense of self-contradiction, of containing the oppressor within oneself. In her article *On Being the Object of Property*, Patricia Williams writes about herself writing about her great-great-grandmother, "picking through the ruins for my roots." What she finds is a paradox: She must claim for herself "a heritage the weft of whose genesis is [her] own disinheritance." Williams's great-great-grandmother, Sophie, was a slave, and at the age of about eleven was impregnated by her owner, a white lawyer named Austin Miller. Their daughter Mary, Williams's great-grandmother, was taken away from Sophie and raised as a house servant.

When Williams went to law school, her mother told her, "The Millers were lawyers, so you have it in your blood." Williams analyzes this statement as asking her to acknowledge contradictory selves:

> [S]he meant that no one should make me feel inferior because someone else's father was a judge. She wanted me to reclaim that part of my heritage from which I had been disinherited, and she wanted me to use it as a source of strength and self-confidence. At the same time, she was asking me to claim a part of myself that was the dispossessor of another part of myself; she was asking me to deny that disenfranchised little black girl of myself that felt powerless, vulnerable and, moreover, rightly felt so.

The theory of black slavery, Williams notes, was based on the notion that black people are beings without will or personality, defined by "irrationality, lack of control, and ugliness." In contrast, "wisdom, control, and aesthetic beauty signify the whole white personality in slave law." In accepting her white self, her lawyer self, Williams must accept a legacy of not only a disinheritance but a negation of her black self: To the Millers, her forebears, the Williamses, her forebears, did not even have selves as such.

Williams's choice ultimately is not to deny either self, but to recognize them both, and in so doing to acknowledge guilt as well as innocence. . . .

This complex resolution rejects the easy innocence of supposing oneself to be an essential black self with a legacy of oppression by the guilty white Other. With such multilayered analyses, black women can bring to feminist theory stories of how it is to have multiple and contradictory selves, selves that contain the oppressor as well as the oppressed.

Strategic Identities and "Difference"

A post-essentialist feminism can benefit not only from the abandonment of the quest for a unitary self, but also from Martha Minow's realization that difference—and therefore identity—is always relational, not inherent. Zora Neale Hurston's work is a good illustration of this notion.

In an essay written for a white audience, *How It Feels to Be Colored Me*, Hurston argues that her color is not an inherent part of her being, but a response to her surroundings. She recalls the day she "became colored"— the day she left her home in an all-black community to go to school: "I left Eatonville, the town of the oleanders, as Zora. When I disembarked from the river-boat at Jacksonville, she was no more. It seemed that I had suffered a sea change. I was not Zora of Orange County any more, I was now a little colored girl." But even as an adult, Hurston insists, her colored self is always situational: "I do not always feel colored. Even now I often achieve the unconscious Zora of Eatonville before the Hegira. I feel most colored when I am thrown against a sharp white background." . . .

Thus, "how it feels to be colored Zora" depends on the answer to these questions:

"Compared to what? As of when? Who is asking? In what context? For what purpose? With what interests and presuppositions? What Hurston rigorously shows is that questions of difference and identity are always functions of a specific interlocutionary situation—and the answers, matters of strategy rather than truth." Any "essential self" is always an invention; the evil is in denying its artificiality.

To be compatible with this conception of the self, feminist theorizing about "women" must similarly be strategic and contingent, focusing on relationships, not essences. One result will be that men will cease to be a faceless Other and reappear as potential allies in political struggle. Another will be that women will be able to acknowledge their differences without threatening feminism itself. In the process, as feminists begin to attack racism and classism and homophobia, feminism will change from being only about "women as women" (modified women need not apply), to being about all kinds of oppression based on seemingly inherent and unalterable characteristics. We need not wait for a unified theory of oppression; that theory can be feminism.

Integrity as Will and Idea

Finally, black women can help [the] feminist movement move beyond its fascination with essentialism through the recognition that wholeness of the self and commonality with others are asserted (if never completely achieved) through creative action, not realized in shared victimization. Feminist theory at present, especially feminist legal theory, tends to focus on women as passive victims. . . . Women are the victims, the acted-upon, the helpless, until by radical enlightenment they are somehow empowered to act for themselves. . . .

This story of woman as victim is meant to encourage solidarity by emphasizing women's shared oppression, thus denying or minimizing difference, and to further the notion of an essential woman—she who is victimized. But as bell hooks has succinctly noted, the notion that women's commonality lies in their shared victimization by men "directly reflects male supremacist thinking. Sexist ideology teaches women that to be female is to be a victim." Moreover, the story of woman as passive victim denies the ability of women to shape their own lives, whether for better or worse. It also may thwart their abilities. . . .

At the individual level, black women have had to learn to construct themselves in a society that denied them full selves. Again, Zora Neale Hurston's writings are suggestive. Though Hurston plays with being her "colored self" and again with being "the eternal feminine with its string of beads," she ends *How It Feels to Be Colored Me* with an image of herself as neither essentially black nor essentially female,

> but simply a brown bag of miscellany propped against a wall. Against a wall in company with other bags, white, red and yellow. Pour out the contents, and there is discovered a jumble of small things priceless and worthless. A first-water diamond, an empty spool, bits of broken glass, lengths of string, a key to a door long since crumbled away, a rusty knife-blade, old shoes saved for a road that never was and never will be, a nail bent under the weight of things too heavy for any nail, a dried flower or two still fragrant. In your hand is the brown bag. On the ground before you is the jumble it held—so much like the jumble in the bags, could they be emptied, that all might be dumped in a single heap and the bags refilled without altering the content of any greatly. A bit of colored glass more or less would not matter. Perhaps that is how

the Great Stuffer of Bags filled them in the first place—who knows?

Hurston thus insists on a conception of identity as a construction, not an essence—something made of fragments of experience, not discovered in one's body or unveiled after male domination is eliminated.

This insistence on the importance of will and creativity seems to threaten feminism at one level, because it gives strength back to the concept of autonomy, making possible the recognition of the element of consent in relations of domination, and attributes to women the power that makes culpable the many ways in which white women have actively used their race privilege against their sisters of color. Although feminists are correct to recognize the powerful force of sheer physical coercion in ensuring compliance with patriarchal hegemony, we must also "come to terms with the ways in which women's culture has served to enlist women's support in perpetuating existing power relations."

However, at another level, the recognition of the role of creativity and will in shaping our lives is liberating, for it allows us to acknowledge and celebrate the creativity and joy with which many women have survived and turned existing relations of domination to their own ends.

Finally, on a collective level this emphasis on will and creativity reminds us that bridges between women are built, not found. The discovery of shared suffering is a connection more illusory than real; what will truly bring and keep us together is the use of effort and imagination to root out and examine our differences, for only the recognition of women's differences can ultimately bring feminist movement to strength. This is hard work, and painful work; but it is also radical work, real work....

NOTES AND QUESTIONS

1. **Essentialism.** The problem of essentialism is important for anyone thinking about women. Harris's point that the experiences of Black women differ from the experiences of white women is well taken. These different experiences will affect white and Black women's understandings of life and their perspectives on various problems. As Harris shows, claiming a single, unitary voice for all women most often results in the privileging of white women's voice, just as the claiming of a single unitary perspective for all humans usually privileges the voice of white men. She argues that the result is twofold. First, the ideals of womanhood are established with stereotypes of white women in mind. This makes it impossible for Black women who are stereotypically thought of as aggressive and sexual temptresses to meet the white woman-derived stereotype of passivity and sexual purity. As a result, their claims of sexual harassment or rape are less likely to be believed because they are not perceived as likely to ever have been true women. In this way, the adoption of a single woman's voice results in the expulsion of non-privileged women from the category "woman." Second, essentialism in feminist thinking skews the analysis by omitting race (or class or age, etc.) For example, analyses of rape or sexual harassment from a white woman's feminist perspective are unlikely to consider the role that prosecutions for sexual offenses have had in maintaining racial hier-

archies. This history of using claims of rape or sexual harassment as a means of keeping non-white men in their place often creates a deep ambivalence in women of color who are faced with the need to assist in prosecutions of men from their own communities who have traditionally been subordinated in part through such prosecutions. Essentialist approaches to describing women's situation can thus be criticized both because they exclude many women and because they do not provide a complete analysis of the situation.

Nevertheless, it is also important to be able to think in categories. In an omitted section of the article, Harris actually quotes Martha Minow's statement, "[W]e need simplifying categories, and the unifying category of 'woman' helps to organize experience, even at the cost of denying some of it." Indeed, in another omitted section of the article, Harris says, "I do not mean . . . to suggest that either feminism or legal theory should adopt the . . . [position that] every experience is unique and no categories or generalizations exist at all. Even a jurisprudence based on multiple consciousness must categorize. . . . " If categorization is necessary, how can we avoid the pitfalls of essentialism? Is it possible to imagine simultaneously using and criticizing categories?

2. **Essentialism and Identity.** Harris's criticisms of essentialist approaches to feminist theory are also applicable to our understanding of personal identity. Harris quotes Patricia Williams in discussing her sense of a multiplicitous self. Many others have voiced the same idea. For example, W.E.B. Du Bois wrote: "It is a peculiar sensation, this double-consciousness. . . . One ever feels his two-ness,—an American, a Negro; two souls, two thoughts, two unreconciled strivings; two warring ideals in one dark body . . ." W.E.B. Du Bois, *The Souls of Black Folk* 8–9. Furthermore, these component parts of one's identity assume differing importance depending on the situation. Zora Neale Hurston was relatively unaware of her blackness while at home in Eatonville, but the moment she left Eatonville and found herself in a predominantly white community, she suddenly recognized herself as black.

Can you identify a variety of identities that make up yourself? What about times when you are particularly aware of one identity or another? When are the moments when you are most aware of your sex? Your race? Your religion? Your sexual preference? Your age? If you agree with Harris that you are a multiplicitous self, what are the implications of this for feminist theory?

C.   WOMEN, LAW AND THE WORK/FAMILY CONFLICT

INTRODUCTION

Pregnancy, a biological act unique to women, and childrearing, a cultural activity more frequently undertaken by women than men, are frequently seen as major obstacles to women's participation in the labor market. Workplace responsibilities often conflict with family duties in ways that produce significant stress and substantial barriers to women as they seek to assimilate and to advance in their labor force jobs. There is also evidence that the work/family conflict is responsible, at least in part, for the gross economic disparity between female and male workers. According to both popular and academic accounts, the work/family conflict is an almost intractable problem for women in the workforce. This section presents materials that describe and criticize some aspects of the legal treatment of the work/family conflict. It also includes references to reform efforts actually proposed and theoretically proposable. The overarching question of this section is what should and can the law do to resolve or ameliorate the conflict.

The readings begin with an excerpt from a law review article by Mary Joe Frug, written in 1979, that sets forth an explanation of how and why the work/family conflict is particularly damaging to women. The second piece, a recent case decided by the Massachusetts Supreme Judicial Court, upholds an employer's right to fire the mother of a young child for refusing to work long hours and weekends. She argued that these interfered with her responsibilities as a mother. Together these two readings suggest the extent and character of the work/family conflict as an issue for women and the law.

The bulk of the law provided in this section consists of Supreme Court decisions involving the legal treatment of pregnancy and fertility during the past two decades. As the readings have already indicated, the intensification of the women's movement in the sixties included a concentrated campaign by feminist lawyers to obtain equal legal treatment for women. The extension of legal equality, however, has not proved sufficient to redress the problems posed by the work/family conflict. Although these problems extend well beyond issues relating to pregnancy and childbirth, the pregnancy related cases in the readings illustrate a significant analytical issue that tends to arise in all legal challenges to workplace structures which burden parenting. This issue is the imposition of a sameness/difference paradigm on the interpretation of equality.

The sameness/difference paradigm, as already indicated, refers to a way of thinking about or analyzing a claim of sex inequality as a question of whether women are the same as or different from men. For example, if both women and men could be pregnant, a workplace rule which treated pregnant women punitively would be prohibited by the equality guarantee, which conventionally has required that similar cases be treated similarly. But since men don't get pregnant, employers—according to the paradigm—can penalize workers on account of their pregnancies with impunity. The paradigm can also be extended to childrearing issues by reasoning that since most women assume more childbearing responsibilities than men, women and men are different with respect to childbearing.

Geduldig v. Aiello, 417 U.S. 484, 94 S.Ct. 2485, 41 L.Ed.2d 256 (1974), the first decision in the readings, is a classic illustration of the application of the sameness/difference paradigm. In *Geduldig,* the Supreme Court, despite having extended special protection under the equality guarantee to sex-based classifications in Reed v. Reed, 404 U.S. 71, 92 S.Ct. 251, 30 L.Ed.2d 225 (1971), refused to grant special protection for pregnancy. *Geduldig* unambiguously signalled that the Constitutional sexual equality guarantee would not be available to combat most workplace problems attributable to pregnancy.

The continuing influence of the paradigm is attested to by the two remaining Supreme Court cases in this section. In both California Federal Savings & Loan Ass'n v. Guerra, 479 U.S. 272, 107 S.Ct. 683, 93 L.Ed.2d 613 (1987) and International Union, UAW v. Johnson Controls, 499 U.S. 187, 111 S.Ct. 1196, 113 L.Ed.2d 158 (1991), the sameness/difference paradigm is a critical analytical aspect of the challenges mounted against the pregnancy leave and fetal protection policies. In *Cal Fed*, Justice Marshall, writing for the Court, ingeniously recognized that leaves with reinstatement guarantees that looked like special treatment of women who were similarly situated to men would become equal treatment if the benefits were extended to men. Thus, the Court could avoid declaring the statute unconstitutional under the sameness/difference paradigm by recognizing that the state could interpret it in a manner that would make it constitutional. Although this was just one of two bases for upholding the statute in *Cal Fed*, the Court in *Johnson Controls* invoked the sameness/difference paradigm to hold that since the women could perform their jobs as well as anyone else, they should not be barred from the jobs on the grounds of possible future damage to their possible future fetuses.

As you read through these cases, you should continue to assess whether the sameness/difference paradigm helps women or hurts them. Can you start to identify particular types of cases where it might be helpful and appropriate and other types where it might be injurious to their interests?

Following the pregnancy cases the readings present recent efforts or proposals to deal with the work/family conflict. The Family and Medical Leave Act of 1993 makes leaves available to any eligible *employee* following the birth or adoption of a child. The Act is written in a self-consciously gender-neutral manner. Would you expect large numbers of male employees to request such leaves? The Act is followed by an excerpt from an article by Kathryn Abrams in which she discusses the need to rethink the line between work and family. She also proposes a variety of reforms to make the workplace more flexible, including some—like part-time employment—that have been implemented by some employers. She notes, however, that these reforms are likely to result in a devaluing of the employees who embrace them: employees (mostly women) who take advantage of leaves and part-time opportunities are unlikely to be seen as sufficiently dependable or committed to the job. The reforms' identification with women and women's difference results in the marginalization of the employees who accept the reforms' benefits. This is exactly what some feminist legal scholars of the seventies and eighties had argued. Their position was that extending childbirth or childcare benefits to women would *weaken* the position of women in labor market work by drawing attention to women's *in*equality.

It may be useful here to recall Catharine MacKinnon's essay, *Difference and Dominance*, in the previous section of the materials. It proposed an analysis of sexual inequality which rejected the terms of sameness and difference as the standard for interpreting equality. Although this analysis has not been adopted by the Supreme Court, does it make sense here to think of the denigration of these workplace reforms and of the people who participate in them as an effect of male dominance?

Another reason why we may think of these workplace reforms as having relatively little transformative potential is the widespread acceptance of the public/private distinction. One might be able to agree with MacKinnon's interpretation of sex equality and still maintain that workplace reforms designed to address parenting problems inject the state too far into the private sphere of family life. Parenting, from the perspective of the public/private distinction, is a private, voluntary activity which the state, through its laws, should avoid, not regulate. Similarly, the terms of an employee's relationship with her (or his) employer, if not otherwise regulated by such laws as minimum wage laws, Blue laws, etc., should be set by private contracts between the employer and the employee. The importance of the public/private distinction is likely to become clear if you think about the *Upton* case included earlier in these materials. Should the Court have held that the employer's right to discharge at will was limited by the mother's need to spend time with her child? Would it be appropriate for the Court to rule on how much time she should spend with the child? What about on whether that time had to be actually with the child, or could be spent doing errands without the child? The power of the public/private distinction is also likely to become clear if we ask whether the state should mandate parental leaves? Should it require that fathers take leaves?

Richard Posner's essay, *Conservative Feminism,* illustrates how the public/private distinction can be deployed as a basis for opposing workplace reform efforts that MacKinnon's equality theory would legitimate. The last reading in the section, Fran Olsen's article, *The Myth of State Intervention in the Family*, provides an elaborate critique of the public/private distinction. While reading the materials in this section, one should evaluate both the sameness/difference paradigm and the public/private distinction as potential barriers to legislative reform. Posner's essay is a particularly inviting subject for focus here because of the way in which the sameness/difference paradigm sneaks in to support his argument against public regulation of either the workplace or family life. Is Posner proposing reforms that involve further regulation of the workplace or the family, or is he proposing that the state avoid intervening in both? What would it mean for the state not to intervene? This is the topic of the essay by Olsen. She argues that the ideas of intervention and nonintervention are applied inconsistently, and that they are fundamentally incoherent. If the ideas of intervention and nonintervention are indeed incoherent, can the public/private distinction be maintained?

Mary Joe Frug, Securing Job Equality for Women: Labor Market Hostility to Working Mothers

59 B.U. L. Rev. 55 (1979).

...The labor force is organized as if workers do not have family responsibilities. The traditional work schedule is both too inflexible and too long for a parent with primary child care responsibility. Preschool age children need full-time care; school age children need care not only during school vacations, but also during after-school hours. Although surrogate child care, either in a day care center or a private home, can resolve some of the scheduling conflicts between home and office demands, workers cannot always find or afford suitable care. Even when they can obtain such care, parents must still cope with emergencies such as illnesses which keep a child at home. In addition, children need more than mere tending; they and their parents need to spend time with one another that is meaningful, relaxing and pleasurable to all. The conventional full-time workday, when combined with unavoidable household duties, leaves little time for this parenting function. Too often when time is available both parent and child are too exhausted to use it advantageously.

Although many working men have children under eighteen, and although a very small but increasing number of men are single parents, the barriers operating against the successful participation of parents in the labor market primarily disadvantage women. Despite the increasing breakdown of the traditional division of roles which sent men into the labor market while keeping women at home, many women who work outside the home continue to shoulder their old jobs within the home as well. Even in families in which both parents are in the labor force and in "dual-career" families, in which both parents are pursuing professional careers, mothers still uniformly bear greater child-rearing responsibilities than fathers. Because women have predominant parenting responsibilities in our society, they, more than men, are handicapped by the structure of the labor market.

The accommodations that working mothers make in order to reconcile child-rearing responsibilities with labor market participation are reflected in the labor market gap between the sexes. Approximately one-third of all working mothers work part-time. Although part-time work allows women the time and flexibility they need to fulfill their family duties, it is dramatically underpaid in comparison with full-time employment. Moreover, it is characterized by inadequate fringe benefits or credits toward promotion, tenure, or salary adjustments. Furthermore, part-time work is usually available only in occupations offering minimal employee responsibility and little opportunity for advancement or self-enrichment. Thus, while part-time work resolves the conflict between childrearing and labor force participation, it does so by requiring workers—mostly women—to sacrifice normal employment expectations in exchange for less time on the job.

Similarly, mothers who work full-time adjust to the labor market barriers against parents by compromising their employment opportunities. Many choose jobs with flexible scheduling, usually available in occupations that are poorly paid and offer minimal fringe benefits. Others have had to choose jobs with less challenge or responsibility. Still others may be willing and able to assume as much responsibility as people without children, but their need to spend regular and predictable time with their children inevitably causes them to lose career opportunities to those without such demands—those who are willing and able to stay after five without notice, to work on holidays, or to travel unexpectedly. Thus, professional women are more often found among teachers, who can keep the same schedules as their children, than among school administrators. They more often practice law in trusts and estates, where they can control their work schedules, than in litigation, where they cannot. Non-professional women are concentrated in secretarial work and department store sales, where their absences can be easily covered by substitutes, and where they can go in and out of positions with little loss, since the jobs offer so little gain.

As long as the labor market is hostile to parents, and as long as roles in the American family continue to be allocated on the basis of gender, the labor market gap between the sexes will continue. If that disparity is unacceptable, as I think it is, then it is appropriate to determine how the disparity can be reduced. Arguably, women could overcome the barriers that the labor market structure erects against successfully combining work outside the home with parental duties by neglecting or giving up child-rearing. The labor market has required most men to forego the full pleasures and responsibilities of family life in order to participate fully in the labor market, but this requirement is hardly an acceptable way to secure job equality. Many children of absentee fathers have been damaged by the inattention they have received from men whose jobs have kept them from joining more than minimally in family activities. Furthermore, the absentee fathers themselves have lost the opportunity for individual growth and development that comes from participating in family life. Just as it is in society's interest to end the difficulties that the labor market has caused fathers, it is not in society's interest to extend to women the requirement of family sacrifice traditionally imposed on men.

Another approach to eliminating the disparity between the sexes would be to change the allocation of family roles, thereby allowing more women the freedom men now have to compete unburdened in the labor market and giving men freedom to care for their children if they choose. However, a reallocation of this sort would require a massive governmental intrusion into family life. Assuming social engineering of this magnitude is desirable and could be achieved without changing the labor market structures that hinder working parents, such a change would not effectively deal with the child-rearing problems of the dual-career family or the conflicts of the single working parent. Furthermore, changing the allocation of family roles is inescapably linked to lowering labor market hostility to parents. By preventing women who have primary child care responsibilities from becoming equal wage earners, the labor market now operates to ensure that women will continue to have the primary child care role. Therefore, changing the labor market to make working more compatible with childrearing seems unavoidable if women are to enjoy actual job equality in the future.

As the foregoing illustrates, job equality is significantly impaired by labor market barriers to working mothers. Through Title VII of the Civil Rights Act of 1964 and through the equal protection guarantee of the Constitution our society is already committed to securing equal employment opportunity for individuals regardless of sex.... [T]he major goal of this article is to analyze whether such provisions can adequately tackle the task of reforming the labor market structure to reduce hostility to working mothers.... [T]he issues that would be basic in any litigational challenge to employment barriers operating against working women will be presented in the context of a restrictive employment condition in the legal profession—the unspoken understanding in many law firms and in some areas of government legal practice that one must work more than forty hours per week. If a parent does not want to relinquish substantial opportunity to care for and be with her children, or if she cannot free herself from child care responsibilities, a limited weekly commitment to the labor market is essential. However, in law practice, limiting the hours one is available for work adversely affects one's ability to be promoted or to obtain significant and stimulating assignments. While both male and female lawyers may have interests or responsibilities which they resist or resent relinquishing because of the hours requirement, there is no reason to believe that the unlimited time obligation disproportionately affects either sex with respect to these conflicts—be they golf, needlepoint, gardening, or tournament bridge. However, since most working mothers, unlike similarly situated men, must take primary care of their children, the unlimited time commitment disproportionately affects women.

Like other employment conditions which restrict working mothers, such as the forty-hour work week itself, the rigid nine-to-five working day, or illness and vacation benefits that do not accommodate dependents' needs, the unlimited time requirement does not explicitly discriminate against women. The requirement was probably not adopted in order to subordinate women, but rather resulted from habit and because it was thought to be profitable for a law firm. Moreover, it is an employment condition that lawyers have long complacently accepted in order to obtain the prestige and financial returns of law practice. Therefore, even though long working hours disadvantage many women who either must or want to fulfill certain child care responsibilities, the question is whether such a requirement, applicable to both sexes and deeply established as a reasonable business practice, constitutes unlawful discrimination under current law....

[A] successful challenge to some labor market barriers to working mothers can be made under present law, but that litigation is unlikely to achieve the dramatic labor market restructuring that is necessary to eliminate the existing disparity of achievement between men and women in the work force. Indeed, it is likely that new legislation will be needed to achieve the fundamental changes in the labor market necessary to ensure full job equality for working mothers. . . .

Upton v. JWP Businessland

Supreme Judicial Court of Massachusetts, 1997.
425 Mass. 756, 682 N.E.2d 1357.

HERBERT P. WILKINS, CHIEF JUSTICE.

The plaintiff, a former at-will employee of the defendant and a divorced single parent, appeals from the entry of summary judgment for the defendant. She asserts that the defendant discharged her when, because of the need to be with her young son, she was unwilling to work long hours. She argues that such a discharge is contrary to public policy and entitles her to damages. . . . We affirm the judgment. . . .

At the time of her discharge, the plaintiff was the mother of a young son whom she cared for herself and supported entirely from her earnings. She commuted from Cape Cod to work for the defendant in Canton. When she was hired in April, 1991, she was told that her hours of work would be 8:15 A.M. to 5:30 P.M., with the need to work late on one or two days each month. The plaintiff arranged child care accordingly. In fact, the requirements of her job kept her until 6:30 P.M. to 7 P.M. from the outset and even later as the job progressed. In late July, 1991, the plaintiff was told that she would have to work until 9 or 10 P.M. each evening and all day Saturday for at least several months. The plaintiff informed her employer that she would not be able to work such hours because of her responsibilities as a mother. She was discharged two weeks later.

The general rule is that an at-will employee may be terminated at any time for any reason or for no reason at all. Liability may be imposed on an employer, however, if an at-will employee is terminated for a reason that violates a clearly established public policy. . . .

The plaintiff seeks to recover for a termination that was not, on its face, made because she did something that public policy strongly encourages (such as serving on a jury) or because she refused to engage in conduct that public policy strongly discourages (such as refusing to lie on behalf of her employer). There is no clearly established public policy which requires employers to refrain from demanding that their adult employees work long hours. Nor is any public policy directly served by an employee's refusal to work long hours. Because no public purpose is served by the conduct for which the plaintiff asserts she was discharged, this case is unlike those cases in which we have held that the employer may be liable for the discharge of an at-will employee.

To advance her claim that her termination violated public policy, the plaintiff relies on the Commonwealth's strong policy favoring the care and protection of children. Her theory is that an employer may not properly discharge an employee whose refusal to work long hours is based on her sense of obligation to be with her young child. She argues that meeting the defendant's demands regarding work hours would cause her to neglect her child in contravention of public policy.

The plaintiff asserts that cases involving eligibility for unemployment compensation directly support her theory. The judge correctly concluded that the Commonwealth's broad policies of protecting the family unit and promoting the best interests of children do not transform the discharge of an at-will employee who cannot work particular hours required by her employer into a discharge in violation of a well-defined public policy. The judge noted that, although the Legislature has established rights to unemployment compensation for certain former employees, compensation is not available in every instance in which an at-will employee experiences a conflict between job requirements and parental responsibilities. A policy that says that, if domestic responsibilities limit a person's availability to work, unemployment compensation may nevertheless be available does not translate into a policy that an employer is liable to a former employee for discharging her in comparable circumstances. The Legislature has directed that unemployment compensation should be available to such a person, but it has not provided that such an employee has an action for wrongful discharge.

The Legislature has not announced a public policy position in the area of unemployment compensation that is as broad as the one that the plaintiff urges us to identify. Nor has any court to our knowledge allowed recovery against an employer who terminated an at-will employee who refused to work newly imposed hours due to an irreconcilable conflict between her new work schedule and the obligations of parenting. There is no public policy which mandates that an employer must adjust its expectations, based on a case-by-case analysis of an at-will employee's domestic circumstances, or face liability for having discharged the employee.... Liability to an at-will employee for a discharge in violation of public policy must be based on general principles, and not on the special domestic circumstances of any particular employee.

The plaintiff argues briefly that the defendant was estopped from firing her because she relied to her detriment on the defendant's representations regarding her expected hours of work. To avoid the entry of summary judgment against her, an at-will employee asserting estoppel would have to show that she reasonably relied on an unambiguous promise. The summary judgment record shows no such promise, only that the plaintiff asked about regular work hours and was so told. No promise in a contractual sense is shown.

We sympathize with the difficulties of persons in the position of the plaintiff who face the challenge of reconciling parental responsibilities with the demands of employment. However, employer liability under common-law principles is not an appropriate means of addressing the problem in the at-will employment context....

Geduldig v. Aiello

Supreme Court of the United States, 1974.
417 U.S. 484, 94 S.Ct. 2485, 41 L.Ed.2d 256.

JUSTICE POTTER STEWART delivered the opinion of the Court.

For almost 30 years California has administered a disability insurance system that pays benefits to persons in private employment who are temporarily unable to work because of disability not covered by workmen's compensation. The appellees brought this action to challenge the constitutionality of a provision of the California program that, in defining "disability," excludes from coverage certain disabilities resulting from pregnancy. . . .

California's disability insurance system is funded entirely from contributions deducted from the wages of participating employees. Participation in the program is mandatory unless the employees are protected by a voluntary private plan approved by the State. Each employee is required to contribute one percent of his salary, up to an annual maximum of $85. These contributions are placed in the Unemployment Compensation Disability Fund, which is established and administered as a special trust fund within the state treasury. . . . In return for his one-percent contribution to the Disability Fund, the individual employee is insured against the risk of disability stemming from a substantial number of "mental or physical illness[es] and mental or physical injur[ies]." Cal.Unemp.Ins.Code § 2626. It is not every disabling condition, however, that triggers the obligation to pay benefits under the program. As already noted, for example, any disability of less than eight days' duration is not compensable, except when the employee is hospitalized. Conversely, no benefits are payable for any single disability beyond 26 weeks. Further, disability is not compensable if it results from the individual's court commitment as a dipsomaniac, drug addict, or sexual psychopath. Finally, § 2626 of the Unemployment Insurance Code excludes from coverage certain disabilities that are attributable to pregnancy. It is this provision that is at issue in the present case. . . .

[Appellee Jacqueline] Jaramillo, experienced a normal pregnancy, which was the sole cause of her disability. . . . [A]ppellees Aiello, Armendariz, and Johnson, whose disabilities were attributable to causes other than normal pregnancy and delivery, became entitled to benefits under the disability insurance program, and their claims have since been paid. . . . Thus, the [only] issue before the Court on this appeal is whether the California disability insurance program invidiously discriminates against Jaramillo and others similarly situated by not paying insurance benefits for disability that accompanies normal pregnancy and childbirth. . . .

It is clear that California intended to establish this benefit system as an insurance program that was to function essentially in accordance with insurance concepts. Since the program was instituted in 1946, it has been totally self-supporting, never drawing on general state revenues to finance disability or hospital benefits. . . . Over the years California has demonstrated a strong commitment not to increase the contribution rate above the one-percent level. The State has sought to provide the broadest possible disability protection that would be affordable by all employees, including those with very low incomes. Because any larger percentage or any flat dollar-amount rate of contribution would impose an increasingly regressive levy bearing most heavily upon those with the lowest incomes, the State has resisted any attempt to change the required contribution from the one-percent level. The program is thus structured, in terms of the level of benefits and the risks insured, to maintain the solvency of the Disability Fund at a one-percent annual level of contribution.

In ordering the State to pay benefits for disability accompanying normal pregnancy and delivery, the District Court acknowledged the State's contention "that coverage of these disabilities is so extraordinarily expensive that it would be impossible to maintain a program supported by employee contributions if these disabilities are included." There is considerable disagreement between the parties with respect to how great the increased costs would actually be, but they would clearly be substantial. For purposes of analysis the District Court accepted the State's estimate, which was in excess of $100 million annually....

Each of ... [the program's] "variables"—the benefit level deemed appropriate to compensate employee disability, the risks selected to be insured under the program, and the contribution rate chosen to maintain the solvency of the program and at the same time to permit low-income employees to participate with minimal personal sacrifice—represents a policy determination by the State. The essential issue in this case is whether the Equal Protection Clause requires such policies to be sacrificed or compromised in order to finance the payment of benefits to those whose disability is attributable to normal pregnancy and delivery.

We cannot agree that the exclusion of this disability from coverage amounts to invidious discrimination under the Equal Protection Clause. California does not discriminate with respect to the persons or groups which are eligible for disability insurance protection under the program. The classification challenged in this case relates to the asserted underinclusiveness of the set of risks that the State has selected to insure. Although California has created a program to insure most risks of employment disability, it has not chosen to insure all such risks, and this decision is reflected in the level of annual contributions exacted from participating employees. This Court has held that, consistently with the Equal Protection Clause, a State "may take one step at a time, addressing itself to the phase of the problem which seems most acute to the legislative mind.... The legislature may select one phase of one field and apply a remedy there, neglecting the others.... " *Williamson v. Lee Optical Co.*, 348 U.S. 483, 489 (1955). Particularly with respect to social welfare programs, so long as the line drawn by the State is rationally supportable, the courts will not interpose their judgment as to the appropriate stopping point....

It is evident that a totally comprehensive program would be substantially more costly than the present program and would inevitably require state subsidy, a higher rate of employee contribution, a lower scale of benefits for those suffering insured disabilities, or some combination of these measures. There is nothing in the Constitution, however, that requires the State to subordinate or compromise its legitimate interests solely to create a more comprehensive social insurance program than it already has.

The State has a legitimate interest in maintaining the self-supporting nature of its insurance program. Similarly, it has an interest in distributing the available resources in such a way as to keep benefit payments at an adequate level for disabilities that are covered, rather than to cover all disabilities inadequately. Finally, California has a legitimate concern in maintaining the contribution rate at a level that will not unduly burden participating employees, particularly low-income employees who may be most in need of the disability insurance.

These policies provide an objective and wholly non-invidious basis for the State's decision not to create a more comprehensive insurance program than it has. There is no evidence in the record that the selection of the risks insured by the program worked to discriminate against any definable group or class in terms of the aggregate risk protection derived by that group or class from the program.[20] There is no risk from which men are protected and women are not. Likewise, there is no risk from which women are protected and men are not.

The appellee simply contends that, although she has received insurance protection equivalent to that provided all other participating employees, she has suffered discrimination because she encountered a risk that was outside the program's protection. For the reasons we have stated, we hold that this contention is not a valid one under the Equal Protection Clause of the Fourteenth Amendment. . . .

WILLIAM BRENNAN, J., with whom MR. JUSTICE WILLIAM DOUGLAS and MR. JUSTICE THURGOOD MARSHALL join, dissenting. . . .

20. The dissenting opinion to the contrary, this case is thus a far cry from cases like *Reed v. Reed,* 404 U.S. 71, 92 S.Ct. 251, 30 L.Ed.2d 225 (1971), and *Frontiero v. Richardson,* 411 U.S. 677, 93 S.Ct. 1764, 36 L.Ed.2d 583 (1973), involving discrimination based upon gender as such. The California insurance program does not exclude anyone from benefit eligibility because of gender but merely removes one physical condition—pregnancy—from the list of compensable disabilities. While it is true that only women can become pregnant it does not follow that every legislative classification concerning pregnancy is a sex-based classification like those considered in *Reed,* supra, and *Frontiero,* supra. Normal pregnancy is an objectively identifiable physical condition with unique characteristics. Absent a showing that distinctions involving pregnancy are mere pretexts designed to effect an invidious discrimination against the members of one sex or the other, lawmakers are constitutionally free to include or exclude pregnancy from the coverage of legislation such as this on any reasonable basis, just as with respect to any other physical condition.

The lack of identity between the excluded disability and gender as such under this insurance program becomes clear upon the most cursory analysis. The program divides potential recipients into two groups—pregnant women and nonpregnant persons. While the first group is exclusively female, the second includes members of both sexes. The fiscal and actuarial benefits of the program thus accrue to members of both sexes.

In my view, by singling out for less favorable treatment a gender-linked disability peculiar to women, the State has created a double standard for disability compensation: a limitation is imposed upon the disabilities for which women workers may recover, while men receive full compensation for all disabilities suffered, including those that affect only or primarily their sex, such as prostatectomies, circumcision, hemophilia, and gout. In effect, one set of rules is applied to females and another to males. Such dissimilar treatment of men and women, on the basis of physical characteristics inextricably linked to one sex, inevitably constitutes sex discrimination. . . .

In the past, when a legislative classification has turned on gender, the Court has justifiably applied a standard of judicial scrutiny more strict than that generally accorded economic or social welfare programs. Compare *Reed v. Reed,* 404 U.S. 71 (1971), and *Frontiero v. Richardson,* 411 U.S. 677 (1973), with *Dandridge v. Williams,* 397 U.S. 471 (1970), and *Jefferson v. Hackney,* 406 U.S. 535 (1972). Yet, by its decision today, the Court appears willing to abandon that higher standard of review without satisfactorily explaining what differentiates the gender-based classification employed in this case from those found unconstitutional in *Reed* and *Frontiero.* The Court's decision threatens to return men and women to a time when "traditional" equal protection analysis sustained legislative classifications that treated differently members of a particular sex solely because of their sex.

I cannot join the Court's apparent retreat. I continue to adhere to my view that "classifications based upon sex, like classifications based upon race, alienage, or national origin, are inherently suspect, and must therefore be subjected to strict judicial scrutiny." *Frontiero v. Richardson,* supra, at 688. When, as in this case, the State employs a legislative classification that distinguishes between beneficiaries solely by reference to gender-linked disability risks, "[t]he Court is not . . . free to sustain the statute on the ground that it rationally promotes legitimate governmental interests; rather, such suspect classifications can be sustained only when the State bears the burden of demonstrating that the challenged legislation serves overriding or compelling interests that cannot be achieved either by a more carefully tailored legislative classification or by the use of feasible, less drastic means." *Kahn v. Shevin,* 416 U.S. 351, 357–358 (1974) (BRENNAN, J., dissenting).

The State has clearly failed to meet that burden in the present case. The essence of the State's justification for excluding disabilities caused by a normal pregnancy from its disability compensation scheme is that covering such disabilities would be too costly. To be sure, as presently funded, inclusion of normal pregnancies "would be substantially more costly than the present program." But whatever role such monetary considerations may play in traditional equal protection analysis, the State's interest in preserving the fiscal integrity of its disability insurance program simply cannot render the State's use of a suspect classification constitutional. For while "a State has a valid interest in preserving the fiscal integrity of its programs[,] ... a State may not accomplish such a purpose by invidious distinctions between classes of its citizens.... The saving of welfare costs cannot justify an otherwise invidious classification." *Shapiro v. Thompson,* 394 U.S. 618, 633 (1969).... Moreover, California's legitimate interest in fiscal integrity could easily have been achieved through a variety of less drastic, sexually neutral means....

NOTES AND QUESTIONS

1.   **General Electric Co. v. Gilbert.** In 1976, the Supreme Court decided General Electric v. Gilbert, 429 U.S. 125, 97 S.Ct. 401, 50 L.Ed.2d 343, in which the plaintiffs argued that G.E.'s disability plan discriminated against women under Title VII because it did not cover pregnancy-related claims. This case was similar to *Geduldig* except that *G.E.* involved a private firm sued under Title VII, instead of a state sued for violating the Equal Protection Clause. The Supreme Court held that this distinction did not change the outcome, and, as in *Geduldig,* the female plaintiff lost in *G.E.*. Justice Rehnquist, writing for the Court in *G.E.*, used cases interpreting the Equal Protection Clause as a means of giving content to Title VII's concept of "discrimination." Given its reliance on the Equal Protection cases, it is not surprising that the Court in *G.E.* found that "an exclusion of pregnancy from a disability-benefits plan providing general coverage is not a gender-based discrimination at all." According to the Court, the exclusion of pregnancy from the plan's coverage was not a mere pretext for discriminating against women; pregnancy might be distinguished from covered conditions on the grounds that it was "not a 'disease' at all" or on the basis that it was frequently a "voluntarily undertaken and desired condition." What assumptions about the conditions under which women become pregnant are imbedded in this last claim? Why does the Court emphasize that pregnancy is not a disease? Do you think that it is easier for the Court to portray pregnancy as voluntary by emphasizing the difference between pregnant women and non-pregnant people? Does the creation of these two particular categories imply that pregnancy is not something that is naturally or automatically connected with being a woman?

The Court also relied in its decision on the fact that there was "no proof that the [plan's] package is ... worth more to men than to women ..." However, as Justice Brennan argued in dissent, the plaintiff's contention was that the plan left more expensive disabilities uncovered for women than for men. In this way it treated women worse than men. Is this just a matter of whether you see the proverbial glass as half full or half empty? If so, why should the glass be viewed from G.E.'s point of view instead of the female plaintiff's? The Court made two arguments in support of its perspective. First, there is no requirement that the employer provide a disability insurance program despite the fact that then too employees would face different disability risks depending on whether they might become pregnant or not. Second, the employer could have provided increased wages instead of a disability plan and a woman who wished to purchase an all inclusive plan would then have to pay more than a man who did so. Are these arguments convincing to you? Does the fact that the employer chose to provide a plan affect your answer?

2.   **The Pregnancy Discrimination Act.** Most people who read *Geduldig* and *G.E.* are struck by the Court's claim that discrimination on the basis of pregnancy is not discrimination on the basis of sex. As the Court said in *Geduldig*'s footnote 20 pregnancy-based classifications divide the world into two groups: "pregnant women and nonpregnant persons." Since the second group included members of both sexes, the Court concluded there was no discrimination on the basis of sex. Unfortunately for the Court (and fortunately for women) this bit of sophistry did not convince many people in the mid–1970s. It is hard to think about the category "pregnant women" without thinking that the people in that category are in it because of their sex.

Congress agreed with the Court's critics, and, after *General Electric*, it passed the Pregnancy Discrimination Act (PDA) of 1978, 42 U.S.C. § 2000e(k), amending Title VII. The Act specifically defines discrimination because of sex under Title VII to include discrimination on the basis of "pregnancy, childbirth or related medical conditions," and requires that "women affected by pregnancy [or] childbirth be treated the same for all employment-related purposes . . . as other persons not so affected . . . " The PDA does not prohibit negative employment decisions against women who are pregnant. Pregnant women still must prove discrimination using either the disparate impact or disparate treatment theories. For a case in which a plaintiff with severe morning sickness was unable to do this, *see* Troupe v. May Department Stores Co., 20 F.3d 734 (7th Cir. 1994). The court there noted, "Employers can treat pregnant women as badly as they treat similarly affected but nonpregnant employees."

The term "pregnancy, childbirth or related medical conditions" in the PDA is not self-defining. In thinking about sameness and difference issues, Herma Hill Kay has argued in favor of treating women exactly like men are treated, except during times of pregnancy:

> The woman's ability to work, measured against her prior performance, may vary with the physical and emotional changes she experiences during pregnancy. . . . In order to maintain the woman's equality of opportunity during her pregnancy, we should modify as far as reasonably possible those aspects of her work where her job performance is adversely affected by the pregnancy.

Equality and Difference: The Case of Pregnancy, 1 Berkeley Women's L. J. 1 (1985).

What is her definition of pregnancy? Are the emotional changes to which she refers a part of a woman's pregnancy? What about morning sickness? A tendency in some women to tears, exhaustion or cravings? Should we define pregnancy and its related medical conditions only in terms of medicine, biology and science, or should we include the culturally constructed attributes of pregnancy? Does the distinction between a biological and a culturally constructed definition of pregnancy make any sense?

In general, the courts have narrowly construed the phrase "pregnancy ... or related medical conditions." They have often acted as if they can discern a bright line between the "fact" of pregnancy and its cultural ramifications. Whereas some Western European countries require women to take a maternity leave to convalesce after the birth of a child, U.S. courts have repeatedly held that child rearing leaves are neither required by nor protected by the PDA. *See* Schafer v. Board of Public Education, 903 F.2d 243 (3d Cir. 1990) (collective bargaining agreement that provides child rearing leave only for women violates Title VII), Fisher v. Vassar College, 70 F.3d 1420 (2d Cir. 1995) (promotion decisions under Title VII may negatively consider employee's long absence from work force in order to raise children), Maganuco v. Leyden Community High School District 212, 939 F. 2d 440 (7th Cir. 1991) (district's policy prohibiting the tacking of paid sick leave with unpaid leaves, including maternity leave, was permitted under Title VII), *but see* Harness v. Hartz Mountain Corp., 877 F.2d 1307 (6th Cir. 1989) (maternity leave of up to one year for pregnant employees or for mothers who have just given birth permissible under Title VII). Similarly, mothers' desires to breast-feed their newborns are not protected. "The PDA," according to one court, " ...focuses on the medical condition of the mother—not the needs of the child." McNill v. New York City Department of Correction, 950 F.Supp. 564 (S.D.N.Y. 1996); *see also* Fejes v. Gilpin Ventures, 960 F. Supp. 1487 (D. Colo. 1997) (breast-feeding not protected by PDA). But, why shouldn't we consider lactation to be a medical condition related to the woman's recent pregnancy?

Given the courts' biological approach to "pregnancy ... or related medical conditions," it may not seem surprising that a woman cannot be discharged from work for having an abortion, *see* Turic v. Holland Hospitality, Inc., 85 F.3d 1211 (6th Cir. 1996). But what about for talking about the possibility of the abortion at work and causing a general brouhaha? According to *Turic*, she cannot be dismissed for that either.

The courts have found the question of infertility treatment considerably more complicated. In Krauel v. Iowa Methodist Medical Center, 95 F.3d 674 (8th Cir. 1996), the court interpreted the statutory term "related medical conditions" to be limited by "pregnancy" and held that infertility treatments did not fall under the PDA. The court therefore found that the plaintiff had not been discriminated against when the employer-funded health plan refused coverage for the treatments. In contrast, in Erickson v. Board of Governors, 911 F. Supp. 316 (N.D.Ill. 1995), the employer had argued that there would not be discrimination against infertile women because they were unlikely to impose the additional costs of pregnancy on the employer. Therefore infertility should not come under the protection of the PDA. The court, however, noted that the whole goal of fertility treatments is to create a pregnancy. Thus, one could expect women undergoing treatment to be subject to the same discrimination as pregnant women. *See also* Pacourek v. Inland Steel Co., 858 F.Supp. 1393 (N.D.Ill. 1994), and Cleese v. Hewlett–Packard Co., 911 F.Supp. 1312 (D.Or. 1995). Which of these positions is more persuasive to you? In what ways is your answer connected to your understanding of the word "pregnancy?" Does your answer depend on a biological definition of pregnancy? How much, if any, of the cultural context in which pregnancies occur would you take into account?

For further thoughts on the relationship between pregnancy, biology and the definition of woman, *see* Tracy E. Higgins, *"By Reason of their Sex,"* 80 Cornell L. Rev. 1536 (1995); Dan Danielsen, *Representing Identities: The Legal Treatment of Pregnancy and Homosexuality*, 26 New Eng. L. Rev. 1453 (1992); Katherine M. Franke, *The Central Mistake of Sex Discrimination Law*, 144 U.Pa. L. Rev. (1995).

3. **The Continuing Vitality of Geduldig.** The PDA may have changed Title VII's definition of discrimination on the basis of sex, but it did not alter the Court's belief that the establishment of categories based on pregnancy was not sex-based discrimination. In Bray v. Alexandria Women's Health Clinic, 506 U.S. 263, 113 S.Ct. 753, 122 L.Ed.2d 34 (1993), abortion clinics had brought suit under 42 U.S.C. § 1985(3) to enjoin Operation Rescue from preventing patients from entering and leaving the abortion facilities. Suit under § 1985(3) requires a showing of a class-based animus. The Court held that actions aimed against women obtaining abortions are not actions aimed against women as a class, and it cited *Geduldig* for the proposition that not every "legislative classification concerning pregnancy is a sex-based classification." It seemed obvious to many commentators that disability plans that discriminated against pregnancy discriminated on the basis of sex. Is it equally obvious to you that discrimination against those who obtain abortions is discrimination on the basis of sex? If not, why not?

In recent welfare reform legislation, Congress has also indicated that it does not see anything wrong with discrimination against pregnant women. The Personal Responsibility and Work Opportunity Reconciliation Act of 1996 requires most unmarried pregnant teenagers and teen mothers to live with their own parents or other approved adults. There is no similar requirement for non-pregnant teens or for teenage girls without children. So long as discrimination against pregnant women is not understood to be sex-based discrimination, this provision will only have to be shown to have a rational basis to survive attack under the equal protection clause of the Fourteenth Amendment.

For an article that considers the continuing effect of *Geduldig*, see Shannon E. Liss, *The Constitutionality of Pregnancy Discrimination*, 23 N.Y.U. Rev. L. & Soc. Change 59 (1997).

California Federal Savings and Loan Ass'n v. Guerra

Supreme Court of the United States, 1987.
479 U.S. 272, 107 S.Ct. 683, 93 L.Ed.2d 613.

JUSTICE THURGOOD MARSHALL delivered the opinion of the Court....

California's Fair Employment and Housing Act (FEHA) is a comprehensive statute that prohibits discrimination in employment and housing.

In September 1978, California amended the FEHA to proscribe certain forms of employment discrimination on the basis of pregnancy. Cal.Gov't Code Ann. § 12945(b)(2). Subdivision (b)(2)—the provision at issue here— is the only portion of the statute that applies to employers subject to Title VII. It requires these employers to provide female employees an unpaid pregnancy disability leave of up to four months. Respondent Fair Employment and Housing Commission, the state agency authorized to interpret the FEHA, has construed § 12945(b)(2) to require California employers to reinstate an employee returning from such pregnancy leave to the job she previously held, unless it is no longer available due to business necessity. In the latter case, the employer must make a reasonable, good-faith effort to place the employee in a substantially similar job. The statute does not compel employers to provide *paid* leave to pregnant employees. Accordingly, the only benefit pregnant workers actually derive from § 12945(b)(2) is a qualified right to reinstatement.

Title VII of the Civil Rights Act of 1964 also prohibits various forms of employment discrimination, including discrimination on the basis of sex. However, in *General Electric Co. v. Gilbert,* 429 U.S. 125, 97 S.Ct. 401, 50 L.Ed.2d 343 (1976), this Court ruled that discrimination on the basis of pregnancy was not sex discrimination under Title VII. In response to the *Gilbert* decision, Congress passed the Pregnancy Discrimination Act of 1978 (PDA). The PDA specifies that sex discrimination includes discrimination on the basis of pregnancy.[6]

Petitioner California Federal Savings & Loan Association (Cal Fed) is a federally chartered savings and loan association based in Los Angeles; it is an employer covered by both Title VII and § 12945(b)(2). Cal Fed has a facially neutral leave policy that permits employees who have completed three months of service to take unpaid leaves of absence for a variety of reasons, including disability and pregnancy. Although it is Cal Fed's policy to try to provide an employee taking unpaid leave with a similar position upon returning, Cal Fed expressly reserves the right to terminate an employee who has taken a leave of absence if a similar position is not available.

Lillian Garland was employed by Cal Fed as a receptionist for several years. In January 1982, she took a pregnancy disability leave. When she was able to return to work in April of that year, Garland notified Cal Fed, but was informed that her job had been filled and that there were no receptionist or similar positions available. Garland filed a complaint with respondent Department of Fair Employment and Housing, which issued an

---

6. The PDA added subsection (k) to § 701, the definitional section of Title VII. Subsection (k) provides, in relevant part:

"The terms 'because of sex' or 'on the basis of sex' include, but are not limited to, because of or on the basis of pregnancy, childbirth, or related medical conditions; and women affected by pregnancy, childbirth, or related medical conditions shall be treated the same for all employment-related purposes, including receipt of benefits under fringe benefit programs, as other persons not so affected but similar in their ability or inability to work, and nothing in section 703(h) of this title shall be interpreted to permit otherwise." ...

administrative accusation against Cal Fed on her behalf. Respondent charged Cal Fed with violating § 12945(b)(2) of the FEHA. Prior to the scheduled hearing before respondent Fair Employment and Housing Commission, Cal Fed, joined by petitioners Merchants and Manufacturers Association and the California Chamber of Commerce, brought this action in the United States District Court for the Central District of California. They sought a declaration that § 12945(b)(2) is inconsistent with and preempted by Title VII and an injunction against enforcement of the section. . . .

Petitioners argue that the language of the federal statute itself unambiguously rejects California's "special treatment" approach to pregnancy discrimination, thus rendering any resort to the legislative history unnecessary. They contend that the second clause of the PDA forbids an employer to treat pregnant employees any differently than other disabled employees. Because " '[t]he purpose of Congress is the ultimate touchstone' " of the pre-emption inquiry, however, we must examine the PDA's language against the background of its legislative history and historical context. As to the language of the PDA, "[i]t is a 'familiar rule, that a thing may be within the letter of the statute and yet not within the statute, because not within its spirit, nor within the intention of its makers.' "

It is well established that the PDA was passed in reaction to this Court's decision in *General Electric Co. v. Gilbert*, 429 U.S. 125, 97 S.Ct. 401, 50 L.Ed.2d 343 (1976). "When Congress amended Title VII in 1978, it unambiguously expressed its disapproval of both the holding and the reasoning of the Court in the *Gilbert* decision." By adding pregnancy to the definition of sex discrimination prohibited by Title VII, the first clause of the PDA reflects Congress' disapproval of the reasoning in *Gilbert*. Rather than imposing a limitation on the remedial purpose of the PDA, we believe that the second clause was intended to overrule the holding in *Gilbert* and to illustrate how discrimination against pregnancy is to be remedied. Accordingly, subject to certain limitations, we agree with the Court of Appeals' conclusion that Congress intended the PDA to be "a floor beneath which pregnancy disability benefits may not drop—not a ceiling above which they may not rise."

The context in which Congress considered the issue of pregnancy discrimination supports this view of the PDA. Congress had before it extensive evidence of discrimination *against* pregnancy, particularly in disability and health insurance programs. The Reports, debates, and hearings make abundantly clear that Congress intended the PDA to provide relief for working women and to end discrimination against pregnant workers. In contrast to the thorough account of discrimination against pregnant workers, the legislative history is devoid of any discussion of preferential treatment of pregnancy beyond acknowledgments of the existence of state statutes providing for such preferential treatment. Opposition to the PDA came from those concerned with the cost of including pregnancy in health and disability-benefit plans and the application of the bill to abortion, not from those who favored special accommodation of pregnancy. . . .

Title VII, as amended by the PDA, and California's pregnancy disability leave statute share a common goal. The purpose of Title VII is "to achieve equality of employment opportunities and remove barriers that have operated in the past to favor an identifiable group of . . . employees over other employees." Rather than limiting existing Title VII principles and objectives, the PDA extends them to cover pregnancy. As Senator Williams, a sponsor of the Act, stated: "The entire thrust . . . behind this legislation is to guarantee women the basic right to participate fully and equally in the workforce, without denying them the fundamental right to full participation in family life."

Section 12945(b)(2) also promotes equal employment opportunity. By requiring employers to reinstate women after a reasonable pregnancy disability leave, § 12945(b)(2) ensures that they will not lose their jobs on account of pregnancy disability. California's approach is consistent with the dissenting opinion of JUSTICE BRENNAN in *Gilbert,* which Congress adopted in enacting the PDA. JUSTICE BRENNAN stated:

> "[D]iscrimination is a social phenomenon encased in a social context and, therefore, unavoidably takes its meaning from the desired end products of the relevant legislative enactment, end products that may demand due consideration of the uniqueness of the 'disadvantaged' individuals. A realistic understanding of conditions found in today's labor environment warrants taking pregnancy into account in fashioning disability policies."

By "taking pregnancy into account," California's pregnancy disability-leave statute allows women, as well as men, to have families without losing their jobs.

We emphasize the limited nature of the benefits § 12945(b)(2) provides. The statute is narrowly drawn to cover only the period of *actual physical disability* on account of pregnancy, childbirth, or related medical conditions. Accordingly, unlike the protective labor legislation prevalent earlier in this century, § 12945(b)(2) does not reflect archaic or stereotypical notions about pregnancy and the abilities of pregnant workers. A statute based on such stereotypical assumptions would, of course, be inconsistent with Title VII's goal of equal employment opportunity. . . .

Moreover, even if we agreed with petitioners' construction of the PDA, we would nonetheless reject their argument that the California statute requires employers to violate Title VII. Section 12945(b)(2) does not prevent employers from complying with both the federal law (as petitioners construe it) and the state law. This is not a case where "compliance with both federal and state regulations is a physical impossibility," or where there is an "inevitable collision between the two schemes of regulation." Section 12945(b)(2) does not compel California employers to treat pregnant workers *better* than other disabled employees; it merely establishes benefits that employers must, at a minimum, provide to pregnant workers. Employers are free to give comparable benefits to other disabled employees, thereby treating "women affected by pregnancy" no better than "other persons not so affected but similar in their ability or inability to work." Indeed, at oral argument, petitioners conceded that compliance with both statutes "is theoretically possible." . . .

Petitioners argue that "extension" of the state statute to cover other employees would be inappropriate in the absence of a clear indication that this is what the California Legislature intended.

. . . This argument is beside the point. Extension is a remedial option to be exercised by a court once a statute is found to be invalid. . . .

JUSTICE BYRON WHITE, with whom THE CHIEF JUSTICE WILLIAM REHNQUIST and JUSTICE LEWIS POWELL join, dissenting. . . .

The PDA gave added meaning to discrimination on the basis of sex:

"The terms 'because of sex' or 'on the basis of sex' [in § 703(a) of this Title] include, but are not limited to, because of or on the basis of pregnancy, childbirth or related medical conditions; and women affected by pregnancy, childbirth, or related medical conditions shall be treated the same for all employment-related purposes, including receipt of benefits under fringe benefit programs, as other persons not so affected but similar in their ability or inability to work. . . ."

The second clause quoted above could not be clearer: it mandates that pregnant employees "shall be treated the same for all employment-related purposes" as nonpregnant employees similarly situated with respect to their ability or inability to work. This language leaves no room for preferential treatment of pregnant workers. . . .

Contrary to the mandate of the PDA, California law requires every employer to have a disability leave policy for pregnancy even if it has none for any other disability. An employer complies with California law if it has a leave policy for pregnancy but denies it for every other disability. On its face, § 12945(b)(2) is in square conflict with the PDA and is therefore preempted. Because the California law permits employers to single out pregnancy for preferential treatment and therefore to violate Title VII, it is not saved by § 708 which limits pre-emption of state laws to those that require or permit an employer to commit an unfair employment practice.

The majority nevertheless would save the California law on two grounds. First, it holds that the PDA does not require disability from pregnancy to be treated the same as other disabilities; instead, it forbids less favorable, but permits more favorable, benefits for pregnancy disability. The express command of the PDA is unambiguously to the contrary, and the legislative history casts no doubt on that mandate. . . .

The parties and their *amici* argued vigorously to this Court the policy implications of preferential treatment of pregnant workers. In favor of

preferential treatment it was urged with conviction that preferential treatment merely enables women, like men, to have children without losing
their jobs. In opposition to preferential treatment it was urged with equal
conviction that preferential treatment represents a resurgence of the 19th–
century protective legislation which perpetuated sex-role stereotypes and
which impeded women in their efforts to take their rightful place in the
workplace. It is not the place of this Court, however, to resolve this policy
dispute. Our task is to interpret Congress' intent in enacting the PDA.
Congress' silence in its consideration of the PDA with respect to preferential treatment of pregnant workers cannot fairly be interpreted to abrogate
the plain statements in the legislative history, not to mention the language
of the statute, that equality of treatment was to be the guiding principle of
the PDA. . . .

The Court's second, and equally strange, ground is that even if the
PDA does prohibit special benefits for pregnant women, an employer may
still comply with both the California law and the PDA: it can adopt the
specified leave policies for pregnancy and at the same time afford similar
benefits for all other disabilities. This is untenable. California surely had no
intent to require employers to provide general disability leave benefits. It
intended to prefer pregnancy and went no further. Extension of these
benefits to the entire work force would be a dramatic increase in the scope
of the state law and would impose a significantly greater burden on
California employers.

That is the province of the California Legislature. . . .

NOTES AND QUESTIONS

1. **Sameness or Difference, Yet Again.** The *Cal Fed* case raised, in a
classic form, the important questions of whether women should be treated
the same as men—and thus not reinstated after a leave if no similar
position is available—or treated differently—and thus reinstated. Like the
litigation over *E.E.O.C. v. Sears,* discussed in the last section, the *Cal Fed*
litigation divided feminists.

The decision in *Cal Fed* could be understood as holding that the PDA
was intended to create a "floor beneath which pregnancy disability benefits
may not drop—not a ceiling above which they may not rise." This would
mean an employer would be prohibited from treating pregnant women
worse than men and nonpregnant women are treated, but that pregnant
women could be treated better. Do you think this "sky's the limit"
approach is a good one as a matter of policy? Alternatively, the case can be
read as holding that the California statute does not violate Title VII
because it does not require California employers to treat pregnant women
differently from other employees; the benefits required to be given to
pregnant women by the statute can also be made available to others. What
do you think of this reasoning? Reasoning like this has the potential to
improve the working conditions of all workers, not just women. Despite this
strong political advantage, is this interpretation open to Justice White's

criticism that California had no intent to provide disability benefits to all? Should this matter? After all, the case's holding does implement statutory intent in that California did intend to provide the benefits to pregnant women. If the Pregnancy Discrimination Act is interpreted to prohibit different treatment of pregnant women than of non-pregnant women and men, then the only way to accomplish the state legislature's goal would be to extend the benefits to all.

Although people may argue over the holding in *Cal Fed*, there is no question that it did not require states to accommodate women's pregnancies in the way California had. As if to make this point absolutely clear, the Court decided *Wimberly v. Labor and Indus. Relations Commission,* 479 U.S. 511, 107 S.Ct. 821, 93 L.Ed.2d 909 (1987), within days of its decision in *Cal Fed. Wimberly* involved a J.C. Penney's employee who requested a leave of absence due to pregnancy, and was given a leave with no guarantee of replacement. After the child was born, she requested reinstatement and was told that there were not any positions open. Wimberly therefore applied for unemployment benefits. According to the applicable Missouri statute, a claimant was disqualified if he or she had "left his work voluntarily without good cause attributable to his work or to his employer." Missouri interpreted this to rule out any benefits for departures due to pregnancy. The Federal Unemployment Tax Act, which establishes minimum standards for state unemployment benefit programs requires that a state not deny compensation solely on the basis of pregnancy. Thus, Wimberley challenged the Missouri decision in her case as contravening the federal mandate.

The Court in *Wimberly* ruled that the state could apply a neutral rule, such as the "voluntarily without good cause" rule, even if it "incidentally disqualifies pregnant or formerly pregnant claimants." It held that "the State cannot single out pregnancy for disadvantageous treatment, but it is not compelled to afford preferential treatment." Taking *Wimberly* together with *Cal Fed*, it is clear that the Court will allow states to provide special treatment for pregnant women, but will not require them to do so.

Although it is generally agreed that *Cal Fed* does not require employers to provide special accommodations for their pregnant employees, is it possible to argue that failure to accommodate the known needs of a pregnant woman indicates intent to discriminate? For example, what if the employer assigns her to a job it knows she cannot do because of her pregnancy? Is that discrimination if other employees are also assigned to the job through the same selection process? In Kelber v. Forest Electric Corp., 799 F. Supp. 326 (S.D.N.Y. 1992), the court said, "Nothing ... justifies an employer deliberately giving a pregnant employee an assignment which she cannot and should not perform simply because the employer wants to treat her 'the same as' male or non-pregnant female employees."

2. **The ADA and Pregnancy.** The Americans with Disabilities Act (ADA), 42 U.S.C. § 12101 et seq., requires covered employers to provide reasonable accommodations for an employee with disabilities, so long as the

employee will be able to perform the job's essential functions with the accommodations. In this way, the ADA contains an explicit requirement for special treatment. At most, Title VII and the PDA have been interpreted as permitting special treatment, as in *Cal Fed,* and often, they are understood to require equal treatment, as in many of the cases cited in these notes. If pregnancy were to be included as a disability under the ADA, pregnant women would be entitled to the special treatment that they are often denied under Title VII and the PDA.

A disability under the ADA is defined, in part, as a "physical or mental impairment that substantially limits one or more of the major life activities of . . . [an] individual." Although it would be possible to understand this definition to include pregnancy, the Equal Employment Opportunity Commission's regulations specifically exclude pregnancy from coverage. Indeed, during hearings to enact the regulations, feminists did not argue for the inclusion of pregnancy. Most courts that have faced the issue have also adopted this interpretation. *But see* Bragdon v. Abbott, —— S.Ct. ——, 1998 WL 332958 (reproduction is a major life activity).

Did feminists make a tactical mistake in 1991 when they agreed that pregnancies should not be covered by the ADA? It is important to remember that the equal treatment feminists had long argued that pregnancy was not a sickness, and that pregnant women did not need to give up their jobs and remain confined in their homes. Did they err in not reversing their previous position and in not contending that pregnancy should be a disability under the ADA? For an argument in favor of considering pregnancy as a covered disability, *see* Colette G. Matzzie, Note, *Substantive Equality and Antidiscrimination: Accommodating Pregnancy under the Americans with Disabilities Act,* 82 GEO. L. J. 193 (1993).

If the ADA were to be applied to pregnant workers, then employers would be required to provide reasonable accommodations for these workers' needs. Title VII is rarely interpreted to require this. For example, in Troupe v. May Department Stores Co., 20 F.3d 734 (7th Cir. 1994), the court clearly stated that the department store was not required to accommodate the plaintiff's morning sickness-induced lateness, if it did not make accommodations for men who had illnesses like arthritis that might cause them to be late frequently. While Title VII's anti-discrimination approach may work adequately for professional women who are pregnant, it may be less successful in protecting the jobs of non-professional working women like the plaintiff in *Troupe.* As with professional women, the prohibition on firing pregnant women merely because of their pregnancy is important to non-professional women. But, conditions on the job will be equally important. Pregnant women working assembly lines may need additional breaks to go to the bathroom, rest, or eat small snacks. They may also need relief from heavy lifting or other physically straining requirements. If these accommodations are not forthcoming, they may be forced to choose between resigning from their jobs or endangering the pregnancy. For more on this subject, *see* Laura Schlichtmann, Comment, *Accommodation of Pregnancy–Related Disabilities on the Job,* 15 Berkeley J. Employment & Lab.L. 335 (1994).

Recently some pregnant plaintiffs have successfully argued for accommodations under the ADA by distinguishing between their troubled pregnancies and "normal" pregnancies. Plaintiffs in these cases have experienced morning sickness, back pain, and leaking and spotting as a result of their pregnancies. *See* Cerrato v. Durham, 941 F.Supp. 388 (S.D.N.Y. 1996), Garrett v. Chicago School Reform Board, 1996 WL 411319 (N.D. Ill.), and Patterson v. Xerox Corp., 901 F. Supp. 274 (N.D. Ill. 1995). Do these conditions strike you as attendant to normal pregnancies or were these pregnancies abnormal? Does the strategy of differentiating normal from problematic pregnancies reinforce the courts' narrow interpretation of pregnancy under the PDA?

3. **European Law and Pregnancy.** Like the U.S., the European Court of Justice (ECJ) has adopted an equality (sameness) approach to dealing with issues of sex discrimination in general. However, European Community (EC) law specifically exempts pregnancy from this standard. It traditionally has been interpreted as allowing individual member states to establish maternity leaves specially for women, and such leaves are the norm. As of 1991, for example, Germany provided 14 weeks of leave at 100% of salary, while Italy provided 20 weeks at 80%. Indeed, starting in 1994, EC law required member states to provide women with a minimum of 14 weeks of paid maternity leave. This goes beyond the U.S. Supreme Court's opinion in *Cal Fed* which would permit states to establish such a program, but not require it.

Some European childbirth leave provisions raise once again the question of the border between biology and socially constructed gender roles. For example, German law requires women to take an eight week convalescence leave after the birth of a child. Do you think a mandatory maternity leave is desirable? Is it justifiable on biological grounds? Women may then take another four months of paid leave. In one case, a father wanted to take the four month paid leave while his wife returned to her job after the eight week convalescence leave. The ECJ rejected the father's claim of sex discrimination when the government refused to pay him benefits. It said that the four month leave protected the "special relationship between a woman and her child" following pregnancy. It feared that otherwise she would submit to pressures to return to work "prematurely." Germany's four month leave for women only was covered by the pregnancy exemption to the equal treatment requirement. Are the biological processes related to pregnancy the reason for protecting this leave? Or is it some idea about women's role in raising children? For further information on European law and pregnancy leaves, *see* Samuel Issacharoff and Elyse Rosenblum, *Women and the Workplace*, 94 Colum. L. Rev. 2154, 2200–14 (1994); Ruth Colker, *Pregnancy, Parenting, and Capitalism*, 58 Ohio St. L.J. 61 (1997).

International Union, UAW v. Johnson Controls, Inc.

Supreme Court of the United States, 1991.
499 U.S. 187, 111 S.Ct. 1196, 113 L.Ed.2d 158.

JUSTICE HARRY BLACKMUN delivered the opinion of the Court.

In this case we are concerned with an employer's gender-based fetal-protection policy. May an employer exclude a fertile female employee from certain jobs because of its concern for the health of the fetus the woman might conceive?

Respondent Johnson Controls, Inc., manufactures batteries. In the manufacturing process, the element lead is a primary ingredient. Occupational exposure to lead entails health risks, including the risk of harm to any fetus carried by a female employee.

Before the Civil Rights Act of 1964 became law, Johnson Controls did not employ any woman in a battery-manufacturing job. In June 1977, however, it announced its first official policy concerning its employment of women in lead-exposure work:

> "[P]rotection of the health of the unborn child is the immediate and direct responsibility of the prospective parents. While the medical profession and the company can support them in the exercise of this responsibility, it cannot assume it for them without simultaneously infringing their rights as persons. . . .

> ". . . Since not all women who can become mothers wish to become mothers (or will become mothers), it would appear to be illegal discrimination to treat all who are capable of pregnancy as though they will become pregnant."

Consistent with that view, Johnson Controls "stopped short of excluding women capable of bearing children from lead exposure," but emphasized that a woman who expected to have a child should not choose a job in which she would have such exposure. The company also required a woman who wished to be considered for employment to sign a statement that she had been advised of the risk of having a child while she was exposed to lead. The statement informed the woman that although there was evidence "that women exposed to lead have a higher rate of abortion," this evidence was "not as clear . . . as the relationship between cigarette smoking and cancer," but that it was, "medically speaking, just good sense not to run that risk if you want children and do not want to expose the unborn child to risk, however small. . . . "

Five years later, in 1982, Johnson Controls shifted from a policy of warning to a policy of exclusion. Between 1979 and 1983, eight employees became pregnant while maintaining blood lead levels in excess of 30 micrograms per deciliter. This appeared to be the critical level noted by the Occupational Health and Safety Administration (OSHA) for a worker who was planning to have a family. The company responded by announcing a broad exclusion of women from jobs that exposed them to lead:

> " . . . [I]t is [Johnson Controls'] policy that women who are pregnant or who are capable of bearing children will not be placed into jobs involving lead exposure or which could expose them to lead through the exercise of job bidding, bumping, transfer or promotion rights."

The policy defined "women ... capable of bearing children" as "[a]ll women except those whose inability to bear children is medically documented." It further stated that an unacceptable work station was one where, "over the past year," an employee had recorded a blood lead level of more than 30 micrograms per deciliter or the work site had yielded an air sample containing a lead level in excess of 30 micrograms per cubic meter.

In April 1984, petitioners filed in the United States District Court for the Eastern District of Wisconsin a class action challenging Johnson Controls' fetal-protection policy as sex discrimination that violated Title VII of the Civil Rights Act of 1964. Among the individual plaintiffs were petitioners Mary Craig, who had chosen to be sterilized in order to avoid losing her job, Elsie Nason, a 50–year–old divorcee, who had suffered a loss in compensation when she was transferred out of a job where she was exposed to lead, and Donald Penney, who had been denied a request for a leave of absence for the purpose of lowering his lead level because he intended to become a father. Upon stipulation of the parties, the District Court certified a class consisting of "all past, present and future production and maintenance employees" in United Auto Workers bargaining units at nine of Johnson Controls' plants "who have been and continue to be affected by [the employer's] Fetal Protection Policy implemented in 1982."

The District Court granted summary judgment for defendant-respondent Johnson Controls. Applying a three-part business necessity defense derived from fetal-protection cases in the Courts of Appeals for the Fourth and Eleventh Circuits, the District Court concluded that while "there is a disagreement among the experts regarding the effect of lead on the fetus," the hazard to the fetus through exposure to lead was established by "a considerable body of opinion;" that although "[e]xpert opinion has been provided which holds that lead also affects the reproductive abilities of men and women ... [and] that these effects are as great as the effects of exposure of the fetus ... a great body of experts are of the opinion that the fetus is more vulnerable to levels of lead that would not affect adults"; and that petitioners had "failed to establish that there is an acceptable alternative policy which would protect the fetus." The court stated that, in view of this disposition of the business necessity defense, it did not "have to undertake a bona fide occupational qualification's (BFOQ) analysis."

The Court of Appeals for the Seventh Circuit, sitting en banc, affirmed the summary judgment by a 7–to–4 vote. The majority held that the proper standard for evaluating the fetal-protection policy was the defense of business necessity; that Johnson Controls was entitled to summary judgment under that defense; and that even if the proper standard was a BFOQ, Johnson Controls still was entitled to summary judgment.

The Court of Appeals first reviewed fetal-protection opinions from the Eleventh and Fourth Circuits. *See* Hayes v. Shelby Memorial Hospital, 726 F.2d 1543 (11th Cir. 1984), and Wright v. Olin Corp., 697 F.2d 1172 (4th Cir. 1982). Those opinions established the three-step business necessity inquiry: whether there is a substantial health risk to the fetus; whether transmission of the hazard to the fetus occurs only through women; and whether there is a less discriminatory alternative equally capable of preventing the health hazard to the fetus. The Court of Appeals agreed with the Eleventh and Fourth Circuits that "the components of the business necessity defense the courts of appeals and the EEOC have utilized in fetal protection cases balance the interests of the employer, the employee and the unborn child in a manner consistent with Title VII." The court further noted that, under *Wards Cove Packing Co. v. Atonio,* 490 U.S. 642, 109 S.Ct. 2115, 104 L.Ed.2d 733 (1989), the burden of persuasion remained on the plaintiff in challenging a business necessity defense, and—unlike the Fourth and Eleventh Circuits—it thus imposed the burden on the plaintiffs for all three steps.

Applying this business necessity defense, the Court of Appeals ruled that Johnson Controls should prevail. Specifically, the court concluded that there was no genuine issue of material fact about the substantial health-risk factor because the parties agreed that there was a substantial risk to a fetus from lead exposure. The Court of Appeals also concluded that, unlike the evidence of risk to the fetus from the mother's exposure, the evidence of risk from the father's exposure, which petitioners presented, "is, at best, speculative and unconvincing." Finally, the court found that petitioners had waived the issue of less discriminatory alternatives by not adequately presenting it. It said that, in any event, petitioners had not produced evidence of less discriminatory alternatives in the District Court.

Having concluded that the business necessity defense was the appropriate framework and that Johnson Controls satisfied that standard, the court proceeded to discuss the BFOQ defense and concluded that Johnson Controls met that test, too. The en banc majority ruled that industrial safety is part of the essence of respondent's business, and that the fetal-protection policy is reasonably necessary to further that concern. Quoting *Dothard v. Rawlinson,* 433 U.S. 321 (1977), the majority emphasized that, in view of the goal of protecting the unborn, "more is at stake" than simply an individual woman's decision to weigh and accept the risks of employment.

Judges Cudahy and Posner dissented and would have reversed the judgment and remanded the case for trial. Judge Cudahy explained: "It may (and should) be difficult to establish a BFOQ here but I would afford the defendant an opportunity to try." ... Judge Posner stated: "I think it is a mistake to suppose that we can decide this case once and for all on so meager a record." He, too, emphasized that, under Title VII, a fetal-protection policy which explicitly applied just to women could be defended only as a BFOQ....

JUSTICE BYRON WHITE concurred in part and concurred in the judgement and filed opinion in which CHIEF JUSTICE WILLIAM H. REHNQUIST and JUSTICE ANTHONY KENNEDY joined. JUSTICE ANTONIN SCALIA, filed an opinion concurring in the judgment.

NOTES AND QUESTIONS

1. **The Effects of Johnson Controls.** Johnson Controls' holding, banning fetal protection policies that bar potentially fertile women from

specific job positions, has been generally effective. Prior to the Court's decision, there was considerable litigation over fetal protection policies. That litigation has ended. Furthermore, the EEOC has had very few post-*Johnson Controls* cases. There is some evidence, however, that employers have moved from the blatant type of policy enunciated in *Johnson Controls* to more subtle policies that require extra notice and counseling of reproductive risks for women only.

Fetal protection policies appeared to exist primarily in relatively well paying, male-dominated industries. Industries that were female-dominated and lower paying never imposed such bans on women despite high levels of toxicity to the reproductive processes. For example, the particular battery-making process involved in *Johnson Controls* had historically involved men's jobs. In contrast, laundries employ large numbers of women, use potentially toxic chemicals, are relatively low-paying, and have rarely had fetal protection policies. Thus, elimination of even the most blatant of these policies should provide substantially more employment opportunities for blue collar women.

For further discussions of the effects of fetal protection policies, see Mary Becker, *Reproductive Hazards after Johnson Controls*, 31 Houston L. Rev. 43 (1994); Ruth Colker, *Pregnancy, Parenting, and Capitalism,* 58 Ohio St. L.J. 61 (1997); Suzanne U. Samuels, *The Lasting Legacy of International Union, U.A.W. v. Johnson Controls*, 12 Wis. Women's L.J. 1 (1997); Nadine Taub, *At the Intersection of Reproductive Freedom and Gender Equality*, 6 UCLA Women's L. J. 443 (1996).

2. **Questions Raised by Johnson Controls.** *Johnson Controls* raises two important questions: First, if it costs more to employ pregnant women than pregnant men, can an employer defend on the grounds that a discriminatory policy is a BFOQ? Second, what is the extent of the employer's exposure through tort liability?

In *Johnson Controls*, the Court held that the plaintiff had made out a prima facie case of disparate treatment sex discrimination. (Why did the Court find this to be a disparate treatment case instead of a disparate impact case?) The defense to a disparate treatment case is a bona fide occupational qualification (BFOQ). According to the statute, § 703(e)(1), a sex-based BFOQ exists if it is "reasonably necessary to the normal operation of that particular business enterprise" to have an employee of a particular sex. As far back as 1971 the courts had held that a BFOQ did not exist if it did not go to the essence of the employer's business. *See* Diaz v. Pan American World Airways, Inc., 442 F.2d 385 (5th Cir. 1971) (holding that alleged preference for female flight attendants by a predominantly male clientele was not sufficient to uphold a BFOQ, because the benefit received by the clientele was "tangential" as opposed to essential to the business) and Wilson v. Southwest Airlines Co., 517 F. Supp. 292 (N.D.Tex. 1981) (holding that being female did not go to the essence of the employer's business despite an advertising campaign that connected the airline with fun and sex appeal). While these decisions made clear that for a sex-based policy to qualify as a BFOQ it must relate to the essence of the employer's business, they did not help in defining "essence."

Thus, in *Johnson Controls,* the Court had to decide whether an employer could claim that "safety" went to the essence of its business. Safety had been accepted as a grounds for a BFOQ in Dothard v. Rawlinson, 433 U.S. 321, 97 S.Ct. 2720, 53 L.Ed.2d 786 (1977), but the Court rejected it here. As the Court noted, fertile women are as able as others to make batteries. For the Court, this left decisions about the well-being of any future children to the women themselves, not the employer. Does it make sense to differentiate for purposes of the BFOQ between the safety of a fetus and the safety of clients or others who have a role in the employer's business? Suppose there was evidence of serious fetal damage from the toxic materials. Would that mean that the employer could exclude pregnant women (as opposed to those who might become pregnant) from the battery-making process?

The Court's analysis leaves as many questions as it answers. Was Johnson Controls' claim that fetal safety went to the essence of its business really a claim about the potential costs of liability for fetal injury? Isn't the essence of the employer's business to make money? If the employer could prove that it would be subject to crippling tort liability as a result of fetal damage from the mothers' participating in the battery-making, would that justify a fetal protection policy as a BFOQ? Notice that there are four concurring Justices who believe that this would be the case.

The second question raised by *Johnson Controls* relates to the employer's potential tort liability. Does Title VII preempt state tort liability? One test for preemption asks whether it is impossible to comply with both state and federal law. Is it? Does Justice Marshall's opinion in *Cal Fed* help you to think about this? A second preemption test applies if the federal law creates a complete scheme of regulation, is identical in its subject matter to the federal law, and if the matter has traditionally been subject to federal regulation. Again, it is questionable whether this standard could be used in this situation to preempt state tort law.

If tort liability is not preempted is it likely to be a major issue? Notice that the record in the case did not indicate any problems or abnormalities among the babies born to the eight employees who had become pregnant. If the employer has not been negligent in exposing the employees to toxic materials, how likely is liability? If the employer has been negligent, why shouldn't it be held liable? Negligence is a standard that is hard to pin down, as well as one that can change over time. Is that necessarily undesirable, however? Shouldn't the employer have the responsibility of running its business as a reasonable person would under the circumstances? Of course, it is also possible that a court might hold an employer that uses toxic materials strictly liable for injuries caused by those materials. Strict liability is usually justified on the basis of enterprise liability or the employer's better position to spread the costs of the accident. Is there any reason why these would not apply in this setting? Should we let the risks of tort liability scare us away from barring fetal protection policies like the one in *Johnson Controls*? Or should Johnson Controls, like any other employer, go out of business if the costs attached to its manufacturing process exceed the benefits?

For additional discussion of the preemption and tort liability issues, see Susan S. Grover, *The Employer's Fetal Injury Quandary after Johnson Controls*, 81 Ky. L. J. 639 (1992/1993); David L. Kirp, *Fetal Hazards, Gender Justice, and the Justices*, 34 Wm. & Mary L. Rev. 101 (1992); Yxta M. Murray, Note, *Employer Liability After Johnson Controls*, 45 Stan. L. Rev. 453 (1993).

Family and Medical Leave Act of 1993

Public Law 103–3, 103d Congress.
107 Stat. 6, February 5, 1993.

AN ACT

To grant family and temporary medical leave under certain circumstances.

Be it enacted by the Senate and House of Representatives of the United States of America in Congress assembled,

SEC. 2.   FINDINGS AND PURPOSES.

(a) FINDINGS.—Congress finds that—

(1) the number of single-parent households and two-parent households in which the single parent or both parents work is increasing significantly;

(2) it is important for the development of children and the family unit that fathers and mothers be able to participate in early childrearing and the care of family members who have serious health conditions;

(3) the lack of employment policies to accommodate working parents can force individuals to choose between job security and parenting;

(4) there is inadequate job security for employees who have serious health conditions that prevent them from working for temporary periods;

(5) due to the nature of the roles of men and women in our society, the primary responsibility for family caretaking often falls on women, and such responsibility affects the working lives of women more than it affects the working lives of men; and

(6) employment standards that apply to one gender only have serious potential for encouraging employers to discriminate against employees and applicants for employment who are of that gender.

(b) PURPOSES.—It is the purpose of this Act—

(1) to balance the demands of the workplace with the needs of families, to promote the stability and economic security of families, and to promote national interests in preserving family integrity;

(2) to entitle employees to take reasonable leave for medical reasons, for the birth or adoption of a child, and for the care of a child, spouse, or parent who has a serious health condition;

(3) to accomplish the purposes described in paragraphs (1) and (2) in a manner that accommodates the legitimate interests of employers;

(4) to accomplish the purposes described in paragraphs (1) and (2) in a manner that, consistent with the Equal Protection Clause of the Fourteenth Amendment, minimizes the potential for employment discrimination on the basis of sex by ensuring generally that leave is available for eligible medical reasons (including maternity-related disability) and for compelling family reasons, on a gender-neutral basis; and

(5) to promote the goal of equal employment opportunity for women and men, pursuant to such clause.

TITLE I—GENERAL REQUIREMENTS FOR LEAVE

SEC. 101.   DEFINITIONS.

As used in this title: ...

(2) ELIGIBLE EMPLOYEE.—

(A) IN GENERAL.—The term "eligible employee" means an employee who has been employed—

(i) for at least 12 months by the employer with respect to whom leave is requested under section 102; and

(ii) for at least 1,250 hours of service with such employer during the previous 12–month period. . . .

(4) EMPLOYER—

(A) IN GENERAL.—The term "employer"—

(i) means any person engaged in commerce or in any industry or activity affecting commerce who employs 50 or more employees for each working day during each of 20 or more calendar workweeks in the current or preceding calendar year; ...

(7) PARENT.—The term "parent" means the biological parent of an employee or an individual who stood in loco parentis to an employee when the employee was a son or daughter. ...

(11) SERIOUS HEALTH CONDITION.—The term "serious health condition" means an illness, injury, impairment, or physical or mental condition that involves—

(A) inpatient care in a hospital, hospice, or residential medical care facility; or

(B) continuing treatment by a health care provider.

(12) SON OR DAUGHTER.—The term "son or daughter" means a biological, adopted, or foster child, a stepchild, a legal ward, or a child of a person standing in loco parentis, who is—

(A) under 18 years of age; or

(B) 18 years of age or older and incapable of self-care because of a mental or physical disability.

(13) SPOUSE.—The term "spouse" means a husband or wife, as the case may be.

SEC. 102. LEAVE REQUIREMENT.

(a) IN GENERAL.—

(1) ENTITLEMENT TO LEAVE.—Subject to section 103, an eligible employee shall be entitled to a total of 12 workweeks of leave during any 12–month period for one or more of the following:

(A) Because of the birth of a son or daughter of the employee and in order to care for such son or daughter.

(B) Because of the placement of a son or daughter with the employee for adoption or foster care.

(C) In order to care for the spouse, or a son, daughter, or parent, of the employee, if such spouse, son, daughter, or parent has a serious health condition.

(D) Because of a serious health condition that makes the employee unable to perform the functions of the position of such employee.

(2) EXPIRATION OF ENTITLEMENT.—The entitlement to leave under subparagraphs (A) and (B) of paragraph (1) for a birth or placement of a son or daughter shall expire at the end of the 12–month period beginning on the date of such birth or placement.

(b) LEAVE TAKEN INTERMITTENTLY OR ON A REDUCED LEAVE SCHEDULE.—

(1) IN GENERAL.—Leave under subparagraph (A) or (B) of subsection (a)(1) shall not be taken by an employee intermittently or on a reduced leave schedule unless the employee and the employer of the employee agree otherwise. Subject to paragraph (2), subsection (e)(2),

and section 103(b)(5), leave under subparagraph (C) or (D) of subsection (a)(1) may be taken intermittently or on a reduced leave schedule when medically necessary. The taking of leave intermittently or on a reduced leave schedule pursuant to this paragraph shall not result in a reduction in the total amount of leave to which the employee is entitled under subsection (a) beyond the amount of leave actually taken.

(2) ALTERNATIVE POSITION.—If an employee requests intermittent leave, or leave on a reduced leave schedule, under subparagraph (C) or (D) of subsection (a)(1), that is foreseeable based on planned medical treatment, the employer may require such employee to transfer temporarily to an available alternative position offered by the employer for which the employee is qualified and that—

(A) has equivalent pay and benefits; and

(B) better accommodates recurring periods of leave than the regular employment position of the employee.

(c) UNPAID LEAVE PERMITTED.—Except as provided in subsection (d), leave granted under subsection (a) may consist of unpaid leave....

(d) RELATIONSHIP TO PAID LEAVE.—

(1) UNPAID LEAVE.—If an employer provides paid leave for fewer than 12 workweeks, the additional weeks of leave necessary to attain the 12 workweeks of leave required under this title may be provided without compensation.

(2) SUBSTITUTION OF PAID LEAVE.—

(A) IN GENERAL.—An eligible employee may elect, or an employer may require the employee, to substitute any of the accrued paid vacation leave, personal leave, or family leave of the employee for leave provided under subparagraph (A), (B), or (C) of subsection (a)(1) for any part of the 12–week period of such leave under such subsection.

(B) SERIOUS HEALTH CONDITION.—An eligible employee may elect, or an employer may require the employee, to substitute any of the accrued paid vacation leave, personal leave, or medical or sick leave of the employee for leave provided under subparagraph (C) or (D) of subsection (a)(1) for any part of the 12–week period of such leave under such subsection, except that nothing in this title shall require an employer to provide paid sick leave or paid medical leave in any situation in which such employer would not normally provide any such paid leave.

(e) FORESEEABLE LEAVE.—

(1) REQUIREMENT OF NOTICE.—In any case in which the necessity for leave under subparagraph (A) or (B) of subsection (a)(1) is foreseeable based on an expected birth or placement, the employee shall provide the employer with not less than 30 days' notice, before the date the leave is to begin, of the employee's intention to take leave under such subparagraph, except that if the date of the birth or placement requires leave to begin in less than 30 days, the employee shall provide such notice as is practicable.

(2) DUTIES OF EMPLOYEE.—In any case in which the necessity for leave under subparagraph (C) or (D) of subsection (a)(1) is foreseeable based on planned medical treatment, the employee—

(A) shall make a reasonable effort to schedule the treatment so as not to disrupt unduly the operations of the employer, subject to the approval of the health care provider of the employee or the health care provider of the son, daughter, spouse, or parent of the employee, as appropriate; and

(B) shall provide the employer with not less than 30 days' notice, before the date the leave is to begin, of the employee's intention to take leave under such subparagraph, except that if the date of the treatment requires leave to begin in less than 30 days, the employee shall provide such notice as is practicable.

(f) SPOUSES EMPLOYED BY THE SAME EMPLOYER.—In any case in which a husband and wife entitled to leave under subsection (a) are employed by the same employer, the aggregate number of workweeks of leave to which both may be entitled may be limited to 12 workweeks during any 12–month period, if such leave is taken—

(1) under subparagraph (A) or (B) of subsection (a)(1); or

(2) to care for a sick parent under subparagraph (C) of such subsection. . . .

SEC. 104.   EMPLOYMENT AND BENEFITS PROTECTION.

(a) RESTORATION TO POSITION.—

(1) IN GENERAL.—Except as provided in subsection (b), any eligible employee who takes leave under section 102 for the intended purpose of the leave shall be entitled, on return from such leave—

(A) to be restored by the employer to the position of employment held by the employee when the leave commenced; or

(B) to be restored to an equivalent position with equivalent employment benefits, pay, and other terms and conditions of employment.

(2) LOSS OF BENEFITS.—The taking of leave under section 102 shall not result in the loss of any employment benefit accrued prior to the date on which the leave commenced.

(3) LIMITATIONS.—Nothing in this section shall be construed to entitle any restored employee to—

(A) the accrual of any seniority or employment benefits during any period of leave; or

(B) any right, benefit, or position of employment other than any right, benefit, or position to which the employee would have been entitled had the employee not taken the leave....

(b) EXEMPTION CONCERNING CERTAIN HIGHLY COMPENSATED EMPLOYEES.—

(1) DENIAL OF RESTORATION.—An employer may deny restoration under subsection (a) to any eligible employee described in paragraph (2) if—

(A) such denial is necessary to prevent substantial and grievous economic injury to the operations of the employer;

(B) the employer notifies the employee of the intent of the employer to deny restoration on such basis at the time the employer determines that such injury would occur; and

(C) in any case in which the leave has commenced, the employee elects not to return to employment after receiving such notice.

(2) AFFECTED EMPLOYEES.—An eligible employee described in paragraph (1) is a salaried eligible employee who is among the highest paid 10 percent of the employees employed by the employer within 75 miles of the facility at which the employee is employed.

(c) MAINTENANCE OF HEALTH BENEFITS.—

(1) COVERAGE.—Except as provided in paragraph (2), during any period that an eligible employee takes leave under section 102, the employer shall maintain coverage under any "group health plan" ... for the duration of such leave at the level and under the conditions coverage would have been provided if the employee had continued in employment continuously for the duration of such leave....

Kathryn Abrams, Gender Discrimination and the Transformation of Workplace Norms

42 Vand. L. Rev. 1183 (1989).

...If women with children are to attain equality in the workplace, then we must challenge the notion of a natural or pre-ordained line dividing work and family. This demarcation is the clearest example of a norm that exists because the workplace was built by and around men. Because men traditionally have not had primary responsibility for rearing children, it was possible for male employers to structure jobs to demand extensive, uncompromised commitment. They could ignore the impact that such demands placed on workers' families, because most workers had wives who could take up the slack. Many employers persist in these assumptions, although workers are no longer exclusively male, and although few workers have wives on whom they can rely for full-time child care....

Moving the boundary between work and family is itself no mean feat. The assumption that one member of a family works while the other attends the children conditions, to varying degrees, contemporary views of what it means to pursue a 'career,' the day-to-day requirements imposed by employers, and the expectations of clients or consumers. Changing this assumption will be financially costly as well as disorienting. Employers will have to determine which jobs or tasks can be shared or accomplished through flexible scheduling, grant fringe benefits to part-time workers, and re-educate clients to greater confidence in the new arrangements. For their part, women in the workplace will have to think more clearly and comprehensively about the affirmative vision of work and its relation to family that they want to propound.

Moreover, until men begin to share equally in child care responsibilities, moving this boundary will require employers to accept certain differences that may emerge in men's and women's work patterns. In opposing discrimination against women, advocates have been most successful when they have asked men simply to treat women as if they were indistinguishable from men. In redrawing the line between work and family, advocates seek a different goal. They ask employers to see some women—and ultimately, some men—that is different from most men, but they ask them not to devalue the difference that they see. They ask employers to evaluate commitment according to a standard more complex than the single-minded shouldering of innumerable tasks that has been the primary gauge....

Women are only beginning the ongoing task of elaborating the norms that will create a new work-family boundary. Nonetheless, it is possible to formulate alternatives to the separate spheres conception, and to the demand for conformity to a male career path characteristic of the dubious employer. Some of these alternative norms have been espoused by feminist scholars and activists in other areas, and now may be applied to the workplace; others can be drawn from the historical experience of women at work. These norms may be, and have been, embraced by both men and women. I identify them as 'socially female,' only because they draw upon life experiences and analytic approaches more typical of women.

Many of these norms embody a different view of the worker, and of her relationship to her job. First, the worker is not viewed simply as the performer of a particular set of tasks; nor is it assumed that her commitments run exclusively or uncompromisedly to the employer. Such assumptions are common in the contemporary workplace, and perhaps are consistent with the model of a married male employee, whose wife attends to the nonwork-related aspects of his life. These assumptions, however, are not appropriate to jobs staffed by single workers and two-career couples. Moreover, they are inconsistent with the way many women view their fellow employees.

Scholars such as Carol Gilligan have noted the reluctance of many women to rely on abstract characterizations and hierarchies of controlling principles in describing people and their personal choices. Schooled by a distinct process of sexual socialization, many women are more inclined to insist on complex, contextualized understandings of those around them. The notion that ordinary people, who have connections and obligations to a range of others, could be expected to make choices systematically in a single direction, without reference to the particular conflict that they face, might seem unnecessarily rigid.... A workplace informed by the perceptions of women might recognize its employees' competing obligations, and offer them more flexibility for resolving the conflicts that arise.

This flexibility also flows from a second perspective that women might bring to work: a desire for a workplace that elicits workers' satisfaction, while it respects their humanity. Some feminists trace this desire to women's ongoing connection with a domestic world in which each person is valued and supported. This background has made it difficult for some women to think about work without thinking about the well-being of their coworkers.... These views question an approach to work and family that compels many workers to perform their tasks exhausted by competing demands, and distracted by their inability to care for their families' needs.

One final element of many women's experience supports a more accommodating response to work-family conflict: the ability to appreciate and value different kinds of contributions and commitments to the workplace. Historically, women have shown greater variation in their contribution and commitment to the workplace than have their male counterparts. Looking at the present century, women have structured their employment to accommodate the family demands during peacetime, and have mobilized to fill the varied and demanding jobs vacated during periods of war. In addition, the working patterns of women with families have contrasted with those of early feminists and social reformers, who often declined to marry and committed themselves exclusively to their professional pursuits. Contemporary women demonstrate and observe around them even greater variation in their commitment to a job or career. Thus, even women without a self-conscious feminist background are likely to hold a less monolithic view of a valuable contribution to the workplace than their male colleagues. Women whose views are informed by the insights of feminist scholarship have other reasons for resisting a single model of professional contribution. They recognize the danger of devaluing difference that comes from adherence to a single model of performance, and they look critically at the assumptions that shape rigid conceptions of quality. All these factors contribute to a view that workers can strike many balances between competing obligations that would be suitable not only from the standpoint of their lives, but also from the standpoint of the employer's performance.

1. *Nonprofessional Employees*

The concrete changes that might be produced by these norms vary in part with the job in question. For nonprofessional workers, the greatest need is for flexibility in accommodating competing commitments. Employers may not see a basic conflict between the obligations of a secretary or office manager and those of a parent. Yet they rarely structure such jobs in ways that permit employees to respond to family demands. Very few grant leave days for the care of sick children, and some discourage or forbid employees to use their own sick days for this purpose. Flex-time working arrangements are not available on a regular basis; part-time arrangements are available but rarely afford benefits. Few employers provide on-site child care or vouchers for off-site services, and even the most progressive generally limit themselves to much-touted child care information and referral services. . . .

Legislation could take numerous forms and involve many levels of government. The federal government, for example, requires its agencies to provide flex-time options for their employees, when feasible. Congress might extend the reach of this program by requiring flex-time or part-time programs of all employers who receive government funds or perform government contracts, or of all employers of a certain size. . . .

2. *Professional Employees*

The barriers facing professional employees who are primary parents are in some respects distinct. On the one hand, they do not face many of the hardships endured by nonprofessional workers. They are unlikely to be replaced if they extend maternity leave, and they may not face official restrictions on sick leave. They do not live so near the edge of poverty that affordable child care is difficult to find, or that family benefits requiring salary reductions are impossible to consider. Yet they face obstacles that nonprofessional employees rarely encounter. Many professional jobs are organized hierarchically. If an employee is to sustain her professional self-esteem—and in some cases, retain her job with a particular employer—then she must progress from one level of achievement and responsibility to the next. Professional jobs also have a strong tradition of male occupants and unlimited demands. Though the former condition largely is responsible for the latter, many employers view comprehensive commitment as inherent in the nature of the work, and consider it a useful tool for gauging employees' potential.

Creating a professional workplace that accommodates primary parents thus requires two distinct types of efforts. First, employers must recognize the need for flexibility and for the accommodation of competing demands. Second, employers must learn not to devalue the more flexible employment alternatives that they create. The latter task, in fact, may prove to be the more difficult. In the few recent efforts professional employers have made to accommodate working parents, many employees have been obliged to purchase flexibility at the price of professional recognition and advancement.

Alternatives to full-time commitment in professional fields are not yet so common as to exhibit standard patterns. A great deal of part-time work still must be arranged on an individual basis with the employer. While this response permits flexibility, it may also isolate the employee who seeks accommodation and may create anxiety about the effect of the arrangement on her career. In some cases this anxiety appears well grounded. Many employers offering part-time work view it as an expedient that alters the character of the employee's contribution and reduces her potential for advancement. Rather than extending the time horizon for promotion of a part-time employee, some employers require that part-time employees leave the promotion track altogether; others make clear ex ante that alternative work patterns affect the employee's chances of promotion. Part-time or shared-work arrangements seem to be regarded as forms of work that are different in quality, not just quantity. Employees who elect them are viewed not as promising professionals with temporarily conflicting obligations, but as people who have made a crucial choice to participate in the profession in a marginal way.

These judgments may be driven in part by the fact that part-time alternatives diverge from the male-centered, professional norm of unrestricted commitment to work. Yet the fact that such arrangements are requested, almost exclusively, by women who wish to commit time to family seems to exacerbate the problem. A group of employees, who to the employer's mind remain marginal participants in the workplace, seek an alteration in a central workplace norm for the purpose of childrearing—an activity that may be straightforwardly devalued and is at least thought to be incompatible with serious work. The persistence of these subordinating views produces an impasse, in which simply establishing new programs is not enough. When advocates do not attempt to reshape male-centered attitudes even as they create new programs, then we see accommodative programs that are viewed as badges of professional dishonor by those who sponsor them.

This conundrum leads to two conclusions about the means of transforming workplace norms. First, legislation cannot be the sole response in the professional setting, because some of the most salient barriers cannot be lowered by legislative fiat. The major problem lies not in achieving the formal accommodation, but in ending devaluation of these alternatives, so that women with parental responsibilities may achieve respect within their profession. While legislation might make such alternatives more broadly available, it cannot prevent their devaluation without also controlling the promotions process—a move that legislators and employers are likely to resist. These difficulties mean that professional women must rely on voluntary programs either to supplement or to take the place of legislation. The challenge, then, is to create programs that will help re-educate employers and other employees, as they are giving working parents the greater flexibility they require.

One program, recently introduced by IBM, provides a useful point of departure. This program permits any professional employee, male or female, to take up to three years leave, with job security and full seniority guaranteed on return. Employees may take this leave to raise a family, or to pursue a 'once-in-a-lifetime' opportunity.... Crucially, the program ... reduces the stigma associated by many in the workplace with committing substantial time to parenting. It does so by decoupling childrearing from gender, and by creating an inplicit analogy between raising a family and taking advantage of a 'once-in-a-lifetime' opportunity.... Finally, the limited character of the leave highlights the important but poorly understood fact that a substantial family commitment need not define a type of worker, but simply may describe one period of a worker's life.

Despite these advantages, certain limitations implicit in this program restrict its usefulness in re-educating employers and their workforces. The fact that it is a leave program——that all those who are pursuing other commitments are out of the workplace at the time they are doing so-perpetuates the current expectation that all those in the workplace will commit themselves unrestrictedly to its demands. This characteristic deprives employees of the opportunity to see coworkers struggling with different balances between work and other commitments. It also permits the company to ignore the burdens imposed on employees who are not on leave, and to neglect alternative ways of structuring existing jobs....

Another alternative that would be particularly effective in reducing the stigma attached to combining work and family responsibilities is a mandatory leave program. A firm could require that every employee take off one year in five (or, similar to universities, one year in seven), or spend one year out of every five working on a part-time basis. Once firms learned how to train temporary workers, how to divide responsibilities among two or more employees, and how to handle seniority and promotion issues for employees who do not make an uninterrupted full-time commitment, this approach would not necessarily be more difficult than granting leaves on a case-by-case basis. It might even permit more advance planning, because some employees would be able to schedule their time away in advance. When leave or part-time work becomes something that literally everyone in the firm does, it would be difficult to view it as a sign of decreased commitment, or as a barrier to future success....

NOTES AND QUESTIONS

1. **Evaluating the Family and Medical Leave Act.** The Act states its goals in §§ 2(a) and (b). Taking it on its own terms, how well do you think it meets these objectives? For example does it provide parents with a "reasonable leave ... for the birth or adoption of a child?" Does it encourage fathers and mothers to participate in the raising of a young

child? In answering these questions, consider the amount of leave available each year to each parent.

How does the fact that leave under the Family and Medical Leave Act (FMLA) can be unpaid affect your evaluation of its adequacy? Who will be able to take leave and who will not? In general, women earn seventy-five cents on every dollar earned by men. In two-parent families, is it more likely the parents will decide the mother should take the leave or the father? In single parent families, how useful will unpaid leave be? Does the FMLA provide a benefit that is only of significant value to well-paid two parent families? In thinking about well-paid employees, it is important to keep in mind that the employer is required to restore most employees to their previous positions after a leave, but this requirement does not apply to the employer's most highly paid employees. Is this likely to remove some of the incentive to take leaves for just those parents, especially single parents, who might have been able to afford to do so?

Leaves for the birth or adoption of a child may not be taken on a reduced leave schedule, although leaves for health purposes may. Is this likely to impact negatively on parents who might want to work part-time for a period of time longer than 12 weeks?

By definition, only fairly large employers are covered by the Act. Who would you expect to be negatively impacted by this? Certainly there will be some professional offices, but also a large number of employees of low pay, low skill, non-unionized employers.

The Act indicates that Congress chose gender neutral-standards because standards that apply only to one gender may encourage discrimination against those employees. How might this work? Do you think that the FMLA is likely to be perceived as a gender-neutral law or as a "woman's law?"

Not surprisingly, evidence from the U.S. and Western Europe indicates that women take advantage of parenting leaves significantly more frequently than men. This remains true (although the statistics narrow somewhat) if the leaves are paid. Why do you think this is the case? What would need to be changed in the corporate culture in order to make men more likely to take leaves?

2. **Beyond the FMLA.** What kinds of changes should we look to next to reduce the conflict that parents face between work and family? President Clinton has suggested more flexibility in leaves, allowing employees to take (unpaid) leave time for such events as parent-teacher conferences or children's doctor's visits.

Kathryn Abrams proposes a number of options that would make the workplace more flexible. She argues that, especially for professional employees, these reforms cannot simply be legislated. To do so will not affect the devaluation of those who take advantage of the reforms. Do you agree? Should women lobby for legislation that would require employers to make child care, flex-time, and part-time work available to parents? Should this legislation then prohibit discrimination against those who take advantage of the new benefits? Would this be too much interference with the employer's ability to run the business? Others have proposed allowing parents to refuse overtime work, even with extra pay, in order to be with their children. Finally, what about Abrams's proposal for mandatory leaves? Should employees be required to take leaves periodically? Again, is this proposal too intrusive on the employer's running of the business?

All of these proposals involve further regulation of private enterprise. In addition, they are aimed at influencing decisions made within the confines of the family. Should the government be in the business of telling employers how to provide for the needs of their employee-parents? Should it be in the business of providing incentives to equalize parenting burdens within the family? What about mandating parental leave for all parents? If you are in favor of large amounts of government intervention to help move the line between work and family, what types of intervention would help single parent families?

For further discussions of this topic, see Nancy E. Dowd, *Family Values and Valuing Family*, 30 Harv. J. On Legis. 335 (1993); Mary Joe Frug, *Securing Job Equality for Women*, 59 B.U. L. Rev. 55, 94–103 (1979); Lise Vogel, *Considering Difference*, 2 Social Politics 111 (1995).

3. **Parental Leave Policies in Europe.** Sometimes it is useful to look to other countries' policies as a source for inspiration. Italy, for example, provides a three month leave for either parent at eighty-percent pay, which can be followed by an additional six month leave at thirty-percent pay. Sweden also provides leave at eighty-percent pay, but its leave is for up to eight months after a child's birth. More innovatively, several countries provide for more extended leaves if the babies are born under difficult circumstances, e.g. prematurely or with a sibling already at home. (In some cases these leaves are only available to the mother.) Perhaps the most innovative program is Sweden's. When studies revealed that fathers there were reluctant to take the paid leaves provided, Sweden mandated leaves for them.

In general European leave programs are for longer periods than the leave provided by the FMLA, and European programs also usually provide some pay. The FMLA, however, is gender-neutral in its language, while many European countries also have pre-or post-birth leaves that are only available to the mother.

For information on parental leaves in Europe, *see* Ruth Colker, *Pregnancy, Parenting, and Capitalism*, 58 Ohio St. L.J. 61 (1997); Mikel A. Glavinovich, *International Suggestions for Improving Parental Leave Legislation in the United States*, 12 Ariz. J. Int'l & Comp. L. 147 (1996); Carol D. Rasnic, *The United States' 1993 Family and Medical Leave Act*, 10 Conn. J. Int'l L. 105 (1994).

Richard Posner, Conservative Feminism
1989 The Univ. of Chicago Legal Forum 191.

. . . [W]hat is "conservative feminism"? It is, I suggest, the idea that women are entitled to political, legal, social, and economic equality to men, in the framework of a lightly regulated market economy. It is the libertarian approach to issues of feminist jurisprudence, provided that "libertarian" is understood to refer to a strong commitment to markets rather than to some natural-rights or other philosophical underpinning of such a commitment. The implications of such an approach are not limited to narrowly "economic" issues such as comparable worth.... The implications extend, as we shall see, to the headiest heights of jurisprudential speculation, where the question whether women have a fundamentally different outlook on law from men is being debated....

There should be no legal barriers to the employment of women. Laws that forbade women to work in dangerous occupations, or to work as long hours as men, were for the most part either paternalistic or designed to reduce competition faced by male workers. This was eventually recognized, and the laws have been repealed; but a subtler barrier to female employment remains. I refer to the fact that house-wives' imputed earnings are not taxed. This may seem an esoteric and impractical—if not downright provocative—topic with which to begin an examination of feminist jurisprudence; but we shall see that it illustrates the limitations of more familiar forms of feminist jurisprudence and social thought.

It is plain that housewives do useful work, in the sense of work for which families pay—as by forgoing the income that the housewife could earn in the market.[4] A lower-bound estimate of its value is, indeed, the amount housewives would earn in a world without income taxes if they entered the market. (It is a lower bound because a given woman might be more productive in the household than in the market.) Because the housewife's "earnings" in the home are not taxed, however, women will stay at home even when they would be worth more in the market. For example, suppose the value of a housewife's work is $40,000 a year; her earnings in the market (net of all expenses associated with market work—commuting costs, etc.) would be $50,000; and she would be in the 28 percent income tax bracket if she did enter the market. Then her after-tax income would be lower in the market than at home, and she will stay home even though she is worth more in the market....

[T]he distortion caused by the failure to tax housewives' real (though nonpecuniary) earnings is an important question for research. Why then is it not a question in which feminists are interested? Perhaps because economic analysis is thought to cut against women's interests. Or perhaps because the proposal of a tax on housewives' imputed earnings is thought to imply increasing the tax burden on women—indeed to invite comparison to a proposal to tax slaves on the ground that they produce real though nonpecuniary income. The comparison is superficial. To isolate the effect of a tax reform designed to reduce the misallocative effects of the existing system of taxation, the analyst must assume that the overall tax burden is

---

4. One estimate is that a full-time housewife contributes, on average, 40 percent of the full (that is, pecuniary plus nonpecuniary) income of the household. But the reader should be warned of the variety of estimates of housewives' imputed earnings, and of the lurking methodological problems.

not to be increased; that any new tax will be offset by a reduction in an existing tax.... Suppose a housewives' tax would be offset by a reduction in the federal income tax rate. Then taxes paid by working women and their husbands would fall; so would taxes paid by the husbands of housewives. The effect on husbands' income is relevant even if we do not care anything about men's welfare. Because much consumption within the household is joint, each spouse benefits from the income earned by the other, and an increase in husbands' income will therefore benefit wives as well. For both reasons (the fall in the taxes paid by working women and the fall in the taxes paid by working husbands), there is no ground for supposing that a tax on housewives' imputed income would increase the tax burden borne by women. It would, however, eliminate tax incentives from the decision whether to work within or outside the home. In doing so it would have the incidental but relevant effect of making men more comfortable with the idea of their wives' working outside the home. But the most important point is that the economic or libertarian perspective (these are not identical, of course, but they are connected) shows that things are not always as they seem; legislation superficially inimical to women's interests may actually serve those interests—and vice versa as we shall see. Feminists who are not libertarians may not like the vocabulary, methods, and assumptions of economics, but if they refuse to consider the economic consequences of policies affecting women they may end up hurting rather than helping women. ...

Where the libertarian is apt to part company with the liberal or radical feminist in the field of employment is over the question whether employers should be forced to subsidize female employees, as by being compelled to offer maternity leave or pregnancy benefits, or to disregard women's greater longevity than men when fixing pension benefits. To the extent that women workers incur higher medical expenses than men (mainly but not entirely due to pregnancy), or live longer in retirement on a company pension, they cost the employer more than male workers do. So the employer should not be required to pay the same wage *and* provide the same package of fringe benefits. (Of course, to the extent that women impose lower costs—for example, women appear to be more careful about safety than men, and therefore less likely to be injured on the job—they are entitled to a correspondingly higher wage or more extensive fringe benefits.) This is not to suggest—which would be absurd—that women are blameworthy for getting pregnant or for living longer than men. It is to suggest merely that they may be more costly workers and that, if so, the disparity in cost should be reflected in their net compensation. If this disparity is not reflected, then male workers are being discriminated against in the same sense in which women would be discriminated against if they received a lower wage than equally productive (and no less costly) male workers. What is sauce for the goose should be sauce for the gander. More than symmetry is involved; we shall see in a moment that laws designed to improve the welfare of women may boomerang, partly though not wholly because of the economic interdependence of men and women.

I anticipate three objections to my analysis. The first is that in speaking of employers subsidizing women I am taking as an arbitrary benchmark the costs and performance of male workers. I am not. Consider an employer who is female in a hypothetical female-dominated society and whose entire labor force is also female, so that for her the benchmark in setting terms of employment is female. A man applies for a job. He asks for a higher wage on the ground that experience shows that the average male employee's medical costs are lower than the average female employee's medical costs. If the employer refuses to pay him the higher wage, then, assuming that this worker is just as good as the employer's average female worker, the employer is discriminating against him. This should answer the second objection—that nature should not be allowed to determine social outcomes. I agree that natural law does not compel the conclusion that women should be penalized in the marketplace or anywhere else for living longer or for incurring greater medical costs on average than men. But neither is there any reason why men should be penalized for not living as long as women by being forced to pay for women's longer years of retirement. The matter should be left to the market.

The third objection to my analysis is that, in suggesting that the employer be allowed to make cost-justified differentiations based on sex, I am necessarily implying that he should be permitted to treat employees as members of groups whose average characteristics the particular employee may not share, rather than as individuals. That is true. Some women die before some men, just as some women are taller than some men. The difference is that while it is obvious on inspection whether a given woman is taller than a given man—and therefore it would be absurd for an employer to implement a (let us assume valid) minimum-height requirement of 5 feet 8 inches by refusing to accept job applications from women, it is not obvious which women employees will not live as long as which men employees or will not take as much leave or incur as high medical expenses. Any cost-based differentiation in these areas must be based on probabilistic considerations, of which sex may be the most powerful in the sense of having the greatest predictive power....

It is not even clear, moreover, that women benefit, on balance, from laws that forbid employers to take into account the extra costs that female employees can impose. Such laws discourage employers from hiring, promoting, and retaining women, and there are many ways in which they can discriminate in these respects without committing detectable violations of the employment-discrimination laws. Sometimes there is no question of violation, as when an employer accelerates the substitution of computers for secretaries in response to an increase in the costs of his female employees.

There is an additional point. Most women are married—and many who are not currently married are divorced or widowed and continue to derive a benefit from their husband's earnings. The consumption of a married woman is ... a function of her husband's income as well as of her own (in the divorce and widowhood cases as well, for the reason just noted).

Therefore a reduction in men's incomes as a result of laws that interfere with profit-maximizing and cost-minimizing decisions by employers will reduce women's welfare as well as men's. Moreover, women who are not married are less likely to have children than women who are married; and where employer benefits are child-related—such as pregnancy benefits and maternity leave—their effect is not merely to transfer wealth from men to women but from women to women.... Feminists who support rules requiring employers to grant pregnancy benefits and maternity leave may therefore, and I assume unknowingly, be discouraging women from remaining single or childless. Feminists of all persuasions would think it outrageous if the government required fertile women to have children, yet many feminists support an oblique form of such a policy—a subsidy to motherhood. They do this, I suspect, because they have not considered the economic consequences of proposals that *appear* to help women.

The principle of equal pay for equal work makes perfectly good economic sense, provided that equal work is understood, consistently with the previous discussion, to mean equal in cost to the employer as well as in benefit to the employer (productivity). It does not follow, however, that women are bound to have the same average wage rate as men even if there is no difference in medical or other costs or those differences are offset by other factors. Whether, despite being just as "good" as men, women will have the same average wage rate depends critically on whether they are willing to make the same commitment to the labor force as men do. A woman who takes several years out of the work force to stay home with her young children cannot expect to have the same average wage as a man who works continuously. Since her expected working life is shorter, she will invest less in her human capital (earning capacity); and part of a wage is a return to that investment.

Feminists who are not libertarians may retort that the propensity of women rather than men to take leave from work to raise their children is itself a subtle consequence of sex discrimination, "sex role socialization," or related factors. Whether it is nature or culture that is responsible for the fact that on average male self-esteem is more involved in career than female self-esteem is a profoundly difficult question on which I can claim no expertise; but certainly it would be rash to reject nature out of hand. It is possible that women are more devoted to children than men are and more talented at child rearing and that these differences reflect a genuine comparative advantage possessed by women as a result of millions of years of evolution, rather than just "brainwashing" by men and male-dominated women. The human infant requires prolonged nurture, and there may well have been efficiency advantages, under the exceedingly primitive conditions that obtained throughout all but the most recent history of the human race, to a sexual division of labor in which one spouse specializes in nurture and the other in hunting and in protection from enemies. To an unknown extent, that division may be "hard-wired" into our brains.

Even if these speculations are correct, they are correct about the average woman versus the average man rather than about every woman and every man. Within each there is a distribution of attitudes toward children. And the two distributions intersect. Many women are less devoted to children and less skillful at raising children than many men. The point of intersection is undoubtedly influenced by cultural factors that are changeable, as well as by biological factors that may be changeable if at all only at great cost.... But the point cuts in both directions. The fact—if it is a fact—that the predominant role of women in child-rearing is culturally contingent rather than biologically determined does not imply that it can easily be changed by governmental intervention or that we should greet governmental regulation of the family structure with open arms. The idea that government should try to alter the decisions of married couples on how to allocate time to raising children is a strange mixture of the Utopian and the repulsive. The division of labor within marriage is something to be sorted out privately rather than made a subject of public intervention. Liberal and radical feminists can if they want urge women to stay in the labor force and have no children or fewer children, or persuade their husbands to assume a greater role in child rearing. Others can urge the contrary. The ultimate decision is best left to private choice....

Frances E. Olsen, The Myth of State Intervention in the Family

18 U. Mich. J.L. Reform 835 (1985).

Most people concede that there are times when state officials should intervene in the private family. Doctrines of family privacy are no longer thought to justify societal neglect of beaten wives or abused children. Yet society continues to use the ideal of the private family to orient policy. It seems important therefore to examine the concept of state intervention in the private family. In this essay, I argue that the private family is an incoherent ideal and that the rhetoric of nonintervention is more harmful than helpful.

Although most people accept in general the assertion that the state should not intervene in the family, they qualify the assertion with the caveat that the state should sometimes intervene in order to correct inequality or prevent abuse. I refer to this widely-accepted caveat as the "protective intervention argument" against nonintervention in the family.

This essay presents a different argument against the policy of nonintervention in the family. It suggests that the terms "intervention" and "nonintervention" are largely meaningless. The terms do not accurately describe any set of policies, and as general principles, "intervention" and "nonintervention" are indeterminate. I refer to this argument as the "incoherence argument." ...

The protective intervention argument [states that] ... [s]ometimes the family misfunctions; instead of being a haven that protects and nurtures family members, the family may become a center of oppression and exploitation. When this happens the state should step in to prevent abuse and to protect the rights of the individual family members. Both the market version and the family version of this protective intervention argument presuppose that it would be possible for the state to remain neutral, but present reasons that the state should not do so. . . .

[N]onintervention in the family [is a] false ideal[]. As long as a state exists and enforces any laws at all, it makes political choices. The state cannot be neutral or. remain uninvolved, nor would anyone want the state to do so. The staunchest supporters of laissez faire always insisted that the state protect their property interests and that courts enforce contracts and adjudicate torts. They took this state action for granted and chose not to consider such protection a form of state intervention. . . .

Similarly, the staunchest opponents of state intervention in the family will insist that the state reinforce parents' authority over their children. Familiar examples of this reinforcement include state officials returning runaway children and courts ordering incorrigible children to obey their parents or face incarceration in juvenile facilities. These state actions are not only widely supported, they are generally not considered state intervention in the family. Another category of state policies is even less likely to be thought of as intervention. Supporters of nonintervention insist that the state protect families from third-party interference. Imagine their reaction if the state stood idly by while doctors performed non-emergency surgery without the knowledge or permission of a ten-year-old patient's parents, or if neighbors prepared to take the child on their vacation against the wishes of the parents, or if the child decided to go live with his fourth grade teacher. Once the state undertakes to prevent such third-party action, the state must make numerous policy choices, such as what human grouping constitutes a family and what happens if parents disagree. These choices are bound to affect the decisions people make about forming families, the distribution of power within the family, and the assignment of tasks and roles among family members. The state is responsible for the background rules that affect people's domestic behaviors. Because the state is deeply implicated in the formation and functioning of families, it is nonsense to talk about whether the state does or does not intervene in the family. Neither "intervention" nor "nonintervention" is an accurate description of any particular set of policies, and the terms obscure rather than clarify the policy choices that society makes.

THE PROTECTIVE INTERVENTION ARGUMENT

To understand the incoherence argument, it is useful to examine in more detail the protective intervention argument—the argument that nonintervention would be possible but is not always a good idea. The protective intervention argument is an argument in favor of selective intervention. In exceptional situations, the state should intervene in the family to protect the interests of society and of the family members who may be at risk; aside from such exceptional situations, state intervention should ordinarily be limited to routine matters such as setting formal requirements for marriage licenses and providing public schooling for children.

According to the usual version of the protective intervention argument, state intervention beyond routine matters should be carefully limited. Excessive or unnecessary intervention jeopardizes people's freedom and interferes with family intimacy. Because of the risks inherent in state intervention, say proponents of protective intervention, safeguards should be devised to protect against government abuse and to prevent unnecessary expansion of state intervention. As long as proper safeguards exist, however, state intervention can be useful—an important force for good.

Families Can Malfunction

The argument in favor of selective state intervention is based on the notion that although families ought to be safe, supportive, and loving, some families at some times are not. The family is supposed to be a warm, nurturant enclave governed by an ethic of altruism and caring—a haven protecting its members from the dangers of an authoritarian state and from the anarchistic intrusions of private third parties. Proponents of protective intervention recognize that in some unfortunate situations, the family can cease to be a haven and become instead, "a center of oppression, raw will and authority, violence and brutality, where the powerful economically and sexually subordinate and exploit the powerless."

State Protection of Individuals

When a family malfunctions it may be important for the state to protect an individual from the private oppression that members of families sometimes inflict on each other. The protective intervention argument justifies state intervention in the family to protect children from abuse or serious neglect. State officials can remove children from their families if the children have been physically or sexually abused. In cases of child neglect, the state may send social workers into the children's homes or remove the children, temporarily or permanently, for their protection. Such state protection can include ordering medical care, even against the parents' religious scruples. These policies are generally considered to be a form of state intervention in the family, but accepted as intervention that is justified, indeed necessary.

Until recent years, state protection for battered wives was also considered state intervention in the family—again, perhaps justified intervention, but intervention nonetheless. The protective intervention argument characterizes such state protection as a beneficial and necessary form of intervention into a family that has problems. Few people today would openly oppose state enforcement of rape and battery laws against spouses. . . .

This protective intervention argument begins to blend into the incoherence argument when people dispute whether such protection should be considered intervention at all. Some people would assert that when the family relationship has broken down, so has any justifiable claim to family privacy, and that state protection of the individual no longer constitutes intervention into the family. Indeed, proponents of this view might argue that it would be state intervention to try to keep the family together—for example, not to allow estranged spouses to get a divorce. In such arguments, the idea that the privacy of the family unit should be protected from state intervention begins to be replaced by the notion that what merits protection is the privacy of the individual regarding sexuality, procreation, and the formation of intimate, family-like relationships. I consider this concept of individual privacy to be part of the protective intervention argument—that state intervention is sometimes justified—because although the privacy argument redefines state intervention, it still considers intervention and nonintervention coherent, meaningful concepts. . . .

THE INCOHERENCE ARGUMENT

The incoherence argument goes further and I believe is more fundamental than the protective intervention argument. The protective intervention argument treats nonintervention as a fully possible but sometimes unwise choice; the incoherence argument questions the basic coherence of the concepts intervention and nonintervention. The state defines the family and sets roles within the family; it is meaningless to talk about intervention or nonintervention, because the state constantly defines and redefines the family and adjusts and readjusts family roles. Nonintervention is a false ideal because it has no coherent meaning.

For example, suppose a good-natured, intelligent sovereign were to ascend the throne with a commitment to end state intervention in the family. Rather than being obvious, the policies she should pursue would be hopelessly ambiguous. Is she intervening if she makes divorces difficult, or intervening if she makes them easy? Does it constitute intervention or nonintervention to grant divorce at all? If a child runs away from her parents to go live with her aunt, would nonintervention require the sovereign to grant or to deny the parents' request for legal assistance to reclaim their child? Because complete agreement on family roles does not exist, and because these roles undergo change over time, the state cannot be said simply to ratify preexisting family roles. The state is continuously affecting the family by influencing the distribution of power among individuals. . . .

In recent years, the state has been expected to treat the members of the family—especially the husband and wife—more as equals. Complete juridical equality would require a new concept of state intervention and nonintervention. At least two radically different concepts are possible, though neither would be acceptable to most people and, as I will demonstrate, neither is coherent. One possibility, which I refer to as the Market Model, is based on enforcement of all laws[.] Under this model, all rights and obligations would be enforced between family members the same way laws are enforced between strangers. In this manner the state could avoid direct support for family hierarchy. Nonintervention under [this] Market Model would be incoherent for the same reasons laissez faire is incoherent: enforcement of any property, tort, or contract law whether between family members or strangers, requires political choices that necessarily affect the power of the individuals and groups involved and the direction of both their intimate and their commercial relations.

A second possible model of state "nonintervention" in a juridically equal family is non-enforcement or delegalization—no rights or obligations to be enforced between family members. I refer to this construct as the State of Nature Model. Unlike the situation regarding the market, something approaching this model is acceptable to many as a form of "nonintervention" in the family. It can be demonstrated, however, that nonintervention under the State of Nature Model is also incoherent. First, because the "state of nature" would exist only within the family, the state would have to decide the boundaries of family. In addition, if the state of nature within the family were partial instead of complete, the state would have to decide which rights and obligations it would enforce within the family. These decisions require political choices that necessarily affect the roles and power within a family. Once the state undertakes to enforce some but not all rights and obligations, the state cannot avoid policy choices that will affect family life. No logical basis exists for identifying these state choices as either intervention or nonintervention....

The notion of nonintervention in the family is in a sense ... [im]plausible[.] [T]he state does not treat members of a family as juridical equals.... Laws establish who is married to whom and who shall be considered the child of whom.

The existence of this "legal-positivist" view of the family should not, however, obscure the coexisting and competing "natural law" belief that the family exists as a natural human formation, not created but merely recognized (or not recognized) by the state. Such a notion is implicit in the sense shared by most of us that some families exist that are not legally recognized....

Nonintervention and the Egalitarian Family

In theory it would be possible for the state to avoid taking a stand in favor of juridical hierarchy within the family. There are at least two ways the state could settle lawsuits involving families that would avoid ratifying family hierarchy. One would be to treat the family as a miniature state of nature by refusing to enforce any lawsuits between family members; the other would be to treat marriage as nothing more than an express contract and parentage as irrelevant, and enforce all lawsuits between family members just as though the litigants were not related. A consideration of these two contrasting extremes will further illustrate the difficulty with the concept of "nonintervention."

1. *State of Nature Model*—The state might seem to be able to remain neutral among family members by steadfastly refusing to enforce any tort, contract, or criminal law between members of a family. This approach, if carried to the extreme, would create a "state of nature" within the family, and could be said to take seriously the notion that families should work out their own problems. If a wife were being beaten, it would be up to her to

deal with the problem; the state would not "intervene." If she dealt with the problem by shooting her husband, the state would be expected to continue its policy of "nonintervention." . . .

The State of Nature Model would not really enable the state to remain neutral or uninvolved in the family. Even if the state of nature were complete within the family, the state would still have to decide who constituted a family and how to deal with lawsuits involving third parties and members of the family. Also, a complete state of nature would not fit contemporary views of nonintervention in the family. A partial state of nature within the family might be acceptable to many people; but if the state of nature were partial, decisions about what laws to enforce among family members would require additional political choices that would affect authority and roles within families.

2. *Market Model*—A second way the state might seem to be neutral among family members is based on the opposite strategy of enforcement. The state could treat each member of a family as a juridical equal and treat their family status as irrelevant. Marriage and parentage would become private relationships, not recognized by the state. Courts would treat as irrelevant the fact that litigants were married to one another or that one was the parent of the other, and enforce lawsuits as between any unrelated people or strangers. This approach essentially ignores the family relationship and treats family members just as strangers are treated. Such a policy would not fit contemporary views of nonintervention in the family, especially as regards children. For example, under the Market Model, parents who disciplined their children by sending them to their rooms might be guilty of kidnaping and the children could have a valid cause of action for false imprisonment. Parents would have neither an obligation to support children nor a right to keep them from living away from home. Children and parents would be free to cut their own deals. Contracts entered into between children and their parents, or between any other family members, would be just as enforceable as contracts between any unrelated individuals. . . .

The concept of nonintervention based on the Market Model is not only unacceptable to most people, but it is also . . . [not] coherent[.] All the arguments put forth by the legal realists to show the incoherence of laissez faire apply to nonintervention under the Market Model. The neutrality of the Market Model would be formal neutrality only, even as between adults. The particular tort, contract, and criminal laws the state chose to create and enforce would affect the relative power of individuals and thus the bargains they could negotiate with their spouses, children, or other relatives. For example, strong battery laws are likely to help wives and children; weakened self-defense doctrines limit their ability to protect themselves, and would seem to help husbands. . . .

THE EXPERIENCE OF STATE INTERVENTION

The assertion I have made—that the concepts of state intervention and nonintervention in the family are essentially meaningless—might ring hollow to an impoverished mother struggling to keep the state from taking her children away from her. More tragically, my assertion could sound absurd or seem totally meaningless to many innocent children who live in fear of the juvenile authorities. Hundreds of youngsters, the quality of whose lives has already been diminished by poverty and neglect, have been forced into silence and concealment. The spector of state intervention in the family denies to many of them even the partial relief they might get from sharing their pain and humiliation with a friendly neighbor or sympathetic teacher. Many such children exist, and to them state intervention can seem real and frightening. . . .

The experience of state intervention in the family can involve either affirmative coercive behavior by state officials, such as physically forcing a child away from his or her parent, or a refusal by state officials to come to the aid of one claiming a family right, such as the state's failure to order foster parents to relinquish a child to her natural parent. From the child's perspective, the transfer of custody to natural parents the child barely knows would seem to be as serious intervention as it would be to take her away from a natural parent.

The experience of intervention depends upon having some expectation disappointed or some sense of entitlement violated. Disappointment and violation are very real experiences. Unfortunately, they cannot be avoided by a simple policy of nonintervention in the family. . . .

Because the notion of state intervention depends upon a conception of proper family roles and these roles are open to dispute, almost any policy may be experienced by someone as state intervention. In many situations, someone's expectations will be disappointed or sense of entitlement violated no matter what action the state takes or refuses to take. One can often argue that in a particular case nonintervention really means whatever one wants the state to do; any policy one dislikes might be labeled intervention.

For example, from one perspective, the state intervenes in the family when it provides contraceptives to minors. The "squeal rule" proposed by the Reagan administration, although not preventing the distribution of contraceptives, would have required that parents be notified that contraceptives had been given to their children. This was supposed to reduce state intervention in the family and to enable parents to counsel their children about the problems of adolescent sex. Opponents feared it would deter the youngsters from obtaining contraceptives (but not from engaging in sex), and argued that this particular intervention in the family was justified.

From another perspective, the "squeal rule" does not reduce state intervention (whether for good or ill), but is itself a crude, abusive form of intervention. The state achieves a virtual monopoly on effective birth control by impoverishing young women and forbidding inexpensive over-the-counter sales of prescription contraceptives. It then proposes to use this monopoly to intrude into the parent-child relationship and pass along information to the parents that the parents have neglected to obtain the old-fashioned way—by talking with their children. The state thus rewards neglectful parents and removes from them an incentive to maintain supportive communication with their children. It encourages parents to neglect their child's sex education and to ignore the pressures put upon their child until after the child has become sexually active and the state so notifies them.

Nonintervention arguments can be leveled against laws and regulations that refuse to treat unmarried couples enough like a family or against laws that treat them too much like a family. Nonintervention arguments can be used to keep children from being put into foster care, to remove them from foster care, or to keep them from being removed from foster care. Nonintervention arguments can even be leveled against a policy of enforcing contracts between unwed couples. While one can sympathize with anyone who is disappointed by a state policy, it is hard to see that anything is actually gained by characterizing the cause of that disappointment as state intervention.

WHY IT MATTERS

The protective intervention argument, that the state should intervene in the family when necessary, has gained so much acceptance ... that one might wonder why we need the incoherence argument, that intervention and nonintervention are meaningless concepts. First, it is not the case that the exception has swallowed the rule. Under the protective intervention argument, the state is treated as having a policing function—to detect and correct those rare circumstances that disturb and disrupt the family, without questioning any of the basic individualistic foundations of society. The assertion that the state can and should avoid "intervention" in the family plays an important but generally unrecognized ideological role. Further, focusing on "nonintervention" tends to mush and confuse the ethical and political choices we make. It directs our attention to a false issue and obscures genuine issues of ethics and policy. Finally, both laissez faire and nonintervention in the family have sprung up in modern versions—law-and-economics in place of laissez faire and the individual right to privacy in place of nonintervention in the family. These new forms, one labeled conservative, the other liberal, are flawed in the same way the originals—laissez faire and nonintervention—are flawed. The standard liberal criticism of law-and-economics and the standard conservative criticism of the right to privacy are both versions of the protective intervention argument. In each instance, I believe the incoherence argument presents a more important critique....

D. "COMPARABLE WORTH": LAW AND THE WAGES FOR "WOMEN'S WORK"

INTRODUCTION

State and federal employment discrimination laws require equal pay for equal or even substantially similar work. They draw on feminist theories of equal treatment. Women, however, frequently do not hold the same jobs as men. Instead, women are disproportionately concentrated in a narrow range of low paying jobs, such as nursing, school teaching, clerical positions and department store sales. Indeed, women, on average, work in jobs where more than two-thirds of the workers are women. *See* National Committee on Pay Equity, Pay Equity: An Issue of Race, Ethnicity and Sex (1987). Although males and females in these jobs receive equal pay for their work, the jobs themselves are not as remunerative as a much broader range of jobs that men have traditionally dominated, such as construction work, over-the-road driving and management positions. As a consequence of this so-called "occupational segregation," in 1990 the average woman working full time all year earned only seventy-one cents for every dollar earned by the average man working the same amount. By 1997, this had risen to seventy-five cents on the dollar. Not only is the market segregated by gender; some "women's jobs" are staffed overwhelmingly by white women and others by women of color. For example, white women tend to dominate clerical positions with contact with the public. Black and Native American Women are concentrated in service occupations. Machine operators tend to be disproportionately Latina, while Asian women are often disparately employed in service and technical positions.

The question this section poses is the extent to which current laws can challenge a nation-wide pay structure in which work that women do is generally segregated by race and sex, and is usually less well compensated than work that men (especially white men) do. The name for this challenge is "comparable worth," and the legal issue it invokes is whether employment discrimination laws can or should require employers to re-value their compensation schemes in order to eliminate the undervaluation of "women's work".

The readings begin with two studies of the incidence and character of occupational segregation. They are intended to provide background on the structure of the employment market so that you can assess the legal efforts to remedy the market's inequities. One crucial question that both studies raise is whether women choose "women's work." If they do choose the work, how much of that choice is a result of socialization? The studies are followed by two decisions regarding the application of employment discrimination law to comparable worth issues. How much promise do the Equal Pay Act and Title VII hold for remedying the market's pay disparities? Neither court opinion addresses the concept of comparable worth directly, but neither indicates that the plaintiffs made a mistake by not relying on it. Comparable worth is usually viewed as too radical a solution to the problem because of the interference it requires with private enterprise and the market's wage setting role. The final reading in this section, an essay by Johanna Brenner, provides a critique of the comparable worth strategy from a socialist-feminist perspective. Instead of arguing that comparable worth is too radical a strategy, she argues that it is insufficiently radical.

At a minimum, these materials should provide an introduction to the legal questions involved in the comparable worth campaign. In addition, we hope this section will stimulate ideas about the reasons for occupational segregation and why the segregation did not diminish more dramatically in the face of the 1980s' legal challenges under both the Equal Pay Act and Title VII. State and federal employment discrimination laws require covered employers to hire and promote women without regard to sex. Why, then, do women choose—if they *do* choose—to work in jobs which pay less than other jobs?

This question is related to the public/private distinction, in that one barrier to the use of employment discrimination laws for the purposes of achieving comparable worth is the objection that the problem of occupational segregation lies within the private sphere of individual subjectivity, the sphere of private life choices which the laws should not regulate. A further twist on the public/private distinction is the historical claim that "the market" is also within the private sphere, and that it too should be shielded from government regulation. Pursuant to this interpretation of the public/private distinction, comparable worth reform would require an unprecedented or undesirable judicial interference with "the market".

Comparable worth has not yet divided feminists as sharply as the work/family conflict, but it is an issue which could provoke considerable controversy. Insofar as comparable worth poses a fundamental challenge to current economic and social structures, it raises a question of how political feminists will have to be in order to pursue the advancement of women in work.

Deborah L. Rhode, Occupational Inequality

1988 Duke L.J. 1207.

... Over the last quarter century, women's employment opportunities have increased substantially. Women now constitute forty-five percent of the labor force. Progress has been accelerated by the enactment of the Equal Pay Act of 1963, which prohibits sex-based discrimination in wages; Title VII of the 1964 Civil Rights Act, which prohibits sex-based discrimination in hiring, advancement, termination, training, and related terms of employment; and Executive Order 11,375, which requires federal contractors to establish affirmative action programs for women.

Despite such enactments and the broader cultural transformation they reflect, wide disparities in the sexes' vocational status have persisted. In 1955, the annual wages of full-time women workers were approximately sixty-four percent of the annual wages of males. Over the next several decades, that percentage declined, dipping to fifty-eight percent in 1968, and then climbed back to current levels of sixty-four percent (seventy percent, if expressed in terms of weekly wages). However, those ratios understate overall gender disparities in earnings, since less than half of all employed women work full-time for the full year, and disproportionate numbers lack employment-related benefits such as health and pension coverage. Even among full-time workers, the average female college graduate still earns less than the average white male with a high-school degree. The average black female college graduate in a full-time position receives ninety-six percent of the average white female college graduate's salary, a figure roughly equivalent to the pay of a white male high-school dropout. Women also experience disproportionate levels of involuntary part-time work and unemployment, with levels particularly high among minorities.

These salary and employment disparities reflect broader patterns of occupational segregation and stratification. Most women employees are crowded into a small number of existing job categories, and about three-fifths are in occupations that are at least seventy-five percent female. Even in gender-integrated occupations, men and women generally hold different positions and receive different pay and promotion opportunities. Most jobs still tend to be stratified by race and ethnicity as well as by sex, and women of color remain at the bottom of the occupational hierarchy.

Despite significant trends toward greater gender-integration, projections suggest that at current rates of change, it could take between seventy-five and one hundred years to achieve a sexually balanced workplace. The most dramatic progress to date has been in formerly male-dominated professions such as law, medicine, and management: women's representation, which ranged between three to seven percent in the early 1960s, increased to levels of thirty or forty percent by the late 1980s. However, at the highest levels of professional status and financial achievement, significant disparities have remained. For example, in the late 1980s, females were still only half as likely as males to be partners in law firms, held only eight percent of state and federal judgeships, and occupied only two percent of corporate executive positions in Fortune 500 companies. Underrepresentation of women of color was significantly greater at all professional levels.

Gains in blue-collar employment have been even less pronounced. Although the absolute number of women in such occupations has increased significantly since the 1970s, their proportionate representation has not substantially changed. Female employees have an increasingly visible presence in some blue-collar jobs, such as bus driver (forty-nine percent) and bartender (forty-eight percent), but reports in the 1980s numbered their share of skilled trade positions at only about twenty percent. So, too, women's increasing interest in "men's work" has not been matched by a comparable increase in men's enthusiasm for "women's work." Within the most heavily female-dominated job sectors, such as clerical work, male representation has not significantly changed.

Defenders of the conventional equal opportunity approach to employment discrimination typically dismiss these asymmetries as artifacts of cultural lag or employee choice, and, in either case, as matters beyond the scope of legitimate legal concern. From this perspective, much of the existing gender gap is a transitory phenomenon, the result of conduct no longer permitted under contemporary antidiscrimination doctrine. Formal prohibitions on gender bias in educational and employment practices will, in time, prove sufficient to guarantee equal opportunity. Given the available remedies for discriminatory treatment, any remaining disparity in occupational status allegedly can be attributed to individual choice, capabilities, and commitment; it is not a ground for further legal intervention.

Yet the vast majority of research suggests that the obstacles confronting women workers are considerably more intractable than the equal opportunity approach acknowledges. In identifying these obstacles, we should note at the outset certain complexities in the concept of occupational equality. It is not self-evident that proportional representation in all employment sectors is the ultimate ideal. To assume that, under conditions of full equality, women will make precisely the same occupational choices as men is to accept an assimilationist perspective that many feminists renounce. But as long as there remains a strong negative correlation between the concentration of women in a given occupation and its relative earnings and status, the persistence of gender segregation is a major concern. We can leave questions about the precise degree of sex-role differentiation in the ideal society open without losing sight of the disadvantages confronting women in this one.

Analysis of those disadvantages should distinguish problems along two dimensions. Workforce inequalities reflect the relatively low status and pay in female-dominated occupations, as well as the factors discouraging women's entry and advancement in alternative employment contexts. These phenomena in turn depend on complex interrelationships among individual choices, social norms, discriminatory practices, and institutional structures.
. . .

Although individual choice plays an important role in virtually all theories of occupational inequality, the nature of that role is the subject of considerable dispute. According to human capital models of labor force participation, gender differences in earnings and occupational status are largely attributable to differences in career investments. In essence, these models assume that women seek to balance work and family commitments by selecting female-dominated occupations that tend not to require extended training, long hours, inflexible schedules, or skills that deteriorate with absence. Under these theories, the solution to women's workplace inequality lies with women themselves. In their crudest form, human capital approaches lead to a kind of Marie Antoinette response to occupational stratification: if women want positions with greater pay, prestige, and power, they should make different career investments; if female nurses want pay scales equivalent to male hotel clerks', let them become hotel clerks.

Human capital approaches are problematic on several levels. Estimates vary widely concerning the percentage of the wage gap that is attributable to human capital factors such as education, experience, hours worked, and so forth. However, most studies have concluded that these characteristics cannot account for more than half of current gender disparities. On the whole, women who make comparable investments in time, training, and experience still advance less far and less quickly than men.

Even in their most sophisticated forms, human capital approaches leave a vast range of questions unanswered. What accounts for cross-cultural variations and historical changes in occupational segregation? Why do females choose to be nurses rather than hotel clerks, or, for that matter, truck drivers, whose job skills are even less likely to deteriorate with absence? Why do unskilled hotel clerks earn more than highly educated nurses? Why don't male employees with family responsibilities disproportionately choose jobs requiring shorter hours? Answers to these questions require a more complex account of cultural norms and institutional constraints....

At the turn of the century, Charlotte Perkins Gilman warned against making any assumptions about what kinds of work men and women would freely choose until generation after generation could grow up under equal conditions. American society remains a considerable distance from that ideal, and occupational choices have been colored by cultural expectations. At very early ages, children begin absorbing cues about appropriate sex-role traits and occupations, and only recently has that socialization process prompted serious concern. For example, not until the 1970s did public attention focus on stereotypes in children's books. What then became apparent was the crudest form of gender generalization. In the world traditionally presented to preschoolers, homemaking was women's sole occupation; in one representative survey, fairies and water maidens were the only apparent alternatives. Most fictional stories centered on males. Female characters appeared mainly in supporting roles; boys had adventures, while girls went shopping or lost bunnies that boys found.

Despite substantial progress over the last decade, the legacy of such gender stereotypes persists. Most research indicates that by early adolescence, males and females have acquired different career expectations. In general, women continue to express lower expectations for occupational success than men and attach higher priorities to relational aspects of employment (such as opportunities to help others) than to opportunities for formal recognition (in terms of money, status, or power).

For many individuals, career decisions have been less the product of fully informed and independent preferences than the result of preconceptions about "women's work," which are shaped by cultural stereotypes, family and peer pressure, and the absence of alternative role models. Many families have discouraged career choices that would conflict with domestic duties, require geographic mobility, or entail greater prestige or income for wives than for husbands. Such patterns can be especially pronounced among some minority groups, where males' education may carry greater priority than females'. Women who have deviated from traditional norms in job selection have generally received less social approval than those who have not. Job training, counseling, and recruitment networks have also channeled women toward conventional occupations, and socioeconomic barriers have limited employment aspirations. Although increasing numbers of women are expressing the same vocational preferences as men, a majority still choose traditional, female-dominated occupations. Having made such choices, many women have found it too costly—financially, psychologically, or logistically—to shift careers in response to more complete information about other options. Family obligations, seniority structures, and financial constraints have converged to entrench the effects of sex-role socialization.

These socialization processes are reinforced by the mismatch between characteristics associated with femininity and characteristics associated with vocational achievement. The aggressiveness, competitiveness, dedication, and emotional detachment thought necessary for advancement in the most prestigious and well-paid occupations are incompatible with traits commonly viewed as attractive in women: cooperativeness, deference, sensitivity, and self-sacrifice. Similar discontinuities have been apparent in blue-collar contexts requiring physical strength, "toughness," or other seemingly masculine attributes. Despite substantial progress toward gender equality over the last several decades, these sexual stereotypes have been remarkably resilient. Women remain subject to the familiar double bind: they are criticized for being too feminine or not feminine enough. Those who conform to accepted stereotypes appear to lack the initiative necessary for occupational success, while those who are more assertive are judged arrogant, aggressive, or abrasive. A "third sex" in vocational contexts has yet to emerge.

Different socialization patterns have also led women to structure their priorities in ways that mesh poorly with occupational dynamics. Although cultural commitments to equal opportunity in vocational spheres have steadily increased, they have not translated into equal obligations in domestic spheres. Most contemporary studies have indicated that women still perform about seventy percent of the family tasks in an average household. Employed wives spend about twice as much time on homemaking tasks as employed husbands. Women also head ninety percent of the nation's single-parent households, which impose special burdens. The problems are particularly acute for women of color, who are most likely to have such responsibilities and least able to afford help in meeting them.

As subsequent discussion suggests, individual choices have also been constrained by unconscious discrimination and workplace structures. The result is a convergence of self-perpetuating social signals that reinforce occupational inequalities. Males' and females' different career investments have been heavily dependent on their perceptions of different opportunities. Women have long faced relatively low wages in traditional vocations and substantial barriers to advancement in non-traditional pursuits. Under such circumstances, it has been economically rational for working couples to give priority to the husband's career, to relocate in accordance with his job prospects, and to assign wives a disproportionate share of family obligations. The gender division of labor in the home and workplace have been mutually reinforcing patterns. Subordinate occupational status has encouraged women to make lower career investments and to assume greater domestic responsibilities, both of which help to perpetuate that subordination. Breaking this cycle will require treating individual choices not as fixed and independent phenomena, but as responses to cultural forces that are open to redirection. . . .

Why ... have women remained crowded in certain sectors of the labor market, and why have those sectors commanded relatively low status and prestige? Why do females in predominately male occupations have lower pay scales and fewer promotion opportunities despite comparable qualifications?

In seeking answers to such questions, commentators have accumulated increasing evidence concerning various forms of discrimination: deliberate, statistical, and unconscious. On the most overt level, as economists such as Gary Becker have argued, market forces do not necessarily discourage deliberate bias against women or minorities when employers have developed a "taste for discrimination." Such tastes, founded on personal prejudice, customer or co-worker preference, or favoritism toward male "breadwinners," have been identified in a wide range of contexts. Before passage of antidiscrimination legislation in the early 1960s, many employers were surprisingly public about their private biases. During the nineteenth century, intermingling between male and female workers was often viewed as "actively operative for evil." Although twentieth-century employers have appeared less concerned about the moral dimensions of occupational integration, many have viewed it as economically inefficient or culturally inappropriate. As late as 1970, some job advertisements openly specified "males preferred," and many workplaces had separate job titles, pay scales, and promotion channels for males and females performing substantially the same work.

Although changing attitudes and statutory mandates have made overt discrimination increasingly rare, some of its legacy remains. Continuing assumptions have been that male workers will resist female colleagues or supervisory personnel, that male consumers of certain services or products will not relate well to female employees, and that women lack the capacity or commitment for positions calling for physical strength, extended training, or managerial skills. Litigation in the late 1980s still revealed claims such as those advanced by owners of tuna fishing boats that excluded women. According to these owners, the presence of female employees would "destroy morale and distract the crew"; their boats would "catch fewer fish if a woman is on board." Similar biases have left women of color doubly disadvantaged.

In theory, a well-functioning free market should serve to erode such discriminatory patterns, since employers who do not indulge arbitrary prejudices should have a competitive advantage. In practice, however, occupational segregation and differential reward structures, once established, can be highly resistant to change. The more insulated the labor market from competitive forces, the more resilient these biases may prove.

Even reasonably competitive markets will permit what economists label "statistical discrimination," that is, discrimination premised on generalizations that are inaccurate in a large percentage of cases, but are cheaper to indulge than to ignore. For example, if an employer believes that female workers have a higher turnover rate than males, and that it is expensive or difficult to screen for job commitment in advance, then it makes sense to channel women toward relatively low-status, low-paid positions where they are easily replaced. Although recent data suggest that men and women with comparable qualifications and holding comparable jobs do not in fact have different turnover rates, the residual effects of statistical discrimination often linger. Once jobs become "typed" as male or female, socialization processes tend to perpetuate those labels.

A final, and in contemporary society perhaps the most intransigent, form of discrimination operates at unconscious levels. Employer decision-making has reflected the same gender biases and stereotypes that have constrained employees' vocational choices. Psychological research suggests that most decisionmakers rate more positively those who conform to stereotypical notions of masculine and feminine behavior than those who do not. Individuals are also more likely to recall evidence that supports rather than challenges such stereotypes. Given the discontinuities between traits associated with femininity and those associated with vocational achievement, female performance is often undervalued. Since research involving racial bias reveals similar patterns, women of color face special obstacles.

More specific clinical and longitudinal research makes the point directly. For example, surveys of a wide variety of decisionmakers have revealed that identical resumes are rated significantly lower if an applicant is a woman rather than a man. In analogous studies, both male and female subjects have often given lower ratings to the same art or scholarly works when the artist or author is thought to be a woman. Men's success is more likely to be attributed to ability and females' to luck, a pattern that has obvious implications for employment decisionmaking.

Such unconscious bias affects not only opportunities for individual workers, but also reward structures for women as a group. This point was well illustrated by a survey of the federal government's Dictionary of Occupational Titles, which rates the complexity of tasks in some 30,000 jobs and has influenced many public and private employers' compensation schemes. Among the occupations rating lowest in the 1975 Dictionary edition were foster mother, nursery-school teacher, and practical nurse—all of which were thought equally or less demanding than parking lot attendant and "offal man," whose respective responsibilities were to park cars and to "shovel[ ] ice into [a] chicken offal container." Although repeated critiques prompted substantial progress in a later Dictionary edition, the legacy of earlier biases remains pervasive in many employment settings....

Unconscious gender prejudices not only affect evaluation of female performance, but also affect performance itself. Low expectations of achievement frequently become self-fulfilling prophecies. Those who expect inadequate performance tend to signal their assumptions in subtle ways, and this negative feedback leads to anxiety, mistakes, and diminished aspirations. Such consequences then reinforce the initial adverse expectations, and a self-perpetuating cycle continues....

More overt, although often unintentional, forms of collegial bias have comparable consequences. Women in a wide range of employment settings remain outside the informal networks of support, guidance, and information exchange that are critical to advancement. Such problems often begin in educational or job training programs and increase in workplace environments. Related problems involve sexual harassment, which not only impairs performance and restricts advancement, but also discourages women from entering male-dominated environments. All of these problems are especially acute for women of color, who face unconscious discrimination on two fronts, and whose small numbers make mentoring and role modeling especially difficult. . . .

Not only has gender bias shaped employment opportunities and salary patterns, it has also affected the way workplace structures have adapted to women's participation. . . . The majority of women work in occupational environments designed by and for men. The way in which the workplace has been structured, advancement criteria defined, and domestic responsibilities allocated have all tended to perpetuate gender inequalities.

In contemporary American society, any individual who seeks to balance significant work and family commitments confronts substantial obstacles. Since, as noted earlier, women continue to assume an unequal share of homemaking obligations, they also experience an unequal share of workplace difficulties. The most obvious problems involve the length and rigidity of most work schedules, the absence of adequate parental leave provisions, and inadequacies in child care services. . . .

For women, the inadequacy of flexible scheduling options, temporary leave provisions, and child care services carry significant occupational consequences. Short-term losses result when female employees find it necessary to forgo promotional and training opportunities, or to leave a particular job, together with its seniority and benefit provisions. Long-term costs result from women's discontinuous work history, which makes advancement within high-paying job sectors more difficult. For most women, the choice is to curtail either employment or family commitments, and whichever option they elect, the result is to perpetuate a decisionmaking structure insulated from their concerns. Those who advance to the positions with greatest power over policies governing parental leaves, working schedules, child care, and related issues are those least likely to have experienced significant work-family conflicts. To promote equality between the sexes and to improve the quality of life for both of them will require fundamental changes in employment policies. . . .

Evelyn Nakano Glenn, From Servitude to Service Work

From The Second Signs Reader (Joeres and Laslett eds. 1996).

Recent scholarship on African American, Latina, Asian American, and Native American women reveals the complex interaction of race and gender oppression in their lives. These studies expose the inadequacy of additive models that treat gender and race as separate and discrete systems of hierarchy. In an additive model, white women are viewed solely in terms of gender, while women of color are thought to be "doubly" subordinated by the cumulative effects of gender plus race. Yet achieving a more adequate framework, one that captures the interlocking, interactive nature of these systems, has been extraordinarily difficult. Historically, race and gender have developed as separate topics of inquiry, each with its own literature and concepts. Thus features of social life considered central in understanding one system have been overlooked in analyses of the other.

One domain that has been explored extensively in analyses of gender but ignored in studies of race is social reproduction. The term *social reproduction* is used by feminist scholars to refer to the array of activities and relationships involved in maintaining people both on a daily basis and intergenerationally. Reproductive labor includes activities such as purchasing household goods, preparing and serving food, laundering and repairing clothing, maintaining furnishings and appliances, socializing children, providing care and emotional support for adults, and maintaining kin and community ties. . . .

Here I want to talk about two forms of waged reproductive work that racial-ethnic women have performed disproportionately: domestic service in private households and institutional service work.

Domestic service as the racial division of reproductive labor

Both the demand for household help and the number of women employed as servants expanded rapidly in the latter half of the nineteenth century. This expansion paralleled the rise of industrial capital and the elaboration of middle-class women's reproductive responsibilities. Rising standards of cleanliness, larger and more ornately furnished homes, the sentimentalization of the home as a "haven in a heartless world", and the new emphasis on childhood and the mother's role in nurturing children all served to enlarge middle-class women's responsibilities for reproduction at a time when technology had done little to reduce the sheer physical drudgery of housework.

By all accounts middle-class women did not challenge the gender-based division of labor or the enlargement of their reproductive responsibilities. Indeed, middle-class women—as readers and writers of literature; as members and leaders of clubs, charitable organizations, associations, reform movements, and religious revivals; and as supporters of the cause of abolition—helped to elaborate the domestic code. Feminists seeking an expanded public role for women argued that the same nurturant and moral qualities that made women centers of the home should be brought to bear in public service. In the domestic sphere, instead of questioning the inequitable gender division of labor, they sought to slough off the more burdensome tasks onto more oppressed groups of women.

... [A]t least through the first half of the twentieth century, "most white middle class women could hire another woman—a recent immigrant, a working class woman, a woman of color, or all three—to perform much of the hard labor of household tasks." Domestics were employed to clean house, launder and iron clothes, scrub floors, and care for infants and children. They relieved their mistresses of the heavier and dirtier domestic chores. White middle-class women were thereby freed for supervisory tasks and for cultural, leisure, and volunteer activity or, more rarely during this period, for a career.

. . . [T]he use of domestic servants also helped resolve certain contradictions created by the domestic code. [T]he early twentieth-century housewife confronted inconsistent expectations of middle class womanhood: domesticity and "feminine virtue." Domesticity—defined as creating a warm, clean, and attractive home for husband and children—required hard physical labor and meant contending with dirt. The virtuous woman, however, was defined in terms of spirituality, refinement, and the denial of the physical body. Additionally, in the 1920s and 1930s there merged a new ideal of the modern wife as an intelligent and attractive companion. If the heavy parts of household work could be transferred to paid help, the middle-class housewife could fulfill her domestic duties, yet distance herself from the physical labor and dirt and also have time for personal development.

Who was to perform the "dirty work" varied by region. In the Northeast, European immigrant women, particularly those who were Irish and German, constituted the majority of domestic servants from the mid-nineteenth century to World War I. In regions where there was a large concentration of people of color, subordinate-race women formed a more or less permanent servant stratum. Despite differences in the composition of the populations and the mix of industries in the regions, there were important similarities in the situation of Mexicans in the Southwest, African Americans in the South and Japanese people in northern California and Hawaii. Each of these groups was placed in a separate legal category from whites, excluded from rights and protections accorded full citizens. This severely limited their ability to organize, compete for jobs, and acquire capital. The racial division of private reproductive work mirrored this racial dualism in the legal, political and economic systems. . . .

The racial division of public reproductive labor

. . . [T]he increasing commodification of social reproduction since World War II has led to a dramatic growth in employment by women in such areas as food preparation and service, health care services, child care, and recreational services. The division of labor in public settings mirrors the division of labor in the household. Racial-ethnic women are employed to do the heavy, dirty, "back-room" chores of cooking and serving food in restaurants and cafeterias, cleaning rooms in hotels and office buildings, and caring for the elderly and ill in hospitals and nursing homes, including cleaning rooms, making beds, changing bed pans, and preparing food. In these same settings white women are disproportionately employed as lower-level professionals (e.g., nurses and social workers), technicians, and administrative support workers to carry out the more skilled and supervisory tasks. . . .

Visual observation of any hospital reveals the hierarchical race and gender division of labor: at the top are the physicians, setting policy and initiating work for others; they are disproportionately white and male. Directly below, performing medical tasks and patient care as delegated by physicians and enforcing hospital rules, are the registered nurses (RNs), who are overwhelmingly female and disproportionately white. Under the registered nurses and often supervised by them are the licensed practical nurses (LPNs), also female but disproportionately women of color. At about the same level are the technologists and technicians who carry out various tests and procedures and the "administrative service" staff in the offices; these categories tend to be female and white. Finally, at the bottom of the pyramid are the nurse's aides, predominantly women of color; housekeepers and kitchen workers, overwhelmingly women of color; and orderlies and cleaners, primarily men of color. They constitute the "hands" that perform routine work directed by others. . . .

This article began with the observation that the racial division of reproductive labor has been overlooked in the separate literatures on race and gender. The distinct exploitation of women of color and an important source of difference among women have thereby been ignored. How, though, does a historical analysis of the racial division of reproductive labor illuminate the lives of women of color and white women? What are its implications for concerted political action? In order to tackle these questions, we need to address a broader question, namely, how does the analysis advance our understanding of race and gender? Does it take us beyond the additive models I have criticized?

The social construction of race and gender

Tracing how race and gender have been fashioned in one area of women's work helps us understand them as socially constructed systems of relationships—including symbols, normative beliefs, and practices—organized around perceived differences. This understanding is an important counter to the universalizing tendencies in feminist thought. When feminists perceive reproductive labor only as gendered, they imply that domestic labor is identical for all women and that it therefore can be the basis of a common identity of womanhood. By not recognizing the different relationships women have had to such supposedly universal female experiences as motherhood and domesticity, they risk essentializing gender—treating it as static, fixed, eternal, and natural. They fail to take seriously a basic premise of feminist thought, that gender is a social construct.

If race and gender are socially constructed systems, then they must arise at specific moments in particular circumstances and change as these circumstances change. We can study their appearance, variation, and modification over time. I have suggested that one vantage point for looking at their development in the United States is in the changing division of labor in local economies. A key site for the emergence of concepts of gendered and racialized labor has been in regions characterized by dual labor systems.

As subordinate-race women within dual labor systems, African American, Mexican American, and Japanese American women were drawn into domestic service by a combination of economic need, restricted opportunities, and educational and employment tracking mechanisms. Once they were in service, their association with "degraded" labor affirmed their supposed natural inferiority. Although ideologies of "race" and "racial difference" justifying the dual labor system already were in place, specific ideas about racial-ethnic womanhood were invented and enacted in everyday interactions between mistresses and workers. Thus ideologies of race and gender were created and verified in daily life.

Two fundamental elements in the construction of racial-ethnic womanhood were the notion of inherent traits that suited the women for service and the denial of the women's identities as wives and mothers in their own right. Employers accepted a cult of domesticity that purported to elevate the status of women as mothers and homemakers, yet they made demands on domestics that hampered them from carrying out these responsibilities in their own households. How could employers maintain such seemingly inconsistent orientations? Racial ideology was critical in resolving the contradiction: it explained why women of color were suited for degrading work. Racial characterizations effectively neutralized the racial-ethnic woman's womanhood, allowing the mistress to be "unaware" of the domestic's relationship to her own children and household. The exploitation of racial-ethnic women's physical, emotional, and mental work for the benefit of white households thus could be rendered invisible in consciousness if not in reality.

With the shift of reproductive labor from household to market, face-to-face hierarchy has been replaced by structural hierarchy. In institutional settings, stratification is built into organizational structures, including lines of authority, job descriptions, rules, and spatial and temporal segregation. Distance between higher and lower orders is ensured by structural segregation. Indeed, much routine service work is organized to be out of sight.... It also makes them and their work invisible, however. In this situation, more privileged women do not have to acknowledge the workers or to confront the contradiction between shared womanhood and inequality by race and class. Racial ideology is not necessary to explain or justify exploitation, not for lack of racism, but because the justification for inequality does not have to be elaborated in specifically racial terms: instead it can be cast in terms of differences in training, skill, or education.

Because they are socially constructed, race and gender systems are subject to contestation and struggle. Racial-ethnic women continually have challenged the devaluation of their womanhood. Domestics often did so covertly. They learned to dissemble, consciously "putting on an act" while inwardly rejecting their employers' premises and maintaining a separate identity rooted in their families and communities.... [I]nstitutional service workers can resist demeaning treatment more openly because they have the support of peers. Minority-race women hospital workers have been in the forefront of labor militancy, staging walkouts and strikes and organizing workplaces. In both domestic service and institutional service work, women have transcended the limitations of their work by focusing on longer-term goals, such as their children's future.

Beyond additive models: Race and gender as interlocking systems

As the foregoing examples show, race and gender constructs are inextricably intertwined. Each develops in the context of the other; they cannot be separated. This is important because when we see reproductive labor only as gendered, we extract gender from its context, which includes other interacting systems of power. If we begin with gender separated out, then we have to put race and class back in when we consider women of color and working-class women. We thus end up with an additive model in which white women have only gender and women of color have gender plus race.

The interlock is evident in the case studies of domestic workers and nurse's aides. In the traditional middle-class household, the availability of cheap female domestic labor buttressed white male privilege by perpetuating the concept of reproductive labor as women's work, sustaining the illusion of a protected private sphere for women and displacing conflict away from husband and wife to struggles between housewife and domestic.

The racial division of labor also bolstered the gender division of labor indirectly by offering white women a slightly more privileged position in exchange for accepting domesticity. Expanding on Judith Rollins's notion that white housewives gained an elevated self-identity by casting Black domestics as inferior contrast figures, Phyllis Palmer suggests the dependent position of the middle-class housewife made a contrasting figure necessary. A dualistic conception of women as "good" and "bad," long a part of western cultural tradition, provided ready-made categories for casting white and racial-ethnic women as oppositional figures. The racial division of reproductive labor served to channel and recast these dualistic conceptions into racialized gender constructs. By providing them an acceptable self-image, racial constructs gave white housewives a stake in a system that ultimately oppressed them.

The racial division of labor similarly protects white male privilege in institutional settings. White men, after all, still dominate in professional and higher management positions where they benefit from the paid and unpaid services of women. And as in domestic service, conflict between men and women is redirected into clashes among women. This displacement is evident in health care organizations. Because physicians and administrators control the work of other health workers, we would expect the main conflict to be between doctors and nurses over work load, allocation of tasks, wages, and working conditions. The racial division of nursing labor allows some of the tension to be redirected so that friction arises between registered nurses and aides over work assignments and supervision.

In both household and institutional settings, white professional and managerial men are the group most insulated from dirty work and contact with those who do it. White women are frequently the mediators who have to negotiate between white male superiors and racial-ethnic subordinates. Thus race and gender dynamics are played out in a three-way relationship involving white men, white women, and women of color. . . .

NOTES AND QUESTIONS

1. **Market Stratification, Race and Gender.** The excerpt from Rhode's article highlights the gender stratification of the market. Notice that a large percentage of women are employed in job categories that are predominantly female. Market forces should work to eliminate this stratification since irrational discrimination is inefficient. Why does this not happen? According to Rhode, women's choices as to jobs, education and training account for less than half of the current gender differences in pay. She attributes the differences to socialization patterns. How are these distinct from women's choices? Is the choice-based explanation one to which an equality feminist or a cultural feminist might subscribe? Is Rhode's socialization explanation more consistent with the position of dominance feminists like MacKinnon?

If choice theories are consistent with the work of either equality or cultural feminists, and if Rhode's approach draws on the work of Mac-Kinnon, what feminist school might be aligned with Glenn's work? Glenn describes the ways in which the market is not only stratified by sex, but also by race. Feminists have often been accused of forgetting the racialization of the work force. Such amnesia results in a tendency to essentialize women's work experiences. This phenomenon was also noted by Angela Harris in her article in the previous section. In reality, Glenn shows, white women perform the more intellectualized of social reproductive tasks, while women of color perform the messy, dirty aspects of this work.

Glenn also argues that white women have been partially responsible for the maintenance of this system. In exchange for accepting their subordination to white men, white women become the "good" women to women of color's "bad." This differentiation between the positions of white women and women of color then permits conflict between white men and white women to be redirected into conflict between white women and women of color. The result is that white women play a direct role in the subordination of women of color.

Does this sound accurate to you? Consider the institutions that you know best—perhaps your law school. Can you identify the different roles played by women of color and by white women?

Glenn does not take into account the fact that racial stereotypes differ for different racial and ethnic groups. How would you expect this to affect the stratification of the market? If the stereotype of Asian women is that they are quiet and meek—"Japanese don't make good executives"—would you expect to find them in different job categories than African Americans who are seen as "organiz[ing] against authority" or "engag[ing] in political intrigue?" Glenn discusses market stratification as if racism works the same against all non-whites. Do you believe this is the case, or has she not seen the distinctions because she has studied communities like Atlanta and Hawaii that tend to have predominately Black or Asian communities, but not both? Many metropolitan areas have more than one non-white, racial or ethnic community represented in their populations. While this may be true, it does not mean that Glenn's analysis is not useful. One could argue that it is because of her analysis with its emphasis on the different experiences of white women and women of color that we are able to see that racism and sexism work together to structure women's experiences in the market, and that this makes it easier for us to see that different forms of racism might work in different ways. Do you agree?

2. **The Family/Market Dichotomy and Market Stratification.** Glenn's article argues that both in the family and in the market women are given the jobs that involve social reproductive work—the work of caring and providing for others. In the home, this is the cooking, cleaning, and nurturing that usually falls to women. In the medical setting, she identifies this work as the work done by nurses. How does this operate within the legal profession? Do women lawyers tend to gravitate to fields that could be considered social reproductive areas? Does Glenn's argument strike you as accurate? Why should an administrative position in nursing be considered as social reproductive work?

Beyond this, what is the connection between the fact that women are performing these tasks and the low status of the tasks? Is it that women get assigned the low status tasks or is it that they become low status by virtue of being performed by women? Nineteenth century women's advocates who argued in favor of a separate sphere within the family for women did not see women's work as demeaning. *See* Reva B. Siegel, *Home as Work*, 103 Yale L. J. 1073 (1994). For them, women's position was every bit as exalted as men's. On the other hand, this has tended not to be the position taken in regard to work done by people of color.

Dorothy Roberts argues that the denigration of women's work, both in the market and at home, influences the development of legal rules relating to work. The work of Black women in caring for their own families is heavily devalued. As a result, politicians (and probably others in this society) believe that any market job for these women would be preferable. Roberts describes a cartoon that shows a politician representing welfare reform talking to a woman on welfare and her children.

> Politician: "You are a bad mother."
>
> Welfare Mother: "Why?"
>
> Politician: "You hang around the house taking care of the kids. We'll cut you off if you don't take a job."
>
> Welfare Mother: "Doing what?"
>
> Politician: "Taking care of someone else's kids."

Roberts identifies numerous ways in which disregard for the value of Black women's work with their own families has influenced the agenda for welfare reform. Can you think of other areas in which the law works to maintain market stratification? Consider, e.g., which job categories are most likely to be exempt from protective labor legislation. Consider also many employers' practices of not paying social security for their domestic employees, or (perhaps at the employee's request) not reporting the income. *See* Dorothy E. Roberts, *Spiritual and Menial Housework,* 9 Yale J. L. & Feminism 51, 73 (1997).

3. **Law and Remedies for Market Stratification.** Should the legal system intervene to reduce the amount of racial and gender stratification that currently exists in the market? Some people, like Richard Posner, author of *Conservative Feminism* in the previous section of the materials, might argue that the matter should be left to the market. If the costs for hiring female workers are higher than the costs for hiring male ones, the law should permit employers to pay women less than men. This would explain some of the market's stratification. Similarly, Richard Epstein argues in *Forbidden Grounds* (1992) that Title VII's prohibition on race and sex-based discrimination may contribute to the density of women and in particular, women of color, in the lower ranks of the work force. To the extent that women have lower skill and education levels than men, employers may be discouraged from hiring them for the same positions as more skilled white men because the employers may fear that the statute will require that the women be treated the same as the men. If the women actually are less skilled than the men, then they will be worth less to the employer. Epstein, like Posner, argues that the whole question ought to be left to the market.

Cultural feminists, in contrast, might rely on the idea of choice to explain the stratification of the market. As Rosalind Rosenberg argued in the *Sears* case, women choose their employment opportunities with the work environment in mind. According to her, they are less interested in high pressured entrepreneurial positions than men. If women choose less lucrative, social reproductive work why should the legal system intervene to thwart their choices?

Both of these positions rely on the use of the public/private dichotomy. Posner and Epstein use it to defend the market—a private arena—against state intervention, while cultural feminists argue for the privacy of individual choices. In contrast, postmodern feminists like Frances Olsen, might argue that this is one more situation in which the idea of non-intervention in the market is incoherent. The market would not exist without state intervention to enforce contractual and property rights. If this is the case, then the question is not whether to intervene, but in what ways.

The remaining materials in this section discuss various efforts to eliminate the intertwined race and gender stratification of the market. As you read them, consider them in light of the comments above.

County of Washington v. Gunther

Supreme Court of the United States, 1981.
452 U.S. 161, 101 S.Ct. 2242, 68 L.Ed.2d 751.

JUSTICE WILLIAM BRENNAN delivered the opinion of the Court. ...

This case arises over the payment by petitioner County of Washington, Ore., of substantially lower wages to female guards in the female section of the county jail than it paid to male guards in the male section of the jail.... Respondents filed suit against petitioners in Federal District Court under Title VII, seeking backpay and other relief.[3] They alleged that they were paid unequal wages for work substantially equal to that performed by male guards, and in the alternative, that part of the pay differential was attributable to intentional sex discrimination. The latter allegation was based on a claim that, because of intentional discrimination, the county set the pay scale for female guards, but not for male guards, at a level lower than that warranted by its own survey of outside markets and the worth of the jobs.

After trial, the District Court found that the male guards supervised more than 10 times as many prisoners per guard as did the female guards, and that the females devoted much of their time to less valuable clerical duties. It therefore held that respondents' jobs were not substantially equal to those of the male guards, and that respondents were thus not entitled to equal pay. The Court of Appeals affirmed on that issue, and respondents do not seek review of the ruling.

The District Court also dismissed respondents' claim that the discrepancy in pay between the male and female guards was attributable in part to intentional sex discrimination. It held as a matter of law that a sex-based wage discrimination claim cannot be brought under Title VII unless it would satisfy the equal work standard of the Equal Pay Act of 1963. ...

We emphasize at the outset the narrowness of the question before us in this case. Respondents' claim is not based on the controversial concept of "comparable worth," under which plaintiffs might claim increased compensation on the basis of a comparison of the intrinsic worth or difficulty of their job with that of other jobs in the same organization or community. Rather, respondents seek to prove, by direct evidence, that their wages were depressed because of intentional sex discrimination, consisting of setting the wage scale for female guards, but not for male guards, at a level lower than its own survey of outside markets and the worth of the jobs warranted. The narrow question in this case is whether such a claim is precluded by the last sentence of § 703(h) of Title VII, called the "Bennett Amendment." ...

The Bennett Amendment to Title VII ... provides:

3. Respondents could not sue under the Equal Pay Act because the Equal Pay Act did not apply to municipal employees until passage of the Fair Labor Standards Amend- ments of 1974. Title VII has applied to such employees since passage of the Equal Employment Opportunity Act of 1972.

"It shall not be an unlawful employment practice under this subchapter for any employer to differentiate upon the basis of sex in determining the amount of the wages or compensation paid or to be paid to employees of such employer if such differentiation is authorized by the provisions of section 206(d) of title 29."

To discover what practices are exempted from Title VII's prohibitions by the Bennett Amendment, we must turn to § 206(d)—the Equal Pay Act—which provides in relevant part:

"No employer having employees subject to any provisions of this section shall discriminate, within any establishment in which such employees are employed, between employees on the basis of sex by paying wages to employees in such establishment at a rate less than the rate at which he pays wages to employees of the opposite sex in such establishment for equal work on jobs the performance of which requires equal skill, effort, and responsibility, and which are performed under similar working conditions, except where such payment is made pursuant to (i) a seniority system; (ii) a merit system; (iii) a system which measures earnings by quantity or quality of production; or (iv) a differential based on any other factor other than sex." . . .

Petitioners argue that the purpose of the Bennett Amendment was to restrict Title VII sex-based wage discrimination claims to those that could also be brought under the Equal Pay Act, and thus that claims not arising from "equal work" are precluded. Respondents, in contrast, argue that the Bennett Amendment was designed merely to incorporate the four affirmative defenses of the Equal Pay Act into Title VII for sex-based wage discrimination claims. Respondents thus contend that claims for sex-based wage discrimination can be brought under Title VII even though no member of the opposite sex holds an equal but higher paying job, provided that the challenged wage rate is not based on seniority, merit, quantity or quality of production, or "any other factor other than sex." . . .

The language of the Bennett Amendment suggests an intention to incorporate only the affirmative defenses of the Equal Pay Act into Title VII. . . . The Equal Pay Act is divided into two parts: a definition of the violation, followed by four affirmative defenses. . . . The second part . . . in essence "authorizes" employers to differentiate in pay on the basis of seniority, merit, quantity or quality of production, or any other factor other than sex, even though such differentiation might otherwise violate the Act. It is to these provisions, therefore, that the Bennett Amendment must refer.

Petitioners argue that this construction of the Bennett Amendment would render it superfluous. Petitioners claim that the first three affirmative defenses are simply redundant of the provisions elsewhere in § 703(h) of Title VII that already exempt bona fide seniority and merit systems and systems measuring earnings by quantity or quality of production, and that the fourth defense—"any other factor other than sex"—is implicit in Title VII's general prohibition of sex-based discrimination.

We cannot agree. The Bennett Amendment was offered as a "technical amendment" designed to resolve any potential conflicts between Title VII and the Equal Pay Act. Thus, with respect to the first three defenses, the Bennett Amendment has the effect of guaranteeing that courts and administrative agencies adopt a consistent interpretation of like provisions in both statutes. Otherwise, they might develop inconsistent bodies of case law interpreting two sets of nearly identical language.

More importantly, incorporation of the fourth affirmative defense could have significant consequences for Title VII litigation. Title VII's prohibition of discriminatory employment practices was intended to be broadly inclusive, proscribing "not only overt discrimination but also practices that are fair in form, but discriminatory in operation." *Griggs v. Duke Power Co.,* 401 U.S. 424, 431 (1971). The structure of Title VII litigation, including presumptions, burdens of proof, and defenses, has been designed to reflect this approach. The fourth affirmative defense of the Equal Pay Act, however, was designed differently, to confine the application of the Act to wage differentials attributable to sex discrimination. Equal Pay Act litigation, therefore, has been structured to permit employers to defend against charges of discrimination where their pay differentials are based on a bona fide use of "other factors other than sex." Under the Equal Pay Act, the courts and administrative agencies are not permitted to "substitute their judgment for the judgment of the employer ... who [has] established and applied a bona fide job rating system," so long as it does not discriminate on the basis of sex.... We therefore conclude that only differentials attributable to the four affirmative defenses of the Equal Pay Act are "authorized" by that Act within the meaning of § 703(h) of Title VII....

Our interpretation of the Bennett Amendment draws additional support from the remedial purposes of Title VII and the Equal Pay Act.... Under petitioners' reading of the Bennett Amendment, only those sex-based wage discrimination claims that satisfy the "equal work" standard of the Equal Pay Act could be brought under Title VII. In practical terms, this means that a woman who is discriminatorily underpaid could obtain no relief—no matter how egregious the discrimination might be—unless her employer also employed a man in an equal job in the same establishment, at a higher rate of pay. Thus, if an employer hired a woman for a unique position in the company and then admitted that her salary would have been higher had she been male, the woman would be unable to obtain legal redress under petitioners' interpretation. Similarly, if an employer used a transparently sex-biased system for wage determination, women holding jobs not equal to those held by men would be denied the right to prove that the system is a pretext for discrimination.... Congress surely did not intend the Bennett Amendment to insulate such blatantly discriminatory practices from judicial redress under Title VII....

Petitioners argue strenuously that the approach of the Court of Appeals places "the pay structure of virtually every employer and the entire economy ... at risk and subject to scrutiny by the federal courts." They raise the specter that "Title VII plaintiffs could draw any type of comparison imaginable concerning job duties and pay between any job predominantly performed by women and any job predominantly performed by men." But whatever the merit of petitioners' arguments in other contexts, they are inapplicable here, for claims based on the type of job comparisons petitioners describe are manifestly different from respondents' claim. Respondents contend that the County of Washington evaluated the worth of their jobs; that the county determined that they should be paid approximately 95% as much as the male correctional officers; that it paid them only about 70% as much, while paying the male officers the full evaluated worth of their jobs; and that the failure of the county to pay respondents the full evaluated worth of their jobs can be proved to be attributable to intentional sex discrimination. Thus, respondents' suit does not require a court to make its own subjective assessment of the value of the male and female guard jobs, or to attempt by statistical technique or other method to quantify the effect of sex discrimination on the wage rates.

We do not decide in this case the precise contours of lawsuits challenging sex discrimination in compensation under Title VII. It is sufficient to note that respondents' claims of discriminatory undercompensation are not barred by § 703(h) of Title VII merely because respondents do not perform work equal to that of male jail guards. . . .

JUSTICE WILLIAM REHNQUIST, with whom the CHIEF JUSTICE WARREN BURGER, JUSTICE POTTER STEWART, and JUSTICE LEWIS POWELL join, dissenting. . . .

The Court today holds a plaintiff may state a claim of sex-based wage discrimination under Title VII without even establishing that she has performed "equal or substantially equal work" to that of males as defined in the Equal Pay Act. Because I believe that the legislative history of both the Equal Pay Act of 1963 and Title VII clearly establishes that there can be no Title VII claim of sex-based wage discrimination without proof of "equal work," I dissent. . . .

Because the Court never comes to grips with petitioners' argument, it is necessary to restate it here. Petitioners argue that Congress in adopting the Equal Pay Act specifically addressed the problem of sex-based wage discrimination and determined that there should be a remedy for claims of unequal pay for equal work, but not for "comparable" work. Petitioners further observe that nothing in the legislative history of Title VII, enacted just one year later in 1964, reveals an intent to overrule that determination. Quite the contrary, petitioners note that the legislative history of Title VII, including the adoption of the so-called Bennett Amendment, demonstrates Congress' intent to require all sex-based wage discrimination claims, whether brought under the Equal Pay Act or under Title VII, to satisfy the "equal work" standard. Because respondents have not satisfied the "equal work" standard, petitioners conclude that they have not stated a claim under Title VII. . . .

Because the decision does not rest on any reasoned statement of logic or principle, it provides little guidance to employers or lower courts as to what types of compensation practices might now violate Title VII. The Court correctly emphasizes that its decision is narrow, and indeed one searches the Court's opinion in vain for a hint as to what pleadings or proof other than that adduced in this particular case would be sufficient to state a claim of sex-based wage discrimination under Title VII. ...[T]he Court today does not and apparently cannot enunciate any legal criteria by which suits under Title VII will be adjudicated ... All we know is that Title VII provides a remedy when, as here, plaintiffs seek to show by direct evidence that their employer intentionally depressed their wages. And, for reasons that go largely unexplained, we also know that a Title VII remedy may not be available to plaintiffs who allege theories different than that alleged here, such as the so-called "comparable worth" theory. One has the sense that the decision today will be treated like a restricted railroad ticket, "good for this day and train only." ...

Equal Employment Opportunity Commission v. Madison Community Unit School District No. 12

United States Court of Appeals, Seventh Circuit 1987.
818 F.2d 577.

RICHARD POSNER, CIRCUIT JUDGE.

The Equal Employment Opportunity Commission brought this suit against the school district of Madison, Illinois, charging that the district was paying female athletic coaches in its high school and junior high school less than male coaches, in violation of the Equal Pay Act of 1963. That Act, so far as relevant to this case, forbids an employer to

discriminate ... between employees on the basis of sex by paying wages to employees ... at a rate less than the rate at which he pays wages to employees of the opposite sex ... for equal work on jobs the performance of which requires equal skill, effort, and responsibility, and which are performed under similar working conditions, except where such payment is made pursuant to ...
(iv) a differential based on any other factor other than sex.

29 U.S.C. § 206(d)(1). Carol Cole and Luvenia Long, two of the four women who are the alleged victims of the discrimination, intervened in the EEOC's suit and added counts under Title VII of the Civil Rights Act of 1964, 42 U.S.C. §§ 2000e et seq. (employment discrimination), and section 1 of the Civil Rights Act of 1871, now 42 U.S.C. § 1983 (deprivation of federal rights—in this case, the right to equal protection of the laws—under color of state law).

After a bench trial, the district judge held that the defendant had violated the Equal Pay Act, and had done so willfully, thus extending the statute of limitations to allow the award of three years of back pay rather than just two. See 29 U.S.C. § 255(a). But he refused to double these damages; the Act gives the district judge discretion not to double if the violation of the Act was "in good faith and [with] ... reasonable grounds for believing that [the defendant's] act or omission was not a violation." 29 U.S.C. §§ 260, 216(b). The judge dismissed the section 1983 equal-protection count and the Title VII "disparate treatment" (= intentional discrimination) charge on the ground that the discrimination had not been intentional, but he found a "disparate impact" violation of Title VII and held that Cole and Long were entitled to an injunction against it. The parties later negotiated a consent decree which settled the Title VII injunction claim and is not challenged in this appeal. Finally, the judge awarded Cole and Long some $28,000 in attorney's fees under the Equal Pay Act and Title VII.

The school district has appealed, challenging everything but the consent decree. The EEOC has cross-appealed, seeking to have the damages doubled. Finally, Cole and Long challenge the district court's finding that there was no intentional discrimination; they hope to get both comprehensive compensatory damages and punitive damages for their equal protection claim, and not just the back pay they were awarded under the Equal Pay Act.

The trial brought out the following facts:

Long was paid substantially less for coaching girls' track than Steptoe, a man, was paid for coaching boys' track. Although the boys' track program included more students and had more meets than the girls', Steptoe had two assistant coaches compared to Long's one, and as a result Long and Steptoe devoted approximately equal time to their coaching jobs. Long also coached the girls' tennis team, and Jakich, a man, the boys' tennis team; and Jakich was paid more than Long even though there were no significant differences between the teams in number of students, length of season, or number of practice sessions; however, the boys' team played almost twice as many matches as the girls' team. Long was also assistant coach of the girls' basketball team one year and received lower pay than Tyus, the male assistant coach of the boys' track team. The district judge found that the work of the two assistant coaches was substantially equal and required the same skill, effort, and responsibility—except that Long worked longer hours than Tyus.

Cole, who coached the girls' volleyball, girls' basketball, and girls' softball teams, was paid less for coaching volleyball than the male coach of the boys' soccer team, less for coaching basketball than the male coach of the boys' soccer team, and less for coaching softball than the male coach of the boys' baseball team. Also, as assistant coach of the girls' track team she was paid less than the assistant coach of the boys' track team. In all of these cases the judge found that the work of the female coach and her male counterpart was the same in skill, effort (including time), and responsibility. Any potential differences in effort and responsibility stemming from the fact that the boys' teams were sometimes larger and played longer seasons were, he found, offset by the fact that the head coaches of the boys' teams had more assistants than their female counterparts.

The picture with respect to the other two female coaches on whose behalf the EEOC sued is similar.

The first question we must decide is whether the pairs of jobs that the district judge compared in finding unequal pay are sufficiently similar to be "equal work" within the meaning of the Equal Pay Act. The Act is not a general mandate of sex-neutral compensation. It does not enact "comparable worth"—the principle that wages should be based on "objective" factors, rather than on market conditions of demand and supply which may depress wages in jobs held mainly by women relative to wages in jobs held mainly by men. A female secretary paid less than a male janitor cannot complain under the Equal Pay Act that the disparity in their wages is not justified by "objective" factors such as differences in skill, responsibility, and effort. ... The Act requires equal pay only when men and women are performing "equal work on jobs the performance of which requires equal skill, effort, and responsibility, and which are performed under similar working conditions." 29 U.S.C. § 206(d)(1). The working conditions of a janitor are different from those of a secretary, and so are the skills and responsibilities of the two jobs. The Act does not prohibit paying different wages even if the result is to pay a woman less than a man and by doing so "underpay" her because the difference in the wage rate is greater than necessary to compensate the male for any greater skill, effort, or responsibility required by, or any inferior working conditions encountered in, his job.

Thus the jobs that are compared must be in some sense the same to count as "equal work" under the Equal Pay Act; and here we come to the main difficulty in applying the Act: whether two jobs are the same depends on how fine a system of job classifications the courts will accept. If coaching an athletic team in the Madison, Illinois school system is considered a single job rather than a congeries of jobs, the school district violated the Equal Pay Act prima facie by paying female holders of this job less than male holders, and the only question is whether the district carried its burden of proving that the lower wages which the four female coaches received were lower than the wages of their male counterparts because of a factor other than sex. If on the other hand coaching the girls' tennis team is considered a different job from coaching the boys' tennis team, and a fortiori if coaching the girls' volleyball or basketball team is considered a different job (or jobs) from coaching the boys' soccer team, there is no prima facie violation. So the question is how narrow a definition of job the courts should be using in deciding whether the Equal Pay Act is applicable.

We can get some guidance from the language of the Act. The Act requires that the jobs compared have "similar working conditions," not the same working conditions. This implies that some comparison of different jobs is possible. It is true that similarity of working conditions between the jobs being compared is not enough to bring the Act into play—the work must be "equal" and the jobs must require "equal" skill, effort, and responsibility, as well as similar working conditions. But since the working conditions need not be "equal," the jobs need not be completely identical.

Estimating and comparing the skill, effort, responsibility, and working conditions in two jobs are factual determinations. We can overturn them, therefore, only if they are clearly erroneous. The district judge found (among other things) that coaching a girls' tennis team is sufficiently like coaching a boys' tennis team, coaching a girls' softball team is sufficiently like coaching a boys' hardball team, and, indeed, coaching a girls' volleyball or basketball team is sufficiently like coaching a boys' soccer team, to allow each pair of jobs to be described as involving equal work, as requiring equal skill, effort, and responsibility, and as being performed under similar working conditions. If these assessments are not clearly erroneous, we must uphold them, regardless of what we might think the correct assessment as an original matter.

There are pitfalls in allowing any comparisons between different jobs, and they are illustrated by this case. One is a tendency to focus entirely on the measurable differences and ignore the equally or more important but less readily measurable ones. The witnesses in this case concentrated on the amount of skill and time required for coaching girls' and boys' teams and paid little attention to responsibility. It may be true that because the boys' teams tend to have more assistant coaches than the girls' teams, the head coaches of the boys' teams put in no more time than the head coaches of the girls' teams even when the boys' teams are larger and play more matches. But normally there is greater responsibility (one of the dimensions in which the statute requires equality between the jobs compared) if you have a staff than if you don't. That is one reason why the president of a company is paid more than a junior executive who, lacking staff assistance, may work longer hours. . . .

Another difference tends to be ignored when effort, which is hard to measure, is equated to time, which is easy to measure. Boys and girls differ on average in strength, speed, and perhaps other dimensions of athletic ability; there may also be important differences in their attitudes toward athletic competition. . . . The differences between boys and girls in athletic aptitude and interest may make coaching a boys' team harder—or easier—than coaching a girls' team; there can be no confidence that the two jobs require equal effort. The district judge set aside this consideration by ruling that a difference in the sex of students, customers, etc. can't be used to justify a pay difference under the Equal Pay Act. But this is wrong. The reference to "factor other than sex" refers to the sex of the employee, not the sex of the employer's customers, clients, or suppliers. Suppose that the school district happened to have just male, or just female, coaches and paid coaches more for coaching boys' teams than girls' teams. Men paid less than other men for coaching, or women paid less than other women, could not complain of a violation of the Equal Pay Act. . . . The Act did not seek to eliminate whatever differences between the sexes might make it harder to coach a boys' team than a girls' team. If it is harder (we are not saying it is harder—we are just discussing possibilities), the statutory requirement of equal effort is not met and the differential in pay is outside the scope of the Act.

Nevertheless, we are unwilling to hold that coaches of girls' and boys' teams can never be found to be doing equal work requiring equal skill, effort, and responsibility and performed under similar working conditions. Above the lowest rank of employee, every employee has a somewhat different job from every other one, even if the two employees being compared are in the same department. So if "equal work" and "equal skill, effort, and responsibility" were taken literally, the Act would have a minute domain. Of course, opponents of an equal pay act may have been strong enough to block the passage of a strong bill—and, to some extent, they were. Remarkably, considering that the Act was enacted almost a quarter of a century ago, its proponents wanted to enact the principle of "comparable worth." But they were beaten back. In the words of Congressman Goodell, "Last year when the House changed the word 'comparable' to 'equal' the clear intention was to narrow the whole concept. We went from 'comparable' to 'equal' meaning that the jobs involved should be virtually identical, that is, they would be very much alike or closely related to each other."

But the words "very much alike," "closely related," or, as the cases sometimes say, "substantially equal"—even the words "virtually identical"—are not synonymous with "identical." There is a gray area, which we must be vigilant to police, between "very much alike," which is within the scope of the Act, and "comparable," which is outside; for it is plain that Congress did not want to enact comparable worth as part of the Equal Pay Act of 1964. . . .

The courts have thus had to steer a narrow course. The cases do not require substantial identity. The line is a fine, perhaps imperceptible, one. . . .

Whatever answer we might give, if we were the finders of fact, to the question whether coaching a girl's tennis team and coaching a boy's tennis team are sufficiently alike to be equal work within the meaning of the Act, we cannot, on the record compiled in this case (a potentially important qualification), deem the district court's determination clearly erroneous. His error in thinking that a difference in the sex of the teams could not be used to ground a difference in the pay of their coaches is immaterial. The record contains no evidence that the sex of the team affects the skill, effort, responsibility, or working conditions of coaching. And while it is odd that the greater number of assistant coaches of boys' compared to girls' teams should be thought a factor tending to equate the jobs of the head coaches of boys' and girls' teams rather than to show that coaching a boys' team is a more responsible position, there is also no evidence that—in the Madison school system, anyway—having an assistant coach is viewed as anything more than a timesaver for the head coach. And there is evidence that head coaches of boys' teams have more assistants in relation to the number of boys on the team than head coaches of girls' teams have in relation to the number of girls. . . .

For those of us whose knowledge of athletic coaching is confined to newspaper and television accounts of the travails of professional and college coaches, the idea of homogenizing the coaching profession in the manner attempted by the plaintiffs and accepted by the district judge is discordant. But we must, by an effort of imagination, place ourselves in a different world, that of small-town high-school and junior-high-school athletics, where the coach's task is not to compete for money in a high-pressure environment but to impart elementary athletic skills and norms of sportsmanship to adolescents. Given these modest goals, a finding that the coaching of boys' and of girls' tennis involves inconsequential differences in skill, effort, responsibility, and working conditions is not so improbable that we can set it aside, under the deferential clear-error standard that governs appellate review of findings of fact, by substituting our personal impressions for the evidence introduced at trial. . . .

Although we conclude that there is no objection in principle to comparing different coaching jobs, the record of the present case does require us to distinguish between coaching boys' and girls' teams of the same sport and coaching boys' and girls' teams of different sports. The judge equated coaching girls' basketball and girls' volleyball to coaching boys' soccer (and, in the assistant-coach comparisons, girls' basketball with boys' track), without regard for the fact that Madison treats coaching a different sport as a different coaching job irrespective of the sex of either the coach or the team. In the 1980 academic year, for example, the boys' track coach received $1,140 each while the boys' soccer coach received only $840 and the boys' tennis coach even less—$780. (These are headcoach salaries; the salary for the assistant coach of the boys' track team was $835 and for the assistant coach of the boys' soccer team $600; there was no assistant tennis coach.) In other words, there is not a single job classification such as "head coach" or "assistant coach"; the wage varies by the sport. The judge was therefore arbitrary in assuming that if the coach of the girls' volleyball team or basketball team had been male, he would have been paid as much as the boys' soccer coach. (The plaintiffs concede, as we said, that coaching the boys' basketball team is not comparable to coaching the girls' basketball team.) We are willing to assume that hardball and fast-pitch softball—similar sports played under similar rules—are the same sport for purposes of the Equal Pay Act. But given the wage differentials among the male coaches, we cannot make this assumption for volleyball and soccer, or for basketball and soccer. Another consideration is the arbitrariness of the particular comparisons suggested by the plaintiffs. In 1980 Long, as girls' track coach, received the same wage as the male coach of the boys' soccer team. How was the school district to know that a court would think basketball and soccer or volleyball and soccer a closer pair than track and soccer? We vacate the findings of the district judge with respect to a violation of the Equal Pay Act in the comparison between boys' soccer and girls' volleyball, boys' soccer and girls' basketball, and boys' track and girls' basketball.

With this exception we conclude that the plaintiffs did establish a prima facie case of violation of the Equal Pay Act, and we move on to consider defenses, of which only one ("factor other than sex") is relevant. Madison argues that the sex of the teams is a factor other than sex, and though the district court thought this wrong, we disagree as we have said; the factor other than sex to which the Act refers is a factor other than the employee's sex. But this point cannot help Madison. We do not understand it to be arguing that it has carried its burden of proving "factor other than sex" as an affirmative defense. Its quarrel is with the district court's suggestion that the sex of the teams can't be taken into account in determining whether the coaching jobs are equal work; it can be. Furthermore, the language of the statute ("except where such payment is made pursuant to ... a differential based on any factor other than sex") makes clear that the pay differential must be caused by the other factor, and not by the sex of the employees who receive the different pay. If Madison, having decided for reasons unrelated to the sex of the coaches that coaches of male teams should be paid more than coaches of female teams, neither prohibited nor even discouraged women from coaching male teams, the difference in pay between male coaches of boys' teams and female coaches of girls' teams would be due to a decision unrelated to the sex of the coaches. But Madison discouraged women, including Cole and Long, from applying to coach boys' teams, which not only adds a reason related to the sex of the coaches for a difference in pay between men and women to a reason related solely to the sex of the team members, but also casts doubt on the bona fides of the school district's claim to have based the difference in the pay of coaches of male and of female teams solely on the sex of the team members. There was contrary evidence: a woman once was hired to coach the boys' tennis team and was paid the same as her male predecessor; several times men were hired to coach girls' teams and paid the same as female coaches of those teams. But such job offers were very rare prior to the EEOC's investigation, and the district judge was entitled to find their evidentiary significance outweighed by the evidence that women were discouraged from applying to coach boys' teams.

The reason for discouraging women from coaching boys' teams was that the school authorities were concerned about the "locker room problem." This may or may not be a good reason (a question touched on later), but it does suggest that women receive less pay than men for doing what the district court found was equal work within the meaning of the Equal Pay Act because they are women; their sex makes them ineligible to receive the higher wage that men receive for equal work. Even if the school district is entitled to insist that coaches and coached be of the same sex, if the work of each coach is the same and the reason for the difference in pay is the difference in the sex of the coach, the Equal Pay Act is violated. An employer cannot divide equal work into two job classifications that carry unequal pay, forbid women to compete for one of the classifications, and defend the resulting inequality in pay between men and women by reference to a "factor other than [the] sex" of the employees. Cf. 29 C.F.R. § 800.114(a). It would not be the sexual segregation that had caused the inequality in pay, but a decision to pay men more for doing the same work as women (albeit with a "clientele" of a different sex from the women's "clientele"). . . .

So the school district violated the Equal Pay Act; . . . That disposes of the Equal Pay Act issues, and we move on to Title VII. Title VII expressly forbids discrimination "against any individual with respect to his compensation," 42 U.S.C. § 2000e–2(a)(1), and is therefore a natural vehicle for a suit claiming that a member of a protected group, such as a black or a woman, is being paid less than another employee on account of race or sex. Where the plaintiff is a woman, however, and where her only complaint is discrimination in pay, there is a considerable overlap between Title VII and the Equal Pay Act. So we must try to be precise about what Title VII did and did not add to the Equal Pay Act counts in this case. . . .

The judge's finding was based on the "disparate impact" approach to proving a violation of Title VII: a practice that, although not intended to discriminate against a protected group, has a disproportionate adverse impact on that group is unlawful unless there is a powerful justification for the practice. The alternative approach, of course, is to prove intentional discrimination ("disparate treatment"), but the district court found that Madison had not engaged in intentional discrimination. We shall have to consider whether the district court was justified in upholding the Title VII claim on a theory of disparate impact and, if not, whether the court's finding that there was no disparate treatment is justifiable.

Merely paying different wages for different jobs (coaching basketball and coaching soccer being, as we have held, different jobs and therefore outside the boundaries of the Equal Pay Act) cannot violate the prohibition against sex discrimination in Title VII on the basis of disparate impact. . . .Comparable worth is not actionable under Title VII. (It may also be compelled by the Bennett Amendment to Title VII—the last sentence in 42 U.S.C. § 2000e–2(h)—but, . . . we need not decide that question.) The term "comparable worth" is, as noted earlier in this opinion, short-hand for the view that paying higher wages in jobs held mostly by men than in jobs held mostly by women is discriminatory and improper unless the difference is justified by demonstrable differences in skill, responsibility, effort, or working conditions; it is no defense that men and women in the same jobs receive the same wages and that women are neither excluded from the higher-paying jobs by some criterion that cannot be justified on sex-neutral grounds of business need, nor otherwise steered into the lower-paying jobs by tactics for which the employer is responsible. Insofar as they are challenging different wages in coaching jobs that we have held to be different jobs (such as coaching basketball and coaching soccer), yet neither relying on a theory of intentional discrimination nor attacking some criterion that excludes them from the higher-paying coaching jobs, Cole and Long are making a comparable worth claim—a claim that the different wages in the different jobs are not justified by differences in skill, responsibility, etc. [Earlier case law] blocks this claim. Granted, there is some evidence of steering, as we saw earlier; but the plaintiffs—who apparently do not want to coach boys' teams—do not seek any relief against steering.

The defeat of the disparate-impact attack on different wages for different work is not fatal, however, if Cole and Long have shown, contrary to the district court's view, that they are victims of deliberate discrimination in being paid less than men in both similar and dissimilar coaching jobs. If an employer, knowing that a particular job is predominantly (or entirely) occupied by women, and wanting to pay women less than men, does pay them less, his conduct is actionable under Title VII even if the women are doing a different kind of work than the men. See County of Washington v. Gunther, 452 U.S. 161, 101 S.Ct. 2242, 68 L.Ed.2d 751 (1981). Cole and Long argue that the district judge's finding that the discrimination against them was unintentional is clearly erroneous. We disagree. Although there is evidence as we have said that the school district steered women into the lower-paid, female coaching jobs, and such steering could of course violate Title VII, the district judge was not required to find, and did not find, that the scattered evidence of steering added up to intentional discrimination. While the school district failed to prove that the pay disparities were due to factors other than sex, it doesn't follow that Cole and Long carried their burden of proving that the disparities were pursuant to a deliberate effort to pay women less than men because they are women. The burden of persuasion in a Title VII case remains on the plaintiff, although the burden of proving that unequal pay for equal work is due to a factor other than sex and hence does not violate the Equal Pay Act is on the defendant because the exception for a factor other than sex is an affirmative defense under that Act. . . .

[A] possible way of fitting the case to the Title VII mold, however, would be to view the reluctance of the Madison school authorities to hire women to coach boys' teams as evidence of a discriminatory practice vulnerable to a claim of disparate impact. Setting to one side as we do throughout this opinion the bearing of the Bennett Amendment, a challenge to a practice that relegates women to lower-paying jobs need not run afoul of the rule that "comparable worth" is not actionable under Title VII; for the practice can be enjoined without putting the district judge in the business of fixing wages. But this case was not tried as a case of job exclusion as distinct from pay disparity; evidence of job exclusion was presented only to undermine the school district's argument that the difference in the pay of the male and female coaches merely reflected the sex of the teams they coached. When a plaintiff claims, not that two different jobs should carry the same pay, but that he should not be kept out of the higher-paying job by some criterion which even if not deliberately discriminatory has no business justification strong enough to outweigh its discriminatory impact, he states a claim for relief under the disparate-impact approach. Only when he wants to remain in his job but have its salary raised is he in danger of having his claim dismissed as being one for comparable worth. Cole and Long are not complaining that they were not allowed to coach boys' teams; so far as we know they don't want to coach boys' teams; they just want the same pay for coaching girls' teams as coaches of boys' teams receive. Their complaint is pay disparity rather than job exclusion.

This conclusion may seem inconsistent with our earlier discussion of the "locker room problem." If the school district discourages women from coaching boys' teams, this might seem to be, prima facie, sex discrimination, and the issue would then be whether the locker room problem was serious enough to make being a man a bona fide qualification for coaching boys' teams. This would be a permissible approach if Cole and Long were complaining about not being allowed to coach boys' teams, but they are not. They are complaining about being paid less for coaching girls' teams than men were paid for coaching boys' teams. Madison has tried to use the sex of the teams to show that the work of male and female coaches was not the same, and has failed. Cole and Long have tried to use the locker room problem to show that they are victims of intentional discrimination and (bearing the burden of proof) have failed, too. The locker room problem cannot be used to show that they were excluded from job opportunities; they didn't want to coach boys' teams. . . .

NOTES AND QUESTIONS

1.   **Equal Pay Act.** Colloquially, the Equal Pay Act, 29 U.S.C. § 206(d)(1), requires equal pay for equal work for employees, regardless of sex. "Equal work" is work which requires "equal skill, effort, and responsibility[,] . . . performed under similar working conditions." Notice that while the levels of skill, effort and responsibility must be equal, the working conditions need only be similar. Since the working conditions need not be equal, the work required by the jobs to be compared need not be identical, just "very much alike."

In order to determine if the two jobs being compared are sufficiently equal, the court must undertake a detailed investigation of the skills, effort, responsibility and working conditions of each. Is coaching a boys' team necessarily the same for purposes of the Equal Pay Act as coaching a women's team in the same sport? In a different sport? Do you think the fact that men's teams often bring in considerably more revenue than women's teams in the same sport should be considered? *See* Stanley v. University of Southern California, 13 F.3d 1313 (9th Cir.1994) (revenue is a relevant factor). Often, men's teams have more assistant coaches and bring in more revenue because spectators prefer to watch men's sports than women's. Should spectator preferences be able to determine the salary levels for coaches when customer preferences cannot justify a BFOQ in a Title VII action? The same issue arises in law firms. Should a firm be able to pay a higher salary to a male "rain-maker" attorney than to a female "non rain-maker" engaged in the same type and level of practice? *See* Byrd v. Ronayne, 61 F.3d 1026 (1st Cir.1995) (ability to bring in revenue may be taken into consideration in setting compensation).

The requirement that a plaintiff locate a specific employee of the other sex who is paid more is often problematic. Courts have not allowed employees to look at the salary structure and create a hypothetical employee who would be similar to the plaintiff-employee, but of the other sex. *See*

Houck v. Virginia Polytechnic Institute, 10 F.3d 204 (4th Cir.1993). In many employment settings, there is no employee of the other sex who has the same education, training, number of years on the job, etc. The absence of a comparable employee means that one cannot bring an action under the Equal Pay Act. This is more likely to be a problem for employees in professional settings or for those employed by relatively small employers than it is for employees in clerical or blue collar settings or those employed with many other employees.

An employer may defend against a claim that it has not provided equal pay for equal work on the grounds that the payments are made in accordance with a seniority system, a merit system, a system that measures earnings by output, or "a differential based on any other factor other than sex." It is this latter defense that is most controversial.

In some ways this defense overlaps the issue of whether the two jobs are the same, as in the discussion of coaching men's and women's teams. This could be analyzed either in terms of the characteristics of the work, or in terms of a factor other than the employee's sex. In other settings, however, the prima facie case and the defense are clearly distinct. Some employers have asserted that even when the jobs are the same, they should be able to pay different wages because of the need to match the employee's last salary before taking the job or an offer that the employee has received from another employer. This almost always benefits the male employee since men are often able to command higher wages than women in the market. Is an employee's previous salary a "factor other than sex" or should it be excluded because of its close connection to sex? *See* Dey v. Colt Construction and Development Co., 28 F.3d 1446 (7th Cir.1994) (use of prior salary in setting compensation is factor other than sex) and Irby v. Bittick, 44 F.3d 949 (11th Cir.1995) (use of prior salary does not justify a pay differential). At many universities, faculty in professional schools are paid more than faculty in liberal arts schools. Is this permissible because the work is not "equal?" If the differential makes out a prima facie case of violation of the Equal Pay Act, can the university defend on the grounds that the market would pay professionals considerably more than historians and sociologists and therefore the pay differentials are based on a factor other than sex?

Another interesting situation arises in cases in which the employer institutes a voluntary plan to rectify the historically low salaries it had paid to women in its employ. Must the employer make the benefits under the plan available to men also, especially if the plan may result in some woman being paid more than the comparable man? *See* Ende v. Board of Regents of Regency Universities, 757 F.2d 176 (7th Cir.1985) (plan need not be applied to men); *see also* Smith v. Virginia Commonwealth University, 84 F.3d 672 (4th Cir.1996) (similar action brought under Title VII).

Given what you now know about the Equal Pay Act, how powerful a remedy do you think it is for redressing the market stratification that Glenn discusses in her article? Would you expect that there would be many male nurses aides against whom a female aide could compare herself? Is there anything in the Equal Pay Act that prevents an employer from creating all-female job categories? (Such categories may violate Title VII if the employee can show that the categories are created either as a result of disparate treatment or disparate impact.) Is there anything in the Equal Pay Act that prevents the type of racial stratification that Glenn describes?

2. **Title VII.** Whereas the Equal Pay Act only provides a cause of action to female employees who can show that a man in a virtually identical job is paid more, Title VII had the potential for allowing suit even in situations where there is no man in a comparable position. It should be enough to bring suit under Title VII to show that the plaintiffs were discriminated against in terms of their pay because they were women. A violation of Title VII can ordinarily be shown either through use of disparate impact theory or disparate treatment. Do you think that by allowing the use of a "factor other than sex" as a defense to Title VII pay actions the Court in *County of Washington v. Gunther* eliminated the possibility of disparate impact actions for wages set in conformity with prevailing market rates? If these rates have a disparate impact on women, have the plaintiffs made out a prima facie case under Title VII? Courts have tended to reject claims based on the disparity that results from the use of market-based wages. *See* American Federation of State, County, and Municipal Employees, AFL-CIO v. Washington, 770 F.2d 1401 (9th Cir.1985) and Donnelly v. Rhode Island Board of Governors, 929 F.Supp. 583 (D.R.I.1996) (permissible plan for setting salaries "mirrors," but does not "mechanical[ly] appl[y]" market rates). Note that the court in *Madison Community Unit School District* took this point for granted, although it does suggest another strategy the plaintiffs could have followed to show disparate impact. What is this other strategy? Why did the plaintiffs not use it? If women do fare less well in the market, why should use of the market as a standard not be considered to have a disparate impact? It is so considered when height or strength requirements are involved. If an employer were not permitted to use the market as a basis for setting compensation, what would it use? Would elimination of the market as a basis for wages mean that an employer would have to develop a schedule of the skills, experience, and training necessary for each job? Would this be a move in the direction of comparable worth?

It is possible to use the disparate treatment model to establish a violation of Title VII in cases in which women employees face sex discrimination in terms of their compensation. Once the employee has shown a prima facie case of discrimination by showing that she was a member of the protected class, that she met the employer's requirements, and that nonmembers of the class were treated more favorably, the burden shifts to the employer to produce a nondiscriminatory explanation for the differential treatment. If the employer is successful at this, the burden shifts back to the employee to show that the employer's explanation is pretextural and that the employer's real motive was to discriminate. Thus, disparate treatment cases require the employee to show that the employer intended to discriminate. How might the plaintiffs prove this in *Gunther*? Does the fact that the County had not acted to equalize positions that its own study had determined to be comparable but unequally compensated show intent to discriminate? Would this make Title VII a vehicle for litigating comparable worth claims? An effort to use a study of pay for comparable jobs was rejected in *American Federation of State, County and Municipal Employees, AFL–CIO (AFSCME) v. State of Washington*, 770 F.2d 1401 (9th Cir. 1985). The *AFSCME* court was concerned that a contrary decision might penalize employers for undertaking studies of pay inequities in their workforces. Why did the plaintiffs' disparate treatment argument fail in *Madison Community Unit School District*?

If, despite all the odds, a plaintiff were to succeed in using Title VII as the basis of a pay discrimination action, what would the remedy be? Certainly a court could enjoin future violations. The plaintiffs, however, would probably also be interested in receiving back pay. How could this be computed? Under the Equal Pay Act, the existence of a male employee in a substantially equal position makes it possible to determine what the woman employee's wages would have been if the violation of the statute had not occurred. This is difficult in cases under Title VII in which there need not be any other comparable employee. Nor is the market likely to establish a standard since in a competitive industry, the employer's wages should be market-driven. Could one use studies of jobs that involve comparable, although not necessarily equal, skills, responsibilities, training and working conditions? Would this turn Title VII into an action to obtain comparable worth?

3. **Labor Law.** A third legal strategy for improving the lot of employed women is to rely on the protections afforded to organized labor. Labor organizing has been a traditional means of improving working conditions. One of the more interesting campaigns of recent years was the successful effort in the 1980s to organize Harvard University's clerical and technical employees, a group that was predominantly female. The workers' complaints centered on the ways in which their employers were exploiting them as women—asking them to run personal errands or to get cups of coffee. The male employers simply did not see the problems with these requests. The union supporters organized by relying on underground support networks instead of expert staff organizers. Instead of focusing the organizing effort on labor's customary goals of improving wages and working conditions, the organizers concentrated on the workers' feelings of powerlessness and on the creation of their networks of employees. They said that reading the work of Carol Gilligan was liberating: "We always thought the guys were right and we weren't. The idea that we could be different was liberating." The union ultimately won the organizing campaign. In their post-certification bargaining with Harvard, they emphasized joint decision-making structures, instead of a rule-based framework.

One commentator has criticized this strategy for bargaining with Harvard because a new administration at Harvard withdrew from the joint decision-making structures. The non-adversarial, cultural feminist tactics that worked in organizing the union may not have been transferrable to its dealings with the university administration. Jean Alonso, *Women's Ways of Organizing*, Women's Review of Books, October, 1997 at 16.

How likely is it that the labor organizing strategy will reduce the stratification of the work force? How might this work? How might Catharine MacKinnon's work have influenced the Harvard organizers' strategy?

4. **The Rights Debate.** Postmodernists and proponents of the critical legal studies movement have criticized the idea that subordinated groups can seek protection through the creation of rights. They argue that rights are based on contradictory premises (such a freedom to act and security from the injurious actions of others). This makes rights easily manipulable by those in power in the legal system. Perhaps it was the recognition of this manipulability that caused the organizers of the Harvard Union of Clerical and Technical Workers to reject the usual guarantees provided by a grievance procedure and job specifications in favor of joint decision-making mechanisms. On the other hand, feminists and members of racial and ethnic minority groups have often argued that, while rights may not be a fail-proof protective mechanism, it is the best one available. Given their subordinated position, they are sure to lose out in the absence of rights.

The Equal Pay Act and Title VII are both based on the idea of a right to equal treatment. As we have discovered, this right can be understood in different ways. One could argue that women have the right to be paid the same as men because they do the same work as men, or one could argue that because women are likely to interrupt their work life more frequently than men that men are worth more to an employer and have a right to be paid more. Can you construct the "rights" argument both for and against the plaintiffs in both *Gunther* and *Madison Community*? Do you think advocates for women in the marketplace should continue to argue for the creation of more rights, even if these rights only protect them imperfectly? Or do you think they should abandon the rights-based strategy for something else? What might that something else be? If you wanted to follow Catharine MacKinnon's insights where would you start? Where might a postmodern feminist begin to improve the situation of women in the workplace?

There are a number of excellent articles on the debate over the value of a rights strategy. Good places to start in the argument that rights are incoherent are, Karl Klare, *Labor as Ideology*, 4 Indus. Rel L. J. 450 (1981); Duncan Kennedy, *Critical Labor Law Theory*, 4 Indus. Rel. L. J.503 (1981); Frances Olsen, *Statutory Rape*, 63 Tex. L. Rev. 387 (1984). For arguments in favor of rights, nonetheless, see Elizabeth M. Schneider, *The Dialectics of Rights and Politics*, 61 N.Y.U. L. Rev. 589 (1986); Patricia J. Williams, *The Alchemy of Race and Rights* 146–65 (1991).

5. **Comparable Worth.** Comparable worth is the idea that wages should be based on an objective comparison of the required skills and training for different jobs, rather than on market factors. Courts have generally rejected the notion that Title VII implies any so thorough a revision of the structure of the economy. Notice, for example, that the Court in *Gunther*

clearly states that the action there is not based on the concept of comparable worth.

Despite this, the *Gunther* Court did reject the petitioner's reading of the Bennett Amendment because it meant that "a woman who is discriminatorily *underpaid* could obtain no relief ... unless her employer also employed a man in an equal job.... " (Emphasis added) Does this imply that the idea of "underpayment" of someone has meaning even in the absence of a comparison case as required under the Equal Pay Act? If so, how would you determine if someone was underpaid? Is this an opening for comparable worth ideas?

Comparable worth is often seen as a radical idea because it would divorce payment in the workplace from the market's norms. In doing so, it emphasizes that the determination of a particular job's value is a political decision which makes statements about the worth of women's work. *See* Linda M. Blum, *Between Feminism and Labor* 15–19 (1991); Paul Weiler, *The Wages of Sex*, 99 Harv. L. Rev. 1728, 1765–71 (1986). Johanna Brenner, in the excerpt that follows, argues that comparable worth would reinforce the existing ideology that fair wages are established by the market based on a meritocratic hierarchy. Do you agree? What effect if any would the acceptance of comparable worth have on the race and gender stratification of the market? Even if it could force better pay for women, would it result in the integration of job categories that are currently predominantly female? Predominantly female of a specific race or ethnic background?

Johanna Brenner, Feminist Political Discourses: Radical Versus Liberal Approaches to the Feminization of Poverty and Comparable Worth

1 Gender and Soc'y. 447 (1987).

Feminization of poverty and comparable worth have become feminist issues in the United States in part to include in feminist politics the central concerns of working-class women and women of color.... [Yet] I contend that situated within a liberal political discourse, both the feminization of poverty and comparable worth campaigns, in practice, and often in rhetoric, fail to bridge class and race divisions among women and, instead, reinforce the separation of feminism from the movements of other subordinated groups. While appearing to speak to problems that women share, they have tended to unite only through a denial of race and class differences. My point is not that these campaigns and the issues they raise are mistaken. Rather, it is that the current organization of these campaigns, in particular the policy demands and their accompanying justifications, may not constructively address differences in the situation and needs of all classes of women. I will suggest an alternative framework that does not court the danger of strengthening the ideological and social underpinnings of women's subordination....

A liberal discourse on equality centers on the ideal of meritocracy. Liberal political thought accepts the notion of inequality and hierarchy: some will have more, some less; some will command, others follow; some will create, others only implement. Equality is defined as equal opportunity, and thus, from a liberal perspective, fairness exists when the distribution of individuals within unequal positions reflects their individual qualities—their differential motivation, talent, intelligence, and effort—and not their gender, race, religion, or family background....

The compelling character of this view is not surprising, since its crucial assumptions about social organization and human nature are widely accepted in advanced capitalist society. These assumptions are that there are large and significant differences among individuals in talent and potential; that a complex industrial society requires hierarchies; that competition and differential rewards for various positions within the hierarchies will motivate the most talented people to fill the most central and important positions. A radical critique challenges these assumptions, claiming that most individuals are capable of making valuable contributions to society and, collectively, of governing it.

In contrast to the assumptions underlying liberal political thought, socialists (and many radical and socialist feminists) have contended that hierarchy brings out the worst, not the best, in individuals, and that while those at the bottom suffer particularly, everyone is distorted and narrowed by competitive striving. They also contend that collective decision making and responsibility are workable alternative forms of social organization, even in an advanced industrial society, and that such forms promote the full development of individual talents and offer the greatest individual freedom.

The second fundamental assumption of liberal political thought is that dependence belongs in the private sphere—there is no place for dependent individuals either in the notion of economic contact or in the concept of the citizen. Indeed, political citizenship is defined by independence, by the capacity to make choices based on individual self-interest, free from control by others on whom one is dependent. Similarly, wage laborers own their own persons and can sell their labor power as independent contractors....

The contribution of women within the family in reproducing the male breadwinner and replacing his labor over a generation is of course hidden in liberal economic theory. The dependence of the whole society, the economy, and political system, on the family and women's work within the family is ignored. As Linda Gordon argues, "Liberal political and economic theory rests on assumptions about the sexual division of labor and on notions of citizens as heads of families." A society of "freely contracting" male citizens relies on the prior existence of the non-contractual relationships of the family. Women and children (and other nonearners) are regarded as dependents of men. How they fare depends on the "effort" and "pluck" of their male protector. Barrett and McIntosh argue that "in order to elevate the morality of the market into an entire social ethic it is necessary to ignore all those members of society who do not themselves enter the market.... Those who cannot earn a living are subsumed under those who can." Women's dependence within the family makes them noncitizens and their family commitments make them politically suspect.

Welfare-state intervention is justified within a political framework that retains the notion of the independent citizen. Just as the society has an obligation to promote the conditions for a free and fair exchange between competing individuals but no obligation to secure their livelihood, the society has a collective obligation to care only for those individuals who cannot legitimately be asked to care for themselves and who, through no fault of their own, cannot be cared for within the family system. Welfare policy has generally been constructed so as to restore the male-breadwinner family, not to substitute for it. Thus men and women have had a very different relationship to the welfare state and different ways of legitimating their claims to state support. Women have had to prove they are morally deserving (their dependence is assumed); while men have to prove they are legitimately dependent (their independence is assumed). For example, the rules and regulations of workman's compensation, disability programs, and unemployment insurance, developed primarily in response to the demands and needs of male workers, require that workers prove either that they are no longer "able-bodied" (in the first two instances) or that they are without work through no fault of their own....

The radical alternative to the liberal framework has argued for interdependence and the legitimate claim of each individual on the community to meet his or her needs for good and productive work, physical sustenance, emotional support, and social recognition. Radical and socialist feminists have further argued that men are as dependent on women's unpaid labor (including women's emotional work) as women are on men's income and that parenthood is a social contribution and should be recognized as such. Socialist feminists have envisioned a society in which the right to contribute and the right to be cared for are equally shared by men and women. This depends on a reformulation of individual and collective responsibilities and the redistribution of material resources such that the care of dependent individuals is no longer primarily a private responsibility of the family.

Feminists have of course been divided on how to approach the state: whether to demand "a fair field and no favor" or "protection". The comparable worth campaign is organized around the first approach—it is essentially a campaign to rectify distortions of the market, which has failed to reward women according to the value of their work. It therefore appeals directly to the liberal principle of meritocracy. The feminization-of-poverty campaign is organized around the second approach—it aims to rectify men's failure to provide for their wives through refusal of child and spousal support (in the case of divorced women) or through lack of life insurance (in the case of widows). Women's claims on the state for support are justified by their lack of a male breadwinner. In the rest of this article, I will discuss the ways in which the feminization of poverty and comparable worth campaigns reflect a liberal political discourse, outline the likely consequences, and suggest an alternative approach....

Because it has been taken up by trade unions and because it has met resistance from employers, employer organizations, and conservatives, comparable worth advocates have tended to assume that the issue has radical or potentially radical force.... Comparable worth is often referred to as the civil rights issue of the 80s. Yet the significance of comparable worth as a remedy to women's low pay and to occupational segregation is limited. Its application has been most effective in public-worker settings because these workers are often unionized and because it is possible for these unions to bring pressure through legislatures or elected officials....

While a demand for recognition of the value of their work and higher pay is a possible strategy for all women workers, raising wages by equating women's and men's wages in comparable jobs will not work in industries, such as insurance, in which men are employed mostly at the top and middle and women at the bottom. Affirmative action remains crucial to encouraging women's employment in nontraditional occupations and management. Furthermore, as even its supporters point out, comparable worth will not improve the access of women of color to jobs and education.

As a political discourse, comparable worth's fundamental claim to legitimacy reinforces an existing ideology: the necessity and validity of meritocratic hierarchy. Rather than questioning the market as an arbiter of wages, comparable worth, as two of its most prominent advocates say, attempts to:

> pay a fair market wage to jobs historically done by women. This means that the wage rate should be based on the productivity-based job content characteristics of the jobs and not on the sex of the typical job incumbent.... Comparable worth advocates seek to disentangle and remove discrimination from the market.

Job evaluations use wage surveys to fix a dollar value to the factor points for benchmark jobs, which are then used to establish a salary scale. Job evaluations measure only the traits of jobs; the money value of the traits is determined by the wages prevailing in the labor market. Thus comparable worth aims primarily to rationalize the existing sorting and selecting of individuals into unequal places and does *not* eliminate market criteria from job evaluation.

From this point of view, comparable worth is a relatively conservative approach to women's low pay in that it situates its rationale firmly within the hegemonic liberal political discourse. A radical approach to women's low pay would not only challenge the existing inequalities between women's and men's pay for comparable jobs, but would also contest the notion that people's income should be determined primarily by where they fit in an occupational hierarchy. If jobs are assessed in terms of their necessity to an integrated labor process, it is equally important that *all* jobs be done consistently and well. Anyone who contributes his or her best efforts in a particular job is as deserving as any other individual.

Western contemporary society will not accept "from each according to his/her ability, to each according to his/her need" as a standard of fairness.

Nonetheless, the claim that everyone who labors deserves to live decently has been, particularly in periods of working-class mobilization, a central value. Of course, historically, the trade union movement appealed to the right of the working *man* to make a family wage. Perhaps because the strategy has served to institutionalize women's marginalization in wage labor, feminists have preferred to address the problem of women's low pay in terms other than women's life needs as individuals and as mothers. Perhaps also because it relies on broadly shared meritocratic values, comparable worth may appear to be a practical approach to raising women's pay. But so long as comparable worth efforts remain within that liberal discourse, they risk eventually increasing racial and occupational divisions among working women.

The heart of the comparable worth strategy is the job evaluation.... To evaluate the probable impact of comparable worth, then, we need to consider who will participate in the negotiations over the factors and factor weights and with what sorts of assumptions. Since less than one-fifth of the U.S. workforce and only 13 percent of all U.S. women workers are unionized, we can expect that in most cases, technical experts and management will formulate the evaluation policies. We can further expect that existing cultural biases in factors and factor weights will be replicated....

Estimating the impact of comparable worth adjustments under different conditions, Aldrich and Buchele found the earnings gap between women workers by quintiles would be reduced by at most 6.5 percent. Since women are not distributed proportionately by race within job categories, large inequalities by race will remain, but appear to be reflections of differential merit and thus ultimately difficult to challenge.

Comparable worth may also exacerbate hierarchies in women's jobs. For example, hospital administrations do not currently award differential salaries among nursing specialities, although there is a clear hierarchy of rewards to medical specialities. Remick predicts that job evaluation systems may expose "internal squabbles that will have to be dealt with by the nursing profession." At hearings conducted by the U.S. Equal Employment Opportunities Commission in 1980, the American Nurses Association testified to the similarities between intensive care unit nurses and doctors. Comparable worth adjustments may encourage nurses with such specialities to claim higher pay.

Comparable worth may very well open up discussion of how society values work, but that discussion must be framed by a broader challenge to the prevailing culture. The superior value of mental over manual skills and the greater importance of supervisory over other kinds of responsibility should not be assumed but questioned. Otherwise, we can expect comparable worth to readjust women's and men's pay but to change very little, perhaps even to solidify, the existing divisions in the work force: divisions between whites and minority workers, between designated professionals and nonprofessionals, between white-collar and blue-collar workers. These divisions cut across gender and have been an important source of trade-union disunity. Yet any radical potential for "politicizing the wage-setting process" depends on the strength of worker organization. . . .

Job evaluation studies often find men's job classes "overpaid" for the content of their jobs, especially craft jobs, which tend to be held by white men. Since market realities may be felt to require relatively higher wages in order to recruit and hold those workers and it may be illegal to equalize pay scales by lowering men's wages, most plans attempt to achieve equity over a long run by gradually increasing women's wages. Some plans freeze men's wages; others simply raise men's wages more slowly, for example, giving all workers a cost-of-living raise and women workers an equity bonus. . . .

A less divisive strategy is to adjust women's wages to a level commensurate with the intrinsic value of their work. In the strike by women clericals at Yale, the union demanded higher pay on the ground that the women made an important contribution to the university, a contribution that has historically been undervalued because they were women. The union did not center its strategy on a direct comparison with men's wages or claims about the comparative value of men's and women's work. The women were well-organized; the unionized, predominantly blue-collar men had nothing to lose and much to gain from a united work force, so the men were willing to honor the women's picket line for the entire ten weeks of the strike. The women reciprocated and supported the men when their contract came up, which allowed the men to make gains that they had unsuccessfully struck for in the past. In short, although the women's and men's pay scales were adjusted separately, not in relation to each other, the gender gap was narrowed.

In sum, comparable worth seems to offer an immediate remedy to a pressing problem, but it may institutionalize divisions among women and between women and men that will make future collective campaigns difficult. While some supporters of comparable worth themselves signal potential dangers, such as the dominance of technocrats and managers in wage setting or divisions among women workers, they tend to minimize the risks and overestimate its radical potential. It seems to me that unless a very different kind of organizing is done concerning the issue, this potential is not likely to be realized.

Comparable worth has been presented as a demand for removing discrimination and improving women's position within an existing system. The demand for equity could, however, be put forward as part of a broader set of longer-range goals that challenge the terms of the system itself. A radical strategy would argue for raising the pay of the lowest-paid workers, most of whom are women and minorities, on the grounds that everyone who contributes his or her labor deserves a comfortable and secure existence. This strategy would not only protest the undervaluation of women's work but also argue that existing salary differentials among jobs, especially between management and nonmanagement jobs, are unnecessarily large. And it would argue that if we are looking at the work people do, then we should ask whether that work is productive, safe, and interesting, and whether it allows people to use their talents and skills and to develop new ones. . . .

E.   WOMEN AND EDUCATION

INTRODUCTION

Until early in this century most educational institutions were dedicated to teaching either men or women, but not both. As late as mid-century, many of the most elite remained single-sex. The materials in this section raise two issues relating to the move to co-education. The first portion of the readings asks when, if ever, it is Constitutionally permissible for public institutions to operate programs that are all male or all female. The second portion of the readings focuses on how we can provide equal opportunities for women in school athletic programs.

The readings in this section provide a bridge that links the issues addressed in the earlier sections on women and work to the issues that will be discussed in relation to sexual harassment in the next section and domestic violence and pornography later in the book. These sections all raise questions about the liberal vision of equality. They suggest that this vision is inadequate to describe some of the settings in which we as women find ourselves. Are cultural feminists' ideas, dominance feminists' theories or postmodern approaches more useful than the liberal stance?

In the first portion of this section, two Supreme Court cases, Mississippi University for Women v. Hogan and United States v. Virginia, address the question of whether sex-segregated educational programs are constitutional. Like some of the cases in the section on the Work/Family Conflict, these cases discuss the standard by which sex-discrimination is tested. They also raise related social issues of whether women should be treated differently by educational institutions because women learn differently, either for biological or cultural reasons. Which theoretical approaches do you think fit these materials best?

The materials dealing with school sports programs raise similar issues about the applicable legal standard and women's differences from men. These materials raise additional questions about the role of sports in our cultural lives. Are sports a site of male aggression? How much of the acculturation that occurs on sports teams involves learning the norms of masculinity? If male bonding occurs on sports teams, is it premised on being anti-female? To the extent that athletic activity is linked to masculinity in modern America, how can women participate in sports? It is here that the liberal's vision of equality is problematic. If women are taught not to participate in sports because to do so is not feminine, what does it mean to treat women equally in terms of providing athletic opportunities? Do any of the other feminist approaches provide more assistance in thinking about this issue?

Mississippi University for Women v. Hogan

Supreme Court of the United States, 1982.
458 U.S. 718, 102 S.Ct. 3331, 73 L.Ed.2d 1090.

JUSTICE SANDRA DAY O'CONNOR delivered the opinion of the Court.

This case presents the narrow issue of whether a state statute that excludes males from enrolling in a state-supported professional nursing school violates the Equal Protection Clause of the Fourteenth Amendment.

The facts are not in dispute. In 1884, the Mississippi Legislature created the Mississippi Industrial Institute and College for the Education of White Girls of the State of Mississippi, now the oldest state-supported all-female college in the United States. The school, known today as Mississippi University for Women (MUW), has from its inception limited its enrollment to women.[1]

In 1971, MUW established a School of Nursing, initially offering a 2–year associate degree. Three years later, the school instituted a 4–year baccalaureate program in nursing and today also offers a graduate program. The School of Nursing has its own faculty and administrative officers and establishes its own criteria for admission.

Respondent, Joe Hogan, is a registered nurse but does not hold a baccalaureate degree in nursing. Since 1974, he has worked as a nursing supervisor in a medical center in Columbus, the city in which MUW is located. In 1979, Hogan applied for admission to the MUW School of Nursing's baccalaureate program. Although he was otherwise qualified, he was denied admission to the School of Nursing solely because of his sex. School officials informed him that he could audit the courses in which he was interested, but could not enroll for credit.

Hogan filed an action in the United States District Court for the Northern District of Mississippi, claiming the single-sex admissions policy of MUW's School of Nursing violated the Equal Protection Clause of the Fourteenth Amendment. Hogan sought injunctive and declaratory relief, as well as compensatory damages. . . .

We begin our analysis aided by several firmly established principles. Because the challenged policy expressly discriminates among applicants on

---

1. The charter of MUW, basically unchanged since its founding, now provides:

"The purpose and aim of the Mississippi State College for Women is the moral and intellectual advancement of the girls of the state by the maintenance of a first-class institution for their education in the arts and sciences, for their training in normal school methods and kindergarten, for their instruction in bookkeeping, photography, stenography, telegraphy, and typewriting, and in designing, drawing, engraving, and paint-

ing, and their industrial application, and for their instruction in fancy, general and practical needlework, and in such other industrial branches as experience, from time to time, shall suggest as necessary or proper to fit them for the practical affairs of life."

Mississippi maintains no other single sex public university or college. Thus, we are not faced with the question of whether States can provide "separate but equal" undergraduate institutions for males and females.

the basis of gender, it is subject to scrutiny under the Equal Protection Clause of the Fourteenth Amendment. *Reed v. Reed,* 404 U.S. 71, 75, 92 S.Ct. 251, 253, 30 L.Ed.2d 225 (1971). That this statutory policy discriminates against males rather than against females does not exempt it from scrutiny or reduce the standard of review.

Although the test for determining the validity of a gender-based classification is straightforward, it must be applied free of fixed notions concerning the roles and abilities of males and females. Care must be taken in ascertaining whether the statutory objective itself reflects archaic and stereotypic notions. Thus, if the statutory objective is to exclude or "protect" members of one gender because they are presumed to suffer from an inherent handicap or to be innately inferior, the objective itself is illegitimate. See *Frontiero v. Richardson,* 411 U.S. 677, 684–685, 93 S.Ct. 1764, 1769–70, 36 L.Ed.2d 583 (1973) (plurality opinion).

If the State's objective is legitimate and important, we next determine whether the requisite direct, substantial relationship between objective and means is present. The purpose of requiring that close relationship is to assure that the validity of a classification is determined through reasoned analysis rather than through the mechanical application of traditional, often inaccurate, assumptions about the proper roles of men and women.

Applying this framework, we now analyze the arguments advanced by the State to justify its refusal to allow males to enroll for credit in MUW's School of Nursing.

The State's primary justification for maintaining the single-sex admissions policy of MUW's School of Nursing is that it compensates for discrimination against women and, therefore, constitutes educational affirmative action.[13] As applied to the School of Nursing, we find the State's argument unpersuasive.

In limited circumstances, a gender-based classification favoring one sex can be justified if it intentionally and directly assists members of the sex that is disproportionately burdened. See *Schlesinger v. Ballard,* 419 U.S. 498, 95 S.Ct. 572, 42 L.Ed.2d 610 (1975).... Mississippi has made no showing that women lacked opportunities to obtain training in the field of nursing or to attain positions of leadership in that field when the MUW School of Nursing opened its door or that women currently are deprived of such opportunities.

Rather than compensate for discriminatory barriers faced by women, MUW's policy of excluding males from admission to the School of Nursing tends to perpetuate the stereotyped view of nursing as an exclusively

13. In the reply brief, the State understandably retreated from its contention that MUW was founded to provide opportunities for women which were not available to men. Apparently, the impetus for founding MUW came not from a desire to provide women with advantages superior to those offered men, but rather from a desire to provide white women in Mississippi access to state-supported higher learning. In 1856, Sally Reneau began agitating for a college for white women. Those initial efforts were unsuccessful, and, by 1870, Mississippi provided higher education only for white men and black men and women.

woman's job.[15] By assuring that Mississippi allots more openings in its state-supported nursing schools to women than it does to men, MUW's admissions policy lends credibility to the old view that women, not men, should become nurses, and makes the assumption that nursing is a field for women a self-fulfilling prophecy.

The policy is invalid also because it fails the second part of the equal protection test, for the State has made no showing that the gender-based classification is substantially and directly related to its proposed compensatory objective. To the contrary, MUW's policy of permitting men to attend classes as auditors fatally undermines its claim that women, at least those in the School of Nursing, are adversely affected by the presence of men. . . . The uncontroverted record reveals that admitting men to nursing classes does not affect teaching style. . . . In sum, the record in this case is flatly inconsistent with the claim that excluding men from the School of Nursing is necessary to reach any of MUW's educational goals.

Thus, considering both the asserted interest and the relationship between the interest and the methods used by the State, we conclude that the State has fallen far short of establishing the "exceedingly persuasive justification" needed to sustain the gender-based classification. Accordingly, we hold that MUW's policy of denying males the right to enroll for credit in its School of Nursing violates the Equal Protection Clause of the Fourteenth Amendment. . . .

CHIEF JUSTICE WARREN BURGER, dissenting.

I agree generally with Justice Powell's dissenting opinion. I write separately, however, to emphasize that the Court's holding today is limited to the context of a professional nursing school. Since the Court's opinion relies heavily on its finding that women have traditionally dominated the nursing profession, it suggests that a State might well be justified in maintaining, for example, the option of an all-women's business school or liberal arts program. . . .

JUSTICE LEWIS POWELL, with whom JUSTICE WILLIAM REHNQUIST joins, dissenting.

The Court's opinion bows deeply to conformity. Left without honor—indeed, held unconstitutional—is an element of diversity that has characterized much of American education and enriched much of American life. The Court in effect holds today that no State now may provide even a single institution of higher learning open only to women students. It gives no heed to the efforts of the State of Mississippi to provide abundant opportunities for young men and young women to attend coeducational institutions, and none to the preferences of the more than 40,000 young women who over the years have evidenced their approval of an all-women's

---

15. Officials of the American Nurses Association have suggested that excluding men from the field has depressed nurses' wages. Hearings before the United States Equal Employment Opportunity Commission on Job Segregation and Wage Discrimination 510–511, 517–518, 523 (Apr.1980). To the extent the exclusion of men has that effect, MUW's admissions policy actually penalizes the very class the State purports to benefit.

college by choosing Mississippi University for Women (MUW) over seven coeducational universities within the State. The Court decides today that the Equal Protection Clause makes it unlawful for the State to provide women with a traditionally popular and respected choice of educational environment. It does so in a case instituted by one man, who represents no class, and whose primary concern is personal convenience.

It is undisputed that women enjoy complete equality of opportunity in Mississippi's public system of higher education. Of the State's 8 universities and 16 junior colleges, all except MUW are coeducational. At least two other Mississippi universities would have provided respondent with the nursing curriculum that he wishes to pursue. . . .

Nor is respondent significantly disadvantaged by MUW's all-female tradition. His constitutional complaint is based upon a single asserted harm: that he must *travel* to attend the state-supported nursing schools that concededly are available to him. The Court characterizes this injury as one of "inconvenience." . . . Thus the Court, to redress respondent's injury of inconvenience, must rest its invalidation of MUW's single-sex program on a mode of "sexual stereotype" reasoning that has no application whatever to the respondent or to the "wrong" of which he complains. At best this is anomalous. And ultimately the anomaly reveals legal error— that of applying a heightened equal protection standard, developed in cases of genuine sexual stereotyping, to a narrowly utilized state classification that provides an *additional* choice for women. Moreover, I believe that Mississippi's educational system should be upheld in this case even if this inappropriate method of analysis is applied.

Coeducation, historically, is a novel educational theory. From grade school through high school, college, and graduate and professional training, much of the Nation's population during much of our history has been educated in sexually segregated classrooms. At the college level, for instance, until recently some of the most prestigious colleges and universities—including most of the Ivy League—had long histories of single-sex education. As Harvard, Yale, and Princeton remained all-male colleges well into the second half of this century, the "Seven Sister" institutions established a parallel standard of excellence for women's colleges. . . .

The sexual segregation of students has been a reflection of, rather than an imposition upon, the preference of those subject to the policy. It cannot be disputed, for example, that the highly qualified women attending the leading women's colleges could have earned admission to virtually any college of their choice. Women attending such colleges have chosen to be there, usually expressing a preference for the special benefits of single-sex institutions. Similar decisions were made by the colleges that elected to remain open to women only.

The arguable benefits of single-sex colleges also continue to be recognized by students of higher education. . . . As summarized in A. Astin, Four Critical Years 232 (1977), the data established that "[b]oth [male and female] single-sex colleges facilitate student involvement in several areas: academic, interaction with faculty, and verbal aggressiveness.... Men's and women's colleges also have a positive effect on intellectual self-esteem. Students at single-sex colleges are more satisfied than students at coeducational colleges with virtually all aspects of college life.... The only area where students are less satisfied is social life."

Despite the continuing expressions that single-sex institutions may offer singular advantages to their students, there is no doubt that coeducational institutions are far more numerous. But their numerical predominance does not establish—in any sense properly cognizable by a court—that individual preferences for single-sex education are misguided or illegitimate, or that a State may not provide its citizens with a choice.

The issue in this case is whether a State transgresses the Constitution when—within the context of a public system that offers a diverse range of campuses, curricula, and educational alternatives—it seeks to accommodate the legitimate personal preferences of those desiring the advantages of an all-women's college. In my view, the Court errs seriously by assuming—without argument or discussion—that the equal protection standard generally applicable to sex discrimination is appropriate here. That standard was designed to free women from "archaic and overbroad generalizations...." *Schlesinger v. Ballard,* 419 U.S. 498, 508, 95 S.Ct. 572, 577, 42 L.Ed.2d 610 (1975). In no previous case have we applied it to invalidate state efforts to *expand* women's choices. Nor are there prior sex discrimination decisions by this Court in which a male plaintiff, as in this case, had the choice of an equal benefit....

By applying heightened equal protection analysis to this case, the Court frustrates the liberating spirit of the Equal Protection Clause. It prohibits the States from providing women with an opportunity to choose the type of university they prefer. And yet it is these women whom the Court regards as the *victims* of an illegal, stereotyped perception of the role of women in our society. The Court reasons this way in a case in which no woman has complained, and the only complainant is a man who advances no claims on behalf of anyone else. His claim, it should be recalled, is not that he is being denied a substantive educational opportunity, or even the right to attend an all-male or a coeducational college. It is *only* that the colleges open to him are located at inconvenient distances....

The record in this case reflects that MUW has a historic position in the State's educational system dating back to 1884. More than 2,000 women presently evidence their preference for MUW by having enrolled there. The choice is one that discriminates invidiously against no one....

In sum, the practice of voluntarily chosen single-sex education is an honored tradition in our country, even if it now rarely exists in state colleges and universities. Mississippi's accommodation of such student choices is legitimate because it is completely consensual and is important because it permits students to decide for themselves the type of college education they think will benefit them most. Finally, Mississippi's policy is substantially related to its long-respected objective.

A distinctive feature of America's tradition has been respect for diversity. This has been characteristic of the peoples from numerous lands who have built our country. It is the essence of our democratic system. At stake in this case as I see it is the preservation of a small aspect of this diversity. But that aspect is by no means insignificant, given our heritage of available choice between single-sex and coeducational institutions of higher learning. The Court answers that there is discrimination—not just that which may be tolerable, as for example between those candidates for admission able to contribute most to an educational institution and those able to contribute less—but discrimination of constitutional dimension. But, having found "discrimination," the Court finds it difficult to identify the victims. It hardly can claim that women are discriminated against. A constitutional case is held to exist solely because one man found it inconvenient to travel to any of the other institutions made available to him by the State of Mississippi. In essence he insists that he has a right to attend a college in his home community. This simply is not a sex discrimination case. The Equal Protection Clause was never intended to be applied to this kind of case.

United States v. Virginia

Supreme Court of the United States, 1996.
518 U.S. 515, 116 S.Ct. 2264, 135 L.Ed.2d 735.

JUSTICE RUTH BADER GINSBURG delivered the opinion of the Court.

Virginia's public institutions of higher learning include an incomparable military college, Virginia Military Institute (VMI). The United States maintains that the Constitution's equal protection guarantee precludes Virginia from reserving exclusively to men the unique educational opportunities VMI affords. We agree. . . .

Founded in 1839, VMI is today the sole single-sex school among Virginia's 15 public institutions of higher learning. VMI's distinctive mission is to produce "citizen-soldiers," men prepared for leadership in civilian life and in military service. VMI pursues this mission through pervasive training of a kind not available anywhere else in Virginia. Assigning prime place to character development, VMI uses an "adversative method" modeled on English public schools and once characteristic of military instruction. VMI constantly endeavors to instill physical and mental discipline in its cadets and impart to them a strong moral code. The school's graduates leave VMI with heightened comprehension of their capacity to deal with duress and stress, and a large sense of accomplishment for completing the hazardous course.

VMI has notably succeeded in its mission to produce leaders; among its alumni are military generals, Members of Congress, and business executives. The school's alumni overwhelmingly perceive that their VMI training helped them to realize their personal goals. VMI's endowment reflects the loyalty of its graduates; VMI has the largest per-student endowment of all public undergraduate institutions in the Nation.

Neither the goal of producing citizen-soldiers nor VMI's implementing methodology is inherently unsuitable to women. And the school's impressive record in producing leaders has made admission desirable to some women. Nevertheless, Virginia has elected to preserve exclusively for men the advantages and opportunities a VMI education affords. . . .

VMI produces its "citizen-soldiers" through "an adversative, or doubting, model of education" which features "[p]hysical rigor, mental stress, absolute equality of treatment, absence of privacy, minute regulation of behavior, and indoctrination in desirable values." As one Commandant of Cadets described it, the adversative method "dissects the young student," and makes him aware of his "limits and capabilities," so that he knows "how far he can go with his anger, . . . how much he can take under stress, . . . exactly what he can do when he is physically exhausted."

VMI cadets live in spartan barracks where surveillance is constant and privacy nonexistent; they wear uniforms, eat together in the mess hall, and regularly participate in drills. Entering students are incessantly exposed to the rat line, "an extreme form of the adversative model," comparable in intensity to Marine Corps boot camp. Tormenting and punishing, the rat line bonds new cadets to their fellow sufferers and, when they have completed the 7–month experience, to their former tormentors.

VMI's "adversative model" is further characterized by a hierarchical "class system" of privileges and responsibilities, a "dyke system" for assigning a senior class mentor to each entering class "rat," and a stringently enforced "honor code," which prescribes that a cadet " 'does not lie, cheat, steal nor tolerate those who do.' "

VMI attracts some applicants because of its reputation as an extraordinarily challenging military school, and "because its alumni are exceptionally close to the school." "[W]omen have no opportunity anywhere to gain the benefits of [the system of education at VMI]." . . .

In 1990, prompted by a complaint filed with the Attorney General by a female high-school student seeking admission to VMI, the United States sued the Commonwealth of Virginia and VMI, alleging that VMI's exclusively male admission policy violated the Equal Protection Clause of the Fourteenth Amendment. . . .

The District Court ruled in favor of VMI . . . and rejected the equal protection challenge pressed by the United States. . . . The District Court reasoned that education in "a single-gender environment, be it male or female," yields substantial benefits. VMI's school for men brought diversity to an otherwise coeducational Virginia system, and that diversity was "enhanced by VMI's unique method of instruction." If single-gender education for males ranks as an important governmental objective, it becomes obvious, the District Court concluded, that the only means of achieving the objective "is to exclude women from the all-male institution—VMI." . . .

Thus, "sufficient constitutional justification" had been shown, the District Court held, "for continuing [VMI's] single-sex policy."

The Court of Appeals for the Fourth Circuit disagreed and vacated the District Court's judgment.... The appeals court greeted with skepticism Virginia's assertion that it offers single-sex education at VMI as a facet of the State's overarching and undisputed policy to advance "autonomy and diversity." ...

The parties agreed that "some women can meet the physical standards now imposed on men," and the court was satisfied that "neither the goal of producing citizen soldiers nor VMI's implementing methodology is inherently unsuitable to women." The Court of Appeals, however, accepted the District Court's finding that "at least these three aspects of VMI's program—physical training, the absence of privacy, and the adversative approach—would be materially affected by coeducation." Remanding the case, the appeals court assigned to Virginia, in the first instance, responsibility for selecting a remedial course. The court suggested these options for the State: Admit women to VMI; establish parallel institutions or programs; or abandon state support, leaving VMI free to pursue its policies as a private institution. In May 1993, this Court denied certiorari. ...

In response to the Fourth Circuit's ruling, Virginia proposed a parallel program for women: Virginia Women's Institute for Leadership (VWIL). The 4–year, state-sponsored undergraduate program would be located at Mary Baldwin College, a private liberal arts school for women, and would be open, initially, to about 25 to 30 students. Although VWIL would share VMI's mission—to produce "citizen-soldiers"—the VWIL program would differ, as does Mary Baldwin College, from VMI in academic offerings, methods of education, and financial resources.

The average combined SAT score of entrants at Mary Baldwin is about 100 points lower than the score for VMI freshmen. Mary Baldwin's faculty holds "significantly fewer Ph.D.'s than the faculty at VMI," and receives significantly lower salaries. While VMI offers degrees in liberal arts, the sciences, and engineering, Mary Baldwin, at the time of trial, offered only bachelor of arts degrees....

Experts in educating women at the college level composed the Task Force charged with designing the VWIL program; Task Force members were drawn from Mary Baldwin's own faculty and staff. Training its attention on methods of instruction appropriate for "most women," the Task Force determined that a military model would be "wholly inappropriate" for VWIL.

VWIL students would participate in ROTC programs and a newly established, "largely ceremonial" Virginia Corps of Cadets, but the VWIL House would not have a military format, and VWIL would not require its students to eat meals together or to wear uniforms during the school day. In lieu of VMI's adversative method, the VWIL Task Force favored "a cooperative method which reinforces self-esteem." In addition to the standard bachelor of arts program offered at Mary Baldwin, VWIL students would take courses in leadership, complete an off-campus leadership externship, participate in community service projects, and assist in arranging a speaker series.

Virginia represented that it will provide equal financial support for in-state VWIL students and VMI cadets, and the VMI Foundation agreed to supply a $5.4625 million endowment for the VWIL program. Mary Baldwin's own endowment is about $19 million; VMI's is $131 million.... The VMI Alumni Association has developed a network of employers interested in hiring VMI graduates. The Association has agreed to open its network to VWIL graduates, but those graduates will not have the advantage afforded by a VMI degree....

Virginia returned to the District Court seeking approval of its proposed remedial plan, and the court decided the plan met the requirements of the Equal Protection Clause....

A divided Court of Appeals affirmed the District Court's judgment. This time, the appellate court determined to give "greater scrutiny to the selection of means than to the [State's] proffered objective." ...

"[P]roviding the option of a single-gender college education may be considered a legitimate and important aspect of a public system of higher education," the appeals court observed; that objective, the court added, is "not pernicious." Moreover, the court continued, the adversative method vital to a VMI education "has never been tolerated in a sexually heterogeneous environment." The method itself "was not designed to exclude women," the court noted, but women could not be accommodated in the VMI program, the court believed, for female participation in VMI's adversative training "would destroy ... any sense of decency that still permeates the relationship between the sexes."

Having determined, deferentially, the legitimacy of Virginia's purpose, the court considered the question of means. Exclusion of "men at Mary Baldwin College and women at VMI," the court said, was essential to Virginia's purpose, for without such exclusion, the State could not "accomplish [its] objective of providing single-gender education."

The court recognized that, as it analyzed the case, means merged into end, and the merger risked "bypass[ing] any equal protection scrutiny." The court therefore added another inquiry, a decisive test it called "substantive comparability." The key question, the court said, was whether men at VMI and women at VWIL would obtain "substantively comparable benefits at their institution or through other means offered by the [S]tate." Although the appeals court recognized that the VWIL degree "lacks the historical benefit and prestige" of a VMI degree, it nevertheless found the educational opportunities at the two schools "sufficiently comparable." ...

... [T]his case present[s] two ultimate issues. First, does Virginia's exclusion of women from the educational opportunities provided by VMI—extraordinary opportunities for military training and civilian leadership development—deny to women "capable of all of the individual activities required of VMI cadets," the equal protection of the laws guaranteed by the

Fourteenth Amendment? Second, if VMI's "unique" situation,—as Virginia's sole single-sex public institution of higher education—offends the Constitution's equal protection principle, what is the remedial requirement? . . .

We note, once again, the core instruction of this Court's pathmarking decision[] in . . . *Mississippi Univ. for Women*: Parties who seek to defend gender-based government action must demonstrate an "exceedingly persuasive justification" for that action. . . . Since *Reed* [*v. Reed,* 404 U.S.71], the Court has repeatedly recognized that neither federal nor state government acts compatibly with the equal protection principle when a law or official policy denies to women, simply because they are women, full citizenship stature—equal opportunity to aspire, achieve, participate in and contribute to society based on their individual talents and capacities. . . .

Without equating gender classifications, for all purposes, to classifications based on race or national origin, the Court, in post—Reed decisions, has carefully inspected official action that closes a door or denies opportunity to women (or to men). To summarize the Court's current directions for cases of official classification based on gender: Focusing on the differential treatment or denial of opportunity for which relief is sought, the reviewing court must determine whether the proffered justification is "exceedingly persuasive." The burden of justification is demanding and it rests entirely on the State. The State must show "at least that the [challenged] classification serves 'important governmental objectives and that the discriminatory means employed' are 'substantially related to the achievement of those objectives.' "The justification must be genuine, not hypothesized or invented post hoc in response to litigation. And it must not rely on overbroad generalizations about the different talents, capacities, or preferences of males and females.

The heightened review standard our precedent establishes does not make sex a proscribed classification. Supposed "inherent differences" are no longer accepted as a ground for race or national origin classifications. Physical differences between men and women, however, are enduring: "[T]he two sexes are not fungible; a community made up exclusively of one [sex] is different from a community composed of both."

"Inherent differences" between men and women, we have come to appreciate, remain cause for celebration, but not for denigration of the members of either sex or for artificial constraints on an individual's opportunity. Sex classifications may be used to compensate women "for particular economic disabilities [they have] suffered," to "promot[e] equal employment opportunity," to advance full development of the talent and capacities of our Nation's people.[7] But such classifications may not be used,

---

7. Several amici have urged that diversity in educational opportunities is an altogether appropriate governmental pursuit and that single-sex schools can contribute importantly to such diversity. Indeed, it is the mission of some single-sex schools "to dissipate, rather than perpetuate, traditional gender classifications." We do not question the State's prerogative evenhandedly to support diverse educational opportunities. We address

as they once were, to create or perpetuate the legal, social, and economic inferiority of women.

Measuring the record in this case against the review standard just described, we conclude that Virginia has shown no "exceedingly persuasive justification" for excluding all women from the citizen-soldier training afforded by VMI. . . .

Virginia . . . asserts two justifications in defense of VMI's exclusion of women. First, the Commonwealth contends, "single-sex education provides important educational benefits," and the option of single-sex education contributes to "diversity in educational approaches." Second, the Commonwealth argues, "the unique VMI method of character development and leadership training," the school's adversative approach, would have to be modified were VMI to admit women. We consider these two justifications in turn. . . .

Single-sex education affords pedagogical benefits to at least some students, Virginia emphasizes, and that reality is uncontested in this litigation. Similarly, it is not disputed that diversity among public educational institutions can serve the public good. But Virginia has not shown that VMI was established, or has been maintained, with a view to diversifying, by its categorical exclusion of women, educational opportunities within the State. . . .

Virginia next argues that VMI's adversative method of training provides educational benefits that cannot be made available, unmodified, to women. Alterations to accommodate women would necessarily be "radical," so "drastic," Virginia asserts, as to transform, indeed "destroy," VMI's program. Neither sex would be favored by the transformation, Virginia maintains: Men would be deprived of the unique opportunity currently available to them; women would not gain that opportunity because their participation would "eliminat[e] the very aspects of [the] program that distinguish [VMI] from . . . other institutions of higher education in Virginia."

The District Court forecast from expert witness testimony, and the Court of Appeals accepted, that coeducation would materially affect "at least these three aspects of VMI's program—physical training, the absence of privacy, and the adversative approach." And it is uncontested that women's admission would require accommodations, primarily in arranging housing assignments and physical training programs for female cadets. It is also undisputed, however, that "the VMI methodology could be used to educate women." The District Court even allowed that some women may prefer it to the methodology a women's college might pursue. "[S]ome women, at least, would want to attend [VMI] if they had the opportunity,"

specifically and only an educational opportunity recognized by the District Court and the Court of Appeals as "unique," an opportunity available only at Virginia's premier military institute, the State's sole single-sex public university or college. Cf. Mississippi Univ. for Women v. Hogan, ("Mississippi maintains no other single-sex public university or college. Thus, we are not faced with the question of whether States can provide 'separate but equal' undergraduate institutions for males and females.").

the District Court recognized, and "some women," the expert testimony established, "are capable of all of the individual activities required of VMI cadets." The parties, furthermore, agree that "some women can meet the physical standards [VMI] now impose[s] on men." In sum, as the Court of Appeals stated, "neither the goal of producing citizen soldiers," VMI's raison d'etre, "nor VMI's implementing methodology is inherently unsuitable to women." ...

The United States does not challenge any expert witness estimation on average capacities or preferences of men and women. Instead, the United States emphasizes that time and again since this Court's turning point decision in Reed v. Reed, 404 U.S. 71 (1971), we have cautioned reviewing courts to take a "hard look" at generalizations or "tendencies" of the kind pressed by Virginia. State actors controlling gates to opportunity, we have instructed, may not exclude qualified individuals based on "fixed notions concerning the roles and abilities of males and females."

It may be assumed, for purposes of this decision, that most women would not choose VMI's adversative method. . . . [I]t is also probable that "many men would not want to be educated in such an environment." Education, to be sure, is not a "one size fits all" business. The issue, however, is not whether "women—or men—should be forced to attend VMI"; rather, the question is whether the State can constitutionally deny to women who have the will and capacity, the training and attendant opportunities that VMI uniquely affords. . . .

Virginia and VMI trained their argument on "means" rather than "end," and thus misperceived our precedent. Single-sex education at VMI serves an "important governmental objective," they maintained, and exclusion of women is not only "substantially related," it is essential to that objective. By this notably circular argument, the "straightforward" test Mississippi Univ. for Women described was bent and bowed.

The State's misunderstanding and, in turn, the District Court's, is apparent from VMI's mission: to produce "citizen-soldiers." . . . Surely that goal is great enough to accommodate women, who today count as citizens in our American democracy equal in stature to men. Just as surely, the State's great goal is not substantially advanced by women's categorical exclusion, in total disregard of their individual merit, from the State's premier "citizen-soldier" corps. Virginia, in sum, "has fallen far short of establishing the 'exceedingly persuasive justification,' " that must be the solid base for any gender-defined classification. . . .

In the second phase of the litigation, Virginia presented its remedial plan—maintain VMI as a male-only college and create VWIL as a separate program for women. . . . The Fourth Circuit . . . deferentially reviewed the State's proposal and decided that the two single-sex programs directly served Virginia's reasserted purposes: single-gender education, and "achieving the results of an adversative method in a military environment." . . . The United States challenges this "remedial" ruling as pervasively misguided. . . .

A remedial decree, this Court has said, must closely fit the constitutional violation; it must be shaped to place persons unconstitutionally denied an opportunity or advantage in "the position they would have occupied in the absence of [discrimination]." The constitutional violation in this case is the categorical exclusion of women from an extraordinary educational opportunity afforded men. A proper remedy for an unconstitutional exclusion, we have explained, aims to "eliminate [so far as possible] the discriminatory effects of the past" and to "bar like discrimination in the future."

Virginia chose not to eliminate, but to leave untouched, VMI's exclusionary policy. For women only, however, Virginia proposed a separate program, different in kind from VMI and unequal in tangible and intangible facilities. Having violated the Constitution's equal protection requirement, Virginia was obliged to show that its remedial proposal "directly address[ed] and relate[d] to" the violation, i.e., the equal protection denied to women ready, willing, and able to benefit from educational opportunities of the kind VMI offers. . . .

VWIL affords women no opportunity to experience the rigorous military training for which VMI is famed. Instead, the VWIL program "deemphasize[s]" military education, and uses a "cooperative method" of education "which reinforces self-esteem." . . . VWIL students receive their "leadership training" in seminars, externships, and speaker series, episodes and encounters lacking the "[p]hysical rigor, mental stress, . . . minute regulation of behavior, and indoctrination in desirable values" made hallmarks of VMI's citizen-soldier training. Kept away from the pressures, hazards, and psychological bonding characteristic of VMI's adversative training, VWIL students will not know the "feeling of tremendous accomplishment" commonly experienced by VMI's successful cadets.

Virginia maintains that these methodological differences are "justified pedagogically," based on "important differences between men and women in learning and developmental needs," "psychological and sociological differences" Virginia describes as "real" and "not stereotypes." . . .

In contrast to the generalizations about women on which Virginia rests, we note again these dispositive realities: VMI's "implementing methodology" is not "inherently unsuitable to women," "some women . . . do well under [the] adversative model," "some women, at least, would want to attend [VMI] if they had the opportunity," "some women are capable of all of the individual activities required of VMI cadets," and "can meet the physical standards [VMI] now impose[s] on men." It is on behalf of these women that the United States has instituted this suit, and it is for them that a remedy must be crafted,[19] a remedy that will end their exclusion from a state-supplied educational opportunity for which they are fit, a decree that will "bar like discrimination in the future." . . .

---

19. Admitting women to VMI would undoubtedly require alterations necessary to afford members of each sex privacy from the other sex in living arrangements, and to adjust aspects of the physical training programs. . . .

In myriad respects other than military training, VWIL does not qualify as VMI's equal. VWIL's student body, faculty, course offerings, and facilities hardly match VMI's. Nor can the VWIL graduate anticipate the benefits associated with VMI's 157–year history, the school's prestige, and its influential alumni network. . . .

Virginia, in sum, while maintaining VMI for men only, has failed to provide any "comparable single-gender women's institution." Instead, the Commonwealth has created a VWIL program fairly appraised as a "pale shadow" of VMI in terms of the range of curricular choices and faculty stature, funding, prestige, alumni support and influence.

Virginia's VWIL solution is reminiscent of the remedy Texas proposed 50 years ago, in response to a state trial court's 1946 ruling that, given the equal protection guarantee, African Americans could not be denied a legal education at a state facility. See Sweatt v. Painter, 339 U.S. 629 (1950). Reluctant to admit African Americans to its flagship University of Texas Law School, the State set up a separate school for Herman Sweatt and other black law students. As originally opened, the new school had no independent faculty or library, and it lacked accreditation. . . .

Before this Court considered the case, the new school had gained "a faculty of five full-time professors; a student body of 23; a library of some 16,500 volumes serviced by a full-time staff; a practice court and legal aid association; and one alumnus who ha[d] become a member of the Texas Bar." This Court contrasted resources at the new school with those at the school from which Sweatt had been excluded. The University of Texas Law School had a full-time faculty of 16, a student body of 850, a library containing over 65,000 volumes, scholarship funds, a law review, and moot court facilities.

More important than the tangible features, the Court emphasized, are "those qualities which are incapable of objective measurement but which make for greatness" in a school, including "reputation of the faculty, experience of the administration, position and influence of the alumni, standing in the community, traditions and prestige." Facing the marked differences reported in the Sweatt opinion, the Court unanimously ruled that Texas had not shown "substantial equality in the [separate] educational opportunities" the State offered. Accordingly, the Court held, the Equal Protection Clause required Texas to admit African Americans to the University of Texas Law School. In line with Sweatt, we rule here that Virginia has not shown substantial equality in the separate educational opportunities the State supports at VWIL and VMI. . . .

The Fourth Circuit plainly erred in exposing Virginia's VWIL plan to a deferential analysis, for "all gender-based classifications today" warrant "heightened scrutiny." Valuable as VWIL may prove for students who seek the program offered, Virginia's remedy affords no cure at all for the opportunities and advantages withheld from women who want a VMI education and can make the grade. In sum, Virginia's remedy does not match the constitutional violation; the State has shown no "exceedingly persuasive justification" for withholding from women qualified for the experience premier training of the kind VMI affords. . . .

JUSTICE ANTONIN SCALIA, dissenting.

. . . Much of the Court's opinion is devoted to deprecating the closed-mindedness of our forebears with regard to women's education, and even with regard to the treatment of women in areas that have nothing to do with education. Closed-minded they were—as every age is, including our own, with regard to matters it cannot guess, because it simply does not consider them debatable. The virtue of a democratic system with a First Amendment is that it readily enables the people, over time, to be persuaded that what they took for granted is not so, and to change their laws accordingly. That system is destroyed if the smug assurances of each age are removed from the democratic process and written into the Constitution. So to counterbalance the Court's criticism of our ancestors, let me say a word in their praise: they left us free to change. The same cannot be said of this most illiberal Court, which has embarked on a course of inscribing one after another of the current preferences of the society (and in some cases only the counter-majoritarian preferences of the society's law-trained elite) into our Basic Law. Today it enshrines the notion that no substantial educational value is to be served by an all-men's military academy—so that the decision by the people of Virginia to maintain such an institution denies equal protection to women who cannot attend that institution but can attend others. Since it is entirely clear that the Constitution of the United States—the old one—takes no sides in this educational debate, I dissent. . . .

I shall devote most of my analysis to evaluating the Court's opinion on the basis of our current equal-protection jurisprudence, which regards this Court as free to evaluate everything under the sun by applying one of three tests: "rational basis" scrutiny, intermediate scrutiny, or strict scrutiny. These tests are no more scientific than their names suggest, and a further element of randomness is added by the fact that it is largely up to us which test will be applied in each case. Strict scrutiny, we have said, is reserved for state "classifications based on race or national origin and classifications affecting fundamental rights." It is my position that the term "fundamental rights" should be limited to "interest[s] traditionally protected by our society," but the Court has not accepted that view, so that strict scrutiny will be applied to the deprivation of whatever sort of right we consider "fundamental." We have no established criterion for "intermediate scrutiny" either, but essentially apply it when it seems like a good idea to load the dice. So far it has been applied to content-neutral restrictions that place an incidental burden on speech, to disabilities attendant to illegitimacy, and to discrimination on the basis of sex.

I have no problem with a system of abstract tests such as rational-basis, intermediate, and strict scrutiny (though I think we can do better than applying strict scrutiny and intermediate scrutiny whenever we feel like it). Such formulas are essential to evaluating whether the new restrictions that a changing society constantly imposes upon private conduct comport with that "equal protection" our society has always accorded in the past. But in my view the function of this Court is to preserve our society's values regarding (among other things) equal protection, not to revise them; to prevent backsliding from the degree of restriction the Constitution imposed upon democratic government, not to prescribe, on our own authority, progressively higher degrees. For that reason it is my view that, whatever abstract tests we may choose to devise, they cannot supersede—and indeed ought to be crafted so as to reflect—those constant and unbroken national traditions that embody the people's understanding of ambiguous constitutional texts. More specifically, it is my view that "when a practice not expressly prohibited by the text of the Bill of Rights bears the endorsement of a long tradition of open, widespread, and unchallenged use that dates back to the beginning of the Republic, we have no proper basis for striking it down." . . .

The all-male constitution of VMI comes squarely within such a governing tradition. Founded by the Commonwealth of Virginia in 1839 and continuously maintained by it since, VMI has always admitted only men. And in that regard it has not been unusual. For almost all of VMI's more than a century and a half of existence, its single-sex status reflected the uniform practice for government-supported military colleges. Another famous Southern institution, The Citadel, has existed as a state-funded school of South Carolina since 1842. And all the federal military colleges—West Point, the Naval Academy at Annapolis, and even the Air Force Academy, which was not established until 1954—admitted only males for most of their history. Their admission of women in 1976 (upon which the Court today relies), came not by court decree, but because the people, through their elected representatives, decreed a change. In other words, the tradition of having government-funded military schools for men is as well rooted in the traditions of this country as the tradition of sending only men into military combat. The people may decide to change the one tradition, like the other, through democratic processes; but the assertion that either tradition has been unconstitutional through the centuries is not law, but politics-smuggled-into-law.

And the same applies, more broadly, to single-sex education in general, which . . . is threatened by today's decision with the cut-off of all state and federal support. Government-run nonmilitary educational institutions for the two sexes have until very recently also been part of our national tradition. "[It is] [c]oeducation, historically, [that] is a novel educational theory. From grade school through high school, college, and graduate and professional training, much of the Nation's population during much of our history has been educated in sexually segregated classrooms." These traditions may of course be changed by the democratic decisions of the people, as they largely have been.

Today, however, change is forced upon Virginia, and reversion to single-sex education is prohibited nationwide, not by democratic processes but by order of this Court. Even while bemoaning the sorry, bygone days of "fixed notions" concerning women's education, the Court favors current notions so fixedly that it is willing to write them into the Constitution of the United States by application of custom-built "tests." This is not the interpretation of a Constitution, but the creation of one. . . .

As is frequently true, the Court's decision today will have consequences that extend far beyond the parties to the case. What I take to be the Court's unease with these consequences, and its resulting unwillingness to acknowledge them, cannot alter the reality. . . .

Under the constitutional principles announced and applied today, single-sex public education is unconstitutional. . . . [T]he rationale of today's decision is sweeping: for sex-based classifications, a redefinition of intermediate scrutiny that makes it indistinguishable from strict scrutiny. Indeed, the Court indicates that if any program restricted to one sex is "uniqu[e]," it must be opened to members of the opposite sex "who have the will and capacity" to participate in it. I suggest that the single-sex program that will not be capable of being characterized as "unique" is not only unique but nonexistent.

In any event, regardless of whether the Court's rationale leaves some small amount of room for lawyers to argue, it ensures that single-sex public education is functionally dead. The costs of litigating the constitutionality of a single-sex education program, and the risks of ultimately losing that litigation, are simply too high to be embraced by public officials. . . .

There are few extant single-sex public educational programs. The potential of today's decision for widespread disruption of existing institutions lies in its application to private single-sex education. Government support is immensely important to private educational institutions. . . .

The issue will be not whether government assistance turns private colleges into state actors, but whether the government itself would be violating the Constitution by providing state support to single-sex colleges. . . . The only hope for state-assisted single-sex private schools is that the Court will not apply in the future the principles of law it has applied today. That is a substantial hope, I am happy and ashamed to say. After all, did not the Court today abandon the principles of law it has applied in our earlier sex-classification cases? And does not the Court positively invite private colleges to rely upon our ad-hocery by assuring them this case is "unique"? I would not advise the foundation of any new single-sex college (especially an all-male one) with the expectation of being allowed to receive any government support; but it is too soon to abandon in despair those single-sex colleges already in existence. It will certainly be possible for this Court to write a future opinion that ignores the broad principles of law set forth today, and that characterizes as utterly dispositive the opinion's perceptions that VMI was a uniquely prestigious all-male institution, conceived in chauvinism, etc., etc. I will not join that opinion. . . .

NOTES AND QUESTIONS

1. **The Equal Protection Clause and Sex Discrimination.** The Supreme Court does not accord discrimination on the basis of sex the same

strict scrutiny under the Equal Protection Clause that it gives to race-based classifications. Reed v. Reed, 404 U.S. 71, 92 S.Ct. 251, 30 L.Ed.2d 225 (1971), began the application of "intermediate" scrutiny to sex-based categories. To be constitutional, sex-based categories must serve important governmental objectives and be substantially related to the achievement of those objectives, Craig v. Boren, 429 U.S. 190, 97 S.Ct. 451, 50 L.Ed.2d 397 (1976).

This is the test that Justice O'Connor used in Mississippi University for Women v. Hogan (MUW). What was the important governmental interest claimed by the state? Why was the Court not convinced? Do you agree with the Court that maintaining an all-women's nursing school is not a form of affirmative action, but rather that it perpetuates stereotypes that nursing is a woman's job? Why didn't Justice Powell see it this way? Did he see the existence of a single sex MUW as harming or helping women? Do you think that the Court was rejecting single sex education across the board? In what situations might it find single sex education to be constitutional? According to the Court, not only did the state fail to show an important state interest, it also failed to show that the sex-based classification was sufficiently related to its claimed objective. All in all, the state had not established an "exceedingly persuasive justification" for its sex-based classification.

Did Justice Ginsburg in *VMI* use the same analysis as Justice O'Connor used in *MUW*? Certainly, the Commonwealth of Virginia never tried to argue that maintaining VMI as an all male institution was a form of affirmative action. In *VMI*, however, is the Court raising the level of scrutiny? In analyzing the Court's opinion in *VMI*, consider the following. The Court repeatedly refers to the need for the state to demonstrate an "exceedingly persuasive justification" for its sex-based classification. Is this a new test for constitutionality? If so, what is its relationship to the intermediate level of scrutiny used in *MUW*? The Court specifically referred to that test also. Furthermore, what do you make of the fact that Justice Ginsburg's opinion noted the similarity between this situation and the one in Sweatt v. Painter, 339 U.S. 629, 70 S.Ct. 848, 94 L.Ed. 1114 (1950)? *Sweatt* is one of the early racial integration cases. Does Justice Ginsburg's analogy to *Sweatt* imply that the same strict scrutiny standard that is used in race discrimination cases should be used in sex discrimination? Justice Scalia in his dissent claimed that the majority opinion's emphasis on the fact that some women might be capable of benefitting from VMI's adversative training indicates the adoption of "strict scrutiny." This is because it is similar to the "least restrictive means" test often used in strict scrutiny cases. If all of this causes you to think the Court is moving in the direction of adopting strict scrutiny in sex discrimination cases, what do you make of the fact that the *VMI* Court specifically noted that sex is not a "proscribed classification" and that classifications based on sex are different from those based on race or national origin?

The Eleventh Circuit, in Engineering Contractors Association v. Metropolitan Dade County, 122 F.3d 895 (1997), decided that *VMI* did not change the level of scrutiny to be applied to sex-based classifications. For an argument to the contrary see Candace Saari Kovacic–Fleischer, United States v. Virginia*'s New Gender Equal Protection Analysis*, 50 Vand. L. Rev. 845 (1997).

2. **Sameness and Difference Revisited.** Justice Ginsburg is certainly one of the strongest advocates of treating women the same as men. Prior to being appointed to the bench, she litigated cases like Califano v. Goldfarb, 430 U.S. 199, 97 S.Ct. 1021, 51 L.Ed.2d 270 (1977) (women's survivors entitled to same social security benefits as men's) and Frontiero v. Richardson, 411 U.S. 677, 93 S.Ct. 1764, 36 L.Ed.2d 583 (1973) (husbands of members of the military entitled to the same benefits as wives), in which she argued in favor of equal treatment. Has she modified this position in terms of the remedy that she suggested in *VMI*? The Court was not satisfied with the proposed VWIL because it would not have afforded women the same treatment as the men received at VMI. Yet, the Court was also unwilling to accept VMI's argument that it should not be required to admit women because to do so would require "drastic" changes in its program. As it said in footnote 19, "admitting women to VMI would undoubtedly require alterations necessary to afford members of each sex privacy from the other sex in living arrangements, and to adjust aspects of the physical training programs." Is this a recognition of the need to accommodate women's differences? Would admitting women to VMI without requiring some changes be setting the new women students up for failure because the system was created around male needs and capacities? Does this indicate a new equal protection standard for women which is either intermediate or strict scrutiny, with a remedial difference?

3. **The Rationales behind Single-sex Education.** In *VMI*, the Court rejected the state's claim that single sex education at VMI should be found constitutional because it promoted an important state policy of affording a range of educational opportunities to its citizens. The Court rejected this rationale on the grounds that the state had not shown that VMI was either created or maintained for the purpose of promoting diverse educational opportunities within the Commonwealth. For a thorough discussion of the history of VMI, *see* Dianne Avery, *Institutional Myths, Historical Narratives and Social Science Evidence*, 5 S. Cal. Review of L. & Women's Stud. 189 (1996). What would the state have needed to prove to the Court that it had created or supported VMI as a single-sex institution so as to provide a variety of educational programs? Remember that the Court stated, "However 'liberally' this plan serves the State's sons, it makes no provision whatever for her daughters." Would the presence of a parallel single-sex institution for women have been sufficient? Could the Commonwealth have created an institution that this Court would have found to be truly parallel?

Is the Court rejecting all single-sex, publicly funded education? Suppose that the state had claimed that women are more likely to volunteer in class, become institutional leaders, and take on challenges if they are not competing with men. Suppose that, because of this, it created an all-women's high school or college? Would such a program be constitutional under *MUW* and *VMI*? In 1996, District Four, in East Harlem, New York, opened a junior high school for girls named the Young Women's Leadership School. It stressed math and science, subjects in which girls have traditionally not performed well. The District's expectation was that girls would do better in these subjects if there were no boys in the classroom. If the Young Women's Leadership School was sued by the parents of a boy who wanted to attend, how would you expect the suit to be decided?

All-girls' schools or classes within coeducational schools are often defended either on the grounds that in coed settings boys win all the leadership positions and dominate the class's airtime, or on the grounds that girls learn better in settings that emphasize responsibilities to others over individual rights, understanding over testing, and collaboration over debate. However, there is some reason to think that these claims for all-girls' schools or courses are very specific to the lives of middle class white girls. Some studies show that lower class white and African American girls do not "lose their voices" as they enter adolescence. Think about your own experiences. Do any of these positions ring true? Can you identify the cultural feminist and dominance feminist positions on which these claims are based? Would you advocate holding sex discriminatory classifications in education to strict scrutiny or do you think that schools should have to accommodate women's "special needs"?

Just as there are advocates for all-girls educational settings, so there are supporters of all-boys schools. Although all-boys schools have had a much harder time surviving in recent years, some educators have been in favor of them as a way of teaching boys the positive aspects of the masculine ideal. In 1991, Detroit tried to create three, all-male high schools. These academies, primarily for African Americans, were intended to focus on male responsibility and to have an Afrocentric curriculum. They were developed in response to the high unemployment, dropout and homicide rates among young Black males. Despite this, the District Court held that the city had not proven that sex segregation was required to achieve the legitimate educational goals of the academies. Garrett v. Board of Educ., 775 F. Supp. 1004 (E.D.Mich.1991). If a sufficiently cogent case could not be made in this situation, do you think it is likely that the courts will find any factual setting convincing enough to warrant upholding single-sex education? *Garrett* was decided under the intermediate scrutiny test of *MUW*. Does that mean that single-sex programs are unlikely to pass constitutional muster even without the higher scrutiny that *VMI* may lead toward?

While some defend all-girls' schools or classes on the grounds that they will allow girls to develop their special capacities, others claim that single-sex education will simply reinscribe the worst aspects of gender stereotypes. Consider bell hooks's position in the following paragraph:

> Much of the recent emphasis on the need for special schools for black boys invests in a rhetoric of patriarchal thinking that uncritically embraces sexist-defined notions of manhood as the cure for all that ails black males. No one talks about the need

for black girls to have positive black male role models that would offer them the kind of affirmation and care that could enhance their self-esteem. No one insists that young black males need positive black female role models whom they respect and treat with regard. All the rhetoric that privileges the self-esteem of black male children over that of girls maintains and perpetuates the assumption that sexist-defined sex roles are healthy, are the key to creating a non-dysfunctional black family.... This seems especially significant since it was Daniel Patrick Moynihan who first suggested in his racist formulations of a theory of black matriarchy a sexist paradigm that would explain black male dysfunction by suggesting that they were castrated and emasculated by strong black females who prevented them from realizing manhood.... It is tragically ironic that black folks who once clearly saw the racism in this attempt to blame the problems black men face living in a white supremacist society on black females are now employing a similar mode of analysis.

bell hooks, *Killing Rage*, 89–90.

Do you agree with hooks that single sex education "uncritically embraces sexist-defined" gender ideals? Is this equally true regardless of whether the single-sex education is for boys or girls? Does hooks's analysis help us to recognize that there are positive and negative images of men (assertive and drifters) and that these images vary depending on race, class, national origin, sexual orientation, etc.? Can you articulate some of the conflicting gender images of women? How do these vary by race, ethnic group, religion, etc.?

After thinking about all of this, what is your position on the desirability of single-sex education?

For background information on the arguments for and against same sex education, *see* Mary F. Belenky, et al., *Women's Ways of Knowing* (1986); bell hooks, *Killing Rage* 89–91 (1995); Karen J. Maschke, *Educational Equity* (1997); Audrey T. McCluskey, *The Historical Context of the Single-Sex Schooling Debate Among African Americans*, 17 Western J. Black Stud. 193 (1993); Deborah Rhode, *Association and Assimilation*, 81 Nw. U. L. Rev. 106, 128–145 (1986); Roberta Tovey, *A Narrowly Gender-Based Model of Learning May End Up Cheating All Students*, Harvard Education Letter, July/August 1995 at 3.

Deborah L. Rhode, **Beginning at Birth**

From D. Rhode, Speaking of Sex.
(Cambridge: Harvard University Press, 1997).

...Athletics is one of the most powerful sources of gender socialization. An estimated thirty million young people participate in sports, and current programs institutionalize inequality. These programs offer fewer opportunities to female athletes than to males and promote damaging stereotypes of masculinity and femininity. Yet, ironically, our recent progress obscures the problems that remain. Opportunities for women athletes have improved so dramatically that we no longer notice what chances they are still missing.

Over the past quarter-century, the passage of antidiscrimination legislation, together with broader cultural changes in gender roles, has transformed women's sports. The number of female athletes in high school interscholastic competition increased from 300,000 (7 percent of all participants) in the early 1970s to over two million (38 percent) in the early 1990s. Girls who, in earlier eras, would have made do with gym classes in ring toss and rhythmic hula hooping now have options ranging from ice hockey to boxing. Women's field hockey teams that once practiced in parking lots can sometimes fill stadiums. Not always large stadiums; but as the 1996 Olympics demonstrated, at least some female athletic events rival their male counterparts in popular appeal.

Yet this striking progress masks equally striking inequalities. In high school, boys still receive disproportionate resources and have greater choices of sports. Girls have finally gotten "a foot in the door" of the gym, but often this happens only when boys aren't using it. At surveyed colleges where women constitute more than half the student body, they account for only a third of the athletes, a fourth of athletic dollars, and less than a fifth of recruiting expenditures. Women coach fewer than half of women's teams and about 1 percent of men's teams, and almost never head athletic programs. Women of color are even more sparsely represented at all coaching and administrative levels. By the mid–1990s, only one of some 600 institutions met the standard of gender equity established by the National Collegiate Athletic Association (NCAA): "fair and equitable distribution of overall athletic opportunities, benefits, and resources," and an absence of gender-based discrimination against athletes, coaches, and administrators.

What accounts for persistent inequalities is a matter of dispute. To many men, the disparities in opportunity simply reflect disparities in interest. From the perspective of most male athletic directors, further efforts to even out resources are unjust and ineffective, and jeopardize important revenue-producing programs like football and basketball. As one commentator puts it, "Equality of interest can never be legislated or enforced." Until society "undergoes a radical transformation," gender disparities will remain "a fact of American life."

Of course, this is the very claim that opponents of antidiscrimination guarantees have been making for the last two decades. Had that argument prevailed in legislative arenas, many female athletes would still be stuck with hula hoops. Until more proportionate opportunities are in place, we cannot really gauge male and female interest levels. Moreover, contrary to popular assumptions, men's football and basketball do not generate significant profits in the vast majority of athletic programs. Although successful male teams may increase revenue indirectly, by building community and alumni support, a school's competitive status is unlikely to suffer if *all* institutions attempt to narrow gender inequalities.

These inequalities involve more than resources. Many athletic programs indirectly compound gender bias in other ways, by giving female teams derivative and stereotypical names and by placing exaggerated importance on cheerleading. Female sporting events often feature zoologically bizarre competitions between beaverettes, lady panthers, and teddy bears. In most schools, these athletes receive less recognition than their cheerleading classmates. The number of cheerleaders continues to rise: in the mid–1990s it increased 20 percent, to well over three million. Although their routines have grown more athletic, their role remains derivative. Cheerleading is still an add-on to the main event. It involves girls applauding boys, and it rewards appearance as much as ability.

The resilience of traditional feminine stereotypes is equally apparent in our rankings of women's sports. It is hardly coincidental that the most popular female competitors are in areas like skating and gymnastics, which emphasize grace and beauty rather than power and aggression. These stereotypical preferences carry a cost. Spectators' preferences for pixie-like female gymnasts have placed those competitors at substantial physical risk. Because the sport now rewards extremely agile, lightweight athletes, girls begin intense training at young ages while their bodies are still developing. The result is a high incidence of injury, often with permanently debilitating consequences. The need to maintain abnormally low weights has also encouraged almost two-thirds of female gymnasts to develop eating disorders. By contrast, men's gymnastics, which rewards strength as well as agility, permits older competitors of normal weight, and carries far fewer risks.

Our preferences for stereotypically feminine athletes also impose substantial costs on lesbian athletes, coaches, and administrators. It is not surprising that rumors of lesbianism can severely damage athletic careers. What is striking, however, is the effort that often goes into avoiding such rumors. Some lesbian coaches have acquired husbands, and some female athletes have cultivated ludicrously seductive images. In one memorable example, college basketball players cast themselves as Playboy Bunnies, and posed in uniforms with floppy ears and rabbit tails. Widespread worries about sexual "deviance" prevent many athletes from expressing their sexual orientation—a fundamental aspect of human identity. And lesbian labels, whether accurate or not, often serve to punish as well as deter gender equity activists.

Yet while current athletic programs are still hostage to traditional understandings of femininity, they have at least loosened its constraints. Many girls now grow up with a sense of physical power and a taste for competition that undermines conventional stereotypes. Boys, however, receive no similarly mixed messages. Male athletics often exalts the worst aspects of traditional masculine stereotypes; it rewards aggression, brutality, and conquest.

From very early ages, most boys feel strong pressure to excel at sports. By adolescence, athletic achievement is the most crucial factor in determining status among classmates. We expect this experience to build character, foster teamwork, and promote health. We discount the ways that competition frequently ritualizes and rewards violence. In sports like football, boxing, and hockey, brutal body contact is an inherent part of the game. In many others, "borderline" violence is a common occurrence. Penalties for gratuitous aggression often are not severe enough to prevent it, particularly when fans enjoy the spectacle. There is more than a little truth to the clichés about hockey fans who go to see the fights and are slightly disappointed when a hockey game breaks out.

Media commentators and athletic coaches compound the problem. Dwelling on the "hits" and "hurts" is a common practice among sports reporters. A *New York Times Magazine* cover story recently increased the celebrity of Ulf Samuelson, the "most hated man in hockey." His achievements, which include permanently disabling several competitors, have resulted in a $2 million salary and no lack of professional opportunities. According to a senior league official, "There are twenty-six team managers, and twenty-five complain about him. And all twenty-five would take him in a heartbeat." If coaches prefer "winning ugly" to losing gracefully, many players feel pressure to oblige. Others enjoy the excuse to express their "manhood." As one professional hockey player puts it, "If you take the fighting out, what comes next ...? Pretty soon we will all be out there in dresses and skirts."

Such views help explain the frequency of physical injuries, homophobic attitudes, and misogynistic assumptions among male athletes. More than one-third of high school football players suffer serious injuries, and three-fourths of those who go on to professional leagues end up with permanent disabilities. Males who are reluctant to play through pain or who fail to show "appropriate" aggressiveness risk ridicule as "fags," "queers," "sissies," and "pussies." Telling a player that he "throws like a girl" or leaving sanitary napkins in his locker sends obvious messages about both the meaning of masculinity and the inferiority of women.

Given these messages, it is scarcely surprising that male athletes are disproportionately involved in sexual violence. In one representative study, college athletes were 40 percent more likely to be reported for rape than the average male student. Assaultive behavior receives ample encouragement from celebrities like Mike Tyson, who acknowledged: "I like to hurt women when I make love to them." Even athletes who don't endorse violence often contribute to attitudes that underlie it. When role models like Magic Johnson claim to have "accommodated as many floozies as I could," and Wilt Chamberlain reports scoring with "20,000 different ladies," these players reinforce prevailing views that women, like trophies, are objects for conquest.

Yet despite the systematic studies and the celebrated cases of athletes involved in sexual abuse, many men deny the problem. To competitors like professional football player Dan Wilkensen who face prosecution on such charges, these are "private matters," unworthy of public attention and unrelated to more systematic patterns. According to NCAA spokesmen, "it's unfair to single out athletes" for blame because only a small number are involved in reported offenses, and women who date high-profile sports "studs" should know what to expect. From the perspective of male coaches, it is equally unfair to blame sports for problems that have deeper cultural roots. As one National Football League administrator summarized prevailing views: "An athlete's attitude toward women comes not from his sport but from his life." But for players whose lives are bound up in sports, locker room values inevitably spill over to other settings. And reported offenses reflect only a small part of the problem. Most victims see no point in bringing charges of harassment or date rape that more often result in humiliation and retaliation against the complainant than in serious sanctions against the athlete.

To make significant changes in sports culture is no insignificant task. But there are some obvious places to start. Promoting greater equality in athletic opportunities will require stronger enforcement of Title IX of the Civil Rights Act, which prohibits sex-based discrimination by schools receiving federal funds. Reducing violence and sexual abuse will require increased penalties. Serious violations should result in serious sanctions, such as forfeitures of games, removal of players, and significant monetary fines. What counts as a "serious" abuse also needs to change. A penalty structure that imposes higher fines for abusing equipment than for sexually harassing female reporters contributes more to the problem than to the solution. Sports leaders should also encourage and participate in the growing number of programs aimed at reducing sexual violence, gender bias, and homophobia among athletes. Finally, more attention, both positive and negative, should center on conduct apart from winning. Coaches and players who engage in abusive behavior should not be rewarded with raises, commercial endorsements, and recognition in sporting halls of fame.

Eliminating gender bias in athletics means not just equalizing opportunities but also transforming them—and developing less combative and commercial alternatives. More athletes need to see sportsmanship as a core value, not a corny anachronism invoked at banquets and ignored in dugouts. If we want to change our cultural definitions of masculinity and femininity, we need also to change our cultural values in sports.

Cohen v. Brown University

United States Court of Appeals, First Circuit, 1996.
101 F.3d 155, cert. denied, ___ U.S. ___, 117 S.Ct. 1469, 137 L.Ed.2d 682 (1997).

HUGH H. BOWNES, SENIOR CIRCUIT JUDGE.

This is a class action lawsuit charging Brown University, its president, and its athletics director (collectively "Brown") with discrimination against women in the operation of its intercollegiate athletics program, in violation of Title IX of the Education Amendments of 1972.... The plaintiff class comprises all present, future, and potential Brown University women students who participate, seek to participate, and/or are deterred from participating in intercollegiate athletics funded by Brown.

This suit was initiated in response to the demotion in May 1991 of Brown's women's gymnastics and volleyball teams from university-funded varsity status to donor-funded varsity status. Contemporaneously, Brown demoted two men's teams, water polo and golf, from university-funded to donor-funded varsity status. As a consequence of these demotions, all four teams lost, not only their university funding, but most of the support and privileges that accompany university-funded varsity status at Brown....

[A]fter hearing fourteen days of testimony, the district court granted plaintiffs' motion for a preliminary injunction, ordering, inter alia, that the women's gymnastics and volleyball teams be reinstated to university-funded varsity status, and prohibiting Brown from eliminating or reducing the status or funding of any existing women's intercollegiate varsity team until the case was resolved on the merits. ("Cohen I "). A panel of this court affirmed the district court's decision ... ("Cohen II "). On remand, the district court determined after a lengthy bench trial that Brown's intercollegiate athletics program violates Title IX and its supporting regulations. ("Cohen III "). This appeal followed ...

As a Division I institution within the National Collegiate Athletic Association ("NCAA") with respect to all sports but football, Brown participates at the highest level of NCAA competition. Brown operates a two-tiered intercollegiate athletics program with respect to funding: although Brown provides the financial resources required to maintain its university-funded varsity teams, donor-funded varsity athletes must themselves raise the funds necessary to support their teams through private donations. The district court noted that the four demoted teams were eligible for NCAA competition, provided that they were able to raise the funds necessary to maintain a sufficient level of competitiveness, and provided that they continued to comply with NCAA requirements. The court found, however, that it is difficult for donor-funded varsity athletes to maintain a level of competitiveness commensurate with their abilities and that these athletes operate at a competitive disadvantage in comparison to university-funded varsity athletes....

Brown's decision to demote the women's volleyball and gymnastics teams and the men's water polo and golf teams from university-funded varsity status was apparently made in response to a university-wide cost-cutting directive. The district court found that Brown saved $62,028 by demoting the women's teams and $15,795 by demoting the men's teams, but that the demotions "did not appreciably affect the athletic participation gender ratio."

Plaintiffs alleged that, at the time of the demotions, the men students at Brown already enjoyed the benefits of a disproportionately large share of both the university resources allocated to athletics and the intercollegiate participation opportunities afforded to student athletes. Thus, plaintiffs contended, what appeared to be the even-handed demotions of two men's and two women's teams, in fact, perpetuated Brown's discriminatory treatment of women in the administration of its intercollegiate athletics program.

In the course of the preliminary injunction hearing, the district court found that, in the academic year 1990–91, Brown funded 31 intercollegiate varsity teams, 16 men's teams and 15 women's teams, and that, of the 894 undergraduate students competing on these teams, 63.3% (566) were men and 36.7% (328) were women. During the same academic year, Brown's undergraduate enrollment comprised 52.4% (2,951) men and 47.6% (2,683) women. The district court also summarized the history of athletics at Brown, finding, inter alia, that, while nearly all of the men's varsity teams were established before 1927, virtually all of the women's varsity teams were created between 1971 and 1977, after Brown's merger with Pembroke College. The only women's varsity team created after this period was winter track, in 1982. . . .

At the time of trial, Brown offered 479 university-funded varsity positions for men, as compared to 312 for women; and 76 donor-funded varsity positions for men, as compared to 30 for women. In 1993–94, then, Brown's varsity program—including both university-and donor-funded sports—afforded over 200 more positions for men than for women. Accordingly, the district court found that Brown maintained a 13.01% disparity between female participation in intercollegiate athletics and female student enrollment, and that "[a]lthough the number of varsity sports offered to men and women are equal, the selection of sports offered to each gender generates far more individual positions for male athletes than for female athletes." . . .

Title IX provides that "[n]o person in the United States shall, on the basis of sex, be excluded from participation in, be denied the benefits of, or be subjected to discrimination under any education program or activity receiving Federal financial assistance." As a private institution that receives federal financial assistance, Brown is required to comply with Title IX.

Title IX also specifies that its prohibition against gender discrimination shall not "be interpreted to require any educational institution to grant preferential or disparate treatment to the members of one sex on account of an imbalance which may exist" between the total number or percentage of persons of that sex participating in any federally supported program or activity, and "the total number or percentage of persons of that sex in any community, State, section, or other area." 20 U.S.C.A. § 1681(b) (West 1990). Subsection (b) also provides, however, that it "shall not be construed to prevent the consideration in any . . . proceeding under this chapter of statistical evidence tending to show that such an imbalance exists with respect to the participation in, or receipt of the benefits of, any such program or activity by the members of one sex." . . .

The agency responsible for administering Title IX is the United States Department of Education ("DED"), through its Office for Civil Rights ("OCR"). The regulation at issue in this case, 34 C.F.R. § 106.41 (1995), provides:

(a) General. No person shall, on the basis of sex, be excluded from participation in, be denied the benefits of, be treated differently from another person or otherwise be discriminated against in any interscholastic, intercollegiate, club or intramural athletics offered by a recipient, and no recipient shall provide any such athletics separately on such basis.

(b) Separate teams. Notwithstanding the requirements of paragraph (a) of this section, a recipient may operate or sponsor separate teams for members of each sex where selection of such teams is based upon competitive skill or the activity involved is a contact sport. However, where a recipient operates or sponsors a team in a particular sport for members of one sex but operates or sponsors no such team for members of the other sex, and athletic opportunities for members of that sex have previously been limited, members of the excluded sex must be allowed to try-out for the team offered unless the sport involved is a contact sport. For the purposes of this part, contact sports include boxing, wrestling, rugby, ice hockey, football, basketball and other sports the purpose or major activity of which involves bodily contact.

(c) Equal Opportunity. A recipient which operates or sponsors interscholastic, intercollegiate, club or intramural athletics shall provide equal athletic opportunity for members of both sexes. In determining whether equal opportunities are available the Director will consider, among other factors:

(1) Whether the selection of sports and levels of competition effectively accommodate the interests and abilities of members of both sexes;

(2) The provision of equipment and supplies;

(3) Scheduling of games and practice time;

(4) Travel and per diem allowance;

(5) Opportunity to receive coaching and academic tutoring;

(6) Assignment and compensation for coaches and tutors;

(7) Provision of locker rooms, practice and competitive facilities;

(8) Provision of medical and training facilities and services;

(9) Provision of housing and dining facilities and services;

(10) Publicity. . . .

In 1978, several years after the promulgation of the regulations, OCR published a proposed "Policy Interpretation," the purpose of which was to clarify the obligations of federal aid recipients under Title IX to provide equal opportunities in athletics programs. . . . The Policy Interpretation establishes a three-part test . . . [to] be considered in determining compliance under 34 C.F.R. § 106.41(c)(1). . . . [T]he . . . three-part test . . . follows:

(1) Whether intercollegiate level participation opportunities for male and female students are provided in numbers substantially proportionate to their respective enrollments; or

(2) Where the members of one sex have been and are underrepresented among intercollegiate athletes, whether the institution can show a history and continuing practice of program expansion which is demonstrably responsive to the developing interest and abilities of the members of that sex; or

(3) Where the members of one sex are underrepresented among inter-collegiate athletes, and the institution cannot show a continuing practice of program expansion such as that cited above, whether it can be demonstrat-ed that the interests and abilities of the members of that sex have been fully and effectively accommodated by the present program.

The district court held that, "because Brown maintains a 13.01% disparity between female participation in intercollegiate athletics and fe-male student enrollment, it cannot gain the protection of prong one." Nor did Brown satisfy prong two. While acknowledging that Brown "has an impressive history of program expansion," the district court found that Brown failed to demonstrate that it has "maintained a continuing practice of intercollegiate program expansion for women, the underrepresented sex." The court noted further that, because merely reducing program offerings to the overrepresented gender does not constitute program expan-sion for the underrepresented gender, the fact that Brown has eliminated or demoted several men's teams does not amount to a continuing practice of program expansion for women. As to prong three, the district court found that Brown had not "fully and effectively accommodated the interest and ability of the underrepresented sex 'to the extent necessary to provide equal opportunity in the selection of sports and levels of competition available to members of both sexes.' " . . .

Brown contends that an athletics program equally accommodates both genders and complies with Title IX if it accommodates the relative interests and abilities of its male and female students. This "relative interests" approach posits that an institution satisfies prong three of the three-part test by meeting the interests and abilities of the underrepresented gender only to the extent that it meets the interests and abilities of the overrepre-sented gender.

Brown maintains that the district court's decision imposes upon uni-versities the obligation to engage in preferential treatment for women by requiring quotas in excess of women's relative interests and abilities. With respect to prong three, Brown asserts that the district court's interpreta-tion of the word "fully" "requires universities to favor women's teams and treat them better than men's [teams]. . . . forces them to eliminate or cap men's teams. . . . [and] forces universities to impose athletic quotas in excess of relative interests and abilities."

The prior panel considered and rejected Brown's approach, observing that "Brown reads the 'full' out of the duty to accommodate 'fully and effectively.' " . . . [P]rong three "demands not merely some accommoda-tion, but full and effective accommodation. If there is sufficient interest and ability among members of the statistically underrepresented gender, not slaked by existing programs, an institution necessarily fails this prong of the test."

Brown's interpretation of full and effective accommodation is "simply not the law." We agree with the prior panel and the district court that Brown's relative interests approach "cannot withstand scrutiny on either legal or policy grounds," because it "disadvantages women and undermines the remedial purposes of Title IX by limiting required program expansion for the underrepresented sex to the status quo level of relative interests." After Cohen II, it cannot be maintained that the relative interests approach is compatible with Title IX's equal accommodation principle as it has been interpreted by this circuit.

Brown argues that the district court's interpretation of the three-part test requires numerical proportionality, thus imposing a gender-based quota scheme . . .

[T]he three-part test . . . does not require preferential or disparate treatment for either gender. Neither the Policy Interpretation's three-part test, nor the district court's interpretation of it, mandates statistical balancing; "[r]ather, the policy interpretation merely creates a presumption that a school is in compliance with Title IX and the applicable regulation when it achieves such a statistical balance."

. . . As previously noted, Cohen II expressly held that "a court assessing Title IX compliance may not find a violation solely because there is a disparity between the gender composition of an educational institution's student constituency, on the one hand, and its athletic programs, on the other hand." The panel then carefully delineated the burden of proof, which requires a Title IX plaintiff to show, not only "disparity between the gender composition of the institution's student body and its athletic program, thereby proving that there is an underrepresented gender," but also "that a second element—unmet interest—is present," meaning that the underrepresented gender has not been fully and effectively accommodated by the institution's present athletic program. Only where the plaintiff meets the burden of proof on these elements and the institution fails to show as an affirmative defense a history and continuing practice of program expansion responsive to the interests and abilities of the underrepresented gender will liability be established. Surely this is a far cry from a one-step imposition of a gender-based quota.

Brown simply ignores the fact that it is required to accommodate fully the interests and abilities of the underrepresented gender, not because the three-part test mandates preferential treatment for women ab initio, but because Brown has been found (under prong one) to have allocated its athletics participation opportunities so as to create a significant gender-based disparity with respect to these opportunities, and has failed (under prong two) to show a history and continuing practice of expansion of opportunities for the underrepresented gender. Brown's interpretation conflates prongs one and three and distorts the three-part test by reducing it to an abstract, mechanical determination of strict numerical proportionality. In short, Brown treats the three-part test for compliance as a one-part test for strict liability.

Brown also fails to recognize that Title IX's remedial focus is, quite properly, not on the overrepresented gender, but on the underrepresented gender; in this case, women. Title IX and its implementing regulations protect the class for whose special benefit the statute was enacted. It is women and not men who have historically and who continue to be under-represented in sports, not only at Brown, but at universities nationwide.

The prior panel held that "[t]he fact that the overrepresented gender is less than fully accommodated will not, in and of itself, excuse a shortfall in the provision of opportunities for the underrepresented gender." Instead, the law requires that, absent a demonstration of continuing program expansion for the underrepresented gender under prong two of the three-part test, an institution must either provide athletics opportunities in proportion to the gender composition of the student body so as to satisfy prong one, or fully accommodate the interests and abilities of athletes of the underrepresented gender under prong three....

We think it clear that neither the Title IX framework nor the district court's interpretation of it mandates a gender-based quota scheme. In our view, it is Brown's relative interests approach to the three-part test, rather than the district court's interpretation, that contravenes the language and purpose of the test and of the statute itself. To adopt the relative interests approach would be, not only to overrule Cohen II, but to rewrite the enforcing agency's interpretation of its own regulation so as to incorporate an entirely different standard for Title IX compliance. This relative interests standard would entrench and fix by law the significant gender-based disparity in athletics opportunities found by the district court to exist at Brown, a finding we have held to be not clearly erroneous. According to Brown's relative interests interpretation of the equal accommodation principle, the gender-based disparity in athletics participation opportunities at Brown is due to a lack of interest on the part of its female students, rather than to discrimination, and any attempt to remedy the disparity is, by definition, an unlawful quota. This approach is entirely contrary to "Congress's unmistakably clear mandate that educational institutions not use federal monies to perpetuate gender-based discrimination," and makes it virtually impossible to effectuate Congress's intent to eliminate sex discrimination in intercollegiate athletics....

Brown also claims error in the district court's failure to apply Title VII standards to its analysis of whether Brown's intercollegiate athletics program complies with Title IX. The district court rejected the analogy to Title VII, noting that, while Title VII "seeks to determine whether gender-neutral job openings have been filled without regard to gender[,] Title IX ... was designed to address the reality that sports teams, unlike the vast majority of jobs, do have official gender requirements, and this statute accordingly approaches the concept of discrimination differently from Title VII." ...

It is imperative to recognize that athletics presents a distinctly different situation from admissions and employment and requires a different analysis in order to determine the existence vel non of discrimination. While the Title IX regime permits institutions to maintain gender-segregated teams, the law does not require that student-athletes attending institutions receiving federal funds must compete on gender-segregated teams; nor does the law require that institutions provide completely gender-integrated athletics programs. To the extent that Title IX allows institutions to maintain single-sex teams and gender-segregated athletics programs, men and women do not compete against each other for places on team rosters. Accordingly, and notwithstanding Brown's protestations to the contrary, the Title VII concept of the "qualified pool" has no place in a Title IX analysis of equal opportunities for male and female athletes because women are not "qualified" to compete for positions on men's teams, and vice-versa. In addition, the concept of "preference" does not have the same meaning, or raise the same equality concerns, as it does in the employment and admissions contexts.

Brown's approach fails to recognize that, because gender-segregated teams are the norm in intercollegiate athletics programs, athletics differs from admissions and employment in analytically material ways. In providing for gender-segregated teams, intercollegiate athletics programs necessarily allocate opportunities separately for male and female students, and, thus, any inquiry into a claim of gender discrimination must compare the athletics participation opportunities provided for men with those provided for women. For this reason, and because recruitment of interested athletes is at the discretion of the institution, there is a risk that the institution will recruit only enough women to fill positions in a program that already under represents women, and that the smaller size of the women's program will have the effect of discouraging women's participation.

In this unique context, Title IX operates to ensure that the gender-segregated allocation of athletics opportunities does not disadvantage either gender. Rather than create a quota or preference, this unavoidably gender-conscious comparison merely provides for the allocation of athletics resources and participation opportunities between the sexes in a non-discriminatory manner. As the Seventh Circuit observed, "Congress itself recognized that addressing discrimination in athletics presented a unique set of problems not raised in areas such as employment and academics."

In contrast to the employment and admissions contexts, in the athletics context, gender is not an irrelevant characteristic. Courts and institutions must have some way of determining whether an institution complies with the mandate of Title IX and its supporting regulations to provide equal athletics opportunities for both genders, despite the fact that the institution maintains single-sex teams, and some way of fashioning a remedy upon a determination that the institution does not equally and effectively accommodate the interests and abilities of both genders. . . .

We find no error in the district court's refusal to apply Title VII standards in its inquiry into whether Brown's intercollegiate athletics program complies with Title IX. We conclude that the district court's application of the three-part test does not create a gender-based quota and is consistent with Title IX, 34 C.F.R. § 106.41, the Policy Interpretation, and the mandate of Cohen II. . . .

Brown has contended throughout this litigation that the significant disparity in athletics opportunities for men and women at Brown is the result of a gender-based differential in the level of interest in sports and that the district court's application of the three-part test requires universities to provide athletics opportunities for women to an extent that exceeds their relative interests and abilities in sports. Thus, at the heart of this litigation is the question whether Title IX permits Brown to deny its female students equal opportunity to participate in sports, based upon its unproven assertion that the district court's finding of a significant disparity in athletics opportunities for male and female students reflects, not discrimination in Brown's intercollegiate athletics program, but a lack of interest on the part of its female students that is unrelated to a lack of opportunities.

We view Brown's argument that women are less interested than men in participating in intercollegiate athletics, as well as its conclusion that institutions should be required to accommodate the interests and abilities of its female students only to the extent that it accommodates the interests and abilities of its male students, with great suspicion. To assert that Title IX permits institutions to provide fewer athletics participation opportunities for women than for men, based upon the premise that women are less interested in sports than are men, is (among other things) to ignore the fact that Title IX was enacted in order to remedy discrimination that results from stereotyped notions of women's interests and abilities.

Interest and ability rarely develop in a vacuum; they evolve as a function of opportunity and experience. The Policy Interpretation recognizes that women's lower rate of participation in athletics reflects women's historical lack of opportunities to participate in sports. . . .

[T]here exists the danger that, rather than providing a true measure of women's interest in sports, statistical evidence purporting to reflect women's interest instead provides only a measure of the very discrimination that is and has been the basis for women's lack of opportunity to participate in sports. Prong three requires some kind of evidence of interest in athletics, and the Title IX framework permits the use of statistical evidence in assessing the level of interest in sports. Nevertheless, to allow a numbers-based lack-of-interest defense to become the instrument of further discrimination against the underrepresented gender would pervert the remedial purpose of Title IX. We conclude that, even if it can be empirically demonstrated that, at a particular time, women have less interest in sports than do men, such evidence, standing alone, cannot justify providing fewer athletics opportunities for women than for men. Furthermore, such evidence is completely irrelevant where, as here, viable and successful women's varsity teams have been demoted or eliminated. . . .

Brown's relative interests approach is not a reasonable interpretation of the three-part test. This approach contravenes the purpose of the statute and the regulation because it does not permit an institution or a district court to remedy a gender-based disparity in athletics participation opportunities. Instead, this approach freezes that disparity by law, thereby disadvantaging further the underrepresented gender. Had Congress intended to entrench, rather than change, the status quo—with its historical emphasis on men's participation opportunities to the detriment of women's opportunities—it need not have gone to all the trouble of enacting Title IX. . . .

It does not follow from our statutory and constitutional analyses that we endorse the district court's remedial order. Although we decline Brown's invitation to find that the district court's remedy was an abuse of discretion, we do find that the district court erred in substituting its own specific relief in place of Brown's statutorily permissible proposal to comply with Title IX by cutting men's teams until substantial proportionality was achieved. . . .

[W]e first examine the compliance plan Brown submitted to the district court in response to its order. We then consider the district court's order rejecting Brown's plan and the specific relief ordered by the court in its place.

Brown's proposed compliance plan stated its goal as follows:

The plan has one goal: to make the gender ratio among University-funded teams at Brown substantially proportionate to the gender ratio of the undergraduate student body. To do so, the University must disregard the expressed athletic interests of one gender while providing advantages for others. The plan focuses only on University-funded sports, ignoring the long history of successful donor-funded student teams.

In its introduction, Brown makes clear that it "would prefer to maintain its current program" and that the plan submitted

is inconsistent with Brown's philosophy to the extent that it grants advantages and enforces disadvantages upon student athletes solely because of their gender and curbs the historic role of coaches in determining the number of athletes which can be provided an opportunity to participate. Nevertheless, the University wishes to act in good faith with the order of the Court, notwithstanding issues of fact and law which are currently in dispute.

Brown states that it "seeks to address the issue of proportionality while minimizing additional undue stress on already strained physical and fiscal resources."

The general provisions of the plan may be summarized as follows: (i) Maximum squad sizes for men's teams will be set and enforced. (ii) Head coaches of all teams must field squads that meet minimum size requirements. (iii) No additional discretionary funds will be used for athletics. (iv) Four new women's junior varsity teams—basketball, lacrosse, soccer, and tennis—will be university-funded. (v) Brown will make explicit a de facto junior varsity team for women's field hockey.

The plan sets forth nine steps for its implementation, and concludes that "if the Court determines that this plan is not sufficient to reach proportionality, phase two will be the elimination of one or more men's teams."

The district court found Brown's plan to be "fatally flawed" for two reasons. First, despite the fact that 76 men and 30 women participated on donor-funded varsity teams, Brown's proposed plan disregarded donor-funded varsity teams. Second, Brown's plan "artificially boosts women's varsity numbers by adding junior varsity positions on four women's teams." As to the propriety of Brown's proposal to come into compliance by the addition of junior varsity positions, the district court held:

Positions on distinct junior varsity squads do not qualify as "intercollegiate competition" opportunities under the Policy Interpretation and should not be included in defendants' plan. As noted in Cohen, "intercollegiate" teams are those that "regularly participate in varsity competition." Junior varsity squads, by definition, do not meet this criterion. Counting new women's junior varsity positions as equivalent to men's full varsity positions flagrantly violates the spirit and letter of Title IX; in no sense is an institution providing equal opportunity if it affords varsity positions to men but junior varsity positions to women. . . .

After rejecting Brown's proposed plan, but bearing in mind Brown's stated objectives, the district court fashioned its own remedy:

. . . In order to bring Brown into compliance with prong one under defendants' Phase II, I would have to order Brown to cut enough men's teams to eradicate approximately 213 men's varsity positions. This extreme action is entirely unnecessary. The easy answer lies in ordering Brown to comply with prong three by upgrading the women's gymnastics, fencing, skiing, and water polo teams to university-funded varsity status. In this way, Brown could easily achieve prong three's standard of "full and effective accommodation of the underrepresented sex." This remedy would entail upgrading the positions of approximately 40 women. In order to finance the 40 additional women's positions, Brown certainly will not have to eliminate as many as the 213 men's positions that would be cut under Brown's Phase II proposal. Thus, Brown will fully comply with Title IX by meeting the standards of prong three, without approaching satisfaction of the standards of prong one. . . .

We agree with the district court that Brown's proposed plan fell short of a good faith effort to meet the requirements of Title IX as explicated by this court in Cohen II and as applied by the district court on remand. Indeed, the plan is replete with argumentative statements more appropriate for an appellate brief. It is obvious that Brown's plan was addressed to this court, rather than to offering a workable solution to a difficult problem.

It is clear, nevertheless, that Brown's proposal to cut men's teams is a permissible means of effectuating compliance with the statute. Thus, although we understand the district court's reasons for substituting its own specific relief under the circumstances at the time, and although the district court's remedy is within the statutory margins and constitutional, we think that the district court was wrong to reject out-of-hand Brown's alternative plan to reduce the number of men's varsity teams. After all, the district court itself stated that one of the compliance options available to

Brown under Title IX is to "demote or eliminate the requisite number of men's positions." Our respect for academic freedom and reluctance to interject ourselves into the conduct of university affairs counsels that we give universities as much freedom as possible in conducting their operations consonant with constitutional and statutory limits.

Brown therefore should be afforded the opportunity to submit another plan for compliance with Title IX. . . .

There can be no doubt that Title IX has changed the face of women's sports as well as our society's interest in and attitude toward women athletes and women's sports. . . . In addition, there is ample evidence that increased athletics participation opportunities for women and young girls, available as a result of Title IX enforcement, have had salutary effects in other areas of societal concern.

One need look no further than the impressive performances of our country's women athletes in the 1996 Olympic Summer Games to see that Title IX has had a dramatic and positive impact on the capabilities of our women athletes, particularly in team sports. These Olympians represent the first full generation of women to grow up under the aegis of Title IX. The unprecedented success of these athletes is due, in no small measure, to Title IX's beneficent effects on women's sports, as the athletes themselves have acknowledged time and again. What stimulated this remarkable change in the quality of women's athletic competition was not a sudden, anomalous upsurge in women's interest in sports, but the enforcement of Title IX's mandate of gender equity in sports.

Affirmed in part, reversed in part, and remanded for further proceedings. . . .

Note: Cheering on Women and Girls in Sports: Using Title IX to Fight Gender Role Oppression

110 Harv. L. Rev. 1627 (1997).

Women and girls across the United States, spurred by the opportunities created by Title IX of the Education Amendments of 1972, are playing sports in record numbers. More than 135,000 women currently participate in college sports, up from 30,000 in 1971. Close to 2.4 million girls play organized high school sports, up from 300,000 in 1971. A much greater number of young girls play in recreational sports leagues.

Although this trend has recently received extensive popular media coverage, feminist legal theorists have yet to give sustained attention to the ways in which women's and girls' participation in sports challenges the systemic gender role oppression that perpetuates gender inequality. Rather, they have focused either on how women can best use or modify Title IX to create more sports opportunities or on how women can bring their unique perspectives to sports, thereby insulating themselves from those aspects of sports which further male domination. Thus, these theorists are stuck in the classic struggle between liberal and difference feminism, which characterizes other debates about women's relationships to society and the law. These views of sports as a vehicle either to gain access to male structures or to emphasize women's unique perspectives ignore the role sports can play both in enriching women's everyday lives and in changing the ways girls and boys are socialized.

This Note develops a theory of empowerment and resocialization through sports—a theory that recognizes the multiple ways in which sports shape society, and provides concrete means to challenge gender role oppression. . . .

Fighting the Backlash

The United States sent more female athletes to the 1996 Summer Olympics than ever before. News media coverage focused on this development, symbolized by the image of four-foot-nine, eighty-pound gymnast Kerri Strug, who, urged on by her burly coach, sacrificed her body to perform her last vault for the gold-medal-winning United States women's gymnastics team. Footage and photographs of Strug completing her last vault, being carried from the arena, and receiving her medal appeared repeatedly alongside footage and photographs of the gold-medal-winning United States women's basketball, softball, and soccer teams. Strug's ginger foot was constantly present, reminding the American public that female frailty, delicacy, and dependency exists even amid the power and strength exhibited by female athletes.

This portrayal of Strug suggests that, despite the record number of female participants in last summer's Olympics, the American public has not yet become comfortable with the ways in which female athletes challenge traditional notions of femininity and masculinity. Female athletes in the United States have historically faced resistance, even outright hostility, for not confining themselves to "feminine" activities. Most often, this resistance has manifested itself through the nullification of female strength: female athletes were often ignored or sexualized, with the result that their threat to masculinity was negated. Rather than eliminating the nullification of female strength, Title IX increased the need for nullification as a means of preserving the traditional gender order.

Indeed, as an increasing number of women and girls participate in sports, they are experiencing a social backlash, arising in part from a desire to preserve an ideology of male superiority that women threaten by invading the domain of the "strong" sex. This backlash takes three forms. First, women's sports continue to be minimized and trivialized by unequal media coverage and community support. Second, female athletes are increasingly sexualized by the media, local communities, and even themselves in an effort to minimize the threat they pose to traditional concepts of femininity and masculinity. Finally, female athletes are increasingly portrayed as gaining sports opportunities only at the expense of funding for male athletes. A feminist legal theory of sports can help women and girls fight this backlash and gain the attention, respect, and funding they deserve. . . .

The Beginning of a Theory of Empowerment and Resocialization Through Sports

The power of Title IX lies in its ability to change both women's and girls' everyday lives and the ways men and women interact in society. The backlash identified above, to the contrary, has the potential to preserve traditional gender roles and relations, thereby diffusing the power of Title IX. Feminist legal approaches to sports can help women and girls overcome this threat and reap the potential benefits of Title IX.

Limits of Current Theoretical Approaches

. . .Advocates of the passage of Title IX were motivated in large part by liberal feminist theory. Indeed, Title IX was like almost all of the other feminist reforms of the 1960s and early 1970s, in that its goals were to provide access to traditionally male structures, and to provide equality of opportunity once inside. Proponents argued that, whenever schools and colleges offered boys' and men's sports, girls and women should have sports opportunities in proportion to their numbers. Further, proponents suggested that equal access requires that girls' and women's sports receive funding, facilities, coaching, and other support on a par with boys' and men's sports.

At the same time, though, the liberal feminist approach to sports, as embodied in the passage and enforcement of Title IX, provides little justification for why girls and women should play sports, beyond the fact that boys and men do. Indeed, sports seemed valuable to the proponents of Title IX only because sports were a male preserve from which women were excluded. Liberal feminists have not explained why women and girls should want to participate in the structure of high school and college sports—a structure that had defined itself in part by excluding women and, for many years, people of color. Moreover, they have not considered that women and girls may experience sports differently from men and boys because of their historical exclusion and that, once inside, women and girls may simply perpetuate exclusionary practices against other groups as well as themselves.

Feminists who take either a difference or dominance feminist approach to sports have attempted to answer some of these questions. Many of their answers consist of critiques of liberal feminist legal approaches to sports. Both difference and dominance feminists argue that Title IX has done nothing to change the structures, practices, or policies of sports at the vast majority of high schools and colleges. Rather, they argue, Title IX simply lets women and girls join in.

Further, difference and dominance feminists argue that those who do join in are complicit in structures, practices, and policies that discriminate against women in at least three ways. First, Title IX benefits white women more than it does women of color, because white women attend college in much larger numbers than do women of color. Moreover, many colleges and universities have complied with Title IX by adding women's sports, such as golf, squash, and tennis, which are played predominantly by white women. Second, Title IX has squeezed out many female coaches and administrators by making the coaching and administration of women's sports more prestigious, and hence more attractive to male coaches and administrators. Finally, and most importantly, Title IX has done little to change an athletic culture that polarizes the sexes and perpetuates male domination. Athletic success is still equated with masculinity, and women and girls must "choose between being a successful girl and being a successful athlete." When taken together, these facts suggest that Title IX has not dramatically altered the underlying sentiments that kept women and girls out of sports in the first place.

In addition to difference and dominance feminists' critique of the liberal feminist approach, difference feminists have posited affirmative reasons that women and girls should participate in sports, reasons beyond the mere fact that men and boys play sports. They argue that sports nurture and reinforce the cooperation and relationship skills that women already possess. If women are given opportunities to participate in sports on their own terms, as opposed to the male model that Title IX de facto adopted, they can exhibit these cooperation and relationship skills to the world and serve as models for an alternative social structure that is built on these qualities. Women can thereby transform the "ideology of meritocracy" that equates success, in sports and beyond, with masculine strength and domination.

However, the difference feminist approach does not address how sports can be valuable to individual women and girls. If sports only reinforce skills that women and girls already possess, they do not need to engage in sports to reap these benefits. Moreover, difference feminists do not believe that individual women benefit from the symbolism that often accompanies women's and girls' participation in structures that previously excluded them. Indeed, unless women's and girls' participation can transform those structures, participation only taints the skills that women already possess. Therefore, the difference feminist approach does not provide any reason that individual girls can benefit from playing with or like the boys.

Toward a Theory of Empowerment Through Sports

Women and girls can in fact benefit from playing with and like men and boys. To some extent, women and girls can profit from breaking down stereotypes that continue to keep them out of sports. But even more directly, they can empower themselves by developing the confidence and self-esteem that they will need to succeed in school, the workplace, and the rest of their lives.

Sports help many women and girls gain more confidence in their everyday interactions. As most girls enter adolescence, they begin to believe that they are valued more for their relationships with others than for their intrinsic beings. Girls therefore learn to silence personal opinions and preferences in an effort to avoid conflict that could threaten their personal relationships. In the process, they come to define themselves in relation to others and to lose confidence in themselves as independent beings. Participation in sports can help girls overcome this disabling crisis in confidence. Sports can increase girls' feeling of self-worth by providing them a forum in which to learn how to assert themselves and, in team sports, to do so when others are relying on them. Moreover, sports can help girls realize and accept that, although some aspects of life are unavoidable, others are within their own control. Sports can therefore serve as an important means of survival in a society that attempts to define individual women and girls in relation to others.

Another way sports can increase the confidence of women and girls is by helping them develop better relationships with their bodies. Generally, men and women learn to experience their bodies differently. Most boys are socialized to play rough and take physical risks; girls, to play it safe and not hurt themselves. This mentality is rooted in the high value society places on women's, as opposed to men's, physical appearance. Girls are taught to maintain their appearance and to protect themselves from any activity that could mar it. As such, girls traditionally are discouraged from playing sports, and many girls lack the individual desire to play sports, especially once they reach adolescence. This lack of participation, in turn, leads to a vicious circle. Because women and girls see few of their peers playing sports, they assume that they are too weak and frail to play. Yet women and girls who actually play sports realize both that they are not weak and that they can survive any departures from bodily perfection. Sports can therefore help girls to value their bodies, and the power of their bodies, even when those bodies are not what they consider to be physically perfect.

Toward a Theory of Resocialization Through Sports

In addition to providing a source of individual survival strategies and empowerment, sports can also give women and girls the ability to transform existing social structures. First, by participating in sports, women and girls can learn valuable teamwork skills. This cooperative aspect of playing team sports can help women and girls work better with others, both in the classroom and in professional institutions generally.

Second, if more girls play sports with boys at an early age, boys and girls will necessarily view each other differently from the way they currently do. If girls always participate with the boys in youth soccer leagues and the like, men may come to see women's participation in professional institutions as a given. Girls may also learn to view boys as less intimidating, which would provide them with the confidence and skills necessary to succeed within professional institutions in later life. Moreover, this increased confidence will reinforce men's acceptance of women's participation. And once the people within these institutions have changed, the institutions themselves will be more susceptible to change. Hence, integrating sports at an early age has the potential to change the nature of gender hierarchy.

Using the Theory to Achieve the Goals of Title IX

Recently, colleges and universities have complained that the enforcement of Title IX has gone far enough. Title IX has encouraged colleges and universities to create and expand sports opportunities for women, with the result that thirty-six percent of college athletes nationwide are women. This percentage roughly equals the percentage of high school athletes who are girls. College and universities argue that they have met the athletic interests of their female students and should not be required under Title IX to provide them with any additional sports opportunities. Indeed, one university recently argued that forcing it to do so would smack of quotas and would unjustly harm male students who are genuinely interested in playing sports.

Four circuit courts, however, have ruled otherwise. These courts have held that Title IX requires colleges and universities to provide sports opportunities to women at a level that is "substantially proportionate" to the number of women in the student body. Colleges and universities must therefore do more than simply meet the relative interests of its male and female students. Rather, the courts have held that, whenever gender disparities in sports offerings exist, colleges and universities must prove that such disparities are not the product of historic discrimination or stereotyped notions of women's interests and abilities. Indeed, colleges and universities must prove that the women at their respective institutions display a relative lack of interest in sports which is unrelated to both a historic and a current lack of sports opportunities.

In effect, the "substantially proportionate" approach recognizes that women's attitudes toward sports are socially constructed and have been limited by discrimination and gender stereotypes. Congress passed Title IX to combat such discrimination and stereotypes, thereby changing the social environment in which girls and women develop, or do not develop, interests in sports. As the First Circuit recently stated: "What stimulated [the recent] remarkable change in the quality of women's athletic competition was not a sudden, anomalous upsurge in women's interest in sports, but the enforcement of Title IX's mandate of gender equity in sports."

As such, the "substantially proportionate" approach goes beyond the liberal feminist "equality of opportunity" model, which many Title IX supporters espouse, by requiring that college women be provided a greater level of sports opportunities than indicated by their relative level of interest. Rather, as long as their interests have been shaped by a discriminatory, sexist society, these women need a proportionate number of opportunities to play, regardless of their misleadingly low interest level. Title IX thus has become not just a tool to overcome stereotypes and allow women to act on their desires to play sports, but also a means to curtail the practice of socializing girls and women not to become athletes in the first place....

NOTES AND QUESTIONS

1. **Title IX's Accommodation Strategy.** One of the interesting aspects of Title IX is that the implementing regulations specifically permit schools

to operate separate teams for men and women "where selection for such teams is based upon competitive skill or the activity involved is a contact sport," 34 C.F.R. § 106.41(b)(1995). Although this acceptance of sex segregated teams is phrased as an exception to a more general principle that no one should be denied the right to participate in a sports activity on the basis of sex, the exception has devoured most of the rule. The term "contact sports" includes many of the major sports such as basketball, football, and ice hockey. Furthermore, all intercollegiate sports qualify for exemption under the "competitive skill" exception. This makes it unnecessary for colleges (and in many cases high schools) to field coeducational teams.

Instead of providing women with opportunities to participate on the same teams as men, Title IX focuses on ensuring that women have equal opportunities to participate in their own ways, 34 C.F.R. § 106.41(c). Commentators have defended this by arguing that if women were given the chance to compete for places on men's teams, very few women would be successful. Whether for biological or cultural reasons, men tend to be faster and stronger than women, and thus, are more likely to win spots on competitively chosen teams. The result would be that most women would not make the team, and those who did would frequently end up on the bench. What is Justice Ginsburg's answer to a similar argument in *VMI*? Which approach seems more appropriate to you? Are there convincing reasons to distinguish the situation in *VMI* from the position of intercollegiate sports?

Assuming that Congress was correct as a matter of policy in its approach to Title IX, is this approach Constitutional? Brown University did challenge the Constitutionality of the act and its implementing regulations. The First Circuit responded to this challenge in a portion of the opinion which was omitted from the excerpt in this book; Chief Judge Torruella's dissent also discussed the issue at length. In *Cohen II*, the First Circuit had found Title IX to be constitutional on the grounds that Congress has broad power under the Fifth Amendment to remedy past discrimination. It cited Metro Broadcasting, Inc. v. FCC, 497 U.S. 547, 110 S.Ct. 2997, 111 L.Ed.2d 445 (1990) as support for this proposition. Between *Cohen II* and the First Circuit's 1997 opinion, the Supreme Court decided Adarand Constructors v. Pena, 515 U.S. 200, 115 S.Ct. 2097, 132 L.Ed.2d 158 (1995). In *Adarand*, the Supreme Court rejected the proposition that a Congressional minority set-aside was Constitutional, despite the fact that it was clearly intended to benefit minority contractors. The *Adarand* Court held that all racial classifications, benign or otherwise, must be subjected to strict scrutiny.

The First Circuit found that *Adarand* was not applicable to Title IX which involved gender discrimination and intermediate level scrutiny, not racial discrimination and strict scrutiny. Do you agree that benign classifications that are impermissible under strict scrutiny might be acceptable under intermediate scrutiny? What aspects of the rationale behind intermediate scrutiny might support such a position? What would be the effect of *VMI* on this analysis? If *VMI* has increased the level of scrutiny how would that affect your analysis? Even if intermediate scrutiny remains intact after *VMI*, was the proposed VWIL program a solution designed to accommodate the fact that most women are not able to compete physically with men? If so, is it analogous to separate teams under Title IX? Or, was the VWIL program proposed because of stereotypes of women's psychological make-up, and thus irrelevant to the separate teams issue?

2. **Team Participation and Choice.** Women have historically participated in sports at lower rates than men. For example, at Brown University, almost 20% of the men took part in intercollegiate varsity athletics, while less than 12% of the women did. How can we account for this discrepancy? Rhode argues that boys receive clear messages from sports that are consistent with cultural ideals of masculinity. Girls, in contrast, receive much more ambivalent messages. For girls, sports are consistent with social stereotypes of femininity only to the extent that they involve grace and beauty, or the sexualization of women. According to Carlin Meyer

> [Sports teach boys] that winning is everything, and that to win, competitiveness and aggression are essential skills—skills that are effectively mobilized by fostering male bonding through emphasizing and vilifying its opposite, femininity. Men learn "a masculinity based upon status-seeking through successful athletic competition and through aggressive verbal sparring which is both homophobic and sexist." Denigration of women and gay men is endemic; masculinity in sports depends on not being or appearing "feminine." "In sport, to be told by coaches, fathers, or peers that one throws 'like a girl' or plays like a 'sissy' or a 'woman' is among the most devastating insults a boy can receive.... "

Carlin Meyer, *Sex, Sin and Women's Liberation*, 72 Tex. L. Rev. 1097, 1163–64 (1994).

Is Meyer's point the same as Rhode's, or is Meyer arguing that sports culture defines itself in opposition to women, thus making it impossible for women to participate as women? How you answer this will affect the remedy that you think is appropriate. In addition to stronger enforcement of Title IX, Rhode would focus on penalizing aggressive actions. Meyer does not discuss a remedy, but do you think she would expect fines to affect the status of sports and its connection to aggressive masculinity? The author of the Harvard Note has yet another theory as to how we can change the relationship between gender stereotypes and sports. Do you agree with her "Theory of Empowerment through Sports?"

In *Cohen*, the court specifically rejected Brown University's claim that an athletics program complies with Title IX if it provides sports opportunities for an equal proportion of interested men and women. Thus, the university argued that if only 80% of the interested men are able to find openings on teams, then it should only need to find positions for 80% of the interested women. Instead, the court upheld the Department of Education's Policy Interpretation that required either participation opportunities for men and women proportionate to their respective enrollment in the institution, or a continuing expansion of program opportunities, or the "full[] and effective[]'' accommodation of the interests of members of the sex that has historically been underrepresented. Why require "full and effective" accommodation of the underrepresented sex in sports, instead of simply requiring that men's and women's interests be proportionately met? Is it fair to require that there must be sporting opportunities for all women who want them if there are only opportunities for 80% of the men who do?

Does this approach to Title IX seem likely to change the close relationship between sports and stereotypes of masculinity? Will it be likely to stimulate increased interest by women in sports? Do you think that women's interest in participating in sports is affected by the understanding of the connections between sports and masculinity? Will forcing schools to serve *all* interested women be likely to change these connections over time?

For further discussion of the choices that women make (in the context of employment decisions, not sports participation), see Vicki Schultz, *Telling Stories about Women and Work*, 103 Harv. L. Rev. 1750 (1990) (excerpted below in the section on Sex Role Stereotypes).

F.   SEX ROLE STEREOTYPES AND THE LIMITS OF LEGAL WORKPLACE REFORM

INTRODUCTION

Despite the apparently unqualified legal command against sex discrimination in the workplace, the preceding sections have indicated how specific workplace obstacles that affect women continue to hinder the advancement of women in their wage market jobs. By focusing on two cases that involve race and sexual orientation, and by providing a variety of readings that bear on these topics, this section provides an opportunity to review, and to stimulate further, generalized explanations for the failure of employment discrimination laws to eliminate sex-related barriers in the workforce.

The two cases in this section both involve employment practices that seem indisputably linked to sex, yet were found by federal Courts of Appeal to fall outside the scope of legal protection. Padula v. Webster, 822 F.2d 97 (D.C. Cir. 1987), in which a lesbian challenged FBI policy against hiring homosexuals, raises the issue of the relationship between the legal regulation of sexual desire and the employment status of women. Chambers v. Omaha Girls Club, 834 F.2d 697 (8th Cir. 1987), involves the moral significance of out-of-wedlock pregnancy for Black women, as well as the question of whether "women of color" should be a distinct category for protection under Title VII, different from sex or race.

Each of the cases in this section could be read as a technical, *sui generis* interpretation of discrimination law. But we suggest that reading these cases together can illuminate why and how workplace regulation laws shelter and foster particular forms of sex-role conduct in individuals. They reveal how employment discrimination laws' failure to eliminate obstacles to women in the workforce is connected to an unarticulated but discernible commitment to what one could call either the social construction of gender or the preservation of sex role stereotypes.

The remaining readings in the section link assumptions regarding gender identity formation to doctrinal patterns in employment discrimination law. Adrienne Rich's essay, "Compulsory Heterosexuality and Lesbian Existence," provides a systemic analysis of how a broad range of cultural factors function to privilege heterosexuality. The essay is useful in evaluating how discrimination on the basis of sexual preference can constitute discrimination on the basis of sex. In another essay, Kim Crenshaw demonstrates, through her description of three employment discrimination claims involving Black women, how specific discrimination rules overlook harms that Black women suffer by relying on what she calls single axis analysis. This singularity of approach, she suggests, protects some roles (white middle class femaleness) but neglects others. Kathryn Abrams' article uses some of Crenshaw's insights to argue that people are more complex than envisioned by discrimination law. She claims that our complicated identities are not biologically derived, but rather result from legal and social practices. She also reconceives discrimination as a process of devaluation. Finally, Vicki Schultz's description of the choice/coercion paradigm in Title VII cases explains how occupational segregation is immunized from litigation reform as a consequence of legal assumptions regarding personality formation.

Padula v. Webster

United States Court of Appeal, District of Columbia Circuit, 1987.
822 F.2d 97.

LAURENCE H. SILBERMAN, CIRCUIT JUDGE:

Appellant Margaret A. Padula alleges that the Federal Bureau of Investigation ("FBI" or "Bureau") refused to employ her as a special agent because of her homosexuality, in violation of both Bureau policy and the equal protection guarantee of the Constitution. Ruling on a motion for summary judgment, the district court rejected both these challenges, concluding that the hiring decision was committed to the FBI's discretion by law and did not infringe upon appellant's constitutional rights. We affirm.

The FBI's policy towards employing homosexuals has been in some flux. Eight years ago, the Bureau formally represented to this court that it "has always had an absolute policy of dismissing proven or admitted homosexuals from its employ." ... Several law schools, concerned with possible discrimination toward their homosexual students during the job recruitment season, requested clarification of the FBI's policy. John Mintz, an Assistant Director of the FBI and the FBI's Legal Counsel, assumed responsibility for answering these queries. On July 31, 1980, he wrote ...:

> The FBI's focus in personnel matters has been and continues to be on conduct rather than status or preference and we carefully consider the facts in each case to determine whether the conduct may affect the

employment. At the same time, we recognize individual privacy rights of applicants and employees.

... In the summer of 1982, Padula applied for a position as a special agent with the FBI. On the basis of a written examination and an interview, the FBI ranked her 39th out of 303 qualified female applicants and 279th out of 1273 male and female applicants. Following these screening tests, the FBI conducted a routine background check. In addition to revealing favorable information about the applicant's abilities and character, the background investigation disclosed that appellant is a practicing homosexual. At a followup interview, Padula confirmed that she is a homosexual—explaining that although she does not flaunt her sexual orientation, she is unembarrassed and open about it and it is a fact well known to her family, friends and co-workers.

On October 19, 1983, the Bureau notified Padula that it was unable to offer her a position; her subsequent attempt to obtain reconsideration of the decision was denied. It was explained to her that her application had been evaluated in the same manner as all others, but had been rejected due to intense competition. Seventeen months later, Padula filed suit in the United States District Court for the District of Columbia....

Padula alleges that the FBI refused to hire her solely because of her homosexuality and that this action denied her the equal protection of the law guaranteed by the fourteenth amendment. She urges us to recognize homosexuality as a suspect or quasi-suspect classification. A suspect classification is subjected to strict scrutiny and will be sustained only if "suitably tailored to serve a compelling state interest," whereas under heightened scrutiny given to a quasi-suspect class, the challenged classification must be "substantially related to a legitimate state interest." ... The issue presented us is only whether homosexuals, when defined as persons who engage in homosexual conduct, constitute a suspect or quasi-suspect classification and accordingly whether the FBI's hiring decision is subject to strict or heightened scrutiny.

The Supreme Court has used several explicit criteria to identify suspect and quasi-suspect classifications. In *San Antonio School Dist. v. Rodriguez,* 411 U.S. 1, 93 S.Ct. 1278, 36 L.Ed.2d 16 (1973), the Court stated that a suspect class is one "saddled with such disabilities, or subjected to such a history of purposeful unequal treatment, or relegated to such a position of political powerlessness as to command extraordinary protection from the majoritarian political process." The immutability of the group's identifying trait is also a factor to be considered. However, the Supreme Court has recognized only three classifications as suspect: race, alienage, and national origin, and two others as quasi-suspect: gender and illegitimacy. Appellant, asserting that homosexuals meet all the requisite criteria, would have us add homosexuality to that list. Appellees, on the other hand, contend that two recent cases, *Bowers v. Hardwick,* ___ U.S. ___, 106 S.Ct. 2841 (1986) and *Dronenburg v. Zech,* 741 F.2d 1388 (D.C.Cir. 1984), are insurmountable barriers to appellant's claim. We agree.

In *Dronenburg*, a naval petty officer claimed violation of his constitutional rights to privacy and to equal protection of the laws because he was discharged from the Navy for engaging in homosexual conduct. A panel of this court rejected the claim, holding that "we can find no constitutional right to engage in homosexual conduct and, ... as judges, we have no warrant to create one." Although the court's opinion focused primarily on whether the constitutional right to privacy protected homosexual conduct, the court reasoned that if the right to privacy did not provide protection "then appellant's right to equal protection is not infringed unless the Navy's policy is not rationally related to a permissible end." The unique needs of the military, the court concluded, justified discharge for homosexual conduct.

Dronenburg anticipated by two years the Supreme Court's decision in *Hardwick*, in which the Court upheld a Georgia law criminalizing sodomy against a challenge that it violated the due process clause. In *Hardwick*, the Court explained that the right to privacy as defined in its previous decisions inheres only in family relationships, marriage and procreation and does not extend more broadly to all kinds of private sexual conduct between consenting adults. Putting the privacy precedent aside, the Court further concluded that a right to engage in consensual sodomy is not constitutionally protected as a fundamental right since it is neither "implicit in the concept of ordered liberty," nor "deeply rooted in this Nation's history and tradition." ...

Padula argues that both *Dronenburg* and *Hardwick* are inapposite because they addressed only the scope of the privacy right, not what level of scrutiny is appropriate under equal protection analysis. But as we have noted, *Dronenburg* did involve an equal protection claim. Although the court did not explicitly consider whether homosexuals should be treated as a suspect class, it seemed to regard that question settled by its conclusion that the Constitution does not afford a privacy right to engage in homosexual conduct. In *Hardwick*, to be sure, plaintiffs did not rely on the equal protection clause, but after the Court rejected an extension of the right to privacy, it responded to plaintiffs' alternate argument that the Georgia law should be struck down as without rational basis (under the due process clause) since it was predicated merely on the moral judgment of a majority of the Georgia electorate. The Court summarily rejected that position, refusing to declare the Georgian majoritarian view "inadequate" to meet a rational basis test. We therefore think the courts' reasoning in *Hardwick* and *Dronenburg* forecloses appellant's efforts to gain suspect class status for practicing homosexuals. It would be quite anomalous, on its face, to declare status defined by conduct that states may constitutionally criminalize as deserving of strict scrutiny under the equal protection clause. More importantly, in all those cases in which the Supreme Court has accorded suspect or quasi-suspect status to a class, the Court's holding was predicated on an unarticulated, but necessarily implicit, notion that it is plainly unjustifiable (in accordance with standards not altogether clear to us) to discriminate invidiously against the particular class.... If the Court was unwilling to object to state laws that criminalize the behavior that defines the class, it is hardly open to a lower court to conclude that state sponsored discrimination against the class is invidious. After all, there can hardly be more palpable discrimination against a class than making the conduct that defines the class criminal.

That does not mean, however, that any kind of negative state action against homosexuals would be constitutionally authorized. Laws or government practices must still, if challenged, pass the rational basis test of the equal protection clause. A governmental agency that discriminates against homosexuals must justify that discrimination in terms of some government purpose.... The FBI, as the Bureau points out, is a national law enforcement agency whose agents must be able to work in all the states of the nation. To have agents who engage in conduct criminalized in roughly one-half of the states would undermine the law enforcement credibility of the Bureau. Perhaps more important, FBI agents perform counterintelligence duties that involve highly classified matters relating to national security. It is not irrational for the Bureau to conclude that the criminalization of homosexual conduct coupled with the general public opprobrium toward homosexuality exposes many homosexuals, even "open" homosexuals, to the risk of possible blackmail to protect their partners, if not themselves. We therefore conclude the Bureau's specialized functions, like the Navy's in *Dronenburg*, rationally justify consideration of homosexual conduct that could adversely affect that agency's responsibilities....

NOTES AND QUESTIONS

Lesbians, Gays and the Military. The *Padula* case and the controversy over the F.B.I.'s employment of homosexuals foreshadowed the debate over the service of gays and lesbians in the military. Courts are split on whether to uphold or overturn the military's discharges of known homosexuals. Thus, in Steffan v. Perry, 41 F.3d 677 (D.C.Cir. 1994) (en banc), the court upheld such a discharge, finding that the military could rationally infer that illegal sexual conduct would be likely to follow from homosexual status. In contrast, in Meinhold v. United States Department of Defense, 34 F.3d 1469 (9th Cir. 1994), the court rejected the rationality of just such an inference. In the most recent of these cases, Able v. United States, 968 F.Supp. 850 (E.D.N.Y. 1997), the court held the "Don't Ask, Don't Tell" policy invalid under the Fifth Amendment's equal protection clause. The government had claimed that the policy helped foster unit cohesion, promoted the privacy of heterosexuals, and reduced sexual tensions in the military. Invoking a new "active" rational basis test, the court found that all three of these justifications fell short.

Do you think that discrimination against lesbians in the military (or elsewhere) is an issue of discrimination against women or of discrimination against homosexuals? Or are the two interwoven in a way that makes the discrimination identifiably both, and yet different from discrimination against straight women or gay men? Does it affect your thinking to know that women in the military have traditionally been stereotyped as lesbians?

During the 1980s, 20–30% of the women in the military may have been lesbians. The result has been a heightened sensitivity on the part of the military to the possible presence of lesbian servicewomen. In 1987 and 1988, 26% of the homosexuals discharged were women, despite the fact that women made up only 10% of the military. *See* Holly Baldwin, *"Don't Ask, Don't Tell,"* 10 Berkeley Women's L.J. 148 (1995).

Does all this activity against lesbians in the military exercise a disciplinary function aimed at enforcing heterosexual, feminine norms? The next reading, by Adrienne Rich, should be helpful in thinking about this question.

Adrienne Rich, Compulsory Heterosexuality and Lesbian Existence

From A. Rich, Blood, Bread and Poetry: Selected Prose 1979-1985
(Norton, 1986).

I am concerned here with two ... matters ...: first, how and why women's choice of women as passionate comrades, life partners, co-workers, lovers, tribe, has been crushed, invalidated, forced into hiding and disguise; and second, the virtual or total neglect of lesbian existence in a wide range of writings, including feminist scholarship. Obviously there is a connection here. I believe that much feminist theory and criticism is stranded on this shoal....

In her essay "The Origin of the Family," Kathleen Gough lists eight characteristics of male power in archaic and contemporary societies that I would like to use as a framework: "men's ability to deny women sexuality or to force it upon them; to command or exploit their labor to control their produce; to control or rob them of their children; to confine them physically and prevent their movement; to use them as objects in male transactions; to cramp their creativeness; or to withhold from them large areas of the society's knowledge and cultural attainments." (Gough does not perceive these power-characteristics as specifically enforcing heterosexuality; only as producing sexual inequality.) Below, Gough's words appear in italics; the elaboration of each of her categories, in brackets, is my own.

Characteristics of male power include the power of men:

1. *to deny women* [our own] *sexuality*

[by means of clitoridectomy and infibulation; chastity belts; punishment, including death, for female adultery; punishment, including death, for lesbian sexuality; psychoanalytic denial of the clitoris; strictures against masturbation; denial of maternal and postmenopausal sensuality; unnecessary hysterectomy; pseudo-lesbian images in media and literature; closing of archives and destruction of documents relating to lesbian existence];

2. *or to force it* [male sexuality] *upon them*

[by means of rape (including marital rape) and wife beating; father-daughter, brother-sister incest; the socialization of women to feel that male sexual "drive" amounts to a right; idealization of heterosexual romance in art, literature, media, advertising, and so forth; child marriage; arranged marriage; prostitution; the harem; psychoanalytic doctrines of frigidity and vaginal orgasm; pornographic depictions of women responding pleasurably to sexual violence and humiliation (a subliminal message being that sadistic heterosexuality is more "normal" than sensuality between women)];

3. *to command or exploit their labor to control their produce*

[by means of the institutions of marriage and motherhood as unpaid production; the horizontal segregation of women in paid employment; the decoy of the upwardly mobile token woman; male control of abortion, contraception, and childbirth; enforced sterilization; pimping; female infanticide, which robs mothers of daughters and contributes to generalized devaluation of women];

4. *to control or rob them of their children*

[by means of father-right and "legal kidnapping"; enforced sterilization; systematized infanticide; seizure of children from lesbian mothers by the courts; the malpractice of male obstetrics; use of the mother as "token torturer" in genital mutilation or in binding the daughter's feet (or mind) to fit her for marriage];

5. *to confine them physically and prevent their movement*

[by means of rape as terrorism, keeping women off the streets; purdah; foot-binding; atrophying of women's athletic capabilities; haute couture, "feminine" dress codes; the veil; sexual harassment on the streets; horizontal segregation of women in employment; prescriptions for "full-time" mothering; enforced economic dependence of wives];

6. *to use them as objects in male transactions*

[use of women as "gifts," bride-price; pimping; arranged marriage; use of women as entertainers to facilitate male deals, for example, wife-hostess, cocktail waitress required to dress for male sexual titillation, call girls, "bunnies," geisha, *kisaeng* prostitutes, secretaries];

7. *to cramp their creativeness*

[witch persecutions as campaigns against midwives and female healers and as pogroms against independent, "unassimilated" women; definition of male pursuits as more valuable than female within any culture, so that cultural values become embodiment of male subjectivity; restriction of female self-fulfillment to marriage and motherhood; sexual exploitation of women by male artists and teachers; the social and economic disruption of women's creative aspirations; erasure of female tradition]; and

8. *to withhold from them large areas of the society's knowledge and cultural attainments*

[by means of noneducation of females (60 percent of the world's illiterates are women); the "Great Silence" regarding women and particularly lesbian existence in history and culture; sex-role stereotyping that deflects women from science, technology, and other "masculine" pursuits; male social/professional bonding that excludes women; discrimination against women in the professions].

These are some of the methods by which male power is manifested and maintained. Looking at the schema, what surely impresses itself is the fact that we are confronting not a simple maintenance of inequality and property possession, but a pervasive cluster of forces, ranging from physical brutality to control of consciousness, that suggests that an enormous potential counterforce is having to be restrained.

Some of the forms by which male power manifests itself are more easily recognizable as enforcing heterosexuality on women than are others. Yet each one I have listed adds to the cluster of forces within which women have been convinced that marriage and sexual orientation toward men are inevitable, even if unsatisfying or oppressive components of their lives. The chastity belt; child marriage; erasure of lesbian existence (except as exotic and perverse) in art, literature, film; idealization of heterosexual romance and marriage—these are some fairly obvious forms of compulsion, the first two exemplifying physical force, the second two control of consciousness. While clitoridectomy has been assailed by feminists as a form of woman-torture, Kathleen Barry first pointed out that it is not simply a way of turning the young girl into a "marriageable" woman through brutal surgery; it intends that women in the intimate proximity of polygynous marriage will not form sexual relationships with each other; that—from a male, genital-fetishist perspective—female erotic connections, even in a sex-segregated situation, will be literally excised....

In her brilliant study *Sexual Harassment of Working Women: A Case of Sex Discrimination*, Catharine A. MacKinnon delineates the intersection of compulsory heterosexuality and economics.... She cites a wealth of material documenting the fact that women are not only segregated in low-paying service jobs (as secretaries, domestics, nurses, typists, telephone operators, child-care workers, waitresses) but that "sexualization of the woman" is part of the job.... And, MacKinnon notes, the woman who too decisively resists sexual overtures in the workplace is accused of being "dried-up" and sexless, or lesbian. This raises a specific difference between the experiences of lesbians and homosexual men. A lesbian, closeted on her job because of heterosexist prejudice, is not simply forced into denying the truth of her outside relationships or private life; her job depends on her pretending to be not merely heterosexual but a heterosexual *woman,* in terms of dressing and playing the feminine, deferential role required of "real" women....

Given the nature and extent of heterosexual pressures, the daily "eroticization of women's subordination" as MacKinnon phrases it, I question the more or less psychoanalytic perspective that the male need to control women sexually results from some primal male "fear of women" and of women's sexual insatiability. It seems more probable that men really fear, not that they will have women's sexual appetites forced on them, or that women want to smother and devour them, but that women could be indifferent to them altogether, that men could be allowed sexual and emotional—therefore economic—access to women *only* on women's terms, otherwise being left on the periphery of the matrix. . . .

[W]hatever its origins, when we look hard and clearly at the extent and elaboration of measures designed to keep women within a male sexual purlieu, it becomes an inescapable question whether the issue we have to address as feminists is not simple "gender inequality," nor the domination of culture by males, nor mere "taboos against homosexuality," but the enforcement of heterosexuality for women as a means of assuring male right of physical, economical, and emotional access. One of many means of enforcement is, of course, the rendering invisible of the lesbian possibility, an engulfed continent that rises fragmentedly to view from time to time only to become submerged again. Feminist research and theory that contributes to lesbian invisibility or marginality is actually working against the liberation and empowerment of women as a group.

The assumption that "most women are innately heterosexual" stands as a theoretical and political stumbling block for many women. It remains a tenable assumption, partly because lesbian existence has been written out of history or catalogued under disease; partly because it has been treated as exceptional rather than intrinsic; partly because to acknowledge that for women heterosexuality may not be a "preference" at all but something that has had to be imposed, managed, organized, propagandized, and maintained by force is an immense step to take if you consider yourself freely and "innately" heterosexual. Yet the failure to examine heterosexuality as an institution is like failing to admit that the economic system called capitalism or the caste system of racism is maintained by a variety of forces, including both physical violence and false consciousness. To take the step of questioning heterosexuality as a "preference" or "choice" for women—and to do the intellectual and emotional work that follows—will call for a special quality of courage in heterosexually identified feminists but I think the rewards will be great: a freeing-up of thinking, the exploring of new paths, the shattering of another great silence, new clarity in personal relationships.

I have chosen to use the terms *lesbian existence* and *lesbian continuum* because the word *lesbianism* has a clinical and limiting ring. *Lesbian existence* suggests both the fact of the historical presence of lesbians and our continuing creation of the meaning of that existence. I mean the term *lesbian continuum* to include a range—through each woman's life and throughout history—of woman-identified experience; not simply the fact that a woman has had or consciously desired genital sexual experience with another woman. If we expand it to embrace many more forms of primary intensity between and among women, including the sharing of a rich inner life, the bonding against male tyranny, the giving and receiving of practical and political support ... we begin to grasp breadths of female history and psychology that have lain out of reach as a consequence of limited, mostly clinical, definitions of "lesbianism."

Lesbian existence comprises both the breaking of a taboo and the rejection of a compulsory way of life. It is also a direct or indirect attack on male right of access to women. But it is more than these, although we may first begin to perceive it as a form of nay-saying to patriarchy, an act of resistance. It has of course included role playing, self-hatred, breakdown, alcoholism, suicide, and intrawoman violence; we romanticize at our peril what it means to love and act against the grain, and under heavy penalties; and lesbian existence has been lived (unlike, say, Jewish or Catholic existence) without access to any knowledge of a tradition, a continuity, a social underpinning. The destruction of records and memorabilia and letters documenting the realities of lesbian existence must be taken very seriously as a means of keeping heterosexuality compulsory for women, since what has been kept from our knowledge is joy, sensuality, courage, and community, as well as guilt, self-betrayal, and pain.

Lesbians have historically been deprived of a political existence through "inclusion" as female versions of male homosexuality. To equate lesbian existence with male homosexuality because each is stigmatized is to deny and erase female reality once again. To separate those women stigmatized as "homosexual" or "gay" from the complex continuum of female resistance to enslavement, and attach them to a male pattern, is to falsify our history. Part of the history of lesbian existence is, obviously, to be found where lesbians, lacking a coherent female community, have shared a kind of social life and common cause with homosexual men. But this has to be seen against the differences: women's lack of economic and cultural privilege relative to men; qualitative differences in female and male relationships, for example, the prevalence of anonymous sex and the justification of pederasty among male homosexuals, the pronounced ageism in male homosexual standards of sexual attractiveness, and so forth. In defining and describing lesbian existence I would hope to move toward a dissociation of lesbian from male homosexual values and allegiances. I perceive the lesbian experience as being, like motherhood, a profoundly *female* experience, with particular oppressions, meanings, and potentialities we cannot comprehend as long as we simply bracket it with other sexually stigmatized existences. Just as the term *parenting* serves to conceal the particular and significant reality of being a parent who is actually a mother, the term *gay* serves the purpose of blurring the very outlines we need to discern, which are of crucial value for feminism and for the freedom of women as a group.

As the term lesbian has been held to limiting, clinical associations in its patriarchal definition, female friendship and comradeship have been set apart from the erotic, thus limiting the erotic itself. But as we deepen and broaden the range of what we define as lesbian existence, as we delineate a lesbian continuum, we begin to discover the erotic in female terms: as that which is unconfined to any single part of the body or solely to the body itself, as an energy not only diffuse but, as Audre Lorde has described it, omnipresent in "the sharing of joy, whether physical, emotional, psychic," and in the sharing of work; as the empowering joy which "makes us less willing to accept powerlessness, or those other supplied states of being which are not native to me, such as resignation, despair, self-effacement, depression, self-denial." . . .

If we consider the possibility that all women—from the infant suckling her mother's breast, to the grown woman experiencing orgasmic sensations while suckling her own child, perhaps recalling her mother's milk-smell in her own; to two women, like Virginia Woolf's Chloe and Olivia, who share a laboratory; to the woman dying at ninety, touched and handled by women—exist on a lesbian continuum, we can see ourselves as moving in and out of this continuum, whether we identify ourselves as lesbian or not. . . . It allows us to connect aspects of woman-identification as diverse as the impudent, intimate girl-friendships of eight- or nine-year-olds and the banding together of those women of the twelfth and fifteenth centuries known as Beguines who "shared houses, rented to one another, bequeathed houses to their room-mates . . . in cheap subdivided houses in the artisans' area of town," who "practiced Christian virtue on their own, dressing and living simply and not associating with men," who earned their livings as spinners, bakers, nurses, or ran schools for young girls, and who managed—until the Church forced them to disperse—to live independent both of marriage and of conventual restrictions. . . .

[W]hen we turn the lens of vision and consider the degree to which, and the methods whereby, heterosexual "preference" has actually been imposed on women, not only can we understand differently the meaning of individual lives and work, but we can begin to recognize a central fact of women's history: that women have always resisted male tyranny. A feminism of action, often, though not always, without a theory, has constantly reemerged in every culture and in every period. We can then begin to study women's struggle against powerlessness, women's radical rebellion, not just in male-defined "concrete revolutionary situations" but in all the situations male ideologies have not perceived as revolutionary. . . . [W]e begin to observe behavior, both in history and in individual biography, that has hitherto been invisible or misnamed; behavior that often constitutes, given the limits of the counterforce exerted in a given time and place, radical rebellion. And we can connect these rebellions and the necessity for them with the physical passion of woman for woman that is central to lesbian existence: the erotic sensuality that has been, precisely, the most violently erased fact of female experience.

Heterosexuality has been both forcibly and subliminally imposed on women, yet everywhere women have resisted it, often at the cost of physical torture, imprisonment, psychosurgery, social ostracism, and extreme poverty. . . . Nor can it be assumed that women . . . who married, stayed married, yet dwelt in a profoundly female emotional and passional world, "preferred" or "chose" heterosexuality. Women have married because it was necessary, in order to survive economically, in order to have children who would not suffer economic deprivation or social ostracism, in order to remain respectable, in order to do what was expected of women because coming out of "abnormal" childhoods they wanted to feel "normal," and because heterosexual romance has been represented as the great female adventure, duty, and fulfillment. We may faithfully or ambivalently have obeyed the institution, but our feelings—and our sensuality—have not been tamed or contained within it. There is no statistical documentation of the numbers of lesbians who have remained in heterosexual marriages for most of their lives. . . . This *double-life*—this apparent acquiescence to an institution founded on male interest and prerogative—has been characteristic of female experience: in motherhood, and in many kinds of heterosexual behavior, including the rituals of courtship; the pretense of asexuality by the nineteenth-century wife; the simulation of orgasm by the prostitute, the courtesan, the twentieth-century "sexually liberated" woman. . . .

The lie is many-layered. In Western tradition, one layer—the romantic—asserts that women are inevitably, even if rashly and tragically, drawn to men; that even when that attraction is suicidal (e.g., Tristan und Isolde, Kate Chopin's The Awakening) it is still an organic imperative. In the tradition of the social sciences it asserts that primary love between the sexes is "normal," that women *need* men as social and economic protectors, for adult sexuality, and for psychological completion; that the heterosexually constituted family is the basic social unit; that women who do not attach their primary intensity to men must be, in functional terms, condemned to an even more devastating outsiderhood than their outsiderhood as women. Small wonder that lesbians are reported to be a more hidden population than male homosexuals. The black lesbian/feminist critic, Lorraine Bethel, writing on Zora Neale Hurston, remarks that for a black woman—already twice an outsider—to choose to assume still another "hated identity" is problematic indeed. Yet the lesbian continuum has been a lifeline for black women both in Africa and the United States. . . .

Another layer of the lie is the frequently encountered implication that women turn to women out of hatred for men. Profound skepticism, caution, and righteous paranoia about men may indeed be part of any healthy woman's response to the woman-hatred embedded in male-dominated culture, to the forms assumed by "normal" male sexuality, and to *the failure even of "sensitive" or "political" men to perceive or find these troubling*. Yet woman-hatred is so embedded in culture, so "normal" does it seem, so profoundly is it neglected as a social phenomenon, that many women, even feminists and lesbians, fail to identify it until it takes, in their own lives, some permanently unmistakable and shattering form. Lesbian existence is also represented as mere refuge from male abuses, rather than as an electric and empowering charge between women. . . .

By the same token, we can say that there is a *nascent* feminist political content in the act of choosing a woman lover or life partner in the face of institutionalized heterosexuality. But for lesbian existence to realize this political content in an ultimately liberating form, the erotic choice must deepen and expand into conscious woman-identification—into lesbian/feminism.

The work that lies ahead, of unearthing and describing what I call here lesbian existence, is potentially liberating for all women. It is work that must assuredly move beyond the limits of white and middle-class Western women's studies to examine women's lives, work, and groupings within every racial, ethnic, and political structure. There are differences, moreover, between lesbian existence and the lesbian continuum—differences we can discern even in the movement of our own lives. The lesbian continuum, I suggest, needs delineation in light of the double-life of women, not only women self-described as heterosexual but also of self-described lesbians. We need a far more exhaustive account of the forms the double-life has assumed. Historians need to ask at every point how heterosexuality as institution has been organized and maintained through the female wage scale, the enforcement of middle-class women's "leisure," the glamorization of so-called sexual liberation, the withholding of education from women, the imagery of "high art" and popular culture, the mystification of the "personal" sphere, and much else. We need an economics that comprehends the institution of heterosexuality, with its doubled workload for women and its sexual divisions of labor, as the most idealized of economic relations.

The question inevitably will arise: Are we then to condemn all heterosexual relationships, including those that are least oppressive? I believe this question, though often heartfelt, is the wrong question here. We have been stalled in a maze of false dichotomies that prevents our apprehending the institution as a whole: "good" versus "bad" marriages; "marriage for love" versus arranged marriage; "liberated" sex versus prostitution; heterosexual intercourse versus rape; Liebeschmerz versus humiliation and dependency. Within the institution exist, of course, qualitative differences of experience; but the absence of choice remains the great unacknowledged reality, and in the absence of choice, women will remain dependent on the chance or luck of particular relationships and will have no collective power to determine the meaning and place of sexuality in their lives. As we address the institution itself, moreover, we begin to perceive a history of female resistance that has never fully understood itself because it has been so fragmented, miscalled, erased. It will require a courageous grasp of the politics and economics, as well as the cultural propaganda, of heterosexuality to carry us beyond individual cases or diversified group situations into the complex kind of overview needed to undo the power men everywhere wield over women, power that has become a model for every other form of exploitation and illegitimate control.

Chambers v. Omaha Girls Club, Inc.

United States Court of Appeals, Eighth Circuit, 1987.
834 F.2d 697.

ROGER L. WOLLMAN, CIRCUIT JUDGE.

Crystal ... Chambers' claims arise from her dismissal as an employee at the Omaha Girls Club on account of her being single and pregnant in violation of the Club's "role model rule." The primary issue in this appeal is whether the Club's role model rule is an employment practice that is consistent with Title VII because it is justifiable as a business necessity or a bona fide occupational qualification.

The Omaha Girls Club is a private, non-profit corporation that offers programs designed to assist young girls between the ages of eight and eighteen to maximize their life opportunities. Among the Club's many activities are programs directed at pregnancy prevention. The Club serves 1,500 members, ninety percent of them black, at its North Omaha facility and 500 members, fifty to sixty percent of them black, at its South Omaha facility. A substantial number of youngsters who are not Club members also participate in its programs. The Club employs thirty to thirty-five persons at its two facilities; all of the non-administrative personnel at the North Omaha facility are black, and fifty to sixty percent of the personnel at the South Omaha facility are black.

The Club's approach to fulfilling its mission emphasizes the development of close contacts and the building of relationships between the girls and the Club's staff members. Toward this end, staff members are trained and expected to act as role models for the girls, with the intent that the girls will seek to emulate their behavior. The Club formulated its "role model rule" banning single parent pregnancies among its staff members in pursuit of this role model approach.

Chambers, a black single woman, was employed by the Club as an arts and crafts instructor at the Club's North Omaha facility. She became pregnant and informed her supervisor of that fact. Subsequently, she received a letter notifying her that because of her pregnancy her employment was to be terminated. Shortly after her termination, Chambers filed charges with the Nebraska Equal Opportunity Commission (NEOC) alleging discrimination on the basis of sex and marital status. The NEOC found no reasonable cause to believe that unlawful employment discrimination had occurred. Chambers then brought this action in the district court seeking injunctions and damages.... The district court examined Chambers' allegations of employment discrimination ... under both the disparate impact and disparate treatment theories. We review in turn the court's conclusions and Chambers' arguments under each of these theories.

A plaintiff seeking to prove discrimination under the disparate impact theory must show that a facially neutral employment practice has a significant adverse impact on members of a protected minority group. The burden then shifts to the employer to show that the practice has a manifest relationship to the employment in question and is justifiable on the ground of business necessity. Even if the employer shows that the discriminatory employment practice is justified by business necessity, the plaintiff may prevail by showing that other practices would accomplish the employer's objectives without the attendant discriminatory effects. The district court found that "because of the significantly higher fertility rate among black females, the rule banning single pregnancies would impact black women more harshly.'' Thus, Chambers established the disparate impact of the role model rule. The Club then sought to justify the rule as a business necessity....

The district court found that the role model rule is justified by business necessity because there is a manifest relationship between the Club's fundamental purpose and the rule. Specifically, the court found:

> The Girls Club has established by the evidence that its only purpose is to serve young girls between the ages of eight and eighteen and to provide these women with exposure to the greatest number of available positive options in life. The Girls Club has established that teenage pregnancy is contrary to this purpose and philosophy. The Girls Club established that it honestly believed that to permit single pregnant staff members to work with the girls would convey the impression that the Girls Club condoned pregnancy for the girls in the age group it serves. The testimony of board members ... made clear that the policy was not based upon a morality standard, but rather, on a belief that teenage pregnancies severely limit the available opportunities for teenage girls. The Girls Club also established that the policy was just one prong of a comprehensive attack on the problem of teenage pregnancy. The Court is satisfied that a manifest relationship exists between the Girls Club's fundamental purpose and its single pregnancy policy.

The court also relied in part on expert testimony to the effect that the role model rule could be helpful in preventing teenage pregnancy. Chambers argues, however, that the district court erred in finding business necessity because the role model rule is based only on speculation by the Club and has not been validated by any studies showing that it prevents pregnancy among the Club's members....

We ... cannot say that the district court's finding of business necessity is clearly erroneous. The district court's conclusion on the evidence is not an impermissible one. Although validation studies can be helpful in evaluating such questions, they are not required to maintain a successful business necessity defense. Indeed, we are uncertain whether the role model rule by its nature is suited to validation by an empirical study....

Chambers argues further, however, that the district court erred in discounting alternative practices that the Club could have used to ameliorate the discriminatory effects of the role model rule. Chambers contends that the Club either could have granted her a leave of absence or transferred her to a position that did not involve contact with the Club's members. The Club responds that neither of these alternatives was available in this case. The Club has a history of granting leaves of up to six weeks, but the purposes of the role model rule would have required a five to six month leave for Chambers, given that the pregnancy would have become visually apparent probably within three or four months. Moreover, employing a temporary replacement to take Chamber's position would itself have required six months of on-the-job training before the replacement would have been able to interact with the girls on the level that the Club's approach requires. The use of temporary replacements would also disrupt the atmosphere of stability that the Club attempts to provide and would be inconsistent with the relationship-building and interpersonal interaction entailed in the Club's role model approach. Furthermore, transfer to a "noncontact position" apparently was impossible because there are no positions at the Club that do not involve contact with Club members. The district court found that the Club considered these alternatives and determined them to be unworkable. We are unable to conclude that the district court's finding that there were no satisfactory alternatives to the dismissal of Chambers pursuant to the role model rule is clearly erroneous....

Unlike the disparate impact theory, the disparate treatment theory requires a plaintiff seeking to prove employment discrimination to show discriminatory animus. The plaintiff must first establish a prima facie case of discrimination. The burden of production then shifts to the employer to show a legitimate, nondiscriminatory reason for the challenged employment practice. If the employer makes such a showing, then the plaintiff may show that the reasons given by the employer were pretextual. No violation of Title VII exists, however, if the employer can show that the challenged employment practice is a bona fide occupational qualification (bfoq).

The district court found that Chambers had succeeded in establishing a prima facie case of discrimination but concluded that the Club's role model approach is a legitimate, nondiscriminatory reason for the role model rule. The court then found that Chambers was unable to show that the Club's reason for the rule was a pretext for intentional discrimination. The court also stated in passing that the role model rule "presumably" is a bfoq....

Although the district court did not clearly conclude that the role model rule qualified as a bfoq, several of the court's other findings are persuasive on this issue. The court's findings of fact, many of which are relevant to the analysis of a potential bfoq exception, are binding on this court unless clearly erroneous. The facts relevant to establishing a bfoq are the same as those found by the district court in the course of its business necessity analysis.... [T]he district court found that the role model rule has a manifest relationship to the Club's fundamental purpose and that there were no workable alternatives to the rule. Moreover, the district court's finding of business necessity itself is persuasive as to the existence of a bfoq. This court has noted that the analysis of a bfoq "is similar to and overlaps with the judicially created 'business necessity' test." ... Inasmuch as we already have affirmed the district court's finding of business necessity as not clearly erroneous, we feel compelled to conclude that "[i]n the particular factual circumstances of this case," the role model rule is reasonably necessary to the Club's operations. Thus, we hold that the role model rule qualifies as a bona fide occupational qualification....

Theodore McMillian, Circuit Judge, dissenting....

Today, the court, contrary to Title VII, upholds the Omaha Girls Club's (OGC) discharge of Chambers, a black, unmarried pregnant woman because of her pregnancy. Chambers, an arts and crafts instructor at OGC, was held to be a "negative role model" for the OGC members, who are girls and young women between the ages of eight and eighteen....

The Equal Employment Opportunity Commission and many courts interpreted this provision barring gender-based discrimination to prohibit discrimination based on pregnancy.... However, the Supreme Court in *General Electric v. Gilbert*, 429 U.S. 125 (1976), determined that an employer could exclude pregnant employees from receiving benefits under a disability plan. The Court reasoned that the exclusion was not gender-based but was condition-based.

In 1978, Congress responded to the Supreme Court's decision in *General Electric v. Gilbert* by amending Title VII to "prohibit sex discrimination on the basis of pregnancy." The new amendment, entitled the Pregnancy Discrimination Act, added a new subsection "k" to the definition section of Title VII.... This provision "made clear that, for all Title VII purposes, discrimination based on a woman's pregnancy is, on its face, discrimination because of her sex."

An employer may justify discrimination otherwise prohibited by Title VII by showing either a business necessity or a bona fide occupational qualification (BFOQ) for the discriminatory policy or practice.... The district court, and now this court, accepts without any proof OGC's assumption that the presence of an unwed pregnant instructor is related to teenage pregnancies. OGC failed to present surveys, school statistics or any other empirical data connecting the incidence of teenage pregnancy with the pregnancy of an adult instructor. OGC also failed to present evidence that other girls clubs or similar types of organizations employed such a rule. OGC instead relied on two or three highly questionable anecdotal incidents to support the rule.... Although there are no cases that have considered precisely the issue raised in this case, a few courts have considered the role model defense in school settings and all have rejected the schools' role model defenses....

The district court in the present case, although correctly articulating the BFOQ and business necessity tests, failed to actually apply the tests. Instead of requiring OGC to demonstrate a reasonable relationship between teenage pregnancy and the employment of single pregnant women, the district court accepted the beliefs and assumptions of OGC board members.... Neither an employer's sincere belief, without more, (nor a district court's belief), that a discriminatory employment practice is related and necessary to the accomplishment of the employer's goals is sufficient to establish a BFOQ or business necessity defense.... The district court, recognizing that there was no data to support such a relationship, should have held that OGC failed to carry its burden of showing a BFOQ or business necessity.

Even if I were to accept for purposes of argument that OGC established a relationship between the single pregnancy policy and the work of the club, the BFOQ and the business necessity exceptions must still fail.... Unlike the district court and the panel majority, I am unimpressed by OGC's rejection of alternatives with less discriminatory impact. OCG's personnel policy provided leave of absences for up to six weeks for pregnancies and other sicknesses and longer leaves upon approval of the board. It is clear that OGC could have accommodated its stated mission and the pregnancy of Crystal Chambers by granting her a leave of absence or by placing her in a noncontact position. Administrative inconvenience is not a sufficient justification for not utilizing these less discriminatory alternatives. . . .

Kimberle Crenshaw, Demarginalizing the Intersection of Race and Sex

1989 U. of Chi. Legal Forum 139.

One of the very few Black women's studies books is entitled *All the Women Are White, All the Blacks Are Men, But Some of Us are Brave.* I have chosen this title as a point of departure in my efforts to develop a Black feminist criticism because it sets forth a problematic consequence of the tendency to treat race and gender as mutually exclusive categories of experience and analysis.[1] . . . I want to examine how this tendency is perpetuated by a single-axis framework that is dominant in antidiscrimination law and that is also reflected in feminist theory and antiracist politics.

I will center Black women in this analysis in order to contrast the multidimensionality of Black women's experience with the single-axis analysis that distorts these experiences. . . . With Black women as the starting point, it becomes more apparent how dominant conceptions of discrimination condition us to think about subordination as disadvantage occurring along a single categorical axis. I want to suggest further that this single-axis framework erases Black women in the conceptualization, identification and remediation of race and sex discrimination by limiting inquiry to the experiences of otherwise-privileged members of the group. In other words, in race discrimination cases, discrimination tends to be viewed in terms of sex- or class-privileged Blacks; in sex discrimination cases, the focus is on race- and class-privileged women.

This focus on the most privileged group members marginalizes those who are multiply-burdened and obscures claims that cannot be understood as resulting from discrete sources of discrimination.

---

1. The most common linguistic manifestation of this analytical dilemma is represented in the conventional usage of the term "Blacks and women." Although it may be true that some people mean to include Black women in either "Blacks" or "women," the context in which the term is used actually suggests that often Black women are not considered. See, for example, Elizabeth Spelman, The Inessential Woman 114B15 (Beacon Press, 1988) (discussing an article on Blacks and women in the military where "the racial identity of those identified as 'women' does not become explicit until reference is made to Black women, at which point it also becomes clear that the category of women excludes Black women"). It seems that if Black women were explicitly included, the preferred term would be either "Blacks and white women" or "Black men and all women."

... One way to approach the problem of intersectionality is to examine how courts frame and interpret the stories of Black women plaintiffs.... To illustrate the difficulties inherent in judicial treatment of intersectionality, I will consider three Title VII cases: *DeGraffenreid v. General Motors,* [413 F.Supp. 142 (E.D.Mo.1976)], *Moore v. Hughes Helicopter,* [708 F.2d 475 (4th Cir.1983)], and *Payne v. Travenol,* [673 F.2d 798 (5th Cir. 1982)]....

In *DeGraffenreid*, five Black women brought suit against General Motors, alleging that the employer's seniority system perpetuated the effects of past discrimination against Black women. Evidence adduced at trial revealed that General Motors simply did not hire Black women prior to 1964 and that all of the Black women hired after 1970 lost their jobs in a seniority-based layoff during a subsequent recession. The district court granted summary judgment for the defendant, rejecting the plaintiffs' attempt to bring a suit not on behalf of Blacks or women, but specifically on behalf of Black women. The court stated:

> [P]laintiffs have failed to cite any decisions which have stated that Black women are a special class to be protected from discrimination. The Court's own research has failed to disclose such a decision. The plaintiffs are clearly entitled to a remedy if they have been discriminated against. However, they should not be allowed to combine statutory remedies to create a new "super-remedy" which would give them relief beyond what the drafters of the relevant statutes intended. Thus, this lawsuit must be examined to see if it states a cause of action for race discrimination, sex discrimination, or alternatively either, but not a combination of both.

Although General Motors did not hire Black women prior to 1964, the court noted that "General Motors has hired ... female employees for a number of years prior to the enactment of the Civil Rights Act of 1964." Because General Motors did hire women—albeit *white women*—during the period that no Black women were hired, there was, in the court's view, no sex discrimination that the seniority system could conceivably have perpetuated.

After refusing to consider the plaintiffs' sex discrimination claim, the court dismissed the race discrimination complaint and recommended its consolidation with another case alleging race discrimination against the same employer....

> The legislative history surrounding Title VII does not indicate that the goal of the statute was to create a new classification of 'black women' who would have greater standing than, for example, a black male. The prospect of the creation of new classes of protected minorities, governed only by the mathematical principles of permutation and combination, clearly raises the prospect of opening the hackneyed Pandora's box.

Thus, the court apparently concluded that Congress either did not contemplate that Black women could be discriminated against as "Black women" or did not intend to protect them when such discrimination occurred.[12] The court's refusal in *DeGraffenreid* to acknowledge that Black women encounter combined race and sex discrimination implies that the boundaries of sex and race discrimination doctrine are defined respectively by white women's and Black men's experiences. Under this view, Black women are protected only to the extent that their experiences coincide with those of either of the two groups....

Moore v. Hughes Helicopters, Inc. presents a different way in which courts fail to understand or recognize Black women's claims. Moore is typical of a number of cases in which courts refused to certify Black females as class representatives in race *and* sex discrimination actions. In *Moore*, the plaintiff alleged that the employer, Hughes Helicopter, practiced race and sex discrimination in promotions to upperlevel craft positions and to supervisory jobs. Moore introduced statistical evidence establishing a significant disparity between men and women, and somewhat less of a disparity between Black and white men in supervisory jobs.

Affirming the district court's refusal to certify Moore as the class representative in the sex discrimination complaint on behalf of all women at Hughes, the Ninth Circuit noted approvingly:

> ... Moore had never claimed before the EEOC that she was discriminated against as a female, *but only* as a Black female.... [T]his raised serious doubts as to Moore's ability to adequately represent white female employees.

The curious logic in *Moore* reveals not only the narrow scope of antidiscrimination doctrine and its failure to embrace intersectionality, but also the centrality of white female experiences in the conceptualization of gender discrimination.... The court rejected Moore's bid to represent all females apparently because her attempt to specify her race was seen as being at odds with the standard allegation that the employer simply discriminated "against females."

---

12. Interestingly, no case has been discovered in which a court denied a white male's attempt to bring a reverse discrimination claim on similar grounds—that is, that sex and race claims cannot be combined because Congress did not intend to protect compound classes. White males in a typical reverse discrimination case are in no better position than the frustrated plaintiffs in *DeGraffenreid*: If they are required to make their claims separately, white males cannot prove race discrimination because white women are not discriminated against, and they cannot prove sex discrimination because Black males are not discriminated against. Yet it seems that courts do not acknowledge the compound nature of most reverse discrimination cases. That Black women's claims automatically raise the question of compound discrimination and white males' "reverse discrimination" cases do not suggest that the notion of compoundedness is somehow contingent upon an implicit norm that is not neutral but is white male. Thus, Black women are perceived as a compound class because they are two steps removed from a white male norm, while white males are apparently not perceived to be a compound class because they somehow represent the norm.

The court failed to see that the absence of a racial referent does not necessarily mean that the claim being made is a more inclusive one. A white woman claiming discrimination against females may be in no better position to represent all women than a Black woman who claims discrimination as a Black female and wants to represent all females. The court's preferred articulation of "against females" is not necessarily more inclusive—it just appears to be so because the racial contours of the claim are not specified.... For white women, claiming sex discrimination is simply a statement that but for gender, they would not have been disadvantaged. For them there is no need to specify discrimination as *white* females because their race does not contribute to the disadvantage for which they seek redress. The view of discrimination that is derived from this grounding takes race privilege as a given.

Discrimination against a white female is thus the standard sex discrimination claim; claims that diverge from this standard appear to present some sort of hybrid claim. More significantly, because Black females' claims are seen as hybrid, they sometimes cannot represent those who may have "pure" claims of sex discrimination. The effect of this approach is that even though a challenged policy or practice may clearly discriminate against all females, the fact that it has particularly harsh consequences for Black females places Black female plaintiffs at odds with white females.

Moore illustrates one of the limitations of antidiscrimination law's remedial scope and normative vision. The refusal to allow a multiply-disadvantaged class to represent others who may be singularly-disadvantaged defeats efforts to restructure the distribution of opportunity and limits remedial relief to minor adjustments within an established hierarchy. Consequently, "bottom-up" approaches, those which combine all discriminatees in order to challenge an entire employment system, are foreclosed by the limited view of the wrong and the narrow scope of the available remedy....

In *Moore*, the court's denial of the plaintiff's bid to represent all Blacks and females left Moore with the task of supporting her race and sex discrimination claims with statistical evidence of discrimination against Black females alone. Because she was unable to represent white women or Black men, she could not use overall statistics on sex disparity at Hughes, nor could she use statistics on race. Proving her claim using statistics on Black women alone was no small task, due to the fact that she was bringing the suit under a disparate impact theory of discrimination.

The court further limited the relevant statistical pool to include only Black women who it determined were qualified to fill the openings in upper-level labor jobs and in supervisory positions.... The court's rulings on Moore's sex and race claim left her with such a small statistical sample that even if she had proved that there were qualified Black women, she could not have shown discrimination under a disparate impact theory. *Moore* illustrates yet another way that antidiscrimination doctrine essentially erases Black women's distinct experiences and, as a result, deems their discrimination complaints groundless....

Black female plaintiffs have also encountered difficulty in their efforts to win certification as class representatives in some race discrimination actions. This problem typically arises in cases where statistics suggest significant disparities between Black and white workers and further disparities between Black men and Black women. Courts in some cases have denied certification based on logic that mirrors the rationale in *Moore*: The sex disparities between Black men and Black women created such conflicting interests that Black women could not possibly represent Black men adequately. In one such case, *Payne v. Travenol*, two Black female plaintiffs alleging race discrimination brought a class action suit on behalf of all Black employees at a pharmaceutical plant. The court refused, however, to allow the plaintiffs to represent Black males and granted the defendant's request to narrow the class to Black women only. Ultimately, the district court found that there had been extensive racial discrimination at the plant and awarded back pay and constructive seniority to the class of Black female employees. But, despite its finding of general race discrimination, the court refused to extend the remedy to Black men for fear that their conflicting interests would not be adequately addressed; the Fifth Circuit affirmed.

Notably, the plaintiffs in *Travenol* fared better than the similarly situated plaintiff in *Moore*: They were not denied use of meaningful statistics showing an overall pattern of race discrimination simply because there were no men in their class. The plaintiffs' bid to represent all Black employees, however, like Moore's attempt to represent all women employees, failed as a consequence of the court's narrow view of class interest.

Even though *Travenol* was a partial victory for Black women, the case specifically illustrates how antidiscrimination doctrine generally creates a dilemma for Black women. It forces them to choose between specifically articulating the intersectional aspects of their subordination, thereby risking their ability to represent Black men, or ignoring intersectionality in order to state a claim that would not lead to the exclusion of Black men. When one considers the political consequences of this dilemma, there is little wonder that many people within the Black community view the specific articulation of Black women's interests as dangerously divisive....

Perhaps it appears to some that I have offered inconsistent criticisms of how Black women are treated in antidiscrimination law: I seem to be saying that in one case, Black women's claims were rejected and their experiences obscured because the court refused to acknowledge that the employment experience of Black women can be distinct from that of white women, while in other cases, the interests of Black women were harmed because Black women's claims were viewed as so distinct from the claims of either white women or Black men that the court denied to Black females representation of the larger class. It seems that I have to say that Black women are the same and harmed by being treated differently, or that they are different and harmed by being treated the same. But I cannot say both.

This apparent contradiction is but another manifestation of the conceptual limitations of the single-issue analyses that intersectionality challenges. The point is that Black women can experience discrimination in any number of ways and that the contradiction arises from our assumptions that their claims of exclusion must be unidirectional.... Black women can experience discrimination in ways that are both similar to and different from those experienced by white women and Black men. Black women sometimes experience discrimination in ways similar to white women's experiences; sometimes they share very similar experiences with Black men. Yet often they experience double-discrimination—the combined effects of practices which discriminate on the basis of race, and on the basis of sex. And sometimes, they experience discrimination as Black women—not the sum of race and sex discrimination, but as Black women....

Unable to grasp the importance of Black women's intersectional experiences, not only courts, but feminist and civil rights thinkers as well have treated Black women in ways that deny both the unique compoundedness of their situation and the centrality of their experiences to the larger classes of women and Blacks. Black women are regarded either as too much like women or Blacks and the compounded nature of their experience is absorbed into the collective experiences of either group or as too different, in which case Black women's Blackness or femaleness sometimes has placed their needs and perspectives at the margin of the feminist and Black liberationist agendas.

While it could be argued that this failure represents an absence of political will to include Black women, I believe that it reflects an uncritical and disturbing acceptance of dominant ways of thinking about discrimination. Consider first the definition of discrimination that seems to be operative in antidiscrimination law: Discrimination which is wrongful proceeds from the identification of a specific class or category; either a discriminator intentionally identifies this category, or a process is adopted which somehow disadvantages all members of this category. According to the dominant view, a discriminator treats all people within a race or sex category similarly. Any significant experimental or statistical variation within this group suggests either that the group is not being discriminated against or that conflicting interests exist which defeat any attempts to bring a common claim. Consequently, one generally cannot combine these categories. Race and sex, moreover, become significant only when they operate to explicitly *disadvantage* the victims; because the *privileging* of whiteness or maleness is implicit, it is generally not perceived at all.

Underlying this conception of discrimination is a view that the wrong which antidiscrimination law addresses is the use of race or gender factors to interfere with decisions that would otherwise be fair or neutral. This process-based definition is not grounded in a bottom-up commitment to improve the substantive conditions for those who are victimized by the interplay of numerous factors. Instead, the dominant message of antidiscrimination law is that it will regulate only the limited extent to which race or sex interferes with the process of determining outcomes. This narrow objective is facilitated by the top-down strategy of using a singular "but for" analysis to ascertain the effects of race or sex. Because the scope of antidiscrimination law is so limited, sex and race discrimination have come to be defined in terms of the experiences of those who are privileged *but for* their racial or sexual characteristics. Put differently, the paradigm of sex discrimination tends to be based on the experiences of white women; the model of race discrimination tends to be based on the experiences of the most privileged Blacks. Notions of what constitutes race and sex discrimination are, as a result, narrowly tailored to embrace only a small set of circumstances, none of which include discrimination against Black women.

To the extent that this general description is accurate, the following analogy can be useful in describing how Black women are marginalized in the interface between antidiscrimination law and race and gender hierarchies: Imagine a basement which contains all people who are disadvantaged on the basis of race, sex, class, sexual preference, age and/or physical ability. These people are stacked—feet standing on shoulders—with those on the bottom being disadvantaged by the full array of factors, up to the very top, where the heads of all those disadvantaged by a singular factor brush up against the ceiling. Their ceiling is actually the floor above which only those who are *not* disadvantaged in any way reside. In efforts to correct some aspects of domination, those above the ceiling admit from the basement only those who can say that "but for" the ceiling, they too would be in the upper room. A hatch is developed through which those placed immediately below can crawl. Yet this hatch is generally available only to those who—due to the singularity of their burden and their otherwise privileged position relative to those below—are in the position to crawl through. Those who are multiply-burdened are generally left below unless they can somehow pull themselves into the groups that are permitted to squeeze through the hatch.

As this analogy translates for Black women, the problem is that they can receive protection only to the extent that their experiences are recognizably similar to those whose experiences tend to be reflected in antidiscrimination doctrine. If Black women cannot conclusively say that "but for" their race or "but for" their gender they would be treated differently, they are not invited to climb through the hatch but told to wait in the unprotected margin until they can be absorbed into the broader, protected categories of race and sex.

Despite the narrow scope of this dominant conception of discrimination and its tendency to marginalize those whose experiences cannot be described within its tightly-drawn parameters, this approach has been regarded as the appropriate framework for addressing a range of problems. In much of feminist theory and, to some extent, in antiracist politics, this framework is reflected in the belief that sexism or racism can be meaningfully discussed without paying attention to the lives of those other than the race-, gender- or class-privileged. As a result, both feminist theory and antiracist politics have been organized, in part, around the equation of racism with what happens to the Black middle-class or to Black men, and the equation of sexism with what happens to white women.

Looking at historical and contemporary issues in both the feminist and the civil rights communities, one can find ample evidence of how both communities' acceptance of the dominant framework of discrimination has hindered the development of an adequate theory and praxis to address problems of intersectionality. This adoption of a single-issue framework for discrimination not only marginalizes Black women within the very movements that claim them as part of their constituency but it also makes the illusive goal of ending racism and patriarchy even more difficult to attain....

NOTES AND QUESTIONS

1. **Reflections on Intersectionality.** Was Crystal Chambers a victim of the Eighth Circuit's failure to recognize the fact that she was simultaneously both Black and a woman? In analyzing the disparate impact and disparate treatment claims, does the Court ultimately consider issues of race separately from issues of gender?

Part of Chambers's problem is that the Omaha Girls Club has a different idea of how a woman should act than she does. The Girls Club's policy indicates that it does not believe that single women should become pregnant because to do so will limit the opportunities available to them. Do you think that this idea has racial images of how women should act imbedded in it? For example, is it significant that a larger percentage of young, single Black women become pregnant than of young, single white women? Is it significant that sociologists have found that in many urban Black communities single mothers have developed strategies for sharing the work and the available resources so as to be able to cope with single motherhood? *See* Carol B. Stack, *All Our Kin* (1974). Could it be that the Girls Club's standard for womanhood is a "white" standard? If this were so, it would mean that Chamber's claims of discrimination should not be decided solely in terms of race or sex, but should simultaneously consider the overlay of race and sex.

How could a court do this without imposing its own views of what ought to be the model of Black womanhood for that particular community? Should the court have been more sensitive to the fact that the evidence revealed that a considerable majority of the *non-administrative* Girls Club staff were Black? Does this imply that a majority of the policy-makers, the administrative staff and the Board of Directors were not Black? On the other hand, what about the fact that the Club serves 1,500 members, 90% of whom are Black? Might they be participating specifically because they (or their parents) approve of the Club's stand on single women's pregnancies? Is this a matter of choice on their part?

These questions lead us back into considering the ways that the law constructs our consciousnesses and identities. The two essays that follow emphasize this point. Using their analysis, can you identify the role that cases like *Chambers* play in constructing a subordinated identity for Black women? Do you agree with this analysis?

Kathryn Abrams, Title VII and the Complex Female Subject

92 Mich. L. Rev. 2479 (1994).

... Title VII ... [c]ases highlighting complex subjectivity have increasingly appeared in court, as persons claiming intersectional forms of discrimination, or manifesting identities that are ambivalent in relation to the existing statutory categories, have sought relief under Title VII. Many courts have been unwilling to accommodate these understandings within Title VII doctrine, requiring that claimants disaggregate and choose among the elements of their identities; others have awarded relief to complex claimants but failed to give an account of the discrimination they face that would help integrate such claims into the mainstream of Title VII doctrine. One factor contributing to these failures is that courts have made little effort to make explicit either the assumptions that underlie complex subjects' claims of discrimination or the barriers that Title VII doctrine currently presents to them ...

[S]cholars [Kimberle Crenshaw and Judy Scales–Trent] bring to legal analysis elements of increasingly influential post-structuralist social theory. They combine, in different ways, post-structuralism's emphasis on the multiplicity and intersection of constructing "discourses" and its depiction of a multifocal, decentered self, whose articulation is variable and dependent on context.

Crenshaw argues that both feminism and antiracism have failed to account for the distinctive experiences of black women. Predicated almost exclusively on the experiences or perceptions of white women and black men, these movements have shaped a legal doctrine in which black women do not exist—and a legal system in which they suffer notorious difficulty making their injuries intelligible to decisionmakers. As she describes the legal failure to comprehend the "intersectionality" of race and gender discrimination, Crenshaw also describes a black female subject who is constructed by multiple influences—racism, sexism, and the failure of feminist and antiracist discourses to account for her position. She illuminates this process of construction in her discussion of rape. Like black men, black women are shaped by the coercive violence of white men; like white women, they often experience it through sexual assault. But unlike either, black women must confront a legal system that for generations has refused their testimony as to matters of sex and still mediates it by reference to a library of particularized stereotypes; they also must face liberatory movements that submerge the distinctive circumstances of black women by focusing on types of victimization characteristic of white women or race-based sexual terrorism targeting black men. This system of intersecting yet marginalizing influences creates a subjectivity that is multifocal; against the backdrop of the available but always insufficient categories, it seems to be in constant movement.... Crenshaw describes a subjectivity that displays, in different moments, affinities with black men, affinities with white women, and solidarity with the marginalization and the experience of other black women.

Scales–Trent offers a slightly different emphasis. She is concerned not only with the failure of established legal categories to comprehend intersectional experience but also with the failure of any categories to capture the ambivalence and contradiction of those who apparently reside comfortably within them. Writing as a person who "[is] black and look[s] white in a society which does not handle anomalies very well," she describes, through narrative prose poetry, the effects this socially created problem of fit has had on her own subjectivity. She must constantly bear the weight of choosing to be either black or white or confront the sense of dislocation produced when that choice is made for her. Frequently she feels that she belongs nowhere. Distinctively revealing as Scales-Trent's experience may be, she does not present it as exceptional. On the contrary, she stresses the connections it has helped her forge with other groups that live both in and out of salient categories—for example, Native Americans no longer on their tribal reservations—and with groups that repeatedly shape their identities through conscious, performative choices, including lesbians. Scales–Trent's invitation to the reader to consider her experiences as having cross-categorical resonance suggests two larger points about the complexity of subjectivity—points that are also made by Crenshaw and other antiessentialist writers.

The first point is that the multifocal quality of subjectivity, and one's movement between different elements of that subjectivity in expressing one's "identity," is not unique to marginalized groups. The sense of being shaped by multiple, sometimes conflicting practices—exposure to classical music and to gospel—may take on a particular valence in Scales-Trent's case because it is the legacy of an interracial family, but it is not unique to her position as a "white black woman," or even as a black woman. . . . A rich, multiply inflected form of subjectivity prevails across a range of social groups, if observers are prepared to see it. It is only under the influence of categorical frameworks, such as that of Title VII, or conceptions of a unified self, such as those that have prevailed from the Enlightenment to the early years of identity politics, that such a subject appears complex.

Yet although a range of subjects may be possessed of this kind of complexity, the reluctance of many actors, in both life and law, to depart from more unitary conceptions of subjectivity does not have the same consequences for all of them. This is the second insight, and the one more often stressed by antiessentialist scholars. The striations and tensions, the juxtaposed elements that mark virtually anyone's subjectivity tend to be muted in the lives of more privileged groups. The privilege associated with some characteristics—for example, whiteness, maleness, heterosexuality—may permit many people, including those who bear these characteristics, to ignore them, thus reducing the range of influences that are perceived as constructing the subjectivity of group members. The power of certain groups may also permit them to normalize a particular tension or multiplicity in their members' subjectivities, making them less subject to the anxieties provoked by a perception of complexity. Crenshaw notes, for example, that the intersectional identity of black women has often prompted courts to view them as problematic antidiscrimination plaintiffs, whereas the intersectional identity of white men as affirmative action plaintiffs has posed few barriers to recovery. The social and legal reliance on unitary conceptions of subjectivity, therefore, does more than apply a simplifying lens to a range of subjects. It imposes a special burden on subjects who lack such indices of privilege—whose constructive or constitutive influences place them at cumulatively greater distance from the groups who prescribe the norm. . . .

The Complex Subject in Title VII Law

In a growing number of cases, courts have been obliged to confront subjects whose self-characterizations, and consequently whose claims, do not fit readily into the categories prescribed by Title VII. . . . In the first [group of cases], the construction of the subject by multiple, intersecting influences leads her to manifest a complex identity or subjectivity that the categories of the statute do not reflect. The claimant in these cases faces a difficulty similar to that described by Crenshaw: she argues that she has suffered discrimination not only on the basis of "race" and of "sex"—both categories independently recognized by the statute—but on the basis of "race and sex," an intersectional form of discrimination about which the statute is largely silent.

In the second set of cases, the difficulty is closer to that described by Scales–Trent: the subjectivity of the claimant is not so much intersectional as ambivalent. The plaintiff claims discrimination on the basis of race or of gender in the standard, singular manner. Yet the claimant fits uneasily within the category established for statutory protection because she manifests not only characteristics associated with the category but also characteristics associated with the category statutorily presumed to be its opposite: this would be the case, for example, for a black person, like Scales–Trent, who might be viewed as white, or for a man who expresses a "socially female" response to sexualized talk or conduct in the workplace. Moreover, in many of these cases, the perpetrator and the victim of discrimination fall technically within the same statutory category, further complicating the courts' analysis. . . .

At first glance, the . . . cases involving the assertion of intersectional discrimination—usually on the basis of race and gender—seem to congregate around two poles. The negative pole is represented by the deservedly notorious DeGraffenreid v. General Motors Assembly Division, [413 F. Supp. 142 (E.D. Mo. 1976)]. In this case the court was asked to determine whether the plaintiffs could maintain a disparate impact challenge to a "last-hired, first-fired" policy on the basis of their status as black women, or whether they would have to challenge the policy on the basis of either race or gender. The plaintiffs had alleged that because of past and ongoing discrimination on the basis of both race and gender, they were uniquely disadvantaged by the defendants' seniority-based policy. The court rejected any notion that "black women are a special class to be protected from discrimination," concluding from the absence of legislative history or applicable precedent that "they should not be allowed to combine statutory remedies to create a new 'super-remedy' which would give them relief beyond what the drafters of the relevant statutes intended." Then, relying in part on the outcomes of contemporaneous Title VII litigation on the basis of race and of gender, the court concluded that General Motors was not liable for discrimination on the basis of gender and dismissed the case without prejudice so the plaintiffs could join an ongoing action challenging the seniority provisions on the basis of race.

The more promising pole is represented by a later case, Jefferies v. Harris County Community Action Assn., [615 F.2d 1025 (5th Cir. 1980)]. In Jefferies, a disparate treatment challenge to the defendants' failure to promote and ultimate termination of the plaintiff, the court acknowledged the possibility of race and gender discrimination that is intersectional, in the sense that it "can exist even in the absence of discrimination against black men or white women." The court considered this ground in addition to the plaintiff's challenges on the bases of race and of sex, despite the fact that the district court had failed to make any findings based on the intersectional claim. The court held that a remedy for "race and sex" discrimination was justified by the language of the statute and its legislative history.... Perhaps most importantly, the court interpreted the "sex-plus" cases as establishing precedent for protection against intersectional discrimination. In these cases, courts held that employers cannot enact rules that discriminate against subclasses of women, distinguished not simply by gender but by an additional characteristic such as weight or marital or parental status. According to these courts, considering this type of discrimination to elude the "sex" category of the statute would permit "the rankest sort of discrimination against women." It would be illogical, the Jefferies court concluded, if women were protected when the additional factor was a statutorily neutral characteristic but not when the additional factor was also statutorily protected. Hence the court remanded the case for consideration in terms of "race and sex" discrimination, noting that for purposes of establishing the prima facie case and pretext, "black males and white females ought to be treated as persons outside Jefferies' class."

This apparently dichotomous judicial approach, however, is not the end of the story. On the one hand, after Jefferies, most courts have been reluctant to follow DeGraffenreid in dismissing intersectional claims out of hand. On the other, Jefferies itself has not proved a durable precedent in securing judicial recognition of intersectional claims. It has been followed in a number of cases, including the much-discussed Chambers v. Omaha Girls Club, in which the court acknowledged the possibility of a disparate impact action based on discrimination against either black women or single black women before concluding that defendant's "role model" policy was based on business necessity. Jefferies has also been restrictively construed, however....

Some responsibility for this retreat, however, must fall on the Jeffries court, for that opinion offers scant elaboration of the innovation it effects. Although it states that discrimination against particular subgroups of women should be viewed as statutorily pernicious and that black women may suffer discrimination when black men and white women suffer none, Jeffries provides little substantive description of the discrimination it seeks to prevent. . . .

[S]exual harassment doctrine, like that relating to hiring, firing, and promotion, reflects some steps toward the recognition of complex claimants. The acknowledgment in ... [some cases] that black women may be differently situated than white women with respect to proving a sexual harassment claim reflects a recognition that even as women—that is, those who are claiming sexual harassment—claimants are constructed by race as well as gender. But the incomplete and flawed elaboration of that understanding by the courts has created difficulties. The emphasis on aggregation of evidence has raised an inference—operating as a limit, even though it is never explicitly defended—that discrimination against black women should be viewed primarily as an additive phenomenon. Moreover, in failing to discuss particular epithets and the kinds of discriminatory understandings they convey, courts have forgone an important opportunity to show an intersectional dynamic at work. Terms like "nigger," "bitch," or "Buffalo Butt" are unlikely ever to be used against either black men or white women; they convey a kind of racialized sexual hostility, or sexualized racial hostility, that cannot be disaggregated into its component parts. The failure to discuss the nature of the discriminatory animus at work in such examples has meant that triers of fact cannot see the racial element in what has been styled as sex discrimination. . . . This failure has shaped unnecessary losses for black women plaintiffs, as well as a reluctance on the part of many claimants to plead "race and sex" harassment.

Thus, although some courts have felt compelled to acknowledge the intersectional position of black women by allowing a "race and sex" claim under Title VII, they have not consolidated that protection by providing an account of the discrimination that this group faces. They may invoke, though not explain, an aggregative understanding of "race and gender" discrimination. Even this partial description comes at a price: it requires plaintiffs to separate evidence into "race" and "gender" categories and select a primary focus in presenting their case. Moreover, the failure to explain how intersectional discrimination in these cases relates to more conventional understandings of discrimination can make the claims of black women seem narrow or partial, while the claims of white women—who also occupy an intersectional position—appear inclusive or universal. Finally, the courts' view of intersectionality in these cases as an anomaly, rather than as a way of re-conceiving the subjectivity of any claimant, leads them to cabin rather than to investigate its influence. . . .

The claimants featured in the second set of cases manifest a different kind of complex subjectivity: it is produced, not by the intersection of two categorical traits, but by the juxtaposition of qualities thought to occupy polar positions within the same categorical dichotomy. Plaintiffs may be blacks with light skin, men who behave in "socially female" ways, women who respond to sexual harassment in a manner more typical of men. The ways in which courts respond to such claimants are not dissimilar from those described above. Courts do not consistently deny relief to such claimants, so plaintiffs have been victorious even in cases in which the perpetrators of their discrimination come from the same statutory categories. Yet courts often fail to acknowledge such complex claimants as the victims of discrimination, and the persuasiveness and stability of even positive outcomes has been undermined by a failure to elaborate the discrimination that such cases reflect. . . .

A look at two leading cases of this type, Walker v. Internal Revenue Service, [713 F. Supp. 403 (N.D. Ga. 1989)], and Hansborough v. City of Elkhart Parks and Recreation Department, [802 F. Supp. 199 (N.D. Ind. 1992)], reveals the analytic knots in which courts have tied themselves, seeking to respond to the complexity they present.

Walker was a suit by a light-skinned black woman, alleging discrimination perpetrated by a dark-skinned black woman. After a "strained" relationship in which the plaintiff was frequently singled out for criticism regarding insubstantial or imagined faults, she was fired by her supervisor for tardiness, incompetence, and attitude problems. She alleged that her termination was attributable to her supervisor's bias against light-skinned black people. The court rejected a magistrate's recommendation that the defendant be granted summary judgment because a Title VII action was not available to a light-skinned black person claiming discrimination by a dark-skinned black person.

The court accepted the plaintiff's characterization of the case as discrimination on the basis of "color," rather than race. It relied first on statutory interpretation to conclude that it was appropriate to treat race and color as distinct, and then on a series of section 1981 cases that appeared to support the court's recourse to color by permitting actions between people who were technically of the same race but differed in "ancestry or ethnic characteristics. . . . It then concluded that the fact that the plaintiff and the defendant were both black did not, as a matter of law, prevent the plaintiff from suing under Title VII: whether the plaintiff's allegations are justified, despite the fact that the defendant belongs to the same race, is a question of fact that must be determined by the fact finder."

In Hansborough v. City of Elkhart Parks & Recreation Department, which concerned a claim of discriminatory termination, the court framed the question, not in terms of color, but in terms of race. . . . Relying apparently on the atypicality of the claimed discrimination, however— among the interactions of people of the same race, or among the concerns of Title VII's framers—the court held that a plaintiff who alleges intraracial discrimination bears a "relatively unique and difficult burden of proof." Hansborough, who offered no such evidence regarding the employer in general or his supervisor in particular, failed to carry this burden.

These cases resolve the categorical questions presented without confronting the kind of discrimination involved. This is particularly true in Walker, which uses the category color to step around the question. Reliance on color is not irrational in a case where the distinction between the two black parties is one of skin tone, or color. The court's insistence, however, on treating color as a category distinct from, and unshaped by the incidents of, race is more problematic. It suggests that the court may be less interested in clarifying its understanding than in evading the paradoxical racial relationship between the parties. Differences in color may be relevant to blacks in an aesthetic sense that has little to do with interracial discrimination.... Yet when differences in color become a source of antagonism between blacks, the reasons cannot be so easily separated from race. In this society, whites have made Caucasian race—and, by inference, fair skin—a source of privilege. That blacks may internalize these meanings and apply them against other blacks seems paradoxical but is sometimes true: this pattern was, in fact, the subject of expert testimony when Walker returned for fact-finding. Yet it is an issue that the court avoids raising or delineating when it acknowledges the availability of an intraracial claim. The court's attempt to steer clear of these turbulent waters by resurrecting and isolating the quiescent statutory category of color seems peculiar and strained.

Although Hansborough resolves to decide the question on the basis of race, it too reaches an odd explanatory impasse.... Both decisions suggest that the problem highlighted ... cases is one of shifting antagonisms between ethnic sub-populations of the same racial group. The Walker court completes the analogy, citing the "sharp and distinctive contrasts amongst native black African peoples (sub-Saharan) both in color and in physical characteristics." But Walker is not a case between blacks who trace their lineages to different African subcultures; Hansborough describes no apparent differences between the plaintiff and the alleged perpetrators. The subgroup differences, categorical ambivalences, and displaced antagonisms that might fuel discrimination among blacks are never framed or discussed....

The sexual harassment cases present a similar difficulty in the context of gender: the possibility that one can both be and not be a member of a protected group—the possibility that one can suffer group-based discrimination perpetrated by a member of the group in question. In the sexual harassment cases, the social constructedness—and ultimate instability—of the statutory categories is even clearer: what causes the plaintiff to fit uneasily within the established category is not a physical characteristic, such as skin color, but the plaintiff's own behavior. In the most striking of these cases, the plaintiffs are men who fit awkwardly within their ostensible gender category because of their discomfort with sexualized talk and conduct in the workplace....

These cases suggest that courts are far more sympathetic to male sexual harassment claimants when they present the image of a normative, unambiguously male subject who receives unexpected sexual attention from another male in the workplace. This is attributable in part to ... the fact that plaintiffs such as ... Goluszek [in Goluszek v. Smith, 697 F.Supp. 1452 (N.D. Ill. 1988)] challenge accepted notions of what it means to be a man, or a male victim of discrimination. Their combination of male characteristics—XY chromosomes, male genitalia—and what are usually thought to be female characteristics—sexual naivete or aversion to sexualized talk—seems to make the courts as uncomfortable as it makes their co-workers. The courts express this discomfort by asking whether discrimination against these claimants can be considered discrimination against men. Fueled in part by their skepticism about the male discrimination claim—reflected in the intermittent insistence on a nexus with social disempowerment—and in part by their skepticism about these males, they want a clear and unitary definition of gender discrimination against men. The holy grail in these cases is a kind of mirror image of gender discrimination against women: at the very least, the courts require some form of animus that treats men as a unified group. What the courts explicitly decline to do is to look beneath biological or unitary classifications at the more complex social interactions they seek to describe and regulate. Were they to do so, they might see that not all men share unambivalently in the qualities socially connected with maleness and that discrimination by men against men does not parallel gender discrimination against women but is, in fact, strongly colored by it. What Goluszek ... suffered was either a form of gender discrimination against women—derision of some of the same qualities that make women targets for sexual harassment—or a form of gender discrimination against men that disciplines not the group but a distinct subset for abandoning the qualities associated with men for the more socially stigmatized characteristics associated with women. Despite their targeting of a different group of objects, these forms of discrimination have more in common with broadly recognized forms of gender discrimination against women, including those associated with sexual harassment, than these courts are inclined to admit. . . .

In large part, courts have failed to come to terms with the complex, and often unstable, arrangement of seemingly contradictory characteristics that comprise the subjectivity of any individual. Walker can be both black and white; she may seem white to her supervisor, Ms. Lewis, but black to the white CEO of the company. Goluszek can be biologically male and socially female; this combination of traits can appear more discordant in the context of a sexualized workplace than in Goluszek's family or church. Rather than seeing such shifting combinations as predictable characteristics of human beings, many courts treat them as anomalies to be swept under the carpet with empty analogies in Walker or Hansborough, or met with the demand for groupwide showings in the sexual harassment cases. As with the cases involving intersectional plaintiffs, these complex notions of subjectivity are not permitted to recast the courts' image of the Title VII claimant, nor are they linked to a theory of discrimination that could locate them within the world of wrongs Title VII is intended to right. . . .

[U]nderstandings of discrimination under Title VII partake, to a greater or lesser extent, of several assumptions. These assumptions help to explain the outcomes in those cases involving complex claimants surveyed above. First, Title VII doctrine assumes that the members of a protected group are easily identifiable. Characteristics such as race and gender are understood to be biologically given, and biological transmission is in turn associated with fixity and lack of ambiguity. There is always the possibility of a claimant who reflects a mixed biological legacy, as in Walker, or whose appearance does not reflect what is conventionally understood to be his biological endowment.... But such cases are regarded as exceptional and are usually dispatched by recourse to some readily applicable rule. Thus, even in the context of sexual harassment, the biological understanding of protected characteristics makes it difficult for courts to see in claims of men like ... Goluszek the kinds of gender discrimination Title VII proscribes.

Second, in order to be considered discrimination against group X, the employer's judgment—which may posit employment-related incapacity or generalized inferiority (disparate treatment, sexual harassment) or reflect insensitivity to the group's social circumstances (disparate impact)—must be applicable to the group as a whole. Discriminatory judgments are understood to apply to the group as a whole when they are applicable to all subgroups or are aimed at persons who are not distinguished by any group-based characteristics other than that designated X. Because all people have many such characteristics, these paradigmatic persons are likely to be those whose non-X characteristics are accorded sufficient privilege to render them invisible for statutory purposes—for example, white women are only distinguished by gender, but Latina women are distinguished by race and gender....

Third, actions or judgments that are most readily understood to be discrimination against group X are made by members of another group. Discriminatory judgments arise from irrational animus, ignorance, or error. There is little reason to believe that a person would be ignorant, mistaken, or intolerant of qualities he possesses himself, particularly when his attitudes are not understood to be integrally shaped by any broader social structures. Thus, when a judgment against a person in group X is made by another person in group X, it is assumed to be the result of personal antagonism, rather than group-based beliefs.... The courts have strayed from this assumption in particular cases: Walker, for example, permitted a departure because the category X—race—could be subdivided and adjudicated according to another protected category—color. But the necessity of this reclassification, or of the imposition of additional burdens of proof in cases such as Goluszek and Hansborough, suggests the importance of the general rule: cases that depart from the assumption of discrimination as an intergroup phenomenon are treated as anomalous and are circuitously or unsatisfactorily explained.

A fourth assumption, reflected more fully in the dominant understanding of discrimination, is that discriminatory actions or judgments are workplace-specific barriers that hinder employment opportunity, rather than parts of a larger system of discrimination that shapes the consciousness of those subject to it or intersects with other systems of discrimination. Under the equality theory that informs disparate treatment law, individuals are formed prior to social interaction. If these individuals are perpetrators of discrimination, they assume discriminatory attitudes through ignorance, irrationality, or conscious choice; if they are victims, they encounter these attitudes as impediments to their at least partially autonomous progress through the workplace. In neither case do these attitudes, in any important sense, constitute the self-conception or subjectivity of those who hold them. Judges and advocates who embrace this view make no effort to link discriminatory judgments in the workplace to those that operate outside, beyond observing that they may be animated by similar ignorance or prejudiced irrationality. To look for social patterns that are not specifically traceable to the judgments of particular individuals is to depart from the focus on individual human agency that is assumed to be the predicate of legal responsibility....

Modifying the four assumptions enumerated above requires legal advocates and decision-makers to revise their views of two critical concepts: the nature and operation of discriminatory judgments, and the characteristics that statutory categories are intended to protect. Underlying each of these reconceptualizations, however, is a vision of the social construction of the subject, and the role of discrimination in that process, that must also be implemented in order fully to accommodate the complex subject.

a. *The nature and operation of discriminatory judgments.* The first set of necessary changes concern the nature and operation of discriminatory judgments: how they arise, how they are connected to other structures of oppression or systems of belief, how they shape those who hold them and those to whom they are applied. In order for courts squarely to address the claims of the complex subject, they must reconceive discrimination, not as a judgment of contrasting capacity that is offered to justify differentiation, but as a judgment of devaluation that effects disempowerment. Catharine MacKinnon has played a pivotal role in shifting the emphasis in discussions of gender discrimination from a focus on women's differences from men to a focus on men's domination of women through sexual objectification. While this analysis has informed some portions of sexual harassment doctrine, it has yet to reach the basic understandings beneath many areas of Title VII law. The question in these areas is still whether an employer has expressed a judgment of differential capacity, not how such judgments shape the institutional position and self-conception of affected employees. As decision-makers shift their focus to judgments of devaluation that justify and effect disempowerment, including judgments of differential capacity, it will be easier to observe themes and patterns in devaluative imagery that will enhance the understanding of intersectional discrimination....

Understanding discrimination as devaluation, however, means more than noting the varied forms that it takes. It also means understanding the way it effects the disempowerment of its subjects. This understanding in turn requires a more constructivist view of the formation of the subject, as well as of the effects of discrimination. The dominant approach posits a world of fully formed beings, who either embrace or are thwarted by opinions of differential capacity. The move toward discrimination as devaluation requires an understanding of the way discrimination helps form the subject. Devaluative imagery employed in the workplace rests on and resonates with a complicated system of cultural myths, images, and stereotypes, which are reflected in many other social institutions and practices. An employer who refers to a female worker as a "nice piece" or derides her as a "dumb bitch" is not originating novel images; he is invoking images with elaborate resonance in the familial, social, or educational experience of most women in this society. Sustained exposure to these images in a variety of contexts shapes our vision of ourselves.... Viewed in this way, employment discrimination represents, not a chosen course of institutionally specific conduct, but a reiterative practice that further enmeshes us in, and shapes us according to, oppressive social patterns.

Reconceiving discrimination in these ways would offer many insights germane to the circumstances of complex claimants. It would suggest, first, that there is no ground for privileging, in an anti-discrimination regime, discriminatory judgments that are general in their application to a group. Although some of the images through which women are devalued and socially or politically dominated apply to the entire group, much of the power of gender discrimination as a system arises from its particularity and variability—its capacity to encompass and explain many different groups of women. Thus judgments that apply to some women—be they sexually active women or mothers or black women—are equally important to the system of discrimination, and especially gender discrimination, despite their particularity. Second, reconceiving discrimination would help explain how some compound forms of discrimination are intersectional rather than merely aggregative. The stereotype of the promiscuous black woman is a vehicle for race discrimination, in that it racializes its sexual subject by reference to a dehumanizing image; and it is a vehicle for gender discrimination, in that it ascribes a form of stigmatized sexuality to the female portion of a particular race. But it is also a terrain on which race and gender discrimination come together to reinforce and, by particularizing, reshape each other.

b. *Protected categories and characteristics.* A social constructivist emphasis also underlies the second change that would be necessary to incorporate the complex subject in Title VII law: a change in the understanding of the characteristics that statutory categories protect. The assumption implicit in the Title VII regime is that membership in protected categories is biologically conferred and therefore unambiguous and stable over time. Legal actors must come to understand that biologically based qualities acquire their meaning through a process of social construction—through the practices and self-understandings of group members, the corrosive images of systems of discrimination, and a range of other influences—and the complexities of this process create far more variation and ambiguity than current doctrine assumes.

Understanding characteristics such as gender or race as given meaning largely through social interaction has several implications. First, membership in a protected category arises, not simply through possession of a biological trait, but also through manifestation of social practices or qualities that have come to be associated with it. As a result, there is more ambiguity as to who belongs in particular categories, because there are more indices of what constitutes group membership or identity and more ways in which these social and biological indices can intersect with each other. Second, discrimination can be quite various in the kinds of attributes that it targets: while some forms of discrimination follow the biological trait, others are tied to its social manifestations, and still others track the intersection of the biological with the social. Women are sometimes stigmatized on the basis of their sex—that is, simply because they are not men—but they may also be stigmatized for manifesting characteristics that are socially female. Men may also be stigmatized if they combine biological masculinity with socially female characteristics, such as emotionalism or sensitivity to sexual conduct. Women, on the other hand, may be less severely stigmatized if they manifest socially male characteristics, such as an exclusive career focus in the workplace. But biological "outsiders" are not always assured of protection by assuming the characteristics of the socially dominant group. The interest of many social groups in preserving the meanings made intelligible by social practices, and the interest of dominant groups in preserving the power conferred on them by the comparative valuation of such practices, means that sanctions may be imposed on biological group members who attempt to escape from the social characteristics ascribed to their groups. These factors mean that who may be considered a woman or a black for purposes of Title VII scrutiny is a multifaceted question, capable of contextually variable answers.

The understandings elaborated above would permit courts to respond more fully to categorically ambivalent claimants. First, they would make clear that categorical ambivalence, such as that described by Scales-Trent, is not an anomaly but a form of subjectivity that occurs all the time. Because they possess biological and social characteristics that admit of ambivalence within themselves and in combination, it is not unusual for people to manifest, in juxtaposition or combination, qualities assigned to different sides of a race or gender dichotomy. Nor, moreover, is it unusual to see discrimination aimed at different bases of a raced or gendered identity. A brief perusal of any set of sexual harassment cases suggests that women are sometimes harassed in response to their biological sex, at other times harassed in response to their manifestation of socially female characteristics, and at still other times targeted for their divergence from socially female characteristics. Courts have rarely felt compelled to look into these distinctions, because the recurrent factor, biological sex, is taken—often incorrectly—to explain all varieties of abuse. If they were to do so, they would see patterns of discrimination that would justify enforcement in cases like Goluszek. The illumination of such practices as stigmatizing the social practice—notwithstanding its separation from the biological characteristic—or disciplining departures from race or gender norms can help place discrimination against categorically ambivalent claimants within the wider discriminatory patterns that Title VII targets. . . .

Vicki Schultz, Telling Stories About Women and Work
103 Harv. L. Rev. 1750 (1990).

How do we make sense of that most basic feature of the world of work, sex segregation on the job? That it exists is part of our common understanding. Social science research has documented, and casual observation confirmed, that men work mostly with men, doing "men's work," and women work mostly with women, doing "women's work."[13] We know also the serious negative consequences segregation has for women workers. Work traditionally done by women has lower wages, less status, and fewer opportunities for advancement than work done by men. Despite this shared knowledge, however, we remain deeply divided in our attitudes toward sex segregation on the job. What divides us is how we interpret this reality, the stories we tell about its origins and meaning. Why does sex segregation on the job exist? Who is responsible for it? Is it an injustice, or an inevitability?

In *EEOC v. Sears, Roebuck & Co.,* the district court interpreted sex segregation as the expression of women's own choice.... The EEOC's statistical studies showed that Sears had significantly underhired women sales applicants for the more lucrative commission sales positions, even after controlling for potential sex differences in qualifications.

Although the statistical evidence exposed a long-standing pattern of sex segregation in Sears' salesforce, the judge refused to attribute this pattern to sex discrimination. The judge concluded that the EEOC's statistical analyses were "virtually meaningless," because they were based on the faulty assumption that female sales applicants were as "interested" as male applicants in commission sales jobs. Indeed, the EEOC had "turned a blind eye to reality," for Sears had proved that women sales applicants preferred lower-paying noncommission sales jobs. The judge credited various explanations for women's "lack of interest" in commission sales, all of which rested on conventional images of women as "feminine" and nurturing, unsuited for the vicious competition in the male-dominated world of commission selling. In the court's eyes, Sears had done nothing to segregate its salesforce; it had merely honored the preexisting employment preferences of working women themselves....

Title VII promised working women change. But, consciously or unconsciously, courts have interpreted the statute with some of the same assumptions that have historically legitimated women's economic disadvantage. Most centrally, courts have assumed that women's aspirations and identities as workers are shaped exclusively in private realms that are independent of and prior to the workworld. By assuming that women form stable job aspirations before they begin working, courts have missed the ways in which employers contribute to creating women workers in their images of who "women" are supposed to be. Judges have placed beyond the law's reach the structural features of the workplace that gender jobs and

---

13. Although the degree of sex segregation declined modestly during the 1970's, work remains highly segregated by sex. Throughout the 1980's, for example, roughly 60% of all men and women workers would have been required to switch to occupations atypical for their sex to achieve sex integrated occupations. As recently as 1985, over two-thirds of working women were employed in occupations in which at least 70% of the workers were female. These estimates of occupational segregation understate the degree of sex segregation, because even workers employed in apparently sex-neutral occupations often work in industries, firms, departments, and jobs that are highly segregated by sex.

people, and disempower women from aspiring to higher-paying nontraditional employment. . . .

The story of how courts have dealt with sex segregation in the workplace is necessarily a story about how they have treated statistical evidence in Title VII cases. The purpose of statistical evidence is to demonstrate that women or minorities are significantly underrepresented in the employer's workforce or in certain jobs, thereby proving the existence of the patterns of segregation that the plaintiffs seek to dismantle. From the beginning of title VII enforcement, judges recognized that plaintiffs would often be forced to rely on statistical evidence " 'to uncover clandestine and covert discrimination.' " But almost as quickly as plaintiffs began to use statistical evidence, employers began to devise strategies to undermine its probative value.

One central strategy has been the lack of interest argument. Since 1967, employers have sought to justify patterns of sex and race segregation in their workforces by arguing that these patterns resulted not from any actions they had taken, but rather from women's and minorities' own lack of interest in higher-paying nontraditional jobs. The lack of interest argument attacks the meaningfulness even of statistical evidence showing egregious, long-standing patterns of segregation. For if these patterns are the expression of women's or minorities' independent work preferences, then employers cannot be blamed. Whether such preferences are attributable to biological influences or to pre-work socialization, the point is that employers are not responsible. . . .

An analysis of lower court decisions shows that the courts have relied on two mutually exclusive explanations for sex segregation in the workplace. The conservative explanation accepts the lack of interest argument and attributes sex segregation to women workers' own "choice," while the more liberal explanation rejects the lack of interest argument and attributes segregation to employer "coercion." Even though these interpretations lead to different results, the fact that they are conceptualized as mutually exclusive reveals that they share a common assumption that women form their choices about work, independently of employer action or coercion, in private pre-work realms. . . .

Both conservative and liberal courts have refused to acknowledge that segregation has arisen because employers have historically restricted women to lower-paying, female-dominated jobs. Judges' failure to recognize the influence of historical discrimination on women's work aspirations has led them to adopt an anti-institutional, individualistic approach to evaluating evidence and conceptualizing discrimination in sex segregation cases. The definition of discrimination is limited to taking specific actions to bar women from exercising what are imagined to be preexisting preferences for nontraditional work. The role of Title VII is limited to ensuring that employers do not place formal barriers in the way of women who have managed to form and express preferences for nontraditional work under existing workplace arrangements. To a large extent, however, the structures of the workworld that disempower most working women from ever aspiring to nontraditional work are left unexamined.

This approach was not inevitable. Before the first sex discrimination case raising the lack of interest argument was decided, the courts had already decided a landmark series of race discrimination cases addressing the same argument. In these early race discrimination cases, the courts applied evidentiary standards that presumed that continuing patterns of racial segregation were attributable to historical labor market discrimination, rather than to minorities' independent preferences for lower-paying, less-challenging jobs. This approach recognized that human choices are never formed in a vacuum and that people's work aspirations are inevitably shaped by the job opportunities that have historically been available to them, as well as by their experiences in the work structures and relations of which they have been a part. . . . To counter the lack of interest argument, judges developed a doctrine that I will call the futility doctrine. This doctrine held that even if minorities had failed to apply in representative numbers, this did not signal any lack of interest in the work, but rather a sense of futility created by the employer's history of discrimination. . . .

Early courts applied the futility doctrine in a way that acknowledged the history of racial disadvantage in the labor market. . . . [T]he courts created an almost irrebuttable presumption that any failure by minorities to apply for more desirable jobs was due to the employer's own historically discriminatory practices. . . . [T]his body of doctrine reflected a strong judicial commitment to the view that minorities' work aspirations posed no impenetrable barrier to their full integration into jobs traditionally reserved for whites. This commitment, in turn, reflected an underlying assumption that minorities' current work interests were neither permanent nor inevitable, but rather only provisional preferences formed and expressed in the context of a historically racist workworld. If these work interests had been formed by employers' historically discriminatory practices, then they could also be altered through employers' persistent efforts. Courts universally pressed forward in the belief that employers could "persuade the doubtful and the skeptical that the discriminatory bars have been removed," and thus free minorities to aspire to work many had never before dreamed of being able to do. By acknowledging that people's work aspirations and identities are shaped in the context of what larger institutional and legal environments define as possible, early courts refused to allow employers to escape responsibility for the collective history of labor market discrimination by pinning the blame on its victims. . . .

The lack of interest argument [in sex discrimination cases] depends on the proposition that women are systematically less interested than men in nontraditional work. Its purpose is to refute statistical evidence showing that the employer has underhired women relative to their representation among some eligible pool of workers. . . . Within the interpretive framework embraced by both conservative and liberal courts, employers' practices are defined as discriminatory only insofar as they prevent individual women from realizing preexisting preferences for nontraditional work—and not because those practices are part of a larger workplace environment in which many women have never been able to dream of the possibility of doing such work....

[Below], I examine how judges have used the "choice" and "coercion" explanations to legitimate accepting or rejecting the lack of interest argument.... I refer to the rhetorical justification used by courts who have accepted the lack of interest argument as the conservative story of choice, and to the one used by courts who have rejected that argument as the liberal story of coercion....

The conservative story of choice is the familiar one told by the *Sears* court: women are "feminine," nontraditional work is "masculine," and therefore women do not want to do it. The story rests on an appeal to masculinity and femininity as oppositional categories. Women are "feminine" because that is the definition of what makes them women. Work itself is endowed with the imagined human characteristics of masculinity or femininity based on the sex of the workers who do it. "Femininity" refers to a complex of womanly traits and aspirations that by definition precludes any interest in the work of men. Even though the story always follows this same logic, the story changes along class lines in the way it is told. Cases involving blue-collar work emphasize the "masculinity" of the work, drawing on images of physical strength and dirtiness. Cases involving white-collar work focus on the "femininity" of women, appealing to traits and values associated with domesticity.

In the blue-collar context, the story begins by describing the work in heavily gendered terms. Courts invoke oppositional images of work as heavy versus light, dirty versus clean, and explicitly align the left side of the equation with masculinity (while implicitly aligning the right side with femininity).... Once the court described the work in reified, masculine terms, women's lack of interest followed merely as a matter of "common sense." "The defendant manufactures upholstered metal chairs," said one court. "Common sense tells us that few women have the skill or the desire to be a welder or a metal fabricator, and that most men cannot operate a sewing machine and have no desire to learn." ... In these blue-collar cases, courts almost never state their specific assumptions about women workers' traits or attitudes. Just what is it about women's "personal interests" that causes them not to want to be welders ...? Interestingly, employers and courts almost never invoke women's family roles as the reason for their lack of interest in male-dominated blue-collar jobs. They appeal instead to a much broader, naturalized conception of femininity that draws on physical images of weakness and cleanliness and applies even to women without family responsibilities.

... In the white-collar context, courts invoke social and psychological characteristics rather than physical images. In particular, employers invoke women's domestic roles to explain their lack of interest in traditionally male white-collar work, and conservative courts accept these explanations. In *Gillespie v. Board of Education,* [528 F.Supp. 433 (E.D.Ark. 1981), aff'd on other grounds, 692 F.2d 529 (8th Cir. 1982).], the court explained why women teachers did not want to be promoted to administrative positions as follows:

> [M]ales who are pursuing careers in education are often the principal family breadwinners. Women ..., on the other hand, have frequently taken teaching jobs to supplement family income and leave when this is no longer necessary or they are faced with the exigencies of raising a family. We regard this as a logical explanation and find as a matter of fact that there has been no discrimination in the North Little Rock School District.

In some cases the appeal to women's domestic roles is less direct, but even broader in its implications. In *Sears*, for example, the court invoked women's experience in the family as the underlying cause of a whole host of "feminine" traits and values that lead them to prefer lower-paying non-commission sales jobs. According to the court:

> Women tend to be more interested than men in the social and cooperative aspects of the workplace. Women tend to see themselves as less competitive. They often view noncommission sales as more attractive than commission sales, because they can enter and leave the job more easily, and because there is more social contact and friendship, and less stress in noncommission selling....

In the end, the logic of the story of choice converges in both blue-collar and white-collar cases. It makes no difference that in blue-collar cases gender is described in physical imagery, while in white-collar cases gender is described in social and psychological terms. In both contexts, the story portrays gender as so complete and natural as to render invisible the processes through which gender is socially constructed by employers. The story is powerful because it appeals to the widely held perception that the sexes are different. It extends this perception into an account of gendered job aspirations: if women have different physical characteristics or have had different life experiences from men, then they must have different work interests, too. There is no room for the possibility that women are different from men in certain respects, yet still aspire to the same types of work. If gender is all-encompassing, it is also so natural as to be unalterable. Women's preferences for "feminine" work are so central to the definition of womanhood itself that they remain unchanged (and unchangeable), regardless of what women experience at work. Because there is no room for change, employers do not and cannot contribute to shaping women's job preferences.

The flip side of the coin is that work itself is somehow inherently "masculine" or "feminine," apart from anything employers do to make it that way. With the world neatly compartmentalized into gendered people and jobs, sex segregation becomes easy to explain.... Courts ... often describe women's jobs as "more desirable" than men's jobs, even where women's jobs pay lower wages, afford less prestige, and offer fewer opportunities for advancement than men's. The implicit point of reference for evaluating the desirability of the work, is, of course, the courts' own construction of women's point of view: no court would describe women's work as more desirable to men. The moral of the conservative story is that working women choose their own economic disempowerment....

Like their conservative counterparts, liberal courts assume that women form their job preferences before they begin working. This shared assumption, however, drives liberal courts to a rhetoric that is the opposite of conservative rhetoric. Whereas the conservative story has a strong account of gender that implies a preference for "feminine" work, the liberal story has no coherent account of gender. To the contrary, liberal courts suppress gender difference, because the assumption of stable, preexisting preferences means that they can hold employers responsible for sex segregation only by portraying women as ungendered subjects who emerge from early life realms with the same experiences and values, and therefore the same work aspirations, as men.

The liberal story centers around the prohibition against stereotyping.... This anti-stereotyping reasoning is the classic rhetoric of gender neutrality: it invokes the familiar principle that likes are to be treated alike. The problem lies in determining the extent to which women are "like" men.... Below the surface, ... this reasoning reflects a basic ambiguity (and ambivalence) about the extent of gender differences. For the anti-stereotyping rule may be interpreted to admit that women are *as a group* less interested than men in nontraditional work, and to assert only that some *individual* women may nonetheless be exceptions who do not share the preferences of most women. Under such an individualized approach, the employer is forbidden merely from presuming that *all* women are so "different" from men that they do not aspire to nontraditional work....

[A]t a conceptual level, the liberal suppression of gender difference actually reinforces the conservative story. Because the liberal story assumes that women form their job preferences through pre-workworld socialization, it accepts the notion that only women who are socialized the same as men desire such work. To secure legal victory under the liberal approach, women must present themselves as ungendered subjects without a distinctive history, experience, culture, or identity. But this approach only validates the conservative notion that women who are "different" ("feminine") in non-work aspects automatically have "different" ("feminine") work preferences, as well.

The EEOC's position in *Sears* illustrates this dynamic. The EEOC emphasized that contrary to the district court's findings, it had *not* assumed that female sales applicants were as interested as males in commission sales jobs. Instead, the EEOC had recognized that the women were less interested than the men, and it had controlled for sex differences in interest by isolating the subgroup of female applicants who were similar to the males on a number of different background characteristics and who therefore could be presumed to be equally interested in commission sales. The EEOC argued that "men and women who are alike with respect to [these] ... characteristics ... would be similar with respect to their interest in commission sales." Judge Cudahy, in a dissent from the Seventh

Circuit's opinion, agreed. Although he condemned the majority and the district court for "stereotyping" women, his acceptance of the EEOC's argument suggests that only women whose job interests were being inaccurately stereotyped were those whose earlier life experiences resembled men's. Judge Cudahy's and the EEOC's position assumed that the women had formed specific preferences for commission or noncommission saleswork before they applied at Sears. Indeed, Judge Cudahy expressed this assumption explicitly, emphasizing that the EEOC's case would have been much stronger if it had produced "even a handful of witnesses to testify that Sears had frustrated their *childhood dreams* of becoming commission sellers." Once this assumption was accepted, it was impossible to analyze seriously the extent to which Sears had shaped its workers' preferences. The only alternative was to identify the illusive group of women whose personal histories were so similar to men's that one might safely presume that they had been socialized to prefer the same jobs.

This liberal approach faces two strategic difficulties that leave working women vulnerable to the conservative explanation for segregation. The first may be termed a credibility problem. Insofar as the liberal story relies on an image of women as "ungendered," it is less believable than the conservative story. Like most people, judges tend to find implausible the suggestion that women have the same characteristics, experiences, and values as men. Employers are able to turn this perception to their advantage by arguing that even feminists have acknowledged that our sexist society socializes girls and women into "feminine" roles. In *Sears,* for example, the historian retained by Sears was able to cite the feminist consciousness-raising movement to the company's advantage, asserting that the very need for consciousness-raising was premised on the "recognition that men and women have internalized different personality traits and different attitudes." In the end, it made no difference that the EEOC had controlled for sex differences in background, for the judge believed that even women whose life experiences resembled men's remained sufficiently "different" that they lacked interest in commission sales jobs. The conservative story thus capitalizes on the widely held perception of sexual difference to imply that, because girls are conditioned to conform to "feminine" sex roles, adult women will automatically aspire to "feminine" work. . . .

This leads to the second, related problem with the liberal story. Because it denies gender difference, the liberal approach misses the ways in which employers draw upon societal gender relations to produce sex segregation at work. The liberal prohibition against stereotyping assumes that the problem is that the employer has inaccurately identified the job interests of (at least some exceptional) women who have already formed preferences for nontraditional work. By stopping at this level of analysis, however, liberal courts fail to inquire into or discover the deeper processes through which employers actively shape women's work aspirations along gendered lines. . . .

[A] rich body of recent sociological research . . . [presents] an alternative account of sex segregation in the workplace. Unlike the liberal story, this account recognizes the reality of gender in social life. It acknowledges that women and men are subjected to different expectations and experiences growing up, and that, as a result, they tend to express preferences for different types of work early in their lives. But unlike the conservative story, the new account does not find sex-role conditioning so monolithic or so powerful that it dictates irrevocably gendered job aspirations. Girls may be taught to be "feminine," but this does not imply that adult women will aspire only to traditionally female work throughout their adult lives. Rather, women's work preferences are formed, created, and recreated in response to changing work conditions.

This new account traces gendered work attitudes and behaviors to organizational structures and cultures in the workplace. Like all workers, women adapt their work aspirations and orientations rationally and purposefully, but always within and in response to the constraints of organizational arrangements not of their own making. Providing women the formal opportunity to enter nontraditional jobs is a necessary but insufficient condition to empower them to claim those jobs, because deeper aspects of work systems pose powerful disincentives for women to enter and remain in nontraditional employment. . . .

The new account suggests a more transformative role for the law in dismantling sex segregation at work. Once we realize that women's work aspirations are shaped not solely by amorphous "social" forces operating in early pre-work realms, but primarily by the structures of incentives and social relations within work organizations, it becomes clear that title VII can play a major role in producing the needed changes. Title VII cases challenging segregation seek to alter (at least indirectly) the very structural conditions that prevent women from developing and realizing aspirations for higher-paid, more challenging nontraditional jobs. . . .

The current judicial framework proceeds from the view that women bring to the labor market stable, fixed preferences for certain types of work. . . . I will refer to this view as the pre-labor market explanation for workplace segregation by sex. . . . [But] workplace segregation cannot be attributed solely to women's pre-labor market preferences. Even if young women's early preferences perfectly predicted the sex-type of their first jobs, the sex-type of the occupations to which they aspire changes substantially over time. Indeed, most young women aspire to both female-dominated and male-dominated occupations at some point or another during their early careers. In addition, women's early aspirations bear almost no relationship to the sex-type of the occupations they hold over time. If sex segregation were attributable to the fact that women emerged from early life experiences with stable preferences for work of a certain sex-type, we would not expect to see so many women moving between female-dominated and male-dominated occupations. . . .

If sociological evidence refutes the view that workplace segregation is a function of women's early socialization, it also challenges the theoretical account of gender implicit in that view. By positing that women have chosen traditionally female work, the pre-labor market explanation initially appears to portray women as agents actively involved in constructing their own work aspirations and identities. Instead, this explanation eliminates women's capacity for agency. To explain segregation as a function of women's own choice, one must presume that the content of early sex-role conditioning is so coherent and its hold on women so permanent that it predetermines what they do throughout their lives.... In fact, the content of early socialization is neither monolithic nor uniform. Girls receive ambiguous and inconsistent signals that encourage them in some stereotypically masculine behavior as well as stereotypically feminine behavior. In addition, children do not always conform to even the clearest parental expectations, but respond to parental and other messages with their own interpretations. In light of these factors, it is not surprising that women emerge from early socialization with work attitudes and preferences that are open and subject to revision. Neither life nor people are static....

At one level, these observations seem astonishingly simple. It seems obvious that socialization does not grind to a halt when young women emerge from childhood, but continues behind the office door or factory gate to influence their attitudes and aspirations as adult workers. This simple point has profound implications, however. It challenges much of what has been taken for granted about how gender is reproduced in our society.... As one researcher put it, early socialization is a necessary but insufficient condition to account for sex segregation at work. Keeping women in their place economically requires a lifelong system of social control that must be exercised powerfully within the workplace itself....

The central insight of this perspective is that adults' work attitudes and behavior are shaped by the positions they occupy within larger structures of opportunity, rewards, and social relations in the workplace. Perhaps for this reason, this perspective has been coined "the new structuralism." But it should not be mistaken for deterministic theories that portray people as having no capacity for agency, for it emphasizes that people act reasonably and strategically within the constraints of their organizational positions in an effort to make the best of them. Indeed, this perspective endows people with an ongoing capacity for agency that is missing from early socialization theories. People's work aspirations and behavior are "the result of a sense-making process involving present experiencing and future projecting, rather than of psychological conditioning in which the dim past is a controlling force." ...

The new account of gender and work thus exposes the myths underlying the conservative "choice" explanation. What is more, it does so in a way that moves beyond, and holds more transformative potential than, the existing liberal alternative. The new account has three implications for legal analysis that, taken together, transform the current judicial framework for interpreting sex segregation.

First, the new account frees courts to reject the conservative "choice" explanation without resorting to the liberal suppression of gender difference. Once judges acknowledge that women's early work preferences remain tentative and temporary, they need not deny the force of gender in social life to hold employers responsible for sex segregation in their workforces.... To put it more positively, courts may acknowledge that women have a distinctive history, culture and identity, without concluding as a corollary that they are marginal workers content to do only unremunerative, unchallenging jobs. The new account thus frees courts to portray "women" and "workers" as involving no contradiction in terms.

Second, the new account demands deeper judicial scrutiny of the way employers have structured their workplaces. Once the assumption that women approach the labor market with fixed job preferences is abandoned, it will no longer do to conceptualize discrimination in terms of whether the employer has erected specific "barriers" that prevent individual women from exercising their preexisting preferences. Employers do not simply erect "barriers" to already formed preferences: they create the workplace structures and relations out of which those preferences arise in the first place.... Judges should be skeptical about employers' claims to have made efforts to attract women to nontraditional work. Such efforts are likely to be ineffective unless they enlist the participation of community organizations that serve working women and employ creative strategies to describe the work in terms that will appeal to women. Moreover, even extensive recruiting efforts will fail if the firm manages only to convey an all too accurate picture of organizational life that serves more as a warning than a welcome to women....

[T]he third and most fundamental implication of the new account is that the judicial system is itself inevitably implicated in creating women's work preferences. Once we understand that women form their job preferences in response to employers' practices, it becomes clear that courts participate in shaping women's work aspirations all the time. Preference shaping is an unavoidable part of the job judges do when they decide title VII cases challenging workplace segregation. Every time a plaintiff brings such a case, the legal system is confronted with a decision whether to affirm or alter the status quo. When courts accept the lack of interest argument, they permit employers to organize their workplaces in ways that disable women from forming an interest in nontraditional work. When courts impose liability instead, they prompt employers to restructure their workplaces in ways that empower women to aspire to nontraditional jobs. Judicial decisions that reject the lack of interest argument also create a climate in which it is more likely that employers not involved in litigation will undertake genuine affirmative action through creative efforts to dismantle old patterns of sexual hierarchy. That such efforts can alter women's aspirations is clear from the reports of nontraditional women workers. Thus, judges' decisions are embedded in the fabric of organizational life through which women's hopes and dreams as workers are woven....

G.   SEXUAL HARASSMENT: LEGAL REGULATION OF SEX IN THE WORKPLACE

INTRODUCTION

For many women, the presence of sex and sexuality in the workplace is not only demeaning and stressful but disabling; it can prevent them from functioning effectively in their jobs.

For many radical feminists, of whom Catharine MacKinnon is the most well known in legal scholarship, the social and economic subordination of women is brought about by cultural forces, which separately and together eroticize domination and define women as sexual objects. Women, according to this account, acquire our identity as women through sex. Unlike men, we are reduced, in what we are, to sex. Moreover, because being dominated is sexy, female identity is also inextricably, relentlessly linked to submission and subordination. This sexualization theory, as an account of how and why women are oppressed, underlies the path-breaking efforts MacKinnon contributed to the development of sexual harassment law, *see* Catharine A. MacKinnon, *Sexual Harassment of Working Women* (1979). One of MacKinnon's insights was to see sexual harassment as one of the ways in which men's eroticization of domination worked to perpetuate women's economic subordination.

The readings begin with several articles that discuss the phenomenon of sexual harassment from a variety of different perspectives. The excerpt from *Surviving Sexual Contradictions*—a book by Muriel Dimen, a psychoanalyst and postmodern feminist—disputes the claim that women are mere objects of male sexualizing. Dimen's description and theorization of a complicated reaction to street hassling contends that, although men can (and often do) degrade and demean women through sex, women can also be the (non-degraded) subjects of sexual activities. The next piece in this section is an excerpt from an Australian sociologist's book, *Secretaries Talk*. In it, Rosemary Pringle argues that sexuality permeates the workplace and cannot be totally banished as a manifestation of sexual harassment. On occasion, she argues, secretaries use sexuality as a tool of empowerment. Although some of the shortcomings of sexual harassment law are undoubtedly predicated on an unwillingness to allow women equal status in the workplace, one question raised by Dimen's and Pringle's pro-desire theses is whether some limits should be placed on sexual harassment law in order to preserve some form of non-invidious eroticism in the workplace.

The excerpt from Diana Vellos's article, *Immigrant Latina Domestic Workers and Sexual Harassment*, is included in order to focus attention on the interplay of sexual harassment, race and ethnicity, and economic status. Although all working women are subject to sexual harassment, our experiences of this harassment differ depending on our backgrounds. Katherine Franke's article, *What's Wrong with Sexual Harassment*, focuses our attention on the disciplinary aspects of sexual harassment. The act of sexually harassing a woman not only demeans and degrades that individual, but also provides a means of enforcing norms of "proper" male and female conduct. Franke's work questions the common assumption that sexual harassment stems from sexual desire. In doing so, it expands the definition of sexual harassment to include same sex cases in which insufficiently macho men are harassed by men enforcing a norm of what it means to be male.

These articles are followed by excerpts from several cases. The first, Meritor Savings Bank, FSB v. Vinson, 477 U.S. 57 (1986), represented the culmination of the hard fought campaign to have the courts recognize sexual harassment as sex discrimination. Prior to this, some courts had simply dismissed sexual harassment as the individual misconduct of particular men who behaved boorishly around some women. It was just one of the costs that women had to bear for entering the (men's) marketplace. *Meritor* recognized a claim for "hostile environment" sexual harassment—that the sexual harassment might create an environment that adversely affected the terms and conditions of women's employment. In doing so, however, it raised questions about what would constitute a hostile environment. Harris v. Forklift Systems, 510 U.S. 17 (1993), decided six years later, addressed the question of just how upsetting the conduct must be to the harassed woman. Neither of these cases dealt directly with the ways in which sexual harassment might interact with biases based on race, ethnic background, or sexual orientation. Oncale v. Sundowner Offshore Services, 118 S.Ct. 998 (1998), addressed the question of whether Title VII prohibits harassment in the same sex setting. This returns us to the question of what sexual harassment is. Is it based on sexual desire and domination? On enforcement of gender norms? Or is it, as Vicki Schultz suggests in her new article, a form of sex discrimination aimed at subordinating women and maintaining male dominance in the workplace?

Finally, this section includes portions of two law review articles discussing the interaction of Title VII's sexual harassment law and the First Amendment. Demeaning, derogatory, sexist comments constitute much of sexual harassment. Physical assaults are not necessary to intimidate either male or female victims or to make them feel disheartened, devalued and worthless. As dominance feminists like Catharine MacKinnon have long claimed, words can wound. Words alone can be a means of ensuring that women remain in their proper place. Recently, some commentators have argued that the First Amendment protects even sexist speech in the workplace from governmental regulation via Title VII. Like the same-sex sexual harassment cases, these articles raise the issue of whether sexual harassment can be used as a radical tool to reform ideas about gender.

Muriel Dimen, Prologue: A Woman on the Streets (Any Day, Any Time)

From M. Dimen, Surviving Sexual Contradictions
(MacMillan, 1986).

I am a thirty-seven-year-old, heterosexual, white woman from a middle-class, upstanding, nonchurchgoing, half-WASP and half-Jewish family. I am a sociology professor at a New York City college and a psychotherapist. My life-style would be defined as "bohemian" by my mother's friends, and my concept of fashion can only be described as New York eclectic. I am divorced and childless and live with my cat and my plants in New York City.

I am walking home, and a slightly drunk and slightly disheveled man is following me, saying, "Mamma, oh mamma, baby please, I wanna fuck you, I give good tongue, oh sweetheart, *please.*"

I am annoyed. "Oh, leave me alone. Haven't you anything better to do?"

He sniggers, then turns away.

After I enter the lobby of my building, I wonder, *What was that man trying to do? Did he want to degrade me, attack me, stimulate me sexually, flatter me, or simply tease me? Should I be angry or feel sorry for him?* And I ask, *Why me, anyway?*

The voices in my head immediately provide answers:

What do you expect when you dress like that? My mother responds rhetorically.

But it happens even when I'm wearing my down parka and my overalls, I explain in bewilderment, adding with some outrage, *How dare he talk to me? He doesn't even know me.*

Let me at him, I'll kill the bastard, growls my father.

Oh Daddy, stop it, I reply, embarrassed by his passion.

You know you love it, insists my own analyst.

Maybe, I admit grudgingly, like a patient cornered on the couch.

You must have a pretty poor opinion of yourself if you get turned on by someone like that, comments an advice columnist.

I guess so, I say, feeling a little humiliated.

You can't ignore what's going on around you. You have to hear what's directed toward you on the street, because it's dangerous out there, the indignant, rational feminist in me asserts in no uncertain terms. *One out of two women is the victim of rape or attempted rape at least once in her life. You have to be alert.*

Maybe, I posit. Soothed and vindicated, I stand a little straighter.

I think your reaction is disgusting, pronounces the politically correct social theorist in me. *This man is a product of his environment, his class, race, ethnicity. He is attacking not you but your middle-class privilege.*

I'm sorry, I'm sorry, I plead, filled with guilt.

Perhaps he's compensating because he feels so weak himself, the psychoanalyst side of me counsels emphatically. *He gets rid of his self-hatred by projecting it onto you, and at the same time he can make verbal love to the all-powerful mother whose comfort he longs for.*

Yes, yes, okay, but still . . . , I argue in increasingly louder tones to these contradictory voices, *Still, I don't know him. He doesn't know me. Is the noise coming from a person like the noise of an ambulance siren? Do I have to hear it so that I can get out of the way and not get run over?*

Don't let it upset you, dear, temporizes the voice of the next-door neighbor of my childhood and adolescence (who used to get me or one of my teenage friends into his den on some pretext or other to engage in intense, flirtatious discussions with the door closed). *Just ignore him. Don't give him the benefit of your attention. Don't dignify men like him with a response. You'll only encourage them.*

You don't understand, I shout back at him, frustrated almost to tears. *My brain hears, my desire is stirred, I lose control of my body. My body is no longer mine. On the street my body is theirs. I can define myself all I want, but in their eyes I am a body on the street, two tits and no head and a big ass. My body becomes a cunt, and although I'm not physically raped, psychically I am, and I ache from it.*

And yet, and yet . . . , I go on more quietly to all the voices in my head, *I am moved, touched, even aroused by a man who I think is a creep. I don't understand how this can happen, and neither do you. . . .*

A woman walks down a city street. A man whom she does not know makes an obscene noise or gesture. She counters with a retort or ignores him and walks on. . . . But beneath the surface is a complexity of feeling, thought, and intention that, despite two decades of feminist theorizing and two millennia of women writing about women, we have just begun to decode. Hidden in this complexity are the personal and political contradictions of women's lives, making the experience of street hassling the quintessential moment of femininity in our culture.

What femininity gives with one hand, it takes away with the other. Here's the knot: On the one hand, a woman wants, simply, to be. On the other, she wants to be who she is—a woman. To be a woman, however, makes it extremely difficult simply to be, that is, to be a human being, because women live in the heart of a contradiction. They are treated as unconscious, passive objects but are required to respond as sentient people who acknowledge and participate in a transformation into something that is other-than-human. They become negatives, not-men, and are therefore less than human, a condition that is linguistically, ideologically, and socially construed as masculine. *Mankind* encompasses all human beings; *he* is the abstract, genderless individual, the self. In this construction, "man" becomes Self, and "woman" Other, a self who does not belong to herself.

To be Other is to be the Subject-as-Object. In our culture, social arrangements put women in a perpetually un-self-possessed state, and they are never allowed to forget that both their psyches and their bodies are always liable to trespass. Street hassling is a characteristic example of the predicament of the Subject-as-Object: A man can, without invitation, approach a woman, because the social interaction between women and men is premised on the belief that biology determines behavior. Someone who has a penis has the power, the unspoken privilege, to say anything to—even to touch—someone who lacks a penis and who consequently lacks reciprocal power. Were a woman to initiate a sexually toned conversation with a man she does not know, she must expect that she would be taken seriously. In contrast, the street hassler expects her to ignore his intrusion, to act as if she were not aware of him. Yet her very awareness is what makes her not a mere Object, but a Subject-as-Object.

Despite the success women have had in the corporate world, despite the public acknowledgment of the legitimacy of women's complaints about sexist attitudes, despite women's increased assertiveness and pride in their femininity—despite all the achievements of women's liberation—women are still the Subject-as-Object. Indeed, in the light of feminism's achievements, their status as Subject-as-Object becomes visible. In our culture, men have traditionally been regarded as Subjects, women as Objects. However, if any evidence had been needed to convince the public mind that women were not passive, inert things but active, conscious human beings, feminism has provided it. Not only feminist activists but feminist-inspired women in all fields of endeavor, and of all classes, races, and sexualities, have come to public attention for their activity, will, and independence of mind. The events of the last two decades should therefore have made it impossible for the public eye to view women as Objects any longer. That women continue to be so viewed despite their manifest subjectivity is demonstrated by their unabated vulnerability to street hassling, which in turn reveals the essential contradiction of their lives: Neither Subject nor Object, they are, paradoxically, both. . . .

Women are not men's slaves, nor are they presently at the beck and call of their fathers or husbands. Their position is far more ambiguous than that. They know, as subjects, that they must recognize that they are treated as objects, into which they must sometimes also transform themselves. In order to live from day to day, they must both accept and reject what they know, that they are and are not people. A person is someone whom others treat with a respectful awareness of personal boundaries and dignity, to whom an address, for example, is a request, not a demand, for attention. According to this definition, then, a woman is not a person. At the same time, this is what she is supposed to be, and this contradiction is what she is supposed to swallow with a smile on her face.

The experience of being the Subject-as-Object is an ordinary one in our society. Men have it as well as women. It happens when they go to work for someone else. For at least eight hours a day, they are directly or indirectly subordinate to another's decisions, even while they are supposed to exercise their own judgment about their work. Although this prosaic experience is culturally defined as an anomaly for men and thereby as altogether anomalous, it is taken as a matter of course for women. Women who work for wages find themselves in the same predicament as men, but, unlike men, they do not escape it when the workday ends. They are the Subject-as-Object everywhere they go. . . .

Women's perpetually contradictory existence is based on the way that our society constructs power and in so doing informs desire. The power that women and men have, like the power of any social group, is of two sorts, political and personal. The first is based on the material things of existence, on the economic and political wherewithal to satisfy the demands of physical and social survival. Political power comes from having both a livelihood and a part in the running of society.

The second sort of power rests on the ability to give meaning to life. Personal power requires the symbolic and psychological tools—ideas, a set of values, a sense of entitlement, and forms in which to express these, such as language, music, or art—to define what the world is, what one wants from the world, and how one will get what one desires. . . .

Like the other major social systems that distribute power in our culture—class, race, and sexual preference—gender does so inequitably, giving more power to some people and less to others. Gender makes men into first-class citizens and women into second-class citizens. Women in general have less political power than men, even though differences of class, race, and sexual preference empower some women more than others. Women frequently have to be twice as good as men to get the same job, and, in many industries, they are the last hired and the first fired. Women receive less pay than men for comparable work and move through the salary ranks more slowly. They have not only had to fight for the "universal" rights of "man," such as suffrage and the minimum wage, they have yet to establish the unquestionable legitimacy of rights deemed particular to women but in fact of universal significance, such as reproductive and sexual freedom.

Nevertheless, even when women's political power seems in hand—when they hold down jobs or move up in corporate hierarchies, run for office or win class-action suits—their personal power is still compromised by the way that gender defines their desire. Our culture has two patterns for desire, one for males and another for females. The first pattern honors, masculinizes, and makes adult the felt experience of "I want." The second demeans, feminizes, and infantilizes the state of being wanted, the felt experience of "I want to be wanted," an experience that is in fact active—to want anything at all is to assert a desire—but that slips easily into a sense of passive, dependent need.

Man then comes to mean the active one-who-wants, woman the passive one-who-wants-to-be-wanted. Even though both men and women experience—consciously or unconsciously—both patterns for desire, "man" is conceptualized as the subject of his own desire and master of the other's. In contrast, "woman" is thought to have no desire of her own. Rather, she is desirable, the one-who-wants-to-be-wanted-by-the-one-who-wants.…

Children take in both patterns, for every human psyche contains images of both Self and Other. Merely from the conscious and unconscious behavior of the adults around them, infants sense these two patterns long before they can be said to "know" or "learn" anything at all. However, they do not simply learn a one-dimensional message to the effect that they are either male or female. In the course of socialization, children absorb the contrast between male and female. Through twinned processes of identification and disidentification, they come to know both that they are one gender and that they are not the other. Absorbing adults' behavior and language through interpenetrating waves of consciousness and unconsciousness, each child identifies with the pattern appropriate to the sex assigned at birth and disidentifies with the other. Each recognizes the assigned pattern as belonging to Self and the pattern not assigned as belonging to Other.

The consequences of this doubled process of self-recognition differ for girls and boys. Through socialization, the boy comes to experience "I want" as Self and "I want to be wanted" as Other. The girl comes to connect being wanted with Self and wanting with Other. In response to the surrounding culture, the boy will tend to train himself to be the active Subject who initiates his own desire and to minimize any wishes to be the Object who longs to be desired. The girl, in contrast, will tend to make herself into the receptor of others' desires, the Object who waits to know what other people want of her, all the while holding in reserve the Subject that she is also expected and longs to be.

The reason he forgets his wishes for objectification and she remembers hers for subjectivity is that the pattern for boys is more highly valued than the pattern for girls. In our culture, it is better to be a Subject who wants than an Object who wants-to-be-wanted. Subjects are first-class citizens, while Objects are second-class. First-class citizenship is accorded those who, impelled by their active desire, create things that transcend mortal existence, which is what Subjects are thought to do. Second-class citizenship is the lot of Objects, those whose existence is seen to be as unproductive and uninteresting as dead leaves.

And here the gendered pattern for personal power and the gendered design for political power fit together. Men's first-class political power enables them to create things that endure and thereby validates their first-class personal power. Thus, in the public domain outside the home where they are dominant, men earn hard cash, make material things that last a long time, and conceive ideas that outlive them.

In contrast, women's second-class political power ensures and ratifies their second-class personal power. In the home, where they are thought to belong despite whatever money they earn outside it, women create products, such as breakfast, lunch, dinner, and people, which are perishable and are therefore thought to be inferior, even though, like the fallen leaves that furnish the nutrients for new trees growing in the forest, they are essential to the round of life. . . .

Being the Subject-as-Object is maddening. It is to be both Self and Other, and to be torn between them. In such a divided state of mind, one's perceptions of others, of one's relations to them, and of oneself become untrustworthy. This chaotic moment can seem like madness, to which one responds with a desperate struggle to understand and explain. When, then, a woman turns into the Subject-as-Object, as in street hassling, she can feel as though she were losing her mind. As if to prevent her from going crazy, thoughts and feelings rush in, materializing into a ghostly chorus, each voice shrieking a contradictory explanation for what just happened or a conflicting instruction about what to do about it.

Thus maddened, the street-hassled woman gets mad. Although she may not initiate, she can certainly retaliate. She may talk back to the street hassler. She may mock him and, in the stories she tells to herself and to others, caricature him.

Yet her retaliation is Pyrrhic. Just as the street hassler strips her of her presence and dignity, so she strips him of his. . . .

Behaving in kind, being active—and the only other choice at the moment is to do nothing at all, to be passive—means to support a society in which no one can be a full human being, in which all men and women become objects to one another. When human experience is split between wanting and wanting-to-be-wanted, which are two sorts of longing that every person feels, and when the first part of the division is seen as masculine and good, while the second is feminine and bad—then every life will, overtly or covertly, be a struggle to be the first, not the second. Anyone who embodies the first seems admirable; anyone embodying the second merits contempt. When the street hassler emits obscene noises, he spits out and onto the woman any trace of the despicable state of wanting-to-be-wanted. Any female can, simply because of her gender, be a proxy for him. And he, in turn, proxies for all those other men whose socialization or subculture disallow such direct expression of masculinity-by-rejection-of-femininity. In street hassling, the man retains a semblance of humanity, albeit a violent version of it, while the woman loses even that, rejects her dangerous femininity as well, and becomes as if inert, absent.

It is in this very context that the woman's seemingly passive turn-on turns out to be active. If femininity prevents a woman from asserting "I want" directly, she will do it circuitously. Through the tortuous path of tuning in to and identifying with the street hassler's wants, she can recognize and recapture her own. For even wanting-to-be-wanted is, finally, a form of wanting. Her silenced but living desire resonates with the street hassler's sexual noises, as rude as they are: Her answering arousal to his lewd playfulness speaks past their mutual disavowal. It addresses what they share, their desire, the genderless longing that each feels, the "it" that each wants.

Here, then, is where feeling "like a woman" is a sign of life, not death. When all the voices in a woman's mind tell her to become Other by distorting her appearance or her knowledge of social reality or her experience of her own will or her feelings about her lust, her arousal tells her that she is a Self who lives and breathes. Her turn-on tells her that, despite every pressure to become an Object, her subjectivity nevertheless survives. She continues to want, she is an "I." Her desire reminds her that the man who objectifies her is not a piece of wood but is as human as she. And, finally, her arousal certifies that her anger is also alive and well, for both lust and ire are fueled by desire, without which there is no feeling at all.

Rosemary Pringle, Sexuality at Work

From R. Pringle, Secretaries Talk: Sexuality, Power and Work
(Verso, 1988).

Sex is like paperclips in the office: commonplace, useful, underestimated, ubiquitous. Hardly appreciated until it goes wrong, it is the cement in every working relationship. It has little to do with sweating bosses cuddling their secretaries behind closed doors—though lots of that goes on. It is more adult, more complicated, more of a weapon.

Brenda Jones, NT, December 1972

... If the boss-secretary relation is organised around sexuality and family imagery, this seems to place it outside the modern bureaucratic structures that are a feature of all large organisations. The relationship is often conceptualised either as archaic or as marginal to the workings of bureaucracy "proper". It is argued here that, on the contrary, the boss-secretary relationship is the most visible aspect of a pattern of domination based on desire and sexuality. Far from being an exception, it vividly illustrates the workings of modern bureaucracies. Gender and sexuality are central not only in the boss-secretary relation but in *all* workplace power relations....

According to [Max] Weber's "ideal type," bureaucracies are based on impersonality, functional specialisation, a hierarchy of authority and the impartial application of rules. There are welldefined duties for each special-ised position and recruitment takes place on criteria of demonstrated knowledge and competence. Authority is held in the context of strict rules and regulations and graded hierarchically with the supervision of lower offices by higher ones. Authority established by rules stands in contrast to the "regulation of relationships through individual privileges and bestowals of favour" which characterised traditional structures. Above all there is a separation of the public world of rationality and efficiency from the private sphere of emotional and personal life.

The boss-secretary relationship runs against every one of these crite-ria. By having direct access to the powerful, secretaries are outside the hierarchy of authority. Far from being specialised, they can be called upon to do just about anything, and their work may overlap with that of their bosses. The relationship is based on personal rapport, involves a degree of intimacy, day-to-day familiarity and shared secrets unusual for any but lovers or close friends, and is capable of generating intense feelings of loyalty, dependency and personal commitment. How are we to explain this least "bureaucratic" of relationships? Is it merely an exception or does its existence suggest problems with the way bureaucracy itself has been theorised?

... Theorists of bureaucracy have long recognised that the personal intrudes into the workplace all the time; even that it is necessary to have an informal arrangement alongside the formal structure to motivate people and to make things actually work. It is acknowledged that, far from being a limitation on bureaucracy, informal relations and unofficial practices actu-ally contribute to efficient operations. The "human relations" theorists of the 1920's and 30's showed that people want more from their work than just pay and that the existence of cohesive bonds between co-workers is a prerequisite for high morale and optimum performance.

In these accounts the existence of "the personal" in the workplace is seen as consistent with bureaucratic organisation and even as supportive of it. While the human-relations theorists added an informal dimension, they did not challenge the theorising of the formal bureaucratic structures. In some ways they reinforced the idea of managerial rationality: while *workers* might be controlled by sentiment and emotion, *managers* were supposed to be rational, logical and able to control their emotions. The division between reason and emotion was tightened in a way that marked off managers from the rest. Where the secretary might have been seen as a source of order in the office, she too came to be positioned as the bearer of sexuality and emotion, while the boss was represented as cool and rational. The success-ful manager was the "man" who could control his emotions, and women were perceived as "temperamentally unfit" for management because they were too emotional.... [W]hile the rational-legal or bureaucratic form presents itself as gender-neutral, it actually constitutes a new kind of patriarchal structure. The apparent neutrality of rules and goals disguises the class and gender interests served by them.... The values of instrumen-tal rationality are strongly associated with the masculine individual, while the feminine is associated with that "other" world of chaos and disorder. This does not mean that men are in fact "rational" or that women are "emotional" but rather that they learn to recognise themselves in these conceptions.

... [I]t is possible to see secretaries not as marginal but as paradig-matic of how ... power operates. Thus the boss-secretary relation need not be seen as an anomalous piece of traditionalism or of an incursion of the private sphere, but rather a site of strategies of power in which sexuality is an important though by no means the only dimension. Far from being marginal to the workplace, sexuality is everywhere. It is alluded to in dress and self-presentation, in jokes and gossip, looks and flirtations, secret affairs and dalliances, in fantasy, and in the range of coercive behaviours that we now call sexual harassment. Rather than being exceptional in its sexualization, the boss-secretary relation is an important nodal point for the organisation of sexuality and pleasure. This is no less true when the boss happens to be a woman.

Sex at work is very much on display. It is undoubtedly true that for both men and women sexual fantasies and interactions are a way of killing time, of giving a sense of adventure, of livening up an otherwise boring day. As Michael Korda put it, "the amount of sexual energy circulating in any office is awe-inspiring, and given the slightest sanction and opportunity it bursts out"....

In [Michel] Foucault's account, sexuality in the workplace is not simply repressed or sublimated or subjected to controlled expression. It is actively produced in a multiplicity of discourses and interactions. Modern Western societies have accumulated a vast network of discourses on sex and plea-sure. We expect to find pleasure in self-improvement in both our work and nonwork activities. Purposive activity operates not through the denial of pleasure but its promise: we will become desirable.

Foucault is concerned with the processes by which individuals come to think of themselves as "sexual subjects". Sex has become not merely another object of knowledge but the basis of "identity". The greater the valorisation of the individual as the ideal subject, the greater the demand for techniques of individual training and retraining. The emphasis on individual choice is consonant with the maximising of disciplinary controls. "Controls" operate not to repress but to prolong, intensify and refine the possibilities of pleasure: "Pleasure and power do not cancel or turn back against one another; they seek out, overlap, reinforce one another. They are linked together by complex mechanisms and devices of excitation and incitement." ... Foucault finds some grounds for optimism in the fact that resistance is ever present. While this may mean that resistance is merely an inherent part of the exercise of power it must also create the possibility of displacing that power. People are never just victims but free subjects faced with choices and real alternatives.

The dual possibilities of "resistance" make it appealing for considering the situation of secretaries. Secretaries have been represented as sellouts, as victims, stooges of management, or alternatively as the potential bearers of a proletarian consciousness based on their deskilling and reduction in status. Rather than simply placing them on one side or the other, Foucault's analysis suggests a more fluid and confused situation:

> Instead there is a plurality of resistances, each of them a special case: resistances that are possible, necessary, improbable; others that are spontaneous, savage, solitary, concerted, rampant, or violent; still others that are quick to compromise, interested, or sacrificial ... the points, knots, or focuses of resistance are spread over time and space at varying densities, at times mobilizing groups or individuals in a definitive way, inflaming certain points of the body, certain moments in life, certain types of behaviour ...

Far from being victims secretaries necessarily engage in resistance. This does not mean that they constitute a revolutionary group but neither are they totally inscribed within existing power relations. . . .

While it has opened up discussion of sexuality and power in the workplace, sexual harassment is not an adequate way of conceptualising the issues. It is not sufficient merely to assert that secretaries are workers (as much feminist literature has done) and that sexuality and femininity have no place at work. There is an important additional step of deconstructing the boss-secretary relationship and analysing the place of gender and sexuality in workplace organisation. Opposition to sexual harassment is only one component of a sexual politics in the workplace. It needs to be supplemented with analyses of the ways in which sexual pleasure might be used to disrupt male rationality and to empower women. Merely to attempt to drive sexuality from the workplace leaves the ideology of separate spheres effectively unchallenged. . . .

New technology is often represented as marking the end of the special relation between boss and secretary. Management consultants, employers, journalists and particularly computer retailers argue that in the new paperless office secretaries will either be redundant or transformed into all-round communications workers with sophisticated computer skills. Automation will break down "traditional" relationships, removing the "drudgery", and offering secretaries new opportunities. Marxist accounts are less sanguine but they too predict the end of the "traditional" secretary. They concede that a small proportion of the workforce is becoming "hyper-skilled" but consider the vast majority are headed for proletarianisation or unemployment. The "sexy secretary" with her "bourgeois" pretensions is here overtaken by the *proletarian* figure experiencing similar conditions to those of factory workers. Her gender is subordinated to her changing class position. She loses control of her own work processes and becomes subject to time and motion studies. As the work becomes deskilled and routinised, health problems emerge that were once more typical of the factory than the office. In this account, secretaries disappear into the broader category of office workers, part of a new working class....

Liberal feminists are optimistic about the possibilities for secretaries to move into the management hierarchy and point out that far from being unemployed, secretaries are in short supply. Marxist feminists find themselves in a dilemma. Capitalist relations are seen to break down the old "feudal" elements of the boss-secretary relationship while increasing exploitation.... Though the above approaches differ in significant ways, all represent the boss-secretary relation as an archaic remnant of "traditional" society that will be swept away by the extension of the bureaucratic model to all aspects of workplace organisation. They view sex in the workplace as at best frivolous and time-wasting and potentially at least a form of harassment. "Modernisation" involves the application of a single, rational and objective standard to everyone. Sex discrimination legislation, equal employment opportunity and affirmative action programs may be seen as a logical extension and application of "modernist" principles. Feminists of all kinds have supported such programs. Whatever their limits, their presence signals a whole new climate. "Modernism" has become the official, though not necessarily the dominant discourse....

Feminists have been wary of the "servility" of secretaries, their femininity, their tendency to align themselves with management, their loyalty to their bosses and reluctance to insist on decent working conditions—their willingness, for example, to work long hours for no overtime. At best secretaries appear in feminist debates as "victims", whether of technology, bosses, sexual harassment or of their own lack of assertiveness. This has created something of a gulf between feminists in general and those activist secretaries who have struggled for change. If feminists as a whole have embraced "degendering" strategies it has not been so easy for secretaries to do so.

Secretaries cannot simply withdraw from the stereotypes and insert themselves into a "degendering" approach, nor do they necessarily want to. While most share the feminist concerns for equal pay and equality of opportunity, they perceive feminists as either wanting to be "like men" or hating men. Feminists are seen as both strident and joyless, obsessed with "finding a rapist behind every filing cabinet". In seeking to remove sexuality and femininity from the workplace they threaten to remove not only dangers but also pleasures. Secretaries do not necessarily want to take on "masculine" work profiles and career goals, develop new skills, or perpetually be off on training courses in order to become part of management.

What the secretaries express is dissatisfaction and scepticism about an approach that attempts to set up one path for all workers. Though their militancy is limited, they want a range of options based on recognition of skills, better pay, and working conditions that give them (rather than the employers) flexibility and security.... Arguments about the relationship between "equality" and "difference" have been central to feminist theory for more than a decade but have had surprisingly little impact on practical politics or workplace struggles. Despite the emphasis placed on sexuality, the sexual investments that secretaries and other groups of women have in the existing system have not been understood or acknowledged.

Sexuality cannot be "banished" from the workplace. Attempts to treat it as an "intruder" are basic to the negative representation of women/sexuality/secretaries. It is by insisting on its presence, making it visible, asserting women's rights to be subjects rather than objects of sexual discourses, that bureaucracy can be challenged. This does not mean organising orgies in the office, encouraging sexual harassment or sitting on the boss's knee! All of these things would imply that women's pleasure is first and foremost in pleasing men. It is actually quite difficult to imagine a secretary sitting on the boss's knee in a way that was purely for her own pleasure and not pandering to his desire.

Making sexuality visible will involve an exploration of what it means to be sexual *subjects* rather than objects. Our culture has such a fear of female sexuality that its autonomous expression is viewed as horrendous: Salome demanding the head of John the Baptist. Given such images, it is hard even to begin to imagine what subjectivity can mean for women. But there is a growing body of feminist work on female sexuality that is relevant. While some feminists have concentrated on the coercive aspects of sexuality: rape, incest, domestic violence, paedophilia, sexual harassment and so on, others have claimed that the priority given to danger and coercion has led to a marginalisation of female pleasure....

Given the difficulties involved in establishing women's subjectivity, it is important to be accepting of female sexuality as it is currently constituted. Rather than assuming, for example, that secretaries are always the pathetic victims of sexual harassment, it might be possible to consider the power and pleasure they currently get in their interactions with people and raise the question of how they can get what they want on their own terms.... The acknowledgement of such pleasure may do something to bridge the negative representations that feminists and secretaries currently have of each other.

Establishing female subjectivity is only part of what is involved in making sexuality visible in the workplace. Just as important is exposing the masculinity that lurks behind gender-neutrality and forcing men to be responsible for their own sexual behaviour.... Men's experience of themselves as unitary and autonomous is achieved through the repression of the "feminine". Given that "identity" is at best a precarious achievement, it may be that masculine identity is particularly vulnerable. While women have long been aware of the "fragility" of the male ego, the implications for the larger structure of "male" rationality are only just beginning to be explored. For women, the lesser likelihood of perceiving themselves as centre-stage, and their more decentred notions of self, may emerge as strengths rather than weaknesses. Should women struggle for autonomous identities or celebrate their fragmentation? The political consequences are complex.

While "post-modernism" has as yet had little to say about the work-place it has been critical of the universalising tendencies of modern culture, the failure to acknowledge or celebrate difference and plurality. It is concerned with the politics of play and pleasure and its main strategies are exaggeration and parody. It delights in being "over the top".... [T]he "Olympia" montage created by a community artist working with a group of Sydney secretaries in 1985 attempts to subvert existing definitions of secretaries. Instead of rejecting or moralising about these images she recreates them in loving detail and plays with them. Here the naked reclining figure of Olympia the prostitute is brought together with every imaginable image of secretary, as sex object, femme fatale, temptress, worker, wife, mother holding the boss in the palm of her hand and so on. The whole thing is lit up with flashing lights; it is flamboyant, garish, loud, and above all celebratory. It is constructed to create the possibility of multiple interpretations and indeed everyone who looks at it sees some-thing different. Whether it subverts or reproduces the discourses it paro-dies is an open question. The author cannot guarantee meaning or ensure that her audience will not take the parody seriously!

In their office humour and sometimes in public expression secretaries use parody of themselves and their bosses to powerful effect. Much pleasure is derived from imitating, exaggerating and ridiculing the existing stereo-types. These interventions are necessarily localised, sporadic, spontaneous and may amount to little more than a letting off of steam. To dispense with other political strategies in favour of parody would be a regressive move. Yet it is not unduly romanticising to suggest that parody has a place in the critical assessment of what "modernism" has to offer and in the creation of a larger-scale politics of change.

Diana Vellos, Immigrant Latina Domestic Workers and Sexual Harassment

5 Am. U. J. Gender & L. 407 (1997).

... Domestic service creates a unique social setting in which people from different social, economic, racial and ethnic backgrounds interact in an informal and intimate setting. This social setting must be studied because it raises a challenge to any feminist notion of sisterhood. Domestic service accentuates the contradiction of race and class in feminism, with the privileged women of one class using the labor of another class of women to escape aspects of sexism. A growing number of middle-class and upper-middle class women escape the "double day" syndrome by hiring poor women of color to do housework and child care....

Census figures show that the percentage of women employed in the domestic labor market has decreased steadily since the turn of the century. Even though the percentages have decreased, the racial and ethnic composition has remained much the same. Women of color and immigrant women are still over-represented in the occupation. It seems that the racial and ethnic stratification present in domestic service at the turn of the century still exists today. There has been a shift, however, from native-born to foreign-born women of color in the domestic labor force. In El Paso, Texas, for example, the hiring of maids from Mexico is so common that locals refer to Monday as the border patrol's "day off" because the agents ignore the women crossing the border to return to their employers' homes after their weekend off.

One explanation for the shift from native-born to foreign-born women of color entering into domestic service is that domestic work is thought of more and more as a "low-skill, low-status occupation, and young women, especially black women, are increasingly shying away from it." It is also important to note that most of the work that immigrant women perform is the work that others refuse to accept. Many American workers would be reluctant to sacrifice their privacy and independence and live in someone else's home. Many Americans would see the work as demeaning or as a form of servitude.

Domestic service has long been described as an entry level position for foreign-born women and their children which offers social mobility to move on to higher-status and better-paying jobs. For example, white, European immigrants were able to use domestic service as a transitional occupation. For women of color, though, this occupation does not provide a bridge or transition to other, better jobs. Women of color experience domestic service as an "occupational ghetto"....

EEOC v. Hacienda Hotel [881 F.2d 1504 (9th Cir. 1989)] raises ...interesting issues surrounding undocumented women workers and sexual harassment. *Hacienda Hotel* is a case in which the EEOC alleged that the hotel general manager, executive housekeeper, and chief of engineering engaged in unlawful employment practices against female house-keeping department employees. The unlawful employment practices included sexually harassing women, terminating them when they became pregnant, failing to accommodate their religious beliefs, and retaliating against them for opposing Hacienda's discriminatory practices. The suit involved five current and former Hacienda maids, all but one of whom were undocumented workers.

When some of the women became pregnant, comments such as "that's what you get for sleeping without your underwear," "stupid women who have kids," "dog," "whore," and "slut" were made by the managing staff of the hotel. Other comments such as "women get pregnant because they like to suck men's dicks" were also made to pregnant workers. These women workers were also terminated due to their pregnancies, after being informed that they were too fat to clean rooms. On many occasions, the chief of engineering threatened to have workers fired if they did not submit to his sexual advances. The chief of engineering also made sexually harassing comments to the women domestics at the hotel. Mercedes Flores, one of the immigrant domestics who brought suit, stated that the chief of engineering regularly offered her money and an apartment to live in if she would "give him [her] body". He also assured her that she would never be fired if she would have sex with him.

The Ninth Circuit Court found that Hacienda's practice of terminating pregnant employees violated Title VII and that the hotel was liable for sexual harassment by its supervisors. This factual situation is different from that experienced by undocumented live-in workers who work in private homes. The women in the Hacienda Hotel had each other for support and corroboration. The stories of each of the women strengthened the story of each individual woman. Domestics working in private homes do not have other people to validate or strengthen their stories, and are isolated from other individuals who would be willing and able to attest to their exploitation. Typically, it is the undocumented domestic worker's word against the employer['s] who usually appears to be an upstanding member of society.

Harassment of immigrant women is common. One District Attorney's office and a community group in a Northern California town concluded, based on their investigation in a local case of sexual abuse, that such episodes happen quite often. [Consider f]or instance, Maria de Jesus Ramos Hernandez, who traveled from Mexico to the United States to work for a chiropractor, in order to raise money for an operation to cure her daughter's birth defect. Almost immediately, her employer began to sexually abuse her. She did not immediately report the attacks or run away because she was alone and isolated, with no place to go. She felt she "could not deny him pleasure . . . because of what he paid her." Ramos Hernandez did not immediately report the abuse for many reasons. She was afraid that the doctor would kill her (and no one would even notice she was missing); she had no money, identification, or knowledge of English; she did not think that the police would believe her word against that of a doctor; and she felt that she would be blamed.

Ramos Hernandez's story is similar in many ways to the abuse that other immigrant women face working in the home. Her story helps explain why undocumented women are unable to take action to end the harassment they experience. To respond aggressively to the harassment, they must confront their learned cultural values, including self-blame and passivity. Their inability to understand the situation is further complicated because their cultures have different views of sexuality, which may not include the concept of sexual harassment.

Maria Ontiveros noted that the race and gender of immigrant women shape and enhance the harasser's actions. Harassers choose these women because they lack power relative to other workers, and because they are often perceived as passive and unable to complain. Racism and sexism blend together in the mind of the harasser, so that comments made and actions taken against immigrant women workers embody unique characteristics of their racially stereotyped sexuality. In many ways undocumented working women are targets of discriminatory harassment because of their race. . . .

Many undocumented domestics try to get their immigration status legalized through employer sponsorship. They realize that their illegal status makes them vulnerable to exploitation. If undocumented domestics were legally allowed to work in the United States, they would have more leverage against abusive employers. Threats of deportation would no longer have value.

Romero illustrates this exact point:

Isabel Garcia–Media recalled an employer who threatened to call the immigration when she refused "to clean her house and iron two big plastic bags full of clothes—do everything for $5." She responded by pulling out her resident alien card and telling the employer to call whomever she wanted....

Since legal documentation is so desirable, why are more employers of domestic workers not putting in the paperwork? Many employers fear liability for not paying taxes or providing benefits to their undocumented domestic workers throughout the years. Also, the immigration process is extremely long and burdensome. It is possible to sponsor a housekeeper for an immigrant visa (green card), but the process is so lengthy under the present law that most immigration lawyers advise against beginning the process.... It is important to note that if undocumented individuals work in the United States without authorization, they are barred from adjusting their status in the United States and must leave the country in order to obtain a green card based upon employer sponsorship. The best estimates available state that it will take ten to fifteen years under the current system for a domestic worker, beginning the process today, to obtain a green card. Employers should also know that they cannot lawfully employ an undocumented worker until she obtains an immigrant visa or employment authorization from the INS.

During this long process, an undocumented worker risks seizure and deportation. The sponsoring employer also risks investigation, prosecution, and fines between $250 and $2000. Consequently, many undocumented workers feel trapped in ... abusive working environment[s] while awaiting their legal documentation. Some domestic workers have endured harsh working situations for years simply to obtain a green card. If an undocumented domestic worker chose to leave her employer, she would give up her opportunity for a green card.

Many employers use their ability to help an undocumented domestic worker get her green card to exploit the worker and coerce her into doing more work and performing sexual favors. Employers' rewards and inducements often bind the worker in an emotional and economic trap. Simply the promise to help an employee get a green card obligates the worker beyond the boundaries of the contractual work arrangement. One woman recalled trying to leave a live-in job once she had obtained a green card. "The employer would break down crying, begging her to stay, telling her it was unfair to leave after all they had done for her."

Another problematic issue for undocumented domestics working in private homes is that penalties for employers are minimal and often not enforced. Many immigration attorneys inform their clients that those who hire undocumented workers do violate an immigration law, but not a criminal law. This is a civil violation similar to a traffic violation. It becomes obvious that the immigration laws are not strictly enforced, particularly against employers of nannies or household workers....

The situation which undocumented domestics face is complex because issues of racism, sexism, classism and ... [national origin] are all involved. Undocumented domestics are extremely vulnerable to exploitation both sexually and economically. The current immigration system must be changed so that undocumented domestic workers will have opportunities to work without the fear of deportation and abuse. The services they provide are in grave demand. Accordingly, the women who give these services should be given the dignity they deserve to work and live....

Katherine M. Franke, What's Wrong With Sexual Harassment?

49 Stan. L. Rev. 691 (1997).

Introduction

What exactly is wrong with sexual harassment? Why is it sex discrimination? ...While our intuitions may lead us to conclude that when a man directs offensive sexual conduct at a female colleague, sex discrimination is afoot, the Supreme Court has not offered a theory as to why this is the case.... Although the Supreme Court has not provided such a theory, feminist theorists and lower courts have attempted to do so. Over time, three principal justifications have emerged for considering workplace sexual harassment a violation of Title VII's proscriptions against discrimination "on the basis of sex": (1) it is conduct that would not have been undertaken but for the plaintiff's sex; (2) it is conduct that violates Title VII precisely because it is sexual in nature; and (3) it is conduct that sexually subordinates women to men.... These theories misdirect attention from the real problem: sexual harassment is a sexually discriminatory wrong because of the gender norms it reflects and perpetuates.

According to the theory I develop herein, the sexual harassment of a woman by a man is an instance of sexism precisely because the act embodies fundamental gender stereotypes: men as sexual conquerors and women as sexually conquered, men as masculine sexual subjects and women as feminine sexual objects.... Sexual harassment is a ...disciplinary practice that inscribes, enforces, and polices the identities of both harasser and victim according to a system of gender norms that envisions women as feminine, (hetero)sexual objects, and men as masculine, (hetero)sexual subjects. This dynamic is both performative and reflexive in nature. Performative in the sense that the conduct produces a particular identity in the participants, and reflexive in that both the harasser and the victim are affected by the conduct. . . .

The Jurisprudential History of Sexual Harassment Doctrine

The concept of sexual harassment as a kind of sex discrimination entered the legal imagination relatively recently. After a period of unsuccessful litigation in which sexual harassment claims were dismissed under a kind of "boys will be boys" view of the harm, feminist advocates provoked a paradigm shift in the late 1970s and early 1980s in which the sexism in sexual harassment was recognized in the law.

. . . [F]eminists argued that Title VII's proscriptions against sex discrimination should be understood to prohibit not only sex harassment [harassment based on sex, such as calling female employees "girls" but calling male employees "men"], but sexual harassment—that is, conduct of a sexual nature. While it may seem self-evident today that one can legitimately infer discriminatory motives when a man engages in unwelcome conduct of a sexual nature toward a woman, why is this so? In the individual case of hostile environment sexual harassment, why should we conclude that sex discrimination has occurred, rather than wholly inappropriate workplace sexual misconduct actionable under appropriate state tort or contract laws? Is sexual harassment transparently sexist, thereby amounting to a kind of per se violation of Title VII? Does it violate Title VII because it targets female and not male employees? Or does it inflict a kind of harm that is discriminatory in its impact on women workers? To pose these sorts of questions is to examine the significance of the sexually explicit content of sexual harassment. . . .

Construed according to formal equality principles, the wrong of sex discrimination amounts to the dissimilar treatment of otherwise similarly situated workers. Thus, where women are treated differently than men in the workplace, they are being discriminated against because of their sex: "The critical issue, Title VII's text indicates, is whether members of one sex are exposed to disadvantageous terms or conditions of employment to which members of the other sex are not exposed." . . .

The inclination to reduce the "because of sex" element of a sexual harassment prima facie case to "but for" causation is particularly appealing . . . where the harasser is either proven to be or believed to be gay. In fact, in most of the same-sex sexual harassment cases involving a gay harasser, . . . courts have held that the conduct violated Title VII because the harasser's sexual orientation provided conclusive evidence of "but for" causation:

> If a plaintiff complains of unwelcome homosexual advances, the offending conduct is based on the . . . [harasser's] sexual preference and necessarily involved the plaintiff's gender, for an employee of the nonpreferred gender would not inspire the same treatment. Thus, unwelcome homosexual advances, like unwelcome heterosexual advances, are actionable under Title VII.

Thus, while "but for" causation is implicit in the conclusion that different-sex sexual harassment is discriminatory, it is often articulated explicitly in same-sex cases as a way to limit actionable harassment only to that undertaken by homosexuals. . . .

The doctrine of formal equality has led many theorists to make the argument that sexual harassment violates the principle "that people who are the same should be treated the same." Others have made a different argument: Sexual harassment violates Title VII because it is sexual.

Susan Estrich, who has written extensively on the social meaning and legal treatment of rape, has approached the problem of sexual harassment by addressing the issue of "where and how 'sexuality' fits into sexual harassment." According to Estrich, the "but for" formula of sex discrimination "ignores the 'sexual' aspect of sexual harassment and the unique meaning of such harassment in a male-female context. . . . What makes sexual harassment more offensive, more debilitating, and more dehumanizing to its victims than other forms of discrimination is precisely the fact that it is sexual." Greatly facilitating this interpretation of Title VII is a nominal complexity in the wording of the statute that appears, at first blush, to be "merely" linguistic: In the English language, the word "sex" has two very different meanings. It means gender and gender identity, as in "the female sex" or "the male sex." But sex also refers to sexual activity, lust, intercourse, and arousal, as in "to have sex." This semantic merging reflects a cultural assumption that sexuality is reducible to sexual intercourse and that it is a function of the relations between women and men. This cultural fusion of gender with sexuality has given rise to the idea that a theory of sexuality may be derived directly out of a theory of gender.

Yet, if "the sexual aspect" is going to do much of the work in a jurisprudence that regards sexual harassment as a kind of sex discrimination, then where is the sexism in sex?

For Estrich, the fact that the conduct is sexual in nature is not merely an accidental aspect of the harm, but rather, lies at the core of what makes the conduct sex discrimination. Sex in the workplace is regarded almost as a toxic pathogen by Estrich for reasons also embraced by other feminists. For these theorists of sexual harassment, the sexual aspect of sexual harassment does all the hegemonic work and has the effect and purpose of sexualizing women workers by reducing their humanity generally, and their status as workers specifically, to objects of male sexual pleasure.

[Catharine] MacKinnon is in complete agreement with these insights. For MacKinnon, the harm of sexual harassment lies, in significant part, in the fact that it is an instrument of sex-role stereotyping. She observes that "a sex stereotype is present in the male attitude, expressed through sexual harassment, that women are sexual beings whose privacy and integrity can be invaded at will, beings who exist for men's sexual stimulation or gratification."

More than anything else, Catharine MacKinnon's life work has been committed to making the connection between sexism, sex, and power.

While few courts have gone as far as MacKinnon and Estrich to hold that male sexual behavior is, in some sense, fundamentally sexist, most courts do treat sex harassment differently from sexual harassment. The sexual content of the harassing behavior makes a difference to them just as it does to many feminist theorists. But what is this difference? . . .

In Vandeventer v. Wabash National Corp., [887 F.Supp. 1178 (N.D.Ind. 1995)] . . . the male plaintiff alleged that a male co-worker used obscene language toward him. . . . The court . . . state[d] that when a man touches a woman in a sexual manner, it can be presumed that he does so because of her sex, but that such a presumption should not be drawn from intra-male sexual behavior. Something else must be shown in order to establish the "because of sex" element of the prima facie same-sex sex harassment case. According to the Vandeventer court, merely calling the plaintiff a "dick sucker" was not enough, because "[t]his was a common epithet, not a sexual advance." . . .

In contrast, however, if a man calls a female coworker a "fucking cunt" this term is not considered a mere epithet. And without question, if a male employee asked a female employee to "suck my dick," no court would hesitate to find a violation of Title VII. Thus, the transparency of the sexism in different-sex harassment does not transfer to same-sex harassment cases. Something more than sexual conduct must be proved to render the conduct sex discrimination. . . .

[N]either the different-sex nor same-sex cases satisfactorily answer the question: What is sexist about sex? In the different-sex cases, for the most part, the link is simply presumed. Yet, in the same-sex cases, many courts observe that Title VII does not and should not be read to collapse sex and sexism—something more is needed for sexual conduct to be considered sexually discriminatory. Both MacKinnon and Estrich want to provide that something more. Estrich's concern with the social construction of male and female sexuality stems from deep skepticism about when or whether sexual conduct between men and women in the workplace can ever take place in the absence of coercion. She finds merit in the assertion that "there is no such thing as truly 'welcome' sex between a male boss and a female employee who needs her job." To those who say that a male supervisor's advances are not sexual harassment unless the woman objects, Estrich replies: "At the very least, we might demand that such men look for 'love' outside of work, or at least ask for it first." Both Estrich and MacKinnon share a grave doubt that sexual conduct could ever be equally offensive to male and female employees alike.

Based on this, Estrich makes a rather austere recommendation:

As things stand now, we protect the right of a few to have "consensual" sex in the workplace (a right most women, according to the studies, do not even want), at the cost of exposing the overwhelming majority to oppression and indignity at work. Is the benefit to the few so great as to outweigh the costs to so many more? I think not. For my part, I would have no objection to rules which prohibited men and women from sexual relations in the workplace, at least between those who worked directly for the other.

According to this view, men should keep their hands off women in the workplace and refrain from sex-talk that reflects "the most traditional and most sexist attitudes." Further, sexual relations between co-workers, even if "consensual," should be deemed per se inappropriate in the workplace.
. . .

The argument has been made that sexual harassment is a kind of sex discrimination either because it violates formal equality principles, or because it is sexual. A third approach advances another way to understand sexual harassment as a kind of discrimination based on sex: it is a practice that subordinates women to men. For MacKinnon, the inequality, or anti subordination, approach understands the sexes to be not simply socially differentiated but socially unequal. In this broader view, all practices which subordinate women to men are prohibited. . . .

MacKinnon believes that the inequality or anti-subordination approach best explains the harm of sexual harassment when applied to women's working lives, and has the greatest potential to transform sexually discriminatory workplace practices through the use of law. She relies heavily upon a subordination account of sexual harassment by defining it in terms of what it does: Sexual harassment perpetuates the interlocked structure by which women have been kept sexually in thrall to men and at the bottom of the labor market. Two forces of American society converge: men's control over women's sexuality and capital's control over employees' work lives. . . .

For MacKinnon sexual harassment is sex discrimination because it helps create and further inequality among the sexes. In her view, "[s]exual harassment is a clear social manifestation of male privilege incarnated in the male sex role that supports coercive sexuality reinforced by male power over the job." At times she disavows the notion that biology predetermines male aggression, arguing that biological males are taught to express their sexuality as power and to express power in sexual ways. In this regard, sexual harassment is sex discrimination because "[s]exual harassment is discrimination 'based on sex' within the social meaning of sex, as the concept is socially incarnated in sex roles." When making this argument, MacKinnon understands male sexuality as eroticized domination: power is sexualized, sex is power. While MacKinnon states that the male perspective is a social, not a biological, construct, she more frequently writes of subordination as something that men inevitably do to women.

While the formal equality and sex-equals-sexism approaches to sexual harassment have been adopted by a number of courts, the anti-subordination approach has found less judicial acceptance. . . . Robinson v. Jacksonville Shipyards, Inc., [760 F.Supp.1486 (M.D. Fla 1991)] represents the jurisprudential high water mark in this area. The court in Robinson, more than almost any other court, was willing to regard the shipyards' sexually polluted work environment [full of pictures of naked women and other sexually graphic material] as an expression of a kind of coercive male sexuality from which female workers could not escape short of quitting their jobs. More typical are cases in which notions of subordination presumably animate the court's willingness to infer that sexual conduct was undertaken because of sex. One might conclude from the Meritor decision that the Court embraced the notion that sexual harassment is about sex-based power, while refusing MacKinnon's fundamental insight that the subordination of women is always sexual.

Not surprisingly, the antisubordination principle has acted as a road-block to same-sex sexual harassment plaintiffs. Where a man directs offensive sexual conduct at a woman in the workplace, the conduct reproduces a subordinating dynamic that it is widely believed Title VII was intended to address. But when a man directs offensive conduct of a sexual nature at another man, it fails to reproduce that same historical script, or so the argument goes. For this reason, virtually all of the courts that have refused to find a cause of action for same-sex sexual harassment have reasoned either that the conduct did not create an anti-male environment, or that as a matter of law men cannot be sexually harassed by other men because they are not a discrete and vulnerable group. . . .

Men, therefore, cannot be the victims of sexual harassment because their sexual objectification, either at the hands of women or other men, would not mirror this subordinating social hierarchy. Sexual epithets, thus, "do not demean men as a group, but only demean the recipient by implying that, although he is male, he is not properly a member," or that his male pedigree is otherwise questionable. This less sophisticated form of the anti subordination principle underlies the courts' findings in many same-sex harassment cases that the conduct complained of does not and cannot violate Title VII. . . .

All three accounts of sexual harassment as a form of sex discrimination have, at one time or another, convinced courts that the sexual harassment of working women violates Title VII. At the same time, all three paradigms have proven inadequate in providing an account of how sexual harassment might be a kind of sex discrimination. I believe that the inferences courts now draw in traditional male/female sexual harassment cases make sense. They represent an appropriately efficient method by which female plaintiffs can prove that they have been discriminated against because of their sex. What concerns me is that these inferences are drawn in the absence of an underlying theoretical account of the wrong of sexual harassment. The absence of a coherent doctrine both in traditional different-sex cases, and in more novel same-sex cases has significant consequences, and is ultimately dangerous for the larger project of ending gender-based discrimination and bias. In the following section, I show how the three dominant accounts of sexual harassment do not do the work they promise to do, and that they deflect attention from the real gender-based harm that makes sexual harassment a form of sex discrimination. . . .

A Critique of the Prevailing Conceptions of Sexual Harassment as Sex Discrimination

The sexual nature of the offending conduct figures prominently in all three of the dominant accounts of the wrong of sexual harassment. And so it should, given that it is the sexual content of the harassment that sets it apart from all other forms of workplace harassment, and that distinguishes it from sex discrimination more generally. But by locating sex at the center of the analysis, all three accounts make a serious mistake. They obscure the degree to which sex is the method, but sexism is the meaning of sexual harassment. That is, sex is "[the] means through which power is articulated." Even as courts have embraced, either expressly, or implicitly, some feminist conceptualizations of sexual harassment as sex discrimination, they have simplified, distorted, and selectively (mis)appropriated the arguments made by feminists in favor of recognizing a Title VII cause of action for sexual harassment. . . .

First, I will explain how formal equality—understood as "but for" causation—inappropriately reduces the harm of sexual harassment to the simple expression of sexual desire. The seriousness of this error is starkly revealed in the same-sex cases where it has been magnified and fixed in ways that will haunt both same and different-sex cases in the future. Next, the simple equation of sex with sexism—a dynamic that figures prominently in some of the cases many feminists consider "good" cases—portends dangerous consequences for female sexual agency within and without the workplace. Finally, while I regard the anti-subordination view of sexual harassment as the most principled account of the wrong of sexual harassment, this theory must abandon the notion that sexual subordination is something that men, and only men, can do to women, and only women. . . .

The "but for" formulation of the wrong of sexual harassment, implicit in most different-sex cases, yet explicit in the same-sex cases, has been regarded as an uncontroversial and even principled way of understanding the "because of sex" element of the prima facie sexual harassment case. That courts have turned to the "but for" formulation in order to resolve same-sex sexual harassment cases should come as no surprise, but should give us pause. It is an expedient way of approaching same-sex cases because it derives from the assumption in different-sex cases that sexual harassment is undertaken because of the harasser's unfettered libido. However, in both the same and different-sex contexts, this account fails to address why sexual harassment is a kind of sex discrimination. . . .

To regard sexual harassment as a form of sex discrimination because the harasser would not have undertaken the conduct "but for" the sex of the victim is to understand the harasser to have engaged in sexual harassment primarily because he finds the target physically attractive, would like to have sex with her or him, and/or derives libidinous pleasure from sexualizing their otherwise professional relationship. Interestingly enough, on this view, the harasser's sexual orientation, either assumed or proven, plays a central role in determining whether the offending sexual conduct was "because of sex." In fact, in these cases "but for" causation collapses into sexual orientation. Under this view, a harasser only sexually harasses members of the class of people that he or she sexually desires. As such, "because of sex," primarily means "because of the harasser's sexual orientation," and only secondarily means "because of the victim's sex." . . .

But we can say more. Sexual harassment cannot and should not be understood as sex discrimination just because it may be an expression of sexual desire. Rather, sexual conduct, whether or not motivated by desire, becomes sex discrimination when it operates as a means of enforcing gender norms. To the extent that desire plays a role in actionable sexual harassment, it does so secondarily.

What then, is wrong with understanding sexual harassment as an expression of sexual desire? A great deal. First, the "but for" conception of sexual harassment is deeply heterosexist in its assumptions. (Hetero)sex implicitly defines the framework within which the court assesses the sexism of sexual harassment. This slippage in the general understanding of sexual harassment as being about sex, not sexism, has the effect of reenacting and reinforcing the fundamental heterosexist assumption that all or virtually all intersexual interactions have some sexual aspect to them, and that all intrasexual interactions are presumed devoid of sexual desire or interest.

The heterosexism of the "but for" theory of harassment is apparent in its conflation of sex with sexism in different sex cases. While it may be true that when a male supervisor looks at a female employee and presumes his relation to her is sexual, he is merely putting into explicit practice the fundamental assumption of heterosexism: that sexuality and relations between the sexes are synonymous. The presumption that any relation to the opposite sex is sexual necessarily follows from that assumption. Paradigmatic sexual harassment is literally the enactment of a conflation between the two senses of sex.

The mistake, therefore, lies in ignoring not just the sexist, but the heterosexist point of view that animates our understanding of the harasser's behavior in cases of this kind. When feminist theorists and the courts accede to this conflation, and worse, make it the centerpiece of their theories of sexual harassment, they build into the theory these underlying heterosexist assumptions. . . .

This mistake reproduces itself in many of the same-sex harassment cases. For many courts, where the harasser is gay, the motivation behind his behavior sufficiently mirrors that of the heterosexual male harasser; therefore the conduct is actionable under Title VII. Yet, as the doctrine is now developing in some jurisdictions, in same-sex cases the plaintiff must actually prove that the defendant was gay in order to benefit from the presumption that the conduct, if sexual, was undertaken "because of sex." . . .[T]he plaintiff can overcome the presumption that same-sex sexual conduct is not motivated by desire—and therefore not undertaken because of sex—only with direct proof of the defendant's homosexuality. . . .

Against background assumptions that assume heterosexuality and conflate "because of sex" with "because of sexual desire," the sexism and heterosexism underlying the harassment of nonmasculine men by hypermasculine men is rendered invisible to the courts. [Some] same-sex sexual harassment cases present this exact problem—cases where men were sexually harassed because they failed to live up to societal expectations of proper masculinity. In ... [a] case of this kind, Goluszek v. H.P. Smith, [1993 WL 358160 (N.D. Ill.)], Anthony Goluszek worked in the defendant's paper plant as an electronic maintenance mechanic. The court described Mr. Goluszek as a man who "ha[d] never been married nor ha[d] he lived anywhere but at his mother's home." He came from "an unsophisticated background" and had led an "isolated existence" with "little or no sexual experience." Goluszek "blushe[d] easily" and [was] abnormally sensitive to comments pertaining to sex.

Shortly after Mr. Goluszek began work, his male co-workers began to make fun of him.... Among the other harassment the plaintiff experienced were comments that he needed to "get married and get some of that soft pink smelly stuff that's between the legs of a woman," periodic questions as to whether "he had gotten any 'pussy' or had oral sex," and forcibly being shown pictures of nude women.

In response to these as well as other sexual and nonsexual harassment, Goluszek filed a Title VII action against his employer claiming that he had been subjected to a sexually hostile work environment. The trial court rejected Goluszek's claim, concluding that "the defendant's conduct was not the type of conduct Congress intended to sanction when it enacted Title VII." ...

In ... [Goluszek and other similar] cases, the male plaintiffs were sexually harassed by their "appropriately" masculine male coworkers because of the plaintiffs' failure to conform to a norm of masculinity that assumed certain hetero-patriarchal parameters: heterosexuality, sexual experience, sexual interest in and desire to objectify women, and an inclination to engage in the social customs of manliness. Never was it alleged, or for that matter believed, that the men who harassed Goluszek ... [and the other plaintiffs] wanted to have sex with their victims. Yet to hold that the absence of desire precludes discrimination is to ignore the critical role that gender stereotypes played in these cases: the sexual harassment of these men amounted to a form of discipline and punishment because they were insufficiently masculine. In these same-sex cases, the possibility of sexism in the absence of desire is unimaginable, and certainly unactionable....

While cognitive psychological studies indicate that the equation of sexual harassment with sexual desire represents a descriptive error, it may reflect a racial bias as well. Theorists such as Kimberle Crenshaw have argued that the claim that rape is fundamentally an expression of male sexuality employed toward the end of controlling female sexuality "eclipse[s] the use of rape as a weapon of racial terror." MacKinnon's inclination to reduce rape to violent sexuality, and violent sexuality alone, ignores the historical role that the rape of black women by white men played in advancing a fundamentally racist and sexist agenda: "When Black women were raped by white males, they were being raped not as women generally, but as Black women specifically: their femaleness made them sexually vulnerable to racist domination, while their Blackness effectively denied them any protection."

Rape and sexual harassment must not be understood in static terms that allow for fixed meanings regardless of the context in which they occur. Theoretical or judicial analyses of sexual harassment rarely mention the racial identity of the victim or the perpetrator. Just as Crenshaw notes that rape can be used by white men to racially subordinate Black women, so too can sexual harassment operate as a means of enforcing racial subordination in the workplace. Thus, sexual harassment may mean different things depending upon the races of the perpetrator and the victim as well as context.

For all these reasons, it would be both a theoretical and a descriptive mistake to characterize offensive workplace sexual conduct primarily as the expression of sexual desire. Rather, sexual harassment is best understood as the expression, in sexual terms, of power, privilege, or dominance. What makes it sex discrimination, as opposed to the actions of "a philanderer, a terrible person, and a cheapskate," or a racist for that matter, is not the fact that the conduct is sexual, but that the sexual conduct is being used to enforce or perpetuate gender norms and stereotypes....

Finally, I offer one last, although no less important, objection to the manner in which sexuality figures in sex discrimination. Unlike some writers, I, for one, am not prepared to say that the expression of sexuality in the workplace is presumptively illegitimate. Shutting down all sexual behavior seems like an overreaction to the problem of sexual harassment, and requires some very disturbing assumptions about the possibility of female sexual agency: since the law has done a bad job of differentiating welcome from unwelcome sexual conduct, better to declare it all unwelcome.

This paternalistic approach to the problem draws into question women's capacity to either consent or object to certain kinds of workplace sexual activity. The requirement that the plaintiff prove the sexual conduct was unwelcome clearly presupposes a degree of female agency in these contexts. Yet, sexual content and unwelcomeness are not enough to make offensive workplace sexual behavior sex discrimination—something more needs to be proven, or at least inferred, for the wrong to be a sexually discriminatory wrong. Recall that to state a hostile environment claim under Title VII a plaintiff must show that the behavior complained of was both unwelcome sexual conduct and exhibited "because of sex." Sexual conduct in the workplace has a special sting for women, not because our sensibilities render us particularly vulnerable to sex, but because the conduct literally sexualizes us. It embodies stereotypic gender norms that become true by virtue of their enactment. When we frame our arguments in terms of sex being "disproportionately more demeaning" to women than to men, or that sex is dangerous for women in some generalized sense, we must be careful not to reinforce Victorian notions of women's special vulnerability to all things sexual. Instead, we should remain focused on a conception of sexual harassment that reveals the constitutive, disciplinary role of sexual harassment....

Finally, the anti-subordination view of sexual harassment, while providing the something more that is lacking in the anti-sex and "but for" paradigms, seems to over determine the nature of the harm as something males do to females. Catharine MacKinnon and Ruth Colker have answered the call to provide a theory of sexual harassment that identifies "what practices are subordinating rather than simply differentiating." A theory of sexual differentiation alone is not an adequate theory of discrimination. What is needed, on this account, is an analysis of the structural problem of enforced inferiority of women. The structural problem that forms the foundation of MacKinnon's inequality approach is one that takes inequality between "the sexes" as a given: "[A]ll practices which subordinate women to men are prohibited." Under the anti-subordination approach, Title VII's application to practices that subordinate some men to other men end up being explained away uneasily.

Two fundamental questions emerge from the subordination account of sexual harassment. First, should we assume that all or most sexual activity initiated by men in the presence of women reproduces subordinating gender norms? If so, why? Second, what does the theory say about same-sex sexual harassment or harassment by women of men? The power of MacKinnon's insights applies almost exclusively to contexts where women are sexually harassed by men. For MacKinnon, the social and historical construction of male and female sexuality and identity does all the work of transforming sexual harassment into sex discrimination. The hierarchical inequality of the sexes is crucial to this analysis. . . .

To my mind, the subordination account conceptualizes the wrong of sexual harassment better than either the anti-sex or "but for" formulations. The anti-subordination principle best conceives sexual harassment as a sexually discriminatory wrong, but it does so by relying too heavily on the premise that this is something that men, as a biological category, do to women, as a biological category. The anti-subordination principle could be greatly improved by conceptualizing the problem as one of gender subordination defined in hetero-patriarchal terms. Thus, sexual harassment is understood as a mechanism by which an orthodoxy regarding masculinity and femininity is enforced, policed, and perpetuated in the workplace. Unwelcome and offensive conduct by men directed at women that has the effect of reducing women's identity to that of a sex object while figuring men's identity as that of a sex subject is one example of gender subordination. But so is the sexual harassment of Goluszek [and others], . . .—men who were insufficiently masculine and as a result were punished by their male co-workers with a campaign of unwelcome, offensive, and hostile conduct of a sexual nature. As such, Goluszek's . . . male coworkers were policing proper masculinity in men, just as [hetrosexual harassment] polic[es] proper femininity in women. . . .

Like MacKinnon, I agree that the subordination account of sexual harassment provides better purchase on the nature of this problem and avenues for relief than do either the formal equality or sex-equals-sexism approaches. But what is the wrong of sexual subordination? MacKinnon

...and others understand it as a gendered hierarchy based upon the enforced inferiority of women to men. Underlying this gendered inferiority is an ideology that is designed to reduce women to victimized, highly sexual, less competent sub-humans who do not enjoy full agency.

Rather than confine the subordination analysis to the methods by which men oppress women, I want to ask a more systemic question: Does the underlying ideology that feminizes and sexualizes women also have an effect upon who men are or can be? As I see it, the wrong of gender-based subordination lies in its power as an overarching regulatory practice that has as its goal the production of feminine women as (hetero)sexual objects and masculine men as (hetero)sexual subjects. Sexual harassment can be a very effective means of accomplishing these hetero-patriarchal objectives, whether by enacting these norms—as in the case of men harassing female subordinates in the workplace—or by punishing gender nonconformists.... It is easy to come away from much of the anti-subordination literature understanding sexism as something that men exclusively visit upon women. Yet sexism, understood in the terms I urge, is something that affects and regulates us all, male and female. This is not to say that it affects us all in the same way, but rather in ways which harm some women and some men in similar fashions.... [T]he net effect of this kind of conduct extends beyond any particular case in that it solidifies what "real men" and "real women" should be....

Conclusion

... The wrong of sexual harassment must consist of something more than that the conduct would not have occurred "but for" the sex of the target, that the conduct was sexual in nature, or that it was something men do to women. The "something more" I suggest is that we regard sexual harassment as a tool or instrument of gender regulation. It is a practice, grounded and undertaken in the service of hetero-patriarchal norms. These norms, regulatory, constitutive, and punitive in nature, produce gendered subjects: feminine women as sex objects and masculine men as sex subjects. On this account, sexual harassment is sex discrimination precisely because its use and effect police hetero-patriarchal gender norms in the workplace.

I do not suggest that we reject existing doctrine, but rather that we work to develop a theoretical justification for inferring sex discrimination in traditional different-sex claims. This theoretical work will also provide the tools to consider whether same-sex sexual harassment raises the same kind of concerns as those present in the more central cases. All that I urge is renewed attention to the "based upon sex" element of the plaintiff's case, such that we view the wrong of sexual harassment in systemic terms, rather than in terms that elevate a method of proof ("but for") over the nature of the harm itself, or that conflate sex with sexism. To understand sexual harassment as a regulatory practice that constitutes gendered subjects by inscribing, enforcing, and policing hetero-patriarchal gender norms is to provide a better account of what sexual harassment is and what it does—in both different-sex and same-sex cases. Most importantly, this approach better explains why sexual harassment is a kind of sex discrimination.

NOTES AND QUESTIONS

1. **Should Sexuality be Banned from the Workplace?** If it were possible to ban sexual relations from the workplace, would you be in favor of doing so? How would feminists from different schools of thought respond to this question? As Katherine Franke indicates, Susan Estrich endorses a ban, "at least between those who work[] directly for the other." Do you agree? Why such a limited ban? Why should sexualized conduct in the workplace necessarily be disempowering to women? On the other hand, Rosemary Pringle is interested in the ways in which sexual pleasure can be used to empower women. In what ways does she think that subordinate women can use their sexuality as a form of power? Does this mean women, like the secretaries she discusses, should be able to harass their bosses? Does Muriel Dimen's portrayal of the variety of ways that women respond to sexual harassment help to illuminate the complicated relationship between sexual harassment and power?

2. **The Public/Private Split and Sexual Harassment.** In what ways do our ideas about public and private realms affect our responses to sexual harassment? Dimen argues that women are second class citizens and that this is directly connected to their seeing themselves in terms of others' desires. Men, the first class citizens, are trained to do the desiring. Men's political power gives them more personal power, while women are left to do the cooking and cleaning. Is this analysis helpful in explaining the powerlessness that women often feel when confronted with sexual harassment even from just one man in a setting in which he does not have formal authority over them?

Cynthia Grant Bowman, in *Street Harassment and the Informal Ghettoization of Women*, 106 Harv. L. Rev. 517, 531 (1993), describes the phenomenon of street hassling:

> The target of street harassment is literally every woman between the age when her body begins to develop sexually and that undefined point when she is no longer assumed to be a sexual being because she is "too old." Different women may experience street harassment in different ways, though. For a very young girl, it is one of her first lessons in what it means to be a sexual being—a confusing and shame-producing experience. According to Robin West[, "]street hassling is also the earliest—and therefore the defining—lesson in the source of a girl's disempowerment. If they haven't learned it anywhere else, street hassling teaches girls that their sexuality implies their vulnerability. It is damaging to be pointed at, jeered at, and laughed at for one's sexuality, and it is infantilizing to know you have to take it.["]

According to Bowman, street hassling, plays a public role in disciplining women and teaching them their places. Do you agree?

3.   **Race, Ethnicity, National Origin and Sexual Harassment.** As the article by Diana Vellos demonstrates, race, ethnicity, and national origin play a large role in making women particularly vulnerable to sexual harassment. Non-white women, women who do not speak English, or women whose immigrant status is not secure may feel particularly isolated and not know where to look for assistance in stopping the harassment. As Vellos indicates, women from these backgrounds may be in marginal, low-skill jobs that they are worried about losing if they complain. Furthermore, they may not be able to afford periods of unemployment.

Culture also may play a role in exacerbating harassment. Women from some Asian cultures may worry that their families will lose face if they charge their bosses or co-workers with sexually harassing them. Some Latin American cultures retain the idea that the "good" woman always repulses sexual advances. This makes it difficult for women to indicate when sexualized conduct is truly unwelcome and when it is acceptable. During the confirmation hearings for Justice Clarence Thomas, Professor Anita Hill accused him of having sexually harassed her years earlier when they were both at the EEOC. Thomas and Hill are both Black. A Black sociologist, Orlando Patterson, defended Thomas, arguing that his harassing comments were a "down-home style of courting" that Black women should recognize and find flattering. The implication was both that Thomas's conduct needed to be measured against a culturally specific standard, and that Hill was subject to criticism for having acted "white" in objecting to the conduct. As this illustrates, the situation may be particularly complicated for non-white women who are subject to harassment: complaining may work to ostracize them from their own communities.

The experience of sexual harassment may also be different for non-white women, recent immigrants, and women who are members of ethnic minorities because stereotypes about their communities may make them particular targets for sexual harassment. Harassers may engage in more pervasive conduct against Black women who are thought to be sexually "available" or Latina women who are believed to be "hot" than against "cool, prudish" white North Americans. Similarly, some women may be reluctant to "turn in" men of their own communities either because these men have traditionally suffered more at the hands of law enforcement than white men have or because turning them in may reinforce stereotypes of sexualized Black or Latino men.

For a series of excellent essays on the Hill/Thomas hearings, see *Racing Justice, En-gendering Power* (Toni Morrison ed. 1992).

Meritor Savings Bank, FSB v. Vinson

Supreme Court of the United States, 1986.
477 U.S. 57, 106 S.Ct. 2399, 91 L.Ed.2d 49.

JUSTICE WILLIAM REHNQUIST delivered the opinion of the Court.

This case presents important questions concerning claims of workplace "sexual harassment" brought under Title VII of the Civil Rights Act of 1964.

In 1974, respondent Mechelle Vinson met Sidney Taylor, a vice president of what is now petitioner Meritor Savings Bank (bank) and manager of one of its branch offices. When respondent asked whether she might obtain employment at the bank, Taylor gave her an application, which she completed and returned the next day; later that same day Taylor called her to say that she had been hired. With Taylor as her supervisor, respondent started as a teller-trainee, and thereafter was promoted to teller, head teller, and assistant branch manager. She worked at the same branch for four years, and it is undisputed that her advancement there was based on merit alone. In September 1978, respondent notified Taylor that she was taking sick leave for an indefinite period. On November 1, 1978, the bank discharged her for excessive use of that leave.

Respondent brought this action against Taylor and the bank, claiming that during her four years at the bank she had "constantly been subjected to sexual harassment" by Taylor in violation of Title VII. She sought injunctive relief, compensatory and punitive damages against Taylor and the bank, and attorney's fees.

At the 11-day bench trial, the parties presented conflicting testimony about Taylor's behavior during respondent's employment. Respondent testified that during her probationary period as a teller-trainee, Taylor treated her in a fatherly way and made no sexual advances. Shortly thereafter, however, he invited her out to dinner and, during the course of the meal, suggested that they go to a motel to have sexual relations. At first she refused, but out of what she described as fear of losing her job she eventually agreed. According to respondent, Taylor thereafter made repeated demands upon her for sexual favors, usually at the branch, both during and after business hours; she estimated that over the next several years she had intercourse with him some 40 or 50 times. In addition, respondent testified that Taylor fondled her in front of other employees, followed her into the women's restroom when she went there alone, exposed himself to her, and even forcibly raped her on several occasions. These activities ceased after 1977, respondent stated, when she started going with a steady boyfriend.

Respondent also testified that Taylor touched and fondled other women employees of the bank, and she attempted to call witnesses to support this charge. But while some supporting testimony apparently was admitted without objection, the District Court did not allow her "to present wholesale evidence of a pattern and practice relating to sexual advances to other female employees in her case in chief, but advised her that she might well be able to present such evidence in rebuttal to the defendants' cases." Respondent did not offer such evidence in rebuttal. Finally, respondent testified that because she was afraid of Taylor she never reported his harassment to any of his supervisors and never attempted to use the bank's complaint procedure.

Taylor denied respondent's allegations of sexual activity, testifying that he never fondled her, never made suggestive remarks to her, never engaged in sexual intercourse with her, and never asked her to do so. He contended instead that respondent made her accusations in response to a business-related dispute. The bank also denied respondent's allegations and asserted that any sexual harassment by Taylor was unknown to the bank and engaged in without its consent or approval.

The District Court denied relief, but did not resolve the conflicting testimony about the existence of a sexual relationship between respondent and Taylor. It found instead that

"[i]f [respondent] and Taylor did engage in an intimate or sexual relationship during the time of [respondent's] employment with [the bank], that relationship was a voluntary one having nothing to do with her continued employment at [the bank] or her advancement or promotions at that institution."

The court ultimately found that respondent "was not the victim of sexual harassment and was not the victim of sexual discrimination" while employed at the bank....

Title VII of the Civil Rights Act of 1964 makes it "an unlawful employment practice for an employer ... to discriminate against any individual with respect to his compensation, terms, conditions, or privileges of employment, because of such individual's race, color, religion, sex, or national origin." ... Respondent argues, and the Court of Appeals held, that unwelcome sexual advances that create an offensive or hostile working environment violate Title VII. Without question, when a supervisor sexually harasses a subordinate because of the subordinate's sex, that supervisor "discriminate[s]" on the basis of sex. Petitioner apparently does not challenge this proposition. It contends instead that in prohibiting discrimination with respect to "compensation, terms, conditions, or privileges" of employment, Congress was concerned with what petitioner describes as "tangible loss" of "an economic character," not "purely psychological aspects of the workplace environment." In support of this claim petitioner observes that in both the legislative history of Title VII and this Court's Title VII decisions, the focus has been on tangible, economic barriers erected by discrimination.

We reject petitioner's view. First, the language of Title VII is not limited to "economic" or "tangible" discrimination. The phrase "terms, conditions, or privileges of employment" evinces a congressional intent " 'to strike at the entire spectrum of disparate treatment of men and women' "in employment. Petitioner has pointed to nothing in the Act to suggest that Congress contemplated the limitation urged here.

Second, in 1980 the EEOC issued Guidelines specifying that "sexual harassment," as there defined, is a form of sex discrimination prohibited by Title VII. As an "administrative interpretation of the Act by the enforcing agency," these Guidelines, " 'while not controlling upon the courts by reason of their authority, do constitute a body of experience and informed judgment to which courts and litigants may properly resort for guidance,' "*General Electric Co. v. Gilbert,* 429 U.S. 125, 141B142 (1976). The EEOC Guidelines fully support the view that harassment leading to non-economic injury can violate Title VII.

In defining "sexual harassment," the Guidelines first describe the kinds of workplace conduct that may be actionable under Title VII. These include "[u]nwelcome sexual advances, requests for sexual favors, and other verbal or physical conduct of a sexual nature." Relevant to the charges at issue in this case, the Guidelines provide that such sexual misconduct constitutes prohibited "sexual harassment," whether or not it is directly linked to the grant or denial of an economic *quid pro quo,* where "such conduct has the purpose or effect of unreasonably interfering with an individual's work performance or creating an intimidating, hostile, or offensive working environment."

In concluding that so-called "hostile environment" (*i.e.,* non *quid pro quo*) harassment violates Title VII, the EEOC drew upon a substantial body of judicial decisions and EEOC precedent holding that Title VII affords employees the right to work in an environment free from discriminatory intimidation, ridicule, and insult. *Rogers v. EEOC,* 454 F.2d 234 (5th Cir.1971), cert. denied, 406 U.S. 957, 92 S.Ct. 2058, 32 L.Ed.2d 343 (1972), was apparently the first case to recognize a cause of action based upon a discriminatory work environment. In *Rogers,* the Court of Appeals for the Fifth Circuit held that a Hispanic complainant could establish a Title VII violation by demonstrating that her employer created an offensive work environment for employees by giving discriminatory service to its Hispanic clientele. The court explained that an employee's protections under Title VII extend beyond the economic aspects of employment:

> "[T]he phrase 'terms, conditions or privileges of employment' in [Title VII] is an expansive concept which sweeps within its protective ambit the practice of creating a working environment heavily charged with ethnic or racial discrimination.... One can readily envision working environments so heavily polluted with discrimination as to destroy completely the emotional and psychological stability of minority group workers...."

Courts applied this principle to harassment based on race, religion, and national origin. Nothing in Title VII suggests that a hostile environment based on discriminatory *sexual* harassment should not be likewise prohibited. The Guidelines thus appropriately drew from, and were fully consistent with, the existing case law.

Since the Guidelines were issued, courts have uniformly held, and we agree, that a plaintiff may establish a violation of Title VII by proving that discrimination based on sex has created a hostile or abusive work environment. As the Court of Appeals for the Eleventh Circuit wrote in *Henson v. Dundee,* 682 F.2d 897, 902 (1982):

> "Sexual harassment which creates a hostile or offensive environment for members of one sex is every bit the arbitrary barrier to

sexual equality at the workplace that racial harassment is to racial equality. Surely, a requirement that a man or woman run a gauntlet of sexual abuse in return for the privilege of being allowed to work and make a living can be as demeaning and disconcerting as the harshest of racial epithets."

Of course, as the courts in both *Rogers* and *Henson* recognized, not all workplace conduct that may be described as "harassment" affects a "term, condition, or privilege" of employment within the meaning of Title VII. For sexual harassment to be actionable, it must be sufficiently severe or pervasive "to alter the conditions of [the victim's] employment and create an abusive working environment." Respondent's allegations in this case—which include not only pervasive harassment but also criminal conduct of the most serious nature—are plainly sufficient to state a claim for "hostile environment" sexual harassment.

The question remains, however, whether the District Court's ultimate finding that respondent "was not the victim of sexual harassment" effectively disposed of respondent's claim. The Court of Appeals recognized, we think correctly, that this ultimate finding was likely based on one or both of two erroneous views of the law. First, the District Court apparently believed that a claim for sexual harassment will not lie absent an *economic* effect on the complainant's employment.... Since it appears that the District Court made its findings without ever considering the "hostile environment" theory of sexual harassment, the Court of Appeals' decision to remand was correct.

Second, the District Court's conclusion that no actionable harassment occurred might have rested on its earlier "finding" that "[i]f [respondent] and Taylor did engage in an intimate or sexual relationship ..., that relationship was a voluntary one." But the fact that sex-related conduct was "voluntary," in the sense that the complainant was not forced to participate against her will, is not a defense to a sexual harassment suit brought under Title VII. The gravamen of any sexual harassment claim is that the alleged sexual advances were "unwelcome." While the question whether particular conduct was indeed unwelcome presents difficult problems of proof and turns largely on credibility determinations committed to the trier of fact, the District Court in this case erroneously focused on the "voluntariness" of respondent's participation in the claimed sexual episodes. The correct inquiry is whether respondent by her conduct indicated that the alleged sexual advances were unwelcome, not whether her actual participation in sexual intercourse was voluntary.

Petitioner contends that even if this case must be remanded to the District Court, the Court of Appeals erred in one of the terms of its remand. Specifically, the Court of Appeals stated that testimony about respondent's "dress and personal fantasies," which the District Court apparently admitted into evidence, "had no place in this litigation." The apparent ground for this conclusion was that respondent's voluntariness *vel non* in submitting to Taylor's advances was immaterial to her sexual harassment claim. While "voluntariness" in the sense of consent is not a defense to such a claim, it does not follow that a complainant's sexually provocative speech or dress is irrelevant as a matter of law in determining whether he or she found particular sexual advances unwelcome. To the contrary, such evidence is obviously relevant. The EEOC Guidelines emphasize that the trier of fact must determine the existence of sexual harassment in light of "the record as a whole" and "the totality of circumstances, such as the nature of the sexual advances and the context in which the alleged incidents occurred." Respondent's claim that any marginal relevance of the evidence in question was outweighed by the potential for unfair prejudice is the sort of argument properly addressed to the District Court. In this case the District Court concluded that the evidence should be admitted, and the Court of Appeals' contrary conclusion was based upon the erroneous, categorical view that testimony about provocative dress and publicly expressed sexual fantasies "had no place in this litigation." While the District Court must carefully weigh the applicable considerations in deciding whether to admit evidence of this kind, there is no *per se* rule against its admissibility.

Although the District Court concluded that respondent had not proved a violation of Title VII, it nevertheless went on to consider the question of the bank's liability. Finding that "the bank was without notice" of Taylor's alleged conduct, and that notice to Taylor was not the equivalent of notice to the bank, the court concluded that the bank therefore could not be held liable for Taylor's alleged actions. The Court of Appeals took the opposite view, holding that an employer is strictly liable for a hostile environment created by a supervisor's sexual advances, even though the employer neither knew nor reasonably could have known of the alleged misconduct. The court held that a supervisor, whether or not he possesses the authority to hire, fire, or promote, is necessarily an "agent" of his employer for all Title VII purposes, since "even the appearance" of such authority may enable him to impose himself on his subordinates.

The parties and *amici* suggest several different standards for employer liability. Respondent, not surprisingly, defends the position of the Court of Appeals. Noting that Title VII's definition of "employer" includes any "agent" of the employer, she also argues that "so long as the circumstance is work-related, the supervisor is the employer and the employer is the supervisor." Notice to Taylor that the advances were unwelcome, therefore, was notice to the bank.

Petitioner argues that respondent's failure to use its established grievance procedure, or to otherwise put it on notice of the alleged misconduct, insulates petitioner from liability for Taylor's wrongdoing. A contrary rule would be unfair, petitioner argues, since in a hostile environment harassment case the employer often will have no reason to know about, or opportunity to cure, the alleged wrongdoing.

The EEOC, in its brief as *amicus curiae,* contends that courts formulating employer liability rules should draw from traditional agency principles. Examination of those principles has led the EEOC to the view that where a supervisor exercises the authority actually delegated to him by his employer, by making or threatening to make decisions affecting the employment status of his subordinates, such actions are properly imputed to the employer whose delegation of authority empowered the supervisor to undertake them. Thus, the courts have consistently held employers liable for the discriminatory discharges of employees by supervisory personnel, whether or not the employer knew, should have known, or approved of the supervisor's actions.

The EEOC suggests that when a sexual harassment claim rests exclusively on a "hostile environment" theory, however, the usual basis for a finding of agency will often disappear. In that case, the EEOC believes, agency principles lead to

"a rule that asks whether a victim of sexual harassment had reasonably available an avenue of complaint regarding such harassment, and, if available and utilized, whether that procedure was reasonably responsive to the employee's complaint. If the employer has an expressed policy against sexual harassment and has implemented a procedure specifically designed to resolve sexual harassment claims, and if the victim does not take advantage of that procedure, the employer should be shielded from liability absent actual knowledge of the sexually hostile environment (obtained, *e.g.,* by the filing of a charge with the EEOC or a comparable state agency). In all other cases, the employer will be liable if it has actual knowledge of the harassment or if, considering all the facts of the case, the victim in question had no reasonably available avenue for making his or her complaint known to appropriate management officials."

As respondent points out, this suggested rule is in some tension with the EEOC Guidelines, which hold an employer liable for the acts of its agents without regard to notice. The Guidelines do require, however, an "examin[ation of] the circumstances of the particular employment relationship and the job [f]unctions performed by the individual in determining whether an individual acts in either a supervisory or agency capacity."

This debate over the appropriate standard for employer liability has a rather abstract quality about it given the state of the record in this case. We do not know at this stage whether Taylor made any sexual advances toward respondent at all, let alone whether those advances were unwelcome, whether they were sufficiently pervasive to constitute a condition of employment, or whether they were "so pervasive and so long continuing . . . that the employer must have become conscious of [them]."

We therefore decline the parties' invitation to issue a definitive rule on employer liability, but we do agree with the EEOC that Congress wanted courts to look to agency principles for guidance in this area. While such commonlaw principles may not be transferable in all their particulars to Title VII, Congress' decision to define "employer" to include any "agent" of an employer, surely evinces an intent to place some limits on the acts of employees for which employers under Title VII are to be held responsible. For this reason, we hold that the Court of Appeals erred in concluding that employers are always automatically liable for sexual harassment by their supervisors. For the same reason, absence of notice to an employer does not necessarily insulate that employer from liability.

Finally, we reject petitioner's view that the mere existence of a grievance procedure and a policy against discrimination, coupled with respondent's failure to invoke that procedure, must insulate petitioner from liability. While those facts are plainly relevant, the situation before us demonstrates why they are not necessarily dispositive. Petitioner's general nondiscrimination policy did not address sexual harassment in particular, and thus did not alert employees to their employer's interest in correcting that form of discrimination. Moreover, the bank's grievance procedure apparently required an employee to complain first to her supervisor, in this case Taylor. Since Taylor was the alleged perpetrator, it is not altogether surprising that respondent failed to invoke the procedure and report her grievance to him. Petitioner's contention that respondent's failure should insulate it from liability might be substantially stronger if its procedures were better calculated to encourage victims of harassment to come forward. . . .

JUSTICE THURGOOD MARSHALL, with whom JUSTICE WILLIAM BRENNAN, JUSTICE HARRY BLACKMUN, and JUSTICE JOHN PAUL STEVENS join, concurring in the judgment.

I fully agree with the Court's conclusion that workplace sexual harassment is illegal, and violates Title VII. . . . [T]he Court's opinion, however, leaves open the circumstances in which an employer is responsible under Title VII for such conduct. Because I believe that question to be properly before us, I write separately.

The issue the Court declines to resolve is addressed in the EEOC Guidelines on Discrimination Because of Sex, which are entitled to great deference. . . . The Commission, in issuing the Guidelines, explained that its rule was "in keeping with the general standard of employer liability with respect to agents and supervisory employees. . . . [T]he Commission and the courts have held for years that an employer is liable if a supervisor or an agent violates the Title VII, regardless of knowledge or any other mitigating factor." I would adopt the standard set out by the Commission.

An employer can act only through individual supervisors and employees; discrimination is rarely carried out pursuant to a formal vote of a corporation's board of directors. Although an employer may sometimes adopt company-wide discriminatory policies violative of Title VII, acts that may constitute Title VII violations are generally effected through the actions of individuals, and often an individual may take such a step even in defiance of company policy. Nonetheless, Title VII remedies, such as reinstatement and backpay, generally run against the employer as an entity. The question thus arises as to the circumstances under which an employer will be held liable under Title VII for the acts of its employees.

The answer supplied by general Title VII law, like that supplied by federal labor law, is that the act of a supervisory employee or agent is imputed to the employer. Thus, for example, when a supervisor discriminatorily fires or refuses to promote a black employee, that act is, without more, considered the act of the employer. The courts do not stop to consider whether the employer otherwise had "notice" of the action, or even whether the supervisor had actual authority to act as he did. Following that approach, every Court of Appeals that has considered the issue has held that sexual harassment by supervisory personnel is automatically imputed to the employer when the harassment results in tangible job detriment to the subordinate employee.

The brief filed by the Solicitor General on behalf of the United States and the EEOC in this case suggests that a different rule should apply when a supervisor's harassment "merely" results in a discriminatory work environment.... The Solicitor General's position is untenable. A supervisor's responsibilities do not begin and end with the power to hire, fire, and discipline employees, or with the power to recommend such actions. Rather, a supervisor is charged with the day-to-day supervision of the work environment and with ensuring a safe, productive workplace. There is no reason why abuse of the latter authority should have different consequences than abuse of the former. In both cases it is the authority vested in the supervisor by the employer that enables him to commit the wrong: it is precisely because the supervisor is understood to be clothed with the employer's authority that he is able to impose unwelcome sexual conduct on subordinates. There is therefore no justification for a special rule, to be applied *only* in "hostile environment" cases, that sexual harassment does not create employer liability until the employee suffering the discrimination notifies other supervisors. No such requirement appears in the statute, and no such requirement can coherently be drawn from the law of agency....

Harris v. Forklift Systems, Inc.

Supreme Court of the United States, 1993.
510 U.S. 17, 114 S.Ct. 367, 126 L.Ed.2d 296.

JUSTICE SANDRA DAY O'CONNOR delivered the opinion of the Court.

In this case we consider the definition of a discriminatorily "abusive work environment" (also known as a "hostile work environment") under Title VII of the Civil Rights Act of 1964....

Teresa Harris worked as a manager at Forklift Systems, Inc., an equipment rental company, from April 1985 until October 1987. Charles Hardy was Forklift's president.

The Magistrate found that, throughout Harris' time at Forklift, Hardy often insulted her because of her gender and often made her the target of unwanted sexual innuendos. Hardy told Harris on several occasions, in the presence of other employees, "You're a woman, what do you know" and "We need a man as the rental manager"; at least once, he told her she was "a dumb ass woman." Again in front of others, he suggested that the two of them "go to the Holiday Inn to negotiate [Harris'] raise." Hardy occasionally asked Harris and other female employees to get coins from his front pants pocket. He threw objects on the ground in front of Harris and other women, and asked them to pick the objects up. He made sexual innuendos about Harris' and other women's clothing.

In mid-August 1987, Harris complained to Hardy about his conduct. Hardy said he was surprised that Harris was offended, claimed he was only joking, and apologized. He also promised he would stop, and based on this assurance Harris stayed on the job. But in early September, Hardy began anew: While Harris was arranging a deal with one of Forklift's customers, he asked her, again in front of other employees, "What did you do, promise the guy ... some [sex] Saturday night?" On October 1, Harris collected her paycheck and quit.

Harris then sued Forklift, claiming that Hardy's conduct had created an abusive work environment for her because of her gender. The United States District Court for the Middle District of Tennessee, ... held that Hardy's conduct did not create an abusive environment. The court found that some of Hardy's comments "offended [Harris], and would offend the reasonable woman," but that they were not

"so severe as to be expected to seriously affect [Harris'] psychological wellbeing. A reasonable woman manager under like circumstances would have been offended by Hardy, but his conduct would not have risen to the level of interfering with that person's work performance. Neither do I believe that [Harris] was subjectively so offended that she suffered injury.... Although Hardy may at times have genuinely offended [Harris], I do not believe that he created a working environment so poisoned as to be intimidating or abusive to [Harris]." ...

The United States Court of Appeals for the Sixth Circuit affirmed....

We granted certiorari to resolve a conflict among the Circuits on whether conduct, to be actionable as "abusive work environment" harassment (no quid pro quo harassment issue is present here), must "seriously affect [an employee's] psychological wellbeing" or lead the plaintiff to "suffe[r] injury." ...

Title VII of the Civil Rights Act of 1964 makes it "an unlawful employment practice for an employer ... to discriminate against any individual with respect to his compensation, terms, conditions, or privileges of employment, because of such individual's race, color, religion, sex, or national origin." As we made clear in Meritor Savings Bank, FSB v. Vinson, 477 U.S. 57, 106 S.Ct. 2399, 91 L.Ed.2d 49 (1986), this language "is not limited to 'economic' or 'tangible' discrimination. The phrase 'terms, conditions, or privileges of employment' evinces a congressional intent 'to strike at the entire spectrum of disparate treatment of men and women' in employment," which includes requiring people to work in a discriminatorily hostile or abusive environment. When the workplace is permeated with "discriminatory intimidation, ridicule, and insult," that is "sufficiently severe or pervasive to alter the conditions of the victim's employment and create an abusive working environment," Title VII is violated.

This standard, which we reaffirm today, takes a middle path between making actionable any conduct that is merely offensive and requiring the conduct to cause a tangible psychological injury. As we pointed out in Meritor, "mere utterance of an ... epithet which engenders offensive feelings in a employee," does not sufficiently affect the conditions of employment to implicate Title VII. Conduct that is not severe or pervasive enough to create an objectively hostile or abusive work environment—an environment that a reasonable person would find hostile or abusive—is beyond Title VII's purview. Likewise, if the victim does not subjectively perceive the environment to be abusive, the conduct has not actually altered the conditions of the victim's employment, and there is no Title VII violation.

But Title VII comes into play before the harassing conduct leads to a nervous breakdown. A discriminatorily abusive work environment, even one that does not seriously affect employees' psychological wellbeing, can and often will detract from employees' job performance, discourage employees from remaining on the job, or keep them from advancing in their careers. Moreover, even without regard to these tangible effects, the very fact that the discriminatory conduct was so severe or pervasive that it created a work environment abusive to employees because of their race, gender, religion, or national origin offends Title VII's broad rule of workplace equality. The appalling conduct alleged in Meritor, and the reference in that case to environments " 'so heavily polluted with discrimination as to destroy completely the emotional and psychological stability of minority group workers,' " merely present some especially egregious examples of harassment. They do not mark the boundary of what is actionable.

We therefore believe the District Court erred in relying on whether the conduct "seriously affect[ed] plaintiff's psychological well-being" or led her to "suffe[r] injury." Such an inquiry may needlessly focus the factfinder's attention on concrete psychological harm, an element Title VII does not require. Certainly Title VII bars conduct that would seriously affect a reasonable person's psychological well-being, but the statute is not limited to such conduct. So long as the environment would reasonably be perceived, and is perceived, as hostile or abusive, there is no need for it also to be psychologically injurious.

This is not, and by its nature cannot be, a mathematically precise test. We need not answer today all the potential questions it raises.... But we can say that whether an environment is "hostile" or "abusive" can be determined only by looking at all the circumstances. These may include the frequency of the discriminatory conduct; its severity; whether it is physically threatening or humiliating, or a mere offensive utterance; and whether it unreasonably interferes with an employee's work performance. The effect on the employee's psychological well-being is, of course, relevant to determining whether the plaintiff actually found the environment abusive. But while psychological harm, like any other relevant factor, may be taken into account, no single factor is required. . . .

Forklift, while conceding that a requirement that the conduct seriously affect psychological well-being is unfounded, argues that the District Court nonetheless correctly applied the Meritor standard. We disagree. Though the District Court did conclude that the work environment was not "intimidating or abusive to [Harris]," it did so only after finding that the conduct was not "so severe as to be expected to seriously affect plaintiff's psychological wellbeing," and that Harris was not "subjectively so offended that she suffered injury." The District Court's application of these incorrect standards may well have influenced its ultimate conclusion, especially given that the court found this to be a "close case."

We therefore reverse the judgment of the Court of Appeals, and remand the case for further proceedings consistent with this opinion.

So ordered.

Justice Antonin Scalia, concurring.

Meritor Savings Bank, FSB v. Vinson, 477 U.S. 57 (1986), held that Title VII prohibits sexual harassment that takes the form of a hostile work environment. The Court stated that sexual harassment is actionable if it is "sufficiently severe or pervasive 'to alter the conditions of [the victim's] employment and create an abusive working environment.' " Today's opinion elaborates that the challenged conduct must be severe or pervasive enough "to create an objectively hostile or abusive work environment—an environment that a reasonable person would find hostile or abusive."

"Abusive" (or "hostile," which in this context I take to mean the same thing) does not seem to me a very clear standard—and I do not think clarity is at all increased by adding the adverb "objectively" or by appealing to a "reasonable person['s]" notion of what the vague word means. Today's opinion does list a number of factors that contribute to abusiveness, but since it neither says how much of each is necessary (an impossible task) nor identifies any single factor as determinative, it thereby adds little certitude. As a practical matter, today's holding lets virtually unguided juries decide whether sex-related conduct engaged in (or permitted by) an employer is egregious enough to warrant an award of damages. One might say that what constitutes "negligence" (a traditional jury question) is not much more clear and certain than what constitutes "abusiveness." Perhaps so. But the class of plaintiffs seeking to recover for negligence is limited to those who have suffered harm, whereas under this statute "abusiveness" is to be the test of whether legal harm has been suffered, opening more expansive vistas of litigation.

Be that as it may, I know of no alternative to the course the Court today has taken. One of the factors mentioned in the Court's nonexhaustive list—whether the conduct unreasonably interferes with an employee's work performance—would, if it were made an absolute test, provide greater guidance to juries and employers. But I see no basis for such a limitation in the language of the statute. Accepting Meritor's interpretation of the term "conditions of employment" as the law, the test is not whether work has been impaired, but whether working conditions have been discriminatorily altered. I know of no test more faithful to the inherently vague statutory language than the one the Court today adopts. For these reasons, I join the opinion of the Court.

JUSTICE RUTH BADER GINSBURG, concurring.

Today the Court reaffirms the holding of Meritor Savings Bank, FSB v. Vinson, 477 U.S. 57 (1986): "[A] plaintiff may establish a violation of Title VII by proving that discrimination based on sex has created a hostile or abusive work environment." The critical issue, Title VII's text indicates, is whether members of one sex are exposed to disadvantageous terms or conditions of employment to which members of the other sex are not exposed. As the Equal Employment Opportunity Commission emphasized, the adjudicator's inquiry should center, dominantly, on whether the discriminatory conduct has unreasonably interfered with the plaintiff's work performance. To show such interference, "the plaintiff need not prove that his or her tangible productivity has declined as a result of the harassment." It suffices to prove that a reasonable person subjected to the discriminatory conduct would find, as the plaintiff did, that the harassment so altered working conditions as to "ma[k]e it more difficult to do the job." Davis concerned race-based discrimination, but that difference does not alter the analysis; except in the rare case in which a bona fide occupational qualification is shown, Title VII declares discriminatory practices based on race, gender, religion, or national origin equally unlawful.*

The Court's opinion, which I join, seems to me in harmony with the view expressed in this concurring statement.

Oncale v. Sundowner Offshore Services, Inc.

Supreme Court of the United States, 1998.
___ U.S. ___, 118 S.Ct. 998, 140 L.Ed.2d 201.

JUSTICE ANTONIN SCALIA delivered the opinion of the Court.

This case presents the question whether workplace harassment can violate Title VII's prohibition against "discriminat[ion] . . . because of . . . sex," when the harasser and the harassed employee are of the same sex. . . .

The District Court having granted summary judgment for respondent, we must assume the facts to be as alleged by petitioner Joseph Oncale. The precise details are irrelevant to the legal point we must decide, and in the interest of both brevity and dignity we shall describe them only generally. In late October 1991, Oncale was working for respondent Sundowner

---

* Indeed, even under the Court's equal protection jurisprudence, which requires "an exceedingly persuasive justification" for a gender-based classification, it remains an open question whether "classifications based upon gender are inherently suspect." See Mississippi Univ. for Women v. Hogan, 458 U.S. 718, 724, 102 S.Ct. 3331, 3336, 73 L.Ed.2d 1090, and n. 9 (1982).

Offshore Services on a Chevron U.S. A., Inc., oil platform in the Gulf of Mexico. He was employed as a roustabout on an eight-man crew which included respondents John Lyons, Danny Pippen, and Brandon Johnson. Lyons, the crane operator, and Pippen, the driller, had supervisory authority. On several occasions, Oncale was forcibly subjected to sex-related, humiliating actions against him by Lyons, Pippen and Johnson in the presence of the rest of the crew. Pippen and Lyons also physically assaulted Oncale in a sexual manner, and Lyons threatened him with rape.

Oncale's complaints to supervisory personnel produced no remedial action; in fact, the company's Safety Compliance Clerk, Valent Hohen, told Oncale that Lyons and Pippen "picked [on] him all the time too," and called him a name suggesting homosexuality. Oncale eventually quit C asking that his pink slip reflect that he "voluntarily left due to sexual harassment and verbal abuse." When asked at his deposition why he left Sundowner, Oncale stated "I felt that if I didn't leave my job, that I would be raped or forced to have sex."

Oncale filed a complaint against Sundowner ...alleging that he was discriminated against in his employment because of his sex.... [T]he district court held that "Mr. Oncale, a male, has no cause of action under Title VII for harassment by male co-workers." On appeal ...the Fifth Circuit ... affirmed....

Title VII's prohibition of discrimination "because of ... sex" protects men as well as women, and in the related context of racial discrimination in the workplace we have rejected any conclusive presumption that an employer will not discriminate against members of his own race.... If our precedents leave any doubt on the question, we hold today that nothing in Title VII necessarily bars a claim of discrimination "because of ... sex" merely because the plaintiff and the defendant(or the person charged with acting on behalf of the defendant) are of the same sex.

Courts have had little trouble with that principle in cases ...where an employee claims to have been passed over for a job or promotion. But when the issue arises in the context of a "hostile environment" sexual harassment claim, the state and federal courts have taken a bewildering variety of stances. Some ...have held that same-sex sexual harassment claims are never cognizable under Title VII. Other decisions say that such claims are actionable only if the plaintiff can prove that the harasser is homosexual (and thus presumably motivated by sexual desire). Still others suggest that workplace harassment that is sexual in content is always actionable, regardless of the harasser's sex, sexual orientation, or motivations.

We see no justification in the statutory language or our precedents for a categorical rule excluding same-sex harassment claims from the coverage of Title VII. As some courts have observed, male-on-male sexual harassment in the workplace was assuredly not the principal evil Congress was concerned with when it enacted Title VII. But statutory prohibitions often go beyond the principal evil to cover reasonably comparable evils, and it is ultimately the provisions of our laws rather than the principal concerns of our legislators by which we are governed. Title VII prohibits "discriminat[ion] ... because of ... sex" in the "terms" or "conditions" of employment. Our holding that this includes sexual harassment must extend to sexual harassment of any kind that meets the statutory requirements.

Respondents and their amici contend that recognizing liability for same-sex harassment will transform Title VII into a general civility code for the American workplace. But that risk is no greater for same-sex than for opposite-sex harassment, and is adequately met by careful attention to the requirements of the statute. Title VII does not prohibit all verbal or physical harassment in the workplace; it is directed only at "discriminat[ion] ... because of ... sex." We have never held that workplace harassment, even harassment between men and women, is automatically discrimination because of sex merely because the words used have sexual content or connotations. "The critical issue, Title VII's text indicates, is whether members of one sex are exposed to disadvantageous terms or conditions of employment to which members of the other sex are not exposed."

Courts and juries have found the inference of discrimination easy to draw in most male-female sexual harassment situations, because the challenged conduct typically involves explicit or implicit proposals of sexual activity; it is reasonable to assume those proposals would not have been made to someone of the same sex. The same chain of inference would be available to a plaintiff alleging same-sex harassment, if there were credible evidence that the harasser was homosexual. But harassing conduct need not be motivated by sexual desire to support an inference of discrimination on the basis of sex. A trier of fact might reasonably find such discrimination, for example, if a female victim is harassed in such sex-specific and derogatory terms by another woman as to make it clear that the harasser is motivated by general hostility to the presence of women in the workplace. A same-sex harassment plaintiff may also, of course, offer direct comparative evidence about how the alleged harasser treated members of both sexes in a mixed-sex workplace. Whatever evidentiary route the plaintiff chooses to follow, he or she must always prove that the conduct at issue was not merely tinged with offensive sexual connotations, but actually constituted "discrimina[tion] ... because of ... sex."

And there is another requirement that prevents Title VII from expanding into a general civility code: As we emphasized in Meritor and Harris, the statute does not reach genuine but innocuous differences in the ways men and women routinely interact with members of the same sex and of the opposite sex. The prohibition of harassment on the basis of sex requires neither asexuality nor androgyny in the workplace; it forbids only behavior so objectively offensive as to alter the "conditions" of the victim's employment. "Conduct that is not severe or pervasive enough to create an objectively hostile or abusive work environment—an environment that a reasonable person would find hostile or abusive—is beyond Title VII's purview." We have always regarded that requirement as crucial, and as sufficient to ensure that courts and juries do not mistake ordinary socializing in the workplace—such as male-on-male horseplay or intersexual flirtation—for discriminatory "conditions of employment."

We have emphasized, moreover, that the objective severity of harassment should be judged from the perspective of a reasonable person in the plaintiff's position, considering "all the circumstances." In same-sex (as in all) harassment cases, that inquiry requires careful consideration of the social context in which particular behavior occurs and is experienced by its target. A professional football player's working environment is not severely or pervasively abusive, for example, if the coach smacks him on the buttocks as he heads onto the field—even if the same behavior would reasonably be experienced as abusive by the coach's secretary (male or female) back at the office. The real social impact of workplace behavior often depends on a constellation of surrounding circumstances, expectations, and relationships which are not fully captured by a simple recitation of the words used or the physical acts performed. Common sense, and an appropriate sensitivity to social context, will enable courts and juries to distinguish between simple teasing or roughhousing among members of the same sex, and conduct which a reasonable person in the plaintiff's position would find severely hostile or abusive....

Because we conclude that sex discrimination consisting of same-sex sexual harassment is actionable under Title VII, the judgment of the Court of Appeals for the Fifth Circuit is reversed, and the case is remanded for further proceedings consistent with this opinion....

Justice Clarence Thomas, concurring.

I concur because the Court stresses that in every sexual harassment case, the plaintiff must plead and ultimately prove Title VII's statutory requirement that there be discrimination "because of ... sex."

NOTES AND QUESTIONS

1. **Quid Pro Quo and Hostile Environment Sexual Harassment.**
The early sexual harassment cases recognized a cause of action for "quid pro quo" harassment. This is harassment in which the sexual favors are understood to be provided either to obtain an employment benefit (e.g., a promotion) or to avoid a threatened adverse action (e.g., a firing). In these cases, the plaintiff provides the sexual favors in return for a change in a "term [or] condition . . . of employment" as the phrase is used in Title VII. In hostile environment cases, by contrast, economic losses or benefits are not involved. Instead, a cause of action exists if the defendant's sexual harassment creates a hostile environment in the workplace. This too can represent discrimination in a "term [or] condition . . . of employment." In *Meritor*, the Supreme Court recognized hostile environment sexual harassment for the first time. Given the opinions in *Meritor* and *Harris*, how does the Court define "hostile environment?"

In Burlington Industries, Inc. v. Ellerth, ___ U.S. ___, 1998 WL 336326 (1998), the Supreme Court addressed again the question of what constitutes actionable sexual harassment. The plaintiff, Kimberly Ellerth, claimed that her supervisor had repeatedly made "boorish and offensive remarks," and on at least three occasions had connected these with threats to deny job benefits to her. The most overt incident involved comments about her breasts, followed by a recommendation that she "loosen up" and a warning that he could "make [her] life very hard or very easy at Burlington." The supervisor did not carry through with any of his threats, however. Thus, it was not clear whether to consider this harassment to be quid pro quo or hostile environment harassment.

The Court, in *Burlington Industries*, moved in the direction of eliminating the distinction between quid pro quo and hostile environment sexual harassment. The distinction, it said, "is helpful, perhaps, in making a rough demarcation between cases in which threats are carried out and those where they are not or are absent altogether, but beyond this [the terms quid pro quo and hostile environment] are of limited utility." It went on to say, "The principal significance of the distinction [between quid pro quo and hostile environment claims] is to instruct that Title VII is violated by either explicit or constructive alterations in the terms or conditions of employment and to explain the latter must be severe or pervasive."

Traditionally, the distinction between these two types of sexual harassment claims was important because an employer was held strictly liable for a supervisor's quid pro quo harassment. The extent of employer liability for a supervisor's hostile environment harassment was less clear. The next note discusses employer liability.

2. **Employer Liability.** On June 26, 1998, the U.S. Supreme decided two cases that raised issues of the employer's liability for a supervisor's sexually harassing conduct of a subordinate. These cases are Faragher v. City of Boca Raton, 1998 WL 336322, and Burlington Industries. Inc. v. Ellerth,

1998 WL 336326 (discussed above). The Court's holdings in the two cases are identical:

An employer is subject to vicarious liability to a victimized employee for an actionable hostile environment created by a supervisor with immediate (or successively higher) authority over the employee. When no tangible employment action is taken, a defending employer may raise an affirmative defense to liability or damages ... The defense comprises two necessary elements: (a) that the employer exercised reasonable care to prevent and correct promptly any sexually harassing behavior, and (b) that the plaintiff employee unreasonably failed to take advantage of any preventive or corrective opportunities provided by the employer or to avoid harm otherwise.

These two cases establish that the employer can be held liable for a supervisor's harassment in both quid pro quo and hostile environment settings even if the employer was unaware of the harassment. Is this strict liability or negligence? The court's use of the term "vicarious liability" would imply strict liability, but the affirmative defense uses reasonableness language like negligence law.

In arriving at this holding, the Court specifically rejected the defendant's argument that an employer should only be held liable if the supervisor had affirmatively invoked his or her authority in harassing the employee. Such an invocation of authority occurs automatically in quid pro quo cases. The Court said, "[N]eat examples illustrating the line between the affirmative and merely implicit uses of power are not easy to come by in considering management behavior.... How far from the course of ostensible supervisory behavior would a company officer have to step before his orders would not reasonably be seen as actively using authority?" Despite its qualms about line-drawing, the Court did say, "No affirmative defense is available ... when the supervisor's harassment culminates in a tangible employment action.... " Does this reinstate the distinction between quid pro quo cases in general and at least some hostile environment cases?

The Court was reluctant to hold employers automatically liable for their supervisors' harassing conduct in all cases if there was no tangible employment action, and thus it created the affirmative defense. If you were counseling an employer after *Faragher* and *Burlington Industries*, what would you recommend doing to avoid liability? In *Faragher*, the Court remanded the case for reinstatement of the District Court's judgment in favor of the plaintiff because the defendant had not disseminated its sexual harassment policy to the employees. Thus, *Faragher* strongly suggests not just that a sexual harassment policy must exist, but also that it must be fully disseminated. In *Burlington Industries*, the case was remanded to give Burlington the opportunity to prove the affirmative defense. Kimberly Ellerth admitted that Burlington maintained a sexual harassment policy and that she was aware of it. Does that mean that Burlington will necessarily succeed in asserting a claim of an affirmative defense? What if the policy requires the employee to lodge a grievance with the very supervisor who has been harassing the employee? Should failure to use the policy count as a reasonable basis for not taking advantage of a corrective opportunity offered by the employer? What if the employee is to lodge a grievance with a supervisor who is also subordinate to the harassing supervisor?

Justice Thomas, in his dissent in *Burlington Industries*, accuses the Court of "willful policymaking, pure and simple." Indeed, there is nothing in Title VII that would indicate an affirmative defense like the one the Court articulated. Should the Court not have articulated the framework of a defense as it did? Could it have decided the issue of employer liability without identifying the crucial components of an affirmative defense? Would that have been preferable for the employer? For the employees? For the allocation of power between legislatures and courts?

Burlington Industries and *Faragher* leave several questions about employer liability unanswered. Is the employer vicariously liable for harassment by a supervisor who has no authority over the employee being harassed? Surely such a supervisor could still make the environment pretty hostile. What about harassment by co-workers? In cases prior to *Burlington Industries* and *Faragher*, courts often used a negligence standard as the basis for determining employer liability, holding the employer liable if it knew or should have known of the harassment and did not remedy it appropriately. It is possible that in the future the line between vicarious and negligence liability will not depend on whether the harassment was quid pro quo or hostile environment but rather on whether or not the harasser had authority over the victim.

Another question that *Burlington Industries* and *Faragher* leave unanswered is the extent of employer liability for non-employees' harassment of employees. These cases often arise in the context of waitresses or employees in the entertainment industry. For example, in Folkerson v. Circus Circus Enterprises, Inc., 107 F. 3d 754 (9th Cir. 1997), the court held that an employer could be held liable for customers' sexual harassment of an employee if the employer either ratified or acquiesced in the harassment by not taking appropriate corrective actions when it knew or should have known of the harassment. In that case, however, the court found that the employer had taken reasonable steps to prevent the harassment. Would you expect cases like *Folkerson* to survive *Burlington Industries* and *Faragher*?

The issue of customers' harassment of employees arose recently in the context of the Hooters' restaurant chain. Hooters is a "family restaurant" which offers the customer "natural female sex appeal," on the side. Hooters required its waitresses to wear tight T-shirts and very short nylon running shorts. One commentator, Sandra Snaden, noted that these were rumored to come only in sizes "small and extra small." Another commentator, Jennie Rhee pointed out:

> The name Hooters ostensibly refers to the restaurant mascot, a seemingly innocuous owl. Yet the Hooters owl is most notable for its two very large eyes, which bear a strong resemblance to a pair of female breasts. The two Os in the Hooters logo appear with the dotted eyes of

the owl peering out, strikingly reminiscent of areolas and nipples. The restaurant's motto is "Hooters_More Than A Mouthful."

Beginning in 1993, waitresses from a number of Hooters restaurant locations sued the chain for sexual harassment by both customers and employees. These cases were ultimately settled without resolving the question as to whether the employer could be held liable for harassment by a customer. Does the fact that Hooters emphasized the sexualized environment in its restaurants make this an easy case? Or does it make you think that the waitresses should have known what they were getting into when they accepted their jobs? Should there be a defense to sexual harassment that resembles assumption of the risk in tort law? Would this be consistent with the tort-like defense articulated in *Burlington Industries* and *Faragher*? If you accept the idea of assumption of the risk as a defense, should it also be available in cases of supervisor harassment involving women who participate in sexualized banter and who "give as good as they get"? For more on the Hooters cases, *see* Jeannie Sclafani Rhee, *Redressing for Success*, 20 Harv. Women's L. J. 163 (1997) and Sandra L. Snaden, *Note: Baring It All at the Workplace*, 28 Conn. L. Rev. 1225 (1996).

3. **Sexual Harassment in the Schools.** Studies and public reports indicate a significant problem of sexual harassment in the schools. A 1993 study by the American Association of University Women reported that 4 out of 5 students in grades eight through eleven were sexually harassed while in school. One quarter of these students reported being harassed "often." College students also report high rates of sexual harassment. For more details on frequency studies, *see* Alexandra A. Bodnar, *Comment, Arming Students for Battle*, 5 S. Cal Rev. L. & Women's Stud. 549 (1996).

There has been an outpouring of litigation in this area recently. This is due, at least in part, to the Supreme Court's recognition in *Franklin v. Gwinnett County Public Schools*, 503 U.S. 60 (1992), that aggrieved plaintiffs could pursue private actions under Title IX for monetary damages. A cause of action under Title IX has some advantages over one under Title VII. First, Title VII applies only to the employment relationship. Thus, it would not cover the harassment of a student by either another student or by a teacher. Second, damages under Title VII, which (except for back pay) were not available until the Civil Rights Act of 1991, are capped at $300,000 for large employers and even less for smaller ones. No similar cap exists under Title IX. Some courts, however, have held that Title VII provides the exclusive remedy for claiming sexual harassment in employment contexts, even within educational settings, *Lakoski v. James*, 66 F.3d 751 (5th Cir. 1995). This would apply to the harassment of a teacher by a principal, but not to harassment of a student by a teacher.

Just as there was considerable disagreement as to the basis for holding an employer liable for a supervisor's harassment under Title VII, so there was disagreement as to whether and on what grounds a school district could be held liable for a teacher's harassment of a pupil. On June 22, 1998, the Supreme Court addressed this issue in Gebser v. Lago Vista Independent School District, ___ U.S. ___, 118 S.Ct. 1989 (1998), a case in which a teacher, Frank Waldrop, had sexual relations with a ninth grade student, Alida Gebser, for over a year. The Court held that a damages remedy will not lie under Title IX unless an official who at a minimum has authority to address the alleged discrimination and to institute corrective measures on the recipient's behalf has actual knowledge of discrimination in the recipient's programs and fails adequately to respond. . . . We think, moreover, that the response must amount to deliberate indifference to discrimination.

Thus, the Court rejected any liability based on imputed or constructive knowledge. The knowledge must be "actual." Who would you expect would be considered an official with "authority to address the alleged discrimination and institute corrective measures?" Suppose a student had said to a non-harassing teacher, "I think Mr. Waldrop is bothering Alida." Would this be actual knowledge? Would the teacher who was informed be someone with the required degree of authority? Who aside from the school board has the necessary authority? Suppose that the informing student told the school's principal, "Mr. Waldrop is sexually harassing Alida," but that the principal then became engrossed in several other pressing problems and simply forgot to investigate whether Alida was being harassed. Would this constitute "deliberate indifference" on the principal's part? Do you think that you should be able to prove "deliberate indifference" by showing that the school district had never published or disseminated a sexual harassment policy?

After *Gebser, Burlington Industries*, and *Faragher*, the standard for employer liability is much more difficult to meet for children who are sexually harassed at school than it is for adults who are sexually harassed on the job. Does this make sense to you given that one might argue that children are less likely than adults to be able to defend themselves against harassment? One of the ways that adults might defend themselves is by switching jobs. Most children do not have a comparable opportunity to leave their school. The *Gebser* Court justified the difference between Title VII and Title IX by describing Title IX as a very different statute than Title VII. Title VII, the Court said, creates an outright prohibition on discrimination whereas Title IX is contractual in nature, "conditioning an offer of federal funding on a promise by the recipient not to discriminate. . . . " In the latter situation, the Court found it essential that a recipient of the funds not be held liable for damages unless it had notice of potential liability. Do you agree that Title IX is contractual in nature? If it were, would it follow from this that a school district was entitled in sexual harassment cases to actual notice to a person in a position of authority whereas an employer under Title VII is vicariously liable for supervisors' sexual harassment? If you do not agree with this argument, do you think that the fact that public schools are covered by Title IX should account for the difference? Private employers can pass the costs of Title VII liability on to their customers, whereas public school districts cannot.

One of the questions left unanswered by *Gebser* is whether a school district is liable for one student's sexual harassment of another. Some courts have held that since the harassing students were not agents of the school, the school could not be liable unless the plaintiffs could prove that the school had treated their complaints as it did because of their sex. *See* Rowinsky v. Bryan Independent School District, 80 F.3d 1006 (5th Cir. 1996). This is a particularly difficult standard for a plaintiff to meet because most claims of sexual harassment come from girls. If boys are not complaining about sexual harassment, a girl cannot show that her claim has been ignored because of her sex. Other courts have used a negligence standard, implying the school would be liable if it knew or should have known of the harassment and failed to take appropriate action. In Murray v. New York University College of Dentistry, 57 F.3d 243 (2nd Cir. 1995), a student sued her school for harassment by a patient. The court found that the school was not on notice of the harassment. Nevertheless, the court implied that, had there been proper notice, it would have used the negligence standard. Do you think that either of these approaches to student harassment of another student will survive *Gebser*?

4. **Understanding Oncale.** The *Oncale* decision makes clear that same sex sexual harassment claims are actionable under Title VII. This was important because the Fifth Circuit had rejected that position in its opinion in *Oncale*. The Supreme Court's opinion stresses that in order to be actionable, the discriminatory conduct must be "because of . . . sex." What this means, however, is not clear. Justice Scalia responds to the fear that sexual harassment litigation will become a means of enforcing a civility code by emphasizing that the conduct must be sufficiently severe to alter the conditions of the victim's employment. The Court states, "Common sense, and an appropriate sensitivity to social context, will enable courts and juries to distinguish between simple teasing or roughhousing among members of the same sex, and conduct which a reasonable person in the plaintiff's position would find severely hostile or abusive." Do you share the Court's confidence in a fact-finder's ability to determine what constitutes discrimination on the basis of sex with very little more as guidance?

One of the few additional bits of guidance that the Court does provide to the trial courts is that the harassment need not have been motivated by sexual desire in order to qualify as discrimination on the basis of sex. The Court admits that harassment in heterosexual cases appears to be because of sex because we assume it is founded in the heterosexual (usually male) harasser's desire. Similarly, if the harasser in a same sex case is homosexual, we can make the same assumption about the role of desire. This explains the Court's denial of certiorari in BVP Management Associates v. Fredette, 118 S.Ct. 1184, 140 L.Ed.2d 315 (1998), within days of the *Oncale* decision. In *BVP Management* the Eleventh Circuit had held in favor of a male who was the subject of his male homosexual supervisor's repeated on-the-job sexual propositions.

It is harder to understand the Supreme Court's action in vacating for further consideration in light of *Oncale* the judgment in Belleville v. Doe, 118 S.Ct. 1183, 140 L.Ed.2d 313. *Belleville* involved sixteen year old twin boys who took a summer job with the city cutting grass, and were subjected to harassment by the other workers on the job because one of the twins wore an earring and the other was somewhat overweight. The boys were repeatedly referred to as "bitch," "queer," and "fag." The other workers asked the one with the earring if he was a boy or a girl. While most of the taunting was verbal, at one point one of the other workers said he was going to find out if this twin was a boy or a girl. He grabbed the teen-ager's testicles, and then announced, "Well, I guess he's a guy." There was no indication that this harassing behavior was based on the older workers' sexual desire for either of the twins, and according to *Oncale* that should not have mattered. The Seventh Circuit in its opinion in *Belleville* took pains to emphasize that it believed that a fact-finder could find that the twins had been harassed because of their sex. It argued that this should be apparent both from the sexual nature of the harassment and also because the twins' conduct as men did not conform with their co-workers' ideas of how men should act. This position is consistent with the position taken by Katherine Franke in the excerpt above.

This raises the question of what the Supreme Court had in mind when it vacated the judgment in *Belleville*. Do you think that it was disagreeing with the Seventh Circuit's understanding of what the term "because of ...sex" means? Is the Supreme Court rejecting the position that Title VII prohibits harassment that is used to enforce gender norms? Is it asking the Seventh Circuit to rethink the proof of harassment claims in single sex workplaces where comparisons to treatment of the other sex are not possible? Or, do you think the Supreme Court was indicating that the Seventh Circuit should reconsider the situation in *Belleville* to ensure that the harassment was sufficiently severe to alter the conditions of the teens' employment? These same questions will be important in *Oncale* on remand. How do you think the Fifth Circuit should handle the *Oncale* case when it reappears in front of the court?

Vicki Schultz, Reconceptualizing Sexual Harassment

107 Yale L.J. 1683 (1998).

... How should we understand sex-based harassment on the job? Its existence is now part of the national consciousness. Over the past twenty years, feminists have succeeded in naming "sexual harassment" and defining it as a social problem....

That feminists (and sympathetic lawyers) have inspired a body of popular and legal opinion condemning harassment in such a brief period of time is a remarkable achievement. Yet the achievement has been limited because we have not conceptualized the problem in sufficiently broad terms. The prevailing paradigm for understanding sex-based harassment places sexuality—more specifically, male-female sexual advances—at the center of the problem. Within that paradigm, a male supervisor's sexual advances on a less powerful, female subordinate represent the quintessential form of harassment.

Although this sexual desire-dominance paradigm represented progress when it was first articulated as the foundation for quid pro quo sexual harassment, using the paradigm to conceptualize hostile work environment harassment has served to exclude from legal understanding many of the most common and debilitating forms of harassment faced by women (and many men) at work each day. The prevailing paradigm privileges conduct thought to be motivated by sexual designs—such as sexual advances—as the core sex-or gender-based harassment. Yet much of the gender-based hostility and abuse that women (and some men) endure at work is neither driven by the desire for sexual relations nor even sexual in content.

Indeed, many of the most prevalent forms of harassment are actions that are designed to maintain work—particularly the more highly rewarded lines of work—as bastions of masculine competence and authority. Every day, in workplaces all over the country, men uphold the image that their jobs demand masculine mastery by acting to undermine their female colleagues' perceived (or sometimes even actual) competence to do the work. . . .

To a large extent, the courts have restricted the conception of hostile work environment harassment to male-female sexual advances and other explicitly sexualized actions perceived to be driven by sexual designs. In doing so, courts have created a framework that is underinclusive. By defining the essence of harassment as sexual advances, the paradigm has obscured—and excluded—some of the most pervasive forms of gender hostility experienced on a day-to-day basis by many women (and men) in the workplace. . . .

In *Harris v. Forklift Systems, Inc.*, [510 U.S. 17 (1993)] the Supreme Court had an opportunity to expand the legal understanding of hostile work environment harassment. Theresa Harris was the rental manager in a company that sold, leased, and repaired forklift equipment. She was one of only two female managers; the other was the daughter of the company president, Charles Hardy. During Harris's tenure, Hardy subjected her to various treatments undermining her authority as a manager, such as denying her an individual office, a company car, and a car allowance; paying her on a different basis from the other managers; refusing to give her more than a cursory annual review; and forcing her to bring coffee into meetings, which he never asked male managers to do. Hardy made it plain that he considered women inadequate as managers. He frequently denigrated the plaintiff in front of other employees with such remarks as, "You're a woman, what do you know"; "You're a dumb ass woman"; and "We need a man as the rental manager." Hardy made other comments that demeaned Harris as a professional, suggesting that the two of them go to the Holiday Inn to negotiate her raise and intimating that she must have promised sex to a client in order to obtain an account. In addition, Hardy denigrated Harris's managerial role by subjecting her to the same sort of sophomoric, sexually oriented conduct that he directed at lower-level women employees (but not male employees), such as asking her to retrieve coins from his front pocket and making suggestive comments about her clothing.

Despite Hardy's conduct, the district court adopted the magistrate's conclusion that the harassment did not rise to the level of a hostile work environment. The Sixth Circuit affirmed. Harris's appeal to the Supreme Court emphasized only one aspect of the case: Harris urged that the lower court had erred in requiring her to prove that the harassment had seriously affected her psychological well-being or otherwise caused her psychological injury. The Supreme Court found for Harris, rejecting the lower court's narrow subjective psychological harm requirement and holding that a plaintiff need show only that a reasonable person would have perceived, as Harris did, that the harassment was sufficiently severe or pervasive to create a hostile or abusive work environment.

In focusing on the abstract standards, however, both the Supreme Court and the lawyers failed to address the real problem in the case: the lower court's application of those standards from an overly narrow, sexualized perspective. The magistrate made the classic analytical move made by courts that have adopted the sexual desire-dominance paradigm: disaggregation. He began by parceling out the sexual and nonsexual conduct into separate claims. The nonsexual conduct, such as denying Harris a car, car allowance, office, and annual review, was not considered part of the harassment claim, but was examined under a separate claim of disparate treatment. For purposes of the hostile work environment claim, the magistrate concluded that only Hardy's "sexually crude comments" met the EEOC guidelines' definition of actionable harassment. After limiting his focus to these comments, the magistrate then trivialized them by emphasizing that they did not sufficiently resemble the sexual advances at the core of the sexual desire-dominance paradigm. The Holiday Inn comment, for instance, was a bad joke, "but it was not a sexual proposition." . . . Winning cases "involved sexual harassment . . . in the form of *requests for sexual relations or actual offensive touching.*" Thus, it was the comparison of Harris's mistreatment to an imagined case of sexual advances that led the magistrate and the lower courts to conclude that the mistreatment was not sufficiently injurious to be actionable.

Harris provided a clear opportunity to transcend this unduly restrictive focus. The case presented a chance to expand the concept of hostile work environment harassment to include all conduct that is rooted in gender-based expectations about work roles and to recognize that harassment functions as a way of undermining women's perceived competence as workers. From such a perspective, Charles Hardy's conduct looks like the central sex discrimination that Title VII was intended to dismantle. Taken together, Hardy's conduct—from the "sexual" conduct that reduced Harris to a sexual object as she struggled to fulfill her work role, to the nonsexual but gender-biased conduct that denigrated her capacity to serve as a manager, to the facially gender-neutral conduct that denied her the perks, privileges, and respect she needed to do her job well—had the purpose and effect of undermining Harris's status and authority as a manager on the basis of her sex. These actions fit a classic pattern of harassment often directed at women who try to claim male-dominated work as their own. Yet, neither the Supreme Court, the Sixth Circuit, the district court,

Harris's counsel, nor most amici curiae saw the case in these terms or even perceived the magistrate's narrow obsession with the lack of direct sexual advances on Harris as problematic. . . .

The disaggregation of sexual and nonsexual conduct was not inevitable, for hostile work environment harassment emerged as a variant of disparate treatment. . . . Despite the origin of hostile work environment harassment in the law of disparate treatment, courts have developed analyses that distinguish the two causes of action and endow each with a life of its own; to many courts, the two claims have become "factually and legally distinct." . . . [S]ome courts have held that disparate treatment claims are confined to supervisor actions that effect a tangible job detriment. Other courts have gone even further to demand proof that the alleged misconduct constituted an "ultimate employment decision," such as hiring, firing, pay, or promotion denial. The cause of action for hostile work environment harassment, however, was devised precisely to cover situations that do not affect the plaintiffs' jobs in any tangible or ultimate sense. As a result, there is no requirement that alleged hostile work environment harassment affect an ultimate employment decision. Instead, plaintiffs are required to prove two alternative elements: First, they must show that the harassment is "sufficiently severe or pervasive to alter the conditions of the victim's employment and create an abusive working environment"; and second, they must also prove that the employer is responsible legally for the challenged misconduct. . . .

The problem with disaggregation should be obvious by now. It weakens the plaintiff's case and distorts the law's understanding of the hostile work environment by obscuring a full view of the culture and conditions of the workplace. Both the hostile work environment and the disparate treatment claims are trivialized. When removed from the larger discriminatory context, the sexual conduct can appear insignificant. For this reason, courts often conclude that the harassment was not sufficiently severe or pervasive to alter the conditions of employment and create a hostile or abusive work environment.

By the same token, when women are denied the training, information, and support they need to succeed on the job, or when they are subjected to threatening or alienating acts that undermine their confidence and sense of belonging, they can easily be made to appear (or even become) less than fully proficient at their jobs. This lack of proficiency then becomes the nondiscriminatory reason that justifies the hostile treatment that has undermined their competence. Furthermore, when separated from sexual advances and other sexual conduct, the nonsexual actions may appear to be gender-neutral forms of hazing with which the law should not interfere. For these reasons, courts frequently rule against plaintiffs on the ground that acts were not directed at them because of their sex.

What is more, some nonsexual forms of hostility escape judicial scrutiny altogether. They appear as insufficiently sexual to be analyzed as hostile work environment harassment, and too remotely related to a tangible job benefit to constitute disparate treatment. . . .

[One] explanation for the courts' emphasis on sexual conduct as the core of sex-based harassment ... [is that] [h]ighlighting sexual abuse has allowed judges to feel enlightened about protecting women from sexual violation while relieving them of the responsibility to redress broader gender-based forms of disadvantage at work. Even though a sexuality-based standard has not yielded predictable results, singling out sexual abuse may permit judges the illusion that they are addressing a problem that can be isolated from other workplace conditions. Indeed, the disaggregation of sexual harassment from other forms of sex discrimination presumes precisely such a separation. To confront the fact that sexual misconduct may be only one—indeed, perhaps only a relatively minor—manifestation of a larger pattern of nonsexual harassment and discrimination raises the disquieting prospect that the world of work is systematically gender-biased. Judges may understandably wish to avoid confronting such a problem....

Courts have not understood, however, that the gender stratification of work—who does what type of work, under what conditions, and for what reward—is at least as influential as sexual relations in producing women's disadvantage. Although judges understand that women are victimized as sexual objects, they have not been able to see that women are also systematically harassed, discriminated against, and marginalized as workers in ways that render them unequal on the job and, as a result, in many other realms of life. The assumptions underlying th[is] ... structure ... may seem natural, but they are the product of larger political currents. To most judges, sexual advances seem intuitively gender-based because cultural-radical feminists, and the sexual desire-dominance paradigm they inspired, have articulated how women are harmed through sexual relations. Yet, in part because no political tradition has expressed with the same force the ways in which women are rendered unequal through workplace relations, judges have difficulty perceiving the characteristic problems that confront working women as gender-based....

To begin constructing a more accurate account of hostile work environment harassment means recognizing the importance of the realm of paid work in creating women's second-class status. Contrary to the assumption of the cultural-radical feminist tradition that inspired the development of harassment law, men's desire to exploit or dominate women sexually may not be the exclusive, or even the primary, motivation for harassing women at work. Instead, a drive to maintain the most highly rewarded forms of work as domains of masculine competence underlies many, if not most, forms of sex-based harassment on the job. Harassment has the form and function of denigrating women's competence for the purpose of keeping them away from male-dominated jobs or incorporating them as inferior, less capable workers.

... I refer to the new account as a "competence-centered" paradigm, for it understands harassment as a means to reclaim favored lines of work and work competence as masculine-identified turf—in the face of a threat posed by the presence of women (or lesser men) who seek to claim these prerogatives as their own. This account provides a more comprehensive understanding of the customary cases of male-female harassment by supervisors and co-workers and also allows us to understand some less conventional forms of harassment, such as harassment of female supervisors by their male subordinates. . . .

Both scholarly research and everyday experience reveal that the world of work plays a pivotal role in producing gender inequality between men and women. This is not surprising. In advanced industrial societies, wage work is a primary source of material security and psychological well-being: A job provides both the means to meet life's concrete needs and a position that confers a sense of place in the world. As scholars have begun to recognize, work not only bestows a livelihood and sense of community, but also provides the basis for full citizenship, and even for personal identity. Like it or not, we are what we do.

If the job makes the person, experience in the job world molds people along gendered lines. As numerous researchers have documented, one of the most striking features of the world of work is the extent to which it is stratified by sex. Almost universally, men and women work at different jobs. At each level of the occupational and educational ladder, the jobs women do tend to pay less and to offer lower status and less opportunity for advancement than those that men do. Especially at the lower ends of the economic spectrum, women work at jobs that offer fewer prospects for challenge, creativity, and physical mobility. Jobs traditionally occupied by women are more likely to be governed by petty, paternalistic forms of authority. Women's inferior position in the world of work confers disadvantages that burden women throughout other realms of life.

The linkages between work and gender are deep—so deep that we tend to think of most types of work as essentially "masculine" or "feminine." These linkages may run especially deep for men. At least since the onset of industrialization, paid work has provided a main source of authority and identity for men. . . . Breadwinning, mastery, and mobility are central to mainstream masculinity. Without them, it is difficult to see what "separate[s] . . . the 'men' from the 'girls.' "

It is not surprising, therefore, that numerous studies have shown that men tend to define their manhood in terms of their status as breadwinners and as masters of uniquely masculine skills. Nor is it surprising that incumbent male workers have sought to defend their occupational turf from incursion by women by branding them as incompetent. The long history of entrenched sex segregation of work has encouraged male workers to adopt proprietary attitudes toward their jobs. The major purpose of Title VII is to dismantle sex segregation by integrating women into work formerly reserved for men. Yet, desegregating the workforce has proved to be a daunting task, for men can create hostile and sexist work environments as a way to retain the better types of work for themselves. Indeed, research shows that women who work in male-dominated settings are more likely than other women to experience hostility and harassment at work. Not all the men in a work setting—nor even the majority—need to participate in the harassment. It takes only a few, particularly if they are able to secure the acquiescence of supervisors, to make the job environment hostile and alienating to any woman who dares to upset the "natural" order of segregation.

Research also confirms what the earlier analyses of the hostile work environment harassment cases suggest: For many, if not most, women workers, neither sexual desire nor sexual advances are the core of the problem.... As one female pipefitter explained:

> Some of the men would take the tools out of my hands. You see it is just very hard for them to work with me because they're really into proving their masculinity and being tough. And when a woman comes on a job that can work, get something done as fast and efficiently, as well, as they can, it really affects them. Somehow if a woman can do it, it ain't that masculine, not that tough.

By driving women out of nontraditional jobs, harassment reinforces the idea that women are inferior workers who cannot meet the demands of a "man's job" More subtly, for women who stay in nontraditional jobs, harassment exaggerates gender differences to remind them that they are "out of place" in a "man's world." By simultaneously labeling the women "freaks" or "deviants" and pressuring them to conform to the dominant culture, men preserve the image of their jobs as masculine work that no real woman would do. By marking nontraditionally employed women workers as exceptions to their gender—yet still women and therefore never quite as competent or as committed as the men—harassment enables men to continue to define their work (and themselves) in masculine terms.

In this analysis, hostile work environment harassment is an endemic feature of the workplace that is both engendered by, and further entrenches, the sex segregation of work.... [H]arassment provides male workers "a mechanism for achieving exclusion and protection of privilege" in connection with work. Motivated by both material considerations and equally powerful psychological ones, harassment provides a means for men to mark their jobs as male territory and to discourage any women who seek to enter. By keeping women in their place in the workplace, men secure superior status in the home, in the polity, and in the larger culture as well.

Contrary to many prevailing assumptions, workplace harassment is not a mere reflection of unequal gender relations that have already been created elsewhere, such as in the domestic sphere. The problem is not that men are not yet accustomed to working alongside women as equals and therefore revert to hierarchical and abusive relations learned in other settings. It is, instead, that by portraying women as less than equal at work, men can secure superior jobs, resources, and influence—all of which afford men leverage over women at home and everyplace else. Work and workplace relations are active shapers of gender difference and identity, and harassment is a central mechanism through which men preserve their work and skill as domains of masculine mastery....

Just as the sexual desire-dominance paradigm creates problems of under inclusiveness, it may also create problems of over inclusiveness by influencing courts and companies to characterize some benign forms of sexual expression as hostile work environment harassment. . . . [It] risks encouraging courts and companies to overreach in an effort to protect women's sexual sensibilities from mere discussions of sexuality that do not threaten their equality in the workplace. Perhaps predictably, courts appear more likely to engage in such overreaching where the discussion involves sexuality perceived as deviant.

By reorienting the focus of harassment law toward conduct that promotes gender stratification, the new paradigm helps rectify this problem.

Contrary to the assumption of the sexual desire-dominance paradigm, gender inequality is not synonymous with sexual relations. Just as gender-based oppression occurs outside the realm of the sexual, so too does the sphere of sexuality encompass more than simply oppression. Sexual relations (heterosexual or otherwise) do not inherently enact male dominance over women. Indeed, to characterize sexuality as such risks allowing heterosexual women to become the arbiters of others' sexual expression—including that of marginalized sexual minorities—even where that expression does not hinder women's full participation in the workplace. . . .

In *Pierce v. Commonwealth Life Insurance* Co., [40 F.3d 796 (6th Cir. 1994),] a male manager, Tom Pierce, was accused of sexual harassment after participating in an exchange of sexually explicit cards with a female office administrator, Debbie Kennedy. One of the cards Pierce sent read, "Sex is a misdemeanor. De more I miss, demeanor I get." The other was a cartoon valentine that read, "There are many ways to say 'I love you' . . . but f—ing is the fastest." According to Pierce and others in the office, Kennedy had also sent Pierce cards with sexually explicit messages and had engaged in other off-color behavior toward Pierce and other employees. In response to Kennedy's claim of sexual harassment, Pierce was disciplined. He was summarily demoted, with a significant reduction in pay, and transferred to another office on the ground that he had violated the company's sexual harassment policy. After spending thirty years with the company, Pierce was bid farewell by having "[his] personal belongings from the office . . . dropped off to him at a 'Hardee's' roadside fast food restaurant."

. . . [I]t is possible that the facts were less sympathetic to Pierce than they appear. Pierce was, after all, a manager, while Kennedy was not. Pierce was responsible for managing three offices and for enforcing the company's sexual harassment policy. The company claimed that he already had been counseled about two sexual harassment complaints in the past ten years—a record that Pierce denied. In light of his position of authority, Pierce's sending the two sexually explicit cards to Kennedy may suggest that his conduct veered perilously close to being actionable. Even if so, however, the reasoning that led the company to such a conclusion is unsound—and disturbing. The company relied on the sexually explicit character of Pierce's actions, without ever examining whether such actions denigrated Kennedy's competence or otherwise disadvantaged her or other women in the office on the basis of their gender. In fact, in an amazing bit of reasoning that conflates *all* forms of sexual interaction, Pierce's superiors told him that he might as well have been a "murderer, rapist or child molester, that [what he did] wouldn't be any worse."

Such reasoning is dangerous. It invites companies to discipline or discharge workers for the wrong reasons. It is unclear how often companies rely on the threat of harassment suits to discipline workers for engaging in sexual expression, but some alarming stories have been reported. In one account, a male social worker was fired for imitating David Letterman and approaching a new female co-worker with the comment, "I'm gonna flirt with ya." In another, a lesbian psychology professor's guest lecture on female masturbation prompted a sexual harassment lawsuit by a married, male Christian student, who claimed that he felt "raped and trapped" by the lecture. . . .

However subtly, the sexual desire-dominance paradigm enables (or even encourages) these kinds of complaints by emphasizing the "sexual" nature of harassment. These kinds of complaints tend to legitimate opposition to harassment law on the part of those who are concerned about protecting sexual expression or who, for less salutary reasons, oppose placing the power of accusation in the hands of women workers. Although some of the reported sexual harassment complaints may raise First Amendment concerns, that is not my focus here. My concern, instead, is the effect on gender relations. It gives feminism a bad name when men (or women) are fired for merely talking about sex at work. In my view, it is misguided to attempt to banish all hints of sexuality from the workplace. For one thing, it will not work. One does not have to be a Freudian to acknowledge that the old Taylorist belief that sexuality could be banished from the realm of the modern organization was incorrect; sexuality permeates organizations and, so long as organizations are made up of human beings, will continue to flourish in one form or another.

Even if all sexual interaction could be eradicated from the work world, this would not necessarily be desirable. Sexuality should not be conceptualized solely as a sphere of gender domination, but also as a potential arena of women's empowerment. If some men use sexual behavior as a weapon of gender struggle at work, one solution is for women to refuse to cede sexuality as a source of male domination and to use it to turn the tables on oppressive men. History provides examples of women who successfully mobilized sexual conduct or expression as a way of undermining authoritarian male control in the workplace. Even more fundamentally, women and sympathetic men can work together to integrate the workforce. Research suggests that where men and women work alongside each other in balanced numbers, harassment is less of a problem. Workers in such settings report that sexual talk and joking occurs with frequency, but is not experienced as harassment.

To some readers, it will seem too risky to acknowledge that the prevailing paradigm may encourage some overreaching. . . . [But] eliminating the current emphasis on the sexual content of harassment does not mean that sexual expression would always go unscrutinized. For one thing, the cause of action for quid pro quo harassment would remain unaffected by my approach; where a supervisor seeks to condition job benefits on sexual favors, the company would continue to be liable. For purposes of hostile work environment harassment, courts and companies would continue to review sexually explicit behavior, but they would examine it along with any challenged nonsexual behavior to determine whether all such activity, taken together, created a discriminatory work environment. Part of the relevant inquiry would be an examination of the larger workplace context—most importantly, the employers' past and present record of recruiting, hiring, promoting, evaluating, and paying women (and gender nonconforming men) on an equal basis. Male supervisors' or co-workers' deployment of sexual expression and activity in traditionally segregated job settings may raise alarm bells that would not sound in more integrated settings particularly where such sexual activity is accompanied by other actions that denigrate the harassers' competence.

Courts should examine such structural linkages between sex-based harassment and other forms of gender stratification, rather than focusing so much attention on the sexual content of the alleged misconduct alone. Women should not have to present themselves as Sunday-school teachers in order to comport with the image of the good victim. But neither should women (or men) be able to sue because they are offended by someone else's sexual conversation or gestures. A competence-centered paradigm alleviates this problem by focusing attention away from sexuality as such and toward gender inequality in work roles. That is where Title VII's focus properly lies....

NOTES AND QUESTIONS

1. **Desire-dominance or Competency Paradigm for Sexual Harassment?** Schultz suggests that we refocus attention in sexual harassment suits from a search for predatory sexual behavior on the part of the harasser to the harasser's efforts to undermine the victim's perceived or actual ability to perform competently in the job. Schultz makes a number of claims in support of her position. First, she argues that harassment in the form of sexual advances constitutes only a part of the harassment that women experience on the job and that it, like other forms of harassment, serves to mark women as incompetent in their jobs. Does thinking about sexual harassment in this way add to your understanding of the cases in these materials or of media depictions of workplace harassment? Second, Schultz asserts that a significant portion of men's identities as men derives from their position and status in the world of work rather than from a desire to dominate women sexually. Again, does thinking about sexual harassment in this way add to (or detract from) your understanding of sexual harassment in specific settings? Third, she disagrees with those feminists who assert that an element from the private sphere—sexual desire—has inappropriately insinuated itself into employment relations and is reproducing there the dominance that men experience within the family.

Instead, Schultz argues that men's position at work—achieved by undermining women's competence—endows them with the power to dominate women outside of work also. Is this claim helpful in thinking about men's position outside of the workplace?

Finally, in assessing Schultz's argument we must ask how important sexual desire has actually become to a finding of sexual harassment. Do you agree with Schultz's analysis of the Court's opinion in *Harris v. Forklift Systems?* Did the *Harris* Court miss an opportunity to expand sexual harassment law to include the undermining of women's performances on the job, and did it instead reinforce the dependence of sexual harassment law on the existence of sexual advances? In contrast, is there support for Schultz's position in the *Oncale* Court's statement that "harassing conduct need not be motivated by sexual desire to support an inference of discrimination on the basis of sex"?

2. **The Role of Sexuality in the Workplace**. Schultz' work raises again the issue of what place, if any, sexuality should have in the workplace. Should the mere mention of sex be considered sexual harassment? Do you think that Pierce, in *Pierce v. Commonwealth Life Insurance*, discussed by Schultz, engaged in sexual harassment? Would your answer change if it were clear that Pierce had not previously engaged in any sexually harassing conduct? What if he were not a manager, but rather an employee on the same level as Kennedy, his target? Do the sexual desire-dominance and competency paradigms lead in different directions in settings like these? Do you agree with Schultz when she says, "Gender inequality is not synonymous with sexual relations"?

Schultz's objection to the effort to remove all mention of sex from the workplace comes from her concern over its effects on gender relations. Other commentators have worried that sexual harassment law may force the removal of talk about sex and gender roles from the workplace and that this may interfere with employees' free speech rights. The excerpts that follow discuss this claim.

Eugene Volokh, Freedom of Speech and Workplace Harassment

39 UCLA L. Rev. 1791 (1992).

> ... In essence, while Title VII does not require an employer to fire all "Archie Bunkers" in its employ, the law does require that an employer take prompt action to prevent such bigots from expressing their opinions in a way that abuses or offends their co-workers. By informing people that the expression of racist or sexist attitudes in public is unacceptable, people may eventually learn that such views are undesirable in private, as well. Thus, Title VII may advance the goal of eliminating prejudices and biases in our society.

Said about almost any other variety of opinion, this statement—by a federal appeals court—would be a civil libertarian's nightmare. Imagine a law requiring that "an employer take prompt action to prevent [Communists] from expressing their opinions in a way that abuses or offends their co-workers," or a law that, "by informing people that the expression of [unpatriotic] attitudes in public is unacceptable" will eventually teach them "that such views are undesirable in private, as well." Most would agree that such a law would raise grave First Amendment concerns, even if applied only to speech in the workplace.

But harassment law—the body of law under Title VII and related state statutes that govern harassing speech in the workplace—has faced remarkably few First Amendment challenges. Few courts applying harassment law even discuss free speech issues, and many commentators have almost taken the constitutionality of harassment law for granted. In part this may be because the need for harassment law is so broadly accepted; it seems intolerable and paradoxical to guarantee equal job opportunity to women and minorities, but to permit them to be driven from their jobs by discriminatory harassment. And in part it may be because much harassing workplace speech seems in our collective judgment to be relatively "valueless": repeated unwanted sexual propositions, bigoted slurs, and the like.

But recent cases have begun to show the price we pay for leaving harassment law's First Amendment implications unexamined. Some courts and state administrative agencies have found religious proselytizing—which is generally seen as core protected speech—to be religious harassment when conducted at work.... In one case, the Equal Employment Opportunity Commission ("EEOC") alleged that a manufacturer's ads that referred to the manufacturer's Japanese competition using "accurate depictions of ... samurai, kabuki, and sumo" were "racist" and "offensive to people of Japanese origin," and thus created a hostile work environment for Japanese employees. One court has implied that a male homosexual's discussion of his sexual preference, and of political issues related to homosexuality, with a male employee might constitute sexual harassment. Other courts have held that "harassment" could include an employee telling a female co-worker that women make bad doctors because they are unreliable when they menstruate, a policeman putting a poster on his locker that says that women do not belong on the police force, an employee saying that "[i]f most niggers would decide to go to work we wouldn't have to pay high taxes," or an employee telling a Catholic co-worker that Catholics are stupid because they have too many children....

Much of this speech is offensive and unprofessional, and perhaps some of it should not receive full First Amendment protection when said in the workplace. Much of harassment law—specifically, the restrictions on offensive speech directed at a particular employee—is ... indeed constitutional. But this conclusion should only follow a serious First Amendment analysis, both so that harassment law itself does not suppress worthy workplace speech, and so that it does not set a dangerous precedent for the future....

Harassment law suppresses speech not by directly penalizing employees who say offensive things, but by threatening employers with liability if they do not punish such employees themselves. This indirect speech restriction is every bit as potent as a direct one. Companies, fearing liability, implement policies prohibiting a particular kind of speech and providing for disciplinary measures. Employees, fearing discipline, avoid expressing the proscribed speech. The employees are as deterred by this as they would be by the threat of a lawsuit aimed directly at them. And this suppression of harassing employee speech by employers was precisely the aim of the EEOC and of many of the courts that developed harassment law. . . .

The incentive for employers to suppress speech is particularly great because the employer is liable for its employees' offensive speech—with the passage of the Civil Rights Act, possibly also liable for emotional distress damages and punitive damages—but derives no benefit from it. In this respect, harassment law differs from, say, libel law, in which liability is imposed on the speaker itself (the newspaper). The newspaper may be chilled by the possibility of a libel judgment if a story about a private figure turns out to be false, but the newspaper's interest in reporting the story counteracts the chilling effect to some extent. There is no similar force working against the chilling effect of harassment law. A prudent employer who is faced with even a small possibility of liability would quite likely demand that its employees avoid even arguably harassing speech.

Of course, some employers may ignore the threat of liability and fail to regulate their employees' speech: most of the harassment cases involve employers like this. But many employers, especially the sensible ones who know the law and care about avoiding liability, will indeed regulate employee speech. Although harassment law may not suppress all harassing speech by employees, it will certainly suppress some. . . .

Though harassment law imposes liability only when speech is sufficiently severe and pervasive to create a hostile work environment, it also indirectly suppresses speech that is not so severe and pervasive. Courts frequently assert that harassment law does not impose liability for isolated slurs, propositions, and the like, but, despite this, harassment law can suppress even such isolated or infrequent instances of offensive speech.

This is because employers—the frontline enforcers of harassment law's speech restrictions—cannot restrict speech that creates a hostile work environment without suppressing other speech as well. To begin with, the "sufficiently severe and pervasive so as to create a hostile work environment" standard is extremely vague. Perhaps this must be so; it may be impossible to specify exactly how much of each kind of offensive speech is necessary to lead to liability. But, like all vague standards, the harassment law standard has a substantial "chilling effect": to be safe, an employer must suppress speech that might qualify as severe and pervasive enough to constitute harassment, even though, if litigated, the speech might not meet the legal standard. And this chilling effect is compounded by the fact, discussed above, that employers derive no benefit from their employees' offensive speech, but must bear liability for it; this gives employers a great incentive to suppress even borderline speech.

Furthermore, the only practical way for an employer to avoid liability based on the sum of all offensive statements is by instituting a policy that will bar each individual statement. An employer cannot say to each employee: "It is all right for you to make offensive statements, but only so long as the total effect of all your statements and the other employees' statements does not create a hostile environment." The employer can either bar all such statements, or tolerate them all and risk possible liability. And, once a policy of banning all offensive speech of a particular kind is established, the only way to ensure that employees comply with it is by enforcing it in each instance of such offensive speech.

It is hard to tell exactly how these effects play out in practice, because employers' oversuppression of speech generally does not end up in court. But if one puts oneself in the shoes of a typical employer, or a typical employer's lawyer, one can make some reasonable conjectures. Say, for instance, that a female employee comes to her manager and says that she is bothered by the swimsuit calendars—or even calendars with reproductions of classical nudes—that many of her co-workers have in the workplace, and threatens to sue. The company's lawyer cannot predict whether a factfinder would find that the calendars create a hostile environment; the calendars are not what most would normally call "pornography," but at least some might consider them to be demeaning to women. But even if the risk of liability for the company is small, the benefit it derives from the calendars is nonexistent. A prudent manager would therefore demand that its employees take down the calendars, even though it may be likely that the calendars do not create a hostile environment. Furthermore, though it may be almost certain that one or two such calendars will not create a hostile environment, the employer cannot just let one or two employees keep their calendars. The only way for it to ensure compliance with its new policy is to demand that all such calendars be taken down.

A similar scenario would arise even if the speech that an employee complains of was core protected speech, such as anti-Equal Rights Amendment posters on people's doors, discussions in the lunchroom of how God wants women to stay at home, or overheard conversations about how American Jews are disloyal to America and care only about Israel. Even if the employer suspects that the speech is not severe or pervasive enough to create a hostile environment, it can never be sure of this; the only thing of which it can be sure is that it derives no benefit from the speech, but might be held liable for it. And the only way it can enforce a prohibition on this sort of speech is by punishing people for each individual instance of such speech, even if the instance may not, by itself, be sufficient to create a hostile work environment. . . .

Harassment law also suppresses isolated instances of offensive speech through the remedies that courts impose once a hostile work environment has been found. For instance, in Robinson v. Jacksonville Shipyards, Inc., [760 Supp. 1486 (M.D. Fla. 1991)], the court held that sexually explicit and derogatory remarks addressed to defendant's female employees, coupled with the pervasive sexually explicit materials posted throughout the workplace, created a hostile work environment. As a remedy, the court ordered defendant to implement a sexual harassment policy that, among other things, prohibited:

> [D]isplaying pictures, posters, ... reading materials, or other materials that are sexually suggestive, sexually demeaning, or pornographic, or bringing into the JSI work environment or possessing any such material to read, display or view at work....

> [R]eading or otherwise publicizing in the work environment materials that are in any way sexually revealing, sexually suggestive, sexually demeaning or pornographic.

All violations of this policy were to result in a "written warning, suspension or discharge upon the first proven offense," and "suspension or discharge upon the second proven offense."

Note how the order transformed the standard of liability for harassment. Before the lawsuit was decided, the employer was liable only for those actions of its employees that created a hostile work environment. If, for instance, only one or two employees had a few "sexually suggestive" or "sexually demeaning" materials in the workplace, the employer might feel relatively safe from liability....

Under the order, on the other hand, any display that falls within the terms of the order must lead to discipline, even if the display is an isolated incident which does not create a hostile work environment, or if the display is innocent enough that it could never even contribute to creating such an environment. Under this order, the employer would quite literally have to (under pain of contempt sanctions) discipline an employee who displays a Renaissance nudes calendar. The prohibition on possessing sexually suggestive reading materials would even require the employer to punish someone who brings a sexually suggestive novel to work to read on his lunch break....

Some have argued that the First Amendment just does not apply with the same force in the workplace as it does elsewhere. One commentator, for instance, thought it "obvious" that "speech that is appropriately protected when it occurs within public discourse is also appropriately regulated as racial or sexual harassment when it occurs within the context of an employment relationship." Another stated that "[w]hen racist and sexist speech is part of a transactional setting, such as harassment in the workplace, it may be regulated." Courts seem to have been influenced by this perception as well....

The Supreme Court in [NLRB v.] Gissel [Packing Co., 395 U.S. 575, 89 S.Ct. 1918, 23 L.Ed.2d 547 (1969)] recognized that both employees and employers have First Amendment rights in the workplace, so long as the communications "do not contain a 'threat of reprisal or force or promise of benefit.' " "[A]n employer's free speech right to communicate his views to his employees is firmly established and cannot be infringed...." ...

But where no promise or threat is present, workplace speech, both by employers and employees, is fully protected.... Harassment law cannot fit within Gissel's threat-or-promise exception. Except for, possibly, sexual propositions made by a supervisor to a subordinate, no other forms of harassing speech could be viewed as threats or promises of benefit.

Some commentators have argued—outside the labor speech context— that hate speech is indeed threatening, or at least is perceived as threatening by the victim. But this is pushing the definition of threat much further than Gissel would allow.... Gissel did not allow courts to presume automatically that any employer statements were threatening; it merely gave courts more license to view such speech as threatening even though it would have been too ambiguous to be seen as threatening in other contexts. Even if the threat-or-promise exception could be made to apply to fellow-employee speech as well as to employer speech, it would not justify suppression of speech in the absence of at least some evidence of threat.... Offensive as pornography may be to some, it is hard to view it as inherently threatening, at least until some evidence is shown in the particular case that the employee was actually threatened (rather than just offended) by it. Similarly, harassment that is largely the work of a single co-worker, who has little power over the victim, should rarely be threatening, though it could easily be very offensive. It may be true that some of the victims of bigoted harassment—especially those who are conscious of a long history of persecution—might perceive such harassment as inherently threatening, but one can also say that some employees might perceive any antiunion commentary by an employer as threatening. Gissel's "threat" exception does not reach far enough to cover either situation....

One court, and a number of recent commentators, have argued that harassment law is constitutional because employees are a "captive audience," unable to flee offensive speech. But, though the Court has indeed allowed some speech restrictions aimed at protecting captive audiences in the home, it has never found that employees in the workplace are "captive"....

Furthermore, the ability to leave is only important if the offense can be avoided by leaving after the speaker has started speaking. But this is usually not true: if one is offended by hearing the word "motherfucker" (or "nigger"), then the offense occurs when the word is spoken and heard, whether or not one can leave and avoid hearing more. An employee in the workplace would be no more captive to someone saying "all niggers should be sent back to Africa," or to someone calling him a derogatory name, than he would be to the same words spoken in public.

Similarly, employees are no more and no less captive to offensive pictures or writings than are people in the street. In both cases, one can only avert one's eyes after one has seen the offensive material and thereby sustained the injury. And, again in both cases, the very process of keeping one's eyes averted reminds one of the offensive message—thinking "I shouldn't look over there because there is a man wearing a 'Fuck the Draft' jacket"—keeps the offensive message in one's mind just as surely as staring at the jacket would. The captivity is the same in the workplace as elsewhere.

One might argue that people are more captive to offensive speech in the workplace because they must necessarily be exposed to the speech every day. Someone may be insulted by a passer-by ... or see some offensive nudity on a drive-in theater's screen, but he can just walk away, and perhaps in the future avoid the places where the offensive speech is likely to recur; an employee who wants to keep her job cannot avoid returning to the workplace....

In fact, if captivity consists of an inability to avoid offensive speech, in today's society we are all "captive" to profanity. We may walk away from someone who is using it, but we cannot avoid it altogether—we hear it wherever we go. This is, regrettably, also true of bigoted abuse. In many places, blacks will be called names wherever they go; obese or disfigured people may be insulted wherever they go. Even in public, they may be able to avoid an individual insulter (though not without being insulted first), but they cannot avoid the insults altogether.

Some might contend this is a good argument for extending the captive audience doctrine not only to the workplace, but to other places, too. In this view, bigoted epithets—or any other kind of personal abuse, such as insults of the disfigured—and other kinds of offensive language should be barred everywhere, precisely because the listeners are captive to them. But if this is done, it can only be done by rejecting ... [decided cases]. As things stand today, the captive audience doctrine cannot be applied to employees in the workplace....

Showing that harassment law does not fit within any existing First Amendment exceptions is, of course, hardly the end of the story. Harassment law may restrict speech, but it does so to achieve a very important goal—an equal work environment for employees regardless of their race, sex, religion, or national origin. Even once all the established exceptions have been found inapplicable, this interest that harassment law serves must be frankly and fairly balanced against the value of the free speech that harassment law suppresses.

The Supreme Court has frequently recognized the need for such balancing....

The state has a very strong interest in ensuring equality in the workplace. Workplace harassment can, if it is severe enough, drive employees from their jobs, but even if it does not do this, it forces some groups of employees to work under real psychological burdens that other groups need not bear. Although the Court has generally held that avoiding offense to the listener is not an acceptable motive for regulating speech, workplace harassment often involves such egregious insults and abuse that all but the toughest-skinned listeners would be very deeply affected, emotionally and sometimes even physically. If workplace harassment could not be prohibited, the promise of equal employment opportunity could prove to be an empty promise for many: an employer might be required to hire minorities or women, but its employees could drive them away.

If this state interest were indeed strong enough to justify the suppression of all speech that creates a hostile work environment, then the analysis would be simple: all harassment law would be constitutional. But this cannot be so.... [S]ome line must be drawn to separate the speech that may be suppressed because it can contribute to a hostile work environment, and the speech that may not be suppressed despite its possible contribution to a hostile work environment.

One obvious place to draw this line is at the office door. Even if allowing speech restrictions outside the workplace is too much of a burden on First Amendment values, perhaps, some have argued, allowing speech restrictions within the workplace is less of a burden. The workplace, after all, is for working, not for political discourse, and in any event banning bigoted speech in the workplace "does not censor such speech everywhere and for all time." Besides, some might say, people on the job are already not free to speak, because they are subject to censorship by their employer; the extra restrictions imposed by law are correspondingly less intrusive....

But such an argument ignores the reality of people's social and political lives. The average American does not go to public demonstrations, or burn flags outside the Republican party convention, or write books, or go to political discussion groups. A great part, maybe even the majority, of most Americans' political speech happens in the workplace, where people spend more of their waking hours than anywhere else except (possibly) their homes. And this is especially true of any issues that have to do with the workplace: equal opportunity, affirmative action hiring, the rights of women, and the like. If a policeman feels that women make bad police officers, or if a worker feels that affirmative action programs are just another way in which the white race is being repressed, the logical place for them to talk about it is in the workplace.

This also shows the fallacy of justifying harassment law by saying that the employees can still spread their bigoted opinions outside the workplace. The Court has consistently rejected this argument when content-based distinctions were involved, and it is particularly untenable in this case, where the opportunities for an employee to communicate to his co-workers outside the workplace are theoretical at best. Telling an employee that he cannot talk politics to his co-workers at the office generally means that he cannot talk politics to them at all.

It is true that political speech in the workplace cannot lead to harassment law liability unless someone actually overhears it and is offended by it. But this danger is always present whenever anyone puts up a poster, and it is almost equally present for spoken conversations. Allowing people to express certain viewpoints only when the speakers know that no possibly offended co-worker can overhear them will have an immense chilling effect. Many employees have no access to truly private areas; anywhere they want to talk, in the lunchroom or in the workplace, they run the risk of being overheard. . . .

Of course, harassment law may not chill the discussion of some political topics, but many political topics do involve racial, sexual, national, or religious issues. Discussions about affirmative action, religion, women's rights, abortion, or election campaigns (especially ones involving racial issues), are quite likely to involve statements that may offend one group or another. If some employees criticize affirmative action, and say that it "gives to less qualified minorities jobs that should belong to more qualified whites," then minority employees who overhear these statements may certainly feel offended, and feel that the work environment has become hostile. Intemperate comments on foreign policy—such as the trade tensions between America and Japan—can be very offensive to some national groups. Racially polarized union elections can easily produce offensive comments or leaflets. . . .

Protecting core political speech from harassment law is especially important because many of harassment law's speech restrictions are viewpoint-based restrictions, the kind that the Court has most strongly condemned. One person in the lunch room may speak eloquently and loudly about how women are equal to men, and harassment law will not stop him. But when another tries to respond that women are inferior—belong in the home, are unreliable during their menstrual periods, or should not be allowed on the police force—harassment law steps in. It seems to be both extremely dangerous in this case, and an extremely dangerous precedent for the future, to let the government control the parameters of public debate in this way. . . .

The case for suppressing bigoted epithets, even when not directed at a particular employee, is easier than the case for suppressing "core political speech." Such epithets are, arguably, both more offensive and less valuable than nonvulgar (though bigoted) speech. It is possible that, even if the balance between the state interest and the free speech interest tips in favor of free speech for core political speech, it would tip against it for the epithets.

But there are good reasons to protect even bigoted epithets (so long as they are undirected). First, the insight of Cohen v. California [403 U.S. 15 (1971)]—that censoring the vulgarism often means censoring the political message—is equally apt in the workplace. "Fuck the Draft" is not the same as "I Do Not Like the Draft," or "The Draft Is Bad"; "niggers are ruining this country" is not the same as "blacks are ruining this country." During the first years of Margaret Thatcher's premiership in England, "Ditch the Bitch" was a popular anti-Thatcher slogan, though it was condemned as offensive by British feminists; "Ditch Thatcher" would have been less offensive, but would hardly have carried the same message.

Second, harassment law censors bigoted epithets precisely because of their political message, the message that members of particular groups are inferior and unwelcome. . . . In harassment law, bigoted epithets are banned when and only when they are used to convey an offensive message, and the ban is traceable directly to their political content. When harassment law suppresses epithets, it is because of their political content, not because of their lack of political content.

Third, drawing distinctions between "valuable" reasoned speech and "low-value" unreasoned speech is difficult and dangerous. Some Justices have indeed drawn some such distinctions in the past, but extending this distinction further is unwise, because it is very hard to establish just what speech is valuable and reasonable and what speech is vulgar (and therefore "low-value").... The vagueness of the terms "vulgar," "offensive," and "no essential part of any exposition of ideas" may lead to the suppression of even core political speech, simply because the majority or the elite find it to be offensive....

Suppressing pornography is also easier to justify than suppressing core political speech, and the Court has indeed allowed greater restrictions on pornography in general. But there are several reasons why even restrictions on workplace pornography are not a good idea.

To begin with, even if pornography can be suppressed, it cannot be suppressed because it makes men who see it think of women in some "improper" way. Robinson v. Jacksonville Shipyards, Inc. used exactly this argument, saying that pornography makes male employees view female employees not as equal co-workers, but as sex objects, and that this leads to a work environment hostile to women; but even if one accepts this factual premise, it is a totally unacceptable reason to suppress speech. If there is one principle at the root of the First Amendment, it is that speech cannot be suppressed because it may change the listeners' opinions; suppressing speech for this reason is "thought control" in its most literal sense. Even the strongest of state interests in equality cannot justify suppressing speech because it makes people think women are inferior.

Even if pornography is restricted not because it makes men think a particular way, but because it offends women more than it does men—because its offensiveness, and not its message, creates a hostile work environment—several problems still remain. To begin with, if pornography is particularly offensive to women because it expresses the message that women are only sex objects, and should be viewed as men's playthings and not as equals, then pornography becomes political speech, suppressed precisely because of the viewpoint it expresses. The Court has been tolerant of pornography regulations only because they were not viewed as attempts to suppress a particular viewpoint....

These are all difficult questions, and their difficulty is part of the reason that this Comment argues against allowing government regulation of undirected pornography in the workplace....

Restrictions on directed speech, unlike restrictions on undirected speech, only prevent people from communicating their opinions to co-workers who do not want to listen. They do not keep an employee from trying to convince willing listeners, or from putting up a poster that conveys his message to the workplace at large. If the main reason we value free speech is that it allows people to spread their ideas, then the value of directed speech, aimed solely at an unwilling listener, is modest indeed. A black employee who is told that he is a "nigger" is unlikely to become convinced of anything. . . .

Employees can still discuss their opinions with willing listeners, and people who disagree with the opinions will still have a chance to argue against them. Suppressing directed harassing speech will merely keep speakers from seeking out an employee who they know will be offended, and expressing their opinions to her face. . . .

[T]here are three reasons to sustain restrictions on offensive directed speech despite their not being viewpoint-neutral. First, unlike restrictions on undirected speech, they do not make it substantially harder for particular viewpoints to make their way into the "marketplace of ideas." Restrictions on directed speech . . . suppress only speech that is highly unlikely to convince the listener. The spread of antiblack diatribes would not be substantially slowed by a requirement that they not be targeted at blacks.

Second, there may be no practical alternative to harassment law that still serves the state interest in ensuring equality of working conditions, but does it in a content-neutral or viewpoint-neutral way. . . .

Third, the very important state interest that is present here . . . may justify even viewpoint-based restrictions that would be unacceptable in the absence of the interest. . . .

The problem of workplace harassment and harassment law's response to it raise two equally frightening specters. One is a workplace so filled with abuse, insult, or unwanted sexual attention that employees are driven from their jobs or forced to work in an intolerable atmosphere. But the other is a workplace in which the exposure of certain "unacceptable" viewpoints on certain political issues—such as religion, affirmative action, or the Equal Rights Amendment—is banned because of the employer's fear of legal liability. Completely unrestricted free speech, such as we enjoy in the public arena, cannot be the answer to this; but neither can the admittedly strong interest in equal access to the workplace justify suppression of all speech that might frustrate this interest. Some accommodation must be made, and both sides must pay some price.

The right place to draw the line, this Comment has argued, is between directed speech—offensive speech that is targeted at a particular employee because of the employee's race, sex, religion, or national origin—and undirected speech, such as overheard conversations between willing employees, or printed matter posted in the workplace. Directed speech can be suppressed with minimum impact on First Amendment interests, because targeted offensive speech is quite unlikely to convince or edify the listener; in most cases, it is likely only to offend. But undirected speech cannot be suppressed without keeping employees from spreading their political and social opinions to other, willing, listeners. For many, the workplace is the only place where they can effectively talk religion or politics, and the First

Amendment cannot tolerate such speech suppression in the workplace, especially when it is only particular points of view that are suppressed.

Tolerating even undirected offensive speech exacts a price, and some have recently begun to challenge its acceptability. Some argue that we have not paid enough attention to the offensiveness and dangerousness of bigoted speech, and that the First Amendment should sometimes yield to equality and social harmony. But the First Amendment has often exacted a high price; it has forced us to tolerate speech that urges revolution, that undermines the nation's war effort, or that advocates what some see as immoral and dangerous personal behavior. We value the First Amendment because the price the alternative exacts—the power of the government to impose an orthodoxy of speech and thought, or to cleanse public discourse of ideas it finds dangerous and threatening—is even higher.

Suzanne Sangree, Title VIII Prohibitions Against Hostile Environment Sexual Harassment and the First Amendment: No Collision in Sight

47 Rutgers L. Rev. 461 (1995).

Scholars are directing substantial attention to the apparent conflict between Title VII hostile environment sex harassment litigation and the free speech protections of the First Amendment. Two scholars in particular, Eugene Volokh and Kingsley Browne, have constructed detailed arguments that Title VII prohibitions against hostile environment harassment violate the First Amendment and must be severely curtailed to preserve free speech. Essentially they argue that hostile environment law as currently applied impermissibly targets speech because of the content and viewpoint of its message: i.e. that women are inferior workers, fit only to work in the home or to be men's playthings. . . .

To date, Volokh and Browne have defined the parameters of the debate concerning hostile environment law and the First Amendment. Each argues that hostile environment regulation under Title VII and analogous state and local law provisions must be drastically scaled back in order to preserve First Amendment values. . . .

My disagreement with the assessment that hostile environment harassment prohibitions must be significantly curtailed is at bottom a philosophical disagreement. Volokh and Browne value most highly the right of workers to say what their employers will allow at the workplace, without the government interfering to curb speech which disadvantages women. They accord less value to the interest of eradicating sex discrimination from the workplace. Thus each proposes ways to curtail Title VII to allow more speech, despite recognizing that speech often contributes to discriminatory harassment and that more harassment will be allowed. Their standards, while protecting more speech, would necessarily give free reign to more harassment than is presently tolerated. . . .

Volokh's description of core protected speech ignores the critical role that context plays in determining the extent to which speech is protected. According to Volokh, if a statement has a political message, it is high value speech which must be accorded the greatest First Amendment protection.... Volokh does not acknowledge that whether speech is protected depends not only on its content but also depends on its context. The First Amendment is not a rigid series of cubicles in which one may cabin expression; it is meant to foster democratic values in real life situations. Stating, "I am going to kill the President" with evidence of a seriousness of purpose to do so raises the words to the level of a threat and is a crime. The exact words stated in a context indicating political hyperbole make them core protected speech. By ignoring context, Volokh overstates the quality and quantity of protected speech that hostile environment regulations chill.

First Amendment doctrine regarding threats of violence, extortion and criminal coercion highlights the importance of context for determining constitutional protection of speech. First Amendment law also delineates social values which may outweigh the right to free expression in certain circumstances. In R.A.V. v. City of St. Paul, [505 U.S. 377 (1992),] Justice Scalia explained that regulation of threats of violence is consistent with the First Amendment to "protect[] individuals from fear of violence, from the disruption that fear engenders, and from the possibility that the threatened violence will occur." Threats of violence violate an individual's personal security, cause psychological distress and may result in a modification of one's lifestyle to guard against the violence. Thus, First Amendment jurisprudence recognizes that serious threats of violence are socially harmful even when the speaker has no present intent of carrying out the threat. To distinguish "true threats" of violence, which are punishable, from political rhetoric or vituperative statements, courts evaluate both the content and the context of the threatening statements, often taking into account social and historical factors....

The legitimacy of a law penalizing coercive speech which interferes with personal security, property rights and personal freedom takes on special meaning in the context of employment. As the Supreme Court stated in NLRB v. Gissel Packing Co. and its progeny, employees are highly susceptible to coercion by their employers.... The particularities of the employment context for First Amendment analysis are also illuminated by the values protected by the captive audience doctrine. The First Amendment right to free expression is restricted when a "captive audience cannot avoid the objectionable speech," and to allow the speech would violate the listeners' right to undisturbed peace.... [F]ew audiences are more captive than employees at the workplace. When sexual discrimination pervades a workplace, whether it be caused by conduct, speech, images, or a combination of these, female employees cannot avoid it. The existence of a state of captivity weighs toward the validity of prohibiting hostile environment sexual discrimination in the workplace, even when it is effectuated by speech....

[Volokh and Browne also] discount or ignore several countervailing forces that discourage employer overregulation of speech. Contrary to the critics' minimalization of this factor, employee morale is recognized to directly benefit employers and to be undermined by overly restrictive work environments. Indeed, the fact that employers have generally not banned all nonwork related speech from workplaces, despite their power to do so, demonstrates that employers recognize the potentially adverse impact of speech restrictions on employee morale. Since men comprise a strong majority of the workforce, employers are unlikely to overzealously regulate speech in the workplace in a way that would injure the morale of male workers. Another countervailing factor for public employers is that employees subjected to draconian speech codes can sue for First Amendment violations. Thus, employers will balance these countervailing interests when establishing and enforcing harassment policies.

Forces encouraging underregulation of sexual harassment also operate subconsciously. The American workplace is highly stratified by sex. Men control the workplace, and their perceptions of what constitutes acceptable behavior generally define workplace rules of conduct. Women have historically been excluded from many work settings and relegated often to unpaid positions as domestic workers and childrearers. Despite documentation that sex harassment was costly to employers in terms of worktime lost, medical treatment required, and employee turnover, employers did not voluntarily eliminate sex harassment to maximize competitiveness for cultural and historical reasons. The same historical and cultural factors perpetuate the incidence of sexual harassment in the workplace today, even though employers obtain no economic benefit from such harassment in the workplace. . . .

Contrary to the fear expressed by Volokh and Browne that hostile environment law has had a pronounced chilling effect on protected speech, Title VII discourages an insubstantial amount of such speech. To the contrary, courts have developed a context-specific doctrine which recognizes the impact of threats and coercion on women employees in a male-dominated economy. Considering both the First Amendment's aversion to coercion and threats which interfere with personal rights and the recognition that these social harms operate more subtly in the employment context, it is clear the First Amendment is not harmed by hostile environment law. Moreover, the First Amendment interest in promoting citizens' participation in the polity is served by enabling women to participate on more equal terms in the economy. Just as equality is the foundation of a free economy, so is equality the foundation of democracy. . . .

Harassment law, like Title VII generally, may chill some protected speech. Hostile environment law may even chill more protected speech than other aspects of Title VII because employers may be held responsible for hostile environment harassment by co-workers. However, the degree of chilling is not substantial either in quantity or quality and is vastly outweighed by the invidious discrimination prohibited by hostile environment law.

The protected speech at issue also has alternative fora for expression. While most workers do spend the bulk of their waking hours in the workplace, nonwork fora are available to protest state authority, and to effectuate government change. Workers and employers dissatisfied with Title VII may organize to influence the EEOC or to lobby Congress to amend Title VII. Indeed employers' associations and unions are extremely active on Capitol Hill and were influential in shaping the Civil Rights Act of 1991, the latest amendment to Title VII.

Implementing Volokh's or Browne's suggestions would result in a drastic curtailment of prohibitions on hostile environment harassment because, as they partially acknowledge, such claims would be rendered much more difficult to prove. Moreover, Volokh's and Browne's analyses cannot logically be limited to hostile environment law, and may potentially invalidate quid pro quo harassment and discrimination law altogether.

Speech which effectuates discrimination in employment undermines First Amendment interests by imposing economic coercion which disadvantages women solely on the basis of gender. Without discrimination protections, women's historic disadvantage in the workplace would continue unabated. To a greater extent than now, women would accept low-paying, dead-end jobs because those are the only ones available and they must eat and feed their families. Women would also be forced to endure abusive work environments more often. Forcing women to endure such work conditions severely disadvantages women and creates an unfair economic advantage for men. Such unfair advantage is antithetical to democracy. It does not contribute to the exposition of ideas or the search for truth. It does not enable self-governance or social stability; it only serves to disable democratic participation. Such coercion does not contribute to self-expression or self-development, except perhaps to satisfy men who enjoy tormenting women. Indeed, verbal harassment can have devastating effects on victims' self-esteem and job retention or advancement. Consequently, harassment interferes with basic prerequisites for full citizenship in a democracy. Harassment relegates its victims to second class citizenship by disabling them economically and socially. The interest in eliminating such disadvantage to women promotes a well-functioning participatory democracy. Such a democracy is fundamental to the First Amendment. Interpretation of the application of the First Amendment should promote the goal of a participatory democracy. Finally, when considering Title VII's potential for conflict with First Amendment protections, there are good reasons to follow the Supreme Court's lead that "invidious private discrimination may be characterized as a form of exercising freedom of association (or expression) protected by the First Amendment, but it has never been accorded affirmative constitutional protections."

NOTES AND QUESTIONS

1. **Sexual Harassment Law and the First Amendment.** Eugene Volokh argues that sexually harassing comments are a form of speech and

therefore, protected by the First Amendment. Indeed, not only are they speech, but often they are speech that articulates a political position, albeit in an offensive manner. Furthermore, he argues that none of the exceptions to the First Amendment justify the regulation of sexually harassing speech. In contrast, Suzanne Sangree argues that sexual harassment law actually promotes the democratic values that are fundamental to the First Amendment. Do you think the First Amendment is endangered or advanced by the existence of a Title VII action against sexual harassment actions?

The debate over the First Amendment and Title VII's prohibition on sexually harassing conduct has generated considerable academic commentary, but relative little case law. Many sexual harassment cases, like *Meritor*, involve sexual assaults in addition to verbal harassment. In these cases, the assault can be seen as the basis of the harassment action, with the verbal harassment going to show the defendant's intent to discriminate on the basis of sex. For most commentators, these cases are fairly easy. But *see*, Kingsley R. Browne, *Title VII as Censorship*, 52 Ohio St. L. J. 481 (1991) (voicing concern about the prejudicial effect of admitting harassing statements.) Other cases, like *Harris*, involve only non-physical harassment.

• *Protected Speech* In order for speech to be protected by the First Amendment it must be the type of speech that the Amendment embraces. If it is, then the court must balance the interests advanced by the First Amendment with the interests that the government is trying to advance by regulating the speech. Sangree argues that speech in the workplace is subject to less protection than the same speech might be elsewhere. Deborah Epstein takes up this argument in *Can a "Dumb Ass Woman" Achieve Equality in the Workplace?* 84 Geo. L.J. 399, 424–25 (1996):

> Professor Volokh claims that "employees are no more and no less captive to offensive [expression] than are people in the street." Professor Browne suggests that workers constitute a captive audience in the workplace only if one believes that individuals lack free will, "have little control over their lives[,] and are thus 'captives' wherever they might be." These arguments are particularly inaccurate in the case of working women, who because of the very discrimination that Title VII is designed to eliminate, face particularly daunting hurdles if they decide to leave their jobs and attempt to find new ones. To put it simply, women who cannot afford to be unemployed cannot avoid harassing speech in the workplace. Female employees therefore constitute the quintessential captive audience. The Constitution does not and should not force a woman into a Hobson's choice between quitting her job or facing a work environment in which she is subjected to severe or pervasive harassing speech that is not inflicted on her male counterparts.

How "captive" do you believe women are in their jobs? To what degree do you think that the answer to this will depend on whether the woman is a white, highly trained professional or one of the immigrant Latinas described above by Vellos in *Immigrant Latina Domestic Workers?* When do you think women have a choice as to their jobs? What about men? Is the issue of choice here similar to the issue of choice as it was discussed in the *Sears* case and materials following it?

For an argument that harassing speech should not be seen as protected speech, but rather as a means of accomplishing discrimination, *see* Charles R. Calleros, *Title VII and Free Speech*, 1996 Utah L. Rev. 227 (1996).

● *The First Amendment and balancing* If the First Amendment protects sexually harassing speech, a court must then balance that against the interests the government was asserting in limiting the speech. Sangree avoids this step by claiming that restrictions on harassing speech will actually promote democracy, and with it, the First Amendment. Why should restrictions on the First Amendment work to promote the interests the Amendment protects? Could you argue that sexually harassing speech has the effect of silencing its victims who will be free to speak once the harassing speech is eliminated? *See* Mari J. Matsuda, *Public Response to Racist Speech*, and Charles R. Lawrence III, *If He Hollers Let Him Go*, in *Words that Wound* (Matsuda, Lawrence, Delgado, and Crenshaw, eds. 1993).

Deborah Epstein, in *Can a "Dumb Ass Woman" Achieve Equality in the Workplace?*, argues that the balance leans in favor of restricting sexually harassing speech. She claims that such speech interferes with workers' equality of opportunity, protected by the Fourteenth Amendment. Sexually harassing speech has an adverse effect on women's performance on the job, making it more difficult for them to perform; it endangers their physical and psychological health; and, it causes them to be viewed as sexual objects. She concludes, "Although Title VII's hostile environment restrictions may be far from perfect, they represent the best possible balance between these two fundamental rights...." Many of the claims made here will be taken up later in this book in the section on pornography. What is the harm in causing women to be viewed as sexual objects? It may be helpful in considering this to review Katherine Franke's arguments as to the disciplinary role served by sexually harassing comments.

Volokh has proposed that speech specifically directed at an individual could be subject to restrictions, but that speech aimed at the world in general ("girlie" calendars, overheard conversations) be considered protected. Would this shield women from the harms that Epstein identified?

2. **The Workplace as a Forum for Discussion**. Volokh argues that one reason we should be especially careful to protect robust speech within the workplace is that in today's world, people's public lives often revolve around the workplace. Why is this an argument in favor of unregulated speech in the workplace? Cynthia Estlund argues in *Freedom of Expression in the Workplace and the Problem of Discriminatory Harassment*, 75 Tex. L. Rev. 687 (1997), that it is exactly the public nature of the workplace that calls for some limits on speech. Estlund provides an admittedly somewhat idealized image of the workplace as "an important location for the forging

of personal bonds that transcend family, neighborhood, and often racial and ethnic identity and for the formation of habits and values of civic virtue." Given this, she says,

> The workplace provides a uniquely configured forum for speech on general public issues, on the regulation of the workplace, and on work place governance. But it is largely the fact of workplace diversity, as enforced by the equality norm, that constitutes the workplace as a uniquely valuable setting for speech and as an important satellite forum for public discourse. The workplace can thus perform its function within the system of freedom of expression only if it is subject to some constraints of equality, civility, tolerance, and respect that help foster reasoned deliberation. These observations do not resolve the paradox of workplace discourse, but they push toward a less libertarian approach than that which prevails in the core of public discourse.

Thus, for Estlund, it is the public nature of the workplace that causes her to argue that not only should offensive speech directed at a particular individual be considered unprotected, but also speech which, independently of the position expressed, is manifestly offensive on the basis of sex and cannot reasonably be avoided by the offended listeners.

Volokh, Sangree, Epstein and Estlund offer a variety of solutions to the question of how sexually harassing speech in the workplace should be treated. Volokh would only permit regulation of offensive speech targeted at a specific individual; he argues that all other sexually harassing speech in the workplace should be deemed protected. Sangree and Epstein, in contrast, argue that Title VII's prohibition on speech that creates a hostile environment should be upheld. Although they come to this conclusion from different directions, each argues that the First Amendment does not require constricting Title VII's guarantees of workplace equality. Estlund's proposal stakes out a middle ground between Sangree and Epstein on the one side and Volokh on the other. She favors leaving unavoidable, manifestly offensive sexually harassing comments unprotected. Which of these, if any, do you support? How is your position influenced by your idea of the proper role of the workplace in promoting democracy or as establishing a private realm governed by the employer and collective bargaining?

If the ability to regulate sexually offensive and harassing speech is premised on the workplace's role as a forum for public discourse, should rules for regulation be different in educational institutions? Should the rules for educational institutions be different if you see the workplace as a private entity?

3. **Politics and the Regulation of Sexually Harassing Speech.** As the Sangree article and the descriptions of Epstein's and Estlund's articles show, many people are sympathetic to an agenda that limits sexually harassing speech. Is this position tied to a leftist-leaning political stance? Consider the following situation:

As part of its program, a public high school held a mandatory assembly for sophomores to make them aware of the dangers of AIDs. The program consisted of several sexually explicit skits, in which chosen students participated along with the organizers of the assembly. The students claimed that the organizers used profane and slang expressions to describe body parts and excretory functions; advocated oral sex, masturbation, homosexuality, and the use of condoms for premarital sex; simulated masturbation; characterized one student's loose pants as "erection pants"; had a male student lick an oversized condom which was then pulled over his head by a female student; informed a male student that he was not having enough orgasms; and, overall, made eighteen references to orgasms, six to male genitals, and eight to female genitals.

In the week or two immediately following the program a number of students used it for a model, and repeatedly acted out the skits on other students in the hallways.

How do you think a court should rule if two students who were required to attend this assembly sued on the grounds that it created a hostile learning environment and therefore constituted sexual harassment under Title IX? Consider whether the harassment was "because of" the plaintiffs' sex, whether the assembly created a hostile environment as discussed in *Harris*, whether a subjective or objective standard should be used in determining if this was a hostile environment, whether it should matter that the suit was brought under Title IX instead of Title VII and whether that makes a difference in the applicable substantive law, and whether the First Amendment protects the speech involved. Use the articles at the beginning of this section on sexual harassment to help you to think about these issues.

The court that actually decided the case did not discuss all of these issues, but it did consider it significant that "the plaintiffs do not allege that they were required to participate in any of the offensive skits or that they were the direct objects of . . . [the] sexual comments," Brown v. Hot, Sexy and Safer Productions, Inc., 68 F.3d 525, 541 (1st Cir. 1995)

PROBLEM ON SEXUAL HARASSMENT

You are the attorney for Coal Creek College (CCC). CCC's President has asked you to formulate a sexual harassment policy for the college. CCC is a private, undergraduate institution with approximately 1100 students. The college is coeducational. In the past five years, CCC has experienced a significant dip in the number of applications for admission that it has received. As a result, recruiters have stepped up their efforts and are now recruiting world wide. Twenty percent of the freshman class that entered in the fall of 1998 is foreign. Among these are a number of students, female and male, from East Africa, Southeast Asia, Saudi Arabia, and Brazil. Almost all of CCC's students live in dorms all four years.

CCC does not currently have a sexual harassment policy, although the administration has occasionally dealt with sexual harassment under rules relating to "conduct unbecoming a student." One male student was expelled five years ago for sexually attacking a woman student on campus. Last year, in an incident that gained a lot of attention, a group of women claimed that they were being verbally harassed by a number of men on campus. When the administration did not react to their liking, they posted signs all over the campus saying, "[Name of particular student] harasses women." Not surprisingly the male targets of these posters objected. Ultimately the administration took no action against the men—who were referring to women as "dumb broads," "a good piece of ass," etc., behind their backs—or against the women who tacked up the posters. However, the request to you to formulate a policy is clearly an effort to avoid another series of incidents like those of last year.

You should be sure to consider the following as you draft your policy.

1. Should the policy cover sexual harassment between administrators and students, faculty and students, staff and students, administrators and faculty or staff? Or should it cover only intra-student harassment, with the other types left to a different policy?

2. Should the policy cover only heterosexual harassment or should it cover same-sex harassment also? If the latter, need it be based on sexual desire?

3. How will you define sexual harassment? Will it be different in the classroom, the dormitory, or on the campus green? Should racist comments addressed to women be considered sexual harassment—e.g., "You black hippo." What about physical aggression, e.g. shoving, directed against a woman, but without words indicating that the violence is intended to be sexualized? Should you ban all expressions of sexuality?

4. What types of procedures will you recommend for hearing the case? How formal should the process be? Should the target of the harassment be permitted to make charges without having her or his identity revealed? Who should have the burden of developing the evidence—the institution or the target? Should there be a preliminary "probable cause" type of hearing before anything else gets set in motion or should the target be able to set the process in motion simply by making allegations?

5. What should the range of penalties be? Should there be some means of ensuring that the target and the alleged harasser do not continue to meet on campus during the time the process is pending?

*

CHAPTER TWO

WOMEN AND THE FAMILY

A. MARRIAGE AND ALTERNATIVES TO MARRIAGE

INTRODUCTION

A romantic contract—or a patriarchal institution; a model for all intimate adult relationships—or a prison confining both real people and human imaginations—which is the best description of marriage?

Historically, first religious and then secular laws specified both who could marry and what legal and economic consequences follow marriage. The prevailing rules in the United States call for a monogamous union between two people, one of whom is a man and one of whom is a woman. Married individuals then become obligated to fulfill the roles of wife and husband.

In the past, those roles assigned to the husband the control over property, power to enter into contracts, and duty to assure economic support for the wife and children at least as to items necessary for subsistence. In his *Commentaries on the Laws of England*, William Blackstone explained the doctrine of martial unity: upon marriage, the husband and wife became one person in the law; the legal existence of the woman was suspended during the marriage. The husband served as the family's representative to the state through property, contract, and suffrage rights. The common law tradition from England also specified powers of the husband over the property and services of his wife and children, along with powers to discipline them. The married woman obtained a dower interest in her husband's property, but it was a mere expectancy, not a right. The married woman undertook duties to serve her husband and children in the domestic sphere.

From the middle of the 19th century to the present, law reform efforts in the United States pressed for a more egalitarian marriage structure. Social and political movements pressed states to adopt Married Women's Property Acts to extend to women rights to control their property, to draft wills, and even to retain their own earnings. A constitutional amendment in 1920 granted women the right to vote. Divorce and alimony reforms in the later part of the century altered traditional assumptions of the wife's dependency. With the expanding presence of women in the paid labor force, legal protections for their equal participation in work, and increasing avenues to challenge violence and abuse within the home, a combination of legal, social, and economic changes altered the traditional roles of husband and wife.

Even before these reforms, however, whether black-letter law matched social practices and the experiences of individuals was hardly certain. Consider the contrast between the 1873 opinion by Justice Bradley in a Supreme Court decision rejecting Myra Bradwell's challenge to an Illinois statute denying women the right to practice law, and Bradwell's own life. Justice Bradley's concurring opinion reasoned that "[t]he constitution of the family organization, which is founded in the divine ordinance, as well as in the nature of things, indicates the domestic sphere as that which properly belongs to the domain and functions of womanhood. The harmony, not to say identity, of interests and views which belong, or should belong, to the family institution is repugnant to the identity of woman adopting a distinct and independent career from that of her husband." Bradwell v. State, 83 U.S. (16 Wall.) 130, 141, 21 L.Ed. 442 (1873)(Bradley, J., concurring). Yet, in fact, Myra Bradwell had already, at the time of the suit, become the publisher of The Chicago Legal News, the leading legal newspaper in the Midwest. Sixty of the leading lawyers of Chicago petitioned the state governor to appoint her notary public while the case was pending in the Supreme Court. At least these lawyers did not enforce the narrow view of married women's roles contemplated by Justice Bradley. *See* generally Martha Minow, *Forming Underneath Everything That Grows: Toward a History of Family Law*, 1985 Wis. L. Rev. 819.

Nonetheless, many people believe that the formal legal rules governing marriage and family roles deeply affect what people imagine and how people actually feel constrained. Philosopher Susan Moller Okin provides a thorough examination of issues posed by marriage even in its modern form.

I. JUSTICE AND MARRIAGE

Susan Moller Okin, Vulnerability by Marriage

From S. Okin, Justice, Gender, and the Family (NY: Basic Books, 1989).

...It is not easy to think about marriage and the family in terms of justice. For one thing, we do not readily associate justice with intimacy, which is one reason some theorists idealize the family. For another, some of the issues that theories of justice are most concerned with, such as differences in standards of living, do not obviously apply among members of a family. Though it is certainly not the case in some countries, in the United States the members of a family, so long as they live together, usually share the same standard of living. As we shall see, however, the question of who earns the family's income or how the earning of this income is shared, has a great deal to do with the distribution of power and influence within the family, including decisions on how to spend this income. It also affects the distribution of other benefits, including basic security. Here, I present and analyze the facts of contemporary gender-structured marriage in the light of theories about power and vulnerability and the issues of justice they inevitably raise. I argue that marriage and the family, as currently practiced in our society, are unjust institutions. They constitute the pivot of a societal system of gender that renders women vulnerable to dependency, exploitation, and abuse. When we look seriously at the distribution between husbands and wives of such critical social goods as work (paid and unpaid), power, prestige, self-esteem, opportunities for self-development, and both physical and economic security, we find socially constructed inequalities between them, right down the list....

... Few people would disagree with the statement that marriage involves, in some respects, especially emotionally, *mutual* vulnerability and dependence. It is, clearly, also a relationship in which some aspects of unequal vulnerability are not determined along sex lines. For example, spouses may vary in the extent of their love for and emotional dependence on each other; it is certainly not the case that wives always love their husbands more than they are loved by them, or vice versa. Nevertheless, as we shall see, in crucial respects gender-structured marriage *involves women in a cycle of socially caused and distinctly asymmetric vulnerability*. The division of labor within marriage (except in rare cases) makes wives far more likely than husbands to be exploited both within the marital relationship and in the world of work outside the home. To a great extent and in numerous ways, contemporary women in our society are *made* vulnerable by marriage itself. They are first set up for vulnerability during their developing years by their personal (and socially reinforced) expectations that they will be the primary caretakers of children, and that in fulfilling this role they will need to try to attract and to keep the economic support of a man, to whose work life they will be expected to give priority. They are rendered vulnerable by the actual division of labor within almost all current marriages. They are disadvantaged at work by the fact that the world of wage work, including the professions, is still largely structured around the assumption that "workers" have wives at home. They are rendered far more vulnerable if they become the primary caretakers of children, and their vulnerability peaks if their marriages dissolve and they become single parents.

Part of the reason that many nonfeminist social theorists have failed to recognize this pattern is that they confuse the socially caused (and therefore avoidable) vulnerability of women with the largely natural (and therefore largely unavoidable) vulnerability of children. This goes along with the usually unargued and certainly unfounded assumption that women are inevitably the primary caretakers of children. But as I shall show, women are made vulnerable, both economically and socially, by the interconnected traditions of female responsibility for rearing children and female subordination and dependence, of which both the history and the contemporary practices of marriage form a significant part.

It may be argued that it makes no sense to claim that something as ill-defined and variable as "modern marriage" is unjust, since marriages and families take so many forms, and not all marriages result in the dependence and vulnerability of their female members. There is some validity to this objection, and I shall try to counter it by making qualifications and pointing out exceptions to some of the general points I shall make. Part of

the peculiarity of contemporary marriage comes from its very lack of
definition. The fact that society seems no longer to have any consensual
view of the norms and expectations of marriage is particularly apparent
from the gulf that exists between the continued *perception* of most men and
women that it is still the primary responsibility of husbands to "provide
for" their wives by participating in wage work and of wives to perform a
range of unpaid "services" for their husbands, and the *fact* that most
women, including mothers of small children, are both in the labor force *and*
performing the vast majority of household duties. In addition, the persistent perception of the male as provider is irreconcilable with both the
prevalence of separation and divorce and the fact that, more and more,
women and children are not being provided for after divorce. Between the
expectations and the frequent outcome lies an abyss that not only is unjust
in itself but radically affects the ways in which people behave within
marriage. There is no way to alleviate the continuing inequality of women
without more clearly defining and also reforming marriage. It seems
evident, both from the disagreements between traditionalists and feminists
and from the discrepancy between people's expectations of marriage and
what in fact often happens to those who enter into it that there exists no
clear current consensus in this society about what marriage is or should be.

Marriage has a long history, and we live in its shadow. It is a clear case
of Marx's notion that we make our history "under circumstances directly
encountered, given and transmitted from the past." Certainly, gender is
central to the way most people think about marriage. A recent, detailed
study of thousands of couples, of different types—married and unmarried,
heterosexual, gay and lesbian—confirms the importance of gender to our
concept of marriage. Philip Blumstein and Pepper Schwartz's findings in
American Couples demonstrate how not only current family law but the
traditional expectations of marriage influence the attitudes, expectations,
and behavior of married couples. By contrast, the lack of expectations about
gender, and the lack of history of the institution of marriage, allow gay and
lesbian couples more freedom in ordering their lives together and more
chance to do so in an egalitarian manner. As the study concludes: "First,
while the heterosexual model offers more stability and certainty, it inhibits
change, innovation, and *choice* regarding roles and tasks."

Second, the heterosexual model, which provides so much efficiency, is
predicated on the man's being the dominant partner. "The unmarried
couples interviewed did not, in general, assume so readily that one partner
would be the primary economic provider or that they would pool their
income and assets." Homosexual couples, because of the absence of both
marriage and the "gender factor," made even fewer such assumptions than
did cohabiting heterosexual couples. They were almost unanimous, for
example, in refusing to assign to either partner the role of homemaker. By
contrast, many of the married respondents still enthusiastically subscribed
to the traditional female/male separation of household work from wage
work. While the authors also found the more egalitarian, two-paycheck
marriage "emerging," they conclude that "the force of the previous tradition still guides the behavior of most modern marriages."

It is important to recollect, in this context, how recently white married women in the United States have begun to work outside the home in significant numbers. Black women have always worked, first as slaves, then mostly—until very recently—as domestic servants. But in 1860, only 15 per cent of all women were in the paid labor force and, right up to World War II, wage work for married women was strongly disapproved of. In 1890, only 5 percent of married women were in the labor force, and by 1960 the rate of married women's labor force participation had still reached only 30 percent. Moreover, wage work has a history of extreme segregation by sex that is closely related to the traditional female role within marriage. The largest category of women workers were domestic servants as late as 1950, since which time clerical workers have outnumbered them. Service (mostly no longer domestic) is still very predominantly female work. Even the female-dominated professions, such as nursing, grade-school teaching, and library work, have been "pink-collar labor ghettos [which] have historically discouraged high work ambitions that might detract from the pull of home and children." Like saleswomen and clerical workers, these female professionals "tend to arrive early in their 'careers' at a point above which they cannot expect to rise." In sum, married women's wage work has a history of being exceptional, and women's wage work in general has been—as much of it still is—highly segregated and badly paid.

The traditional idea of sex-differentiated marital responsibility, with its provider-husband and domestic-wife roles, continues to be a strong influence on what men and women think and how they behave. Husbands, at least, tend to feel this way even when their wives do work outside the home; and when there is disagreement about whether the wife should work, it is more often the case that she wants to but that he does not want to "let" her. Thirty-four percent of the husbands and 25 percent of the wives surveyed by Blumstein and Schwartz did not think that couples should share the responsibility for earning a living. These percentages rise sharply when children are involved: 64 percent of husbands and 60 percent of wives did not think that the wife should be employed if a couple has small children. Given the emphasis our society places on economic success, belief in the male provider role strongly reinforces the domination of men within marriage. Although, as we shall see, many wives actually work longer hours (counting paid and unpaid work) than their husbands, the fact that a husband's work is predominantly paid gives him not only status and prestige, both within and outside the marriage, but also a greater sense of entitlement. As a consequence, wives experiencing divorce, especially if they have been housewives and mothers throughout marriage, are likely to devalue their own contributions to the marriage and to discount their right to share its assets. "Many divorcing women still see the money their husbands have earned as 'his money.'" In ongoing marriages too, it is not uncommon for husbands to use the fact that they are the primary bread-winners to enforce their views or wishes....

Even though the proportion of young women who plan to be housewives exclusively has declined considerably, women's choices about work are significantly affected from an early age by their expectations about the effects of family life on their work and of work on their family life. As is well known, the participation of women in the labor force, especially women with small children, has continued to rise. But, although a small minority of women are rapidly increasing the previously tiny percentages of women in the elite professions, the vast majority of women who work outside the home are still in low-paying jobs with little or no prospect of advancement. This fact is clearly related to girls' awareness of the complexity they are likely to face in combining work with family life. As the authors of one study conclude: "the occupational aspirations and expectations of adolescents are highly differentiated by sex ... [and this] differentiation follows the pattern of sexual segregation which exists in the occupational structure." They found not only that the high school girls in their large-scale study were much less likely than the boys to aspire to the most prestigious occupations, but that the girls who had such aspirations displayed a much lower degree of confidence than the boys about being able to attain their goals....

Regardless of educational achievement, women are far more likely than men to work in administrative support jobs, as a secretary, typist, or bookkeeper, for example, which in most cases hold no prospects for advancement. Almost 30 percent of employed women worked in this category in 1985, compared with fewer than 6 percent of men. A study of workplaces during the late 1960s and the 1970s (*after* the 1963 Equal Pay Act and Title VII of the 1964 Civil Rights Act) found the sex segregation of specific jobs and occupational ladders in both manufacturing and nonmanufacturing firms to be so pervasive that more than 90 percent of women would have had to change jobs in order for women to share equally the same job titles as men. Frequently, workplaces had only one or two job titles that included members of both sexes. On top of all this, recent research has shown that large discrepancies exist between male and female wages for the same job title. While female secretaries earned a median wage of $278 per week in 1985, the median for male secretaries was $365; moreover, in twenty-four other narrowly defined occupations in which females earned *less* than they would have as secretaries, males earned *more* in every case than a female secretary. Indeed, some firms designate particular jobs as male and others designate the same jobs as female, and the wage rates differ accordingly. It seems, therefore, that "the wage level for a particular job title in a particular establishment is set *after the employer decides whether those jobs will be filled by women or men.*"...

It is no wonder, then, that most women are, even before marriage, in an economic position that sets them up to become more vulnerable during marriage, and most vulnerable of all if their marriage ends and—unprepared as they are—they find themselves in the position of having to provide for themselves and their children. ...

... In many marriages, partly because of discrimination at work and the wage gap between the sexes, wives (despite initial personal ambitions and even when they are full-time wage workers) come to perceive themselves as benefiting from giving priority to their husbands' careers. Hence they have little incentive to question the traditional division of labor in the household. This in turn limits their own commitment to wage work and their incentive and leverage to challenge the gender structure of the workplace. Experiencing frustration and lack of control at work, those who thus turn toward domesticity, while often resenting the lack of respect our society gives to full-time mothers, may see the benefits of domestic life as greater than the costs....

   ... *A cycle of power relation and decisions pervades both family and workplace, and the inequalities of each reinforce those that already exist in the other.* ...

Housework and the Cycle of Vulnerability

   It is no secret that in almost all families women do far more housework and childcare than men do. But the distribution of paid and unpaid work within the family has rarely—outside of feminist circles—been considered a significant issue by theorists of justice. Why should it be? If two friends divide a task so that each takes primary responsibility for a different aspect of it, we would be loath to cry "injustice" unless one were obviously coercing the other. But at least three factors make the division of labor within the household a very different situation, and a clear question of justice. First, the uneven distribution of labor within the family is strongly correlated with an innate characteristic, which appears to make it the kind of issue with which theorists of justice have been most concerned. The virtually automatic allocation to one person of more of the paid labor and to the other of more of the unpaid labor would be regarded as decidedly odd in any relationship other than that of a married or cohabiting heterosexual couple. One reason for this is that, as we shall see, it has distinct effects on the distribution of power. While the unequal distribution of paid and unpaid work has different repercussions in different types of marriages, it is always of significance. Second, though it is by no means always absolute, the division of labor in a traditional or quasi-traditional marriage is often quite complete and usually long-standing. It lasts in many cases at least through the lengthy years of child rearing, and is by no means confined to the preschool years. Third, partly as a result of this, and of the structure and demands of most paid work, the household division of labor has a lasting impact on the lives of married women, especially those who become mothers. It affects every sphere of their lives, from the dynamics of their marital relationship to their opportunities in the many spheres of life outside the household. The distribution of labor within the family by sex has deep ramifications for its respective members' material, psychological, physical, and intellectual well-being. One cannot even begin to address the issue of why so many women and children live in poverty in our society, or why women are inadequately represented in the higher echelons of our political and economic institutions, without confronting the division of labor between the sexes within the family. Thus it is not only itself an issue of justice but it is also at the very root of other significant concerns of justice, including equality of opportunity for children of both sexes, but especially for girls, and political justice in the broadest sense. ...

Predominantly Wage–Working Wives and Housework

Despite the increasing labor force participation of married women, including mothers, "working wives still bear almost all the responsibility for housework." They do less of it than housewives, but "they still do the vast bulk of what needs to be done," and the difference is largely to be accounted for not by the increased participation of men, but by lowered standards, the participation of children, purchased services such as restaurant or frozen meals, and, in elite groups, paid household help. Thus, while the distribution of paid labor between the sexes is shifting quite considerably onto women, that of unpaid labor is not shifting much at all, and "the couple that shares household tasks equally remains rare." The differences in total time spent in all "family work" (housework and child care plus yard work, repairs, and so on) vary considerably from one study to another, but it seems that fully employed husbands do, *at most*, approximately half as much as their fully employed wives, and some studies show a much greater discrepancy. . . .

. . . Wives are likely to start out at a disadvantage, because of both the force of the traditions of gender and the fact that they are likely to be already earning less than their husbands at the time of marriage. In many cases, the question of who is responsible for the bulk of the unpaid labor of the household is probably not raised at all, but *assumed*, on the basis of these two factors alone. Because of this "nondecision" factor, studies of marital power that ask only about the respective influence of the partners over decisions are necessarily incomplete, since they ignore distributions of burdens and benefits that may not be perceived as arising from decisions at all. . . .

If we are to aim at making the family, our most fundamental social grouping, more just, we must work toward eradicating the socially created vulnerabilities of women that stem from the division of labor and the resultant division of power within it. As I shall argue in the final chapter, in order to do anything effective about the cycle of women's socially created vulnerability we must take into account the current lack of clarity in law, public policy, and public opinion about *what marriage is*. Since evidently we do not all agree about what it is or should be, we must think in terms of building family and work institutions that enable people to structure their personal lives in different ways. If they are to avoid injustice to women and children, these institutions must encourage the avoidance of socially created vulnerabilities by facilitating and reinforcing the equal sharing of paid and unpaid work between men and women, and consequently the equalizing of their opportunities and obligations in general. They must also ensure that those who enter into relationships in which there is a division of labor that might render them vulnerable are fully protected against such vulnerability, both within the context of the ongoing relationship and in the event of its dissolution.

NOTES AND QUESTIONS

1. **Law and Marriage**. Does Okin persuasively demonstrate that current laws surrounding marriage create problems for women? What sources

besides family law contribute to the economic disadvantages and segregation of women in the workplace, or to the tendency of women to carry the bulk of the burden of housework?

2. **Legal Reforms and Justice**. Does Okin imply any law reforms that would promote justice within or after marriages? What would such law reforms look like? What would it take to secure sufficient political support to reform gender inequalities in marital relationships?

II.   THE DEBATE OVER GAY MARRIAGE

The purposes and qualities of marriage have come under sharp public scrutiny in the face of a national debate over whether same-sex couples should be allowed to marry. This debate is of crucial concern not only to those interested in the status of gays and lesbians, but also to those troubled by the legacies of male domination in the structure of marriage. Indeed, in Baehr v. Lewin, the landmark litigation challenging under Hawaii's constitution the state's heterosexuality requirement for marriage, the Hawaii Supreme Court entertained and accepted an argument based on the protections against sex discrimination.

In response to developments in Hawaii, Congress passed The Defense of Marriage Act to ensure that article IV, § 1 of the U.S. Constitution ("Full Faith and Credit shall be given in each State to the public Acts, Recordes, and Judicial Proceedings of every other State") could not be used to compel other states to recognize same-sex Hawaiian marriages. The Act was signed by President Clinton in 1996. Both the Hawaii decision and the congressional response raise issues of policy and legality. What should be the boundaries on a state's ability to decide who may marry, and what is a lawful marriage? What is the proper allocation of federal and state control over such questions? Does the "Full Faith and Credit" clause of the U.S. Constitution permit states to refuse to recognize marriages lawfully performed in other states? Why did Congress become so quickly mobilized to assure such power to the states? What views about intimate relationships and the law's role in them are, and should be, adopted? Is the equality of women hurt or hindered by the developments in the law of same-sex marriages?

Beyond these issues are more basic questions about whether marriage is a desirable status for same-sex couples or for any person who seeks to establish and maintain an intimate relationship. The writings inspired by the gay marriage debate afford rich and sophisticated analyses of these issues.

Baehr v. Lewin

Supreme Court of Hawaii, 1993.
74 Haw. 530, 852 P.2d 44.

STEVEN H. LEVINSON, JUDGE, in which RONALD T.Y. MOON, CHIEF JUDGE joins.

. . . [T]he precise question facing this court is whether we will extend the present boundaries of the fundamental right of marriage to include same-sex couples or, put another way, whether we will hold that same-sex couples possess a fundamental right to marry. In effect, as the applicant couples frankly admit, we are being asked to recognize a new fundamental right. There is no doubt that "[a]s the ultimate judicial tribunal with final unreviewable authority to interpret and enforce the Hawaii Constitution, we are free to give broader privacy protection ... than that given by the federal constitution." ... However, we have also held that the privacy right found in article I, section 6 is similar to the federal right and that no "purpose to lend talismanic effect" to abstract phrases such as "intimate decision" or "personal autonomy" can "be inferred from [article I, section 6], any more than ... from the federal decisions." ...

In the case that first recognized a fundamental right to privacy, *Griswold v. Connecticut*, ... the Court declared that it was "deal[ing] with a right ... older than the Bill of Rights[.]" ... And in a concurring opinion, Justice Goldberg observed that judges "determining which rights are fundamental" must look not to "personal and private notions," but

> to the "traditions and [collective] conscience of our people" to determine whether a principle is "so rooted [there] ... as to be ranked as fundamental." ... The inquiry is whether a right involved "is of such a character that it cannot be denied without violating those 'fundamental principles of liberty and justice which lie at the base of all our civil and political institutions.' " ...

Applying the foregoing standards to the present case we do not believe that a right to same-sex marriage is so rooted in the traditions and collective conscience of our people that failure to recognize it would violate the fundamental principles of liberty and justice that lie at the base of all our civil and political institutions. Neither do we believe that a right to same-sex marriage is implicit in the concept of ordered liberty, such that neither liberty nor justice would exist if it were sacrificed. Accordingly, we hold that the applicant couples do not have a fundamental constitutional right to same-sex marriage arising out of the right to privacy or otherwise.
. . .

Marriage is a state-conferred legal status, the existence of which gives rise to rights and benefits reserved exclusively to that particular relationship. This court construes marriage as " 'a partnership to which both partners bring their financial resources as well as their individual energies and efforts.' " ... So zealously has this court guarded the state's role as the exclusive progenitor of the marital partnership that it declared, over seventy years ago, that "common law" marriages—*i.e.*, "marital" unions existing in the absence of a state-issued license and not performed by a person or society possessing governmental authority to solemnize marriages—would no longer be recognized in the Territory of Hawaii....

The applicant couples correctly contend that the [Department of Health's] refusal to allow them to marry on the basis that they are members of the same sex deprives them of access to a multiplicity of rights and benefits that are contingent upon that status. Although it is unnecessary in this opinion to engage in an encyclopedic recitation of all of them, a number of the most salient marital rights and benefits are worthy of note. They include: (1) a variety of state income tax advantages, including deductions, credits, rates, exemptions, and estimates ... (2) public assistance from and exemptions relating to the Department of Human Services ... (3) control, division, acquisition, and disposition of community property ... (4) rights relating to dower, curtesy, and inheritance ... (5) rights to notice, protection, benefits, and inheritance ... (6) award of child custody and support payments in divorce proceedings ... (7) the right to spousal support ... (8) the right to enter into premarital agreements ... (9) the right to change of name ... (10) the right to file a nonsupport action ... (11) post-divorce rights relating to support and property division ... (12) the benefit of the spousal privilege and confidential marital communications ... (13) the benefit of the exemption of real property from attachment or execution ... and (14) the right to bring a wrongful death action....

The equal protection clauses of the United States and Hawaii Constitutions are not mirror images of one another. The fourteenth amendment to the United States Constitution somewhat concisely provides, in relevant part, that a state may not "deny to any person within its jurisdiction the equal protection of the laws." Hawaii's counterpart is more elaborate. Article I, section 5 of the Hawaii Constitution provides in relevant part that "[n]o person shall ... be denied the equal protection of the laws, *nor be denied the enjoyment of the person's civil rights or be discriminated against in the exercise thereof because of* race, religion, *sex,* or ancestry" (emphasis added). Thus, by its plain language, the Hawaii Constitution prohibits state-sanctioned discrimination against any person in the exercise of his or her civil rights on the basis of sex.... Rudimentary principles of statutory construction render manifest the fact that, by its plain language, HRS Sect. 572–1 restricts the marital relation to a male and a female. " '[T]he fundamental starting point for statutory interpretation is the language of the statute itself.... [W]here the statutory language is plain and unambiguous,' " we construe it according " 'to its plain and obvious meaning.' " ... Accordingly, on its face and (as Lewin admits) as applied, HRS Sect. 572–1 denies same-sex couples access to the marital status and its concomitant rights and benefits....

Relying primarily on four decisions construing the law of other jurisdictions, Lewin contends that "the fact that homosexual [sic—actually, same-sex] partners cannot form a state-licensed marriage is not the product of impermissible discrimination" implicating equal protection considerations, but rather "a function of their biologic inability as a couple to satisfy the definition of the status to which they aspire." ... Put differently, Lewin proposes that "the right of persons of the same sex to marry one another does not exist because marriage, by definition and usage, means a special relationship between a man and a woman." ...

We believe Lewin's argument to be circular and unpersuasive....

The facts in *Loving* and the respective reasoning of the Virginia courts, on the one hand, and the United States Supreme Court, on the other, both discredit the reasoning . . . and unmask the tautological and circular nature of Lewin's argument that HRS Sect. 572–1 does not implicate article I, section 5 of the Hawaii Constitution because same-sex marriage is an innate impossibility. Analogously to Lewin's argument and the rationale of the Jones court, the Virginia courts declared that interracial marriage simply could not exist because the Deity had deemed such a union intrinsically unnatural . . ., and, in effect, because it had theretofore never been the "custom" of the state to recognize mixed marriages, marriage "always" having been construed to presuppose a different configuration. With all due respect to the Virginia courts of a bygone era, we do not believe that trial judges are the ultimate authorities on the subject of Divine Will, and, as *Loving* amply demonstrates, constitutional law may mandate, like it or not, that customs change with an evolving social order. . . .

"Whenever a denial of equal protection of the laws is alleged, as a rule our initial inquiry has been whether the legislation in question should be subjected to 'strict scrutiny' or to a 'rational basis' test." . . .

Our decision in *Holdman* is key to the present case in several respects. First, we clearly and unequivocally established, for purposes of equal protection analysis under the Hawaii Constitution, that sex-based classifications are subject, as a *per se* matter, to some form of "heightened" scrutiny, be it "strict" or "intermediate," rather than mere "rational basis" analysis. Second, we assumed, *arguendo*, that such sex-based classifications were subject to "strict scrutiny." Third, we reaffirmed the longstanding principle that this court is free to accord greater protections to Hawaii's citizens under the state constitution than are recognized under the United States Constitution. And fourth, we looked to the *then current* case law of the United States Supreme Court for guidance.

Of the decisions of the United States Supreme Court cited in *Holdman*, *Frontiero v. Richardson, supra* was by far the most significant. . . .

The disagreement among the eight-justice majority lay in the level of judicial scrutiny applicable to instances of statutory sex-based discrimination. The Brennan plurality agreed with the Frontieros' contention that "classifications based upon sex, like classifications based upon race, alienage, and national origin, are inherently suspect and must therefore be subjected to close judicial scrutiny." . . . Thus, the Brennan plurality applied the "strict scrutiny" standard to its review of the illegal statutes. Justice Stewart concurred in the judgment, "agreeing that the statutes . . . work[ed] an invidious discrimination in violation of the Constitution." . . .

Particularly noteworthy in *Frontiero*, however, was the concurring opinion of Justice Powell, joined by the Chief Justice and Justice Blackmun (the Powell group). The Powell group agreed that "the challenged statutes constitute[d] an unconstitutional discrimination against servicewomen," but deemed it "unnecessary for the Court *in this case* to characterize sex as a suspect classification, with all of the far-reaching implications of such a holding." . . .

Central to the Powell group's thinking was the following explanation:

There is another ... reason for deferring a general categorization of sex classifications as invoking the strictest test of judicial scrutiny. *The Equal Rights Amendment, which if adopted will resolve the substance of this precise question*, has been approved by Congress and submitted for ratification by the states. If this Amendment is duly adopted, it will represent the will of the people accomplished in the manner prescribed by the Constitution. By acting prematurely and unnecessarily, ... the Court has assumed a decisional responsibility at the very time when state legislatures functioning within the traditional democratic process are debating the proposed Amendment. It seems ... that this reaching out to pre-empt by judicial action a major political decision which is currently in process of resolution does not reflect appropriate respect for duly prescribed legislative processes....

The Powell group's concurring opinion therefore permits but one inference: had the Equal Rights Amendment been incorporated into the United States Constitution, at least seven members (and probably eight) of the *Frontiero* Court would have subjected statutory sex-based classifications to "strict" judicial scrutiny.

In light of the interrelationship between the reasoning of the Brennan plurality and the Powell group in *Frontiero*, on the one hand, and the presence of article I, section 3—The Equal Rights Amendment—in the Hawaii Constitution, on the other, it is time to resolve once and for all the question left dangling in *Holdman*. Accordingly, we hold that sex is a "suspect category" for purposes of equal protection analysis under article I, section 5 of the Hawaii Constitution and that HRS Sect. 572–1 is subject to the "strict scrutiny" test. It therefore follows, and we so hold, that (1) HRS Sect. 572–1 is presumed to be unconstitutional (2) unless Lewin, as an agent of the State of Hawaii, can show that (a) the statute's sex-based classification is justified by compelling state interests and (b) the statute is narrowly drawn to avoid unnecessary abridgements of the applicant couples' constitutional rights....

As a final matter, we are compelled to respond to Judge Heen's suggestion that denying the appellants access to the multitude of statutory benefits "conferred upon spouses in a legal marriage ... is a matter for the legislature, which can express the will of the populace in deciding whether such benefits should be extended to persons in [the applicant couples'] circumstances." ... In effect we are being accused of engaging in judicial legislation. We are not. The result we reach today is in complete harmony with the *Loving* Court's observation that any state's powers to regulate marriage are subject to the constraints imposed by the constitutional right to the equal protection of the laws....

If it should ultimately be determined that the marriage laws of Hawaii impermissibly discriminate against the appellants, based on the suspect category of sex, then that would be the result of the interrelation of existing legislation.

[W]hether the legislation under review is wise or unwise is a matter with which we have nothing to do. Whether it ... work[s] well or work[s] ill presents a question entirely irrelevant to the issue. The only legitimate inquiry we can make is whether it is constitutional. If it is not, its virtues if it have any, cannot save it; if it is, its faults cannot he invoked to accomplish its destruction. If the provisions of the Constitution be not upheld when they pinch as well as when they comfort, they may as well be abandoned....

NOTES AND QUESTIONS

1. *Baehr*: **The Case and Its Consequences.** The Hawaii Supreme Court's decision in *Baehr* is notable not only for what it decided, but also for what it refused to decide. In challenging the Hawaii statute's restriction of marriage to couples of opposite sexes, the plaintiffs claimed that the statute violated both their fundamental right to privacy as well as their right to equal protection under the Hawaiian Constitution. Significantly, while the court held that the statute amounted to a form of sex discrimination under the state constitution's equal protection clause, the court refused to recognize the existence of a right to same-sex marriage flowing out of a fundamental right to privacy.

As a result of this decision, *Baehr* was remanded to the trial court for a determination of whether the state could prove that the statute furthered a compelling state interest. In December 1996, the trial court found that it could not, and the state appealed to the Hawaii Supreme Court. That appeal is currently pending, and the trial judge has stayed his decision until the outcome of the appeal. What could opponents of gay marriage in Hawaii do if the state supreme court affirms the recent trial in *Baehr*?

2. **The Legislative Response.** As noted above, Congress responded to *Baehr* by passing the Defense of Marriage Act. Excerpts from its text appear below. Many states, also fearing the implications of the "Full Faith and Credit" clause, have introduced legislation seeking to ban same-sex marriage. And, in Hawaii itself, opponents of same-sex marriage in the state legislature approved an amendment to the state constitution in April 1997 stating that "the legislature shall have the power to reserve marriage to opposite-sex couples"; that amendment will appear on the ballot in November 1998. Moreover, in July 1997, the state legislature passed "reciprocal beneficiary" legislation (HRS Sect. 572 C) extending certain benefits to same-sex couples (as well as roommates and siblings)—thereby attempting to remove one of the reasons for seeking a same-sex marriage. Under the new law, any two adults who cannot marry legally will have inheritance rights, the right to own joint property, and the right to share medical insurance. However, in September 1997, in deciding a suit filed by seven companies, a U.S. district court approved a settlement between the plaintiffs and the state attorney general limiting the state's interpretation

of the new law so as to not require private employers to extend health benefits to so-called reciprocal beneficiaries, citing preemption by the Employee Retirement Income Security Act ("ERISA"). Whether the legislature will be able to rewrite the law to reflect federal law remains to be seen.

The Defense of Marriage Act

Public Law 104–199, 104th Congress.
110 Stat. 2419, September 21, 1996.

AN ACT

To define and protect the institution of marriage.

Be it enacted by the Senate and House of Representatives of the United States of America in Congress assembled,

SECTION 1. SHORT TITLE.

This Act may be cited as the "Defense of Marriage Act."

SEC. 2. POWERS RESERVED TO THE STATES.

(a) IN GENERAL.—Chapter 115 of title 28, United State Code, is amended by adding after section 1738B the following:

"§ 1738C. CERTAIN ACTS, RECORDS, AND PROCEEDINGS AND THE EFFECT THEREOF

"No State, territory, or possession of the United States, or Indian tribe, shall be required to give effect to any public act, record, or judicial proceeding of any other State, territory, possession, or tribe respecting a relationship between persons of the same sex that is treated as a marriage under the laws of such other State, territory, possession, or tribe, or a right or claim arising from such relationship."

. . .

SEC. 3. DEFINITION OF MARRIAGE.

(a) IN GENERAL. Chapter 1 of title 1, United States Code, is amended by adding at the end the following:

"§ 7. DEFINITION OF 'MARRIAGE' AND 'SPOUSE'

"In determining the meaning of any Act of Congress, or of any ruling, regulation, or interpretation of the various administrative bureaus and agencies of the United States, the word 'marriage' means only a legal union between one man and one woman as husband and wife, and the word 'spouse' refers only to a person of the opposite sex who is a husband or a wife.'' . . .

Nan D. Hunter, Marriage, Law, and Gender: A Feminist Inquiry

1 Law & Sexuality 9 (1991).

. . .

Reflecting on the problems and possibilities inherent in the concept of same-sex marriage is especially intriguing as we enter the 1990s. This is not because the idea is new. In a series of cases, constitutional challenges to the exclusion of lesbian and gay male couples from the matrix of rights and responsibilities that comprise marriage were brought and failed more than fifteen years ago. Nor is it because there is a substantial body of newly developed constitutional doctrine that would undergird litigation to establish such a claim. It is because there is a rapidly developing sense that the legalization of marriage for lesbian and gay Americans is politically possible at some unknown but not unreachable point in the future, that it shimmers or lurks—depending on one's point of view—on the horizon of the law.

This sense of possibility has in turn triggered multiple debates. The mainstream public debate centers on whether the current exclusionary laws promote a moral good in preserving "traditionalism" in family relationships or perpetuate the moral evil of injustice. Within the lesbian and gay community, an intense debate has also arisen, not about whether the exclusionary laws are good, but about whether seeking the right to marry should be a priority. Proponents of a campaign for marriage rights have framed their arguments largely in terms of equality for lesbians and gay men, and have employed a body of rights discourse that has animated the major civil rights struggles of this century. Opponents have relied on two primary arguments. First, they have invoked a feminist critique of marriage as an oppressive institution, which lesbians and gay men should condemn, not join. Second, these activists have drawn on the politics of validating difference, both the difference of an asserted lesbian and gay identity and culture that resist assimilation as well as the differences between persons who would marry and those (homosexual or heterosexual) who would elect to forego marriage and, thereby, it is argued, become even more stigmatized. Analogous tensions between equality-based strategies and difference-based strategies have buffeted feminist theory for the last decade.

The question of whether the law should recognize same-sex marriage has its own intrinsic importance, both as a matter of law and as a liberationist goal. This essay, however, seeks to position that issue in a different theoretical context by framing the question primarily as one of gender systems, rather than of minority rights. I argue in Part II that legalizing lesbian and gay marriage would have enormous potential to destabilize the gendered definition of marriage for everyone, a consideration that is missing from most of the current debate. The cultural and legal impact of such an achievement would resonate far more widely than simply within the lesbian and gay community. Some feminist critiques of marriage posit an unalterable and forever oppressive institution, implicitly assuming that the gendered terms can never change. The possibility of legalizing lesbian and gay marriage, however, creates the possibility of disrupting precisely that linkage between gender and definition. In Part III, I describe current attempts to pluralize the law of intimate relationships, focusing primarily on domestic partnership laws that adopt a functionalist approach to identifying relationships that are the equivalent of marriage. I argue that both sets of proposals for reform—legalization of lesbian and gay marriage and the adoption of domestic partnership provisions—are incomplete unless the other option also exists, and that they need to be analyzed as part of the feminist inquiry into how both private and public law reinforce power imbalance in family life. Lastly, in Part IV, I suggest that a specifically nonlegal political discourse is needed. New discursive terms could communicate that legalization of lesbian and gay marriage is not only a rights claim by a particular minority, but part of a much broader effort to subvert a social system of gender-based power differentials.

Marriage as Nature

Decisional law on the issue of lesbian and gay marriage is most striking for its brevity and tautological jurisprudence. In each case, the justices of the respective court (not one of whom dissented) seem somewhat astonished at even having to consider the question of whether the limitation of marriage to opposite-sex couples is constitutionally flawed. These cases tell us nothing about equality or privacy doctrine. Instead, their holdings are grounded in statements about what the courts believe marriage is. Their significance lies in their thorough conflation of gender, nature, and law.

Marriage is, after all, a complete creation of the law, secular or ecclesiastical. Like the derivative concept of illegitimacy, for example, and unlike parenthood, it did not and does not exist without the power of the state (or some comparable social authority) to establish, define, regulate, and restrict it. Beyond such social constructs, individuals may couple, but they do not "marry." Moreover, although marriage may have ancient roots, its form has not been unchanging. It is an historically contingent institution, having existed with widely differing indicia and serving shifting social functions in various cultures. Marriage can be defined empirically as "a socially approved union between unrelated parties that gives rise to new families and, by implication, to socially approved sexual relations. But beyond that minimal definition, there is no linguistically valid explanation of what marriage entails." Yet in each of the rulings in a lesbian or gay marriage challenge, the courts have essentialized as "nature" the gendered definitional boundaries of marriage.

It was the assumption that gender is an essential aspect of marriage that enabled these courts to so easily rebuff the analogy to *Loving v. Virginia*, which held that the equal protection clause forbade the criminalization of marriage between persons of different races. The Minnesota Supreme Court drew "a clear distinction between a marital restriction based merely upon race and one based upon the *fundamental* difference in sex." The Washington court in *Singer [v. Hara]* similarly dismissed *Loving* as inapposite because irrelevant to the definition of marriage. Having done so, it was then free, in its analysis of the plaintiffs' sex discrimination claim, to reason that, because neither men nor women could marry a person of the same sex, there was no sex discrimination, thus repeating the identical separate-but-equal logic rejected by the Supreme Court in *Loving*. By so casually distinguishing *Loving*, both courts simultaneously essentialized gender and ignored the history of the essentialization of race in marriage law.

The constructed basis of this essentialized definition is illustrated by the fact that, for most of American history, race also defined who could marry. Under the slave codes, African–American slaves could not lawfully marry, either other slaves or any other person, of any race. After slavery was abolished, laws establishing race as a defining element of marriage did not disappear, nor were they limited to a handful of states. Not until 1948 did the California Supreme Court declare that state's antimiscegenation law unconstitutional, the first such ruling in the nation. Statutes prohibiting miscegenation, carrying penalties of up to ten years in prison, were in effect in twenty-nine states in 1953. The Motion Picture Production Code, a voluntary but effective self-regulator of the content of Hollywood films, forbade depiction of interracial sex or marriage until 1956. *Loving* was not decided until 1967, nearly twenty years after the California ruling.

Race, as a biological characteristic, is a fact of nature. Race also exists, however, as a social category, onto which multiple meanings and power relationships are inscribed. What changed between the time of the slave codes and the decision in *Loving* was not the biological, but the social, aspects of race. Today, the state formally defines eligibility for marriage on the basis of sex, a biological category. In reality, however, the definition of marriage is grounded on gender, the social category. The key to this distinction lies in how gender-determined *roles* were once invoked, with equal assurance, as the "nature" of marriage.

For many decades, courts proclaimed and enforced the precept that marriage necessitated not only an authority and dependence relationship, but one that was gendered. One's status as either husband or wife determined all duties and obligations, as well as one's right to name, domicile, physical integrity, property, and other attributes of personhood. When faced with nonconforming individuals, courts struck down their attempts to alter these gender-determined aspects of marriage in terms that underscored the perceived fixedness of the male authority/female dependence "nature" of marriage.

The legal landscape on which the possibility of lesbian and gay marriage is being debated may not differ greatly from that of twenty years ago in its treatment of homosexuality, but it is a different world as to regulation of the terms and conditions of marriage. Two decades of feminist litigation efforts have established virtual equality in formal legal doctrine. The Supreme Court has repeatedly stricken sex-based classifications in family law, whether of the male as the economic provider for women and children or of the female as solely the wife and mother.

What feminist litigation has not been able to do is achieve social and economic equality. In such areas as no-fault divorce, alimony, and child support, the enforcement by law of a presumed equality that usually does not exist has, in fact, operated to the detriment of many women. The terms of marriage as a legal institution (as in, for example, the right to a separate name or domicile) have changed dramatically; it is the social power relations between men and women, inside or outside of marriage, that have changed much less significantly.

The legalization of lesbian and gay marriage would not, of course, directly shift the balance of power in heterosexual relations. It could, however, alter the fundamental concept of the particular institution of marriage. Its potential is to disrupt both the gendered definition of marriage and the assumption that marriage is a form of socially, if not legally, prescribed hierarchy.

With the erosion of legally enforceable authority and dependence statuses as a central defining element of marriage, all that remains of gender as the formal structural element of marriage are the foundational constructs of "husband" and "wife." The once elaborate *de jure* assignations of gender status in marriage have now been reduced to only their most minimal physical manifestation, the gendered pair of spouses. Claims for the legalization of lesbian and gay marriage raise the question of what, without gendered content, could the social categories of "husband" and "wife" mean.

Seizing on the same definitional concerns as those expressed by the courts, conservatives have ridiculed the challenge to husband and wife constructs posed by the idea of lesbian and gay marriage in order to mobilize the social anxiety that that possibility precipitates. Taunts such as "Who would be the husband?" have a double edge, however, if one's project is the subversion of gender. Who, indeed, would be the "husband" and who the "wife" in a marriage of two men or of two women? Marriage enforces and reinforces the linkage of gender with power by husband/wife categories, which are synonymous with the social power imbalance between men and women. Whatever the impact that legalization of lesbian and gay marriage would have on the lives of lesbians and gay men, it has fascinating potential for denaturalizing the gender structure of marriage law for heterosexual couples.

Marriage between men or between women could also destabilize the cultural meaning of marriage. It would create for the first time the possibility of marriage as a relationship between members of the same social status categories. However valiantly individuals try to build marriages grounded on genuine equality, no person can erase his or her status in the world as male or female, or create a home life apart from culture. Same-sex marriage could create the model in law for an egalitarian kind of interpersonal relation, outside the gendered terms of power, for many marriages. At the least, it would radically strengthen and dramatically illuminate the claim that marriage partners are presumptively equal.

Beyond "nature," the other most likely argument in defense of exclusionary marriage laws is also, at bottom, gender-based. The *Singer* court found that, even if the denial of same-sex marriage did constitute sex discrimination, it fell within the exception to Washington state's Equal Rights Amendment, which permits differential treatment based on the unique physical characteristics of the sexes. The court reasoned that "marriage exists as a protected legal institution primarily because of societal values associated with the propagation of the human race," and that "it is apparent that no same-sex couple offers the possibility of the birth of children by their union." Inability to bear children, however, has never been a bar to marriage, nor is it a ground for divorce. Persons who lack the ability or the intent to procreate are nonetheless allowed to marry. The real interest behind the procreation argument probably lies in discouraging childrearing by homosexual couples. That concern stems from the fear that the children will be exposed, not to negligent or inept parenting, but to the wrong models of gender, implicitly marked as legitimate.

To date, the debate about whether the marriage law should change to include lesbian and gay couples has been almost universally framed, both in the larger public and within the lesbian and gay community, as revolving around a claim of rights for particular persons now excluded from marriage. The implicit corollary is that this issue affects only lesbians and gay men. That is much too restricted a focus. The extent of the opposition to the legalization of lesbian and gay marriage indicates not mere silliness or stupidity, as it would if the change were of little consequence to the larger world, nor is it solely a manifestation of irrational prejudice. Legalization of lesbian and gay marriage poses a threat to gender systems, not simply to antilesbian and antigay bigotry.

What is most unsettling to the status quo about the legalization of lesbian and gay marriage is its potential to expose and denaturalize the historical construction of gender at the heart of marriage. Those who argue that marriage has always been patriarchal and thus always will be make the same historical mistake, in mirror image, as the courts that have essentialized the "nature" of marriage. There is no "always has been and ever shall be" truth of marriage. Nor is the experience of marriage and family life problematic to women in similar or identical ways. Certainly marriage is a powerful institution, and the inertial force of tradition should not be underestimated. But it is also a social construct. Powerful social forces have reshaped it before and will continue to do so.

Although the theory used in future litigation to secure legalization of lesbian and gay marriage will likely be grounded on an equality or a due process privacy or associational claim for lesbians and gay men, the impact, if such a challenge prevails, will be to dismantle the legal structure of gender in every marriage.

Marriage as Function and Contract

During the same period of the last fifteen years, when legalization of lesbian and gay marriage has been attempted and so far has failed, a variety of other proposals for pluralizing the law of intimate relationships have been advanced. These new approaches have responded to profound demographic changes that have reshaped the social experience of marriage. Marriage is still central to the adult life experience of a large majority of Americans, but there has been a dramatic alteration in its role and timing. A majority of Americans will spend more of their lifetimes outside, rather than as part of, married-couple households. Cohabitation, often for a significant period of time, frequently precedes marriage and/or remarriage. The number of unmarried cohabiting heterosexual couples increased by more than five hundred percent from 1970 to 1989. The average American marriage does not last a lifetime, but a much more modest 9.6 years. The American divorce rate doubled between 1966 and 1976, peaked in 1981, and has dropped somewhat since, but remains much higher than it was twenty years ago. Concomitant with that shift, there has been an enormous growth in the remarriage rate, so much so that one-third of all marriages are remarriages. As of 1989, the number of Americans who had never married, by the age of forty-five, remained low: 6 percent for women and 8 percent for men. The rate of nonmarriage differed significantly by race. Of all Americans at age forty-five, 7.3 percent had never married; for African–Americans, the comparable figure was 14.4 percent.

For many Americans, then, the formation of couples and coupled households will, over the course of a lifetime, include both nonmarital cohabitant unions as well as marriages, often multiple times. The response of the law has been contradictory. The law still penalizes cohabiting couples, both directly and indirectly. The courts also, however, have undertaken the adjudication of increasing numbers of civil disputes initiated by persons in relationships comparable to marriage. In that context, two distinct lines of doctrine have emerged.

In situations involving the dissolution of the relationship and disputes between the two partners, many courts have adopted contract law principles to decide the allocation of economic assets and responsibilities based on the terms of the agreement expressed or implied between the parties.

The focus of such an analysis is on the intent of the parties. In opting for a contract measure, virtually all of these courts have explicitly rejected the possibility of declaring a constructive marriage and applying a jurisdiction's divorce law. To do so, they have reasoned, would be to frustrate a presumed desire of the parties not to marry and to subvert the interest of the state in preserving a clear boundary between marriage and nonmarriage.

In situations involving the eligibility of the nonmarital family unit or its members for benefits from the state or from third parties, courts have developed a different approach, a jurisprudence of functionalism. In the functionalist approach, courts seek to identify by objective criteria those relationships that are the "functional and factual equivalent" of marriage. A functionalist approach to family law underlay the recognition of common-law marriage, which was widespread in the nineteenth century, and was used to mitigate the effects of a race-bound definition of marriage in cases involving slaves. The leading functionalist case to have reached the U.S. Supreme Court involved an extended multigenerational household, which the Court ruled had to be considered as one family to determine eligibility to live in a neighborhood zoned for single-family units.

Functionalism can also operate to the detriment of nonmarital couples, as when governmental benefits are denied on the grounds that the couple should be treated as married, even when they are not, because they are presumed to be enjoying the same economies of shared expenses.

The high water mark of functionalism to date with regard to homosexual couples was the ruling of the New York Court of Appeals in *Braschi v. Stahl Associates* that a gay couple must be treated as a family for purposes of the provision in New York's rent control law that protected surviving "members of the family" from eviction in the event of the death of the named tenant. In interpreting the rent control law, the court reasoned that

> [it] should not be rigidly restricted to those people who have formalized their relationship by obtaining, for instance, a marriage certificate or an adoption order. The intended protection against sudden eviction should not rest on fictitious legal distinctions or genetic history, but instead should find its foundation in the reality of family life.

The court went on to articulate a set of criteria for determining whether a "family" existed:

> [T]he exclusivity and longevity of the relationship, the level of emotional and financial commitment, the manner in which the parties have conducted their everyday lives and held themselves out to society, and the reliance placed upon one another for daily family services.... [I]t is the totality of the relationship as evidenced by the dedication, caring and self-sacrifice of the parties [that] should, in the final analysis, control.

Domestic partnership laws represent the most successful attempt to date to merge the two lines of doctrine into codified rights and benefits laws. The status of domestic partner is not limited by sexual orientation; both lesbian and gay as well as straight couples may register. Politically, domestic partnerships serve as a mechanism for achieving legal protection for lesbian and gay couples without seeking legalization of lesbian and gay marriage. Such provisions have been adopted in ten municipalities. Domestic partnership laws present a way of solving, by legislation, two problems that arose in the case-by-case development of functionalist and contract principles: the uncertainty of definitional boundaries for a nonmarital relationship and the risk of fraudulent claims. The statutes set out objective definitions that specify which relationships can qualify for domestic partner status and that establish a mechanism, usually a registration system, for verifying whether a particular couple has self-declared as a partnership. The procedure for terminating a partnership involves filing a notice with the registry.

The domestic partnership laws enacted to date have established benefits primarily in the areas of bereavement and sick leave for municipal employees based on the illness or death of a partner; tenancy succession and other housing-related benefits; and health insurance benefits for partners of municipal employees. All have been enacted by municipal, rather than state or federal jurisdictions, and so cannot alter provisions of the state or federal laws that accord benefits based on marriage in areas such as tax, inheritance, or most public benefits.

Moreover, most domestic partnership laws emphasize their functionalist, rather than their contractual, aspects. Their focus, and the bulk of the political support for them, concerns the creation of a claim for entitlement by the nonmarried couple to rights or benefits offered by a third party to married couples. Most also, however, contain language that at least arguably establishes a contract between the two persons themselves. The most recent of the laws, adopted by San Francisco voters, is the most explicit in this regard.

The terms of the implied contract provisions of domestic partnership laws are far more libertarian than the state-imposed terms of marriage, however, and more limited than the scope of implied contracts potentially recognizable under *Marvin* [*v. Marvin*], and its progeny. Domestic partnerships cover only reciprocal obligations for basic support while the two individuals remain in the partnership. There is no implied agreement as to the ownership or division of property acquired during the term of the partnership, nor is there any basis for compelling one partner to support the other for any length of time, however short, after the partnership is dissolved.

These laws thus go the farthest toward removing the state from regulation of intimate relationships. The issue of whether the state should be expelled raises an old and continuing debate. Feminists have exposed the law's long-professed tradition of noninterference in certain aspects of family life as a mask for the ceding of control to those who wield greater power in the domestic sphere. Some feminists have attacked the contract doctrine embodied in *Marvin* for applying a market ideology that will inevitably disfavor those with less power in the market. These writers favor the imposition of constructive marriage as to certain terms, especially regarding support and property, when unmarried couples end a relationship. They argue that permitting judges to infer that a marriage exists, rather than simply attempting to discern the intent of the parties, operates as a necessary guarantor of balance between socially unequal parties. . . .

For feminists both inside and outside the lesbian and gay rights movement, the current focus on the possibility of legalization for lesbian and gay marriage provides an opportunity to develop ways to address the issues of hierarchy and power that underlie this debate. The politics of both gender and sexuality are implicated. The social stigma that attaches to sexuality outside of marriage produces another hierarchy, parallel to the hierarchy of gender. Simply democratizing or degendering marriage, without also dislodging that stigma, would be at best a partial reform.

Faced with such difficult issues, advocates for change should consider formulating specifically rhetorical strategies that can be utilized in long-term political efforts, in addition to the rights claims that ground litigation. A concept of "gender dissent" might form one such theme. In contrast to much of the equality rhetoric used in the lesbian and gay marriage debate, "gender dissent" does not imply a desire merely to become accepted on the same terms within an unchallenged structure of marriage. Nor does it connote identity based on sexual orientation; anyone can dissent from a hierarchy of power. Rather, it conveys an active intent to disconnect power from gender and an adversary relationship to dominance. Its specific expression could take a variety of forms, appropriate to differing contexts and communities. The goal of such a strategy would be enhancement of an openness to change and maximization of the potential for future and ever broader efforts to transform both the law and the reality of personal relationships. . . .

Paula L. Ettelbrick, Since When Is Marriage a Path to Liberation?

OUT/LOOK , no.6 (Fall 1989), p.8

. . .

. . . Marriage runs contrary to two of the primary goals of the lesbian and gay movement: the affirmation of gay identity and culture and the validation of many forms of relationships. . . .

The fight for justice has as its goal the realignment of power imbalances among individuals and classes of people in society. A pure "rights" analysis often fails to incorporate a broader understanding of the underlying inequities that operate to deny justice to a fuller range of people and groups. . . . At this point in time, making legal marriage for lesbian and gay couples a priority would set an agenda of gaining rights for a few, but would do nothing to correct power imbalances between those who are married (whether gay or straight) and those who are not. Thus, justice would not be gained.

Justice for gay men and lesbians will be achieved only when we are accepted and supported in this society *despite* our difference from the dominant culture and the choices we make regarding our relationships. . . .

Being queer means pushing the parameters of sex, sexuality, and family, and in the process transforming the very fabric of society. Gay liberation is inexorably linked to women's liberation. Each is essential to other.

The moment we argue, as some amongst us insist on doing, that we should be treated as equals because we are really just like married couples and hold the same values to be true, we undermine the very purpose of our movement and begin the dangerous process of silencing our different voices. As a lesbian, I am fundamentally different from nonlesbian women. That's the point. Marriage, as it exists today, is antithetical to my liberation as a lesbian and as a woman because it mainstreams my life and voice. I do not want to be known as "Mrs. Attached–To–Somebody–Else." Nor do I want to give the state the power to regulate my primary relationship....

The thought of emphasizing our sameness to married heterosexuals in order to obtain this "right" terrifies me. It rips away the very heart and soul of what I believe it is to be a lesbian in this world. It robs me of the opportunity to make a difference. We end up mimicking all that is bad about the institution of marriage in our effort to appear to be the same as straight couples.

By looking to our sameness and de-emphasizing our differences, we do not even place ourselves in a position of power that would allow us to transform marriage from an institution that emphasizes property and state regulation of relationships to an institution that recognizes one of many types of valid and respected relationships.... We would be perpetuating the elevation of married relationships and of "couples" in general, and further eclipsing other relationships of choice.

Ironically, gay marriage, instead of liberating gay sex and sexuality, would further outlaw all gay and lesbian sex that is not performed in a marital context. Just as sexually active nonmarried women face stigma and double standards around sex and sexual activity, so too would nonmarried gay people....

Undoubtedly, whether we admit it or not, we all need to be accepted by the broader society.... Those closer to the norm or to power in this country are more likely to see marriage as a principle of freedom and equality. Those who are more acceptable to the mainstream because of race, gender, and economic status are more likely to want the right to marry. It is the final acceptance, the ultimate affirmation of identity.

On the other hand, more marginal members of the lesbian and gay community (women, people of color, working class and poor) are less likely to see marriage as having relevance to our struggles for survival. After all, what good is the affirmation of our relationships (that is, marital relationships) if we are rejected as women, people of color, or working class? ...

If the laws changed tomorrow and lesbians and gay men were allowed to marry, where would we find the incentive to continue the progressive movement we have started that is pushing for societal and legal recognition of all kinds of family relationships? To create other options and alternatives? . . . To get the law to acknowledge that we may have more than one relationship worthy of legal protection? . . .

Nitya Duclos, Some Complicating Thoughts on Same–Sex Marriage

1 Law & Sexuality 31 (1991).

. . .

Shifting Perspectives

The greater part of the answer to a question is found in the way that the question itself is phrased. Questions tend to get phrased in conformity with dominant ideology, in ways that take for granted the existing social order and its institutions. All of us unconsciously assume the existence of the norms into which we have been socialized. However, to the extent we belong to groups that have been ill-treated by the dominant group in a society, we are not likely to be understood from dominant perspectives nor are our needs likely to be met by institutions that were not designed for us. We should therefore resist our socialized tendencies to pose questions in ways that accept the dominant framework as natural and inevitable.

Too often when writing or talking about same-sex marriage, the basic question seems to be something like, "Should homosexuals be allowed to enter a legal marriage?" The hidden subject of this sentence is the state; it gets to give or withhold permission. Lesbians and gay men get lumped together into "homosexuals," an abstract and over-simplified sexualized label. Marriage is reified; it assumes a shape fixed by ideological and legal norms that "homosexuals" may or may not fit; the complexity and dynamism of this longstanding legal relationship is collapsed into the point of entry (marrying). The question is posed from the dominant perspective; the yes/no answer it commands presupposes a singularity (or essence) in the categories "homosexual" and "marriage" that does not actually exist.

This is not to say that the question does not need to be posed from the dominant perspective. Clearly, framing the issue in those terms is important, because the dominant perspective constitutes the framework within which the answers to questions acquire the force of law. And, in my view, the answer to the dominant perspective question is obviously "yes." It is a glaring injustice to preclude lesbian women and gay men from marrying their partners. But to take this answer as the whole answer is to accept the dominant perspective as the only perspective. Given that the same-sex marriage bar is a bad thing for the state to impose, lesbians and gay men still need to ask whether marriage is a good thing for them to seek.

Shifting perspectives means changing the subject of the sentence and opening up the field of responses. We could ask something like, "Will lesbians and gay men or some of them benefit from legal recognition and regulation of their relationships through the marriage system?" This puts lesbians and gay men front and center as people with whom and for whom we are concerned. It specifies that legal recognition is one form of recognition and that the issue involves the *regulation* of those relationships by law. It expressly removes from consideration any doubt that lesbians and gay men *have* relationships—something that earlier question left open. And it asserts that marriage is a system of legal and social rules, not elemental but socially constructed and open to change.

Embracing Complexity

The shift from "homosexual" to "lesbians and gay men" is a first step. Expanding from one category to two is hardly sufficient, however. Neither "the" lesbian community nor "the" gay community exist any more than "the" homosexual community or "the" family. These are not homogeneous groups, and being a lesbian or a gay man does not automatically confer representative authority for the whole group of lesbians and/or gay men. Responsibility to these communities requires appreciation of the great diversity *within* lesbian and gay communities. We need to call to mind as many of the complex ways in which lesbians and gay men differ as possible, since these differences affect not only their views and expectations but also their likely experiences of marriage and its corollary, divorce.

Paying attention to only relatively standard categories of difference, namely, race, class, and gender, creates a small wealth of differences. Differences such as sexual identity, culture, religion, age, and disability substantially increase the degree of diversity, as do education and political affiliations. There are also other differentiating characteristics that, although less universally recognized as such, are especially important in the context of this issue. Consider, for example:

- Is the person single or involved in a relationship? If in a relationship, what kind of relationship is it and how does the person feel about it (about to break up? just beginning?)?

- Is the person a parent, including genetic parents, gestational parents, and functional parents? If a parent, does the person live alone with his or her child(ren) or with a co-parent? Does the parent have legal custody of or access to the child(ren)? What is the age(s) and sex(es) of the child(ren)? What kind of relationship does the parent have with the child(ren)?

- Is or has the person been legally married? If married, has he or she ever gone through a legal divorce? How does the person feel about these experiences?

- In what kind of community does the person live? What are his or her relationships with parents, siblings, and other family members? What kind of support network does the person have?

Obviously, the list could go on and on. Facing this multiplicity of differences is difficult for it is clearly impossible to ascertain each constituency's views on the issue or to analyze the likely impact of legal recognition of their relationship(s). The purpose is not to paralyze reform or to defeat activist efforts, but to stimulate a greater awareness of the need to think about and talk to (some) others and, when mapping out legal and political strategies or making predictions, to test them with many different people in mind.

A second component of embracing the complexity of the issue involves deconstructing marriage. Specifying the components of marriage is a crucial step toward identifying what it is about marriage that is desired or will benefit various constituencies within lesbian and gay communities. Marriage is not a monolith, although we are socialized to think of it as such. It is an extremely complex social, economic, legal, and religious institution, with deep emotional (but certainly not the same) significance to most individuals. It is closely tied to concepts of family and sexuality, both of which generate a strongly held set of social taboos in contemporary Canadian and American societies.

Marriage includes a state licensing procedure at the point of entry that permits the state to control who can and cannot marry and to raise money from marriage license fees. It also includes divorce, a process that permits the state to control exit from the institution and to raise more money. A complex series of economic benefits and burdens flow from the status of being married, both in the public sphere and in the private sphere. For example, some people who are married get tax breaks, but marital or "family" status also disentitles some people from access to benefits provided through the social welfare system. In the classic "private" context, being married leads to extended employment benefits but it may also hurt a spouse's ability to obtain credit. Marriage confers social legitimacy on relationships, it expresses a conformity with social norms that is good or bad in different communities and at different times, and it provides some people with psychological and emotional security within their relationships. The marriage system also includes the whole set of social, economic, legal, and emotional consequences of divorce. Legal systems governing marital property, spousal and child support, custody, and access all confer a host of benefits and burdens upon those who have been married.

All of these features, and others, constitute the institution of marriage as it presently exists in our society. When lesbian women, gay men, and others argue in favor of recognition of same-sex marriage, however, they do not always have the whole marriage system or the whole group of lesbians and gay men in mind. Asking an anti-essentialist question about same-sex marriage requires identifying what kinds of things lesbians and gay men want out of marriage, and then working through how the institution is likely to respond to those needs, considering the many different people within lesbian and gay communities. Only after this kind of analysis, it seems to me, should conclusions be drawn about whether struggling for the right to a marriage license (as compared to other kinds of reform) is a good strategy and for whom.

Those who advocate recognition of same-sex relationships through the legal system of marriage frequently assert roughly four distinct yet interrelated objectives that lesbian and gay people seek in marriage. Two of these are more abstract and two are more concrete. First, some people advocate marriage for primarily altruistic, political reasons, arguing that legal recognition of lesbian and gay relationships as marriages will revolutionize marriage and force society to confront and rethink its collective views of sex and sexuality. Second, some people argue that public validation and legitimation of same-sex relationships as equally worthy of respect can be realized through recognition of a legal right to marry. Third, some people see in marriage a range of socioeconomic benefits that could make a big difference in the lives of lesbian and gay families. Fourth, some people see in marriage a way of legitimating their relationships in the eyes of courts so that it is easier for them to keep their children.

Political Reform The argument that legally recognizing same-sex relationships as marriages will force our society to confront its deeply rooted sexist, heterosexist, and repressed beliefs about human sexuality and stimulate a complete rethinking of sexual relations is, I think, a brave but ultimately misdirected political strategy. It is courageous because it conceives of lesbian and gay couples who seek to marry as catalysts for and possibly the victims of radical social change—victims, since fundamental social changes are never accomplished without human cost. However, I worry whether the existence of a group of married lesbians and gay men can really revolutionize the institution of marriage. My concern arises from the fact that this argument is precisely the same as that used by reactionary groups *against* legal recognition of same-sex relationships as marriages. Perhaps the lesbian or gay activist's confidence in the radicalizing potential of same-sex marriage reflects an unconscious acceptance of homophobic rhetoric, which assumes the inevitability of marriage, distracting attention from more radical projects of social reorganization. After all, marrying is on its face an assimilationist move, and, although society is not universal in its responses to change, it is likely to be regarded as such by most people. Without a compelling strategy that maps out *how* acquiring a right to legally marry will trigger desired social changes, I find it more probable that current views of sex and sexuality will persist and that the public will continue to marry and divorce, noting only with passing interest that lesbians and gay men can now do the same.

Finally, legal recognition of same-sex relationships as marriages or as equivalent to marriages may not simply prove ineffective to attain the political goal of sexual liberation, it may also prove harmful to this effort. In particular, the creation of fixed alternative categories of legal matrimonial relationships may contribute to the entrenchment of mutually exclusive and immutable categories of sexual orientation. In the process, less "mainstream" sexual identities may suffer further marginalization.

Public Legitimation The second argument in favor of legal recognition of same-sex relationships as marriages, that allowing same-sex marriage will publicly legitimate lesbian and gay relationships, is expressly assimilationist. That is, its advocates do not seek the transformation of the institution of marriage so much as its extension to same-sex couples, in the name of equality. While it is obvious that the current marriage system flagrantly discriminates against lesbians and gay men and should be condemned for this, as I have argued earlier, it does not automatically follow that acquiring the right to marry is a sufficient solution for lesbians and gay men. What is undeniably conceptually offensive to liberal ideology should not be conflated with what is actually harmful to people: it is important to know who is hurt by not being able to marry and divorce, and how, and whether getting married and divorced will actually address these harms.

The assumption in the "public legitimation" argument that marriage is a good thing should be questioned. Historically, the experience of marriage has been generally destructive for half of those who have married: women. Marriage has condoned and sustained class and racial segregation within a sexist context, it has stripped propertied women of their possessions, and it continues to play a significant role in the feminization of poverty. Marriage has also sheltered and legitimized violence against women and children. It is true that all of this damage has occurred while marriage has been restricted to opposite-sex couples and that individuals in same-sex relationships do not suffer gendered economic inequality relative to each other. However, this does not mean that lesbian and gay couples will be able to avoid these ills of marriage any more easily than straight couples. We have all been socialized into the mores of our sexist, racist, classist, and heterosexist society and a lesbian or gay male identity is not a reliable shield against them. Although same-sex relationships are not the same as opposite-sex relationships, they nonetheless still exist within the context of powerful social ideologies that ingrain gendered, classed, and racial patterns of exploitation. Lesbian or gay male partners may differ from each other on the basis of class, race, age, education, and other differentiating characteristics, which, because of their position in the social hierarchy, also tend to alter the balance of power within relationships. Battery is not unknown in lesbian and gay relationships. Some same-sex couples divide household responsibilities along lines that reflect traditional gender patterns—and it is hard not to do so in a system that makes this division of labor economically advantageous whenever there are young children in the household. Marriage strengthens the force of dominant ideologies both in its symbolic and social influences, and in more concrete ways. For example, pressure to conform to traditional gendered roles increases when judges rely so heavily on these ideologies in arbitrating the consequences of termination of marital or marriage-like relationships.

The process of seeking such legal reform can also be damaging. Cases in which lesbians and gay men seek recognition of their family or spousal status have been based on trying to establish that lesbian and gay relationships conform to prevailing legal ideologies of family and marriage. The effort of making out a case of "sameness" has costs both for those who try to fit the mold and for those who clearly cannot. Even if some lesbian and gay marriages will not reproduce the pattern of subordination and domination that characterizes heterosexual marriages, struggling for a right to marry legitimates and entrenches the institution—which has adverse consequences for heterosexually identified women.

Another assumption underlying the "public legitimation" argument for legal recognition of same-sex marriage is that marriage is voluntary. The equality that is sought is the right to *choose* to marry so that acquiring the right simply increases the field of options for lesbian and gay couples. But the premise of choice in this formulation is misleading. One of the major trends in family law in Canada in recent years has been the assimilation of more and more *unmarried* heterosexual couples into the legal marriage system. That is, it is increasingly difficult for individuals living within heterosexual relationships to avoid being considered "married" by the state with respect to support obligations, pension and other employment benefits, and so on. If lesbians and gay men who wish to marry gain the "right" to choose to marry, cohabiting lesbians and gay men who wish to choose otherwise may find this increasingly difficult.

The goals of lesbians and gay men who seek to marry for this reason are equality and public validation of their relationships. Both are undeniably important goals that touch on the deep structure of the injustice that society has inflicted on lesbians and gay men. The community approval of a loving relationship as one deserving of public recognition and respect that the marriage ceremony signifies would likely ameliorate the social inequality and stigmatization felt by lesbians and gay men to some extent. But it is important not to overestimate the magnitude of the consequences flowing from the issuance of a marriage license. The very necessary struggle for formal equality does not guarantee any degree of substantive equality. There is still lots of room for *de facto* double standards, and lesbian and gay marriages could easily come to occupy one of the lower tiers of an already hierarchical social marriage system. Possession of a marriage license may not be sufficient for lesbian and gay couples to marry within particular religions, and a legal change of status may not be a persuasive means of gaining family acceptance and support for the relationship. Moreover, for some lesbians and gay men, gaining legal recognition of their relationships will not address the most significant reasons for their experiences of inequality and oppression. The problem is that a claim for a "right" to marry is at best an argument for legal *toleration* of same-sex relationships, but such tolerance falls short of social respect.

Socioeconomic Benefits The next two rationales for seeking legal recognition of same-sex relationships leave the realm of ideals and come down to earth. They are pragmatic, not theoretical, and they seek in marriage material benefits from which same-sex couples are currently excluded.

Clearly there are some socioeconomic benefits to marriage, and it is unjust to exclude same-sex couples from them. However, the socioeconomic benefits sought by advocates of same-sex marriages do not apply equally to everyone nor do they all flow automatically from marriage. In addition, marital status carries with it certain economic burdens that disproportionately affect some people. Just what these various benefits and burdens are and how they affect different people should be calculated before concluding that marriage will improve the economic position of lesbian and gay couples. In conducting this analysis, whether the benefit or burden applies to married couples exclusively or also to unmarried cohabitants in heterosexual relationships, as well as whether it applies to "spouses" or to "families" must also be considered. Finally, the benefits and burdens that flow from the termination of marriage should not be omitted. To give a sense of the complexity of this enterprise, here is a list of some of the socioeconomic benefits and burdens that marriage brings:

Benefits

- public pensions
- immigration preferences for family members, married spouses, and engaged persons
- municipal benefits such as "family" zoning ordinances
- dependent married spouse tax deduction
- health insurance (lower "family" rates)
- eligibility for prisoner "family" and conjugal visiting programs
- adoption (administrative policies favoring married couples)
- intestate succession laws favoring "spouses"
- testator's "family" maintenance legislation (when the deceased has not adequately provided for his or her "family")
- right to sue for the wrongful death of a "spouse"
- no criminal liability for married spouses who would otherwise be considered accessories after the fact
- compensation for "families" of deceased crime victims
- interspousal transfer of property by will or trust
- protection against eviction upon death of a tenant for "spouses" or "family" members
- right to receive worker's compensation payments upon death of worker "spouse"
- "spousal" and "family" employment benefits in collective agreements, legislation, or private employers' benefit packages (*e.g.*, bereavement leave for death of a "spouse's" relative)
- power to make medical decisions for an incapacitated "spouse" or "family" member
- "family" discounts for clubs and other recreational activities

Burdens

- "spouse in the house" rules for state welfare assistance (counting as claimant's income any income received by opposite-sex cohabitant)
- prohibition against income-splitting for tax purposes
- disentitlement from state benefits on the basis of availability of financial claims against former married or unmarried cohabitant

- termination of state benefits upon marriage
- income tax income attribution rules for interspousal transfers loss of "status" upon marriage for First Nations women in Canada
- criminal liability for failure to provide "dependents" with the necessities of life
- disentitlement from government student loans on the basis of "spouse's" income
- conflict of interest legislation anti-nepotism rules in employment
- "spouse's" credit history taken into account in credit rating
- discounting of a "spouse's" income in bank's mortgage calculations on the assumption that she is likely to leave the workforce to care for children

With respect to economic benefits if the relationship ends, there is widespread acknowledgment that the current system of legal regulation of the economic consequences of divorce and separation is inequitable both in cases of direct legal intervention and in the approximately ninety percent of cases that are settled out of court. The people the system works worst for (in economic terms) are women with children; however, most people who encounter it feel it is unjust. In this context, it is hard to know whether legal provisions governing the economic aspects of marital termination are a benefit or a burden. For example, spousal support payments may seem to be a burden to the payor and a benefit to the payee. However, the payor's burden is significantly offset by being able to deduct support payments for income tax purposes; extremely high default rates and very low enforcement rates may mean that a spouse or former spouse is worse off than a nonspouse who may receive less from the state but can rely on getting it. Finally, it should be remembered that acquiring marital status will not end all socioeconomic discrimination on the basis of sexual orientation.

It is beyond the scope of this paper to calculate how these various benefits and burdens will likely affect different same-sex couples. What should be clear from this discussion, however, is that statements that lesbians and gay men benefit socioeconomically from being able to marry will likely have only some lesbians or gay men—and some benefits or burdens—in mind. On the basis of this brief catalogue of socioeconomic consequences of marriage, I would guess that those individuals who most benefit from the socioeconomic advantages of marriage are members of the middle class. Those who rely for most of their income on state benefits are more likely to be economically penalized for marrying. Given that class relations are interpenetrated by gender and race relations, I suspect that, for example, white gay men as a group will likely benefit more from marriage than will black lesbian women, in purely socioeconomic terms.

Children Marriage has sometimes been advocated as a way for lesbian or gay parents to keep their children, particularly when the challenge to custody is made by a heterosexual individual or couple, or in situations in which a genetically related parent denies the parental claims of a former lesbian partner. Marriage might also be seen as a way of safeguarding one's children from the state on the assumption that children living with unmarried lesbian or gay parents are more likely to be found by the state to be children in need of protection under the standard tests in child protection legislation.

This argument rests on the assumption that possession of a marriage certificate will legitimize the sexual relationship between the adults in the household in the eyes of the court so that the judge will not consider the lesbian or gay relationship to be a threat to the "best interests of the children" (the governing principle in all child custody cases). But is the absence of a marriage certificate really the problem? The history of judicial treatment of same-sex relationships in the custody context constitutes such appalling evidence of deep-seated and visceral anti-lesbian and anti-gay feeling in the judiciary that it seems naive to think such attitudes can be wiped out by a marriage certificate. In fact, the enormous social signifi-cance vested in a marriage certificate may provoke greater hostility on the part of homophobic judges toward married lesbians and gay men. Even when the judge is not overtly homophobic, heterosexist bias may well manifest itself in matters, such as assessment of credibility, that are critical to success in a contested custody case. It is also important to remember that alongside the catalogue of anti-lesbian and anti-gay rulings, judicial titillation and inappropriate inquiry into sexual relationships, and offensive moral pronouncements about the lives of litigants in custody cases involv-ing lesbians and gay men, lies a similarly reprehensible list of judicial actions in cases involving heterosexually identified married women at-tempting to retain custody of their children.

In fact, the excessive judicial scrutiny, moral pronouncements, and serious constraints on behavior that characterize custody cases regardless of how the litigants' sexual orientation is described to the court may be more reflective of the defects in our system of custody dispute resolution in general than of the importance of a marriage certificate.

Custody disputes arise in a wide variety of contexts—for example, a lesbian may be seeking custody of children against their biological father, or she may be opposing his relatives, or she may be litigating against a former lesbian partner with whom she has had children (and she may or may not be the biological mother), or she may be opposing her lover's relatives—and they are always agonizingly painful, stressful, and expensive. In the vast majority of cases, both parties clearly meet the minimum standards of parenting ability required by law, and the judge is required to select between people who desperately want custody of the child(ren) on the basis of the child(ren)'s "best interests." No one knows what that means. In the face of this vast discretionary power to do what is "best" for the child(ren) and overwhelming pressure to decide cases as quickly as possible, judges rely on "commonsense," conventional morality, and a whole host of considerations that reflect the prejudices of privileged groups in our society to which virtually all judges belong. Thus, while not being married may well be a mark against some parents (whether gay, lesbian, or heterosexually identified), being a lesbian or a gay man will likely also be a negative factor—as will being a working mother, belonging to a nontraditional religion, and so on. As long as the custody dispute resolution system remains unchanged, there will be an informal hierarchy of preferred parents, reflecting judges' assumptions about who is a good parent. Married lesbians and gay men will simply take their place in the ranks (likely above unmarried lesbians and gay men and below heterosexual parents). Trying to conform to the evolving, judicial standard of "good lesbian mother" may require a further gloss if it becomes possible to be a married lesbian mother, but the stereotype will remain and may even gain strength if same-sex partners can (and so can be expected to) marry.

Given the serious inadequacies of the custody dispute resolution system, it may be wise to pause before seeking a reform that would inevitably bring lesbian and gay parents into greater contact with it. Although it is true that custody disputes often arise outside the context of marriage, the termination of a marriage necessarily involves the intervention of a court to scrutinize and resolve custody arrangements. And the adversarial nature of the system exerts a powerful influence at a time when individuals, regardless of their sexual identities, are terribly vulnerable to feelings of antagonism against their former partners. Contact with the marriage dissolution system, especially when young children are involved, heightens conflict, exacerbates emotional strain, and costs a lot of money, to the detriment of everyone. Adding a new and growing category of custody disputes between divorcing same-sex couples may well increase the magnitude of the problem rather than ameliorate the injustices already experienced by lesbian and gay parents.

It is true that lesbian and gay parents are currently at greater risk in custody litigation, both against heterosexually identified persons and biological parents; it is shocking that an absentee genetic father has more legal rights to his genetic offspring than does the lesbian co-parent who lives with, cares for, and loves the child along with its genetic mother. Similarly, it is manifestly unfair that a lesbian parent who is not genetically related to her child has no legal rights as against a former partner who is a genetic parent. The injustice and psychological harms in these situations should galvanize reformers to action. But turning to custody law and the courts in the absence of substantial legislative reform, with only a marriage certificate in hand, may not make a very big difference.

I do not believe that it is coincidental that those whom marriage is most likely to benefit are those who are already fairly high up in the hierarchy of privilege that pervades society at large. Thus, another possible consequence of legal recognition of same-sex marriage is that differences of power and privilege within lesbian and gay communities might be exacerbated.

When to seek a "right" to marry and how to do it, if at all, are complicated questions that do not admit of easy answers. In this essay, I have attempted to show just how complicated these questions are. By pausing to consider the many different situations of lesbian and gay people and by carefully dissecting the various elements of the institution of marriage, genuinely progressive reform is possible. While the legal institution of marriage is one of society's most basic institutions and one from which lesbians and gay men should never have been barred, I think the message of this paper is that we should all be wary of package deals.

Kathy Duggan, I Earned This Divorce

The New York Times, July 25, 1996, p. A23.

The woman who once stood with me before an altar, promising to share her life with me, is now holding my computer hostage until I give her the VCR. Though the Defense of Marriage Act, passed last week by the House, bars federal recognition of gay marriages, I find myself wishing our marriage was legal for a reason I never anticipated. I want a divorce.

I don't just mean I want to end my marriage. I did that two years ago. I'm single now, having learned how to cook for one and attend weddings alone.

What I want is a forum where I can act out all the anger, frustration and disappointment of a failed relationship. One where I can hand responsibility for the haggling over our possessions to a professional—a lawyer who can be ruthless on my behalf when I'm likely to just dissolve into tears and say, "No, really, you take the flatware." I want a ritual that takes apart our relationship as deliberately as we put it together.

Mary and I were the perfect couple. Unfortunately, together we made lousy individuals. From the start, people often got us confused. We chalked it up to being the same height and having similar coloring, but the truth is our identities were slowly merging into one.

Oblivious to the consequences of our fused identities, in September 1991 we gathered family and friends at a ceremony in my girlhood church, had a backyard reception and then left for a honeymoon in Provincetown, Massachusetts.

Though we knew we were just as married as any husband and wife, we chose not to use the language of heterosexual marriages. We believed that to use such words as "wedding," "marriage" and "wife" would trivialize that there was no legal or religious recognition.

So we decided on life partner and labeled the relationship a domestic partnership. (I'm still stunned by how many people thought we had opened a small business together.) We struggled over a suitable alternative to the word "wedding." For lack of anything better, we finally just called our ritual exchange of vows "the ceremony."

Taking sacred vows did not help our individuality problems. After two and a half years, I left Mary and found myself in a semantic void. I could call her my ex-lover, but I rarely called her my lover when we were together—the illicit undertones the word carries were the last thing I wanted. "Former life partner" sounds like something Shirley MacLaine would say.

When a relationship that was only marginally recognized comes to an end, it is almost as though it never existed. When filling out forms, I can no more check the box labeled "divorced" than I could have once checked "married." Invisible as we may have been as a couple, Mary and I at least had each other to affirm our relationship.

Some gay men and lesbians have come up with ceremonies of dissolution to mark the radical changes in their lives, but I couldn't imagine planning such an event. For heterosexual couples, the legal process of filing for divorce can serve that function. Oh, sure, Mary and I attended to a few legal matters. But telling coworkers, "Well, we shredded the health-care proxies last night," just doesn't carry the same weight as saying, "Well, I signed the divorce papers last night."

I sometimes jokingly refer to Mary as my first wife. I hope to marry again, and I hope that by the time I do, my partner and I will be able to do it legally. Right now though, I want a divorce.

III. ALTERNATIVES TO MARRIAGE

Some couples choose to cohabit without marriage; some end up cohabiting because they cannot marry by law or by religious belief (due to pre-existing marriages). Some people like the idea of crafting the terms for intimate relationships through their own written contracts. Some turn to contract in order to formalize the terms of unions that lack legal recognition. Some municipalities have provided through ordinances an alternative to marriage by recognizing other intimate unions, usually called domestic partnerships. Are individual women helped or hurt by legal recognition of non-marital cohabitation? Are women helped or hurt by the creation of domestic partnership ordinances? How about privately negotiated agreements to govern intimate relationships?

A. Non–Marital Cohabitation

Michelle Marvin v. Lee Marvin

California Supreme Court, 1976.
18 Cal.3d 660, 134 Cal.Rptr. 815, 557 P.2d 106.

MATHEW TOBRINER, JUSTICE.

In the instant case plaintiff and defendant lived together for seven years without marrying; all property acquired during this period was taken in defendant's name. When plaintiff sued to enforce a contract under which she was entitled to half the property and to support payments, the trial court granted judgment on the pleadings for defendant, thus leaving him with all property accumulated by the couple during their relationship. Since the trial court denied plaintiff a trial on the merits of her claim, its decision ... must be reversed....

In *Trutalli v. Meraviglia* (1932) 12 P.2d 430 we established the principle that nonmarital partners may lawfully contract concerning the ownership of property acquired during the relationship. We reaffirmed this principle in *Vallera v. Vallera* (1943) 134 P.2d 761, 763, stating that "If a man and a woman [who are not married] live together as husband and wife under an agreement to pool their earnings and share equally in their joint accumulations, equity will protect the interests of each in such property."
. . .

Defendant [responds] that the alleged contract is so closely related to the supposed "immoral" character of the relationship between plaintiff and himself that the enforcement of the contract would violate public policy. He points to cases asserting that a contract between nonmarital partners is unenforceable if it is "involved in" an illicit relationship, or made in "contemplation" of such a relationship. A review of the numerous California decisions concerning contracts between nonmarital partners, however, reveals that the courts have not employed such broad and uncertain standards to strike down contracts. The decisions instead disclose a narrower and more precise standard: a contract between nonmarital partners is unenforceable only *to the extent* that it *explicitly* rests upon the immoral and illicit consideration of meretricious sexual services. . . .

. . . [A]dults who voluntarily live together and engage in sexual relations are nonetheless as competent as any other persons to contract respecting their earnings and property rights. Of course, they cannot lawfully contract to pay for the performance of sexual services, for such a contract is, in essence, an agreement for prostitution and unlawful for that reason. But they may agree to pool their earnings and to hold all property acquired during the relationship in accord with the law governing community property; conversely, they may agree that each partner's earnings and the property acquired from those earnings remains the separate property of the earning partner. So long as the agreement does not rest upon illicit meretricious consideration, the parties may order their economic affairs as they choose, and no policy precludes the courts from enforcing such agreements.

[The court held that Michelle Marvin had made out a proper claim of express contract, based on her allegations that she and Lee Marvin had entered into an oral agreement under which she would provide her services as "companion, homemaker, housekeeper and cook" in return for financial support from Lee Marvin. The court also held that Michelle Marvin could amend her complaint to add further causes of action for "implied contract" and "equitable relief."]

. . . We conclude that the judicial barriers that may stand in the way of a policy based upon the fulfillment of the reasonable expectations of the parties to a nonmarital relationship should be removed. As we have explained, the courts now hold that express agreements will be enforced unless they rest on an unlawful meretricious consideration. We add that in the absence of an express agreement, the couples may look to a variety of other remedies in order to protect the parties' lawful expectations.

The courts may inquire into the conduct of the parties to determine whether the conduct demonstrates an implied contract or implied agreement of partnership or joint venture, or some other tacit understanding between the parties. The courts may, when appropriate, employ principles of constructive trust or resulting trust. Finally, a nonmarital partner may recover in quantum meruit for the reasonable value of household services rendered less the reasonable value of support received if he can show he has rendered services with the expectation of monetary reward. . . .

NOTE

A Postscript to *Marvin*. Marvin v. Marvin had a long and tortured history. Following this decision, the case was remanded to trial court which, in 1979, found on the evidence that the parties had had neither an express nor an implied contract to share property and, furthermore, that the plaintiff was not entitled to the equitable remedies of a resulting or a constructive trust. (The court did not consider the remedy of quantum meruit, as the plaintiff had dismissed her causes of action based on that ground.) Recognizing, however, that the California Supreme Court had instructed it to employ whatever equitable remedy might be appropriate under the circumstances, and aware that the plaintiff was then receiving unemployment insurance benefits and that the value of the defendant's property at the time of separation had exceeded $1 million, the trial court awarded plaintiff $104,000 for rehabilitation purposes. This figure was calculated by taking the highest salary the plaintiff had ever received as a singer—$1,000 per week—and multiplying it over two years. However, following an appeal by the defendant, the California Court of Appeals, in 1981, held that the award was not within the issues as framed by the pleadings and modified the judgment by deleting this award.

Although Michelle Marvin was ultimately unable to recover on any of the grounds recognized by the California Supreme Court in *Marvin,* the court's holding has exerted considerable influence on other states, many of which have allowed formerly cohabiting partners to recover on contractual or quasi-contractual claims. And, as the following excerpt from Alderson v. Alderson illustrates, the California courts since *Marvin* have themselves been willing to apply the principles articulated in *Marvin* even to allow a former cohabitant to recover a one-half interest in the parties' property as well as to set aside quitclaim deeds signed by her.

Alderson v. Alderson

Court of Appeal, First Dist., California, 1986.
180 Cal.App.3d 450, 225 Cal.Rptr. 610.

ROBERT MERRILL, ASSOCIATE JUSTICE.

Appellant Steve Alderson appeals from a March 31, 1982, judgment dividing certain real property equally between himself and respondent

Jonne Alderson. . . . He also appeals from a January 28, 1983, order appointing a receiver for his real property. . . .

I

Jonne Koenig and Steve Alderson first met in December 1966 in Reno, Nevada. Jonne was living with her parents at the time and was employed at a local bank. During the ensuing year, Jonne and Steve fell in love and talked of marriage.

In September 1967, Jonne moved from Reno to Portland, Oregon, for the purpose of marrying Steve who had moved there a month earlier. The marriage plans, however, for various unspecific reasons, did not material-ize. Instead, Jonne and Steve embarked on a period of nonmarital cohabita-tion which lasted twelve years.

The couple initially rented a house in Portland. Steve worked as a civil engineer. Jonne found a job as a receptionist. The parties' earnings were placed in joint bank accounts. The two filed a joint federal income tax return as a married couple in 1967.

In September 1968 the couple moved to Eugene, Oregon, because of Steve's job and purchased their first home. The decision to purchase the property was made jointly. The parties intended the acquisition to be both a home and an investment. Title was taken in Steve's name only. Neverthe-less, the downpayment on the property came from the parties' joint savings account and, according to Jonne's testimony, it was her understanding that she and Steve owned the property together.

Jonne secured another office position in Eugene. And in December 1969 the couple had the first of three children that were to be born to them.

The Eugene, Oregon move and purchase began a string of moves and realty acquisitions for the pair over the next eleven years. Between 1968 and 1979, the two acquired a total of fourteen properties, most of which were purchased purely for investment purposes. Eleven of the fourteen properties were located in California where the couple eventually settled. Purchase of the properties was again made by joint decision of the parties. Down payments for these purchases came from the couple's joint savings account and/or loans from Jonne's parents. Jonne and Steve acquired title to seven of the properties as husband and wife or as married persons. With three of the properties, they acquired joint title without designation as to marital status.

Jonne, who continued to work off and on during this period, contribut-ed her earnings toward these realty purchases. Additionally, she collected the rents, paid the bills and kept the books for all the rental properties. She also helped to repair and fix up the properties. She later testified that she viewed the properties as "our houses." She said: "We both worked and sacrificed different things so that we had the money to buy them and to keep them." "We had higher expectations than some because we wanted property; we wanted investments; we wanted things for the future for the kids."

During the entire twelve-year period Jonne and Steve lived together, they held themselves out be a married couple to everyone including family and friends. Jonne assumed Steve's surname of Alderson as her own, as did the three children. The couple maintained joint bank accounts throughout the period and filed joint federal income tax returns.

At the end of this period, in December 1979, the parties separated. Jonne moved from the family home, she said, because Steve "told me to get out." Prior to leaving, Jonne signed quitclaim deeds "for all of the houses." She said she did so under duress. She testified that Steve made various threats of what he would do to her if she did not sign. "Steve told me that I would never get any property. He would see me dead before I got any of them." Jonne said she was afraid for her own safety and so she "just signed [the deeds] to get out." Jonne received no payment for signing the deeds.

II

On October 14, 1980, Jonne filed her second amended complaint against Steve. The first cause of action alleged that Steve was the father of Jonne's three minor children, and sought child support and attorney's fees. The second and third causes of action alleged that Jonne and Steve lived together as husband and wife for a twelve-year period although they were not married. During this period the parties had three children and jointly accumulated substantial property, including ten parcels of real property. (At trial, it was determined that the parties actually had eleven properties at the time of separation; three other properties had been sold prior to separation.) According to the complaint, the parties impliedly agreed to equally share the property acquired during the course of their relationship. The second cause of action also alleged that Steve had coerced Jonne into signing quitclaim deeds to the real property. The complaint sought to set aside the quitclaim deeds and to equally divide the property.

In a fourth cause of action, Jonne alleged that Steve had recently committed an assault and battery on her and had broken her arm. (The assault apparently took place sometime after the filing of the first amended complaint. Steve was later convicted of having violated Pen.Code Sect. 243, a misdemeanor, based on this assault.) The complaint sought compensatory and punitive damages. In the fifth cause of action, Jonne sought injunctive relief against harassment by appellant under Code of Civil Procedure section 527.6.

In his answer to the complaint filed on November 10, 1980, Steve denied paternity of two of the three children. He denied all of the other material allegations of the complaint. Steve also set forth affirmative defenses asserting that (1) Jonne had sexual intercourse with other men; (2) the alleged agreement to share property violated the statute of frauds; (3) estoppel; and (4) self-defense.

On February 13, 1981, a stipulation for entry of judgment was filed in which defendant admitted paternity of all three children. On February 1, 1982, an "Order Specifying Issues Without Substantial Controversy ..." was filed in which the following issue was deemed established against Steve: "On or about September 7, 1980, defendant Steve Colden Alderson did willfully and unlawfully use force and violence upon the person of plaintiff, and as a result thereof did inflict serious bodily injury upon the plaintiff." This order was based upon Steve's municipal court conviction for violation of Penal Code section 243.

By stipulation it was ordered that the first, second and third causes of action (i.e., paternity, child support and division of property) were to be tried separately from the fourth (assault and battery) and fifth (injunctive relief) causes of action.

On March 4, 1982, trial of the first, second and third causes of action commenced without jury. All of the issues concerning paternity, child support and child visitation were settled by stipulation, including an acknowledgment by Steve that he was the father of all three children. After hearing the evidence, the court, on March 31, rendered judgment for Jonne on the property issues. The court declared that Jonne was entitled to an undivided one-half interest in the parties' property, quieted title to the real property in both of the parties, and set aside the quitclaim deeds. The trial court denied Steve's request for a statement of decision as untimely under Code of Civil Procedure section 632. By stipulation, the court reserved jurisdiction to divide the property. In a stipulated order filed on May 25, 1982, the parties equally divided the property. The stipulation was made without prejudice to Steve's right to appeal from the judgment.

On June 16, 1982, Steve filed a notice of appeal from both the March 31, 1982, judgment and the stipulated order of May 25, 1982. On August 10, 1982, this court dismissed the appeal from the stipulated order of May 25, 1982.

On July 9, 1982, trial of the bifurcated fourth and fifth causes of action was held. Judgment was rendered again in favor of Jonne and included $15,000 in compensatory damages, plus $4,000 for punitive damages. This judgment is not the subject of an appeal.

III

In her complaint, Jonne, in essence, alleges an implied contract between the parties to equally share the property acquired during the course of their relationship. In ruling in her favor, the trial court impliedly found this allegation to be true.

In this appeal, Steve does not appear to dispute the court's finding. Nevertheless, he maintains that the trial court's ruling upholding the contract must be overturned because the contract was illegal and thus unenforceable. Under Marvin v. Marvin (1976) 18 Cal.3d 660, 134 Cal.Rptr. 815, 557 P.2d 106, he says, "[it] is clear that a contract between two unmarried persons living together will not be enforced if an inseparable part of the consideration for the contract is an agreement to provide sexual services." Steve adds: "The record below is uncontradicted that the agreement between appellant and respondent integrally contemplated that the parties would provide sexual services to each other." We find no merit in Steve's contention.

In *Marvin*, a woman brought an action against a man with whom she had lived for approximately six years, in which she alleged that she and defendant entered into an oral agreement that during the time they lived together they would combine their efforts and earnings and share equally the property accumulated through their individual or combined efforts, and that plaintiff would reader services to defendant as companion, homemaker, housekeeper and cook, give up her career as an entertainer and singer, and that defendant would provide for all her financial support for the rest of her life. Plaintiff further alleged that at the end of the six-year period, defendant compelled her to leave his household. He continued to support her for about one and one-half years, but thereafter refused to provide further support and refused to recognize that she had any interest in the considerable amount of property that had been accumulated during the years they resided together.

Plaintiff prayed for declaratory relief, asking the court to determine her contract and property rights and also to impose a constructive trust upon one-half of the property acquired during the course of the relationship. The trial court granted defendant's motion for judgment on the pleadings.

The Supreme Court reversed. The high court held that the terms of the contract as alleged by plaintiff in *Marvin* furnished a suitable basis upon which the trial court could render declaratory relief, and the trial court therefore erred in granting defendant's motion for judgment on the pleadings. The court held generally that while the provisions of the Family Law Act do not govern the distribution of property acquired during a nonmarital relationship, the courts should enforce express contracts between nonmarital partners except to the extent that the contract is explicitly founded on the consideration of meretricious sexual services. Said the court: "The fact that a man and woman live together without marriage, and engage in a sexual relationship, does not in itself invalidate agreements between them relating to their earnings, property, or expenses. Neither is such an agreement invalid merely because the parties may have contemplated the creation or continuation of a nonmarital relationship when they entered into it. Agreements between nonmarital partners fail only to the extent that they rest upon a consideration of meretricious sexual services." . . . "[A] contract between nonmarital partners, even if expressly made in contemplation of a common living arrangement, is invalid only if sexual acts form an inseparable part of the consideration for the agreement." . . .

"In summary, we base our opinion on the principle that adults who voluntarily live together and engage in sexual relations are nonetheless as competent as any other persons to contract respecting their earnings and property rights. Of course, they cannot lawfully contract to pay for the performance of sexual services, for such a contract is, in essence, an agreement for prostitution and unlawful for that reason. But they may agree to pool their earnings and to hold all property acquired during the relationship in accord with the law governing community property; conversely they may agree that each partner's earnings and the property acquired from those earnings remains the separate property of the earning partner. So long as the agreement does not rest upon illicit meretricious consideration, the parties may order their economic affairs as they choose, and no policy precludes the courts from enforcing such agreements." ...

Although not directly called upon to do so, the *Marvin* court further addressed the issue of the property rights of a nonmarital partner in the absence of an express contract. Rejecting what it called "judicial barriers that ... stand in the way of a policy based upon the fulfillment of the reasonable expectations of the parties to a nonmarital relationship," the court held that "[c]ourts may inquire into the conduct of the parties to determine whether that conduct demonstrates an implied contract or implied agreement of partnership or joint venture [citation], or some other tacit understanding between the parties. The courts may, when appropriate employ principles of constructive trust ... or resulting trust.... Finally, a nonmarital partner may recover in quantum meruit for the reasonable value of household services rendered less the reasonable value of support received if he can show that he rendered services with the expectation of monetary reward. ..." ...

In the instant case, the trial court ruled in favor of Jonne and held that she was entitled to an undivided half interest in the parties' properties. In so ruling, the court impliedly found that the parties' conduct over the twelve-year period they were together, evidenced an implied contract between them to share equally any and all property acquired during the course of their relationship, as alleged in the complaint. The court also impliedly found this contract to be legal and enforceable under *Marvin* and not resting on "a consideration of meretricious sexual services." Our review of these findings, necessarily begins and ends with the question of whether or not they are supported by substantial evidence. After fully examining the record before us, we have determined that they are.

Evidence that the parties impliedly agreed to share equally in their acquisitions includes the following: Jonne's testimony to this effect, the fact that the parties held themselves out socially, as well as otherwise, as husband and wife; the fact that Jonne and the couple's three children, in fact, took Steve's surname; the fact that the pair pooled their financial resources and then drew upon the same to purchase the subject properties; the fact that the decision to purchase said properties was, in most cases, made jointly; the fact of Jonne's participation in the properties other than financial (she kept the books on the properties, helped repair and fix up the properties, paid the bills and collected the rents); and finally, the fact that title to ten of the properties was taken by Jonne and Steve jointly and in the case of seven of these purchases, was taken as husband and wife.

Evidence that consideration for the implied agreement between the parties did not rest on meretricious sexual service includes the absence of any evidence to the contrary and Jonne's own testimony.[1] Said testimony

1. "[D]efense Counsel: Q. Mrs. Alderson, in your complaint, you described that you had a contract with Mr. Alderson by which you would share the ownership of all of the property you acquired during the time you lived together, is that a fair statement of what you are saying in the case?

"A. Yes.

"Q. According to the terms of your contract you were going to do something for the property you were to acquire, is that correct?

"A. I was going to do something?

"Q. Yes. You each were going to do things for each other, is that correct?

"A. You mean both to work and—

"Q. Yes

"A. Uh huh.

"Q. For instance, you were going to cook for you and Mr. Alderson, is that right?

"A. I was. I was his wife. I mean, whatever a wife does.

"Q. Okay. Well, let me list the things that a wife does and ask you if that's what you understood you were going to do as part of this contract, all right. Did you understand that as put of your contact you were going to cook?

"A. I—as far as a contract, written, saying I did this and he did this, we just were living together as we were married. We did anything that any other married couple did and we pooled together resources, we saved money, we didn't buy things so we had money to buy houses.

"Q. Let me ask this: Was it your understanding that you were going to stay home and cook for the time that you lived together as long as you didn't work, and Mr. Alderson was going to go out and earn the money?

"A. There was no such understanding. If I had a job, I worked and we—it was our money. If I didn't have a job, I had children to take care of.

"Q. Let me explain what I am driving at. In every contract the parties have some understanding as to what each are going to do. If I hire someone to paint my house, my understanding is that he is going to paint the house and his understanding is that I pay him, say, a thousand dollars. And I am asking you whether you had an understanding that you were supposed to do certain things, or were expected to do certain things and if you don't do those things, then this would be an extreme disappointment by Mr. Alderson. That's what I am trying—driving at. If you had not cooked and refused to cook at all times, would your living arrangement have continued?

"A. Yes, I mean it would—if I had a broken arm and couldn't cook, I wouldn't expect him to leave me.

"Q. Would you expect him to give you half of everything—

"A. Yes, there were many things, if you took one specific thing away; there was so many other things that we both did, one wouldn't make any difference, or two or three.

"Q. All right. You told me that you had a contract with Mr. Alderson, is that correct, or did you have a contract?

"A. I don't know what you mean by contract, an agreement written on paper?

"Q. No.

"A. Verbal contract?

"Q. Yes.

"A. We were living together. We were living—I mean we were married and anything any other married couples do, we were just the same. We had higher expectations than some because we wanted property; we wanted investments; we wanted things for the future for the kids.

"Q. Let me ask this: As far as your understanding went you were going to be getting half of everything Mr. Alderson earned, is that correct?

"A. It was ours. There was no—I mean, if I left the house there was no talk of my leaving as far as me getting half and him getting half, was both of ours. If something happened to him it was all mine, if something happened to me, it was all his. . . .

"Q. Let me ask about the—about the role of a wife. As you performed your duty in the house, did that include being the cook for the family, the housekeeper, the companion established that the implied agreement between Jonne and Steve was very generous. The parties never bothered to actually spell out the terms of their agreement or the consideration therefor. Jonne testified that her part of the consideration was to be Steve's wife and to do "whatever a wife does." However, she also said, "if you took one specific thing away, there [were] so many other things that we both did, one wouldn't make any difference, or two or three."

Such an agreement can hardly be deemed the type disapproved in *Marvin*. A contract based on "many ... things", no one of which is in itself crucial, is not the same as one based upon a consideration of meretricious sexual services. Before a nonmarital contract is to be deemed unenforceable under *Marvin*, it must be found to explicitly rest upon a consideration of meretricious sexual services and even then the contract will fail "only to the extent" that it does so. Here, there is no evidence that the agreement between Jonne and Steve, or any part thereof, explicitly rests upon such a consideration.

Nor does the fact that the couple engaged in sexual relations and that Jonne perceived this as part of her "role" alter this conclusion. As the *Marvin* court pointed out, the fact that a man and woman live together without marriage, and engage in a sexual relationship does not in itself invalidate agreements between them relating to their earnings, property or expenses.... In today's society when so many couples are living together without the benefit of marriage vows, it would be illogical to deny them the ability to enter into enforceable agreements in respect to their property rights. ...

IV

At trial, Jonne admitted signing the quitclaim deeds around the time she left Steve in December 1979. She said she signed them because Steve told her he "would see me dead before I got any of [the properties]." She said she feared for her own physical safety and so she "just signed them to get out."

Evidence that tended to corroborate her claim of duress included testimony to the effect that Steve had been violent during the time the couple lived together. ...

Clare Dalton, An Essay In The Deconstruction of Contract Doctrine

94 Yale L. J. 997 (April, 1985).

. . .

The Cases

State courts have increasingly confronted cases involving various aspects of the cohabitation relationship, and their decisions have attracted a

of Mr. Alderson, the lover of Mr. Alderson and mother of the children?

"A. Yes.

"Q. Were all of those essential parts of being a wife, as you understood them?

"A. Yes."

fair amount of scholarly attention. I focus on two such decisions: that of the California Supreme Court in *Marvin v. Marvin* and that of the Illinois Supreme Court in *Hewitt v. Hewitt*.

In *Marvin*, Justice Tobriner addressed the question of whether plaintiff Michelle Triola, who had lived with the defendant, Lee Marvin, for seven years, could recover support payments and half the property acquired in Lee Marvin's name over the course of the relationship. The court found that the plaintiff, in alleging an oral contract, had stated a cause of action in express contract, and further found that additional equitable theories of recovery might be applicable. On remand, the trial court found that there existed neither an express contract nor unjust enrichment, but awarded the plaintiff equitable relief in the nature of rehabilitative alimony. The court of appeals then struck this award on the theory that relief could be granted only on the basis of express contract or quasi-contract.

The alleged oral agreement provided that plaintiff and defendant would, while they lived together, combine their efforts and earnings and share equally any property accumulated. They agreed to present themselves publicly as husband and wife. Triola also undertook to serve as the defendant's companion, homemaker, housekeeper, and cook. A later alleged modification to the contract provided that Triola would give up her own career in order to provide these services; in return, Marvin promised to support Triola for the rest of her life. The relationship ended when Marvin threw Triola out.

The plaintiff in *Hewitt* was in many respects a more sympathetic figure than Michele Triola. When she and Mr. Hewitt were both college students, she became pregnant. He then proposed that they live together as man and wife, presenting themselves as such to their families and friends, and that he thereafter share his life, future earnings, and property with her. She borrowed money from her family to put him through professional school, worked with him to establish his practice, bore him three children and raised them, and otherwise fulfilled the role of a traditional wife. After over fifteen years he left her. She sought an equal division of property acquired during the relationship and held either in joint tenancy or in the defendant's name.

The appeals court ruled that she could have an equitable share of the property if she were able to prove her allegation of an express oral contract, although it did not preclude the possibility of alternative equitable theories of recovery in appropriate circumstances. The Supreme Court of Illinois reversed, basing its decision principally on considerations of public policy.

Express and Implied Agreement

The opinions in the cohabitation cases indicate that the distinction between the intention-based express contract and the public institution of quasi-contract may be central to the question of whether to grant relief. As I have earlier argued, however, techniques for interpreting the express contract are indistinguishable from techniques used to determine the presence of a quasi-contractual relationship. If the interpretive techniques employed highlight factors external to the parties and their actual intentions, even express contracts seem very public. If, in contrast, the techniques used have as their stated goal the determination of the parties' intentions, then quasi-contracts appear no less private or consensual than express contracts. The cohabitation opinions employ both public-sounding and private-sounding arguments to reach a variety of conclusions. In some cases courts determine that the parties are bound by *both* real and quasi-contract obligations, in others that they are bound by neither, in yet others that they are bound by one but not the other. The arguments do not determine these outcomes—they only legitimate them.

In these cases, as in the earlier-discussed *Hertzog* [v. Hertzog, 29 Pa. 465 (1857)], there is a common presumption that agreements between intimates are not contractual. While this model of association was developed in husband-wife and parent-child cases, non-marital cohabitations are assumed, for these purposes, to have the same kind of relationship. As in *Hertzog*, express words are taken to be words of commitment but not of contract; conduct that in other circumstances would give rise to an implied-in-fact contract is instead attributed to the relationship. These cases also reach a conclusion only intimated in *Hertzog*: They find no unjust enrichment where one party benefits the other.

One possible explanation for this presumption against finding contracts is that it accords with the parties' intentions. It can be argued that cohabitants generally neither want their agreements to have legal consequences, nor desire to be obligated to one another when they have stopped cohabitating. It can further be presented as a matter of fact that their services are freely given and taken within the context of an intimate relationship. If this is so, then a subsequent claim of unjust enrichment is simply unfounded.

This intention-based explanation, however, coexists in the opinions—indeed sometimes coexists within a single opinion—with two other, more overtly public, explanations that rest on diametrically opposed public policies. The first suggests that the arena of intimate relationships is too private for court intervention through contract enforcement to be appropriate. In *Hewitt*, for example, the Illinois Supreme Count suggests that "the situation alleged here was not the kind of arm's length bargain envisioned by traditional contract principles, but an intimate arrangement of a fundamentally different kind."

While it has some intuitive appeal, the argument that intimate relationships are too private for court enforcement is at odds with the more general argument that all contractual relationships are private and that contract enforcement merely facilitates the private relationship described by contract. To overcome this apparent inconsistency, we must imagine a scale of privateness on which business arrangements, while mostly private, are still not as private as intimate arrangements. But then the rescue attempt runs headlong into the other prevailing policy argument, which separates out intimate arrangements because of their peculiarly public and regulated status. Under this view, it is the business relationship that by and large remains more quintessentially private.

According to this second argument, the area of non-marital agreements is too public for judicial intervention. The legislature is the appropriate body to regulate such arrangements; courts may not help create private alternatives to the public scheme. In *Hewitt*, the supreme court directly follows its appeal to the intimate nature of the relationship with an acknowledgement of the regulated, and hence public, character of marriage-like relations. With respect to intimate relations conceived as public, the judiciary can then present itself as either passive or active. The argument for passivity is that judges should "stay out" of an arena already covered by public law. The argument for activity is that judges should reinforce public policy by deterring the formation of deviant relationships, either because they fall outside the legislative schemes organizing familial entitlements and property distribution, or because they offend public morality.

Neither the private nor the public arguments for the absence of contract in this setting are conclusive. Both private and public counterarguments are readily available. If the absence of contract is presented as flowing from party intention, competing interpretations of intention can be used to argue the presence of contract. If, within a more public framework, the court categorizes the concerns implicated by the relationship as private, then an argument can be made that within the boundaries expressly established by legislation, the parties should be free to vary the terms of their relationship without interference by the state. If the focus is the place of cohabitation agreements within the publicly-regulated sphere of intimate relationships, then an argument can be made that certain kinds of enforcement in fact extend and implement public policy rather then derogate from it.

Judges' differing interpretations of virtually identical agreements seem to depend quite openly on either their views of what policy should prevail or their own moral sense. Rarely does a judge even appear to make a thorough attempt to understand what the parties had in mind. For Justice Underwood in *Hewitt*, for example, nothing but "naivete" could explain the assertion that there are involved in these relationships contracts separate and independent from the sexual activity, and the assumption that those contracts would have been entered into or would continue without that activity.

Justice Tobriner in *Marvin*, on the other hand, rejects the idea that the sexual relationship between parties to a cohabitation contract renders the contract as a whole invalid. He explicitly uses the divide between objective and subjective, form and substance, to carve out a much larger space for enforceable agreements than that envisaged by Underwood. Tobriner's test has two components: Contracts between non-marital partners are enforceable unless they *explicitly* rest "upon the immoral and illicit consideration of meretricious sexual services." Furthermore, such contracts are unenforceable only *"to the extent"* that they rest on this meretricious consideration.

Tobriner is not so naive as to suppose that the Triola–Marvin agreement did not contemplate a sexual relationship. But he feels that the "subjective contemplation of the parties" is too "uncertain and unworkable" a standard. He relies instead on formal criteria of intent—on the manifestations of agreement alleged by Triola—to determine if his two-part test of enforceability has been met. For the purposes of this analysis Tobriner describes the agreement as follows: "[T]he parties agreed to pool their earnings, . . . they contracted to share equally in all property acquired, and . . . defendant agreed to support plaintiff." None of this strikes Tobriner as necessitating a conclusion that sex invalidates the agreement.

Of course the formal criteria are themselves empty of significance until given meaning by judicial analysis. The very same language construed by Tobriner had been given very different effect in an earlier decision. In *Updeck v. Samuel*, a California District Court of Appeal considered the statement that the woman would make a permanent home for the man and be his companion as indicating precisely the sexual character of the relationship. Unwilling or unable to disapprove *Updeck*, Tobriner is forced to distinguish this case in a fashion that directly undercuts the legitimacy of his stated reliance on form or manifestation. He argues that the *Updeck* agreement was found invalid because the court "[v]iew[ed] the contract as calling for adultery." But the very act of "viewing" the contract, or interpreting its terms, involves an explanation of substance. The court in *Updeck* supplied sexual substance, while Tobriner supplies economic substance. *Jones v. Daly*, a case subsequent to *Marvin*, provides another striking illustration of the manipulability of form. In *Jones*, which involved a homosexual partnership, a California Court of Appeal denied relief on the ground that an agreement, in other respects almost identical to the *Marvin* agreement, contained the word "lover."

[As]   the courts wrestle with these interpretive questions, we see them apparently infusing a public element, external to the parties' own view of their situation, into their assessment of cohabitation agreements. We also can see how this is a necessary result of the tension between manifestation and intent, of the way in which intent requires embodiment in manifested forms, even while the forms require an infusion of substance before they can yield meaning. Indeed, to accuse judges of moving from the private to the public sphere is only to accuse them of the inevitable. If there is force behind the accusation, it is not *that* they have made the transition from private to public, but that they have made the transition *unselfconsciously*, and that the particular values, norms, and understandings they incorporate are different from the ones we would have favored, or different from the ones we think would correspond with those of one or both of the parties to the agreement.

Consideration: Its Substance

Consideration doctrine offers yet other opportunities for the conflation of public and private, and the introduction of competing values, norms, and understandings into the resolution of these cohabitation cases. Just as in the area of interpretation, the crucial additions are judicial conceptions of sexuality, and of woman's role in her relationship with man. Two aspects of consideration doctrine recur in the cases. Each illustrates the proposition that formal consideration doctrine cannot be implemented without recourse to substance. Substance, here as elsewhere, can be provided by assessments of objective value or by investigations into subjective intent. It is with respect to these substantive inquiries that ideas about sexuality and relationship come to play so potentially important a part.

The first use of consideration doctrine in this context shows up in the disinclination of courts to enforce contracts based on "meretricious" consideration. Courts frequently search beyond the express language of the agreement in order to "find" that sex is at the heart of the deal—specifically that the woman is providing sexual services in return for the economic security promised by the man. Insofar as this investigation depends on divining what the parties had in mind, consideration turns on subjective intent. For these purposes, it matters not at all that "intent" has been derived from the judge's own feelings about such relationships, even when the express language of the parties would appear to point in an opposite direction.

The treatment of meretricious consideration also illustrates how consideration may depend on a finding of objective value. When courts refuse to enforce contracts based on the exchange of sexual services for money, they are, for longstanding policy reasons, declining to recognize sexual services as having the *kind* of value that they will honor. This decision, based on an objective measure of value, is no different from the decision that "nominal" consideration will not support a contract. There, too, courts disregard intention in the name of a policy that depends upon societal recognition of certain sorts of values and delegitimation of others.

The second aspect of consideration doctrine of interest in this context is the traditional conclusion that the woman's domestic services cannot provide consideration for the promises made to her by the man. This is usually linked to the idea that the relationship itself is not one the parties see as having a legal aspect. The standard explanation is that the woman did not act in expectation of gain, but rather out off affection, or that she intended her action as a gift.

Tobriner in the *Marvin* decision rejects this conclusion by recasting the issue as one properly belonging in the selfish world of business. Unless homemaking services are considered lawful and adequate consideration for a promise to pay wages, the entire domestic service industry will founder. Just as plainly, such services can provide the consideration for an agreement concerning property distribution. Tobriner thus appeals to the substance of objective value: There is a market in which domestic services receive a price; when intimates arrange that one will deliver those same services to the other, that promise is therefore capable of supporting a return promise.

Even as Tobriner uses ideas of objective value, however, his reasoning reveals that the ultimate rationale for this aspect of consideration doctrine depends upon arguments of subjective intent. Like the promise in the *Michigan* case [Wisconsin and Mich. Ry. Co. v. Powers, 191 U.S. 379 (1903)], the services could constitute consideration if they were offered with the intention of bargain or exchange. It is only the altruistic context, revealing the beneficent intention, which invalidates them.

Thus, while one route of access into this issue threatens to expose the public determination of what values the law will and will not recognize, that route is apparently closed off by the reminder that it is private intention, not public power, that assigns value. But then the very public role abjured in the context of objective value is placed out instead through the "finding" of intent according to criteria that are essentially and inevitably public rather than private.

The Question of Power

Under duress and unconscionability doctrines, policing the "fair" exchange is tied irretrievably to asking whether each party entered into the contract freely, whether each was able to bargain in equally unconstrained ways, and whether the deal was a fair one. I suppose that any of us would find these questions even harder to answer in the context of intimate relationships than in other contexts—harder in that we would require a much more detailed account of the particulars before we could hazard an opinion, and harder in that even this wealth of detail would be likely to yield contradictory interpretations. Yet we acknowledge the importance of these questions in the area of intimate relations; we do not imagine either that most couples wind up with a fair exchange, or that most couples have equal bargaining power vis-a-vis one another.

The doctrinal treatment of cohabitation agreements, however, like the treatment of contracts in general, usually pays little attention to questions of power and fairness. Duress and unconscionability are the exceptions that prove the rule. Those doctrines identify the only recognized deviations from the supposedly standard case of equal contracting partners. Intimate partners are conceived of as fitting the standard model. One consequence of this conception is that courts can justify the failure to enforce cohabitation arrangements as mere nonintervention, overlooking the fact that the superior position in which nonaction tends to leave the male partner is at least in part a product of the legal system. Another is that courts can idealize the private world in which their "nonintervention" leaves the parties, disregarding the ways in which that world is characterized by inequality and the exercise of private power. Yet another is that courts can talk blithely about the intentions of "the parties" in a fashion that ignores the possibility that one party's intentions are being respected at the expense of the other's.

Not all of the cohabitation contract opinions ignore the issues of fairness and power. They are more likely to receive explicit attention when a judge frankly invokes "public policy" instead of relying exclusively on contract doctrine. They appear, for example, when the Illinois appeals court in *Hewitt* explains why enforcement of such agreements promotes rather than undermines the institution of marriage. When a judge casts his opinion in traditional doctrinal terms, using intention, for example, or consideration, then any sensitivity he has to questions of power and fairness must be translated—translated, for example, into a willingness to assume that the parties did intend to enter a relationship of reciprocal obligation or that the woman has provided services that require compensation. Frequently this involves construing the male partner's intentions *as if* he were the concerned and equal partner the law assumes him to be. Again, these devices parallel those used by courts across the range of contract decisions. But only when judges move outside the framework of traditional contract doctrine will they be in a position to grapple with the full range of problems posed by these disputes.

There are several ways to begin a richer examination of the cohabitation cases. First, we can learn from the truths underlying contract doctrine while rejecting the idea that doctrine alone can lead us to correct answers. The dichotomies of public and private, manifestation and intent, form and substance, do touch on troubling questions that are central to our understanding of intimate relationships and the role of the state in undermining or supporting them. The problem with doctrinal rhetoric is twofold. First, it recasts our concerns in a way that distances us from our lived experience of them. Second, the resolution of the cases that the application of doctrine purports to secure offers us a false assurance that our concerns can be met—that public can be reconciled with private, manifestation with intent, form with substance.

Once we realize that doctrinal "resolutions" are achieved only by sleight of hand, consideration of the identified dichotomies helps us to explore more fully the cohabitation agreement. What is the nature of this relationship, or what range of cohabitation arrangements precludes us from making general statements about the nature of the relationship? To what extent do these relationships need protection from authority, and to what extent do they require nurturing by authority? To what extent do they reflect the shared expectations of their participants, and to what extent the imposition of terms by one party on another? How can we harbor intimacy within institutions that offer the flexibility to accommodate individual need, while at the same time providing a measure of predictability and stability? What stake does the society have in limiting the forms of association it will recognize? Given our dependence on our social and cultural context, what freedom does any of us have to reimagine the terms of human association?

Study of the play between public and private, objective and subjective, shows us that these same dichotomies organize not only the strictly doctrinal territory of contract interpretation or consideration, but also the broader "policy" issues that are folded into the cases. Questions of judicial competence, for example, turn out to involve precisely the question of whether a private sphere can be marked off from the public sphere.

Similarly, whether enforcement of cohabitation agreements is a pro-mar-
riage or an anti-marriage position turns out to depend on questions of
intention and power. Even as this analysis illuminates the policy dimension
of the cases, it refutes the claim that the addition of policy considerations
can cure doctrinal indeterminacy.

If neither doctrine nor the addition of policy can determine how
decision-makers choose outcomes in particular cases, the next question is
whether the opinions contain other material that illuminates the decision-
making process. The dimension of these cohabitation cases that cries out
for investigation is the images they contain of women, and of relationship.
And since images of women and of relationship are the central concern of
feminist theory, I have used that theory as the basis for my inquiry. This
does not, of course, foreclose the possibility that other inquiries, in this or
other settings, might prove equally possible and promising once doctrine is
opened up to make room for them.

I am not claiming that judges decide cohabitation cases on the basis of
deeply held notions about women and relationship in the sense that these
notions provide a determinate basis for decision. For this to be true,
attitudes toward women and relationship would have to be free from
contradiction in a way that doctrine and policy are not. I believe instead
that these notions involve the same perceived divide between self and other
that characterizes doctrine, and are as internally contradictory as any
doctrine studied in this article. My claim, therefore, is only that notions of
women and relationship are another source of influence, and are therefore
as deserving of attention as any other dimension of the opinions. These
notions influence how judges frame rule-talk and policy-talk; in a world of
indeterminacy they provide one more set of variables that may persuade a
judge to decide a case one way or another, albeit in ways we cannot predict
with any certainty.

One introductory caveat is in order. To say that "the opinions" convey
images of woman and relationship is to miss the distinction between images
that appear to inhere in the doctrine as it has developed, and images woven
into the texture of opinions seemingly at the initiative of a particular judge.
I think this distinction is worth noting, even though in practice it cannot
always be made. It becomes clearest, perhaps, when a judge struggles
against images he sees embedded in the doctrine, and offers new images
that in turn provide him with new doctrinal choices.

One powerful pair of contradictory images of woman paints the female
cohabitant as either an angel or a whore. As angel, she ministers to her
male partner out of noble emotions of love and self-sacrifice, with no
thought of personal gain. It would demean both their services and the spirit
in which they were offered to imagine that she expected a return—it would
make her a servant. As whore, she lures the man into extravagant promises
with the bait of her sexuality—and is appropriately punished for her
immorality when the court declines to hold her partner to his agreement.

Although the image of the whore is of a woman who at one level is
seeking to satiate her own lust, sex—in these cases—is traditionally pre-

sented as something women give to men. This is consistent both with the view of woman as angel, and with the different image of the whore as someone who trades sex for money. In either event, woman is a provider, not a partner in enjoyment. When a judge invokes this image, he supports the view that sex contaminates the entire agreement, and that the desire for sex is the only reason for the male partner's promises of economic support. If sex were viewed as a mutually satisfying element of the arrangement, it could be readily separated out from the rest of the agreement. In most cases, the woman's career sacrifices and childrearing and homemaking responsibilities would then provide the consideration for the economic support proffered by the man.

Marriage is often presented in the cases as the only way in which men and women can express a continuing commitment to one another. This suggests that when men do not marry women, they intend to avoid all responsibility for them. Women therefore bear the burden of protecting themselves by declining the irregular relationship. At the same time, the institution of marriage as an expression of caring is portrayed as so fragile that only the most unwavering support by the state will guarantee its survival. This could mean that other expressions of caring would entirely supplant marriage without vigilant enforcement of the socially endorsed forms of relationship, although that would be inconsistent with the portrayal of marriage as the only expression of commitment. Alternatively, it could mean that men and women would not choose to enter relationships of caring without pressure from the state.

These nightmarish images have much in common with what other disciplines tell us men think about women and relationship. The conception of women as either angels or whores is identified by Freud, and supported by feminist accounts. The evil power of female sexuality is a recurrent subject of myth and history. The contrast of men fearing relationship as entrapping, and women fearing isolation, is the subject of Carol Gilligan's work in the psychology of moral development; others have explored the origins of that difference in the context of psychoanalytic theory. Raising these images to the level of consciousness and inquiry therefore seems to me an important aspect of understanding this particular set of cases. It is also a way of stepping beyond the confines of current doctrine and beginning to think about other ways of handling the reciprocal claims cohabitants may make of one another.

B.   Domestic Partnership

Chapter 2.119 Domestic Partnerships

Municipal Code of the City of Cambridge, MA

2.119.010 Recognition and scope.

A.   The City Council recognizes the diverse composition of its citizenry and values its people. The City Council acknowledges that the people's lives have evolved from when laws governing family relationships were enacted.

Perpetuation of the traditional definitions of "family" excludes a significant segment of the Cambridge population, deprives them of recognition and validation, and denies certain rights that should be afforded to persons who share their homes, their hearts and their lives. The City, recognizing its commitment to nondiscrimination and fair treatment of its citizens and employees, adopts this chapter acknowledging domestic partnerships.

B.   The chapter allows persons in committed relationships who meet the criteria established by the City as constituting domestic partnerships to register at the office of the City Clerk and obtain a certificate attesting to their status. The chapter recognizes certain rights of access for domestic partners. This chapter, in conformance with the Human Rights Ordinance, which bars discrimination on the basis of sexual orientation, marital status and family status, also equalizes the treatment of City employees. (Ord. 1144 (part), 1992).

2.119.020 Definitions.

As used in this chapter:

A.   "Competent to contract" means eighteen years of age or older, and mentally competent to contract.

B.   "Dependent" means a minor who lives within the household of a domestic partnership and is:

1.   A biological child or adopted child, or foster child of a domestic partner, if the child is not provided with medical insurance coverage by the Commonwealth;

2.   A dependent as defined under IRS regulations; or

3.   A ward of a domestic partner as determined in a guardianship proceeding.

C.   "Domestic partner" means a person who meets the criteria set out in subsection D of this section or who is registered as such in another jurisdiction.

D.   "Domestic partnership" means the entity formed by two persons who meet the following criteria and jointly file a registration statement proclaiming that:

1.   They are in a relationship of mutual support, caring and commitment and intend to remain in such a relationship; and

2.   They reside together; and

3.   They are not married; and

4.   They are not related by blood closer than would bar marriage in the Commonwealth of Massachusetts; and

5.   They are each other's sole domestic partner; and

6.   They are competent to contract; and

7.   They consider themselves to be a family.

E. Subsequent to the filing of a registration form, the existence of a "family" relationship may be shown by evidence relevant to the following factors:

1. The manner in which the people live their daily lives;

2. How they hold their relationship out to the world;

3. Their emotional and financial commitment;

4. Their reliance on each other for daily family services;

5. The longevity and exclusivity of their relationship; and

6. Any other factors which may be relevant.

F. "Mutual support" means that the domestic partners each contributed in some fashion, not necessarily equally or financially, to the maintenance and support of the domestic partnership.

G. "Reside together" means living together in a common household. A partner may be temporarily absent from the common household, so long as she or he has the intent to return. A partner may own or maintain an additional residence. (Ord. 1144 (part), 1992).

2.119.030 Registration and termination.

A. Persons who meet the criteria set out in subsection D of Section 2.119.020 may make an official record of their domestic partnership by filing a domestic partnership registration form with the City Clerk. The domestic partnership registration shall include the name and date of birth of each of the domestic partners, the address of their common household, and the name and dates of birth of any dependents of the domestic partnership, and shall be signed, under the pains and penalties of perjury, by both domestic partners.

B. Domestic partners may amend the domestic partnership registration to add or delete dependents or change the household address. Amendments to the domestic partnership registration shall be signed, under the pains and penalties of perjury, by both domestic partners.

C. A domestic partnership is terminated by the death of a domestic partner or by the filing of a termination statement by a domestic partner.

1. The death of a domestic partner automatically terminates a domestic partnership.

2. A domestic partnership may be terminated by a domestic partner who files with the City Clerk, by hand or by certified mail, a termination statement. The person filing the termination statement must declare under pains and penalties of perjury that the domestic partnership is terminated and that a copy of the termination statement has been mailed by certified mail to the other domestic partner at his or her last known address. The person filing the termination statement must include on such statement the address to which the copy was mailed.

D. The termination of a domestic partnership shall be effective immediately upon the death of a domestic partner. The voluntary termination of a domestic partnership by a partner shall be effective seven days after the receipt of a termination statement by the City Clerk. Prior to becoming effective, the person who filed the termination statement may withdraw the termination statement in person at the office of the City Clerk. If the termination statement is withdrawn, the domestic partner shall give notice of the withdrawal, by certified mail, to the other domestic partner.

E. If a domestic partnership is terminated by the death of a domestic partner, there shall be no required waiting period prior to filing another domestic partnership. If a domestic partnership is terminated by one or both domestic partners, neither domestic partner may file another domestic partnership until six months have elapsed from termination. (Ord. 1144 (part), 1992).

2.119.040 City Clerk—Fees.

A. The City Clerk shall collect a reasonable fee for filing a domestic partnership registration. The initial amount for this fee shall be fifteen dollars and it shall be adjusted as necessary to remain consistent with the fee for an application for a marriage license.

B. The City Clerk shall collect a fee of five dollars for certified copies of domestic partnership documents, other than the copy of the certificate of domestic partnership issued by the City Clerk to the domestic partners, as provided for in section 2.119.050. (Ord. 1144 (part), 1992).

2.119.050 City Clerk—Records.

A. Upon receipt of a domestic partnership registration and filing fee, the City Clerk shall issue a certificate of domestic partnership and shall mail to the household of the domestic partnership one certified copy of the certificate and two wallet-sized cards indicating the existence of the domestic partnership, the names of the domestic partners and the names of the dependents of the domestic partnership, if any.

B. The City Clerk shall maintain records of domestic partnerships registered in the city, including forms filed and certificates issued. The City Clerk shall provide forms to persons requesting them in accordance with section 2.119.120.

C. The City Clerk shall allow public access to domestic partnership records to the same extent and in the same manner as marriage licenses. (Ord. 1144 (part), 1992).

2.119.060 Rights of Domestic Partners.

Persons who have registered their domestic partnership at the office of the City Clerk pursuant to section 2.119.030 are entitled to the following rights:

A. A domestic partner shall have the same visitation rights as a spouse or parent of a patient at the Cambridge City Hospital and all other health care facilities in the city. A dependent shall have the same visitation rights as a patient's child.

2.   The term "health care facilities" includes, but is not limited to, hospitals, convalescent facilities, mental health care facilities, and other short- and long-term care facilities under the City's jurisdiction.

B.   A domestic partner shall have the same visitation rights at all correctional facilities in Cambridge as a spouse or parent of a person in custody. A dependent shall have the same visitation rights afforded to the child of a person in custody.

2.   The term "correctional facilities" includes, but is not limited to, holding cells, jails and juvenile correction centers under the City's jurisdiction.

C.   A domestic partner, who is also the parent or legal guardian of a child, may file a form at or send a letter to the child's school to indicate that the parent's domestic partner shall have access to the child's records, access to school personnel in matters concerning the child, and access to the child, including the right to remove such child from the school for sickness or family emergency. The school shall afford such person access as directed by the child's parent.

2.   When a domestic partnership is terminated pursuant to Section 2.119.030, it is the responsibility of the parent or guardian to notify the school, in writing, of the termination of rights of the former domestic partner.

3.   The term "school" includes, but is not limited to, high schools, vocational schools, junior high and middle schools, elementary schools, preschool programs, after-school programs and day care programs. (Ord. 1144 (part), 1992).

2.119.070 Employment benefits.

A.   The city and school department shall provide the same health and other employment fringe benefits to employees with domestic partners as to employees with spouses. As used in this chapter, "employees" refers to active and retired employees of the City and the Cambridge School Department eligible for benefits pursuant to state or municipal law, employment policies or collective bargaining agreements.

B.   Employees must file a declaration of domestic partnership, signed under the pains and penalties of perjury, with their department administrator or department of personnel of the City or School Department, as appropriate, in order to obtain benefits under this chapter. On such declaration, employees shall agree to promptly notify the City or School Department, as appropriate, of any change in the status of their domestic partnership. There shall be no fee for such declaration. Employees shall not be obligated to file a domestic partnership registration form with the City Clerk.

C.   The City and School Department shall provide medical insurance coverage to an employee's domestic partner as it does to an employee's spouse, and to the dependent(s) of an employee's domestic partnership as it does to an employee's child(ren). An employee may opt to decline medical insurance coverage for her or his domestic partner, without foregoing the right to obtain medical insurance coverage for her or his domestic partner at a later date.

D.   Upon termination of a domestic partnership by an employee, the domestic partner shall be covered by medical insurance for a period of sixty days following the termination of the domestic partnership. If the employee leaves employment with the City or School Department prior to the expiration of the sixty days, the medical insurance shall lapse on the date that the former employee's insurance lapses.

E.   Upon termination of a domestic partnership by the death of an employee, the surviving domestic partner's medical insurance coverage shall lapse as it would for the spouse of a married employee, upon the death of such employee.

F.   Employees shall be granted a leave of absence, with pay, for the death of a domestic partner or family member of a domestic partner to the same extent as for a spouse or family member of a spouse. Use of the term "in-law" in employee handbooks shall include the relatives of a domestic partner.

G.   Employees shall be granted sick leave to care for a domestic partner to the same extent permitted to care for a spouse, and to care for a dependent of a domestic partnership to the same extent permitted to care for a child.

H.   Employees shall be entitled to take parental leave to take care of a child born to their domestic partner or a newly adopted child to the same extent as a married person. (Ord. 1144 (part), 1992).

2.119.080 Limitation of liabilities.

A.   Nothing in this chapter shall be interpreted to contravene the general laws of the Commonwealth.

B.   Nothing contained in this chapter shall be construed to impose liability upon a domestic partner for the health or medical expenses of his or her domestic partner, with the sole exception of the medical insurance contributions assumed by a City or School Department employee who is a member of a domestic partnership.

C.   Nothing in this chapter shall be construed to create additional legal liabilities greater than those already existing under law or to create new private causes of action. (Ord. 1144 (part), 1992).

2.119.090 Reciprocity.

All rights, privileges and benefits extended to domestic partnerships registered pursuant to this chapter shall also be extended to domestic partnerships registered pursuant to similar laws in other jurisdictions. (Ord. 1144 (part), 1992).

2.119.100 Retaliation.

No person shall discriminate or retaliate against a person who seeks the benefit of this chapter, registers or makes a declaration pursuant to its provisions, or assists another person in obtaining the benefits of this chapter. Any person who so discriminates or retaliates shall be penalized in accordance with the provisions of the Cambridge Human Rights Ordinance, Cambridge Code Chapter 2.76. (Ord. 1144 (part), 1992).

2.119.110 Severability.

The provisions of this chapter are severable. If any of its provisions are held invalid by a court of competent jurisdiction, all other provisions shall continue in full force and effect. (Ord. 1144 (part), 1992).

2.119.120 Forms.

A.   The City Clerk shall distribute copies of the following forms to those persons who request them:

1.   Domestic partnership registration;

2.   Domestic partnership information sheet;

3.   Termination of domestic partnership;

4.   School authorization form.

B.   The Department of Personnel shall distribute copies of the following forms to those persons who request them:

1.   Declaration of domestic partnership;

2.   Amendment to declaration of domestic partnership.

C.   The School Department shall distribute copies of the following forms to persons who request them:

1.   School authorization form;

2.   Revocation of school authorization form.

D.   The City Clerk, the Department of Personnel, School Department and all other affected City agencies, offices and departments shall provide and distribute any other relevant forms that are or become necessary. (Ord. 1144 (part), 1992).

2.119.130 Effect on other sections of code.

When the term "spouse" is used in other City ordinances, it shall be interpreted to include a domestic partner. When the term "family" is used in other City ordinances, it shall be interpreted to include domestic partnerships. (Ord. 1144 (part), 1992).

City of Atlanta v. Morgan

Supreme Court of Georgia, 1997.
268 Ga. 586, 492 S.E.2d 193.

CAROL HUNSTEIN, JUSTICE.

This is an appeal from an order of the Fulton County Superior Court declaring the City of Atlanta's 1996 Domestic Partnership Benefits Ordinance unconstitutional under the Georgia Constitution Art. III, Sec. VI, Par. IV(a) and (c), and the Municipal Home Rule Act of 1965, OCGA Sec. 36–35–1 et seq., as a special law enacted in an area for which provision has been made by an existing general law. Because we find that the benefits ordinance is consistent with State law, we reverse.

On September 3, 1996 the Atlanta City Council passed Ordinance 96–O–1018 which provides certain insurance benefits for dependents of City of Atlanta employees who qualify and are registered as domestic partners under Sec. 94–131 et seq. of the Atlanta City Code, the City's domestic partner registry ordinance. This benefits ordinance was enacted in response to our opinion in City of Atlanta v. McKinney, 265 Ga. 161(2), 454 S.E.2d 517 (1995), in which we upheld the constitutionality of the registry in Sec. 94–131 but held unconstitutional the City's original benefits ordinance (Ordinance 93–O–1057) because in it the City had recognized domestic partnerships as "a family relationship" and provided employee benefits to domestic partners "in a comparable manner . . . as for a domestic spouse," thereby expanding the definition of "dependent" in a manner inconsistent with State law and in violation of both the Georgia Constitution and OCGA Sec. 36–35–6(b). *McKinney*, supra at (1) and (2). The issue in *McKinney*, as in this appeal, was whether the City acted within its authority to provide benefits to its employees and their dependents by defining "dependent" consistent with State law. Id. at (2).

OCGA Sec. 36–35–4(a) authorizes a municipality to provide insurance benefits to its employees and their dependents. Although this section of the Municipal Home Rule Act grants specific authority to provide such benefits to the dependents of a municipal employee, it does not provide a definition of the term "dependent." In order to determine whether the definition provided in the City's benefits ordinance is consistent with State law, we must, therefore, look to the ordinary meaning of the term as well as the way in which it is defined in other statutes. See generally OCGA Sec. 1–3–1(b); Fisch v. Randall Mill Corp., 262 Ga. 861(1), 426 S.E.2d 883 (1993); Risser v. City of Thomasville, 248 Ga. 866, 286 S.E.2d 727 (1982); see also *McKinney*, supra at 164(2), 454 S.E.2d 517.

The City's benefits ordinance defines a "dependent" as "one who relies on another for financial support" and provides that an employee's domestic partner shall be dependent if:

(i) The employee makes contributions to the domestic partner of cash and supplies, and the domestic partner relies upon and uses those contributions to support himself/herself in order to maintain his or her standard of living. The contributions may be at irregular intervals and of irregular amounts, but must have existed for at least six months, and must be continuing.

(ii) The employee is obligated, based upon his/her commitment set forth in the Declaration of Domestic Partnership, to continue the financial support of the domestic partner for so long as the domestic partnership shall be in effect.

(iii) The domestic partner is supported, in whole or in part, by the employee's earnings, and has been for at least the last six months.

Ordinance 96–O–1018 (a)(1)(B).

Based on our review of other definitions of "dependent" in Georgia case law, we conclude that the ordinance definition of "dependent" is consistent with both the common, ordinary meaning of the term "dependent" and the definition attributed to that term as it is used in the Georgia statutes. In Smith v. Smith, 254 Ga. 450, 451, 330 S.E.2d 706 (1985), this Court looked to Funk and Wagnalls Standard Dictionary to define "dependent" for purposes of the Georgia Long–Arm Statute, OCGA Sec. 9–10–91(5). Funk and Wagnalls defines "dependent" as "[r]elying on someone or something for support." See also Webster's Third New International Dictionary, p. 604 (1967) ("dependent" is "one relying on another for support"); The American Heritage Dictionary of the English Language, 3d ed., p. 501 (1992) ("dependent" is "[o]ne who relies on another especially for financial support"). The same definition was recognized by this Court in *McKinney* as one definition of the term "dependent" found in Georgia statutes specifically providing a definition of that term. See *McKinney*, supra at 164(2), 454 S.E.2d 517 (identifying State statutes which define the term "dependent" as "a spouse, child, or one who relies on another for financial support"). This definition is also consistent with cases in the Court of Appeals and opinions of the Attorney General of Georgia, which have determined that "a 'dependent' is one who looks to another for support, one dependent on another for the ordinary necessities of life." Glens Falls Indemnity Co. v. Jordan, 56 Ga.App. 449, 452–453(1), 193 S.E. 96 (1937). Accord Insurance Co. of North America v. Cooley, 118 Ga.App. 46, 48, 162 S.E.2d 821 (1968); Op. Ga. Att'y Gen. 94–14 (1994). Moreover, the City followed our holding in *McKinney* and carefully avoided the constitutional flaw in its previous benefits ordinance by eliminating from Ordinance 96–O–1018's definition of "dependent" any language recognizing any new family relationship similar to marriage.

Contrary to Morgan's argument, the requirement that "dependents" must also be registered with the City as domestic partners under Sec. 94–131 et seq., the registry ordinance, does not unconstitutionally expand the definition of "dependent" as provided in Ordinance 96–O–1018. As we noted earlier, the registry ordinance is a separate municipal ordinance which has been held to be constitutional. *McKinney*, supra at (1). Looking at Ordinance 96–O–1018, the only ordinance the constitutionality of which is in issue in this case, the City is authorized to provide benefits to those dependents who are financially reliant upon a City employee. OCGA Sec. 36–35–4. That the City chose to further narrow the group of individuals to whom it would offer certain insurance benefits by placing additional qualifications upon the receipt of such benefits does not alter and clearly does not expand the State law definition of "dependent." The City acted within its authority when it chose to provide insurance benefits to the dependents of a City employee. OCGA Sec. 36–35–4(a). It is within the City's discretion as a governing authority to determine whether to provide such benefits to all, some, or none of its employees' dependents. See Athens–Clarke County v. Walton Electric Membership Corp., 265 Ga. 229, 231(2), 454 S.E.2d 510 (1995) (municipality authorized by statute to grant franchise may "condition the grant of the franchise upon requirements the municipality deems wise"); Goodman v. City of Atlanta, 246 Ga. 79, 79–80(2), 268 S.E.2d 663 (1980) and DuPre v. City of Marietta, 213 Ga. 403, 405, 99 S.E.2d 156 (1957) (power granted to municipalities "is broad enough to authorize them to exercise poor judgment so long as it is their judgment and it is not capricious and arbitrary. . . . It is not permissible for courts to substitute [their] judgment for that of the mayor and council in such matters"); Local 574, Int'l Ass'n of Firefighters v. Floyd, 225 Ga. 625, 628, 170 S.E.2d 394 (1969) (powers granted municipalities "may be executed by the City in any manner it chooses, in the exercise of its nondelegable discretion").

The dissent's objection to the benefits ordinance is based entirely on objections to the language of the registry ordinance which, according to controlling precedent, is constitutional. *McKinney*, supra at (1). Indeed the dissent repeats the same arguments rejected by this Court in *McKinney*. Id. at 167–170, 454 S.E.2d 517, Carley, J., dissenting. The benefits ordinance, the only ordinance at issue on this appeal, provides insurance benefits to dependents of City employees and consistent with State law defines the term "dependent," as one "who is supported, in whole or in part, by the employee's earnings" and who uses such contributions to maintain his or her standard of living. Ordinance 96–O–1018(a)(1)(B)(i) and (iii). The City's decision to further limit the group of individuals to whom insurance benefits are offered by reference to Sec. 94–131 et seq. can in no way be considered part of the definition of "dependent" as provided in Ordinance 96–O–1018 or to define a new family relationship contrary to State law.

As we recognized in *McKinney*:

> [S]tate law grants cities power related to the administration of municipal government. See OCGA Sec. 36–34–2. This grant of authority does "not define the means by which the cities would and could manage their affairs" or "prohibit municipal governing authorities from choosing how such powers shall be exercised. [Cit.]"

McKinney, supra at 165(3), 454 S.E.2d 517; see Sadler v. Nijem, 251 Ga. 375, 378, 306 S.E.2d 257 (1983). Having determined that the ordinance defines "dependent" consistent with State law and, therefore, having concluded it is not in violation of either the Georgia Constitution or the Municipal Home Rule Act, we will not interfere with the exercise of discretion by the City to offer insurance benefits to fewer than all of its employees' dependents.

Judgment reversed.

All the Justices concur, except CARLEY and THOMPSON, JJ, who dissent.

GEORGE H. CARLEY, JUSTICE, dissenting.

In my opinion, the City's Domestic Partnership Benefits Ordinance is unconstitutional because it is in direct conflict with state law, and the trial court correctly so held. Accordingly, I respectfully dissent to the majority's reversal of the judgment of the trial court.

The City is authorized to provide insurance benefits to its employees' dependents. OCGA Sec. 36–35–4(a). The City has no authority, however, to define "dependents" in a manner which is inconsistent with state law. City of Atlanta v. McKinney, 265 Ga. 161, 164(2), 454 S.E.2d 517 (1995). " '[I]t may be said in general terms that a "dependent" is one who looks to another for support, one dependent on another for the ordinary necessities of life. . . . ' " Glens Falls Indemnity Co. v. Jordan, 56 Ga.App. 449, 452–453(1), 193 S.E. 96 (1937). The City's ordinance does not comport with this definition, but defines a "dependent" as one who relies upon its employees "in order to maintain his or her standard of living" and who complies with the City's domestic partnership registry ordinance. Thus, the City's ordinance does not purport to provide insurance coverage only for those who must rely upon its employees for their "support" or "the ordinary necessities of life," but to furnish such coverage for those who have entered voluntarily into a "domestic partnership" with its employees and who have agreed to a combination of resources for their mutual support.

In Georgia, a municipality "may not enact ordinances defining family relationships. The Georgia General Assembly has provided for the establishment of family relationships by general law. [Cits.]" City of Atlanta v. McKinney, supra at 164(2), 454 S.E.2d 517. The City's "domestic partnership" ordinance defines in detail a new relationship which is very similar to marriage. See OCGA Secs. 19–3–1, 19–3–2. In City of Atlanta v. McKinney, supra at 163(1), 454 S.E.2d 517, this Court upheld the constitutionality of the City's registry ordinance because "we construe[d] [it] as creating only a registration system and not any legal rights.". . . In a clear departure from this prior holding, the majority today views the ordinance as creating much more than a mere registration system. Contrary to the letter, spirit and intent of City of Atlanta v. McKinney, supra, the majority now construes the ordinance as creating a legal right to insurance coverage as a "dependent" under OCGA Sec. 36–35–4(a). However, the Georgia Constitution clearly precludes the City from doing so. With regard to the creation of legal rights arising from domestic relations, the general state law of marriage and divorce preempts the municipal domestic partnership benefit ordinance. Georgia Const. of 1983, Art. III, Sec. VI, Par. IV(a); OCGA Sec. 36–35–6(a); City of Atlanta v. McKinney, supra at 164(2), 454 S.E.2d 517. The Municipal Home Rule Act, OCGA Secs. 36–35–1 et seq., "indicates that the state does 'not wish to give our cities the power to enact a distinctive law of contract.' [Cit.]" City of Atlanta v. McKinney, supra at 164(2), 454 S.E.2d 517. "[C]ities in this state may not enact ordinances defining family relationships." City of Atlanta v. McKinney, supra at 164(2), 454 S.E.2d

517. Thus, the City has no authority, through its ordinance, to create a contract, comparable to that of marriage, and to confer upon the parties to that contract the same rights and responsibilities, such as the right to mutual support, as are enjoyed by those who enter into a marriage sanctioned by the state.

The City's ordinance disclaims the creation of marital relationship and the intent to alter or affect Georgia laws regulating private or civil relationships. However, phraseology cannot save a municipal ordinance which is unconstitutional. The "special laws" provision of the Georgia Constitution, which prohibits a municipality from enacting an ordinance defining a family relationship, "would be nullified if by play upon words and definitions the courts should hold valid a special law when there existed at the same time of its enactment a general law covering the same subject-matter." City of Atlanta v. Hudgins, 193 Ga. 618, 623(1), 19 S.E.2d 508 (1942). Here, by utilizing the same type of semantic maneuver rejected in Hudgins, the City seeks to create a legal right to insurance coverage for those who enter into a domestic partnership with its employees. In City of Atlanta v. McKinney, supra at 163(1), 454 S.E.2d 517, we clearly held that the creation of such a legal right would be unconstitutional and I dissent to the majority's failure to adhere to that controlling precedent, which mandates the affirmance of the trial court's holding that the City's Domestic Partners Benefits Ordinance is unconstitutional.

Cindy Tobisman, Marriage vs. Domestic Partnership: Will We Ever Protect Lesbians' Families?

12 Berkeley Women's L.J. 112 (1997).

. . .

Separate and Unequal: Domestic Partnership is Insufficient

The *Baehr* decision has spawned the development of domestic partnership law across the United States. These domestic partnership policies are not, however, viable substitutes for marriage.

Major corporations [including AT & T, Bank of America, Apple Computer, and Levi Strauss & Co.], schools and the California Bar Association continue to promote and adopt domestic partnership plans that extend spousal benefits to their employees' gay and lesbian partners. Over thirty municipalities, beginning with Berkeley in 1984, and including San Francisco, New York City, and Seattle have done the same, establishing in some cases a system of civic registrations for same-sex couples. In 1994, Vermont became the first state to extend health insurance coverage to the same-sex partners of its state workers.

Although domestic partnerships receive public support that gay and lesbian access to marriage lacks, domestic partnerships fail to provide lesbian-headed families and their children with the broad range of substantive protections afforded to families through legal marriage. At work, for instance, while domestic partnerships may afford a lesbian the ability to take advantage of certain "invisible cost" benefits, such as bereavement leave if her domestic partner is killed, it does not assure that she will be afforded health care benefits. Furthermore, the benefits afforded to the partners differ from company to company, and municipality to municipality. The lack of uniformity or mutual recognition of domestic partnerships means that a lesbian cannot leave her job if her partner is incapacitated and dependent on health care provided through work.

The shortcomings of domestic partnership laws have become apparent in Scandinavian countries, where domestic partnership law is more developed than in the United States. For instance, although domestic partners in Denmark and Sweden receive economic benefits such as health coverage, they are not eligible to receive joint custody or to adopt. Furthermore, they are not considered married for purposes of international treaties, may not claim the benefits of marriage laws defining marital status in term of biological gender (e.g. presumption of paternity laws), and may not participate in artificial insemination.

As is apparent in these Scandinavian countries, the shortcomings of domestic partnerships particularly involve the creation and protection of lesbians' families. In their quest for legal recognition of their relationships, the plaintiff couples in *Baehr* seek protections which married couples take for granted, such as those related to the bearing and raising of children. Without the protection of marriage, lesbian-headed couples have faced tragedy. Courts have denied life partners life insurance benefits, the right to elect against a will, and the right to petition for custody or visitation of children they helped raise. . . .

The injustices promulgated by the lack of recognition and protection for lesbian-headed families dictate against the use of domestic partnership laws as a substitute for full marital rights. Although domestic partnership registries are a step in the right direction, they fail to provide substantive protection for the families of lesbians and gay men. Furthermore, because marriage has remained largely the province of the individual states, federal domestic partnership legislation likely would be ineffective to provide substantive protections for families.

C.   Intimate Contracts

Lenore Weitzman, The Case for Intimate Contracts

From L. Weitzman, The Marriage Contract: A Guide to Living With Lovers and Spouses (NY: The Free Press, 1981).

. . . From the perspective of a couple about to enter a relationship, a contract offers four major legal advantages, which are discussed in the first section of this chapter. First, in contrast to the outdated framework of traditional legal marriage, a contract allows couples to formulate an agreement that conforms to contemporary society. Second, it permits an escape from the sex-based legacy of legal marriage and aids couples who wish to establish an egalitarian relationship. Third, it affords couples the freedom and privacy to order their personal relationships as they wish. Finally, it allows those who have not married (such as unwed cohabitants) and those who are barred from legal marriage (such as same-sex couples and groups of more than two individuals) to formalize their relationship.

In the discussion that follows, the contracting parties may be referred to as "a couple" or "a man and a woman" for linguistic convenience; however, it is important to bear in mind that the model is equally applicable to same-sex couples and to groups.

In addition to its legal advantages, the contractual model provides social and psychological benefits. Contracts facilitate open and honest communication, and help prospective partners to clarify their expectations. Once this is done, the contract creates a normative guide for future behavior. In addition, a contract can help a couple to identify and resolve potential conflicts in advance, and can provide a useful system for dealing with other conflicts that arise in an ongoing marriage. Finally, contracts increase predictability and security. . . .

Escape from the Outmoded Legal Tradition

One major advantage of a personal contract is that it affords those who want to legitimate their relationship an alternative to the outmoded scheme imposed by traditional legal marriage. In Part II we surveyed the myriad ways in which the traditional law imposes a socially anachronistic model that fails to meet the changing needs of couples in contemporary society. A personal contract provides an avenue of escape from this legal straitjacket and a means of structuring relationships in accord with a couple's individual situation and needs. For example, instead of the legal assignment of the major responsibility for family support to the husband, a contract could recognize the support commitments of both parties. It could also structure other commitments to take into account the time and work pressures in a dual-career family. Similarly, in contrast to the law's delegation of home and child care responsibilities, to the wife, a contract might structure the sharing of these responsibilities. It might also help a young couple plan for the possibility of a divorce, and guide previously married couples in the allocation of responsibilities to former spouses and the children of former marriages.

Under the present legal system, most couples face a choice "between two evils: either to accept the strictures and disabilities arising out of legal marriage, or to run the legal gauntlet that attends an irregular union." A contract, however, not only allows them to avoid that choice, it provides a positive alternative—the option of creating a personally-tailored structure to facilitate their goals and desires. A contract gives their requirements and aspirations legitimacy and aids those couples who want to renounce the out-dated assumptions of legal marriage.

Promotion of an Egalitarian Relationship

A contract promotes egalitarian relationships in two ways. First, a contract allows a couple to reject the patriarchal system of rights and obligations imposed by the legal institution of marriage. Second, the contracting process is, by its very nature, an egalitarian enterprise.

Part I of this book discusses the systematic ways in which the law imposes a hierarchical (and patriarchal) structure on intimate relationships by designating the husband as head of the family and by granting him rights and privileges denied the wife. Couples intent upon creating a partnership of equals have, for over a century, turned to contracts for redress. For example, as early as 1855 Lucy Stone and Henry Blackwell explicitly rejected the superior status that the law bestowed upon the husband by writing their own contract:

> While we acknowledge our mutual affection by publicly assuming the relationship of husband and wife, we deem it a duty to declare that this act on our part implies no sanction of, nor promise of voluntary obedience to, such of the present laws of marriage as refuse to recognize the wife as an independent, rational being, while they confer upon the husband an injurious and unnatural superiority.

Modern-day feminists have similarly embraced the marriage contract as a means of establishing an egalitarian relationship in defiance of the law's sex-based inequalities. For example, a 1973 contract featured in *Ms.* magazine begins with a similar rejection of the law's view of the rights and obligations of husbands and wives:

> Harriet and Harvey desire to enter a marriage relationship, duly solemnized under the laws of the State of Washington, the rights and obligations of which relationship differ from the traditional rights and obligations of married persons in the State of Washington which would prevail in the absence of this CONTRACT. The parties have together drafted this MARRIAGE CONTRACT in order to define a marriage relationship sought by the parties which preserves and promotes their individual identities as a man and a woman contracting to live together for mutual benefit and growth.

Thus, marriage contracts provide married couples who believe in the principles of equal partnership and self-determination with a legitimate means of modifying the sex-based marital rights and obligations imposed by law.

A second way in which a contract promotes an egalitarian relationship is inherent in the structure of the contracting process. A contract is based on the premise of equality, for it requires the voluntary consent of two independent parties. Each must have a say in the drafting of provisions and each must freely consent to be bound by them. Neither party can unilaterally impose a provision on the other; the second party's acquiescence is always necessary. In fact, ... a contract cannot be legally enforced if one party has used fraud or duress to obtain the other's agreement. The only permissible foundation for a valid contract its the willing consent of each party.

Privacy and Freedom in Ordering Personal Relationships

Even if the rights and duties imposed by the law were sexually neutral, and even if they conformed more closely to the norms of contemporary society, they still could not encompass the great diversity of individual arrangements that people might construct if they were allowed to structure their own relationships. Contracts would still be necessary to permit individuals to arrange satisfying relationships according to their own needs and desires.

The belief that individuals should have the freedom and privacy to arrange their personal affairs as they wish (as long as they do not endanger others) is fundamental to the philosophy of those who advocate intimate contracts. Indeed the disagreements between advocates and opponents of intimate contracts tend to hinge on the advocates' stress on personal freedom and marital privacy in contrast to societal concerns. As [Laura] Rausmussen aptly observes, opponents of intimate contracts regard marriage primarily as a public institution, while proponents view it as a private relationship. Those who view it as a public institution stress the ways in which uniformity promotes social stability. Those who see it as a private relationship counter that social stability (and social welfare) are better served by permitting individually satisfying contractual agreements. "Recent judicial and legislative support for individual freedom, privacy, and equality of rights under the law," seem to have buttressed the latter position and the legal support for individual contracts.

Legitimation and Structuring of Cohabiting, Homosexual, and Other Nontraditional Relationships

The legal status of homosexual couples and persons in relationships of more than two individuals ... and of those heterosexual couples who live together without marriage ... is similar in that all may suffer a series of legal disabilities as a result of their nonconforming life-styles. As no state has yet seen fit to accord them the same privileges as those who conform to the traditional legal norms, the only way they can legitimate their relationships and establish their rights and obligations is through a contract.

In the absence of a contract, couples who have no legal relationship are likely to be severely disadvantaged by the denial of a variety of benefits, both public and private, that are automatically accorded to married persons. While some of these benefits of marriage are status benefits in that they are accorded only to those who have the status of a spouse (e.g. the widow's right to a forced share of her husband's estate), in many cases the same results may be achieved through private contract. For example, cohabitors may contract to make mutual wills so that they can inherit from each other, or contract to share in jointly acquired property held in one partner's name, or contract to designate each other as the beneficiary of a life insurance policy. In addition, because a contract formalizes a relationship by specifying each person's rights and obligations, it serves a legitimizing function—and provides the attendant social and psychological advantages that accompany the legitimation of a relationship that one regards as of primary importance. . . .

Clarification of Expectations

The contracting process itself helps the parties articulate and clarify their goals and expectations. It stimulates straightforward, open communication, as each partner reveals his or her needs, hopes, goals, and plans. Couples about to enter a new relationship are likely to benefit from this planning and drafting process because it provides a natural forum for revealing and discussing both parties' expectations for their life together.

In fact, the benefits of facing major life questions in the drafting process might alone justify the contract as a means of facilitating family communication. Once open communication has been established as a norm, a couple is more likely to share feelings and concerns as situations and attitudes change.

Creation of a Normative Blueprint for Behavior

A contract enables the parties to establish a clear normative standard for behavior. This serves two important functions. First, when important agreements are written down in "black and white" they can constantly be read and referred to by the parties. Many of the marital disagreements that result from simple oversight or thoughtlessness can be resolved without rancor by simple reference to the contract, which stands as a constant reminder of all that was mutually agreed upon.

In addition, the contract serves as a written statement of the goals of the relationship. To this end, its existence provides the parties with a good deal of guidance and security, for they know what to expect of the partner and what the partner expects of them. A clearly spelled-out standard of conduct and prescription of duties and obligations constitutes a more or less specific description of what the relationship should be or must be if it is to continue.

Obviously the existence of a contract alone cannot ensure its fulfillment, nor can it guarantee a happy and stable relationship. However, one who agrees in writing to perform certain duties is likely to be willing in fact to perform those duties, just as one who publicly expresses an attitude is likely to behave in a manner consistent with that attitude.

This brings up the second advantage of specifying behavioral expectations: they make it easier to act in accordance with one's ideals. We know that many couples who give lip service to the ideal of an egalitarian relationship nevertheless find it difficult to translate their ideals into concrete arrangements (such as household task assignments, years to be supported in school, hours with the children, dollars of discretionary income). Those who do specify these practical matters have a concrete guideline for transforming ideals into day-to-day actions. The specification gives couples a concrete standard against which to monitor and measure their own behavior and thereby keep themselves on track. This is especially important to couples in a legal marriage where it is easier to slip into traditional roles and routines without realizing it. For example, a mother accustomed to being her child's primary parent may find it hard to resist her mate's pleas for "help" with the child care duties he has agreed to perform.

Advance Identification of Potential Problems

The contracting process helps couples to identify potential conflicts before they enter a relationship. There is no doubt that marriage (and any other intimate relationship) provides fertile ground for the development of disagreement and conflict. Open and honest communication in contract discussions can play an important role not only in alleviating conflict, but in helping parties to identify and deal with areas of potential trouble in advance. Attorney Karl Fleischmann asserts that all couples about to marry can benefit from a prenuptial discussion of the values and goals that each will bring to the marriage and the difficulties they foresee or have already encountered in reconciling divergent ideas. He then proposes the resolution of these differences by written agreement. By way of example, he notes that men are particularly prone to view earning money as their primary goal, even when this satisfaction is achieved at the family's expense. An exploration of the values of economic vs. personal goals can bring potential philosophical differences into the open and may help to resolve them before they become a source of conflict.

Fleischmann further advocates the involvement of a professional (that is, an attorney, marriage counselor, or therapist) in these discussions, even though the contractors do not feel they need help. Fleischmann argues that a professional adviser may unmask a problem in the process of drafting what appears to be a straightforward contract, just as the lawyer asked to draw up a simple will may uncover a complex tax consideration. He added, however, that an absence of professional assistance, whether by choice or by circumstance, should not deter couples from drawing their own marriage contracts.

Couples who write their own contracts can gain an important degree of control over their relationships, as can those who draw up their own wills. Nevertheless, Fleischmann cautions, "lay instruments" in both cases entail the risk that the writers' intentions may be frustrated by the writers' lack of legal knowledge and requirements.

Resolution of Conflict in an Ongoing Relationship

Before a marriage reaches the stage where it is in serious trouble there are usually periods of rising (but unresolved) conflict. If a contract has established a mechanism for resolving differences at an early stage, many disputes can be resolved before they grow to proportions that seriously threaten the relationship.

One pioneering effort in this direction has been undertaken by the Conciliation Court of Los Angeles County under the direction of Meyer

Elkin. The Conciliation Court was originally established to try to "save troubled marriages" by reconciling couples who had filed for divorce. Now, however, any couple may receive counseling to resolve disagreements before they lead to dissolution proceedings. In addition, parents of children under 18 who have filed for a dissolution or legal separation receive special encouragement to use the counseling services.

Significantly, the major tool used in these counseling sessions is a "Marriage Agreement." This agreement, or contract, is negotiated by the parties with the assistance of the marital counseling staff of the court and covers "practically every facet of married life." All counseling is short-term, from one to six sessions, and is geared to resolving immediate problems. According to James Crenshaw, negotiating the contract helps the couple communicate and "redefine their respective roles and responsibilities in the marriage." When the parties are satisfied with the terms, the document is signed by each partner and the Conciliation Court judge; it then has the status of a court order and is technically enforceable through contempt citations. However, the court has rarely exercised this enforcement power, preferring to rely on the psychological and emotional force of the agreement.

During the first thirteen years of its existence the Conciliation Court counseled more than fifteen thousand families. The effectiveness of the marriage agreement is, according to the court's report, indicated by the fact that 75 percent of those couples who negotiated an agreement were still living together one year after reconciliation.

Contracts have also been used successfully in the therapeutic realm. Many therapists believe that marriage and other intimate relationships are, in large part, contractual relationships; that is, they are based on a set of expectations and understandings between two parties. And while these understandings are rarely articulated, and even more rarely reduced to writing, they nevertheless form the structure of the parties' relationship.

The therapeutic model aims at making each party aware of the contractual basis of the relationship. This insight enables each party to make his or her expectations explicit, which in turn helps the other partner meet those expectations. The therapists argue that the success of any marriage depends in large part on the extent to which the partners are aware of, and attempt to fulfill, each other's contractual expectations. As psychiatrist Clifford Sager and his colleagues explain:

> We use the term marriage contract to refer to the individual's expressed and unexpressed, conscious and unconscious, concepts of his obligations within the marital relationship and to the benefits he expects to derive from marriage in general, and his spouse in particular. But what must be emphasized, above all, is the reciprocal aspect of the contract: what each partner expects to give, and what he expects to receive from his spouse in exchange, is crucial to this concept. Contracts deal with every conceivable aspect of family life: relationships with friends, achievements, power, sex, leisure time, money, children, etc. *The degree to which a marriage*

can satisfy each partners contractual expectations in these areas is an important determinant of the quality of that marriage.

A major complication arises when each spouse is aware of most of his or her own needs and wishes—of the terms of his or her own "contract"— but neither is equally aware of the other's expectations; in this case important expectations on both sides go unfulfilled. "The disappointed partner may react with rage and depression and may provoke marital discord just as though a real agreement had been broken." This response is particularly likely to occur when one partner feels strongly that he or she has fulfilled his or her obligations, but the other has not.

Sager and his colleagues try to elucidate and clarify the spouses' implicit contract terms so they can be dealt with in therapy. When each person's implicit expectations are made explicit the couple is able to negotiate a mutual agreement on the terms of their contract. In addition, once the contract is made explicit the parties have a legitimate forum for expressing concern about unmet expectations.

Another group of therapists and marriage counselors have used the contract negotiation process to resolve a wider range of family problems. For example, Scoresby et al. have developed a procedure for formulating a family action plan (somewhat similar to the contracts used in transactional analysis) to deal with family crises and continuing problems. This type of contract is arrived at through discussion and negotiation between spouses (or among all members of the family, if children are involved), and has been implemented by families on their own with only a minimum of guidance.

Increased Security, Predictability, and Commitment

Many people enter marriage with little or no awareness of the obligations and limitations to which they are committing themselves. A contract ensures that the people entering a relationship know "exactly what they are getting into." This knowledge provides the parties with the security that stems from predictability: the assurance that one's own performance of certain responsibilities will be complemented by the partner's performance of another set of responsibilities. In addition, common sense dictates that parties to a contract will be more committed to rights and responsibilities freely chosen than to obligations that the state has imposed on all husbands and wives. It also follows that the parties will be more likely to comply with the obligations of a freely negotiated contract than with a court order that seeks to enforce duties they may consider unwarranted or unfair. Thus one important result of the contract is a mutually reinforcing sense of security and commitment.

B. DIVORCE AND ITS ECONOMIC CONSEQUENCES

INTRODUCTION

Do the rules governing divorce and its consequences foster or impede the independence of women? This very question suggests a theme underlying the entire subject joining women and law. That is, what is the relationship between the ideological function and the practical effects of law? How, if at all, can a rule "promote equality"? Conflicting arguments regarding law reform proposals implicitly involve conflicting views about the relationships among law, individual consciousness, and human behavior.

The introduction of no-fault divorce followed many kinds of criticisms of the fault-based systems. Did any of these criticisms stem from concerns for women's needs? Or was the "gender" dimension of no-fault reform only advanced by advocates for men who believed that women received too much financial advantage under that regime? After no-fault divorce was adopted in California in 1969, every other state quickly followed suit, to some degree. Many states retained, however, some forms of fault-based divorce as an alternative to the no-fault option. By the 1990s, new critical voices argued that divorce had become too easy. The most recent development— covenant marriage reforms—push for restricting access to divorce. Does this development hurt women's struggles for independence and equality, or assist women who otherwise risk abandonment by men and consignment to reduced economic well-being? What underlying interests and concerns help to explain these cycles of reform and criticism? Assessing these questions calls ultimately for empirical research about the actual effects of laws in practice and also cultural criticism about the views that frame and are framed by law and law reform.

I. THE NO–FAULT REVOLUTION

Walton v. Walton

Court of Appeal, Fourth District, California, 1972.
28 Cal.App.3d 108, 104 Cal.Rptr. 472.

MARCUS KAUFMAN, ACTING PRESIDING JUSTICE.

Wife appeals from an interlocutory judgment granting Husband's petition for dissolution of marriage and denying Wife's request for legal separation.

Facts

The parties were married on or about August 7, 1948 and separated approximately 21 years later on August 7, 1969. On October 6, 1970, Husband filed a petition for dissolution of marriage on the ground of irreconcilable differences which have caused the irremediable breakdown of the marriage (Civ.Code, § 4506(1)). On October 2, 1970, Wife filed her response seeking legal separation on the same ground, irreconcilable differences which have caused the irremediable breakdown of the marriage (Civ.Code, § 4506(1)). Prior to trial Wife moved the court to dismiss Husband's petition on grounds that certain provisions of The Family Law Act enacted in 1969 (Stats.1969, ch. 1608), particularly Civ.Code, sections 4506(1) and 4507, are violative of the California and federal constitutions on several bases. The motion was denied, the matter proceeded to trial, and the court rendered an interlocutory judgment of dissolution of the marriage placing custody of the minor children of the parties with Wife, providing for spousal and child support and dividing the marital property. . . .

Impairment of Contract

Wife's contention that dissolution of her marriage on the ground of irreconcilable differences as prescribed in The Family Law Act constitutes an unconstitutional impairment of her contract rights is untenable. In the first place, marital rights and obligations are not contractual rights and obligations within the meaning of article I, section 10 of the United States Constitution or article I, section 16 of the California Constitution. . . . Marriage is much more than a civil contract; it is a relationship that may be created and terminated only with consent of the state and in which the state has a vital interest. . . .

Secondly, even if marital obligations were treated as contractual obligations protected by the constitutional prohibitions, a statutory change in the grounds for divorce would not constitute an unconstitutional impairment thereof. "Marriage, as creating the most important relation in life, as having more to do with the morals and civilization of a people than any other institution, has always been subject to the control of the legislature. That body prescribes the age at which parties may contract to marry, the procedure or form essential to constitute marriage, the duties and obligations it creates, its effects upon the property rights of both, present and prospective, and the acts which may constitute grounds for its dissolution." . . . When persons enter into a contract or transaction creating a relationship infused with a substantial public interest, subject to plenary control by the state, such contract or transaction is deemed to incorporate and contemplate not only the existing law but the reserve power of the state to amend the law or enact additional laws for the public good and in pursuance of public policy, and such legislative amendments or enactments do not constitute an unconstitutional impairment of contractual obligations. . . .

Deprivation of Property Without Due Process of Law

Similarly, Wife's contention that the dissolution of her marriage on the ground of irreconcilable differences under The Family Law Act unconstitutionally deprives her of vested interest in her married status cannot be sustained. Certainly a wife has a legitimate interest in her status as a married woman, but, separate and apart from marital property and support rights as to which Wife makes no contention, we entertain some doubt whether her interest in her status as a married woman constitutes property within the purview of the due process clauses. . . .

Even if Wife is said to have some constitutionally protected vested right, she has not been deprived thereof without due process of law. "Vested rights, of course, may be impaired 'with due process of law' under many circumstances. The state's inherent sovereign power includes the so called 'police power' right to interfere with vested property rights whenever reasonably necessary to the protection of the health, safety, morals, and general well being of the people. . . . The constitutional question, on principle, therefore, would seem to be, not whether a vested right is impaired by a marital ... law change, but whether such a change reasonably could be believed to be sufficiently necessary to the public welfare as to justify the impairment." ...

The primary purpose of Civil Code, section 4507 is to indicate that the determination of the existence of irreconcilable differences specified in Civil Code, section 4506(1) is to be made by the court, that is, that this determination is to be a judicial determination, not a ministerial one. The general legislative history of The Family Law Act is chronicled in the Report of 1969 Divorce Reform Legislation of the Assembly Committee on Judiciary (4 Assem.J. (1969) 8054). ...

Civil Code, section 4507 had its genesis in Assembly Bill 530 and, in our view, along with Civil Code, sections 4508 and 4511, was intended to ensure that the determination of the existence of irreconcilable differences remained a judicial determination, not a ministerial one.

The second purpose of Civil Code, section 4507 is to make clear that the irreconcilable differences sufficient to justify dissolution of marriage must be substantial as opposed to trivial or minor. ... As stated in the Report of 1969 Divorce Reform Legislation of the Assembly Committee on Judiciary (4 Assem.J. (1969) at p. 8058): "The test of irreconcilability will be met when, according to Civil Code Section 4507, the differences sought to be proved are 'substantial reasons for not continuing the marriage and which make it appear that the marriage should be dissolved.'" Thus, reading Civil Code, sections 4506(1) and 4507 together, irreconcilable differences which have caused the irremediable breakdown of the marriage refers to the existence of substantial marital problems which have so impaired the marriage relationship that the legitimate objects of matrimony have been destroyed and as to which there is no reasonable possibility of elimination, correction or resolution.

Unfair and Unjust Impact of the Family Law Act

Under this head, it is asserted that elimination of the fault concept in dissolution proceedings is unjust and unfair because it permits a spouse guilty of morally reprehensible conduct to take advantage of that conduct in terminating marriage against the wishes of an entirely unoffending spouse. While this may be true and while such a result may be offensive to those steeped in the tradition of personal responsibility based upon fault, this contention presents no issue cognizable in the courts. After thorough study, the Legislature, for reasons of social policy deemed compelling, has seen fit to change the grounds for termination of marriage from a fault basis to a marriage breakdown basis. ...

Affirmed.

NOTES AND QUESTIONS

1. **History**. Until the late 19th century, divorce was rare; marriage was "until death do we part." States then started to recognize fault-based grounds to end marriages—grounds such as adultery, insanity, and deser-

tion. Gradually, by the end of the 19th century, many states had expanded the fault grounds to include cruelty, even emotional cruelty, drunkenness, nonsupport, vagrancy, and infecting the wife with a venereal disease. Defendants could defend, and prevent divorce, by establishing mutual antipathy, collusion, or resumption of marital cohabitation. Pressure to reform and enlarge grounds for divorce mounted as people developed higher expectations of happiness in marriage.

The no-fault divorce reform, undertaken first in California, shifts the focus on legal involvement in the termination of marriages from morality to economics. Its supporters sought to eliminate the adversarial nature of divorce and thereby reduce the hostility, damage, and trauma of the fault-based divorce regime for the parties and for their children. Some advocates sought gender equality for men, and claimed that the prior regime permitted lawyers to "suck the blood, not to mention the money, of former husbands." Herma Hill Kay, *The California Background*, quoted in Lenore Weitzman, The Divorce Revolution: The Unexpected Social and Economic Consequences for Women and Children in America 17 (1985). Others supported the reform as part of a larger effort to eliminate gender distinctions in family roles, entitlements, and obligations in marriage and in divorce.

2. **Walton.** Why would someone like Mrs. Walton oppose the divorce? She apparently did not contest that she and her husband had irreconcilable differences and in fact sought a legal separation. What would remaining married offer her? Would that status—and should that status—affect her standard of living, access to resources, or parenting arrangements?

3. **Weitzman's Critique.** Lenore Weitzman published an influential—and controversial—empirical study finding a devastating, negative impact of the California divorce reform on women and children. *See* Weitzman, *supra*. Although her methodology and interpretations have been questioned, task forces investigating the possibility of gender bias in nine states have found that gender bias detrimental to women permeates property division and child support following divorce. *See* Cynthia Starnes, *Divorce and the Displaced Homemaker*, 60 U. Chi. L. Rev. 67, 93 (1993).

Herma Hill Kay, a law professor involved in both the reform and the effort to evaluate it, wrote a comment in 1987 evaluating the consequences of no-fault reform in California; Professor Mary Ann Glendon wrote a comparative study placing the no-fault movement in international context. Consider how these historical and comparative approaches strike you now and also whether they sufficiently attend to the interests of women.

Herma Hill Kay, Equality and Difference: A Perspective on No-fault Divorce and Its Aftermath
56 U. Cincinnati L. Rev. 1 (1987).

. . .

The Social and Economic Aftermath of No–Fault Divorce
Even though the proponents of no-fault divorce did not visualize it as a change designed to ensure equality between the divorcing spouses, many of

them saw the reform effort as a progressive and enlightened move away from outmoded and unnecessary legal restrictions. In California there was a surprising lack of public opposition to the varying proposals that emerged over the period between 1963 and 1969. While Catholic religious opposition existed in New York in 1965 to the plan to add a no-fault ground based on separation to the existing fault-based grounds, in California representatives of the same religious group supported the Governor's Commission in its recommendation for a Family Court. The only organized interest group involved in the California reform effort was an association of divorced men who felt they had been treated unfairly and who thought divorce should be removed from the courts. No feminist groups were available to participate: the modern women's movement was just emerging in 1963, when the California Assembly began its inquiry into divorce. Once women's groups became aware of the proposed change from fault to no-fault divorce, many supported the concept.

As no-fault divorce spread across the country, however, and as social scientists began to investigate the impact of the new laws, the attitude of some feminists began to change. Particularly in the common law states, observers began to insist that new financial provisions were needed to accompany the no-fault laws in order to protect women and children. A debate emerged over whether property should be divided equally or distributed in equitable shares following divorce.

Meanwhile, legal commentators monitoring the emerging case law in California noted a disturbing tendency of trial court judges to cut back on already meager alimony awards and to limit even those awards to brief periods of time. California appellate courts found themselves reversing spousal support awards as inadequate, and accompanying their orders remanding the judgments for reconsideration with a stern message to trial court judges denying that the no-fault laws had been intended as a mechanism for the impoverishment of former wives. Proposals began to be advanced for broadening the definition of what constituted "property" subject to division. The California Assembly Committee on Judiciary issued a supplemental report clarifying its original intent regarding the equal division requirements in order to eliminate unanticipated confusion among lawyers and judges about its application.

A vague sense that something had gone wrong was crystallized for many observers in Fall 1985 by the publication of Dr. Lenore Weitzman's study of the impact of the California Family Law Act. Her message was a mixed one: on the one hand, she found that the no-fault philosophy had been accepted as an improvement over the fault system by California judges and lawyers, and that it was seen as "fair" by most divorcing couples. On the other hand, she found that the equal division requirement had lowered property awards to women below the higher unequal awards some women had received under the earlier law, and, where there was insufficient offsetting property, had been interpreted by judges to require sale of the family home in order to effectuate an equal division. ...

Weitzman shares common ground with Martha Fineman and others in her observation that the removal of fault from the divorce system altered the framework for bargaining between divorcing spouses. Under the fault system, the bargaining advantage lay with the "innocent" spouse. If that person were the wife, and if she wished to preserve the marriage, she could simply refuse to press her cause of action against the guilty husband. Of course, in cases where the parties had separated, her refusal served to prevent the husband's "[r]estoration to the freedom of the marriage market," as Professor Max Rheinstein put it. In a no-fault system, even one based on a period of separation, the "guilty" spouse could simply wait out the period and the "innocent" spouse could not prevent a divorce. Thus, as Weitzman notes, in a no-fault divorce system, the advantage lies with the spouse who wants to end the relationship, not the one who wants to continue it.

Many proponents of no-fault divorce would not disagree with this analysis. Taking the "blackmail" out of divorce was not an unintended consequence of the reform movement. The California Governor's Commission on the Family, as well as the Commissioners on Uniform State Laws, rejected the idea that marriage should be used as a device for extortion. What was not intended was that the shift to a no-fault approach should itself deprive either women or men of the capacity to negotiate a fair agreement.

Despite her criticisms, Weitzman does not propose a return to the fault system of divorce. Instead, she identifies four situations which, in her view, present the most serious cases of injustice under the no-fault laws. She then proposes changes in the law to remedy each situation. What follows is a brief summary of her analysis.

(1) First, Weitzman cites the situation of children, who, despite the influence of the fathers' rights movement, and the trend toward joint custody, are still living with their mothers following divorce in most cases. She proposes higher child support awards and a more effective support enforcement mechanism.

(2) Weitzman finds the situation of the older, long-married housewife without paid employment experience outside the home particularly troubling. To protect her, Weitzman proposes that the property and support awards be structured so as to equalize the standards of living between her household and that of her former husband. Weitzman also advocates that women of this group, particularly those for whom the family home is a major asset of the marriage, should be allowed to continue living in the family home after divorce. This recommendation holds even if no children remain in the custody of the divorced wife, and applies as an exception to any equal division rule.

(3) Weitzman's data show that mothers with sole custody of children who live as single heads of households are economically disadvantaged relative to their former husbands. She urges that these women be allowed to continue to live in the family home with the children for a period of time as a form of child support. She also suggests early, high balloon payments

of spousal support to enable these women to secure job training for positions that will allow them to become relatively self-supporting.

(4) Weitzman's fourth unfair case is less precisely defined. She points to the disadvantaged situation of the forty-year-old divorced woman who works at a relatively low-level job. This woman may have sacrificed her own career development to help her husband advance in his chosen profession. Weitzman recommends a division of the husband's career assets as part of the property award; compensating to the woman for detriment to her own career; and job training.

Weitzman argues that the disadvantages to women and children reflected in these four cases can be traced most immediately to the change from a fault to a no-fault system of divorce. In the introduction to her book, Weitzman thus previews her research.

Yet these modern and enlightened reforms have had unanticipated, unintended, and unfortunate consequences. In the pages that follow we shall see how gender-neutral rules—rules designed to treat men and women "equally" have in practice served to deprive divorced women (especially older homemakers and mothers of young children) of the legal and financial protections that the old law provided. Instead of recognition for their contributions as homemakers and mothers, and instead of compensation for the years of lost opportunities and impaired earning capacities, these women now face a divorce law that treats them "equally" and expects them to be equally capable of supporting themselves after divorce.

Toward the end of her book, however, Weitzman recognizes that the disadvantage to women upon divorce results in larger part from choices made during marriage that reflect traditional notions of sex roles. Noting that a major defect in the divorce reform effort was the failure of many reformers to realize that they could not simply legislate equality between men and women "without changing the social realities that promote equality," Weitzman concludes:

> It is now obvious that equality cannot be achieved by legislative fiat in a society in which men and women are differently situated. As long as women are more likely than men to subordinate their careers in marriage, and as long as the structure of economic opportunity favors men, and as long as women contribute to their husband's earning capacities, and as long as women are likely to assume the major responsibilities of child rearing, and as long as we want to encourage the care and rearing of children, we cannot treat men and women as "equals" in divorce settlement. We must find ways to safeguard and protect women, not only to achieve fairness and equity, but also to encourage and reward those who invest in and care for our children and, ultimately, to foster true equality for succeeding generations.

Weitzman's critique of the aftermath of the California Family Law Act is a powerful one. Her data show clearly that California trial judges, left to their own devices without the special training and experience that a unified

Family Court system might have provided, administered the new laws without adequate regard to the different life situations and economic circumstances of divorced women and men. Even so, I question whether the judicial attitudes that produced the unfair results Weitzman documents can be attributed entirely to the legal change from fault to no-fault divorce. Weitzman herself suggests that other factors were significant when she observes that

> the reformers [did not] anticipate the profound impact of the women's movement on the consciousness of all the participants in the divorce process. Since the California legal reforms came before the forceful organizational efforts of the women's movement in the 1970s, the reformers did not realize that the concept of "equality," and the sex-neutral language of the new law, would be used by some lawyers and judges as a mandate for "equal treatment" with a vengeance, a vengeance that can only be explained as a backlash reaction to women's demands for equality in the larger society. Thus the reformers did not forsee [sic] that the equality they had in mind for a childless divorcee of twenty-five would be used to terminate alimony for a fifty-five-year-old housewife who had never held a paying job.

More broadly, as Max Rheinstein has argued, the relinquishment of the ideal of marriage as a union indissoluble except for fault was itself made possible by a gradual shift in Western civilization away from what he called the "Christian-conservative" ideology toward the "eudemonistic-liberal" one. Similarly, Carl Schneider has recently identified four forces in American culture and institutions that he believes have shaped contemporary family law: "[T]he legal tradition of noninterference in family affairs, the ideology of liberal individualism, American society's changing moral beliefs, and the rise of 'psychologic man.'" He suggests that the combination of these forces has changed the locus of moral decision-making about the family from the legal system to the family itself. He cites the emergence of no-fault divorce as among the "clearest examples" of his hypothesis.

If, as Rheinstein and Schneider contend, no-fault divorce was the indirect product of broad social change, their analysis would suggest as well that the judges who interpreted the no-fault laws were themselves affected by these profound changes. Under that view, the shift from fault to no-fault divorce provided the trigger that enabled the judges to identify and apply (or misapply) those changing patterns to the divorce cases they decided, but the social and cultural changes themselves preceded the legal reforms.

Weitzman does not conclude from her research that California or the other states that have followed California in adopting a no-fault standard as the sole basis for divorce should now return to a fault system, nor would I offer such a recommendation. But Weitzman pointedly refrains from suggesting that states that have adopted a combined fault/no-fault approach should press forward to abolish their fault grounds. Instead, she implies that the retention of fault grounds might offer some protection to women and children in other states against the disadvantages she has found to exist in California.

I am not persuaded that the retention of fault in divorce has this effect. I suspect, rather, that despite the continued existence of fault grounds on the statute books of thirty-five states and the District of Columbia, women do not fair substantially better after divorce in those jurisdictions than they do in the fifteen pure no-fault states. The social and cultural changes mentioned earlier that facilitated the national acceptance of no-fault divorce are not limited to the fifteen pure no-fault states. Their influence is national, although their impact may have been felt earlier and accepted more readily in California than elsewhere. I would expect that judicial attitudes similar to those Weitzman has documented in California exist in other states as well, regardless of the continued existence of fault grounds for divorce.

I cannot test this hypothesis against a national body of data describing judicial practice comparable to that Weitzman has produced for California, for no such data are yet available. Some roughly comparable empirical work has been undertaken, however, in three states that fall into the group of fifteen jurisdictions that have combined their fault-based grounds for divorce with a conservative approach to no-fault divorce based on separation, rather than on a factual showing of marital breakdown. These studies provide some preliminary confirmation of the hypothesis that perpetuation of fault in divorce does not protect women against financial disadvantage. For example, Wishik's study in Vermont covered all divorce cases decided between October 1982 and February 1983 in four Superior Court Districts, a total of 227 cases. Wishik does not distinguish between those cases decided on fault grounds and those decided on no-fault grounds, but rather considers them without regard to grounds. She concludes that "Vermont women appear ... to be even worse off after divorce than women are in California, for instance, and in some respects to be worse off than women are on the average nationally."

Two other studies, conducted in New Jersey and New York, were not limited to divorce, but were broadly designed to document the treatment of women by the court system. Both studies, however, include data on the impact of divorce on women that indicate that women in both states are economically disadvantaged by divorce. The New York Task Force had available to it a study by two matrimonial lawyers of seventy reported cases applying New York's Equitable Distribution Law. The authors concluded that "with few exceptions the courts are not treating the wife as an equal partner." Neither the New York nor the New Jersey report distinguished between divorces based on fault and those granted on no-fault grounds. Weitzman cites these two studies in support of her conclusion that women generally fare better in property awards in states like California that require an equal division of marital property than they do in states like New Jersey and New York that follow a system of equitable distribution. She does not, however, draw the further inference that these studies suggest: namely, that the presence of fault as an alternative basis for divorce is not sufficient to protect women against economic disadvantage.

Moreover, the four "unjust" cases that Weitzman uses to illustrate the most serious problems of no-fault divorce are not limited to California and those states that have followed its lead into a pure no-fault approach. To be sure, her unfair cases do appear in other pure no-fault states. But they arise as well in the other two groups of states: those that combine fault with the modern breakdown of marriage approach to no-fault divorce, and those that more cautiously use a traditional no-fault approach such as a period of separation or incompatibility. Wives do not appear to obtain more favorable treatment in the latter two groups of states than they obtain in pure no-fault states. Thus, financial hardship affecting children, Weitzman's first unfair situation, is not limited to no-fault states. As she herself demonstrates, the unfairness that results from inadequate and unenforced child support awards is a national problem affecting children of divorce everywhere. Others agree. Her second case, that of the older, long-married housewife and mother who has no paid employment experience, portrays a classic victim of divorce whose plight is also identified by others. Appellate courts in all three groups of states have found it necessary to remind trial court judges of their obligation to protect the older divorced homemaker's financial security. The difficult situation of the young mother burdened with the care of children, Weitzman's third case, is also well-known in the divorce literature. Her circumstances are in part a function of the unfairness identified in case one: without adequate and reliable child support payments, she has neither the time nor the resources to build a higher standard of living for herself and her children. Like that of the children in case one, her problem is a national one. Weitzman's fourth case encompasses a variety of situations in which decisions made during marriage have had the effect of limiting the wife's capacity for self-support. One such situation has been identified in all three groups of states: that of the wife who worked to support the family while her husband undertook professional training. While states vary in their approaches to the "Ph.T." (Putting Hubby Through) problem, their solutions do not vary according to whether fault remains part of their approach to divorce.

Finally, even if the continued recognition of marital fault as an alternative basis for divorce or as a factor in the financial determination were shown to enable women to obtain higher settlements, I would still want to ask whether that outcome is worth the cost of perpetuating the blackmail and other abuses that accompanied the fault system. I do not conclude from Weitzman's study that the change from fault to no-fault divorce was a mistake. Nor, I repeat, does she. Rather, we both perceive that the immediate task lying ahead is that of correcting the judicial attitudes that produced the unfair applications of the no-fault laws, or, failing that, of reducing the scope of judicial discretion by changing particular aspects of those laws in an effort to obtain fair results for both divorcing spouses despite those attitudes. Beyond that concrete and immediate task, however, I believe a more basic challenge lies ahead: we must explore new ways of looking at the family, ways that will perhaps reduce the inequality

between women and men when their familial relationship comes to an end.
. . .

Mary Ann Glendon, From No–Fault to No–Responsibility Divorce

From M.A. Glendon, Abortion and Divorce in Western Law: American Failures, European Challenges (Cambridge, MA: Harvard University Press, 1987).

Countries that differ from each other culturally and politically and are at quite disparate levels of economic development have moved, as if in concert, toward making marriage more freely terminable. Yet a closer examination here, as in the area of abortion, shows the United States taking a somewhat particular and extreme position. When the grounds of divorce are compared, one finds that only Sweden resembles the United States in the degree to which its legal system has accepted unilateral no-fault divorce. When a comparison is made of the legal treatment of the economic consequences of divorce, however, it is apparent that in most places, including Sweden, freer terminability of marriage by no means connotes freedom from economic responsibilities toward former dependents. In fact, the United States appears unique among Western countries in its relative carelessness about assuring either public or private responsibility for the economic casualties of divorce.

NOTES AND QUESTIONS

1. **No Responsibility?** Professor Glendon titles her discussion "From No–Fault to No–Responsibility Divorce?" How would you answer her question?

2. **Bringing Fault Back In?** Some feminists have argued that bringing back a requirement of fault before divorce would help women regain some control and some bargaining power in the resolution of disputes over financial and childcare arrangements following divorce. Professor Barbara Woodhouse, for example, urges revival of fault notions because of their narrative power, emphasis on contextual considerations, and possible link to equitable remedies. The language of fault could enable women to name and seek redress for sexual abuse, economic exploitation and violence, while making it possible to attribute consequences for good and bad conduct during a marriage. Professor Katherine Bartlett responds with concerns that the use of fault concepts in divorce could hurt women while maintaining the image of private responsibility rather than public norms in the context of divorce. She also argues that fault-based divorce invites distortion and polarization. Their exchange appears in *Sex, Lies, and Dissipation: The Discourses of Fault in a No–Fault Era*, 82 Georgetown L. J. 2525 (1994).

3. **Advice to Practitioners.** Imagine you have joined the local Women's Bar Association and are drafting its position paper on the proper place of

fault notions in divorce. What advice would you give to practitioners who represent women with the choice of filing for fault-based or no-fault divorce? What stance should the Women's Bar Association take on possible future legislative reforms to enlarge fault grounds and/or restrict access to no-fault divorce?

4. **Covenant Marriage.** Alongside the sociologists, communitarians, and feminist theorists who have criticized no-fault divorce laws, members of conservative religious and political groups argue that no-fault divorce has contributed to the decline in "family values" and the rise in the divorce rate in this country over the last two decades. In recent years, these two groups have joined forces to introduce legislation in several states—including Idaho, Michigan, Georgia, Iowa, Pennsylvania, and Colorado—designed to roll back what is perceived as the negative consequences of no-fault divorce laws. These bills have proposed such measures as requiring mutual consent in all no-fault divorces and requiring mutual consent in no-fault divorces where minor children are involved. In the summer of 1997, legislators in Louisiana passed a law creating a new, alternative form of marriage that would permit divorce only in certain narrow circumstances such as adultery, abuse, abandonment, lengthy marital separation, or imprisonment for a felony. If chosen by a couple prior to marriage, this new type of marriage, known as "covenant marriage," would preclude that couple from later divorcing on no-fault grounds. However, couples who do not choose covenant marriages could later seek a no-fault divorce. Proponents of the law argued that covenant marriage would improve family stability by forcing couples to engage in serious conversations abut their marital commitments *prior* to marriage and by offering a more serious form of marriage to couples who so choose.

Will bringing fault back in to divorce be a positive development for women and children, or will this political backlash against no-fault divorce ultimately impose even greater harm on women and children?

II. DIVISION OF PROPERTY

The traditional common law rule turned all property held by a woman over to her husband upon marriage; she in turn obtained only a dower or curtesy interest upon her husband's death. The Married Women's Property Acts of the 19th century extended control to women over their separate property, based on title, but permitted no further claims to property held by the husband or generated through the course of the marriage. As divorce became a more common practice, this framework exposed to view the inequality of women's property rights under marriage. Under the common law rule, after divorce the wife would receive only that property to which she had separate title; the traditional homemaker had no claim therefore to her husband's earnings or the fruits of those earnings. That wife might have been eligible for alimony (now more commonly called spousal support), which might be understood as a kind of property settlement or else as enforcement of the husband's promise at the time of marriage to assure the wife's economic support. But the traditional rules did not entitle a divorcing wife to a share of the assets obtained during the marriage. Occasionally, courts would create under equity a "constructive trust" to provide some financial resources to former wives who would otherwise be left destitute. But most states viewed this basic framework as unfair and untenable, and, today, no state forbids division of property formally held in the name of the husband.

A few states, influenced by Spanish and French traditions brought to American colonies, employ a "community property" regime which treats all property acquired by either husband or wife during the marriage as available for division after divorce, and some also permit division of separate property brought into the marriage by one spouse.

Other states have been influenced by this equality ideal and have adopted the norm of equitable distribution of property upon divorce. These states treat the task of division as one calling for a fair and just distribution, rather than an equal division, and generally grant considerable discretion to judges to perform the property division. Very different results would emerge if the judge responds to party need instead of an assessment of each party's contribution to the acquisition of assets.

How do these different regimes affect women? What conception of women's needs, entitlements, or desert does and should guide the development of property division practices following divorce? Both general theoretical accounts and more specific discussions of the tasks of classifying assets, valuing them, and distributing them are relevant to these questions, as the readings that follow suggest.

Martha Fineman, Property Distribution, Need, and Women's Equality

From M. Fineman, The Illusion of Equality: The Rhetoric and Reality of Divorce Reform (Chicago: University of Chicago Press, 1991).

While property distribution may in fact reflect concern about a spouse's future needs, such concern is increasingly considered inappropriate as the image of marriage becomes more that of partnership than of dependency. Need may be implicit in some of the factors utilized for division, but typically the stated rules explicitly reflect notions of *entitlement* based on earnings or, more recently, on marital contributions whether economic or homemaking. . . .

Currently, a variety of specific distribution factors are typically noted in common law, state statutes, or court opinions in states with general statutory directives. These factors include:

1. The length of the marriage;

2. The property brought to the marriage by each party;

3. The "contribution" of each party to the marriage, often with the explicit admonition that appropriate economic value is to be given to contributions of homemaking and child-care services;

4. The contribution by one party to the education, training, or increased earning power of the other;

5. Whether one of the parties has substantial assets not subject to division by the court;

6. The age and physical and emotional health of the parties;

7. The earning capacity of each party, including educational background, training, employment skills, work experience, and length of absence from the job market;

8. Custodial responsibilities for children;

9. The time and expense necessary to acquire sufficient education or training to enable a party to become self-supporting at a standard of living reasonably comparable to that enjoyed during the marriage.

Increasingly, some consideration is given to the desirability of awarding the family home, or the right to live there for a reasonable period, to the party having custody of any children. In addition, other economic circumstances may be considered. These include vested or invested pension benefits, future interests, the tax consequences to each party, and the amount and duration of an order granting maintenance payments.

If a written agreement was made by the parties before or during the marriage concerning any arrangement for property distribution, such agreements are often presumed binding upon the court unless inequitable. Some statutory systems that enumerate the various factors explicitly end with a general catch-all for judicial discretion that allows consideration of such other factors as the court may in each individual case determine to be relevant. . . .

There are at least four potential conceptual categories into which one could place the various factors considered in property distributions: title, fault, need, and contribution. These conceptual categories represent rationales or justifications for allocation decisions and may be ordered according to when they first were utilized. This sequencing has been used to suggest that there has been a progression from the simple, common-law emphasis on title to the more complex understanding of the function and purpose of the distribution system as reflecting the valuing of both monetary and nonmonetary contributions to the marriage.

While there has been a movement away from the strict common-law system based on title to the modern notion of a partnership based on equally valued though different-in-kind contributions to the marriage, I believe there is a serious problem with characterizing the movement from title to partnership and contribution as "progress." Progress implies that we have either outgrown the basis for the old concepts or that our initial perceptions were in error and now must be revised. A progression thesis might, therefore, characterize fault and need as "transitional" concepts— inelegant patches that allowed judges to do justice under a strict title system prior to the enlightened presentation of marriage as partnership.

I am not convinced, however, that the circumstances that generated arguments for a distribution system focused on needs that no longer exist. Further, I am concerned that the material circumstances of divorcing women and children are being detrimentally ignored by supplanting a focus on needs with a focus on contribution as the primary distributive concept. The ascendancy of contribution may present a nice, neat instance of conceptual progress to legal academics and law reformers, but for many divorcing spouses, as well as for the practicing professionals to whom they turn for advice, adverse material circumstances and the needs they generate have not been left behind.

While the considerations do not seem to be determinative in modern distribution schemes, need and, to a lesser extent, fault are still viable alternatives to contribution as conceptual frameworks for the creation and implementation of various specific distribution factors. When fault and need were first introduced into consideration, they were welcomed as helping to ameliorate the hardships of the title system. But, in contemporary divorce practice, both have increasingly come under attack because they carry negative symbolic connotations. In the context of "no-fault" divorce reform, for example, continued reference to fault as an explicit allocation category would obviously be problematic.

Further, the concept of *need* presents even more complex conceptual difficulties. As a relevant consideration, however, need is not a consideration as easily moved beyond and left behind as fault. Historically, the courts could respond to the existence of dependency, since marriage was viewed as a status relationship. The husband and father was obligated to provide support for the needs of his wife and children, and this obligation did not necessarily cease with divorce and could be extended beyond divorce through awards of alimony, through property division provisions, or through both. However, modern attacks on the legitimacy of the patriarchal family have had an unplanned legal impact: the erosion of the traditional notion that the husband is predominantly and perpetually responsible for the financial well-being of all members of the family. Attempts to cast family structure in more egalitarian terms have assisted in transforming our approach to the rules governing the economic aspects of divorce. The earlier status-based model of marriage has been replaced by an individualistic or equality model under which obligations to spouses ideally end with the marriage, and any ongoing economic obligation that is recognized as appropriate, such as child support or payment of existing marital debts, is considered a shared and equal responsibility. ...This individualistic approach, coupled with the undeniable fact that more resources are necessary when an adult has to care for children in addition to herself, means that the allocation of private resources at divorce has a profound economic and social impact because it affects the future ability of a custodial parent to care adequately for her children.

I assume that private decisions about child custody at divorce and actual assumed responsibility for children after divorce will typically be gender-related for generations to come. As a result, the wife, the parent statistically more likely to be at a disadvantage in the market, will more likely also be the parent who must adjust career activities to accommodate childrearing. This adjustment will result in potentially immeasurable costs to her career and personal development.

Finally, I assume that alimony awards will continue to be extremely rare and that child-support awards will continue to be systematically low and/or only sporadically enforced. Thus, given the predominant view of the children's future economic well-being as a private or family function, and given that enforcement of support orders might be a problem, a custodial parent cannot comfortably rely on future contributions from her ex-spouse in providing for the children, nor can she rely on any other source of support outside her own efforts.

Dependency has not disappeared, however. I believe that marriage often conceals or masks the poverty of women in this country and that divorce removes this mask. The care of children produces dependency, not only for the children, but also for the primary caretaker. The needs that this dependency generates must be met either by society as a whole or by individuals with legally significant connections to children. Moreover, it must be recognized that this dependency does not end when the child reaches eighteen or any other magic age. Children's needs may change with the passage of time, but the caretaker has assumed ongoing responsibilities with present as well as future economic consequences, such as a reduced amount of money in a social security or pension fund or an increased susceptibility to requests for "loans" once the children are fully grown and supposedly "independent."

The laws governing the economic aspects of divorce should be grounded in the realization that some family relationships tend to last. This is particularly true of the primary caretaking parent and her children. The obligations that such a parent may feel are not legal but moral or emotional ones. A parent who desires to assist a newly "adult" child may not be required to do so by law, but that does not mean that the law should be insensitive to (or unsupportive of) the parent's sensibilities when assessing the most socially useful allocation of property at divorce. . . .

Assessment of the various specific distribution factors listed above reveals that four may be categorized under the concept of *contribution* while the other five fit more neatly within the concept of *need*. The fact that within any system the factors are often combined and exist simultaneously reflects the tension between the two incompatible contemporary images of marriage: the modern egalitarian partnership and the older, status-based, dependency model. These represent polar ends on the spectrum of the way society views marriage and the position of women within it, as well as the major transformation that has occurred in this regard.

The partnership image gives rise to the idea of contribution—each person contributes a different but valuable set of benefits to the good of the whole, and the whole should be divided to reflect these contributions if it is dissolved. Under this view, need has no role to play in a true partnership of equals. In fact, contribution rhetoric is often placed in opposition to another vision of marriage—that of dependency. The dependency image, in contrast to contribution, anticipates that a woman has been "victimized" in marriage. She is viewed as having sacrificed career goals and ambitions for the marriage. At divorce she is dependent, and that dependency will continue. She therefore has economic needs that should be recognized and compensated. In this context need is cast as a negative, something demeaning and to be overcome. Dependency and need are dramatized as products of women's victimization by men and marriage and are not rhetorically associated with the dependency and needs of children.

In our contemporary society, the concept of need must necessarily create some ambivalence for those who accept equality as the social and legal ideal. The predominance of the equality model evident in much of the commentary and law reform efforts illustrates that there is a strong preference for the legal presentation of women as equal partners within marriage and as independent, equal economic actors outside of it.

Liberal feminist legal reformers, for example, have adhered for the most part to the ideal of egalitarian marriage in addressing the economic questions in divorce. In some states, the equality norm is formally embodied in provisions which establish an initial presumption that all property of the spouses is to be equally divided upon divorce. This rule-equality presumption is consistent with the organizing concept of marriage as an equal partnership. While need is not forgotten, the partnership model is urged because of its symbolic significance in reflecting the preferred or correct vision of women and also, secondarily, because it addresses need. Through ideological fiat, the dependent woman is considered to be benefited in being brought "up" to partnership status and made an "equal."

That factors based on both the dependency and partnership models of marriage exist simultaneously within any distribution system does not suggest that the application of these factors will necessarily reflect an explicit, principled balancing process. Rather, it seems that within the context of any distribution task, there may be unavoidable concessions to dependency within a preferred framework that focuses on contribution and equality.

If one rejects the comprehensiveness of either or both of the conflicting images of marriage that the stereotypes of woman as equal and woman as dependent represent, one must confront the reality that many women whose mixed circumstances may require remedial rules are neglected. The stereotypes of dependency and partnership are polar opposites. Thus no single, typical result can be fairly reconciled with the goal of doing justice to both. A woman who operates in both the marriage and the market as an "equal" might be better off under the old common-law system, where she keeps her separate property, and her ex-husband is liable only for child support. The true dependent, by contrast, might by her very circumstances have been able to claim all of the property and still be found in need of continued support for herself. In either case, it would seem that what is desirable in the way of reform is the creation of a range of acceptable economic outcomes which could accommodate a variety of differences among women in various circumstances. The focus on the stereotypes of dependency and equality and the futile attempt to reconcile them tend to narrow rather than expand the definition of acceptable results. . . .

The dominance of equality means it will . . . provide the preferred method for valuing contributions and thus will further obviate the need for anything resembling detailed fact-finding or consideration of individualized circumstances regarding the actual amount of contribution. Because divorce is an economic adjustment between partners, with the ideal solution being an equal division of the assets and liabilities amassed as a result of their equally-valued contribution, the use of contribution eliminates the need for individualized inquiry. Based on a fictitious past, on some socially derived, idealized notion of all spouses' actions and conduct during marriage, contribution operates at the expense of inquiry into possible future needs.

As already noted, the partnership model is not an absolute one, and specific factors are often available which can be employed to allow deviation from the equality ideal. Various individual circumstances may exist that could indicate the necessity of making an unequal allocation of assets and/or liabilities at divorce to handle future needs. Theoretically, even in the face of an initial equal-division presumption, the existence of need-based factors provides the potential for deviation from the distribution norm of equality.

Unfortunately, in the statutory schemes and case law, the need factors are neither sufficiently developed nor sufficiently clear to offset the partnership model with its easily grasped contribution factors. While it is true that other statutory provisions dealing with child support and maintenance are designed in part to alleviate need, these provisions present practical problems which make them ineffective in many instances.

Some of these problems were created by the reform movement because the equality ideal was also extended to responsibilities. Women now share equal responsibility with their ex-husbands for the economic well-being of the children, a result which on its face is desirable and fair. However, as with property division, equality in shouldering child-support obligations may mean equally splitting the monetary costs, not contributing according to ability nor valuing nonmonetary contributions. There is an unreality about the use of equality in such circumstances. It does not allow us to focus clearly on predictable future circumstances which will have profound implications for single-parent families. Thus, even without a specific mandate that the court presume that property is to be divided equally, judges and lawyers will tend to adopt this standard because of the social and professional conditioning that presents modern marriage as an equal partnership.

Alteration of the partnership model is likely to be possible only if the spouse arguing for such a deviation can meet the burden of establishing that her circumstances (needs) are clearly exceptional. The wholesale acceptance of the partnership model means, however, that the burdens of production, proof, and persuasion will be placed upon the one who argues that the rule-equality concept is inadequate given her specific circumstances.

Furthermore, even if a wife could initially meet the burden of demonstrating that her needs should outweigh the equal-contribution assumptions, her husband could argue the presence or absence of other factors in an attempt to counter the assertion that deviation is appropriate. Because the factors are not weighted or ranked, one factor or set of factors may be balanced against another in the decision-making process. As a result, unless one spouse can assert that she occupies all, or most, of the categories (an unlikely scenario since they are inherently incompatible), her spouse may use the remaining factors to push the allocation toward the rule-equality norm.

The difficulty of attempting to deviate from the equality presumption is further complicated by the fact that, in using and developing the factors, decision-makers have themselves failed to distinguish those grouped under the concept of contribution from those supported by need. Although they are really referencing different models and different sets of concerns, contribution arguments may be used to offset an appeal for unequal division based on need.

For example, a woman may argue that since her education or employment skills and the presence of small children make it unlikely that she can become self-supporting at a standard of living reasonably comparable to that enjoyed during the marriage, she needs more than 50 percent of the property. Her husband need not dispute these assertions but only argue that the marriage lasted only a few years, implying that she has not assisted in the accumulation of assets or that he has aided her by assuming financial and domestic responsibilities while she went to school or work, and these equally unweighted contribution factors may be applied in his favor to negate her need-based arguments. Since he is able to argue that some of the provisions apply to him, these are likely to cancel out her arguments, and the norm of equal division will probably prevail.

It should be recognized that the arguments are presented on different conceptual bases. She is arguing *need*, while he is responding with *contribution*, which does not meet or defeat the thrust of her assertions. To the extent that contribution is defined by the equality or partnership model, only the greatly disadvantaged—the polar model of dependency—will have a chance at deviation.

In addition, since the factors are not weighted or ranked, even when employed they will be only partially effective in negating the preference for the rule-equality model. Since equality is established as the norm, justification becomes more difficult for more than nominal deviations from equal division of assets. Therefore, even in cases where deviation is considered appropriate, the combination of the failure to weigh the factors and the expressed preference for equal division is likely to lessen the distance from the equality ideal and, consequently, the incentive for attempting deviation at all. . . .

The logical ramifications of symbolic adherence to equality may be significant. A commitment to equality initially encourages its proponents to minimize or deny differences between the individuals they perceive to be in superior positions and those who are in socially subordinate positions. Contribution is an equalizing concept, while need demands an acknowledgment and evaluation of differences.

Overreliance on symbolic concerns may create several difficulties, however. The contribution concept may impede the development of instrumental rules that directly address practical problems. For example, arguing that housework and child care are equal to monetary contributions and are therefore entitled to equal recognition when property is divided can be viewed as one way of dealing with need in the overall context of the equality concept. The need concept is disguised but not abandoned. This is only satisfactory, however, if the conceptual limitation on the contribution notion (one-half, or an equal share) results in decisions which satisfy need in an overwhelming majority of cases. If it cannot, the equality solution is inadequate for the problem of need. In fact, need cannot be alleviated by equal divisions so long as other factors between men and women remain unequal.

The concept of need is often the unstated argument that underlies all the arguments in the area of property division. Because it is disguised, though, the solutions which are proposed necessarily fail to deal effectively with the problem of need. To emerge from a divorce in a position that even begins to put them on an economic par with their ex-husbands, many women need to receive more in property division than the strict equality concept applied to a narrower and more traditionally appropriate definition of marital property will allow. The triumph of the rule-equality concept in this area has been by the sacrifice of equity.

Since sharing responsibility is often translated into assuming equal responsibility, the result is unrealistic, even cruel, given the practical situation of many women. The problem is not that the idea of sharing financial responsibility between husband and wife is inherently unreasonable or unfair, but rather that sharing expectations must be tempered by reference to evidence indicating that equality in the financial circumstances of men and women does not exist. *Shared* responsibility, therefore, should not be equated with *equal* responsibility.

Simplistic, rule-equality changes in divorce laws premised on an unrealized egalitarian marriage ideal will tend to further impoverish women and their children. Under such laws, divorced women are to assume sole economic responsibility for themselves and joint economic responsibility for their children. Theoretically, this requirement is fair because divorced women will assume this responsibility under the same terms and conditions as their ex-spouses. Equal treatment in divorce, however, can only be fair if spouses have access to equal resources and have equivalent needs. Realistically, many women do not have such economic advantages. In addition, they continue to care for children.

III.   DEFINING MARITAL PROPERTY

A basic problem in divorce involves identifying the properties that should be subject to division upon divorce. This is a problem in states that specify that only community or marital property is subject to division upon divorce. Who is nominally the holder of the property cannot answer the question under a broader view of marital partnership and mutual contributions. Yet absent a statute authorizing division of all assets owned by each spouse, courts must engage in a process of characterizing the assets that are divisible.

Consider one hotly contested example. Should the expected future income from the professional degree or license earned by one partner during the marriage be treated as property, properly divisible upon divorce? Most states have rejected this view. One thoughtful treatment of the minority answer in the affirmative appears in the case of O'Brien v. O'Brien.

O'Brien v. O'Brien

Court of Appeals of New York, 1985.
66 N.Y.2d 576, 498 N.Y.S.2d 743, 489 N.E.2d 712.

RICHARD SIMONS, JUDGE.

In this divorce action, the parties' only asset of any consequence is the husband's newly acquired license to practice medicine. The principal issue presented is whether that license, acquired during the marriage, is marital property subject to equitable distribution under Domestic Relations Law Sec. 236(B)(5). Supreme Court held that it was and accordingly made a distributive award in the defendant's favor. It also granted attorney's fees (114 Misc.2d 233). On appeal to the Appellate Division, a majority of that court held that plaintiff's medical license is not marital property and that defendant was not entitled to an award for the expert witness fees. It modified the judgment and remitted the case to Supreme Court for further proceedings, specifically for a determination of maintenance and a rehabilitative award (106 A.D.2d 223, 485 N.Y.S.2d 548). . . .

We now hold that plaintiff's medical license constitutes "marital property" within the meaning of Domestic Relations Law Sec. 236(B)(1)(c) and that it is therefore subject to equitable distribution pursuant to subdivision 5 of that part. That being so, the Appellate Division erred in denying a fee, as a matter of law, to defendant's expert witness who evaluated the license.

I

Plaintiff and defendant married on April 3, 1971. At the time both were employed as teachers at the same private school. Defendant had a bachelor's degree and a temporary teaching certificate but required 18 months of postgraduate classes at an approximate cost of $3,000, excluding living expenses, to obtain permanent certification in New York. She claimed, and the trial court found, that she had relinquished the opportunity to obtain permanent certification while plaintiff pursued his education. At the time of the marriage, plaintiff had completed only three and one-half years of college but shortly afterward he returned to school at night to earn his bachelor's degree and to complete sufficient premedical courses to enter medical school. In September 1973 the parties moved to Guadalajara, Mexico, where plaintiff became a full-time medical student. While he pursued his studies defendant held several teaching and tutorial positions and contributed her earnings to their joint expenses. The parties returned to New York in December 1976 so that plaintiff could complete the last two semesters of medical school and internship training here. After they returned, defendant resumed her former teaching position and she remained in it at the time this action was commenced. Plaintiff was licensed to practice medicine in October 1980. He commenced this action for divorce two months later. At the time of trial, he was a resident in general surgery.

During the marriage both parties contributed to paying the living and educational expenses and they received additional help from both of their families. They disagreed on the amounts of their respective contributions but it is undisputed that in addition to performing household work and managing the family finances defendant was gainfully employed throughout the marriage, that she contributed all of her earnings to their living and educational expenses and that her financial contributions exceeded those of plaintiff. The trial court found that she had contributed 76% of the parties' income exclusive of a $10,000 student loan obtained by defendant. Finding that plaintiff's medical degree and license are marital property, the court received evidence of its value and ordered a distributive award to defendant.

Defendant presented expert testimony that the present value of plaintiff's medical license was $472,000. Her expert testified that he arrived at this figure by comparing the average income of a college graduate and that of a general surgeon between 1985, when plaintiff's residency would end, and 2012, when he would reach age 65. After considering Federal income taxes, an inflation rate of 10% and a real interest rate of 3% he capitalized the difference in average earnings and reduced the amount to present value. He also gave his opinion that the present value of defendant's contribution to plaintiff's medical education was $103,390. Plaintiff offered no expert testimony on the subject.

The court, after considering the life-style that plaintiff would enjoy from the enhanced earning potential his medical license would bring and defendant's contributions and efforts toward attainment of it, made a distributive award to her of $188,800, representing 40% of the value of the license, and ordered it paid in 11 annual installments of various amounts beginning November 1, 1982 and ending November 1, 1992. The court also directed plaintiff to maintain a life insurance policy on his life for defendant's benefit for the unpaid balance of the award and it ordered plaintiff to pay defendant's counsel fees of $7,000 and her expert witness fee of $1,000. It did not award defendant maintenance.

A divided Appellate Division, relying on its prior decision in Conner v. Conner, 97 A.D.2d 88, 468 N.Y.S.2d 482 and the decision of the Fourth Department in Lesman v. Lesman, 88 A.D.2d 153, 452 N.Y.S.2d 935, appeal dismissed 57 N.Y.2d 956, concluded that a professional license acquired during marriage is not marital property subject to distribution. It therefore modified the judgment by striking the trial court's determination that it is and by striking the provision ordering payment of the expert witness for evaluating the license and remitted the case for further proceedings.

On these cross appeals, defendant seeks reinstatement of the judgment of the trial court. Plaintiff contends that the Appellate Division correctly held that a professional license is not marital property but he also urges that the trial court failed to adequately explain what factors it relied on in making its decision, that it erroneously excluded evidence of defendant's marital fault and that the trial court's awards for attorneys and expert witness fees were improper.

II

The Equitable Distribution Law contemplates only two classes of property: marital property and separate property (Domestic Relations Law Sec. 236(B)(1)(c),(d)). The former, which is subject to equitable distribution, is defined broadly as "all property acquired by either or both spouses during the marriage and before the execution of a separation agreement or the commencement of a matrimonial action, regardless of the form in which title is held" (Domestic Relations Law 236(B)(1)(c); see 236(B)(5) (b),(c)). Plaintiff does not contend that his license is excluded from distribution because it is separate property; rather, he claims that it is not property at all but represents a personal attainment in acquiring knowledge. He rests his argument on decisions in similar cases from other jurisdictions and on his view that a license does not satisfy common-law concepts of property. Neither contention is controlling because decisions in other States rely principally on their own statutes, and the legislative history underlying them, and because the New York Legislature deliberately went beyond traditional property concepts when it formulated the Equitable Distribution Law (see generally, 2 Foster–Freed–Brandes, Law and the Family—New York ch. 33, at 917 et seq. [1985 Cum.Supp.]). Instead, our statute recognizes that spouses have an equitable claim to things of value arising out of the marital relationship and classifies them as subject to distribution by focusing on the marital status of the parties at the time of acquisition. Those things acquired during marriage and subject to distribution have been classified as "marital property" although, as one commentator has observed, they hardly fall within the traditional property concepts because there is no common-law property interest remotely resembling marital property. "It is a statutory creature, is of no meaning whatsoever during the normal course of a marriage and arises full-grown, like Athena, upon the signing of a separation agreement or the commencement of a matrimonial action. [Thus] [i]t is hardly surprising, and not at all relevant, that traditional common law property concepts do not fit in parsing the meaning of 'marital property'." ... Having classified the "property" subject to distribution, the Legislature did not attempt to go further and define it but left it to the courts to determine what interests come within the terms of section 236(B)(1)(c).

We made such a determination in Majauskas v. Majauskas, 61 N.Y.2d 481, 474 N.Y.S.2d 699, 463 N.E.2d 15, holding there that vested but unmatured pension rights are marital property subject to equitable distribution. Because pension benefits are not specifically identified as marital property in the statute, we looked to the express reference to pension rights contained in section 236(B)(5)(d)(4), which deals with equitable distribution of marital property, to other provisions of the equitable distribution statute and to the legislative intent behind its enactment to determine whether pension rights are marital property or separate property. A similar analysis is appropriate here and leads to the conclusion that marital property encompasses a license to practice medicine to the extent that the license is acquired during marriage.

Section 236 provides that in making an equitable distribution of marital property, "the court shall consider: . . . (6) any equitable claim to, interest in, or direct or indirect contribution made to the acquisition of such marital property by the party not having title, including joint efforts or expenditures and contributions and services as a spouse, parent, wage earner and homemaker, and to the career or career potential of the other party [and] . . . (9) the impossibility or difficulty of evaluating any component or asset or any interest in a business, corporation or profession" (Domestic Relations Law Sec. 236(B)(5)(d)(6), (9) . . .). Where equitable distribution of marital property is appropriate but "the distribution of an interest in a business, corporation or profession would be contrary to law" the court shall make a distributive award in lieu of an actual distribution of the property (Domestic Relations Law Sec. 236(B)(5)(e) . . .). The words mean exactly what they say: that an interest in a profession or professional career potential is marital property which may be represented by direct or indirect contributions of the non-title-holding spouse, including financial contributions and nonfinancial contributions made by caring for the home and family.

The history which preceded enactment of the statute confirms this interpretation. Reform of section 236 was advocated because experience had proven that application of the traditional common-law title theory of property had caused inequities upon dissolution of a marriage. The Legislature replaced the existing system with equitable distribution of marital property, an entirely new theory which considered all the circumstances of the case and of the respective parties to the marriage (Assembly Memorandum, 1980 N.Y.Legis.Ann., at 129–130). Equitable distribution was based on the premise that a marriage is, among other things, an economic partnership to which both parties contribute as spouse, parent, wage earner or homemaker (id., at 130; see, Governor's Memorandum of Approval, 1980 McKinney's Session Laws of N.Y., at 1863). Consistent with this purpose, and implicit in the statutory scheme as a whole, is the view that upon dissolution of the marriage there should be a winding up of the parties' economic affairs and a severance of their economic ties by an equitable distribution of the marital assets. Thus, the concept of alimony, which often served as a means of lifetime support and dependence for one spouse upon the other long after the marriage was over, was replaced with the concept of maintenance which seeks to allow "the recipient spouse an opportunity to achieve [economic] independence" (Assembly Memorandum, 1980 N.Y.Legis.Ann., at 130).

The determination that a professional license is marital property is also consistent with the conceptual base upon which the statute rests. As this case demonstrates, few undertakings during a marriage better qualify as the type of joint effort that the statute's economic partnership theory is intended to address than contributions toward one spouse's acquisition of a professional license. Working spouses are often required to contribute substantial income as wage earners, sacrifice their own educational or career goals and opportunities for child rearing, perform the bulk of household duties and responsibilities and forego the acquisition of marital assets that could have been accumulated if the professional spouse had been employed rather than occupied with the study and training necessary to acquire a professional license. In this case, nearly all the parties' nine-year marriage was devoted to the acquisition of plaintiff's medical license and defendant played a major role in that project. She worked continuously during the marriage and contributed all of her earnings to their joint effort, she sacrificed her own educational and career opportunities, and she traveled with plaintiff to Mexico for three and one-half years while he attended medical school there. The Legislature has decided, by its explicit reference in the statute to the contributions of one spouse to the other's profession or career (see, Domestic Relations Law Sec. 236(B)(5)(d)(6), (9); (e)), that these contributions represent investments in the economic partnership of the marriage and that the product of the parties' joint efforts, the professional license, should be considered marital property.

The majority at the Appellate Division held that the cited statutory provisions do not refer to the license held by a professional who has yet to establish a practice but only to a going professional practice. ... There is no reason in law or logic to restrict the plain language of the statute to existing practices, however, for it is of little consequence in making an award of marital property, except for the purpose of evaluation, whether the professional spouse has already established a practice or whether he or she has yet to do so. An established practice merely represents the exercise of the privileges conferred upon the professional spouse by the license and the income flowing from that practice represents the receipt of the enhanced earning capacity that licensure allows. That being so, it would be unfair not to consider the license a marital asset.

Plaintiff's principal argument, adopted by the majority below, is that a professional license is not marital property because it does not fit within the traditional view of property as something which has an exchange value on the open market and is capable of sale, assignment or transfer. The position does not withstand analysis for at least two reasons. First, as we have observed, it ignores the fact that whether a professional license constitutes marital property is to be judged by the language of the statute which created this new species of property previously unknown at common law or under prior statutes. Thus, whether the license fits within traditional property concepts is of no consequence. Second, it is an overstatement to assert that a professional license could not be considered property even outside the context of section 236(B). A professional license is a valuable property right, reflected in the money, effort and lost opportunity for employment expended in its acquisition, and also in the enhanced earning capacity it affords its holder, which may not be revoked without due process of law. ... That a professional license has no market value is irrelevant. Obviously, a license cannot be alienated as may other property and for that reason the working spouse's interest in it is limited. The Legislature has recognized that limitation, however, and has provided for an award in lieu of its actual distribution (see, Domestic Relations Sec. Law 236(B)(5)(e)).

Plaintiff also contends that alternative remedies should be employed, such as an award of rehabilitative maintenance or reimbursement for direct financial contributions. ... The statute does not expressly authorize retrospective maintenance or rehabilitative awards and we have no occasion to decide in this case whether the authority to do so may ever be implied from its provisions (but see, Cappiello v. Cappiello, 66 N.Y.2d 107, 495 N.Y.S.2d 318, 485 N.E.2d 983). It is sufficient to observe that normally a working spouse should not be restricted to that relief because to do so frustrates the purposes underlying the Equitable Distribution Law. Limiting a working spouse to a maintenance award, either general or rehabilitative, not only is contrary to the economic partnership concept underlying the statute but also retains the uncertain and inequitable economic ties of dependence that the Legislature sought to extinguish by equitable distribution. ...

Turning to the question of valuation, it has been suggested that even if a professional license is considered marital property, the working spouse is entitled only to reimbursement of his or her direct financial contributions (see, Note, Equitable Distribution of Degrees and Licenses: Two Theories Toward Compensating Spousal Contributions, 49 Brooklyn L. Rev. 301, 317–322). By parity of reasoning, a spouse's down payment on real estate or contribution to the purchase of securities would be limited to the money contributed, without any remuneration for any incremental value in the asset because of price appreciation. Such a result is completely at odds with the statute's requirement that the court give full consideration to both direct and indirect contributions "made to the acquisition of such marital property by the party not having title, including joint efforts or expenditures and contributions and services as a spouse, parent, wage earner and homemaker" (Domestic Relations Law 236(B)(5)(d)(6)). If the license is marital property, then the working spouse is entitled to an equitable portion of it, not a return of funds advanced. Its value is the enhanced earning capacity if affords the holder and although fixing the present value of that enhanced earning capacity may present problems, the problems are not insurmountable. . . .

NOTES AND QUESTIONS

1. **Are Professional Degrees Property Divisible Upon Divorce?** Other than New York, only a few Michigan appellate courts have adopted the view that a professional degree is property divisible upon divorce. Other jurisdictions, like Massachusetts, have strongly rejected this approach, although some do require courts to take into consideration one spouse's contribution to the acquisition of the degree by the other. For example, in some jurisdictions, courts may award "reimbursement" for the expenses incurred in putting the former spouse through school. This was the approach taken in Mahoney v. Mahoney, 91 N.J. 488, 453 A.2d 527 (1982), a case in which the wife had financially supported her husband while he received his M.B.A. The court, while refusing to characterize the degree as property, introduced the concept of "reimbursement alimony," stating that such a concept

> accords with the Court's belief that regardless of the appropriate-ness of permanent alimony or the presence or absence of marital property to be equitably distributed, there will be circumstances where a supporting spouse should be reimbursed for the financial contributions he or she made to the spouse's successful profession-al training. Such reimbursement alimony should cover all financial contributions towards the former spouse's education, including household expenses, educational costs, school travel expenses, and any other contributions used by the supported spouse in obtaining his or her degree or license. . . . Marriage should not be a free ticket to professional education and training without subsequent obligations. This Court should not ignore the scenario of the young professional who after being supported through graduate school leaves his mate for greener pastures. One spouse ought not to receive a divorce complaint when the other receives a diploma. *Id.* at 502–503.

The *Mahoney* decision makes clear that the Court intended reimburse-ment alimony to apply only to financial contributions and only to those financial contributions from which the parties mutually expected to benefit. Does this view undervalue the nonmonetary contributions performed by a homemaker? Also, imagine the case in which a financially successful executive's spouse returns to school after many years of homemaking. Under the logic of *Mahoney*, should the spouse who returned to school be required to reimburse the other for his or her contributions toward the degree?

2. **Pensions.** Similar issues arise with employment-related benefits, such as pensions. Although many states call for the division of one spouse's pension benefits upon divorce, some do not. States also divide over whether

to distribute the present value of a future pension or instead to divide the pension payments when they become due.

3. **Businesses**. When one or both of the divorcing spouses owns a business or a business interest, disputes may arise over whether and how to divide the value of that asset. Should the goodwill value (expectation of continuing patronage and economic success) be divisible? The courts are split on this question, and also differ on valuation methods. What theory of gender relations during marriage would support division of this asset—that the non-owner supplied important assistance at home that should be treated as an investment? What theory of gender relations at home would push against dividing this asset? What should be the result if marriage is conceived as a partnership to which spouses may give equal though different contributions?

4. **Traditional Homemaker**. A special problem arises in devising a method for dividing property where one spouse, usually the man, worked outside the home during the marriage, and the other, usually the woman, became a homemaker and spent time raising children. Where the parties to a marriage planned that traditional allocation of roles, how should property be divided upon divorce?

5. **Reliance Theory**. Bea Ann Smith argues that a partnership theory of marriage will never meet the needs of a dependent spouse upon divorce because many marriages do not produce easily divisible property, and the primary source of wealth—in human capital—is not easily divisible. Therefore, "[t]o soften the harsh economic consequences of divorce, we need a scheme for sharing the ongoing liabilities and responsibilities created by roles assumed during marriage, whether or not marital property has accumulated. ...It is not enough to distribute marital assets without also redistributing the economic consequences flowing from marital reliance." Bea Ann Smith, *The Partnership Theory of Marriage: A Borrowed Solution Fails*, 68 Texas L. Rev. 689 (1990). Therefore, Smith urges use of a detrimental reliance notion to help allocate economic resources upon divorce.

IV. SPOUSAL SUPPORT

Traditional common law practices assigned a support duty to a husband that carried on after separation. As divorce became more common, this support duty continued, at least in theory, under the name of alimony (and, more recently, spousal support or maintenance) and was justified on the presumption of financial need. In practice, however, actual orders and payments of spousal support have always been quite rare for the population as a whole.

One of the landmark Supreme Court challenges to sex differences in the law occurred in Orr v. Orr, 440 U.S. 268, 99 S.Ct. 1102, 59 L.Ed.2d 306 (1979), which rejected as a violation of the Equal Protection clause of the Fourteenth Amendment a state statute imposing a duty to pay alimony on divorced husbands for wives in financial need, but not on divorced wives with husbands in financial need. Today, a small but growing number of divorced men—estimated at between 5 and 10 percent—are now getting alimony from their former wives. Explains sociologist Kathryn Rettig: "Women are getting better, higher-paying jobs at the same time that men's wages are decreasing ... If women want equality under the law, they have to take the responsibility" for supporting dependent spouses. *See* Margaret A. Jacobs, *More Men Get Alimony, and More Women Get Mad*, Wall Street Journal, July 30, 1997, at p. B1.

Three questions have become increasingly pressing as states have had to replace traditional schemes for alimony in order to eliminate the old rules explicitly restricting the alimony duty to men. First, should the duty to provide support be permanent, until the death of either party, or temporary, and if so, based on what end-point? Some commentators have argued that long-term maintenance for women fosters dependency and undermines women's equality with men. They have suggested that divorce laws should emphasize achieving a fair division of marital property and should de-emphasize spousal support in an effort to allow women to achieve a clean break. For such a perspective, see Herma Hill Kay, *An Appraisal of California's No–Fault Divorce Law*, 75 Calif. L. Rev. 291, 313, 318 (Jan. 1987). Do you believe that permanent or long-term support for divorced women is desirable or undesirable from a feminist perspective? Furthermore, do you believe that it is possible to generalize on this issue or, rather, that the length of alimony awards should be considered on a case-by-case basis? Finally, if you take the latter position, what types of situations do you believe would merit the imposition of long-term or permanent maintenance?

A second, and related, question concerns the size and content of the alimony award: How should it be calculated, and should the calculation be made in conjunction with child support and property division? Since the answer to this question turns largely on the rationale for awarding alimony in the first place, a third question has emerged: How can spousal support ever be justified? Here is a sampling of some responses:

Ellman's Theory of Alimony. Professor Ira Ellman criticizes justifications for alimony based on contractual notions of party preferences because such preferences are rarely known in fact. Inspired by efficiency analysis, he offers an alternative theory designed to encourage socially beneficial sharing behavior in marriage "by requiring compensation for lost earning capacity arising from that behavior." Ira Ellman, *The Theory of Alimony*, 77 Calif. L. Rev. 1, 12 (1989). According to Ellman,

> A system of alimony that compensates the wife who has disproportionate postmarriage losses arising from her marital investment protects marital decisionmaking from the potentially destructive pressures of a market that does not value marital investment as much as it values career enhancement. The system of alimony generated by this theory is also consistent with equitable notions: It protects the spouse who has made a marital investment, thinking that her marriage was a shared enterprise, from a unilateral decision by her spouse to cease sharing ... This conception of alimony differs fundamentally from prevailing law. It casts alimo-

ny as an entitlement earned through marital investment, and as a tool to eliminate distorting financial incentives, and not as a way of relieving need. An alimony law based upon this conception would therefore ask whether the wife invested in her marriage and is thereby economically disadvantaged upon divorce; it would not inquire into need per se. The wife who invested little or whose need arose from events unrelated to her marriage would have no claim against her former husband. Her relief, if she was in need, would be a societal obligation. By the same token, the wife who suffers economically from a divorce as a result of her marital investment would have a claim even if her financial situation did not place her in "need." *Id.*, at 51.

If the alimony award does not meet the cost of raising children after divorce, then child support awards should reflect that amount, not alimony awards. *Id.*, at 74. A central idea here is that members of a couple can rationally decide to specialize, and assign to one party the task of earning a living and to the other party the non-market work in the home, but this specialization works only when the marriage continues. A cautious spouse who worries about marital breakup might reject this optimal specialization path; alimony provides some assurance that even marital breakup can preserve the gains of specialization during the marriage.

Singer's Reply. Professor Jana Singer replies that economic efficiency should not guide a theory of alimony because it treats wealth maximization as the primary purpose of marriage. Jana B. Singer, *Alimony and Efficiency: The Gendered Costs and Benefits of the Economic Justification for Alimony*, 82 Geo. L. J. 2423 (1994). In addition, the theory values marriages with role specialization, which was traditionally linked to conventional gender roles. Singer raises doubts about whether such specialization is in fact efficient, and even if efficient, whether it is desirable. As an alternative, Singer supports a theory of alimony predicated on marriage as an equal partnership and enhancement of human capital as the most valuable asset produced during most marriages. *Id.*, at 2454. If the divorce produces a net economic loss, that loss should be shared equally by both spouses. Singer acknowledges that this approach might lead to post-divorce economic obligations that deter subsequent marriages for the higher-earning spouse, and she comments that this might not be a bad result. This kind of regime should also, in Singer's view, encourage people to invest more in the ongoing marriage.

Income Sharing. Professor Jane Rutherford advocates income sharing following divorce "in which the incomes of the former couple would be added and divided by the number of people to be supported." Jane Rutherford, *Shared Income in Divorce*, 58 Fordham L. Rev. 539 (1990). This approach embraces equality of results in order to foster sharing in families, to protect the spouse who was devoted to homemaking during the marriage, to avoid fault-based considerations, and to eliminate the economic disadvantages of divorce for many women. Rather than producing a specific alimony award, this formula would automatically adjust to changing circumstances.

Property Not Alimony. Professor Joan Williams argues that the challenge for gender equality should not be cast in terms of devising a new rationale and scheme for alimony, but instead eliminating the vestiges of the husband's control over marital property. Joan Williams, *Is Coverture Dead: Beyond a New Theory of Alimony*, 82 Geo. L. J. 2227 (1994). Accordingly, Williams proposes that the same community property presumption of joint entitlement applicable to income earned during the marriage should apply to income earned after the dissolution where the marriage produced children or where one spouse supported the other spouse's costs of schooling. She also suggests combining child support and alimony into a single calculation of post-divorce income to assure the primary caretaker and children from the marriage a standard of living equal to that of the non-custodial parent.

What is the picture of the family implicit in these competing theories? What is the image of the marriage, and the presumed class and racial status of the participants? Professor Perry's article offers a perspective on these questions.

Twila L. Perry, Alimony: Race, Privilege, and Dependency in the Search for Theory

82 Georgetown L. J. 2481 (1994).

... This article draws from the intersection of theories of alimony, feminist legal theory, and the racial critique of feminist legal theory. The goal of the article is to explore the implications of the search for a theory of alimony for those women who, as a practical matter, are least likely to benefit from this effort—women who are neither well-to-do nor white.

Statistics indicate that Black women are awarded alimony at a significantly lower rate than white women. In 1987, over eighteen percent of currently divorced or separated white women had been awarded alimony at the time of their divorces, while less than eight percent of Black women had received such an award. It also appears that women in higher income marriages are more likely to receive alimony than women in lower income marriages. In light of this data, it is important that we examine the implications of women scholars devoting substantial attention to an issue that is of practical importance to relatively few women, and especially so few women of color. What are the implications for women of color and other poor women of this search for a theory of alimony? Does it serve to reinforce the differences between women of different classes and races? Or are there ways in which a discourse that seems relevant only to privileged women can be helpful to the struggles of a wider range of women in whose lives gender, race, and class oppression are often experienced simultaneously? Can efforts aimed at developing a theory of alimony both enrich and draw upon other scholarly work directed toward improving the conditions of subordinated groups?

... [T]he marriage paradigm that has, to a great extent, shaped the discourse on developing a theory of alimony ... has little relevance to the realities faced by most poor women of color and ..., accordingly, most of the approaches to alimony based on it have little practical relevance to the lives of these women. I define the issue, however, as more than one of mere irrelevance or exclusion—I argue that the search to develop a theory of alimony may have serious negative implications for poor women of color, especially Black women. Specifically, the paradigmatic model of marriage and divorce has the potential to reinforce the subordination and marginalization of Black women in two ways: first, by reinforcing privilege or an image of privilege for middle and upper-middle class white women in both marriage and divorce, and second, by reinforcing a hierarchy among women in which their value is determined by the presence or absence of legal ties to men, particularly affluent men. ...

The Paradigm Marriage and the Lives of Black Women

Although much of the writing about theories of alimony may not envision most divorces as occurring among the rich and famous, it at least assumes a middle or upper-middle class marriage. The marital arrangements assumed in most discussions of alimony may be described as the "paradigm marriage."

In the paradigm marriage, the wife sacrifices or slows down her career to attend to the interests of her husband and children. It used to be the case that many married women remained out of the workforce in order to care for their families. Today, with the majority of women in the workforce, the paradigm marriage may be better represented by the wife who stays home for a few years, works part-time for a few years, or generally slows down her career in order to make more time for her domestic responsibilities. The consequences of both models, however, may be similar. The husband's career is benefitted by his freedom from time-consuming family responsibilities. The wife makes her decision in the belief that she is investing in a long-term marriage. She believes that her marriage is for life and that at a later stage, when she is older and the children are grown, she will benefit from her sacrifices by sharing an economically comfortable life with her husband. However, if the couple divorces, the wife is left in a troubling position. She has less earning power than her former husband. She has less ability to find another spouse. Usually, she has custody of the children, a fact that will impede her ability to pursue a demanding, potentially lucrative career. She has a generally lower social and economic position and fewer prospects than she had during the marriage.

This paradigm becomes the framework in which we think about the problem of alimony. We visualize a man financially capable of providing money, both during and after marriage. We think of a woman who has had the choice to work, to stay home, or to slow down her career in order to care for her family. We often tend to think of the woman as the "victim" of divorce—cast out by a man who has tired of her after she has rendered many years of dedicated service and made him the focus of her life. The goal becomes to find a way to ensure that the man remains financially responsible so as to lessen the former wife's economic fall. We may not give much thought to the implications of our discussion for women who live their lives outside of the paradigm and whose lives have been characterized by employment and independence rather than homemaking and dependency.

The whole notion of separate spheres and the "cult of domesticity" that defined women as naturally suited for motherhood rather than public life has not been a part of Black women's experience in this country. Black women have never been excluded from the public sphere as workers and have generally not been the object of the law's notion of protection. Thus the concept of limiting women to domestic roles evidenced in Supreme Court opinions such as *Bradwell v. Illinois* or *Muller v. Oregon* has never applied to the lives of most Black women, a group that has historically defied the norm that defines motherhood as incompatible with wage labor. During slavery, Black women engaged in physical labor while white women's roles were more that of companion or mother. After slavery, Black women continued to be workers, entering the labor force in numbers that far exceeded those of white women. By 1880, fifty percent of Black women were in the labor force, as compared to only fifteen percent of white women. And although today the majority of married women have jobs, Black women continue to hold jobs outside of the home in greater numbers than white women.

Nor does the present structure of most marriages of Black couples fit the paradigm generally assumed in discussion of the theory of alimony. Whereas historically many white women have been able to enhance their standards of living by "marrying well," this has seldom been the case for most Black women. Because Black men typically earn less than white men, for most Black families, having the mother in the workforce has always been a necessity. Black women are less likely than white women to have the option of choosing part-time work in order to spend more time with their children, and, obviously, Black women are less likely than white women to be confronted with the "dilemma" of having to decide whether to leave a promising job to follow a husband whose company has transferred him or who has found a job opportunity elsewhere.

Research on Black women also suggests that they may not experience the divide between mothering and working outside of the home in precisely the same way as white women. Indeed, in much of the literature on the socialization of Black women, a common theme is that Black women were taught by their mothers that, rather than aspiring to be financially cared for by a man, they should expect their lives to include working and mothering simultaneously. Thus, Gloria Joseph explains that "Black females are socialized by adult figures in early life to become heads of their own households." And Patricia Hill Collins comments that

[t]hree themes implicit in White perspectives on motherhood are particularly problematic for Black women.... First, the assumption that mothering occurs within the confines of a private, nuclear family household where the mother has almost total responsibility for child-rearing is less applicable to Black families. While the ideal of the cult of true womanhood has been held up to Black women for emulation, racial oppression has denied Black families sufficient resources to support private, nuclear family households. Second, strict sex-role segregation, with separate male and female spheres of influence within the family, has been less commonly found in African–American families than in White middle-class ones. Finally, the assumption that motherhood and economic dependency on men are linked and that to be a "good" mother one must stay at home, making motherhood a full-time "occupation," is similarly uncharacteristic of African–American families.

As a result of these sometimes different experiences of marriage and motherhood, Black women and middle or upper-middle class white women may have somewhat different perspectives on the relationship between caring for home and children and expecting economic rewards at a later point in their marriage. This is not to suggest that Black women are unconcerned about their husband's careers or do not hope for a happy marriage or a comfortable life with their husbands as they grow older. What I am suggesting, however, is that Black women's views of their roles as mothers may be more independent from how they view their roles as wives, at least as compared to women who are white and middle or upper-middle class. . . .

As a result of the different situations between most white women and Black women during marriage, the expectations, sexual politics, and economic realities at divorce may also be different. For a Black woman, however intense her emotional devastation may be at the end of a marriage, she probably has less of an expectation of economic compensation than a middle class or upper-middle class white woman might have. Black families have much less tangible economic wealth than white families have, and Black men, on the average, earn substantially less than white men earn. Indeed, in some cases, particularly when the husband has been sporadically employed or unemployed, a wife who has been the primary economic provider for her family may find her economic situation unchanged or even improved upon divorce because there is one less person who is dependent on her for financial support.

Approaches seeking to establish a theory of alimony are based on the paradigm of a husband who is, at least relatively, economically powerful and a wife who has had the option of staying home or slowing down her career in support of the family. Because the paradigm marriage does not fit most Black marriages, the theories of alimony based on it are, for the most part, inapplicable to most Black marriages.

For example, the law and economics approach to alimony is premised on the traditional paradigm. That approach focuses on how to structure family law so as to provide incentives that will encourage specialization of labor in the family. The marital relationship is seen as one in which it is desirable for the parties to make what are considered to be "economically rational" decisions about the division of labor in the home. It may be preferable, in this view, for one spouse to make an investment in the home and the other an investment in the market. It seems obvious that the assumptions of this model have very little relevance to poor people of color where, as it has been noted, necessity may require less clear role definitions or that both spouses be employed full-time in order to make ends meet.

Even those models of alimony not based on the paradigm of the powerful man and the dependent woman have little relevance for most Black couples. For example, the professional degree scenario I mentioned earlier is one that would occur less frequently among Black couples because proportionately there are many fewer Black than white professionals. Proposals based on sharing income after divorce assume both the paradigm marriage and a higher earning spouse (presumably the husband) with a salary sufficient to be shared after divorce, which are assumptions with limited applicability to Blacks. . . .

Implications of Current Discussions Concerning a Theory of Alimony

Ensuring economic justice for upper-middle class women in the event of divorce is not unimportant. Fairness is contextual, and some of these women suffer devastating losses, both economic and emotional. The losses are particularly large for older women who have spent many years as full-time homemakers. It is not necessary to adopt or embrace a general view of women as "victims" to recognize that some of these women have had their domestic labor seriously exploited during marriage.

However, at the same time that scholars seek to achieve economic justice for middle and upper-middle class women whose economic futures may be jeopardized by divorce, they should also consider the implications of their alimony discussion on the many women in this society who will never have the option to become full-time homemakers, to work part-time, or to otherwise slow down their careers to provide more care for their husbands or children. For these women, many but not all of whom are Black or other women of color, working is not an option—it is a necessity. The jobs these women work at are often low-paying, unglamorous positions with limited possibilities for advancement.

Consequently, although it is important to recognize that middle and upper-middle class women may be exploited during marriage, it is equally important to recognize that this exploitation is often accompanied by an element of privilege that may operate both during marriage and after divorce. It is also important to recognize that privileging more advantaged women by awarding alimony can easily reinforce hierarchies that view women as being deserving or undeserving of economic support based solely on their attachment to men. In this hierarchy, where women who have been attached to affluent men are viewed the most sympathetically, Black women, who are the most unlikely to be attached to affluent mates, will always occupy the bottom rung of the ladder. . . .

Another danger of focusing on theories of alimony relevant primarily to privileged women is that it reinforces society's unfortunate tendency to divide women into categories of those who are deserving of economic support and those who are not. Professor Martha Fineman has made significant contributions to the thinking in this area. She has argued that the law has tended to develop various categories in which we place mothers, characterizing them as either deserving or undeserving. Professor Fineman describes a hierarchy of mothers based on their relationships to men, with widows thought of as most deserving, followed by divorced women, followed by unmarried women—especially those who have children—at the bottom of the pile. There is a danger that the search for a theory of alimony reinforces a similar hierarchy.

Let us take the example of two women, neither of whom has ever held a job in her adult life. The first woman was married right out of college to a young man with a promising career. The other woman never married but had three children and ended up receiving public assistance. Both women have been out of the workforce caring for their children at home for the last several years. In one case, the husband has now decided that he wants to end the marriage. In the other case, the government has decided to take more severe measures against mothers receiving public assistance and to force them into workfare programs.

It is likely that many people would be sympathetic to the privileged woman, believing that she is deserving of continued economic support. If circumstances required that she work after divorce, the feeling would probably be that she should be trained for a job that has long-term potential for financial and personal growth. There would be concern about the decline in her economic status as a result of the divorce. There would also probably be concern about her loss of status and about possible resulting psychological harm. On the other hand, many people would feel that the welfare mother should take any job, however low-paying and dead-end, even if it causes her to lose important benefits, such as medical care for her and her children.

It is interesting that many people would probably see it as a noble thing for a talented upper-middle class woman to forgo career opportunities in order to stay home and care for her children, but at the same time take the position that the welfare mother should go out and get a job. The former is viewed as having sacrificed her career in order to spend time with her children, the latter is seen as just plain lazy. We need to think not only about why these two women are likely to be perceived so differently, but also about what the commonality is in our views of them.

It certainly could be argued that if a woman chooses to stay home with her children, the costs of this arrangement should not be borne by society. Thus, some people would argue that it is an acceptable choice for the married woman to stay home because her decision is paid for privately and not by the public. However, the explanation for why the two situations are perceived so differently is probably much deeper than this. For many people, a woman's economic dependency is acceptable as long as that dependency is on a man.

Thus, it could be argued that there is a common thread in these two situations: the yardstick by which both of these women are measured is their relationship to men. A woman who has been supported by a man for twenty years is seen as deserving of continued economic support; a woman who has been supported by the government rather than by a man for the same period is not. Both women may have been superb homemakers and wonderful, attentive mothers, yet only one is viewed as deserving.

In short, we are willing to reward, with partial lifetime financial support, those women who have been "good wives." Women are either punished or rewarded not because of their willingness to forgo work to take care of their children, because some upper-middle class women and some women on welfare may be willing to do this. Instead, what we are willing to reward is the woman who has been willing to tend faithfully to the needs of a man.

The implications of the different perceptions of the two women go even further than just the question of how the women are perceived and valued. Promoting the permanency of a system that protects and rewards privileged women when they stay at home also reinforces a system in which the needs of the children of the well-to-do and the children of the poor are valued differently. We are willing to support a system that provides for the children of affluent fathers the option of remaining at home, cared for by their mothers, while inadequately funded public day-care centers are thought to be enough for the children of poor men. In the case of children, as is true for women, value is assigned on the basis of the status of the adult males in their lives.

Reinforcing a system in which the value of women is determined primarily by the status of the men to whom they are attached can also have profound implications for the relationships between white and Black women. As Patricia Hill Collins has noted, "[r]elationships among Black and white women are framed by the web of sexual politics that seduces white women with an artificial sense of specialness and vests them with the power to sustain that illusion." She also has noted that Black women often feel that far too many white women are unwilling to acknowledge—let alone challenge—the actions of white men because, in part, they have benefitted from them. Indeed, it is that attachment to powerful white men that has enabled white women to participate in the subordination of Black women ever since slavery, and it is those white women with higher family income levels—where alimony would most likely be received in the event of a divorce—who are in the best position to subordinate. These are the women most likely to have the opportunity to employ Black women to do domestic work in their homes, where a complex relationship of racial domination and subordination is often played out. It is, in part, this relationship, as well as Black women's awareness of a past rooted in slavery, that stands as one of the barriers to the formation of effective coalitions between white and Black women.

Issues for Feminist Theory

Alimony creates an image of privilege for white middle and upper-middle class women and does in fact provide a privilege of choice for some of these women. But to a large degree, the institution of alimony is a myth; it appropriately might be called a fraud. Although most people are probably unaware of this fact, the reality is that the vast majority of divorced women have never been awarded alimony. Those who did receive it have not gotten much and often received awards of limited duration. It also seems increasingly likely that none of the theories that have been advanced to justify alimony is likely to adequately protect the economic interests of most women who subordinate their careers to those of their husbands. Alimony may present fascinating intellectual problems for scholars of family law, but, as an institution, it has never been wide-spread, and, at present, it may well be on the way out.

Thus, the institution of alimony and the search for a theory to justify it present two serious concerns for feminists. The first concern has already been discussed: Alimony is troubling because it contributes to the racial hierarchy among women in this society. The second concern is that alimony's promotion of the "cult of true womanhood" encourages privileged women to become economically dependent on men and then often fails to protect them adequately in the event of divorce. . . .

A theory of alimony should be constructed as part of a broader consideration of the question of the relationship between women and work. This means more than advocating a redefinition of traditional roles in the home so that men contribute more to household chores and childrearing. It also means more than demanding a change in the system of wage labor that is currently quite unresponsive to the needs of working mothers. The discussion must go beyond debates about the politics of equality as compared to the "politics of difference." The question is not just how to ultimately achieve gender equality; the question is what are the responsibilities of feminists to women of all races and classes and to the project of creating a more humane and economically just society for everyone.

Let us suppose, for example, that feminists conclude alimony should be eliminated because it encourages dependency. Elimination would mean that, over a period of time, women would more likely put more emphasis on their careers. But this also should not be the end of the matter. A critical question to be asked is how the need for upper-middle class women to work while taking care of their families affects women of other classes and races.

At the present time, the majority of married women are in the workforce. However, many studies have demonstrated that wives who work outside of the home still continue to do a disproportionate amount of child care and housework. Employed wives work an average of forty-four percent more hours than do housewives. These women can operate under great stress and clearly their lives are not easy. They confront a dilemma: how to excel at their jobs outside of the home while ensuring that their children are attended to and that their husbands do not become too unhappy. The solution has often been to hire domestic help. . . .

The current arrangement, whereby middle and upper-middle class white women pursuing careers avail themselves of the work of low-paid women of color and other poor women, is problematic for the feminist movement. It is true that the ability of these women to pursue their careers and maintain acceptable home lives is dependent upon their ability to obtain domestic help. It is equally true that they have an interest in paying as little as they can for that help. They are therefore unlikely to become advocates for childcare workers. Consequently, although obtaining jobs outside of the home may assist in the liberation of white women, it fails to challenge an important context for racial subordination—the domestic service relationship between Black and white women that has existed in this country since slavery. Indeed, such liberation can easily serve to reinforce this unequal relationship.

This is not to suggest that scholars seeking to develop a theory of alimony should feel an obligation to address every problem that affects women of different races and classes. The development of a theory of alimony alone has proven to be an extraordinarily difficult undertaking. However, I have three responses to the argument that taking into account the needs of diverse groups of women as we think about alimony, work, and dependency is beyond the scope of the present effort.

First, women scholars have long discussed the wider implications of women entering the workforce in significant numbers and have argued for the need to restructure the workplace so as to make it more accommodating to the needs of families. It would not be an undue extension of this discussion to also address the question of how the decision of privileged women to work affects the women who are likely to be the caretakers of their homes and children. While professional women work for improvements in their own working conditions, they must remain mindful of the working conditions of the women who work for them—women who are also raising families of their own. Indeed, it would seem to be a much easier undertaking for middle and upper-middle class women to alter the working conditions of the women who work for them than to institute widespread changes in family policy in the workplace.

Second, ignoring the plight of domestic workers seems inconsistent with the underlying idea of fairness that is at the center of the search for a theory of alimony. At its core, the search for a theory of alimony is a search for economic justice for women at the end of marriages in which they have cared for the home and children while their husbands pursued their careers. For Black women who care for the children of upper-middle class white women while these women work, the question is also one of economic justice—but for the period when they are performing domestic services rather than after. To deny the importance of economic justice for women who perform domestic services to assist other women while promoting it for women who have served men seems not only unfair, but troubling for another reason that should be of concern to feminists. It suggests that domestic services are valued if they are done to please and to make life comfortable for men, but that they are not similarly valued when they are performed by one woman for another. The feminist goal of changing a system that values men more than it values women would seem to require acknowledgment of claims of economic justice for women who work for other women.

Third, a lesson from the past illustrates the need for feminists to take a long-term rather than a short-term view of the issues that affect women. During the period divorce was moving from the fault system to a no-fault system, the women's movement was not very involved in the transition, in part because it was overextended and understaffed and in part because the implications of the reforms were not clear. It was only years later that the devastating economic effects of no-fault divorce on women were understood. The lesson of this experience is that an expansive, long-term vision of women's needs and interests is not only desirable, but crucial. Although in any movement, limitations of time and focus are not to be minimized, we should be mindful that what is ignored in the short-term may prove to be extremely important over time. As the number of women who work outside the home increases and the society becomes more and more ethnically diverse, an effective women's movement will have to address the needs of many women, rather than the needs of a few. . . .

Feminists must, however, recognize that the search for a theory of alimony also reinforces privilege—or at least that image of privilege—in a group that is predominantly white and middle or upper-middle class, in a world where women of color and other poor women often live lives of economic desperation. To the extent that alimony reinforces the subordination of poor and minority women, it fuels a divisiveness that undermines and weakens the women's movement. Feminists must also recognize that to the extent women are protected when they play the role of full-time homemaker they will continue to see it as a viable option. The result is continued economic dependence on men. A feminist theory of alimony must address the economic and psychological dependency of women on men and must confront, head on, the implications of patriarchy. . . .

C.   FEMINIST LEGAL THEORY II

INTRODUCTION

This section serves the function of the earlier section on feminist legal theory. It contains feminist essays which are meant to stimulate reflection about the effect of alternate feminist approaches on the analyses of specific doctrinal topics. Equitable distribution and child custody issues, for example, principally affect the family lives of heterosexual and middle-class women. Consequently, an analysis of how those family law doctrines affect women's economic positions and their sexual practices can overlook the role of class and differing feminine cultures in the application of these doctrines. Similarly, concentration on these doctrines can obscure the role of factors other than family law in constructing the opportunities and limitations women experience in family life.

This chapter's examination of legal issues affecting women in their families parallels the first chapter's examination of legal issues affecting women in the workplace. Both chapters focus on the role of law in combating institutional barriers that inhibit women: discrimination in the workplace; traditional social practices in the family. But both chapters also focus on the role of law in creating barriers in the form of limiting who women are and what they should be like at work or in the family.

The section begins with essays by Nancy Chodorow, a socialist feminist, and Maxine Zinn, a race-conscious feminist, which provide fresh perspectives on the general problems of child rearing and family support that underlie the doctrinal issues posed in the first two sections of this chapter. The next article, by Martha Minow and Mary Lyndon Shanley, surveys competing political theories and their relevance for family governance attentive to concerns for women's equality and relationships. The final article, by Lynda Marin, reveals the intimate and even erotic dimensions of the mother-child bond. Each of the articles should raise questions for readers about what is, or should be, the agenda of feminists in the area of family law as well as how law constructs women.

Nancy Chodorow, Mothering, Male Dominance, and Capitalism

From Z. Eisenstein, Capitalist Patriarchy and the Case for Socialist Feminism (NY: Monthly Review Press, 1979).

Women mother. In our society, as in most societies, women not only bear children. They also take primary responsibility for infant care, spend more time with infants and children than do men, and sustain primary emotional ties with infants. When biological mothers do not parent, other women, rather than men, take their place. Though fathers and other men spend varying amounts of time with infants and children, fathers are never routinely a child's primary parent. These facts are obvious to observers of everyday life.

Because of the seemingly natural connection between women's child-bearing and lactation capacities and their responsibility for child care, and because of the uniquely human need for extended care in childhood, women's mothering has been taken for granted. It has been assumed to be inevitable by social scientists, by many feminists, and certainly by those opposed to feminism. As a result, the profound importance of women's mothering for family structure, for relations between the sexes, for ideology about women, and for the sexual division of labor and sexual inequality both inside the family and in the nonfamilial world is rarely analyzed.

Uniquely among early social theorists, Frederick Engels divided the material basis of society into two spheres, that of material production and that of human reproduction. ...Anthropologist Gale Rubin, in an important recent contribution to the development of feminist theory, pushes further Engels' conception that two separate spheres organize society, and she reforms and expands it in an even more sociological vein. Marx and Marxists, she points out, have convincingly argued two things about any society's organized economic activity, its "mode of production." One is that this activity is a fundamental determining and constituting element (some would say *the* fundamental determining and constituting element) of the society. The second is that it does not emanate directly from nature (is, rather, socially constructed), nor is it describable in solely technological or mechanically economic terms. Rather, a mode of production consists of the technology *and* social organization through which a society appropriates and transforms nature for purposes of human consumption and transforms the experience of human needs to require further manipulations of nature.

Rubin suggests, in an analytic system parallel to this Marxian view, that every society contains, in addition to a mode of production, a "sex-gender system"—"systematic ways to deal with sex, gender, and babies." The sex-gender system includes ways in which biological sex becomes cultural gender, and of gender-organized social worlds, rules and regulations for sexual object choice, and concepts of childhood. The sex-gender system is, like a society's mode of production, a fundamental determining and constituting element of society, socially constructed, and subject to historical change and development. ...

Kinship and family organization consist in and reproduce socially organized gender and sexuality. ...In addition to assigning women primary parenting functions, our sex-gender system, as all systems to my knowledge, creates two and only two genders out of the panoply of morphological and genetic variations found in infants, and maintains a heterosexual norm. It also contains historically generated and societally more specific features: its family structure is largely nuclear, and its sexual division of labor locates women first in the home and men first outside of it. It is male dominant and not sexually egalitarian, in that husbands traditionally have right to control wives and power in the family; women earn less than men and have access to a narrower range of jobs; women and men tend to value men and men's activities more; and in numerous other ways that have been documented and redocumented since well before the early feminist movement. Our mode of production is more and more exclusively capitalist. ...

The distinction that we easily draw, however, between the economy ("men's world") and the family ("women's world"), and the analytic usefulness in our separation of the mode of production and the sex-gender system, does not mean that these two systems are not empirically or structurally connected. Rather, they are linked (and almost inextricably intertwined) in numerous ways. Of these ways, women's mothering is that pivotal structural feature of our sex-gender system—of the social organization of gender, ideology about women, and the psychodynamic of sexual inequality—that links it most significantly with our mode of production. ...

In all societies there is a mutually determining relationship between women's mothering and the organization of production. Women's work has been organized to enable women to care for children, though childbirth, family size, and child-tending arrangements have also been organized to enable women to work. Sometimes, as seems to be happening in many industrial societies today, women must care for children and work in the labor force simultaneously.

Historically and crossculturally, women's mothering has become a fundamentally determining feature of social organization. Michelle Rosaldo has argued that women's responsibility for child care has led, for reasons of social convenience rather than biological necessity, to a structural differentiation in all societies of a "domestic" sphere that is predominantly women's and a "public" sphere that is men's. The domestic sphere is the sphere of the family. It is organized around mothers and children. Domestic ties are particularistic—based on specific relationships between members— and often intergenerational, and are assumed to be natural and biological. The public sphere is nonfamilial and extra-domestic. Public institutions, activities, and forms of association are defined and recruited normatively, according to universalistic criteria in which the specific relationships among participants are not a factor. The public sphere forms "society" and "culture"—those intended, constructed forms and ideas that take humanity beyond nature and biology. And the public sphere, therefore "society" itself, is masculine. . . .

The structural differentiation between public and domestic spheres has been sharpened through the course of industrial capitalist development, producing a family form centered on women's mothering and maternal qualities. In precapitalist and early capitalist times, the household was the major productive unit of society. Husband and wife, with their own and/or other children, were a cooperative producing unit. A wife carried out her childcare responsibilities along with her productive work, and these responsibilities included training girls—daughters, servants, apprentices—for this work. Children were early integrated into the adult world of work, and men took responsibility for the training of boys once they reached a certain age. This dual role—productive and reproductive—is characteristic of women's lives in most societies and throughout history. Until very recently, women everywhere participated in most forms of production. Production for the home was in, or connected to, the home.

With the development of capitalism, however, and the industrialization that followed, production outside the home expanded greatly, while production within the home declined. Women used to produce food and clothing for the home. Cloth, and later food and clothing, became mass-produced commodities. Because production for exchange takes place only outside the home and is identified with work as such, the home is no longer viewed as a workplace. Home and workplace, once the same, are now separate.

This change in the organization of production went along with and produced a complex of far-reaching changes in the family. In addition to losing its role in production, the family has lost many of its educational, religious, and political functions, as well as its role in the care of the sick and aged. These losses have made the contemporary nuclear family a quintessentially relational and personal institution, the personal sphere of society. The family has become the place where people go to recover from work, to find personal fulfillment and a sense of self. It remains the place where children are nurtured and reared.

This split between social production, on the one hand, and domestic reproduction and personal life, on the other, has deepened the preindustrial sexual division of spheres. Men have become less and less central to the family, becoming primarily "bread-winners." They maintained authority in the family for a time, but as their autonomy in the nonfamilial world decreased, their authority in the family itself has declined, and they have become increasingly nonparticipant in family life itself. ...Women [have] lost their productive economic role both in social production and in the home.

This extension and formalization of the public-domestic split brought with it increasing sexual inequality. As production left the home and women ceased to participate in primary productive activity, they lost power both in the public world and in their families. Women's work in the home and the maternal role are devalued because they are outside of the sphere of monetary exchange and unmeasurable in monetary terms, and because love, though supposedly valued, is valued only within a devalued and powerless realm, a realm separate from and not equal to profits and achievement. Women's and men's spheres are distinctly unequal, and the structure of values in industrial capitalist society has reinforced the ideology of inferiority and relative lack of power vis-a-vis men which women brought with them from preindustrial, precapitalist times.

At the same time, women's reproductive role has changed. Two centuries ago marriage was essentially synonymous with childrearing. One spouse was likely to die before the children were completely reared, and the other spouse's death would probably follow within five years of the last child's marriage. Parenting lasted from the inception of a marriage to the death of the marriage partners. But over the last two centuries, fertility and infant mortality rates have declined, longevity has increased, and children spend much of their childhood in school. ...

Just as the actual physical and biological requirements of childbearing and child care were decreasing, women's mothering role gained psychological and ideological significance and came increasingly to dominate women's lives, outside the home as well as within it. In this society it is not assumed, as it has been in most societies previously, that women as mothers and wives do productive or income-producing work as part of their routine contribution to their families. The factual basis for this assumption is fast being eroded—as the number of wives and both married and single mothers in the paid labor force soars—but the ideology remains with us. Whatever their marital status and despite evidence to the contrary for both married and unmarried women, women are generally assumed to be working only to supplement a husband's income in nonessential ways. This assumption justifies discrimination, less pay, layoffs, higher unemployment rates than men, and arbitrary treatment. In a country where the paid labor force is more than 40 percent female, many people continue to assume that most women are wives and mothers who do not work. In a situation where almost two thirds of the women who work are married and almost 40 percent have children under eighteen, many people assume that "working women" are single and childless.

The kind of work women do also tends to reinforce stereotypes of women as wives and mothers. This work is relational and often an extension of women's wife-mother roles in a way that men's work is not. Women are clerical workers, service workers, teachers, nurses, salespeople. If they are involved in production, it is generally in the production of nondurable goods like clothing and food, not in "masculine" machine industries like steel and automobiles. All women, then, are affected by an ideological norm that defines them as members of conventional nuclear families. . . .

We explain the sexual division of labor as an outgrowth of physical differences. We see the family as a natural, rather than a social, creation. In general, we do not see the social organization of gender as a product or aspect of social organization at all. The reification of gender, then, involves the removal of all imputation of historicity and all sense that people produce and have produced its social forms.

An ideology of nature that sees women as closer to nature than men, or as anomalies neither natural nor cultural, remains fundamental. In our society, moreover, the particular ideology of nature that defines the social organization of gender generally, and women's lives in particular, bases itself especially upon interpretations and extensions of women's mothering functions and reproductive organs. . . . Thus, the virtues of mother and wife collapsed into one, and that one was maternal: nurturant, caring, and acting as moral model. This rising image of women as mother, moreover, idealized women's sexlessness, pointing further to the assimilation of wife to mother in the masculine psyche. . . .

During the present century the ideology of natural gender differences and of women's natural maternal role has lost some of its Victorian rigidity. The dichotomy between what is social and public, however, and what is domestic and natural takes on ever increasing psychological weight. In a society so thoroughly characterized by, and organized around, socially constructed, universalistic variables (a market in labor, alienation, bureaucratic norms, citizenship, and formal equality of access to the political sphere and before the law), we retain at least one sphere where membership and attribution seem to be entirely independent of social construction. People continue to explain the sexual division of labor and the social organization of gender as an outgrowth of physical differences and to see the family as a natural, rather than a social, creation.

The ideology of women as natural mothers has also been extended within the home. In the last fifty years the average birthrate has fallen, but during the same period studies show that women have come to spend more time in child care. Women in the home used to do productive work and more physical labor along with their mothering. They used to have more children, which meant they were involved in actual physical care and nursing for most of their adult lives. In preindustrial societies, and in traditional communities, children and older people often helped and continue to help in child care. Now homes contain few children, and these children enter school at an early age. They are not available as aides to their mothers. . . .

Ironically, biological mothers have come to have more and more exclusive responsibility for child care just as the biological components of mothering have lessened—as women have borne fewer children and bottle feeding has become available. Post–Freudian psychology and sociology has provided new rationales for the idealization and enforcement of women's maternal role, as it has emphasized the crucial importance of the mother-child relationship for the child's development.

This crucial mothering role contributes not only to child development but also to the reproduction of male supremacy. Because women are responsible for early child care and for most later socialization as well, because fathers are more absent from the home, and because men's activities generally have been removed from the home while women's have remained within it, boys have difficulty attaining a stable, masculine gender role identification. They fantasize about and idealize the masculine role, and their fathers and society define it as desirable. Freud first described how a boy's normal oedipal struggle to free himself from his mother and become masculine generated "the contempt felt by men for a sex which is the lesser." Psychoanalyst Grete Bibring argues from her own clinical experience that "too much of mother," resulting from the contemporary organization of parenting and extra-familial work, creates men's resentment and dread of women, and their search for nonthreatening, undemanding, dependent, even infantile women—women who are "simple, and thus safe and warm." Through these same processes, she argues, men come to reject, devalue, and even ridicule women and things feminine. Thus, women's mothering creates ideological and psychological modes which reproduce orientations to, and structures of, male dominance in individual men and builds an assertion of male superiority into the very definition of masculinity. . . .

Women's mothering has traditionally been and continues to be a pivotal feature in the social organization and social reproduction of gender and sexual inequality. In our time it is also pivotal to the reproduction of the capitalist mode of production and the ideology which supports it. To begin with, of course, women, now as always, reproduce the species biologically. But this is a biological universal. In the present context, it is the daily and generational reproduction specific to our contemporary economic system that is of interest.

There are several aspects to reproduction. The capitalist organization of production sustains conditions that ensure a continually expanding labor force whose wages and salaries can maintain its members and their families but are not sufficient to enable them to become capitalists. Legitimating ideologies and institutions—the state, schools, media, families—contribute to the reproduction of capitalism. Finally, workers themselves, at all levels of the production process, are reproduced, both physically and in terms of requisite capacities, emotional orientation, and ideological stances. The family is a primary locus of this last form of reproduction, and women, as mothers and wives, are its primary executors. Women's role and work activities in the contemporary family contribute to the social reproduction specific to capitalism.

With the development of capitalism and the separation of work and family life, women continued to have primary home responsibilities as a heritage from the precapitalist past and as an extension of the domestic-public division found in this earlier period. This did not mean that the factory system and industrialization automatically drew men, and not women, into its labor force: women and children were prominent among the first factory workers. In the United States, most men engaged in agricultural production as the factory system was developing, and in England women and children were a cheaper source of labor than men. Moreover, the first factories produced cloth, which had been previously produced in the home by women. Significantly, however, the development of labor outside the home (a development that would subsequently be reversed) did not affect the division of labor within it. Women of all classes retained, and continue to retain, home responsibilities. . . .

[A]ffective work, which women's magazines sometimes call ego-building, is one part of that work of women in the home that reconstitutes labor power in capitalist society. This work includes the actual physical labor of housework, which Parsons and other traditional family theorists also ignore. Mariarosa dalla Costa takes the socialist-feminist argument to its extreme and illuminates it through metaphor, if not through reality, in her argument that the home in capitalist society is a factory producing capitalism's most crucial commodity—labor power. . . .

The family has always transmitted orientations to authority. However, the nature of this orientation changed with the structure of authority in the economic world. During the period of early capitalist development more fathers had some economic power. This paternal authority expressed itself in the family as well, and sons, through a classic oedipal struggle, could internalize their father's authority—that is, could internalize bourgeois inner direction and self-motivation and accept power as it was. As the household became restricted to immediate family members, conditions were set for internalization: "Childhood in a limited family [became] an habituation to authority." This was an appropriate response to the requirements of wage labor: "In order that they may not despair in the harsh world of wage labor and its discipline, but do their part, it is not sufficient merely to obey the pater familias; one must desire to obey him." Fathers, with the growth of industrialization, became less involved in family life. They did not simply leave home physically however. As more fathers became dependent wage laborers, the material base for their familial authority was also eroded.

...[I]n reaction fathers have developed authoritarian modes of acting, but because there is no longer a real basis for their authority there can be no genuine oedipal struggle. Instead of internalizing paternal authority, sons engage in an unguided search for authority in the external world. In its most extreme form, this search for authority creates the characterological foundation for fascism. More generally, however, it leads to tendencies to accept the mass ideological manipulation characteristic of late capitalist society and the loss of autonomous norms or internal standards as guides for the individual. ...

Thus woman's mothering role and position as primary parent in the family, and the maternal qualities and behaviors which derive from it, are central to the daily and generational reproduction of capitalism. Women resuscitate adult workers, both physically and emotionally, and rear children who have particular psychological capacities which capitalist workers and consumers require. ...But all this is a question of history, convenience, and profitability. It is not a logical requirement. As more and more women enter the work force, the extra-domestic economic sector may take over more aspects of physical reproduction.

As I have suggested, however, the reproduction of workers is not exclusive or even primarily a physical or physiological question in capitalist society. Capitalist achievement, and properly submissive, organized, and regular work habits in workers, have never been purely a matter of money. Inner direction, rational planning and organization, and a willingness to come to work at certain hours and work steadily, whether or not money is needed that day, certainly facilitated the transition to capitalism. Additional psychological qualities play a major part in late capitalism: specific personality characteristics and interpersonal capacities are appropriate to the bureaucrat, the middle manager, the technician, the service worker, and the white-collar worker. The increasingly nuclear, isolated neolocal family in which women do the mothering is suited to the reproduction in children of personality commitments and capacities appropriate to these forms of work and domination.

This *internal* connection, rather than a connection of capitalist convenience, is also true of wives' maternal support of husbands and of their denial of threatening (because active) sexuality. Thus, a wife's role draws not only upon the heterosexual (what we might consider specifically "wifely" as opposed to "motherly") elements of ideology about and expectations of women. Sex is undoubtedly a source of masculine self-esteem, and sexual dominance helps a man to take out frustrations encountered on the job and to exercise in his own sphere the control he feels exercised over him. Women's dependent and passive behavior toward their husbands, however, also masks the nurturant controlling that is going on. As long as women continue to provide emotional support and "ego-building" to their husbands, they are mothering them. ...

The developments I have been discussing gain meaning one from the other. Women's mothering, as a nearly universal feature of family structure, has given particular characteristics to the social organization and valuation of gender as we know it in all societies, and we have inherited our organization of parenting, as well as our sex-gender system, from our pre-capitalist past. At the same time, particular attributes of the organization and valuation of gender have gained salience in our own society. The organization of gender and male dominance as we experience them are historical products and must be understood historically. Women's mothering has continued to be basic to women's lives and the organization of the family and fundamental to the genesis of ideology about women.

But the development of industrial capitalism has modified this, has given particular meanings to women's mothering and male dominance, and enhanced their significance in particular ways. The same repressions, denials of affect and attachment, rejection of the world of women and things feminine, appropriation of the world of men, identification with the idealized absent father—all a product of women's mothering—create masculinity and male dominance in the sex-gender system and also create men as participants in the capitalist work world.

Women's mothering as a basis of family structure and of male dominance has thus developed an internal connection to the reproduction of capitalism. But while it contributes to the reproduction of sexual inequality, the social organization of gender, and capitalism, it is also in profound contradiction to another consequence of recent capitalist development—the increasing labor force participation of mothers. We cannot predict how or if this contradiction will be resolved. History, ideology, and an examination of industrial countries which have relied on women in the labor force for a longer period and have established alternate childcare arrangements suggest that women will still be responsible for child care, unless we make the reorganization of parenting a central political goal.

Maxine Baca Zinn, Family, Race and Poverty in the Eighties

14 Signs 856 (1989).

The 1960s Civil Rights movement overturned segregation laws, opened voting booths, created new job opportunities, and brought hope to Black Americans. As long as it could be said that conditions were improving, Black family structure and life-style remained private matters. The promises of the 1960s faded, however, as the income gap between whites and Blacks widened. Since the middle 1970s, the Black underclass has expanded rather than contracted, and along with this expansion emerged a public debate about the Black family. Two distinct models of the underclass now prevail—one that is cultural and one that is structural. Both of them focus on issues of family structure and poverty.

The Cultural Deficiency Model

... [P]roponents of the culture-of-poverty thesis contend that the poor have a different way of life than the rest of society and that these cultural differences explain continued poverty. Within the current national discussion are three distinct approaches that form the latest wave of deficiency theories.

The first approach—culture as villain—places the cause of the swelling underclass in a value system characterized by low aspirations, excessive masculinity, and the acceptance of female-headed families as a way of life.

The second approach—family as villain—assigns the cause of the growing underclass to the structure of the family. While unemployment is often addressed, this argument always returns to the causal connections between poverty and the disintegration of traditional family structure.

The third approach—welfare as villain—treats welfare and anti-poverty programs as the cause of illegitimate births, female-headed families, and low motivation to work. In short, welfare transfer payments to the poor create disincentives to work and incentives to have children out of wedlock—a self-defeating trap of poverty. . . .

The logic of the culture-of-poverty argument is that poor people have distinctive values, aspirations, and psychological characteristics that inhibit their achievement and produce behavioral deficiencies likely to keep them poor not only within generations but also across generations, through socialization of the young. In this argument, poverty is more a function of thought processes than of physical environment. As a result of this logic, current discussions of ghetto poverty, family structure, welfare, unemployment, and out-of-wedlock births connect these conditions in ways similar to the 1965 Moynihan Report. Because Moynihan maintained that the pathological problem within Black ghettos was the deterioration of the Negro family, his report became the generative example of blaming the victim. Furthermore, Moynihan dismissed racism as a salient force in the perpetuation of poverty by arguing that the tangle of pathology was "capable of perpetuating itself without assistance from the white world."

The reaction of scholars to Moynihan's cultural-deficiency model was swift and extensive although not as well publicized as the model itself. Research in the sixties and seventies by Andrew Billingsley, Robert Hill, Herbert Gutman, Joyce Ladner, Elliot Leibow, and Carol Stack, to name a few, documented the many strengths of Black families, strengths that allowed them to survive slavery, the enclosures of the South, and the depression of the North. Such work revealed that many patterns of family life were not created by a deficient culture but were instead "a rational adaptational response to conditions of deprivation."

A rapidly growing literature in the eighties documents the disproportionate representation of Black female-headed families in poverty. Yet, recent studies on Black female-headed families are largely unconcerned with questions about adaptation. Rather, they study the strong association between female-headed families and poverty, the effects of family disorganization on children, the demographic and socioeconomic factors that are correlated with single-parent status, and the connection between the economic status of men and the rise in Black female-headed families. While most of these studies do not advance a social pathology explanation, they do

signal a regressive shift in analytic focus. Many well-meaning academics who intend to call attention to the dangerously high level of poverty in Black female-headed households have begun to emphasize the family structure and the Black ghetto way of life as contributors to the perpetuation of the underclass. ...According to this refurbished version of the old Moynihan Report, a breakdown in family values has allowed Black men to renounce their traditional breadwinner role, leaving Black women to bear the economic responsibility for children. The argument that the Black community is devastating itself fits neatly with the resurgent conservatism that is manifested among Black and white intellectuals and policymakers.
. . .

The idea that poverty is caused by psychological factors and that poverty is passed on from one generation to the next has been called into question by the University of Michigan's Panel Study of Income Dynamics (PSID), a large-scale data collection project conceived, in part, to test many of the assumptions about the psychological and demographic aspects of poverty. This study has gathered annual information from a representative sample of the U.S. population. Two striking discoveries contradict the stereotypes stemming from the culture-of-poverty argument. The first is the high turnover of individual families in poverty and the second is the finding that motivation cannot be linked to poverty. Each year the number of people below the poverty line remains about the same, but the poor in one year are not necessarily the poor in the following year. "Blacks from welfare dependent families were no more likely to become welfare dependent than similar Blacks from families who had never received welfare. Further, measures of parental sense of efficacy, future orientation, and achievement motivation had no effects on welfare dependency for either group." This research has found no evidence that highly motivated people are more successful at escaping from poverty than those with lower scores on tests. Thus, cultural deficiency is an inappropriate model for explaining the underclass. ...

Today, nearly six out of ten Black children are born out of wedlock, compared to roughly three out of ten in 1970. In the 25–34–year age bracket, today the probability of separation and divorce for Black women is twice that of white women. The result is a high probability that an individual Black woman and her children will live alone. The so-called "deviant" mother-only family, common among Blacks, is a product of "the femininization of poverty," a shorthand reference to women living alone and being disproportionately represented among the poor. The attention given to increased marital breakups, to births to unmarried women, and to the household patterns that accompany these changes would suggest that the bulk of contemporary poverty is a family-structure phenomenon. Common knowledge—whether true or not—has it that family-structure changes cause most poverty, or changes in family structure have led to current poverty rates that are much higher than they would have been if family composition had remained stable.

Despite the growing concentration of poverty among Black female-headed households in the past two decades, there is reason to question the conventional thinking. Research by Mary Jo Bane finds that changes in family structure have less causal influence on poverty than is commonly thought. Assumptions about the correlation and association between poverty and family breakdown avoid harder questions about the character and direction of causal relations between the two phenomena. Bane's longitudinal research on household composition and poverty suggests that much poverty, especially among Blacks, is the result of already-poor, two-parent households that break up, producing poor female-headed households. This differs from the event transition to poverty that is more common for whites: "... Reshuffled poverty as opposed to event-caused poverty for blacks challenges the assumption that changes in family structure have created ghetto poverty. This underscores the importance of considering the ways in which race produces different paths to poverty."

A two-parent family is no guarantee against poverty for racial minorities. Analyzing data from the PSID, Martha Hill concluded that the long-term income of Black children in two-parent families throughout the decade was even lower than the long-term income of non-Black children who spent most of the decade in mother-only families: "Thus, increasing the proportion of Black children growing up in two-parent families would not by itself eliminate very much of the racial gap in the economic well-being of children; changes in the economic circumstances of the parents are needed most to bring the economic status of Black children up to the higher status of non-Black children." ...

An important variant of the family-structure and deficient-culture explanations, one especially popular among political conservatives, is that welfare undermines incentives to work and causes families to break up by allowing Black to have babies and encouraging Black men to escape family responsibilities. This position has been widely publicized by Charles Murray's influential book, Losing Ground. According to Murray, liberal welfare policies squelch work incentives and thus are the major cause of the breakup of the Black family. In effect, increased AFDC benefits make it desirable to forgo marriage and live on the dole.

Research has refuted this explanation for the changes in the structure of families in the underclass. Numerous studies have shown that variations in welfare across time and in different states have not produced systematic variation in family structure. ...

They [also] highlight two facts that raise questions about the role of welfare policies in producing female-headed households. First, the real value of welfare payments has declined since the early 1970s, while family dissolution has continued to rise. Family-structure changes do not mirror benefit-level changes. Second, variations in benefit levels across states do not lead to corresponding variations in divorce rates or numbers of children in single-parent families. ...In sum, the systematic research on welfare and family structure indicates that AFDC has far less effect on changes in family structure than has been assumed.

Opportunity Structures in Decline

A very different view of the underclass has emerged alongside the popularized cultural-deficiency model. ...Focusing on the opportunity structure of society, these concrete studies reveal that culture is not responsible for the underclass.

Within the structural framework there are three distinct strands. The first deal with transformations of the economy and the labor force that affect Americans in general and Blacks and Hispanics in particular. The second is the transformation of marriage and family life among minorities. The third is the changing class composition of inner cities and their increasing isolation of residents from mainstream social institutions.

All three are informed by new research that examines the macrostructural forces that shape family trends and demographic patterns that expand the analysis to include Hispanics. ...

Massive economic changes since the end of World War II are causing the social marginalization of Black people throughout the United States. The shift from an economy based on the manufacture of goods to one based on information and services has redistributed work in global, national, and local economies. While these major economic shifts affect all workers, they have more serious consequences for Blacks than whites, a condition that scholars call "structural racism." Major economic trends and patterns, even those that appear race neutral, have significant racial implications. ...

The decline of manufacturing jobs has altered the cities' roles as opportunity ladders for the disadvantaged. ...Today inner cities are shifting away from being centers of production and distribution of physical goods toward being centers of administration, information, exchange, trade, finance, and government service. Conversely, these changes in local employment structures have been accompanied by a shift in the demographic composition of large central cities away from European white to predominantly Black and Hispanic, with rising unemployment. The transfer of jobs away from central cities to the suburbs has created a residential job opportunity mismatch that literally leaves minorities behind in the inner city. Without adequate training or credentials, they are relegated to low-paying, nonadvancing exploitative service work or they are unemployed. Thus, Blacks have become, for the most part, superfluous people in cities that once provided them with opportunities. ...

While cities once sustained large numbers of less skilled persons, today's service industries typically have high educational requisites for entry. Knowledge and information jobs in the central cities are virtually closed to minorities given the required technological education and skill level. Commuting between central cities and outlying areas is increasingly common; white-collar workers commute daily from their suburban residences to the central business districts while streams of inner-city residents are commuting to their blue-collar jobs in outlying nodes. ...[R]acial discrimination and inadequate incomes of inner-city minorities now have the additional impact of preventing many from moving out of the inner city in order to maintain their access to traditional sources of employment. The dispersed nature of job growth makes public transportation from inner-city neighborhoods impractical, requiring virtually all city residents who work in peripheral areas to commute by personally owned automobiles. . . .

The connection between declining Black employment opportunities (especially male joblessness) and the explosive growth of Black families headed by single women is the basis of William J. Wilson's analysis of the underclass. Several recent studies conducted by Wilson and his colleagues . . . have documented the relationship between increased male joblessness and female-headed households. By devising an indicator called "the index of marriageable males," they reveal a long-term decline in the proportion of Black men, and particularly young Black men, who are in a position to support a family. Their indicators include mortality and incarceration rates, as well as labor-force participation rates, and they reveal that the proportion of Black men in unstable economic situations is much higher than indicated in current unemployment figures.

Wilson's analysis treats marriage as an opportunity structure that no longer exists for large numbers of Black people. Consider, for example, why the majority of pregnant Black teenagers do not marry. . . . According to Wilson, . . . [this] is tied directly to the changing labor-market status of young Black males. He cites the well-established relationship between joblessness and marital instability in support of his argument that "pregnant teenagers are more likely to marry if their boyfriends are working." Out-of-wedlock births are sometimes encouraged by families and absorbed into the kinship system because marrying the suspected father would mean adding someone who was unemployed to the family's financial burdens. Adaptation to structural conditions leaves Black women disproportionately separated, divorced, and solely responsible for their children. The mother-only family structure is thus the consequence, not the cause, of poverty. . . .

Not only is inner-city poverty worse and more persistent than it was twenty years ago, but ghettos and barrios have become isolated and deteriorating societies. . . . Without working-class or middle-class role models these families have little in common with mainstream society. . . . If successfully employed persons do not live nearby, then the informal methods of finding a job, by which one worker tells someone else of a opening and recommends her or him to the employer, are lost. Concentration and isolation describe the processes that systematically entrench a lack of opportunities in inner cities. . . .

Hispanic poverty, virtually ignored for nearly a quarter of a century, has [also] recently captured the attention of the media and scholars alike. . . . Not only have Hispanic poverty rates risen alarmingly, but like Black poverty, Hispanic poverty has become increasingly concentrated in inner cities. Hispanics fall well behind the general population on all measures of social and economic well-being: jobs, income, educational attainment, housing, and health care. Poverty among Hispanics has become so persistent that, if current patterns continue, Hispanics will emerge in the 1990s as the nation's poorest racial-ethnic group. . . . The association between national economic shifts and high rates of social dislocation among Hispanics provides further evidence for the structural argument that economic conditions rather than culture create distinctive forms of racial poverty. . . .

The structural model described above advances our understanding of poverty and minority families beyond the limitations of the cultural model. It directs attention away from psychological and cultural issues and towards social structures that allocate economic and social rewards. . . . On matters of gender, however, the structural model would benefit from discussion, criticism, and rethinking. This is not to deny the structural model's value in linking poverty to external economic conditions but, rather, to question the model's assumptions about gender and family structure and to point to the need for gender as a specific analytic category.

Although several key aspects of the structural model distinguish it from the cultural model, both models are remarkably close in their thinking about gender. Patricia Hill Collins . . . exposes the gender ideologies that underlie cultural explanations of racial inferiority. Those same ideologies about women and men, about their place in the family and their relationship to the public institutions of the larger society, reappear, albeit in modified ways, in the structural model.

Collins shows how assumptions about racial deficiency rest on cultural notions about unfit men and women. In contrast, the structural approach focuses on the social circumstances produced by economic change. It therefore avoids drawing caricatures of men who spurn work and unmarried women who persist in having children. Yet both models find differences between mainstream gender roles and those of the underclass. Indeed, some of the most striking and important findings of the structural approach focus on this difference. Clearly, the reasons for the difference lie in the differing economic and social opportunities of the two groups, yet the structural model assumes that the traditional family is a key solution for eliminating racial poverty. Although the reasons given for the erosion of the traditional family are very different, both models rest on normative definitions of women's and men's roles. Two examples reveal how the structural perspective is locked into traditional concepts of the family and women's and men's places within it.

Wilson identifies male joblessness and the resulting shortage of marriageable males as the conditions responsible for the proliferation of female-headed households. His vision of a solution is a restoration of marital opportunities and the restoration of family structures in which men provide for their families by working in the labor force and women have children who can then be assured of the economic opportunities afforded by two-parent families. He offers no alternative concept of the family, no discussion of lesbian families or other arrangements that differ from the standard male-female married pair. Instead of exploring how women's opportunities and earning capacities outside of marriage are affected by macrostructural economic transformations, instead of calling "for pay equity, universal day care and other initiatives to buttress women's capacities for living independently in the world ... Wilson goes in exactly the opposite direction."

Ellwood's comprehensive analysis of American family poverty and welfare, *Poor Support: Poverty in the American Family*, contains a discussion that says a great deal about how women, men, and family roles are viewed by authoritative scholars working within the structural tradition. Looking at the work of adults in two-parent families, Ellwood finds that all families must fulfill two roles—a nurturing/child-rearing role and a provider role—and that in two-parent families these responsibilities are divided along traditional gender lines. Therefore, Ellwood raises the question: "Do we want single mothers to behave like husbands or like wives? Those who argue that single mothers ought to support their families through their own efforts are implicitly asking that they behave like husbands." While Ellwood's discussion is meant to illustrate that single mothers experience difficulty in having to fulfill the dual roles of provider and nurturer, it confuses the matter by reverting to a gendered division of labor in which women nurture and men provide. By presenting family responsibilities as those of "husbands" and "wives," even well-meaning illustrations reproduce the ideology they seek to challenge.

Structural approaches have failed to articulate gender as an analytic category even though the conditions uncovered in contemporary research on the urban underclass are closely intertwined with gender. In fact, the problems of male joblessness and female-headed households form themselves around gender. Although these conditions are the result of economic transformations, they change gender relations as they change the marital, family, and labor arrangements of women and men. Furthermore, the economic disenfranchisement of large numbers of Black men, what Clyde Franklin calls "the institutional decimation of Black men," is a gender phenomenon of enormous magnitude. It affects the meanings and definitions of masculinity for Black men, and it reinforces the public patriarchy that controls Black women through their increased dependence on welfare. Such gender issues are vital. They reveal that where people of Color "end up" in the social order has as much to do with the economic restructuring of gender as with the economic restructuring of class and race. ...

Martha Minow and Mary Lyndon Shanley, Revisioning the Family: Relational Rights and Responsibilities

From M. Shanley & V. Narayan, eds., Reconstructing Political Theory: Feminist Perspectives (Oxford: Polity, 1997).

... Although there have always been significant differences among liberal political theorists concerning the nature of the family and its relation to civil society, certain general features of liberal theory's understanding of proper family relationships and of the relation between the family and the state infused works of liberal political theorists and lawyers from the seventeenth century through the nineteenth. The family was a natural and therefore a "private" association, consisting of a male, a female, and their biological children. In this family the husband/father exercised authority over his wife and children (and in many instances his servants, tenants, and slaves), was responsible for the economic support of members of the household, and represented them in the public sphere. The mother/wife was responsible for managing household life and expenditures, seeing to the physical care of household residents, and providing emotional support and nurture to family members. The responsibility for both the moral education and the economic support of children fell to their parents (but servants, tenants, and slaves did not have claims for such support and education).

This depiction of the family as a natural association that gave authority over children to their parents and over servants to the head-of-household was deeply gendered: the husband had authority over the wife, and the father was the head-of-household. Liberal theory also assumed that there was a clear division between the private realm of the family, created by nature through human sexual mating and reproduction, and the public realm of politics, created by convention through the social contract. Hence at one and the same time liberalism assumed that government authority and law properly regulated public, not private, matters, and that the representative of the household in the public realm—the citizen—was male.

There were, of course, always disjunctions between the picture of the family in political theory and law and the actual lives of families. In the United States, domestic relations law until the mid-nineteenth century did not encompass the family life of slaves, who instead were governed by slave codes and property laws. Children born out of wedlock, widows, and abandoned wives and their children as well as those who explicitly rejected conventional family life and instead pursued solitary or communal households also fell outside the legal norms of the patriarchal family in nineteenth-century US law.

The disjunction between the picture of the family in political theory and law and many people's lived or desired experiences increased from the mid-nineteenth century to our own day. Abolitionist efforts before the Civil War brought the experiences of slaves into debates over political rights; both experience in abolition activities and rhetorical analogies between slavery and marriage enabled white women reformers to seek changes in the legal status of married women and to seek direct political participation through the vote. In both respects the women's rights reformers rejected the picture of the wife's legal personality as subsumed in the husband's and sought to secure her independent rights to hold property, enter into contracts, and express political preferences. Notions of romantic love and the propriety of individual choice of marriage partner led to the view that if marriage was created by the consent of the parties to live in a certain way, and if one of them violated that agreement, then their union could be dissolved. The growing acceptance of formal legal adoption from the mid-nineteenth century on reflected the notion that binding relationships between parent and child could be created by volition and consent as well as by biology, although adoption did try to mirror the "natural family" through efforts to match race and religion and to seal from view the adoptee's family of origin.

Legal and political reforms responded to changing work patterns, tides of immigration, and continuing racial tensions throughout the first half of the twentieth century. As unmarried women and immigrant women sought waged work in rapidly urbanizing and industrial America, their activities challenged the seeming inevitability of the male-headed household, as did the volunteer projects of more privileged women. Anti-racism efforts first against lynching and then against racial segregation laid the foundations for challenges to antimiscegenation laws and race-matching in adoption by the middle of the twentieth century. Migrations from rural to urban areas and from the South to the North, along with continuing immigration, produced diverse communities and extensive personal experiences with change. World War II drew many women into traditionally male employment roles and also gave many African–American and other minority men experiences serving the country that contrasted sharply with their continuing treatment as second-class citizens at home. By mid-century, the Black civil rights movement and the women's liberation movement insisted that the law reflect the collapse of ascriptive status and redefine the meaning of "equality" with respect to both race and sex.

The "second wave" of feminism underscored the depth of challenge to the conception of the male-headed nuclear family as "natural." The power of husbands over wives was no longer treated as natural, and patriarchal control increasingly faced serious challenges in both public and private settings. Egalitarian notions also affected popular and legal views of children. In place of earlier practices that treated children as analogous to property controlled by parents, laws and judicial decisions restricted the power of parents over children in areas such as child labor, extended a certain set of fundamental liberties to children, and invited children's views in matters such as custody following divorce.

Cumulatively, these developments have a common theme: political theorists could no longer view the family as a prepolitical entity, and legal theorists faced complicated judgments over the extent to which families were private and immune from the intervention of the state. The various conceptualizations of family underlying many of the debates on family policy and law reflect the complexity of human aspirations that include the desire to enjoy both autonomy and interrelationship, to savor both independence and intimacy. But while the challenge to the notion that the family is a natural and private association of a heterosexual couple and their biological children has been widespread, scholarship did not arrive at consensus on any alternative legal understanding of "family." Three legal approaches have attempted to deal with these complexities of family life and family law during the past 25 years—contractarian, communitarian and rights-based; we examine each in turn and show why we consider the last, when formulated to take account of family relationships, the most promising foundation for a theory of family law.

Contract-based Theories of Family: The Primacy of Individual Volition

Ever since Sir Henry Maine characterized the development of modern law as a movement from status to contract, these concepts have been juxtaposed as competing bases for legal regimes: one must choose between ascriptive roles and obligations on the one hand, or freely chosen roles and obligations on the other. Hence proponents of a contractual ordering of family life point out the consistency between their views and one of the deepest aspirations of liberal society: the right of individuals to have their freedom limited only by self-assumed obligations.

Given the burdens that ascriptive notions about women's "nature" and proper roles have placed on women seeking equality in both the family and public life, it is not surprising that some feminists see contract as an instrument to provide women greater freedom, self-determination, and equality without subjecting either women or men to traditional sex roles. Unlike traditional marriage law's assumptions about the sexual division of labor in both household and larger society, contractual ordering could allow spouses to decide for themselves how to order their personal as well as their financial relationship during their marriage and in the event of divorce.

Contracts could also provide for pluralism and a diversity in family life impossible to achieve under a uniform domestic relations law. If marriage were regulated by contract, for example, there would seem to be no reason why two individuals of the same sex should be prohibited from entering such a contract. Arguing both for contractual ordering and for legal recognition of same-sex marriage, Lenore Weitzman asserts that "there is a serious question as to whether the state has any legitimate interest interfering with contracts regarding non-commercial sexual relations between consenting adults," although she acknowledges that legal recognition of same-sex marriages might be hampered by the fact that homosexual relations are "still prohibited by the criminal codes of most states." Marjorie Shultz finds that the repeated refusals by the states to formalize unions of same-sex couples by legal marriage "reflect a hesitancy to pursue fully the implications of pluralism and privacy. Where diverse individual outcomes are valued and pluralism is necessary, some form of private ordering of conduct and values is the appropriate regulatory structure." The point of marriage is to create clear expectations and binding obligations to promote stable interpersonal relationships. It is reasonable to ask the state to enforce agreements that would underpin the material aspects of such relationships, but it is not a legitimate concern of the state who may marry whom, or how spouses should order the personal and material aspects of their relationship.

Proponents of contractual ordering of reproduction see it, like contract marriage, as a way of breaking down gender stereotypes and increasing the scope of human choice in establishing families. Contracts could facilitate diverse ways of bringing children into a family, including children born through contract pregnancies ("surrogate mother" arrangements) and through sperm donation from known donors; such arrangements might help gay and lesbian couples, and single persons, become parents; make possible a genetic relationship between at least one parent and the child; and stipulate in advance of conception the degree of contact, if any, to be had between the "surrogate" or sperm donor and the child. Contracts might be used to regulate the degree of contact between biological parent(s) and offspring in open adoptions; in some accounts, contracts could make adoption a market transaction. Some feminists welcome contract pregnancy as a way to illustrate that childbearing and child-rearing are quite distinct human functions and that child-rearing need not be and should not be assigned exclusively to the woman who bears the child (or to women rather than men, for that matter). From this perspective, contract pregnancy seems to expand choice for both the woman who bears the child and for the commissioning parent(s). Carmel Shalev argues that one aspect of autonomy is "the deliberate exercise of choice with respect to the individual's reproductive capacity," and that pregnancy contracts should be strictly enforced out of respect for women's decision-making capacity.

While private ordering has liberating aspects, it also entails more worrisome implications. The assumption that bargains will be freely struck masks configurations of social power that provide the backdrop to any contracts. Generations of labor leaders have pointed out the fallacy of assuming that workers and employers are equal bargaining agents. With respect to the marriage contract, one of John Stuart Mill's great insights in The Subjection of Women was his observation that the decision to marry for the vast majority of women could scarcely be called "free." Given women's low wages, scarcity of jobs, and lack of opportunity for higher or even secondary education, marriage was for them a "Hobson's choice," that or none. Even the "I do" of someone very much in love and desirous of marriage does not in-and-of-itself guarantee freedom. With respect to contract pregnancy, the notion that the "labor" of pregnancy and childbirth can be sold like any other bodily labor sweeps away "any intrinsic relation between the female owner, her body, and reproductive capacities." As Carole Pateman points out, this objectification of women's bodies and reproductive labor could be more alienating than liberating, while to extol the "freedom" of a woman who agrees to bear a child because she needs the money ignores the restraints or compulsions of economic necessity.

As contract provides no guarantee of freedom to those entering marriage or pregnancy contracts, it similarly offers no guarantee of an equal relationship between the parties to the contract. Leaving decisions about property distribution to contracts between the marriage partners does not insure that such agreements will be more fair than statutory stipulations regarding equitable distribution. Similarly, descriptions of contract pregnancy as nothing more than womb rental in a supposedly neutral market masks the profoundly gendered nature of the structures that surround such transactions. Contractual ordering does not alter those background economic and social conditions that create relationships of domination and subordination between men and women as well as between rich and poor.

Contractual ordering also fails to deal with the fact that certain dependencies that develop in intimate relationships cannot be adequately addressed by contract. Persons who may be considered independent actors at the time a contract is signed make whole series of decisions—not only career decisions but other life choices as well—the consequences of which can neither be anticipated nor allocated between the parties when they occur. "Surrogate" mothers who attempt to revoke their agreements often describe the emergence of an unanticipated sense of relationship that emerged unbidden during the course of pregnancy. To speak of the "freedom" of the contracting woman as residing in her intention as an "autonomous" agent misunderstands the relationship between woman and fetus, and the influence of that relationship on the woman's sense of herself.

The model of the individual on which proposals for contracts-in-lieu-of-marriage and pregnancy contracts rest—that of a self-possessing individual linked to others only by agreement—fails to do justice to the complex interdependencies involved in family relations and child-rearing. Proposals to replace family law by private ordering reflect the serious limitations of a version of liberalism that understands freedom as the ability to determine and pursue one's goals without interference from government or other individuals, and obligation as arising only from specific acts of the will. It also does away with any recognition of a public interest in the ordering of family relationships. Contractual ordering regards individuals as what Hegel called "immediate self-subsistent persons," abstracted from their social relationships. The bases of marriage, reproductive activity, and family life thus become indistinguishable from those of civic and economic association. From this perspective, as Carole Patemen has pointed out, "Marriage and the family are ... treated as if they were an extension of civil society and so constituted by, and their relationships exhausted by, contract." Contractual ordering is not so much a movement away from status as its negation or mirror image: "The undifferentiated social bonds of a hierarchy of ascription are replaced by the undifferentiated, universal bond of contract."

In its capacity to replace the outmoded, hegemonic, and frequently oppressive understandings of gender norms of traditional statutory and common law rules infusing family law, contract seems a tool of liberation to many advocates of gender equality and pluralism of family forms. But this tool is too crude to deal with the complex relationships of family life. Although persons may freely decide to marry, marriage itself is a social practice; stipulations governing the rights and responsibilities of spouses and parents reflect shared understandings of propriety and fairness which may be subject to debate, but should not be set aside by idiosyncratic agreements. Too often other people are deeply affected by the contracts over whose terms they have no say. Rejecting the contractarians' notion of marriage as a partnership to be shaped by the will of the parties, genetic material and babies as marketable resources, and gestation as comparable to any other waged labor, other legal and political theorists emphasize the influence of community and the socially constructed nature of both families and their individual members.

Community-based Theories of Family: The Importance of Social Norms and Traditions of the Good

Unlike contract-based theorists, who leave family definition and responsibilities to the private ordering of individuals, community-based theorists regard families as expressions of personal and social relationships larger than individuals and not resting primarily on agreement. Community-based theorists reject the picture of the self adopted by contractarians, who start with the autonomous individual and neglect both the context of larger social relationships and "communal notions of equity and responsibility" in relationships. These theorists all emphasize that families are not simply private associations but also crucial institutions that help compose civil society and the polity.

Some community-based theorists turn to traditional sources to articulate the content of social norms and the shape of relationships endorsed by the community. Others stress a commitment by the society to pursue the common good rather than a regime of entirely private, individual choices. Some expressly embrace the title "communitarian" in search of public values larger than the preferences of individuals and more than a mere aggregation of those preferences. They value civil society and criticize liberalism's tendency to ignore or reject history, tradition, or collective decisions about the good life.

Community-based theorists stress that no person becomes autonomous without first going through an extended period of dependency. "Selves" are formed through the intense relationships of infancy and childhood. Community-based theorists also remind us that individuals are shaped by membership in particular ethnic, regional, and religious communities whose values may depart from the values of society's majority. Where contract-based theories would urge freedom for individuals to embrace their own values under a state neutral about all values except individuals' freedom to contract, community-based theories regard it as neither possible nor desirable "that the state should refrain from coercive public judgments about what constitutes the good life for individuals." William Galston rejects the assumption that the only political alternatives are private individual choice and repressive state-imposed norms. There is, he argues, "a third way: a nonneutral, substantive liberalism committed to its own distinctive conception of the good, broadly (though not boundlessly) respectful of diversity, and supported by its own canon of the virtues," including tolerance, the work ethic, and the "disposition and the capacity to engage in public discourse."

Many feminists endorse at least parts of the community-based critiques of contractarian versions of liberal individualism. They agree with the critique of autonomous individualism that neglects or distorts how human identities are formed; they add that this picture is deeply gendered in both imagining a male self and neglecting historically female work in nurturing children and dependents. In a moving essay on family life Jean Elshtain points out the way in which the notion of the autonomous individual has not only denied the importance of community but has also denigrated women's traditional sphere of activity and ignored the contribution "women's work" has made to sustaining both families and civil society. Any viable human community, she notes, must include persons "devoted to the protection of vulnerable human life. That, historically, has been the mission of women. The pity is not that women reflect an ethic of social responsibility but that the public world has, for the most part, repudiated such an ethic."

Feminist community-based theorists agree that political life should hold more than the fulfillment of ends chosen independently by individuals, and that more than calculated self-interest can and should bind together the political community. But while they join other communitarians in the critique of marriage as merely a contract, they are skeptical about turning to traditional articulations of shared norms about how spouses and parents should act toward one another as a basis for understanding spousal responsibilities. These shared norms have been too thoroughly permeated by gender inequality to act as a model for contemporary marriage law. In such discussions, feminists no less than other community-based theorists face difficult disagreements about which norms and values the community should endorse and law should enforce.

Once the topic for debate is the content of values deserving public endorsement and enforcement, disagreements can grow intense even among people who share a critique of the excesses of individualism. Elshtain, for example, argues not only that "the family is a prerequisite for any form of social life" but also that "a particular ideal of the family is imperative to create a more humane society." Much contemporary debate over families involves disagreements about what precisely the terms of that particular ideal should be, and whose intimate relationships should be excluded from public support or even punished.

Consider the question whether same-sex couples should be allowed to marry. Community-based theorists join in agreeing that this is not a question to be left to the parties themselves, as contractarians would have it. Nor do community-based theorists ask, as rights-based theorists do, whether individuals regardless of sexual orientation should enjoy a right against state control over intimate relationships. Community-based theorists instead view questions such as same-sex marriage as questions for the community to decide, based on tradition, normative theories of the good, or other collective judgments. The result is considerable disagreement. ...

The arguments on both sides refer to values, traditions, and substantive ends, many of which overlap and converge; nothing internal to this debate can resolve it. Community-based theorists invite such debates given their commitment to the substantive good. They further present conflicts over how to ground the values that should prevail and even how to justify critiques of the excesses of individualism. Some, such as [Mary Ann] Glendon, would combat excessive individualism by norms of individual responsibility and state obligation to protect families. Others, such as Galston, pursue community-based norms from a functional or instrumental perspective; social power should be deployed to reduce divorce, for example, in order to lessen the chances that children of divorce fail to grow into independent and contributing members of the society, economic community, and polity. Still others focus on the need to revitalize traditions such as the centrality of status.

Having embraced as a political task the substantive choices about families and intimate roles and duties, community-based theorists have to confront deep divisions about policy choices and the values implicated by them. The community-based theories proceed with the view that one way of life is to be preferred or some are to be disfavored. Not only does this run counter to the liberty and tolerance usually advocated in pluralist societies, it also invites potentially unresolvable and intense conflicts about what should and should not be preferred, and may exacerbate social and political divisions along religious and cultural lines. Religious and cultural views and practices vary regarding what kind of family form is desirable, who is a good parent, what range of choice should be granted over reproduction and to whom, and what duties adult children owe their parents. The community-based theories lack the easy accommodation for pluralism afforded by contract-based theories that leave many such matters to private agreement. We think they also lack a similar accommodation for pluralism afforded by rights-based theories that endorse individual freedoms.

The vision of individual freedoms and equality in a rights-based approach to family law, we believe, presents the possibility of recognizing the importance of family privacy and diversity without relying on private ordering or community traditions to preserve those values. Such an approach also recognizes the political and negotiated nature of social norms and values, including many rights. One problem with "rights-talk" applied to family policy and law has been the tendency to see familial rights as protections for individual freedom, rather than as rights that create, foster, and protect valued relationships. Because they deal with persons in relationship, they must take account of inequalities and dependencies among family members. It is impossible to have an adequate account of certain rights pertaining to family relationships—such as the right to divorce; maternal and paternal rights; rights to custody, visitation, and child support—without paying adequate attention to these various normative dimensions of family relationships. We believe that a theory of relational rights and responsibilities offers a promising avenue for a new foundation for conceptualizing "families" and formulating family policy and law.

Rights-based Theories of Family: The Tension Between Individualism and Family Relationship

Community-based theories seem to invite disputes over what kinds of families and family values society should endorse (whereas contract-based approaches seem to promote pluralism of family forms and intimate choices) yet they may fail to protect individuals against oppressive bargains and ongoing patterns of social inequality. Advocates of rights-based approaches to family law seem to hope that they will be able to promote pluralism while also putting forward as societal values certain basic freedoms guaranteed to each individual. These rights-based approaches are rooted both in classical liberalism and in US constitutionalism.

Extending individual rights to the realm of families is a relatively new phenomenon: prior to the mid-twentieth century, the Supreme Court seldom confronted disputes claiming constitutionally protected rights associated with family formation or dissolution, definitions of kinship or affiliation, and obligations of care and support based on family ties. Instead, those matters remained subject to state regulation, and often the states in turn relied on traditions, religious or otherwise. The states did define terms for family formation and dissolution but also tended to exempt families from otherwise prevailing rules of contract, tort, and criminal law. In these respects, US courts followed a tradition of noninterference in family lives, at least when that tradition coincided with state purposes and values. The states did require parents to comply with compulsory school laws for their children, and often scrutinized the living conditions, household composition, and child-rearing practices of poor, immigrant, African–American, and Native American families, which at times led to the removal of children from their family homes.

In the mid-twentieth century, litigation involving various "rights" of family members began to impart a federal, constitutional dimension to family law. The Supreme Court pronounced constitutional bases for a right to marry (*Loving v. Virginia* 1967); the right to procreate (*Skinner v. Oklahoma* 1942; *Griswold v. Connecticut* 1965); the right not to procreate (*Griswold v. Connecticut* 1965; *Eisenstadt v. Baird* 1972; *Roe v. Wade* 1973); the right to retain or establish paternal ties (*Stanley v. Illinois* 1972; *Caban v. Mohammed* 1979). The Court rejected claims for a right to engage in consensual homosexual activity (*Bowers v. Hardwick* 1986), and restricted claims of parental status outside of marriage (*Lehr v. Robertson* 1983; *Michael H. v. Gerald D.* 1989). The Court also recognized as worthy of constitutional protection certain claims of parental decision-making power (*Wisconsin v. Yoder* 1972; *Parham v. J.R.* 1979) and family privacy (*Moore v. City of East Cleveland* 1977).

Two fundamental conceptions of rights undergird these decisions. The first views the family as a unitary entity, entitled to protection from state scrutiny or interference; the second locates rights in distinct individuals who should be guarded from state obstruction in intimate choices and behaviors. Both approaches offer a critical purchase on otherwise prevailing governmental actions, but the second in particular begins to challenge legal assumptions about proper family relationships. Elizabeth Schneider has documented efforts to marshal individual rights against assault by spouses, and against the screen of family privacy that had shielded such practices from arrest, prosecution, and punishment. Nan Hunter, Sylvia Law, and more recently William Eskridge have asserted individual rights to marry that should extend to couples of the same sex, not only to recognize gay and lesbian rights but also to combat gender hierarchies that harm women even in heterosexual marriages. Nancy Polikoff argues that courts should recognize that both partners in a lesbian couple should have parental rights with regard to children living in their household. Despite this widespread invocation of rights, commentators do not always agree about what rights are relevant and which should prevail in any particular case. Earl Maltz, for example, does not think that there is a constitutional protection for same-sex marriage. John Robertson advocates recognition of a right to use medical technology and to purchase genetic and gestational services from others. In contrast, Margaret Jane Radin invokes "the right of inalienability" to empower individuals to resist the incursions of the market especially in the context of genetic material and "surrogate," or contract mother arrangements.

The most pronounced conflict, however, pits the vision of individuals enjoying rights against the picture of the family as a unitary entity entitled to rights against state intrusion. Many of the asserted individual rights specifically prevail upon the state to pry behind closed doors of family homes either to protect individuals from harm or to enable them to alter the otherwise prevailing pattern of relationships. Thus, the right to be free from abuse in marriage brings the state into the household by justifying actual police investigations and more basically by instituting a norm of mutual respect between spouses. The right to choose contraception or abortion enables not just a couple but an individual to make choices without the interference of others, including the intimate partner.

Another approach to the critique of the family as a unitary entity has emerged from feminist engagement with the work of John Rawls. Although Rawls notably neglects the internal ordering of families, his work has strengthened the intellectual resources for rights-based theories. *A Theory of Justice* develops a strong foundation for notions of individual rights even when they challenge traditions and conventions. Rawls's work has also led to debates about what the rights pertaining to family members might be, and whether a rights-based discourse is, in the end, adequate for a political or legal theory of the family. Notably, Susan Okin criticizes Rawls for failing to take gender seriously in formulating the principles of justice and for failing to carry these principles fully into the context of families. Attacking the common law notion that the family is a unitary entity that should be shielded from the state's prying eye, Okin argues that the traditional liberal defense of family privacy has made it difficult to recognize the gender inequality that permeates social and legal arrangements affecting women's lives in both families and civil society. Okin maintains further that when Rawls identifies "the monogamous family" as one of the major social institutions that is to be guided by his two principles of justice, he fails to acknowledge that most families violate the principle of equal liberty and the principle that any inequalities should work to the benefit of the least well-off. No one uncertain about what sex he or she will have, Okin argues, would accept the prevailing gender structures of society and the family as just.

This argument by Okin makes tremendous strides toward a theory of justice addressing families. It demands that such a theory explore the ways that gender-based practices affect the distribution of power and goods both in families and in larger social institutions, and in the interaction between both realms. Similarly, Okin opens the way toward consideration of state recognition for relationships between same-sex couples as part of a larger effort to eliminate the significance of gender roles. . . .

We agree with these feminist critics of rights theory that a political theory inattentive to relationships of care and connection between and among people cannot adequately address many themes and issues facing families. Many community-based theories share with the feminist theories of care a rejection of the model of the self-sufficient and self-interested individual. However, in their rejection of that model, community-based theorists critical of the liberal tradition often do not distinguish contractarian from rights-based approaches in political theory and law. But these approaches are distinguishable. Contractarian views acknowledge human relationships but treat them all as chosen and susceptible to market or market-like bargains. Little scope for public articulation of values persists in a contract-based regime beyond preservation of the institution of contract and perhaps rejection of extreme bargains. Rights-based views instead require public articulation of the kinds of freedoms that deserve protection and the qualities of human dignity that warrant societal support. Moreover, whether acknowledged or not, rights articulate relationships among people. Every freedom of action guaranteed to an individual demands as a correlate constraints of respect by other individuals. In the context of family matters, rights-based theories need to acknowledge more fully their relational dimensions and draw on the insights of those who study care-taking.

This route—enriching rights-based theories with strong attention to relationships and their preconditions—holds more promise for family law than either contractarian or communitarian approaches. Contract-based theories promote individual freedoms but neglect social values and concerns about inequality and dignity; community-based theories articulate shared values but risk constraining individual freedoms and social pluralism and may prompt greater social conflict. While rights-based theories invigorate as social values respect for certain individual freedoms, they historically lack a rich understanding of relationships, including the preconditions, responsibilities, and consequences of human relationships. In the next section we consider whether and how a notion of relational rights, informed by theories of care-taking, might address a variety of difficult issues confronting family policy and law.

Relational Rights and Responsibilities: Elements of an Adequate Theory of Family Law

Sociological changes, rapid developments in reproductive technology, and the collapse of the common law paradigm of the family as a unitary, hierarchical, and indissoluble entity make it imperative to think anew about what social policy and law should take to be the constitutive or defining features of "family." Among the difficult policy issues that challenge current underpinnings of contemporary family law are those concerning what role genetic ties should play in establishing parental rights; the relevance or irrelevance of sexual orientation in establishing legal marriage and parental rights; the extent to which the law should allow legal family ties to be established through sale of genetic material (sperm, ova) and gestational services; the importance, if any, of racial or religious identity to decisions regarding custody, foster care, or adoption; and the relative responsibilities of government and family members to pay for childcare, respite care, and care of ill or disabled family members. The hard choices each of these issues poses for policymakers indicate the extent to which family law and family policy reflect both human social practices and institutions, and conscious political choices. These choices require argument, debate, and continual assessment and reassessment in light of experience and values.

But to say that family law is properly the product of political discussion and negotiation is not to say that it cannot be based on principle. It is, rather, to say that in a world in which social and material conditions change over time, the way in which law reflects fundamental principles will change, too.

We believe that any adequate family law must be based on principles that take account of two complex characteristics of family life and the family's relationship to the state. First, the individual must be seen simultaneously as a distinct individual and as a person fundamentally involved in relationships of dependence, care, and responsibility. For example, a woman who agrees to bear a child for someone else must be viewed both as a responsible agent and as someone who, during her pregnancy, has established some relationship to the child. A court deciding who shall have custody of the child she has borne and now wishes to keep must neither reduce the case to the enforcement of a contract nor regard the fact of childbearing alone as determining parental claims. Similarly, when either same-sex or heterosexual couples who share custody of children separate or divorce, rulings determining financial support and child custody or visitation must consider the parties to such actions both as separate adults and as individuals-in-relationship. The law must allow parents to resume their independence and to remarry or form new relationships if they wish, but the law must also enforce the continuing obligations each has to their children. Those obligations are not only for financial support, but may also include requirements that one parent not take actions that would jeopardize the possibility of a continuing relationship between the other parent and the child.

Second, family law and political theory must take account of the fact that families are simultaneously private associations and entities shaped by the political order. Even confining our view to Western societies, the forms family associations take are clearly affected by law. People's views of who might be a possible marriage partner are shaped by the prohibited degrees of kinship and bans on same-sex and polygamous marriages. Laws also have affected who were regarded as parents and children; legal adoption allowed the creation of nonbiological family ties, while bastardy statutes denied any legal significance to the biological tie between offspring and parents. Yet families were clearly not creatures of the state like joint-stock companies and limited partnerships. With the exception of bastardy statutes, the biological tie between an adult and his or her offspring has been taken to establish prima facie parental rights and obligations; few have proposed that children, at birth, be assigned to the best possible caretaker, rather than to their biological parents.

Moreover, peoples' lives as family members are importantly framed and influenced by practices and decisions of the larger society. Some of those practices and decisions impose burdens and allocate benefits according to generally held views about acceptable family and public behaviors; for example, nepotism laws both reflected and enforced norms against married women's working outside the home. Others reflect matters including but not limited to macroeconomics policies that set the acceptable level of unemployment, and therefore the availability of jobs; resources devoted to public transportation; and employment practices that affect equal opportunity regardless of gender, race, or other characteristics. The current practice of contract pregnancy in the United States is shaped both by cultural norms that link maternity and womanhood very closely and that regard biological ties to the children one raises as highly desirable, and by economic structures that have made paid gestational labor an attractive job relative to other available options for some women and couples.

We have argued that neither a contract-based approach nor a community-based approach takes adequate account of these tensions that are inherent in contemporary family life. While a contractarian view of marriage emphasizes the need to accommodate differences among individuals and within relationships, it does not sufficiently acknowledge the non-contractual dimension of family relationships, the social and economic contexts that influence decisions made by family members, and the weight of social and state interests affected by family-like arrangements. While community-based theories understand the importance of tradition and social context in shaping individuals and defining their relationships, they often fail sufficiently to consider individual rights and interests, the status of family as a private association, and the plurality of family-like relationships that might warrant recognition and protection. Community-based theories risk marginalizing perspectives of members of non-traditional groups that have not historically had strong political representation. A conception of relational rights and responsibilities, we believe, would not regard "rights" as belonging to individuals and arising from the imperative of self-preservation, but rather would view rights as claims grounded in and arising from human relationships of varying degrees of intimacy, what Kenneth Karst has called "intimate associations."

Relational rights and responsibilities should draw attention to the claims that arise out of relationships of human interdependence. Those claims entitle people to explore a range of relationships and in so doing to draw sustenance from the larger community. A focus on relational rights and responsibilities might examine the legality of same-sex marriage by considering the place of such proposed relationships in the lives of those immediately involved and those in the surrounding community. Similarly, in thinking about cases in which a gestational mother who is party to a pregnancy contract wishes to keep the child rather than turn him or her over to the other contracting party, attention to relational rights and responsibilities requires consideration of the relationship between the gestational mother and the baby, the potential relationship between the commissioning parent(s) and the baby, and the baby's need for ongoing relationships with adults who assume full parental responsibilities. The issues for resolution thus are not simply the rights of adults who entered a contract, nor of community standards about contracts in such circumstances, but the moral and psychological dimensions of persons whose claims arise out of actual and potential relationships. In other disputes concerning child custody, a focus on relational rights and responsibilities would give great weight to preserving some continuity of relationships.

An adequate theory of family law would also have to recognize the relationship between family life and the political and economic order. Here again a vital conception of relationships and responsibilities would help. Each intimate relationship is in turn embedded in ties among members of neighbors, religious and ethnic groups, fellow citizens, all of which are deeply affected but not entirely determined by the political system and economic circumstances. Connecting these relationships to a vibrant sense of responsibility would engage wide circles of people, including even public-policy makers and voters, who would need to consider what social and economic structures are necessary to permit continuous, caring human relationships especially responsive to those most dependent on such care. As [Eva] Kittay argues, "A society cannot be well-ordered, that is, it cannot be one in which all its members are sustained and included within the ideal of equality, if it fails to be a society characterized by care." The polity cannot take for granted the contribution made by caregivers to maintaining the social and political order, but "must take upon itself the primary responsibility of maintaining structures that will support the principles of care."

Recognizing that individuals are invariably—although to different degrees and at different times—shaped by and accountable for relationships of interdependency would invigorate private and public responses to family issues. Acknowledging the interdependence of family members and the larger polity itself is crucial, although this is simply a beginning, not an end, of the analysis. For then the society, whether through law or other means, must still address what criteria should be used to resolve disputes over what should count within the definition of "family" and what constellation of intimate relations should receive the special resources of public approval and recognition. The resolution of such issues, we argue, requires not only reasoned deliberation, but also politics and a political practice fashioned to produce maximum participation by all members of society. Exclusions and disadvantages based on gender, race, ethnicity, religion, and class historically have been reflected in public policy dealing with families. The creation of a just family policy requires reform not only of family law itself but also the larger political and legal processes by which family law is created and applied, so that people who are presently marginalized may engage fully in the debates and decisions that frame entitlements essential to sustaining viable family lives.

A political and legal theory of family that took into account the two complex aspects of family membership, even if combined with legislative and judicial processes that worked to ensure representation of minority views and maximum participation, would not provide ready, easy, or universally acceptable answers to difficult questions such as those we raise at the beginning of this section. It would, however, provide the analytic, intellectual, and rhetorical resources for approaching such questions. It would help to ensure that the contractarian models of economic life do not take over all other areas of public life or of family relationships, and that a search for common norms would not eliminate pluralism or curtail privacy. It would also put the prerequisites of relationships of care at the center of concern, rather than treat them as incidental effects of individual choices or needs. A theory of relational rights and responsibilities would encompass not only individual freedoms but also rights to enter and sustain intimate associations consistent with public conceptions of the responsibilities those associations entail, underscoring the connection between families and the larger community. Progress in thinking about and addressing the complex issues concerning family life that have arisen from sociological changes in family structures, developments in reproductive technology, and the demise of the common law model of the patriarchal family seems most likely to develop from the conjuncture of a political and legal theory that focuses on the relationships that constitute family life and the preconditions necessary to sustain such relationships, and political practices designed to maximize inclusion, representation, and democratic participation.

Lynda Marin, Mother and Child: The Erotic Bond

From M. Reddy, M. Roth, A. Sheldon, eds., Mother Journeys: Feminists Write About Mothering (Duluth, MN: Spinsters Ink, 1994).

No one is prepared for becoming a mother even though the world is full of discourse on the subject. I became a mother at thirty-eight and by then I thought I knew a few things. I knew for a fact that I would never be adequately prepared, for instance, and that I would just do it the way every other woman probably had, the best way I could. Right from the beginning of the pregnancy I felt myself initiated into the realm of the best-kept secrets. . . .

A secret . . . that has increasingly gained complexity in the last two years, has to do with the erotic bond between my son and me. That the bond is an erotic one is not in itself a secret. This is the secret upon which Freud founded psychoanalysis as we know it—that the child has drives that are sexual and that the first objects of those drives are its parents, most initially its mother('s body), but what we do with that bit of psychoanalytic insight is what we seem to bent on keeping hidden.

Alexander likes to say he is "four-and-three-quarters." I got plenty of warning about this age, about the intensity of the little boy's attachment to the mother and his Oedipal struggle to possess her entirely for himself. . . . But no one had really ever told me, in a way that I could hear at least, what it might feel like to be the mother in the Oedipal conflict. . . . [W]e do not speak of our erotic feelings toward those most desirable of objects, our children. We say our kids are cute, of course, or beautiful or remarkable, and we endlessly detail their behaviors and idiosyncrasies, but rarely do we acknowledge the erotic component of our own feelings in these observations of them. I say "rarely" because just today, when I was trying to explain the topic of this essay to a friend with a six-month-old daughter, she said simply, "It's the most erotic thing *I've* ever felt. You know it's no joke about pretending to eat her right up. I really do want to. It's just uncontainable, this desire. But what can I do? I can't have sex with her. Although nursing takes care of that." That's right, I thought. The physical intimacy of early infancy does mediate those drives in the parent, does "take care of" the uncontainable desire in a way that can't occur at the Oedipal stage. Now that my son is nearly five, I do not have access to his body in the same ways I did when he was younger, nor does have the same access to mine. . . .

I remember a specific moment, a "where-it-all-began" moment when I glimpsed . . . the continuum of desire that contained us both. We were in the kitchen and he was two. . . . "Mommy!" he said, "you want a cookie." And as if my brain were wired through his, I indeed felt hunger for a cookie, as if he had only "read my mind." In the time it took to hand him the cookie, a lot happened. I realized that we had been operating like this for a long time, that the boundarylessness between mothers and preverbal children did not simply shore up with the onset of language but rather found ways to persist inside it. This was the first time I had ever noticed in nearly a year of his acquiring language that he had never used the word I. . . . Not surprisingly, it was around this time that I noticed other people in the family helping him to make the distinction between *I* and *you*. . . . I left it to the others. I was in no hurry to give up what might be the last vestiges of some of the most compelling commingling I have ever felt.

But the leaving it to others felt like a secret I ought to keep. No one likes the idea that a mother enjoys the boundarylessness of relation with her child. That pleasure suggests too intimately her own regressive, infantile underpinnings. More than anything, we need a mother to be an adult. We want to believe that all her own early polymorphous pleasure has now been securely organized around her genitals and directed toward her adult sexual partner. We like to think of a mother's delight in the softness of her child's skin, the firmness of its body, the familiarity of its smell, the singularity of its voice, the sweetness of its breathing as something quite separate from a woman's delight in the body of her lover. We like to make a clear distinction between motherly affection and female passion. If there were not a clear distinction, what would stop mothers from engulfing their children forever in their own hedonistic designs? What hope would culture have?

But what if one of the best-kept secrets is that there is no distinction, really, between motherly affection and female passion? Or rather, that we practice this same love, this erotic energy continuous with our early attachment to our own mother's (or her substitute's) body, in tirelessly deliberate and mediated ways. And we do this exactly because of the lack of boundary between ourselves and our children, exactly because our children are never entirely other. This is the positive side of the narcissistic attachment to children for which mothers are so often criticized. Never is it more clear than with our own children that what we do unto them, we do unto ourselves. If we support their independence and self-reliance, we inevitably gain more freedom and time for ourselves. If we honor their individual expression and spirit, we usually get respected in return. And if we burden them with guilt and shame, we can count on being plagued with those same feelings about ourselves and our parenting. Since the feedback loop is almost immediate, we learn early how to mediate the merging of desire (ours, theirs, and whatever overlaps), how to negotiate the tangle of erotic drives that constitutes the bond between a mother and a child. The other thing we learn is not to talk about it.

Alexander likes to cuddle a lot. *A lot.* . . . By now Alexander's cuddling is a highly developed art. It begins early in the morning when he appears in my room holding Orker the seal, slips into bed beside me, and coaxes one of my sleepy arms around his middle. . . . "Mommy," he says, after about ten or fifteen minutes, "let's be animals." This has been going on for as long as I can remember (perhaps this is what replaced nursing so long ago). He is the baby elephant, bird, snake, fish, seal, horse, dog, or kitty, and I am the mommy of the same species. We go looking for food, we have adventures, we don't get caught, we return home where we cuddle, of course. Sometimes he just collapses against me, his face pressing down on mine, and I breathe him in, breathe him out. Sometimes in these moments he says how much he loves me, but most of the time he is talking to himself, or singing, or just staring off. If his dad tries to enter in, Alexander always pushes him away, even though at other times he is quite loving with him. Then suddenly he will disappear under the covers all the way to the foot of the bed. After a lot of tossing and giggling he reappears, naked, having left his pajamas somewhere down at my feet. He presents himself with noisy fanfare, giddy with his own assumed prohibition. For although nudity is commonplace in our family, he seems to sense that he's on some kind of an edge. He turns his skinny backside to my front and we lie like spoons, half moaning half-humming an exaggerated "Yummmmmm." The sensuality of this moment that we have constructed almost takes my breath away. For the short time that we snuggle like this, I feel as close to perfectly happy as I imagine possible.

Most of the time I'm the one to say we've got to get up, to eat, to dress, to go to school, etc. But when I can't marshall the forces, or when I am lulled into overtime by the pleasure of our play, I sometimes begin to feel uncomfortable. "OK, I'll be the mommy bird and you be the baby and you cry and I'll feed you. Here, nurse the mommy," he says, pointing to his tummy. And although I'm tempted to kiss that spot as a way of playing along (I can't even imagine pretending to nurse him—here a taboo is in full force), I often hear myself responding with things like, "No, I'm sleepy now," or "Yikes, I fell in the river." Nevertheless I let the game go on. I am, of course, partly curious to see how he plays out being the mommy (she's always good at finding food and fighting off hunters). Now suddenly he's the baby and wants to nurse. I laugh him away, but he insists and pretends to grab for my breast. "Cut it out!" I say partly laughing because he's laughing, but partly serious, too, and in this moment thinking quite concertedly about where the boundaries ought to be. "OK, OK," he says, seems to stop, and then dives toward my chest, kissing me on the clavicle. That he kisses me takes me aback. I see that he does the same thing I do— that he doesn't really pretend to nurse either, that he opts for that more adult vestigial gesture of nursing, the kiss. And, like someone who suddenly realizes she is witnessing an historical event in the making, I think IT IS HAPPENING RIGHT NOW. In this moment, unlike any other than I have known, I am actually the mother and the woman, the original object and its displacement. This is the impossible conjoining that patriarchal and hetero-sexual culture so labors to veil, to mystify, to interdict, which I can hardly hang on to long enough to mark before it passes imperceptively like water into air. . . .

I see that what I am holding out for, in these borderline experiments in erotic love with my son (the wording is so sensitive here, and nothing that I can think to say is quite what I mean), is a rewriting of sexuality as I know it. It is not a free-for-all kind of sexuality that powered the imagination of the "sexual revolution" of the '60s and '70s but left us, men and women, just as split in ourselves as ever. It is an inclusive kind of sexuality that recognizes itself basically everywhere. It is not so scary in its infantility because it's just as much a part of adulthood, too. And if we were to recognize that kind of sexuality much more intimately in ourselves all the time (since it's operating here all the time anyway), we would have to pay it close attention, to be careful and caring with it. I imagine our having to add lots of new words to our language to describe it in its multiple manifesta-tions in any interaction, fantasy, work of art, etc., in much the same way we have thought Inuit peoples to have so many words for snow. But I recognize that as innocently as I try to cast it, it's a sexuality that would not support life on the planet as we know it, that is, would not support social hierarchies, multinational corporations, a free market economy, racism, colonization, or any other of the problematic realities that depend on our ability to split off what's safe and good (mother) from what's desirable (woman). . . .

On my desk sits a small photo of myself *circa* four "and-three-quarters." I retrieved it from my stepfather after my mother died thirteen years ago. It had been taken in Iowa where I lived with a foster parent who must have sent it on to my mother in California. I have often wondered at the self-possessed expression on that child's face, her legs crossed and her hands clasped squarely in her lap. It is one of the few photos I have of my childhood and it has become, by now, one of my most familiar images of myself. Recently, though, while late-night working on some translation at my desk, ... I looked at the little girl in the photo and I felt such a surge of desire I must have stopped breathing. I wanted her entirely, to embrace her until she melted into me, to infuse her with all of myself, to enjoy the delicious intimacy of her little body as a day-to-day, minute-to-minute commonplace—her skin, her hair, her smell, her sound. I could almost reproduce her right then and there, a tangible, palpable child.

In a trying-to-make-sense-of-this effort I reminded myself that these were actually feelings I have for Alexander. And it did make sense that on account of family resemblance and age correspondence I had, at that moment, mapped the feelings I have for my actual child onto the photographic image that represents for me my internalized child. But the unmediated desire I felt for that small girl in the photo made me at least suspect that it might be the other way around. What I mean to say is what if, for a reason I can't presume to know, for a split second some of my psycho-social infrastructure slipped just enough to reveal another of the best-kept secrets: that all love whether it be for our children, our lovers, our work, our ideas, is fundamentally the same love, is first and last, coming and going, not even erotic but autoerotic? For isn't erotic love just a further development, a successful splitting off, redirecting, and renaming of that first continuous unbounded connection/pleasure we feel with our mother's body?

Of course, autoeroticism is not such a secret since we can find it strategically positioned, just as I'm suggesting now, in psychoanalytic discourse. The real secret, though, is how "ardorously" culture struggles to forget what eroticism actually is, where it comes from, and why it is absolutely everywhere all the time, especially and necessarily in a mother's love for her child. When we successfully forget that fact, as we require ourselves to do in the name of becoming adults, we severely limit the ways we can experience the connection/pleasure which originally nurtured us into life and which sustains our desire for life forever after. It seems evident that one of the reasons, for instance, that Western culture has so little regard, by and large, for what's left of natural life—for plants and animals and earth and atmosphere—is its successful endeavor to see itself as separate from all that life, to forget the connection/pleasure that informs our very being here.

So what *is* a mother to do? If I had never had a child, my task would be the same. I would still have that little girl internalized and her picture on my desk. I would still need to be parenting her, the child she is, the woman I am, the best way I know how. It's just that having Alexander confronts me more urgently to uncover the secret of what that best way is. ...

One morning recently he sits at the table eating cereal and crooning a love song to mother. Something about how wonderful and sweet I am and how much much much he loves loves loves me. "Goodbye" I interrupt him on my way out the door. "Can I have a hug?" The goodbye hug is a ritual. But this morning he doesn't even hear me. His eyes are so far off in his song that I hesitate to ask again, though I suppose that later on he'll think I didn't say goodbye. So I try once more. But it's no use. "I just love her so much my mommy," I hear as I leave the house. Tossing his car pillow into the backseat to make room next to me for my books and papers, I marvel at that other "mommy," that symbolic creature who, seemingly overnight, has exceeded and displaced me, and who, this morning, has him in thrall. I only hope, for all our sakes, she loves him as undividedly as she can.

D. PARENTING

INTRODUCTION

The biological acts giving rise to the conception, gestation, and birth of a child do not by themselves create parents. It is a legal decision, usually made by default, to assign parental status to the woman who gives birth and to the man who supplied the sperm. The choice involved in such a decision has become transparent in the face of emerging new reproductive strategies, including sperm and egg donation, contract (or surrogate) mothering, in vitro fertilization, and embryo transfer. Because these new technologies—as well as efforts to avoid pregnancy—so deeply involve women's bodies, they are addressed directly in the third chapter of this text.

The legal construction of parenthood itself implicates gender roles in profound ways, as revealed in contemporary rules and debates over adoption, child custody, and child abuse and neglect. In the traditionally dominant cultural practices presumed for the most part in American law, the point is not simply that women mother and men father. The verbs historically marked not merely a distinction in the gender of the person performing the role but also a distinction in the presumed content and scope of the role. Letty Cottin Pogrebin put this difference this way: " 'to father' a child refers to the momentary act of impregnation; 'to mother' a child means to succor and sacrifice." Letty Cottin Pogrebin, *The New Father*, in Family Politics: Love and Power on an Intimate Frontier 195 (1983). Traditionally, to say that a father "takes care of" his family meant he provided for it economically, while a mother's caring behavior historically was measured in terms of a capacity to give comfort and to be present and involved in constant, daily ways.

What should happen when both parents seek to be primary custodian after divorce? Should a man who fulfilled the traditional father role gain as likely a chance for primary custody as the woman who fulfilled the traditional mother role? Should a man who fulfilled the traditional father role have a greater chance to serve as primary custodian if the woman worked outside the home, and thus departed from a traditional conception of the stay-at-home caretaker? Should it matter if the man has remarried and the woman has not? Should standards for neglectful conduct vary for fathers and for mothers? Are women held to higher standards of parenting than men, and should they be?

Furthermore, how does the legal construction of parenthood affect same-sex couples with children? If a child has been parented by a same-sex couple, how should the adults' relationship with the child be recognized by the law?

Before turning directly to these themes, let's examine the place where the state explicitly considers who should become a parent: adoption. What images of parenting, and what inflection based on gender does and should govern adoption judgments? Of what relevance is marital status, sexual orientation, experiences with infertility, or other features of the prospective parent's intimate life?

I. ADOPTION

Elizabeth Bartholet, Parenting Options for the Infertile

From E. Bartholet, Family Bonds: Adoption and the Politics of Parenting (Boston: Houghton Mifflin, 1993).

Shaping Women and Their Choices

Adoption is the choice of last resort for most infertile men and women who want to parent. If asked why this is true, many would say, "Because it is natural to want your own child." But it is hard to know what is natural, given the fact that society weighs in to *make* adoption the last resort. And it is not clear that we should characterize parenting decisions as the product of choice. We are all conditioned from early childhood to equate personhood with procreation and procreation with parenting.

The fertile almost never consider adoption, and the infertile are unlikely to consider it until they have reached the end of a long medical road designed to produce a biological child. This road has lengthened as the medical possibilities have expanded. The infertile seem increasingly eager for what the medical experts have to offer. It is the *treatment* of infertility that has increased in recent years, not its overall *incidence*. Visits to physicians for infertility services increased almost threefold from the 1960s to the 1980s, while infertility rates remained stable. It is generally only after people have explored the possibilities for infertility treatment and either rejected or exhausted the various medical options that they give adoption serious consideration. . . .

The medical profession has a near-monopoly on the information given out as people discover their infertility and explore and exercise options. When people who have been trying to have a baby realize that something may be wrong, they usually consult their family doctor or their gynecologist, and then, if they can afford it, a fertility specialist. The specialist educates them about the range of treatment possibilities and, if they are willing and financially able, begins to lead them down the treatment path. A couple may start with temperature charts and scheduled sex and move on to fertility drug treatment. They may then decide on an exploratory laparoscopy, which can reveal pelvic adhesions on the woman's fallopian tubes. Tubal surgery may follow, and then tests to see whether the tubes remain open. If the woman still does not become pregnant, the couple may explore and pursue IVF or related high-tech treatment methods.

This treatment scenario has become a common one, and as people move through it, their chief advisers at every step are likely to be doctors. The advice doctors give is inevitably biased toward the treatment option. Doctors think of it as their job to know and advise about the various medical possibilities. Few see it as equally their job to explore with patients why they are considering medical treatment, whether continued treatment efforts are worth it, or when enough is enough. Fewer still see it as their job to help patients work through the advantages and disadvantages of treatment as compared with parenting through adoption. Doctors once played a major role in helping infertile patients connect with pregnant patients interested in surrendering their children for adoption. But the specialized fertility experts in today's treatment world have little interest in or knowledge about adoption. . . .

The adoption world does essentially nothing to reach out to the infertile to educate them about adoption possibilities. Indeed, adoption agency rules operate to push the infertile away and thus to prevent them from obtaining the information they need to consider adoption at an early stage. The accepted ethic among adoption workers is that prospective parents must resolve feelings about infertility before they pursue adoption. The idea behind this makes some sense: people *should* try to understand their feelings about infertility and grieve over any loss that that infertility represents before they become adoptive parents. They should not enter into adoption thinking of their adopted child as a second-best substitute for the biologic child they still ache to produce. But it may be impossible to know what part of the pain of infertility relates to a desire to parent, and whether this desire will be satisfied by adoption, without knowing what adoption is about. . . .

If the infertile do manage to get accurate information about their various parenting options, they find that our society gives vastly preferential treatment to people seeking to produce children rather than those seeking to adopt.

First and foremost, those seeking to reproduce operate in a free market world in which they are able to make their own decisions subject only to financial and physical constraints. Those seeking to adopt operate in a highly regulated world in which the government asserts the right to determine who will be allowed to parent.

As a result, those seeking to reproduce retain the sense that they are normal rights-bearing citizens. No one asks them to prove that they are fit to parent. They are perceived as having a God-given right to reproduce if they are capable of doing so. Those in the business of providing infertility services do not see it as their role to regulate access to parenting. The IVF practitioners who made the initial decision to exclude singles from their programs did so in large part because in an era when IVF treatment was highly controversial, the risk-averse course was to limit services to married couples. But IVF programs never enforced their rules excluding singles with the moral fervor typical of the adoption agencies, as my own experience illustrates. Today, as the IVF treatment industry has become more established, many programs are beginning officially to open their doors to singles.

Those entering the world of adoption agencies and home studies quickly realize that they have no right to become adoptive parents. Parental screening is the essence of what traditional adoption is all about, with the government determining through its agents who should be disqualified altogether from the parenting opportunity and then how those who are qualified should be rated for purposes of allocating the available children. There are no privacy rights in this world, either. The entire point of the home study process is to find out whether the most intimate events and relationships of a person's life have produced someone fit to parent. It is true that there are significant differences between the screening process in agency adoptions and that in independent adoptions. Prospective adopters with enough money can buy their way around the traditional agency home study process. But many who would like to adopt do not have this kind of money, and even in independent adoptions, the government demands at least some minimum showing of parental fitness.

The parental screening requirement is a very real deterrent to many who might otherwise consider adoption. People don't like to become helpless supplicants, utterly dependent on the grace of social workers, with respect to something as basic as their desire to become parents. Screening also adds to the financial costs of adoption. Because it takes time, prospective parents must endure the related delays in forming a family. Screening turns the process of becoming a parent into a bureaucratic nightmare in which documents must be endlessly accumulated and stamped and submitted and copied.

Regulation also sends a powerful message about the essential inferiority of adoption as a form of parenting. By subjecting adoptive but not biologic parents to regulation, society suggests that it trusts what goes on when people give birth and raise a birth child but profoundly distrusts what goes on when a child is transferred from a birth to an adoptive parent. The specific nature of adoption regulation constantly reinforces the notion that biologic parenting is the ideal and adoption a poor second best. Adoptive families are thus designed in imitation of biologic families. Prospective parents are screened because as adoptive parents they are suspect. They must be carefully matched with the right children because of the assumed risk that adoptive parenting won't work out. Ideally, they should be matched with the kinds of children they could have produced. And so forth.

Society also discriminates in financial terms, giving preferred treatment to those who choose child production over child adoption. People covered by health insurance are reimbursed for many of the costs involved in infertility treatment, pregnancy, and childbirth. Although insurance plans have so far typically not covered IVF treatment, the trend is in the direction of expanding coverage to include it. Treatment and childbirth expenses that are not covered by insurance are tax-deductible if they exceed a certain percentage of income. By contrast, those who adopt are generally on their own in paying for the adoption, and only limited subsidies are available for those who adopt children with special needs. There is no equivalent to insurance coverage for the expenses involved in adoption, nor are those expenses generally deductible for income tax purposes. Employment benefit policies also favor child production over adoption. Employers that provide health insurance and childbirth leave usually do not provide equivalent benefits for those who become parents through adoption. . . .

A Snapshot of Adoption's Realities

Our society's current laws signal adoption's inferiority to the biologic family and proclaim the dangers allegedly inherent in raising children apart from their birth families. Almost all the rules are designed either to ensure that a child is not improperly removed from the biologic family or that a child is not placed with an inadequate adoptive family. There are no rules, or at least none with any teeth, that give children a right to a nurturing home or that limit how long they can be held in limbo.

Our laws design adoptive families in imitation of biology. The central symbolic event is the issuance of a new birth certificate for the child and the sealing of the old certificate, together with other adoption records. The goal is to ensure that the birth parents, the child, and the adoptive parents can all proceed with their new lives as if the child had never been born to the original parents. The clear implication of this "as if" model of adoption is that adoption is an inferior and not quite real form of family which can at best aspire to look like the real thing.

The central legal event in adoption is issuance of the adoption decree, which completely severs the legal relationship between the child and the birth family, transferring to the adoptive family all rights and responsibilities. Legally as well as symbolically, it is as if the child were born to the adoptive parents. This promotes a rigid separation of the birth from the adoptive family, reinforcing notions that the true family is the closed nuclear family and warding off as much as possible any sense that adoptive relationships might be more contingent and less proprietary than traditional parenting relationships.

The "as if" adoption model produces parental screening policies that confirm traditional prejudices. The home study process favors married couples who look as if they could have produced the child they will adopt. It tends to screen out prospective parents who do not fit traditional notions of what parents should look like; among those disqualified or ranked at the bottom of eligibility lists are singles, older parents, gays and lesbians, and people with disabilities. The rules for matching waiting children with prospective parents are designed to maximize sameness and avoid what is seen as dangerous diversity within families. Originally the goal was literally to match—to give prospective parents children with similar physical features and similar mental characteristics, so that the parents could pretend to the world and even to the child that this was their biologic child. In addition, the idea was (and to a great degree still is) that adoption has the best chance of working if the child is as much like the parent as possible.

After all, how can you expect a smart parent to relate to a not-so-smart child, or a musical parent to relate to a baby jock? What would happen to the talented child in a family of pedestrian minds? In today's adoption world, the matching ideal has given way significantly to reality: there are relatively few healthy babies in this country to match with the mass of eager prospective parents. But interestingly, traditional matching principles are very much alive with respect to race. Powerful policies in force throughout the nation restrict adoption across racial lines, reinforcing notions of the importance of racial barriers. . . .

Screening for parental fitness is a basic part of the agency adoption process. Both public and private agencies conduct home studies designed to assess eligibility for adoptive parenthood. The process also determines the ranking of prospective parents for purposes of child assignment; that is, it determines which parents will be considered for which children within an agency's jurisdiction. As discussed later in this chapter, home studies are not part of the independent adoption process, in which birth parents place their children with adoptive parents either directly or through an intermediary.

Defenders of the home study system claim that screening assesses such important qualities as the capacity to love and nurture an adoptive child. They also claim that the child assignment, or "matching," process involves sophisticated judgments as to which particular parent-child combinations will work best. But the fact is that the screening and matching system is extremely crude and quite inconsistent with its alleged purposes.

The system ranks prospective parents from top to bottom in terms of relative desirability, which is assessed primarily on the basis of easily determined objective factors. These factors reflect the system's bias in favor of a biologic parenting model as well as a socially traditional family model. So heterosexual couples in their late twenties or early thirties with apparently stable marriages are at the top of the ladder. These are the kind of people who could, if not for infertility, produce children, and who should, in the system's view, be parents. Single and older adoptive applicants—those in their late thirties and forties—are placed lower on the ladder, along with people with disabilities. Gays, lesbians, and the seriously disabled are generally excluded altogether.

Although social work practices reflect changing social realities, they tend to lag a generation or so behind. Bureaucratic rules take on a life of their own. Entrenched policies take time to reverse, and the bureaucratic mentality is averse to risk: the safe path for an adoption agency is to select parents on the basis of accepted models. Single adoptive parenting was essentially unheard of until the mid–1960s, when forty children were placed in single parent homes by the Los Angeles Department of Adoptions. Many adoption workers continued to treat single-parent adoption as highly suspect, and questioned whether singles should be found eligible to parent even those children who would not otherwise find adoptive homes. As late as 1969 a respected adoption expert found it necessary to defend single-parent adoptions as "not inherently or necessarily pathogenic." The fact that a large percentage of all children in our society were being raised by single parents took decades to sink into the bureaucratic mind and to have an impact on adoption practices.

The adoption screening system ranks and categorizes children waiting for homes, as well as parents, in order to decide how to make particular parent-child matches. The children are placed on their own desirability list, with healthy infants at the top, somewhat older and less healthy children next, and the oldest and most seriously disabled children at the bottom. Children are also classified according to racial, ethnic, and religious heritage.

In matching children with parents, the system operates primarily on the basis of what looks roughly like a market system, one in which ranking produces buying power. The most "desirable" parents are matched with the most "desirable" children, and the less desirable with the less desirable, on down the list. The "marginally fit" parents are matched with the hardest-to-place children ...

The matching system also demonstrates deference to a biologic model of parenting. As I have noted, in earlier times agencies made a significant effort to give prospective parents children as closely matched as possible in looks and temperament to the birth children they might have had. While this philosophy has been tempered in recent years by virtue of necessity, it still governs with respect to those attributes deemed most important. Older parents are often precluded from adopting children more than thirty-five or forty years younger than themselves on the ground that they would not have been likely to have produced such children themselves. Black parents are given black children, and Catholic parents are given the children surrendered by Catholic birth parents.

Discrimination is thus the name of the game in adoptive parenting. Those who procreate live in a world of near-absolute rights with respect to parenting. Those who would adopt have no rights. They must beg for the privilege of parenting, and do so in a state-administered realm that denies them both the right to privacy and the "civil rights" that we have come to think of as fundamental in the rest of our communal life. ...

The government has traditionally asserted an interest in promoting heterosexual marriage and parenting in the context of such a marriage. But adoptive screening does little to promote this vision of the family. What it does is to drive some gays and lesbians underground to pose as straight adoptive parents, and others, together with older applicants and singles, into the independent adoption world, where they can avoid the screening system. Furthermore, it drives many of those who are fertile but would nonetheless be interested in adoption into the world of biologic parenting. Straight singles and gay singles and couples meet with no real restrictions if they seek to form families by reproduction, either naturally or with the help of reproductive technology. Increasing numbers are becoming parents through the use of sperm donors and, more recently, in vitro fertilization and surrogacy. More and more older prospective parents are resorting to IVF and related methods of infertility treatment. Even assuming that the government has a valid interest in promoting a traditional model of the family, this interest is not served by driving socially unorthodox people away from adoptive and into biologic parenting.

The state's claimed justification for adoptive screening is that it is necessary to serve children's interests. But it is hard to identify any way in which the current system furthers the goal of ensuring children the best homes. What is clear is that it deprives many children altogether of the homes they need.

NOTES AND QUESTIONS

1. **The Challenges of Adopting as an Unmarried Person**. Although many states, including New York, now have statutes explicitly allowing adoption by single persons, prospective adoptive parents who are unmarried still face the biases of social service agencies, adoption agencies, and judges:

> . . . Despite the existence of these statutes, courts are more likely to grant an adoption where there is both a mother and a father in the family unit.

> Marital status may be one valid factor to consider in deciding an adoption because "[i]t is safer to start with two guardians . . . It is undoubtedly greater protection for the future." [quoting from *A. v. M.*, 74 N.J.Super. 104, 125, 180 A.2d 541, 553 (1962).] This conclusion may be outweighed by other factors impacting on the welfare of the child.

> . . . Even though one-parent households are increasingly common, the concern about placing a child in such a family structure persists. The concern centers primarily on the future care of the child if the sole parent becomes financially or physically disabled, or should die while the child is still young. This sentiment is expressed in *In re Adoption of H.* [69 Misc.2d 304, 330 N.Y.S.2d 235 (Fam. Ct. 1972)], where the court states that single parent adoptions should be considered only for hard-to-place children, as an alternative to institutional care, because joint responsibility of a mother and father is preferable. . . .

> The illogical conclusion to be drawn from this is that a parent able to meet the needs and demands of a hard-to-place child—usually physically or emotionally handicapped or both—is not as able to successfully meet the needs and demands of a non-handicapped child. . . .

> The difficulty many single adults encounter in attempting to adopt is the lack of enthusiasm that their marital status evokes from social service agencies. The result is that many single parents go through private placement adoptions.

> Despite the equal eligibility of single and married adults under state adoption statutes, the best interest standard gives the court wide latitude to view marital status as a negative factor. Conse-

quently, the single adult will often find private placement adoption or adoption of a hard-to-place child the only options available.

Myra G. Spencer, *Adoption in the Non–Traditional Family—A Look at Some Alternatives*, 16 Hofstra L. R. 191 (Fall 1987).

2. **Gender Bias and Becoming a Parent**. Because most of the single adults trying to adopt are women, women are disproportionately affected by these personal and institutional prejudices against adoption by single persons. However, those single men who petition to adopt a child may find themselves subject to even greater prejudice, since men are not traditionally regarded as "caregivers" in our society. Should adoption agencies be forbidden from ranking prospective parents based on gender, marital status or sexual orientation?

3. **Surrendering the Child for Adoption**. A child eligible for adoption must be removed by the state from the custody and control of the parents, surrendered voluntarily by the parents, or else the state must establish grounds to dispense with parental consent for adoption. What if the parents are unmarried? What if the biological mother wishes to surrender the child for adoption but the biological father does not? What if the biological mother has in fact never notified the biological father of the fact of the child's birth, or indeed, the fact of the child's conception? Although this very factual circumstance underscores a difference in the relationship of the woman and the man to the child, the courts have increasingly required efforts to equalize the roles of the biological parents in deciding whether to surrender the child for adoption. Thus, in Stanley v. Illinois, 405 U.S. 645, 92 S.Ct. 1208, 31 L.Ed.2d 551 (1972), the Supreme Court rejected as a violation of Fourteenth Amendment Due Process a state statute allowing state officials to remove children of a deceased mother from their home with their unmarried father without a finding of unfitness. An unmarried father may not be presumed unfit to raise children.

4. **Gender Distinctions for Unmarried Parents' Rights**. In Quilloin v. Walcott, 434 U.S. 246, 98 S.Ct. 549, 54 L.Ed.2d 511 (1978), the Supreme Court rejected an Equal Protection challenge to a Georgia statute that always required an unmarried mother's consent to the adoption of her child but required the unmarried father's consent only if he had accepted paternity and responsibility for the child. The Court relied on an apparent difference in the existence of an actual relationship between the parent and the child. Relying on the existence of an actual relationship and acceptance of paternity, the Court found an Equal Protection defect in a New York statute granting the unmarried mother but not the unmarried father a veto over the adoption of their children. Caban v. Mohammed, 441 U.S. 380, 99 S.Ct. 1760, 60 L.Ed.2d 297 (1979). Once again, in Lehr v. Robertson, 463 U.S. 248, 103 S.Ct. 2985, 77 L.Ed.2d 614 (1983), the Court reiterated its emphasis on the existence of an established relationship. It rejected a Due Process argument that the unmarried father, who had failed to sign his name in a registry of putative fathers, deserved special notice prior to an adoption proceeding involving his child. The Court also rejected an Equal Protection challenge to the state statute that ensured prior notice of an

adoption proceeding to any mother surrendering the child but only to a select class of fathers. Those fathers selected for notice by the statute included those who had been identified as such on the child's birth certificate, who had been adjudicated as the father, who had been identified by the mother as the father, who had married the mother within six months of the child's birth, and who had lived openly with the child and the mother while presenting himself as the father. The Court reasoned that these categories implemented the justifiable distinction between those parents with an actual relationship with the child and those without it.

5. **Maternal v. Paternal Rights**. Imagine an unmarried mother who relinquishes custody of her newborn without signing a consent for adoption. Should she have any greater rights prior to the adoption of her child than the unmarried father? Explain your views.

II. "SECOND PARENT" ADOPTIONS

When members of a same-sex couple decide to have a child, how can both adults acquire the status of parents? Historically, state laws made this goal difficult. Members of same-sex couples have usually been discouraged or explicitly forbidden from becoming adoptive parents through state child protection agencies. If one woman involved in a same-sex relationship becomes pregnant and gives birth, she by the default rules in place becomes the mother but her partner does not. Because at birth, each child is assigned at most two parents—the biological mother and the biological father—there has been no place to recognize a third individual as a parent. If the "father" is an anonymous sperm donor, there is no existing second parent, but states traditionally afforded no method for an unmarried partner of the child's mother to become the child's parent.

Many states permit adoption by a stepparent, who has married the child's biological parent. In contrast, the unmarried partner historically could not adopt the child unless both biological parents surrendered the child for adoption or lost their parental rights. *See* In the Interest of Angel Lace M., 184 Wis.2d 492, 516 N.W.2d 678 (Wis. 1994). Several state courts have tried to craft "second-parent adoptions" to deal with this set of problems. To date, the highest courts in three states—Massachusetts, New York, and Vermont—have authorized second-parent adoptions. Additionally, lower courts in a number of other jurisdictions, including Maryland, the District of Columbia, California, Washington, Alaska, and New Jersey, have also allowed second-parent adoptions. However, other states limit those persons eligible to adopt to married persons or unmarried individuals; statutes generally do not envision adoption by two unmarried individuals. New Hampshire and Florida explicitly prohibit adoption by homosexuals.

Adoption of Tammy

Supreme Judicial Court of Massachusetts, 1993.
416 Mass. 205, 619 N.E.2d 315.

JOHN M. GREANEY, JUSTICE.

In this case, two unmarried women, Susan and Helen, filed a joint petition in the Probate and Family Court Department under G.L. c. 210,

§ 1 (1992 ed.) to adopt as their child Tammy, a minor, who is Susan's biological daughter. Following an evidentiary hearing, a judge of the Probate and Family Court entered a memorandum of decision containing findings of fact and conclusions of law. Based on her finding that Helen and Susan "are each functioning, separately and together, as the custodial and psychological parents of [Tammy]," and that "it is the best interest of said [Tammy] that she be adopted by both," the judge entered a decree allowing the adoption. Simultaneously, the judge reserved and reported to the Appeals Court the evidence and all questions of law, in an effort to "secure [the] decree from any attack in the future on jurisdictional grounds." See G.L. c. 2, § 13 (1992 ed.). See also Adoption of Thomas, 408 Mass. 446, 559 N.E.2d 1230 (1990). We transferred the case to this court on our own motion. We conclude that the adoption was properly allowed under G.L. c. 210.

We summarize the relevant facts as found by the judge. Helen and Susan have lived together in a committed relationship, which they consider to be permanent, for more than ten years. In June, 1983, they jointly purchased a house in Cambridge. Both women are physicians specializing in surgery. At the time the petition was filed, Helen maintained a private practice in general surgery at Mount Auburn Hospital and Susan, a nationally recognized expert in the field of breast cancer, was director of the Faulkner Breast Center and a surgical oncologist at the Dana Farber Cancer Institute. Both women also held positions on the faculty of Harvard Medical School.

For several years prior to the birth of Tammy, Helen and Susan planned to have a child, biologically related to both of them, whom they would jointly parent. Helen first attempted to conceive a child through artificial insemination by Susan's brother. When those efforts failed, Susan successfully conceived a child through artificial insemination by Helen's biological cousin, Francis. The women attended childbirth classes together and Helen was present when Susan gave birth to Tammy on April 30, 1988. Although Tammy's birth certificate reflects Francis as her biological father, she was given a hyphenated surname using Susan and Helen's last names.

Since her birth, Tammy has lived with, and been raised and supported by, Helen and Susan. Tammy views both women as her parents, calling Helen "mama" and Susan "mommy." Tammy has strong emotional and psychological bonds with both Helen and Susan. Together, Helen and Susan have provided Tammy with a comfortable home, and have created a warm and stable environment which is supportive of Tammy's growth and over-all well being. Both women jointly and equally participate in parenting Tammy, and both have a strong financial commitment to her. During the work week, Helen usually has lunch at home with Tammy, and on weekends both women spend time together with Tammy at special events or running errands. When Helen and Susan are working, Tammy is cared for by a nanny. The three vacation together at least ten days every three to four months, frequently spending time with Helen's and Susan's respective extended families in California and Mexico. Francis does not participate in parenting Tammy and does not support her. His intention was to assist Helen and Susan in having a child, and he does not intend to be involved with Tammy, except as a distant relative. Francis signed an adoption surrender and supports the joint adoption by both women.

Helen and Susan, recognizing that the laws of the Commonwealth do not permit them to enter into a legally cognizable marriage, believe that the best interests of Tammy require legal recognition of her identical emotional relationship to both women. Susan expressed her understanding that it may not be in her own long-term interest to permit Helen to adopt Tammy because, in the event that Helen and Susan separate, Helen would have equal rights to primary custody. Susan indicated, however, that she has no reservation about allowing Helen to adopt. Apart from the emotional security and current practical ramifications which legal recognition of the reality of her parental relationships will provide Tammy, Susan indicated that the adoption is important for Tammy in terms of potential inheritance from Helen. Helen and her living issue are the beneficiaries of three irrevocable family trusts. Unless Tammy is adopted, Helen's share of the trusts may pass to others. Although Susan and Helen have established a substantial trust fund for Tammy, it is comparatively small in relation to Tammy's potential inheritance under Helen's family trusts.

Over a dozen witnesses, including mental health professionals, teachers, colleagues, neighbors, blood relatives and a priest and nun, testified to the fact that Helen and Susan participate equally in raising Tammy, that Tammy relates to both women as her parents, and that the three form a healthy, happy, and stable family unit. Educators familiar with Tammy testified that she is an extremely well-adjusted, bright, creative, cheerful child who interacts well with other children and adults. A priest and nun from the parties' church testified that Helen and Susan are active parishioners, that they routinely take Tammy to church and church-related activities, and that they attend to the spiritual and moral development of Tammy in an exemplary fashion. Teachers from Tammy's school testified that Helen and Susan both actively participate as volunteers in the school community and communicate frequently with school officials. Neighbors testified that they would have no hesitation in leaving their own children in the care of Helen or Susan. Susan's father, brother, and maternal aunt, and Helen's cousin testified in favor of the joint adoption. Members of both women's extended families attested to the fact that they consider Helen and Susan to be equal parents of Tammy. Both families unreservedly endorsed the adoption petition.

The Department of Social Services (department) conducted a home study in connection with the adoption petition which recommended the adoption, concluding that "the petitioners and their home are suitable for the proper rearing of this child." Tammy's pediatrician reported to the department that Tammy receives regular pediatric care and that she "could not have more excellent parents than Helen and Susan." A court-appointed guardian ad litem, Dr. Steven Nickman, assistant clinical professor of psychiatry at Harvard Medical School, conducted a clinical assessment of Tammy and her family with a view toward determining whether or not it would be in Tammy's best interests to be adopted by Helen and Susan. Dr. Nickman considered the ramifications of the fact that Tammy will be brought up in a "nonstandard" family. As part of his report, he reviewed and referenced literature on child psychiatry and child psychology which supports the conclusion that children raised by lesbian parents develop normally. In sum, he stated that "the fact that this parent-child constellation came into being as a result of thoughtful planning and a strong desire on the part of these women to be parents to a child and to give that child the love, the wisdom and the knowledge that they possess ... [needs to be taken into account] ... The maturity of these women, their status in the community, and their seriousness of purpose stands in contrast to the caretaking environments of a vast number of children who are born to heterosexual parents but who are variously abused, neglected and otherwise deprived of security and happiness." Dr. Nickman concluded that "there is every reason for [Helen] to become a legal parent to Tammy just as [Susan] is," and he recommended that the court so order. An attorney appointed to represent Tammy's interests also strongly recommended that the joint petition be granted.

Despite the overwhelming support for the joint adoption and the judge's conclusion that joint adoption is clearly in Tammy's best interests, the question remains whether there is anything in the law of the Commonwealth that would prevent this adoption. The law of adoption is purely statutory, Davis v. McGraw, 206 Mass. 294, 297, 92 N.E. 332 (1910), and the governing statute, G.L. c. 210 (1992 ed.), is to be strictly followed in all its essential particulars. ... To the extent that any ambiguity or vagueness exists in the statute, judicial construction should enhance, rather than defeat, its purpose. ... The primary purpose of the adoption statute, particularly with regard to children under the age of fourteen, is undoubtedly the advancement of the best interests of the subject child. See G.L. c. 2, §§ 3, 4A, 5A, 5B, 6. ... With these considerations in mind, we examine the statute to determine whether adoption in the circumstances of this case is permitted.

1. The initial question is whether the Probate Court judge had jurisdiction under G.L. c. 210 to enter a judgment on a joint petition for adoption brought by two unmarried cohabitants in the petitioners' circumstances. We answer this question in the affirmative.

There is nothing on the face of the statute which precludes the joint adoption of a child by two unmarried cohabitants such as the petitioners. Chapter 210, § 1, provides that "[a] person of full age may petition the probate court in the county where he resides for leave to adopt as his child another person younger than himself, unless such other person is his or her wife or husband, or brother, sister, uncle, aunt, of the whole or half blood." Other than requiring that a spouse join in the petition, if the petitioner is married and the spouse is competent to join therein, the statute does not expressly prohibit or require joinder by any person. Although the singular "a person" is used, it is a legislatively mandated rule of statutory construction that "[w]ords importing the singular number may extend and be applied to several persons" unless the resulting construction is "inconsistent with the manifest intent of the law-making body or repugnant to the context of the same statute." G.L. c. 4, § 6 (1992 ed.). In the context of adoption, where the legislative intent to promote the best interests of the child is evidenced throughout the governing statute, and the adoption of a child by two unmarried individuals accomplishes that goal, construing the term "person" as "persons" clearly enhances, rather than defeats, the purpose of the statute. Furthermore, it is apparent from the first sentence of G.L. c. 2, § 1, that the Legislature considered and defined those combinations of persons which would lead to adoptions in violation of public policy. Clearly absent is any prohibition of adoption by two unmarried individuals like the petitioners.

While the Legislature may not have envisioned adoption by same-sex partners, there is no indication that it attempted to define all possible categories of persons leading to adoptions in the best interests of children. Rather than limit the potential categories of persons entitled to adopt (other than those described in the first sentence of § 1), the Legislature used general language to define who may adopt and who may be adopted.

. . .

. . . Adoption will not result in any tangible change in Tammy's daily life; it will, however, serve to provide her with a significant legal relationship which may be important to her future. At the most practical level, adoption will entitle Tammy to inherit from Helen's family trusts and from Helen and her family under the law of intestate succession (G.L. c. 210, § 6), to receive support from Helen, who will be legally obligated to provide such support (G.L. c. 209C, § 9; G.L. c. 273, § 1 [1992 ed.]), to be eligible for coverage under Helen's health insurance policies, and to be eligible for social security benefits in the event of Helen's disability or death (42 U.S.C. § 42[d] [1988]).

Of equal, if not greater significance, adoption will enable Tammy to preserve her unique filial ties to Helen in the event that Helen and Susan separate, or Susan predeceases Helen. As the case law and commentary on the subject illustrate, when the functional parents of children born in circumstances similar to Tammy separate or one dies, the children often remain in legal limbo for years while their future is disputed in courts. Polikoff, *This Child Does Have Two Mothers: Redefining Parenthood to Meet the Needs of Children in Lesbian–Mother and Other Nontraditional Families*, 78 GEO. J.L. 459, 508–522 (1990); *Comment, Second Parent Adoption for Lesbian–Parented Families: Legal Recognition of the Other Mother*, 19 U.C. DAVIS L.REV. 729, 741–745 (1986). In some cases, children have been denied the affection of a functional parent who has been with them since birth, even when it is apparent that this outcome is contrary to the children's best interests. Adoption serves to establish legal rights and responsibilities so that, in the event that problems arise in the future, issues of custody and visitation may be promptly resolved by reference to the best interests of the child within the recognized framework of the law. See G.L. c. 209C, § 10. See also Adoption of B.L.V.B., 628 A.2d 1271, ___ (Vt.1993). There is no jurisdictional bar in the statute to the judge's consideration of this joint petition. The conclusion that the adoption is in the best interests of Tammy is also well warranted.

The judge also posed the question whether, pursuant to G.L. c. 210, § 6 (1992 ed.), Susan's legal relationship to Tammy must be terminated if Tammy is adopted. Section 6 provides that, on entry of an adoption decree, "all rights, duties and other legal consequences of the natural relation of child and parent shall ... except as regards marriage, or cohabitation, terminate between the child so adopted and his natural parents and kindred." Although G.L. c. 210, § 2, clearly permits a child's natural parent to be an adoptive parent Sec. 6 does not contain any express exceptions to its termination provision. The Legislature obviously did not intend that a natural parent's legal relationship to its child be terminated when the natural parent is a party to the adoption petition. ...

So ordered.

SANDRA L. LYNCH, JUSTICE (dissenting, with whom FRANCIS P. O'CONNOR, JUSTICE, joins).

At the outset I wish to make clear that my views are not motivated by any disapproval of the two petitioners here or their life-style. The judge has found that the petitioners have provided the child with a healthy, happy, stable family unit. The evidence supports the judge's findings. Nor is my disagreement with the court related to the sexual orientation of the petitioners. I am firmly of the view that a litigant's expression of human sexuality ought not determine the outcome of litigation as long as it involves consenting adults and is not harmful to others. However, the court's decision, which is inconsistent with the statutory language, cannot be justified by a desire to achieve what is in the child's best interests. Indeed, those interests can be accommodated without doing violence to the statute by accepting the alternative to joint adoption suggested by the Probate Court judge ... that is, permitting Helen to adopt Tammy while allowing Susan to retain all her parental rights and obligations. This is essentially what the court accomplishes in part 2 ... of its opinion. By this simple expedient, all of the court's concerns about protecting filial ties and avoiding legal limits are put to rest without invading the prerogatives of the Legislature and giving legal status to a relationship by judicial fiat that our elected representatives and the general public have, as yet, failed to endorse.

The court concludes that the Probate and Family Court has jurisdiction to grant a joint petition for adoption by two unmarried cohabitants because they meet the statutory requirements of G.L. c. 210, § 1, and it is in the child's best interests to be adopted by both. General Laws c. 2, § 1, enumerates who may petition for adoption. In accordance with the statute, a petitioner of full age may petition to adopt. If a person is married and has a competent spouse, the spouse is required to join in the petition to adopt.

See Mitchell v. Mitchell, 312 Mass. 154, 163, 43 N.E.2d 783 (1942); Davis v. McGraw, 206 Mass. 294, 298, 92 N.E. 332 (1910). If a husband and wife fail jointly to petition for adoption, a decree or judgment granting the adoption is void. Lee v. Wood, 279 Mass. 293, 295–296 (1932). A minor may petition for adoption of his or her natural child or may join in the petition of his or her spouse when the child is the natural child of one of the parties. G.L.c. 21, Sec. 1. The court has also interpreted the statute as permitting a biological parent of full age to petition for the adoption of his or her own child. Curran, petitioner, 314 Mass. 91, 95, 49 N.E.2d 432 (1943). There is, however, nothing in the statute indicating a legislative intent to allow two or more unmarried persons jointly to petition for adoption. . . .

The court opines that the use of the singular form "a person" in the first sentence of the statute should not be construed as prohibiting joint petitions by unmarried persons because such an interpretation would not be in the best interests of the child. I have already demonstrated that, whether the petition be singular or joint, has nothing to do with the best interests of the child. The court's reasoning in part 2 of its opinion amounts to a tacit agreement with this position. Furthermore, on examining § 1 as a whole, I find no inconsistent use of the singular form from the first sentence that "[a] person ... may ... adopt ... another person younger than himself," to the final sentence pertaining to nonresidents who wish to adopt. Throughout the section, the singular is preserved. The only time a second petitioner is contemplated is where the initial petitioner has a living, competent spouse. There is nothing in the statute to suggest that joint petitions other than by spouses are permitted.

A biological mother may petition alone for the adoption of her child. Curran, petitioner, supra. Helen also meets the statutory requirements and may petition alone for the adoption of Tammy with Susan's consent. G.L. c. 2, § 2. Despite the admirable parenting and thriving environment for this child, the statute does not permit their joint petition for adoption of Tammy.

In the Matter of the Adoption of T.K.J. and K.A.K., Children

Colorado Court of Appeals, 1996.
931 P.2d 488.

Opinion by JUDGE KAREN S. METZGER.

Petitioners, G.K. and L.J., appeal the judgment which dismissed their petitions seeking the adoption of two children, T.K.J. and K.A.K., for lack of jurisdiction. We affirm.

Petitioners live together as same-sex domestic companions. Each is the natural mother of one of the two children who are the subject of the petition. Each petitioner sought a "co-parent" adoption decree that would, in effect, grant her the rights and duties associated with a "stepparent adoption" for the other petitioner's child, while retaining her parental rights over her natural child.

Before seeking the adoptions, petitioners took steps to preserve an ongoing relationship with each other's child. Each has designated the other as the guardian or conservator for her child. Likewise, each has conferred on the other durable medical and financial powers of attorney and has executed durable powers of attorney for her child, designating the other as agent for purposes of exercising parental decisions. Additionally, petitioners prepared mutual wills and testamentary trusts listing each other as primary beneficiaries and the children as alternate beneficiaries. Thus, regardless of any additional benefits that would have accrued had the adoption petitions been granted, petitioners readily acknowledge that: "This family will remain intact even if the adoptions are not granted."

The district court determined that the children were not "available for adoption" within the meaning of Sec. 19–5–203, C.R.S. (1995 Cum.Supp.) because the petitioners were not married to each other and because each petitioner sought to retain parental rights over her natural child while consenting to the other petitioner's adoption of her child. Accordingly, it concluded that it was without jurisdiction to rule on the petitions, and entered a judgment of dismissal.

Petitioners first contend that the district court erred in determining that, because they were not married and each declined to relinquish her parent-child relationship with her natural child, the children were not available for adoption. We find no error.

Adoption is a creature of statute and is governed by the provisions set out in Sec. 19–5–201, et seq., C.R.S. (1995 Cum.Supp.). In re Petition of S.O., 795 P.2d 254 (Colo.1990). Thus, if a proposed adoption fails to conform to statutory requirements, the effort to adopt must fail, and a trial court has no power to enter a decree of adoption. Lien v. Gertz, 158 Colo. 416, 407 P.2d 328 (1965); Johnson v. Black, 137 Colo. 119, 322 P.2d 99 (1958).

Section 19–5–201 provides that a child may be adopted if he or she is under the age of 18 and is present in the state at the time the petition for adoption is filed. However, the child must be "available for adoption" as defined by Sec. 19–5–203.

As pertinent here, Sec. 19–5–203 provides:

(1) A child may be available for adoption only upon:

(a) Order of the court terminating the parent-child legal relationship in a proceeding brought under article 3 or 5 of this title;

(b) Order of the court decreeing the voluntary relinquishment of the parent-child legal relationship under section 19–5–103 or 19–5–105;

. . .

(d) (1) Written and verified consent of the parent in a stepparent adoption where the other parent is deceased or his parent-child legal relationship has been terminated under paragraph (a) or (b) of this subsection (1);

(II) Written and verified consent of the parent in a stepparent adoption where the other parent has abandoned the child for a period of one year or more or where he has failed without cause to provide reasonable support for such child for a period of one year or more.

. . .

(f) Written and verified consent of the parent or parents as defined in section 19–1–103(21) in a stepparent adoption where the child is conceived and born out of wedlock.

Also relevant to this inquiry Sec. 19–5–211, C.R.S. (1995 Cum.Supp.) which provides in pertinent part that, after a final decree of adoption is entered by the district court:

(2) The natural parents shall be divested of all legal rights and obligations with respect to the child, and the adopted child shall be free from all legal obligations of obedience and maintenance with respect to the natural parents.

(3) Nothing in this part 2 shall be construed to divest any natural parent or child of any legal right or obligation where the adopting parent is a stepparent and is married to said natural parent.

In essence, petitioners argue that, because these statutes are silent on whether a person can adopt the child of a parent to whom the person is not married, without terminating the parent's rights and duties to the child they are ambiguous. Petitioners further contend the resolution of such ambiguity must be in favor of adoption based on the best interests of the children. We disagree.

It has been held that adoption statutes are to be given a liberal construction to carry out their beneficial purpose of promoting the welfare of the child. Stjernholm v. Mazaheri, 180 Colo. 352, 506 P.2d 155 (1973). However, liberal construction does not permit a court to rewrite the statute; instead, this principle may be used only to uphold the beneficial intent of the General Assembly when the wording of the statute creates a doubt. . . .

Thus, we must first look to the statutory language itself and give the words and phrases their commonly accepted and understood meaning. And, if we can give effect to the ordinary meaning of the words adopted by the General Assembly, we must apply the statute as written. Resolution Trust Corp. v. Heiserman, 898 P.2d 1049 (Colo.1995).

Both Sec. 19–5–203 and 19–5–211 are phrased in mandatory language. Section 19–5–203(1) states: "A child may be available for adoption only upon . . ." the fulfillment of certain enumerated conditions. In this context, the word "only" is synonymous with "exclusively" or "solely," see Webster's Third New International Dictionary 1577 (1986), and its use serves to delimit the types of conditions that could make a child available for adoption. Similarly, Sec. 19–5–211 lists certain effects that "shall" result from a final decree of adoption. There is no indication from the statutory context that these requirements should be read as anything other than the mandatory effects of the entry of a decree. . . .

To construe these statutes to permit adoptions such as those attempted here would require that we ignore the mandatory wording of Sec. 19–5–203 and 10–5–211. This we cannot do.

We view both sections as excluding from the reach of the adoption statutes all forms of adoption not otherwise expressly permitted. As reflected in Sec. 19–5–211(2), C.R.S. (1995 Cum.Supp.), the general rule is that a decree of adoption terminates the parental rights and duties of a child's natural parents and bestows those rights and duties on the adoptive parent or parents. Section 19–5–211(3), C.R.S. (1995 Cum.Supp.) provides a singular exception to that rule which applies only in cases of "stepparent" adoption, i.e., when the adopting parent is married to the natural parent. Thus, these express statements of limitation must be read to exclude from the statute's reach all other possible exceptions not enumerated.

Petitioners next argue that Sec. 19–5–203, as it relates to stepparent adoptions, serves only to insure proper notice to a noncustodial parent whose parental rights would be terminated by a stepparent adoption and that the statute cannot be read to prohibit other forms of adoption not enumerated. Reading this section together with other statutes relating to adoption, we disagree. . . .

The other situation is a "stepparent adoption." A stepparent adoption constitutes the only exception to the general rule that an adoption divests both of the adoptee's parents of all legal rights and duties relating to the adoptee. This exception applies only when a custodial parent is married to the adopting parent. See Sec. 19–5–211(3). . . .

Petitioners finally contend that the district court's dismissal of the adoption petition violated the children's constitutional rights to equal protection. Assuming that petitioners have standing to raise this issue, we disagree. . . .

Petitioners assert that intermediate scrutiny is the appropriate standard for determining whether the district court's application of Sec. 19–5–203 violated the children's right to equal protection. We disagree.

Petitioners base this assertion on the premise that classifications based on illegitimacy are functionally indistinguishable from the classification created by the district court's application of Sec. 19–5–203 insofar as both classifications distinguish between children based upon the marital status of their parents.

The classification at issue here does not warrant the application of intermediate scrutiny. Illegitimacy is based on a natural parent's marital status at the time of the child's birth and the district court's application focuses on the adoptive parents' marital status at the time of the adoption petition.

Intermediate scrutiny is appropriate in the context of illegitimacy classifications because of the injustice associated with burdening the child for the sake of punishing the illicit relations of the parents. See Clark v. Jeter, 486 U.S. 456, 108 S.Ct. 1910, 100 L.Ed.2d 465 (1988). It is rooted in a recognition that: "The status of illegitimacy has expressed through the ages society's condemnation of irresponsible liaisons beyond the bonds of marriage." . . .

Sections 19–5–203 and 19–5–211 do treat children differently for purposes of stepparent adoption based on whether the person seeking the adoption is married to a natural parent of the child. However, there is no indication that this disparate treatment is based on societal condemnation of two unmarried persons jointly engaging in the adoption of a child and we cannot infer such to be the case. . . .

Thus, we will evaluate petitioners' equal protection challenge under the rational basis standard. And, applying that standard, we reject petitioners' contention. . . .

Under the rational basis standard, we must first determine whether there is a legitimate governmental purpose underlying the absence of legislation permitting the "co-parent" adoption proposed by petitioners.

Here, we conclude that the General Assembly may reasonably have determined that the best interests of children and the interests of familial stability would be promoted by limiting adoptions to situations in which: (1) the parents are completely divested of their parental rights and duties or (2) the adopting party is married to the custodial parent. See In Interest of Angel Lace M., 184 Wis.2d 492, 516 N.W.2d 678 (1994). The determination whether this legislative decision is or is not in keeping with the changing social mores of the public at large is the role of the democratic process and not of the courts.

Our second inquiry under the rational basis test is whether the disparate treatment is rationally related to the governmental objectives of promoting the best interests of children and familial stability. Under the rational basis standard, the General Assembly is not required to choose between addressing all aspects of a situation or none of them, so long as the choice made by that legislative body is rational. See Duran v. Industrial Claim Appeals Office, supra.

Here, the means chosen by the General Assembly are sufficiently related to the underlying governmental objectives to withstand rational basis scrutiny. See In Interest of Angel Lace M., supra.

The judgment is affirmed.

. . .

III. CUSTODY DISPUTES

With more than 50% of marriages performed each year likely to end in divorce, many children of married couples become the subject of custody decisions. Although most divorcing spouses privately agree, sometimes after initial disputes, about how to resolve the custody question, it is often, understandably, the most difficult and emotional part of divorce. The background rule assumed by a state will influence disputed cases, negotiation between divorcing parties, and even the allocation of parental responsibilities during ongoing marriages. What should that background rule be?

Until the late 19th century, a married father held rights to custody and control over children of the marriage. By the turn of the 20th century, emerging psychological theories, joined with a growing sentimentalization of the maternal role, helped to launch a maternal preference or presumption for custody to the mother for young children, known as children of "tender years." This regime lasted until around 1970, when judges and legislators pressed for a more gender-neutral standard, typically summarized by the phrase "the best interests of the child." This general standard itself encouraged case-by-case consideration of many factors, including the parents' emotional relationships with the child, their religious practices, their life styles, and their financial resources. The best interests standard is very difficult to predict and lends itself to the particular prejudices and preferences of the judge in evaluating two presumably competent parents. Many feminists argue that the best interests standard allowed predominantly male judges to disadvantage the mother in custody fights, especially where the father had remarried.

Another standard that emerged by 1980 is a presumption for joint custody, ensuring decisional power for both parents over important decisions affecting the child's schooling, medical treatment, and religious upbringing. Joint custody in practice could mean joint physical custody, with the child moving between the parental homes, or more commonly, joint legal custody, with the child primarily living in one home and visiting the other. West Virginia developed the "primary caretaker" standard for custody to acknowledge the unequal distribution of parenting tasks during most marriages without re-installing an explicitly gender-based standard in the law. *See* Garska v. McCoy, 278 S.E.2d 357 (W.Va.1981). In that decision, Justice Neely called for a focus on detailed facts of day-to-day caring and nurturing duties including:

"(1) preparing and planning of meals; (2) bathing, grooming and dressing; (3) purchasing, cleaning, and care of clothes; (4) medical care, including nursing and trips to physicians; (5) arranging for social interaction among peers after school, i.e., transporting to friends' houses or, for example, to girl or boy scout meetings; (6) arranging alternative care, i.e., babysitting, day-care, etc.; (7) putting child to bed at night, attending to child in the middle of the night, waking child in the morning; (8) disciplining, i.e., teaching general manners and toilet training; (9) educating, i.e., religious, cultural, social, etc.; and, (10) teaching elementary skills, i.e., reading, writing and arithmetic." *Id.*, at 363.

NOTES AND QUESTIONS

1. **Primary Caretaker Standard.** Is the primary caretaker standard likely to help women seeking primary custody following divorce? Is it likely

instead to encourage men to become more involved in the day-to-day care of their children during the marriage?

2. **Application By Trial Courts.** Mary Becker reports that during the first 10 years after it was announced, the primary parent standard produced 25 cases on appeal, and 68% of these involved "fathers who received custody at the trial court level even though the mother seems to have been the primary caretaker" and a fit parent. Mary Becker, *Maternal Feelings: Myth, Taboo, and Child Custody*, 1 S.Cal. Rev. Law and Women's Studies 133, 193–94 (1992). A fuller excerpt appears below.

3. **Children's Preferences.** When, if ever, should the child's preference be given weight in a disputed custody case? Although consulting with and deferring to the child might seem to accord the child respect, it might also lead parents to try to manipulate the child, or produce a sense of guilt in the child who in effect rejects one parent.

4. **Gender Neutrality.** Should the movement against gender discrimination seek gender-neutral rules for child custody determinations or rules that give mothers an advantage?

5. **Changes?** What changes would you recommend in the language of a typical state statute giving custody? Here is the Massachusetts statute.

Ch. 208, Section 31 (1997)

Massachusetts General Laws.

Section 31. Custody of Children.

For the purposes of this section, the following words shall have the following meaning unless the context requires otherwise. . . .

"Shared legal custody," continued mutual responsibility and involvement by both parents in major decisions regarding the child's welfare including matters of education, medical care and emotional, moral and religious development. . . .

In making an order or judgment relative to the custody of children, the rights of the parents shall, in the absence of misconduct, be held to be equal, and the happiness and welfare of the children shall determine their custody. When considering the happiness and welfare of the child, the court shall consider whether or not the child's present or past living conditions adversely affect his physical, mental, moral or emotional health.

Upon the filing of an action in accordance with the provisions of this section, section twenty-eight of the chapter, or section thirty-two of chapter two hundred and nine and until a judgment on the merits is rendered, absent emergency conditions, abuse or neglect, the parents shall have temporary shared legal custody of any minor child of the marriage; provided, however, that the judge may enter an order for temporary sole legal custody of one parent if written findings are made that such shared custody would not be in the best interest of the child. Nothing herein shall be construed to create any presumption of temporary shared physical custody.

In determining whether temporary shared legal custody would not be in the best interest of the child, the court shall consider all relevant facts including, but not limited to, whether any member of the family has been the perpetrator of domestic violence, abuses alcohol or other drugs or has deserted the child and whether the parties have a history of being able and willing to cooperate in matters concerning the child.

If, despite the prior or current issuance of a restraining order against one parent pursuant to chapter two hundred and nine A, the court orders shared legal or physical custody either as a temporary order or at a trial on the merits, the court shall provide written findings to support such shared custody order.

There shall be no presumption either in favor of or against shared legal or physical custody at the time of the trial on the merits.

At the trial on the merits, if the issue of custody is contested and either party seeks shared legal or physical custody, the parties, jointly or individually, shall submit to the court at the trial a shared custody implementation plan setting forth the details of shared custody including, but not limited to, the child's education; the child's health care; procedures for resolving disputes between the parties with respect to child-raising decisions and duties; and the periods of time during which each party will have the child reside or visit with him, including holidays and vacations, or the procedure by which such periods of time shall be determined.

At the trial on the merits, the court shall consider the shared custody implementation plans submitted by the parties. The court may issue a shared legal and physical custody order and, in conjunction therewith, may accept the shared custody implementation plan submitted by either party or by the parties jointly or may issue a plan modifying the plan or plans submitted by the parties. The court may also reject the plan and issue a sole legal and physical custody award to either parent. A shared custody implementation plan issued or accepted by the court shall become part of the judgment in the action, together with any other appropriate custody orders regarding the responsibility of the parties for the support of the child. . . .

Where the parents have reached an agreement providing for the custody of the children, the court may enter an order in accordance with such agreement, unless specific findings are made by the court indicating that such an order would not be in the best interests of the children. . . .

Mary Becker, Maternal Feelings: Myth, Taboo, and Child Custody

1 S.Cal. Rev. Law and Women's Studies 133 (1992).

. . . In this article, I advocate a maternal *deference* standard: judges should defer to the fit mother's judgment of the custodial arrangement that would be best. I offer two types of arguments for this standard. The first argument is based on an examination of the reported cases in West Virginia under the primary caretaker standard over the last ten years. These cases suggest that commentators have been naive in their belief that the primary caretaker standard could sufficiently protect primary-caretaking mothers and their children. Even in West Virginia, primary-caretaking mothers risk losing custody if they litigate in many situations, such as when the father has done more than the average father and both parents have worked for wages. Perhaps some of these problems could be addressed by reforms to the primary caretaker standard as it has evolved in West Virginia. But the second problem with the primary caretaker standard cannot be so easily remedied.

The second problem is that the standard completely ignores both the caretaking done only by women (pregnancy, childbirth, and nursing) and the emotional work of raising a child, except to the extent that physical caretaking is a proxy for emotional caretaking and its accompanying bond. But even in families in which both parents work, and in which the father shares physical care more or less equally, the mother is emotionally closer to the child in the vast majority of families. In part, the intensity of the maternal-child relationship is the result of deep emotional ties formed during pregnancy, infancy, and when the child is very young. It is during these periods that the relationship between the child and the caretaking mother is most emotionally intense. And it is precisely during these periods that fathers are least likely to caretake equally on even a physical level.

Of course, judges cannot be expected to make accurate case-by-case determinations of which parent is emotionally closer to a particular child. Only a systemic preference for awarding custody to mothers can give the appropriate weight to the greater emotional intensity of the relationships between women and children. . . .

. . . I leave the development of constitutional arguments for a different article.

. . . [M]othering and fathering continue to be different activities; mothers tend to be more intensely involved in their children's lives and tend to have greater empathy for their children. This difference has life long economic consequences since caretaking within families is not in itself remunerative and impedes one's ability to earn wages elsewhere.

. . . As a result of ignoring women's emotional child care, ordinary women suffer the intense pain of losing children with whom they have emotionally intense relationships, and children lose the opportunity to live with the parent with whom they are emotionally closest. . . .

. . . [W]hile the primary caretaker standard is much better for women than the discretionary best interest standard, it is not good enough. . . .[T]he primary caretaker standard does not adequately account for the emotional labor of child care. . . .

In most heterosexual couples, the mother's relationship with the child has a primacy of meaning with respect to the child without parallel for the father. For fathers, the primary and emotionally more intense relationship is likely to be with the mother. These differences seem to originate at a deep level of the psyche. Women and men were mothered by women. For women, the mother-child dyad is most obviously recreated in a relationship with a child. A romantic union is a less distinct reflection of that original mother-child dyad. As a result, women's ego boundaries are likely to be most permeable with respect to their children.

The parent-child relationship does not have the same meaning for heterosexual men. They cannot create the mother-child dyad by being the mother in a relationship with a child because they must not be the mother; the essence of their masculinity is not to be the mother. For heterosexual men, the mother-child dyad is most clearly approximated in their relationship with their wives, who represent the caring and all-loving mother. Indeed, the original union is improved upon: the wife is now economically dependent on the man in most heterosexual couples and this time he is the one in control. Thus, for the heterosexual male adult, the primary mother-child union is represented in his relationship with his wife, which is an inverted version of the original flawed union, rather than in his relationship with his child.

Further evidence of the difference between the relationship of mothers and fathers with their children is the triangle created by the infant and the heterosexual couple. Husbands are often jealous of the child's relationship with the mother because it interferes with the husband's relationship with the wife both during pregnancy and after birth. The jealousy is especially strong during the child's infancy. During infancy of the first child, many fathers tend to feel disappointed and abandoned as the mother focuses much of her attention on the child, decreasing her mothering of the father and becoming less available sexually. Women are not as often jealous in a symmetrical way. In most families the very notion that the mother might be jealous of the father's relationship with the child because it interfered with her relationship with the father would make no emotional sense. The mother is more likely to be jealous of the father's relationship with the child because she feels it interferes with her own relationship with the child. But the mother is more likely to resent the emotional and physical drain of the constant demands of the infant, sapping her energy and challenging her existence as an independent, autonomous being with physical and emotional integrity. Thus, the jealous mother is most likely to be jealous of the father's freedom and independence. . . .

In this section, I make two related points. First, child care is still overwhelmingly provided by women. In most families, child care is still regarded as the mother's responsibility. When the father cares for children, he "helps" her. Second, the assignment of caretaking responsibility to women reflects women's greater emotional commitment to child care. It is generally not true that couples simply divide labor in an "efficient" manner, and women therefore specialize in domestic work while men specialize in the wage-labor market. Even women who earn more than husbands in the wage-labor market are likely to be primary caretakers of their children. . . .

I propose that we consider a maternal deference standard. When the parents cannot agree on a custody outcome, the judge should defer to the mother's decision on custody provided that she is fit, using the "fitness" standard applicable when the state is arguing for temporary or permanent separation of parents and children in intact families. This standard would operate much like the traditional maternal preference for children of tender years. It would not, however, be limited to young children. And it would be formally expressed in terms of a *deference*, rather than a *preference*. In this section, I discuss and assess the arguments for and against this standard. . . .

. . . A maternal deference standard (a) recognizes women's reproductive labor, competence, and authority, (b) has the potential to yield the proper result in custody disputes more often than current standards to the benefit of caretaking women and their children, (c) could improve the economic situation of divorced women and children in many families in which actual custody remains unaffected, and (d) would give fathers an incentive to change their behavior within marriage. . . .

Arguments Against Maternal Deference

Two powerful arguments can be made against judicial deference to mothers at divorce. First, such a rule is unfair to the unusual father who has been an equal caretaker on emotional, as well as physical levels. Second, such a rule will not guarantee better outcomes, and may have a number of negative strategic consequences, thus impeding needed social change.

a. *Unfairness to the unusual father* A rule deferring to mothers as long as they are fit will be unfair to fathers who have done half, or more than half, of the emotional and physical caretaking and whose wives nevertheless want custody. Such fathers will be unfairly treated under a maternal deference standard. If, however, only about 8% of fathers, as estimated above, do nearly half or more of child care, the error rate under a maternal deference standard would not be high. Even in this group of families, fathers are likely to be less involved than wives or, at best, equally involved.

b. *Maternal deference will have a number of negative strategic effects and cannot guarantee better results*. The articulation of this standard will not necessarily mean that women will win more often. Judges may reword their opinions awarding custody to fathers to comply with the new standard by finding mothers unfit.

Moreover, the new standard may have a number of negative effects. The standard will reinforce traditional stereotypes of proper maternal behavior. It may universalize a sentimental version of the experience of some women as the essence of being a woman. And it may encourage employers, legislators, and judges to be tolerant of sex-specific rules no matter how harmful to women, damaging women's opportunities in the wage-labor market. A maternal deference standard could give new life to the notion that biology is destiny, and to the importance of biological links.

Thus, for example, tolerance for a maternal deference standard may also lead to tolerance for policies excluding fertile women from jobs considered hazardous to fetal health. More fundamentally, focusing on women's pleasures and pains in a world of inequality may be inconsistent with many of the changes needed for equality between the sexes and inconsistent with individual women's long term needs.

Balancing the Pros and Cons

The costs of implementing a maternal deference standard are real and cannot be ignored. But there is no definitive way to know from an arm chair whether a maternal deference standard would hurt more than it would help. In the end, the reader must make her own assessment of the costs and benefits. The maternal deference standard will be unfair to the unusual father who carries the child in his mind, as well as caring for the child physically, and whose relationship with the child is more intense than the mother's. The standard will reinforce traditional stereotypes, and may increase tolerance of sex specific rules. Additionally, the focus on women's hedonic lives may be self defeating.

There is, however, no ideal custody rule. It is true that favoring mothers will be unfair to unusual fathers. But any rule will be unfair to some people in the absence of perfect decisionmakers. In light of the capacities of judges, which do not extend to being able to determine with any degree of reliability who has been the emotional and physical caregiver, any standard fair to mothering fathers will be unfair to more mothers, mothers who have done more than half the physical and emotional child care.

When I began this project, I thought that perhaps one could have a standard that started with a presumption for mothers, but allowed the father to rebut the presumption by showing that he was substantially more involved in the children's lives, with the requirement that this be proven by objective evidence in the form of his having worked outside the home for fewer hours a week than the mother. But, in fact, fathers who work less than full time, in sharp contrast to mothers who work less than full time, are likely to spend less time with their children. In light of the judicial bias against mothers there may be no way to protect women, who are most often the caretakers, that is also fair to the unusual father who caretakes more than his wife.

Given women's economic and emotional vulnerability to paternal threats to contest custody, the legal standard should protect the large number of women and children vulnerable under current standards at the cost of unfairness to the atypical father. Some of the costs are not, however, as great as they might seem at first glance. I make three points here. First, the approach I suggest need not be biologically based. Second, the focus on women's hedonic lives is appropriate in thinking about a custody standard at divorce. And third, it is far from clear whether a gender neutral standard or sex specific standard would be better in terms of fostering social change. Experimentation is appropriate, and should include my proposal.

a. *Biology and maternal deference* A maternal deference standard need not be based entirely on notions of biology as all important. The standard could protect women whose mothering did not begin with a genetic link. Indeed, my own understanding of the difference between men's and women's relationships with children grew out of my relationship with a child with whom I live, but did not bear. I live with my divorced sister and her three children. With respect to the older two, I am a step parent, and thus fully appreciate how difficult such relationships are. To the youngest, I am a parent. I have been intensely involved with her all her life, and she thinks of me as a parent. Although I am somewhat less involved emotionally with the child than her mother—for example, I found separation when she was an infant much easier than did her mother—I am much closer to her than her father.

The arguments I make in this article can be used to strengthen the rights of women generally with respect to children they have mothered regardless of genetic link. For example, these arguments could be used on behalf of a surrogate who has carried a child during pregnancy and should be recognized as having a stronger connection to a child than the father or mother who provided only the genetic material. Similarly, in the event Mr. and Dr. Stern divorce in the future, the arguments could be used to support an award of custody to the woman who is raising Baby M., Dr. Stern, rather than to the father, Mr. Stern, who provided half of the genetic material but has not mothered his child. These arguments could be used to support the right of the nonbiologically related lesbian mother to visitation when lesbian parents separate. These arguments can, therefore, weaken as well as reinforce notions that biology, or the genetic link, is the essence of the parent-child relationship. This danger is therefore limited, and not as serious as it might seem at first glance.

b. *Hedonic focus appropriate for a custody standard* As noted earlier, a focus on women's hedonic lives will often be dangerous for women in a world of inequality. Challenge and achievement are often uncomfortable, particularly when one has been educated in romance, rather than socialized to consider development of one's abilities as the key to fulfillment. A hedonic focus is nonetheless appropriate for custody standards at divorce because by this point individual women have made intense emotional commitments that cannot be ignored without inflicting deep pain. Children are of such central importance to women's emotional lives that preserving these relationships at divorce should be primary. Social engineering to change women's commitment to children should occur much earlier before women have made the commitments ignored by gender neutral custody rules. This point is developed further in the paragraphs that follow.

c. *Fostering social change* A maternal deference standard *will* tend to reinforce traditional stereotypes, may encourage important decisionmakers to think of women as the caretakers of children rather than as serious wage workers, and may lead to sex-specific legislation even more harmful to women. Social change at divorce *might* be good for women, or at least for younger generations of women in the aggregate. But the benefits to younger generations of women are at best tenuous. It is true that if older women caretake less after divorce they will be regarded as more serious wage workers. As a result, there may be some positive changes in attitudes toward younger women wage workers. But if younger women continue to caretake *during* marriage, it is unlikely that these positive effects will be significant. Employers of women who are doing most of the caretaking are likely to appreciate that fact regardless of the legal standard for custody at divorce.

Perhaps women will *stop* caretaking during marriage due to the great risks of investing so much in children whom one might lose. As feminists, is this the kind of change we want to foster? The strategy would be at odds with the desires and hedonic lives of most women alive today. Most women are more committed to their children than men are. Three out of four mothers do not want equality with respect to participation of mothers and fathers in caring for children. It may be, of course, that these mothers do not want their husbands equally involved in parenting because they see these fathers as inadequate: too impatient, too indifferent, too self-centered. The may be right. To the extent that women caretake for this reason, they *are* caretaking because of their greater emotional connection to their children. But for that stronger connection, they would not see the problem, nor their own caretaking as the solution.

Would a maternal deference standard lead to tolerance of harmful sex-specific legislation, and thus increase inequality? As many feminists have now noted in a variety of other contexts, ignoring the differences between women and men with sex neutral rules can also foster inequality. Failing to recognize and respect the emotional commitments of women, and accord them appropriate weight, while protecting the investments men make, is itself a form of inequality. Ignoring or denying women's reproductive labor, giving men an option to appropriate it at divorce, is itself a form of subordination.

Without experimentation, we cannot know whether a maternal deference standard would lead to increased tolerance of harmful sex-specific legislation. The question is a pragmatic one and cannot be answered in the abstract. Only some experience with such a standard, and observation of the ability of judges to distinguish desirable from undesirable sex-specific rules, can yield an answer. In the context of disability leave at childbirth, tolerance of sex-specific policies have not led to judicial decisions upholding harmful legislation, such as employer policies excluding fertile women from jobs perceived to be hazardous to fetal health.

At the same time, a standard explicitly recognizing and valuing women's reproductive labor could be desirable in two ways. It could change outcomes at divorce with respect to custody and economic security and, more broadly, it could contribute to changing social attitudes toward women's reproductive work. The standard I suggest might be part of a new appreciation of women's reproductive labor throughout society, and might, therefore, have some effect on judges, and more broadly, increase the visibility and value of women's caretaking. We should experiment by deferring to mothers. If my suggestion does not work, then we must find other ways to protect women's reproductive labor at divorce. . . .

NOTES AND QUESTIONS

1. **Evaluating Maternal Deference.** How do you evaluate the pluses and minuses of Becker's proposal for a maternal deference standard in the child custody context? What political problems would it raise if debated in the state legislature? What constitutional problems?

2. **Rating Custody Standards.** Are more determinate standards (such as maternal deference or primary caretaker) better for women than indeterminate standards (such as best interests of the child)? Better for children?

IV. CUSTODY AND MOTHERS' SEXUALITY

There is a familiar double standard in American society; a man who engages in sexual activity outside of marriage is doing what a man needs to do, while a woman who does so is immoral. Does this double standard appear in judicial assessments of child custody disputes? How do and how should courts deal with the claim by a parent competing for custody that the other parent's sexual relationships injure the child? Should it matter if these are heterosexual, same-sex or interracial relationships, monogamous or multiple, casual or serious?

Jarrett v. Jarrett

Supreme Court of Illinois, 1979.
78 Ill.2d 337, 36 Ill.Dec. 1, 400 N.E.2d 421, cert. denied, 449 U.S. 927, 101 S.Ct. 329, 66 L.Ed.2d 155 (1980).

ROBERT C. UNDERWOOD, JUSTICE:

On December 6, 1976, Jacqueline Jarrett received a divorce from Walter Jarrett in the circuit court of Cook County on grounds of extreme and repeated mental cruelty. The divorce decree, by agreement, also awarded Jacqueline custody of the three Jarrett children subject to the father's right of visitation at reasonable times. Seven months later, alleging changed conditions, Walter petitioned the circuit court to modify the divorce decree and award him custody of the children. The circuit court granted his petition subject to the mother's right of visitation at reasonable times, but a majority of the appellate court reversed and we granted leave to appeal.

During their marriage, Walter and Jacqueline had three daughters, who, at the time of the divorce, were 12, 10 and 7 years old. In addition to custody of the children, the divorce decree also awarded Jacqueline the use of the family home, and child support; Walter received visitation rights at all reasonable times and usually had the children from Saturday evening to Sunday evening. In April 1977, five months after the divorce, Jacqueline informed Walter that she planned to have her boyfriend, Wayne Hammon, move into the family home with her. Walter protested, but Hammon moved in on May 1, 1977. Jacqueline and Hammon thereafter cohabited in the Jarrett home but did not marry.

The children, who were not "overly enthused" when they first learned that Hammon would move into the family home with them, asked Jacqueline if she intended to marry Hammon, but Jacqueline responded that she did not know. At the modification hearing Jacqueline testified that she did not want to remarry because it was too soon after her divorce; because she did not believe that a marriage license makes a relationship; and because the divorce decree required her to sell the family home within six months after remarriage. She did not want to sell the home because the children did not want to move and she could not afford to do so. Jacqueline explained to the children that some people thought it was wrong for an unmarried man and woman to live together but she thought that what mattered was that they loved each other. Jacqueline testified that she told some neighbors that Hammon would move in with her but that she had not received any adverse comments. Jacqueline further testified that the children seemed to develop an affectionate relationship with Hammon, who played with them, helped them with their homework, and verbally disciplined them. Both Jacqueline and Hammon testified at the hearing that they did not at that time have any plans to marry. In oral argument before this court Jacqueline's counsel conceded that she and Hammon were still living together unmarried.

Walter Jarrett testified that he thought Jacqueline's living arrangements created a moral environment that was not a proper one in which to raise three young girls. He also testified that the children were always clean, healthy, well dressed and well nourished when he picked them up, and that when he talked with his oldest daughter, Kathleen, she did not object to Jacqueline's living arrangement. . . .

Both parties to this litigation have relied on sections 602 and 610 of the new Illinois Marriage and Dissolution of Marriage Act which provide:

"Sec. 602. Best interest of child.

(a) The court shall determine custody in accordance with the best interest of the child. The court shall consider all relevant factors including:

(1) the wishes of the child's parent or parents as to his custody;

(2) the wishes of the child as to his custodian;

(3) the interaction and interrelationship of the child with his parent or parents, his siblings and any other person who may significantly affect the child's best interest;

(4) the child's adjustment to his home, school and community; and

(5) the mental and physical health of all individuals involved.

(b) The court shall not consider conduct of a present or proposed custodian that does not affect his relationship to the child."

"Sec. 610. Modification.

(a) No motion to modify a custody judgment may be made earlier than 2 years after its date, unless the court permits it to be made on the basis of affidavits that there is reason to believe the child's present environment may endanger seriously his physical, mental, moral or emotional health.

(b) The court shall not modify a prior custody judgment unless it finds, upon the basis of facts that have arisen since the prior judgment or that were unknown to the court at the time of entry of the prior judgment, that a change has occurred in the circumstances of the child or his custodian and that the modification is necessary to serve the best interest of the child. In applying these standards the court shall retain the custodian appointed pursuant to the prior judgment unless: . . .

(3) the child's present environment endangers seriously his physical, mental, moral or emotional health and the harm likely to be caused by a change of environment is outweighed by its advantages to him. . . .

(c) . . ."

The relevant standards of conduct are expressed in the statutes of this State: Section 11–8 of the Criminal Code of 1961 provides that "[a]ny person who cohabits or has intercourse with another not his spouse commits fornication if the behavior is open and notorious." In *Hewitt v. Hewitt* (1979), 77 Ill.2d 49, 61–62, 31 Ill.Dec. 827, 394 N.E.2d 1204, we emphasized the refusal of the General Assembly in enacting the new Illinois Marriage and Dissolution of Marriage Act to sanction any nonmarital relationships and its declaration of the purpose to "strengthen and preserve the integrity of marriage and safeguard family relationships."

Jacqueline argues, however, that her conduct does not affront public morality because such conduct is now widely accepted, and cites 1978 Census Bureau statistics that show 1.1 million households composed of an unmarried man and woman, close to a quarter of which also include at least one child. This is essentially the same argument we rejected last term in *Hewitt v. Hewitt*, and it is equally unpersuasive here. The number of people living in such households forms only a small percentage of the adult population, but more to the point, the statutory interpretation urged upon us by Jacqueline simply nullifies the fornication statute. The logical conclusion of her argument is that the statutory prohibitions are void as to those who believe the proscribed acts are not immoral, or, for one reason or another, need not be heeded. So stated, of course, the argument defeats itself. The rules which our society enacts for the governance of its members are not limited to those who agree with those rules—they are equally binding on the dissenters. The fornication statute and the Illinois Marriage and Dissolution of Marriage Act evidence the relevant moral standards of this State, as declared by our legislature. The open and notorious limitation on the former's prohibitions reflects both a disinclination to criminalize purely private relationships and a recognition that open fornication represents a graver threat to public morality than private violations. Conduct of that nature, when it is open, not only violates the statutorily expressed moral standards of the State, but also encourages others to violate those standards, and debases public morality. While we agree that the statute does not penalize conduct which is essentially private and discreet, Jacqueline's conduct has been neither, for she has discussed this relationship and her rationalization of it with at least her children, her former husband and her neighbors. It is, in our judgment, clear that her conduct offends prevailing public policy.

Jacqueline's disregard for existing standards of conduct instructs her children, by example, that they, too, may ignore them and could well encourage the children to engage in similar activity in the future. That factor, of course, supports the trial court's conclusion that their daily presence in that environment was injurious to the moral well-being and development of the children.

It is true that, as Jacqueline argues, the courts have not denied custody to every parent who has violated the community's moral standards, nor do we now intimate a different rule. Rather than mechanically denying custody in every such instance, the courts of this State appraise the moral example currently provided and the example which may be expected by the parent in the future. ...[P]ast moral indiscretions of a parent are not sufficient grounds for denying custody if the parent's present conduct establishes the improbability of such lapses in the future. This rule focuses the trial court's attention on the moral values which the parent is actually demonstrating to the children. ...[T]he appellate courts of this State have repeatedly emphasized this principle, particularly when the children were unaware of their parent's moral indiscretion.

... At the time of this hearing, however, and even when this case was argued orally to the court, Jacqueline continued to cohabit with Wayne Hammon and had done nothing to indicate that this relationship would not continue in the future. Thus the moral values which Jacqueline currently represents to her children, and those which she may be expected to portray in the future, contravene statutorily declared standards of conduct and endanger the children's moral development. ...

The mother argues ... that section 610 of the Illinois Marriage and Dissolution of Marriage Act requires the trial court to refrain from modifying a prior custody decree unless it finds that the children have suffered actual tangible harm. The statute, however, directs the trial court to determine whether "the child's present environment *endangers* seriously his physical, mental, moral or emotional health." (Emphasis added.) In some cases, particularly those involving physical harm, it may be appropriate for the trial court to determine whether the child is endangered by considering evidence of actual harm. In cases such as this one, however, such a narrow interpretation of the statute would defeat its purpose. At the time of the hearing the three Jarrett children, who were then 12, 10 and 7 years old, were obviously incapable of emulating their mother's moral indiscretions. To wait until later years to determine whether Jacqueline had inculcated her moral values in the children would be to await a demonstration that the very harm which the statute seeks to avoid had occurred. Measures to safeguard the moral well-being of children, whose lives have already been disrupted by the divorce of their parents, cannot have been intended to be delayed until there are tangible manifestations of damage to their character.

While our comments have focused upon the moral hazards, we are not convinced that open cohabitation does not also affect the mental and emotional health of the children. Jacqueline's testimony at the hearing indicated that when her children originally learned that Wayne Hammon would move in with them, they initially expected that she would marry him. It is difficult to predict what psychological effects or problems may later develop from their efforts to overcome the disparity between their concepts of propriety and their mother's conduct. Nor will their attempts to adjust to this new environment occur in a vacuum. Jacqueline's domestic arrangements are known to her neighbors and their children; testimony at the hearing indicated that Wayne Hammon played with the Jarrett children and their friends at the Jarrett home and also engaged in other activities with them. If the Jarrett children remained in that situation, they might well be compelled to try to explain Hammon's presence to their friends and, perhaps, to endure their taunts and jibes. In a case such as this the trial judge must also weigh these imponderables, and he is not limited to examining the children for current physical manifestations of emotional or mental difficulties. . . .

Since the evidence indicated that Jacqueline had not terminated the troublesome relationship and would probably continue it in the future, the trial court transferred custody to Walter Jarrett, an equally caring and affectionate parent whose conduct did not contravene the standards established by the General Assembly and earlier judicial decisions. Its action in doing so was not contrary to the manifest weight of the evidence. . . .

JOSEPH H. GOLDENHERSH, CHIEF JUSTICE, with whom THOMAS J. MORAN, JUSTICE, joins, dissenting: . . .

This record shows clearly that the children were healthy, well adjusted, and well cared for, and it should be noted that both the circuit and appellate courts made no finding that plaintiff was an unfit mother. The majority, too, makes no such finding and based its decision on a nebulous concept of injury to the children's "moral well-being and development." I question that any competent sociologist would attribute the increase of "live in" unmarried couples to parental example. . . .

As a legal matter, simply stated, the majority has held that on the basis of her presumptive guilt of fornication, a Class B misdemeanor, plaintiff, although not declared to be an unfit mother, has forfeited the right to have the custody of her children. This finding flies in the face of the established rule that, in order to modify or amend an award of custody, the evidence must show that the parent to whom custody of the children was originally awarded is unfit to retain custody, or that a change of conditions makes a change of custody in their best interests. This record fails to show either. . . .

THOMAS J. MORAN, JUSTICE, with whom GOLDENHERSH, CHIEF JUSTICE, joins, dissenting:

. . . [T]he majority's finding of a violation of the seldom-enforced fornication statute effectively foreclosed any further consideration of the custody issue. Instead of focusing solely on the best interest of the children . . . [,] the majority has utilized child custody as a vehicle to punish Jacqueline for her "misconduct." Such selective enforcement of a statute is inappropriate and, especially in the child-custody context, unfortunate. . . .

Bottoms v. Bottoms

Supreme Court of Virginia, 1995.
249 Va. 410, 457 S.E.2d 102.

CHRISTIAN COMPTON, JUSTICE.

This is a child custody dispute between a child's mother and maternal grandmother. The sole issue is whether the Court of Appeals erred in deciding that the child's best interests would be served by awarding custody to the mother. We conclude that the Court of Appeals erred, and reverse. . . .

In March 1993, appellant Pamela Kay Bottoms filed a petition against her daughter, appellee Sharon Lynne Bottoms, . . . seeking an award of custody of the daughter's son, born in July 1991. In the petition, the grandmother alleged that the "infant is currently living in an environment which is harmful to his mental and physical well being." . . . At the conclusion of the hearing, the trial court ruled that custody of the child should be awarded to the grandmother, with restricted visitation rights granted the mother.

The mother appealed to the Court of Appeals. A three-judge panel unanimously reversed and vacated the trial court's order . . . . We awarded the grandmother this appeal from the Court of Appeals' June 1994 order.

"In all child custody cases, including those between a parent and a non-parent, 'the best interests of the child are paramount and form the lodestar for the guidance of the court in determining the dispute.' " . . . In a custody dispute between a parent and non-parent, "the law presumes that the child's best interests will be served when in the custody of its parent." . . .

Although the presumption favoring a parent over a non-parent is strong, it is rebutted when certain factors, such as parental unfitness, are established by clear and convincing evidence. The term "clear and convincing evidence" is . . . intermediate, being more than a mere preponderance, but not to the degree of proof beyond a reasonable doubt as in criminal cases; it does not mean clear and unequivocal. The burden to show unfitness is upon the one seeking to alter the parent's right to custody.

In custody cases, the welfare of the child takes precedence over the rights of the parent. But, when the contest is between parent and non-parent, this rule is conditioned upon the principle that a parent's rights "are to be respected if at all consonant with the best interests of the child."

. . .

[T]he appellate court should view the facts in the light most favorable to the party prevailing before the trial court. Accordingly, we shall summarize the facts in the light most favorable to the grandmother, resolving all conflicts in the evidence in her favor.

This child's mother, born in February 1970, "dropped out" of school in the twelfth grade. Until she was 18 years of age, she resided at home with her mother, who is a divorcee, and her mother's boyfriend.

Upon leaving home, the child's mother was supported by and lived with a cousin, a friend, and a sister respectively. In December 1989, the child's mother married Dennis Doustou, whom she had been dating for several years. She left Doustou after eight months of marriage, and resumed living with the cousin for a while. The child was born during the separation in July 1991. The parties were divorced, and the mother was awarded custody of her child. The child's father has expressed little interest in his son and pays no child support.

The maternal grandmother, born in January 1951, resides in the Richmond area. Her boyfriend ceased living with her shortly before the juvenile court hearing, and has not returned. The grandmother did not complete her high school education, and has worked as a nurse's aide and manager of a shoe store. She currently is employed as a "nanny," taking care of two children.

During the two-year period before the trial court hearing, the child had spent 70 percent of the time with the grandmother and 30 percent with his mother. The grandmother has kept the child for "weeks at a time" and during "every weekend since he's been born." On at least three occasions during that period, the mother left the child with the grandmother without informing her of the mother's whereabouts or how she could be reached "in the event something happened to the child."

Following the mother's separation from Doustou, she continued a "relationship" with another man that had begun during her marriage. She contracted a venereal disease during this relationship that prevents her from having additional children. During the child's first year, the mother "slept with two or three different guys, maybe four, in the same room" with the child "where his crib was." At the time, the mother "lived two blocks away" from the grandmother, and the mother kept the child's "suitcase packed" for visits to the grandmother's home. The mother said that she has "had trouble" with her temper, and that when the child was about "a year" old, she "popped him on his leg too hard a couple of times," and left her fingerprints there. She has had "counseling" in an effort to control her temper.

At "some point subsequent to" the child's birth, the mother lived in a dwelling with yet another man who supported her for more than a year. After the mother "left" this man, she "lived with" a lesbian "couple."

Except for brief employment as a grocery store cashier, the mother had been unemployed during most of the three-year period prior to the trial court hearing. She was receiving "welfare money" which often was spent to "do her fingernails before the baby would get any food."

During May 1992, ten months before the juvenile court hearing, 16 months before the trial court hearing, and when her son was ten months old, the mother met April Wade, a lesbian. Wade, born in April 1966, had been discharged from the U.S. Army in 1986. Wade is a "recovering alcoholic."

The mother and Wade "moved in together" in September 1992. From that time, with the exception of a two-week period, the mother and Wade have lived in "a lesbian relationship." According to the mother, the relationship involves hugging and kissing, patting "on the bottom," sleeping in the same bed, "fondling," and "oral sex." The mother testified that she loves Wade and that they "have a lifetime commitment."

At the time of the juvenile court hearing, the mother, the child, and Wade were living in a two-bedroom apartment with "Evelyn," another lesbian. "At one time," the child's bed was in a room where the mother and Wade slept, having "sex in the same bed." At one point in her testimony, however, when asked "how many times did you do it when the child was sleeping in the same bedroom," the mother responded, "None." She said that she and Wade displayed other signs of affection "in front of" the child.

Wade, employed as a gift shop manager, supports the mother. The pair live in an apartment complex .... Wade has become "a parent figure" to the child, who calls Wade "Da Da."

Two months before the petition for custody was filed, the mother revealed her lesbian relationship to the grandmother. This disclosure alienated the two.

During the period after the juvenile court hearing, when regimented visitation with the mother began, the child demonstrated certain traits. For example, when the child returned to the grandmother from being with the mother, he would "stomp" his foot, tell himself to "go to the corner," and then would stand in the corner of the room, facing the wall. He curses, saying "shit" and "damn," language never used in the grandmother's home. On one occasion, when the mother and Wade "came to pick him up," the child "held his breath, turned purple. He didn't want to go with her," according to the grandmother. During a period in mid–1993, each time the mother "would come pick him up," the child would scream and cry.

Wade has admitted she "hit" the child. Also, on one occasion, when an argument developed between the mother and Wade, on the one hand, and the grandmother, on the other, about the timing of the exchange of the child for visitation, Wade said during the quarrel, "I might end up killing somebody." According to the grandmother, the child is "always neglected." For example, when the child returns to the grandmother's home, she testified that he "can't even sit down in the bathtub. That's neglect from changing his diaper. He's so red."

At the conclusion of the hearing, the guardian ad litem made a closing statement to the trial judge. Saying that he "took this appointment very seriously," the guardian ad litem stated he had "done extensive reading in many areas," including "the effect homosexuality will have on the rearing of children." He stated that he had "talked with psychiatrists in the field," and met "at length" with the mother, the grandmother, Wade, and the child, and "interviewed all of these parties as best I could." He asked another attorney, a woman, to assist him in order to obtain "another perspective." The guardian ad litem said that he and his associate "literally" spend the entire month before the hearing on the case.

In evaluating the case, the guardian ad litem said he is "a pretty open-minded guy" without any biases, "especially involving a homosexual issue." He stated that the child's father "should be ashamed of himself" for having no interest in the child and for contributing "nothing towards financial support of the child."

He stated that Wade is "a very nice person," but "she has a lot of baggage that she brings along with her" causing him to question her "stability." He observed that Wade genuinely "loves the child," but in view of her "rather sketchy" employment history, he was "curious as to how she will support the child if custody goes with" Wade and the mother.

Commenting on the mother, the guardian ad litem said he has "no question that she loves [the child] very much," but he found her to be a "very ... immature young lady." He noted that she has "never really contemplated anything," has "jumped from relationship to relationship, from one place to another," and has "never really put roots down." Observing that "she has no employment to speak of, no skills, no education" and that her "future in the job market ... is rather bleak," nevertheless, the guardian ad litem said, she is the child's natural mother, and "the love between a natural mother and child is something that's almost sacred." He stated that he "firmly" believed that the mother's love for the child "is an honest love" and "that she comes to this court with clean hands in that regard."

Referring to the grandmother, he said he found "her to be an equally very nice person, a very sincere person." He said he regarded her "as a bit more than" a third-party stranger, and that she had had "more than a typical grandmother relationship with the child." He noted she "has taken care of this child the majority of the child's life," and "has provided for the child financially, fed the child, clothed the child," and "taken the child to the doctor."

The guardian ad litem observed, "The homosexual issue does not alarm me," stating his belief "that a homosexual should be allowed to raise a child." One matter "did concern" him about the mother. He referred to evidence that the mother separated herself from Wade after the juvenile court hearing, on the advice of counsel, to "help ... with the custody fight," but returned to live with her two weeks later on the advice of new counsel. When asked why she is presently living with Wade if she thought living apart would help her regain custody, the mother responded, "I was taking a chance." The guardian ad litem observed that the mother felt her individual "rights" were as important as her child's.

Summarizing, and noting "that custody is something that's flexible and can change if the circumstances change," the guardian ad litem suggested to the court that the child's best interests, "at this time under this actual situation," would be served by awarding custody to the grandmother.

The trial judge, announcing his decision from the bench at the conclusion of the hearing, said the dispute "presents the question ... whether the child's best interest is served by a transfer of the custody of the child from [his] mother to [his] maternal grandmother." Stating that the mother's conduct is "illegal," and constitutes a felony under the Commonwealth's criminal laws, and that "her conduct is immoral," the court recognized the "presumption in the law in favor of the custody being with the natural parent."

Mentioning the evidence of lesbianism and specified "other evidence" in the case not involving homosexual conduct, the trial court concluded from "all the facts and circumstances ... of the case," that "custody will be with the grandmother."

The Court of Appeals concluded that "the evidence fails to prove" that the mother "abused or neglected her son, that her lesbian relationship with April Wade has or will have a deleterious effect on her son, or that she is an unfit parent." "To the contrary," said the Court of Appeals, the evidence showed that the mother "is and has been a fit and nurturing parent who has adequately provided and cared for her son. No evidence tended to prove that the child will be harmed by remaining with his mother." The court held "the trial court abused its discretion by invoking the state's authority to take the child from the custody of his natural mother ... and by transferring custody to a non-parent, ... the child's maternal grandmother."

We disagree. The Court of Appeals failed to give proper deference upon appellate review to the trial court's factual findings, and misapplied the law to the facts viewed from a proper appellate perspective.

The evidence plainly is sufficient, when applying the clear and convincing standard and when viewing the facts from the correct appellate perspective, to support the trial court's findings that the parental presumption has been rebutted, that the mother is an unfit custodian at this time, and that the child's best interests would be promoted by awarding custody to the grandmother.

Among the factors to be weighed in determining unfitness are the parent's misconduct that affects the child, neglect of the child, and a demonstrated unwillingness and inability to promote the emotional and physical well-being of the child. Other important considerations include the nature of the home environment and moral climate in which the child is to be raised.

We have held, however, that a lesbian mother is not per se an unfit parent. Conduct inherent in lesbianism is punishable as a ... felony in the Commonwealth; thus, that conduct is another important consideration in determining custody.

And, while the legal rights of a parent should be respected in a custody proceeding, those technical rights may be disregarded if demanded by the interests of the child.

In the present case, the record shows a mother who, although devoted to her son, refuses to subordinate her own desires and priorities to the child's welfare. For example, the mother disappears for days without informing the child's custodian of her whereabouts. She moves her residence from place to place, relying on others for support, and uses welfare funds to "do" her fingernails before buying food for the child. She has participated in illicit relationships with numerous men, acquiring a disease from one, and "sleeping" with men in the same room where the child's crib was located. To aid in her mobility, the mother keeps the child's suitcase packed so he can be quickly deposited at the grandmother's.

The mother has difficulty controlling her temper and, out of frustration, has struck the child when it was merely one year old with such force as to leave her fingerprints on his person. While in her care, she neglects to change and cleanse the child so that, when he returns from visitation with her, he is "red" and "can't even sit down in the bathtub."

Unlike *Doe* [*v. Doe*, 222 Va. 736, 284 S.E.2d 799 (1981)], relied on by the mother, there is proof in this case that the child has been harmed, at this young age, by the conditions under which he lives when with the mother for any extended period. For example, he has already demonstrated some disturbing traits. He uses vile language. He screams, holds his breath until he turns purple, and becomes emotionally upset when he must go to visit the mother. He appears confused about efforts at discipline, standing himself in the corner facing the wall for no apparent reason.

And, we shall not overlook the mother's relationship with Wade, and the environment in which the child would be raised if custody is awarded the mother. We have previously said that living daily under conditions stemming from active lesbianism practiced in the home may impose a burden upon a child by reason of the "social condemnation" attached to such an arrangement, which will inevitably afflict the child's relationships with its "peers and with the community at large." We do not retreat from that statement; such a result is likely under these facts. Also, Wade has struck the child and, when there was a dispute over visitation, she has threatened violence when her views were not accepted. . . .

Accordingly, we hold that the trial court, based on all the facts and circumstances, correctly ruled on the custody in question. . . .

In Re Custody of Temos

Superior Court of Pennsylvania, 1982.
304 Pa.Super. 82, 450 A.2d 111.

EDMUND SPAETH, JUDGE:

On this appeal the mother of two children asks that we reverse an order awarding custody of the children to their father. The children are a 7–1/2 year old girl and a 6 year old boy. They have spent most of their lives with the mother and under her care have done well. In awarding custody of them to their father the lower court particularly relied on three factors: that the mother "maintained a close relationship with a married man"; that the mother was involved in two questionable financial transactions; and that since the parties' divorce, "the mother has become increasingly career-oriented [and] has placed heavy reliance on baby-sitters." These factors were not a reason to order a change in custody. The married man is black and the mother and father are white. The lower court regarded this difference in race as a factor that "ought" to be considered. It ought not have been. The evidence does not show either that the mother's relationship with a married man or her need to work has had any adverse effect on the children, or that the financial transactions were in fact questionable. We believe that the best interests of the children will be served by continuing the mother's custody of them. We therefore reverse.

The parties were married on November 24, 1973. It was the mother's first marriage, the father's second. Their daughter, Jessica, was born on March 23, 1975, and their son, Andrew, on August 7, 1976. The parties lived in Bath, near Allentown, Pennsylvania, although the father was required by his employment in the construction industry to be away from home for extended periods. In 1977 the mother returned to work as an operating room technician at a local hospital.

In March 1979 the mother told the father that she wanted a divorce. . . . In May 1980 the parties signed a separation and property settlement agreement, providing among other matters, that the father would have "permanent custody" of the children and the mother, "temporary custody," and that the father would buy the family home in Bath. On July 9, 1980, the parties were divorced. On July 10, 1980, the father and his wife-to-be and her two children by her prior marriage moved into the home at Bath. The father obtained custody of the children but only for one week, because the mother refused to return them after a visit with her. The father and mother each filed an action in the lower court seeking custody of the children. These actions eventually resulted in an agreement that the mother would have custody of the children for ten months of the year and the father, custody for two months in the summer. The agreement was entered in the lower court as a stipulated order of December 4, 1980.

The mother has not remarried. In December 1980 she bought a home in Allentown, and she continues to work at the local hospital, where she is now a supervisor of supply processing and distribution. The father remarried in August 1980. About then, his employer sent him to work in Utah and he has remained there. . . .

In March 1981 Andrew went to live with the father in Utah; Jessica remained with the mother in Allentown. This change was with the parties' agreement. In August 1981 the mother asked the father to return both children. Her position was that she and the father had agreed that Andrew should return if he was unhappy living with the father; that he was unhappy; and that under the stipulated order of December 4, 1980, the children were to be returned to the mother after their summer visit with the father. The father returned Jessica but refused to return Andrew. The mother filed a petition in the lower court asking that the father be held in contempt of the order of December 4, 1980. The father filed preliminary objections challenging the court's jurisdiction. On October 5, 1981, the mother flew to Utah with her mother, met Andrew on his way to school, and brought him back to Allentown. On November 23, 1981, the father filed a petition in the lower court asking that he be awarded custody of the children, and the mother filed a petition asking that her custody, as provided by the order of December 4, 1980, be confirmed. The lower court held a hearing on March 16 and 17, 1982, and on June 15, 1982, it awarded custody of the children to the father. . . .

Incident to the hearing the lower court ordered home study reports. The report regarding the mother's home was prepared by a case worker from the Lutheran Home of Topton. The report states:

> Mrs. Temos has lived in her home at the above address since December 1980. The three bedroom townhouse, for which she pays a $392.92 monthly mortgage, is located in a development near Emmaus. The homes in the neighborhood appear well-kept, as does that of Mrs. Temos. There are many young children in the neighborhood, and Jessica and Andrew . . . name a long list of playmates and friends they have in the neighborhood. There is a good-sized fenced-in yard behind the house, in which the children can play. There also is a park/playground about a block from the house. As per mother's orders, they take turns cleaning up their toys in the yard at the end of each day. The family also has a small dog and a cat, for which the children help to care.
>
> The house is very nicely decorated and was very clean on the interviewer's announced and unannounced visits. The children have their own bedrooms. Mrs. Temos said that she plans to remain at this residence. It is less than ten minutes from her place of employment.

With respect to the mother's personal qualities, the home study report states:

> Mrs. Temos impressed this interviewer as being a responsible, motivated, and caring person and mother. She exhibited some very effective and consistent parenting skills with her children. Her children seem to be her number one priority. Mrs. Temos is not involved in any outside activities except for a work-related association that requires one meeting per month. She has shown stability and progression in her job. She appears open and honest and has definitely transferred some good values to her children. She also has remained cooperative and supportive of continuing monthly visits between the children and their paternal grandparents.

The home study report also states that "Jessica and Andrew seemed to be healthy, happy, and well-adjusted children. They were very talkative and sociable and appeared at ease when communicating with their interviewer." This favorable opinion was shared by the children's teachers. ...

In its opinion the lower court makes virtually no reference to the testimony which we have just summarized. ...Instead of recognizing and giving weight to the beneficial effects on the children of the care and home that the mother has provided, the lower court concentrated its attention on certain aspects of the mother's life that it disapproved of.

After an opening chronological summary of the parties' marital and employment histories, the lower court states:

> Cathy Temos admittedly maintains a close relationship with a married man, Wilburt Banks ("Wilburt"), a technologist in a New York hospital, who resides in the Bronx, New York, and is black. They met at a work-related conference. They admittedly spend two-to-three weekends a month together, sharing the same bed, at the mother's Allentown town house and have persistently done so for the last year and a half. Their bedroom is across the hall from the children's bedroom. Although the children have done well in school, their absences are suspiciously more frequent when Wilburt visits. On several occasions, the children, their mother and Wilburt visited and slept in Wilburt's one-bedroom New York apartment. Wilburt has recently experienced financial difficulties. Cathy Temos has supported Wilburt's efforts to skirt the bankruptcy court by allowing his car to be titled in her name in Pennsylvania. Moreover, there is evidence that she also supports her babysitter's efforts to skirt the welfare authorities by paying her cash while the sitter receives a grant for her own children. While it appears that the children consider their relationship with Wilburt in a favorable light, it can be said rather assuredly and we have so concluded that the manner in which she and her male friend have pursued their relationship will hardly add to the positive development of the children. While not by itself determinative of the outcome of this case, this non-marital relationship is a factor properly considered in arriving at our decision. Although Wilburt testified that two weeks before the hearings began in this

case he filed a divorce action, and stated that when he is financially able to do so he will pursue a divorce, uncertainties exist as to whether he and Cathy Temos will eventually wed each other. He observed that it will be difficult to do so but that he is willing to relocate here and seek a position in the business world. Wilburt has two teenage daughters from his marriage; they both reside with their mother.

The court then states:

> While faced with no other choice when their marriage ended, the mother has become increasingly career-oriented. She has placed heavy reliance on baby-sitters.

The court then refers to the home studies, summarizing each very briefly as favorable (we have quoted the court's summary of the study of the mother's home; its summary of the study of the father's home is very similar). The court then refers to its interview with the children.

In concluding its opinion the court states:

> Clearly both parents love Jessica and Drew and have deep concern for their future welfare.

> We concluded, however, that it is the father who can provide the most favorable setting for the physical, intellectual, moral and spiritual well-being of these children and the constancy of love, direction and discipline. He enjoys a stable, loving marriage with a wife who is willing and able to share their home with the children.

The court adds that it is

> not unmindful that changing their residence from Pennsylvania to Utah may cause Jessica and Drew some temporary discomfort ... [but] once they are settled they will have the opportunity to grow up in a normal, stable and secure environment. ...

[W]e have concluded that here, custody of the children should be awarded to the mother. We may explain our conclusion by discussing (a) why the factors relied upon by the lower court do not support the court's award to the father; (b) certain other factors urged upon us by counsel for the father; and (c) what seems to us to be the dispositive factors. ...

It will be convenient first to discuss the lower court's view of the financial transactions, for the discussion may be brief. ...[T]here is no evidence that the [automobile] transaction represented a fraud on creditors.... As the record stands, the lower court's statement that Mr. Banks tried "to skirt the bankruptcy court" is no more than speculative.... There is no evidence either that ... the babysitter did collect public assistance while being paid as a babysitter, or that if she did, the mother knew it. Moreover, having ruled that whether the babysitter was collecting assistance was "irrelevant" "and has nothing to do with the case," the lower court should not then have made the matter relevant by citing it against the mother....

We may now turn to issues of greater importance: the lower court's consideration of the fact that Mr. Banks was black, that he was married, and that the mother had to work. . . .

In a child custody case, race is not a "consideration," or "concern," or "factor." Questions about race are in no respect "appropriate." In stating that race "ought to be" a consideration, the lower court was fundamentally mistaken.

To be sure, the court was not mistaken in its statement that "it's obvious" that "[race is] something that is involved in the case." For it *is* obvious that racial prejudice exists. And while no evidence suggests that the children have so far encountered racial prejudice, no doubt because of their mother's, and their own, relationship with a black man they may some day be taunted, excluded, or otherwise treated meanly. But that has nothing to do with deciding who should have custody of them.

A court may not assume that because children will encounter prejudice in one parent's custody, their best interests will be served by giving them to the other parent. If the children are taunted and hurt because they live with a black man, with love and help they may surmount their hurt and grow up strong and decent—the sort of children any parent would be proud of.

We know that may not happen. No feature of our society, neither religious intolerance nor economic greed, is more damaging than racial prejudice. Perhaps the children will not surmount their hurt. But a court must never *yield* to prejudice because it cannot *prevent* prejudice. . . .

In addition to considering Mr. Banks' race, the lower court was concerned with the fact that while spending weekends with the mother and children he has been married to another woman. This concern combined with, and reinforced, the court's concern that because the mother was unmarried and had to work, she had to depend upon babysitters. . . .

[W]e have repeatedly held that if one of the parties is involved in a non-marital relationship, the court must not presume that the relationship will have a bad effect on the children. Instead, the court must examine the facts of the particular relationship and on the basis of those facts determine what effect the relationship *has* had on the children. The court may find that a parent's non-marital relationship has had a bad effect on the children, or that the relationship demonstrates that the parent is so immature or emotionally unstable as to be unfit to raise the children, and such a finding will of course support an award of custody to the other parent. But the *mere fact* of a non-marital relationship—evidence of the relationship *without more*—will not support an award. . . .

Nothing in the evidence suggests, however, that the relationship has had a bad effect on the children. The father argues nevertheless that the fact of the mother's relationship with Mr. Banks counts against her having custody without reference to, or any proof of, bad effect on the children. . . .Implicit in the father's argument, and in the lower court's statements, is the suggestion that not to condemn nonmarital relationships is somehow to approve them, that while some "old stodgy" judges adhere to old fashioned virtues, others yield to, if indeed they do not accept, modern standards of sexual conduct. This line of thought misreads, and misses the point of, the cases.

We don't know what will become of the mother's relationship with Mr. Banks—whether it will "cement" or "uncement." We admit to some skepticism about its future. Although both parties testified that they intended to marry, Mr. Banks has started divorce proceedings only recently; his work is and for some eighteen years has been in New York; and he would apparently not move to Allentown unless he could find work there. It may well be that the parties will end by never marrying. But that is no reason why the mother should not have custody of the children. Is a court to say to an unmarried parent, You may not have custody of your children because you have had a sexual relationship with someone—*even though* the evidence shows that no harm has been done the children? That would serve no useful purpose. It would severely punish the parent for transgressing the court's personal standards of morality. But the punishment would be idle, and idle punishment is no one's business, certainly not a court's. No evidence, or experience, suggests that the parent's standards, or the standards of other single parents, would be changed to conform to the court's— although perhaps secretiveness or marriages of convenience would be encouraged. Neither does any evidence, or experience, suggest that the children would be helped; if their parents were driven into secretiveness or a marriage of convenience, matters might be made worse for them. In any event, a custody decree is not meant to punish a parent, or anyone else; its only purpose is to help the children. ...This purpose must never be forgotten. ...

It remains to discuss the weight the lower court gave to the fact that the mother must work. ...It is not apparent what the lower court intended by its statement that "the mother has become increasingly career-oriented." It is true that the evidence shows that the mother has been promoted at work, and thus, that she had made progress in her career. We assume, however, that the court did not mean that a working woman should *not* seek promotion. To "become increasingly career-oriented" seems to us to be a compliment, not censure—to be one way of saying that the mother has become increasingly interested in trying to do better and more responsible and challenging work. To be sure, if a parent's desire for promotion were to result in interfering with the parent's ability to care for the children, then that would be evidence against awarding custody to the parent. For example, a parent who insisted upon accepting a promotion even though the promotion would require extended absences from home might very well not be entitled to custody. Choices have to be made, and it is fair question for the court to ask whether a parent cares more about achieving a promotion or being able to devote time to the children. But here there is no evidence that as the mother has become increasingly career-oriented, the children have suffered. The evidence is to the contrary. The mother has bought a home ten minutes from work. She is able to take the children to school most mornings. Her hours are regular: she is home well before supper, and rarely has to work overtime. And she does not have to work weekends or holidays.

Because the mother must work, she does, it is true, have to use a babysitter. . . . The father's working hours are substantially the same as the mother's. By awarding the children to the father the lower court did not ensure that they would have any more time with the father than they now have with the mother. It only ensured that they would have a few hours a day with the father's wife instead of with a babysitter.

It is apparent from its opinion that the lower court regarded this change as important. According to the court, the change would enable the children to "have the opportunity to grow up in a normal, stable and secure environment." We find no evidence in support of this conclusion.

Although we do not know how many children are cared for by a parent and a stepparent, statistics do tell us that the single-parent household has become more "normal" in recent years than it had been in the past. . . . Nor is there any reason to suppose that a two-parent environment is more "stable and secure" than a one-parent environment. The fact that most children *used* to be raised by a working father and a non-working mother is not a reason. Most children used to be raised that way because divorce and working mothers were both unusual. . . . As with every other aspect of a child custody case, the court may not resort to generalizations, especially not generalizations derived from the past. It must focus on the case before it.

Here the evidence is that the father could provide the children with an environment excellent in many respects, and in material terms, better than the environment the mother can provide. The home study report describes the father's home and neighborhood as follows:

Glenn and Darlene Temos reside in a white, brick home at 8488 Escalante Drive in Sandy, Utah. The neighborhood is zoned exclusively for one-family dwellings. It is located near Willow Creek Country Club. Most of the homes in this area are brick of rather large size and were built about 15 years ago. The residents are primarily homeowners with above-average income. The culture of Utah is considered to be child-centered with a population that is leading the nation in the birth rate per capita. Education and family life is a value the majority of the community share. The homes in the Temos' neighborhood appear to have owners who take pride in their gardens, green lawns, and artistically-landscaped yards.

The exterior of the Temos' home is as well-maintained as the neighboring homes. The interior of their home is very clean and tidy. The furnishings are comfortable, of excellent quality and carefully color-coordinated to create a pleasant visual experience. The home has a large, front room with a fireplace, a dining room-kitchen with an adjoining eating area, a television-recreation room; three bedrooms and one bath are downstairs. There is a master bedroom suite created by combining two bedrooms and another bedroom with two baths upstairs. There are storage rooms for food and toys, plus a laundry room.

Further:

> The data from collateral sources was consistent with information presented by Glenn and Darlene Temos during the home visit. It appeared that Glenn and Darlene Temos have good judgment and are sincerely convinced that Andrew's and Jessica's present environment in their natural mother's home is not conclusive [sic] to healthy emotional development. . . .

> Glenn and Darlene Temos had more positive factors and fewer negative factors than any other parents evaluated by this worker in the past 17 years. It is this worker's opinion that Jessica and Andrew Temos would thrive emotionally, socially, educationally, and physically in their father's home. Glenn Temos expressed his desire to have legal custody of his children and have them maintain a relationship with their mother.

In addition, we may add, the father makes $850 per week, or over $44,000 per year.

Some of the evidence detracts from this favorable picture. This is the father's third marriage. The question therefore arises whether it will prove more stable than his first two. The home study report of the father's home is perhaps less persuasive because less disinterested, less objective, than the report of the mother's home. The caseworker who studied the father's home criticizes the mother's qualities as a parent because of her relationship with Mr. Banks. The fact that she chose to condemn a woman she had never met on the basis of hearsay from two obviously biased sources raises some questions about her judgment and, therefore, of the accuracy of her report. . . .

We are satisfied that the father's home and financial circumstances are most desirable, that he loves his children, that he and his wife would give them good care. This said, it is equally apparent that the mother's home and financial circumstances are entirely adequate, that she too loves the children, and that she too would give—and has given—them good care. Comparing the two homes, we find no basis for the lower court's statement that the father's home would be any more "normal, stable and secure" than the mother's. . . .

Van Driel v. Van Driel

Supreme Court of South Dakota, 1994.
525 N.W.2d 37.

ROBERT A. MILLER, CHIEF JUSTICE.

Appellant James Mark Van Driel (James) appeals the trial court's award of primary physical custody of his minor children to their mother, appellee Lori Ann Van Driel (Lori), citing their mother's lesbian relationship and the parties' status as joint legal custodians as grounds for reversal. . . .

James and Lori were married on May 23, 1981. In 1989 or 1990, the couple separated. During this period of separation, Lori became involved in a lesbian relationship and began sharing a residence with her lesbian partner.

James and Lori divorced on January 3, 1991. Pursuant to a settlement agreement, James and Lori shared joint legal and physical custody of their two children, an eight-year-old daughter and a five-year-old son. Under this arrangement, the children lived with each parent on an alternating weekly basis.

Approximately three weeks after the finalization of her divorce, Lori "exchanged vows" with her lesbian partner, with the intent to enter into a permanent and monogamous relationship. Considering Lori's lesbian relationship, James objected to Lori having custody, fearing the children would be ridiculed by their peers and would react negatively in the future to their mother's sexual orientation. . . . In a memorandum opinion, the trial court awarded primary physical custody to Lori, subject to reasonable and liberal visitation with James.

During the summer of 1993, Lori arranged to move to Minnesota due to the closing of the plant in Mitchell, South Dakota, where she had worked. James filed a motion for reconsideration of the custody determination, citing Lori's lesbian relationship and her move to Minnesota as grounds for reconsideration. . . .

When a divorce decree is based on an agreement of the parties, the issue of custody may be considered in a subsequent custody modification hearing without a showing of "substantial change of circumstances." The party seeking modification must show that the best interests and welfare of the children requires a change of custody. . . .

James argues that Lori's cohabitation with a woman in a lesbian relationship was per se not in the best interests of the children, and the trial court's designation of Lori as the primary custodian parent constituted an abuse of discretion for this reason. We disagree.

The trial court found that both James and Lori were loving and caring parents who had the best interests of their children at heart. Although James suggests that Lori's relationship with another woman is immoral per se, "immoral conduct by one parent does not automatically render that parent unfit to have custody of the children and require an award of custody to the other parent." The parent's conduct must be shown to have had some harmful effect on the children. Furthermore, the issue properly before us is whether the trial court abused its discretion in awarding primary custody of these children to their mother. We are called upon to make a judicial review of the trial court's decision rather than a moral evaluation of the parties' conduct. . . . Personal conceptions of morality held by the members of this Court have no place in the resolution of this controversy.

James mistakenly relies on Chicoine [v. Chicoine, 479 N.W.2d 891 (S.D.1992)] . . .

This Court's ruling [in *Chicoine*] was triggered by evidence that the mother had experienced a myriad of psychological problems, had taken the children to gay bars, had allowed the children to sleep with her and her partner while the mother was unclothed, had kissed and caressed her partner in front of the children despite protests by her oldest son, and had continued a sexual encounter rather than comfort her child after the child had discovered her engaged in sexual activity.

In contrast, there is no evidence of this type of behavior in this case. The record indicates that Lori and her partner are affectionate and attentive toward the children, while being discreet about the sexual aspects of their own relationship. Contrary to James' fears, there was no evidence that the children were ridiculed by classmates or the larger community because of their mother's sexual orientation or that the children were repulsed or embarrassed by, or otherwise showed adverse reactions to, their mother's living arrangement. Indeed, the children's own statements, as reported by the clinical psychologist, indicated that they would prefer living with their mother. Finally, a custody evaluation issued by a clinical psychologist who was retained by both parties recommended that the court award physical custody of the children to Lori. This recommendation was based on a wealth of information, including interviews, psychological tests, and clinical observations of the parties and the children, collateral contact with the parties' friends and family, and psychological literature concerning the effect of gay or lesbian parents on child development. In light of all of this evidence, this Court cannot conclude that the trial court's custody decision was an abuse of discretion. . . .

V. WORK AND FAMILY CONFLICTS REVISITED: CUSTODY, CHILD CARE, AND THE WORKING MOTHER

Perhaps you have seen the bumper sticker: "All Mothers Are Working Mothers." It exposes the oddity and ambiguity in the conventional use of the phrase "working mothers" to refer to mothers who work for pay outside the home. It also reveals how "mother," unmodified, is usually assumed to refer to a woman who stays at home to care for her children. This simple point about a convention of language may offer insight into disputes over child custody in which a woman's efforts to provide substitute child care while she is working or at school can be viewed as inadequate parenting. How can the work-family balance be assessed in contested custody disputes to ensure gender equality and protection for children's interests?

Ireland v. Smith

Court of Appeals of Michigan, 1995.
214 Mich.App. 235, 542 N.W.2d 344.

ROMAN S. GRIBBS, JUDGE.

Plaintiff appeals as of right in Docket No. 177431 from a circuit court order changing custody of the parties' daughter to defendant. Defendant has filed a cross appeal. In a consolidated appeal, Docket No. 182369, plaintiff also appeals by leave granted an order of the chief judge of the circuit court denying plaintiff motion for disqualification of the trial judge. Numerous amici curiae briefs have been filed and considered. We affirm in part, reverse in part, and remand for further proceedings.

On April 22, 1991, plaintiff gave birth to a daughter. At the time, both plaintiff and defendant-father were sixteen years old. They never married or lived together. Defendant signed papers agreeing to place the child for adoption, and she was placed in foster care. Within about three weeks, however, plaintiff decided to raise the child herself. At the time of the child's birth, and until September 19, 1993, both parties lived with their respective families. Plaintiff lived with her mother and younger sister, who helped her raise the child. Defendant continued to live with his parents. Both parties continued in high school with apparently normal pursuits, including sports, cheerleading, dating, and partying, and both eventually graduated. Defendant did not attempt to see his daughter during the first year of her life. Since that time, defendant has visited the child regularly.

In the fall of 1993, plaintiff and the child moved to Ann Arbor, where plaintiff began attending the University of Michigan on a scholarship. Plaintiff and the child lived in an apartment in the university family housing unit. When plaintiff attended class, the child was cared for in university-approved day care. Plaintiff and the child came back to plaintiff's mother's home during the spring of 1994 for this custody trial, and plaintiff returned to the University of Michigan with her daughter in September 1994. Defendant has continued to live in his parents' home throughout these proceedings.

On January 29, 1993, plaintiff filed an action for child support. Defendant then petitioned for custody. The trial court conducted a several-day evidentiary hearing in May and June 1994, and issued a written opinion on June 27, 1994, transferring custody to defendant. The trial court found that there was an established custodial environment in plaintiff and found the parties equal or the proofs neutral with regard to all but one of the factors contained in the Child Custody Act, M.C. Sec. 722.21 et seq.; M.S.A. Sec. 25.312(1) et seq. Because defendant argues on cross appeal that the trial court was correct in its disposition but erred in virtually all its findings, we will review each aspect of the trial court's decision.

A court may not change the established custodial environment of a child unless clear and convincing evidence is presented that it is in the best interest of the child. Baker v. Baker, 411 Mich. 567, 309 N.W.2d 532 (1981). Section 7(1)(c) of the Child Custody Act explains that "[t]he custodial environment of a child is established if over an appreciable time the child naturally looks to the custodian in that environment for guidance, discipline, the necessities of life, and parental comfort." M.C.L. Sec. 722.27(1)(c); M.S.A. Sec. 25.312(7)(1)(c).

Whether a custodial environment is established is a question of fact. ... Findings of fact in a child custody case are reviewed under the great weight of the evidence standard. M.C.L. Sec. 722.28; M.S.A. Sec. 25.312(8). Fletcher v. Fletcher, 447 Mich. 871, 526 N.W.2d 889 (1994). Under that standard, the trial court's findings will be sustained unless the evidence clearly preponderates in the opposite direction. ...

The trial court's findings in this case that there was an established custodial environment in plaintiff is not contrary to the great weight of the evidence. As the trial judge noted, the child has lived with her mother for her entire life. Although plaintiff's mother and sister acted as a support group for plaintiff and the child, plaintiff has been a consistent part of the child's life since the beginning. Most of the necessities of life have been provided by plaintiff's mother. Neither plaintiff nor defendant earns a living wage, and defendant's parents acknowledge that they have not provided any financial support for plaintiff or the child, although they have purchased numerous items for the child's use while she is in their home. Defendant did not seek visitation for more than a year after the child was born. Although his visits since then have been regular and satisfactory, he has never had the sole obligation of taking care of the child for any extended period. Defendant contends that plaintiff's mother, sister, and friends have done more to raise the child than plaintiff. However, defendant, who lives with his parents, also has a support group for his involvement with the child during visitation. Since September 1993, plaintiff has lived alone with the child for most of the year and, and as the trial court notes in its thorough opinion, has matured considerably in her commitment to parenting. The trial court's finding that there was an established custodial environment with plaintiff is affirmed.

Because there was an established custodial environment in this case, the trial court is prohibited from changing custody unless clear and convincing evidence demonstrates that a change in custody would be in the child's best interest. *Baker*, supra at 577, 309 N.W.2d 532. ... The trial court's determination regarding best interest is made by weighing the "sum total" of twelve statutory factors. M.C.L. Sec. 722.23; M.S.A. Sec. 25.312(3). A court's ultimate finding regarding a particular factor is a factual finding that can be set aside if it is against the great weight of evidence. A trial court's discretion in weighing the evidence is "not unlimited; rather, it must be supported by the weight of the evidence." *Fletcher*, supra at 881, 526 N.W.2d 889. Questions of law are reviewed by this Court for legal error. When a trial court "incorrectly chooses, interprets, or applies the law, it commits legal error that the appellate court is bound to correct." Id.

In this case, as required by the Child Custody Act, the trial court made findings of fact regarding each of the following statutory factors contained in M.C.L. Sec. 722.23; M.S.A. Sec. 25.312(3).

"(a) The love, affection, and other emotional ties existing between the parties involved and the child." The trial court found that the child has a strong attachment to both parents and that both parents now "exhibit a strong degree of love and affection for the child." The trial court found that this factor does not weigh in either party's favor and we agree. The evidence does not "clearly preponderate" against the trial court's finding that this factor is neutral.

"(b) The capacity and disposition of the parties involved to give the child love, affection, and guidance and to continue the education and raising of the child in his or her religion or creed, if any." As the trial court noted in its findings, neither party demonstrated significant parenting ability during the child's early life. Since shortly after high school graduation, however, plaintiff has demonstrated a "new maturity and determination." Defendant has shown himself to be "very capable" in caring for the child during visitation. We are aware that defendant presented at the hearing a great deal of testimony purporting to show that defendant's child-rearing techniques were preferable to plaintiff's. We commend the trial court's recognition that the parties' parenting styles are not identical and that "it is anticipated that each one would, in their own way, bring to the child their concept of nurturing, guidance and love." Both parties share the Roman Catholic faith and, although both "practice their faith as they see fit," they agree that the child will be raised in their faith. The trial court's finding that the parties are equal with regard to this factor is not contrary to the great weight of the evidence.

"(c) The capacity and disposition of the parties involved to provide the child with food, clothing, medical care or other remedial care recognized and permitted under the laws of this state in place of medical care, and other material needs." The trial court found that the day-to-day costs of raising the child have been paid by the maternal grandmother. However, the trial court correctly found that the grandparents' contributions to expenses did not weigh in favor of either party. Although both parties work part-time, "these child-parents are in no position to adequately support their baby." The evidence supports the trial court's finding that the parties are equal with regard to this factor.

"(d) The length of time the child has lived in a stable, satisfactory environment, and the desirability of maintaining continuity." The child has lived virtually all her life with plaintiff, most of the time in plaintiff's family home. As the trial court indicated in its opinion, defendant presented "derogatory comments relating to conditions that existed in the plaintiff's home prior to the summer of 1993." The trial court also found that the evidence showed that the conditions improved "with the maturity of the plaintiff," and that, in any event, the plaintiff is now living independently of her mother most of the time. The trial court's conclusion that this factor "carries little, if any, weight in favor of either party" is not contrary to the evidence.

"(e) The permanence, as a family unit, of the existing or proposed custodial home or homes." In evaluating this factor, the trial court extensively considered each party's child-care plans and living arrangements. The trial court contrasted the child's care by a grandparent with child care by a university-approved provider, and contrasted plaintiff's university housing with defendant's childhood home with his parents. The trial court acknowledged that defendant's plans for his own future education, housing, or employment were "not completely clear," but concluded that, in the meantime, defendant's home, with his parents, was a "regular home and a regular program," and therefore preferable to plaintiff's university life style.

We find no support in the record for the trial court's speculation that there is "no way that a single parent attending an academic program at an institution as prestigious as the University of Michigan, can do justice to their studies and to raising of an infant child." The evidence shows that the child has thrived in the university environment. Defendant concedes that he has no complaint about the university day care, and the trial court recognized that the child has had a "meaningful experience" there. The trial court found plaintiff's day-care arrangements "appropriate," but concluded that defendant's plan to have his mother baby-sit was better for the child because she was a "blood relative" rather than a "stranger." Both parties will necessarily need the help of other people to care for their child as they continue their education and employment, and eventually their careers. In light of undisputed evidence that plaintiff's child-care arrangements are appropriate and working well, the evidence does not support the trial court's judgment that defendant's proposed, but untested, plans for the child's care would be better.

Moreover, an evaluation of each party's arrangements for the child's care while her parents work or go to school is not an appropriate consideration under this factor. We find the trial court committed clear legal error in considering the "acceptability" of the parties' homes and child-care arrangements under this factor, which is directed to the "permanence, as a family unit," of the individual parties. "This factor exclusively concerns whether the family unit will remain intact, not an evaluation about whether one custodial home would be more acceptable than the other." Fletcher v. Fletcher, 200 Mich.App. 505, 517, 504 N.W.2d 684 (1993). Our Supreme Court affirmed this Court's opinion in *Fletcher* on this issue, 447 Mich. 871, 884–885, 526 N.W.2d 889, stating: "We agree with the Court of Appeals. The facts relied upon and expressed by the judge relate to acceptability, rather than permanence, of the custodial unit."

Because the trial court's finding with regard to this factor was the basis for a change in the child's established custodial environment, the error is not harmless. Were we permitted to do so, we would reverse the trial court's decision and resolve the matter. However, review de novo of a custodial disposition is expressly prohibited by *Fletcher*, 447 Mich. at 889, 526 N.W.2d 889. Although it appears from the record that both of the child's "custodial units" are equally committed to permanence, we are no longer permitted to reach a speedy resolution. Particularly in a case such as this, in our view it ill serves the best interest of the child to remand for further proceedings. Nonetheless, *Fletcher* requires that we remand to the trial court for reevaluation of this factor. Id.

On remand, the trial court is to consider "up-to-date information" regarding this factor, as well as the fact that the child has "been living with the plaintiff during the appeal and any other changes in circumstances arising since the trial court's original custody order." Id. . . . The trial court is not, however, to entertain or revisit further "evidence" concerning events before the trial in May and June, 1994. See id.

"(f) The moral fitness of the parties involved." The trial court noted that both parties were apparently "sexually indiscriminate" during high school, and concluded that "neither one of these parties deserve any medals for their youthful activities." The evidence supports the trial court's finding that neither party benefits under this factor and that both parties have shown considerable growth during the past year.

"(g) The mental and physical health of the parties involved." The evidence does not clearly preponderate against the trial court's finding that this factor does not weigh in favor of either party. As the trial court stated, "the parties appear to be youthfully healthy and at this time have a good mental outlook on their future."

"(h) The home, school, and community record of the child." Although there was testimony from the child's day-care provider that the child was well adjusted and clean, the trial court's conclusion that the child is too young to have a significant school and community record is affirmed.

"(i) The reasonable preference of the child, if the court considers the child to be of sufficient age to express preference." The trial court found that, after seeing the child, "it was apparent that due to the infant's youth that no meaningful preference could be ascertained." The trial court's finding is not contrary to the evidence.

"(j) The willingness and ability of each of the parties to facilitate and encourage a close and continuing parent-child relationship between the child and the other parent." The record amply supports the trial court's conclusion that "pettiness, jealousy, etc., is still going to be on the scene and that the situation would require constant court monitoring." The trial court's finding that both parties have contributed to the "considerable discord," and are equal on this factor, is supported by the evidence.

"(k) Domestic violence, regardless of whether the violence was directed against or witnessed by the child." Although there was evidence of violence between the parties, the trial court found the issue of domestic violence "not pertinent here." While we agree that the trial court's choice of words was unfortunate, it is apparent from the record that the trial court carefully considered the issue and found the parties neutral with regard to this factor after reviewing the vastly conflicting evidence. The evidence presented in this case does not clearly preponderate against the trial court's finding.

"(l) Any other factor considered by the court to be relevant to a particular child custody dispute." The parties do not dispute the trial court's finding that no other factors were relevant in this case.

As noted previously, we affirm the trial court's finding that there was an established custodial environment in plaintiff. We also affirm the trial court's finding that the parties are equal, or the proofs neutral, with regard to eleven of the twelve statutory factors. We find no record support for the trial court's finding that factor e favored defendant, and find that it was clear legal error to consider, under factor e, which party's arrangement was preferable for the child's care while her parent was working or at school. Because we are no longer permitted, under *Fletcher*, to resolve this matter here, we remand for reevaluation of factor e. Only changes in circumstances since the previous custody hearing are to be considered on remand by the trial court. . . .

NOTES AND QUESTIONS

1. **Custodial Environment.** In Ireland v. Smith, the mother clearly had an "established custodial environment" and the father did not. How, if at all, should the analysis change if prior to the divorce, both parents shared the home with the child, and after the divorce, both parents planned to be away from the child for the same amount of time?

2. **Past Patterns.** Should the custody determination give deference to past patterns of care and time allocations with the children, even if those patterns will change following the divorce? *See* Elizabeth Scott, *Pluralism, Parental Preference, and Child Custody*, 80 Cal. L. Rev. 615 (1992).

3. **When Father Remarries and Mother Does Not.** If the father remarries and his new wife does not work outside the home, some judges might find that household more beneficial than the one with the single mother who works outside the home. How does this view undermine gender equality? How, if at all, do gender concerns affect a potential custody contest between the noncustodial mother and the stepmother who has had custody of the children but has now separated from the father? *See* Zuziak v. Zuziak, 169 Mich.App. 741, 426 N.W.2d 761 (Mich.Ct.App.1988) (finding that trial court erred in placing child with mother rather than stepmother after stepmother and father separated and divorced).

4. **Time and the Working Parent**. How should courts, and the parties themselves, think about the time working parents do or should have available to be with children following divorce? Below, Professor D. Kelly Weisberg addresses the special time problems for professional women such as Marcia Clark, who came under both media criticism and a custody challenge as she prosecuted O.J. Simpson.

5. **Welfare Reform and the Double Bind.** On August 22, 1996, President Clinton signed into law the Personal Responsibility and Work Opportunity Reconciliation Act, Pub. L. 104–193, Stat. 2105. This piece of "welfare reform" places a five-year limit on individuals' lifetime receipt of welfare benefits and requires states to have 50 percent of recipients engaged in paid employment, unpaid work experience, or community service for at least 20 hours per week by the year 2000. What will be the effect of this federal legislation on single mothers with children who receive aid?

Will new resources for day care and after-school care emerge to enable such women to hold full-time jobs? Will that kind of substitute care jeopardize custody by mothers? One author noted these concerns:

> One question not answered in current welfare "reform" proposals is what happens to the children of mothers who cannot find work, or work-related essentials such as child care, when benefits are denied or exhausted after five years. State child protection services are currently not equipped to deal with large classes of parents entirely unable to provide their children with the necessities of life. A likely result is that many children will be removed from their parents and placed in either foster care or institutions. . . .
>
> Moreover, in divorce cases, some states' "best interests of the child" standard appears to contain a bias against mothers who work outside the home. In several recent, highly publicized decisions, judges in New York, Michigan, Mississippi and the District of Columbia have used maternal employment as a reason to grant custody to fathers.
>
> In these states, a mother whose husband does not have the resources, or seeks custody after refusing, to pay child support, faces an impossible situation in custody disputes, particularly if she has ever received AFDC [Aid to Families with Dependent Children] before. The Court makes a presumption against her if she places the child in day care, but she has no option to raise the child at home. Once again, she would be likely to lose the child on grounds that have nothing to do with her "fitness." This situation could be particularly damaging for children since at least forty-five percent of current and former AFDC recipients are victims of repeated domestic abuse. Given a choice between an allegedly abusive father and a mother with a strong chance of losing her children to foster care or an orphanage within five years, it is impossible to predict what kinds of tragic decisions judges may make.

Benjamin L. Weiss, *Single Mothers' Equal Right to Parent: A Fourteenth Amendment Defense Against Forced–Labor Welfare "Reform,"* 15 Law and Inequality 215, 238–241 (Winter 1997).

D. Kelly Weisberg, Professional Women and the Professionalization of Motherhood: Marcia Clark's Double Bind

6 Hastings Women's L.J. 295 (1995).

. . . The quantity of time that a parent has available to spend with a child neither dictates the quality of that interaction nor guarantees that the available time will, in fact, be spent with the child. For example, research on mother-child versus father-child relationships reveals that husbands of working wives spend considerably less time than the working mothers in child-care activities. Fathers' interactions differ qualitatively, too. Fathers tend to interact more with their young children in play rather than in the performance of routine caretaking tasks. Research has also suggested that, at the time of divorce, fathers often overestimate the time they say they want to spend with their children. A certified family law specialist told a committee studying gender bias in the legal profession that a father will "quite frequently" suggest that joint physical custody is important to him:

> [H]e wants not only quality time, but quantity time with his children.... Now, one thing that I'm finding quite often is that dad says that, and dad gets that.... All of a sudden he's on a more traditional, once every other weekend, once a month, maybe on Christmas, all of a sudden the children aren't hearing from dad at all....

Research that documents visitation patterns over time supports this finding. At the end of the third year after a divorce, there was a declining rate of visitation by fathers in terms of overnight visits, daytime visitation, and regular visitation during the school year.

In addition, a focus on the quantity of time that a child spends with a parent may detract from more important considerations. For example, in *Renee B. [v. Michael B.*, 204 A.D.2d 57, 611 N.Y.S.2d 831 (N.Y. App.Div. 1994)] a court-appointed expert determined that the unemployed father would be a better custodian than the mother, because of his greater availability. In awarding custody to the father, the appellate court gave little weight to the father's character, which had been described by the trial judge as, "cold, pedantic, and humorless, and above all, with a pervasive quality of controlled anger." The judge continued, "[e]ven when directly discussing his daughter, there was little sense of the warmth and empathy for her that her mother displayed." In Sharon Prost's case [Prost v. Greene, 652 A.2d 621 (D.C.Ct.App. 1995), aff'd 675 A.2d 471 (D.C.Ct.App. 1996)], by focusing on her availability, the trial court minimized allegations of domestic violence by Prost's husband (which had been serious enough to merit a civil protection order). Surely, a parent who spends limited "high quality time" with a child is a more appropriate custodian than a parent who has socially undesirable qualities.

Moreover, it is important to note that societal views have evolved concerning children's need for quantity time. Sociologist Arlie Hochschild writes that in the second half of the nineteenth century, when a woman's place was in the home, child-care experts agreed that the child needed a mother's constant care at home. As women's roles have changed, however, so has our concept of children's needs: "Nowadays, a child is increasingly imagined to need time with other children, to need 'independence-training,' not to need 'quantity time' with a parent but only a small amount of 'quality time.'"

A second problem regarding consideration of time as a factor in custody decision-making is that a reliance on availability "freezes" the status quo. In other words, it measures the *present time constraints* of one parent against the *present availability* of the other parent to determine fulfillment of the *present time needs* of a child. Yet, any, or all, of these factors may change significantly over time.

Consideration of a parent's current career demands assumes that these constraints are reflective of the career as a whole. In the cases of many of the professional women above, this assumption may not be warranted. For example, although the ordinary demands of a prosecutor may be high, the notoriety of the O.J. Simpson trial makes this trial a singular event. Similarly, for Sharon Prost, the Senate confirmation hearing of Justice Thomas also presented unique time demands. Likewise, Linda Tresnak [In re Marriage of Tresnak, 297 N.W.2d 109, 110 (Iowa 1980)] was at the beginning of her law school career, a time when the demands upon her would, most likely, be highest. Thus, a reliance on present availability fails to recognize that the present situation may be a momentary stage in a lifelong career.

Reliance on time as a factor also freezes the availability of the non-custodial parent. Gordon Clark, for example, asserts that he is home every night by 6:15 p.m. This ignores the possibility that, in time, he might be promoted into a more demanding position, accept a different job, or become involved in a new amorous relationship that would take up more of his time. Similarly, as is the case for two other ex-husbands discussed above, a parent's availability might be related to temporary unemployment or a current position with flexible hours; both of these work situations are subject to change.

Reliance on present availability also disregards the changing needs of children and fails to recognize that children's demands on a parent's time vary as a function of each developmental stage. For example, once children reach school age, they are absent from home for a large portion of the parent's work day. Moreover, school children's after-school lives may quickly fill with extracurricular activities and friendships, thus lessening their need and desire to be with a parent.

A third criticism of reliance on availability as a factor in custody decision-making rests on an unspoken assumption that *availability* is an objective and easily measurable criteria. This assumption is, however, open to challenge. Conscious and unconscious biases by the parties themselves, as well as by decision-makers, may pervade the evaluation of availability. Several other issues also complicate the measurement of availability: What should be measured? Child care only? Or, child care and house work (work performed for the family)? If child care, then what types of tasks? One problem in emphasizing the more visible caretaking activities is that this tends to minimize all the "invisible" work that mothers might perform (such as arranging for baby-sitting or housekeeper services, scheduling doctors' appointments, scheduling play dates, determining a child's need for new clothes and haircuts, helping with school work, planning domestic chores and events, making grocery lists, and paying bills).

Sociologist Arlie Hochschild has made visible the extent of the child care and house work that working women perform. Her classic study of fifty working couples in California from 1980 to 1988 reveals that working mothers work "a second shift"; in other words, they work at their job and then come home and perform another shift doing housework and child care. Hochschild estimates that mothers' second shifts amount to their working an extra month of twenty-four-hour days per year.

Moreover, Hochschild suggests that working mothers may actually do more family work (housework and child care) than non-working mothers. Furthermore, Hochschild points out that those working women who earn more than their husbands tend to participate to a greater extent than other working women in the division of labor. Hochschild attributes this to the women's subconscious desire to restore power to their husbands.

Sharon Prost's case illustrates the possibility of bias in the measurement of "invisible" caretaking tasks. The appellate court determined that Prost was so devoted to her career that she neglected her "health, her children and her family." To the contrary, Prost remarked:

> I think they [the children] view me as their parent who takes care of really their most basic needs. I did their laundry, cut their nails every work [sic], I'd give them haircuts. From the little details of the day to the broader aspects of, you know, going to camp or whatever, I was just [there]....

Prost maintains that she read the children bedtime stories and tucked them into bed. She adds, "[m]ost of our best times are just spent hanging out."

Much of the work Prost performed by tending to the children's "basic needs" was "invisible" to the judge who focused on the father because he was the principal cook for the family. The judge ignored several other aspects of Prost's availability—for example, her proximity to her son's day care. Instead, the judge faulted her for allowing her husband to take the child home from day care when she worked late and for placing Prost's mother's name (rather than the child's father's name) on the parent notification card as an alternate emergency contact.

In addition, the judge ignored the fifteen months before trial during which Prost was the children's primary caretaker. Also, both the trial court judge and the appellate judge discounted the work Prost performed during their son's infancy (such as nursing and tending to him at night). Summarizing the trial court's opinion, the appellate court stated:

> The trial judge made detailed findings of fact attempting to resolve the conflicting evidence. The judge found ... [s]pecifically, except *during the first several months of Matthew's life,* [that] Prost and Greene were "full and equal caretakers of Matthew from his birth [in 1987] through at least February 1989."

Research on gender bias in the courts reveals that this de-emphasis on a mother's primary caretaking may be part of a pattern:

[I]t appears that as soon as physical custody is contested, any weight given to a history of primary caretaking disappears. Mothers who have been primary caretakers throughout their child's life are subjected to differential and stricter scrutiny, and may lose custody if the role of primary caretaker has been assumed, however briefly and for whatever reason, by someone else.

Measurement of availability is complicated by other subtle factors. Mothers and fathers may attach different meanings to the attentiveness required by child care. Or, mothers and fathers may have different standards regarding child care or housework which may affect their availability to their children. For example, one parent may care more about how the house looks or how clean the children are, and thereby perform more child care or household tasks accordingly.

Further, it becomes important to notice how certain tasks are weighed in the measurement of availability. An evaluation of availability in some of the cases above appears to rest on gender-based assumptions about the traditional roles of mother and father. Thus, the appellate court judge faults Sharon Prost for not making dinner for her family and for not eating with them. He gives her husband credit for food preparation. This judge obviously presupposes a very traditional family model with traditional gender roles.

Similarly, the court-appointed mental health expert in *Renee B.* faults Renee for not being available to the daughter after school. It matters little that she wakes the daughter and gives her breakfast. Gordon Clark faults his ex-wife, similarly, for coming home at 10 p.m. Yet, we do not know if she, like Renee, spends time with the children in the morning.

These opinions reveal underlying gender-based assumptions about the expected roles of mother and father that may be out of place in contemporary family life. The families of professional women may function differently. They may, for instance, alter their children's schedule in order to spend more time with them.

Further, subjective bias often emerges in the weight given to the amount and type of work that fathers, as compared to mothers, perform. Commentators have pointed out a judicial tendency to overrate fathers' contributions to caretaking:

> Case analysis reveals a tendency to overrate small paternal contributions to parenting because they are still so noticeable, and to concomitantly over-emphasize lack of total maternal parenting. In other words, the emphasis in evaluating mothers is on what they do not do, because they are expected to do everything. By this standard, men will always look good for doing more than nothing and women will always look bad for doing less than everything.

The court in *Prost*, for example, pointed to the father's "regular involvement in school functions" while disregarding the mother's "own equal involvement in [the son's] schooling." While Prost's husband was unemployed for almost two years, the couple still hired a live-in baby-sitter to care for the children. He took over from the baby-sitter at 5:00 or 5:30. As Prost commented:

> If he was unemployed, at home all day, the question—the lens wasn't, "Well, why wasn't he taking the children during the day?" It was, "Isn't he wonderful? . . . so what he did was wonderful, but everything I did was from a lens of how little I did."

Similarly, in *Renee B.*, the court-appointed expert testified that the unemployed father was more available. His gender bias against working mothers is apparent in his written report:

> Ms. RB is an attorney and has a full-time job. She is available to dress Rebecca in the morning and to give her breakfast. In contrast, Mr. MB [father] is much more available to spend time with Rebecca after school [and] at times of sickness, accidents, and other possible emergencies. . . . Although MB's greater availability is, in part, a manifestation of a long history of occupational difficulties, from Rebecca's point of view her father is much more available than her mother and this puts Mr. MB at an advantage
> . . .

Subsequently, the mental health expert charged that Renee, "is not herself available each day after school. . . . [H]er work situation does have the effect of reducing Rebecca's time with her . . . The expert's testimony reflects the traditional role expectation that mothers are to be home when their children return from school."

Because of stereotypical gender role expectations, custody decision-makers may not expect fathers to be involved in child care. As a result, fathers' time commitments in housework and child care are accorded considerable weight.

A final criticism of reliance on time as a relevant factor in custody decision-making is the subjectivity of the assessment by the parties themselves. Their measurement may be not unbiased, especially given the likelihood of intra-parental conflict and hostility upon divorce. As one commentator points out, "[i]n all events, because the [time] test would require a prediction of the amount of time each parent would spend with the child, it would be very difficult to apply and would invite exaggeration and dishonesty in litigation." This commentator presupposes that parents consciously might misrepresent the time they spend on caretaking.

Hochschild's findings suggest, however, that unconscious motivations may also play a role in a parent's measurement of child care contributions. That is, Hochschild suggests that some families participate in "family myths," delusions that serve some unconscious function. One such myth is that the marriage is egalitarian and that the husband's workload (in terms of housework and child care) is equal to that of the wife. Specifically, Hochschild identifies relationships in which (despite an observable gender-based inequality in the division of labor), *both* the husband the wife refer to the division of labor as "equal . . . because equality was so important to [the wife]."

In sum, parental availability is a problematic criterion by which to measure the suitability of a custodial parent. A reliance on time places undue emphasis on quantity rather than quality. Reliance on this factor inappropriately freezes the status quo in a way that may not be in the child's best interests. Also, the evaluation process reveals subjective bias, such as gender bias and stereotyped role expectations, on the part of the decision-makers and the parties.

The Feminist Double Bind

Another perspective on the experience of Marcia Clark (and those of the professional women herein) is that it exemplifies gender bias in custody decision-making. Divorced professional mothers are being treated differently than similarly situated men. These working women are expected to be perfect mothers. If they cannot excel in both their work-life and family-life, they are penalized and made to choose between them. Fathers are confronted neither with the expectation of parental perfectibility nor the demand that they make a choice.

The conflicting role expectations for the working mother versus father have roots in nineteenth century gender ideology. On one hand, imagery portrays the hardworking father as *a good provider*. Mothers, on the other hand, suffer from the effects of the social movement of the professionalization of motherhood.

Reviewing the feminist literature on mothering, Nancy Chodorow and Susan Contratto identify and articulate the theme of maternal perfection:

> [This includes] a sense that mothers are totally responsible for the outcomes of their mothering. . . . Belief in the all-powerful mother spawns a recurrent tendency to blame the mother on the one hand, and a fantasy of maternal perfectibility on the other. . . .

Chodorow and Contratto label this the "myth of the perfect mother." This myth results in a paradoxical treatment of mothers: idealization and blame.

Chodorow and Contratto do not delve into the historical source of this treatment. The source, however, is highly relevant to the legal treatment of the professional woman/mother. The idealization of mothers derives from nineteenth century beliefs about womanhood. Historian Barbara Welter identifies "the cult of true womanhood" that surfaced after 1820. According to this view, the "true woman" was supposed to possess certain attributes, such as submissiveness and domesticity.

Woman's place was in the home as wife and mother. She was supposed to busy herself with domesticity, the most prized virtue. Women's literature regarded housework as uplifting. "[M]any a marriage is jeopardized because the wife has not learned to keep house." It was woman's job to make the home a cheerful, comfortable place. This "mystique," according to Welter, "of what woman was and ought to be persisted. . . . " Other social forces, including industrialization and urbanization, contributed to the idea of the home as a sanctuary from the outside world.

In the late nineteenth century, women who sought careers, such as women physicians, were the object of ridicule and were "a frequent inspiration to cartoonists." They were regarded as deviant; the popular view was that "any female who did succeed at medicine must be not a lady at all, but some kind of freak." In the twentieth century, the working woman would confront remnants of this ideology.

By the 1920s and 1930s, the professional woman continued to receive censure. For example, Deborah Rhode quotes the advice of a therapist to women:

> Dr. W.B. Wolfe captured the sentiments of many therapists in the late 1920s and early 30s with his queries to the seemingly "successful" professional woman. Would she be content to "take her Ph.D. to bed with [her] on cold nights, or [would she] warm [her] bones with gilt-edged stocks?" Success or no success, "there [was] in all the world no substitute for the job of motherhood."

In the late nineteenth and early twentieth century, a diverse range of "scientific" experts advised women on the virtues of domesticity and motherhood. Motherhood witnessed a professionalization, spurred by the birth of domestic science and a recognition of the growing importance of childhood. In a speech addressed to women, President Theodore Roosevelt illustrated this deification of motherhood:

> The good mother, the wise mother ... is more important to the community than even the ablest man; her career is more worthy of honor and is more useful to the community than the career of any man, no matter how successful, can be.... But ... the woman who, whether from cowardice, from selfishness, from having a false and vacuous ideal shirks her duty as wife and mother, earns the right to our contempt, just as does the man who, from any motive, fears to do his duty in battle when the country calls him.

A "mothers' movement" at the end of the century provided an eager audience for the experts who were transforming child rearing into a science. This mothers' movement, paradoxically, contained elements of a feminist backlash; leaders of this movement reproached those women who rejected domesticity for a career.

In contrast to the elevation of domesticity and motherhood for women, a corresponding nineteenth century transformation associated men with imagery of *the good provider*. Sociologist Jessie Bernard explains that the structure of our traditional family took shape in the early nineteenth century, beginning in the 1830s. The industrial revolution spurred the development of a specialized male role. Formerly, in a subsistence economy, both the husband and the wife contributed significantly to the division of labor. With the transition to a market economy, however, men were expected to provide to the best of their ability for their family.

Gender identity for men was associated with the public sphere of work. The good provider role envisioned "a hardworking man who spent most of his time at his work." Also, the role encompassed the idea that "[h]is work might have been demanding, but he expected it to be. . . . "

Bernard identifies the "costs" of the good provider ideology for our conceptualization of husbands:

> The most serious cost was perhaps the identification of maleness not only with the work site but especially with success in the role. . . . To be a man one had to be not only a provider but a good provider. Success in the good-provider role came in time to define masculinity itself.

Another "cost" of the good provider role, Bernard explains, was the exclusion of the attribute of "emotional expressivity." The man was not expected to provide emotional comfort, nurturance, or tenderness: "[T]he good provider was often, in a way, a kind of emotional parasite. Implicit in the definition of the role was that he provided goods and material things. Tender loving care was not one of the requirements."

This aspect of the good provider role began to change in the 1970s. Society placed new demands on husbands, including increased expressivity and the sharing of household responsibilities and child care. Men's behavior in the family began to evolve based on these new expectations.

The increase of working wives in the labor force in this century signals that women now share the provider role: "[N]ow that she is entering the labor force in large numbers, she can once more resume her ancient role, this time, like her male counterpart the provider, by way of a monetary contribution." With this transformation in the division of labor, women's work patterns increasingly resemble men's; men's work patterns more closely resemble women's.

Thus, the good provider role has declined in importance for the husband-father, and new male role expectations in regard to housework and child care have emerged. No correlative decline has occurred, however, in the role expectations for the working wife-mother. Although she now shares with her husband the role of provider for the family, she is still expected to conform to the role of the perfect mother.

Nineteenth century gender ideology regarding the role of women haunts society today in its treatment of women lawyers in the context of custody disputes. Custody decision-makers in several of the cases discussed above were influenced by traditional gender role expectations. The very qualities that contribute to a woman lawyer's success militate against her in a custody dispute when her mothering role is evaluated. An exploration of several common gender stereotypes is useful in explaining how these stereotypes are used to the detriment of women lawyers.

1. Gender Stereotype: Women are Responsible for Family Maintenance Tasks.

One stereotype is that the woman, even if she works, is expected to perform traditional gender-based tasks, such as food preparation. The trial judge in *Prost* is appalled that Prost rarely cooks for the family. It was a "special event" when Prost came home early to cook dinner. Also, the trial court was influenced by testimony that Prost often ate dinner alone, late in the evening, while sitting on the kitchen floor, talking on the phone. Even on occasions when Prost cooked dinner, she ate "standing at the stove or elsewhere in the kitchen, rather than at the table with the children."

The image conveyed is that Prost is an inadequate wife and mother. She lacks the requisite domestic attributes. Also, she is an uncaring mother by neglecting her children's primary needs. She fails to provide requisite psychological support and foster family cohesion. Furthermore, she is "selfish" (being on the telephone, presumably engaged in personal conversations) for not sacrificing her needs in favor of her children's.

The judge could have arrived at an alternate explanation for Prost's behavior, of course. After a hard day at the office, a working mother needs transition time, both to "decompress" and to perform all the necessary scheduling (family and personal) that she was unable to do during the work day. As a busy professional, eating may have no special significance to her. She may often eat food while she works as a way of making use of precious minutes. Moreover, an attribute which may have contributed to her successful career is that she performs several tasks at the same time: "[I]n a multitasking world, many feel they are wasting time unless they combine eating with another activity." Further, food preparation may simply not be one of the many skills that this woman possesses or enjoys.

In contrast to Prost, law student Linda Tresnak succeeds, on appeal, because of her domesticity. She is "a fastidious housekeeper." The appellate court, approvingly, notes that even as a full-time student, she returned home each weekend "to clean house, help with the laundry, cook meals, and prepare foods to be served during the week." Ironically, her success may have depended, in part, on her husband's lack of domesticity.

2. Gender Stereotype: The Mother Must Perform Certain Symbolic Child Care Tasks.

According to this stereotype, the mother must be the parent who performs those child care tasks with special significance. These appear to include: (1) picking up the child from school or preschool; (2) being home when the child returns after school; (3) putting the children to bed; and (4) choreographing special family events.

Sharon Prost is faulted because her husband brings her son home from work when she works late. Renee B. is criticized by the court-appointed psychologist for not being available to the daughter after school, for "farm[ing] out" her daughter to friends' houses and relying on them for baby-sitting. Marcia Clark's husband charges her with returning home after 10 p.m., implicitly criticizing her failure to put the children to bed.

Conversely, Sharon Prost's husband is given credit for hosting a son's birthday party in their home while his wife was working. The appellate court in *Tresnak*, reversing the trial court's denial of custody, commends Linda Tresnak for her participation in vacation and recreation activities; she "fishes, reads, bakes cookies, bicycles and swims" with her sons.

These images harken back to the "myth of the perfect mother." They idealize the mother and a mother's loving care. Her presence is regarded as essential to the child's development. If the mother does not perform these child care tasks, she is blamed for this shortcoming. Moreover, her absence at these important times is a symbol of her psychopathology, *per se* evidence of her unfitness as a custodian. Her psychopathology is also manifest in other ways, discussed below.

3. Gender Stereotype: A Woman's Zealous Commitment to Work is a Form of Psychopathology.

In many of the above cases, the woman's devotion to her career is viewed as an additional element of unfitness. The trial judge characterizes Prost as "driven to succeed" and "intensely dedicated to achievement." The judge criticizes her for returning to work "immediately" after her son was born despite a difficult pregnancy. In awarding custody to the father, the court notes that Prost is "simply more devoted to and absorbed by her work and career than anything else. . . . "

Similarly, Renee B. is characterized as psychologically unstable. In denying her custody, the appellate court based its decision on the opinion of a court-appointed expert who said that Renee's "general superior intellectual capacities [eclipsed] the more subtle manifestations of psychopathology." He characterized Renee as "paranoid" and "delusional."

Yet, as the trial record reveals, when the expert is cross-examined, he agrees that all of Renee's concerns have a factual basis. Her husband admitted that he slept in the same bed with the daughter and that he taped all of the telephone conversations between the daughter and Renee. These examples reveal vestiges of the nineteenth century view of working women. The fact that a woman works, and is committed to her work, signifies that there must be something wrong with her.

4. Gender Stereotype: Mother Must Be the Constant Loving Nurturer. She Must Be Flexible and Accommodating to Family Members.

The above-mentioned cases further reveal the expectation that the mother be a constant warm, loving source of affection for the family members. She must be flexible and accommodating to their needs and desires. The professional women described above do not fit these stereotypes. For example, a court-appointed psychologist criticizes Renee B. for her attempts at humor when describing her daughter's temper tantrums. To the psychologist, Renee is revealing herself as an uncaring mother.

Sharon Prost is criticized for her "rigidity" and "inflexibility" in terms of her unwillingness to adjust her ex-husband's visitation; she became irritated that her husband "barged in" on her scheduled weekend with the children. Similarly, Marcia Clark's ex-husband criticizes her for being furious when he unexpectedly kept the children overnight on short notice.

Renee B. is charged with being "temperamental" and "attempt[ing] to exclude [her ex-husband] from the child's life," as the result of an incident where school personnel threw the ex-husband off school premises and asked him never to return. Likewise, Prost is criticized for "demonstrat[ing] insensitivity" to her husband's periods of unemployment and resultant depression. The traits and actions of these two women do not accord with the stereotypes of a submissive, nurturing wife and mother.

Yet, several of these actions are understandable in light of the requisite attributes and career demands of a professional woman. The professional woman is required to be well-organized and to adhere to a schedule. Impromptu, last-minute changes could upset a carefully-crafted accommodation of child care arrangements and work. Also, being temperamental, rigid, and inflexible might be positive attributes for a litigator or corporate attorney who needs to zealously represent clients. Actions which might not be characterized as parental shortcomings for a male professional take on a different significance for women:

> For the professional man, frequent absences from home, tardiness for dinner, and "overtime" work are not only expected but also accepted as evidence that he is . . . a good parent and spouse. Such is not the case for the professional woman.

Another common expectation is that the woman should adjust to her husband's career. For example, during the Tresnak marriage, the Tresnaks moved twice in order to accommodate Jim's teaching career. Yet, paradoxically, the trial court objected to Linda attending law school, in part, because she would have to move the children to a different state for three years, and then, possibly move them again to start her career.

In short, these cases reveal that decision-makers have expectations of mothers that they do not have of fathers. Gender ideology of the perfect mother leads us to blame these working women when they fail to meet these expectations. This blame sometimes results in the harshest of penalties, custody deprivation.

Conclusion

This article has highlighted a small number of cases in which women have been denied custody because of their demanding careers. Admittedly, the number of divorced women affected by this problem is unknown. Cases in which custody or visitation is contested make up only a small percentage of custody cases. To date, empirical research does not reveal the extent to which career demands serve as the grounds for the contest. This study underscores the need to conduct such research.

This article, however, accurately identifies an issue confronting at least some divorced women. This issue may well assume greater proportions in the future. More women are entering the professions; more women are entering the legal profession, in particular. Many women are likely to be divorced mothers, and a high percentage of divorced mothers work.

This article will now suggest several tentative implications of this research, bearing in mind the methodological caveat regarding the unknown magnitude of the problem. First, this piece lends support to the recognition of gender bias in the legal treatment of working mothers. Commentators have theorized that such bias may be operative. This research augments the number of cases reflecting such bias.

Survey data also substantiate the existence of gender bias. In particular, empirical research reveals that judicial decisions reflect traditional attitudes toward working mothers. One study reports that half of the judges surveyed expressed such stereotypical beliefs as, "[m]others should be home when their school-age children get home from school." Almost half also agreed that, "[a] preschool child is likely to suffer if his/her mother works." Noting that parenting by mothers is scrutinized more closely than that by fathers when custody is contested, these researchers concluded: "Double standards are particularly a problem in the areas of *work outside the home*, temporary relinquishment of custody, and dating and cohabitation."

Gender bias may stem from decision-makers' own beliefs about traditional roles for mothers and fathers. Alternatively, gender bias may result from decision-makers' personal experiences with marriage and divorce. Another possible explanation is that it may derive from an anti-feminist backlash:

> [M]any people feel threatened by the vitality and productivity of the people who accomplish the demands of multiple roles. In a society in which until very recently people believed that the typical American woman was incapable of balancing a checkbook or driving a van, women's new competence as bank officers and truck drivers may encounter resistance.

This sentiment may be directed especially toward women in high-level careers. People may feel that it is quite "inappropriate" that women are employed in these prestigious positions, and they resent the status and money that these women earn.

A possible remedy to combat gender bias in the family courts is "consciousness raising" for legal and social service personnel. The Massachusetts Gender Bias Committee recommended the development of such programs, which would be made mandatory for "probate [family] judges, family service officers, and court clinic staff." The Committee also recommended Continuing Legal Education courses on gender bias for attorneys generally. Although it is not easy to change deep-rooted beliefs, such programs certainly would constitute a step in the right direction.

Another remedy is to encourage the divorcing parties to attempt to work out their differences themselves without litigation. This would take the matter of custody out of the hands of possibly biased decision-makers. Admittedly, although this suggestion might prove workable for some parties, in cases of disputes that are "100 year wars," it is unlikely to be successful.

Using mediation by a neutral third party is yet another suggestion. This idea, however, is similarly no panacea. Mediators, too, may have gender bias. This becomes especially problematic if mediators make recommendations to the court, a practice permitted in some jurisdictions. Mandatory mediation also may constrain the parties to reach a resolution without full consideration of long-range consequences. Further, mediation does not work well in cases when the parties have unequal bargaining power, especially in cases of battering.

Second, this article suggests that custody determinations based on gender-neutral, "objective" criteria may have significant shortcomings. That is, reliance on the factor of time or the related factor of parental availability is a mine-field strewn with problems of subjectivity and speculation. Moreover, gender-based stereotypes regarding the proper roles for men and women may enter into measurement of "neutral" factors. The existence of attitudes deriving from a time when men were the sole breadwinners and women were homemakers/mothers may result in mothers being censured for a failure to conform to an idealized standard, whereas fathers may be accorded considerable approval for their contributions because they have deviated from traditional role expectations.

If parental availability is to enter into custody decision-making, either explicitly or implicitly, then we must exercise considerable caution in our evaluation. We need to be especially careful in our evaluation of families with dual career parents. Determinations of primary caretaker are complicated when both parents work. These families may have negotiated a division of labor that is far from traditional; the concept of "primary" caretaker may not be meaningful when applied to these families.

We also need to recognize that "parental availability" may function as strategic behavior in the divorce bargaining process. That is, fathers may demand sole or joint custody, or increased visitation, because they hope to lessen the amount of their child support. It may have been more than coincidental that Gordon Clark's request for primary custody came on the heels of his ex-wife's request for increased support.

Some statutes link child support awards to custody arrangements, either explicitly or implicitly. This linkage results in the allocation of support being based on the number of nights the child sleeps in the parent's home. In a custody contest, then, each parent is motivated by financial factors to emphasize the extent of his/her child-care responsibilities, especially the time he/she spends with the child. Commentators have urged that the statutory linkage of support and custody be modified or repealed in order to decrease the likelihood that child support be utilized as a bargaining chip in custody disputes.

Decoupling support and visitation may also be in the children's interests in that it might help the children maintain contact with both parents.

For example, a mother would not feel that any increase in visitation with the child's father will lessen her child support.

Third, this study, although limited to the lives of a few professional women, brings into focus the difficulties some professional women experience regarding the work/family conflict and suggests a need for improved workplace accommodations. Women make significant efforts to meet the demands of both their private and professional lives. Their efforts are all the more commendable given that, despite their employment in the public sphere, women still perform the majority of child-rearing and housework in the private sphere.

We need to explore the empirical basis (or lack thereof) for the occasional judicial condemnation of working women. Psychological research fails to substantiate that maternal employment has harmful effects on children. To the contrary, data reveal the positive consequences for children of a mother's employment. Research indicates that maternal employment correlates with an increase of children's cognitive and social development; more flexibility in their sex-role perceptions; expansion of children's stereotypical masculine and feminine personality traits; and better personality adjustment. Working mothers provide role models for daughters and expanded occupational options for sons. Further, studies report that mothers who work full-time are happier and healthier than those who are unemployed or employed part-time, which also has a positive effect on children's development.

If, indeed, maternal employment has positive consequences for children, then we need more support for women to deal with the work/family conflict. For example, we need an improved parental and family leave policy on the part of government and private sector employers. The federal family leave policy has been criticized for many reasons: the allotted amount of time for leave is inadequate; it has no provisions for wage replacement or the accrual of seniority benefits; and it limits benefits to certain parents.

In addition, more employers need to offer part-time work or flexible schedules in order to accommodate the childbearing and child-rearing periods when family demands are highest. Better coordination of school schedules, the work day, and holidays is necessary. Good day care facilities, especially in-house day care or day care referral, are essential. The government might encourage employers to accommodate family needs by the provision of tax incentives.

Sociologist Cynthia Fuchs Epstein urges that the workplace and family "be considered an interactive unit." "Above all," she writes, "what we need from government is symbolic leadership that helps to legitimate the role of the employed mother, and, in so doing, weaken the contradictory norms that make life for working women ... more difficult." She adds, "[t]his is not only a 'woman's problem,' but a social problem."

VI. CUSTODY AND VISITATION DISPUTES IN LESBIAN RELATIONSHIPS

When married couples separate and divorce, they each have claims to the custody of and visitation with their children. When unmarried couples separate, they too each have claims to the custody of and visitation with their children based on the constitutional accord to parent-child relationships. What should happen when a same-sex couple separates, and the biological parent opposes any shared custody or visitation between the children and the former adult partner? If there has been an adoption, *see supra* at Section D.II. (discussing second-parent adoptions), then both parents have standing to claim custody and visitation (and both have child support obligations). In the absence of an adoption, however, courts are divided over whether to accord the person who is not a biological parent any standing to be heard in a request for custody or visitation.

Here are three contrasting treatments of the issue by different state courts:

Titchenal v. Dexter

Supreme Court of Vermont, 1997.
___ Vt. ___, 693 A.2d 682.

FREDERIC W. ALLEN, CHIEF JUSTICE.

The issue in this case is whether the superior court may apply its equitable powers to adjudicate a visitation dispute that cannot be brought in statutory proceedings within the family court's jurisdiction. We affirm the superior court's decision that it does not possess the authority to adjudicate such matters.

The dispute arose after the breakup of a relationship between two women who had both participated in raising a child adopted by only one of them. . . . In 1985, plaintiff Chris Titchenal and defendant Diane Dexter began an intimate relationship. They purchased a home together, held joint bank accounts, and jointly owned their automobiles. They both contributed financially to their household, and each regarded the other as a life partner.

At some point, the parties decided to have a child. When their attempts to conceive via a sperm donor failed, they decided to adopt a child. In July 1991, defendant adopted a newborn baby girl, who was named Sarah Ruth Dexter–Titchenal. The parties held themselves out to Sarah and all others as her parents. The child called one parent "Mama Chris" and the other parent "Mama Di." For the first three and one-half years of Sarah's life, until the parties' separation, plaintiff cared for the child approximately 65% of the time. Plaintiff did not seek to adopt Sarah because the parties' believed that the then-current adoption statute would not allow both of them to do so.

Eventually, the parties' relationship faltered, and by November 1994 defendant had moved out of the couple's home, taking Sarah with her. For the first five months following the parties' separation, Sarah stayed with plaintiff between Wednesday afternoons and Friday evenings. By the spring of 1995, however, defendant had severely curtailed plaintiff's contact with Sarah and had refused plaintiff's offer of financial assistance.

In October 1995, plaintiff filed a complaint requesting that the superior court exercise its equitable jurisdiction to establish and enforce regular, unsupervised parent-child contact between her and Sarah. The court granted defendant's motion to dismiss, refusing to recognize a cause of action for parent-child contact absent a common-law or statutory basis for the claim. . . .

Plaintiff urges us to grant "nontraditional" family members access to the courts by recognizing the legal rights of de facto parents. According to plaintiff, the state's parens patriae power to protect the best interests of children permits the superior court to adjudicate disputes over parent-child contact outside the context of a statutory proceeding. Thus, under the scheme advocated by plaintiff and amicus curiae, the family court would adjudicate disputes concerning parental rights and responsibilities and parent-child contact within the parameters and criteria set forth in statutory divorce, parentage, dependency and neglect, nonsupport and separation, relief-from-abuse, and at times guardianship and adoption proceedings, see 4 V.S.A. Sections 454–455 (establishing jurisdiction of family court), while the superior court would exert its equitable powers to consider such disputes arising outside of these proceedings.

We find no legal basis for plaintiff's proposal. Courts cannot exert equitable powers unless they first have jurisdiction over the subject matter and parties. . . . Equity generally has no jurisdiction over imperfect rights arising from moral rather than legal obligations; not every perceived injustice is actionable in equity—only those violating a recognized legal right. . . .

Notwithstanding the plaintiff's claims to the contrary, there is no common-law history of Vermont courts interfering with the rights and responsibilities of fit parents absent statutory authority to do so. Although there is some support for the proposition that state courts have equity jurisdiction under their parens patriae power to adjudicate custody matters, such authority is generally invoked in the context of dependency or neglect petitions. . . .

. . . Realizing that the family court lacks jurisdiction to adjudicate her claims, see In re R.L., 163 Vt. 168, 171, 657 A.2d 180, 183 (1995) (family court is court of limited jurisdiction, and its jurisdictional grant must be strictly construed), plaintiff seeks equitable relief in the superior court, notwithstanding that (1) Vermont courts have intervened in custody and visitation matters only within the context of statutory proceedings, and (2) expansion of the courts' role in these matters has come only through legislative enactments or this Court's construction of statutes affecting parental rights and responsibilities. See, e.g., [In re] B.L.V.B., 160 Vt. [368,] 369–72, 628 A.2d at 1272–74 [(1993)] (construing adoption statute to hold that when family unit is comprised of biological mother and her partner, and adoption is in children's best interest, terminating biological mother's parental rights is unnecessary and unreasonable); Paquette [v. Paquette], 146 Vt. [83,] 86, 92, 499 A.2d at 26, 30 [(1985)] (construing divorce and

separation statutes to empower court to award custody of child to stepparent when circumstances warrant).

Plaintiff acknowledges that no specific statutory or constitutional
provisions require the superior court to assume jurisdiction over her claim,
but she argues that public policy compels such a result, given her status as
Sarah's de facto parent. We do not agree. The superior court's refusal to
extend its jurisdiction here does not create circumstances "cruel or shocking to the average [person's] conception of justice." Payne, 147 Vt. at 493,
520 A.2d at 588. Persons affected by this decision can protect their
interests. Through marriage or adoption, heterosexual couples may assure
that nonbiological parental rights and responsibilities or parent-child contact in the event a relationship ends. Nonbiological partners in same-sex
relationships can gain similar assurances through adoption.

In this case, plaintiff contends that she did not attempt to adopt Sarah
at the time defendant did because the parties believed that Vermont's then-
current adoption laws would not permit it. See 15 V.S.A. Section 431
(repealed 1996) ("A person or husband and wife together . . . may adopt
any other person. . . . "). The language of the statute, however, certainly
did not preclude plaintiff from seeking to adopt Sarah; indeed, as of
December 1991, when Sarah was only five months old, at least one
Vermont probate court had allowed the female partner of a child's adoptive
mother to adopt the child as a second parent. See B.L.V.B., 160 Vt. at 373
n. 3, 628 A.2d at 1274 n. 3. Further, in June 1993, more than a year before
plaintiff alleges that the parties' relationship ended, this Court construed
the earlier adoption statute as allowing a biological mother's female partner to adopt the mother's child without the mother having to terminate her
parental rights. . . .

In 1996, the Legislature enacted a new adoption statute embracing our
holding in B.L.V.B. and allowing unmarried adoptive partners to petition
the family court regarding parental rights and responsibilities or parent-
child contact. See 15A V.S.A. § 1–102(b) (if family unit consists of parent
and parent's partner, and adoption is in child's best interest, partner of
parent may adopt child without terminating parent's rights); 15A V.S.A.
§ 1–112 (family court shall have jurisdiction to hear and dispose of issues
pertaining to parental rights and responsibilities and parent-child contact
in accordance with statutory divorce proceedings when two unmarried
persons who have adopted minor child terminate their domestic relationship); see also 15 V.S.A. Section 293(a) (amended version allows parents
and stepparents, whether married or unmarried, to petition family court
regarding parental rights and responsibilities and parent-child contact).
Thus, same-sex couples may participate in child-rearing and have recourse
to the courts in the event a custody or visitation dispute results from the
breakup of a relationship. . . .

Plaintiff scoffs at the notion that various relatives, foster parents, and
even day-care providers could seek visitation through court intervention,
but the cases we have reviewed suggest that the possibilities are virtually
limitless. See In re Hood, 252 Kan. 689, 847 P.2d 1300, 1301 (1993) (day-
care provider claiming right to visitation based on best interest of child and
existence of substantial relationship between herself and child); L. v. G.,

203 N.J.Super. 385, 497 A.2d 215, 219, 222 (Ch.Div.1985) (applying its inherent equitable powers, court concluded that adult siblings have right to visit minor siblings, subject to best interests of minors); Bessette v. Saratoga County Comm'r, 209 A.D.2d 838, 619 N.Y.S.2d 359, 359 (1994) (petition for visitation by former foster parents). Further, as some courts have noted, third parties could abuse the process by seeking visitation to continue an unwanted relationship or otherwise harass the legal parents. See Hood, 847 P.2d at 1304 (danger of parents being harassed by third-party visitation petitions is policy consideration that weighs against expanding classes of persons who may seek visitation). . . .

We recognize that, in this age of the disintegrating nuclear family, there are public-policy considerations that favor allowing third parties claiming a parent-like relationship to seek court-compelled parent-child contact. In our view, however, these considerations are not so clear and compelling that they require us to acknowledge that de facto parents have a legally cognizable right to parent-child contact, thereby allowing the superior court to employ its equitable powers to adjudicate their claims. Given the complex social and practical ramifications of expanding the classes of persons entitled to assert parental rights by seeking custody or visitation, the Legislature is better equipped to deal with the problem. . . .

J.A.L. v. E.P.H.

Superior Court of Pennsylvania, 1996.
453 Pa.Super. 78, 682 A.2d 1314.

PHYLLIS W. BECK, JUDGE:

We are asked to decide whether appellant J.A.L., the former lesbian life partner of appellee E.P.H., has standing to petition for partial custody of the child born to E.P.H. during their relationship. We conclude that the trial court erred in denying standing to J.A.L. . . .

Appellant J.A.L. and appellee E.P.H. entered into a lesbian relationship in 1980 and begin living together as life partners in 1982, purchasing a home together in 1988. From quite early in the relationship, E.P.H. wished to have a child. Following several years of discussion, the parties agreed that E.P.H. would be artificially inseminated to attempt to conceive a child whom the parties would raise together. Together, E.P.H. and J.A.L. selected a sperm donor and made arrangements for a contract between E.P.H. and the donor whereby the donor relinquished his parental rights in any child E.P.H. might bear.

In August 1980, the insemination process began. The inseminations occurred in J.A.L.'s and E.P.H.'s home. For each insemination, the donor would produce the sperm in one room and J.A.L. would receive the sperm and take them to E.P.H. in another room, where J.A.L. would perform the insemination. This procedure was repeated several times each month until E.P.H. became pregnant in October, 1989, then resumed in 1990 after E.P.H. had a miscarriage in December, 1989. In September, 1990, E.P.H.

again became pregnant. During the pregnancy, J.A.L. accompanied E.P.H. to doctor's visits and attended childbirth classes with her. E.P.H. successfully carried the child to term, and J.A.L., as well as two friends of E.P.H., was present at the birth of the child, G.H., in June, 1991. In registering the child's birth, E.P.H. gave J.A.L.'s surname as the child's middle name; E.P.H. subsequently had the child's middle name legally changed.

During E.P.H.'s pregnancy, E.P.H. and J.A.L. consulted with an attorney regarding the status of the child. The attorney prepared drafts of several documents for the parties' consideration. The first document was a Nomination of Guardianship in which E.P.H. named J.A.L. as the guardian of the child in the event of E.P.H.'s death or disability. The document included the following statement:

> This nomination is based on the fact that [J.A.L.] and I jointly made the decision that I should conceive and bear a child that we would then jointly raise. It is our intention that [J.A.L.] will establish from birth a loving and parental relationship with the child. Furthermore, my child will live with this adult from birth and will look to her for guidance, support and affection. It would be detrimental to my child to deprive my child of this established relationship at a time when I am unable to provide the security and care necessary to my child's healthy development.

The second document prepared for the parties was an Authorization for Consent to Medical Treatment of Minor, permitting J.A.L. to consent to medical or dental treatment of the child. The attorney also prepared a Last Will and Testament for each party, providing for the other party and the child. E.P.H.'s will also included a clause appointing J.A.L. as the guardian of the child, stating:

> I have specifically and purposefully named [J.A.L.] as primary guardian of my child as I intend for the bond between my partner, [J.A.L.], and my child to be of primary importance and strength. [J.A.L.] and I jointly decided that I would conceive and bear my child. We intend to raise the child together as a family, It is my belief that the continuation of the parent-child relationship between [J.A.L.] and my child will be essential to my child's well-being, and that it will be in the child's best interests to remain with [J.A.L.].

The final document prepared by the attorney was a co-parenting agreement which set forth the parties' intention to raise the child together, to share the financial responsibility for the child, to make decisions about the child jointly, and for J.A.L. to become a de facto parent to the child. The agreement also provided that in the event of the parties' separation, they would share custody, continuing to make major decisions about the child jointly and splitting the financial responsibility for the child's support.

Shortly before the child's birth, the parties executed the nomination of guardian, the authorization for consent to medical treatment and the wills.

J.A.L. refused to execute the co-parenting agreement, which the attorney advised the parties was not enforceable in Pennsylvania.

After the birth, E.P.H. and J.A.L. and the child lived together in the house owned by E.P.H. and J.A.L. E.P.H. was the primary caretaker to the child, but J.A.L. assisted with all aspects of the care of the baby, particularly during the first few weeks after the birth while E.P.H. recovered from a caesarean section. J.A.L. also cared for the baby alone from time to time when E.P.H. went out. During E.P.H.'s maternity leave, J.A.L. provided the primary financial support for the household, and throughout 1991 she continued to provide the majority of the household's income because E.P.H. initially returned to work only part-time.

In late 1991, serious problems developed in the relationship between E.P.H. and J.A.L., and in the spring of 1992, E.P.H. left the parties' home, taking the child with her and informing J.A.L. that she intended to raise the child as a single parent. For the first year of the separation, by agreement of the parties, J.A.L. took the child for visits twice a week, one on a weekday afternoon and the other for a full day on the weekend. During the second year of the separation, E.P.H. reduced the visits, still allowing one afternoon visit per week, but limiting the full-day weekend visits to once every two weeks. On the days of her visits, J.A.L. would pick up the child, who was then one to two years old, either from day care (for the weekday visits) or E.P.H.'s residence (for the weekend visits) and would return the child in the evening. During the visits, J.A.L. would feed the child, arrange for naps, provide toys and activities, and generally care for the child. Both parties testified that the child enjoyed and looked forward to these visits and felt an attachment to J.A.L. E.P.H. also testified that the child has similar visits and relationships with other adult "special friends."

In April, 1994, E.P.H. advised J.A.L. that she no longer wished to have any contact whatsoever with J.A.L. and that she also wished to end the visits between J.A.L. and the child. E.P.H. testified that she took this action because she felt that J.A.L. was trying to establish a parental relationship with the child and to undermine E.P.H. as parent and that this could be harmful to the child. Although J.A.L. sought to continue seeing the child, the parties were unable to come to any agreement to continue J.A.L.'s visits, and in February, 1995, J.A.L. initiated this action for partial custody. ...

The trial court in this case determined that because J.A.L. was neither a biological nor an adoptive parent of the child, she must be viewed as a "third party" in her attempt to obtain partial custody and thus would have standing to seek custody only if she stood in loco parentis to the child. The court went on to conclude that J.A.L. did not stand in loco parentis to the child because E.P.H. never intended to grant her that status and J.A.L. understood that she was considered only to be a friend, not a parent, of the child. Accordingly, the trial court held that J.A.L. lacked standing to seek partial custody of the child. We hold that the trial court's application of the concept of standing in this custody matter was overly technical and mechanistic and that it was error to preclude J.A.L. from seeking a judicial determination of her claim for partial custody of the child. . . .

In the area of child custody, principles of standing have been applied with particular scrupulousness because they serve a dual purpose: not only to protect the interest of the court system by assuring that actions are litigated by appropriate parties, but also to prevent intrusion into the protected domain of the family by those who are merely strangers, however well-meaning. . . . Thus in custody cases it has been held that an action may be brought only by a person having a "prima facie right to custody."
. . .

Biological parents have a prima facie right to custody, but biological parenthood is not the only source of such a right. Cognizable rights to seek full or partial custody may also arise under statutes such as Chapter 53 of the Domestic Relations Code, 23 Pa.C.S. Sections 5311 et seq. (permitting grandparents and great grandparents to seek visitation or partial custody of their grandchildren or great grandchildren), or by virtue of the parties' conduct, as in cases where a third party who has stood in loco parentis has been recognized as possessing a prima facie right sufficient to grant standing to litigate questions of custody of the child for whom he or she has cared. See, e.g., Rosado v. Diaz, 425 Pa.Super. 155, 624 A.2d 193 (1993); Karner v. McMahon, 433 Pa.Super. 290, 640 A.2d 926 (1994).

It is important to recognize that in this context, the term "prima facie right to custody" means only that the party has a colorable claim to custody of the child. The existence of such a colorable claim to custody grants standing only. In other words, it allows the party to maintain an action to seek vindication of his or her claimed rights. A finding of prima facie right sufficient to establish standing does not affect that party's evidentiary burden: in order to be granted full or partial custody, he or she must still establish that such would be in the best interest of the child under the standards applicable to third parties. . . .

The in loco parentis basis for standing recognizes that the need to guard the family from intrusions by third parties and to protect the rights of the natural parent must be tempered by the paramount need to protect the child's best interest. Thus, while it is presumed that a child's best interest is served by maintaining the family's privacy and autonomy, that presumption must give way where the child has established strong psychological bonds with a person who, although not a biological parent, has lived with the child and provided care, nurture, and affection, assuming in the child's eye a statute like that of a parent. Where such a relationship is shown, our courts recognize that the child's best interest requires that the third party be granted standing so as to have the opportunity to litigate fully the issue of whether that relationship should be maintained even over a natural parent's objections.

Although the requirement of in loco parentis status for third parties seeking child custody rights is often stated as though it were a rigid rule, it is important to view the standard in light of the purpose of standing principles generally: to ensure that actions are brought only by those with a genuine, substantial interest. When so viewed, it is apparent that the showing necessary to establish in loco parentis status must in fact be flexible and dependent upon the particular facts of the case. Thus, while unrelated third parties are only rarely found to stand in loco parentis, step-parents who by living in a family setting wit the child of a spouse have developed a parent-like relationship with the child, have often been assumed without discussion to have standing to seek a continued relationship with the child upon the termination of the relationship between the step-parents. . . .

In today's society, where increased mobility, changes in social mores and increased individual freedom have created a wide spectrum of arrangements filling the role of the traditional nuclear family, flexibility in the application of standing principles is required in order to adapt those principles to the interests of each particular child. We do not suggest abandonment of the rule that a petitioner for custody who is not biologically related to the child in question must prove that a parent-like relationship has been forged through the parties' conduct. However, we hold that the fact that the petitioner lived with the child and the natural parent in a family setting, whether a traditional family or a nontraditional one, and developed a relationship with the child as a result of the participation and acquiescence of the natural parent must be an important factor in determining whether the petitioner has standing. . . .

We hold that the evidence of record in this matter, particularly the evidence that J.A.L. and the child were co-members of a nontraditional family, is sufficient to establish that J.A.L. stood in loco parentis to the child and therefore has standing to seek partial custody. Accordingly, we remand for a full custody hearing to determine whether partial custody by J.A.L. is in the child's best interest. . . .

In Re the Custody of H.S.H.-K.

Supreme Court of Wisconsin, 1995.
193 Wis.2d 649, 533 N.W.2d 419.

SHIRLEY S. ABRAHAMSON, JUSTICE.

Sandra Lynne Holtzman appeals from an order of the circuit court for Dane County, George A.W. Northrup, circuit judge, dismissing her petition seeking custody of or visitation rights to H.S., the biological child of Elsbeth Knott. . . .

Two issues of law are presented in this case. The first issue is whether Holtzman's assertions of Knott's parental unfitness and inability to care for the child, or of compelling circumstances requiring a change of custody, are sufficient to proceed on a petition for custody under sec. 767.24(3), Stats. 1991–92. The second issue is whether Holtzman may seek visitation rights to the child.

We agree with the circuit court that Holtzman has not raised a triable issue regarding Knott's fitness or ability to parent her child and has not shown compelling circumstances requiring a change of custody. Therefore the circuit court properly dismissed the custody action commenced under sec. 767.24(3), Stats. 1991–92.

For the reasons set forth, we conclude that the ch. 767 visitation statute, sec. 767.245, Stats. 1991–92, does not apply to Holtzman's petition for visitation rights to Knott's biological child. However, we further conclude that the legislature did not intend that sec. 767.245 be the exclusive means of obtaining court-ordered visitation, or that it supplant or preempt the courts' long recognized equitable power to protect the best interest of the child by ordering visitation under circumstances not included in the statute. Finally, mindful of preserving a biological or adoptive parent's constitutionally protected interests and the best interest of a child, we conclude that a circuit court may determine whether visitation is in a child's best interest if the petitioner first proves that he or she has a parent-like relationship with the child and that a significant triggering event justifies state intervention in the child's relationship with a biological or adoptive parent. To meet these two requirements, the petitioner must prove the component elements of each one.

To demonstrate the existence of the petitioner's parent-like relationship with the child, the petitioner must prove four elements: (1) that the biological or adoptive parent consented to, and fostered, the petitioner's formation and establishment of a parent-like relationship with the child; (2) that the petitioner and the child lived together in the same household; (3) that the petitioner assumed obligations of parenthood by taking significant responsibility for the child's care, education and development, including contributing towards the child's support, without expectation of financial compensation; and (4) that the petitioner has been in a parental role for a length of time sufficient to have established with the child a bonded, dependent relationship parental in nature.

To establish a significant triggering event justifying state intervention in the child's relationship with a biological or adoptive parent, the petitioner must prove that this parent has interfered substantially with the petitioner's parent-like relationship with the child, and that the petitioner sought court ordered visitation within a reasonable time after the parent's interference.

The petitioner must prove all these elements before a circuit court may consider whether visitation is in the best interest of the child. The proceedings must focus on the child. When a non-traditional adult relationship is dissolving, the child is as likely to become a victim of turmoil and adult hostility as is a child subject to the dissolution of a marriage. Such a child needs and deserves the protection of the courts as much as a child of a dissolving traditional relationship. . . .

NOTES AND QUESTIONS

1. **Legal Theories**. In a comprehensive article entitled *This Child Does Have Two Mothers: Redefining Parenthood to Meet the Needs of Children in*

Lesbian–Mother and Other Nontraditional Families, 78 Geo. L. J. 459 (1990), Professor Nancy Polikoff identified several legal doctrines to assist the ex-partner of a biological parent who seeks custody or visitation with a child with whom the adult previously lived. "Equitable estoppel" arguments allow a court to permit a legally unrecognized parent to maintain ongoing parent-child relationships despite the lack of legal tie. Child support, as well as shared custody or visitation, could ensue. *Id.*, at 491–502. Alternatively, "in loco parentis" arguments allow courts to recognize ongoing relationships between a child and a person who has functioned as a parent. *Id.*, at 502–508. In addition, arguments about standing, equitable adoption, or best interests of the child may be framed to urge judicial consideration of unrelated adult's claims.

2. **Statutory reform.** Statutory recognition of second-parent adoption and other nontraditional families is increasing, and ensures greater predictability than ad hoc judicial treatment. *See, e.g.*, Ore. Rev. Stat. 109.119 (Supp. 1989)(recognizing legal rights of adult in an established "child-parent relationship.") Yet the chances for legislative reform are small in many states due to both the limited political clout of supporters and the potentially strong opposition to any alterations of the legal status of traditional families. Even if there is political support, crafting an administra-ble statute poses challenges. If you were drafting a statute, what language would you use? Should it cover only those individuals who were in intimate relationships with a child's parent and cohabited with the parent and child, or roommates as well? Romantic partners who did not cohabit? Can you find language that would not cover nannies or other child-care providers?

VII. THE "BAD MOTHER": REMOVAL OF CHILDREN AND TERMINATION OF PARENTAL RIGHTS

Some parents—including some mothers—seriously injure their children, endanger them, and even kill them. Curbing the general legal protection for family privacy and parental rights, state departments of child protection implement statutes forbidding child abuse and neglect. How do agencies exercise their power to remove children from homes that endanger them or to seek to terminate the rights of parents alleged to be abusive or neglectful? Many observers claim that the agencies too often act with prejudices about poor parents who are members of racial or ethnic minorities; others claim that the agencies fail to offer sufficient protection for children in precisely those kinds of families. It could well be that both problems co-exist in the same state.

A growing number of scholars explore the cultural depictions and constructions of "bad mothers" that are then used to discipline women in many circumstances. *See, e.g.*, Martha Albertson Fineman, The Neutered Mother, The Sexual Family, and Other Twentieth Century Tragedies (1995); Marie Ashe, *The "Bad Mother" in Law and Literature: A Problem of Representation*, 43 Hastings L.J. 1017 (1992); Marie Ashe, *"Bad Mothers," "Good Lawyers," and "Legal Ethics,"* 81 Geo. L.J. 2533 (1993); Bernadine Dohrn, *Bad Mothers, Good Mothers, and the State: Children on the Margins*, 2 U. Chi. L. Sch. Roundtable 1 (1995); Carol Sanger, *Separating from Children*, 96 Colum. L. Rev. 375 (1996).

In this context, consider three specific risks of unfair gender bias. First, women may be held to higher standards of care than men in assessments of abusive or neglectful parent. Second, women who are themselves experiencing violence at the hands of husbands or boyfriends may be found to be inadequate parents because they fail to protect their children from witnessing or experiencing violence at the hands of the abusive male. Third, lawyers working for the state and even lawyers who defend women facing child abuse or neglect charges may appeal to and fuel negative images of mothers, or of particular kinds of mothers. How can these risks be addressed without continuing jeopardy to children's well-being? The question thus is not only what should be the result in a case such as the one that follows, but also what kind of arguments and language should the lawyers, social workers, and judges use to evaluate the children's needs and interests?

Adoption of Kimberly

Supreme Judicial Court of Massachusetts, 1993.
414 Mass. 526, 609 N.E.2d 73.

SANDRA L. LYNCH, JUSTICE.

The mother of two minor children appeals from judgments of the Probate and Family Court, dispensing with the need for her consent to the adoption of her daughters, Kimberly and Joyce, pursuant to G.L. c. 210, Section 3 (1990 ed.). She argues that (1) the judge's findings regarding current parental unfitness and the best interests of the children were not supported by clear and convincing evidence; (2) the failure of the Department of Social Services (department) to provide timely and appropriate services to prevent the dissolution of the family requires reversal of the judge's decision to terminate parental rights; and (3) certain evidentiary rulings constituted reversible error. We transferred the case here on our own motion, and now affirm.

The children at issue, Kimberly and Joyce, have the same natural mother but different fathers. The mother also has another child, Lucy, by the father of Joyce (to whom we shall refer as "Bob"). Since November 1, 1988, Kimberly and Joyce have lived with Kimberly's paternal grandparents, who are the prospective adoptive parents. On January 24, 1989, a District Court judge adjudicated Kimberly and Joyce in need of care and protection pursuant to a petition filed by the department. See G.L. c. 119, Section 24 (1990 ed.). On October 5, 1989, the department filed the instant petitions which, while not consolidated, were heard together. The children's natural fathers did not contest the petitions.

After a three-day trial, the judge found that both girls had been victims of sexual and emotional abuse and neglect and allowed the department's petitions. The judge's order allowed the children to be adopted by the grandparents and granted the mother visitation rights subject to certain conditions.

The mother argues that the evidence relied on by the judge in concluding that she was currently unfit to parent the children was stale and, therefore, was not clear and convincing. She admits that the record supports the judge's findings as to her life-style up to the time that the children were removed from her care, but claims that she has since improved and currently has the ability to assume parental responsibility for the children. The mother also argues that the judge's conclusion that the best interests of the children are served by terminating parental rights is also not supported by clear and convincing evidence. Since parental fitness and the best interests of the child are interrelated inquiries, we address both arguments together. . . .

In order to remove children permanently from a natural parent and to dispense with parental consent to adoption under G.L. c. 210, Section 3, the judge must find, by clear and convincing evidence, that the parent is currently unfit to further the welfare and best interests of the child. . . . However, a judge can "rely upon prior patterns of ongoing, repeated, serious parental neglect, abuse, and misconduct in determining current unfitness." . . . The judge's findings must be left undisturbed absent a showing that they are clearly erroneous. . . .

Many of the judge's findings concerned the mother's life-style prior to when Kimberly and Joyce were removed from her care in 1988. The judge also made findings that the mother may have been improving her ability to care for the children. However, the judge concluded that the mother was unfit to parent her children specifically due to "her continuing and problematic relationship with [Bob, the father of Joyce and Lucy]." The judge found that "[b]oth girls [Kimberly and Joyce] were sexually abused by [Bob] by direct and inappropriate physical contact. This is clear from the Court's own observations of [Kimberly], as well as from the testimony and exhibits . . . One of the many results of this abuse is that both girls are in fear of being in [Bob's] presence, alone or with others, and even seeing possessions associated with [Bob] cause them great anxiety." On the testimony of the children's therapist, the judge also found that, "[u]nder no circumstances should [Joyce and Kimberly] be in the presence of [Bob], or in a place where he may leave his clothing or personal effects." Further, while the judge was unable to find that the mother lived with Bob at the time of the trial, he did find that Bob did not have a permanent address, worked near the mother's residence, visited her residence daily to visit his child Lucy, left many possessions there, and frequently showered, changed clothes, and ate there. In addition, on the basis of a psychological assessment, the judge found that the mother "placed her own needs to continue involvement with [Bob] before the needs of her children," that "the mother was very slow to acknowledge and deal with the impact of the sexual abuse," and that "[t]he mother has a history of having failed to protect these two minor children from abuse and neglect and in fact has contributed to some of what they have suffered." Thus, the judge concluded, "[g]iven that on-going contact and relationship, there is no way that the girls could be returned to the mother's care as they would be continually at risk of contact with [Bob]."

In regard to the children, the judge found that Kimberly "needs consistently stable care with a regular routine, warm, nurturing care where she feels loved and safe with no threat of danger." As to Joyce, the judge found that her "parenting needs are the same of those of [Kimberly] plus she needs a little more understanding for her regression: she needs tolerance and patience." The judge also found that both girls were suffering from posttraumatic stress disorder as a result of the sexual abuse, but that their behavior had improved since living with the grandparents. Thus, the judge concluded that the department's proposed plans for the children, which called for the grandparents to adopt the children, were in the best interests of the children. The judge granted the mother visitation rights, but stated that the children should not be exposed in any way to Bob or his effects, and that the visits should be at the discretion of the grandparents. Because of the evidence of Bob's abuse, the mother's continuing relationship with Bob, and the children's improvement since living with the grandparents, the judge's findings and disposition of these cases were not clearly erroneous.

The mother next contends that the judge's finding that the children "were sexually abused by [Bob] by direct and inappropriate physical contact" was not supported by clear and convincing evidence. She also argues that the finding is clearly erroneous because it conflicts with a finding adopted by the judge that "[Bob] sexually abused [Kimberly] and may have also sexually abused [Joyce]"

We do not reach the mother's argument that the evidence of abuse must be shown by clear and convincing evidence because the ample evidence of abuse clearly met that standard. The mother testified that she believed Bob had abused both of her daughters. One expert testified that she had no question the sexual abuse had occurred. In a report admitted in evidence, another expert who evaluated the children stated that "these two girls give a very definite history of inappropriate sexual activity by [Bob]. This is given against a backdrop that is well defined by everyone as high risk given the substance abuse that is present in the home and the presence of x-rated movies." The grandmother testified that Joyce and Kimberly demonstrated inappropriate sexual activity at home with each other and with dolls. Another witness testified that the children demonstrated similar activity in therapy. This evidence provides a clear and convincing basis for the judge's finding that both girls were abused. . . .

The mother next contends that the department failed to perform its duty to provide timely and appropriate services to prevent the dissolution of this family and, thus, that we should reverse the judge's decision. See G.L. c. 119, Section 1 (1990 ed.); 110 Code Mass.Regs. Section 1.01 (1986). We disagree. While there were findings that indicated one department social worker provided "marginal" services for a five-month period in 1990, the judge also found that those deficiencies were subsequently rectified by a department case manager who reestablished counseling for the mother and visitation with the children. In addition, the findings indicate that the department properly did not return the children to the mother after the care and protection proceeding because she continued her relationship with the man who sexually abused her children. Thus, we hold that the department's treatment of the family was not "so arbitrary and irrational as to warrant a dismissal." Petition of the Dep't. of Pub. Welfare to Dispense with Consent to Adoption, 376 Mass. 252, 269, 381 N.E.2d 565 (1978). ...

NOTES AND QUESTIONS

1. **The Passive Mother of Victimized Children.** The unfitness findings against the mother of Kimberly and Joyce include her failure to protect the girls against sexual abuse by Bob. How exactly should she have protected them, and at what risk to herself? Can her failure to protect her children be distinguished from her failure to acknowledge that they were being harmed by her lover—and are both failures blameworthy? The trial court also found that she put her own needs to continue her involvement with Bob ahead of her children's protection. Is this an independent ground of unfitness in the view of the reviewing court? Should it be?

2. **The Passive Mother Who Is Herself Abused.** Should the legal evaluation change if the mother is herself suffering abuse at the hand of the adult who is abusing her children? Some advocates argue that such a woman may be subject to a psychological paralysis because she is battered; others argue that this very line of defense would enchain the woman in low expectations and passivity rather than recognize and reward efforts at resistance by this or other women. Should a woman risk losing her children because she was unable to guard against child abuse? Or should the state be obliged to protect both mother and children from contact with the abusive father? If the mother did not leave with the child after the first instance of abuse by the father or boyfriend, should that constitute neglect or child endangerment jeopardizing her custody? What if the only abuse was directed at her—and she was unable to shield the children from witnessing the violence she experienced? What if an abused mother in turn abuses the children? Should she lose custody and parental rights? Should she be criminally prosecuted or excused?

3. **Cultural Images of Mothers.** Professor Kristian Miccio argues that when states charge mothers with abuse for failing to protect or stop abuse to themselves, the law codifies beliefs that punish mothers and fail to protect children from abusive fathers and boyfriends. Kristian Miccio, *In the Name of Mothers and Children: Deconstructing the Myth of Passive Battered Mother and the 'Protected Child' in Child Neglect Proceedings*, 58 Alb. L. Rev. 1087 (1995). She argues that mothers are commonly viewed as either selfless and loving or else selfish and cruel; therefore, a mother who fails to be selfless may be found to be neglectful or a failure as a parent.

4. **Termination of Parental Rights.** The ultimate state response to child neglect and abuse is to terminate parental rights. Ideally, this would

free the child for adoption by other adults; in practice, especially with older children, the result is to place or leave the child in foster care with adults who may, or may not, be better parents than the biological parents. In a series of cases, the Supreme Court has developed procedural due process protections for parents at risk of termination of parental rights. See Lassiter v. Department of Social Services of Durham County, 452 U.S. 18, 101 S.Ct. 2153, 68 L.Ed.2d 640 (1981)(directing trial courts to engage in case-by-case analysis of need for counsel for indigent defendants in parental rights termination cases); Santosky v. Kramer, 455 U.S. 745, 102 S.Ct. 1388, 71 L.Ed.2d 599 (1982)(requiring "clear and convincing" proof before termination of parental rights); M.L.B. v. S.L.J., 519 U.S. 102, 117 S.Ct. 555, 136 L.Ed.2d 473 (1996)(due process requires waiver of record preparation fees where record is required prior to appeal from termination of parental rights). Is there, or should there be, a gender discrimination dimension to the development of procedural protections in parental rights termination cases? Are women at greater risk than men of indigency impairing their ability to defend their parental rights or greater risk of facing charges (warranted and unwarranted) of bad parenting?

5. **Better Protecting Children**. Four experts recently debated how society could better protect children from abuse and neglect. Douglas Besharov, a scholar at the American Enterprise Institute for Public Policy Research and professor at the University of Maryland, emphasized the need to improve the process for reporting suspected problems. One step would change the laws requiring reporting to specify the parental behaviors or conditions that are linked to severe and demonstrable harms to children. He also urged recognition that parental crack addiction cannot be cured and therefore children who remain in the home of crack-using parents need ongoing supervisory visits and protection. In addition, because "[m]ost drug-addicted women would be better off if they had greater control over their own fertility," Besharov argued for including family planning as part of child welfare services. Douglas Besharov, Commentary 1, in *Four Commentaries: How We Can Better Protect Children From Abuse and Neglect*, 8 The Future of Children 120, 123 (Spring 1998) [hereinafter cited as *Protect Children*].

Marcia Robinson Lowry, heads Children's Rights, Inc., a national organization working to reform state and county child welfare systems through class-action lawsuits. She identified as a central problem the simplistic debate over whether to try to preserve families or instead to remove children quickly and permanently from dangerous or risky home situations. Instead, the problem is the failure of public agencies to develop the capacity to make individualized decisions about the proper course of action for particular children and families. The proper response, she argued, would be the kind of public scrutiny and reform of local child welfare systems that a class action lawsuit can trigger. Marcia Robinson Lowry, Commentary 2, in *Protect Children*, at 122, 125.

Leroy Pelton, director of the School of Social Work at University of Nevada, criticized child welfare advocates for demonizing the poor and for expanding coercive interventions in the name of benevolently protecting children. Instead, he pressed for greatly narrowing the definitions of abuse and neglect. Also, society should sever the functions of prevention and support—to be fulfilled by child welfare agencies—from the functions of investigation and foster care—to be fulfilled by law enforcement and the civil court system. Leroy H. Pelton, Commentary 3, in *Protect Children*, at 126, 128.

Michael Weber, president of a direct-service agency and former head of the Hennepin County, Minnesota social services program, urged shifting from crisis-orientation to prevention and early intervention. The chief route he recommended uses partnerships to connect child protective systems with a variety of ongoing community supports for families and children. He also recommended sharply distinguishing those parents who pose no imminent threat to the child's safety and instead need help in overcoming social isolation and poor parenting practices from those situations calling for expedited termination of parental rights. Michael W. Weber, Commentary 4 in *Protect Children*, at 129, 131–132.

Which of these views is most persuasive to you, and why? Which is most likely to help both women and children?

5. **The Reality of Bad Mothers.** In the effort to combat unfair prejudices against women or particular women who risk losing their children due to state claims of child protection, how can feminists avoid denying the realities of child abuse, often at the hands of women? What should be the feminist approach to child abuse?

Marie Ashe & Naomi R. Cahn, Child Abuse: A Problem for Feminist Theory

2 Tex. J. Women & L. 75 (1993).

A broad professional and popular awareness of the disturbing and not uncommon reality of child abuse has developed during the past two decades. Responses in legislation and the legal process reflect this awareness. Prosecution of child abuse has greatly accelerated; children's accounts of sexual abuse and other forms of abuse are now recognized as deserving credence; and procedural accommodations have been instituted in many jurisdictions to aid child victims in telling their stories. Increased awareness of child abuse has been accompanied by popular reactions of outrage and horror and by widespread condemnation of its perpetrators.

The accounts of child abuse delivered through popular media and various types of professional literature have tended to tell the story of child abuse with a focus on the experience of child victims and have devoted only very limited attention to the realities and experiences of perpetrators of such abuse. While parents, particularly mothers, are regularly brought under the jurisdiction of trial courts in child dependency proceedings, pursuant to which children are removed temporarily or permanently from their custody, there is a surprising dearth of literature about the complexities of such parents. The developing contemporary understanding of child abuse within and without the legal system, to the degree that it focuses on perpetrators of abuse, tends to reduce to a story of "bad mothers."

This Article attempts to expand the scope of discussion regarding the "bad mother" and suggests ways in which a fuller dialogue may take place. ...We argue that feminist theory has ... largely ignored "bad mothers" and their implications for child abuse. Finally, we urge the commitment of feminist theory to intensive consideration of the realities of the "bad mother."

bell hooks expresses this need for theory when she writes of theory as a "liberatory practice." hooks has identified theory as having its roots in pain and desperation and as offering a "location for healing." In this characterization, hooks echoes the notion of French feminist Julia Kristeva, who has suggested that every question is rooted in pain. The need for theory concerning the "bad mother" is a need that unquestionably arises out of pain—pain that both supports and is supported by inquietude or even horror. We intend this Article to be a preliminary venture in which we struggle to begin to come to terms with the common experience of pain surrounding "bad mothering" and the complex realities of the "bad mother." ...

The "Bad Mother" in Legal Proceedings

This section briefly explores the prosecution of mothers for child abuse and neglect, focusing on cases in which the mother has been battered as well. Another definition of "bad mothers" is constructed by the state proceedings that regulate them.

In the District of Columbia, a city attorney represented a battered woman who was seeking an emergency protection order against her husband to prevent further violence. The day before the court hearing, her sworn testimony asserted that her husband had:

> punched her in the head and face and body, bruising her throat. He then hit her in the back with a chair, smashed her head into some paintings on the wall, stomped on her head with his foot, and swung at her with the legs from a table he had just broken. He told her that wherever she was, he would hunt her down and kill her.... The Petitioner is very afraid and the children are visibly upset ...

> Respondent has a history of hitting and threatening the petitioner.... On her birthday last year he beat her so bad [sic] she could not walk.

After waiting in a large public room for several hours to see an attorney, and then waiting several more hours in the courthouse to see the judge, the Petitioner began arguing with her young children. The children had been making a lot of noise and fighting with each other while they waited. Their mother took off her shoe and threatened to hit one of the children; the child became quiet, and the mother put her shoe back on. The mother then went in to see the judge and was granted an emergency protection order. Her lawyer, whose office also represents the city in child abuse prosecutions, reprimanded the mother and subsequently reported her to the local child abuse authorities on the basis of his observation of her threatening the child.

This sequence of events culminating in the lawyer's report of child abuse instances the adult tendency to produce a story purportedly from the perspective of the child-victim. It clearly does not include a consideration of the story that the mother might tell. Nor does it include what the child's experience of being removed from the family might be. It might be assumed that the function of the child protective services caseworkers is to obtain a fuller story through a process of investigation. It has been the authors' experience, however, that even when a somewhat contextualized story begins to be developed by investigating social workers, that story tends not to include the reality of the risks associated with transferring children from maternal care to foster care. Legal commentary has begun to develop this part of the story. Indeed, many recent lawsuits against state agencies responsible for foster placements have alleged inadequate care and conditions, such that children who are removed may be placed in a situation more abusive than their family homes.

All states and the District of Columbia have various methods of dealing with parents who abuse or neglect their children, including prosecution for the underlying criminal offense, and/or civil actions under abuse and neglect statutes. The civil abuse and neglect procedure is generally triggered by a report to child abuse authorities. When such a report has been made, the state can generally remove the child from the home without a hearing, albeit only for a few days. The state must then establish that it has met the statutory criteria for intervention; upon an adjudication that the state has met its burden of proof, the court can decide upon an appropriate disposition. The focus of the "child protector" system is, of course, to ensure that children are safe; quite often, this seems to result in removal of the child from her family at the earliest legally permissible opportunity.

The definition of "bad mothering" applied in prosecution of child abuse and neglect is a broad one, and few explicit standards curb the discretion of prosecutors. For example, in the District of Columbia, an abused child is defined as "a child whose parent, guardian, or custodian inflicts or fails to make reasonable efforts to prevent the infliction of physical or mental injury upon the child, including excessive corporal punishment, an act of sexual abuse, molestation, or exploitation, or an injury that results from exposure to drug-related activity in the child's home environment."

Such a broad standard allows and requires prosecutors to define appropriate parental behavior according to their discretion. As a result, decisions concerning prosecutions will tend to reflect race, class, and gender biases of prosecutors who have tended to be white, middle-class, and male. Mothering is taken out of its context in abuse prosecution and is judged by a judiciary that assumes middle-class, sexist, and racist norms. Mothers— across classes and cultures—are expected to perform in ways that satisfy those norms.

Criticism of prosecutorial and judicial discretion does not resolve the problem of child abuse in legal and moral terms. It does not by itself offer guidance concerning the distinctions of blameworthiness that might properly be made among parents who abuse their children. It does not answer the question whether the civil or criminal law should, for example, treat battered women who abuse their children differently from men who abuse their children. Various commentators have begun to struggle with these questions. Consider the thoughts of Albert Alschuler:

> Imagine that a brutal man (call him Joel Steinberg) and a lover whom he has physically abused for years (call her Hedda Nussbaum) have participated in the same act of child abuse. Imagine further that the battered woman participant has no defense of insanity or duress but that she comes close. The seriousness of the crime (judged in the abstract) is the same for both offenders. Still, I think that their "dessert" differs greatly and that imposing identical sentences would offend ordinary concepts of "proportionality."

The question that Alschular does not address is why he would hold the woman less culpable than the man.

Not everyone subscribes to the same "ordinary concepts" as Alschuler. Indeed, his opinions differ from those of many judges and social service workers who, studies indicate, are likely to blame mothers for anything that happens to their children. This difference appears to be caused by conflicting images of women: On one hand it seems to be proposed by commentators such as Alschuler that because they are victims of male patriarchy, battered women should not be blamed for hurting their children when they themselves are being battered; on the other hand, many workers in the field apparently assume that because mothers are supposed to be nurturing, their culpability exceeds that of other adults when they are abusive.

Martha Minow has proposed a partial answer to this dilemma of determining responsibility and culpability. Minow has suggested that the context of "bad mothers," which includes complex family dynamics and a society unresponsive to domestic violence, is perhaps to blame for family violence. This proposition provides a context for understanding the mother's actions: why she did not leave the abusive situation; why she did not—or could not—prevent her partner from abusing a child; and why she herself may have abused her child. This interpretation allows us to move beyond mere blaming of the mother herself and permits our focusing on her embeddedness within systems that foster violence. While it does not entirely resolve the issue of how to understand the "bad mother" as moral agent, it reminds us of the need for examination of context, an approach to which much feminist theory has reliably directed attention. . . .

It is our belief that most feminist writers who have attended to the reality of child abuse perpetrated by mothers have minimized the extent of such abuse, ignored its pervasiveness, or attempted to define it away. As we have already suggested, it is not surprising that feminist theorists would attempt such simplified resolutions for political and intellectual reasons. It is also not surprising that feminist theories have only now begun to acknowledge and struggle with the reality of child abuse committed by mothers.

To the degree that liberal, radical, and cultural feminism have all expressed a high valuation of context, each has much to contribute to a new direction in feminist theory more fully appreciative of the realities of "bad mothers." In so-called "failure to protect" situations, for example, contextualized examination can often disclose fairly readily the reasons why a mother may not have intervened to prevent abuse of a child by her boyfriend or husband. Such an examination may disclose, for example, that the mother was being abused herself; that she feared further abuse; that she had a history of prior unsuccessful attempts at intervention; or that she did not fully understand what was occurring. Some feminists have begun the work of examining the contexts within which mothers or pregnant women fail to protect.

The seemingly more difficult challenge to feminist theory presented by mothers who actively abuse their children is one that feminist theory must undertake for both theoretical and practical reasons. Practically, it must be recognized that the sheer pervasiveness of child abuse by mothers absolutely demand some exploration and discussion. It is impossible for feminism to continue to ignore the numbers of women who are abusive to their children. They appear too frequently for us to label them as aberrational or for us to dismiss them as non-representative of women. Many lawyers have represented these women and have had to struggle with feelings of frustration, horror, or denial outside any framework of legal theory that assists either the exploration of these women's experiences or exploration of the lawyers' experiences in representing them.

The theoretical justification for feminism's encountering "bad mothers" relates to the feminist project of reconstructing images of women. Feminism is limited to the degree that it fails to give some account of aspects of women that seem ugly or undesirable. As many feminists have argued, the meaning of woman is not unitary; not only does it go beyond white, middle-class, heterosexual women, it also includes "bad mothers." In its attempt to give an account of alternative women's realities, feminist theory must explore the different forms that those realities take. If feminist theory is "outsider" criticism, "bad mothers" are "outsiders" to feminist theory. A feminism that excludes or reduces any woman is clearly inadequate. What we are urging is that feminism attempt to include these outsiders, and that it do so by attending to and developing the kind of narrative expressions that many writers have seen as most helpful to "outsiders."

Our overview of the image of "bad mother" in literature, and in the stories told by the social sciences, the legal culture, the popular culture, and feminist theory in general, discloses only the barest outlines of a counter-narrative detailing the contextual realities of "bad mothers." The fuller development of new narratives will require the commitment of all story-tellers to persistent inquiry and to persistent self-examination. It will require the willingness of all story-tellers to recognize the partiality of every account, and the willingness of listeners and speakers to raise the political and intellectual questions: "Who is speaking?" and "What is the basis of the speaker's claim to knowledge?" Addressing those questions can open up the possibility of new formulations. For example, social scientists, judges, and lawyers should recognize that the realities of the lives purportedly described or defined by social science always exceed the legal categories into which they are forced. Thus, this recognition should support a shift away from the uncritical reliance of courts on the expert stories about women and their children typical in custody proceedings. Raising the question "Who is speaking?" might similarly operate to expose the class, racial, gender, and other biases that often enjoy free play in the adjudication of child abuse matters. Similarly, a recognition of the erasures accomplished by abstraction in psychological theory could open up the possibility of more direct, more contextualized, and more persuasive storytelling about women. . . .

. . . [The rarity of such stories] demonstrates something that legal advocates for "bad mothers" often have occasion to note, namely, that such women are rarely able to speak effectively for themselves and of themselves, at least within the legal system. We mean not only that such women experience the violence of having to reshape the realities of their experiences to accommodate a legal discourse that demands narrowing and erasure. We mean, beyond that, that they are as constrained as are their judges and prosecutors by the ambivalences that underlie and give rise to binarisms of defining "good" and "bad" motherhood. Thus, it has been our experience that women alleged to have abused or neglected their children are typically unable to self-define except by directly denying what has been alleged, by asserting its opposite. They often seem to see no alternative to reciting counterclaims: "I'm a good mother!" or "I would never hurt my child!" And these counterclaims may be no more meaningful than the original claim of "badness."

The limited ability of "bad mothers" to speak for and about themselves means that the task of representing and interpreting bad mothers will necessarily be a collaborative project. It will be one in which such women will participate in conjunction with people differently situated and, therefore, more able to begin an expansion of the relevant emotional and moral discourse. The new representations will need to examine more fully the mothers' agency, complicity, and victimization. . . .

A gap exists between the experiences of oppressed people and the representation of those experiences by those who purport to understand them and to advocate on their behalf. It behooves us to be mindful of that reality as we struggle to re-present both motherhood and childhood. It is essential that writers interpreting "bad mothers" be willing to recognize the limitations of our own perspectives. At the same time, feminist writers must recognize that even if the representation of motherhood in some absolute sense exceeds our human limitations, that re-presentational task nonetheless presents itself as perhaps our most compelling obligation.

E.   DOMESTIC VIOLENCE

INTRODUCTION

Because the legal response to domestic violence is strongly affected by its site in family life, and because domestic violence is one of the most egregious issues affecting women's bodies, this section constitutes a bridge between this chapter on women and the family and the final chapter on women and their bodies. The readings address five kinds of legal responses: state court civil protection orders and the statutes authorizing them; criminal prosecutions; federal civil rights legislation treating violence against women as a violation of a civil right; the development of a battered woman's defense for women who injure or kill their abusers or find themselves unable to protect children from abuse; and the emergence of tort remedies in civil actions against batterers.

The section begins with an excerpt from *Heroes of Their Own Lives*, by historian Linda Gordon. In the analysis of domestic abuse based on an examination of Boston social welfare agency records, Gordon argues that domestic violence is not a new phenomenon, and that its occurrence over time cannot be attributed to any single cause, such as alcoholism, ethnic culture, or poverty. In addition to providing a detailed description of domestic abuse in which to situate legal responses to it, this reading implicitly questions whether a dispute-focused legal strategy constitutes a feasible model for preventing domestic violence.

To question a dispute-focused model is not to favor mediation. The use of mediation to treat domestic violence is typically no less focused on particular disputes than is litigation. *See* generally Lisa G. Lerman, *Mediation of Wife Abuse Cases: The Adverse Impact of Informal Dispute Resolution on Women*, 7 Harv. Women's L.J. 57 (1984). According to Gordon, dispute-focused strategies are inferior to a legal strategy which would address simultaneously the long-standing economic, cultural, and psychosexual factors that affect a batterer's use of force against a family member. Equally important are the economic, cultural, and psychological factors affecting the victim's response. Kimberlé Crenshaw's article addresses these contextual issues specifically in relation to minority racial and ethnic experiences in the United States.

The account of family violence should not always be frozen in a stark division between abuser and victim. The abuser often becomes contrite and tender toward the victim, or the victim exhibits compassion or concern for the abuser. Then the complexity of intimacy and violence may make it appealing to defer to an old legal distinction between the public and private realms. Bewildered, repulsed, or irritated by the confusion in the situation before them, police and judges may discount a victim's complaint or give an abuser another chance. A sense that the state should not rush in to negotiate family affairs may relieve the representatives of the state of any doubts about their decision to refrain from protecting the victim. Yet nonintervention would function as public support for the domestic partner with superior physical power, who, in heterosexual unions, usually is the male.

The failure to deter domestic abuse sometimes results in a victim injuring or murdering her batterer. Readings in the section address the development and critique of the battered woman's syndrome, developed as a defense for such victims. In addition to addressing the effectiveness of legal responses to domestic violence, this section is also meant to raise questions regarding competing views of its underlying causes. How, if at all, does legal treatment of domestic violence contribute to its incidence and character?

I. BATTERING IN SOCIAL CONTEXT

Linda Gordon, Heroes of Their Own Lives

From L. Gordon, Heroes of Their Own Lives: The Politics and History of Family Violence, (NY: Viking, 1988).

Introduction

In the past twenty-five years, family violence has appeared as a substantial social problem in the United States. Starting with a wave of concern about child abuse in the 1960s, the concern widened to include wife-beating, incest (the sexual abuse of children in the family), and marital rape, as the women's liberation movement of the 1970s drew those crimes to public attention. The actual extent of family violence is controversial; estimates of child abuse vary, for example, from 50,000 to 1.5 million cases a year in the United States. Whatever the real figure, the general awareness of the problem has increased substantially.

For most of these two and a half decades, I was not a family-violence scholar. My responses were probably typical: First, I wondered how anyone could be so bestial as to beat or mutilate their children (beating and mutilation were at first the dominant media representations of child abuse); then, as I gathered how widespread the problem was, I wondered that so many could have so little self-control; then, as I began to meet former victims and perpetrators, I began to suspect that the boundary separating me from those experiences was by no means invulnerable. Finally, the issue provoked my historian's curiosity. I noticed that family violence had had virtually no history; that most who discussed it—experts, journalists, friends—assumed they were discussing a new problem. As my preliminary forays into libraries revealed that it was an old problem, I began to notice the distortions created in the public discussion by the lack of a history.

One example is the tendency of the media to cover only the most cruel cases, creating the impression that these were typical. I learned that, a century ago, the problem had also gained public attention through sensational cases, while the majority of cases were ambiguous, not life-threatening, more often crimes of neglect than of assault. Another example is that many diagnoses of the causes of family violence—e.g., the increasing permissiveness of recent family and sexual life—assume that the problem is unprecedented, which is not the case. By contrast, the ebb-and-flow pattern of concern about family violence over the last century suggests that its incidence has not changed as much as its visibility.

The changing visibility of family violence is, in my opinion, the leading indicator of the necessity of an historical approach to understanding it. Concern with family violence has been a weathervane identifying the prevailing winds of anxiety about family life in general. The periods of silence about family violence are as significant as the periods of concern. Both reveal the longing for peaceful family life, the strength of the cultural image of home life as a harmonious, loving, and supportive environment. One response to this longing has been a tendency to deny, even suppress, the evidence that families are not always like that. Denying the problem serves to punish the victims of family violence doubly by forcing them to hide their problems and to blame themselves. Even the aggressors in family violence suffer from denial, since isolation and the feeling that they are unique make it difficult to ask for the help they want.

About 110 years ago there arose for the first time a different response—an attempt to confront the facts of family violence and to stop or at least control it. The first social agencies devoted to family-violence problems arose in the 1870s, called Societies for the Prevention of Cruelty to Children. They originally focused only on child abuse, but were soon drawn into other forms of family violence as well. It is important to learn and evaluate this history for its contemporary value as well as its historical interest.

The central argument of this book is that family violence has been historically and politically constructed. I make this claim in a double sense. First, the very definition of what constitutes unacceptable domestic violence, and appropriate responses to it, developed and then varied according to political moods and the force of certain political movements. Second, violence among family members arises from family conflicts which are not only historically influenced but political in themselves, in the sense of that word as having to do with power relations. Family violence usually arises out of power struggles in which individuals are contesting real resources and benefits. These contests arise not only from personal aspirations but also from changing social norms and conditions.

The historical developments that influenced family violence—through the behavior of family members and the responses of social-control agencies—include, prominently, changes in the situation of women and children. Another major argument of this book, therefore, is that family violence cannot be understood outside the context of the overall politics of the family. Today's anxiety about family issues—divorce, sexual permissiveness, abortion, teenage pregnancy, single mothers, runaway or allegedly stolen children, gay rights—is not unprecedented. For at least 150 years there have been periods of fear that "the family"—meaning a popular image of what families were supposed to be like, by no means a correct recollection of any actual "traditional family"—was in decline; and these fears have tended to escalate in periods of social stress. Anxieties about family life, furthermore, have usually expressed socially conservative fears about the increasing power and autonomy of women and children, and the corresponding decline in male, sometimes rendered as fatherly, control of family members. For much of the history of the family-violence concern, moreover, these anxieties have been particularly projected onto lower-class families. Thus an historical analysis of family violence must include a view of the changing power relations among classes, sexes, and generations.

Yet family-violence policy is mainly discussed today without an historical dimension, and with its political implications hidden. The result has been a depoliticization of family-violence scholarship, as if this were a social problem above politics, upon which "objective" scientific expertise could be brought to bear. The questions raised by proposed remedies cannot be answered by "neutral" experts, but only by public decisions about the extent and limits of public responsibility.

A few examples may offer an introductory sense of what it means to call family violence a political problem. For over a century there has been a consensus that there must be some limits placed on the treatment family "heads" can mete out to their dependents. But setting and enforcing those limits encounters a fundamental tension between civil liberties and social control. In policing private behavior, one person's right may be established only by invading another person's privacy. Moreover, social control of family violence is made difficult by our dominant social norm that families ought to be economically independent. There is a consensus that children ought to have some minimal guarantees of health and welfare, no matter how poor their parents. Yet there is a consistent tendency to insist that social welfare be a temporary expedient, made uncomfortable, and its recipients stigmatized. These dilemmas must be confronted by political choices; they cannot be ironed out by expert rationalization.

The political nature of family violence is also revealed in the source of the campaign against it. For most of the 110 years of this history, it was the women's-rights movement that was most influential in confronting, publicizing, and demanding action against family violence. Concern with family violence usually grew when feminism was strong and ebbed when feminism was weak. Women's movements have consistently been concerned with violence not only against women but also against children. But this does not mean that anti-family-violence agencies, once established, represented feminist views about the problem. On the contrary, anti-feminism often dominated not only among those who would deny or ignore the problem but also among those who defined and treated it. In some periods the experts confronted wife-beating and sexual assault, male crimes, while in others they avoided or soft-pedaled these crimes and emphasized child neglect, which they made by definition a female crime. In some periods they identified class and in others gender inequalities as relevant, and in still others ignored connections between family violence and the larger social structure.

Political attitudes have also affected research "findings" about family violence. For example, in the last two decades, experts on the problem have tended to divide into two camps. A psychological interpretation explains the problem in terms of personality disorders and childhood experience. A sociological explanatory model attributes the problem primarily to social stress factors such as poverty, unemployment, drinking, and isolation. In fact, these alternatives have been debated for a century, and the weight of opinion has shifted according to the dominant political mood. More conservative times bring psychological explanations to the foreground, while social explanations dominate when progressive attitudes and social reform movements are stronger. The debate is intense because it is not mainly about diagnoses but about their implications for policy. Social diagnoses imply social action and demand resources; psychological diagnoses may point to the need for psychotherapy but also justify criminal penalties and remove family violence from the range of problems called upon to justify welfare spending. When caseworkers lack the resources to help clients materially, they may focus on psychological problems—which are usually present—because at least something can be done about them. Those opposed to the commitment of resources on social spending are more likely to focus on individual psychological deviance as the problem. But both sides have often ignored the gender politics of family-violence issues, and the gender implications of policy recommendations, not only when women or girls were the victims of men, but also when women were the abusers.

Political attitudes have determined the very meanings of family violence. Family violence is not a fixed social illness which, like tuberculosis, can have its causal microorganism identified and then killed. Rather, its definitions have changed substantially since it first appeared as a social problem. Most of the discussion of family violence today assumes that what makes it problematic and requires social action is self-evident. Yet what was considered spanking a century ago might be considered abusive today, and the standards for what constitutes child neglect have changed greatly.

To insist that family violence is a political issue is not to deny its material reality as a problem for individuals—a painful, often terrifying reality. If there were any doubt, the victims', and often aggressors', pleas for help would erase it. But to discuss the violence itself without attention to the conflicts that give rise to it is to avoid the roots of the problem.

It is equally important to look at the history of attempts to control family violence. These efforts illustrate many of the general problems of "social control," a phrase often used to describe processes by which deviant and, presumably, dangerous behavior is disciplined by the larger society. Agencies devoted to the problem of family violence are in many ways typical of the entire welfare state. They have faced great difficulties in maintaining a balance between social order and privacy, between protecting the rights of some individuals and preserving the autonomy of others, and they have often been the means of imposing dominant values on subordinate groups. As with other activities of the state, social control of family violence could hardly be expected to be administered fairly in a society of such great inequalities of power. Yet it is precisely those inequalities that create such desperate need for the intervention of a welfare state.

Thus the example of family violence also produces a more complex view of social control than has been customary among social theorists. One of the most striking findings of this study is how often the objects of social control themselves asked for intervention from child-protection agencies. Clients were troubled by their inability to raise children according to their own standards, or to escape domestic violence themselves, and were eager for outside help. Moreover, once becoming clients, they attempted aggressively to influence agency policy and the definitions of the problems themselves, sometimes successfully. . . .

As we turn now to examine the historical construction and reconstruction of definitions of family violence, one such case history will serve as an example of the interaction of client and social worker. The "Amatos" were clients of the MSPCC [Massachusetts Society for the Prevention of Cruelty to Children] from 1910 to 1916. They had five young children from the current marriage, and Mrs. Amato had three from a previous marriage, two of them still in Italy and one daughter in Boston. Mrs. Amato kept that daughter at home to do housework and look after the younger children while she earned money doing home piece-rate sewing. This got the family in trouble with a truant officer, and they were also accused, in court, of lying, saying that the father had deserted when he was in fact at home. Furthermore, once while left alone, probably in the charge of a sibling, one of the younger children fell out a window and had to be hospitalized, making the mother suspect of negligence.

Despite her awareness of these suspicions against her, Mrs. Amato went to many different agencies, starting with those of the Italian immigrant community and then reaching out to elite (Protestant) social work agencies, seeking help, reporting that her husband was a drunkard, a gambler, a non-supporter, and a wife-beater. The Massachusetts Society for the Prevention of Cruelty to Children agents at first doubted her claims because Mr. Amato impressed them as a "good and sober man," and blamed the neglect of the children on his wife's incompetence in managing the wages he gave her. The Society ultimately became convinced of her story because of her repeated appearance with severe bruises and the corroboration of the husband's father. Mr. Amato, Sr., was intimately involved in the family troubles, and took responsibility for attempting to control his son. Once, he came to the house and gave the son "a warning and a couple of slaps," after which the son improved for a while. Another time he extracted from his son a pledge not to beat his wife for two years.

Mrs. Amato did not trust this method of controlling her husband. She begged the MSPCC agent to help her get a divorce; then she withdrew this request; later she claimed that she had not dared take this step because his relatives threatened to beat her if she tried it. Finally, Mrs. Amato's daughter (from her previous marriage) took action, coming independently to the MSPCC to bring an agent to the house to help her mother. As a result of this complaint Mr. Amato was convicted of assault once and sentenced to six months. During that time Mrs. Amato survived by "a little work" and help from "Italian friends," according to her caseworker. Her husband returned more violent than before; he went at her with an ax, beat the children so much on the head that their "eyes wabbled" [sic], and supported his family so poorly that the children went out begging. This case closed, like so many, without a resolution.

The Amatos, it must be remembered, exist only as they were interpreted for us by social workers in a particular historical period—the Progressive era. I want to press the Amatos into service to help illustrate the historicity and political construction of family violence, by imagining how social workers might have responded to the Amatos differently in different periods. A summary of these changes produces a rough periodization of the history of family violence:

1.   The late nineteenth century, approximately 1875–1910, when family violence agencies were part of the general charity organization and moral reform movement, influenced by feminism.

2.   The Progressive era and its aftermath, approximately 1910–1930, when family violence work was incorporated into professional social work and a reform program relying heavily on state regulation.

3.   The Depression, when intrafamily violence was radically deemphasized in favor of amelioration of economic hardship.

4.   The 1940s and 1950s, when psychiatric categories and intensely "pro-family" values dominated the social work approach to family problems.

5.   The 1960s and 1970s, when feminist and youth movements began a critique of the family which forced open the doors of closets that hid family problems.

. . . In order to avoid violating clients' privacy any more than necessary, I chose not to read any currently ongoing case records, which required ending this research in 1960. It will be helpful, nonetheless, to contrast this historical material with the contemporary context of family-violence discussion. Professional and public responses to family violence have undergone significant changes since 1960. . . . In the 1960s . . . child abuse was seized upon by doctors, particularly pediatricians, its diagnosis and treatment medicalized, also as a means of building the prestige of the group. . . . More importantly, the context of the rediscovery and redefinition of family violence in the last decades was the civil-rights, anti-war, student, and women's movements, all of them challenging family norms in different ways. Combined, these movements raised critical questions about the sanctity of family privacy, the privileged position of the male head of family, and the importance of family togetherness at all costs. The movements created an atmosphere in which child abuse, wife-beating, and incest could again be pulled out of the closet. Moreover, the critique of family violence was situated in an atmosphere of criticism of more accepted forms of violence as well—military, political, and cultural. In challenging the ideology of separate public and private spheres, the new social movements also challenged the power of professionals to define and then cure social problems. Their anti-authoritarian interpretive framework stimulated collective citizens' action on family violence. Self-help organizations of family-violence victims and assailants started competing with professionals for hegemony. Mrs. Amato might have gone to a battered women's shelter and discovered her commonality with many other women. She might have been encouraged by the shelter atmosphere, or that of other self-help projects such as Parents Anonymous, to identify her goals and strategies for change. These projects render evident what was previously disguised—the role of victims, "clients," in defining the problem and the remedies. . . .

"The Powers of the Weak": Wife–Beating and Battered Women's Resistance

. . . The basis of wife-beating is male dominance—not superior physical strength or violent temperament (both of which may well have been effects rather than causes of male dominance), but social, economic, political, and psychological power. It is less useful to call male dominance the cause of wife-beating, because we usually mean something more specific when we speak of cause; after all, most men, including many very powerful and sexist men, do not beat women. But it is male dominance that makes wife-beating a social rather than a personal problem. Wife-beating is not comparable to a drunken barroom assault or the hysterical attack of a jealous lover, which may be isolated incidents. Wife-beating is the chronic battering of a person of inferior power who for that reason cannot effectively resist.

Defining wife-beating as a social problem, not merely a phenomenon of particular violent individuals or relationships, was one of the great achievements of feminism. Women always resisted battering, but in the last hundred years they began to resist it politically and ideologically, with considerable success. While that success is far from complete, it is important to recognize the gains, and to give credit where it is due. Wife-beating is now not only illegal but also, to a majority of Americans, shameful. The contemporary alarm about wife-beating is an emblem of this achievement. The fact that many find it unacceptable that wife-beating continues at all is a sign of the greater respect that women have won, in large part as a result of 150 years of feminist conscious-raising. Moreover, women have gained substantially, if unevenly, in the economic and psychological strengths needed to escape abusive men.

If the achievements of feminism in countering wife-beating have been inadequately recognized, those of battered women themselves have been practically invisible. It is not a denial of their victimization to notice also their bravery, resilience, and ingenuity, often with very limited resources, in trying to protect and nurture themselves and their children. Elizabeth Janeway has eloquently called such gifts the "powers of the weak." This chapter argues that in the process of protecting themselves, battered women helped to formulate and promulgate the view that women have a right not to be beaten.

This chapter also examines how male dominance is enforced by, and produces, violence against women. Wife-beating usually arises out of specific domestic conflicts, in which women were by no means always passive, angelically patient, and self-sacrificing. To analyze these conflicts, and women's role in them, does not mean blaming the victim, a common distortion in the literature on wife-beating. That women are assertive in domestic power struggles is not a bad thing; women's suppression of their own needs and opinions is by far the greater danger. Victorian longings for women without egos or aggression should be understood as misogynist myths. Examining the construction of specific marital violence in historical context may contribute to understanding how male supremacy worked and is resisted. . . .

The condemnation of wife-beating and child-beating . . . had made substantial progress by the late nineteenth century. Contrary to some common misconceptions, wife-beating was not generally accepted as a head-of-household right at this time, but was considered a disreputable, seamy practice, and was effectively illegal in most states of the United States by 1870.

Although wife-beating was not widely considered legitimate, neither was public discussion of it. If feminists as well as more conservative moralists preferred it to remain a hidden or at least whispered subject, it is not surprising that child-protection clients also opted for an indirect approach. . . .[O]ne should not suppose that prior to modern feminism women never objected to or resisted beating. A better if rough paradigm with which to understand "tolerance" of wife-beating is as a tense compromise between men's and women's, patrilineal and matrilineal interests. Unlimited family violence was never tolerated, and there were always standards as to what constituted excessive violence. Recently such notions as the "rule of thumb"—that a man might not use a stick thicker than his thumb to beat his wife—have been cited as evidence of the extremes of women's humiliation and powerlessness. On the contrary, such regulation was evidence of a degree of women's power, albeit enforceable mainly through the willingness of others to defend it. But women often did have allies within the patriarchal community. If that much abused word "patriarchy" is to have any usefulness, it must be used to describe a system larger than any individual family, a system which required regulation even of its privileged members. While patriarchal fathers could control their households, they in turn were subject to sanctions—social control—by the community, whose power brokers included not only fellow patriarchs but also women, particularly senior women. The agency clients were accustomed to appealing to fathers as well as mothers, brothers as well as sisters and friends, for support against abusive husbands.

Nevertheless, in the nineteenth and early twentieth centuries, many women clients did not seem to believe they had a "right" to freedom from physical violence. When social workers expressed disgust at the way they were treated, the clients sometimes considered that reaction naive. They spoke of the inevitability of male violence. Their refusal to condemn marital violence in moral terms must be interpreted carefully. It did not mean that these women were passive or accepted beatings. They often resisted assault in many ways: fighting back, running away, attempting to embarrass the men before others, calling the police. And they did express moral outrage if their men crossed some border of tolerability. There is no contradiction here. . . .Because the client women did not conduct a head-on challenge to their husbands' prerogatives does not mean that they liked being hit or believed that their virtue required accepting it. . . .

What was new in the nineteenth-century middle-class reform sensibility was the notion that wife-beating was entirely intolerable. Family reformers proposed, like abolitionists toward slavery and prohibitionists toward drink, to do away with physical violence in marriage altogether. This differed from their attitude toward child abuse, because they did not propose to do away with spanking. By contrast, many poor battered women had a more complex view of the problem then their benefactors: welcoming all the help they could get in their individual struggles against assault, they also needed economic help in order to provide a decent family life for children. Given a choice, they might have preferred economic aid to prosecution of wife-beaters.

Feminist reformers also avoided women's violence toward men, whether offensive or defensive. The Victorian sensibility made them feel they should offer charity only to "true women," peaceful and long-suffering. There were political advantages to their myopia: they kept the focus on battered women and declined to redefine the problem as mutual marital violence; they knew that it was a whole system of male power, not just physical violence, that made women battered. On the other hand, their view of women's proper role ruled out the possibility that women could create independent lives and reject violent husbands. To these nineteenth-century child-savers, women's victimization meant virtue more than weakness; women who submitted to abuse were more praised than those who left their husbands. For example, in the random sample of this study, battered women frequently left or kicked out their husbands, then repeatedly reconciled or reunited with them. In the 1960s such a record would probably have made a social worker question a woman's sincerity and doubt the point of continuing to offer help. In the nineteenth century these women's ambivalence was interpreted as evidence of their commitment to fulfilling wifely duties. . . .

Women's invention of a right not to be beaten came from a dialectic between changing social possibilities and aspirations. When women's best hope was husbands' kindness, because they were economically dependent on marriage, they did not protest violations of their individual rights but rested their case on their importance as mothers. As women's possibilities expanded to include wage-earning, remarriage after divorce, birth limitation, and aid to single mothers, their best hopes escalated to include escape from marital violence altogether. . . .

By far the most striking and consistent women's complaint. . . .through the 1930s focused on their husbands' non-support rather than abuse. . . . The 1930s were the divide in this study, after which the majority of women clients complained directly rather than indirectly about wife-beating. . . .Wife-beating accusations stood out even more because of the virtual disappearance of non-support complaints. This striking inverse correlation between non-support and wife-beating complaints stimulates an economistic hypothesis: economic dependence prevented women's formulation of a sense of entitlement to protection against marital violence, but it also gave them a sense of entitlement to support; by contrast, the growth of a wage labor economy, bringing unemployment, transience, and dispersal of kinfolk, lessened women's sense of entitlement to support from their husbands, but allowed them to insist on their physical integrity. It is a reasonable hypothesis that the Depression, by the leveling impact of its widespread unemployment, actually encouraged women regarding the possibilities of independence.

An oblique kind of supporting evidence for this process of consciousness change is provided by wife-beaters' defenses. Men did not often initiate complaints to agencies, but they frequently responded with counter-complaints when they were questioned. Their grievances were usually defensive, self-pitying, and opportunistic. They remain, however, important evidence of a consensus among men about the services they expected from wives—or about what complaints might be effective with social workers. Men accused of wife-beating usually countered that their wives were poor housekeepers and neglectful mothers, making themselves the aggrieved parties. The men's counter-accusations were, of course, a means of seeking to reimpose a threatened domination. Yet they simultaneously expressed a sense of an injustice, the violation of a traditional and/or contractual agreement, and their dismay at the historical changes that made women less able or willing to meet these expectations.

Often male and female expectations of marital responsibilities were consonant. Women as well as men professed allegiance to male-supremacist understanding of what relations between the sexes should be like. These shared assumptions, however, by no means prevented conflict. Women's assumptions of male dominance did not mean that they quit trying to improve their situations. Husbands expected dominance but also expected women's resistance to it. Clients of both sexes expected marriage and family life to be conflict-ridden—they did not share the bourgeois denial of family disharmony—and demonstrated no shyness in exposing their family hostilities to social workers. Female clients often both "accepted" that men were violent—that is, they did not approve but expected it—and also tried to stop it.

By emphasizing mutual conflict as the origin of wife-beating, I do not mean to suggest an equality in battle. Marital violence almost always resulted in the defeat of women and served to enforce women's subordination. Nor did every act of marital violence emerge from an argument. Contestation could be chronic, structured into the relationship. Male violence often became a pattern, virtually normal, appearing regularly or erratically, without relation to any particular interaction. One man who eventually murdered his wife beat her because their children "had no shoe lacings." Some men simply came home drunk and angry enough to hit anyone in the way. But their drinking ... was often an assertion of privilege, as was their violence an assertion of dominance. ...

While the first-wave women's movement had asserted women's rights to personal freedom even in marriage, it had not provided any organized, institutional means for poor women to secure and defend that right, a power which was necessary for women really to believe in their own entitlement. Until the revival of feminism and the establishment of battered-women's shelters in the 1970s, wife-beating victims had three resources: their own individual strategies of resistance; the help of relatives, friends, and neighbors; and the intervention of child-welfare agencies. None was adequate to the task. The first two easily outweighed by the superior power of husbands and the sanctity of marriage itself, and the last did not well represent the interests of the women themselves. Still, on some occasions victims were able to use these inadequate resources to construct definite improvements, if not permanent solutions.

Women in abusive relationships with men still face great difficulties in extricating themselves. These difficulties in turn weaken their ability to insist that the men's behavior change, since the woman's threat to leave is often her most powerful lever and his only incentive to change. Such difficulties were greater fifty or one hundred years ago, and greater for the poor and uneducated women who dominated in these cases. Their difficulties were essentially those faced by single mothers. The biggest obstacle for most women facing abusive men was that they did not wish to lose their children; indeed, their motherhood was for most of them (including, it must be emphasized, many who were categorized as abusive or neglectful parents) their greatest source of pleasure, self-esteem, and social status. In escaping they had to find a way simultaneously to earn and raise children in an economy of limited jobs for women, little child care, and little or no reliable aid to single mothers. They had to do this with the often low confidence characteristic of women trying to take unconventional action. Moreover, these women of the past had the added burden of defying a social norm condemning marital separation and encouraging submission as a womanly virtue. ...

[One] solution. ... [was] a "separation and maintenance" agreement, as such provisions were then known: ... the state ... [would] guarantee ... [a woman] the right to a separate household and require her husband to pay support. Such plans were the most common desire of the beaten wives in this study. ... Failing to get separation-and-maintenance agreements, and unable to collect support even when it was promised, the remaining option—called desertion—was taken only by the most depressed, disheartened, and desperate women. A moralistic nomenclature no longer common, desertion meant a woman leaving a husband and children. Female desertion was extremely uncommon in these cases, especially in contrast with the prevalence of male desertion. The low female desertion rate revealed the strength of women's attachment to their children. Moreover, the guilt and stigma attached to such action usually meant that women "deserters" simultaneously cut themselves off from friends and kin. All in all, it was unlikely that ridding themselves of the burdens of children would lead to better futures for wife-beating victims.

Another response to beatings was fighting. For differing reasons, both feminists and sexists have been reluctant to recognize or acknowledge women's physical aggression. Yet fighting was common and accepted among poor women of the past, more so than among "respectable" women and contemporary women. . . . Most of the women's violence was responsive or reactive. This distinguished it from men's violence, which grew out of mutual conflict, to be sure, but was more often a regular tactic in an ongoing power struggle. . . . Over time there appeared to be a decline in mutual violence and women's aggression. The apparent decline in women's violence was offset by an increase in women's leaving marriages. A likely hypothesis is that there is a trade-off between women's physical violence and their ability to get separations or divorces.

Although women usually lost in fights, the decline in women's violence was not a clear gain for women and their families. Condemnation of female violence went along with the romanticization of female passivity which contributed to women's participation in their own victimization. Historian Nancy Tomes found that a decline in women's violence in England between 1850 and 1890 corresponded to an increased in women's sense of shame about wife-beating, and reluctance to report or discuss it. In this area feminism's impact on women in violent families was mixed. The delegitimization of wife-beating increased battered women's guilt about their inability to escape; they increasingly thought themselves exceptional, adding to their shame. First-wave feminism, expressing its relatively elite class base, helped construct a femininity that was oppressive to battered women: by emphasizing the superiority of women's peacefulness, feminist influence made women loathe and attempt to suppress their own aggressiveness and anger. . . .

For several reasons a woman-blaming response to wife-beating became more pervasive after the 1930s. Changes in social work procedures created a structural imperative to map the problem onto the client who was present and influenceable. In the early years of child protection, caseworkers tried to reform men. The unembarrassed moralism of the earlier period, combined with the wider range of pre-professional techniques, gave agency workers a choice of tactics to influence male behavior: they hectored, threatened, and cajoled; they used short jail sentences, frequent home visits, including surprise visits, visits to employers and relatives; and they dunned non-supporting men for money. As professionalized casework concentrated on office visits, fewer men were seen. Moreover, women were more introspective and self-critical—more productive in casework. Men infrequently originated cases, were rarely willing to meet with caseworkers, and were more defensive about their own behavior. In search of any ways to influence troubled families, social workers not unnaturally focused on those most open to influence.

More fundamentally, blaming family problems on women was part of a change in family and gender ideology evident by the 1930s. The caseworkers were more affected by the decline of feminism than their clients were, apparently. Ironically, these social-work attitudes were also conditioned by gains in sexual equality. Women were no longer pictured as helpless in the manner of the nineteenth-century victim, and indeed, women were not so helpless, having greater ability to divorce and create separate households or new marriages than they had had earlier. As child neglect became, virtually by definition, a sign of maternal inadequacy, so did marital violence become a sign of wifely dysfunction. "Instead of aligning our agency with the mother," the MSPCC reported in 1959, "we felt it only proper to have the father present his side of the picture. . . . The mother was seen and instead of encouraging her laments about her husband, efforts were made to help her to understand his needs and the strains he was under."

After World War II a particularly intense anxiety about wifely sexual and gender maladjustment became evident. Nor was there parallelism: if men suffered similar maladjustment, no one noticed. Freudian thought influenced many caseworkers in this direction, with its story that women's maturity required self-sacrifice and renunciation. But the social workers' concern about maladjusted women was also an observation of the stresses of actual social and economic change, the conflicts women were experiencing between earning and housekeeping, raised aspirations and continued restriction of opportunity, public rights and continued subordination. They had to counsel women to perform in contradictory ways.

This was the era of the "feminine mystique," not of Victoria. Divorce was a common occurrence. The marital counsel offered by the child protectors and marriage experts combined woman-blaming with toleration for marital separation. A standard social work manual on women in marital conflict categorized problems under the headings: excessive dependence, the need to suffer, rejection of femininity, sex response, interfering relatives, cultural differences, and economic factors; four of the seven referred to women's faults, none to men's faults, and three to extramarital pressures. A classic "feminine mystique" document, the book expresses the contradictions of the age, condemning both excessive dependence, a quality acknowledged to be culturally encouraged—"combines well with femininity"—*and* women's employment. It blamed women for provoking abusive men and then for staying with them; indeed, suspicion is expressed that dependence created battering. . . .

. . . One assault does not make a battered woman; she becomes that because of her socially determined inability to resist or escape: her lack of

economic independence, law enforcement services, and quite likely, self-confidence. Battering behavior is also socially determined, by a man's expectations of what a woman should do for him and his acculturation to violence. Wife-beating arose not just from subordination but also from contesting it. Had women consistently accepted their subordinate status, and had men never felt their superior status challenged, there might have been less marital violence. To focus on women's "provocations," and to examine men's grievances against their wives, is not to blame women but, often, to praise them. It is to uncover the evidence of women's resistance.
. . .

Batterers were not necessarily conscious of their goals. Often they felt so wounded by women's behavior, and so desperately longed for a wife's services, that they experienced their violence as uncontrollable; they felt they had no recourse. Their sense of entitlement was so strong it was experienced as a need. Their wives did not feel so entitled. And when, stimulated often by responsibility for children, they gave up trying to wheedle and pacify, and tried to escape, they found what they had always suspected: a set of obstacles, any of which might have been definitive—poverty, motherhood, isolation, and the hostility or indifference of social control agencies. When the context is supplied, many seemingly ineffective responses to wife-beating, including resignation, pandering, and changes of mind, are revealed to be rational, trial-and-error, even experienced and skilled survival and escape tactics.

Battered women's defeats are losses for everyone. Wife-beating molds not only individual relationships but also the overall social definitions of heterosexual relations. Wife-beating sends "messages" to all who know about it or suspect it; it encourages timidity, fatalism, manipulativeness in women. Men's violence against some women (extra- as well as intrafamilial) reinforces all women's subordination and all men's dominance. This does not mean that wife-beaters got what they wanted. On the contrary, wife-beating, even more than nonfamily violence against women, is often dysfunctional even for the assailants. In many of the cases reviewed here, men longed for the impossible, for sycophantic service and selfless devotion, which they would have hated had they gotten it, and their violence brought them no gain. On the contrary, in most marriages, even in extremely patriarchal societies, men's and women's interests have been complementary as well as adversary, especially because their economic futures were joined. This contradictory nature of marriage and the family—requiring cooperation among unequals—helps explain why wife-beating is not universal. Men benefited more from camaraderie, mutual respect, and friendship. Cooperation, especially in work, promoted men's as well as women's values: prosperity, health, calm, leisure.

If battered women's failures were costly to all, their successes were beneficial to all. The victims' own struggles were hard to see until the last two decades, when battered women organized themselves as part of a feminist movement. In fact, battered women's self-image, interpretation of their problem, and strategies of resistance had always been influenced by organized feminism. In turn, they also influenced social and legal policy, particularly through their interactions with social workers and other authorities: at worst they kept the issue from being completely forgotten, at best they provided a pressure for such solutions as we have today—liberalized divorce, AFDC, prosecution. Even women who have never been struck have benefited from the "disestablishment" of marriage that is now taking place, the process of transforming it from a coercive institution, inescapable and necessary for survival, to a relationship that is chosen.

Kimberlé Crenshaw, Mapping the Margins: Intersectionality, Identity Politics, and Violence Against Women of Color
43 Stan. L. Rev. 1241 (1991).

. . . While it would be misleading to suggest that white Americans have come to terms with the degree of violence in their own homes, it is nonetheless the case that race adds yet another dimension to why the problem of domestic violence is suppressed within nonwhite communities. People of color often must weigh their interests in avoiding issues that might reinforce distorted public perceptions against the need to acknowledge and address intracommunity problems. Yet the cost of suppression is seldom recognized in part because the failure to discuss the issue shapes perceptions of how serious the problem is in the first place.

The controversy over Alice Walker's novel THE COLOR PURPLE can be understood as an intracommunity debate about the political costs of exposing gender violence within the Black community. Some critics chastised Walker for portraying Black men as violent brutes. One critic lambasted Walker's portrayal of Celie, the emotionally and physically abused protagonist who finally triumphs in the end. Walker, the critic contended, had created in Celie a Black woman whom she couldn't imagine existing in any Black community she knew of or could conceive of.

The claim that Celie was somehow an unauthentic character might be read as a consequence of silencing discussion of intracommunity violence. Celie may be unlike any Black woman we know because the real terror experienced daily by minority women is routinely concealed in a misguided (though perhaps understandable) attempt to forestall racial stereotyping. Of course, it is true that representations of Black violence—whether statistical or fictional—are often written into a larger script that consistently portrays Black and other minority communities as pathologically violent. The problem, however, is not so much the portrayal of violence itself as it is the absence of other narratives and images portraying a fuller range of Black experience. Suppression of some of these issues in the name of antiracism imposes real costs. Where information about violence in minority communities is not available, domestic violence is unlikely to be addressed as a serious issue.

The political imperatives of a narrowly focused antiracist strategy support other practices that isolate women of color. For example, activists who have attempted to provide support services to Asian- and African–American women report intense resistance from those communities. At other times, cultural and social factors contribute to suppression. Nilda Rimonte, director of Everywoman's Shelter in Los Angeles, points out that in the Asian community, saving the honor of the family from shame is a priority. Unfortunately, this priority tends to be interpreted as obliging women not to scream rather than obliging men not to hit.

Race and culture contribute to the suppression of domestic violence in other ways as well. Women of color are often reluctant to call the police, a hesitancy likely due to a general unwillingness among people of color to subject their private lives to the scrutiny and control of a police force that is frequently hostile. There is also a more generalized community ethic against public intervention, the product of a desire to create a private world free from the diverse assaults on the public lives of racially subordinated people. The home is not simply a man's castle in the patriarchal sense, but may also function as a safe haven from the indignities of life in a racist society. However, but for this "safe haven" in many cases, women of color victimized by violence might otherwise seek help.

There is also a general tendency within antiracist discourse to regard the problem of violence against women of color as just another manifestation of racism. In this sense, the relevance of gender domination within the community is reconfigured as a consequence of discrimination against men. Of course, it is probably true that racism contributes to the cycle of violence, given the stress that men of color experience in dominant society. It is therefore more than reasonable to explore the links between racism and domestic violence. But the chain of violence is more complex and extends beyond this single link. Racism is linked to patriarchy to the extent that racism denies men of color the power and privilege that dominant men enjoy. When violence is understood as an acting-out of being denied male power in other spheres, it seems counterproductive to embrace constructs that implicitly link the solution to domestic violence to the acquisition of greater male power. The more promising political imperative is to challenge the legitimacy of such power expectations by exposing their dysfunctional and debilitating effect on families and communities of color. Moreover, while understanding links between racism and domestic violence is an important component of any effective intervention strategy, it is also clear that women of color need not await the ultimate triumph over racism before they can expect to live violence-free lives. . . .

Not only do race-based priorities function to obscure the problem of violence suffered by women of color; feminist concerns often suppress minority experiences as well. Strategies for increasing awareness of domestic violence within the white community tend to begin by citing the commonly shared assumption that battering is a minority problem. The strategy then focuses on demolishing this strawman, stressing that spousal abuse also occurs in the white community. Countless first-person stories begin with a statement like, "I was not supposed to be a battered wife." That battering occurs in families of all races and all classes seems to be an ever-present theme of anti-abuse campaigns. First-person anecdotes and studies, for example, consistently assert that battering cuts across racial, ethnic, economic, educational, and religious lines. Such disclaimers seem relevant only in the presence of an initial, widely held belief that domestic violence occurs primarily in minority or poor families. Indeed some authorities explicitly renounce the "stereotypical myths" about battered women. A few commentators have even transformed the message that battering is not *exclusively* a problem of the poor or minority communities into a claim that it *equally* affects all races and classes. Yet these comments seem less concerned with exploring domestic abuse within "stereotyped" communities than with removing the stereotype as an obstacle to exposing battering within white middle- and upper-class communities.

Efforts to politicize the issue of violence against women challenge beliefs that violence occurs only in homes of "others." While it is unlikely that advocates and others who adopt this rhetorical strategy intend to exclude or ignore the needs of poor and colored women, the underlying premise of this seemingly universalistic appeal is to keep the sensibilities of dominant social groups focused on the experiences of those groups. Indeed, as subtly suggested by the opening comments of Senator David Boren (D–Okla.) in support of the Violence Against Women Act of 1991, the displacement of the "other" as the presumed victim of domestic violence works primarily as a political appeal to really white elites. Boren said,

> Violent crimes against women are not limited to the streets of the inner cities, but also occur in homes in the urban and rural areas across the country.
>
> Violence against women affects not only those who are actually beaten and brutalized, but indirectly affects all women. Today, our wives, mothers, daughters, sisters, and colleagues are held captive by fear generated from these violent crimes— held captive not for what they do or who they are, but solely because of gender.

Rather than focusing on and illuminating how violence is disregarded when the home is "othered," the strategy implicit in Senator Boren's remarks functions instead to politicize the problem only in the dominant community. This strategy permits white women victims to come into focus, but does little to disrupt the patterns of neglect that permitted the problem to continue as long as it was imagined to be a minority problem. The experience of violence by minority women is ignored, except to the extent it gains white support for domestic violence programs in the white community. . . .

While Senator Boren's statement reflects a self-consciously political presentation of domestic violence, an episode of the CBS news program *48 Hours* shows how similar patterns of othering nonwhite women are apparent in journalistic accounts of domestic violence as well. The program presented seven women who were victims of abuse. Six were interviewed at some length along with their family members, friends, supporters, and even detractors. The viewer got to know something about each of these women.

These victims were humanized. Yet the seventh woman, the only nonwhite one, never came into focus. She was literally unrecogizable throughout the segment, first introduced by photographs showing her face badly beaten and later shown with her face electronically altered in the videotape of a hearing at which she was forced to testify. Other images associated with this woman included shots of a bloodstained room and blood-soaked pillows. Her boyfriend was pictured handcuffed while the camera zoomed in for a close-up of his bloodied sneakers. Of all the presentations in the episode, hers was the most graphic and impersonal. The overall point of the segment "featuring" this woman was that battering might not escalate into homicide if battered women would only cooperate with prosecutors. In focusing on its own agenda and failing to explore why this woman refused to cooperate, the program diminished this woman, communicating, however subtly, that she was responsible for her own victimization.

Unlike the other women, all of whom, again, were white, this Black woman had no name, no family, no context. The viewer sees her only as victimized and uncooperative. She cries when shown pictures. She pleads not to be forced to view the bloodstained room and her disfigured face. The program does not help the viewer to understand her predicament. The possible reasons she did not want to testify—fear, love, or possibly both— are never suggested. Most unfortunately, she, unlike the other six, is given no epilogue. While the fates of the other women are revealed at the end of the episode, we discover nothing about the Black woman. She, like the "others" she represents, is simply left to herself and soon forgotten.

I offer this description to suggest that "other" women are silenced as much by being relegated to the margin of experience as by total exclusion. Tokenistic, objectifying, voyeuristic inclusion is at least as disempowering as complete exclusion. The effort to politicize violence against women will do little to address Black and other minority women if their images are retained simply to magnify the problem rather than to humanize their experiences. Similarly, the antiracist agenda will not be advanced significantly by forcibly suppressing the reality of battering in minority communities. As the *48 Hours* episode makes clear, the images and stereotypes we fear are readily available and are frequently deployed in ways that do not generate sensitive understanding of the nature of domestic violence in minority communities. . . .

II.   LEGAL RESPONSES TO ABUSE

A series of possible public responses to intimate violence can be, and have been, pursued. Roughly in the chronological order of their appearance in advocacy campaigns in the United States, they are:

1.   do nothing;

2.   advocate public punishments, such as whippings;

2.   constrain access to and use of alcohol on the grounds that it is associated with violence in the home;

3.   seek enforcement of existing criminal laws against assault and battery even when the participants are cohabitants;

4.   pursue civil law suits against police departments for failing to enforce criminal laws to protect victims of violence in their homes;

5.   create emergency residential shelters for victims of violence who vacate their own homes;

6.   defend victims of violence who kill their abusers either by expanding self-defense theories or advocating clemency after conviction;

7.   advocate legislative authority for the grant of civil protection orders, enabling criminal contempt for the violation, that include: orders of no-contact, orders to vacate a residence, orders to stay away from the complaining party for a specified period of time;

8.   advocate mandatory arrests for violation of civil protection orders and policies against prosecutorial abandonment of violence complaints even if the complaining witness declines to cooperate;

9.   push for training police, judges, clerks, and lawyers to understand domestic violence and dynamics of domestic abuse;

10.   justify training and support of advocates for victims of domestic violence to help victims negotiate the civil process and the criminal process;

11.   develop rules to protect the custodial and visitation rights of victims of violence and to treat the violence they have experienced as potential grounds to halting contact between the child and the abuser; and

12.   devise federal civil rights guarantees to create federal court jurisdiction and potential damage awards for violence committed in intimate settings as an interference with commerce and/or fundamental rights.

Compare the processes produced under state statutes authorizing courts to issue civil restraining orders and prosecution of domestic abuse as a crime. What are the strengths and drawbacks of each from the victim's perspective? Similar comparisons should be made with the recent federal Violence Against Women Act and emerging state court tort remedies.

Laurie Wermuth, Domestic Violence Reforms: Policing the Private?

27 Berkeley J. Soc. 27 (1982).

In recent years, reforms of police and criminal justice agencies have attempted to address the problem of family violence. This effort to expand the involvement of state agencies in private conflicts provides an opportunity to examine the extent and nature of state interests in the mediation of the family—in particular, relationships between men and women. This paper focuses on the state's responses to pressure from the women's movement to recognize and criminalize the problem of wife-beating through a description and analysis of two reform efforts. The first attempt instituted police training in crisis intervention skills; the second focused on a multi-agency treatment of the problem. These reforms will be viewed as a response to both internal pressures from within the law enforcement apparatus and to external pressures on that apparatus from the women's movement. The question of whether the reforms initiated a more active state role, or maintained a *laissez-faire* stance, will be discussed in terms of the larger issue of state intervention in private violence against women. Rather than providing victims leverage against their violent husbands and boyfriends, it will be seen that the new governmental "responsiveness" in fact further entrenched their disadvantaged position. . . .

Recent critics of state interventionism imply that governmental agencies attempt to extend their influence and control over private life. According to Christopher Lasch, experts, empowered by the state, have sabotaged the internal structure of the family and undermined the authority of husbands over wives and parents over children. The modern family is disintegrating as a result. From Lasch's argument, we would expect the police to exercise their discretionary powers in such a way as to undermine the status quo in couples' relationships. We would also expect police administration to *expand* the role of police mediation.

Jacques Donzelot also suggests the expansion of state influence and control in private life under the guise of professional help. He perceives, however, not the family's demise, but rather its greater susceptibility to state influence and control. Over roughly the past century and a half, according to Donzelot, the role of the state has been transformed from the traditional government *over* families, to a modern government *through* families. Pressure from state, philanthropic, and professional providers defeated working-class families' resistance to intrusion. A new relationship emerged: In return for families' maintenance of individuals' needs, and parents' cooperation in the control of public disorder, families were rewarded with increased privacy and autonomy over internal affairs. Material self-sufficiency and public order were exchanged for the privacy and individualism of family units. According to Donzelot, then, families serve the state as a source of protection against disorder. Moreover, this means of state control through the family is economical; the state minimizes welfare expenses, while agencies normalize deviance and disruption.

In their views of the family and the state, Lasch and Donzelot fail to recognize that the consequences of state interventionism are not uniform. For example, *within* families, men are treated differently by the police than women; parents and children, the young and the old, similarly experience different treatment. Furthermore, state agencies are diverse, are riddled with inconsistencies, and often work at cross-purposes. Domestic violence reforms, for example, developed services and publicly supported victims of wife-abuse, while simultaneously discouraging the criminal prosecution of husbands. Behind the new therapeutic techniques of the police remains the reality of a *laissez-faire* stance towards private violence against women.

Feminist theorists address this entrenched bias. They view the state as instrumental in the maintenance of two systems of inequality—class and gender. Zillah Eisenstein, for example, characterizes these social relationships as "capitalist patriarchy," in which systems of class and gender inequality are mutually reinforced. Police reluctance to intervene in wife-battery would then be explained in terms of state observance of patriarchal privilege. When state agents *do* intervene, a similar explanation applies; the state takes on a patriarchal role when a husband's use of force becomes excessive; intervention normalizes the individual case in order to protect the institution. Thus, *laissez-faire* practices and intervention are explained in the same way. For present purposes, however, we need to differentiate among state practices and consider the possibility of state intervention which would support the interests of *women*.

None of these theories is complete, but each sheds *some* light on the kinds of responses we have seen to domestic violence; in turn, the specific cases examined below suggest important areas *not* addressed by existing models of state-family relations. . . .

In the mid-sixties, police administrations faced dual pressures. In the wake of the civil rights and anti-war movements, and their accompanying urban unrest, accusations of police brutality brought about demands for police accountability and responsiveness to community needs. Public discontent coincided with internal police concern over the danger and costliness of domestic calls (i.e., requests for police intervention in private disputes). Viewed as a dangerous nuisance, the domestic call was universally detested by rank-and-file officers. The fact that officers were discouraged from taking criminal action and that the solutions they did devise were difficult to monitor, only added to the tendency to neglect this line of duty.

When, in 1967, the Law Enforcement Assistance Administration (LEAA) funded psychologist Morton Bard's plan for a New York police Family Crisis Unit, it was hoped that it would improve officer morale, decrease citizen complaints, and meet administrative needs. Reforming the domestic call in particular posed a dilemma: how could better techniques for controlling private violence be implemented at a time when police were under fire for being overly intrusive and aggressive? Innovations would have to meet practical, professional, and political needs: violence would have to be controlled, the safety of officers improved, and the image of the police enhanced.

Bard's grant to train New York City police in crisis intervention techniques, drew upon psychological theories about the handling of crises to posit a therapeutic model of intervention. He spoke to politicians, social service workers, and police and stressed that family conflict might be an early sign of emotional disorder in one or all participants. Since other agencies could not respond to emergencies, police crisis intervention would provide the most effective delivery of crisis services. Properly trained police, according to Bard, could be the "early detectors" of mental problems, acting as "front line casefinders" for mental health and social work agencies. Police would defuse crises, apply preliminary treatments, and refer clients to agencies. Impressed with Bard's police training program, the LEAA implemented it in six more cities. In addition, it provided funds to several other police departments for the development of similar crisis intervention training and service programs. . . .

The redefinition of domestic calls as "service work" also contributed to the acceptance of crisis intervention training. Although there was some resistance to this reformulation, it was adopted as part of a larger effort to upgrade police image and improve police-community relations. "Service work" complemented the "peace officer" role, thereby downplaying the rougher, tougher "crime fighting" image. The two roles—service and crime fighting—were defined as complementary, since service work prevents more serious crimes: it "strives for some form of resolution . . . [which] may serve to decrease the number of times the police must be called to what were recurring disputes, and may defuse a situation which, experts agree, incubates more serious crimes." According to police administration, service work required skills—quick and sensitive thinking and accurate choices—and in the long run made police work more effective and the community safer. . . .

What kind of mediation of private life did crisis intervention techniques bring? In theory, they were therapeutic skills, to be used by police to better serve all individuals involved. Attention to the domestic call gave it more importance, at least temporarily. However, the redefinition of the problem and its proper treatment confirmed the assumption that family violence is not a criminal matter, but rather a private, interpersonal problem. In practice, these changes had *negative* consequences for women victims of violent husbands and boyfriends. A victim became subject to the same "cooling out" techniques as the assailant; she might be encouraged to "think about the good times" in the relationship, or about "how hard it would be on her own with the kids." Where this approach was used, women were given the message that they were equal participants in the dispute, and that they too were responsible for the violence.

The use of professional skills to mediate conflicts between men and women had the effect of legitimizing a non-criminal treatment of wife-beating. The elevation of crisis management to formal policy precluded other kinds of action, and ruled out culpability. For example, crisis intervention literature and training consistently failed to examine the conditions under which these techniques would be inappropriate, and where, instead, criminal sanctions were warranted.

It was not long, however, before groups outside police institutions began to express discontent with crisis intervention.

. . . In response to public interest, pressure from liberals and the women's movement, and its own chronic difficulties with domestic calls, the Law Enforcement Assistance Administration again turned its attention to family violence. This time the focus was not limited to police response, and it was acknowledged that previous efforts were insufficient. The limitations of crisis intervention and the need for further reform were later summarized in a publication for the Police Executive Research Forum (funded by the LEAA):

> The severity of spouse abuse and wife beating problems that has recently emerged is different from that traditionally thought to be involved in family fights. ...Moreover, the right of a man to discipline and physically punish his wife, permitted under colonial laws, and even state law until the last century, has been rejected.

> The traditional police response to these calls, emphasizing crisis intervention skills and reconciliation of the parties, is inappropriate and unhelpful in cases involving serious injury or repeated abuse, nor is it effective in reducing the number of spouse abuse cases. In fact, it may aggravate the problem by suggesting to assailants that their violent behavior can be overlooked. ...

If an offender has the choice between facing a criminal trial and probation consisting of visits to a therapist, he is likely to choose the latter. Whether this treatment could rehabilitate him if it is accepted under pressure, is questionable. This reveals the limitations of the medical model upon which the prescribed treatment is based. Supposedly a man beats his wife or girlfriend because he is sick or has learned violent behavior from his parents, or, he goes out of control because of an alcohol or drug abuse problem. The issue of his *choice* to use force is ignored, so that the solution is to be found in therapeutic cure, not in punitive sanction.

According to this treatment model, the illness of violent behavior incubates within the family system and is symptomatic of stress and "underlying personal and family conflicts." Victims, therefore, also are encouraged to attend therapy, so they can "see the role that they played in what happened." The violence itself is not identified as the problem, as it would be if perpetrated by a stranger; instead, psychological ill health, interpersonal communication difficulties, and family tensions are the root causes of this "symptomatic" abuse. The conceptualization of the problem inherent in diversion, then, values reconciliation over controls and avoids the consideration of purposeful wrongdoing.

Diversion programs neatly fit Donzelot's description of the "therapeutic state" in operation. Suspects are coerced into therapy in order to avoid criminal sanctions and then become the clients of experts. Through the probation officer, a link to the criminal process is maintained in case these "gentle" measures prove insufficient for keeping the man out of trouble. This arrangement creates an image which is beneficial to the state, given the current popularity of rehabilitation: offenders are rehabilitated rather than punished; this best serves the welfare of the individual and the society. The partnership of independent experts and state officials enhances the legitimacy of each and, as with Donzelot's example of the French juvenile courts, helps disguise the coercive aspects of the system. This is a practical arrangement: therapists act as a self-supporting adjunct of the criminal justice system, and cases are handed over, reducing the work load and easing the overburdened courts. Thus, diversion appears to be a serious and concerned response to the problem of family violence. Offenders are now treated and are processed by higher levels of the system, where before they were simply released. Diversion is an ingenious way to handle (rather than ignore) wife-assault, without criminalizing the offense. Suspects now have the opportunity to be "rehabilitated" without ever being formally charged with a crime, without making a plea, and without the arrest remaining on their record.

What Donzelot's model does not illuminate, however, is the impact on the relationship between the man and the woman. Instead of state agents' taking responsibility, the diversion arrangement puts the woman in the position of enforcer. In addition to calling the police and agreeing to prosecute, it is she who must initiate state action at each ensuing step. Since the violence is treated as symptomatic of relationship and communication problems, she is part of the ailment. This definitional framework makes it possible not only to deflect the victim's attempts to prosecute, but also to include her in the offender's treatment.

Although the man's position in the system is not fortuitous—he becomes subject to controls and the threat of prosecution—his position vis-a-vis the victim *is*. He may continue to use force and threats to silence her reporting of incidents, and he is likely to continue to blame *her* for his trouble with the system. This interaction between the state and the family, then, reinforces male advantage in these relationships, and therefore supports a private context in which force and threat may be used against women. . . .

For Shelter and Beyond

Massachusetts Coalition of Battered Women Services Groups, excerpts from *For Shelter and Beyond, An Educational Manual for Working with Women Who Are Battered*

LEGAL ADVOCACY

Introduction to the Legal System

The legal system is broken into two general categories: civil and criminal. The civil category usually concerns two or more persons who are involved in some matter that has caused harm to one or more of them. For example, if two people are in a car accident, one might sue the other for money, claiming that the other person was at fault. The Commonwealth of Massachusetts doesn't have any interest in this private dispute because it doesn't "affect the stability of the state" or the health, welfare and safety of Massachusetts residents generally. On the other hand, a criminal action (e.g., one person presses assault and battery charges against another), by definition affects these things because the law has been violated. The state issues a complaint against the offender and asks the court to punish (or reform) the offender supposedly to protect the state's interest in preserving the peace and safeguarding its citizens. In a civil action the woman chooses whether or not to file and follow through with the case; in a criminal action, the state decides whether or not to take the case and how to handle it.

This can get very confusing when one court can handle both civil and criminal cases; for example, the district courts handle criminal complaints like assault and battery and civil cases like abuse prevention. The court you're in, therefore, does not automatically determine whether the legal action is civil or criminal. As advocates the two courts that you will regularly use are the district court and the probate court. District courts handle civil and criminal matters; probate courts handle only civil matters. Both district and probate courts handle abuse prevention cases which are civil in nature.

The criminal courts have traditionally ignored criminal cases involving spouses or household members. Most such cases never make it to trial because the woman is intimidated by the abuser or the court into dropping the case. Many cases are dismissed or continued without a finding; of the few that go to trial with sufficient (overwhelming) evidence of guilt, most end in suspended sentences and/or probation. The man is then back on the street—or in the woman's home—in no time at all. The following overview therefore does not deal with the criminal system but rather uses examples from abuse prevention cases which are civil. The generalizations regarding attitudes toward woman—particularly battered women and women of color, whether battered or not—apply equally to civil and criminal court personnel.

Going to Court

Always keep in mind that not every woman needs to go to court; it depends on the circumstances and on what she wants. Many battered women want to go to court because they think that the legal system exists to protect them. Laws, however, were made by and for white, middle-class men, and most people working in the legal system have conservative/traditional ideas about men and women and their respective roles in society—particularly within the family. They accept the view that a man is the head of the household and that family matters are private and confidential. Because they have a vested interest in keeping families together and preserving the status quo, they will often downplay or ignore outright the danger that "staying together" will create for the woman by discouraging her from taking legal action against the abuser.

In district courts many judges and clerks consider abuse cases family matters that do not belong in their courts. Some make abusive comments about the woman living with someone to whom she is not married, or suggest that she's only going to make things worse for herself by taking him to court, or misinform her about the law and her rights. It is not unusual, for instance, for a married woman to be told that she must go to probate court and file for divorce, or for a single woman to be told that she must go to district court, or even that she is not entitled to orders because she is single. The law, in fact, gives both married and single women the right to file and to request protective orders in either the district, probate or superior court. The choice is hers, not the court's.

She must often face the judge in a public courtroom after waiting hours for her case to be called. Even if she has visible bruises and other evidence of battering, she may be asked a number of questions about the battering, and a number of irrelevant questions such as who pays the rent on her apartment, or what did she say or do to anger the abuser. In some cases a clerk or judge may accuse her of exaggerating or even lying about the violence. Some judges are more concerned with protecting a man's due process rights than with preserving a woman's physical safety. She may have come all this way fighting fear, embarrassment, lack of knowledge about the law, and perhaps a difficult clerk, only to be denied orders by the judge. If she gets her orders, she must then try to get the police to enforce them.

Because the legal system is intended primarily to protect the interests of white men of property, women of color often have an even more difficult time getting protective orders. Racist clerks and judges often assume that people of color are more violent than white people, and that some violence in the family should therefore be tolerated. (Similar assumptions are made about working-class people.) Third-world women thus have to deal with the racism of an almost-all-white environment at the courthouse, and then face blatant, overtly racist treatment by clerks and judges. Furthermore, if a woman comes away from that experience with protective orders, she must then deal with the police who are infamous for their hostility and racism toward people of color.

Dealing with the Police

Although having protective orders makes things a little safer, women usually expect the orders to have a much greater impact on the abuser and the police than they generally have. The abuser may ignore the orders and continue to harass the woman; the police may not enforce the orders.

Despite the fact that the Massachusetts Abuse Prevention Act established certain basic responsibilities for the police, many officers have refused to meet them. For instance, the police now have the power to arrest a man who has violated protective orders as long as they have reasonable cause to believe that he violated them (whether or not they witnessed the violation). In most cases however, the police have outrightly refused to arrest even when they've actually witnessed a violation of orders. Similarly, when the police respond to a "domestic disturbance" call they have to inform a victim of abuse of her rights with a simple rights card in English and Spanish which details her legal rights and the officer's responsibilities. Many officers ignore this responsibility by simply telling the woman that they can't do anything and that she has to go to court, without any further information, explanation or support.

Back to Court

When the police refuse to enforce her protective orders, the woman may decide to press criminal charges against the abuser for violation of orders. In some very serious cases a police officer may arrest the abuser and press charges against him. In most cases, however, the woman will have to press charges against the abuser on her own in the district court for the place in which the violation occurred. Women trying to press criminal charges for violation of orders are often shuffled back and forth between probate and district court, each telling her that she must go to the other or between the district court for the area in which the violation occurred. Even if her case is taken seriously and the abuser is prosecuted, the most she can hope for is that he will be put on probation in the majority of abuse cases.

Legal Advocates: Where Do We Fit In?

Legal advocates have often been able to make the system work somewhat better for battered women. They usually are better able to persuade or argue with difficult clerks, fill out court forms, etc., because they are less emotionally involved in the process. An advocate can often make the difference between a woman getting or not getting protective orders by stepping in when she is having difficulty explaining what has happened or what she needs.

The danger of this is that the advocate will take over for the woman and deny her the opportunity to be in control of her situation, or that the advocate will buy the myth that only "professional" or "semi-professional" people can effectively use the legal system. Many clerks and judges avoid dealing directly with battered women because they are elitist and want to deal with "professionals"; from their perspective, an advocate is the next best thing to a lawyer. Don't exclude the woman you're supporting from the process that is much more important to her than to you or the judge.

This is particularly destructive if the woman you're with is a woman of color and you are white. Judges and clerks are particularly disrespectful and contemptuous toward third-world women, and will use any means to exclude them from the process. Be sure that you're not reinforcing that behavior by appearing to be "providing social services" for this "unfortunate" woman who needs the help of white people to "straighten out" her life!

Before agreeing to go to court with a woman, make sure that that is what she wants to do and that she is aware of her options, both legal and non-legal. Explain the law to her and discuss what protective orders are available and what they can do and what they cannot do to help her, so that she can make an informed decision about whether or not to use the law.

If she chooses to go to court, you should discuss the facts with her ahead of time; in telling you about what happened (what the abuser did), the woman will get used to telling the story and be a little less embarrassed/intimidated once she's in court. You can also help the woman to write her affidavit (a written statement of facts signed under the penalties of perjury), if one is required by the court you are using. Explain the basic court procedures involved—where she'll stand, who she should talk to, what the judge or clerk might ask her, etc.

Part of our work is giving emotional support through the very difficult and emotionally draining experience of trying to use the legal system. A little pressure—or even a lot of indifference—could prevent a woman from demanding her legal rights. An advocate can prevent this from happening by supporting her in explaining her situation and intervening for her when the clerk is being pushy and/or giving her the wrong information (an all-too-frequent occurrence).

Dealing with Clerks and Judges as an Advocate

Be friendly and polite; dress well. It can get the woman's case called at a reasonable time, make the interview with the clerk less painful and get respect for you. Seeing you treated with respect can make things easier for the woman.

While it's important to act friendly and respectful to court personnel, it is also important to strike a balance between getting along with them and advocating for the woman. Don't be afraid to point out a mistake or misinformation by the clerk; don't hesitate to demand to see the judge if the clerk is refusing to deal with you. Like police, clerks will sometimes change their behavior toward you when you ask for their name or to see their superior. Gauge your behavior to theirs. When friendly persuasion doesn't work, don't be afraid to demand what the woman is entitled to by law or to express dissatisfaction.

When you get before the judge, explain who you are and that you are there to give the woman emotional support. If the judge excludes you from the process, there's nothing you can do; so if you're not sure what will happen till you actually speak to the judge, warn the woman that she may have to face the judge on her own. Judges are not necessarily any more sensitive or cooperative than clerks, but you and the woman should be aware that they have the power to hold you in contempt of court depending on your behavior.

If the woman gets her orders, make sure that she has a copy of them before you leave the courthouse that day, and that she understands them and knows when to come back to court for the second hearing. Remember that she may need your support even more during the second hearing if the abuser shows up at that time.

Finally, remember that your control of the situation is limited; there are some judges and clerks who will never be reformed. We can't expect to change a whole system and some of its most invested (and corrupted) members in a short time. Do as much as you can to help the woman through the process, but don't be afraid to suggest (remind her of) other options open to her. And even after a rash of courtroom successes, try not to forget that while we can make a difference in individual cases which affect women's lives, we cannot completely reform a system that is constantly reinforcing and perpetuating itself in patriarchal, racist and classist ideas and practices. Laws were established and are maintained by and for white, middle-class men, and it's going to take a long time to change that.

Elena Salzman, Note: The Quincy District Court Domestic Violence Prevention Program: A Model Legal Framework for Domestic Violence Intervention
74 B.U.L.Rev. 329 (March 1994).

... Pursuant to [The Massachusetts Abuse Prevention Act, Mass. Gen.L. ch. 209A (1992)] courts can issue restraining orders, which prohibit the defendant from abusing the plaintiff. ... Section 1 defines "abuse" as "attempting to cause or causing physical harm; placing another in fear of imminent serious physical harm; causing another to engage involuntarily in sexual relations by force, threat or duress."

A Massachusetts court has the power to order a defendant to refrain from contacting the plaintiff. Id. 3(b). The court also can issue a vacate order, which orders the defendant: (1) to leave and remain away from a premises; (2) to surrender any keys to the plaintiff; (3) not to damage any belongings of the plaintiff or any other occupant; (4) not to shut off or cause to be shut off any utilities or mail delivery to the plaintiff; and (5) not to interfere in any way with the plaintiff's right to possess that residence, except by appropriate legal proceedings. ...

If a victim demonstrates a substantial likelihood of immediate danger of abuse, the court may issue one of these orders without notice to the defendant. However, the court must give the defendant an opportunity to be heard on the question of continuing the temporary order and of granting other relief requested by the plaintiff within 10 court business days after such orders are entered. Id. The victim must reappear in court at this time if she seeks to extend the temporary order for the maximum period of one year. This hearing is commonly referred to as the "ten day hearing."

Since 1976, all 50 states have enacted civil laws allowing victims to obtain restraining orders against their batterers. ...

[The previous four paragraphs appear in footnote 25 of the Note and have been included to provide background about M.G.L. ch. 209A.— Editor's Note]

Despite the 1978 enactment of the Massachusetts Abuse Prevention Act, many Massachusetts judges have continued to exhibit traces of a "double standard" for family violence. Somerville District Court Judge Paul Heffernan's response to Pamela Nigro Dunn in 1986 is perhaps the most well-known and egregious example of judicial insensitivity to battered women. Ms. Dunn sought court protection from her husband who had beaten her, choked her, and locked her out of their apartment. When Ms. Dunn petitioned for a restraining order, Judge Heffernan admonished her for requesting legal intervention and squandering judicial time and resources. The Massachusetts Supreme Judicial Court privately reprimanded Judge Heffernan for exhibiting sarcastic, discourteous, and hostile behavior. Despite this episode, some judges continue to exhibit similarly inappropriate courtroom behavior.

The Quincy District Court Domestic Violence Program

The Quincy Program, one of the nation's most successful domestic violence intervention models, rests on three fundamental concepts: integration, communication, and prioritization of domestic violence issues. To accommodate over 1700 petitioners who seek restraining orders in the Quincy District Court each year, the Program classifies domestic violence cases as a priority over other civil matters. Chief Probation Officer Andrew Klein explains that by not choosing to make domestic violence cases a priority, "courts have, in effect, made the choice the other way around." The Quincy Program was the first of its kind in Massachusetts to integrate the traditionally separate roles of clerks, judges, district attorneys, probation officers, police officers, and batterers' treatment counselors. During monthly roundtable discussions, participants developed a powerful and coordinated judicial response to domestic abuse. Although courts in other counties have incorporated many of its components, the Quincy Program continues to be the most comprehensive and effective program in the state.

Judicial Participants

1. The Clerk's Office

When a woman comes to the Quincy District Court seeking a restraining order, her first contact will likely be with a domestic abuse clerk in the Restraining Orders Office. The Quincy Program innovators felt that the establishment of a separate restraining orders office would be more conducive to providing the one-on-one assistance women need to fill out the proper paperwork.

Of the eighty-three courts in Massachusetts that hear domestic violence cases, Quincy is one of only twenty-six that provides full-time, specialized advocacy to women seeking restraining orders. The importance of the domestic abuse clerks cannot be overemphasized. A woman entering the court is often confused, scared, and uncertain. The clerks help to provide the security a woman needs to embark on the intimidating process of requesting a restraining order.

Many of the domestic abuse clerks in Quincy are volunteer interns from law schools and social work programs at local universities. Their duties include disseminating: a sheet listing the critical information the woman should provide to the assisting clerk; a sheet detailing procedures on how to file a drug/alcohol petition; and an informational brochure entitled "Help and Protection for Families Experiencing Violence in the Home," which includes a list of emergency resources.

After the initial intake procedure, domestic abuse clerks refer the woman to the daily briefing sessions hosted by the District Attorney's Office. During these sessions, women not only receive information about referral services and their legal rights, but they also receive emotional support. After the briefing, a clerk accompanies a woman to the courtroom for her emergency hearing, which is usually conducted ex parte, without the batterer or his counsel present. Often the clerk will stand with the woman before the bench to provide moral support.

This individual assistance may explain why three times as many women return for the ten-day restraining order hearing in Quincy than in other area courts. Clerks are able to dispel a woman's misconceptions about the order's efficacy and provide her with information that can increase her safety. The clerks can also assure the woman that the abuse was not her fault.

2.   Judges

The Quincy Program would not be as responsive to women if it were not for judges' cooperation. Local judges helped pioneer the establishment of special procedures for domestic violence cases. Much of the proposed and recently enacted domestic violence legislation uses their approach as a model.

The Quincy Program has established "fast track" procedures for judges to expedite domestic violence hearings. Quincy has established daily morning and afternoon sessions to handle restraining order requests exclusively. If women miss these special sessions, judges should attempt to see them as soon as the petitions are filed, ahead of other pending cases. This contrasts sharply with many area courts in which women must wait hours for an available judge.

Judges can also influence violent relationships through their choice of sanctions for batterers who violate restraining orders. Some of the most stringent punishments include incarceration of batterers with prior criminal convictions and placement of batterers without prior convictions on one year or nine months probation. Often, however, batterers receive suspended sentences or short probation terms.

Quincy has a regular probation revocation session in which the presiding judge evaluates abusers' compliance with court orders. Judges hear new complaints alleging restraining order violations and may revoke probation without waiting for a new criminal trial and conviction. Judges may impose sanctions if they find, by a preponderance of the evidence, that an abuser has violated the order. Because probation violators pose tremendous safety risks to their victims, judges have incorporated this accelerated enforcement procedure into the Quincy Program.

3.   The District Attorney's Office: Family Violence Unit

The District Attorney's Office contributes a more comprehensive range of services than any other participant in the Quincy Program. The Office has full-time domestic violence staff (often called domestic violence counselors), victim/witness advocates, two special domestic violence prosecutors, and numerous volunteer interns who assist in virtually every aspect of the Program's operation.

Consistent with the Quincy Program's emphasis on integration, the District Attorney's Office provides twenty hours of training to the Quincy Police Department each year. The Office trains officers on the proper procedures for incident report writing, disturbance investigation, and evidence collection. When the police record incriminating evidence, the District Attorney's Office can prosecute or "go forward," without the victim's participation. This policy contrasts starkly with the policies of the Lawrence and Dorchester District Courts, where prosecutors will not pursue a case without the woman's testimony.

The Quincy Program includes an innovative tracking system whereby the police department forwards reports of domestic violence disturbances to the District Attorney's Office. A domestic violence counselor then follows-up by sending a letter to each identified victim. In all cases except those involving verbal arguments, Quincy counselors call the woman within a week after the follow-up letter to invite her to attend a restraining order briefing. This process often enables the office to establish contact with a woman before she has decided to come to court.

The domestic violence counselors also hold daily briefing sessions for all restraining order applicants. The counselors provide information on what women will face in court, what options they can request as part of the restraining order, what referral services are available to them, and what rights they have (i.e., filing a criminal complaint). The counselors also advise each woman to tell the judge if she is in fear, if there is a history of physical abuse, or if the abuser has access to weapons. . . .

The District Attorney's Office is involved with women from the initial follow-up letter and briefing, through the process of referrals and group sessions, to the completion of a complaint and appearance before a judge. This comprehensive support helps explain why seventy-four percent of women who file restraining orders return on the ten-day hearing date to request permanent orders. . . .

Nonjudicial Participants

. . . This success would not have been possible without further coordination with nonjudicial participants, including the Quincy Police Department and Emerge.

1. The Quincy Police Department

Pursuant to section 6 of the Massachusetts Abuse Prevention Act, a police officer must use "all reasonable means" to prevent abuse when the officer has reason to believe that a woman has been abused or is in danger of being abused. Accordingly, police must take domestic violence calls seriously.

The Quincy Police Department and the District Attorney's Office jointly created a special tracking system for domestic violence calls, which maintains computer records of all family disturbances, filed by address. Before officers respond to a particular domestic disturbance, this tracking system provides them with information on the presence of weapons, past or present restraining orders, and past arrests. . . .

2.   Emerge: A Batterers' Treatment Program

Between 1987 and 1992, the Quincy Program sent over 350 abusive men to Emerge, a counseling and educational program for batterers. Emerge treats battering as an ingrained social behavior rather than an anger or impulse control problem. Accordingly, Emerge teaches batterers to control future conduct by relearning appropriate social behaviors.

Unfortunately, the rate of "positive termination" is only twenty percent for men who voluntarily enter the program and thirty-five percent for men who are court-referred. These figures reflect the difficulty in curing a chronic batterer of his physical abusiveness.

Emerge employs confrontation group therapy designed to impress upon the batterer the severity of his conduct. Groups of approximately ten batterers meet with two counselors once a week for two hours. In the program's first stage, which lasts eight weeks, counselors give the men a behavior plan to help them initiate changes. In the second stage, counselors focus on overcoming attitudes that perpetuate abuse, encourage men to share their own experiences, and teach respectful, nonabusive ways to interact with women and children to resolve conflicts. Emerge has found that batterers must participate in this program for at least one year to make lasting changes in behavior and attitudes.

The Massachusetts legislature amended the Massachusetts Abuse Prevention Act in 1990 to allow judges to sentence eligible male batterers to certified treatment programs like Emerge. Because of Emerge's success, the Massachusetts Department of Public Health hired it in 1992 to conduct training programs for applicants seeking to qualify as certified treatment programs under the law. There are now at least sixteen other treatment programs throughout Massachusetts, in part because Emerge has sponsored training programs for batterers' treatment counselors. . . .

A Critical Evaluation of the Quincy Program:
Recommendations for Improvements

The Quincy Program has been an inspirational model for other courts. It deserves praise for its innovation and coordination in a field traditionally ignored by the judicial system. Many of the participants concede, however, that certain changes need to occur both in its administration and in its structure. . . .

[Judges remain hesitant to recommend criminal justice system response.] Chief Probation Officer Andrew Klein identifies two fundamental reasons why some judges hesitate to recommend the issuance of criminal complaints. First, he believes that some judges are not accustomed to integrating their traditionally separate civil and criminal roles. It may be counter-intuitive for these judges to think about criminal complaints during a hearing on a civil restraining order petition. Second, clerk-magistrates traditionally had maintained exclusive control over the decision to issue a criminal complaint. Some judges may still believe that these decisions are best handled solely by the clerks because this task is not part of a judge's responsibility.

Judge Whitman [a former Quincy judge] suggests that the fear of disempowering the woman may also account for judges' failure to recommend that the clerk issue a criminal complaint. Issuing a complaint without her permission can make her feel angry, out of control, frightened, and distrustful of the judicial system. Although this judicial sensitivity is commendable, batterers often need stronger control than a civil restraining order can provide. As a result, judges face the difficult task of balancing concerns for a woman's dignity with the likelihood of serious harm against her. . . .

Perhaps the most serious impediment to the safety of battered women arises from judicial insensitivity. Some judges may have an understandable sense of frustration with women who petition multiple times for an order and then consistently fail to return for the ten-day hearing. Regardless of the reason, however, insensitive conduct may dissuade a woman from pursuing a restraining order. . . .

The key to modifying judicial behavior lies in comprehensive and ongoing training programs for judges. Unfortunately, no comprehensive training program is currently in place. The legislature's elimination of funding for court personnel training has been the primary impediment to the creation of such a program. . . .

Future training should incorporate the following specific recommendations. First, training should inform judges about the range of sanctions available and the necessity for stringent measures in domestic violence cases. This basic training will assist judges in " 'assessing a batterer's level of dangerousness and [setting] up a safety plan for the victim.' " Judges should be advised that when sentencing batterers to a treatment program, the sentence should be for at least one year.

Second, judges who hesitate to recommend that clerk-magistrates issue criminal orders must be educated that the combination of civil and criminal complaints synergistically enhances a woman's safety. Further, judicial training should emphasize techniques both for encouraging women to seek criminal complaints and also for reassuring them through this difficult process. When a woman initiates the filing of a criminal complaint, a judge is less likely to disempower her by overriding her choice.

Third, training must focus on educating judges on the dynamics of victimization:

> "Judges ... must understand that violence produces a depen-
> dence as a result of the victimization. In addition, the court
> must recognize that victims must make choices within the
> relationship. These choices sometimes require the victim to
> come into court and vacate the order so as to maintain her
> own or her children's safety. The court and people in the
> system must understand that the abuser and the victim, in
> most part, exist together outside of the court, and the mere
> existence of a judicial order does not necessarily protect the
> victim."

The best judges in domestic violence are those that are sensitive to the
woman's fears and the alleged batterer's rights. A comprehensive, long-
term training program addressing these issues will enable judges to handle
domestic violence cases more effectively.

Angela West, Prosecutorial Activism: Confronting Heterosexism in a Lesbian Battering Case

15 Harv. Women's L.J. 249 (1992).

The phone rang in Division 56 of the Los Angeles Municipal Court. I
had just begun studying the *Metro* section of *The Los Angeles Times* for the
gory details of the weekend's violent crimes when the clerk called my name.
"West," he said gruffly, "they're sending us a battery from Division 30."
Groaning inwardly, I put the paper aside. Duty called. As a Deputy City
Attorney in Los Angeles, my job is to prosecute those who have been
charged with misdemeanor offenses committed within the city limits.

Shortly after the clerk's announcement, the door swung open. Two
women entered and immediately sat down together. ... The report had
described a roommate dispute, but I hadn't had time to read it carefully,
and it certainly seemed as if the dispute had been settled. Then I recognized them. I had noticed them earlier that week outside calendar court.
The had been arguing. The one who turned out to be the defendant had
been gesturing and talking very agitatedly to the other woman, who had
been nodding meekly. Their body language had attracted my attention.
Although women are usually less squeamish with each other than men
about physical closeness and touching, these women stood only about a half
inch apart. The first woman was aggressively angry, but the other woman
did not move back and seemed resigned to the situation. It was immediately clear to me that these women had an intimate relationship. ...

The file contained a sealed envelope. Inside was a Polaroid photo of the
victim (whom I shall call "Michele") with two swollen, purplish black eyes.
The extent of her injury alone would distinguish this case as one of our
more serious cases. ...

I took my time reviewing the file, trying to figure out how to approach
the situation. There they sat, the classic presentation: Michele, very close
by the defendant's side; the defendant, smiling broadly in anticipation of

the imminent demise of the case. I reread the police report. Maybe there *had* been some mistake. I recalled their intimate stance earlier that week in calendar court. The defendant couldn't have meant to do this, I reasoned, as I stared at Michele's black eyes staring back at me from that Polaroid. Women aren't aggressive. Women aren't violent by nature. Women don't hurt other women in relationships—do they? Isn't that one of the major advantages of lesbianism—freedom from domination and from the threat of brute force? Surely there was another reason why this had happened, some reason that I could understand. . . .

I stood up and approached the victim, ready to evaluate how whatever she said would sound to a jury. She flinched and stood up reluctantly upon being elbowed by the defendant. . . . I introduced myself. She told me that there had been a horrible misunderstanding.

"Let's step outside," I suggested.

The Story was that she and Sherry, the defendant, had been shopping on Olvera Street a few weeks ago, when her purse was snatched by "two Mexican guys." She gave chase and was punched in the face by one of them. Discouraged, she had gone home without reporting the theft to the police. Throughout this ordeal, Sherry had been nothing but supportive. . . . Distressed by the loss of a significant amount of money, she had picked a fight with Sherry. After the argument, she had decided to "get Sherry in trouble" by going to the police station the next day and saying that Sherry had hit her. She knew it was wrong, and she was sorry. She tried to smile apologetically. It looked more like a wince.

I thought about the police report. It said that Michele had appeared at the station with two friends and two black eyes, insisting that Sherry be arrested. She told the desk officer that she was tired of Sherry beating her up and hitting her son. Michele told them that the black eyes had been inflicted the night before during a particularly vicious beating, and that her son had been struck when he tried to run between them. Afterwards, Sherry had confiscated Michele's purse with all her money and identification so that she would not be able to leave. . . . Sherry was arrested. A booking search had produced Michele's ID and the contents of her wallet, stuffed into Sherry's pocket.

I then considered another major problem with this case. The desk officer had written that Michele and Sherry were "roommates." I believe that a different assumption would have been made if Michele had described the same set of circumstances involving a man. But since we live in a heterosexual society, the facts, indicating a deeper relationship, were denied or ignored. My guess was that the officer's assumption was based on the fact that Michele was a very attractive, feminine woman, the kind who "could get a man."

The police description of a "roommate" relationship created . . . problems. . . . [T]estimony from an expert on BWS [Battered Woman Syndrome] would not be relevant unless it was alleged and demonstrated at

SHIP TO:

UNIV OF NOTRE DAME   IN
PROF MICHAEL ZUCKERT
POLITICAL SCIENCE DEPT
NOTRE DAME IN 46556

ORDER DATE	ORDER NO.
06-22-99	6678098

BATCH	ACCOUNT NO.	P.O. NO.	PAGE	ATTENTION
9601	999-999-950		1	3025993300-0066678098

SPECIAL INSTRUCTIONS

PACKING SLIP

ISBN	ORDERED	SHIPPED	AUTHOR/DESCRIPTION	
1-56662-557-2	1	1	ESKRIDGE SEXUALITY GENDER TM	0.00
1-56662-705-2	1	1	ESKRIDGE SEX GENDER 98 SUPP	0.00
1-56662-608-0	1	1	FRUG WOMEN & THE LAW 2D	0.00
				0.00

THANK YOU

trial that the assault had taken place in the course of some sort of conjugal relationship. . . .

I realized that my only hope in pursuing the case was to explain away the recanting. I therefore had to get Michele to tell me, and be willing to state in open court, that she and Sherry were in a lesbian relationship. . . .

I anticipated Michele's desire to stay in the closet for two reasons. She had a child, and court proceedings are a matter of public record. The revelation of her sexual preference conceivably could be used against her in a custody proceeding brought by homophobic relatives or the child's father. Furthermore, the police report indicated that the defendant had also struck the child. If evidence to support this abuse came out at trial, the Department of Children's Services might be notified if Michele and Sherry continued to live together. If the child were taken into protective custody, Michele would again be faced with the prospect of losing custody. Besides that, Michele and Sherry are both Black, as am I. My experience indicates that gay men and lesbians of color are reluctant to reveal their homosexuality, which generally is regarded with even greater hostility in minority communities than in society at large. Despite my misgivings, I had to try. I decided to be direct. I fixed Michele with a look that I hoped was both knowing and encouraging. "Look," I began, drawing closer to her, "You guys are . . . together, right?" I asked as conspiratorially as possible.

She hesitated. She looked down and shifted her feet a bit. She looked back up, "Well . . . yes."

I wanted to embrace her. I was elated! She was willing to tell the truth. This case could be proven! . . .

At this point, I encountered the real obstacles.

The PD [public defender] told the judge that I had no case, that the victim had been mugged. The judge, also a Black woman, looked to me for an explanation. If the victim said the defendant was not the mugger, she wanted to know, what was I trying to do?

I told them that the case had been misfiled: This was a lesbian relationship, the incident had been domestic violence, the victim was only recanting as victims often do, and I was going to call in the DV expert.

The judge and the PD both protested. The nature of the relationship was irrelevant and therefore inadmissible. Even if it were admissible, I would have to prove the lesbian relationship, and that would take the focus off the real issue of whether the defendant had hit the victim. And, the judge announced, the testimony regarding BWS could not be offered unless the charge was domestic battery.

I had not expected this obstacle. The case had been misfiled as a simple battery because the police had made a heterosexist assumption. No one had bothered to ascertain the nature of the relationship even when, on its face, the facts of the assault indicated a chronically violent situation. . . . I offered to amend the complaint to allege domestic battery under Section

273.5 [of the California Penal Code]. The PD was way ahead of me: "That's only for violence between a man and a woman." . . .

This, I said hotly, was institutionalized heterosexism and should not be tolerated. After all, there was a victim to protect. This argument caused the judge some discomfort.

More discussion ensued among the three of us. After considerable back-and-forth, it came down to this: The judge ruled that any testimony regarding why the victim might be lying would not be permitted from our standard DV/BWS experts. In her opinion, there was no certainty that the standard testimony was broad enough to apply to a homosexual, specifically lesbian, relationship. Any expert called by the People would have to prove, to the judge's satisfaction, that lesbians were affected by BWS; demonstrate through sufficient statistical evidence that it occurred with some frequency; and prove to be qualified to speak on the subject before a jury.

The judge was concerned with protecting the defendant from a conviction based on unwarranted assumptions. But this ruling posed a major obstacle . . . I worried that I would not find a qualified expert . . . .

Dr. Vallerie Coleman, Ph.D., . . . had written . . . on the incidence of battering in lesbian relationships . . . . When Dr. Coleman told me during our phone conversation that she had concluded that lesbians did suffer from BWS in the course of an abusive relationship, I considered hers to be the last word on the subject.

Dr. Coleman further noted that a battered woman in a lesbian relationship is less likely to admit the abuse than a heterosexual woman, given society's hostility toward the relationship itself. The secrecy and shame connected to the incidents are compounded by extreme reluctance to discuss the relationship with authorities, and even with other lesbians. The lesbian victim's aversion to discussing the situation within her community is also based on feelings that I myself had experienced upon reviewing the file; that lesbians were not supposed to hit their lovers or be physically aggressive. The lesbian community generally feels that dominance and violence within a relationship are only displayed by males; women who conducted themselves in that way would therefore be emulating men. A lesbian in a battering relationship would thus feel several layers of shame: the violence, the simulation of heterosexuality, and the perpetration of the worst kind of tyranny and oppression of women, from which this relationship should have freed her.

Lesbians are often referred to as an "invisible" group. Their lack of visibility is connected both to sexism and societal homophobia. Due to the pervasiveness of violence against women, coupled with women's relative economic disadvantage, the fear of being "out" is greater for lesbians than for gay men. The batterer quite frequently will threaten the victim who wants to end the relationship with disclosure of her lesbianism to family, friends, and employers. For the closeted victim, the terror that such revelations could result in her losing her job and/or children silences her.

I told the judge about Dr. Coleman the next day in chambers, feeling very much like Dorothy bringing back the broomstick of the vanquished Wicked Witch to the great and powerful Oz. . . .

My case-in-chief began with the victim's testimony. She told the mugging story with enough hesitation, furtive looks at the defendant for approval, and inconsistencies (which I took great care to highlight) to make the jurors shift in their seats. Encouraged, I pressed forward with the police officers. They related in detail the victim's apparent fear and desperation at the time they had encountered her, and the defendant's hostile, defiant attitude throughout the arrest and booking process. When I asked them whether they had been aware at the time that they were dealing with a homosexual relationship, they were nonplused, not reacting negatively or indicating that this fact in any way changed their opinion of the victim or the defendant. The fact that the officers did not change facial expressions or body language when discussing the subject of sexual preference was, I thought, a very good example for the jury.

I also brought out the fact that the officers would not have charged the defendant with a mere simple battery if they had known that the violence had taken place in the context of an intimate relationship; that instead they would have arrested the defendant for violation of [California Penal Code] Section 243 [criminalizing battery within a dating relationship]. . . . The one failing on the part of my police witnesses was that they stated that they only charged under that section if the parties specifically told them that they were homosexual. "We don't like to assume those things," said one officer. . . .

Dr. Coleman concluded that, although she had never met the victim, based upon the "hypothetical" situation that I had given her, it was likely that a lesbian in her situation would be afflicted by BWS.

The prosecution rested.

The defense's case consisted of the testimony of the defendant. She reiterated the mugging story, with several digressions that were extremely telling. The purse had been snatched because "Michele doesn't know how to take care of her things." She was aware that Michele had been hurt in the altercation because she had heard her scream and Michele was "always too loud." She had to take care of all the details of treating her injuries because Michele was "kinda ding-y" and "always messed things up." Yes, they had had an argument that week, but she had only yelled at Michele because Michele had "eaten the meat out of her Chinese rice," which indicated that she was "selfish" and "didn't care about anybody but herself." Michele had left to spend the night with a friend; this friend's house was where Michele "always goes" when they had arguments.

The derisive, belittling tone of the defendant's remarks about Michele fit perfectly with Dr. Coleman's description of an abuser's attitude toward a victim. The testimony also made clear that Sherry and Michele regularly had arguments of such intensity that Michele often found it necessary to leave the house for substantial periods of time, even though she had a young child in tow and the apartment was in her name. The defendant also testified that Michele was financially dependent on her, and that she didn't approve of Michele's spending time with her friends because they "wanted" Michele and were "out to get" her. She became hostile and aggressive during my cross-examination, and was evasive when I asked if she ever got mad enough at Michele to hit her.

The defense rested.

The jury deliberated for a day before coming back with a conviction. Interestingly, the lone lesbian juror was the one who had balked at convicting. The other jurors had had to spend most of the time that they were out trying to convince her of Sherry's guilt. She had not wanted to convict "a sister." ... In the jury room, she had seen herself as the lone advocate for gay rights—the problem was that she had focused on the defendant as the object of the crusade rather than on the victim.

Sherry was sentenced to thirty-six months of probation. Although she was convicted for a simple battery, the judge ordered her to attend batterers' counseling. ... The admission of BWS testimony was not only crucial to the conviction itself (a fact later verified to me by the jurors), but also seems to have influenced the judge in sentencing Sherry.

Michele left the court before sentencing and I never saw her again. I did, however, receive two phone calls from her. The first, on the evening the verdict was returned, was in response to the media hoopla surrounding the outcome. ...

The second call came a month later. She was so sorry, Michele began, that she had lied. Sherry had threatened to "get her" if she told the real story. She felt very guilty for making me go through such effort, and she also wanted me to apologize to the judge for lying on the stand. What she wanted to know was, could I do anything to help her? Sherry was "bothering" her again and was now threatening to set fire to her apartment while she slept. She had already vandalized Michele's car. She was so afraid at this point that she was ready to cooperate with the prosecution if we could somehow help her.

I advised her to call the police and make a report. I told her that our DV unit could give her shelter information and that there was a support group ... for abuse victims, facilitated by Dr. Coleman. I told her that there was nothing I could do unless a new case was filed. She thanked me and hung up. I don't know if she ever called any of those people. ...

In the time that has passed since the case, I have had a chance to reflect on the dynamics of Sherry's conviction and to question my initial excitement at the implications of the successful prosecution of a lesbian battering case. I now suspect that there were some negative factors that may have contributed to the jurors' acceptance of the BWS testimony. BWS explains the actions and responses of a victim that are generally thought to be unreasonable, or abnormal. Recanting—especially after repeated battering incidents—and reluctance to terminate the relationship are incredible to many jurors, even after considering the victim's fear of and conjugal affection for the batterer. The expert testimony is received upon the theory that the recanting victim is not "normal" and her actions must necessarily be explained and interpreted by some sort of mental health professional. In order to use this evidence to convict, the jury must believe and accept that the victim is indeed not normal. It certainly seems possible that Michele's lesbianism may have helped the eleven heterosexual jurors to reach this conclusion.

As for Sherry, she may have been the victim of multiple stereotyping. Black females have traditionally been viewed as much more hostile and aggressive than women of other races. This perception probably increased the jurors' willingness to believe that Sherry was capable of the violence with which she was charged. (Nine of the twelve jurors were white.) The stereotype that Black women are "angry" and "domineering" often results in their criminal convictions despite exculpatory evidence—in this case, Michele's recantation. BWS generally is rejected when used to bolster a *defense* for Black women who assault or kill their batterers. However, in this case, when the *prosecution* used BWS *against* the defendant, the jury readily accepted the theory.

The jury had to decide who was the "good" woman and who was the "bad" woman. Sherry was the logical target for homophobia because she was more "butch," more masculine in appearance and behavior, than Michele. Although Michele may have been the victim of homophobia also, it would work to the prosecution's advantage if Michele were perceived as "sick." . . .

I am still convinced that any step that highlights the sameness of gay and lesbian couples and families, and extends to them the legal protections already enjoyed by heterosexuals, is positive. The subject may indeed be uncomfortable for lesbians and gay men interested in "putting on a good face" in hopes of achieving social acceptance, but the fact is that we must demand equal protection under the law. We do not yet have it, and we must begin somewhere. . . .

Excerpts from the Violence Against Women Act

42 USCA § 13981.

(a) Purpose

Pursuant to the affirmative power of Congress to enact this part under section 5 of the Fourteenth Amendment to the Constitution, as well as under section 8 of Article I of the Constitution, it is the purpose of this part to protect the civil rights of victims of gender motivated violence and to promote safety, health, and activities affecting interstate commerce by establishing a Federal civil rights cause of action for victims of crimes of violence motivated by gender.

(b) Right to be free from crimes of violence

All persons within the United States shall have the right to be free from crimes of violence motivated by gender (as defined in subsection (d) of this section).

(c) Cause of action

A person (including a person who acts under color of any statute, ordinance, regulation, custom, or usage of any State) who commits a crime of violence motivated by gender and thus deprives another of the right declared in subsection (b) of this section shall be liable to the party injured, in an action for the recovery of compensatory and punitive damages, injunctive and declaratory relief, and such other relief as a court may deem appropriate.

(d) Definitions

For purposes of this section—

(1) the term "crime of violence motivated by gender" means a crime of violence committed because of gender or on the basis of gender, and due, at least in part, to an animus based on the victim's gender; and

(2) the term "crime of violence" means—

(A) an act or series of acts that would constitute a felony against the person or that would constitute a felony against property if the conduct presents a serious risk of physical injury to another, and that would come within the meaning of State or Federal offenses described in section 16 of Title 18, whether or not those acts have actually resulted in criminal charges, prosecution, or conviction and whether or not those acts were committed in the special maritime, territorial, or prison jurisdiction of the United States; and

(B) includes an act or series of acts that would constitute a felony described in subparagraph (A) but for the relationship between the person who takes such action and the individual against whom such action is taken.

(e) Limitation and procedures

(1) Limitation

Nothing in this section entitles a person to a cause of action under subsection (c) of this section for random acts of violence unrelated to gender or for acts that cannot be demonstrated, by a preponderance of the evidence, to be motivated by gender (within the meaning of subsection (d) of this section).

(2) No prior criminal action

Nothing in this section requires a prior criminal complaint, prosecution, or conviction to establish the elements of a cause of action under subsection (c) of this section.

(3) Concurrent jurisdiction

The Federal and State courts shall have concurrent jurisdiction over actions brought pursuant to this part.

(4) Supplemental jurisdiction

Neither section 1367 of Title 28 nor subsection (c) of this section shall be construed, by reason of a claim arising under such subsection, to confer on the courts of the United States jurisdiction over any State law claim seeking the establishment of a divorce, alimony, equitable distribution of marital property, or child custody decree. . . .

Jane Doe v. John Doe

United States District Court, D. Connecticut, 1996.
929 F.Supp. 608.

JANET B. ARTERTON, DISTRICT JUDGE.

Plaintiff Jane Doe seeks to avail herself of the civil rights remedy provided under the Violence Against Women Act of 1994 ("VAWA" or the "Act"), 42 U.S.C. Section 13981, seeking damages for deprivation of her federal right to be free from her husband's alleged gender-based violence against her. Plaintiff alleges that from 1978 until 1995 the defendant "systematically and continuously inflicted a violent pattern of physical and mental abuse and cruelty upon the plaintiff," including throwing her to the floor, kicking her, throwing sharp and dangerous objects at her, threatening to kill her, and destroying property belonging to the plaintiff. . . . Plaintiff also alleges that the defendant forced her "to be a 'slave' and perform all manual labor, including maintaining and laying out his clothes for his numerous dates with his many girlfriends and mistresses." . . . She claims extreme emotional distress, including battered women's syndrome, post-traumatic stress disorder, and depression. . . .

Defendant's motion to dismiss the complaint challenges the constitutionality of the Civil Rights Remedy provision of the VAWA, claiming that Congress lacked authority under either the Commerce Clause or the Fourteenth Amendment of the United States Constitution to enact this statutory scheme recognizing and enforcing a federal civil right to be free from gender-based violence. . . .

I. Discussion

A. The Violence Against Women Act of 1994

In September 1994, Congress passed the Violence Against Women Act of 1994, a comprehensive statutory enactment designed to address "the escalating problem of violent crime against women," as part of the larger Violent Crime Control and Law Enforcement Act of 1994, P.L. 103–322. S.Rep. 103–138, 103rd Cong., 1st Sess., Violence Against Women Act of 1993, 38 (Sept. 10, 1993). In considering whether a comprehensive federal approach was needed to address systematic, gender-based violent crime, Congress held numerous hearings over a four-year period and amassed substantial documentation on how gender-based violence impacts interstate commerce and interferes with women's ability to enjoy equal protection of the laws. Congressional committees heard testimony from law enforcement officials, anti-domestic violence organizations, rape crisis centers, psychiatrists, other mental health experts, physicians, law professors, staff attorneys from legal advocacy groups, state Attorneys General, and victims of domestic violence. Congress also reviewed U.S. Justice Department statistics and studies of gender bias in state courts commissioned by seventeen state supreme courts. See S.Rep. 138, at 49 n. 52.

After such consideration, the congressional committees found:

> 1. "Violence is the leading cause of injury to women ages 15–44, more common than automobile accidents, muggings, and cancer deaths combined." S.Rep. 138, at 38.
>
> 2. "In 1991, at least 21,000 domestic crimes were reported to the police every week; at least 1.1 million reported assaults—including aggravated assaults, rapes, and murders—were committed against women in their homes that year; unreported domestic crimes have been estimated to be more than three times this total." Id. at 37.
>
> 3. "Every week, during 1991, more than 2,000 women were raped and more than 90 women were murdered—9 out of 10 by men." Id. at 38.
>
> 4. "An estimated 4 million American women are battered each year by their husbands or partners. Approximately 95% of all domestic violence victims are women. About 35% of women visiting hospital emergency rooms are due to injuries sustained as a result of domestic violence. One study of battered women found that 63 percent of the victims had been beaten while they were pregnant." H.R.Rep. 95, 103d Cong., 1st Sess., Violence Against Women Act of 1993, 26 (Nov. 20, 1993).

As part of the VAWA, Congress established a new federal civil right and remedy for victims of gender-based violent crimes. The Act declares that "[a]ll persons within the United States shall have the right to be free from crimes of violence motivated by gender." 42 U.S.C. Section 13981. As remedy for violation of this new civil right, the Act provides for compensatory and punitive damages awards and injunctive relief:

> A person (including a person who acts under color of any statute, ordinance, regulation, custom, or usage of any State) who commits a crime of violence motivated by gender and thus deprives another of the right declared in subsection (b) of this section shall be liable to the party injured, in an action for the recovery of compensatory and punitive damages, injunctive and declaratory relief, and such other relief as a court may deem appropriate.

Id. at Section 13981(c). The term "crime of violence motivated by gender" is defined as "a crime of violence committed because of gender or on the basis of gender, and due, at least in part, to an animus based on the victim's gender." Id. Section 13981(d)(1). The statute does not require a prior criminal complaint, prosecution, or conviction to establish the elements of the cause of action. Id. at Section 13981(e)(2).

Congressional authority to enact the civil rights remedy was asserted as an exercise of the "affirmative power of Congress" under both the Fourteenth Amendment, section 5 and the Commerce Clause, section 8 of Article I of the U.S. Constitution. Id. at 13981(a). Defendant argues, however, that Congress exceeded its powers in enacting VAWA under both the Commerce Clause and the Fourteenth Amendment, claiming that VAWA creates a "plenary federal police power," outside the Constitution's rubric which "creates a Federal Government of enumerated powers," United States v. Lopez, 514 U.S. 549, ___, 115 S.Ct. 1624, 1626, 131 L.Ed.2d 626 (1995), and impermissibly encroaches on the states' separate and distinct powers under the Tenth Amendment. See Id. (citing THE FEDERALIST No. 45, pp. 292–293 (C. Rossiter ed. 1961)).

B. The VAWA's Civil Rights Remedy and the Constitution's Commerce Clause.

Under the Commerce Clause, the Constitution grants to Congress three broad categories of activity which it has the power to regulate: (1) the use of channels of interstate commerce, (2) the instrumentalities of interstate commerce, or persons or things in interstate commerce, and (3) those activities that substantially affect interstate commerce. *Lopez*, 514 U.S. at ___-___, 115 S.Ct. at 1629–30 (citations omitted). The Court's analysis is limited to this third area of regulatory activity in light of the Supreme Court's attention to this prong in *Lopez* on which defendant relies.

In reviewing the constitutionality of a statute under the third prong of permissible regulation under the Commerce Clause, granting Congress power "[t]o regulate Commerce with foreign Nations, and among the several states," U.S. Const. art. I Section 8, cl. 3, "[t]he task of a court that is asked to determine whether a particular exercise of congressional power under the Commerce Clause is relatively narrow," Hodel v. Virginia Surface Mining & Reclamation Ass'n, Inc., 452 U.S. 264, 276, 101 S.Ct. 2352, 2360, 69 L.Ed.2d 1 (1981), and this Court's standard of review is limited to whether a rational basis existed for concluding that a regulated activity sufficiently affected interstate commerce. Id. While the Court's inquiry is an independent one, it will consider congressional findings, including congressional committee findings. *Lopez*, 514 U.S. at ___, 115 S.Ct. at 1631. If the court concludes that Congress had a rational basis for enacting the statutory provision at issue, then the remaining question is whether the means chosen by Congress are " 'reasonably adapted to the end permitted by the Constitution.' " *Hodel*, 452 U.S. at 276, 101 S.Ct. at 2360 (quoting Heart of Atlanta Motel, Inc. v. United States, 379 U.S. 241, 262, 85 S.Ct. 348, 360, 13 L.Ed.2d 258 (1964)).

In United States v. Lopez, supra, on which defendant principally relies, the Supreme Court struck down, as violative of the Commerce Clause, the Gun–Free School Zones Act of 1990 (18 U.S.C. Section 922(a)(1)(A),) which federalized the offense of possession of a firearm within 1,000 feet of a school. Id., at ___, 115 S.Ct. at 1629. In *Lopez*, despite the absence of any Congressional findings for the Supreme Court to review, the Government claimed that the statute regulated an activity which substantially impacted interstate commerce because possession of firearms in a school zone may result in an increase in violent crime which would affect the national economy by increased insurance costs, reduction of the willingness of individuals to travel to areas within the country that are perceived to be unsafe, and by diminution in citizen productiveness from impaired student learning environments. See Id. at ___, at 1632.

The Supreme Court concluded, however, that the activity regulated by the Gun Free Zones Act did not fall within any of the three categories authorizing Congressional action under the Commerce Clause, and that gun possession was already subject to regulation by most states, which have " 'primary authority for defining and enforcing criminal law.' " *Lopez*, 514 U.S. at ___ n. 3, 115 S.Ct. at 1631 n. 3 (quoting Brecht v. Abrahamson, 507 U.S. 619, 634, 113 S.Ct. 1710, 1720, 123 L.Ed.2d 353 (1993)). Thus, the Court held that the "statute by its terms has nothing to do with 'commerce' or any sort of economic enterprise, however broadly one might define those terms," Id. at ___, 115 S.Ct. at 1631, and rejected the Government's "cost of crime" argument as an overexpansive theory which would permit Congress to "regulate not only all violent crime, but all activities that might lead to violent crime, regardless of how tenuously they relate to interstate commerce." Id. at ___, 115 S.Ct. at 1632.

Here, this defendant asserts that the Civil Rights Remedy of VAWA suffers the same constitutional defects as the Gun Free Zones Act. First, defendant maintains that *Lopez* overruled the rationality test for determining whether federal regulation of interstate conduct can be sustained. See *Hodel*, 452 U.S. at 276, 101 S.Ct. at 2360. This Court disagrees. *Lopez* does warn that the Commerce Clause has limits, and that "the scope of the interstate commerce power 'must be considered in light of our dual system of government and may not be extended so as to embrace effects upon interstate commerce so indirect and remote.... ' " *Lopez*, 514 U.S. at ___, 115 S.Ct. at 1628 (quoting N.L.R.B. v. Jones & Laughlin Steel Corp., 301 U.S. 1, 37, 57 S.Ct. 615, 624, 81 L.Ed. 893 (1937)). Along with this warning, however, *Lopez* reaffirmed the rationality test of *Hodel*:

> Since that time, the Court has heeded that warning and undertaken to decide whether a rational basis existed for concluding that a regulated activity sufficiently affected interstate commerce.

Id. at 514 U.S. at ___, 115 S.Ct. at 1629 (citing *Hodel*, 452 U.S. at 276–280, 101 S.Ct. at 2360–2362); See Perez v. United States, 402 U.S. 146, 155–56, 91 S.Ct. 1357, 1362, 28 L.Ed.2d 686 (1971); Katzenbach v. McClung, 379 U.S. 294, 299–301, 85 S.Ct. 377, 381–82, 13 L.Ed.2d 290

(1964); *Heart of Atlanta Motel, Inc.*, 379 U.S. at 252–253, 85 S.Ct. at 354–55.

Defendant next seizes upon dicta in *Lopez* as critical of the same arguments relied on in enacting VAWA, namely the Government's "cost of crime" and "national productivity" arguments, and deduces that similarly VAWA is an impermissible overreaching of congressional authority. Since this Court has concluded that *Lopez* did not overturn or limit the nationality test, and because Congress has demonstrated the need for this legislation, the Court rejects defendant's conclusion which is based upon "selectively relying on Supreme Court statements plucked from their context." U.S. v. Wilson, 73 F.3d 675, 685 (7th Cir.1995).

The Congressional findings and reports qualitatively and quantitatively demonstrate the substantial effect on interstate commerce of gender-based violence, in marked distinction to the Gun Free Zone Act challenged in *Lopez* which lacked such analysis, only theoretical impact arguments.

In its final report on the Violence Against Women Act, the Senate concluded:

> Gender-based crimes and fear of gender-based crimes restricts movement, reduces employment opportunities, increases health expenditures, and reduces consumer spending, all of which affect interstate commerce and the national economy. Gender-based violence bars its most likely targets—women— from full participation in the national economy. For example, studies report that almost 50 percent of rape victims lose their jobs or are forced to quit in the aftermath of the crime. Even the fear of gender-based violence affects the economy because it deters women from taking jobs in certain areas or at certain hours that pose a significant risk of such violence.

S.Rep. 138, at 54.

Moreover, the House Conference found:

> [C]rimes of violence motivated by gender have a substantial adverse effect on interstate commerce, by deterring potential victims from traveling interstate, from engaging in employment in interstate businesses, and from transacting with business, and in places involved, in interstate commerce; crimes of violence motivated by gender have a substantial adverse effect on interstate commerce, by diminishing national productivity, increasing medical and other costs, and decreasing the supply of and the demand for interstate products.

H.Report 103–711, Violent Crime Control and Law Enforcement Act of 1994, 103rd Cong., 2d Sess., 385 (Aug. 21, 1994) U.S. Code Cong. & Admin.News 1994 pp. 1801, 1839, 1853.

The determination of whether a particular activity substantially affects interstate commerce is "ultimately a judicial rather than a legislative question." *Lopez*, 514 U.S. at ___, 115 S.Ct. at 1629 (quoting *Heart of*

Atlanta, 379 U.S. at 273, 85 S.Ct. at 366)(Black, J., concurring). "[S]imply because Congress may conclude that a particular activity affects interstate commerce does not necessarily make it so." Id. 514 U.S. at ___ n. 2, 115 S.Ct. at 1629 n. 2 (quoting *Hodel*, 452 U.S. at 311, 101 S.Ct. at 2391). However, because of the extensive compilation of data, testimony, and reports on which Congress based its findings, this Court is not left to speculate or " 'pile inference upon inference' to perceive an explicit connection between the regulated activity and interstate commerce." United States v. Sage, 906 F.Supp. 84, 92 (D.Conn.1995) (upholding the constitutionality of the Child Support Recovery Act under the Commerce Clause).

Defendant concedes that the gender-based violence that the VAWA was designed to discourage, affects interstate commerce, but asserts that the substantiality of its interstate impact is no more than that of other activities regulated under the states' police powers. While Supreme Court precedent does not articulate a particular standard or test to determine whether a particular activity "substantially affects" interstate commerce, Wickard v. Filburn, 317 U.S. 111, 63 S.Ct. 82, 87 L.Ed. 122 (1942) is instructive as setting forth the outer-limit of Congress' authority to regulate private intra-state conduct. See *Lopez*, 514 U.S. at ___, 115 S.Ct. at 1630

In *Wickard*, a small Ohio farmer, Roscoe Filburn, harvested 23 acres of wheat, 12 acres more than his allotment under the Agricultural Adjustment Act of 1938. After harvesting his wheat, he sold a portion of his crop, fed part of it to livestock on his farm, used some as flour for home consumption, and kept the remainder for seeding future crops. The Secretary of Agriculture assessed him a penalty for his 12 acre excessive harvest under the Agricultural Adjustment Act, which was designed to regulate the volume of wheat moving in interstate commerce as a means of regulating surpluses and shortages to stabilize wheat prices. *Wickard*, 317 U.S. at 114, 63 S.Ct. at 83–84. The Supreme Court concluded that the repetitive impact of activity like farmer Filburn's home wheat consumption was sufficient to demonstrate substantial impact on interstate commerce to uphold the constitutionality of the Agricultural Adjustment Act:

> It can hardly be denied that a factor of such volume and variability as home-consumed wheat would have a substantial influence on price and market conditions. This may arise because being in marketable condition such wheat overhangs the market and, if induced by rising prices, tends to flow into the market and check price increases. But if we assume that it is never marketed it supplies a need of the man who purchases in the open market. Home-grown wheat in this sense competes with wheat in commerce.

Id. at 128, 63 S.Ct. at 90 (emphasis added). See *Lopez*, 514 U.S. at ___, 115 S.Ct. at 1630.

Certainly the repetitive nationwide impact of women withholding, withdrawing or limiting their participation in the workplace or marketplace in response to or as a result of gender-based violence or the threat thereof, is of such a nature to be as substantial an impact on interstate commerce as the effect of excess "home-grown" wheat harvesting which was found to have been properly regulated by Congressional enactment. See Katzenbach v. McClung, 379 U.S. at 303, 85 S.Ct. at 383 (upholding Title II of the Civil Rights Act of 1964 and finding that the refusal of restaurants to serve African–Americans "imposed burdens both on the interstate flow of food and upon the movement of goods in general.").

After careful review of the Congressional history of VAWA, this Court concludes that the statistical, medical, and economic data before the Congress adequately demonstrated the rational basis for Congress' findings that gender-based violence has a substantial effect on interstate commerce. Notwithstanding *Lopez*'s conclusion that "states possess primary authority for defining and enforcing criminal law," *Lopez*, 514 U.S. at ___ n. 3, 115 S.Ct. at 1631 n. 3 (citations omitted), dozens of courts throughout the country, post-*Lopez*, have upheld a variety of federal criminal and civil enactments as constitutional under the Commerce Clause, including those which proscribe interference with access to reproductive health clinics, carjacking, failure to pay child support, possession of a firearm by a felon, intrastate possession and/or sale of narcotics, transfer and possession of machine guns, extortion or robbery that affects interstate commerce, Title III of the Americans with Disabilities Act, the Employee Retirement Income Security Act, the National Labor Relations Act, and the Beef Promotion and Research Act of 1985.

Defendant next argues that enactment of the VAWA encroaches on traditional police powers of the state and impermissibly "federalizes" criminal, family law, and state tort law. The Civil Remedy section of VAWA, however, does nothing to infringe on a state's authority to arrest and prosecute an alleged batterer on applicable criminal charges. VAWA does not encroach on traditional areas of state law; it complements them by recognizing a societal interest in ensuring that persons have a civil right to be free from gender-based violence, and through the Civil Rights Remedy, makes operative the Act's remedial and deterrent purposes, by making violators of this right personally answerable to the victims in compensatory and punitive damages. Defendant's assertion that the Act "federalizes" family law is clearly contradicted by the VAWA's express language under which federal jurisdiction excludes " ... any State law claim seeking the establishment of a divorce, alimony, equitable distribution of marital property, or child custody decree." 42 U.S.C. Section 13981(e)(4).

Moreover, nothing in VAWA precludes a victim of domestic violence from bringing a tort action in state court for assault and battery or intentional infliction of emotional distress. The significance of this Act is its recognition of a federal civil right, with attendant remedies, which is distinct in remedy and purpose from state tort claims. A plaintiff who obtains relief in a civil rights lawsuit "does so not for himself [or herself] alone but also as a 'private attorney general,' vindicating a policy that Congress considered of the highest importance." City of Riverside v. Rivera, 477 U.S. 561, 575, 106 S.Ct. 2686, 2694, 91 L.Ed.2d 466 (1986) (citations omitted). The distinct societal function Congress sought to confer by enacting the VAWA civil remedy was to provide by a plaintiff's verdict "a special societal judgment that crimes motivated by gender bias are unacceptable because they violate the victims' civil rights." S.Rep. 138, at 50. Given the distinctive function of the VAWA civil remedy, there is no impermissible encroachment or federalization of states' traditional police powers.

C. Scope of the Statutory Scheme Chosen by Congress is Reasonably Adapted to its Intended End.

Having concluded that there is a rational basis for Congress to find that gender-motivated violence substantially affects interstate commerce, the remaining issue before the Court is whether the particular statutory scheme chosen by Congress is reasonably adapted to its intended end. *Hodel*, 452 U.S. at 276, 101 S.Ct. at 2360. In enacting VAWA, based in part on the results of states' reports of their self-assessments of deficiencies in their judicial systems in prosecuting injurious gender-based conduct, the House of Representatives found that both existing state and federal criminal laws were inadequate to protect against gender-motivated violence:

> State and Federal criminal laws do not adequately protect against the bias element of crimes of violence motivated by gender, which separates these crimes from acts of random violence, nor do these [laws] adequately provide victims of gender-motivated crimes the opportunity to vindicate their interests; existing bias and discrimination in the criminal justice system often deprives victims of crimes of violence motivated by gender of equal protection of the laws and the redress to which they are entitled.

H.R.Rep. 711, at 385. Further, the Senate found:

> Traditional State law sources of protection have proved to be difficult avenues of redress for some of the most serious crimes against women. Study after study has concluded that crimes disproportionately affecting women are often treated less seriously than comparable crimes affecting men.

S.Rep. 138, at 49.

The United States Supreme Court has recognized that these bias-inspired types of crimes are "thought to inflict greater individual and societal harm ... [because they] are more likely to provoke retaliatory crimes, inflict distinct emotional harms on their victims, and incite community unrest." Wisconsin v. Mitchell, 508 U.S. 476, 487–88, 113 S.Ct. 2194, 2200–01, 124 L.Ed.2d 436 (1993). Given the important nature of the conduct sought to be prevented and the previously-approved private attorney general method of remedy, this court concludes that the statutory scheme which creates a federal civil rights remedy for gender-motivated violence is reasonably adapted to an end permitted by the Constitution. This conclusion is consistent with prior precedent related to other federal civil rights remedies enacted by Congress and upheld by courts as constitutional under the Commerce Clause. See, e.g., *Katzenbach*, supra; *Heart of Atlanta Motel*, supra (upholding Title II of the Civil Rights Act of 1964 under the Commerce Clause); EEOC v. Wyoming, 460 U.S. 226, 243, 103 S.Ct. 1054, 1064, 75 L.Ed.2d 18 (1983) (upholding the Age Discrimination in Employment Act under the Commerce Clause); Pulcinella v. Ridley Township, 822 F.Supp. 204, 211 (E.D.Pa.1993) (Fair Housing Act); Abbott v. Bragdon, 912 F.Supp. 580, 593–595 (D.Me.1995) (Americans with Disabilities Act).

II. Conclusion

Based on the above analysis, it is the Court's conclusion that enactment of the civil rights section of the Violence Against Women Act of 1994 was a permissible constitutional exercise of Congressional authority under the Commerce Clause, and reasonably adapted to its goal of deterring gender-based violence. Having reached this result, it is unnecessary to consider whether the Fourteenth Amendment also authorizes Congress to enact VAWA. For the above reasons, the Court DENIES defendant's motion to dismiss.

NOTES AND QUESTIONS

1. **The Unique Remedy of the Violence Against Women Act**. Unlike state abuse prevention statutes, Subtitle C of the Violence Against Women Act ("VAWA") makes available to victims of gender-motivated violence a *private civil rights remedy* against the perpetrator of the violence. 42 U.S.C. § 13981(b). This right permits the victim to bring a civil rights action against a private individual—even when no state action is present—and allows her to recover both compensatory and punitive damages, as well as injunctive and declaratory relief, from the perpetrator. 42 U.S.C. § 13981(c). In addition to establishing a private cause of action for crimes of violence motivated by gender, the VAWA also authorized spending $1.6 billion over six years for grants to support state and local law enforcement and prosecution efforts to reduce violent crime against women, education and prevention programs, battered women's shelters, and community programs on domestic violence. Moreover, the VAWA established new federal criminal penalties for "hate crimes" motivated by the victim's gender, new federal felonies for interstate domestic violence, and proposed amendments to the Federal Rules of Evidence concerning the admissibility of the past sexual behavior of victims in criminal and civil sex offense cases.

2. **Contested Constitutionality.** Although the district court in *Doe* held that the VAWA was a permissible constitutional exercise of congressional authority under the Commerce Clause, this point of view has not been universal. In fact, in May 1996, just one month before the *Doe* decision, the U.S. District Court for the Western District of Virginia found the VAWA unconstitutional. In deciding Brzonkala v. Virginia Polytechnic State University, 935 F.Supp. 779 (W.D.Va.1996), a case involving the rape of a college student by two members of the college football team, the district court held that the VAWA constitutes an improper use of Congress'

authority under both the Commerce Clause and Section 5 of the Fourteenth Amendment.

With regard to the Commerce Clause, the district court found that, in enacting the VAWA, Congress had relied on extensive factual findings regarding the economic impact of violence against women. However, according to the Court, these findings showed only that gender-based violence affected the national economy, not that it "substantially affected" interstate commerce, as required under United States v. Lopez, 514 U.S. 549, 115 S.Ct. 1624, 131 L.Ed.2d 626 (1995). Nor did the Act restrict its focus to situations involving interstate commerce. Accordingly, the court concluded, Congress had acted beyond its commerce power and had intruded on state law in enacting the VAWA.

However, in December 1997, the U.S. Court of Appeals for the Fourth Circuit reversed and remanded, holding that the district court erred in ruling the VAWA unconstitutional. *See* Brzonkala v. Virginia Polytechnic Institute and State University, 132 F.3d 949 (4th Cir. 1997). In considering whether Congress had exceeded its Commerce Clause authority in enacting the VAWA, the appeals court noted that its job as a reviewing court was simply to determine "whether a rational basis existed for determining that a regulated activity"—here violence against women—substantially affects interstate commerce. *Id.* at 967. The appeals court found that four years of congressional "hearings and consideration of voluminous testimonial, statistical, and documentary evidence" allowed Congress to make "an unequivocal and persuasive finding that violence against women substantially affects interstate commerce." *Id.* at 968.

III. BATTERED WOMAN SYNDROME AND THE DEFENSE OF BATTERED WOMEN

Louise Bauschard & Mary Kimbrough, Voices Set Free

From L. Bauschard & M. Kimbrough, Voices Set Free: Battered Women Speak from Prison, (1986).

To the battered woman, the American dream of marital bliss and "ever after" happiness becomes a ghastly nightmare from which she cannot awaken. She lives in a world of terror and her home is her prison.

If she strikes back—even to save her life or the life of her child—she moves into the labyrinthine world of criminal justice and a prison may become her home.

The subculture of which she thus becomes an unwilling member is growing steadily. The number of women in federal and state prisons, according to Bureau of Justice Statistics, was 12,746 in 1978, 19,019 in 1983, and has now topped 20,000.

Family violence statistics, states the Bureau, "may be seriously underreported." Total reported violent incidents average 450,000 annually, with more than half committed by spouses or ex-spouses.

How many of these are victims of battering is difficult to document precisely because abuse can take many forms. But it is believed to be a sizable number, indicating a strong correlation between a background of battering and the perpetration of a felony. At Renz Correctional Center in Missouri, an estimated seven of ten women are battered women.

But, regardless of her offense or her background, each of these women, as she stepped into this regimented world, became an instant statistic, stripped of her rights, her identity, her family, ignored by all but a few who occasionally visit her, forgotten by the society that put her there.

In the eyes of the law, she is no longer a human being with control of her own destiny.

She is caged by public apathy, often by official ineptness, callousness and prejudice, and by the myths that serve an indifferent society well as plausible explanations for her battering and handy excuses for sentencing her to prison, perhaps for the rest of her life.

She is the invisible woman. But, ironically, she has helped focus public attention and indignation on the plight of all victims of domestic violence. At the 1986 trial of a woman who testified that she killed her husband after many years of physical and mental abuse and was sentenced to 28 years in prison, a grassroots movement, Women Rising in Resistance, suddenly emerged from a St. Louis suburb to publicize what its members were convinced was a miscarriage of justice.

The long-buried monster of domestic violence has been pulled out of the dark slime of secrecy into the sunshine to be seen for what it is.

It is encouraging that, as a result, some legislators, government officials, social workers, judges, lawyers, psychologists and doctors, and even the media, are waking up at last to the horrifying statistic that every 18 seconds another American woman suffers abuse.

But this is not enough.

Many may speak out for the victim who endures abuse. But who speaks for the victim who dares to strike back?

The Women's Self Help Center of St. Louis, marking its tenth anniversary in 1986, has pioneered in this advocacy. But throughout the country fewer than 75 other agencies are focusing their attention on abused women in prison.

While some work with a woman when she seeks protection from her abuser, few, if any, besides the St. Louis agency, give her support and advocacy services when she becomes an offender in the homicide of her partner.

While library shelves are filling up with books on domestic violence, only a few writers have become champions of the women trapped in the criminal justice system. Foremost are Lenore Walker, author of *The Battered Woman;* Ann Jones, *Women Who Kill;* Del Martin, *Battered Wives;* and Terry Davidson, *Conjugal Crime.*

Even fewer have delved into the question of the abused_imprisoned woman's mental health and its relationship to her lifestyle, her acceptance of violence and her crime. . . .

Surely, it is not surprising that the victim's mental and emotional health can be irreparably damaged by the violence that confronts her every day.

She is isolated, she is misunderstood, she is often unable to find someone to listen and help, and if she does, she may not be able to articulate the depth and the scope of the abuse—partly from fear, partly from pride, partly from her inability to express herself. Said a spokesperson from the Bedford Hills, New York, Correctional Facility:

Too often women hide, from themselves and others, the problem of domestic violence, pretending that it does not exist for them.

They do this out of fear of ridicule from family and friends, out of shame and embarrassment, or out of ignorance. An abused woman may not know where to turn for help.

On the other hand, some abused women have sought help, only to have had the system fail them. An abused woman often is frustrated into feeling that she has reached an impasse, and that her only source of help must come from herself.

Devastating consequences often occur when a woman, after repeated attacks of abuse, retaliates with violence.

No matter how severe or frequent those attacks, or how justifiable her retaliatory act of self-defense, the battered woman bears a stigma she cannot shed.

Throughout her history of abuse, when she has asked for help, she often has met only callousness or ignorance on the part of law enforcement, clergy, therapists and courts and she is scarred by public attitudes that too often blame her for the behavior of her abusive partner and convince her that she is not deserving of any support.

If she kills her partner in a last effort to save herself and her children, she is morally flawed and faces total rejection by her community through intense criminal charges and vigorous state prosecution, costing thousands of taxpayers' dollars.

That rejection is bolstered by myths which have persisted in the minds even of some who should be the most compassionate and understanding.

Myth: "Nice" people don't batter others.

Fact: Battering is not a class crime. It occurs in all social and economic strata. And a millionaire's wife can hurt as much as a poor man's.

In her book *Battered Wives,* Del Martin reported that in Fairfax, Virginia, one of the wealthiest counties in America, police received more than 4,000 family disturbance calls in 1 year and that an estimated 30 assault warrants were sought each week by Fairfax County wives.

In one survey of 80 battered women, a counselor found that 17 had attended college, six had graduated, four had graduate degrees. Occupations of the women included social worker, nurse, artist, librarian, psychologist, banker, waitress, and law enforcement officer. The men accused of beating them included a doctor, a librarian, a sanitation worker, a computer programmer, and a career military man.

Counselors and researchers agree that many wealthy and socially prominent victims do not want to go public with their stories. As members of a circle that values highly a man's success in the business and professional world and his prominence as a community leader, these women are afraid of harming their husbands' careers or of not being believed.

Myth: A battered woman is a masochist who enjoys pain.

Fact: This is another handy rationale by which those who have never suffered abuse naively explain a woman's "enjoyment" of being thrown across the room into a wall or beaten with fists until her eyes are black and her jaw is broken and she is bleeding from her wounds.

Many battered women report that police, friends and even relatives, instead of offering help, have asked, "What did you do to provoke him?"

A survey of 100 abused women by J.J. Gaylord, reported in the British Medical Journal, showed that 89 percent fled their homes, 42 percent tried to commit suicide, and 36.6 percent wanted to sever all relations with the abuser.

Myth: She deserves it.

Fact: Unfortunately, this myth has been accepted by the victim as well as the victimizer and the public.

An abused woman has been robbed of her self-esteem. She has been called every vicious and obscene name her abuser can think of. She has been programmed to think of herself as worthless; whatever happens to her must be her fault. She may have lived with abuse even from babyhood, so victimization is her "way of life" and it would not occur to her to object or to become aggressive in return. Because she is in a power relationship in which she is totally dependent on her husband, she accepts the blame, no matter how painful.

Myth: Why doesn't she leave him? She can if she wants to.

Fact: Can she?

A battered woman has many reasons for staying where she is, but four common denominators are fear, economics, willingness to accept the familiar and abusive rather than venture into the unknown, and, last, the abuser's "promise" to change.

A woman in Iowa ran away, only to be tracked down by her husband, beaten severely and bodily carried back to their home, where she was beaten repeatedly and threatened that another "escape" would mean her death.

A woman in California wanted to leave but she had no money, no job skills, nowhere to go. Her husband controlled the checkbook, refused to let her leave the house even to shop or attend church, isolated her from her family and friends. He had threatened to beat their children if she tried to leave. She stayed to endure the beatings to protect them.

"I would ask myself many times," said a New York woman who killed her husband after years of abuse, " 'Why do I stay under such conditions?' My feelings went from, 'He'll change' to 'I love him.' Where would I go? He's sick and he needs my help. Maybe I don't deserve any better."

Psychologist Lenore Walker, who has been an expert witness at the trials of many abused women, has characterized the feelings of many victims as "learned helplessness," an acceptance of themselves as powerless to change their situation, self-portraits of stupid creatures of no value or influence and no control over their own lives.

Dr. Walker coined the phrase "battered woman syndrome" to characterize the battered relationship experienced by victims of domestic violence. Although the courts of 26 states have permitted use of the battered woman syndrome at the trial as a part of the self-defense plea, only two have brought the state legislature to a vote to make it a part of the self-defense body of law.

Interviews with victims now in prison for the killing of abusive partners reveal years-long patterns of abuse. That abuse may be throughout her life. The abuse may be physical, emotional, mental. It may be isolation. It can be, at its most vicious, sexual slavery. It is an insidious power which can destroy a woman's mind and spirit as well as her body, a power ironically wielded by those who profess to love her.

For the battered woman, imprisoned for striking back, that abuse may be never ending.

She probably has been battered as a child, by harsh discipline, neglect or incest. She has been battered as a lover and wife. If she kills her abuser, is arrested and charged with murder or manslaughter, her experience with the police and courts often is abusive.

If she is not actually physically abused in prison—although this is not uncommon—she is battered by the very condition of incarceration. Here, behind the walls, she suffers a continuous erosion of her dignity and self-respect and a constant dehumanization by such prison-defended practices as frequent strip searches and lack of privacy. For the felony offender, the humiliation is even worse. If she is taken out of the prison temporarily to work or have medical attention, she may be handcuffed and shackled and escorted by a coterie of armed guards.

When, or if, an offender is released, it is again society's turn to batter. Having ignored the problem earlier, refusing to become involved, society now refuses to give the ex-offender a productive, well-paying job which will permit her to regain at least a fragment of her dignity and self-respect. . . .

The Victims

... *Now having totally manipulated my brain, my husband began what turned out to be daily rituals, the actual beatings.*

I come from a white, middle-class, well-educated family. I'm 32 years old and I've held federal and county government jobs for 11 years. Perhaps you feel that I don't fit the description of a battered woman, but physical and psychological abuse has no color or social status. I have been the victim of both.

Before the beatings began, I had already acquired emotional scars. In a sense, my husband prepared my mind to accept the physical abuse I was to have. The mental abuse began by him isolating me from my friends, my family and even my children. My husband molded my mind into a dark shadow which existed only to accept his yelling, his possessiveness, his obsession to make me his perfect wife. My family had difficulty understanding why I separated myself from them. They sensed that something was wrong but I never confessed the truth to them. In fact, I became a very convincing liar.

At this time I didn't realize that I was really lying to myself. I didn't seek help from an outside source because the idea of someone else knowing that I took this abuse could cause them to look down on me.

The physical humiliation began shortly afterwards. Now having totally manipulated my brain, my husband began what turned out to be daily rituals, the actual beatings. Throughout the rest of my marriage, I was subjected to his fists, his throwing me against the walls, his crude beatings with furniture and other objects. He was an extremely domineering and demanding man. When his anger grew, he became erratic and lost full control of his strength.

I always maintained a clean and neat household but sometimes between full time employment and my children I couldn't get the chance to vacuum everyday. My husband would come home and start to verbally abuse me and end up hitting me with the vacuum cleaner or me being thrown around from wall to wall.

I can remember that one day, when we were going to a friend's house, he was the last one to leave our house. However, he didn't close the door tightly. When we returned, we found the door wide open.

Naturally, he began yelling at me and I wouldn't dare answer him, yet I knew I had to tell him he was the last one to leave. Well, I should have followed my initial fear of keeping quiet. As soon as I opened my mouth, I got a fist in my face, then I doubled over from the punch in the stomach which actually knocked the wind right out of me. Immediately, I learned that he was always to be right even if I knew differently.

Another time I went out after work with my friends, with my husband's consent, of course. He had even asked me to call home so he wouldn't worry about me coming home late. I called and all was fine. When I got home, I got into bed and as my head hit the pillow I got a fist to my nose and eyes. He was mad because I had called as he asked and had woke him out of a deep sleep.

Like with all the other bruises, I lied to my children, my family and co-workers, and I told them I had banged myself into the edge of the bathroom door.

In all my 11 years of abuse, I always believed that he was truly sorry, as he stated, after each violent attack. I actually convinced myself that he would change because he loved me or I thought he did. My greatest fear then was that my husband would leave me. I had lost my own self-respect, my self-esteem. I had so lost myself in his cruel and violent world that I believed I could not function again without him.

After each battering, I tried to justify in my mind that maybe I deserved this ill treatment.

The last three years of my marriage I was the sole breadwinner. My husband was fired from his state job because of abusive conduct to others. These were probably the worst of all the bad times. I walked in an air of terror and fear that clogged my every breath. My main concern in life was to protect my children and to avoid any further violence from him.

Today my children are being taken care of by my family because I am a criminal in the justice system. I am a CRIMINAL because I refused to take one more beating. . . .

He told me, "If you ever convince me that you are through with me and will leave me, I will have to kill you."

The next morning I got up and started packing. He beat me to death. He took my car keys. He said, "You made me do this. Are you happy now? I love you and you made me beat you up."

Note: She is serving a 50–year sentence without possibility of parole on a charge of first degree murder in the death of her abusive husband. The prosecution charged that she had hired a man to kill him. This man, who admitted the killing—and testified that before the shooting, the wife had told him she had changed her mind and did not want her husband killed—pled guilty to a reduced charge of second degree murder and was sentenced to life imprisonment. He should be eligible for parole in the mid–1990s. Unless the woman's sentence is reversed, she will be in prison until 2032. . . .

I was born in Yugoslavia. We came here when I was 11. I saw my father beat my mother and put her in the hospital I don't know how many times.

I was going through a real hard period in my life. My mom and dad spoke hardly any English. They married my sister off to an older man and that left me.

My dad wouldn't let me bring any friends home. Ever since I can remember, he beat my mom. To me, it was her fault. I thought if she would shut up he would stop. I didn't know that even if she did, he would keep on beating her.

At 18 I met a man I thought was my Prince Charming. That was the most confusing time of my life. It was my downfall. I had these illusions about men. I didn't want to marry someone like my dad. I wanted someone who would come home and have dinner with you, buy you flowers and candy and take you out.

For a couple of months, he was a prince. But then he would lose his temper and slap me. I could live with that because I thought maybe that meant he loved me.

Then he started beating on me and I couldn't live with that. I was too good to him. I was his slave. I would have his supper ready and his shoes shined. But it turned out I was married and he wasn't. I wanted to be around him all the time. But rather than take me with him, he would beat me up.

I got a job and one morning after he had gone to work I moved out. But he would come to where I worked and threaten me. I lost my job and had to move three or four times because he would knock the door down and terrorize me.

My sister was getting beat on by her husband. I thought in this country you didn't have to stand for that.

A few years later I married again. I liked him because he made me laugh. I found some kind of happiness there. He was a great guy but I didn't dream he was doing drugs behind my back. I thought maybe I could help him.

After a few weeks we split up. My dad died and my mother wanted to visit Europe. I got really sick and my mom came back and left me there. My relatives decided I would marry a local man. I made up my mind there was nothing to stop this child from going home.

The day before the wedding I slipped out of the house and caught a bus to the nearest city. I had my act together. It was sheer luck and will power. When I got to the airport, I hid in the bathroom the whole time. I was afraid I would be caught and taken back. I'll never forget the deep breath of relief when the plane took off for America.

Then after I got home I ran into another man. I only knew good things about him. He was nice looking and drove a big car. He was another Prince Charming.

I thought he would take care of me. I was so tired of trying to take care of myself and doing such a lousy job.

It seemed like the whole world changed overnight. He started giving me $100 bills. He bought me a nice car. He was real good to me, treated me better than anyone had treated me in my whole life.

I moved in with him. It was a beautiful home. Things were going real good for us. I would have done anything for him.

He was a contractor and I suggested we start our own construction company and I could keep the books. Overnight we hit it big. They were putting up a subdivision and we got the job. My life went from the ditch to the penthouse. I thought he was the greatest thing ever. For the first time in my life I didn't have to worry.

But I had been taken away from all my friends. I didn't have anyone to talk to.

One night he came home and kicked me out of bed. It was 3 in the morning. He said, "We have to talk. I am tired of babying you. It's time you grew up."

Then he told me about his past and of the men he had killed. It was a bomb. That was the worst day of my life. I felt my whole life was a dream. It completely destroyed my self-image. I felt I didn't have a brain in my head.

From that day on, until I went to prison, I considered myself stupid.

The next morning, I got up and started packing. He beat me to death. He took my car keys and said, "You made me do this. Are you happy now? I love you and you made me beat you."

I cried all day. That evening I remembered there was one way out. Suicide. I couldn't stand any more. I had made him do this to me and I was no good to myself or anyone else.

I went outside and took a whole bottle of pills.

The last I remember was going back into the house and picking up the telephone. I have no idea who I was trying to call. Then I passed out.

That's when he found me. He took me to the hospital and when I came to, a strange man was sitting on my bed. It was a psychiatrist. This man I was living with was there, too. The psychiatrist said, "I'll leave you with your wife." But we still weren't married.

I didn't know what I was doing or what had happened.

He was dressing me and he said, "We've got to get you out of here before they start asking questions. They'll lock you up for trying to kill yourself."

The next time I woke up I was on the roof of a house. He had taken me to work with him because he was afraid to let me out of his sight. I don't know how he got me up the ladder.

He told me to go back to sleep and when I came to I was home in bed.

Then he spanked me and told me, "You can never get away from me."

He instilled such fear in me. I thought I can't even commit suicide right. That destroyed me that much more. But then he brought me flowers and jewelry and he said, "I'll never hurt you again."

I was so ready to forgive him that I went for it.

Several months later, the beatings started again. That's how I ended up a totally battered woman. I was back to feeling stupid. If he beat me up, I figured I had it coming. But I thought if I couldn't change the situation maybe I could control his attitude.

A year later, I got pregnant. I thought if I had a baby, things would be better. But he told me, "You'll have to marry me now." Well, that was another mistake.

I filed for divorce. After the baby was born, one day a man called on the phone and said he had been questioned by the police about blowing up the house and the baby and me. He said to be careful, that my husband was acting crazy.

It scared me real good. I knew that my husband intended to blow up the house. He had told me that because we were fast losing everything we had and he was spending hundreds of dollars a day on drugs. He was gambling and selling everything. The house was all we had left. He had insured it for a lot of money.

I didn't think he would hurt us but then there were little hints like he wouldn't buy health insurance because he said I wouldn't need it.

One day he came to the house with another man and I saw them fiddling with the car. Later, I was driving with the baby and the hood flew up. I told him, "I know you messed with my car." He didn't deny it. He just said, "Well, bitch, I guess the next time you'll be more careful."

I felt I had never known this person. He would sneak into the house in the middle of the night and hold a gun to my head. He would click it and then start laughing. The last few months were a nightmare. I couldn't sleep because I was so scared.

Then he told me, "Look, I am going out of town when this happens to you." He was talking about the house blowing up. He said, "It has to look like a vendetta. I'll call and tell you when to get out."

But something told me he would kill me.

Then I met a man in a bar. I didn't know him but it was so easy to talk to him because he was a stranger. He was the first person who would listen to me.

I was thin and scroungy looking. I looked like I had come out of an insane asylum. And here was this man calmly sitting there and I felt comfortable with him because he acted like he believed me. He had heard of my husband.

I told him I was scared and needed help. He said, "Why don't we go to your house and look at it? I can tell you what to look for." So I took him there. He agreed that my husband could blow it up. He reinforced my fears but at the same time he gave me the support I needed.

I asked him, "Can you help me?"

He said, "The only way to help you is to kill him before he kills you. I'll get back with you."

The next time I saw him was at our house but I had changed my mind. I said I didn't want anyone to get hurt. He said, "Do you mind if I hang around? I don't want him to hurt you."

The next day I told him the same thing, that I didn't want anyone to get hurt.

But then my husband came to the house. He was cursing me. He was sitting there drinking and screaming at me. He started toward me. I didn't know which way to run. The phone rang. He picked up the phone and then I heard a gun go off. . . .

Lenore Walker, Battered Women and Learned Helplessness

2 Victimology 525, (1977–78).

It has become increasingly apparent that the family, especially the nuclear family, is not at all the expected placid, tranquil refuge; rather, it is a fertile ground on which violence can and does occur. In the spring of 1975, I began to interview battered women in order to learn more about violent behavior between couples. . . .To date, . . . I have gathered over 100 non-structured interviews from battered women. . . .

This article will address a psychological rationale for why the battered woman becomes a victim, and how the process of victimization further entraps her, resulting in psychological paralysis to leave the relationship. This psychological rationale is the construct of learned helplessness.

There has been a good deal of recent evidence that powerful social factors have created an atmosphere where society tolerates and perhaps encourages violence against women. Del Martin documents the inadequacies of the justice and social service systems in supporting women's right not to be battered. She and Straus, Steinmetz, and Gelles also cite the role played by early sex role socialization and inequities between males and females in our culture in perpetuating wife abuse. The recent findings that 28 percent of a random sample in this country have been involved in physical violence indicates the magnitude of this problem. Their findings may very well be an underestimate of the incidence of spousal abuse. When the incidence of any phenomenon reaches such high proportions, it must be evaluated as an epidemiological social problem rather than one of individual psychopathology.

Psychologists have typically looked at intrapsychic personality deficits of both the woman and the man in order to understand wife abuse. The myth of the masochistic woman who finds her appropriate mate has been the most popular explanation for the analytical and psychopathological viewpoints. Blaming the victim or her batterer and labeling either one or both mentally ill forms a cognitive set that prevents understanding of such violent love relationships. It is probable that a combination of sociological and psychological variables account for the existence of the battered women syndrome.

It is entirely possible that any woman may find herself in a battering relationship by accident. My interviews with such women indicate that they do not like being beaten; they are not masochistic; and they do not leave because of complex psycho-social reasons. Many stay because of economics, dependency, children, terror, fears, and often they have no safe place to go. Their victimization often provides them with compelling psychological factors which bind them to their symbiotic relationships. Both the men and the women are frightened that they cannot survive alone. . . .

Within the last several years the theory of learned helplessness also has been tested with human subjects. Can people learn early in life that voluntary responses will not control what happens to them? Seligman and researchers have demonstrated that the learned helplessness theory does indeed apply to the human species.

It has been shown that human experience with inescapable aversive events will cause interference with later learning. This has been demonstrated in the laboratory and in reconstructing natural life events. In the laboratory, human motivation is sapped; the ability to perceive success is undetermined; and emotionality is heightened when the subjects experience helplessness. Learned helplessness has been proposed as one model to account for exogenous depression in people. This model is based on instrumental learning, cognitive, and motivational theoretical principles.

The learned helplessness theory has three basic components: information about what should happen (or the contingency); cognitive representation about the contingency (learning, expectation, belief, perception); and behavior. The faulty expectation that how someone will respond will have no effect on what happens occurs in the cognitive representation component. This is the point at which cognitive, motivational, and emotional disturbances originate. Thus, social learning theory accounts for intellectual, perceptual and feeling problems. It is also important to accept that the expectation of powerlessness may or may not be accurate. Thus, if the person does have control over response-outcome variables but believes such control is not possible, then the person responds accordingly with the learned helplessness phenomenon. If such a person believes that she/he does have control over a response-outcome contingency, even if the reality is that the person does not have control, that person's behavior then is not affected. So, the actual nature of controllability is not as important as the belief, expectation or cognitive set. This concept is important for understanding why battered women do not attempt to gain their freedom from a battering relationship. They do not believe they can escape from the batterer's domination. Often their perceptions are accurate, but they need not be for this theory to work. Battered women's behavior appears similar to Seligman's dogs, rats, and people.

Sex role socialization in childrearing can be responsible for inducing a faulty belief system that supports women's feelings of helplessness. It is hypothesized that those women who have the hardest time escaping from the victimization of being a battered woman were subjected to a greater degree of traditional socialization patterns.

Experiments by Kemler and Shepp, and Dweck, Davidson, and Nelson, demonstrate how cognitive disturbances can arise. Dweck's work is particularly interesting. Children in classroom situations are observed interacting with their teachers. Feedback from teachers on accuracy of their learning is different for boys than girls. Boys receive positive feedback based on their academic success, while girls receive inadequate feedback for academic work and greater positive feedback for social behavior. Thus girls learn a cognitive set that says their intellectual achievement is not as important to their survival as their social skills. It seems highly probable that girls, through their socialization in learning the traditional woman's role, also receive more non-contingent behavioral reinforcement from significant people in their lives: teachers, family, and friends. They learn that they have little direct control over their lives no matter what they do. Their key to success is through a man. Maccoby and Jacklin show this to be true in their review of studies on sex role stereotyping effects. . . .

The sex role socialization process may be responsible for the learned helplessness behavior seen in adult women, specifically battered women. They learn that their voluntary responses really don't make that much difference in what happens to them. Thus, it becomes extraordinarily difficult for such women to change their cognitive set to believe their competent actions can change their life situation. Like Seligman's dogs, they need to be shown the way out repeatedly before change is possible. My interview data support this supposition. Approximately 25 percent of the women in this sample admitted to having been physically abused as a child in their family background. However, three-quarters of them indicated a benign, paternalistic, "dresden doll" kind of upbringing. These women stated they learned very early that their competence in areas other than the social arena would not be useful to them in life. The message they received was that in order to be successful and popular with the boys, it was necessary to give their power away. Learned helplessness may be one cause of the lack of leadership among women cited in some literature of the women's movement. . . .

Several studies have pointed to the greater likelihood of learned helplessness developing in women than in men. Radloff has developed a measure of reported symptoms of depression at the Center for Epidemiological Studies at the National Institute of Mental Health. Using this scale, she confirmed the previous findings of Gove and Tudor, Chessler and others that women are more prone to depression than men. This is especially true for married women whether or not they work outside the home. Married women as a group are more depressed than men, although housewives are significantly more depressed than those who also work. This research also found that parental status was significantly related to female depression. Parents whose children no longer live with them (the "empty nest" situation) are not as depressed as we have been led to believe. In fact, the most depressed are those with children living at home under the age of 6. Radloff suggests that analysis of sex-role stereotypes, psychological theories of depression, and epidemiological studies of marital status need to be integrated. She further suggests the applicability of the learned helplessness model. Certainly this area of research needs to be explored further in the context of violent relationships.

It is also probable that helplessness is learned on a relative continuum. There may be different levels of learned helplessness that a woman learns from an interaction of traditional female role standards and individual personality development. The male/female dyadic relationship may be a specific area that is affected by this interactive developmental process. Battered women seem to be most affected by feelings of helplessness in their relationship with men. This is true for battered women who not only are housewives but also women with responsible jobs and careers. Many women are well-educated, ambitious, and function extremely well in high status positions. However, when it comes to their marriage or in other social relationships with men, they resort to traditional, stereotyped behavior. They typically defer to the men to make decisions, even if they have manipulated the choices behind the scenes. Direct communication is conspicuously absent from the battering relationships studied to date.

It is reasonable to expect that battered women will be ambivalent about the women's movement. Those who are successful in business and professions may cling tenaciously to the belief that any woman can achieve success without realizing its heavy cost. Research is needed to measure the attitudes of battered women toward women in general. My preliminary data indicate that battered women value men's approval more than from other women. Battered women are embarrassed that their home life is not as they expected it would be. Traditional socialization taught them that it is their role to make their marriage successful. Many battered women go to great lengths to cover up the violence in order to present a successful picture to the rest of the world. They do not believe that anything they do can make the batterer stop and so, in the manner predicted by the learned helplessness model, they cease all attempts to change their situation.

The feeling of powerlessness to change a battering relationship is also reinforced by the "happy family" cultural stereotype. Battered women usually do not know other battered women. If they do, the same protective conspiracy develops between them as develops between the battering couple. Battered women tend to isolate themselves so that friends and family do not find out how bad their life really is. They lie to others so much that they begin to confuse reality themselves. They make excuses for their men and assume self-blame for many battering incidents. They begin to believe all the negative comments made by the batterers to them. This pattern seems to occur even with successful career women and may be explained partially by the cognitive dissonance between their home life and professional life. Their need for others to view them as successful is stronger than their need to escape from violence. . . .

The need to protect their men and themselves may be partially responsible for the tendency of battered women to retreat from the assistance of helpers even when they themselves have initiated requests for such help. Helpers report becoming exasperated and angry with battered women. The helpers try to bring whatever legal and social assistance is possible under a limited system. This often occurs at considerable effort to the helper. Just when some assistance is found (restraining order, a police call, hospitalization, foster home, psychological help, etc.), the battered woman often turns it down. Understandably, helpers become exasperated when she returns to the dangerous relationship, denying that any harm can come to her. She assures herself and others that she can handle her man and returns to him, leaving others speechless at her behavior. They question her intelligence and sanity. It is probable that battered women do not accept the helper's assistance because they do not believe it will be effective. This can be attributed to the learned helplessness hypothesis in which their cognitive set tells them no one can help them. They see the batterer as all powerful. Thus, there is no safety for them.

The recent advent of refuges where battered women can go to live has been the most successful effort to help such women leave battering relationships. Nevertheless, even in the safety of a hidden refuge, many women reportedly go home to the unchanged battering relationship, only to return again to the refuge. Pizzey reports that many women go home and return to the refuge many times before they make the final decision to leave the relationship. Other refuges and centers in this country have had similar experiences. The British government financially supports crisis houses for the battered woman, as well as "second stage" houses which provide longer term rehabilitation for those women who are not ready to live on their own. Third stage housing is also available for women who wish to live with other battered women on a more permanent basis. These programs have established a therapeutic community for battered women and their children. Both Pizzey's Chiswick Women's Aid and the British government funded National Women's Aid Federation refuges have successfully treated over 6000 such families since 1971. The impression from my data and Gayford's research is that most of the battered women who remain at Chiswick come from the most violent family relationships. Since the 100 federation refuges are located throughout the country, similar data are difficult to collect.

The learned helplessness theory proposes that the only successful treatment to reverse the cognitive, emotional, and motivational deficits is to learn under which conditions responses will be effective in producing results. This new learning is difficult since previous conditioning has created the belief that no responses are effective for battered women. Their often justified fears that one wrong move on their part will set off an explosion in the batterer make new learning frightening to battered women. They also have a lowered response initiative rate. It becomes important to find ways of motivating battered women to attempt new behaviors so that they can experience success. Each new success helps to return to them some individual power. Self-esteem rises as these women take back control of their lives.

Most helpers agree that once battered women leave the relationship and learn new skills to reverse helplessness, they usually also overcome the emotional and motivational deficits. They do not choose to relate to another batterer as the popular myth has it. However, there is less success in overcoming helplessness when women remain with their battering partners and try to change the relationship to a nonbattering one. Morton Flax and I have attempted to apply these theoretical principles in our clinical psychology practice with assaultive couples. Before the specific couple's therapy can begin one must sever the symbiotic dependency bonds that have developed between a couple engaged in battering behavior. It is necessary to treat the couple as two individuals, strengthening their independence and teaching new communication skills, in order to reverse the learned helplessness process. The battered woman needs to relearn the response-outcome contingencies by directly experiencing a sense of power and control over those paradigms which are indeed under her voluntary and independent control. . . .

Once a woman falls into the learned helplessness syndrome her energy is drained. Maintenance of a battering relationship occurs through psychological devastation that results in lowered self-esteem. The existence of a cycle of violence has also been isolated from the stories of battered women. Rather than constant or random battering, there is a definite cycle which has been repeated over a period of time. This cycle appears to have *three distinct phases* which vary in time and intensity both within the same couple and between different couples: the tension building phase; the explosion of acute battering incidents; and the calm, loving respite. So far, it has been difficult to discern how long a couple will remain in any one phase. Predicting the length of the cycle is also not yet possible. There is evidence that situational events can influence the timing.

It is in the third phase of this cycle that the battered woman's victimization becomes completed. She wants to believe that her man's kind and loving behavior will last. It is at this time that she gets a glimpse of her original dream of how wonderful love is. This is her reinforcement for staying in the relationship. She hopes that if the other two phases can be eliminated, the battering behavior will cease and her idealized relationship will magically remain. Since almost all of the rewards of being married occur during this loving phase, this is the most difficult time for her to end the relationship.

The implications for treatment alternatives for battered women and their families are profound when social learning theories are adopted as psychological constructs. Behavioral and cognitive changes are encouraged while motivation and emotion are expected to follow. Safety is the number one priority. Killing and being killed are real possibilities. Psychological assistance can often make a difference.

The learned helplessness theory is important in understanding the psychological paralysis that maintains the victim status of a battered woman. There are other compelling economic and social factors which contribute both to their victimization and to its perpetuation. Battered women have long been accused of masochism. They are thought to enjoy being abused and seen as unwilling to stop the batterer's violence. The learned helplessness theory demonstrates that propensity to being a victim repeatedly is socially learned behavior that can be unlearned through systematic procedures designed to allow battered women actual power and control over their lives.

Martha R. Mahoney, Legal Images of Battered Women: Redefining the Issue of Separation

90 Mich. L. Rev. 1 (1991).

. . .

To illustrate the contrast between women's lives and legal and cultural stereotypes, and to accomplish a translation between women's lives and law, this article offers narratives . . . from the lives of survivors of domestic violence . . . . Seven women's stories have come to me through their own accounts. Five of these have at some time identified themselves as battered women. Three of these women were Stanford Law School students or graduates . . . . One is black, the rest are white. All but two were mothers when the violence occurred. Though our class backgrounds vary, only one was a highly educated professional before the battering incidents described, but several have acquired academic degrees since the marriages ended. . . .

One of these stories is my own. I do not feel like a "battered woman." Really, I want to say that I am not, since the phrase conjures up an image that fails to describe either my marriage or my sense of myself. It is a difficult claim to make for several reasons: the gap between my self-perceived competence and strength and my own image of battered women, the inevitable attendant loss of my own denial of painful experience, and the certainty that the listener cannot hear such a claim without filtering it through a variety of derogatory stereotypes. However, the definitions of battered women have broad contours, at least some of which encompass my experience and the experiences of the other strong, capable women whose stories are included here.

In fact, women often emphasize that they do not fit their own stereotypes of the battered woman:

The first thing I would tell you is that very little happened. I am not one of those women who stayed and stayed to be beaten. It is very important to me not to be mistaken for one of them, I wouldn't take it. Besides, I never wanted to be the one who tells you what it was really like. . . .

Statistics show that domestic violence is extremely widespread in American society. . . . The most conservative figures estimate that women are physically abused in twelve percent of all marriages, and some scholars estimate that as many as fifty percent or more of all women will be battering victims at some point in their lives. . . .

Although these statistics are widely reproduced, there is little social or legal recognition that domestic violence has touched the lives of many people in this society and must be known to many people. Judicial opinions, for example, treat domestic violence as aberrant and unusual: "a unique and almost mysterious area of human response and behavior," "beyond the ken of the average lay [person]." This radical discrepancy between the "mysterious" character of domestic violence and repeatedly gathered statistics reflects massive denial throughout society and the legal system.

Denial is a defense mechanism well recognized in psychology that protects people from consciously knowing things they cannot bear to reckon with at the time. A powerful if undiscussed force affecting the evolution of the law and litigation on battered women, denial exists at both the societal and individual levels. Societal denial amounts to an ideology that protects the institution of marriage by perpetuating the focus on individual violent actors, concealing both the commonality of violence in marriage and the ways in which state and society participate in the subordination of women. . . .

Individual denial protects the images of self and marriage held by individual women and men, as well as being the mechanism through which much societal denial operates. . . . [P]eople need to know that their own marriages are sound, therefore it is important to know that they (or their wives) do not "stay" in the relationship; they "are" in the relationship. Their own relationships define what is normal and appropriate; it is appropriate for their own relationships to continue. The battered woman *must* be different. Therefore, the question "why did she stay?" commonly finds answers that attempt to explain difference: "because she had children" or "because she was frightened" or "because she became pathologically helpless"—not, significantly, because I/you/we "stayed" too.

Do we "stay," or are we simply married? Writing this article forced me to grapple with my own image of battered women, my "credentials" in claiming this identity, and my experience of marriage. As I worked, I found similar conceptions of self and marriage in several of the women who spoke with me. These women described their marriages as "bad" or "unhappy" and then went on to recount attacks that were almost murderous—threats with guns and knives, partial strangling, deliberately running into a woman with a car[.] . . . Women often discussed the relationship at length before they mentioned any violence. Finally, I began to understand that the violence against these women seemed shocking to me—and the violence against me seemed shocking to them—precisely because we heard each others' reports of violence isolated from the context of the marriages. For ourselves, on the other hand, the daily reality of the marriages—none of which included daily or even weekly violent episodes—defined most of our memories and retrospective sense of the relationship: these were "bad" marriages, not ordeals of physical torture. We resisted defining the entire experience of marriage by the episodes of violence that had marked the relationship's lowest points. Our understanding of marriage, love, and commitment in our own lives—as well as our stereotypes of battered women—shaped our discussion.

This question of the line between "normal" marriage and violent marriage is a common one. One activist social worker recounts that when she speaks on domestic violence in any forum, someone *always* asks why women "stay." She says, "When should she have left? At what point? Maybe the time she watched while he smashed up the furniture?" A silence, a shock of recognition, falls over the audience. It is, relatively speaking, *normal* for a woman to watch a man smash up the furniture.

Many of the women in the room have seen something like it—and called it "marriage," and not "staying."

Denial conditions women's perceptions of our own relationships and need for assistance. An extreme example is a woman who founded a shelter for battered women; although her husband was beating her during this period, she never identified with the women she sought to help:

> I just thought that the incidents of violence that I—in order to be a battered woman you had to be really battered. I mean OK, I had a couple of bad incidents, but mostly it was pretty minor, in inverted commas, "violence." I didn't see myself in that category, as a battered woman at all.

Similarly, women may fail to perceive armed attacks that do not result in injury as physical abuse .... This may happen even when the woman calls for help:

> When I finally called the Battered Women's Center for help, I was just looking for advice—my husband had threatened to move back in without my consent while I was recovering from a Cesarian section.... He said "you can't stop me".... I told the counselor that I was just looking for a referral, as I didn't qualify for their help because my marriage had not been violent, although I had left after he attacked me with a loaded shotgun. There was a tiny pause, and then she said gently: "We classify that as extreme violence." ...

The literature on battering notes, clinically and sometimes with condescending undertones, that women tend to "perceive" the onset of violence as atypical. Of course, the *onset* of violence *is* atypical, and therefore our perceptions are in many ways appropriate. Yet we may ignore danger signals and early attacks because we believe that the "battered-ness" is a characteristic of the woman—a characteristic we do not have—rather than a characteristic of her partner or a symptom of a dynamic in the relationship. Denial creates and reinforces the perceptions (1) that battered women are weak, (2) that we are not weak, and (3) that therefore we are safe. ...

The ordinary lives of women leave us vulnerable to violence and oppression both because of our commitments and because of the lack of understanding and protection within the law. Despite the many responsibilities and connections of women's lives, courts and legal scholars widely assume that it is a woman's responsibility to leave the relationship. When women tell the stories of their commitment to relationships, stories which may include love and hope, the legal system often has no way to hear them. ... In fact, the onset of violence often occurs *after* commitment deepens. ...

From the viewpoint of the woman in a violent marriage, "staying" may look very different. One of the women in my support group was strikingly strong and serene. She worked as a legal secretary, earning a good salary for a working woman. She was attractive, intelligent, thoughtful. I simply could not reconcile this woman's presence, composure, and depth with my image of a battered woman. Finally, after a meeting, I took her aside and said, "I know this question must sound just awful, but what on earth are you doing here? You're so strong. . . . " She said:

> Well, my husband is an alcoholic. Things have been really bad these past few years. But we've been married thirteen years. And I have three children. For nine of those years, he was the best husband and father anyone could have asked for. The way I look at it, he has a disease. I *know* that when he's not drinking, he's not like this. I may have to leave. But if I do, I'm giving up on a father for the children, and I'm giving up on him. And I can't just throw away those nine years. So I go to Al–Anon, and I come here. I get the support I need. And I may have to decide to go. But I'm not going to do it lightly.
>
> . . .

Finally, the sense of physical responsibility to the children—inevitably, economic responsibility—is a major constraint. Women and children suffer severe losses upon divorce. Mothers must be very desperate to walk out without knowing how they will all survive. A large number of homeless women and children today have fled violent situations, and women often balance the possible harm to the children through inadequate housing with the harm from maintaining the relationship. Unless the children are threatened directly or indirectly, the woman may well choose for them rather than herself. I a very real way, she is choosing between known and unknown dangers . . . .

Women resist applying the term "battered woman" to ourselves. This is often true even when we approach hotlines and shelters, even when we seek temporary restraining orders against our abusers, even when we talk to each other. I believe that we do this *not only* because of the denial discussed above, but because the stereotypical implications of the term fail to correlate with our self-images in ways that reflect *correct* self-assessment on our parts.

It is a deadly combination, this mixture of (negative) denial and (positive) self-respect that makes women reject an image of degradation and incapacitation. As a woman interviewed at a shelter in England said, "It's difficult to accept yourself as a 'battered wife' as the term isn't right. I have had a lot of marital troubles, which have included violence. Despite all my attempts to make the marriage work, I had no choice but to get away." She defines herself as active, working to solve her problems, reaching out for solutions. These actions conflict with her sense of what a "battered wife" is. Yet her story told of frequent beatings and otherwise fit the stereotypical picture of a battering relationship reasonably well. Her self-esteem and insistence on her own competency may have been double-edged: a woman's rejection of the stereotype may slow her perception of her problems or available resources, or postpone her decision to seek help, since she may not turn immediately to agencies targeting "battered women." . . .

State v. Stewart

Supreme Court of Kansas, 1988.
243 Kan. 639, 763 P.2d 572.

TYLER LOCKETT, JUSTICE.

... Peggy Stewart fatally shot her husband, Mike Stewart, while he was sleeping. She was charged with murder in the first degree. Defendant pled not guilty, contending that she shot her husband in self-defense. Expert evidence showed that Peggy Stewart suffered from the battered woman syndrome. Based upon the battered woman syndrome, the trial judge instructed the jury on self-defense. The jury found Peggy Stewart not guilty.

The State stipulates that Stewart "suffered considerable abuse at the hands of her husband," but contends that the trial court erred in giving a self-defense instruction since Peggy Stewart was in no imminent danger when she shot her sleeping husband. We agree that under the facts of this case the giving of the self-defense instruction was erroneous. We further hold that the trial judge's self-defense instruction improperly allowed the jury to determine the reasonableness of defendant's belief that she was in imminent danger from her individual subjective viewpoint rather than the viewpoint of a reasonable person in her circumstances. ...

Following an annulment from her first husband and two subsequent divorces in which she was the petitioner, Peggy Stewart married Mike Stewart in 1974. Evidence at trial disclosed a long history of abuse by Mike against Peggy and her two daughters from one of her prior marriages. Laura, one of Peggy's daughters, testified that early in the marriage Mike hit and kicked Peggy, and that after the first year of the marriage Peggy exhibited signs of severe psychological problems. Subsequently, Peggy was hospitalized and diagnosed as having symptoms of paranoid schizophrenia; she responded to treatment and was soon released. It appeared to Laura, however, that Mike was encouraging Peggy to take more than her prescribed dosage of medication.

In 1977, two social workers informed Peggy that they had received reports that Mike was taking indecent liberties with her daughters. Because the social workers did not want Mike to be left alone with the girls, Peggy quit her job. In 1978, Mike began to taunt Peggy by stating that Carla, her 12–year–old daughter, was "more of a wife" to him than Peggy.

Later, Carla was placed in a detention center, and Mike forbade Peggy and Laura to visit her. When Mike finally allowed Carla to return home in the middle of summer, he forced her to sleep in an un-air conditioned room with the windows nailed shut, to wear a heavy flannel nightgown, and to cover herself with heavy blankets. Mike would then wake Carla at 5:30 a.m. and force her to do all the housework. Peggy and Laura were not allowed to help Carla or speak to her.

When Peggy confronted Mike and demanded that the situation cease, Mike responded by holding a shotgun to Peggy's head and threatening to kill her. Mike once kicked Peggy so violently in the chest and ribs that she required hospitalization. Finally, when Mike ordered Peggy to kill and bury Carla, she filed for divorce. Peggy's attorney in the divorce action testified in the murder trial that Peggy was afraid for both her and her children's lives.

One night, in a fit of anger, Mike threw Carla out of the house. Carla, who was not yet in her teens, was forced out of the home with no money, no coat, and no place to go. When the family heard that Carla was in Colorado, Mike refused to allow Peggy to contact or even talk about Carla.

Mike's intimidation of Peggy continued to escalate. One morning, Laura found her mother hiding on the school bus, terrified and begging the driver to take her to a neighbor's home. That Christmas, Mike threw the turkey dinner to the floor, chased Peggy outside, grabbed her by the hair, rubbed her face in the dirt, and then kicked and beat her.

After Laura moved away, Peggy's life became even more isolated. Once, when Peggy was working at a cafe, Mike came in and ran all the customers off with a gun because he wanted Peggy to go home and have sex with him right that minute. He abused both drugs and alcohol, and amused himself by terrifying Peggy, once waking her from a sound sleep by beating her with a baseball bat. He shot one of Peggy's pet cats, and then held the gun against her head and threatened to pull the trigger. Peggy told friends that Mike would hold a shotgun to her head and threaten to blow it off, and indicated that one day he would probably do it.

In May 1986, Peggy left Mike and ran away to Laura's home in Oklahoma. It was the first time Peggy had left Mike without telling him. Because Peggy was suicidal, Laura had her admitted to a hospital. There, she was diagnosed as having toxic psychosis as a result of an overdose of her medication. On May 30, 1986, Mike called to say he was coming to get her. Peggy agreed to return to Kansas. Peggy told a nurse she felt like she wanted to shoot her husband. At trial, she testified that she decided to return with Mike because she was not able to get the medical help she needed in Oklahoma.

When Mike arrived at the hospital, he told the staff that he "needed his housekeeper." The hospital released Peggy to Mike's care, and he immediately drove her back to Kansas. Mike told Peggy that all her problems were in her head and he would be the one to tell her what was good for her, not the doctors. Peggy testified that Mike threatened to kill her if she ever ran away again. As soon as they arrived at the house, Mike forced Peggy into the house and forced her to have oral sex several times.

The next morning, Peggy discovered a loaded .357 magnum. She testified she was afraid of the gun. She hid the gun under the mattress of the bed in a spare room. Later that morning, as she cleaned house, Mike kept making remarks that she should not bother because she would not be there long, or that she should not bother with her things because she could not take them with her. She testified she was afraid Mike was going to kill her.

Mike's parents visited Mike and Peggy that afternoon. Mike's father testified that Peggy and Mike were affectionate with each other during the visit. Later, after Mike's parents had left, Mike forced Peggy to perform oral sex. After watching television, Mike and Peggy went to bed at 8:00 p.m. As Mike slept, Peggy thought about suicide and heard voices in her head repeating over and over, "kill or be killed." At this time, there were two vehicles in the driveway and Peggy had access to the car keys. About 10:00 p.m., Peggy went to the spare bedroom and removed the gun from under the mattress, walked back to the bedroom, and killed her husband while he slept. She then ran to the home of a neighbor, who called the police.

When the police questioned Peggy regarding the events leading up to the shooting, Peggy stated that things had not gone quite right that day, and that when she got the chance she hid the gun under the mattress. She stated that she shot Mike to "get this over with, this misery and this torment." When asked why she got the gun out, Peggy stated to the police:

> "I'm not sure exactly what . . . led up to it . . . and my head started playing games with me and I got to thinking about things and I said I didn't want to be by myself again. . . . I got the gun out because there had been remarks made about me being out there alone. It was as if Mike was going to do something again like had been done before. He had gotten me down here from McPherson one time and he went and told them that I had done something and he had me put out of the house and was taking everything I had. And it was like he was going to pull the same thing over again."

Two expert witnesses testified during the trial. The expert for the defense, psychologist Marilyn Hutchinson, diagnosed Peggy as suffering from "battered woman syndrome," or post-traumatic stress syndrome. Dr. Hutchinson testified that Mike was preparing to escalate the violence in retaliation for Peggy's running away. She testified that loaded guns, veiled threats, and increased sexual demands are indicators of the escalation of the cycle. Dr. Hutchinson believed Peggy had a repressed knowledge that she was in a "really grave lethal situation."

The State's expert, psychiatrist Herbert Modlin, neither subscribed to a belief in the battered woman syndrome nor to a theory of learned helplessness as an explanation for why women do not leave an abusive relationship. Dr. Modlin testified that abuse such as repeated forced oral sex would not be trauma sufficient to trigger a post-traumatic stress disorder. He also believed Peggy was erroneously diagnosed as suffering from toxic psychosis. He stated that Peggy was unable to escape the abuse because she suffered from schizophrenia, rather than the battered woman syndrome. . . .

The question reserved is whether the trial judge erred in instructing on self-defense when there was no imminent threat to the defendant and no evidence of any argument or altercation between the defendant and the victim contemporaneous with the killing. We find this question and the related question of the extent to which evidence of the battered woman syndrome will be allowed to expand the statutory justification for the use of deadly force in self-defense are questions of statewide importance.

The State claims that under the facts the instruction should not have been given because there was no lethal threat to defendant contemporaneous with the killing. The State points out that Peggy's annulment and divorces from former husbands, and her filing for divorce after leaving Mike, proved that Peggy knew there were non-lethal methods by which she could extricate herself from the abusive relationship.

Under the common law, the excuse for killing in self-defense is founded upon necessity, be it real or apparent. . . . In *State v. Rose,* 30 Kan. 501, 1 Pac. 817 (1883), we approved an instruction on self-defense which stated in part: "[B]efore a person can take the life of another, it must reasonably appear that his own life must have been in imminent danger, or that he was in imminent danger of some great bodily injury from the hands of the person killed. No one can attack and kill another because he may fear injury at some future time." The perceived imminent danger had to occur in the present time, specifically during the time in which the defendant and the deceased were engaged in their final conflict.

These common-law principles were codified in K.S.A. 21–3211, which provides:

> "A person is justified in the use of force against an aggressor when and to the extent it appears to him and he reasonably believes that such conduct is necessary to defend himself or another against such aggressor's imminent use of unlawful force."

The traditional concept of self-defense has posited one-time conflicts between persons of somewhat equal size and strength. When the defendant claiming self-defense is a victim of long-term domestic violence, such as a battered spouse, such traditional concepts may not apply. Because of the prior history of abuse, and the difference in strength and size between the abused and the abuser, the accused in such cases may choose to defend during a momentary lull in the abuse, rather than during a conflict. However, in order to warrant the giving of a self-defense instruction, the facts of the case must still show that the spouse was in imminent danger close to the time of the killing.

A person is justified in using force against an aggressor when it appears to that person and he or she reasonably believes such force to be necessary. A reasonable belief implies both an honest belief and the existence of facts which would persuade a reasonable person to that belief. A self-defense instruction must be given if there is any evidence to support a claim of self-defense, even if that evidence consists solely of the defendant's testimony.

Where self-defense is asserted, evidence of the deceased's long-term cruelty and violence towards the defendant is admissible. In cases involving battered spouses, expert evidence of the battered woman syndrome is relevant to a determination of the reasonableness of the defendant's perception of danger. Other courts which have allowed such evidence to be introduced include those in Florida, Georgia, Illinois, Maine, New Jersey, New York, Pennsylvania, Washington, and Wisconsin. However, no jurisdictions have held that the existence of the battered woman syndrome in and of itself operates as a defense to murder.

In order to instruct a jury on self-defense, there must be some showing of an imminent threat or a confrontational circumstance involving an overt act by an aggressor. There is no exception to this requirement where the defendant has suffered long-term domestic abuse and the victim is the abuser. In such cases, the issue is not whether the defendant believes homicide is the solution to past or future problems with the batterer, but rather whether circumstances surrounding the killing were sufficient to create a reasonable belief in the defendant that the use of deadly force was necessary.

In three recent Kansas cases where battered women shot their husbands, the women were clearly threatened in the moments prior to the shootings. *State v. Hundley,* 236 Kan. 461, 693 P.2d 475, involved a severely abused wife, Betty Hundley, who shot her husband, Carl, when he threatened her and reached for a beer bottle. Several weeks prior to the shooting, Betty had moved to a motel. Carl continued to harass her and threaten her life. On the day of the shooting, Carl threatened to kill her. That night he forcibly broke into Betty's motel room, beat and choked her, painfully shaved her pubic hair, and forced her to have intercourse with him. Thereafter, he pounded a beer bottle on the night stand and demanded that Betty get him some cigarettes. Betty testified that he had attacked her with beer bottles before. She pulled a gun from her purse and demanded that Carl leave. When Carl saw the gun he stated: "You are dead, bitch, now." Betty fired the gun and killed Carl.

In *State v. Osbey,* 238 Kan. 280, 710 P.2d 676 (1985), Osbey was convicted of first-degree murder of her husband. On the day of the shooting, the husband had a gun and had communicated threats to kill Osbey both to her and others. He had shown the gun to a friend of Osbey's who warned Osbey. After an argument, when the husband was moving out, Osbey threw his chair towards his van. Osbey's husband said, "I'm sick of this shit," picked up some record albums from inside the van, and started towards the house. Osbey ran inside, loaded a gun, and told her husband to stay back because she did not want to hurt him. Her husband said he did not want to hurt her, either, and reached behind the albums he was carrying. Fearing he was reaching for his gun, Osbey shot him.

In *State v. Hodges,* 239 Kan. 63, 716 P.2d 563 (1986), on the night of the shooting, the husband attacked Hodges and beat her head against a doorjamb twenty times. He then said he was going to kill her. Hodges was then kicked and beaten before making her way into another room. When her husband said, "God damn you. Get in here now!" she grabbed a gun, ran to the doorway, and shot him.

On appeal, none of these cases raised the issue of the propriety of the self-defense instruction. Each case involved a threat of death to the wife and a violent confrontation between husband and wife, contemporaneous with the shooting. Here, however, there is an absence of imminent danger to defendant: Peggy told a nurse at the Oklahoma hospital of her desire to kill Mike. She later voluntarily agreed to return home with Mike when he telephoned her. She stated that after leaving the hospital Mike threatened to kill her if she left him again. Peggy showed no inclination to leave. In fact, immediately after the shooting, Peggy told the police that she was upset because she thought Mike would leave her. Prior to the shooting, Peggy hid the loaded gun. The cars were in the driveway and Peggy had access to the car keys. After being abused, Peggy went to bed with Mike at 8 p.m. Peggy lay there for two hours, then retrieved the gun from where she had hidden it and shot Mike while he slept.

Under these facts, the giving of the self-defense instruction was erroneous. Under such circumstances, a battered woman cannot reasonably fear imminent life-threatening danger from her sleeping spouse. We note that other courts have held that the sole fact that the victim was asleep does not preclude a self-defense instruction. In *State v. Norman*, 89 N.C.App. 384, 366 S.E.2d 586 (1988), cited by defendant, the defendant's evidence disclosed a long history of abuse. Each time defendant attempted to escape, her husband found and beat her. On the day of the shooting, the husband beat defendant continually throughout the day, and threatened either to cut her throat, kill her, or cut off her breast. In the afternoon, defendant shot her husband while he napped. The North Carolina Court of Appeals held it was reversible error to fail to instruct on self-defense. The court found that, although decedent was napping at the time defendant shot him, defendant's unlawful act was closely related in time to an assault and threat of death by decedent against defendant and that the decedent's nap was "but a momentary hiatus in a continuous reign of terror."

There is no doubt that the North Carolina court determined that the sleeping husband was an evil man who deserved the justice he received from his battered wife. Here, similar comparable and compelling facts exist. But, as one court has stated: "To permit capital punishment to be imposed upon the subjective conclusion of the [abused] individual that prior acts and conduct of the deceased justified the killing would amount to a leap into the abyss of anarchy." *Jahnke v. State*, 682 P.2d 991, 997 (Wyo.1984). Finally, our legislature has not provided for capital punishment for even the most heinous crimes. We must, therefore, hold that when a battered woman kills her sleeping spouse when there is no imminent danger, the killing is not reasonably necessary and a self-defense instruction may not be given. To hold otherwise in this case would in effect allow the execution of the abuser for past or future acts and conduct.

One additional issue must be addressed. In its *amicus curiae* brief, the Kansas County and District Attorney Association contends the instruction given by the trial court improperly modified the law of self-defense to be more generous to one suffering from the battered woman syndrome than to any other defendant relying on self-defense. We agree and believe it is necessary to clarify certain portions of our opinion in *State v. Hodges*, 239 Kan. 63, 716 P.2d 563.

Here, the trial judge gave the instruction approved in *State v. Simon,* 231 Kan. 572, 575, 646 P.2d 1119 (1982), stating:

"The defendant has claimed her conduct was justified as self-defense.

"A person is justified in the use of force against an aggressor when and to the extent it appears to him and he reasonably believes that such conduct is necessary to defend himself or another against such aggressor's imminent use of unlawful force. Such justification requires both a belief on the part of the defendant and the existence of facts that would persuade a reasonable person to that belief."

The trial judge then added the following:

"You must determine, from the viewpoint of the defendant's mental state, whether the defendant's belief in the need to defend herself was reasonable in light of her subjective impressions and the facts and circumstances known to her."

This addition was apparently encouraged by the following language in *State v. Hodges,* 239 Kan. 63, 716 P.2d 563:

"Where the battered woman syndrome is an issue in the case, the standard for reasonableness concerning an accused's belief in asserting self-defense is not an objective, but a subjective standard. The jury must determine, from the viewpoint of defendant's mental state, whether defendant's belief in the need to defend herself was reasonable."

The statement that the reasonableness of defendant's belief in asserting self-defense should be measured from the defendant's own individual subjective viewpoint conflicts with prior law. Our test for self-defense is a two-pronged one. We first use a subjective standard to determine whether the defendant sincerely and honestly believed it necessary to kill in order to defend. We then use an objective standard to determine whether defendant's belief was reasonable—specifically, whether a reasonable person in defendant's circumstances would have perceived self-defense as necessary. In *State v. Hundley,* 236 Kan. at 467, 693 P.2d 475, we stated that, in cases involving battered spouses, "[t]he objective test is how a reasonably prudent battered wife would perceive [the aggressor's] demeanor."

Hundley makes clear that it was error for the trial court to instruct the jury to employ solely a subjective test in determining the reasonableness of defendant's actions. Insofar as the above-quoted language in *State v. Hodges* can be read to sanction a subjective test, this language is disapproved. . . .

HAROLD HERD, JUSTICE, dissenting:

. . . The cumulative effect of Mike's past history, coupled with his current abusive conduct, justified appellee's belief that a violent explosion was imminent. As he slept, appellee was terrified and thought about suicide and heard voices in her head repeating over and over, "kill or be killed." The voices warned her there was going to be killing and to get away.

She went to the spare bedroom and removed the gun from under the mattress, walked back to the bedroom, and fatally shot Mike. After the first shot, she thought he was coming after her so she shot again and fled wildly outside, barefoot, wearing only her underwear. Ignoring the truck and car outside, although she had the keys in her purse inside, she ran over a mile to the neighbors' house and pled with them to keep Mike from killing her. She thought she had heard him chasing her. The neighbor woman took the gun from appellee's hand and gave her a robe while her husband called the sheriff. The neighbor testified appellee appeared frightened for her life and was certain Mike was alive and looking for her.

Psychologist Marilyn Hutchinson qualified as an expert on the battered woman syndrome and analyzed the uncontroverted facts for the jury. She concluded appellee was a victim of the syndrome and reasonably believed she was in imminent danger. In *State v. Hodges,* 239 Kan. 63, 716 P.2d 563 (1986), we held it appropriate to permit expert testimony on the battered woman syndrome to prove the reasonableness of the defendant's belief she was in imminent danger. Most courts which have addressed the issue are in accord.

The majority implies its decision is necessary to keep the battered woman syndrome from operating as a defense in and of itself. It has always been clear the syndrome is not a defense itself. Evidence of the syndrome is admissible only because of its relevance to the issue of self-defense. The majority of jurisdictions have held it beyond the ordinary jury's understanding why a battered woman may feel she cannot escape, and have held evidence of the battered woman syndrome proper to explain it. The expert testimony explains how people react to circumstances in which the average juror has not been involved. It assists the jury in evaluating the sincerity of the defendant's belief she was in imminent danger requiring self-defense and whether she was in fact in imminent danger.

Dr. Hutchinson explained to the jury at appellee's trial the "cycle of violence" which induces a state of "learned helplessness" and keeps a battered woman in the relationship. She testified appellee was caught in such a cycle. The cycle begins with an initial building of tension and violence, culminates in an explosion, and ends with a "honeymoon." The woman becomes conditioned to trying to make it through one more violent explosion with its battering in order to be rewarded by the "honeymoon phase," with its expressions of remorse and eternal love and the standard promise of "never again." After all promises are broken time after time and she is beaten again and again, the battered woman falls into a state of learned helplessness where she gives up trying to extract herself from the cycle of violence. She learns fighting back only delays the honeymoon and escalates the violence. If she tries to leave the relationship, she is located and returned and the violence increases. She is a captive. She begins to believe her husband is omnipotent, and resistance will be futile at best.

It is a jury question to determine if the battered woman who kills her husband as he sleeps fears he will find and kill her if she leaves, as is usually claimed. Under such circumstances the battered woman is not under actual physical attack when she kills but such attack is imminent, and as a result she believes her life is in imminent danger. She may kill during the tension-building stage when the abuse is apparently not as severe as it sometimes has been, but nevertheless has escalated so that she is afraid the acute stage to come will be fatal to her. She only acts on such fear if she has some survival instinct remaining after the husband-induced "learned helplessness."

Dr. Hutchinson testified the typical batterer has a dichotomous personality, in which he only shows his violent side to his wife or his family. A batterer's major characteristic is the need to blame all frustration on someone else. In a typical battering relationship, she said, the husband and wife are in traditional sex roles, the wife has low self-esteem, and the husband abuses drugs or alcohol. The husband believes the wife is his property and what he does to her is no one's business. There is usually a sense of isolation, with the woman not allowed to speak with friends or children. Overlying the violence is the intimation of death, often created by threats with weapons.

It was Dr. Hutchinson's opinion Mike was planning to escalate his violence in retaliation against appellee for running away. She testified that Mike's threats against appellee's life, his brutal sexual acts, and appellee's discovery of the loaded gun were all indicators to appellee the violence had escalated and she was in danger. Dr. Hutchinson believed appellee had a repressed knowledge she was in what was really a gravely lethal situation. She testified appellee was convinced she must "kill or be killed." ...

The majority claims permitting a jury to consider self-defense under these facts would permit anarchy. This underestimates the jury's ability to recognize an invalid claim of self-defense. Although this is a case of first impression where an appeal by the State has been allowed, there have been several similar cases in which the defendant appealed on other grounds. In each of these cases where a battered woman killed the sleeping batterer, a self-defense instruction has been given when requested by the defendant.

The most recent case on this issue is *State v. Norman,* 89 N.C.App. 384, 393, 366 S.E.2d 586 (1988), which held the trial court erred in refusing to instruct on self-defense where a battered wife shot her husband as he slept. The court stated:

"[W]ith the battered spouse there can be, under certain circumstances, an unlawful killing of a passive victim that does not preclude the defense of perfect self-defense. Given the characteristics of battered spouse syndrome, we do not believe that a battered person must wait until a deadly attack occurs or that the victim must in all cases be actually attacking or threatening to attack at the very moment defendant commits the unlawful act for the battered person to act in self-defense. Such a standard, in our view, would ignore the realities of the condition. This position is in accord with other jurisdictions that have addressed the issue."

There are other cases in which the defendant has been held to have the right to a jury instruction on self-defense where the victim, although not sleeping, was not directly attacking the defendant. . . .

The majority bases its opinion on its conclusion appellee was not in imminent danger, usurping the right of the jury to make that determination of fact. The majority believes a person could not be in imminent danger from an aggressor merely because the aggressor dropped off to sleep. This is a fallacious conclusion. For instance, picture a hostage situation where the armed guard inadvertently drops off to sleep and the hostage grabs his gun and shoots him. The majority opinion would preclude the use of self-defense in such a case. . . .

The majority disapproves *State v. Hodges,* 239 Kan. 63, 716 P.2d 563, where we adopted the subjective test for self-defense in battered wife cases. We adopted the subjective test because there is a contradiction in the terms "reasonably prudent battered wife." One battered into "learned helplessness" cannot be characterized as reasonably prudent. Hence, the *Hodges* modification of *State v. Hundley,* 236 Kan. 461, 693 P.2d 475, was necessary and properly states the law. . . .

Elizabeth Schneider, Describing and Changing: Women's Self–Defense Work and the Problem of Expert Testimony on Battering

9 Women's Rights Law Rptr. 195 (1986).

Examination of the expert testimony cases involving battered women underscores the complexity of the task of expanding defense options for battered women faced with homicide or assault. These cases reveal the tenacity of sex-stereotyping for, despite the purpose for which this legal strategy was conceived, old stereotypes of incapacity are replicated in a new form. Judicial opinions suggest that lawyers who have submitted expert testimony have had this testimony focus primarily on the passive, victimized aspects of battered women's experience, their "learned helplessness," rather than circumstances which might explain the homicide as a woman's necessary choice to save her own life. Even if lawyers are not emphasizing this aspect, judges are hearing the testimony in this way. For both lawyers and judges the term "syndrome" and the psychological description of battered women that predominates in battered woman syndrome descriptions appears to conjure up images of a psychological defense—a separate defense and/or an impaired mental state defense. Moreover, although the rationale for admission of expert testimony on battered woman syndrome was to counteract stereotypes of battered women as solely responsible for the violence, testimony is being presented, heard and sometimes misheard, that goes to the other extreme of depicting battered women as helpless victims and failing to describe the complexity and reasonableness of why battered women act. Courts are reflecting these perspectives in opinions on expert testimony on battered woman syndrome that resonate with familiar stereotypes of female incapacity.

Judicial perceptions of battered woman syndrome as a form of incapacity have problematic consequences for defense of battered women. The critical defense problem in representing battered women who kill and assert self-defense is how to explain the woman's *action* as reasonable. The woman's experience as a battered woman and her inability to leave the relationship—her victimization—is the context in which that action occurs. When battered woman syndrome is presented or heard in a way that sounds like passivity or incapacity, it does not address the basic fact of the woman's action and contradicts a presentation of reasonableness. Indeed, the overall impact of the battered woman syndrome stereotype may be to limit rather than expand the legal options of women who cannot conform to these stereotypes. Judges are not likely to recognize the need for expert testimony in those cases where the woman's actions significantly depart from both the traditional "male" model of self-defense and the passive "battered woman" model. If they do admit the testimony they may see its relevance in terms that, even unwittingly, conform to or reinforce these stereotypes.

For feminist theorists and practitioners the issue of expert testimony is also important because it highlights a broader problem that we face in many different contexts. How do we describe and name a legal problem for women—describe it in detail, in context—and translate it to unsympathetic courts in such a way that it is not misheard and, at the same time, does not remain static? How do we develop legal theory and practice that is not only accurate to the realities of women's experience but also takes account of complexity and allows for change?

The expert testimony cases manifest this problem on the issue of the characterization of battered women's experience in terms of victimization, for battered woman syndrome has been presented, interpreted and heard as victimization. Yet the expert testimony cases by definition pose the dilemma of how we describe *both* victimization and agency in women's lives. How do we translate women's experiences honestly to courts without falling into extremes of victimization *or* fault that can be misheard? In describing what has appeared to be an accurate picture of battered women in order to remedy sex-bias, have we emphasized the victimized, passive, helpless aspects of the battered woman's experience in order to counteract the disabling stereotypes that solely blame her for the violence? In so doing, have we permitted courts to limit the utility of women's self-defense and constrained its theoretical impact as well? . . .

In *State v. Kelly,* the New Jersey Supreme Court held that expert testimony concerning battered woman syndrome was admissible. The court ruled that the testimony was relevant under New Jersey's standard of self-defense, and that the testimony met the standards of New Jersey's rules for admissibility of expert testimony. . . .*Kelly* exemplifies contradictory themes in the development of the issue of expert testimony. The Supreme Court's opinion reveals both the severity and tenacity of the problem of sex-bias in the law of self-defense. The court acknowledges the importance of this testimony to explain, not merely the woman's "subjective" honesty, but also the "objective" reasonableness of her response. At the same time, the Supreme Court seems to perceive the testimony as primarily relevant to the issue of why Gladys Kelly did not leave, rather than the reasonableness of why she acted. . . .

Certainly the court is correct that the question of why the battered woman did not leave (so as to avoid the possibility of death) is a threshold issue in the jury's mind. Her failure to leave raises the question of whether the woman was really battered (for if she was, why did she stay?), as well as the question of whether, by staying, she had in a sense "assumed the risk" of death. However, these questions only present the first issue for the jury. The second issue (and the more pressing one in many cases) is the reasonableness of the battered woman's belief that she was in particular jeopardy at the time that she responded in self-defense. A battered woman who has been the victim of abuse for many years and has survived it before must credibly explain why it was necessary to act on that occasion. Expert testimony, admitted for the purpose of explaining why the battered woman did not leave, does not help the jury answer the question whether she was reasonable in acting violently in order to save her life. It thus does not address the basic defense problem that the battered woman faces. Indeed, if the testimony is limited, or perceived as limited to the issue of why the woman does not leave, it highlights a contradiction implicit in the message of battered woman syndrome—if the battered woman was so helpless and passive, why did she kill the batterer? . . .

The reasonableness of the woman's fear and the reasonableness of her act are *not* issues which the jury knows as well as anyone else. The jury needs expert testimony on reasonableness precisely because the jury may not understand that the battered woman's prediction of the likely extent and imminence of violence is particularly acute and accurate.

The court's lack of emphasis on this aspect of the relevance of the testimony is puzzling. . . . One possible explanation is that the court finds it easier to focus on those aspects of the testimony which characterize the woman as passive and helpless (i.e., her inability to leave) rather than active and violent but reasonable. This highlights the dilemma of battered woman syndrome: explanation of the battered woman's actions from a solely victimized perspective cannot fully explain why she believed it was necessary to act. . . .

Perhaps the fact that the substance of the proffered testimony submitted in many courts has been on battered woman syndrome and "learned helplessness" has unwittingly allowed even sensitive courts to emphasize individual psychological incapacity by admitting the testimony but then perceiving its relevance in a more limited way. Courts appear to be willing to recognize the importance of expert testimony when the rationale for admission is women's individual and collective psychological "weakness." Judicial willingness to find the battered women's perspective acceptable may relate to the fact that the perspective that courts are hearing and to which they are responding is that of damaged women, not of women who perceive themselves to be, and may in fact be, acting competently, assertively and rationally in light of the alternatives. . . .

Description of the battered women's common experiences has become encapsulated in the phrase "battered woman syndrome." . . . "[B]attered woman syndrome" carries with it stereotypes of individual incapacity and inferiority which lawyers and judges may respond to precisely because they correspond to stereotypes of women which the lawyers and judges already hold. Battered woman syndrome does not mean, but can be heard as reinforcing stereotypes of women as passive, sick, powerless and victimized. Although it was developed to merely *describe* the common psychological experiences and characteristics which battered women share, and it is undoubtedly an accurate description of these characteristics, battered woman syndrome can be misused and misheard to enshrine the old stereotypes in a new form. This repeats an historic theme of treatment of women by the criminal law—women who are criminals are viewed as crazy or helpless or both. Thus the description of battered women's "different" experiences, although purely categorical in intent, carries with it the language and baggage of familiar stereotypes of female incapacity. . . .

Self-defense as justification focuses on the act of defending oneself; it rests on a determination that the act was right because of its circumstances. In contrast, a finding of excuse, like insanity or heat of passion, focuses on the actor; it is a finding that the act, although wrong, should be tolerated because of the actor's characteristics or state of mind. Traditionally, since women's acts of violence could not be viewed as reasonable, the inquiry shifted to excuse; women were viewed as incapable. Women's self-defense work has attempted to redraw the lines between justification and excuse, to challenge the stereotypes which might prevent women, lawyers, and judges from viewing the woman's acts as justified. The goal of expert testimony is also to challenge these stereotypes and make it possible for the jury to identify with and understand the circumstances of the act and to thereby see the act as reasonable.

However, the danger of the battered woman syndrome approach is that it revives concepts of excuse. Even the New Jersey Supreme Court's thoughtful and comprehensive analysis of battered woman syndrome in *Kelly* has elements of a classic excuse description; it focuses on the woman's defects, the woman subject to the "syndrome." It implies that she is limited because of *her* weakness and *her* problems. It does not appear to affirm the circumstances of her act. The opinion seems to suggest that admission of expert testimony is primarily important because the battered woman "suffers" from the syndrome and could not be expected to leave her home, not because it is relevant to the reasonableness of her act. The court is willing to extend its "protection" and admit the testimony because the battered woman is perceived as weak. Although the purpose of expert testimony on battered woman syndrome is to explain the reasonableness of the woman's action, the psychological aspect of the description sounds like incapacity and excuse.

By emphasizing a strain of excuse, battered woman syndrome tends to rigidify other dichotomies which, as others have suggested, are roughly correlated with excuse and justification. Excuse suggests that the act is personal to the defendant, a private act, in contrast with a more public and common sense of rightness which justification reflects. Excuse suggests a sense of the subject, while justification implies a more objective statement. Redrawing the boundaries of justification and excuse means recasting the boundaries of the private—public and subjective—objective oppositions, making women's experiences generally, and battered women's experiences and perceptions specifically, more public and legitimate, and also more objective.

The notion of battered woman syndrome contains the seeds of old stereotypes of women in new form—the victimized and the passive battered woman, too paralyzed to act because of her own incapacity. From a defense standpoint, this perspective is potentially counterproductive in that it explains why the woman did not leave but not why she acted. It is in tension with the notion of reasonableness necessary to self-defense since it emphasizes the woman's defects and incapacity. It also does not adequately describe the complex experiences of battered women. The effect is that women who depart from this stereotype, because of their own life situations or because the facts of their cases do not fit this perspective, are not likely to be able to take advantage of judicial solicitude. This has already presented serious defense problems in several cases. The stereotype of the reasonable battered woman who suffers from battered woman syndrome creates a new and equally rigid classification, which has the potential to exclude battered women whose circumstances depart from the model and force them once again into pleas of insanity or manslaughter rather than expanding our understandings of reasonableness. It thus reinforces and rigidifies the traditional boundaries of justification and excuse, rather than redrawing them.

From the standpoint of the jury's determination of whether the woman acted reasonably in self-defense, the explanation of battered woman syndrome is only partial. Giving commonality to an individual woman's experience can make it seem less aberrational and more reasonable. Yet, to the degree that the explanation is perceived to focus on her suffering from a "syndrome," a term which suggests a loss of control and passivity, the testimony seems to be inconsistent with the notion of reasonableness, and the substance of the testimony appears to focus on incapacity.

In addition, battered woman syndrome has sounded to many lawyers and judges like either a separate defense or a defense akin to impaired mental state. Some courts have assumed that expert testimony on battered woman syndrome was being proffered as relevant to an impaired mental state defense. This is undoubtedly not merely the problem of the term itself—which, again, intends to be simply descriptive—but of the stereotypes that it triggers for lawyers and judges. Courts are more likely to hear and respond to a perception of women as damaged than as reasonable, so presentation of testimony on battered woman syndrome responds more to and plays on patriarchal attitudes which courts have exhibited toward women and women defendants generally. . . .

Many courts have accepted the need for expert testimony. But consider what judicial acceptance of this testimony implies. It emphasizes the profound gap between the experiences of battered women and those of the rest of society; it reaffirms the notion of a woman's viewpoint *and* separate experience. It suggests that psychological and social factors are interrelated and that individual experience is necessarily shaped by group identity. It also suggests that women's own description of their experiences lacks credibility, because these experiences differ from the male norm, and because women generally are not viewed as believable.

Courts are effectively recognizing that an expert, a professional, someone not a battered woman, is needed to translate the experiences of large numbers of women in this society to the rest of society's representatives. It is arguable that expert testimony may be necessary only for a transitional period, until women's voices are strong enough to be heard on their own. But experience with the use of experts in the women's movement suggests that there may be risks. Courts may find experts particularly useful in cases involving women not as a complement to, but as a substitute for, women's voices.

On a theoretical level, judicial acceptance of expert testimony has a profound impact because it affirmatively recognizes the substantive experience and content of sex discrimination and validates a "woman-centered" perspective. This collapses the dichotomy between individual experience and group experience by describing the experience as not just the individual's, but that of all battered women generally. At the same time, it is disturbing, for it suggests that only experts can bridge the gap between the individual and collective experience of women and counsel jurors and society that an individual woman's experience has a social validity and commonality and might be reasonable. . . .

Over the last several years, victimization has increasingly become a powerful, pervasive and seductive theme in the women's movement and the women's legal rights movement. It is a theme that has had wide appeal. While I believe that women are victims, and that this perspective on women's experience is important and useful, particularly on issues concerning violence against women, the virtually exclusive focus on victimization by the women's movement in recent years has been problematic. Portrayal of women as solely victims or agents is neither accurate nor adequate to explain the complex realities of women's lives. It is crucial for feminists and feminist legal theorists to understand and explore the role of both victimization and agency in women's lives, and to translate these understandings into the theory and practice that we develop. . . .

Other feminist theorists and legal thinkers have questioned the women's movement's reliance on victimization in a range of contexts, including divorce and pornography. In the specific context of battered women, Susan Schechter has emphasized the dangers of an analysis premised on victimization. She suggests that the characterization of victim has been viewed as posing a complicated political problem for the battered women's movement:

> because the focus on victimization helps to blur the insight that the struggle for battered women's rights is linked to the more general fight for women's liberation. When activists view battering as victimization rather than as an aspect of oppression, they have a tendency to see individual problems rather than collective ones.

In addition, she observes that "victim" may be a label that battered women reject because "it fails to capture their complexity and strength."

At the same time, a notion of the importance of women's agency without a social context of victimization is equally unsatisfactory. The notion of agency carries with it assumptions of liberal visions of autonomy, individual action, individual control and mobility that are also inadequate and incomplete. But women do act, we have acted in history, we act to make choices and shape our lives, we act even when there are few and terrible options. Sometimes, like battered women who kill, we act if only in order to survive.

In the battered woman context, recognition of the need to transcend the dichotomy and exclusivity of characterizations of victim versus agent and develop a theory and practice which encompasses both has consequences for the way we approach and handle the use of expert testimony in battered women's cases. Defense efforts should focus on the battering experience as well as the reasonableness of the woman's actions. Expert testimony on battering should be proffered and admitted, but lawyers should be sensitive to the way in which they understand, characterize and explain the testimony and its relevance, and they should not rely on it to the exclusion of other defense strategies. Battered women who kill need not be portrayed solely as victims with the focus on the battering, but as actors and survivors whose acts are reasonable. The psychological mechanisms that battered women develop, as in battered woman syndrome, can be explained as ways for battered women to cope and survive. If killing in self-defense can be understood as a reasonable act in terms of the context of victimization and other options, both the victimization and agency aspects of battered women's experiences are included. If battered women who kill are described as women who are victims but have fought back in order to survive, their actions in killing their batterers may be more effectively understood as reasonable.

Defense lawyers and experts must emphasize the common experiences of battered women, but must describe both the particular experiences of the individual woman and be sensitive to the sex-stereotypical implications of the testimony. Defense lawyers and experts should emphasize the common aspects of the battered women's experience, both her helplessness and her behavioral adjustments that allow her to survive, her desperate coping, her unique insight and ability to know and anticipate the degree of violence she faces, and her painful understanding of the paucity of alternatives available to women in this culture. This fuller description of battered women's experiences is both more accurate and better explains to judges and juries why a battered woman doesn't leave the house *and* why she kills to save her own life.

Explanation of aspects of both victimization and agency makes it possible for expert testimony to more accurately describe the complexity of battered women's experiences, respond to the hard defense problems presented in these cases, and allow for change by transcending static stereotypes. Feminist legal work must *both* describe *and* allow for change. As lawyers for battered women we must take account of battered women's experiences in being acted upon *and* acting. Our work must simultaneously capture the reality of battered women's lives, translate this reality more fully and effectively to courts, and push toward transforming this reality.

NOTES AND QUESTIONS

1. **New Legal Applications for Battered Woman Syndrome**. Although the concept of "battered woman syndrome" ("BWS") was originally conceived as a legal justification in the defense of women charged with the murder, manslaughter, or assault of their husbands or lovers, in recent years the courts of many states have recognized expanded legal applications for BWS. In Massachusetts, for example, the state appeals court affirmed that expert testimony regarding BWS offered by the Commonwealth was admissible against a male defendant charged with rape and assault to explain the female victim's continuing relationship with him. *See* Commonwealth v. Goetzendanner, 42 Mass.App.Ct. 637, 645, 679 N.E.2d 240, 246 (1997), holding that "the over-all ends of justice would be ill-served if we were to deny the use of evidence of BWS to a victim after she has finally taken matters into her own hands and is placed on trial for killing or assaulting her abuser." In New Jersey, the state superior court has expanded the concept of BWS to allow a victim of domestic violence—whether female or male and in a heterosexual or homosexual relationship—to recover in tort for his or her injuries. *See* Cusseaux v. Pickett, 279 N.J.Super. 335, 652 A.2d 789 (Law Div.1994). *See also* Giovine v. Giovine, 284 N.J.Super. 3, 663 A.2d 109 (1995), excerpts of which appear in the next section. The West Virginia Supreme Court has reversed a trial court's decision to terminate a mother's parental rights for allowing her husband to sexually abuse their daughter in part on the ground that the mother's perceived inability to break from the pattern of abuse was part of BWS. *See* In the Interest of Betty J.W., 179 W.Va. 605, 371 S.E.2d 326 (1988). In California, evidence of BWS has been held admissible to support a woman's defense that she committed crimes under duress from her male partner. *See* People v. Romero, 13 Cal.Rptr.2d 332 (1992), reversed and remanded on other grounds.

2. **Resisting Labels.**   Many women who have experienced abuse at the hands of a husband or lover resist the label of abused woman or battered woman. Why? How should this resistance be addressed by advocates for particular women?

IV. TORT LAW AS A RESPONSE TO BATTERING

Clare Dalton, Domestic Violence, Domestic Torts and Divorce: Constraints and Possibilities

31 New Eng. L. Rev. 319 (1997).

Reading from the latest editions of most torts casebooks would lead you to believe that interspousal immunity is now a dead letter, leaving spouses free to sue one another in tort almost as if they were strangers. It would be a mistake to assume, however, that this makes a tort suit by an abused spouse against an abuser a straightforward affair. Far from it. This Article explores the remaining formidable obstacles to such suits, and what might be done to overcome or dismantle those obstacles, at the level of daily practice or through further legal reform.

A significant problem confronting any plaintiff who is considering a tort claim arising out of domestic violence is her batterer, and the potential danger involved in challenging his abusive behavior. My suggestions strive to be consistently attentive to this reality, but proceed from the premise that further problems inhere first in the tort system itself, and then in the juncture between tort law and the law of divorce, as that interface is currently managed by the legal system. They also proceed from the premise that there is a world of difference between simply removing the overt discrimination against such plaintiffs embodied in the interspousal tort immunity, and making the tort system genuinely hospitable to them. Achieving this latter goal involves significant redesign of a system not developed with such claims in mind. It involves committing the system to assist plaintiffs who have been victims of a partner's violence as they pursue a somewhat particularized set of goals within the particular limitations imposed by their situations. . . .

Stating the Claim

. . . [W]hile broken bones, black eyes, burns, and lacerations may be evidence of battery, and threats levelled directly at the partner may constitute assault, this just begins the list of abuse-related injuries. In many cases a more potent cause of action may be intentional infliction of emotional distress, especially when the emotional toll the abuse has taken is measurable in the symptomatology of post-traumatic-stress disorder. The isolating strategies may be extreme enough to constitute false imprisonment. When an abuser verbally humiliates his partner in public, making false accusations of infidelity, or substance abuse, or tries to poison his partner's professional relationship with a school or an employer by blackening her reputation, she may have an action in defamation. Illegal wiretapping may be civilly actionable.

If children are themselves abused or threatened, physically or sexually, they have their own assault and battery claims. If they witness a parent's violence, the psychological consequences for them may provide a basis for a claim of negligent, reckless, or intentional infliction of emotional distress. If their access to one parent is manipulated by the other as part of his campaign to control his partner, there may be claims, called various names in different jurisdictions, such as child snatching, obstruction of visitation rights, or interference with custody. A child hurt accidentally by violence aimed at his or her parent can pursue a straightforward negligence action.

Could a direct victim of domestic violence argue negligence rather than battery? Why might she want to? Chiefly because negligence claims may find a deeper pocket than the batterer's own—if injuries negligently inflicted are covered by a household or an automobile insurance policy, as they usually are, while intentionally inflicted injuries are not, as is also common. Is it then worth a woman's while to argue that when her husband backed the car down the driveway, pinning her to the garage door, he was driving negligently, while the insurance company argues that his violence was deliberate, and therefore beyond the terms of the policy? I have to confess that my own enthusiasm for tort recovery for victims of battering falters when recovery depends on their participation in a "cover-up." "Covering-up," after all, is what most victims of domestic violence have done for too long before they are able to take action to challenge their abusers. In addition, all too often their abusers have tried to persuade them, after the fact, that they were hurt by accident, rather than deliberately. There is a good deal unsavory about a legal process that mimics this same distortion of reality. Nonetheless, if compensation is the priority, this may be a strategy to consider in some cases.

While it is important to be creative in considering potential tort claims, the ones most commonly employed in the domestic abuse context are certainly assault and battery on the one hand, and intentional infliction of emotional distress on the other. There is more to be said about the choice between these two. But it is worth pausing for a moment to note that the intentional infliction of emotional distress claim, so promising in so many respects, has one vulnerability. It depends on a judge or jury finding that the defendant's behavior is "extreme and outrageous," or "beyond all possible bounds of decency," or "utterly intolerable in a civilized community." This community-based standard provides a good test of how far America has come today in condemning cruel and abusive behavior between intimate partners. . . .

Although the injuries of abuse can be captured quite successfully through existing causes of action, especially if lawyers themselves have a good understanding of the dynamics of abuse, and use both lay and expert witnesses to good effect, an argument can be made for creating a new tort of "partner abuse," which would allow the entire history of combined physical and emotional abuse to be presented to the court in support of a single claim. Recognition of this cause of action, which would in turn support the presentation of cases not as a collection of unfortunate incidents, but as a coherent narrative of domestic abuse, might advance the goal of improving understanding of domestic violence among both lawyers and judges. New Jersey courts have taken this step, recognizing "battered-woman's syndrome as an affirmative cause of action under the laws of New

Jersey." In the first such case, the court explicitly held that "[b]ecause the battered-woman's syndrome is a result of a continuing pattern of abuse and violent behavior that causes continuing damage, it must be treated in the same way as a continuing tort." Elsewhere the concept of a unique cause of action has been treated with suspicion, suggesting that increased understanding of abusive relationships may need to precede any such change, rather than being a consequence of it.

There is one additional danger associated with this strategy, which is that the elements of the new cause of action might be somewhat inflexibly conceived, creating a stereotype of the abusive relationship of which not all victims could take advantage. The unfortunate result of this might be to discredit the claims of some injured by abuse, leaving them in a worse position than they currently enjoy under the present "piecemeal" approach. This problem has hounded the efforts of battered women's advocates to make "battered woman syndrome" relevant to women's claims of self-defense, only to find their clients measured against an inflexible stereotype, and denied the status of "battered woman," with the new legal protection it affords, if they do not fit the stereotype. If the tort of partner abuse were recognized, would a woman who could not meet the elements of that claim, but sued her former partner instead for battery and intentional infliction of emotional distress, be met with the argument that she was merely trying to manipulate the system into providing relief for partner abuse under circumstances in which she did not qualify for that relief?

Ultimately, the strongest argument in favor of a new cause of action is that if partner abuse were understood as a continuing tort, victims of abuse would be free of the artificial constraints imposed by existing statutes of limitation. . . .

Statutes of Limitation

Traditionally, statutes of limitation require that actions for battery or assault be brought within two, or at most three years after the incident on which they are based. The corresponding limitation periods for intentional infliction of emotional distress are sometimes a little more generous— ranging between one and six years. Based on what was said earlier about the nature of abusive relationships and the time it may take for an abused partner to take action, if these limitation periods are imposed without modification, she is likely to be able to sue for only a small portion of her total injury.

The most successful litigation strategy to date has been to argue that partner abuse should be understood as a continuing tort, and a cumulative injury, so that statutes of limitation begin to run only when the abuse stops, which will be when the partners separate, unless the abuser continues to terrorize his partner, either to punish her, or in the hopes of bringing her back into the relationship. But, and this is an important qualification, the argument appears to have been successful, at least at the appellate level, only for claims of intentional infliction of emotional distress, not for claims based on physical injury. With respect to these more concrete incidents of physical abuse, courts have tended to adhere to the shorter limitation periods associated with battery and assault, and to insist on viewing each incident separately.

The consequence of this approach is that the physical and emotional components of the relationship become artificially separated, whereas in truth the threat or reality of physical abuse is one potent source of the cumulative emotional impact of abuse. Do judges expect juries to distinguish, and exclude, emotional injuries associated with incidents of physical violence, while awarding damages based on other emotional injuries? If instead the theory is that all emotional injuries can be included, as part of the cumulative impact of the abuse, it seems illogical to exclude more tangible injuries flowing from the very same incidents. It may be that jury discretion is in practice, what rescues this system from its own illogic. It may also be that judges view this position as a compromise that does rough justice by "splitting the difference" between the justice of plaintiffs' claims, and defendants' arguments that they deserve the traditional protection provided by statutes of limitation against fading memories, lost witnesses, and missing documentation. If it were the goal instead to bring judicial application of statutes of limitation into line with the reality of abusive relationships, some other possibilities might be worth exploring.

The first would be to push a little harder for the recognition of the cumulative and intimately connected impact of both the physical and emotional or psychological dimensions of abuse, so that both, in the particular context of an abusive relationship, could be considered continuing torts. From a conceptual point of view it might seem best to make this point by creating a new tort of partner abuse, which would be characterized precisely by its cumulative or "continuing" character. This has been the strategy followed by the New Jersey courts in recognizing "battered woman's syndrome" as creating an independent cause of action. . . .

Another alternative is to accept the "continuing-tort" fix for emotional injuries, but make some additional arguments, applicable to both physical and emotional injuries, for tolling otherwise applicable statutes of limitation in the context of abuse. One such argument would be that to the extent victims remain in abusive relationships out of the desire to make them work—seeking to end the violence without ending the relationship—they are expressing the very values that supported the old interspousal tort immunity. In essence, they are seeking to restore marital harmony to a relationship disrupted by violence. The immunity was flawed in imposing that value on marital partners, whether or not they shared it. But to the extent an abused partner embraces that value a her own, we should not penalize her by jeopardizing her ability to recover for her injuries if her efforts are sabotaged by further abuse. Rather, the legal system should recognize her efforts by preserving her right to sue.

If instead her failure to take action sooner is the result of intimidation, then her argument for tolling applicable statutes of limitation is an argument based on duress. Even if her abuser does not say in so many words: "Sue me and you are dead," or "Sue me and you'll be sorry," the underlying theory is the same. She fears, with reason, that any action taken to separate herself from her abuser, or confront him with his abuse, will result in serious injury or death to her, and for the time being chooses what appears to be the lesser of two evils. . . .

A third argument is that the abuser's power over his partner prevents her from being able to frame her abuse as a wrong for which he is responsible, and seek to hold him accountable. Like the sexual abuse victim of a therapist, she needs distance from this inherently unequal relationship to see the exploitation for what it is and to summon the independence to challenge it. In the context of therapist abuse, courts place great weight on the professional "tools" that make the patient vulnerable to exploitation, but the equally effective "tools" of the batterer give his victim's claim just as much force. . . .

It would be possible to litigate these arguments separately, as seemed most appropriate in each individual case. It might be more effective, however, to urge that every abusive relationship of any duration will fit into one or more category, and that litigation would be streamlined, and justice better served, by creating a tolling provision universally applicable in partner-abuse cases, whereby any applicable statute of limitation would begin to run only when the abuse ended, whether that occurred at the time of separation, or subsequently. This might be more likely to come from a legislature than from the judiciary. To adopt such a provision would be to recognize that merely abolishing the interspousal tort immunity does not in fact equip spouses to redress their grievances against one another, when those grievances arise out of abuse. The tolling provision recognizes that intimate relationships continue to require somewhat special treatment within the legal system: room for partners with positive aspirations for their relationships to seek to work out their differences, without compromising their claims, and room for partners whose independence has been compromised in their relationship to recover sufficient autonomy to assert their rights as individuals. . . .

Managing the Money

As courts have repeatedly emphasized, a divorce proceeding is usually not a suitable forum in which to present detailed accounts of abuse, with specific price-tags attached. Further, while the distribution of marital assets *may* be governed by a set of criteria broad enough to respond to past abuse, and support obligations *may* also be structured to account for continuing needs and disabilities, both physical and emotional, that are the consequence of abuse, both distribution and support decisions may legitimately be made on the basis of such an array of "factors," that the abuser never fully pays the bill associated with his abuse. This is problematic from both the perspective of justice, and the perspective of accountability. Furthermore, with respect to support, an award may be subsequently modified for reasons that have nothing to do with one partner's wrongdoing toward the other, or her legitimate claim for redress—seriously undercutting the message that he is responsible because of his past conduct, and the injuries he has inflicted. There is the further danger, in the context of a divorce proceeding, that an abuser will use the leverage of access to the children to make his partner scale down her financial claims. This is, of course, a charge against the family law system not limited to those interested in a context in which a woman may be very legitimately concerned for the physical safety of her children.

For all these reasons, the tort system may offer a more satisfactory process of collecting compensation. Here the only issues are the perpetrator's wrongdoing, and the injuries, physical and emotional, he has inflicted. The award can recognize pain and suffering, as well as the tangible elements, such as medical expenses and lost earnings; punitive damages are also a possibility. . . .

Christina Giovine v. Peter J. Giovine

Superior Court of New Jersey, Appellate Division, 1995.
284 N.J.Super. 3, 663 A.2d 109.

STEVEN Z. KLEINER, J.A.D.

On July 1, 1994, plaintiff Christina Giovine filed an eleven count complaint against defendant Peter J. Giovine denominated: "Complaint for divorce, domestic torts, equitable claims and jury trial demand." Plaintiff's complaint alleged habitual drunkenness, . . . and extreme cruelty, . . . as alternative grounds for the dissolution of the marriage. In counts three through six, plaintiff asserted claims for compensatory and punitive damages based upon an assault and battery which allegedly occurred in March 1972 . . .; intentional infliction of emotional injury/distress commencing in March 1972 . . .; "continuous wrong" between March 1972 and May 1993, resulting in "severe emotional and physical damage" . . .; and negligence. . . .

Interspousal tort immunity no longer exists to bar the suit of one spouse against another for injuries sustained by one spouse due to the tortious conduct of the other. Merenoff v. Merenoff, 76 N.J. 535, 557, 388 A.2d 951 (1978).

> [T]he abolition of the doctrine pertained to tortious conduct generally encompassing not only conventional negligence but also intentional acts, as well as other forms of excessive behavior such as gross negligence, recklessness, wantonness, and the like. The only kind of marital conduct excepted from the abolition was that involving marital or nuptial privileges, consensual acts and simple, common domestic negligence, to be defined and developed on a case-by-case approach. [Tevis v. Tevis, 79 N.J. 422, 426–27, 400 A.2d 1189 (1979)(citation omitted).]

If the circumstances surrounding a domestic tort and claim for monetary damages are relevant to a divorce proceeding, the domestic tort must be joined with the divorce proceeding under the "single controversy doctrine" in order to avoid protracted, repetitious and fractionalized litigation. Id. at 434, 400 A.2d 1189.

On appeal, plaintiff contends that the motion judge erred in refusing to follow the decision in Cusseaux v. Pickett, 279 N.J.Super. 335, 652 A.2d 789 (Law Div.1994), which concluded that "battered-woman's syndrome is the result of a continuing pattern of abuse and violent behavior that causes continuing damage." Id. at 345, 652 A.2d 789. As such, "it must be treated in the same way as a continuing tort." Ibid. Battered woman's syndrome would therefore be an exception to N.J.S.A. 2A:14–2, that "[e]very action at law for an injury to the person caused by the wrongful act, neglect or default of any person within this state shall be commenced within 2 years next after the cause of any such action shall have occurred." Ibid. The decision in *Cusseaux* substantially relied upon State v. Kelly, 97 N.J. 178, 478 A.2d 364 (1984).

In *Kelly*, the Supreme Court, relying in part on the research of Lenore E. Walker, THE BATTERED WOMAN (1979), noted that battered woman's syndrome is a recognized medical condition. By definition, a battered woman is one who is repeatedly physically or emotionally abused by a man in an attempt to force her to do his bidding without regard for her rights. ...According to experts, in order to be a battered woman, the woman and her abuser must go through the "battering cycle" at least twice. ...

The battering cycle consists of three stages. ... Stage one, the "tension-building stage," involves some minor physical and verbal abuse while the woman tries to prevent an escalation of the abuse by assuaging the abuser with her passivity. ...Stage two, the "acute battering incident," is characterized by more severe battering due to either a triggering event in the abuser's life or the woman's inability to control the anger and fear she experienced during stage one. ...During stage three, the abuser pleads for forgiveness and promises that he will not abuse again. ...This period of relative calm and normalcy eventually ends when the cycle begins anew. ...

"The cyclical nature of battering behavior helps explain why more women simply do not leave their abusers." Ibid. The caring and attentive behavior of the abuser during stage three fuels the victim's hope that her partner has reformed and keeps her tied to the relationship. ...In addition, some women who grew up in violent families do not leave abusive relationships because they perceive their situations as normal. ... Other cannot face the reality of their situations. ... Some victims "become so demoralized and degraded by the fact that they cannot predict or control the violence that they sink into a state of psychological paralysis and become unable to take any action at all to improve or alter the situation." Ibid. Victims are often afraid to seek help out of shame, fear that no one will believe them, or fear of retaliation by their abusers. ..."They literally become trapped by their own fear." Ibid. ...

Cusseaux established a four-part test to state a cause of action for battered woman's syndrome:

1) involvement in a marital or marital-like intimate relationship; and 2) physical or psychological abuse perpetrated by the dominant partner to the relationship over an extended period of time; and 3) the aforesaid abuse has caused recurring physical or psychological injury over the course of the relationship; and 4) a past or present inability to take any action to improve or alter the situation unilaterally. [Id. at 344, 652 A.2d 789 (footnotes omitted).]

We agree with the premise espoused in *Cusseaux* and conclude that a wife diagnosed with battered woman's syndrome should be permitted to sue her spouse in tort for the physical and emotional injuries sustained by continuous acts of battering during the course of the marriage, provided there is medical, psychiatric, or psychological expert testimony establishing that the wife was caused to have an "inability to take any action to improve or alter the situation unilaterally." Ibid. In the absence of expert proof, the wife cannot be deemed to be suffering from battered woman's syndrome, and each act of abuse during the marriage would constitute a separate and distinct cause of action in tort, subject to the statute of limitations, N.J.S.A. 2A:14–2. Laughlin v. Breaux, 515 So.2d 480, 482–83 (La.Ct.App.1987).

Our disagreement with *Cusseaux* is predicated upon semantics. *Cusseaux* classifies battered woman's syndrome as a continuous tort. The concept of "continuous tort" has been recognized in this state. Morey v. Essex County, 94 N.J.L. 427, 430, 110 A. 905 (E. & A. 1920) (unremitting trespass is a continuous tort); Russo Farms, Inc. v. Vineland Bd. of Educ., 280 N.J.Super. 320, 327–28, 655 A.2d 447 (App.Div. 1995) (claim of inverse condemnation continued to accrue as long as defendant' conduct caused plaintiff's property to be subject to continual flooding due to negligent construction of an adjoining building); Aykan v. Goldzweig, 238 N.J.Super. 389, 392, 569 A.2d 905 (Law Div. 1989) (continuous negligent representation by an attorney is a continuous tort which tolls the statute of limitations until the representation is terminated or the client discovered or should have discovered the injury). This concept was also discussed, although not applied, in Tortorello v. Reinfeld, 6 N.J. 58, 66, 77 A.2d 240 (1950), in reference to a claim that a continuing course of negligent treatment by a physician should be considered a continuous tort, and not an isolated incident of negligent treatment.

We do not adopt the conclusion in *Cusseaux* that battered woman's syndrome is itself a continuous tort. Battered woman's syndrome is more correctly the medical condition resulting from continued acts of physical or psychological misconduct. Because the resulting psychological state, composed of varied by identifiable characteristics, is the product of at least two separate and discrete physical or psychological acts occurring at different times, to overcome the statute of limitations, it is imperative that the tortious conduct giving rise to the medical condition be considered a continuous tort. . . .

... [I]n Kyle v. Green Acres at Verona, Inc., supra, 44 N.J. at 112, 207 A.2d 513, the Supreme Court directed:

A trial court shall itself without a jury hear and determine (1) whether insanity developed on or subsequent to the date of the alleged act of defendant and within the period of limitation and if so, whether that insanity resulted from the defendant's acts; and (2) whether plaintiff's suit was started within a reasonable time after restoration of sanity....

That same mandate will be applicable in the trial of this matter. It will be incumbent upon plaintiff to establish pretrial, by medical, psychiatric or psychological evidence, that she suffers from battered woman's syndrome, which caused an inability to take any action to improve or alter the circumstances in her marriage unilaterally, so as to warrant a conclusion by the trial judge that the statute of limitations should be tolled. ...

STEPHEN SKILLMAN, J.A.D., concurring and dissenting.

I see no need for the creation of a new tort cause of action for "battered woman's syndrome." In addition, I would conclude that plaintiff failed to present any evidence that could justify postponing the accrual of her other tort causes of action. ...

"It is inadvisable to create new causes of action in tort in advance of any necessity for doing so in order to achieve a just result." Neelthak Dev. Corp. v. Township of Gloucester, 272 N.J.Super. 319, 325, 639 A.2d 1141 (App.Div.1994). Consequently, this court should consider whether existing tort causes of action provide an adequate remedy for conduct that may result in battered woman's syndrome before undertaking to create a new cause of action.

Any person who is a victim of violence, or the threat of violence, may recover money damages for assault and/or battery. A person may be liable for battery if "he acts intending to cause a harmful or offensive contact ... or an imminent apprehension of such contact" and a "harmful" or "offensive" contact "directly or indirectly results." 1 Restatement (Second) of Torts Sections 13, 18 (1965). A person who acts with the same intent may be liable for assault even if no contact actually results if the victim is placed in "imminent apprehension" of a harmful or offensive contact. Id. at Section 21. Consequently, any woman who is the victim of an act of battering, or a threat of battering, can bring a tort action against her assailant for each of those acts. Moreover, a battered woman would be entitled to recover not only for any economic losses resulting from those acts, such as medical expenses and lost wages, but also for pain and suffering and disability, see Schroeder v. Perkel, 87 N.J. 53, 66, 432 A.2d 834 (1981), which would include the psychological sequelae of any act of battering. Wilson v. Parisi, 268 N.J.Super. 213, 219–20, 633 A.2d 113 (App.Div.1993).

The trial court's opinion in Cusseaux v. Pickett, 279 N.J.Super. 335, 343, 652 A.2d 789 (Law Div.1994), upon which the majority relies, simply asserts, without any supporting explanation, that "the civil laws of assault and battery [are] insufficient to redress the harms suffered as a result of domestic violence." Although the majority's opinion likewise fails to explain why the law of assault and battery fails to provide adequate means of redress for the victims of domestic violence, it suggests that the creation of an independent tort of battered woman's syndrome would allow recovery in tort for "all acts of cruelty which occurred during the course of [the] marriage," (majority op. at 22, 663 A.2d at 119), even if those acts do not involve any battering. Under this view, plaintiff could seek money damages for the alleged emotional distress and psychological harm resulting from the alleged occasions when defendant came home late at night in an intoxicated condition and verbally abused her.

However, the creation of a cause of action that allowed recovery for incidents of verbal abuse would extend marital tort liability to conduct that would not give rise to legal liability in other contexts. Mere verbal abuse or insult is not generally a basis for the imposition of tort liability. 2 Fowler V. Harper, et al., THE LAW OF TORTS Section 9.2 (1986); Prosser on Torts Section 12 at 59–60 (5th ed. 1984). As observed in a comment to the Restatement of Torts, "some safety valve must be left through which irascible tempers may blow off relatively harmless steam." 1 Restatement (Second) of Torts Section 46 commend d (1965); cf. Ward v. Zelikovsky, 136 N.J. 516, 529, 643 A.2d 972 (1994) (quoting Rodney A. Smolla, Law of Defamation Section 6.12[9], at 6–54) ("[N]ame calling, epithets, and abusive language, no matter how vulgar or offensive, are not actionable" under the law of defamation). Moreover, even assuming that verbal abuse could be sufficiently outrageous and harmful to the target to give rise to a cause of action for intentional infliction of emotional distress, see Price v. State Farm Mut. Auto. Ins. Co., 878 F.Supp. 1567 (S.D.Ga. 1995); Jean C. Love, *Discriminatory Speech and the Tort of Intentional Infliction of Emotional Distress*, 47 WASH & LEE L.REV. 123 (1990), our courts have established rigorous prerequisites for proving this cause of action: Generally speaking, to establish a claim for intentional infliction of emotional distress, the plaintiff must establish intentional and outrageous conduct by the defendant, proximate cause, and distress that is severe. Initially, the plaintiff must prove that the defendant acted intentionally or recklessly. . . .

Second, the defendant's conduct must be extreme and outrageous. The conduct must be "so outrageous in character, and so extreme in degree, as to go beyond all possible bounds of decency, and to be regarded as atrocious, and utterly intolerable in a civilized community." Third, the defendant's actions must have been the proximate cause of the plaintiff's emotional distress. Fourth, the emotional distress suffered by the plaintiff must be "so severe that no reasonable man could be expected to endure it." By circumscribing the cause of action with an elevated threshold for liability and damages, courts have authorized legitimate claims while eliminating those that should not be compensable. [Buckley v. Trenton Saving Fund Soc'y, 111 N.J. 355, 366–67, 544 A.2d 857 (1988) (citations omitted).]

The kind of verbal abuse that defendant allegedly directed at plaintiff, although certainly offensive, was not "so outrageous in character, and so extreme in degree, as to go beyond all possible bounds of decency, and to be regarded a atrocious, and utterly intolerable in a civilized community." Id. at 366, 544 A.2d 857; see Price v. State Farm Mut. Auto. Ins. Co., supra; cf. Ruprecht v. Ruprecht, 252 N.J.Super. 230, 238, 599 A.2d 604 (Ch.Div.1991) (holding that wife's eleven year secret adulterous affair with her employer failed "to reach the level of outrageousness necessary for liability under this tort."). In fact, serious verbal abuse, often reciprocal in nature, is a common feature of deteriorating marriages. Consequently, the verbal abuse that plaintiff ascribes to defendant could not provide the basis for a claim of intentional infliction of emotional distress.

It is clear to me that we should not create a cause of action that would result in potential tort liability between domestic partners in a broader range of circumstances than apply in other contexts. Although close family relationships, such as those between a husband and wife or a parent and child, serve as primary sources of love, affection and support, the emotional significance of such relationships and the constant contact that occurs among family members who live together also produce various forms of tension, discord and verbal abuse. Verbal abuse between spouses is likely to be most frequent, and most nasty, when a marital relationship is deteriorating. As we noted in Peranio v. Peranio, 280 N.J.Super. 47, 56, 654 A.2d 495 (App.Div.1995):

> [T]he dissolution of a marriage is rarely a happy event. All parties suffer and even the most rational are hard pressed to avoid any emotional encounters.

In my view, such emotional encounters within a marriage should not form a basis for the imposition of tort liability unless one of the parties engages in conduct that could support a claim for assault, battery or intentional infliction of emotional distress. See Merenoff v. Merenoff, 76 N.J. 535, 555, 388 A.2d 951 (1978) ("There is a range of activity arising in the course of a marriage relationship beyond the reach of the law of torts."). In fact, the creation of an overly expansive concept of tort liability in the marital setting would conflict with current statutory provisions that have reduced the significance of fault in matrimonial litigation, see Kazin v. Kazin, 81 N.J. 85, 92, 405 A.2d 360 (1979), and would unnecessarily complicate such litigation. Therefore, I would reject plaintiff's effort to gain recognition of a new tort action for battered woman's syndrome.

. . . The majority opinion suggests that a primary objective of creating a new tort cause of action for battered woman's syndrome is to avoid the normal application of the statute of limitations to bar marital tort claims. If that is the underlying reason for the creation of this new tort, it is a classic case of the tail being allowed to wag the dog. If defendant's alleged marital misconduct could be properly characterized as "continuous" or if plaintiff's mental state could be shown to constitute "insanity," the running of the statute of limitations could be tolled regardless of whether plaintiff's cause of action were labeled assault and battery, intentional infliction of emotional distress, or the amorphous new tort of battered woman's syndrome. See Jones v. Jones, 242 N.J.Super. 195, 576 A.2d 316 (App.Div.), certif. denied,

122 N.J. 418, 585 A.2d 412 (1990); Twyman v. Twyman, 790 S.W.2d 819, 820–21 (Tex.Ct.App.1990), rev'd on other grounds, 855 S.W.2d 619 (Tex. 1993). To state the point another way, it seems to me that the elements that a plaintiff must prove to establish a cause of action should be analyzed separately from the question of whether the plaintiff has made the kind of showing required to toll the statute of limitations. . . .

NOTES AND QUESTIONS

1. **Jury Right**. The *Giovine* court also addressed the availability of a jury in cases alleging the tort of battered woman's syndrome. It concluded that courts of equity are often able to adjudicate tort claims asserted in matrimonial litigation, but some tort claims "encompassing complex medical issues or substantial claims of permanent disability, whether physical or psychological, may warrant a jury trial." 284 N.J. Super. at 3–26, 663 A.2d at 109–131. To obtain a jury, the tort claimant must establish by written expert opinion that the trial will introduce proof of such injury or complex medical evidence. In adjudicating tort claims arising from domestic abuse, when would a jury be beneficial and when harmful—to the claimant, to the defendant, to any children involved, or to the larger public?

2. **Damages**. What should be the measure of damages in successful tort claims of battered woman's syndrome? When, if ever, should punitive damages be awarded?

3. **No-fault Divorce**. In what ways does the development of tort remedies for abuse during marriage revive notions of fault that have been eliminated in no-fault divorce regimes? In what ways do the tort remedies express values quite apart from fault notions in divorce?

V.   VIOLENCE IN INTIMATE RELATIONSHIPS

Violence in intimate relationships once seemed so different from other kinds of violence that it was exempted from public sanction under criminal law and tort. As reforms alter that practice and subject intimate partners and family members to legal sanctions for physical and emotional abuse, should there be any special concerns or approaches to distinguish these sanctions from the treatment of violence between neighbors or strangers? This question is especially germane when the intergenerational dimensions of intimate violence come to view. As bell hooks and Martha Minow explore in the closing readings for this chapter, children who watch violence between their parents and other adults learn complicated messages about what to expect and what to accept. What legal responses to intimate violence between adults are most likely to alter the patterns in subsequent generations?

bell hooks, Violence in Intimate Relationships

From b. hooks, Talking Back: Thinking Feminist/Thinking Black (Boston: South End Press, 1989).

We were on the freeway, going home from San Francisco. He was driving. We were arguing. He had told me repeatedly to shut up. I kept talking. He took his hand from the steering wheel and threw it back, hitting my mouth—my open mouth, blood gushed, and I felt an intense pain. I was no longer able to say any words, only to make whimpering, sobbing sounds as the blood dripped on my hands, on the handkerchief I held to tightly. He did not stop the car. He drove home. I watched him pack his suitcase. It was a holiday. He was going away to have fun. When he left I washed my mouth. My jaw was swollen and it was difficult for me to open it.

I called the dentist the next day and made an appointment. When the female voice asked what I needed to see the doctor about, I told her I had been hit in the mouth. Conscious of race, sex, and class issues, I wondered how I would be treated in this white doctor's office. My face was no longer swollen so there was nothing to identify me as a woman who had been hit, as a black woman with a bruised and swollen jaw. When the dentist asked me what had happened to my mouth, I described it calmly and succinctly. He made little jokes about, "How we can't have someone doing this to us now, can we?" I said nothing. The damage was repaired. Through it all, he talked to me as if I were a child, someone he had to handle gingerly or otherwise I might become hysterical.

This is one way women who are hit by men and seek medical care are seen. People within patriarchal society imagine that women are hit because we are hysterical, because we are beyond reason. It is most often the person who is hitting that is beyond reason, who is hysterical, who has lost complete control over responses and actions.

Growing up, I had always thought that I would never allow any man to hit me and live. I would kill him. I had seen my father hit my mother once and I wanted to kill him. My mother said to me then, "You are too young to know, too young to understand." Being a mother in a culture that supports and promotes domination, a patriarchal, white-supremacist culture, she did not discuss how she felt or what she meant. Perhaps it would have been too difficult for her to speak about the confusion of being hit by someone you are intimate with, someone you love. In my case, I was hit by my companion at a time in life when a number of forces in the world outside our home had already "hit" me, so to speak, made me painfully aware of my powerlessness, my marginality. It seemed then that I was confronting being black and female and without money in the worst possible ways. My world was spinning. I had already lost a sense of grounding and security. The memory of this experience has stayed with me as I have grown as a feminist, as I have thought deeply and read much on male violence against women, on adult violence against children.

In this essay, I do not intend to concentrate attention solely on male physical abuse of females. It is crucial that feminists call attention to physical abuse in all its forms. In particular, I want to discuss being physically abused in singular incidents by someone you love. Few people who are hit once by someone they love responded in the way they might to a singular physical assault by a stranger. Many children raised in households where hitting has been a normal response by primary caretakers react ambivalently to physical assaults as adults, especially if they are being hit by someone who cares for them and whom they care for. Often female parents use physical abuse as a means of control. There is continued need for feminist research that examines such violence. Alice Miller has done insightful work on the impact of hitting even though she is at times anti-feminist in her perspective. (Often in her work, mothers are blamed, as if their responsibility in parenting is greater than that of fathers.) Feminist discussions of violence against women should be expanded to include a recognition of the ways in which women use abusive physical force toward children not only to challenge the assumptions that women are likely to be nonviolent, but also to add to our understanding of why children who were hit growing up are often hit as adults or hit others.

Recently, I began a conversation with a group of black adults about hitting children. They all agreed that hitting was sometimes necessary. A professional black male in a southern family setting with two children commented on the way he punished his daughters. Sitting them down, he would first interrogate them about the situation or circumstance for which they were being punished. He said with great pride, "I want them to be able to understand fully why they are being punished." I responded by saying that "they will likely become women whom a lover will attack using the same procedure you who have loved them so well used and they will not know how to respond." He resisted the idea that his behavior would have any impact on their responses to violence as adult women. I pointed to case after case of women in intimate relationships with men (and sometimes women) who are subject to the same form of interrogation and punishment they experienced as children, who accept their lover assuming an abusive, authoritarian role. Children who are the victims of physical abuse—whether one beating or repeated beatings, one violent push or several—whose wounds are inflicted by a loved one, experience an extreme sense of dislocation. The world one has most intimately known, in which one felt relatively safe and secure, has collapsed. Another world has come into being, one filled with terrors, where it is difficult to distinguish between a safe situation and a dangerous one, a gesture of love and a violent uncaring gesture. There is a feeling of vulnerability, exposure, that never goes away, that lurks beneath the surface. I know. I was one of those children. Adults hit by loved ones usually experience similar sensations of dislocation, of loss, of new found terrors.

Many children who are hit have never known what it feels like to be cared for, loved without physical aggression or abusive pain. Hitting is such a widespread practice that any of us are lucky if we can go through life without having this experience. One undiscussed aspect of the reality of children who are hit finding themselves as adults in similar circumstances is that we often share with friends and lovers the framework of our childhood pains and this may determine how they respond to us in difficult situations. We share the ways we are wounded and expose vulnerable areas. Often, these revelations provide a detailed model for anyone who wishes to wound or hurt us. While the literature about physical abuse often points to the fact that children who are abused are likely to become abusers or be abused, there is no attention given to sharing woundedness in such a way that we let intimate others know exactly what can be done to hurt us, to make us feel as though we are caught in the destructive patterns we have struggled to break. When partners create scenarios of abuse similar, if not exactly the same, to those we have experienced in childhood, the wounded person is hurt not only by the physical pain but by the feeling of calculated betrayal. Betrayal. When we are physically hurt by loved ones, we feel betrayed. We can no longer trust that care can be sustained. We are wounded, damaged—hurt to our hearts.

Feminist work calling attention to male violence against women has helped create a climate where the issues of physical abuse by loved ones can be freely addressed, especially sexual abuse within families. Exploration of male violence against women by feminists and non-feminists shows a connection between childhood experience of being hit by loved ones and the later occurrence of violence in adult relationships. While there is much material available discussing physical abuse of women by men, usually extreme physical abuse, there is not much discussion of the impact that one incident of hitting may have on a person in an intimate relationship, or how the person who is hit recovers from that experience. Increasingly, in discussion with women about physical abuse in relationships, irrespective of sexual preference, I find that most of us have had the experience of being violently hit at least once. There is little discussion of how we are damaged by such experiences (especially if we have been hit as children), of the ways we cope and recover from this wounding. This is an important area for feminist research precisely because many cases of extreme abuse begin with an isolated incident of hitting. Attention must be given to understanding and stopping these isolated incidents if we are to eliminate the possibility that women will be at risk in intimate relationships.

Critically thinking about issues of physical abuse has led me to question the way our culture, the way we as feminist advocates focus on the issue of violence and physical abuse by loved ones. The focus has been on male violence against women and, in particular, male sexual abuse of children. Given the nature of patriarchy, it has been necessary for feminists to focus on extreme cases to make people confront the issue, and acknowledge it to be serious and relevant. Unfortunately, an exclusive focus on extreme cases can and does lead us to ignore the more frequent, more common, yet less extreme case of occasional hitting. Women are also less likely to acknowledge occasional hitting for fear that they will then be seen as someone who is in a bad relationship or someone whose life is out of control. Currently, the literature about male violence against women identifies the physically abused woman as a "battered woman." While it has been important to have an accessible terminology to draw attention to the issue of male violence against women, the terms used reflect biases because they call attention to only one type of violence in intimate relationships. The term "battered women" is problematical. It is not a term that emerged from feminist work on male violence against women; it was already used by psychologists and sociologists in the literature on domestic violence. This label "battered woman" places primary emphasis on physical assaults that are continuous, repeated, and unrelenting. They focus in on extreme violence, with little effort to link these cases with the everyday acceptance within intimate relationships of physical abuse that is not extreme, that may not be repeated. Yet these lesser forms of physical abuse damage individuals psychologically and, if not properly addressed and recovered from, can set the stage for more extreme incidents.

Most importantly, the term "battered woman" is used as though it constitutes a separate and unique category of womanness, as though it is an identity, a mark that sets one apart rather than being simply a descriptive term. It is as though the experience of being repeatedly violently hit is the sole defining characteristic of a woman's identity and all other aspects of who she is and what her experience has been are submerged. When I was hit, I too used the popular phrases "batterer," "battered woman," "battering" even though I did not feel that these words adequately described being hit once. However, these were the terms that people would listen to, would see as important, significant (as if it is not really significant for an individual, and more importantly for a woman, to be hit once). My partner was angry to be labeled a batterer by me. He was reluctant to talk about the experience of hitting me precisely because he did not want to be labeled a batterer. I had hit him once (not as badly as he had hit me) and I did not think of myself as a batterer. For both of us, these terms were inadequate. Rather than enabling us to cope effectively and positively with a negative situation, they were part of all the mechanisms of denial; they made us want to avoid confronting what had happened. This is the case for many people who are hit and those who hit.

Women who are hit once by men in their lives, and women who are hit repeatedly do not want to be placed in the category of "battered woman" because it is a label that appears to strip us of dignity, to deny that there has been any integrity in the relationships we are in. A person physically assaulted by a stranger or a casual friend with whom they are not intimate may be hit once or repeatedly but they do not have to be placed into a category before doctors, lawyers, family, counselors, etc., take their problem seriously. Again, it must be stated that establishing categories and terminology has been part of the effort to draw public attention to the seriousness of male violence against women in intimate relationships. Even though the use of convenient labels and categories has made it easier to identify problems of physical abuse, it does not mean the terminology should not be critiqued from a feminist perspective and changed if necessary.

Recently, I had an experience assisting a woman who had been brutally attacked by her husband (she never commented on whether this was the first incident or not), which caused me to reflect anew on the use of the term: "battered woman." This young woman was not engaged in feminist thinking or aware that "battered woman" was a category. Her husband had tried to choke her to death. She managed to escape from him with only the clothes she was wearing. After she recovered from the trauma, she considered going back to this relationship. As a church-going woman, she believed that her marriage vows were sacred and that she should try to make the relationship work. In an effort to share my feeling that this could place her at great risk, I brought her Lenore Walker's THE BATTERED WOMAN because it seemed to me that there was much that she was not revealing, that she felt alone, and that the experiences she would read about in the book would give her a sense that other women had experienced what she was going through. I hoped reading the book would give her the courage to confront the reality of her situation. Yet I found it difficult to share because I could see that her self-esteem had already been greatly attacked, and she had lost a sense of her worth and value, and that possibly this categorizing of her identity would add to the feeling that she should just forget, be silent (and certainly returning to a situation where one is likely to be abused is one way to mask the severity of the problem). Still I had to try. When I first gave her the book, it disappeared. An unidentified family member had thrown it away. They felt that she would be making a serious mistake if she began to see herself as an absolute victim which they felt the label "battered woman" implied. I stressed that she should ignore the labels and read the content. I believed the experience shared in this book helped give her the courage to be critical of her situation, to take constructive action.

Her response to the label "battered woman," as well as the responses of other women who have been victims of violence in intimate relationships, compelled me to critically explore further the use of this term. In conversation with many women, I found that it was seen as a stigmatizing label, one which victimized women seeking help felt themselves in no condition to critique. As in, "who cares what anybody is calling it—I just want to stop this pain." Within patriarchal society, women who are victimized by male violence have had to pay a price for breaking the silence and naming the problem. They have had to be seen as fallen women, who have failed in their "feminine" role to sensitize and civilize the beast in the man. A category like "battered woman" risks reinforcing this notion that the hurt woman, not only the rape victim, becomes a social pariah, set apart, marked forever by this experience.

A distinction must be made between having a terminology that enables women, and all victims of violent acts, to name the problem and categories of labeling that may inhibit the naming. When individuals are wounded, we are indeed often scarred, often damaged in ways that do set us apart from those who have not experienced a similar wounding, but an essential aspect of the recovery process is the healing of the wound, the removal of the scar. This is an empowering process that should not be diminished by labels that imply this wounding experience is the most significant aspect of identity.

As I have already stated, overemphasis on extreme cases of violent abuse may lead us to ignore the problem of occasional hitting, and it may make it difficult for women to talk about this problem. A critical issue that is not fully examined and written about in great detail by researchers who study and work with victims is the recovery process. There is a dearth of material discussing the recovery process of individuals who have been physically abused. In those cases where an individual is hit only once in an intimate relationship, however violently, there may be no recognition at all of the negative impact of this experience. There may be no conscious attempt by the victimized person to work at restoring her or his well-being, even if the person seeks therapeutic help, because the one incident may not be seen as serious or damaging. Alone and in isolation, the person who has been hit must struggle to regain broken trust—to forge some strategy of recovery. Individuals are often able to process an experience of being hit mentally that may not be processed emotionally. Many women I talked with felt that even after the incident was long forgotten, their bodies remain troubled. Instinctively, the person who has been hit may respond fearfully to any body movement on the part of a loved one that is similar to the posture used when pain was inflicted.

Being hit once by a partner can forever diminish sexual relationships if there has been no recovery process. Again there is little written about ways folks recover physically in their sexualities as loved ones who continue to be sexual with those who have hurt them. In most cases, sexual relationships are dramatically altered when hitting has occurred. The sexual realm may be the one space where the person who has been hit experiences again the sense of vulnerability, which may also arouse fear. This can lead either to an attempt to avoid sex or to unacknowledged sexual withdrawal wherein the person participates but is passive. I talked with women who had been hit by lovers who described sex as an ordeal, the one space where they confront their inability to trust a partner who has broken trust. One woman emphasized that to her, being hit was a "violation of her body space" and that she felt from then on she had to protect that space. This response, though a survival strategy, does not lead to healthy recovery.

Often, women who are hit in intimate relationships with male or female lovers feel as though we have lost an innocence that cannot be regained. Yet this very notion of innocence is connected to passive acceptance of concepts of romantic love under patriarchy which have served to mask problematic realities in relationships. The process of recovery must include a critique of this notion of innocence which is often linked to an unrealistic and fantastic vision of love and romance. It is only in letting go of the perfect, no-work, happily-ever-after union idea, that we can rid our psyches of the sense that we have failed in some way by not having such relationships. Those of us who never focused on the negative impact of being hit as children find it necessary to reexamine the past in a therapeutic manner as part of our recovery process. Strategies that helped us survive as children may be detrimental for us to use in adult relationships.

Talking about being hit by loved ones with other women, both as children and as adults, I found that many of us had never really thought very much about our own relationship to violence. Many of us took pride in never feeling violent, never hitting. We had not thought deeply about our relationship to inflicting physical pain. Some of us expressed terror and awe when confronted with physical strength on the part of others. For us, the healing process included the need to learn how to use physical force constructively, to remove the terror—the dread. Despite the research that suggests children who are hit may become adults who hit—women hitting children, men hitting women and children—most of the women I talked with not only did not hit but were compulsive about not using physical force.

Overall the process by which women recover from the experience of being hit by loved ones is a complicated and multi-faceted one, an area where there must be much more feminist study and research. To many of us, feminists calling attention to the reality of violence in intimate relationships has not in and of itself compelled most people to take the issue seriously, and such violence seems to be daily on the increase. In this essay, I have raised issues that are not commonly talked about, even among folks who are particularly concerned about violence against women. I hope it will serve as a catalyst for further thought, that it will strengthen our efforts as feminist activists to create a world where domination and coercive abuse are never aspects of intimate relationships.

Martha Minow, Words and the Door to the Land of Change: Law, Language, and Family Violence

43 Vanderbilt L. Rev. 1665 (1990).

The turn toward narrative by legal scholars may help illuminate the difficulties of speaking about domestic violence against children and against women. Literary accounts and narratives of experience can offer new language to challenge conventional legal understandings, or misunderstandings, of domestic violence. Narratives with evocative, rich details about subjective experiences can be used to persuade people—like judges—who have sufficient power to make a difference actually to do so for people—like children and women—who face persistent risks of violence at the hands of intimate fellow householders.

At least, this is the hope. But does the hope carry any promise for practices beyond the pages of law reviews? Does the turn to storytelling and literature offer any chance that words may halt the violence, or at least strengthen those in a position to punish and deter the violence? Toward this end, I have joined others in a project of continuing education for judges in which we create settings to discuss family violence by using works of fiction. The project began as a response to a problem named in the trade as "judicial burnout." For one day, fifteen to twenty judges came to the campus of Brandeis University to discuss several works of literature.

We begin each session by noting that we have two sets of texts before us—the assigned literature and our own lives—and both will engage us in interpretation for the whole day. I call the judges by their first names. Some of them know one another. Some of them talk with a kind of reserve that may come from not talking often with strangers who call them by their first names.

Sometimes there are moments of empathy engendered by the readings; a character seems quite appealing, or a difficult situation seems recognizable. Sometimes the judges express their irritation with litigants, the press, and society. Sometimes there are surprising insights into texts or intense arguments about the literature and about what judges should do. In one session, several judges begin by criticizing women who come to court seeking temporary restraining orders to halt the physical abuse by their husbands or boyfriends. Two judges spoke: "These women come for the order, and then they never follow up with the hearing and final disposition," and questioned, "Are they serious or not?"

I suggest that we turn to Mary Gordon's short story, *Violation*. The story begins with this statement by an unnamed narrator: "I suppose that in a forty-five-year life, I should feel grateful to have experienced only two instances of sexual violation." I ask the judges, "What do you think is her tone of voice as she says or thinks this?" A judge responds, "I don't know, I found her baffling." Another says, "I think she is passionless. There is no emotion when she says it." We talk some more. How could she feel lucky? Is this an ironic statement, or is it a sober response to the world she has known?

We examine two incidents the narrator describes. In the first one, she recounts her post-college trip to Europe, a conversation with a sailor in a bar, the walk she took with him, and the way he raped her. "She should have known better," says one judge. "She wouldn't have talked with a sailor in a bar at home; it's only that she felt free and adventuresome during her travels," says another. A woman judge, one of the few present, recalls her own experiences traveling and says quietly, "Why should she have to watch what she does, why should she be blamed for what happened?" An intense discussion follows: the judges talk of their daughters, themselves, of the cities they know, of dangers outside.

We turn to the other incident described in the story. An uncle visiting the family comes to the narrator's bed; he is drunk and he makes a sexual overture. After experiencing an inner paralysis, she resists him with humor and then struggles with the knowledge that telling anyone would seem a betrayal of the whole family. One judge comments, "She handled it perfectly." Another says, "I don't understand what is the big deal here." Another responds sharply, "So, it's okay if it happens in the family?" After a series of exchanges, I return to the opening sentence of the story. What do we know, now, about this person; why would she describe herself as lucky? One judge says he feels sad for her because she seems repressed, she seems to have cut off feeling in response to the vents in her life. Another disagrees, but says, "I still don't understand why she never told anyone."

We return to the first incident. After the rape, the narrator has missed her travel connection and checks into a hotel. She describes how she gladly paid extra for a private bath because she could not bear the idea of sharing a bathtub. "It wasn't for myself I minded; I cared for the other people. I knew myself to be defiled, and I didn't want the other innocent, now sleeping guests, exposed to my contamination." We talked about what she felt and why she could not tell anyone. After we converse, one judge volunteers, "I guess it's hard for anyone to come to court after something like this happens." I do not know exactly what prompts the thought, but I am glad for it.

We break for coffee. A judge who has said little or nothing all morning talks to me alone about a very difficult case, one in which the state removed a child from a family partly because the social workers thought the mother was mentally incompetent. They later found out that the mother only spoke a particular East Asian dialect. Meanwhile, the child has been with a foster family for eight months and has developed ties to them. Should the court correct the original injustice, or would this inflict a new injustice from the child's perspective?

After returning from the break, we discuss a story by William Faulkner. It is called *Barn Burning* and the story begins with a hearing before a justice of the peace in which a boy's father is accused of burning down a man's barn. The complainant mentions that the boy knows what happened. The justice of the peace calls on the boy and Faulkner lets us hear the boy think about how his father wants him to lie and how he would have to do so. The justice asks the complainant, "Do you want me to question this boy?" After a pause, the complainant explosively answers "no." Why does he not want the boy questioned? "Because he knows the boy will lie," says one judge. "Because he knows it will be excruciating for the boy to testify, whether he lies or tells the truth," responds another. "Because the father will beat the child, if he doesn't lie," says another judge.

A few pages later in the story, the father beats the child anyway. He "struck him with the flat of his hand on the side of the head, hard but without heat, exactly as he had struck the two mules at the store." We talk about the father and the boy: who are they, what do they think, what is their world like? The judges are deeply sympathetic with the boy. They despise the father. They give him psychiatric labels. We try to examine his social and economic position. As a "poor white," he is angered by his dependency as a sharecropper. He despises blacks, treats his family members like property, and moves constantly to elude the repercussions of his vengeful acts, like barn burning. It is hard to elicit any respect or understanding for him, although I try. We look at why he seems so humiliated by other people's expectations. We debate his motives and his capacity for self-reflection or self-control.

I then ask, "Does the boy ever strike anyone?" "No," says one judge. "Oh yes, he does," says another, pointing to the fist fight the boy started after another boy called his father "Barn burner!" We trace the son's course through the story and our own course with him—how he comes to warn a landowner that his barn is about to be burned down by the father; how he comes to run away; whether this is strength or weakness of character; what we think about his abandonment of his mother and sisters; whether we should admire him; how much the boy knew at the time he ran away; and whether we have access to anything but what he thought years later about these events. What did Faulkner think about it all?

During these discussions, I sometimes sense a shift in the room. I sense a shift in loyalties. I hear imaginations exercised. Sometimes nothing like this happens. I often wonder whether we, the conveners, merely are providing a break from the routine of too many cases for these judges, or worse, a salve before sending the soldiers back to the war. My thoughts wander back and forth. Are they on our side? Am I on theirs? Who is "we," anyway?

After lunch, where I sit at a table with judges who complain about the lack of funding for court personnel and retell war stories about problems with the media, we read and discuss a story called *A Jury of Her Peers*. In this story by Susan Glaspell, a feminist writing in 1917, a farmer has died and his wife is the chief suspect. The story depicts the inquiries made by the prosecutor and the sheriff, both men, who unsuccessfully look for clues to the motive behind the murder. The story presents the contrasting inquiry undertaken by the sheriff's wife and her woman friend when they visit the farm kitchen to gather items for the imprisoned widow. Seeing her world and imagining the details of her life, these women glimpse the widow's relentlessly desperate loneliness and the signs of abuse by her husband. The women find clues indicating an altercation between the husband and wife; they figure out that he had crushed her songbird. The conclude that she had felt her husband crushing the life out of her, and that she had responded by strangling him in his sleep. The women decide to share neither the clues nor their conclusions with the men.

I ask the judges, "Did the women forgive the farmer's wife and protect her for that reason? Or did they feel they could not judge her became they themselves were partly to blame for her isolation? Did they believe that the formal legal system, with no women judges, lawyers, or jurors, never could yield understanding and fair judgment about what happened here?"

No one responds at first. As in all the sessions, the judges are mostly men. There usually is tension in the room, often defensiveness, and sometimes suppressed anger. The judges seem distrustful even before we start. One responds that he is dismayed that a woman could excuse another woman despite concluding that she indeed did commit a murder. Another criticizes the story for suggesting that women see the world differently from men, observe clues that men miss, and judge those clues differently. Another judge objects to the men being portrayed as stick figures. (So were the women, notes a woman judge.) One judge trumpets a temporal difference: we are now enlightened; we now recognize a defense for battered women who attack their batterers. Another objects that this cases does not fit our standard for the battered woman's syndrome defense. I intervene. Let's not talk about what the law says; let's talk about the story. A judge explains that the story made him think about his difficulties judging immigrant families who use extensive corporal punishment with their children. "They are in our country now, they must obey our laws," he says. He then wonders aloud about a man who killed his wife and then received a light sentence after explaining to the judge how his culture viewed her adultery.

I worry about these discussions. Am I simply sponsoring cultural relativism and undermining a commitment to disapprove of family violence? The judges reassure me, and themselves, that their commitment is to enforce the law, regardless of individual or cultural differences. But should we not learn to distinguish minimum norms—such as a right to be protected against physical harm—that warrant legal intervention no matter what competing demands we may endorse concerning tolerance for cultural differences? Then the business of understanding is not inconsistent with the business of judging, and cultivating empathy would not conflict with strengthening judgments about the unacceptability of some acts, especially violent acts. Understanding the complex reasons why people abuse others does not mean condoning that abuse. Perhaps understanding reasons for violence strengthens a commitment to draw violent actors into the human community and subject them to its judgments. I worry still about those who remain silent, even in this room of judges—those whose point of view remains unspoken because it would not be popular. I wonder if anyone in the room has been a participant in family violence but does not speak about it.

I enjoy these sessions, yet I worry about them, too. I relish the thirst the judges show for probing conversation. I delight when I see them scour the texts for meaning. When I hear them talk with intensity, and sometimes humility, I learn about their frustrations. I sometimes see the literature illuminated by their lives, and their lives by the literature. I fear disserving the texts, however, by my sometimes crude readings or by those offered by the students. I fear my fear of this. Do I betray an elitist academic sensibility toward "right" or "sensitive" readings of texts and toward the meaning of doing "justice" to a text? I genuinely hope that engagement with literature can provide occasions for the moral act of taking the perspectives of others. I still worry, however, that in our pride in this enterprise we may neglect the possibility that we do not understand—that silenced discomfort over who is "we" is itself a serious stumbling block to understanding. I see a difference between readings that lead to sage nodding because "we" claim to share an understanding of the text, and readings that lead to struggle and disagreement because I did not see it the way you did, or because you catch a glimpse of a character you know and I do not, or because she reads against the text for what it does not say, or because he believes we are kidding ourselves about what we really would do under similar circumstances?

Perhaps in these struggles, we make a way to talk about violence. Perhaps. If so, we may come closest in those moment of silence in which we—individually and together—realize some of that which we do not know how to say.

Cornelia Spelman, a psychotherapist, recently wrote:

The stuffed clown flies across my office and hits me in the head. "Use *words*," I say to my six-year-old patient, a little girl. "Use words to tell me if you're mad; don't throw the clown."

Spelman explains that a psychotherapist tries to help patients learn the power of words:

Using words to teach and comfort, listening, I am witness and midwife to the slow, painful rebirth of people whom language failed. For them, words have been used by others only to wound and destroy.

A week later the six-year-old was carefully cutting paper. "This," she announced, pointing to a hole she had made in a piece of paper, "is the Door to the Land of Change."

For survivors of family violence, words may be doors to the land of change. Words may provide these survivors with something to hold on to and thus something to aid recovery, something to grasp for a modicum of control and recollection of self. What words can open doors for those not yet victimized and for those who have been standing by?

CLOSING PROBLEM TO CHAPTER TWO

To explore your understanding of and conclusions about the materials and themes in this chapter, consider this closing problem.

Claire, a business executive, and Marion, a freelance writer, are a lesbian couple who have lived together for fifteen years. During that time they have opened joint bank accounts and have jointly purchased a house and a car. Although Claire has always earned considerably more money than Marion, the couple has always pooled their earnings and paid for expenses jointly.

Ten years ago, the pair decided that they wanted to have a child, and Claire became pregnant with sperm from an anonymous donor. Claire subsequently gave birth to a son, named Rick. When Rick was an infant, Marion, with Claire's consent, commenced an action in Family Court to adopt Rick. The adoption statute in their jurisdiction states, in relevant part, the "any person may petition the court for a decree of adoption." However, the adoption statute also states that "after the making of an order of adoption, the natural parents of the adoptive child shall be relieved of all parental duties toward and of all responsibilities for and shall have no rights over such adoptive child or to his property by descent or succession, except that when one of the natural parents is the spouse of the adopter, the rights and relations as between the adoptee, that natural parent, and his [or her] parents and collateral relatives, including mutual rights of inheritance or succession, are in no way altered." The Family Court ultimately denied Marion's petition, ruling that since Claire obviously did not intend to give up her rights to Rick, the adoption was statutorily prohibited.

a) Do you agree with the Family Court's interpretation and application of the adoption statute? If you were Marion's lawyer, what types of arguments could you raise on appeal in opposition to the Family Court's ruling?

Despite Marion's failure to obtain a second-parent adoption, she remained actively involved in caring for Rick. In fact, since Claire's job has always been more demanding than Marion's, Marion assumed most of the parenting responsibilities such as making Rick's meals, bringing him to and picking him up from school, and helping him with his homework. During this period, Marion turned down offers for more lucrative employment because she has feared that they would impinge on the time she spends with Rick. Rick is closely attached to both women.

About two years ago, the couple's relationship began to become troubled. Claire, depressed by the accidental death of her sister, became increasingly verbally abusive toward Marion and, on several occasions after drinking alcohol, even punched and kicked her. Claire has repeatedly ignored Marion's requests to seek professional counseling.

b) You are a lawyer in a family law practice in Claire and Marion's hometown. Marion comes to see you because she is planning to leave Claire. She indicates that she is interested in seeking custody of Rick and wants to know whether you think she will be able to. In this jurisdiction, a parent may obtain custody of a minor if the court deems that such custody would serve the best interests of the child. Additionally, if neither parent is fit and proper to have the custody of the child, the court may transfer custody of that child to a relative. As Marion's lawyer, what arguments could you make on her behalf to help her obtain custody of Rick?

c) If she cannot gain custody of Rick, Marion would at least like to be permitted regular, scheduled visitation. The relevant statute states that "the trial court may grant the right of visitation with respect to any minor child to any person, upon an application of such person. In making such an order, the court shall be guided by the best interest of the child. . . . " What arguments could you make on Marion's behalf to help her obtain the right to visit Rick?

d) Finally, Marion indicates that she is interested in seeking property and/or support from Claire. Assume that this jurisdiction has not yet considered a *Marvin*-type case. What types of arguments would you make to the court to convince it to adopt *Marvin*-like remedies in this case? What do you foresee as the likely counter-arguments presented by Claire?

CHAPTER THREE

WOMEN AND THEIR BODIES

A. THE PREGNANT BODY

Introduction

The legal regulation of women's bodies raises some of the most controversial issues for feminists. Do surrogacy arrangements commodify women's bodies or give women greater reproductive options? Is prostitution a form of "sexual slavery" or an acceptable—even liberating—line of work? Does pornography cause men to treat women as sex objects or does it provide a tool to assist women in redefining their own sexuality? These tensions arise partly because of the body's conflicting meanings for women. According to Carlin Meyers, one of the authors whose work is included here, "activities surrounding the body are at one and the same time sources of oppression and among women's primary arenas of empowerment." The law's treatment of women's bodies, then, is a critical focus for those seeking women's equality and self-determination.

Because reproduction is one of the most regulated aspects of women's bodies, and because the legal regulation of reproduction is strongly affected by its role in family life, this section constitutes another bridge between the preceding chapter on women and the family and the concluding sections on women and their bodies. The readings consider four subjects of reproductive regulation: abortion, maternal conduct during pregnancy, welfare reform measures that deter childbearing, and reproduction-assisting technologies.

The right to an abortion has been one of the most explosive legal and social issues of our time. When Roe v. Wade, 410 U.S. 113 (1973), was decided more than 25 years ago, it received uniformly negative criticism from legal commentators concerned about jurisprudential integrity. The right to privacy by which it was justified was based on dubious Constitutional language and precedent, and privacy seemed like an incongruous authority for a practice that technically could rarely occur "in private." The Court's trimester analysis, which supported gradually intensified degrees of governmental regulation, seemed to come out of thin air, and the trimester logic—that the state's interest in protecting the fetus corresponded with medical ability to support the fetus outside the womb—seemed injudiciously vulnerable to imminent technological developments. For pro-choice advocates, the Supreme Court cut Constitutional protection for abortion too short by rooting *Roe* in privacy doctrine, the injunction against state intervention in the private sphere. The Court went on to hold, in cases succeeding *Roe,* especially in the 1980 case Harris v. McRae, 448 U.S.

297 (1980), that the right to privacy does not compel states to pay for poor women's abortions. Thus, privacy worked to shield women from some abortion restrictions in *Roe,* but privacy has also justified the government's refusal to provide abortions for those who cannot pay for them. The separation of public and private elaborated in *Roe* and in *Harris* was extended by the court in Webster v. Reproductive Health Services, 492 U.S. 490 (1989), to permit states' prohibiting the performance of abortions in public facilities or by public employees. The public/private split was invoked as well in Rust v. Sullivan, 500 U.S. 173 (1996), to uphold the ban on furnishing abortion information and counselling to poor women by federally funded family-planning agencies.

The material on abortion begins with the Supreme Court's decision in Planned Parenthood of Southeastern Pennsylvania v. Casey, 505 U.S. 833 (1992), which while declining to overturn *Roe* allowed states greater leeway in placing restrictions on women's ability to obtain an abortion. *Casey* is followed by three essays about the legal and social significance of abortion rights. Catharine MacKinnon's piece criticizes privacy as the basis for reproductive control and argues that this approach only shields and reinforces women's subordination to men. Reva Siegel argues that restrictions on abortion constitute state action compelling pregnancy and motherhood that offend constitutional guarantees of equal protection. Loretta Ross's essay discusses the controversy over abortion rights in the Black community and advocates the understanding of reproductive freedom as a civil rights issue.

The next set of readings examines two types of legal regulation of pregnant women's conduct for the sake of the fetus—court-ordered medical treatment and the prosecution of women who use drugs during pregnancy. In re A.C., 573 A.2d 1235 (D.C. 1990), posthumously reversed a trial judge's decision ordering a cesarean section performed on a pregnant woman who was dying of cancer. (Both the mother and the child died shortly after the operation.) Whitner v. South Carolina, 492 S.E.2d 777 (S.C. 1997), upheld the child abuse conviction of a woman whose newborn tested positive for cocaine. The article by Dorothy Roberts argues that the prosecutions for prenatal crimes, which are disproportionately directed against poor Black women, effectively punish these women for having babies and reflect racist standards of motherhood. Roberts also advocates a more liberating notion of privacy that incorporates equality concerns. This theme of devalued motherhood is continued in the material on welfare reform "family caps" that attempt to deter women on welfare from having more children. While a federal judge upheld the constitutionality of New Jersey's family cap provision in C.K. v. Shalala, 883 F.Supp. 991 (D.N.J.1995), aff'd 92 F.3d 171 (3d Cir. 1996), Lucy Williams demonstrates how these policies arise from myths about welfare mothers and a right-wing politics of division.

Reproductive technology has developed the capacity to alter significantly the biological processes by which many women become mothers. The opening selection on this topic, which is taken from a feminist symposium on reproductive technologies, provides an overview of non-coital techniques as well as the feminist critiques of their impact on women's social roles. By developing, legitimating, and implementing techniques that enhance fertility and reverse infertility, society might seem to be, finally, compassionately turning science to the service of women. And yet many commentators have concluded that the fertility industry is strengthening the hegemony of biological maternity. By supporting new reproductive techniques, the law may be furthering the objectification of women's bodies. Although contract pregnancy (or "surrogacy") arrangements are much less frequently used than other innovations described by the opening reading, two surrogacy cases—In re Baby M, 537 A.2d 1227 (N.J.1988), and Johnson v. Calvert, 851 P.2d 776 (Cal.1993)—are included because the scope of analysis in the decisions offers a particularly rich context in which to situate a discussion of legal issues related to reproduction-assisting technologies. The final two articles provide additional exploration of the social context in which reproductive technologies operate. Debra Satz rejects several feminist approaches to contract pregnancy that focus on the intrinsic features of women's reproductive labor, arguing instead that contract pregnancy is objectionable because it reinforces women's inequality. Lisa Ikemoto explores the discourses that describe infertility and assign value to the procreation of different groups of women. She ends by suggesting the potential for the transgressive use of these discourses for purposes of self-definition.

I. ABORTION

Planned Parenthood of Southeastern Pennsylvania v. Casey

Supreme Court of the United States, 1992.
505 U.S. 833, 112 S.Ct. 2791, 120 L.Ed.2d 674.

JUSTICE SANDRA DAY O'CONNOR, JUSTICE ANTHONY M. KENNEDY, and JUSTICE DAVID H. SOUTER announced the judgment of the Court and delivered the opinion of the Court with respect to Parts I, II, III, V–A, V–C, and VI, an opinion with respect to Part V–E, in which JUSTICE JOHN PAUL STEVENS joins, and an opinion with respect to Parts IV, V–B, and V–D.

Liberty finds no refuge in a jurisprudence of doubt. Yet 19 years after our holding that the Constitution protects a woman's right to terminate her pregnancy in its early stages, *Roe v. Wade*, that definition of liberty is still questioned. Joining the respondents as amicus curiae, the United States, as it has done in five other cases in the last decade, again asks us to overrule *Roe*.

At issue in these cases are five provisions of the Pennsylvania Abortion Control Act of 1982 as amended in 1988 and 1989. The Act requires that a woman seeking an abortion give her informed consent prior to the abortion procedure, and specifies that she be provided with certain information at least 24 hours before the abortion is performed. For a minor to obtain an abortion, the Act requires the informed consent of one of her parents, but provides for a judicial bypass option if the minor does not wish to or cannot obtain a parent's consent. Another provision of the Act requires that, unless certain exceptions apply, a married woman seeking an abortion must sign a statement indicating that she has notified her husband of her intended abortion. The Act exempts compliance with these three requirements in the event of a "medical emergency." ... In addition to the above provisions regulating the performance of abortions, the Act imposes certain reporting requirements on facilities that provide abortion services.

Before any of these provisions took effect, the petitioners, who are five abortion clinics and one physician representing himself as well as a class of physicians who provide abortion services, brought this suit seeking declaratory and injunctive relief. Each provision was challenged as unconstitutional on its face. The District Court ... held all the provisions at issue here unconstitutional. ... The Court of Appeals for the Third Circuit affirmed in part and reversed in part, upholding all of the regulations except for the husband notification requirement. ...

[W]e acknowledge that our decisions after *Roe* cast doubt upon the meaning and reach of its holding. Further, the Chief Justice admits that he would overrule the central holding of *Roe* and adopt the rational relationship test as the sole criterion of constitutionality. State and federal courts as well as legislatures throughout the Union must have guidance as they seek to address this subject in conformance with the Constitution. Given these premises, we find it imperative to review once more the principles that define the rights of the woman and the legitimate authority of the State respecting the termination of pregnancies by abortion procedures.

After considering the fundamental constitutional questions resolved by *Roe*, principles of institutional integrity, and the rule of stare decisis, we are led to conclude this: the essential holding of *Roe v. Wade* should be retained and once again reaffirmed. It must be stated at the outset and with clarity that *Roe's* essential holding, the holding we reaffirm, has three parts. First is a recognition of the right of the woman to choose to have an abortion before viability and to obtain it without undue interference from the State. Before viability, the State's interests are not strong enough to support a prohibition of abortion or the imposition of a substantial obstacle to the woman's effective right to elect the procedure. Second is a confirmation of the State's power to restrict abortions after fetal viability, if the law contains exceptions for pregnancies which endanger a woman's life or health. And third is the principle that the State has legitimate interests from the outset of the pregnancy in protecting the health of the woman and the life of the fetus that may become a child. These principles do not contradict one another; and we adhere to each.

Constitutional protection of the woman's decision to terminate her pregnancy derives from the Due Process Clause of the Fourteenth Amendment. It declares that no State shall "deprive any person of life, liberty, or property, without due process of law." The controlling word in the case before us is "liberty." Although a literal reading of the Clause might suggest that it governs only the procedures by which a State may deprive persons of liberty, ... the Clause has been understood to contain a substantive component as well. ...

[M]atters ... involving the most intimate and personal choices a person may make in a lifetime, choices central to personal dignity and autonomy, are central to the liberty protected by the Fourteenth Amendment. At the heart of liberty is the right to define one's own concept of existence, of meaning, of the universe, and of the mystery of human life. Beliefs about these matters could not define the attributes of personhood were they formed under compulsion of the State.

These considerations begin our analysis of the woman's interest in terminating her pregnancy but cannot end it, for this reason: though the abortion decision may originate within the zone of conscience and belief, it is more than a philosophic exercise. Abortion is a unique act. It is an act fraught with consequences for others: for the woman who must live with the implications of her decision; for the persons who perform and assist in the procedure; for the spouse, family, and society which must confront the knowledge that these procedures exist, procedures some deem nothing short of an act of violence against innocent human life; and, depending on one's beliefs, for the life or potential life that is aborted. Though abortion is conduct, it does not follow that the State is entitled to proscribe it in all instances. That is because the liberty of the woman is at stake in a sense unique to the human condition and so unique to the law. The mother who carries a child to full term is subject to anxieties, to physical constraints, to pain that only she must bear. That these sacrifices have from the beginning of the human race been endured by woman with a pride that ennobles her in the eyes of others and gives to the infant a bond of love cannot alone be grounds for the State to insist she make the sacrifice. Her suffering is too intimate and personal for the State to insist, without more, upon its own vision of the woman's role, however dominant that vision has been in the course of our history and our culture. The destiny of the woman must be shaped to a large extent on her own conception of her spiritual imperatives and her place in society. ...

[T]he reservations any of us may have in reaffirming the central holding of *Roe* are outweighed by the explication of individual liberty we have given combined with the force of stare decisis We turn now to that doctrine. ...

Although *Roe* has engendered opposition, it has in no sense proven "unworkable." ...

The inquiry into reliance counts the cost of a rule's repudiation as it would fall on those who have relied reasonably on the rule's continued application. Since the classic case for weighing reliance heavily in favor of following the earlier rule occurs in the commercial context, ... one can readily imagine an argument stressing the dissimilarity of this case to one involving property or contract. Abortion is customarily chosen as an unplanned response to the consequence of unplanned activity or to the failure of conventional birth control. ...[R]eproductive planning could take virtually immediate account of any sudden restoration of state authority to ban abortions.

To eliminate the issue of reliance that easily, however, one would need to limit cognizable reliance to specific instances of sexual activity. But to do this would be simply to refuse to face the fact that for two decades of economic and social developments, people have organized intimate relationships and made choices that define their views of themselves and their places in society, in reliance on the availability of abortion in the event that contraception should fail. The ability of women to participate equally in the economic and social life of the Nation has been facilitated by their ability to control their reproductive lives. The Constitution serves human values, and while the effect of reliance on *Roe* cannot be exactly measured, neither can the certain cost of overruling *Roe* for people who have ordered their thinking and living around that case be dismissed. . . .

An entire generation has come of age free to assume *Roe's* concept of liberty in defining the capacity of women to act in society, and to make reproductive decisions. . . . Within the bounds of normal stare decisis analysis, . . . the stronger argument is for affirming *Roe's* central holding, with whatever degree of personal reluctance any of us may have, not for overruling it. . . .

The woman's liberty is not so unlimited, however, that from the outset the State cannot show its concern for the life of the unborn, and at a later point in fetal development the State's interest in life has sufficient force so that the right of the woman to terminate the pregnancy can be restricted. . . .

We conclude the line should be drawn at viability, so that before that time the woman has a right to choose to terminate her pregnancy. We adhere to this principle for two reasons. First, as we have said, is the doctrine of stare decisis. Any judicial act of line-drawing may seem somewhat arbitrary, but *Roe* was a reasoned statement, elaborated with great care. . . .

The second reason is that the concept of viability, as we noted in *Roe*, is the time at which there is a realistic possibility of maintaining and nourishing a life outside the womb, so that the independent existence of the second life can in reason and all fairness be the object of state protection that now overrides the rights of the woman. . . . The viability line also has, as a practical matter, an element of fairness. In some broad sense it might be said that a woman who fails to act before viability has consented to the State's intervention on behalf of the developing child.

The woman's right to terminate her pregnancy before viability is the most central principle of *Roe v. Wade*. It is a rule of law and a component of liberty we cannot renounce.

On the other side of the equation is the interest of the State in the protection of potential life. . . .

Roe v. Wade speaks with clarity in establishing not only the woman's liberty but also the State's "important and legitimate interest in potential life." ... That portion of the decision in *Roe* has been given too little acknowledgement and implementation by the Court in its subsequent cases. ...

Roe established a trimester framework to ... ensure that the woman's right to choose not become so subordinate to the State's interest in promoting fetal life that her choice exists in theory but not in fact. We do not agree, however, that the trimester approach is necessary to accomplish this objective. A framework of this rigidity was unnecessary and in its later interpretation sometimes contradicted the State's permissible exercise of its powers.

Though the woman has a right to choose to terminate or continue her pregnancy before viability, it does not at all follow that the State is prohibited from taking steps to ensure that this choice is thoughtful and informed. Even in the earliest stages of pregnancy, the State may enact rules and regulations designed to encourage her to know that there are philosophic and social arguments of great weight that can be brought to bear in favor of continuing the pregnancy to full term and that there are procedures and institutions to allow adoption of unwanted children as well as a certain degree of state assistance if the mother chooses to raise the child herself. ... It follows that States are free to enact laws to provide a reasonable framework for a woman to make a decision that has such profound and lasting meaning. This, too, we find consistent with *Roe's* central premises, and indeed the inevitable consequence of our holding that the State has an interest in protecting the life of the unborn.

We reject the trimester framework, which we do not consider to be part of the essential holding of *Roe*. ... A logical reading of the central holding in *Roe* itself, and a necessary reconciliation of the liberty of the woman and the interest of the State in promoting prenatal life, require, in our view, that we abandon the trimester framework as a rigid prohibition on all previability regulation aimed at the protection of fetal life. ...

[N]ot every law which makes a right more difficult to exercise is, *ipso facto*, an infringement of that right. ... The fact that a law which serves a valid purpose, one not designed to strike at the right itself, has the incidental effect of making it more difficult or more expensive to procure an abortion cannot be enough to invalidate it. Only where state regulation imposes an undue burden on a woman's ability to make this decision does the power of the State reach into the heart of the liberty protected by the Due Process Clause. ...

These considerations of the nature of the abortion right illustrate that it is an overstatement to describe it as a right to decide whether to have an abortion "without interference from the State." All abortion regulations interfere to some degree with a woman's ability to decide whether to terminate her pregnancy ... and that brings us to ... [a] basic flaw in the trimester framework: even in *Roe's* terms, in practice it undervalues the State's interest in the potential life within the woman.

Roe v. Wade was express in its recognition of the State's "important and legitimate interests in preserving and protecting the health of the pregnant woman [and] in protecting the potentiality of human life." The trimester framework, however, does not fulfill *Roe's* own promise that the State has an interest in protecting fetal life or potential life. ...Before viability, *Roe* and subsequent cases treat all governmental attempts to influence a woman's decision on behalf of the potential life within her as unwarranted. This treatment is, in our judgment, incompatible with the recognition that there is a substantial state interest in potential life throughout pregnancy.

The very notion that the State has a substantial interest in potential life leads to the conclusion that not all regulations must be deemed unwarranted. Not all burdens on the right to decide whether to terminate a pregnancy will be undue. In our view, the undue burden standard is the appropriate means of reconciling the State's interest with the woman's constitutionally protected liberty. ...

A finding of an undue burden is a shorthand for the conclusion that a state regulation has the purpose or effect of placing a substantial obstacle in the path of a woman seeking an abortion of a nonviable fetus. A statute with this purpose is invalid because the means chosen by the State to further the interest in potential life must be calculated to inform the woman's free choice, not hinder it. And a statute which, while furthering the interest in potential life or some other valid state interest, has the effect of placing a substantial obstacle in the path of a woman's choice cannot be considered a permissible means of serving its legitimate ends. ...

Some guiding principles should emerge. What is at stake is the woman's right to make the ultimate decision, not a right to be insulated from all others in doing so. Regulations which do no more than create a structural mechanism by which the State, or the parent or guardian of a minor, may express profound respect for the life of the unborn are permitted, if they are not a substantial obstacle to the woman's exercise of the right to choose. Unless it has that effect on her right of choice, a state measure designed to persuade her to choose childbirth over abortion will be upheld if reasonably related to that goal. Regulations designed to foster the health of a woman seeking an abortion are valid if they do not constitute an undue burden. ...We give this summary:

(a) To protect the central right recognized by *Roe v. Wade* while at the same time accommodating the State's profound interest in potential life, we will employ the undue burden analysis as explained in this opinion. An undue burden exists, and therefore a provision of law is invalid, if its purpose or effect is to place a substantial obstacle in the path of a woman seeking an abortion before the fetus attains viability.

(b) We reject the rigid trimester framework of *Roe v. Wade*. To promote the State's profound interest in potential life, throughout pregnancy the State may take measures to ensure that the woman's choice is informed, and measures designed to advance this interest will not be invalidated as long as their purpose is to persuade the woman to choose childbirth over abortion. These measures must not be an undue burden on the right.

(c) As with any medical procedure, the State may enact regulations to further the health or safety of a woman seeking an abortion. Unnecessary health regulations that have the purpose or effect of presenting a substantial obstacle to a woman seeking an abortion impose an undue burden on the right.

(d) Our adoption of the undue burden analysis does not disturb the central holding of *Roe v. Wade*, and we reaffirm that holding. Regardless of whether exceptions are made for particular circumstances, a State may not prohibit any woman from making the ultimate decision to terminate her pregnancy before viability.

(e) We also reaffirm *Roe's* holding that "subsequent to viability, the State in promoting its interest in the potentiality of human life may, if it chooses, regulate, and even proscribe, abortion except where it is necessary, in appropriate medical judgment, for the preservation of the life or health of the mother."

These principles control our assessment of the Pennsylvania statute, and we now turn to the issue of the validity of its challenged provisions. . . .

. . . Except in a medical emergency, the statute requires that at least 24 hours before performing an abortion a physician inform the woman of the nature of the procedure, the health risks of the abortion and of childbirth, and the "probable gestational age of the unborn child." The physician or a qualified nonphysician must inform the woman of the availability of printed materials published by the State describing the fetus and providing information about medical assistance for childbirth, information about child support from the father, and a list of agencies which provide adoption and other services as alternatives to abortion. An abortion may not be performed unless the woman certifies in writing that she has been informed of the availability of these printed materials and has been provided them if she chooses to view them.

Our prior decisions establish that as with any medical procedure, the State may require a woman to give her written informed consent to an abortion. . . .

In attempting to ensure that a woman apprehend the full consequences of her decision, the State furthers the legitimate purpose of reducing the risk that a woman may elect an abortion, only to discover later, with devastating psychological consequences, that her decision was not fully informed. If the information the State requires to be made available to the woman is truthful and not misleading, the requirement may be permissible. . . .

We also see no reason why the State may not require doctors to inform a woman seeking an abortion of the availability of materials relating to the consequences to the fetus, even when those consequences have no direct relation to her health. . . . [W]e permit a State to further its legitimate goal of protecting the life of the unborn by enacting legislation aimed at ensuring a decision that is mature and informed, even when in so doing the State expresses a preference for childbirth over abortion. ...This requirement cannot be considered a substantial obstacle to obtaining an abortion, and, it follows, there is no undue burden. ...

Whether the mandatory 24–hour waiting period is nonetheless invalid because in practice it is a substantial obstacle to a woman's choice to terminate her pregnancy is a closer question. The findings of fact by the District Court indicate that because of the distances many women must travel to reach an abortion provider, the practical effect will often be a delay of much more than a day because the waiting period requires that a woman seeking an abortion make at least two visits to the doctor. The District Court also found that in many instances this will increase the exposure of women seeking abortions to "the harassment and hostility of anti-abortion protestors demonstrating outside a clinic." As a result, the District Court found that for those women who have the fewest financial resources, those who must travel long distances, and those who have difficulty explaining their whereabouts to husbands, employers, or others, the 24–hour waiting period will be "particularly burdensome."

These findings are troubling in some respects, but they do not demonstrate that the waiting period constitutes an undue burden. ...

We ... disagree with the District Court's conclusion that the "particularly burdensome" effects of the waiting period on some women require its invalidation. A particular burden is not of necessity a substantial obstacle. Whether a burden falls on a particular group is a distinct inquiry from whether it is a substantial obstacle even as to the women in that group. And the District Court did not conclude that the waiting period is such an obstacle even for the women who are most burdened by it. Hence, on the record before us, and in the context of this facial challenge, we are not convinced that the 24–hour waiting period constitutes an undue burden. ...

Section 3209 of Pennsylvania's abortion law provides, except in cases of medical emergency, that no physician shall perform an abortion on a married woman without receiving a signed statement from the woman that she has notified her spouse that she is about to undergo an abortion. The woman has the option of providing an alternative signed statement certifying that her husband is not the man who impregnated her; that her husband could not be located; that the pregnancy is the result of spousal sexual assault which she has reported; or that the woman believes that notifying her husband will cause him or someone else to inflict bodily injury upon her. A physician who performs an abortion on a married woman without receiving the appropriate signed statement will have his or her license revoked, and is liable to the husband for damages. ...

In well-functioning marriages, spouses discuss important intimate decisions such as whether to bear a child. But there are millions of women in this country who are the victims of regular physical and psychological abuse at the hands of their husbands. Should these women become pregnant, they may have very good reasons for not wishing to inform their husbands of their decision to obtain an abortion. Many may have justifiable fears of physical abuse, but may be no less fearful of the consequences of reporting prior abuse to the Commonwealth of Pennsylvania. Many may have a reasonable fear that notifying their husbands will provoke further instances of child abuse; these women are not exempt from § 3209's notification requirement. Many may fear devastating forms of psychological abuse from their husbands, including verbal harassment, threats of future violence, the destruction of possessions, physical confinement to the home, the withdrawal of financial support, or the disclosure of the abortion to family and friends. These methods of psychological abuse may act as even more of a deterrent to notification than the possibility of physical violence, but women who are the victims of the abuse are not exempt from § 3209's notification requirement. . . .

The spousal notification requirement is thus likely to prevent a significant number of women from obtaining an abortion. It does not merely make abortions a little more difficult or expensive to obtain; for many women, it will impose a substantial obstacle. . . .

Respondents attempt to avoid the conclusion that § 3209 is invalid by pointing out that it imposes almost no burden at all for the vast majority of women seeking abortions. They begin by noting that only about 20 percent of the women who obtain abortions are married. They then note that of these women about 95 percent notify their husbands of their own volition. Thus, respondents argue, the effects of § 3209 are felt by only one percent of the women who obtain abortions. . . .

The analysis does not end with the one percent of women upon whom the statute operates; it begins there. Legislation is measured for consistency with the Constitution by its impact on those whose conduct it affects. . . .

For the great many women who are victims of abuse inflicted by their husbands, or whose children are the victims of such abuse, a spousal notice requirement enables the husband to wield an effective veto over his wife's decision. . . . If a husband's interest in the potential life of the child outweighs a wife's liberty, the State could require . . . pregnant married women to notify their husbands before engaging in conduct causing risks to the fetus. After all, if the husband's interest in the fetus' safety is a sufficient predicate for state regulation, the State could reasonably conclude that pregnant wives should notify their husbands before drinking alcohol or smoking. Perhaps married women should notify their husbands before using contraceptives or before undergoing any type of surgery that may have complications affecting the husband's interest in his wife's reproductive organs. . . . A State may not give to a man the kind of dominion over his wife that parents exercise over their children.

Section 3209 embodies a view of marriage . . . repugnant to our present understanding of marriage and of the nature of the rights secured by the Constitution. Women do not lose their constitutionally protected liberty when they marry. The Constitution protects all individuals, male or female, married or unmarried, from the abuse of governmental power, even where that power is employed for the supposed benefit of a member of the individual's family. These considerations confirm our conclusion that § 3209 is invalid.

[The Court also upheld the statute's parental consent provision and recordkeeping and reporting requirements.]

[JUSTICE JOHN PAUL STEVENS, concurred in part and dissented in part]

JUSTICE HARRY BLACKMUN, concurring in part, concurring in the judgment in part, and dissenting in part.

Three years ago, in *Webster v. Reproductive Health Serv.*, four Members of this Court appeared poised to "cast into darkness the hopes and visions of every woman in this country" who had come to believe that the Constitution guaranteed her the right to reproductive choice. All that remained between the promise of *Roe* and the darkness of the plurality was a single, flickering flame. Decisions since *Webster* gave little reason to hope that this flame would cast much light. But now, just when so many expected the darkness to fall, the flame has grown bright.

I do not underestimate the significance of today's joint opinion. Yet I remain steadfast in my belief that the right to reproductive choice is entitled to the full protection afforded by this Court before *Webster*. And I fear for the darkness as four Justices anxiously await the single vote necessary to extinguish the light. . . .

In my view, application of [*Roe's* trimester] analytical framework is no less warranted than when it was approved by seven Members of this Court in *Roe*. Strict scrutiny of state limitations on reproductive choice still offers the most secure protection of the woman's right to make her own reproductive decisions, free from state coercion. No majority of this Court has ever agreed upon an alternative approach. The factual premises of the trimester framework have not been undermined, and the *Roe* framework is far more administrable, and far less manipulable, than the "undue burden" standard adopted by the joint opinion. . . .

The Chief Justice's . . . complete omission of any discussion of the effects that compelled childbirth and motherhood have on women's lives [is shocking]. The only expression of concern with women's health is purely instrumental—for The Chief Justice, only women's *psychological* health is a concern, and only to the extent that he assumes that every woman who decides to have an abortion does so without serious consideration of the moral implications of their decision. In short, The Chief Justice's view of the State's compelling interest in maternal health has less to do with health than it does with compelling women to be maternal. . . .

CHIEF JUSTICE WILLIAM H. REHNQUIST, with whom JUSTICE BYRON WHITE, JUSTICE ANTONIN SCALIA, and JUSTICE CLARENCE THOMAS join, concurring in the judgment in part and dissenting in part.

The joint opinion . . . retains the outer shell of *Roe v. Wade*, but beats a wholesale retreat from the substance of that case. We believe that *Roe* was wrongly decided, and that it can and should be overruled consistently with our traditional approach to ... constitutional cases. We would ... uphold the challenged provisions of the Pennsylvania statute in their entirety. ...

We think ... that the Court was mistaken in *Roe* when it classified a woman's decision to terminate her pregnancy as a "fundamental right" that could be abridged only in a manner which withstood "strict scrutiny." ...

While we disagree with ... [the fundamental right] standard, it at least had a recognized basis in constitutional law at the time *Roe* was decided. The same cannot be said for the "undue burden" standard, which is created largely out of whole cloth by the authors of the joint opinion. It is a standard which even today does not command the support of a majority of this Court. And it will not, we believe, result in the sort of "simple limitation," easily applied, which the joint opinion anticipates. In sum, it is a standard which is not built to last.

Because the undue burden standard is plucked from nowhere, the question of what is a "substantial obstacle" to abortion will undoubtedly engender a variety of conflicting views. For example, ... while striking down the spousal *notice* regulation, the joint opinion would uphold a parental *consent* restriction that certainly places very substantial obstacles in the path of a minor's abortion choice. The joint opinion is forthright in admitting that it draws this distinction based on a policy judgment that parents will have the best interests of their children at heart, while the same is not necessarily true of husbands as to their wives. This may or may not be a correct judgment, but it is quintessentially a legislative one. The "undue burden" inquiry does not in any way supply the distinction between parental consent and spousal consent which the joint opinion adopts. Despite the efforts of the joint opinion, the undue burden standard presents nothing more workable than the trimester framework which it discards today. Under the guise of the Constitution, this Court will still impart its own preferences on the States in the form of a complex abortion code. ...

We have stated above our belief that the Constitution does not subject state abortion regulations to heightened scrutiny. Accordingly, we think that ... [a] woman's interest in having an abortion is a form of liberty protected by the Due Process Clause, but States may regulate abortion procedures in ways rationally related to a legitimate state interest. ...

JUSTICE ANTONIN SCALIA, with whom THE CHIEF JUSTICE, JUSTICE BYRON WHITE, and JUSTICE CLARENCE THOMAS join, concurring in the judgment in part and dissenting in part.

My views on this matter are ... [that t]he States may, if they wish, permit abortion-on-demand, but the Constitution does not *require* them to do so. The permissibility of abortion, and the limitations upon it, are to be resolved like most important questions in our democracy: by citizens trying to persuade one another and then voting. ...A State's choice between two positions on which reasonable people can disagree is constitutional even when (as is often the case) it intrudes upon a "liberty" in the absolute sense. . . .

That is, quite simply, the issue in this case: not whether the power of a woman to abort her unborn child is a "liberty" in the absolute sense; or even whether it is a liberty of great importance to many women. Of course it is both. The issue is whether it is a liberty protected by the Constitution of the United States. I am sure it is not. I reach that conclusion . . . because of two simple facts: (1) the Constitution says absolutely nothing about it, and (2) the longstanding traditions of American society have permitted it to be legally proscribed. . . .

QUESTIONS

1. Do you agree with Justices O'Connor, Kennedy, and Souter that their opinion reaffirmed "the essential holding of *Roe*?" Which aspects of *Roe* did the joint opinion retain and which aspects did it reject? How did their understanding of *Roe* differ from that of Justice Blackmun, its author?

2. The joint opinion replaced *Roe*'s trimester framework with the undue burden test. How can legislatures and courts determine whether or not a statute places an undue burden on a women's ability to get an abortion? Why did the spousal notification provision constitute an undue burden, while the informed consent and 24–hour waiting period requirements did not?

Catharine A. MacKinnon, Privacy v. Equality: Beyond Roe v. Wade

From C. MacKinnon, Feminism Unmodified: Discourses on Life and Law
(Cambridge, MA.: Harvard University Press, 1987.)

Roe v. Wade guaranteed the right to choose abortion, subject to some countervailing considerations, by conceiving it as a private choice, included in the constitutional right to privacy. In this critique of that decision, I first situate abortion and the abortion right in the experience of women. The argument is that abortion is inextricable from sexuality, assuming that the feminist analysis of sexuality is our analysis of gender inequality. I then criticize the doctrinal choice to pursue the abortion right under the law of privacy. The argument is that privacy doctrine reaffirms and reinforces what the feminist critique of sexuality criticizes: the public/private split. The political and ideological meaning of privacy as a legal doctrine is connected with the concrete consequences of the public/private split for the lives of women. This analysis makes *Harris v. McRae,* in which public funding for abortions was held not to be required, appear consistent with the larger meaning of *Roe.* . . .

Most women who seek abortions became pregnant while having sexual intercourse with men. Most did not mean or wish to conceive. In contrast to this fact of women's experience, which converges sexuality with reproduction with gender, the abortion debate has centered on separating control over sexuality from control over reproduction, and on separating both from gender and the life options of the sexes. Liberals have supported the availability of the abortion choice as if the woman just happened on the fetus. The political right, imagining that the intercourse preceding conception is usually voluntary, urges abstinence, as if sex were up to women, while defending male authority, specifically including a wife's duty to submit to sex. Continuing with this logic, many opponents of state funding of abortions, such as supporters of some versions of the Hyde Amendment, would permit funding of abortions when pregnancy results from rape or incest. They make *exceptions* for those special occasions during which they presume women did *not* control sex. From all this I deduce that abortion's proponents and opponents share a tacit assumption that women significantly do control sex.

Feminist investigations suggest otherwise. Sexual intercourse, still the most common cause of pregnancy, cannot simply be presumed coequally determined. Feminism has found that women feel compelled to preserve the appearance—which, acted upon, becomes the reality—of male direction of sexual expression, as if male initiative itself were what we want, as if it were that which turns us on. Men enforce this. It is much of what men want in a woman. It is what pornography eroticizes and prostitutes provide. Rape—that is, intercourse with force that is recognized as force—is adjudicated not according to the power or force that the man wields, but according to indices of intimacy between the parties. The more intimate you are with your accused rapist, the less likely a court is to find that what happened to you was rape. Often indices of intimacy include intercourse itself. If "no" can be taken as "yes," how free can "yes" be?

Under these conditions, women often do not use birth control because of its social meaning, a meaning we did not create. Using contraception means acknowledging and planning the possibility of intercourse, accepting one's sexual availability, and appearing non-spontaneous. It means appearing available to male incursions. A good user of contraception can be presumed sexually available and, among other consequences, raped with relative impunity. (If you think this isn't true, you should consider rape cases in which the fact that a woman had a diaphragm in is taken as an indication that what happened to her was intercourse, not rape. "Why did you have your diaphragm in?") From studies of abortion clinics, women who repeatedly seek abortions (and now I'm looking at the repeat offenders high on the list of the right's villains, their best case for opposing abortion as female irresponsibility), when asked why, say something like, "The sex just happened." Like every night for two and a half years. I wonder if a woman can be presumed to control access to her sexuality if she feels unable to interrupt intercourse to insert a diaphragm; or worse, cannot even want to, aware that she risks a pregnancy she knows she does not want. Do you think she would stop the man for any other reason, such as, for instance, the real taboo—lack of desire? If she would not, how is sex, hence its consequences, meaningfully voluntary for women? Norms of sexual rhythm and romance that are felt interrupted by women's needs are constructed against women's interests. Sex doesn't look a whole lot like freedom when it appears normatively less costly for women to risk an undesired, often painful, traumatic, dangerous, sometimes illegal, and potentially life-threatening procedure than to protect themselves in advance. Yet abortion policy has never been explicitly approached in the context of how women get pregnant, that is, as a consequence of intercourse under conditions of gender inequality; that is, as an issue of forced sex.

. . . In 1973 *Roe v. Wade* found that a statute that made criminal all abortions except those to save the life of the mother violated the constitutional right to privacy. The privacy right had been previously created as a constitutional principle in a case that decriminalized the prescription and use of contraceptives. Note that courts use the privacy rubric to connect contraception with abortion through privacy in the same way that I just did through sexuality. In *Roe* that right to privacy was found "broad enough to encompass a woman's decision whether or not to terminate her pregnancy." In 1977 three justices observed, "In the abortion context, we have held that the right to privacy shields the woman from undue state intrusion in and external scrutiny of her very personal choice."

In 1981 the Supreme Court in *Harris v. McRae* decided that this right to privacy did not mean that federal Medicaid programs had to fund medically necessary abortions. Privacy, the Court had said, was guaranteed for "a woman's *decision* whether or not to terminate her pregnancy." The Court then permitted the government to support one decision and not another: to fund continuing conceptions and not to fund discontinuing them. Asserting that decisional privacy was nevertheless constitutionally intact, the Court stated that "although the government may not place obstacles in the path of a woman's exercise of her freedom of choice, it need not remove those not of its own creation." It is apparently a very short step from that which the government has a duty *not* to intervene in to that which it has *no* duty to intervene in.

. . . By staying out of marriage and the family, prominently meaning sexuality—that is to say, heterosexuality—from contraception through pornography to the abortion decision, the law of privacy proposes to guarantee individual bodily integrity, personal exercise of moral intelligence, and freedom of intimacy. But if one asks whether *women's* rights to these values have been guaranteed, it appears that the law of privacy works to translate traditional social values into the rhetoric of individual rights as a means of subordinating those rights to specific social imperatives. In feminist terms, I am arguing that the logic of *Roe* consummated in *Harris* translates the ideology of the private sphere into the individual woman's legal right to privacy as a means of subordinating women's collective needs to the imperatives of male supremacy.

This is my retrospective on *Roe v. Wade*. Reproduction is sexual, men control sexuality, and the state supports the interest of men as a group. *Roe* does not contradict this. So why was abortion legalized? Why were women even imagined to have such a right as privacy? It is not an accusation of bad faith to answer that the interests of men as a social group converged with the definition of justice embodied in law in what I call the male point of view. . . .

We are defined as women by the uses to which men put us. In this context it becomes clear why the struggle for reproductive freedom has never included a woman's right to refuse sex. In this notion of sexual liberation, the equality issue has been framed as a struggle for women to have sex with men on the same terms as men: "without consequences." In this sense the abortion right has been sought as freedom from the reproductive consequences of sexual expression, with sexuality defined as centered on heterosexual genital intercourse. It is as if biological organisms, rather than social relations, reproduced the species. But if your concern is not how more people can get more sex, but who defines sexuality—pleasure and violation both—then the abortion right is situated within a very different problematic: the social and political problematic of the inequality of the sexes. As Susan Sontag said, "Sex itself is not liberating for women. Neither is more sex . . . The question is, what sexuality shall women be liberated to enjoy?" To address this requires reformulating the problem of sexuality from the repression of drives by civilization to the oppression of women by men. . . . So long as women do not control access to our sexuality, abortion facilitates women's heterosexual availability. In other words, under conditions of gender inequality, sexual liberation in this sense does not free women; it frees male sexual aggression. The availability of abortion removes the one remaining legitimized reason that women have had for refusing sex besides the headache.

. . . The liberal ideal of the private—and privacy as an ideal has been formulated in liberal terms—holds that, so long as the public does not interfere, autonomous individuals interact freely and equally. . . . [T]his private is personal, intimate, autonomous, particular, individual, the original source and final outpost of the self, gender neutral. It is, in short, defined by everything that feminism reveals women have never been allowed to be or to have, and everything that women have been equated with and defined in terms of *men's* ability to have. . . . Its inviolability by the state, framed as an individual right, presupposes that the private is not already an arm of the state. In this scheme, intimacy is implicitly thought to guarantee symmetry of power. Injuries arise in violating the private sphere, not within and by and because of it.

In private, consent tends to be presumed. It is true that a showing of coercion voids this presumption. But the problem is getting anything private to be perceived as coercive. Why one would allow force in private—the "why doesn't she leave" question asked of battered women—is a question given its urgency by the social meaning of the private as a sphere of choice. But for women the measure of the intimacy has been the measure of the oppression. This is why feminism has had to explode the private. This is why feminism has seen the personal as the political. The private is the public for those for whom the personal is the political. In this sense, there is no private, either normatively or empirically. Feminism confronts the fact that women have no privacy to lose or to guarantee. We are not inviolable. Our sexuality is not only violable, it is—hence, we are— seen *in* and *as* our violation. To confront the fact that we have no privacy is to confront the intimate degradation of women as the public order.

In this light, a right to privacy looks like an injury got up as a gift. Freedom from public intervention coexists uneasily with any right that requires social preconditions to be meaningfully delivered. For example, if inequality is socially pervasive and enforced, equality will require intervention, not abdication, to be meaningful. But the right to privacy is not thought to require social change. It is not even thought to require any social preconditions, other than nonintervention by the public. The point of this for the abortion cases is not that indigency—which was the specific barrier to effective choice in *Harris*—is well within the public power to remedy, nor that the state is exempt in issues of the distribution of wealth. The point is rather that *Roe v. Wade* presumes that government nonintervention into the private sphere promotes a woman's freedom of choice. When the alternative is jail, there is much to be said for this argument. But the *Harris* result sustains the ultimate meaning of privacy in *Roe:* women are guaranteed by the public no more than what we can get in private— that is, what we can extract through our intimate associations with men. Women with privileges get rights.

So women got abortion as a private privilege, not as a public right. We got control over reproduction that is controlled by "a man or The Man," an individual man or the doctors or the government. Abortion was not decriminalized; it was legalized. In *Roe* the government set the stage for the conditions under which women gain access to this right. Virtually every ounce of control that women won out of this legalization has gone directly into the hands of men—husbands, doctors, or fathers—or is now in the process of attempts to reclaim it through regulation. This, surely, must be what is meant by reform. . . .

Privacy conceived as a right against public intervention and disclosure is the opposite of the relief that *Harris* sought for welfare women. State intervention would have provided a choice women did *not* have in private. The women in *Harris,* women whose sexual refusal has counted for particularly little, needed something to make their privacy effective. The logic of the Court's response resembles the logic by which women are supposed to consent to sex. Preclude the alternatives, then call the sole remaining option "her choice." The point is that the alternatives are precluded *prior to* the reach of the chosen legal doctrine. They are precluded by conditions of sex, race, and class—the very conditions the privacy frame not only leaves tacit but exists to *guarantee.*

When the law of privacy restricts intrusions into intimacy, it bars change in control over that intimacy. The existing distribution of power and resources within the private sphere will be precisely what the law of privacy exists to protect. It is probably not coincidence that the very things feminism regards as central to the subjection of women—the very place, the body; the very relations, heterosexual; the very activities, intercourse and reproduction; and the very feelings, intimate—form the core of what is covered by privacy doctrine. From this perspective, the legal concept of privacy can and has shielded the place of battery, marital rape, and women's exploited labor; has preserved the central institutions whereby women are *deprived* of identity, autonomy, control and self-definition; and has protected the primary activity through which male supremacy is expressed and enforced. Just as pornography is legally protected as individual freedom of expression—without questioning whose freedom and whose expression and at whose expense—abstract privacy protects abstract autonomy, without inquiring into whose freedom of action is being sanctioned at whose expense.

To fail to recognize the meaning of the private in the ideology and reality of women's subordination by seeking protection behind a right *to* that privacy is to cut women off from collective verification and state support in the same act. I think this has a lot to do with why we can't organize women on the abortion issue. When women are segregated in private, separated from each other, one at a time, a right to that privacy isolates us at once from each other and from public recourse. This right to privacy is a right of men "to be let alone" to oppress women one at a time. It embodies and reflects the private sphere's existing definition of womanhood. This is an instance of liberalism called feminism, liberalism applied to women as if we *are* persons, gender neutral. It reinforces the division between public and private that is *not* gender neutral. It is at once an ideological division that lies about women's shared experience and that mystifies the unity among the spheres of women's violation. It is a very material division that keeps the private beyond public redress and depoliticizes women's subjection within it. It keeps some men out of the bedrooms of other men.

Reva Siegel, Reasoning From the Body: A Historical Perspective on Abortion Regulation and Questions of Equal Protection

44 Stan. L. Rev. 261 (1992).

Abortion-restrictive regulation is state action compelling pregnancy and motherhood, and this simple fact cannot be evaded by invoking nature or a woman's choices to explain the situation in which the pregnant woman subject to abortion restrictions finds herself. A pregnant woman seeking an abortion has the practical capacity to terminate a pregnancy, which she would exercise but for the community's decision to prevent or deter her. If the community successfully effectuates its will, it is the state, and not nature, which is responsible for causing her to continue the pregnancy. Similarly, a woman's choice to engage in sexual relations is no longer significant as a cause of pregnancy, if she would terminate that pregnancy, but for the interposition of communal force. A woman's "choice" to engage in (protected or unprotected) sex may be relevant to the state's justifications for enacting abortion-restrictive regulation, but it does not absolve the state from responsibility for compelling the pregnancy of a woman it prevents from obtaining an abortion. Indeed, if nature or a woman's "choices" play a prominent role in the state's justifications for imposing motherhood upon her, such explanations will obscure the fact that the state's decision to enact abortion restrictions rests on social judgments about the pregnant woman, just as they obscure the fact that such restrictions are an act of communal force against her. The significant role that arguments about women's nature and choices have played in rationalizing abortion-restrictive regulation, today and in the past, should raise suspicions about them: Both types of explanations express normative judgments about women, and do not eliminate the task of analyzing abortion-restrictive regulation as an act of state force against women.

When abortion-restrictive regulation is analyzed as state action compelling motherhood, it presents equal protection concerns that *Roe's* physiological reasoning obscures.... Along with a growing number of commentators, I would like to explore this equality claim as the Court has not. Constitutional analysis of abortion-restrictive regulation need not be confined to an equal protection framework, but the history of such regulation suggests important reasons why such an inquiry should be an integral part of any constitutional review. ...

Is the purpose of abortion-restrictive regulation a legitimate one? *Roe* describes a legislature's purpose in restricting women's access to abortion as protecting unborn life. Yet, from a social standpoint, that purpose can be differently described. A legislature's purpose in enacting restrictions on abortion is to pressure or compel women to carry a pregnancy to term which they would otherwise terminate—as the Court has acknowledged in the funding cases.

It is by no means clear that this legislative purpose is legitimate under equal protection doctrine. A legislature's effort to force women to bear children could easily be characterized as a "statutory objective [that] reflects archaic and stereotypic notions" about women. Motherhood is the role upon which this society has traditionally predicated "gross, stereotyped distinctions between the sexes." Thus, the objective of abortion-restrictive regulation is to force women to assume the role and perform the work that has traditionally defined their secondary social status. ...Of course, state actors may well believe their interest in protecting unborn life justifies their interest in forcing pregnant women to bear children. But, as history attests, the fact that state actors believe they are justified in forcing women to bear children by no means precludes the possibility that they are acting from invidious attitudes about women.... Considered from an antidiscrimination perspective, the state's purpose in adopting restrictions on abortion is deeply suspect—if not illegitimate on its face. ...

Roe describes the purpose of abortion-restrictive regulation as protecting unborn life. If one follows this descriptive convention, compelled motherhood is not the purpose of abortion-restrictive regulation, but instead a particular means to a nominally benign legislative end. And on the face of it, this means-ends relationship satisfies the doctrine's requirement of instrumental rationality: A state that seeks to protect unborn life by compelling women to continue pregnancies they wish to terminate employs means that are substantially and functionally related to important governmental ends.

Yet ... one has to ask, in what ways might assumptions about the proper roles of men and women have moved the state to engage in fetal life-saving by compelling pregnancy? What view of women prompted the state's decision to use them as a means to an end? Given the constitutionally suspect means that laws restricting abortion employ to promote the state's interest in potential life, and especially given their history of overt gender-based justifications, it is patently unreasonable to assume a priori that they are adopted by a process of legislative deliberation free from constitutionally illicit judgments about women. ...

Thus, ... legislators enacting restrictions on abortion may act from judgments about the sexual and maternal conduct of the women they are regulating, and not merely from a concern about the welfare of the unborn. Legislators may condemn abortion because they assume that any pregnant woman who does not wish to be pregnant has committed some sexual indiscretion properly punishable by compelling pregnancy itself. Popular support for excusing women who are victims of rape or incest from the proscriptions of criminal abortion laws demonstrates that attitudes about abortion do indeed rest on normative judgments about women's sexual conduct. Opinion polls ... suggest that the public assumes a woman can be coerced into continuing a pregnancy because the pregnancy is her sexual "fault."

Along distinct, but related lines, legislators may view abortion as repellant because it betrays a lack of maternal solicitude in women, or otherwise violates expectations of appropriately nurturing female conduct. If legislators assume that women are "child-rearers," they will take for granted the work women give to motherhood and ignore what it takes from them, and so will view women's efforts to avoid some two decades of life-consuming work as an act of casual expedience or unseemly egoism. Thus, they will condemn women for seeking abortion "on demand," or as a mere "convenience," judging women to be unnaturally egocentric because they do not give their lives over to the work of bearing and nurturing children—that is, because they fail to act like mothers, like normal women should....

Abortion-restrictive regulation has several characteristics that make it particularly suitable for analysis under ... antisubordination principles. First, abortion-restrictive regulation is sex-based state action: It is regulation directed at women as a class, and not dispersed across the citizenry at large. Second, the most dramatic and visible of its effects—the continuation of an unwanted pregnancy—is an intended consequence of social policy. Indeed, as I have already argued, it is fair to characterize forced childbearing as the principal purpose of abortion-restrictive regulation. Third, abortion-restrictive regulation has historically functioned as caste legislation. Finally, today, as in the past, the injury inflicted on women by compelling them to bear children is a specific form of status harm, one that plays a central role in women's subordination. ...

Laws restricting women's access to abortion are only intermittently discussed in their compulsive aspect. Even then, discussion often seems to assume that such regulation coerces women into performing only the work of childbearing. But if abortion-restrictive regulation is evaluated in light of actual social practice, it is clear that such regulation coerces women to perform, not only the work of childbearing, but the work of childrearing as well.

Hypothetically, a woman compelled to bear a child she does not want could give it up for adoption, abandon it, or pay someone to care for the child until maturity. In this society, however, these are not options that women avail themselves of with great frequency for the simple reason that few women are able to abandon a child born of their body. That society as a whole, or some women in particular, may judge it morally preferable to give a child up to adoption rather than abort a pregnancy is beside the point. Once compelled to bear a child against their wishes, most women will feel obligated to raise it. ...Legislatures that enact restrictions on abortion understand this. They both desire and expect that most women will raise the child they are forced to bear, and in the vast majority of cases, women will. ...

Finally, notwithstanding changing norms of family life, it remains the case that it is women who perform the vast majority of the labor necessary to make infants into adults. Mothers are expected to subordinate their personal interests to children in a way that men are not; most women give themselves over to the nurturance of life in a way that men do not—and face stigmatization, unlike men, if they will not. Consequently, a woman's identity, relations, and prospects are defined by becoming a parent in a way that a man's are not. ...

[T]his society ... continues to view the work of raising children as "women's work." ... [C]hildcare is uncompensated labor, traditionally performed under conditions of economic dependency.... Those who devote their personal energies to raising children are likely to find their freedom to participate in so-called public sphere activities impaired for years on end, for the evident reason that most activities in the realms of education, employment, and politics are defined and structured as incommensurate with that work. Thus, a woman who becomes a parent will likely find that the energy she invests in childrearing will compromise her already con-strained opportunities and impair her already unequal compensation in the work force—all the more so if she raises the child alone, whether by choice, divorce, or abandonment. Considered in cold dollar terms, it is the institu-tion of motherhood that gives a gendered structure to the economics of family life, and a gendered face to poverty in the nation's life. ...

In assessing the social effects of restrictions on abortion, it is impor-tant to observe not only that such regulation compels women to perform the work of bearing and rearing children, but that it lacks any provision that would mitigate or offset the social consequences of enforced motherhood for women. No modern legislature interested in adopting restrictions on abortion has, to my knowledge, offered to compensate women for this work; to protect women's employment and education opportunities while they perform the work of motherhood; or to provide women adequate childcare so that they are not pushed into dependency upon men or the state. Nor has a legislature required that men fathering the children women are forced to bear assume primary responsibility for the work of nurturance and maintenance women typically provide. Thus, when the state enacts restrictions on abortion, it coerces women to perform the work of motherhood without altering the conditions that continue to make such work a principal cause of their secondary social status. . . .

From this perspective, it is apparent that compelled pregnancy will injure women in context-dependent ways. It may be endured by women who have ordered their lives in conformity with traditional norms of motherhood, but it will profoundly threaten the material and psychic welfare of any woman whose life deviates from this traditional norm, whether by choice or socio-economic circumstance. When the state deprives women of choice in matters of motherhood, it deprives women of the ability to lead their lives with some rudimentary control over the sex-role constraints this society imposes on those who bear and rear children. It makes the social reality of women's lives more nearly conform with social stereotypes of women's lives. Considered from this perspective, choice in matters of motherhood implicates constitutional values of equality and liberty both.

Restrictions on abortion thus offend constitutional guarantees of equal protection, not simply because of the status-based injuries they inflict on women, but also because of the status-based attitudes about women they reflect. For centuries, this society has defined women as mothers and defined the work of motherhood as women's work. These are the assumptions which make it "reasonable" to force women to become mothers. Absent these deep-rooted assumptions about women, it is impossible to explain why this society insists that restrictions on abortion are intended to protect the unborn, and yet has never even considered taking action that would alleviate the burdens forced motherhood imposes on women.

Restrictions on abortion reflect the kind of bias that is at the root of the most invidious forms of stereotyping: a failure to consider, in a society always at risk of forgetting, that women are persons, too. . . .

NOTES AND QUESTIONS

1. Although some feminist theorists focus on either sexuality or reproduction as the center of women's subordination, Catharine MacKinnon relates the two. How is women's lack of control over sex relevant to the abortion right? Reva Siegel, on the other hand, demonstrates how abortion law reflects norms of motherhood. Does the focus on male domination of women's sexuality pay too little attention to the importance of motherhood in constructing reproductive policies?

2. Do you find compelling the critique of privacy as the basis for women's reproductive freedom? Are the problems MacKinnon demonstrates inherent in notions of privacy and autonomy or do they stem from the way in which these notions have been interpreted by the courts? What are the advantages of the equality approach advocated by MacKinnon and Siegel?

3. In *Breaking the Abortion Deadlock: From Choice to Consent* (1996), Eileen McDonagh argues that the key right in abortion is not merely a woman's right to choose an abortion without interference by the state but rather her right to consent to be made pregnant by a fertilized ovum. "Nonconsensual pregnancy, like nonconsensual sexual intercourse," writes McDonagh, "is a condition that must be stopped immediately because both processes severely violate one's bodily integrity and liberty." When the government refuses to protect women against the injuries of a wrongful pregnancy it violates women's constitutional right to equal protection by the state from harm imposed by private parties. According to McDonagh, equal protection of pregnant women's bodily integrity and liberty requires not only the right to terminate a nonconsensual pregnancy but also the right to state funding of abortions for all women. Do you think the notion of the fetus as an intruder inflicting harm on the pregnant woman is a useful basis for arguments supporting abortion rights?

Loretta Ross, Raising Our Voices

From M. Gerber Fried, From Abortion to Reproductive Freedom
(Boston: South End Press, 1990).

I had an abortion in 1970, yet I find it difficult to write about abortion. I have escorted friends to get abortions, yet I find it difficult to talk with them about abortion. I have tried to talk them into defending the clinics against anti-abortionists. But I couldn't convince them because they felt scared—scared about carrying out a decision that had been right for them.

They felt they needed to be secretive about their experience, and that was hard. It made them feel ashamed. They did not hear voices validating their decision, supporting their experience, so they questioned their choice. They were lucky if they had a girlfriend to escort them to have an abortion. Often they had only an angry parent or lover, or they went alone. It is not easy for Black women to talk about abortion. It is not easy for Black women to have abortions.

Our abortion experiences have been invisible. News cameras do not find us when we speak out for abortion rights. Instead, the few Black anti-choice voices are given prominence and are presumed to speak for all of us. Black women are said to be anti-choice. But we have spoken silently with our actions. Black women get abortions at twice the rate of white women. But we have had to act without community support because of the conspiracy of silence surrounding abortion.

No Black woman should have to go through an abortion alone. The lack of open discussion about abortion in our communities prevents us from building support for abortion rights within our communities. It prevents us from organizing in our own interests. A silent community cannot commit itself to change. A silent community cannot support sisters doing what they need and choose to do.

White women have begun to break their silence about their abortions. But they do not speak for us. We need to start telling our stories about how illegal abortion killed our mothers and how legal abortion saved our lives. We have to talk to each other as Black women, sister to sister. This will allow us to talk to Black women who are anti-choice, and hopefully we will find that we have more in common with these sisters than we have dividing us. We cannot and will not see each other as enemies. We have to respect each other's opinions, while affirming the essence of freedom for all of us. This freedom is the right to control, at all times, our bodies. We can listen to the sisters who are pro-choice but anti-abortion, and we must support the sisters who are actively pro-choice. . . .

As we break our silence about abortion, we are creating our vision of "choice." Thus far, the abortion debate has largely been between white men and white women. It has centered on abstract arguments about personhood or fetal rights. Even when the debate has managed to take up women's lives, it has focused on the lives of white women. Black women's voices will push the parameters of the abortion debate further.

We want to talk about life and choices—real life, real choices. Our history as slaves has given us a deep understanding of what it means to choose life for ourselves and our children. We made life and death "choices" in wretched human conditions. We must still do so today when many of our people live in poverty: without work, without homes.

When we choose abortion, we choose life for ourselves and for our families. This is not easy when we do not control the circumstances of our lives. But lack of control is not lack of understanding. We make decisions from the full perspective of our lives. We are capable decision makers and reject any claims to the contrary. We know that only we can control our lives by making the choices we think are right for us, and we resist any efforts to prevent us from having that control.

Black women are now learning to talk about abortion. We are internalizing and understanding what it means to be the "sleeping giant" of the pro-choice movement. Each generation of a movement creates its own vision of what the movement should be. We will push its parameters too. We come to the movement with a low level of confidence in a system which has historically exploited people of color. The health care system has never met our needs. The judicial system has systematically discriminated against us. Institutions of power have never represented our concerns. When women of color enter the post-*Webster* abortion rights movement, we are not, therefore, likely to be focused on legislative or legal strategies. Instead, we are asking how we can begin to take abortion and other aspects of our health and reproduction into our own hands.

Black women bring to the pro-choice struggle a herstory of women controlling their own lives. Black women have always used abortion as a means of childspacing. Herbs and potions were used by women in Africa. My elders told me about the roots their grandmothers used in the 19th century. Early 20th–century douche powders were advertised in Black newspapers for "missed cycles." An African sister was recently featured on the radio speaking about the tradition of women teaching themselves about their own bodies. We have lost that tradition in the United States. We can regain it.

Within our own communities, there are those who do not want us to have that control. We should not be surprised, confused, or intimidated when Black anti-choice activists call abortion genocide. Whites who oppose abortion call it genocide for whites. I imagine that anti-choice Jews, Italians, or Native Americans make the same allegations. We should see this for what it is—an attempt to silence us and through that silence to control us, to prevent us from controlling our own lives.

The contemporary effort to control us through our reproduction is not new. In the 1960s, Black women were told to throw away their birth control pills and "have a baby for the Black Revolution." The men would fight racism and we would produce Black babies (males) to carry on the struggle. But Black women did not do as they were told. They were unwilling to accept a political ideology that made *their* freedom expendable in the fight for racial liberation. We must and will make a revolution, but we will not give up control of our bodies and our right to make our own decisions.

I am not rejecting the genocide argument. We do, however, need to make sure the shoe is on the correct foot. The fervor of the anti-abortion movement comes at a time when the white birth rate is declining. Seventy percent of abortions in the United States are obtained by white women between the ages of 20 and 24. These are the wombs that the anti-choice forces are trying to manipulate. I do not think that the mostly white anti-abortion movement really cares how many Black or Puerto Rican children are born except to feel that there are too many of "them." I do think they are deathly afraid of the demographic prediction that by the year 2012 the majority of people in the United States will not be white.

I am also sensitive to the genocide question from within the pro-choice movement. Too often arguments for abortion have appealed to racist notions about "overpopulation" by third world people. The important message for Black women is that we must refuse to be used and abused by someone else's political agenda for our womb. We reject all efforts to do so, whether by anti-abortion or right wing zealots, international family planning agencies, or those within our own communities. . . .

We must also raise our voices within the civil rights movement. While most Blacks, 87 percent, are pro-choice, Black civil rights organizations have not been particularly solid or organized to defend their pro-choice positions. The abortion issue has been used by opponents of abortion to divide and weaken the civil rights coalition and to stall progress on civil rights. . . . Vacillation by the civil rights movement on the question of birth control and abortion rights is a relatively new phenomenon. We need to publicize the pro-choice activities of Black organizations in the first half of the 20th century. Leading Black groups viewed birth control and abortion, even when illegal, as integral to issues of economics, health, race relations, and racial progress. Major organizations and Black newspapers gave sustained coverage to pro-choice organizing and participated actively in the debate on abortion and birth control.

In the 1960s, the Black Power movement re-opened the genocide debate of the 1920s, and this had a profound influence on the civil rights movement which is still being felt today. Reproductive rights were characterized as "white women's issues." We need to challenge this. Reproductive rights are civil rights, fundamental necessities for Black women (and men) to gain control over their lives. . . .

NOTES AND QUESTIONS

1. **Minority Voices**. How does adding the voices of Black and other nonwhite women to the struggle for abortion rights change our understanding of those rights? Does Loretta Ross's statement that "reproductive rights are civil rights" modify the dominant notion of reproductive liberty?

Angela Davis distinguished between women of colors' support of abortion rights and the endorsement of abortion:

> When Black and Latina women resort to abortions in such large numbers, the stories they tell are not so much about the desire to be free of their pregnancy, but rather about the miserable social conditions which dissuade them from bringing new lives into the world. . . . During the early abortion rights campaign, it was too frequently assumed that legal abortions provided a viable alternative to the myriad problems posed by poverty. As if having fewer children could create jobs, higher wages, better schools, etc. This assumption reflected the tendency to blur the distinction between *abortion rights* and the general advocacy of *abortion*. The campaign often failed to provide a voice for women who wanted the *right* to legal abortions while deploring the social conditions that prohibited them from bearing more children.

Angela Davis, *Racism, Birth Control, and Reproductive Rights*, in Marlene Gerber Fried, ed., *From Abortion to Reproductive Freedom* 15 (1990).

2. **Birth Control as Racial Genocide**. Loretta Ross's essay describes a longstanding debate within the Black community about the dangers and benefits of birth control and abortion. One strain of this debate has been the claim that family planning programs are a form of racial genocide. Ross acknowledges that there is support for this fear, but also criticizes the civil rights movement for neglecting the importance of reproductive rights. Do you find that reproductive rights are seen in America as primarily a "white women's issue"?

In *Killing the Black Body: Race, Reproduction and the Meaning of Liberty* (1997), Dorothy Roberts documents a long history of coercive birth control policies and sterilization abuse inflicted on Black women, a history that underlies many Blacks' concerns about genocide. Roberts argues, however, that these policies are dangerous primarily because of the message they send:

> Although some Blacks believe that white-controlled family planning literally threatens Black survival, I take the position that racist birth control policies serve primarily an ideological function. The chief danger of these programs is not the physical annihilation of a race or social class. Family planning polices never reduced the Black birthrate enough to accomplish this end. Rather, the chief danger of these policies is the legitimation of an oppressive social structure. Proposals to solve social problems by curbing Black reproduction make racial inequality appear to be the product of nature rather than power. By identifying procreation as the cause of Black people's condition, they divert attention away from the political, social, and economic forces that maintain America's racial order. This harm to the group compounds the harm to individual members who are denied the freedom to have children.

This critique of coercive birth control policies suggests the need to expand our understanding of reproductive freedom beyond the typical focus on the right to an abortion. How can we integrate both abortion rights and opposition to sterilization and birth control abuse into a coherent notion of women's control over their bodies?

II. MATERNAL CONDUCT DURING PREGNANCY

In Re A.C.

Court of Appeals of the District of Columbia, En Banc, 1990.
573 A.2d 1235.

JOHN A. TERRY, ASSOCIATE JUDGE: . . .

This case came before the trial court when George Washington University Hospital petitioned the emergency judge in chambers for declaratory relief as to how it should treat its patient, A.C., who was close to death from cancer and was twenty-six and one-half weeks pregnant with a viable fetus. After a hearing lasting approximately three hours, which was held at the hospital (though not in A.C.'s room), the court ordered that a caesarean section be performed on A.C. to deliver the fetus. Counsel for A.C. immediately sought a stay in this court, which was unanimously denied by a hastily assembled division of three judges. The caesarean was performed, and a baby girl, L.M.C., was delivered. Tragically, the child died within two and one-half hours, and the mother died two days later.

A.C. was first diagnosed as suffering from cancer at the age of thirteen. In the ensuing years she underwent major surgery several times, together with multiple radiation treatments and chemotherapy. A.C. married when she was twenty-seven, during a period of remission, and soon thereafter she became pregnant. She was excited about her pregnancy and very much wanted the child. Because of her medical history, she was referred in her fifteenth week of pregnancy to the high-risk pregnancy clinic at George Washington University Hospital.

On Tuesday, June 9, 1987, when A.C. was approximately twenty-five weeks pregnant, she went to the hospital for a scheduled check-up. Because she was experiencing pain in her back and shortness of breath, an x-ray was taken, revealing an apparently inoperable tumor which nearly filled her right lung. On Thursday, June 11, A.C. was admitted to the hospital as a patient. By Friday her condition had temporarily improved, and when asked if she really wanted to have her baby, she replied that she did.

Over the weekend A.C.'s condition worsened considerably. Accordingly, on Monday, June 15, members of the medical staff treating A.C. assembled, along with her family, in A.C.'s room. The doctors then informed her that her illness was terminal, and A.C. agreed to palliative treatment designed to extend her life until at least her twenty-eighth week of pregnancy. The "potential outcome [for] the fetus," according to the doctors, would be much better at twenty-eight weeks than at twenty-six weeks if it were necessary to "intervene." A.C. knew that the palliative treatment she had chosen presented some increased risk to the fetus, but she opted for this course both to prolong her life for at least another two weeks and to maintain her own comfort. When asked if she still wanted to have the baby, A.C. was somewhat equivocal, saying "something to the effect of 'I don't know, I think so.'"As the day moved toward evening, A.C.'s condition grew still worse, and at about 7:00 or 8:00 p.m. she consented to intubation to facilitate her breathing.

The next morning, June 16, the trial court convened a hearing at the hospital in response to the hospital's request for a declaratory judgment. The court appointed counsel for both A.C. and the fetus, and the District of Columbia was permitted to intervene for the fetus as *parens patriae*. The court heard testimony on the facts as we have summarized them, and further testimony that at twenty-six and a half weeks the fetus was viable, i.e., capable of sustained life outside of the mother, given artificial aid. A neonatologist, Dr. Maureen Edwards, testified that the chances of survival for a twenty-six-week fetus delivered at the hospital might be as high as eighty percent, but that this particular fetus, because of the mother's medical history, had only a fifty to sixty percent chance of survival. Dr. Edwards estimated that the risk of substantial impairment for the fetus, if it were delivered promptly, would be less than twenty percent. However, she noted that the fetus' condition was worsening appreciably at a rapid rate, and another doctor—Dr. Alan Weingold, an obstetrician who was one of A.C.'s treating physicians—stated that any delay in delivering the child by caesarean section lessened its chances of survival. . . .

There was no evidence before the court showing that A.C. consented to, or even contemplated, a caesarean section before her twenty-eighth week of pregnancy. There was, in fact, considerable dispute as to whether she would have consented to an immediate caesarean delivery at the time the hearing was held. A.C.'s mother opposed surgical intervention, testifying that A.C. wanted "to live long enough to hold that baby" and that she expected to do so, "even though she knew she was terminal." Dr. Hamner testified that, given A.C.'s medical problems, he did not think she would have chosen to deliver a child with a substantial degree of impairment. . . .

After hearing this testimony and the arguments of counsel, the trial court made oral findings of fact. It found, first, that A.C. would probably die, according to uncontroverted medical testimony, "within the next twenty-four to forty-eight hours"; second, that A.C. was "pregnant with a twenty-six and a half week viable fetus who, based upon uncontroverted medical testimony, has approximately a fifty to sixty percent chance to survive if a caesarean section is performed as soon as possible"; third, that because the fetus was viable, "the state has [an] important and legitimate interest in protecting the potentiality of human life"; and fourth, that there had been some testimony that the operation "may very well hasten the death of [A.C.]," but that there had also been testimony that delay would greatly increase the risk to the fetus and that "the prognosis is not great for the fetus to be delivered post-mortem. . . ." Most significantly, the court found:

> The court is of the view that it does not clearly know what [A.C.'s] present views are with respect to the issue of whether or not the child should live or die. She's presently unconscious. As late as Friday of last week, she wanted the baby to live. As late as yesterday, she did not know for sure.

Having made these findings of fact and conclusions of law, . . . the court ordered that a caesarean section be performed to deliver A.C.'s child.

The court's decision was then relayed to A.C., who had regained consciousness. When the hearing reconvened later in the day, Dr. Hamner told the court:

> I explained to her essentially what was going on. . . . I said it's been deemed we should intervene on behalf of the baby by caesarean section and it would give it the only possible chance of it living. Would you agree to this procedure? *She said yes.* I said, do you realize that you may not survive the surgical procedure? *She said yes.* And I repeated the two questions to her again [and] asked her did she understand. *She said yes.* [Emphasis added.]

When the court suggested moving the hearing to A.C.'s bedside, Dr. Hamner discouraged the court from doing so, but he and Dr. Weingold, together with A.C.'s mother and husband, went to A.C.'s room to confirm her consent to the procedure. What happened then was recounted to the court a few minutes later: . . .

> Dr. Weingold: She does not make sound because of the tube in her windpipe. She nods and she mouths words. One can see

what she's saying rather readily. She asked whether she would survive the operation. She asked [Dr.] Hamner if he would perform the operation. He told her he would only perform it if she authorized it but it would be done in any case. She understood that. She then seemed to pause for a few moments and then very clearly mouthed words several times, *I don't want it done. I don't want it done.* Quite clear to me.

. . .

After hearing this new evidence, the court found that it was "still not clear what her intent is" and again ordered that a caesarean section be performed. . . .

From a recent national survey, it appears that over the five years preceding the survey there were thirty-six attempts to override maternal refusals of proposed medical treatment, and that in fifteen instances where court orders were sought to authorize caesarean interventions, thirteen such orders were granted. . . .

[O]ur analysis of this case begins with the tenet common to all medical treatment cases: that any person has the right to make an informed choice, if competent to do so, to accept or forego medical treatment. . . . [C]ourts do not compel one person to permit a significant intrusion upon his or her bodily integrity for the benefit of another person's health. See, e.g., *McFall v. Shimp,* 10 Pa.D. & C.3d 90 (Allegheny County Ct.1978). In *McFall* the court refused to order Shimp to donate bone marrow which was necessary to save the life of his cousin, McFall:

The common law has consistently held to a rule which provides that one human being is under no legal compulsion to give aid or to take action to save another human being or to rescue. . . . For our law to *compel* defendant to submit to an intrusion of his body would change every concept and principle upon which our society is founded. To do so would defeat the sanctity of the individual, and would impose a rule which would know no limits, and one could not imagine where the line would be drawn.

Even though Shimp's refusal would mean death for McFall, the court would not order Shimp to allow his body to be invaded. It has been suggested that fetal cases are different because a woman who "has chosen to lend her body to bring [a] child into the world" has an enhanced duty to assure the welfare of the fetus, sufficient even to require her to undergo caesarean surgery. Surely, however, a fetus cannot have rights in this respect superior to those of a person who has already been born. . . .

This court has recognized as well that, above and beyond common law protections, the right to accept or forego medical treatment is of constitutional magnitude. . . . This court and others, while recognizing the right to accept or reject medical treatment, have consistently held that the right is not absolute. In some cases, especially those involving life-or-death situations or incompetent patients, the courts have recognized four countervailing interests that may involve the state as *parens patriae*: preserving life, preventing suicide, maintaining the ethical integrity of the medical profession, and protecting third parties.

Neither the prevention of suicide nor the integrity of the medical profession has any bearing on this case. Further, the state's interest in preserving life must be truly compelling to justify overriding a competent person's right to refuse medical treatment. ...This is equally true for incompetent patients, who have just as much right as competent patients to have their decisions made while competent respected, even in a substituted judgment framework.

In those rare cases in which a patient's right to decide her own course of treatment has been judicially overridden, courts have usually acted to vindicate the state's interest in protecting third parties, even if in fetal state. See *Jefferson v. Griffin Spalding County Hospital Authority,* (ordering that caesarean section be performed on a woman in her thirty-ninth week of pregnancy to save both the mother and the fetus); *Raleigh Fitkin–Paul Morgan Memorial Hospital v. Anderson* (ordering blood transfusions over the objection of a Jehovah's Witness, in her thirty-second week of pregnancy, to save her life and that of the fetus); *In re Jamaica Hospital* (ordering the transfusion of blood to a Jehovah's Witness eighteen weeks pregnant, who objected on religious grounds, and finding that the state's interest in the not-yet-viable fetus outweighed the patient's interests); *Crouse Irving Memorial Hospital, Inc. v. Paddock* (ordering transfusions as necessary over religious objections to save the mother and a fetus that was to be prematurely delivered).

What we distill from the cases ... is that every person has the right, under the common law and the Constitution, to accept or refuse medical treatment. This right of bodily integrity belongs equally to persons who are competent and persons who are not. Further, it matters not what the quality of a patient's life may be; the right of bodily integrity is not extinguished simply because someone is ill, or even at death's door. To protect that right against intrusion by others—family members, doctors, hospitals, or anyone else, however well-intentioned—we hold that a court must determine the patient's wishes by any means available, and must abide by those wishes unless there are truly extraordinary or compelling reasons to override them. When the patient is incompetent, or when the court is unable to determine competency, the substituted judgment procedure must be followed.

From the record before us, we simply cannot tell whether A.C. was ever competent, after being sedated, to make an informed decision one way or the other regarding the proposed caesarean section. The trial court never made any finding about A.C.'s competency to decide. ...

We think it is incumbent on any trial judge in a case like this, unless it is impossible to do so, to ascertain whether a patient is competent to make her own medical decisions. Whenever possible, the judge should personally attempt to speak with the patient and ascertain her wishes directly, rather than relying exclusively on hearsay evidence, even from doctors. ...

Without a competent refusal from A.C. to go forward with the surgery, and without a finding through substituted judgment that A.C. would not have consented to the surgery, it was error for the trial court to proceed to a balancing analysis, weighing the rights of A.C. against the interests of the state.

There are two additional arguments against overriding A.C.'s objections to caesarean surgery. First, as the American Public Health Association cogently states in its *amicus curiae* brief:

> Rather than protecting the health of women and children, court-ordered caesareans erode the element of trust that permits a pregnant woman to communicate to her physician—without fear of reprisal—all information relevant to her proper diagnosis and treatment. An even more serious consequence of court-ordered intervention is that it drives women at high risk of complications during pregnancy and childbirth out of the health care system to avoid coerced treatment.

Second, and even more compellingly, any judicial proceeding in a case such as this will ordinarily take place—like the one before us here—under time constraints so pressing that it is difficult or impossible for the mother to communicate adequately with counsel, or for counsel to organize an effective factual and legal presentation in defense of her liberty and privacy interests and bodily integrity. . . .

Sometimes . . . a once competent patient will be unable to render an informed decision. In such a case, we hold that the court must make a substituted judgment on behalf of the patient, based on all the evidence. This means that the duty of the court, "as surrogate for the incompetent, is to determine as best it can what choice that individual, if competent, would make with respect to medical procedures." . . .

After A.C. was informed of the court's decision, she consented to the caesarean; moments later, however, she withdrew her consent. The trial court did not then make a finding as to whether A.C. was competent to make the medical decision or whether she had made an informed decision one way or the other. Nor did the court then make a substituted judgment for A.C. Instead, the court said that it was "still not clear what her intent is" and again ordered the caesarean.

It is that order which we must now set aside. What a trial court must do in a case such as this is to determine, if possible, whether the patient is capable of making an informed decision about the course of her medical treatment. If she is, and if she makes such a decision, her wishes will control in virtually all cases. If the court finds that the patient is incapable of making an informed consent (and thus incompetent), then the court must make a substituted judgment. This means that the court must ascertain as best it can what the patient would do if faced with the particular treatment question. Again, in virtually all cases the decision of the patient, albeit discerned through the mechanism of substituted judgment, will control. We do not quite foreclose the possibility that a conflicting state interest may be so compelling that the patient's wishes must yield, but we anticipate that such cases will be extremely rare and truly exceptional. This is not such a case.

. . . We need not decide whether, or in what circumstances, the state's interests can ever prevail over the interests of a pregnant patient. We emphasize, nevertheless, that it would be an extraordinary case indeed in which a court might ever be justified in overriding the patient's wishes and authorizing a major surgical procedure such as a caesarean section. . . . [S]ome may doubt that there could ever be a situation extraordinary or compelling enough to justify a massive intrusion into a person's body, such as a caesarean section, against that person's will. Whether such a situation may someday present itself is a question that we need not strive to answer here. . . .

JAMES A. BELSON, ASSOCIATE JUDGE, concurring in part and dissenting in part:

. . . The state's interest in preserving human life and the viable unborn child's interest in survival are entitled, I think, to more weight than I find them assigned by the majority when it states that "in virtually all cases the decision of the patient . . . will control." I would hold that in those instances, fortunately rare, in which the viable unborn child's interest in living and the state's parallel interest in protecting human life come into conflict with the mother's decision to forgo a procedure such as a caesarean section, a balancing should be struck in which the unborn child's and the state's interests are entitled to substantial weight.

It was acknowledged in *Roe v. Wade* that the state's interest in potential human life becomes compelling at the point of viability. . . . [I]t is important to emphasize, as does the majority opinion, that this case is not about abortion; we are not discussing whether a woman has the legal right to terminate her pregnancy in its early stages. Rather, we are dealing with the situation that exists when a woman has carried an unborn child to viability. When the unborn child reaches the state of viability, the child becomes a party whose interests must be considered.

. . . The balancing test should be applied in instances in which women become pregnant and carry an unborn child to the point of viability. This is not an unreasonable classification because, I submit, a woman who carries a child to viability is in fact a member of a unique category of persons. Her circumstances differ fundamentally from those of other potential patients for medical procedures that will aid another person, for example, a potential donor of bone marrow for transplant. This is so because she has undertaken to bear another human being, and has carried an unborn child to viability. Another unique feature of the situation we address arises from the singular nature of the dependency of the unborn child upon the mother. A woman carrying a viable unborn child is not in the same category as a relative, friend, or stranger called upon to donate bone marrow or an organ for transplant. Rather, the expectant mother has placed herself in a special class of persons who are bringing another person into existence, and upon whom that other person's life is totally dependent. Also, uniquely, the viable unborn child is literally captive within the mother's body. No other potential beneficiary of a surgical procedure on another is in that position. . . .

Whitner v. South Carolina

Supreme Court of South Carolina, 1997.
328 S.C. 1, 492 S.E.2d 777.

JEAN TOAL, JUSTICE.

This case concerns the scope of the child abuse and endangerment statute in the South Carolina Children's Code (the Code), S.C.Code Ann. § 20–7–50 (1985). We hold the word "child" as used in that statute includes viable fetuses.

FACTS

On April 20, 1992, Cornelia Whitner (Whitner) pled guilty to criminal child neglect, S.C.Code Ann. § 20–7–50 (1985), for causing her baby to be born with cocaine metabolites in its system by reason of Whitner's ingestion of crack cocaine during the third trimester of her pregnancy. The circuit court judge sentenced Whitner to eight years in prison. Whitner did not appeal her conviction.

Thereafter, Whitner filed a petition for Post Conviction Relief (PCR), pleading the circuit court's lack of subject matter jurisdiction to accept her guilty plea as well as ineffective assistance of counsel. Her claim of ineffective assistance of counsel was based upon her lawyer's failure to advise her the statute under which she was being prosecuted might not apply to prenatal drug use. The petition was granted on both grounds. The State appeals.

LAW/ANALYSIS

Subject Matter Jurisdiction

The State first argues the PCR court erred in finding the sentencing circuit court lacked subject matter jurisdiction to accept Whitner's guilty plea. We agree.

Under South Carolina law, a circuit court lacks subject matter jurisdiction to accept a guilty plea to a nonexistent offense. For the sentencing court to have had subject matter jurisdiction to accept Whitner's plea, criminal child neglect under section 20–7–50 would have to include an expectant mother's use of crack cocaine after the fetus is viable. All other issues are ancillary to this jurisdictional issue.

S.C.Code Ann. § 20–7–50 (1985) provides:

> Any person having the legal custody of any *child* or helpless person, who shall, without lawful excuse, refuse or neglect to provide, as defined in § 20–7–490, the proper care and attention for such *child* or helpless person, so that the life, health or comfort of such *child* or helpless person is endangered or is likely to be

endangered, shall be guilty of a misdemeanor and shall be punished within the discretion of the circuit court. (emphasis added).

The State contends this section encompasses maternal acts endangering or likely to endanger the life, comfort, or health of a viable fetus.

Under the Children's Code, "child" means a "person under the age of eighteen." S.C.Code Ann. § 20–7–30(1) (1985). The question for this Court, therefore, is whether a viable fetus is a "person" for purposes of the Children's Code. . . .

South Carolina law has long recognized that viable fetuses are persons holding certain legal rights and privileges. In 1960, this Court decided *Hall v. Murphy*. That case concerned the application of South Carolina's wrongful death statute to an infant who died four hours after her birth as a result of injuries sustained prenatally during viability. The Appellants argued that a viable fetus was not a person within the purview of the wrongful death statute, because, *inter alia*, a fetus is thought to have no separate being apart from the mother.

We found such a reason for exclusion from recovery "unsound, illogical and unjust," and concluded there was "no medical or other basis" for the "assumed identity" of mother and viable unborn child. In light of that conclusion, this Court unanimously held: "We have no difficulty in concluding that a fetus having reached that period of prenatal maturity where it is capable of independent life apart from its mother is a person."

Four years later, in *Fowler v. Woodward*, we interpreted *Hall* as supporting a finding that a viable fetus injured while still in the womb need not be born alive for another to maintain an action for the wrongful death of the fetus. . . .

More recently, we held the word "person" as used in a criminal statute includes viable fetuses. *State v. Horne* concerned South Carolina's murder statute. The defendant in that case stabbed his wife, who was nine months' pregnant, in the neck, arms, and abdomen. Although doctors performed an emergency caesarean section to deliver the child, the child died while still in the womb. The defendant was convicted of voluntary manslaughter and appealed his conviction on the ground South Carolina did not recognize the crime of feticide.

This Court disagreed. In a unanimous decision, we held it would be "grossly inconsistent . . . to construe a viable fetus as a 'person' for the purposes of imposing civil liability while refusing to give it a similar classification in the criminal context." Accordingly, the Court recognized the crime of feticide with respect to viable fetuses.

Similarly, we do not see any rational basis for finding a viable fetus is not a "person" in the present context. Indeed, it would be absurd to recognize the viable fetus as a person for purposes of homicide laws and wrongful death statutes but not for purposes of statutes proscribing child abuse. Our holding in *Hall* that a viable fetus is a person rested primarily on the plain meaning of the word "person" in light of existing medical knowledge concerning fetal development. We do not believe that the plain and ordinary meaning of the word "person" has changed in any way that would now deny viable fetuses status as persons.

The policies enunciated in the Children's Code also support our plain meaning reading of "person." S.C.Code Ann. § 20–7–20(C) (1985), which describes South Carolina's policy concerning children, expressly states: "It shall be the policy of this State to concentrate on the *prevention of children's problems* as the most important strategy which can be planned and implemented on behalf of children and their families." (emphasis added). The abuse or neglect of a child at *any* time during childhood can exact a profound toll on the child herself as well as on society as a whole. However, the consequences of abuse or neglect which takes place after birth often pale in comparison to those resulting from abuse suffered by the viable fetus before birth. This policy of prevention supports a reading of the word "person" to include viable fetuses. Furthermore, the scope of the Children's Code is quite broad. It applies "to *all* children who have need of services." When coupled with the comprehensive remedial purposes of the Code, this language supports the inference that the legislature intended to include viable fetuses within the scope of the Code's protection. . . .

Whitner . . . argues an interpretation of the statute that includes viable fetuses would lead to absurd results obviously not intended by the legislature. Specifically, she claims if we interpret "child" to include viable fetuses, every action by a pregnant woman that endangers or is likely to endanger a fetus, whether otherwise legal or illegal, would constitute unlawful neglect under the statute. For example, a woman might be prosecuted under section 20–7–50 for smoking or drinking during pregnancy. Whitner asserts these "absurd" results could not have been intended by the legislature and, therefore, the statute should not be construed to include viable fetuses.

We disagree for a number of reasons. First, the same arguments against the statute can be made whether or not the child has been born. After the birth of a child, a parent can be prosecuted under section 20–7–50 for an action that is likely to endanger the child without regard to whether the action is illegal in itself. For example, a parent who drinks excessively could, under certain circumstances, be guilty of child neglect or endangerment even though the underlying act—consuming alcoholic beverages—is itself legal. Obviously, the legislature did not think it "absurd" to allow prosecution of parents for such otherwise legal acts when the acts actually or potentially endanger the "life, health or comfort" of the parents' born children. We see no reason such a result should be rendered absurd by the mere fact the child at issue is a viable fetus.

Moreover, we need not address this potential parade of horribles advanced by Whitner. In *this* case, which is the only case we are called upon to decide here, certain facts are clear. Whitner admits to having ingested crack cocaine during the third trimester of her pregnancy, which caused her child to be born with cocaine in its system. Although the precise effects of maternal crack use during pregnancy are somewhat unclear, it is well documented and within the realm of public knowledge that such use can cause serious harm to the viable unborn child. There can be no question here Whitner endangered the life, health, and comfort of her child. We need not decide any cases other than the one before us.

We are well aware of the many decisions from other states' courts throughout the country holding maternal conduct before the birth of the child does not give rise to criminal prosecution under state child abuse/endangerment or drug distribution statutes. Many of these cases were prosecuted under statutes forbidding delivery or distribution of illicit substances and depended on statutory construction of the terms "delivery" and "distribution." Obviously, such cases are inapplicable to the present situation. The cases concerning child endangerment statutes or construing the terms "child" and "person" are also distinguishable, because the states in which these cases were decided have entirely different bodies of case law from South Carolina. For example, in *Commonwealth v. Welch*, the Kentucky Supreme Court specifically noted Kentucky law has not construed the word "person" in the criminal homicide statute to include a fetus (viable or not). In *Reyes v. Superior Court the California Court of Appeals* noted California law did not recognize a fetus as a "human being" within the purview of the state murder and manslaughter statutes, and that it was thus improper to find the fetus was a "child" for purposes of the felonious child endangerment statute.

Massachusetts, however, has a body of case law substantially similar to South Carolina's, yet a Massachusetts trial court has held that a mother pregnant with a viable fetus is not criminally liable for transmission of cocaine to the fetus. . . .

The Massachusetts trial court found [state court decisions allowing wrongful death actions on behalf of viable fetuses injured *in utero*] "accord legal rights to the unborn only where the mother's or parents' interest in the potentiality of life, not the state's interest, are sought to be vindicated." In other words, a viable fetus should only be accorded the rights of a person for the sake of its mother or both its parents. . . .

We decline to read *Horne* in a way that insulates the mother from all culpability for harm to her viable child. Because the rationale underlying our body of law—protection of the viable fetus—is radically different from that underlying the law of Massachusetts, we decline to follow the decision of the Massachusetts Superior Court. . . .

Finally, the dissent implies that we have ignored the rule of lenity requiring us to resolve any ambiguities in a criminal statute in favor of the defendant. The dissent argues that "[a]t most, the majority only suggests that the term 'child' as used in § 20–7–50 is ambiguous," and that the ambiguity "is created not by reference to our decisions under the Children's Code or by reference to the statutory language and applicable rules of statutory construction, but by reliance on decisions in two different fields of the law, civil wrongful death and common law feticide."

Plainly, the dissent misunderstands our opinion. First, we do not believe the statute is ambiguous and, therefore, the rule of lenity does not apply. Furthermore, our interpretation of the statute is based primarily on the plain meaning of the word "person" as contained in the statute. We need not go beyond that language. However, because our prior decisions in *Murphy, Fowler, and Horne* support our reading of the statute, we have discussed the rationale underlying those holdings. We conclude that both statutory language and case law compel the conclusion we reach. We see no ambiguity. . . .

Constitutional Issues

Right to Privacy

Whitner argues that prosecuting her for using crack cocaine after her fetus attains viability unconstitutionally burdens her right of privacy, or, more specifically, her right to carry her pregnancy to term. We disagree.

Whitner argues that section 20–7–50 burdens her right of privacy, a right long recognized by the United States Supreme Court. She cites *Cleveland Board of Education v. LaFleur*, 414 U.S. 632 (1974), as standing for the proposition that the Constitution protects women from measures penalizing them for choosing to carry their pregnancies to term.

In *LaFleur* two junior high school teachers challenged their school systems' maternity leave policies. The policies required "every pregnant school teacher to take maternity leave without pay, beginning [four or] five months before the expected birth of her child." A teacher on maternity leave could not return to work "until the beginning of the next regular school semester which follows the date when her child attains the age of three months." The two teachers, both of whom had become pregnant and were required against their wills to comply with the school systems' policies, argued that the policies were unconstitutional.

The United States Supreme Court agreed. It found that "[b]y acting to penalize the pregnant teacher for deciding to bear a child, overly restrictive maternity leave regulations can constitute a heavy burden on the exercise of these protected freedoms." The Court then scrutinized the policies to determine whether "the interests advanced in support of" the policy could "justify the particular procedures [the School Boards] ha[d] adopted." Although it found that the purported justification for the policy—continuity of instruction—was a "significant and legitimate educational goal," the Court concluded that the "absolute requirement[ ] of termination at the end of the fourth or fifth month of pregnancy" was not a rational means for achieving continuity of instruction and that such a requirement "may serve to hinder attainment of the very continuity objectives that they are purportedly designed to promote." Finding no rational relationship between the purpose of the maternity leave policy and the means crafted to achieve that end, the Court concluded the policy violated the Due Process Clause of the Fourteenth Amendment.

Whitner argues that the alleged violation here is far more egregious than that in *La Fleur*. She first suggests that imprisonment is a far greater burden on her exercise of her freedom to carry the fetus to term than was the unpaid maternity leave in *LaFleur*. Although she is, of course, correct that imprisonment is more severe than unpaid maternity leave, Whitner misapprehends the fundamentally different nature of her own interests and those of the government in this case as compared to those at issue in *LaFleur*.

First, the State's interest in protecting the life and health of the viable fetus is not merely legitimate. It is compelling. See, e.g., *Roe v. Wade; Planned Parenthood v. Casey*. The United States Supreme Court in *Casey* recognized that the State possesses a profound interest in the potential life of the fetus, not only after the fetus is viable, but throughout the expectant mother's pregnancy.

Even more importantly, however, we do not think any fundamental right of Whitner's—or any right at all, for that matter—is implicated under the present scenario. It strains belief for Whitner to argue that using crack cocaine during pregnancy is encompassed within the constitutionally recognized right of privacy. Use of crack cocaine is illegal, period. No one here argues that laws criminalizing the use of crack cocaine are themselves unconstitutional. If the State wishes to impose additional criminal penalties on pregnant women who engage in this already illegal conduct because of the effect the conduct has on the viable fetus, it may do so. We do not see how the fact of pregnancy elevates the use of crack cocaine to the lofty status of a fundamental right.

Moreover, as a practical matter, we do not see how our interpretation of section 20–7–50 imposes a burden on Whitner's right to carry her child to term. In *LaFleur*, the Supreme Court found that the mandatory maternity leave policies burdened women's rights to carry their pregnancies to term because the policies prevented pregnant teachers from exercising a freedom they would have enjoyed but for their pregnancies. In contrast, during her pregnancy after the fetus attained viability, Whitner enjoyed the same freedom to use cocaine that she enjoyed earlier in and predating her pregnancy—none whatsoever. Simply put, South Carolina's child abuse and endangerment statute as applied to this case does not restrict Whitner's freedom in any way that it was not already restricted. The State's imposition of an additional penalty when a pregnant woman with a viable fetus engages in the already proscribed behavior does not burden a woman's right to carry her pregnancy to term; rather, the additional penalty simply recognizes that a third party (the viable fetus or newborn child) is harmed by the behavior.

Section 20–7–50 does not burden Whitner's right to carry her pregnancy to term or any other privacy right. Accordingly, we find no violation of the Due Process Clause of the Fourteenth Amendment.

CONCLUSION

For the foregoing reasons, the decision of the PCR Court is REVERSED.

Ernest A. Finney Jr., Chief Justice:

I respectfully dissent, and would affirm the grant of post-conviction relief to respondent Whitner.

. . . It is apparent from a reading of the entire [Children's Code] that the word child in § 20–7–50 means a child in being and not a fetus. A plain reading of the entire child neglect statute demonstrates the intent to criminalize only acts directed at children, and not those which may harm fetuses. First, § 20–7–50 does not impose criminal liability on every person who neglects a child, but only on a person having legal custody of that child. The statutory requirement of legal custody is evidence of intent to extend the statute's reach only to children, because the concept of legal custody is simply inapplicable to a fetus. Second, . . . the vast majority of acts which constitute statutory harm . . . are acts which can only be directed at a child, and not toward a fetus. . . . Read in context, and in light of the statutory purpose of protecting persons of tender years, it is clear that "child" as used in § 20–7–50 means a child in being. . . .

I would affirm.

JAMES E. MOORE, JUSTICE:

I concur with the dissent in this case but write separately to express my concerns with today's decision.

In my view, the repeated failure of the legislature to pass proposed bills addressing the problem of drug use during pregnancy is evidence the child abuse and neglect statute is not intended to apply in this instance. This Court should not invade what is clearly the sole province of the legislative branch. At the very least, the legislature's failed attempts to enact a statute regulating a pregnant woman's conduct indicate the complexity of this issue. While the majority opinion is perhaps an argument for what the law should be, it is for the General Assembly, and not this Court, to make that determination by means of a clearly drawn statute. With today's decision, the majority not only ignores legislative intent but embarks on a course of judicial activism rejected by every other court to address the issue. . . .

In construing this statute to include conduct not contemplated by the legislature, the majority has rendered the statute vague and set for itself the task of determining what conduct is unlawful. Is a pregnant woman's failure to obtain prenatal care unlawful? Failure to quit smoking or drinking? Although the majority dismisses this issue as not before it, the impact of today's decision is to render a pregnant woman potentially criminally liable for myriad acts which the legislature has not seen fit to criminalize. To ignore this "down-the-road" consequence in a case of this import is unrealistic. The majority insists that parents may already be held liable for drinking after a child is born. This is untrue, however, without some further act on the part of the parent. A parent who drinks and then hits her child or fails to come home may be guilty of criminal neglect. The mere fact of drinking, however, does not constitute neglect of a child in being.

The majority attempts to support an overinclusive construction of the child abuse and neglect statute by citing other legal protections extended equally to a viable fetus and a child in being. The only law, however, that specifically regulates the conduct of a mother toward her unborn child is our abortion statute under which a viable fetus is in fact treated differently from a child in being.

The majority argues for equal treatment of viable fetuses and children, yet its construction of the statute results in even greater inequities. If the statute applies only when a fetus is "viable," a pregnant woman can use cocaine for the first twenty-four weeks of her pregnancy, the most danger-ous period for the fetus, and be immune from prosecution under the statute so long as she quits drug use before the fetus becomes viable. Further, a pregnant woman now faces up to ten years in prison for ingesting drugs during pregnancy but can have an illegal abortion and receive only a two-year sentence for killing her viable fetus.

Because I disagree with the conclusion § 20–7–50 includes a viable fetus, I would affirm the grant of post-conviction relief.

Dorothy E. Roberts, Punishing Drug Addicts Who Have Babies: Women of Color, Equality, and the Right of Privacy

104 Harv. L. Rev. 1419 (1991).

. . . A growing number of women across the country have been charged with criminal offenses after giving birth to babies who test positive for drugs. The majority of these women . . . are poor and Black. Most are addicted to crack cocaine. The prosecution of drug-addicted mothers is part of an alarming trend towards greater state intervention into the lives of pregnant women under the rationale of protecting the fetus from harm. This intervention has included compelled medical treatment, greater re-strictions on abortion, and increased supervision of pregnant women's conduct.

Such government intrusion is particularly harsh for poor women of color. They are the least likely to obtain adequate prenatal care, the most vulnerable to government monitoring, and the least able to conform to the white, middle-class standard of motherhood. . . . Finally, their failure to meet society's image of the ideal mother makes their prosecution more acceptable.

To charge drug-addicted mothers with crimes, the state must be able to identify those who use drugs during pregnancy. Because poor women are generally under greater government supervision—through their associa-tions with public hospitals, welfare agencies, and probation officers--their drug use is more likely to be detected and reported. Hospital screening practices result in disproportionate reporting of poor Black women. The government's main source of information about prenatal drug use is hospitals' reporting of positive infant toxicologies to child welfare authori-ties. Hospitals serving poor minority communities implement this testing almost exclusively. Private physicians who serve more affluent women perform less of this screening both because they have a financial stake both in retaining their patients' business and securing referrals from them and because they are socially more like their patients.

Hospitals administer drug tests in a manner that further discriminates against poor Black women. One common criterion triggering an infant toxicology screen is the mother's failure to obtain prenatal care, a factor that correlates strongly with race and income. Worse still, many hospitals have no formal screening procedures, relying solely on the suspicions of health care professionals. This discretion allows doctors and hospital staff to perform tests based on their stereotyped assumptions about drug addicts.

Health care professionals are much more likely to report Black women's drug use to government authorities than they are similar drug use by their wealthy white patients. A study recently reported in *The New England Journal of Medicine* demonstrated this racial bias in the reporting of maternal drug use. Researchers studied the results of toxicologic tests of pregnant women who received prenatal care in public health clinics and in private obstetrical offices in Pinellas County, Florida. Little difference existed in the prevalence of substance abuse by pregnant women along either racial or economic lines, nor was there any significant difference between public clinics and private offices. Despite similar rates of substance abuse, however, Black women were *ten times* more likely than whites to be reported to public health authorities for substance abuse during pregnancy. Although several possible explanations can account for this disparate reporting, both public health facilities and private doctors are more inclined to turn in pregnant Black women who use drugs than pregnant white women who use drugs.

It is also significant that, out of the universe of maternal conduct that can injure a fetus, prosecutors have focused on crack use. The selection of crack addiction for punishment can be justified neither by the number of addicts nor the extent of the harm to the fetus. Excessive alcohol consumption during pregnancy, for example, can cause severe fetal injury, and marijuana use may also adversely affect the unborn. The incidence of both these types of substance abuse is high as well. In addition, prosecutors do not always base their claims on actual harm to the child, but on the mere delivery of crack by the mother. Although different forms of substance abuse prevail among pregnant women of various socioeconomic levels and racial and ethnic backgrounds, inner-city Black communities have the highest concentrations of crack addicts. Therefore, selecting crack abuse as the primary fetal harm to be punished has a discriminatory impact that cannot be medically justified.

Focusing on Black crack addicts rather than on other perpetrators of fetal harms serves two broader social purposes. First, prosecution of these pregnant women serves to degrade women whom society views as undeserving to be mothers and to discourage them from having children. If prosecutors had instead chosen to prosecute affluent women addicted to alcohol or prescription medication, the policy of criminalizing prenatal conduct very likely would have suffered a hasty demise. Society is much more willing to condone the punishment of poor women of color who fail to meet the middle-class ideal of motherhood.

In addition to legitimizing fetal rights enforcement, the prosecution of crack-addicted mothers diverts public attention from social ills such as poverty, racism, and a misguided national health policy and implies instead that shamefully high Black infant death rates are caused by the bad acts of individual mothers. Poor Black mothers thus become the scapegoats for the causes of the Black community's ill health. Punishing them assuages any guilt the nation might feel at the plight of an underclass with infant mortality at rates higher than those in some less developed countries. Making criminals of Black mothers apparently helps to relieve the nation of the burden of creating a health care system that ensures healthy babies for all its citizens. . . .

The systematic, institutionalized denial of reproductive freedom has uniquely marked Black women's history in America. An important part of this denial has been the devaluation of Black women as mothers. A popular mythology that degrades Black women and portrays them as less deserving of motherhood reinforces this subordination. This mythology is one aspect of a complex set of images that deny Black humanity in order to rationalize the oppression of Blacks. . . .

The disproportionate number of Black mothers who lose custody of their children through the child welfare system is a contemporary manifestation of the devaluation of Black motherhood. This disparate impact of state intervention results in part from Black families' higher rate of reliance on government welfare. Because welfare families are subject to supervision by social workers, instances of perceived neglect are more likely to be reported to governmental authorities than neglect on the part of more affluent parents. Black children are also removed from their homes in part because of the child welfare system's cultural bias and application of the nuclear family pattern to Black families. Black childrearing patterns that diverge from the norm of the nuclear family have been misinterpreted by government bureaucrats as child neglect. For example, child welfare workers have often failed to respect the longstanding cultural tradition in the Black community of shared parenting responsibility among blood-related and non-blood kin. The state has thus been more willing to intrude upon the autonomy of poor Black families, and in particular of Black mothers, while protecting the integrity of white, middle-class homes.

This devaluation of Black motherhood has been reinforced by stereotypes that blame Black mothers for the problems of the Black family. . . .White sociologists have held Black matriarchs responsible for the disintegration of the Black family and the consequent failure of Black people to achieve success in America. Daniel Patrick Moynihan popularized this theory in his 1965 report, *The Negro Family: The Case for National Action.* . . .Moynihan attributed the cause of Black people's inability to overcome the effects of racism largely to the dominance of Black mothers. . . .

Informed by the ... devaluation of Black motherhood, we can better understand prosecutors' reasons for punishing drug-addicted mothers. This Article views such prosecutions as punishing these women, in essence, for having babies.... It is important to recognize at the outset that the prosecutions are based in part on a woman's pregnancy and not on her illegal drug use alone. Prosecutors charge these defendants not with drug use, but with child abuse or drug distribution—crimes that relate to their pregnancy. Moreover, pregnant women receive harsher sentences than drug-addicted men or women who are not pregnant. ...

When a drug-addicted woman becomes pregnant, she has only one realistic avenue to escape criminal charges: abortion. Thus, she is penalized for choosing to have the baby rather than having an abortion. ... [I]t is the *choice of carrying a pregnancy to term* that is being penalized.

There is also good reason to question the government's justification for the prosecutions—the concern for the welfare of potential children. ... The history of overwhelming state neglect of Black children casts further doubt on its professed concern for the welfare of the fetus. When a society has always closed its eyes to the inadequacy of prenatal care available to poor Black women, its current expression of interest in the health of unborn Black children must be viewed with suspicion. The most telling evidence of the state's disregard of Black children is the high rate of infant death in the Black community. In 1987, the mortality rate for Black infants in the United States was 17.9 deaths per thousand births—more than twice that for white infants (8.6). ... The main reason for these high mortality rates is inadequate prenatal care. ... The government has chosen to punish poor Black women rather than provide the means for them to have healthy children.

The cruelty of this punitive response is heightened by the lack of available drug treatment services for pregnant drug addicts. Protecting the welfare of drug addicts' children requires, among other things, adequate facilities for the mother's drug treatment. Yet a drug addict's pregnancy serves as an *obstacle* to obtaining this treatment. Treatment centers either refuse to treat pregnant women or are effectively closed to them because the centers are ill-equipped to meet the needs of pregnant addicts. Most hospitals and programs that treat addiction exclude pregnant women because their babies are more likely to be born with health problems requiring expensive care. Program directors also feel that treating pregnant addicts is worth neither the increased cost nor the risk of tort liability. ...

Finally, and perhaps most importantly, ample evidence reveals that prosecuting addicted mothers may not achieve the government's asserted goal of healthier pregnancies; indeed, such prosecutions will probably lead to the opposite result. Pregnant addicts who seek help from public hospitals and clinics are the ones most often reported to government authorities. The threat of prosecution based on this reporting forces women to remain anonymous and thus has the perverse effect of deterring pregnant drug addicts from seeking treatment. For this reason, the government's decision to punish drug-addicted mothers is irreconcilable with the goal of helping them.

Pregnancy may be a time when women are most motivated to seek treatment for drug addiction and make positive lifestyle changes. The government should capitalize on this opportunity by encouraging drug-addicted women to seek help and providing them with comprehensive treatment. Punishing pregnant women who use drugs only exacerbates the causes of addiction—poverty, lack of self-esteem, and hopelessness. Perversely, this makes it more likely that poor Black women's children—the asserted beneficiaries of the prosecutions—will suffer from the same hardships. . . .

Understanding the prosecution of drug-addicted mothers as punishment for having babies clarifies the constitutional right at stake. The woman's right at issue is not the right to abuse drugs or to cause the fetus to be born with defects. It is the right to choose to be a mother that is burdened by the criminalization of conduct during pregnancy. This view of the constitutional issue reveals the relevance of race to the resolution of the competing interests. Race has historically determined the value society places on an individual's right to choose motherhood. Because of the devaluation of Black motherhood, protecting the right of Black women to choose to bear a child has unique significance. . . .

[P]rivacy concepts have two benefits for advocating the reproductive rights of women of color in particular: the right of privacy stresses the value of personhood, and it protects against the totalitarian abuse of government power. First, affirming Black women's constitutional claim to personhood is particularly important because these women historically have been denied the dignity of their full humanity and identity. The principle of self-definition has special significance for Black women. Angela Harris recognizes in the writings of Zora Neale Hurston an insistence on a "conception of identity as a construction, not an essence. . . . [B]lack women have had to learn to construct themselves in a society that denied them full selves." Black women's willful self-definition is an adaptation to a history of social denigration. Rejected from the dominant society's norm of womanhood, Black women have been forced to resort to their own internal resources. Harris contrasts this process of affirmative self-definition with the feminist paradigm of women as passive victims. Black women willfully create their own identities out of "fragments of experience, not discovered in one's body or unveiled after male domination is eliminated."

The concept of personhood embodied in the right of privacy can be used to affirm the role of will and creativity in Black women's construction of their own identities. Relying on the concept of self-definition celebrates the legacy of Black women who have survived and transcended conditions of oppression. The process of defining one's self and declaring one's personhood defies the denial of self-ownership inherent in slavery. Thus, the right of privacy, with its affirmation of personhood, is especially suited for challenging the devaluation of Black motherhood underlying the prosecutions of drug-addicted women.

Another important element of the right of privacy is its delineation of the limits of governmental power. The protection from government abuse also makes the right of privacy a useful legal tool for protecting the reproductive rights of women of color. Poor women of color are especially vulnerable to government control over their decisions. The government's pervasive involvement in Black women's lives illustrates the inadequacy of the privacy critique presented by some white feminist scholars. Catharine MacKinnon, for example, argues that privacy doctrine is based on the false liberal assumption that government nonintervention into the private sphere promotes women's autonomy. The individual woman's legal right of privacy, according to MacKinnon, functions instead as "a means of subordinating women's collective needs to the imperatives of male supremacy."

This rejection of privacy doctrine does not take into account the contradictory meaning of the private sphere for women of color. Feminist legal theory focuses on the private realm of the family as an institution of violence and subordination. Women of color, however, often experience the family as the site of solace and resistance against racial oppression. For many women of color, the immediate concern in the area of reproductive rights is not abuse in the private sphere, but abuse of government power. The prosecution of crack-addicted mothers . . . [is an] example . . . of state intervention that pose[s] a much greater threat for women of color than for white women.

Another telling example is the issue of child custody. The primary concern for white middle-class women with regard to child custody is private custody battles with their husbands following the termination of a marriage. But for women of color, the dominant threat is termination of parental rights by the state. Again, the imminent danger faced by poor women of color comes from the public sphere, not the private. Thus, the protection from government interference that privacy doctrine affords may have a different significance for women of color. . . .

The right to bear children goes to the heart of what it means to be human. The value we place on individuals determines whether we see them as entitled to perpetuate themselves in their children. Denying someone the right to bear children—or punishing her for exercising that right—deprives her of a basic part of her humanity. When this denial is based on race, it also functions to preserve a racial hierarchy that essentially disregards Black humanity. . . .

Imagine that courts and legislatures have accepted the argument that the prosecution of crack-addicted mothers violates their right of privacy. All pending indictments for drug use during pregnancy are dismissed and bills proposing fetal abuse laws are discarded. Would there be any perceptible change in the inferior status of Black women? Pregnant crack addicts would still be denied treatment, and most poor Black women would continue to receive inadequate prenatal care. The infant mortality rate for Blacks would remain deplorably high. In spite of the benefits of privacy doctrine for women of color, liberal notions of privacy are inadequate to eliminate the subordination of Black women. In this section, I will suggest two approaches that I believe are necessary in order for privacy theory to contribute to the eradication of racial hierarchy. First, we need to develop a positive view of the right of privacy. Second, the law must recognize the connection between the right of privacy and racial equality.

The most compelling argument against privacy rhetoric, from the perspective of women of color, is the connection that feminist scholars have drawn between privacy and the abortion funding decisions. Critics of the concept of privacy note that framing the abortion right as a right merely to be shielded from state intrusion into private choices provides no basis for a constitutional claim to public support for abortions. . . . Defining the guarantee of personhood as no more than shielding a sphere of personal decisions from the reach of government—merely ensuring the individual's "right to be let alone"—may be inadequate to protect the dignity and autonomy of the poor and oppressed. . . .

Laurence Tribe . . . has suggested an alternative view of the relationship between the government's negative and affirmative responsibilities in guaranteeing the rights of personhood: "Ultimately, the affirmative duties of government cannot be severed from its obligations to refrain from certain forms of control; both must respond to a substantive vision of the needs of human personality."

This concept of privacy includes not only the negative proscription against government coercion, but also the affirmative duty of government to protect the individual's personhood from degradation and to facilitate the processes of choice and self-determination. This approach shifts the focus of privacy theory from state nonintervention to an affirmative guarantee of personhood and autonomy. Under this post-liberal doctrine, the government is not only prohibited from punishing crack-addicted women for choosing to bear children; it is also required to provide drug treatment and prenatal care. . . .

This affirmative view of privacy is enhanced by recognizing the connection between privacy and racial equality. The government's duty to guarantee personhood and autonomy stems not only from the needs of the individual, but also from the needs of the entire community. The harm caused by the prosecution of crack-addicted mothers is not simply the incursion on each individual crack addict's decisionmaking; it is the perpetuation of a degraded image that affects the status of an entire race. The devaluation of a poor Black addict's decision to bear a child is tied to the dominant society's disregard for the motherhood of all Black women. The diminished value placed on Black motherhood, in turn, is a badge of racial inferiority worn by all Black people. The affirmative view of privacy recognizes the connection between the dehumanization of the individual and the subordination of the group.

Thus, the reason that legislatures should reject laws that punish Black women's reproductive choices is not an absolute and isolated notion of individual autonomy. Rather, legislatures should reject these laws as a critical step towards eradicating a racial hierarchy that has historically demeaned Black motherhood. Respecting Black women's decision to bear children is a necessary ingredient of a community that affirms the personhood of all of its members. The right to reproductive autonomy is in this way linked to the goal of racial equality and the broader pursuit of a just society. This broader dimension of privacy's guarantees provides a stronger claim to government's affirmative responsibilities.

Feminist legal theory, with its emphasis on the law's concrete effect on the condition of women, calls for a reassessment of traditional privacy law. It may be possible, however, to reconstruct a privacy jurisprudence that retains the focus on autonomy and personhood while making privacy doctrine effective. Before dismissing the right of privacy altogether, we should explore ways to give the concepts of choice and personhood more substance. In this way, the continuing process of challenge and subversion—the feminist critique of liberal privacy doctrine, followed by the racial critique of the feminist analysis—will forge a finer legal tool for dismantling institutions of domination. . . .

NOTES AND QUESTIONS

1. **The Interests at Stake**. Both court-ordered medical interventions and the prosecution of prenatal crimes can be seen as part of a trend to regulate pregnant women's conduct for the sake of the fetus. What are the state's and the pregnant woman's interests at stake in these two sets of cases? How do they compare with the interests involved in abortion? Do you find these competing interests equally compelling in forced medical intervention, fetal abuse, and abortion cases?

2. **Maternal Duty**. Compelling pregnant women to undergo medical treatment or punishing them for harmful conduct can be seen as enforcing the woman's duty to care for the fetus. Does a pregnant woman have special duties toward the fetus she is carrying? Should those duties exceed the obligations parents generally owe their children? The court in *In re A.C.* held, however, that the interests of the fetus should almost never be balanced against those of the mother. Is the pregnant woman's autonomy over her body absolute? Is this true even if the mother refuses medical intervention or drug treatment for irrational reasons?

3. **Privacy Doctrine**. The court in *In re A.C.* relied on notions of privacy and bodily autonomy to overturn the trial judge's decision authorizing a forced cesarean section. Does the feminist critique of privacy as a justification for abortion rights raise concerns about the power of privacy as a basis for opposing the legal regulation of maternal conduct during pregnancy? Think about how equality theory would apply to regulations of pregnant women's conduct. On the other hand, do you agree with Dorothy Roberts's argument that there are benefits to retaining at least some aspects of privacy doctrine? Does the extreme, surgical violation of the woman's bodily integrity highlight the continued importance of guaranteeing women's control over their physical bodies?

4. **Race and Forced Treatment**. Roberts's article points out the racial disparity in the prosecution of women who use drugs during pregnancy.

There is similar racial disparity in court-ordered medical treatment of pregnant women. A national survey published in 1987 in the *New England Journal of Medicine* discovered 21 cases in which court orders were sought, of which 18 petitions were granted. Eighty-one percent of the women involved were women of color; all were treated in a teaching-hospital clinic or were receiving public assistance. Veronika E. B. Kolder, Janet Gallagher, and Michael T. Parsons, *Court-Ordered Obstetrical Interventions*, 316 New England Journal of Medicine 1192 (1987). In another essay, Roberts suggests an explanation for the disproportionate use of coercive measures against women of color:

> The racial disparity may be explained partly by physicians' unwillingness to acknowledge the complexity of patients' cultural life, interpreting refusals to follow medical judgments as individual idiosyncracies. Rayna Rapp's finding that low-income Black women often explained their decision to refuse medical intervention during pregnancy in terms of nonmedical systems, such as religion, visions, and folk healing, is confirmed by the facts of some of the forced cesarean cases. . . . Judges and doctors describe women who refuse medical treatment as angry, irrational, fearful, stubborn, selfish, and uncooperative. They dismiss these women's reasons for rejecting doctors' recommendations, reasons which are not expressed in scientific terms, as unfounded and illegitimate. . . .

> Why are doctors more likely to determine that the duty to obtain consent is outweighed in the case of women of color? Race helps to explain why they treat the choices of these women with less respect. Doctors are more likely to deem the judgments of white, middle-class women to be legitimate because these women are considered more closely affiliated with the interests of medical authority. Minority women's motives for challenging their doctors' advice are more suspect; since they are defined as irresponsible mothers, their reasons are more likely to be considered irrational and selfish. . . .

> It also appears that privileged women are more likely to consent to cesarean surgeries, even though they are performed at alarming rates. These women may more readily obey their doctors' orders because they trust their doctors and seek the support and approval of those in medical authority. Women of color, on the other hand, may more readily reject these medical interventions because of an alternative cultural view of birth or because their experience of racism leads them to distrust medical authority. Nancy Ehrenreich suggests that the court-ordered treatment of women of color may constitute a coercive response to their acts of resistance to doctors' control of their reproduction.

Dorothy E. Roberts, *Reconstructing the Patient: Starting with Women of Color*, in Susan M. Wolf, ed., *Feminism and Bioethics: Beyond Reproduc-*

tion 116 (1996). *See also* Nancy Ehrenreich, *The Colonization of the Womb*, 43 Duke L.J. 492 (1993); Lisa C. Ikemoto, *Furthering the Inquiry: Race, Class, and Culture in the Forced Medical Treatment of Pregnant Women*, 59 Tenn. L. Rev. 487 (1992). What role can the resistance of women of color to medical control play in challenging the regulation of pregnant women's bodies?

5. Are you persuaded by Roberts's argument that the prosecutions punish women for their decision to have a baby, as well as her argument that most of the defendants are punished because of their race? If the punishment of drug use during pregnancy is so tied to race, how can we explain the prosecution of some white, Latina, and Indian women for these crimes? Although the conviction and sentencing of Cornelia Whitner might have depended on her race, the South Carolina Supreme Court's decision dramatically affects all pregnant women in the state. How should the racial dimension of the regulation of pregnant women's conduct influence legal strategies to guarantee women's control over their bodies?

III. WELFARE REFORM AND RESTRICTIONS ON CHILDBEARING

C.K. v. Shalala

United States District Court, District of New Jersey, 1995.
883 F.Supp. 991, aff'd, 92 F.3d 171 (3d Cir. 1996).

[NICHOLAS H. POLITAN, JUDGE.]

Plaintiffs, residents of New Jersey currently receiving welfare funding via the Aid to Families with Dependent Children ("AFDC") program, . . . challenge the [Health and Human Services] Secretary's grant of waivers to the state of New Jersey in July 1992 to allow implementation of the state's Family Development Program ("FDP") which, *inter alia*, contains the so-called Family Cap provision, an amendment to existing state law that eliminates the standard increase provided by AFDC for any child born to an individual currently receiving AFDC.

Plaintiffs have . . . moved this Court to enter summary judgment on their behalf and thereby permanently enjoin the Family Cap. . . . They assert that . . . as a matter of law the Family Cap violates . . . the Equal Protection and Due Process Clauses of the United States Constitution. . . .

Plaintiffs have conceded that their challenge to the FDP is predicated mainly on . . . administrative and statutory arguments. . . . Their primary goal, as stated at oral argument, is to secure a remand and reconsideration of their opposition to New Jersey's welfare reforms. However, plaintiffs also attempt to hold the Family Cap against the constitutional touchstones that are the Due Process and Equal Protection Clauses of the Fifth and Fourteenth Amendments . . . and it is to this final inquiry that the Court now turns. . . .

The Supreme Court has held that a program which places a ceiling on welfare benefits will pass constitutional muster provided that it bears a rational relationship to a legitimate state interest. Plaintiffs argue that the Family Cap cannot meet this standard because in their view it "penalizes vulnerable and needy children for their parents' behavior over which they have no control: the circumstances of their conception and birth." ...

[T]he Family Cap is not an example of a state's attempt to influence the behavior of men and women by imposing sanctions on the children born of their illegitimate relationships. The legislation here does not direct the onus of parental conduct against the child, nor does it completely deprive children of benefits which they might otherwise receive but for the conduct of their parents. Rather, New Jersey's cap merely imposes a ceiling on the benefits accorded an AFDC household while permitting any additional child to share in that "capped" family income. ...

As noted above, New Jersey's welfare cap must be rationally related to a legitimate governmental purpose. The state (and indeed, the societal) interest served by the Family Cap has been well chronicled in the record as well as in this Opinion: to give AFDC recipients the same structure of incentives as working people, to promote individual responsibility, and to strengthen and stabilize the family unit.

These interests are clearly legitimate. Placing welfare households on a par with working families is a reasonable and appropriate goal of welfare reform; indeed, as the Supreme Court found in *Dandridge*[*v. Williams*, 397 U.S. 471 (1970)], a "solid foundation for [a] regulation can be found in the State's legitimate interest in encouraging employment and avoiding discrimination between welfare families and the families of the working poor." The Family Cap, by maintaining the level of AFDC benefits despite the arrival of an additional child, puts the welfare household in the same situation as that of a working family, which does not automatically receive a wage increase every time it produces another child. This in turn reflects the reasoned legislative determination that a ceiling on benefits provides an incentive for parents to leave the welfare rolls for the work force, as any "advantage" of welfare in the form of the per child benefit increase is no longer available. This legislatively-inspired impetus to enter or return to employment further illustrates a rational decision by the state not only to encourage personal responsibility but also to assist AFDC beneficiaries in achieving self-sufficiency. In addition, it cannot be gainsaid that the Family Cap sends a message that recipients should consider the static level of their welfare benefits before having another child, a message that may reasonably have an ameliorative effect on the rate of out-of-wedlock births that only foster the familial instability and crushing cycle of poverty currently plaguing the welfare class. ...

It is obvious that in this case, the state's interest in reforming welfare is legitimate. ...It is equally plain from the foregoing discussion that New Jersey has sought to realize its reform goals in a reasonable and rational fashion. Consequently, I must dismiss plaintiffs' contention that the cap does not have a rational relationship to an appropriate state purpose.

Apparently recognizing the obstacles to their challenge to the rationality of the Family Cap, plaintiffs assert that the cap violates their fundamental right to make private procreative choices such that strict scrutiny review must be applied. They argue that the cap cannot meet this increased level of review because the state has no compelling interest in deterring child birth and because the cap is not narrowly tailored to meet this goal. Plaintiffs' claim, distilled to its essence, is that the Family Cap is a governmental attempt to alter recipients' reproductive behavior by denying them benefits should they make procreative decisions disfavored by the state.

It is well-settled that decisions about family composition, conception and childbirth fall into a constitutionally protected zone of privacy. An individual has the right "to be free from unwarranted governmental intrusion into matters so fundamentally affecting a person as the decision whether to bear or beget a child." . . . [W]hile a state may not hinder one's exercise of protected choices, it is not obligated to remove obstacles that it did not create, including a lack of financial resources. In addition, once the government decides to provide public benefits, it may not selectively deny those benefits in order to infringe a constitutional right, including the right to procreative choice free from government influence.

This case, however, does not present a situation where New Jersey has unduly burdened the procreative choice of the plaintiff class, as the Family Cap in no way conditions receipt of benefits upon plaintiffs' reproductive choices. Although plaintiffs may claim that the state's failure to subsidize a recipient's choice to procreate intrudes upon that individual's reproductive freedom, this assertion misses the mark. An AFDC household is still entitled to and will still receive benefits whether or not a member of that household conceives and/or gives birth to an additional child. While benefits heretofore granted a recipient household to which another child is added will no longer be available, that family will not suffer any decrease in aid and in fact will continue receiving benefits at the same level as before. In other words, New Jersey's legislative action does nothing to bar an AFDC recipient from conceiving and/or bringing to term an additional child, but has merely removed the automatic benefit increase associated with an additional child under the federal program. Moreover, it should be noted that if New Jersey eliminated its AFDC program altogether, plaintiffs would be faced with the same choices concerning conception but with an even greater lack of financial resources.

Thus, while this Court recognizes that a woman has a right to be free from governmental intrusion vis-a-vis her procreative choices, "it simply does not follow that a woman's freedom of choice carries with it a constitutional entitlement to the financial resources to avail herself of the full range of protected choices." Accordingly, the Court finds that the Family Cap does not infringe plaintiffs' procreative rights. In addition, the Court finds that New Jersey's welfare reform efforts are rationally related to the legitimate state interests of altering the cycle of welfare dependency that it has determined AFDC engenders in its recipients as well as promoting individual responsibility and family stability. . . .

In conclusion, the Court notes that New Jersey's reform proposal does not attempt to fetter or constrain the welfare mother's right to bear as many children as she chooses, but simply requires her to find a way to pay for her progeny's care. This is not discrimination; rather, this is the reality known to so many working families who provide for their children without any expectation of outside assistance. The legislative choices made by the New Jersey Legislature and approved by the Secretary reflect their judgment that the exercise of fundamental rights by welfare recipients ofttimes brings with it the onset of fundamental responsibilities which the recipients themselves must bear. It cannot be said in arriving at this determination that either authority transgressed the permissible bounds of legislative action. . . .

Lucy A. Williams, The Ideology of Division: Behavior Modification Welfare Reform Proposals

102 Yale L. J. 719 (1992).

[T]he underlying assumptions of Family Cap proposals—that AFDC mothers have many children, that they have free access to medical options for family planning, and that they get pregnant in order to receive additional benefits—are unsound. In fact, as of 1990, the average AFDC family, including adults, had 2.9 members; 72.5% of all families on AFDC had only one or two children, and almost 90% had three or fewer children. These figures are no larger than those found among two-parent families in the general population. Moreover, AFDC family size has declined substantially; in 1969, 32.5% of AFDC families had four or more children, and in 1990, only 9.9% had four or more children. Contrary to the commonly held perception that teen pregnancies are skyrocketing, teen birthrates have dropped dramatically over the last three decades.

Furthermore, for those women who wish to terminate their pregnancies, neither abortion facilities nor government funding are necessarily available. Title X of the Public Health Service Act, the only federal program targeted for the provision of family planning services, was cut by 16% during the 1980's. In addition, even when a woman does obtain birth control, the failure rates for the most reliable forms of contraceptives (i.e., the pill, diaphragms, condoms) range from 6% to 16% per year.

There are many reasons why AFDC mothers become pregnant or choose to remain pregnant. These reasons include occurrences of unplanned pregnancies (whether due to a lack of information, money, or forethought), the belief that a child solidifies a relationship with the father, the assumption that children represent an economic value (e.g., to serve as agricultural workers, to support parents in their old age), the belief that the significant health problems and infant mortality rates associated with poverty increase the risk that a single woman with only one child will become childless, a sense that one's life is so hopeless that having a child gives it value and meaning, and the desire to give a grandchild to one's own mother. Many of these reasons are equally applicable to non-AFDC, middle-class women.

"Normal" women allegedly have children only when they are economically able to support them. This is not true. Most people do not view having a baby as the prize for having made it economically, nor do they have a child to gain an additional tax deduction for a dependent. Just like AFDC recipients, they want to be parents and to share their lives with a child. Of course, some families decide not to have an additional child because they believe that they cannot afford it, but the dollar value placed on whether they can afford it varies widely. Therefore, many upper-income families may have a small number of children because they believe it is critical to provide the child with certain advantages, such as piano lessons or private school education, that never enter the minds of a working class family with more children.

Empirical studies have consistently documented the lack of a correlation between the receipt of AFDC benefits and the child-bearing decisions of unmarried women—even for young, unmarried women. In a recent study of AFDC recipients ..., 100% of the mothers said their ability to receive AFDC had no effect on the decision to have a child. In addition, AFDC families are not larger in those states with larger AFDC grants, and teen birth rates are not higher in the states with higher AFDC grants. The number of female-headed families has continued to grow since the early 1970's, even though AFDC benefits, adjusted for inflation, have decreased by 30%. Women receiving AFDC are less likely than non-AFDC recipients to want an additional child, less likely to have multiple pregnancies, and more likely to practice contraception.

Furthermore, the incremental increase that an AFDC family receives when a new child enters the family is so small that it does not even cover such basic essentials as diapers, clothing, bottles and formula. In Wisconsin, for example, an additional third child adds $100 to the grant; in New Jersey, $64; in Mississippi, $24. Thus if economics were really the driving factor in an AFDC mother's decision to have a child, she would make the "rational" decision not to do so.

If Mississippi's economic disincentive of giving only an additional $24 for another child has not reduced AFDC family size or curbed teenage birth rate, Wisconsin's reducing the grant increment from $77 to $39 is also likely to be ineffective. If poor people do not change their behavior based on the strongest economic motivator—living well below the poverty level—the additional economic incentive of a $70 AFDC reduction is certainly nondeterminative. ...

In the face of uniform data that ... Family Cap and other behavioral modification "welfare reform" proposals will not accomplish their articulated goals, why do policymakers, politicians, and the American public continue to espouse and support them? Why does American society cling to the myth that unlike the majority, welfare recipients have deviant values that

can be manipulated solely by the economics of a meager AFDC grant? ...
The answer to these questions lies in a New Right agenda, which I call an
ideology of division, playing to America's deepest racial fears and to
resentment of the poor, single, unemployed mother. ...

The articulation of the "otherness" of the poor—their amorality and
depravity—is longstanding. But the unique contribution of the American
New Right has been to manipulate public attitudes through the subtle use
of racism, scapegoating and stereotypes. ...Thus the New Right has
achieved popular acceptance for the misuse of AFDC laws, shifting our
attention from national structural problems to the purported social deviance of individual women of color.

In the current variation of "otherness," the average citizen considers
all AFDC recipients as part of the "underclass," i.e., African–American,
long-term welfare recipients who live in inner-city ghettos and regularly
have babies. The stereotype also holds that unlike whites, these undeserving poor have warped values, which do not include the desire for such
things as good schools, jobs, or safe streets. Consequently, the current
"welfare reform" proposals are designed to "re-exclude" these "undeserving" poor, until they modify their behavior and prove they are worthy of
our largesse.

The New Right's success in drawing support from working and middle
class whites indicates the depth and pervasiveness of the myth of deviance
regarding the AFDC African–American underclass. By exploiting a stereotype based on race and demerit, the New Right encourages the average
white citizen to distance herself or himself from the African–American
welfare mother and her children. While a white may support income
transfer programs for the elderly because she or he anticipates growing old
someday, whites know that they will never be African American, fourteen
years old and pregnant. They can freely discount poverty as the moral
failing of urban African-American culture, rather than recognizing it as a
social condition cutting across racial and geographic lines and entrapping
even the morally virtuous. The myth enables whites to nourish their deeply
held belief that they will never be poor because they work hard, keep their
kids in school, and make rational family planning decisions. ...

The New Right has played not only to racial fears and prejudice, but
also to the dream of intact families and the fantasy of women as moral
guardians. ...

A growing number of women now would prefer not to work, but feel
trapped by perceived economic circumstances. Social expectations about
women as domestic caretakers have not adjusted to the realities of working
women. Women are still expected to do the bulk of the child care, home
care, and nurturing, and they are often overwhelmed by the substantial
and conflicting demands on their time.

The New Right's ideology of division channels that dissatisfaction
toward welfare mothers: why should a woman who wants to be a homemaker have to work outside of the home and support through her tax

dollars the AFDC recipient who has the "luxury" of staying at home to raise her children? This sentiment has prompted behavioral modification proposals like ... Family Cap, which seek to punish and devalue the "nonproductive" mother for the ostensible reason that she at least should exercise some control ... and stop getting pregnant.

This attempt to use economic motivation to create changed behavior in AFDC mothers and children leads to "solutions" that are contrary to empirical evidence and thus cannot solve the problems for which they are ostensibly designed. "Welfare reform" programs such as ... Family Cap do not solve burgeoning social problems; they reflect only political expedience and culturally biased mythology.

NOTES AND QUESTIONS

1. Child exclusion provisions or "family caps" are only one of several welfare reform policies that have been advanced to reduce the number of children born to women receiving public assistance. The most benign is to make Norplant and other long-acting contraceptives available to poor women through Medicaid. Every state and Washington, D.C. cover the cost of Norplant insertion under their Medicaid programs. Legislators in some states have proposed offering a cash bonus to women on welfare for using Norplant. The most coercive proposal is to mandate Norplant insertion as a condition of receiving welfare benefits. *See* Roberts, *The Welfare Debate: Who Pays for Procreation?* in *Killing the Black Body*, at 202.

2. Is Judge Politan correct that the New Jersey family cap "merely imposes a ceiling on the benefits accorded an AFDC household?" Or does the provision deny the benefits increase on the basis of the mother's AFDC status? Note that the law only excludes children born or conceived while their families are on welfare; families get full benefits for children they already have when they join the welfare rolls. Does this distinction make a difference to the constitutionality of the law? Does the family cap constitute an undue burden on welfare mothers' choice to have a child? Do the abortion-funding cases support the constitutionality of family caps or are these two types of reproductive regulations distinguishable? *See* Susan Frelich Appleton, *Standards for Constitutional Review of Privacy–Invading Welfare Reforms: Distinguishing the Abortion–Funding Cases and Redeeming the Undue Burden Test*, 49 Vanderbilt L. Rev. 1 (1996).

3. Judge Politan also accepted the argument that family caps equalize the situations of poor families and working families "who provide for their children without any expectation of outside assistance." Do you agree? Is it true that working families receive no government subsidies? What is the basis for the government's obligation, if any, to provide financial assistance to families? On the other hand, do taxpayers have a right to decide whether or not their tax dollars should go to support the procreative decisions of poor women?

4. What role do you think race and class divisions play in the public's support for policies like family caps that regulate welfare mothers' sexuali-

ty and childbearing? Are you convinced by Lucy Williams's argument that these policies are fueled by race and class politics? If these policies apply to all welfare recipients, most of whom are not Black, what is the relevance of public devaluation of Black mothers? On the construction of maternal deviancy in poverty discourses, *see also* Martha A. Fineman, *The Neutered Mother, the Sexual Family and Other Twentieth Century Tragedies* 106 (1995).

IV. REPRODUCTION—ASSISTING TECHNOLOGIES

Isabel Marcus, Rhonda Copelon, Ruth Hubbard, Barbara Katz Rothman, Barbara Omolade, Looking Toward the Future: Feminism and Reproductive Technologies

37 Buf. L. Rev. 203 (1988–1989).

Isabel Marcus: We have arranged a program with a number of conversants so that you can hear different perspectives on an extremely complicated set of issues which demand careful, thoughtful consideration. Our goal is to explore the impact and implications of alternative reproductive technologies for feminism and for feminists. ...

Ruth Hubbard: I have been asked to explain the technologies that underlie the legal, political, and ethical issues that we will be talking about. ...The place to start, even if we are just going to look at the technical issues, is to ask how we got here. Why are we trying to invent new ways of producing babies and why are we developing techniques to assess the health of fetuses before they are born? To understand that, we have to acknowledge several things. One is the medicalization of life in general. We use health and sickness as metaphors: healthy means good, as in "healthy relationships," and sick means bad, as in "a sick society."

More significantly, we look for individualized medical and technical solutions to social problems. The inability to generate or conceive or gestate our own biological children could be tackled socially by expanding the concept of family—the people who are considered grandparents, parents, uncles, and so on. Instead, we insist on a narrow definition of family that doesn't reflect most people's experience. Family is one mother, one father, and one or more children. With present divorce and custody arrangements and single parent families, many and perhaps most children's families consist of a mother and her partner or partners and their children, a father and his partner or partners and children, and lots of grandparents. We also have precedents in adoption, and now in open adoption. Society's treatment of adoption is interesting in this regard because it has tried to become more open and tolerant of less conventional arrangements. But when it comes to the new reproductive technologies and arrangements, in which a child can have five potential parents—a sperm donor, an egg donor, the woman who gestates, and two social parents—we insist that only two of them can be real parents, and the others are ...? We don't know what to call them, but they are not parents. So that is a peculiar contradiction.

The other thing we need to think about carefully is the individualistic concept and language of rights which we have perpetuated in the civil rights and women's rights movements. Our legal structure forces us to talk about rights in individual terms, and so lays the groundwork for justifying some of the new reproductive technologies. It is this structure which leads to statements like: "Every couple (or every woman) has a right to have a child"; "Every couple (or woman) has a right to a healthy child"; and "Every child has a right to be born healthy," which by a peculiar sleight of hand gets transmuted into "A child that is not going to be healthy has no right to be born." So we suddenly have these rights to reproductive technologies, both technologies to help a fertile couple have children and technologies for the prenatal diagnosis of disabilities and diseases.

First, let's think about the new technologies for producing children. Presumably the reason for them is that men, women, or couples find they cannot generate or gestate children. Some say the rate of infertility among both men and women has been increasing, although there is disagreement about this, as well as about the proper criteria of infertility. In any case, about one couple in six cannot conceive a child within one year of regular, unprotected intercourse. This number is relatively evenly divided between couples in which the man cannot produce an adequate amount of sperm or sufficiently mobile sperm, the woman either cannot produce eggs or gestate embryos, or both partners have problems.

Why is infertility increasing, if it is? There are various social reasons, including pollution and workplace hazards such as chemicals and radiation. Lots of women work in technical capacities, in hospitals, as beauticians, and in jobs that have reproductive hazards associated with them. So do many men. Then there is what has been called the sexual revolution. Various forms of contraception, specifically female contraception such as the pill and other hormone contraceptives, can result in temporary or permanent infertility. The IUD can, and often does, lead to infection, which in turn can either prevent conception or impair the ability of the uterus to carry an implant. And sexually transmitted diseases which can cause sterility, such as gonorrhea, chlamydia, and ... pelvic inflammatory disease, have been increasing. We are also told that delayed childbearing plays a role. That is an ideologically loaded subject and there are differences of opinion on the extent to which this is correct. Obviously, if women delay childbearing beyond age forty or forty-five, there are going to be problems. But whether delayed childbearing beyond age thirty or thirty-five creates problems, that's more questionable. There are also social reasons, such as lesbian parenthood and gay parenthood, which lead some people to look to reproductive technologies to get an egg and sperm together.

There are four main technologies in use, two quite old and two new. The oldest is artificial insemination by donor, also called donor insemination by people who don't like the word artificial in there. Here the issues are mostly social and legal. While donor insemination is often performed in a medical setting, people can do it in the privacy of their own home. All that is required is that a man masturbate into a condom or some other container. His sperm is handed over to a woman who uses a turkey baster or a syringe to get the sperm close to her cervix. Then she waits to see whether it takes . . . . .

The second technology, which clearly is not very technological, is what has been called surrogate motherhood. . . . Basically, it involves donor insemination and the issues are economic and social and legal, having to do with pay to the woman and to the mediators and arrangers of this transaction, with the ability to contract, with custody issues, and so on. . . . [T]he two more complicated techniques [are]: *in vitro* fertilization and embryo flushing and transfer. I was very surprised about a year or year-and-a-half ago to have a legal expert in a panel such as this refer to *in vitro* as the simplest of all the procedures. He was, of course, speaking from a legal perspective. It is true that usually the donated egg is from the woman who expects to be the social mother and the donated sperm is from the man who expects to be the social father. Since we are talking about only one possible mother and father, we don't have to ask, "Who are the parents?" Beyond that simplicity, however, it is a technically complicated procedure, considerably more complex than the previous ones. Before the procedure, the woman who donates the egg has to undergo a host of tests. There is usually exploratory surgery to be sure the ovaries are accessible. She is routinely treated with hormones, so-called fertility drugs, to know the time at which the ovary is going to release the eggs and to stimulate it to produce more than one egg. Nowadays it is considered better to fertilize several eggs and transfer several embryos into the uterus at the same time to improve the chances that one will implant. The process of implantation is the weakest link in the *in vitro* sequence.

What you have to consider, then, is a whole set of preliminary procedures that screen the woman to find out whether she is even a reasonable candidate for *in vitro* and screen the man to see if he has enough sperm. These screenings are followed by exploratory surgery and chemical intervention, after which comes the surgical procedure, called laparoscopy, by which the eggs are removed from the ovary. It has to be done under anesthesia which carries its own risks. Once the eggs and sperm have been collected, fertilization occurs in a carefully developed bacteria-free medium, in a small glass dish at the appropriate temperature. . . . In *in vitro* fertilization the embryo is introduced into the uterus . . . around the six-or eight-cell stage. . . .

The fourth technology I mentioned is embryo flushing and transfer, which is used much less than *in vitro* fertilization. Embryo flushing is being developed entirely in private hands, for profit. It is a standard agricultural practice used for cattle and other farm animals. A few days after artificial insemination, the embryo is flushed out through the cervix. That embryo can be frozen and stored for later transfer, or transferred directly to the gestating cow. Or woman. The medical reasons for doing this with people would be, say, if a woman cannot produce eggs and perhaps does not have intact fallopian tubes but has an intact uterus, or she can produce eggs but cannot gestate an embryo. In either case, you can get donation of the embryo, that is, a transfer of the embryo from the woman who has eggs to the woman who can gestate. The point is that the gestating woman is different from the woman who provides the egg. The health risks have to do with the repeated lavage or flushing of the uterus to collect the embryo, which carries with it discomfort and the risk of infection. Since the embryo cannot always be flushed out, the woman who planned to donate her egg to a woman who was going to gestate the baby and be its social mother may find herself pregnant and then have to decide whether to carry the baby to term or have an abortion.

All four of these techniques are costly and, therefore, raise class and racial issues. Donor insemination is the cheapest, although its expense depends on whether one uses a medicalized form or does it privately.... Class and race bias is inevitable not only because of the expense, but because infertility rates are higher among poor people and especially among people of color because of reproductive hazards at work and because the incidence of disease, including venereal disease, is higher than among affluent people. The techniques are clearly being developed for middle and upper middle class people, for those who can pay. That is especially true in this country, the only industrialized country ... that does not have some form of national health insurance which pays for and monitors medical procedures....

Barbara Katz Rothman: ... I would like to look at the development of a range of technologies and put what is happening in the context of our ideology. ...Babies and children, or some babies and some children, are becoming increasingly precious, while motherhood is becoming increasingly less precious. Motherhood is becoming devalued or proletarianized. Biological motherhood, as well as social nurturing motherhood, is being seen as cheap labor. This is most obvious with the surrogate mother. Surrogacy entails the notion that one can rent a womb and can affix an arbitrary price tag on pregnancy, often $10,000. This price has stayed fixed for the past decade. While the cost of everything else has risen, the cost of surrogacy stays the same. This is as clear a case of devaluation as I've ever seen, spelled out in dollars and cents. ...

Not only are we devaluing motherhood in a very clear, economically measurable way, we are also looking at motherhood as a production process, as cheap labor, as work, and we are increasingly applying the standards of work to motherhood. ...Genetic counseling is serving the purpose of quality control, and wrongful life suits are a variety of product liability litigation. Motherhood is now seen as a work process, babies as a product, and we are beginning to see some quality control of the product. We are beginning to think of the baby as a purchasable and perfectable commodity. We are beginning to put different price tags on different products.

The pricing down of motherhood services goes along with the development of work standards. The notion arises that pregnant women have to adhere to certain work protocols, such as not drinking during pregnancy.... Mothers are increasingly not trusted. It has been a long time since anyone has trusted mothers, but the working philosophy used to be that mothers had their babies' best interests at heart.... Now the culture suggests that we don't necessarily want to take care of the babies, that we have to be watched because we really are selfish. Selfish is replacing selfless in the current ideology of motherhood in America.

Our society's approach to reproduction grows out of a patriarchal analysis that seeds are precious and the genetic tie between generations is a very important one. In this analysis, mothers are essentially fungible. You can plant the seeds here. You can plant the seeds there. It doesn't make a lot of difference. They grow a baby. From a woman's point of view, you could get pregnant with this man or you could get pregnant with that man. You still get a big belly. Your breasts still flow with milk. You will produce a baby. You may prefer one man's seed to another, but the essence of creating a baby is not going to be which seed gets planted. From the man's perspective, the only connection is the seed, that genetic tie, not where it is planted. From this patriarchal perspective, the crucial consideration is control of the environment. So now we can make substitutions in the environment for the seed. We can finish the last few months of pregnancy in an incubator or even in a dead mother. We can substitute a glass dish for the nurturing environment of a womb because we don't need the mother. What we have to do is take this seed and gestate it somehow, somewhere, so this particular seed—not that one or that one—so this particular, precious seed, grows into a baby. . . .

Barbara Omolade: In my analysis of the current urgency around mechanical and artificial reproduction, three concepts underlie the social implications of the new reproductive technologies: (1) the continuation and expansion of the racial patriarchy in the United States; (2) the universal urgency to reproduce biologically; and (3) the technological discrepancy between the social and biological reproduction of white people and people of color with its attendant allocation of resources for different groups.

All the issues around reproduction are tied in with power, and with how powerful men function and organize our society. White women and women of color each occupy a separate but interconnected place in the social hierarchy. They are usually unaware of the comprehensive organization of social control. One week, Mary Beth Whitehead is described as not being a capable mother, in part because she demanded to mother the child she was hired to birth. The next week, teenage mothers, especially black teenage mothers, are characterized as inept, incapable, and confused, in part because they demand to have children although they are young. In spite of differences between the experiences of these white and black mothers, both are attacked in the media as unfit. This attack is part of a general attack on motherhood which has been going on since the beginning of the country.

The first concept is the development of the racial patriarchy: a group of men who use racism and racial violence to control men and women of color, and to usurp the traditional patriarchal relationships between men and women. During the earliest stages of United States history, a numerical minority of white European men took political and economic control using military power. They were surrounded by nations of Native Americans, indentured white labor, and African slave labor. The racial patriarchs established a social order in which everyone had a carefully prescribed place: Africans were to become perpetual bonded cheap manual labor; whites were to be semi-free labor (wage earners, independent farmers, and merchants); and Native Americans were to be annihilated. That social order has been held in place by a combination of ideology, social law, and economic control.

The social order that racial patriarchs established has always contained a sexual and sexist component centered around the control of all women's sexuality and reproduction. The first laws of the country were organized around the children of indentured and slave mothers. A 1662 Virginia statute stipulated that "all offspring follow the condition of the mother in the event of a white man getting a Negro with child." The child of a slave mother would be a slave, irrespective of its father. The traditional patriarchal relationship between men and women was broken.

Usually the patriarch in a society is the father, husband, brother, or son of a woman. These men protect, take care of, subjugate, and dominate women, but these are also men with whom women have a primary emotional, biological, and social attachment. The racial patriarchy fosters another set of agendas, especially for women of color. The racial patriarchy has no primary relationship with women of color and, therefore, no interest in protecting women of color. It has only an interest in exploiting these women and their men. On the other hand, the white women of the racial patriarch are held in place by both traditional patriarchal power and by the seeming invincibility of men who exercise control over other men.

The earliest examples of manipulating women's reproductive capacities began in this country over two hundred years ago with slave mothering. What happened to the fetus and infant of a slave mother? Who owned it? If the mother claimed the child because she loved it, that claim was invalid because the child wouldn't be profitable to the racial patriarch who owned it. If a black man fathered the child, he couldn't claim patriarchal protection for that child or his woman because he had little patriarchal power of his own.

With the advent of technologies which can control and manage biological reproduction, the racial patriarchy is able to extend and expand its power over women. The technologies are an expansion of its direct control over white middle and lower class women's reproductive choices, with ominous implications for all women. Women may say, "I want to be a surrogate mother, because I love children and I want to help these infertile couples," but they do not see themselves caught in a more comprehensive plan.

The second aspect of my analysis is the universal urgency to reproduce. All peoples have a racial urgency to reproduce themselves. Every patriarch wants to reproduce the son. Every woman in every culture gets messages to become a mother and thereby support the desires of the patriarch to reproduce. All cultures have tremendous penalties for women who cannot mother. To be a woman is to mother. In most societies, women who can't have children are penalized and stigmatized. Women who are feminist still desire to mother, and feel lack and loss when they haven't become mothers.

Ironically, black women are stigmatized by the racial patriarchy because they have too many babies. But their own men want them to have their children—particularly their sons. There is a conflicting message to women of color. The racial patriarchy gives them one message and through social policies actively prevents women of color from taking care of their children properly. Our men say: "Reproduce babies for the nation."

The urgency to reproduce is intense and often irrational because it is based solely on biological parenting. The social aspects of parenting are often ignored. Adoption, a means of becoming social parents, is viewed as a last resort of the desperate, rather than a socially acceptable expansion of parenting.

The current urgency of the racial patriarch to reproduce is connected to demographics and power. The birth rate of white people is declining compared to the birth rates of people of color. White people are a racial minority. Only a minority of that minority controls the world's resources. ... The racial patriarchs of today fear that there will not be enough white males to whom they can pass the reins of power. The reproductive choices of white women are critical to the biological reproduction of the racial patriarch. Thus, the women's movement, with its emphasis upon reproductive choice and sexual freedom, threatens the very existence of the racial patriarchy and white people. The universal racial urgency to reproduce has been reinforced by the racial patriarchs' desire to control white women's reproductive freedom and choices.

In addition to demographics undermining the international power of white male rule, the women's movement and the civil rights movement began to seriously challenge that power in this country about twenty years ago. Underlying the social and political agendas of these movements were demands for increased domestic spending for housing, childcare, education, and health care, including abortion and prenatal care. Since the rise of conservatism, the agenda has been pushed back, stifled and contained, and replaced in part by an ideological and now biological drive to increase the numbers of traditional nuclear white middle class families, thereby enhancing the mass base of white male power.

The third concept I use in my analysis of reproductive technologies is the conflict between biological reproduction and social reproduction. The racial patriarch has placed biological reproduction at the top of the list and, of course, that biological reproduction is of healthy white children. At the same time, social reproduction of black and other children of color is placed at the very bottom of the list. This is a source of tremendous conflict. Resources are here, but children are starving over there, literally malnourished. The research findings on prenatal care for black women in Harlem are astounding. The prenatal death rates are comparable with those of an undeveloped country. Yet, Harlem and other communities exist in the middle of a highly developed country where scientific knowledge can be used to do anything in the lab, where the capacity to reproduce is daily being expanded. We have an imbalance which leads to fundamental conflicts about the direction of our society, especially the application of our scientific knowledge and technology. The imbalance is linked to the increased underdevelopment of people of color. Part of the increasing rate of unemployment of Hispanic and black men is due to a shift from production to service jobs. Poor single mothers cannot adequately care for their children because they lack adequate resources. Poverty and unemployment among men and women of color are directly related to social and political policies which undermine the development of the black working class. However, the underdevelopment of the black working class is tied directly to the reproduction and development of the white middle class through reproductive technologies. . . .

In the Matter of Baby M

Supreme Court of New Jersey, 1988.
109 N.J. 396, 537 A.2d 1227.

ROBERT N. WILENTZ, C.J.

In this matter the Court is asked to determine the validity of a contract that purports to provide a new way of bringing children into a family. For a fee of $10,000, a woman agrees to be artificially inseminated with the semen of another woman's husband; she is to conceive a child, carry it to term, and after its birth surrender it to the natural father and his wife. The intent of the contract is that the child's natural mother will thereafter be forever separated from her child. The wife is to adopt the child, and she and the natural father are to be regarded as its parents for all purposes. The contract providing for this is called a "surrogacy contract," the natural mother inappropriately called the "surrogate mother."

We invalidate the surrogacy contract because it conflicts with the law and public policy of this State. While we recognize the depth of the yearning of infertile couples to have their own children, we find the payment of money to a "surrogate" mother illegal, perhaps criminal, and potentially degrading to women. Although in this case we grant custody to the natural father, the evidence having clearly proved such custody to be in the best interests of the infant, we void both the termination of the surrogate mother's parental rights and the adoption of the child by the wife/stepparent. We thus restore the "surrogate" as the mother of the child. We remand the issue of the natural mother's visitation rights to the trial court, since that issue was not reached below and the record before us is not sufficient to permit us to decide it *de novo*.

We find no offense to our present laws where a woman voluntarily and without payment agrees to act as a "surrogate" mother, provided that she is not subject to a binding agreement to surrender her child. Moreover, our holding today does not preclude the Legislature from altering the current statutory scheme, within constitutional limits, so as to permit surrogacy contracts. Under current law, however, the surrogacy agreement before us is illegal and invalid. . . .

In February 1985, William Stern and Mary Beth Whitehead entered into a surrogacy contract. It recited that Stern's wife, Elizabeth, was infertile, that they wanted a child, and that Mrs. Whitehead was willing to provide that child as the mother with Mr. Stern as the father.

The contract provided that through artificial insemination using Mr. Stern's sperm, Mrs. Whitehead would become pregnant, carry the child to term, bear it, deliver it to the Sterns, and thereafter do whatever was necessary to terminate her maternal rights so that Mrs. Stern could thereafter adopt the child. Mrs. Whitehead's husband, Richard, was also a party to the contract; Mrs. Stern was not. Mr. Whitehead promised to do all acts necessary to rebut the presumption of paternity under the Parentage Act. Although Mrs. Stern was not a party to the surrogacy agreement, the contract gave her sole custody of the child in the event of Mr. Stern's death. Mrs. Stern's status as a nonparty to the surrogate parenting agreement presumably was to avoid the application of the baby-selling statute to this arrangement.

Mr. Stern, on his part, agreed to attempt the artificial insemination and to pay Mrs. Whitehead $10,000 after the child's birth, on its delivery to him. In a separate contract, Mr. Stern agreed to pay $7,500 to the Infertility Center of New York ("ICNY"). The Center's advertising campaigns solicit surrogate mothers and encourage infertile couples to consider surrogacy. ICNY arranged for the surrogacy contract by bringing the parties together, explaining the process to them, furnishing the contractual form, and providing legal counsel.

The history of the parties' involvement in this arrangement suggests their good faith. William and Elizabeth Stern were married in July 1974, having met at the University of Michigan, where both were Ph.D candidates. Due to financial considerations and Mrs. Stern's pursuit of a medical degree and residency, they decided to defer starting a family until 1981. Before then, however, Mrs. Stern learned that she might have multiple sclerosis and that the disease in some cases renders pregnancy a serious health risk. Her anxiety appears to have exceeded the actual risk, which current medical authorities assess as minimal. Nonetheless that anxiety was evidently quite real, Mrs. Stern fearing that pregnancy might precipitate blindness, paraplegia, or other forms of debilitation. Based on the perceived risk, the Sterns decided to forgo having their own children. The decision had a special significance for Mr. Stern. Most of his family had been destroyed in the Holocaust. As the family's only survivor, he very much wanted to continue his bloodline.

Initially the Sterns considered adoption, but were discouraged by the substantial delay apparently involved and by the potential problem they saw arising from their age and their differing religious backgrounds. They were most eager for some other means to start a family.

The paths of Mrs. Whitehead and the Sterns to surrogacy were similar. Both responded to advertising by ICNY. The Sterns' response, following their inquiries into adoption, was the result of their long-standing decision to have a child. Mrs. Whitehead's response apparently resulted from her sympathy with family members and others who could have no children (she stated that she wanted to give another couple the "gift of life"); she also wanted the $10,000 to help her family. . . .

The two couples met to discuss the surrogacy arrangement and decided to go forward. On February 6, 1985, Mr. Stern and Mr. and Mrs. Whitehead executed the surrogate parenting agreement. After several artificial inseminations over a period of months, Mrs. Whitehead became pregnant. The pregnancy was uneventful and on March 27, 1986, Baby M was born.

Mrs. Whitehead realized, almost from the moment of birth, that she could not part with this child. She had felt a bond with it even during pregnancy. Some indication of the attachment was conveyed to the Sterns at the hospital when they told Mrs. Whitehead what they were going to name the baby. She apparently broke into tears and indicated that she did not know if she could give up the child. She talked about how the baby looked like her daughter, and made it clear that she was experiencing great difficulty with the decision.

Nonetheless, Mrs. Whitehead was, for the moment, true to her word. Despite powerful inclinations to the contrary, she turned her child over to the Sterns on March 30 at the Whiteheads' home.

Later in the evening of March 30, Mrs. Whitehead became deeply disturbed, disconsolate, stricken with unbearable sadness. She had to have her child. She could not eat, sleep, or concentrate on anything other than her need for her baby. The next day she went to the Sterns' home and told them how much she was suffering.

The depth of Mrs. Whitehead's despair surprised and frightened the Sterns. She told them that she could not live without her baby, that she must have her, even if only for one week, that thereafter she would surrender her child. The Sterns, concerned that Mrs. Whitehead might indeed commit suicide, not wanting under any circumstances to risk that, and in any event believing that Mrs. Whitehead would keep her word, turned the child over to her. It was not until four months later, after a series of attempts to regain possession of the child, that Melissa was returned to the Sterns, having been forcibly removed from the home where she was then living with Mr. and Mrs. Whitehead, the home in Florida owned by Mary Beth Whitehead's parents.

The Sterns' complaint, in addition to seeking possession and ultimately custody of the child, sought enforcement of the surrogacy contract. . . . [The trial court] held that the surrogacy contract was valid; ordered that Mrs. Whitehead's parental rights be terminated and the sole custody of the child be granted to Mr. Stern; and, after hearing brief testimony from Mrs.

Stern, immediately entered an order allowing the adoption of Melissa by Mrs. Stern, all in accordance with the surrogacy contract. Pending the outcome of the appeal, we granted a continuation of visitation to Mrs. Whitehead, although slightly more limited than the visitation allowed during the trial. . . .

We have concluded that this surrogacy contract is invalid. Our conclusion has two bases: direct conflict with existing statutes and conflict with the public policies of this State, as expressed in its statutory and decisional law.

One of the surrogacy contract's basic purposes, to achieve the adoption of a child through private placement, though permitted in New Jersey "is very much disfavored." Its use of money for this purpose—and we have no doubt whatsoever that the money is being paid to obtain an adoption and not, as the Sterns argue, for the personal services of Mary Beth Whitehead—is illegal and perhaps criminal. In addition to the inducement of money, there is the coercion of contract: the natural mother's irrevocable agreement, prior to birth, even prior to conception, to surrender the child to the adoptive couple. Such an agreement is totally unenforceable in private placement adoption. Even where the adoption is through an approved agency, the formal agreement to surrender occurs only *after* birth . . ., and then, by regulation, only after the birth mother has been counseled. Integral to these invalid provisions of the surrogacy contract is the related agreement, equally invalid, on the part of the natural mother to cooperate with, and not to contest, proceedings to terminate her parental rights, as well as her contractual concession, in aid of the adoption, that the child's best interests would be served by awarding custody to the natural father and his wife—all of this before she has even conceived, and, in some cases, before she has the slightest idea of what the natural father and adoptive mother are like.

The foregoing provisions not only directly conflict with New Jersey statutes, but also offend long-established State policies. These critical terms, which are at the heart of the contract, are invalid and unenforceable; the conclusion therefore follows, without more, that the entire contract is unenforceable. . . .

The surrogacy contract conflicts with: (1) laws prohibiting the use of money in connection with adoptions; (2) laws requiring proof of parental unfitness or abandonment before termination of parental rights is ordered or an adoption is granted; and (3) laws that make surrender of custody and consent to adoption revocable in private placement adoptions.

Our law prohibits paying or accepting money in connection with any placement of a child for adoption. Violation is a high misdemeanor. Excepted are fees of an approved agency (which must be a non-profit entity) and certain expenses in connection with childbirth.

Considerable care was taken in this case to structure the surrogacy arrangement so as not to violate this prohibition. . . . Nevertheless, it seems clear that the money was paid and accepted in connection with an adoption.

...The surrogacy agreement requires Mrs. Whitehead to surrender Baby M for the purposes of adoption. ...The payment of the $10,000 occurs only on surrender of custody of the child and "completion of the duties and obligations" of Mrs. Whitehead, including termination of her parental rights to facilitate adoption by Mrs. Stern. As for the contention that the Sterns are paying only for services and not for an adoption, we need note only that they would pay nothing in the event the child died before the fourth month of pregnancy, and only $1,000 if the child were stillborn, even though the "services" had been fully rendered. Additionally, one of Mrs. Whitehead's estimated costs, to be assumed by Mr. Stern, was an "Adoption Fee," presumably for Mrs. Whitehead's incidental costs in connection with the adoption.

Mr. Stern knew he was paying for the adoption of a child; Mrs. Whitehead knew she was accepting money so that a child might be adopted; the Infertility Center knew that it was being paid for assisting in the adoption of a child. The actions of all three worked to frustrate the goals of the statute. It strains credulity to claim that these arrangements, touted by those in the surrogacy business as an attractive alternative to the usual route leading to an adoption, really amount to something other than a private placement adoption for money. ...

The termination of Mrs. Whitehead's parental rights, called for by the surrogacy contract and actually ordered by the court, fails to comply with the stringent requirements of New Jersey law. Our law, recognizing the finality of any termination of parental rights, provides for such termination only where there has been a voluntary surrender of a child to an approved agency or to the Division of Youth and Family Services ("DYFS"), accompanied by a formal document acknowledging termination of parental rights, or where there has been a showing of parental abandonment or unfitness. ...

In this case a termination of parental rights was obtained not by proving the statutory prerequisites but by claiming the benefit of contractual provisions. From all that has been stated above, it is clear that a contractual agreement to abandon one's parental rights, or not to contest a termination action, will not be enforced in our courts. The Legislature would not have so carefully, so consistently, and so substantially restricted termination of parental rights if it had intended to allow termination to be achieved by one short sentence in a contract.

Since the termination was invalid, it follows, as noted above, that adoption of Melissa by Mrs. Stern could not properly be granted.

The provision in the surrogacy contract stating that Mary Beth Whitehead agrees to "surrender custody ... and terminate all parental rights" contains no clause giving her a right to rescind. ...Such a provision, however, making irrevocable the natural mother's consent to surrender custody of her child in a private placement adoption, clearly conflicts with New Jersey law. ...

These strict prerequisites to irrevocability constitute a recognition of the most serious consequences that flow from such consents: termination of parental rights, the permanent separation of parent from child, and the ultimate adoption of the child. Because of those consequences, the Legislature severely limited the circumstances under which such consent would be irrevocable. The legislative goal is furthered by regulations requiring approved agencies, prior to accepting irrevocable consents, to provide advice and counseling to women, making it more likely that they fully understand and appreciate the consequences of their acts. . . .

Under the contract, the natural mother is irrevocably committed before she knows the strength of her bond with her child. She never makes a totally voluntary, informed decision, for quite clearly any decision prior to the baby's birth is, in the most important sense, uninformed, and any decision after that, compelled by a preexisting contractual commitment, the threat of a lawsuit, and the inducement of a $10,000 payment is less than totally voluntary. . . .

Worst of all, however, is the contract's total disregard of the best interests of the child. There is not the slightest suggestion that any inquiry will be made at any time to determine the fitness of the Sterns as custodial parents, or Mrs. Stern as an adoptive parent, their superiority to Mrs. Whitehead, or the effect on the child of not living with her natural mother.

This is the sale of a child, or, at the very least, the sale of a mother's right to her child, the only mitigating factor being that one of the purchasers is the father. Almost every evil that prompted the prohibition of the payment of money in connection with adoptions exists here.

The differences between an adoption and a surrogacy contract should be noted, since it is asserted that the use of money in connection with surrogacy does not pose the risks found where money buys an adoption. . . . First, and perhaps most important, all parties concede that it is unlikely that surrogacy will survive without money. Despite the alleged selfless motivation of surrogate mothers, if there is no payment, there will be no surrogates, or very few. . . . Second, the use of money in adoptions does not *produce* the problem—conception occurs, and usually the birth itself, before illicit funds are offered. With surrogacy, the "problem," if one views it as such, consisting of the purchase of a woman's procreative capacity, at the risk of her life, is caused by and originates with the offer of money. . . .

The main difference, that the plight of the unwanted pregnancy is unintended while the situation of the surrogate mother is voluntary and intended, is really not significant. Initially, it produces stronger reactions of sympathy for the mother whose pregnancy was unwanted than for the surrogate mother, who "went into this with her eyes wide open." On reflection, however, it appears that the essential evil is the same, taking advantage of a woman's circumstances (the unwanted pregnancy or the need for money) in order to take away her child, the difference being one of degree. . . .

The point is made that Mrs. Whitehead *agreed* to the surrogacy arrangement, supposedly fully understanding the consequences. Putting aside the issue of how compelling her need for money may have been, and how significant her understanding of the consequences, we suggest that her consent is irrelevant. There are, in a civilized society, some things that money cannot buy. In America, we decided long ago that merely because conduct purchased by money was "voluntary" did not mean that it was good or beyond regulation and prohibition. Employers can no longer buy labor at the lowest price they can bargain for, even though that labor is "voluntary," or buy women's labor for less money than paid to men for the same job, or purchase the agreement of children to perform oppressive labor, or purchase the agreement of workers to subject themselves to unsafe or unhealthful working conditions. There are, in short, values that society deems more important than granting to wealth whatever it can buy, be it labor, love, or life. Whether this principle recommends prohibition of surrogacy, which presumably sometimes results in great satisfaction to all of the parties, is not for us to say. We note here only that, under existing law, the fact that Mrs. Whitehead "agreed" to the arrangement is not dispositive.

The long-term effects of surrogacy contracts are not known, but feared—the impact on the child who learns her life was bought, that she is the offspring of someone who gave birth to her only to obtain money; the impact on the natural mother as the full weight of her isolation is felt along with the full reality of the sale of her body and her child; the impact on the natural father and adoptive mother once they realize the consequences of their conduct. . . .

The surrogacy contract creates, it is based upon, principles that are directly contrary to the objectives of our laws. It guarantees the separation of a child from its mother; it looks to adoption regardless of suitability; it totally ignores the child; it takes the child from the mother regardless of her wishes and her maternal fitness; and it does all of this, it accomplishes all of its goals, through the use of money.

Beyond that is the potential degradation of some women that may result from this arrangement. In many cases, of course, surrogacy may bring satisfaction, not only to the infertile couple, but to the surrogate mother herself. The fact, however, that many women may not perceive surrogacy negatively but rather see it as an opportunity does not diminish its potential for devastation to other women.

In sum, the harmful consequences of this surrogacy arrangement appear to us all too palpable. In New Jersey the surrogate mother's agreement to sell her child is void. Its irrevocability infects the entire contract, as does the money that purports to buy it. . . .

Nothing in this record justifies a finding that would allow a court to terminate Mary Beth Whitehead's parental rights under the statutory standard. It is not simply that obviously there was no "intentional abandonment or very substantial neglect of parental duties without a reasonable expectation of reversal of that conduct in the future," quite the contrary, but furthermore that the trial court never found Mrs. Whitehead an unfit mother and indeed affirmatively stated that Mary Beth Whitehead had been a good mother to her other children.

Although the best interests of the child is dispositive of the custody issue in a dispute between natural parents, it does not govern the question of termination. . . . The parent's rights, both constitutional and statutory, have their own independent vitality. . . . We therefore conclude that the natural mother is entitled to retain her rights as a mother. . . .

Both parties argue that the Constitutions—state and federal—mandate approval of their basic claims. . . . The right asserted by the Sterns is the right of procreation; that asserted by Mary Beth Whitehead is the right to the companionship of her child. We find that the right of procreation does not extend as far as claimed by the Sterns. As for the right asserted by Mrs. Whitehead, since we uphold it on other grounds (i.e., we have restored her as mother and recognized her right, limited by the child's best interests, to her companionship), we need not decide that constitutional issue. . . .

The right to procreate very simply is the right to have natural children, whether through sexual intercourse or artificial insemination. It is no more than that. Mr. Stern has not been deprived of that right. Through artificial insemination of Mrs. Whitehead, Baby M is his child. The custody, care, companionship, and nurturing that follow birth are not parts of the right to procreation; they are rights that may also be constitutionally protected, but that involve many considerations other than the right of procreation. To assert that Mr. Stern's right of procreation gives him the right to the custody of Baby M would be to assert that Mrs. Whitehead's right of procreation does *not* give her the right to the custody of Baby M; it would be to assert that the constitutional right of procreation includes within it a constitutionally protected contractual right to destroy someone else's right of procreation. . . . There is nothing in our culture or society that even begins to suggest a fundamental right on the part of the father to the custody of the child as part of his right to procreate when opposed by the claim of the mother to the same child. . . .

Mr. Stern also contends that he has been denied equal protection of the laws by the State's statute granting full parental rights to a husband in relation to the child produced, with his consent, by the union of his wife with a sperm donor. The claim really is that of Mrs. Stern. It is that she is in precisely the same position as the husband in the statute: she is presumably infertile, as is the husband in the statute; her spouse by agreement with a third party procreates with the understanding that the child will be the couple's child. The alleged unequal protection is that the understanding is honored in the statute when the husband is the infertile party, but no similar understanding is honored when it is the wife who is infertile.

It is quite obvious that the situations are not parallel. A sperm donor simply cannot be equated with a surrogate mother. The State has more than a sufficient basis to distinguish the two situations—even if the only difference is between the time it takes to provide sperm for artificial insemination and the time invested in a nine-month pregnancy—so as to justify automatically divesting the sperm donor of his parental rights without automatically divesting a surrogate mother.

... Having decided that the surrogacy contract is illegal and unenforceable, we now must decide the custody question without regard to the provisions of the surrogacy contract that would give Mr. Stern sole and permanent custody. ...The applicable rule given these circumstances is clear: the child's best interests determine custody. ...There were eleven experts who testified concerning the child's best interests, either directly or in connection with pattern related to that issue. Our reading of the record persuades us that the trial court's decision awarding custody to the Sterns (technically to Mr. Stern) should be affirmed. ...Our custody conclusion is based on strongly persuasive testimony contrasting both the family life of the Whiteheads and the Sterns and the personalities and characters of the individuals. ...

Mrs. Whitehead is entitled to visitation at some point. ...The trial court will determine what kind of visitation shall be granted to her, with or without conditions, and when and under what circumstances it should commence. ...

This case affords some insight into a new reproductive arrangement: the artificial insemination of a surrogate mother. The unfortunate events that have unfolded illustrate that its unregulated use can bring suffering to all involved. Potential victims include the surrogate mother and her family, the natural father and his wife, and most importantly, the child. Although surrogacy has apparently provided positive results for some infertile couples, it can also, as this case demonstrates, cause suffering to participants, here essentially innocent and well-intended. ...

Johnson v. Calvert

Supreme Court of California, 1993.
5 Cal.4th 84, 19 Cal.Rptr.2d 494, 851 P.2d 776.

EDWARD PANELLI, J.

[On January 15, 1990, Anna Johnson entered a surrogacy agreement with Crispina and Mark Calvert, a married couple who desired to have a child. An embryo formed through *in vitro* fertilization using Crispina Calvert's ova and Mark Calvert's sperm was implanted in Johnson, who became pregnant and gave birth to the child on September 19, 1990. When Johnson notified the Calverts in July 1990 that she would refuse to relinquish her parental rights to the child, the Calverts sought a declaration that they were the legal parents of the unborn child. Johnson then filed an action to be declared the mother of the child, and the two cases were eventually consolidated.]

Because two women each have presented acceptable proof of maternity, we do not believe this case can be decided without inquiring into the parties' intentions as manifested in the surrogacy agreement. Mark and

Crispina are a couple who desired to have a child of their own genes but are physically unable to do so without the help of reproductive technology. They affirmatively intended the birth of the child, and took the steps necessary to effect in vitro fertilization. But for their acted-on intention, the child would not exist. Anna agreed to facilitate the procreation of Mark's and Crispina's child. The parties' aim was to bring Mark's and Crispina's child into the world, not for Mark and Crispina to donate a zygote to Anna. Crispina from the outset intended to be the child's mother. Although the gestative function Anna performed was necessary to bring about the child's birth, it is safe to say that Anna would not have been given the opportunity to gestate or deliver the child had she, prior to implantation of the zygote, manifested her own intent to be the child's mother. No reason appears why Anna's later change of heart should vitiate the determination that Crispina is the child's natural mother.

We conclude that although the [Uniform Parentage] Act recognizes both genetic consanguinity and giving birth as means of establishing a mother and child relationship, when the two means do not coincide in one woman, she who intended to procreate the child-that is, she who intended to bring about the birth of a child that she intended to raise as her own-is the natural mother under California law.

Our conclusion finds support in writings of several legal commentators. See Hill, *What Does It Mean to Be a "Parent"? The Claims of Biology as the Basis for Parental Rights*, 66 N.Y.U.L. Rev. 353; Schultz, *Reproductive Technology and Intent–Based Parenthood: An Opportunity for Gender Neutrality* Wis. L. Rev. 297 (1990); Note, *Redefining Mother: A Legal Matrix for New Reproductive Technologies* 96 Yale L.J. 187, 197–202 (1986). Professor Hill, arguing that the genetic relationship per se should not be accorded priority in the determination of the parent-child relationship in the surrogacy context, notes that "while all of the players in the procreative arrangement are necessary in bringing a child into the world, the child would not have been born but for the efforts of the intended parents. . . .[T]he intended parents are the first cause, or the prime movers, of the procreative relationship."

Similarly, Professor Shultz observes that recent developments in the field of reproductive technology "dramatically extend affirmative intentionality. . . .Steps can be taken to bring into being a child who would not otherwise have existed." "Within the context of artificial reproductive techniques," Professor Shultz argues, "intentions that are voluntarily chosen, deliberate, express and bargained-for ought presumptively to determine legal parenthood."

In deciding the issue of maternity under the Act we have felt free to take into account the parties' intentions, as expressed in the surrogacy contract, because in our view the agreement is not, on its face, inconsistent with public policy.

We are unpersuaded that gestational surrogacy arrangements are so likely to cause the untoward results Anna cites as to demand their invalidation on public policy grounds. Although common sense suggests that women of lesser means serve as surrogate mothers more often than do wealthy women, there has been no proof that surrogacy contracts exploit poor women to any greater degree than economic necessity in general exploits them by inducing them to accept lower-paid or otherwise undesirable employment. We are likewise unpersuaded by the claim that surrogacy will foster the attitude that children are mere commodities; no evidence is offered to support it. The limited data available seem to reflect an absence of significant adverse effects of surrogacy on all participants.

The argument that a woman cannot knowingly and intelligently agree to gestate and deliver a baby for intending parents carries overtones of the reasoning that for centuries prevented women from attaining equal economic rights and professional status under the law. To resurrect this view is both to foreclose a personal and economic choice on the part of the surrogate mother, and to deny intending parents what may be their only means of procreating a child of their own genes. Certainly in the present case it cannot seriously be argued that Anna, a licensed vocational nurse who had done well in school and who had previously borne a child, lacked the intellectual wherewithal or life experience necessary to make an informed decision to enter into the surrogacy contract.

Moreover, if we were to conclude that Anna enjoys some sort of liberty interest in the companionship of the child, then the liberty interests of Mark and Crispina, the child's natural parents, in their procreative choices and their relationship with the child would perforce be infringed. Any parental rights Anna might successfully assert could come only at Crispina's expense. As we have seen, Anna has no parental rights to the child under California law, and she fails to persuade us that sufficiently strong policy reasons exist to accord her a protected liberty interest in the companionship of the child when such an interest would necessarily detract from or impair the parental bond enjoyed by Mark and Crispina.

JOYCE KENNARD, J.,

Dissenting.

When a woman who wants to have a child provides her fertilized ovum to another woman who carries it through pregnancy and gives birth to a child, who is the child's legal mother? Unlike the majority, I do not agree that the determinative consideration should be the intent to have the child that originated with the woman who contributed the ovum. In my view, the woman who provided the fertilized ovum and the woman who gave birth to the child both have substantial claims to legal motherhood. Pregnancy entails a unique commitment, both psychological and emotional, to an unborn child. No less substantial, however, is the contribution of the woman from whose egg the child developed and without whose desire the child would not exist.

First, in making the intent of the genetic mother who wants to have a child the dispositive factor, the majority renders a certain result preordained and inflexible in every such case: as between an intending genetic mother and a gestational mother, the genetic mother will, under the majority's analysis, always prevail. The majority recognizes no meaningful contribution by a woman who agrees to carry a fetus to term for the genetic mother beyond that of mere employment to perform a specified biological function.

The majority's approach entirely devalues the substantial claims of motherhood by a gestational mother such as Anna. True, a woman who enters into a surrogacy arrangement intending to raise the child has by her intent manifested an assumption of parental responsibility in addition to her biological contribution of providing the genetic material. But the gestational mother's biological contribution of carrying a child for nine months and giving birth is likewise an assumption of parental responsibility. A pregnant woman's commitment to the unborn child she carries is not just physical; it is psychological and emotional as well. The United States Supreme Court made a closely related point in *Lehr v. Robertson*, explaining that a father's assertion of parental rights depended on his having assumed responsibility for the child after its birth, whereas a mother's "parental relationship is clear" because she "carries and bears the child." This court too has acknowledged that a pregnant woman and her unborn child comprise a "unique physical unit" and that the welfare of each is "intertwined and inseparable." Indeed, a fetus would never develop into a living child absent its nurturing by the pregnant woman. A pregnant woman intending to bring a child into the world is more than a mere container or breeding animal; she is a conscious agent of creation no less than the genetic mother, and her humanity is implicated on a deep level. Her role should not be devalued.

To summarize, the woman who carried the fetus to term and brought a child into the world has, like the genetic mother, a substantial claim to be the natural mother of the child. The gestational mother has made an indispensable and unique biological contribution, and has also gone beyond biology in an intangible respect that, though difficult to label, cannot be denied. Accordingly, I cannot agree with the majority's devaluation of the role of the gestational mother.

Debra Satz, Markets in Women's Reproductive Labor

21 Phil. & Pub. Aff. 107 (1992).

Much of the evolution of social policy in the twentieth century has occurred around conflicts over the scope of markets. To what extent, under what conditions, and for what reasons should we limit the use of markets? Recently, American society has begun to experiment with markets in women's reproductive labor. Many people believe that markets in women's reproductive labor, as exemplified by contract pregnancy, are more problematic than other currently accepted labor markets. I will call this the asymmetry thesis because its proponents believe that there ought to be an asymmetry between our treatment of reproductive labor and our treatment of other forms of labor. Advocates of the asymmetry thesis hold that treating reproductive labor as a commodity, as something subject to the supply-and-demand principles that govern economic markets, is worse than treating other types of human labor as commodities. Is the asymmetry thesis true? And, if so, what are the reasons for thinking it is true?

My aims in this article are to criticize several popular ways of defending the asymmetry thesis and to offer an alternative defense. Other foundations for an arguments against contract pregnancy are, of course, possible. For example, several of the arguments that I examine in this article have sometimes been raised in the context of more general anti-commodification arguments. I do not examine such general arguments here. Instead, I focus my discussion on those arguments against contract pregnancy that *depend* on the asymmetry thesis. I believe that the asymmetry thesis both captures strong intuitions that exist in our society and provides a plausible argument against contract pregnancy.

Many feminists hold that the asymmetry thesis is true because women's reproductive labor is a special kind of labor that should not be treated according to market norms. They draw a sharp dividing line between women's reproductive labor and human labor in general: while human labor may be bought and sold, women's reproductive labor is intrinsically not a commodity. According to these views, contract pregnancy allows for the extension of the market into the "private" sphere of sexuality and reproduction. This intrusion of the economic into the personal is seen as improper: it fails to respect the intrinsic, special nature of reproductive labor. As one writer has put it, "When women's labor is treated as a commodity, the women who perform it are degraded."

Below, I argue that this is the wrong way to defend the asymmetry thesis. While I agree with the intuition that markets in women's reproductive labor are more troubling than other labor markets, in this article I develop an alternative account of why this should be so....

THE SPECIAL BONDS OF MOTHERHOOD

Sometimes what critics of pregnancy contracts have in mind is not the effect of such contracts on the relationship between reproductive labor and a woman's sense of self or her dignity, but its effect on her views (and ours) of the mother-fetus and mother-child bond. On this view, what is wrong with commodifying reproductive labor is that by relying on a mistaken picture of the nature of these relationships, it degrades them. Further, it leads to a view of children as fungible objects. In part 1 of this section I examine arguments against contract pregnancy based on its portrayal of the mother-fetus bond; in part 2 I examine arguments based on contract pregnancy's portrayal of the mother-child bond.

Mothers and Fetuses

Some critics of contract pregnancy contend that the relationship between a mother and a fetus is not simply a biochemical relationship or a matter of contingent physical connection. They claim that the relationship between a mother and a fetus is essentially different from that between a worker and her material product. The long months of pregnancy and the experience of childbirth are part of forming a relationship with the child-to-be. Elizabeth Anderson makes an argument along these lines. She suggests that the commodification of reproductive labor makes pregnancy an alienated form of labor of the women who perform it: selling her reproductive labor alienates a woman from her "normal" and justified emotions. Rather than viewing pregnancy as an evolving relationship with a child-to-be, contract pregnancy reinforces a vision of the pregnant woman as a mere "home" or an "environment." The commodification of reproductive labor thus distorts the nature of the bond between the mother and the fetus by misrepresenting the nature of a woman's reproductive labor. What should we make of this argument?

Surely there is truth in the claim that pregnancy contracts may reinforce a vision of women as baby machines or mere "wombs." Recent court rulings with respect to contract pregnancy have tended to acknowledge women's contribution to reproduction only insofar as it is identical to men's: the donation of genetic material. The gestational labor involved in reproduction is explicitly ignored in such rulings. Thus, Mary Beth Whitehead won back her parental rights in the "Baby M" case because the New Jersey Supreme Court acknowledged her genetic contribution.

However, as I will argue in Section IV below, the concern about the discounting of women's reproductive labor is best posed in terms of the principle of equal treatment. By treating women's reproductive labor as identical to men's when it is not, women are not in fact being treated equally. But those who conceptualize the problem with pregnancy contracts in terms of the degradation of the mother-fetus relationship rather than in terms of the equality of men and women tend to interpret the social practice of pregnancy in terms of a maternal "instinct," a sacrosanct bonding that takes place between a mother and her child-to-be. However, not all women "bond" with their fetuses. Some women abort them.

Indeed, there is a dilemma for those who wish to use the mother-fetus bond to condemn pregnancy contracts while endorsing a woman's right to choose abortion. They must hold that it is acceptable to abort a fetus, but not to sell it. While the Warnock Report takes no stand on the issue of abortion, it uses present abortion law as a term of reference in considering contract pregnancy. Since abortion is currently legal in England, the Report's position has this paradoxical consequence: one can kill a fetus, but one cannot contract to sell it. One possible response to this objection would be to claim that women do not bond with their fetuses in the first trimester. But the fact remains that some women never bond with their fetuses; some women even fail to bond with their babies after they deliver them.

Additionally, are we really sure that we know which emotions pregnancy "normally" involves? While married women are portrayed as nurturing and altruistic, society has historically stigmatized the unwed mother as selfish, neurotic, and unconcerned with the welfare of her child. Until quite recently, social pressure was directed at unwed mothers to surrender their children after birth. Thus, married women who gave up their children were seen as "abnormal" and unfeeling, while unwed mothers who failed to surrender their children were seen as selfish. Such views of the mother-fetus bonding relationship reinforce this traditional view of the family and a woman's proper role within it.

Mothers and Children

A somewhat different argument against contract pregnancy contends that the commodification of women's reproductive labor entails the commodification of children. Once again, the special nature of reproduction is used to support the asymmetry thesis: the special nature of maternal love is held to be incompatible with market relations. Children should be loved by their mothers, yet commercial surrogacy responds to and promotes other motivations. Critics argue that markets in reproductive labor give people the opportunity to "shop" for children. Prospective womb-infertile couples will seek out arrangements that "maximize" the value of their babies: sex, eye color, and race will be assessed in terms of market considerations. Having children on the basis of such preferences reflects an inferior conception of persons. It brings commercial attitudes into a sphere that is thought to be properly governed by love.

What are the reasons that people seek to enter into contract pregnancy arrangements? Most couples or single people who make use of "surrogates" want simply to have a child that is "theirs," that is, genetically related to them. In fact, given the clogged adoption system, some of them may simply want to have a child. Furthermore, the adoption system itself is responsive to people's individual preferences: it is much easier, for example, to adopt an older black child than a white infant. Such preferences may be objectionable, but no one seriously argues that parents should have no choice in the child they adopt nor that adoption be prohibited because it gives rein to such preferences. Instead, we regulate adoption to forbid the differential payment of fees to agencies on the basis of a child's ascribed characteristics. Why couldn't contract pregnancy be regulated in the same way.

Critics who wish to make an argument for the asymmetry thesis based on the nature of maternal love must defend a strong claim about the relationship between markets and love. In particular, they must claim that even regulated markets in reproductive services will lead parents to love their children for the wrong reasons: love will be conditional on the child's having the "right" set of physical characteristics. While I share the view that there is something wrong with the "shopping" attitude in the sphere of personal relations, I wonder if it has the adverse effects that the critics imagine. Individuals in our society seek partners with attributes ranging from a specified race and height to a musical taste for Chopin. Should such singles' advertisements in magazines be illegal? Should we ban dating services that cater to such preferences? Isn't it true that people who meet on such problematic grounds may grow to love each other? I suspect that most parents who receive their child through a contract pregnancy arrangement will love their child as well.

Even if contract pregnancy does not distort our conception of person-hood per se, critics can still associate contract pregnancy with baby-selling. One popular argument runs: In contract pregnancy women not only sell their reproductive services, but also their babies. Because baby-selling is taken to be intrinsically wrong, this type of argument attempts to use an analogy to support the following syllogism: If baby-selling is wrong, and contract pregnancy is a form of baby-selling, then contract pregnancy is wrong. The Warnock Report, for example, makes this charge. Suppose that we grant, as seems plausible, that baby-selling is wrong (perhaps on essentialist grounds). Is this argument successful?

It is important to keep in mind that pregnancy contracts do not enable fathers (or prospective "mothers," women who are infertile or otherwise unable to conceive) to acquire children as property. Even where there has been a financial motivation for conceiving a child, and whatever the status of the labor that produced it, the *child* cannot be treated as a commodity. The father cannot, for example, destroy, transfer, or abandon the child. He is bound by the same norms and laws that govern the behavior of a child's biological or adoptive parents. Allowing women to contract for their repro-ductive services does not entail baby-selling, if we mean by that a proxy for slavery.

Anderson has argued that what makes contract pregnancy a form of baby-selling is the way such contracts treat the "mother's rights over her child." Such contracts mandate that the mother relinquish her parental rights to the child. Furthermore, such contracts can be enforced against the mother's wishes. Anderson argues that forcing a woman to part with her child and to cede her parental rights by sale entails treating the child as a mere commodity, as something that can be sold. Even if this is true, it does not necessarily lead to the conclusion that pregnancy contracts should be banned. There are many similarities between contract pregnancy and adoption. Like adoption, pregnancy contracts could be regulated to respect a change of mind of the "surrogate" within some specified time period; to accord more with an "open" model in which all the parties to the contract retain contact with the child; or by making pregnancy contracts analogous to contracts that require informed consent, as in the case of medical experiments. Pregnancy contracts could be required to provide detailed information about the emotional risks and costs associated with giving up a child.

Finally, some writers have objected to pregnancy contracts on the ground that they must, by their nature, exploit women. They point to the fact that the compensation is very low, and that many of the women who agree to sell their reproductive labor have altruistic motivations. Anderson writes, "A kind of exploitation occurs when one party to a transaction is oriented toward the exchange of 'gift' values, while the other party operates in accordance with the norms of the market exchange of commodities."

Two responses are possible to this line of argument. First, even if it is the case that all or most of the women who sell their reproductive labor are altruistically motivated, it is unfair to argue that the other parties to the contract are motivated solely in accord with market values. The couples who use contract pregnancy are not seeking to make a profit, but to have a child. Some of them might even be willing to maintain an "extended family" relationship with the "surrogate" after the child's birth. Second, even if an asymmetry in motivation is established, it is also present in many types of service work: teaching, health care, and social work are all liable to result in "exploitation" of this sort. In all of these areas, the problem is at least partially addressed by regulating compensation. Why is contract pregnancy different? . . .

REPRODUCTIVE LABOR AND EQUALITY

In the preceding three sections I have argued that the asymmetry thesis cannot be defended by claiming that there is something "essential" about reproductive labor that singles it out for different treatment from other forms of labor; nor by arguing that contract pregnancy distorts the nature of the bonds of motherhood; nor by the appeal to the best interests of the child. The arguments I have examined ignore the existing background conditions that underlie pregnancy contracts, many of which are objectionable. In addition, some of the arguments tend to accept uncritically the traditional picture of the family. Such arguments take current views of the maternal bond and the institution of motherhood as the baseline for judging pregnancy contracts—as if such views were not contested.

If we reject these arguments for the asymmetry thesis, are we forced back to the view that the market is indeed theoretically all-encompassing? Can we reject contract pregnancy, and defend the asymmetry thesis, without claiming either that reproductive labor is essentially not a commodity, or that it necessarily degrades the bonds between mothers and children, or that it is harmful to children?

I think that the strongest argument against contract pregnancy that depends upon the asymmetry thesis is derived from considerations of gender equality. It is this consideration that I believe is tacitly driving many of the arguments; for example, it is the background gender inequality that makes the commodification of women's and children's attributes especially objectionable. My criticism of contract pregnancy centers on the hypothesis that in our society such contracts will turn women's labor into something that is used and controlled by others and will reinforce gender stereotypes that have been used to justify the unequal treatment of women.

Contrary to the democratic ideal, gender inequality is pervasive in our society. This inequality includes the unequal distribution of housework and child care that considerably restricts married women's opportunities in the work force; the fact that the ratio between an average full-time working woman's earning and those of her average male counterpart is 59.3:100, and the fact that divorce is an economically devastating experience for women (during the 1970's, the standard of living of young divorced mothers fell 73%, while men's standard of living following divorce rose 42%). These circumstances constitute the baseline from which women form their preferences and make their "choices." Thus, even a women's choice to engage in commercial surrogacy must be viewed against a background of unequal opportunity. Most work done by women in our society remains in a "female ghetto": service and clerical work, secretarial work, cleaning, domestic labor, nursing, elementary school teaching, and witnessing.

I assume that there is something deeply objectionable about gender inequality. My argument is that contract pregnancy's reinforcing of this inequality lies at the heart of what is wrong with it. In particular, reproduction is a sphere that historically has been marked by inequality: women and men have not had equal influence over the institutions and practices involved in human reproduction. In its current form and context, contract pregnancy contributes to gender inequality in three ways:

1. Contract pregnancy gives others increased access to and control over women's bodies and sexuality. In a provocative book, Carmel Shalev argues that it is wrong to forbid a woman to sell her reproductive capacities when we already allow men to sell their sperm. But Shalev ignores a crucial difference between artificial insemination by donor (AID) and a pregnancy contract. AID does not give anyone control over men's bodies and sexuality. A man who elects AID simply sells a product of his body or his sexuality; he does not sell control over his body itself. The current practices of AID and pregnancy contracts are remarkably different in the scope of intervention and control they allow the "buyer." Pregnancy contracts involve substantial control over women's bodies.

What makes this control objectionable, however, is not the intrinsic features of women's reproductive labor, but rather the ways in which such control reinforces a long history of unequal treatment. Consider an analogous case that has no such consequence: voluntary (paid) military service, where men sell their fighting capacities. Military service, like contract pregnancy, involves significant invasions into the body of the seller: soldiers' bodies are controlled to a large extent by their commanding officers under conditions in which the stakes are often life and death. But military service does not *directly* serve to perpetuate traditional gender inequalities. The fact that pregnancy contracts, like military contracts, give someone control over someone else's body is not the issue. Rather, the issue is that in contract pregnancy the body that is controlled belongs to a woman, in a society that historically has subordinated women's interests to those of men, primarily through its control over her sexuality and reproduction.

Market theorists might retort that contract pregnancy could be regulated to protect women's autonomy, in the same way that we regulate other labor contracts. However, it will be difficult, given the nature of the interests involved, for such contracts not to be very intrusive with respect to women's bodies in spite of formal agreements. The purpose of such contracts is, after all, to produce a healthy child. In order to help guarantee a healthy baby, a woman's behavior must be highly controlled.

Moreover, if the pregnancy contract is a contract for reproductive labor, then, as in other types of labor contracts, compliance—what the law terms "specific performance"—cannot be enforced. For example, if I contract to paint your house, and I default on my agreement, you can sue me for breaking the contract, but even if you win, the courts will not require me to paint your house. Indeed, this is the salient difference between even poorly paid wage labor and indentured servitude. Thus by analogy, if the woman in a pregnancy contract defaults on her agreement and decides to keep the child, the other parties should not be able to demand performance (that is, surrender of the child); rather, they can demand monetary compensation.

This inability to enforce performance in pregnancy contracts may have consequences for the *content* of such contracts that will make them especially objectionable. Recall that such contracts occur over a long period of time, during which a woman may undergo fundamental changes in her willingness to give up the child. The other parties will need some mechanism to ensure her compliance. There are two mechanisms that are likely to produce compliance, but both are objectionable: (a) The contract could be set up so that payment is delivered to the woman only after the child is born. But this structure of compensation closely resembles babyselling; it now looks as if what is being bought is not the woman's services, but the child itself. Thus, if baby-selling is wrong, then we should be very troubled by the fact that, in order to be self-enforcing, contract pregnancy must use incentives that make it resemble baby-selling. (b) The contract could mandate legal and psychological counseling for a woman who is tempted to change her mind. Given that it is hard to imagine in advance what it means to surrender a child, such counseling could involve a great deal of manipulation and coercion of the woman's emotions.

2.   Contract pregnancy reinforces stereotypes about the proper role of women in the reproductive division of labor. At a time when women have made strides in labor force participation, moving out of the family into other social spheres, pregnancy contracts provide a monetary incentive for women to remain in the home. And, while some women may "prefer" to stay at home, we need to pay attention to the limited range of economic opportunities available to these women, and to the ways in which these opportunities have shaped their preferences. Under present conditions, pregnancy contracts entrench a traditional division of labor—men at work, women in the home—based on gender.

Additionally, pregnancy contracts will affect the way society views women: they will tend to reinforce the view of women as "baby machines." It is also likely that they will affect the way women see themselves. Insofar as the sale of women's reproductive capacities contributes to the social subordination of women, and only of women, there are antidiscrimination grounds for banning it.

3.   Contract pregnancy raises the danger, manifested in several recent court rulings, that "motherhood" will be defined in terms of genetic material, in the same way as "fatherhood." Mary Beth Whitehead won back parental rights to Baby M on the basis of her being the genetic "mother." On the other hand, Anna Johnson, a "gestational" surrogate, lost such rights because she bore no genetic relationship to the child. These court rulings establish the principle of parenthood on the basis of genetic

contribution. In such cases, women's contribution to reproduction is recognized only insofar as it is identical to that of men. Genes alone are taken to define natural and biological motherhood. By not taking women's actual gestational contributions into account, the courts reinforce an old stereotype of women as merely the incubators of men's seeds. In fact, the court's inattention to women's unique labor contribution is itself a form of unequal treatment. By defining women's rights and contributions in terms of those of men, when they are different, the courts fail to recognize an adequate basis for women's rights and needs. These rulings place an additional burden on women.

Given its consequences for gender inequality, I think that the asymmetry thesis is true, and that pregnancy contracts are especially troubling. Current gender inequality lies at the heart of what is wrong with pregnancy contracts. The problem with commodifying women's reproductive labor is not that it "degrades" the special nature of reproductive labor, or "alienates" women from a core part of their identities, but that it reinforces a traditional gender-hierarchical division of labor. A consequence of my argument is that under very different background conditions, in which men and women had equal power and had an equal range of choices, such contracts would be less objectionable. For example, in a society in which women's work was valued as much as men's and in which child care was shared equally, pregnancy contracts might serve primarily as a way for single persons, disabled persons, and same-sex families to have children. Indeed, pregnancy contracts and similar practices have the potential to transform the nuclear family. We know too little about possible new forms of family life to restrict such experiments on a priori grounds; but in our society, I have argued that there are consequentialist reasons for making this restriction.

At the same time, there are potential caveats to the acceptability of a regulated form of pregnancy contract even under conditions of gender equality: (1) the importance of background economic inequality; (2) the effect of the practice on race equality; (3) the need to ensure the woman's participation in the overall purpose of the activity; (4) the need to ensure that the vulnerable—children—are protected. We know very little about the prerequisites for psychologically healthy children. We know very little about the effects of pregnancy contracts on parental exit or on the other children of the birth mother. For this reason, even under more ideal circumstances, there is reason to be cautious about the potential use of such contracts. For the time being, I believe that pregnancy contracts should be discouraged. This can be done by making such contracts unenforceable in the courts. Furthermore, in contested cases, the courts should recognize no distinction between genetic and gestational "surrogates" with respect to parental rights. Finally, brokerage of pregnancy contracts should be illegal. These proposals aim to discourage contract pregnancy and to strengthen the position of the "surrogate," who is the most economically and emotionally vulnerable party in any such arrangement....

Lisa C. Ikemoto, The In/fertile, The Too Fertile, And the Dysfertile

47 Hastings L. J. 1007 (1996).

Introduction

I began by thinking about procreative technology. But you cannot think about procreative technology as such. The technology is nearly indistinguishable from the stories about its uses. The stories and the images embedded in the stories shift according to the context. And, as philosopher Helen Longino has noted, "[e]ach contextual setting would yield a different pattern of connections." Since procreative technology is often characterized as infertility treatment, I am interested in questioning the stories of in/fertility. It seems to me that these stories are shaping public policy and law in direct and indirect ways. So, in questioning the stories of in/fertility, I am trying to raise questions about the public policy and law addressing in/fertility.

I use the slash (/) between "in" and "fertility" to signal that the dominant understandings of infertility and the infertile are shaped with respect to our understanding of fertility and the fertile. My inquiry takes for granted that human procreation, and in/fertility in particular, is a culturally significant site upon which political contests play out. So my inquiry, more accurately, is not about the way the technology should be used. It is, rather, an effort to trace the pattern of connections in the in/fertility discourses, formed largely by procreative technology use.

I follow three threads in the stories and images, or discourses, if you will, of in/fertility. The most obvious thread is that of the infertile, who are usually identified as women. Perhaps not surprisingly, given the binary, oppositional nature of master narratives, that thread leads to the thread of the "too fertile," those women whose sexuality and fertility are deemed deviant by dominant norms. The too fertile include unwed adult women, teens, welfare recipients, and/or women of color. In fact, within the in/fertility discourses, all of these women are too fertile. The third thread may be less apparent. While infertile women and too fertile women have been made visible and obvious in the in/fertility discourses, the fertility of those within the third thread—lesbians and gay men—has been made invisible or irrelevant. I use the term "dysfertile" to suggest the dysfunction attributed to lesbians and gay men by the in/fertility discourses. . . .

The Possibilities of Procreative Technology

Thoughtful commentators have leaned toward two particular concerns about the possibilities of reformulating family. One is the intellectual and moral confusion that might result from separating different aspects of the biological relationship between parent and child. More specifically, the concern has been that the separation of coital conception, genetic ties, gestation, and child rearing means that we have to articulate why these connections are significant and we have to weight these connections. There is the chance that in the process we will have to admit that some or all of these connections are not significant. That admission would undermine our existing justifications for protecting the relationships we have been calling "family." It might threaten or at least devalue the psychic significance we attribute to these connections. Or, there is the chance that we will lose something simply by exposing the connections to questioning. The second concern raised about the possibility of reformulating family is for the welfare of children born as a result of procreative technology use. This concern has focused on the psychological risk that might come to a child from learning the means of birth, and from physical defects that may be caused by the intervention of technology.

Consider how these concerns have been discussed in the context of two surrogacy cases, *In re Baby M* and *Johnson v. Calvert*. Both cases were highly publicized. Anthropologist Helena Ragone concluded in her ethnography of surrogacy that the judicial decisions in the *Baby M* case reflected public opinion. I would extend that observation to the *Johnson* case as well. The outcomes in both cases have been explained as similar resolutions of the concerns about identifying the significant biological connections and the welfare of the child. For these reasons, these cases can serve as an introductory text for exploring the nature of the fundamental something at issue in the possibility of reformulating family....

Two differences between [*Johnson*] and *Baby M* proved to be key. In *Baby M*, all the parties were white. In *Johnson v. Calvert*, the three adults were all of different races. Anna Johnson is African American. Crispina Calvert is Filipina. And Mark Calvert is white. The media stories focused on Anna Johnson's blackness and Mark Calvert's whiteness. In these stories, the baby was not described as biracial or Filipino, but was implicitly made white. Like the 1994 stories reporting that a black woman had used a white woman's ova, the stories about *Johnson v. Calvert* did not explain the difference race might make. It was apparently self-explanatory. And as in 1994, race did make a difference; there was unease over the idea of a black woman claiming a "white" child. The California Supreme Court did not mention race in its opinion. The Court recognized the Calverts as the legal parents, thus denying Anna Johnson any legal basis for custody or visitation. The Court's analysis rested on the genetic connection between the Calverts and the child. The message that follows from this holding is that the genetic link is superior to the biological connection formed by pregnancy and childbirth. In the public discussion about the case, the racial identities of the parties made the logic of the preference for genetic link obvious.

In both of these cases, there was never any question that William Stern and Mark Calvert would be recognized as the legal fathers. Nor was their desire for a genetically-related child questioned. The parent question at issue in both cases was, who should be the mother and whose motivation was most appropriate. The fact is that the law in most states protects the parental status of the genetic father except where artificial insemination by anonymous donor has been used. There is also well-established law that presumes that a woman who gives birth to a child is that child's legal mother. The California Supreme Court's decision indicates that the legal status of women as mothers is less well-established and more contingent than that of men as fathers.

A reading of the surrogacy cases, *Johnson v. Calvert* in particular, in light of the history behind the Uniform Parentage Act (UPA) reveals the role of race in the contingent nature of motherhood. We rarely think about the legal basis for motherhood. The fact that a woman gives birth to a child makes the woman's status as mother seem obvious. Yet, the rule that the woman who gives birth to a child is the legal mother has long depended on the woman's race. For example, the maternal presumption was simply not applied to women who were slaves. These black women had no legal claim to their children. Professor Mary Louise Fellows has shown how the maternal presumption and its exceptions result from patriarchal concerns about sexual control of women and racial purity. The holding of *Johnson v. Calvert* has created another exception to the maternal presumption. The Court's preference for the genetic, rather than the experiential basis for parenthood is historically located in the twin goals of racial purity and the sexual control of women. The fact that Anna Johnson is black makes that history visible. The fact that so many find logic in the holding suggests that the goals are not mere relics.

Professor Fellows has also illustrated how the marital presumption—an evidentiary presumption that a child born to a married woman is the child of the husband—operates to "transfer procreative power to white men while simultaneously minimizing and denying the procreative power of African–American women and, in different ways, of white women." In part, the presumption was created on the premise that interracial marriage was forbidden. So, the rule was never applied to white men in relationships with black women. Further, the rule was not applied to married white women who gave birth to children that appeared to be of mixed race. In other words, the law was intended to secure paternity rights to white children. When the presumption was used in an interracial marriage context, the courts often refused to apply the pre-UPA marital presumption, especially if the result would be to recognize an African American child as heir of a white father. One can read the *Johnson* case as continuing the judicial practice of selectively applying the parental status laws to maintain white fatherhood. In other words, the court's holding was not inevitable. Our preference for genetic links has political as well as sociobiological reasons. Here, a decision to recognize Ms. Johnson as the child's legal mother would have given a black woman claim to a white child, made the child nominally black, and would have established a white man's paternity to that child.

Stating the last point in normative terms, motherhood is contingent on white fatherhood in this line of paternity cases. Ms. Johnson's role was reduced to that of biological function. From a feminist standpoint, the preference for the genetic link, rather than that formed by pregnancy and childbirth, is perfectly consistent with a male-centered perspective. In simplistic terms, recognizing or even preferring pregnancy and childbirth as a legally significant basis for establishing parenthood would diminish the power of men as fathers; but preferring the genetic link while devaluing pregnancy and childbirth subordinates women as mothers. The marital presumption cases did not directly devalue pregnancy and childbirth. But they did reduce black women to biological functionaries. These cases erased black woman's status as wife and mother. Motherhood assumes fatherhood. But in these cases, black women merely produced black, not white, children, who could not lay claim to their white fathers.

The concerns about the welfare of the child and biological indeterminacy have been addressed within the public discourses, at least with respect to surrogacy. First, the UPA, in contradiction to its effect, has the avowed purpose of protecting the welfare of the child. Neither the judicial nor public opinions suggested that the outcomes of the surrogacy cases undermined this purpose. Second, procreative technology use has extended the primacy of genetics as the basis for parenthood, and fatherhood in particular. The match between the legal outcome and public opinion in these cases may reflect the social significance attributed to the genetic connection. The significance of that connection seems "natural." But history shows that the significance attributed to genetic links comes from patriarchy and white supremacy. The naturalness of the relationship at issue depends on the race of the parents, and in particular on the race of the mother. In the marital presumption cases, the father-child relationship seemed unnatural because the marital relationship seemed unnatural; the marital relationship seemed unnatural because the woman married to the white man was African American. In *Johnson v. Calvert*, the parent (Anna Johnson)-child relationship seemed unnatural—unnatural because the woman who gave birth to the white child was black. One could state the explanations in reverse racial order. That is, one could say that the father-child relationship in the marital presumption cases seemed unnatural because the father was white, or that the parent-child relationship in *Johnson v. Calvert* seemed unnatural because the child was white. But the fact that the law secured the status of the fathers so that neither William Stern nor Mark Calvert had to defend their paternity shifted the focus to the identity of the mothers.

The uncertainty raised by the possibilities of reformulating family now may be read more accurately as concern about maintaining the security of paternity, particularly for white fathers. The anxiety about using procreative technology to produce new family structures also may have been a more general concern about maintaining the primacy of the "nuclear" or marriage-based family as the most privileged family structure. That concern also explains why procreative technology as infertility treatment emerged as the primary explanation for its use. As infertility treatment, procreative technology use has become a way of reinscribing the marriage-based family on the middle class.

The Technological Reinscription of the Marriage-based Family on the Middle Class

The institutional authority of both medicine and law have been brought to bear on the technological reinscription of the marriage-based family. Within the in/fertility discourses, the normative power of "family" naturalizes the technology, while the excluding power of "family" marks non-marriage-based parent-child relationships as unnatural.

Consider the formal definition of "infertility." It usually states that a couple is infertile if conception has not occurred after one year of unprotected intercourse. The meaning of these words is clear if you read into them dominant assumptions about who should have children. In other words, the definition assumes that the couple is heterosexual. It assumes that they have failed to conceive after a particular type of intercourse—vaginal penetration by the penis, followed by ejaculation. My point about the patriarchal and heterosexist assumptions built into the definition of infertility may seem overwrought. But the effects of the assumptions are real. When we read heterosexuality into the definition of infertility, it becomes impossible for a non-partnered person or lesbian couple to be included among the infertile. Since procreative technology use is primarily understood as infertility treatment, access to the technology usually hinges on the diagnostic power of the definition.

The process of choosing criteria for diagnosis requires designating some experience as more significant than others. That ability to define standards then becomes the power to test. Foucault described the power to test as "normalizing," as that which "introduces the constraints of conformity ... [that] compares, differentiates, hierarchizes, homogenizes, excludes." Here, testing is a means of reinforcing the norms expressed in the test itself. Medicine has used its power to test in ways that reinforce traditional, excluding norms that privilege heterosexual marriage as the basis for family formation. Testing, in this context, is a sign of fitness for parenthood. The contents of the definition deem some not fit for testing nor, by implication, for parenthood.

At fertility clinics, physicians often screen by using fixed social criteria. Marital status, age, and sexual orientation are commonly used to exclude unmarried persons, especially lesbians and gay men, from procreative technology use. Professor Helena Ragone lists these criteria as "extra-program guidelines" for surrogacy programs: "(1) Couples should be asked to provide medical proof of their infertility; (2) Only heterosexual, married couples should be permitted the option of participating in the surrogate mother program; (3) Unmarried heterosexual women or men should not be permitted to engage the services of a surrogate; (4) Lesbians, lesbian couples, gay men, or gay male couples should not be permitted to engage the services of a surrogate." She defines extra-program guidelines as those "primarily designed as a public relations strategy, to protect the industry from potential negative publicity by averting situations that might be perceived as immoral, exploitative, or transgressive." Two obvious points follow from this. First, medicine and the fertility industry [are] consciously accepting dominant norms about preferred family structures, or at least medicine is consciously reconstructing what it perceives to be acceptable. Second, the guidelines make clear that non-marriage based family formation is understood to be transgressive. . . .

Clinic rules that screen patients based on these social criteria reinforce the conflation of marriage, heterosexuality, and procreation. This, in turn, makes each social category seem like an inherent element of the others— marriage as heterosexual, heterosexuality as procreative, and procreation as marital. The apparent inseparability of these concepts makes the definition of infertility and the procreative technology use as infertility treatment less penetrable to questioning. The reservation of procreative technology for use by heterosexual, married couples to achieve parenthood seems unquestionable and therefore, natural.

The class and race dimensions of the boundaries of use emerge in the effects of the clinic rules. Current estimates of the mean charges for in vitro fertilization range from $6,233 to $8,000, although one study showed that, in 1992, charges at six centers ranged from $7,000 to $11,000. The cost per delivery may be $44,000 to $211,940. Anyone who uses in vitro fertilization or a comparable method must have substantial credit or lots of cash. For many, the lack of financial means bars access to procreative technology use. In effect, the high cost screens out low income users. Surrogacy users "as a group are upper-middle-income, educated professionals, in their late thirties and early forties. . . . The average combined family income is in excess of $100,000." In addition, the majority of couples who use surrogacy, in vitro fertilization, and other technologies to achieve fertility are white. Procreative technology use has become a racially-specific, class-based method of family formation.

Procreative technology use is little regulated at law. In other words, the law enables physicians and clinic rules to operate freely. So while there has been much public and scholarly discussion about using law to regulate procreative technology use, the standard approach has been to refrain from legal intervention, and in effect, to delegate the regulatory function to medicine. To the extent that legal rules do govern procreative technology use, most rules affirm current medical industry practices.

Most of the existing legal rules govern use through the potential parents, rather than through the medical professional. And the most common types of legal rules provide legal certainty for married couples who use procreative technology. More specifically, the most common types of legal rules provide married couples with certainty about their status as the legal parents and the status of the child as theirs. In addition, the legal rules, like the clinic rules assume that the potential parents are married couples. For example, approximately one-third of the states have adopted the Uniform Parentage Act provisions to determine the status of a child conceived by artificial insemination. The UPA provides that a child born to a married woman by heterologous artificial insemination is the husband's child, if he consented in writing, and if a physician performed the insemination. It further states that the donor in this situation is not the father. These legal rules support the prevailing view that procreative technology is medical treatment most appropriately used to address married couples' infertility. . . .

The success of characterizing procreative technology as infertility treatment has marked the discourses of in/fertility in at least two ways. First, the technological imperative has become a family formation imperative—at least for married couples, and perhaps also for single persons who "should be" married (i.e. those presumed to be heterosexual). The focus has shifted from the "unnatural" method of family formation that procreative technology might represent to the unnaturalness of childlessness. Second, because "infertility" has come to mean a treatable, and therefore temporary condition, it stands in opposition to "sterility." Sterility signals permanent inability to have a child. Before the advent of infertility as a treatable condition, sterility referred to physical flaws causing childlessness. Now sterility may have a physical or social source. That is, sterility now includes those whom I call the "dysfertile," those rendered childless by their failure to fit the definition of infertile, because they are unmarried and/or lesbian or gay. Within the discourse, sterility is an abnormal state. Because having children is the natural state, and because the assumption that childlessness is temporary has grown stronger, those who are unmarried or married without children are seen as waiting to have children, even expected to use the technology to achieve parenthood. Thus the technology imperative has been transformed from a need to see scientific progress into a social imperative for which it is natural to use technology to achieve.

Within the in/fertility discourses, the work that infertile women perform to become procreative maintains the cultural significance of motherhood and its use as a means of social control. The sacrifices infertile women make to become mothers is taken as proof that they should be mothers and that motherhood is important. Comments made by women using procreative technology indicate that for them, motherhood has personal emotional and social significance. But the emotional and social consequences are read as evidence that maternity is inherent, natural, and desirable for women. That is, a woman's particular hopes and needs are translated into cultural artifact—motherhood—that has symbolic meaning and results in practices that support production.

Motherhood as a cultural system simultaneously reproduces an understanding of women as inherently and inevitably responsible for domestic labor, both physical and moral, and it preserves the assumption that reproductive labor is predominantly feminine while productive labor is predominantly masculine in nature. Motherhood describes women as mothers whether or not they have babies. The ultimate irony is that within the in/fertility discourses, it is women who give birth, but it is men who perform the productive labor. Procreative technology use has provided opportunity to extend largely patriarchal significations of pregnancy and birth. While many women choose procreative technology use over adoption so that they may experience pregnancy and childbirth, pregnancy is also read as evidence that "daddy planted a seed." In addition, procreative technology use further segregates and devalues the significance of pregnancy and birth from the genetic link. So the desire of women who want to experience childbirth and pregnancy is trivialized compared to the goal of using the ova and sperm of the married couple.

If women as mothers perform reproductive labor, they are probably service workers. Service is a "kind of labor that is immediately consumed or exhausted. That is, it cannot be stored, accumulated, or saved. Service is exhausted in its performance." On a simpler level of analysis, mothers serve, and they do it with pleasure. Certainly, this willingness is implied, if not expressed, in the stories and images of infertile women. This description of motherhood places infertile women in a lower class position than the economic status of the infertile would indicate. Middle class women as mothers are simultaneously servants and employers. It is the middle class woman who can and does hire other women to do household labor, thus delegating part of her role as woman and transferring her gender subordination by virtue of her race and class privilege. Yet it is the infertile middle class woman who uses procreative technology to affirm her place as a mother and service worker.

The Infertile

The last part of the discussion suggests that another point on the line is bounded by the identities of infertile women as white, middle class women and those who receive the transfer of subordination. I am not referring to women who are actually hired as domestic labor, but to women characterized as only fit for low status labor by virtue of their race and class. Just as class (middle), race (white), and marital status (married) qualify infertile women as those who should be mothers, class (low income), race (nonwhite), and marital status (single) mark the women on the other side of the line as not fit for motherhood. Their apparent fertility makes them "too fertile." So infertile women can use procreative technology to fulfill their natural role as mothers, while avoiding the most stigmatized and oppressive work of women by hiring others. Poor women of color are deemed destined for low status labor, while their work as mothers is stigmatized.

I can identify infertile women and too fertile women as groups because there were already stories and images attached to these identities. The groups were pre-constructed. The stories and images seem to explain the predicament of women read through these identities. And the explanations implicitly ascribe causal power to race, gender, and class.

Upon reviewing the texts—medical, legal, and media news—that I have used to trace the in/fertility discourses, I find that there are two types of descriptors for in/fertile women. There are vital statistics indicating that in/fertile women who seek treatment are over thirty; and as discussed, in/fertile women are typically white, middle class, and married. The other type of descriptor provides explanations, which then become inextricably linked with the vital statistics. Both the medical and media accounts of procreative technology use refer to the frustration, despair and hope that the infertile experience during the diagnosis and treatment process. These descriptions call for empathy with the infertile. The accounts also refer, usually subtly, to negative views of infertile women held by the public. More specifically, the negative views seem to say that because infertile women are economically privileged, they do not need support or sympathy. These views tend to be described as a response to the demand for legislation requiring insurance coverage of procreative technology use. So one explanatory story links infertile women with class. But what is the rest of the story?

A medical journal article stated, "[p]art of the resistance to paying for a lot of these treatments is the thought that all these women are just upper middle-class women who have a lot of money and they delay childbearing to have a career." A newspaper article quoted a psychotherapist who counsels infertile women: "Part of the myth that really gets me is this idea that women have just kind of postponed pregnancy because of their careers." In other words, the message in the story about infertile women is that they put career before marriage and motherhood. Social historian, Margarete Sandelowski, has traced the tendency within the in/fertility discourse, to conflate voluntary and involuntary infertility and "to suggest that infertile women who seek to achieve motherhood may not really want it." When you think about the opposition within the explanatory story for infertility, the attribution of volition becomes clear. The story sets up selfishness in opposition to motherhood. Motherhood is about selflessness, not only on behalf of children, but also on behalf of society. The explanatory story privileges a particularly domestic, essentialized notion of selflessness and devalues achievements that threaten this image of social order. The story offers a moral about women who have too much control and operates as a response to the feminist call for women's liberation.

The same theme about the price of control runs through a slightly different explanatory story. This story is premised on one assumed and one accepted medical fact. The assumed fact is that contraceptive use by women can cause infertility. The accepted fact is that sexually transmitted disease may result in blocked fallopian tubes or other problems causing infertility. This story is about the liberated woman who sought not only sexual freedom but also freedom from the consequences of her deviant sexuality. The message here is that infertility is the price women must pay for sexual freedom and reproductive control. Remember that by virtue of their race and class, infertile women are the women who should be mothers. The fact that these women have tried to have children reinforces the assumption that the "should be" women are naturally mothers. The explanatory story, particularly when coupled with the prevalence of accounts about successful procreative technology use, becomes a vindication of motherhood as the primary role for women. In these stories, the infertile were always mothers; they were the only ones who did not realize that. It was their exercise of choice and control that denatured them. And it is the use of technology that can restore them to nature.

The Too Fertile

While the problem of infertility has been labelled a medical problem, and read as the result of a problematic social trend, the problem of the too fertile has been clearly labelled first and foremost as a social problem. So law and media texts, not medical texts provide the explanatory stories and images, even though, to some extent, the problem has been medicalized. Here, I rely on the records of recent senate and house debates about "welfare reform" and on news media accounts.

It is interesting that in the media coverage of those moments of conflict discussed above, several reports drew direct comparisons between the granny moms and the too fertile. Consider this comment:

> What has the woman [the 59 year old British woman who had twins] done that merits such ethical concern and public criticism? She isn't an unmarried, 15–year-old high school dropout whose unplanned baby will put her on welfare, perhaps for decades. She isn't 21 and having her fourth baby by four men, none of whom will actively father their children.

> She hasn't been using crack or other illegal drugs during pregnancy, condemning her unborn infant to neurological problems of unpredictable severity. She's not passing along the AIDS virus or forcing fetal alcohol syndrome on her child by her drinking. She's not risking her baby's health by skipping prenatal care. Her twins aren't the unintended and unwanted consequences of careless sex.

The problems ascribed to the too fertile become the standard against which troubling technology use gets measured. In this comparison, the too fertile are simultaneously a problem of nature and of inappropriate intervention. When read within the broader discourse about deviantly fertile women, the too fertile woman's race and class emerge as natural explanations for her hyper-sexuality and promiscuity. On the other hand, in the context of the debate about welfare reform, the woman's dependency and lack of education result from misguided government intervention.

This comment, like recent political debates, combines a series of stories about deviant fertility that have emerged over the years. The identity stories about unwed pregnancy and motherhood consistently have been framed as calls for social control over women. But the crux of the problem and the explanations have changed over time and varied according to race and class....

The current debate about deviant fertility emerged in the late 1980s. But the key moments have occurred in the 1990s. Newspapers published articles about out-of-wedlock pregnancy and childbearing at a higher rate during three moments of this decade. First, then-Vice President Dan Quayle, in May 1992, made use of a story line in Murphy Brown, a popular television sitcom, to emphasize his conclusion that a "poverty of values" caused the mass street violence that took place in Los Angeles that year. In the story line, the main character, a single, white, professional woman, became pregnant and had a child. Second, a June 1994 Census Bureau report showed that the most significant rate of increase in out-of-wedlock pregnancy occurred among white, college-educated women over 20 years of age. In fact, the report proved that most unwed mothers are white. Third, President Clinton and house and senate republicans placed unwed motherhood centrally in their plans for social reform. The centrality of this issue emerged most clearly after the Fall 1994 elections resulted in Republican control of both the house and senate, and the resulting push for an agenda called the Contract with America.

The current debate combines elements of earlier stories, so that the comment made in support of granny moms is not atypical. In other words, one image operating in the in/fertility discourse is that of the teenaged, substance-abusing, welfare-dependent, pre-natal care shirking, disease-ridden woman who has several damaged and ill children each sired by a different man. However, the most visible and stigmatized identities in the discourse are those of women of color who live in poverty. The problem is so strongly linked with race and welfare that the traits of the all-in-one unwed mother are also strongly linked with race and welfare. This has two effects. It simplifies—it shifts attention away from substance-addiction, prenatal care, contraceptive distribution, and AIDS prevention to the women themselves. In addition, the conflation of unwed motherhood among poor women of color with every other visible social ill makes unwed motherhood among white women seem less problematic. . . .

The Dysfertile

Stories about procreative technology use by lesbians and gay men exists largely in the extreme margins of the in/fertility discourses. As discussed, procreative technology use is little regulated at law, and most of the legal rules reinforce marriage and opposite sex parenting. They barely suggest that others might use the technology, or that there might be other family structures. The medical rules also tend to premise technology use on marriage. While some clinic rules permit access to single women, the written medical texts simply do not address procreative technology use by lesbians and gay men. There are a few mainstream media news and popular culture accounts of gay and lesbian procreation. But only a few. So, within the dominant parts of the in/fertility discourses, lesbians and gay men are virtually invisible. One can infer their presence by reading the other parts of the in/fertility discourses through dominant gay and lesbian identity constructs.

Procreation and parenthood are so strongly associated with heterosexuality and marriage that procreation and lesbians and parenthood and gay men seem disassociated. I used the pairings, procreation-lesbian and parenthood-gay men, intentionally. I believe that for women, procreation is mediated largely by the presence of the masculine, and that for men, parenthood is mediated largely by the feminine.

For infertile women, it is marriage and the presence of potential fathers, in part, that qualify them as women, and as women who should be mothers. For too fertile women, it is sexual activity while not married and mothering in the absence of fathers that stigmatize unwed motherhood. So heterosexuality, marital status and procreation are either positively or negatively, but apparently inherently, linked. The independence from men in lesbian sexuality and social intimacy de-links lesbian identity from procreation. Remember that within the in/fertility discourses, woman's work as mother is reproductive labor, and that man performs the productive work. In other words, pregnancy and childbearing have been segregated and trivialized compared to the power attributed to the male seed. So lesbian sexuality denies women access to the seed, and therefore denies them access to the power to procreate.

Anthropologist Ellen Lewin has observed, "[l]esbians, after all, were assumed to be creatures defined by their sexual appetites and thus were seen to be at odds with the kind of selfless devotion expected of mothers." Motherhood defines women who should be or are mothers as nonsexual. The fact that procreative technology use separates sexuality from procreation may have seemed not unnatural because white, middle class women— those who should be mothers—use the technology. They were already defined as nonsexual and simply reproductive. So even when lesbians identify themselves as mothers, they may remain invisible, simply because lesbian identity as reflected in the dominant parts of the discourse stands in opposition to, not within, motherhood.

The invisibility of gay men in the in/fertility discourse may be more acute than that of lesbians. Even though the male seed is understood to be the source of procreative power, male procreation depends on the biological capacity of women to carry and give birth to the child. So it is at least possible to imagine a lesbian woman as pregnant, giving birth, and therefore becoming a mother. But it seems difficult, at best, to imagine how a gay man would have a child. His sexual orientation simultaneously makes sexual intimacy with men and women seem unnatural.

Perhaps more important is that social fatherhood depends on motherhood. It may be that existing stories about unwed fathers disrupt our ability to perceive gay men as fathers. Unwed fathers to children of unwed mothers are marked by their absence from the family structure. Active parenthood outside of marriage, then, seems unlikely. In addition, the ability of men to achieve stability in intimate relationships is also understood to be contingent on the presence of women. Masculinity is partly about the uncontrolled sexual drive of men that inhibits their ability to form stable relationships until they choose or commit to do so. In marriage, men "settle down." Stories about gay men often emphasize their promiscuity. The implication is that two gay men in a relationship are potentially more unstable than men in heterosexual relationships. So the formation of a marriage-like relationship in which to raise a child appears inconsistent with gay male identity. Finally, motherhood attributes qualities we deem necessary to parenting to women. Fatherhood has largely been about balancing the emotional aspects of mothering with authority. But because gay male identity has been feminized, gay men are caught between the twin assumptions that they lack the stability and nurturing capacity to mother and the authority to father children.

Even while I write about the invisibility of lesbians and gay men in the in/fertility discourses, I am conscious of the fact that lesbians and gay men do use procreative technologies to become parents. Despite their extreme marginalization within the in/fertility discourses, both lesbians and gay men are procreative and forming parent-child relationships through technology use. In fact, one can find references to a "lesbian baby boom." So, perhaps it is more accurate to say that lesbians and gay men are becoming parents largely independent of the medical establishment. The question this raises is how do these technology uses and these relationships disrupt dominant concepts used to define procreation and family, and what follows from the disruption. . . .

Consider the links between women and procreative technology. Procreative technology use, within the dominant parts of the discourses, reproduces motherhood as a cultural system that maintains social control of women, essentializes woman with respect to her capacity to bear children, and devalues maternal labor. The technology is also used in ways that reinforce the inscription of gender roles on biological function, and further, to segment those parts and roles so that both body and identity become component parts. Lesbians who use the technologies lay claim to identity parts denied them in the dominant discourse—womanhood and motherhood—by manipulating the splintering effect of the technologies. The result, lesbian motherhood, may be both transgressive and assimilated. The transgressive use of technology, in turn, flips the human/invention distinction on its head. Lesbian use of the technology inscribes lesbian identity on the technology. . . . What this suggests is that the liminal position within the discourses may be manipulated for self-definition.

NOTES AND QUESTIONS

1. **Baby M and Johnson**. Compare the decisions in *In re Baby M* and *Johnson,* particularly the courts' treatment of the surrogate mother's claim to the child. How do you explain the difference between the holdings in the two cases? Do you think the cases are distinguishable solely in terms of genetic relatedness or do you agree with Lisa Ikemoto that the birth mother's race helped to determine the outcome?

2. **Liberating Technology or Patriarchal Tool?** The reproductive technologies described in this section seem to have a liberating potential for women: they enable infertile women or women whose partners are infertile to bear children; they have helped single women and lesbians who are often regarded as unfit to raise children to circumvent legal barriers to motherhood; and they challenge traditional notions of what constitutes a family. Yet many of the readings claim that these technologies do just the opposite: they enforce traditional patriarchal roles that privilege men and objectify women's procreative capacity. Do you think that reproduction-assisting technologies devalue women or enhance women's control over their bodies? If these techniques are oppressive, how should we approach some women's desire to use these technologies to become pregnant or have children?

3. **Exploitation of Surrogate Mothers?** Do you agree with the argument that women who serve as surrogate mothers are exploited? If so, in what sense are they exploited: does their exploitation stem from the differences in bargaining power between them and the wealthier couples they contract with, or from the social forces that push them to assume this

work, or from the inherent devaluation of their reproductive capacity entailed in surrogacy? Do find compelling Debra Satz's argument that the problem with surrogacy is related to its perpetuation of women's inequality rather than to its intrinsic qualities? How does this argument account for the women who choose to be surrogates and find it a fulfilling occupation?

4. **Race and New Reproductive Technologies.** Racism, along with gender inequality, influences the fertility industry. First, Blacks make up a disproportionate number of infertile people who *avoid* reproductive technologies. White women seeking treatment for fertility problems are twice as likely to use high-tech treatments such as IVF and egg donation as Black women. *See* Roberts, *Race and the New Reproduction*, in *Killing the Black Body*. Dorothy Roberts argues that this disparity stems from "a complex interplay of financial barriers, cultural preferences, and more deliberate professional manipulation." Second, as Lisa Ikemoto demonstrates, race helps to determine the cultural significance of new reproductive technologies. Roberts similarly argues that the popularity of these techniques depends in large part on the race of the children they produce:

> The new reproduction also graphically discloses the disparate values placed on children of different races. By trading genes on the market, these technologies lay bare the high value placed on whiteness and the worthlessness accorded blackness. New reproductive technologies are so popular in American culture not simply because of the value placed on the genetic tie, but because of the value placed on the *white* genetic tie. The monumental effort, expense, and technological invention that goes into the new reproduction marks the children produced as especially valuable. It proclaims the unmistakable message that white children merit spending billions of dollars toward their creation. Black children, on the other hand, are the object of welfare reform measures designed to discourage poor women's procreation.

Killing the Black Body, at 269.

5. **Social Policy Options.** How should social policy address the gender, race, and class disparities in the fertility business discussed in the readings? Consider three options: 1) continue to allow people who can afford these services to use them if they desire; 2) ensure greater access to these services by providing public assistance or including them in medical insurance plans; 3) discourage proliferation of these technologies through government regulation or even banning certain practices. Which of these options do you think would benefit women most? Is the Constitution relevant to this question: do individuals have a constitutional right to procreation that encompasses their use of reproduction-assisting technologies and even government assistance?

    On the other hand, can we justify the public cost of high-tech services that benefit a relatively small group of people? A study recently reported in the New England Journal of Medicine calculated the real cost of IVF at approximately $67,000 to $800,000 per successful delivery, taking into account the cost of treatment, delivery, and neonatal intensive care for risky multiple births. Peter J. Neuman et al, *The Cost of Successful Delivery with In Vitro Fertilization*, 331 New Eng. J. Med. 239 (1994). Would research designed to reduce infertility, programs that facilitate adoption, and the general improvement of health care, which would benefit a far broader range of people, be a better investment?

B.   RAPE

INTRODUCTION

The law of rape historically regulated competing male interests in controlling sexual access to females, rather than protecting women's interest in controlling their own bodies and sexuality. One of feminism's most dramatic contributions to legal culture has been the effort to transform the aim of rape law as well as to expand society's understanding of what constitutes rape. This project has not been without conflict. Rape embodies physical harm, the infringement of women's autonomy, and a subordinating sexuality. The feminist critique of rape law has accordingly involved both explaining rape as violence and explaining rape as heterosexual sex.

This section concerns the legal treatment of rape. The readings begin with Katharine Baker's examination of the various reasons why men rape and continue with an excerpt from Susan Estrich's extensive article on rape law. Estrich provides a critique of current rape law and proposals for its reform. Her piece is followed by two cases that illustrate contemporary courts' differing approaches to the force and consent elements of statutory definitions of rape. Kimberlé Crenshaw's essay discusses a dimension of rape law often ignored by courts and feminist reformers—how racism influences the meaning of rape in America, particularly by erasing the sexual violation of minority women. Baker's motivational study, Estrich's legal analysis, Crenshaw's racial critique, and the decisions, taken together, are designed to help us consider how the law can resolve competing views of rape.

The readings also include essays by Catharine MacKinnon, bell hooks, and Fran Olsen. Their essays, like Estrich's, are concerned with the relationship between rape, law, and the oppression of women. All four scholars agree that the legal treatment of sexual violence is currently inadequate and that reform is desirable. However, these writers take different positions on why the law is inadequate and how reform might be achieved. To some extent, the differences among the writers correspond to the positions previously attributed in this book to liberal, radical, race-conscious, and postmodern feminism.

Katharine K. Baker, Once a Rapist? Motivational Evidence and the Relevancy of Rape Law

110 Harv. L. Rev. 563 (1997).

Rape is many things. It is a goal in and of itself. It is an instrument of torture. It is a means of proving masculinity. It is a means of getting sex.

Many men rape. They have all done something very wrong. Most of them have not done something particularly extraordinary.

An estimated 12.1 million women in America have been raped. Little suggests that the incidence of rape is decreasing. Rape's prevalence forces women to live with a fear of violation and attack that is essentially unknown to men. This fear cripples women's ability to move freely and to live life as autonomous individuals. It forces women to find protection, often from men, and it fundamentally restricts women's liberty. Clearly, therefore, there are powerful reasons for enacting rules that help to decrease the incidence of rape by securing more rape convictions....

All rapes are not alike. They are not alike in the eyes of the men who commit them, and they are not alike in the eyes of the jurors and the public who judge them. The degree to which different kinds of rape adversely affect victims is still an open inquiry, but it is all too obvious that the perpetrators of rape and the public-at-large view rape along a complex spectrum of permissibility. All rapes are, in part, about sex and masculinity and domination. But some rapes are predominantly about sex, some rapes are predominantly about masculinity, and some rapes are predominantly about domination. This Article argues that we cannot adequately address either the evidentiary problems in rape cases or the issues central to rape reform unless we begin to recognize and incorporate the rather obvious insight that not all rapes are the same....

Distinctions Among Rapes

... Because much of what we know about rape comes from narrative, I offer eight short accounts of rape. Most of these stories are not new; they have been circulating through the legal scholarship on rape for several years. Some of the stories are here because they are familiar, so that we may analyze what the rules should be in those cases that we already know to be rape. All of the stories are here because they have helped us to feel, and therefore to know, the pervasiveness and destructiveness of rape. They have validated unrecognized pain and given name to crimes that had no definition. They have helped us to understand how the law's abstraction of rape has often ignored the reality of women's experience. These stories are our source for what rape is, and they are our starting point for figuring out what to do about it.

Stranger

On a May evening in Boston, a man held an ice pick to the throat of a woman stopped in her car and said: "Push over, shut up or I'll kill you." She did what he said and when he was finished, she fled from her car and he drove away.

My Lai

In March of 1968, "[t]he systematic shooting of old men, women and children at My Lai began at breakfast time. By 10:30 A.M. most of the wanton destruction of unarmed human beings ... had already been accomplished.... It was at this time that enlisted men ... witnessed their first attempted rape of the day." Several days later, a helicopter pilot looked down on My Lai from the air. He saw a body in the field below. "It was a woman," he said. "She was spread-eagled, as if on display. She had an 11th Brigade patch between her legs—as if it were some type of display, some badge of honor."

New Bedford

In 1983, a woman went to Big Dan's Tavern in New Bedford, Massachusetts, to buy cigarettes and to have a drink. She sat at the bar. After a verbal exchange between the woman and a man named Daniel Silva, who had been playing pool, Silva and a partner picked the woman up and carried her across the room as she screamed and sobbed. More men joined in the attack. Two men pulled down her pants, while another two men held her down. There were nine or ten men in the bar that night. It is not clear how many of them raped her. Those who were not raping her stood by and cheered. The rapes lasted more than two hours.

St. John's University

In 1989, a St. John's University student, "Sandra," accepted a ride home from a rifle-club teammate and fellow student, "Mike," who lived in a house with a group of other men. Sandra and Mike stopped at Mike's house because he said he needed money for gas; he invited Sandra inside to meet his housemates. Once inside, the men offered Sandra a drink. She said that drinking made her sick, but they insisted. She complied with their requests that she drink. At one point, Mike held the cup to her lips and forced her to drink. Sandra soon felt very ill and began to pass out. Mike took off her shirt and bra and began to kiss her. She then passed out completely. She awoke to find Mike's penis in her mouth. When she tried to remove it, he put it back in. She was too intoxicated to get up or move. She continued to drift in and out of consciousness. Other men in the household sodomized her and banged their penises against her head. She awoke to feel the men ejaculating on her chest.

The Train

"Vanessa was thirteen years old and very naive. She thought she had gone to [an older male friend's house] just to talk with somebody she had a crush on. A bunch of the fellas hid in closets and under beds. When she stepped inside and sat down, they sprang from their hiding places and blocked the door so that she couldn't leave. When I got there, two or three dudes were in the back room, trying to persuade her to give it up.... Some had never even had sex before, yet they were trying to act like they knew what to do. I fronted, too. I acted like I was eager to get on Vanessa, because that's how everybody else was acting.... She looked so sad that I started to feel sorry for her. Something in me wanted to reach out and do what I knew was right.... But I couldn't do that. It was too late. This was our first train together as a group. All the fellas were there and everybody was anxious to show everybody else how cool and worldly he was.... We weren't aware of what it symbolized at the time, but that train marked our real coming together as a gang."

Spur Posse

In the spring of 1993, a group of teenage boys in Southern California devised a game of sorts in which each boy was afforded a point every time that he achieved orgasm with a girl. The boys got points whether the girls were dates who consented and/or enjoyed the activity or "[w]hores you just nut and you leave." The typical act involved "just throw[ing] a couple of pumps, and you're done." Most of the girls involved were young teenagers between the ages of ten and sixteen.

Thomas

Anne, a seventeen-year-old freshman at Stanford who had been at college only a few days, stopped by Thomas's room because she heard familiar music. Thomas was a twenty-three year-old varsity athlete. Thomas offered Anne a beer and some peppermint schnapps. She drank them. During a two-hour period, she drank eight glasses of schnapps. She began to feel very sleepy. She lay down. She and Thomas began to kiss. He undressed her. She felt intimidated by Thomas but did not initially ask him to stop. When she became aware that he wanted to "go[ ] beyond holding and kissing," she told him to stop. "I can't do this," she said, "I have a boyfriend." "[H]e doesn't have to know," Thomas said. "I'm a virgin," Anne protested. "No one has to know, your family doesn't have to find out, this can be between you and me. If you want it, it's O.K. I won't hurt you." Thomas proceeded to insert his erect penis into her vagina. Anne felt a sharp pain and said, "Ow, stop." Thomas stopped temporarily. After a few minutes of more kissing and fondling, he inserted his penis again. Again, she said, "Ow, stop." He stopped. Lying there afterwards, Thomas said, "If you don't want it in you, will you at least kiss it?"

John

"We got home.... He'd left something in my refrigerator, so of course he had to come in.... I was saying something innocuous ... and the next thing I know, I've been struck, and I've hit the floor.... And then he's on top of me, ... and he's saying, 'I don't want to hurt you. I don't want to hurt you. Don't scream. Relax and I won't hurt you.' ... I had the feeling that I could get seriously hurt if I screamed.... When it was all over, he just sort of lay there, and then did the classic thing of apologizing. 'I've never done this before. Forgive me.'"

In the past twenty years, feminists and legal scholars have made tremendous strides in recognizing the similarities between these narrative accounts. To the women involved, these acts are rape. They are all horrific violations of women's physical and emotional integrity. They all represent ways in which men maintain power advantages over women by forcing them to live with a ubiquitous fear of rape. The acts in these stories could all be considered felonies or misdemeanors under most state laws. For people who are concerned about stopping rape and freeing women from the severe restrictions that the fear of rape imposes, recognizing the common criminality of these acts is indisputable progress. For purposes of criminal law, evidence law, and effective future rape reform, however, one cannot ignore how these rapes are different. . . . Failure to recognize such distinctions leads to a monolithic construction of rape that focuses on the small percentage of men who commit stereotypical rapes and stifles further attempts to understand why sexualized violence exists. If we are to secure rape convictions that are true and that touch every level of the population, we must recognize distinctions in motivation. . . .

All of the narratives above may depict severe violations of women's autonomy, personhood, and physical and emotional integrity, and they all include a sexual component, but that does not make them all the same thing. The state statutes recognize that there are many different kinds of rape, involving very different kinds of force, manipulation, coercion, and degrees of consent. If there was consensus that all of these rapes were essentially the same act, we would not have the myriad of definitions that now fill the statute books. If there is no consensus that all of these rapes are essentially the same act, it is not at all clear that the commission of one kind of sexual assault is probative of a likelihood to commit another kind of sexual assault. . . .

A Large Class of Normal Human Beings

. . . [T]he last twenty-five years of research clearly demonstrate that the class of rapists is neither small nor particularly likely to be depraved. In a 1988 nationwide survey of more than 6100 college students, one in twelve college men admitted to committing rape. Another study found forty-three percent of college males reporting that they had engaged in coercive sex. The coercion ranged from ignoring women's protests to using physical force. Fifteen percent of this group acknowledged committing acquaintance rape; eleven percent admitted using physical restraint. Twenty-three percent of a random sample of 1846 college-age men responded "yes" to the question: "Have you ever been in a situation where you became so sexually aroused that you could not stop yourself even though the woman didn't want to?" These men may not all have been committing acts that resemble the acts of the soldiers at My Lai or the stranger with an ice pick, but they were all committing rape. "Small" simply does not describe the size of the rapist class.

Numerous studies have also found that men who rape are "normal" to the extent that psychologists fail to find evidence of abnormality. Male levels of sexual aggression do not correlate with elevated scores on the Psychopathic Deviate scale. One well-cited study found that thirty-five percent of college men indicated a likelihood to rape if they were sure that they could get away with it. Psychologists working with rapists in prison report that the incident of mental illness among rapists varies from only two to twenty percent. Researchers have consistently failed to find significant psychological differences between the rapist and nonrapist populations. There is simply no evidence, save the rape itself, suggesting that all or even most rapists are objectively depraved.

Nonetheless, a tendency to rape can be linked to objective variables. Macrosociological research on rape strongly suggests that the prevalence of rape is positively correlated with a variety of social phenomena, including the acceptance of gender inequality, the prevalence of pornography, and the degree of social disorganization in a community. The self-reported likelihood to rape is also strongly related "to acceptance of rape myths, acceptance of violence against women, and sex role stereotyping." States with a high incidence of rape have a rate that is five to ten times greater than states with a low incidence of rape, thus suggesting that the prevalence of rape is linked to community norms. What this suggests, in contradistinction to the legislative assumption and in support of feminist theory on the subject, is that rape is culturally dictated, not culturally deviant. Given the prevalence of the social norms that encourage rape, one can hardly define the class of men who hold these norms as abnormal. . . .

The Motive Question

. . . In order to secure more rape convictions without perpetuating or exacerbating current inequities and myths, we must start focusing both our academic inquiry and legal practice on the question of why men rape. By focusing on the question of why, we accomplish two different goals. First, we pave the way for a more equitable and comprehensive enforcement of rape law by belying the myths of who rapes. Second, we pave the way for more effective and realistic rape-reform measures by furthering our collective understanding of what rape is and why sexualized violence exists.

For too long, juries have essentially ignored the question of why men rape. Instead, juries have assumed, wrongly, that rapists rape because they are crazy and because women ask for it. This neglect of the "why" question is somewhat odd, given the importance of motivational questions in criminal trials. For many crimes, of course, motive is obvious. People rob banks, snatch purses, cheat on their taxes, or blackmail others for money or personal gain. For some crimes, however, particularly crimes that do not involve pecuniary reward, motive can be much more difficult to discern. . . .

Apparently, some commentators find the emphasis on motive, at least in rape cases, misplaced. David Bryden and Roger Park write, without explication, that "[m]otive is not a mystery in a sex crime case." Really? Think back to the narratives offered at the outset of Part II. Is it obvious why the man who raped Susan Estrich did it? Is it obvious why the St. John's University athletes sodomized a comatose guest in their house? What motivated John, the man who apologized after raping his date, to rape her? Is it obvious why Nathan McCall joined that train? Was he motivated by the same thing that John was? Were the soldiers at My Lai motivated by the same thing motivating Thomas, the Stanford athlete who said "[i]f you don't want it in you, will you at least kiss it?" We may be able to develop answers to these questions, and with some analysis I hope to do so. But one can hardly dismiss the motive question in rape law as self-evident, particularly given well-documented and demonstrably false public belief about rapist motivation. What follows is an explication of the "why" question. The answers to the "why" question vary in different situations; rapists do not all rape for the same reasons. We learn essential lessons about what rape is—and why juries respond to it as they do—by delving into the question of why men rape. By analyzing why men rape, we also better understand when prior acts of sexual assault should be admissible.

Sex

1. *Sex and Lovemaking.*—Some men rape because they want sex. Possibly aware of this, a number of academics, in an effort to explain what rape is, have attempted to define what sex should be and what rape is not. Rape is not lovemaking. Lovemaking, according to one such feminist theory, is "the practice of a communicative sexuality, one which combines the appropriate knowledge of the other with respect for the dialectics of desire." Another theory posits that "sexual conduct is mutual and acceptable when animating inducements are the parties' desires for sexual pleasure or for intimacy." One need not dispute the accuracy of these definitions of lovemaking, or their benefit in helping us to understand and restructure sexuality, in order to question their utility in rape-reform efforts. Consider Thomas, the athlete, or the numerous date rapists who seem to expect a dating relationship to continue notwithstanding the fact that they have raped the woman that they want to date. On the evenings of the rapes in question, these men might well have sought to practice communicative sexuality. They may have been looking for shared sexual pleasure and intimacy. That was what motivated them. That was what they wanted. That was what sex was supposed to represent and help them achieve. But, in reality, they had no idea what they were looking for. The abstract goal may have been lovemaking, but it is exceedingly difficult to understand communicative sexuality, sexual pleasure, and intimacy, particularly when one is young and inexperienced.

Rapists are young. Donna Schram found that the majority of sex offenders represented in police data are between eighteen and twenty-five years old. In a San Antonio study, thirty-four percent of the rapists were under age twenty-five; sixty-eight percent were under age thirty. Research documents that coercive behavior in college men is positively correlated with immaturity, irresponsibility, and lack of social conscience. Youth probably commit a disproportionate number of all crimes, but what is important in analyzing rapist motivation is that youthful predisposition for irresponsible and criminal activity coincides with male sexual coming of age.

Immature or inexperienced men, unfamiliar with what lovemaking is but looking for it and cast by culture into the role of pursuer, go experimenting. The experimenting can become coercive because many boys are taught that power, dominance, and violence can be arousing to women. Leaving aside the question whether we ought to regulate or ban pornography, its existence and the prevalence of its distribution clearly affect the extent to which men believe that violence is sensual. Men who believe that women enjoy sexual violence are more likely to use force to obtain sex and are more likely to self-report a willingness to rape. In one study, respondents who were exposed to a depiction of a woman being sexually aroused by assault showed an increased belief that rape and all forced sexual acts could be pleasurable to women. These men perceived rape victims as suffering only minimal trauma. Another study of college men and women found that their exposure to films depicting sexual violence against women increased their acceptance of interpersonal violence against women. Sociological studies confirm that distribution of violent pornography is positively correlated to an increased rape rate. Given these findings, it is not surprising that many men who want to make love end up committing sexual assault.

Even when boys do not presume that power and coercion are pleasurable for women, their use of physical strength to get what they want is comprehensible and common. Consider a typical response to the candy machine that refuses to dispense the candybar for which one has inserted seventy-five cents. One puts in the money, pushes the button, and nothing happens. Maybe one puts in another seventy-five cents; maybe one just pushes the buttons again, this time with more force. Then one pushes the buttons a third time, with even more force. Finally, one slams the palm of one's hand against the machine in an effort to get the candybar to fall. This is a common use of force to get what one wants and feels entitled to. It is usually a pointless and relatively harmless use of force against inanimate objects. The comparable use of force against animate objects is, in contrast, often effective and very harmful.

Many rapes involve comparable uses of force. The kinds of encounters that are marked by brief assertions of power, constant cajoling, or infusion of a great deal of alcohol often involve force, coercion, and domination as an instrumental means of getting sex. In a study of college students, Margaret Hamilton and Jack Yee found that rape is more often a form of instrumental aggression, by which the authors indicate a means of attaining the goal of sexual gratification, than it is a means of expressing anger or hostility toward women. The fact that these rapes involve violence does not mean that, from the perpetrator's perspective, they are not fundamentally about sexual experimentation. Most of these young men do not understand the distinctions between lovemaking and sex and rape. Some of them might even be trying to make love. Although they want to, their dates do not. Precisely because the lines of personhood and autonomy are so confused during sex, men try to force what they want. Intimacy necessarily involves a breaking down of boundaries; it is no surprise that people experimenting with intimacy do not initially understand the rules of trespassing against those boundaries.

2. *Sex and Shoplifting.*—No doubt, many readers are incensed at the candy-machine analogy. Women are not goods. Rape is not theft. Robbery is not the ultimate violation of self next to murder. Goods have no self. Women do. I draw the commodification analogy purposefully, however, not

to endorse commodification as a normatively appropriate way for the law to conceptualize rape and/or sex, but to demonstrate that the commodification framework may best explain both the defendant's state of mind and society's frequent failure to condemn men for rape.

For some, sex is a commodity, and if sex is a commodity, then taking it is theft. The definitions of lovemaking discussed above may attempt to resist the classification of sex as a commodity, but most people rarely, if ever, discuss the personal, intimate, and shared experiences of sex. We live in a culture that rarely discusses sex as anything other than a commodity. Indeed, the more objectified and commodified the conversation, the easier it is for most people—especially young people—to talk about sex. Some people are never able to talk about the intimate aspects of sex, even if they do understand them. It is hardly surprising that most young people neither talk about nor understand sexual intimacy.

Instead, youths, particularly young men, are bombarded by a culture that sexualizes commodities and commodifies women's sexuality. Companies sell products by selling the sexuality of the women endorsing the product. The product and the sex are purposefully conflated. Sex is also purposefully commodified. Men can easily buy sex, even though all but one state prohibit prostitution. Men can also buy pornography and purchase tickets to peep shows. What motivates many rapists may not be substantively different from that which motivates men who go to prostitutes or purchase tickets to peep shows. None of these acts requires mutual enjoyment or emotional intimacy, and they are all called sex. Thus, men are able to satisfy a desire for sex without having to incorporate the complexities of sexually intimate communication.

This cultural endorsement and marketing of sex as a commodified good leads to an increased desire for, and sense of entitlement to, sex. Most men are taught that sexual desire is like hunger: when it is there, you satisfy it. Women are candybars. Of course, food is not free and neither is sex, but precisely because men can and do pay for sex, taking it without consent becomes much less morally reprehensible than other violent crimes. Thus, it is not surprising that one study found that thirty-nine percent of convicted rapists were caught in the course of a robbery. As many of these men conceded, they raped because she was there. They were already breaking the laws of trespass and ownership—why not take one more thing?

Men know that taking sex without consent is wrong, but many men do not perceive it as really bad. The relationship between alcohol and rape demonstrates this point. In one study of college men who had committed sexual assault, seventy-five percent said that they had used alcohol or drugs prior to the assault. Another study of convicted rapists found a comparable seventy-five percent who admitted to using drugs or alcohol prior to the attack. All of the college gang rapes that were analyzed in a 1985 study involved alcohol. This direct relationship between alcohol use and rape exists, despite clear scientific evidence showing that "[a]lcohol disinhibits psychological sexual arousal and suppresses physiological responding."

What may explain the correspondence between alcohol use and rape therefore is not alcohol's affect on sex drive, but rather alcohol's tendency to decrease inhibitions against taking that to which one has no right. Teenagers get drunk and go get sex in the same way that they get high and go to the 7–11 to shoplift candybars. They know it is wrong, but it is not that bad. Most adolescents do not get drunk and go rob banks. They do not get drunk and commit murder. They do get drunk and break little rules. They shoplift and joyride and vandalize. The rule against raping, particularly date raping, is like the rule against shoplifting—it is a little rule.

The above analysis is deeply disturbing. However much men do view women as candybars, women are not candybars. Because women are not candybars, rape is not shoplifting. Rape, at least in the words of one survivor, "is death." It is "a primal experience to which other events might be meaningfully analogized—the 'rape' of the land, the 'rape' of a people. But rape itself cannot be reduced to other painful experiences." The social proscription against inflicting such a horrific experience upon another human being should be a powerful one; it should be a Big Rule, not a little rule. But currently, it may very well not be. This little-rule hypothesis explains, in part, both why people refuse to condemn rape and why juries acquit. Juries do not send men to jail for pocketing candybars.

For more than twenty-five years now, feminists have been writing to tell the world that rape is annihilation, that it is like murder, that it is really, really bad. The reluctance of juries to convict rapists and the public opinion research on rape suggest that most people still refuse to believe this message. People may not be able to see what rape is, however, until they reconceptualize what sex is. It will be hard for people to believe that rape is like murder as long as we maintain a commodified view of sex. If sex is a commodity, taking it is theft.

The commodification of sex and the relative impunity with which society treats extorting that commodity, coupled with the prevalence of sexualized violence and instrumental physical aggression, explain several different kinds of rape. These theories explain the confused and somewhat pathetic date rapists looking for some amorphous concept of lovemaking, and the theories explain why some men want sex and simply take it without entertaining any illusion of lovemaking. Commodification may also, in part, explain what motivated the soldiers at My Lai. The soldiers wanted sex because it was a good, like any other, that they could take from the enemy.

But theories of commodification and instrumental aggression have their limits. They cannot explain why the soldiers at My Lai placed their 11th Brigade patch between the legs of the women whom they left dead, spread-eagled in a field. Nor does either theory explain why the men in New Bedford cheered and goaded the others into performance. Commodification and instrumental aggression do not explain why men who do not want to rape the victim of a train nonetheless do so. These theories seem incomplete as an explanation of why the group of St. John's University students had sex with a woman who was not even conscious, and they do not explain why the Spur Posse gang needed a point system. If the commodified good is its own reward, why bother to keep score?

Relationships Among Men

1. *Uniting.*—The questions just posed are best answered by examining how men use rape to relate to other men. Men often rape women to demonstrate their strength, virulence, and masculinity to other men. For these men, having an audience is critical; intercourse is instrumental. The authors of one of the first extensive studies of men who rape conclude that "[m]en do not rape women out of a sexual desire for other men, but they may rape women, in part, as a way to relate to men." Chris O'Sullivan, studying fraternity rapes, writes that "participation in a group sexual assault is motivated by the relationships among the men, for the purpose of maintaining or creating images and roles within the group."

Thus, the Spur Posse boys developed a point system to distinguish themselves from each other. The more points the boys got, the more respect they commanded within the group. The need to relate to other men also explains the St. John's University incident. Those boys ejaculated on that comatose woman's chest, sodomized her, and whipped their penises across her comatose face to show off to each other. They could not have been trying to control or show off to her; she was unconscious. Nor were they necessarily likely to have assaulted her if they had been acting alone.

One study found that most gang rapes involve an instigator and followers. Forty-three percent of the gang rape offenders studied were followers. Followers only rape in the context of the gang. It is the group and the need to "confirm his masculinity, achieve recognition, and/or retain his acceptance with his co-offenders" that motivates the follower. The men in New Bedford who cheered for their friends and then took their turn at raping the victim were not looking for sex as much as camaraderie. Nathan McCall joined the train not because he wanted sexual gratification, but as he admits, because he wanted to show his fellow gang members how "cool and worldly he was" and because he wanted to be a part of the ceremony that marked the "coming together as a gang."

2. *Dividing.*—Men also rape women in order to establish power over, or distinction from, other men. Again, using women at a purely instrumental level, men rape women who they view to be the property of other men. These rapists rape not because they want or need the good—i.e., the sex or the woman—but because the good belongs to a man whom they wish to insult. Thus, the U.S. soldiers left the 11th Brigade patch in order to impugn the honor of North Vietnamese men. The U.S. soldiers could have gotten their sex without leaving manifest evidence that they had done so. They could have just killed the women in the same way in which they destroyed the village's animals, property, and elderly men. By making the fact of their rapes public, the soldiers added further insult to the enemy. This view explains why rapes during war time often take place in public or are committed in front of civilian witnesses, and it explains why rape and war have gone hand in hand since there has been war. The rapist seeks to

demonstrate the superiority of his team. He does this by raping the property of the enemy.

This use of rape to insult or denigrate other men has particular impact in racial contexts. Perhaps Eldridge Cleaver described it best: "Rape [is] an insurrectionary act. It delighted me that I was defying and trampling upon the white man's law, upon his system of values, and that I was defiling his women.... I felt I was getting revenge." As Cleaver himself admits, he started out raping black women for practice, but what motivated him to keep raping white women was a desire to send a message to white men.

Fear that interracial rapes are motivated by such a desire to divide and denigrate can also partially explain the racist enforcement of rape law. Some members of white culture are particularly offended by interracial rape not because the white woman has suffered a more egregious violation, but because all of white culture, its "law" and "system of values," has been defied. Black men were lynched for raping white women precisely because white men understood that rape was intended to be used as a weapon against white men and white women.

Power and Anger

1. *Power.*—In 1977, Nicholas Groth, Ann Burgess, and Lynda Holmstrom published an influential psychological analysis of rapist motivation. Their thesis, in short, was:

> [I]n all cases of forcible rape three components are present: power, anger and sexuality. The hierarchy and interrelationships among these three factors, together with the relative intensity with which each is experienced and the variety of ways in which each is expressed, may vary.... [But] power or anger dominates and ... rape, rather than being primarily an expression of sexual desire, is, in fact, the use of sexuality to express issues of power and anger.

Recent research refutes the universality of this power typology: Groth and his coauthors limited their studies to more traditional rapes, and later studies conducted with convicted rapists indicate that factors as diverse as an inability to interpret heterosocial messages, an acceptance of interpersonal violence, and a desire for intimacy all operate interactively, not independently, to motivate some men to rape. Nonetheless, no one disputes the role that power and anger play in many rapes.

Rape necessarily involves an assertion of power. As discussed above, some men use this power instrumentally, to get sex, or to get sex in order to relate to other men. Other men use power for its own sake. Power rapists rape because they want to establish control over their victims. They rarely exert more strength than is necessary to force their victims into submission. Rape—the act of controlling—not sex, is critical to their motivation to rape.

This kind of motivation explains a variety of kinds of rape. For instance, the prison rapist may rape to establish himself above his victim in the prison hierarchy; by dominating his victim, he elevates his own position. He may also establish power in the prison community because, like others who share or display their rapes, he sends the message that, "because I rape, I deserve your respect."

Unlike many of the rapes that were described in the previous section, however, power rapists also rape to establish control over their particular victims. The identity of the subject/victim is critical. Power rapists want to control their particular victim. They use rape to do so. As one analyst of prison systems explains, "[t]here aren't many weapons in prison, so the penis becomes a weapon of control.... It is how prisoners assert themselves and show others that they are unassailable." Once prison rapists have other methods of control at their disposal, for instance, when they get out of prison, they do not necessarily continue to rape those over whom they want control. There is no evidence that prison rapists become chronic rapists or that they choose to have sex with other men once they leave prison.

This is not to say that either heterosexual or homosexual power rapes are devoid of a sexual component. Some prison rapists rape to get a "punk" and provide themselves with a sexual outlet. Some heterosexual power rapists rape women to establish sexual control. Consider the comments of several men studied in an analysis of male attitudes toward sexual violence. These men do not self-report for having raped, but they were asked to explain their feelings about rape:

> If I were actually desperate enough to rape somebody, it would be from wanting the person, but also it would be a very spiteful thing, just being able to say, "I have power over you and I can do anything I want with you," because really I feel that *they* have power over me just by their presence.

> When you see a girl walking around wearing real skimpy clothes, she's offending you and I guess rape would be a way of getting even.

> I've always felt powerless to come on to a woman who was being that sexual.... She had all this power.

Although some deeply disturbing notions of power and sexuality must inform these men's understanding of rape, it is also clear that, for these men, rape is different than sex. They would not rape to have sex, nor would they rape to show off to other men. They would rape to assert control, albeit sexual, over a very specific subject—their victim.

This kind of motivation also explains much marital rape. A husband rapes in order to assert control over a wife who is somehow defying his command. His wife may not want to have sex, or she may simply have annoyed him. He rapes her to control her, to make her his subject. Often, the husband also assaults his wife in less sexual ways: he punches her, he throws her downstairs, he shoots bullets at her, he chokes her. Sometimes he just rapes her. Unlike the man in prison, the husband has many weapons in his arsenal; his penis is just one of them. But like the man in prison, he uses his penis to establish control over his victim.

2. *Anger and Sadism.*—Groth and his colleagues also developed an anger rapist typology. The anger rapist assaults his victim completely. He attacks all parts of her body, often forces her to engage in repeated, nonsexual degrading acts, and uses much more violence than is necessary to force her into submission. "The aim of this type of rapist is to vent his rage on his victim and to retaliate for perceived wrongs or rejections he has suffered at the hands of women.... This offender displays a great deal of anger and contempt toward women." The offender "does not seek out a specific victim but instead discharges his anger onto someone who is immediately available." Some anger rapists reach the point of what Groth calls sadism. In these situations, "[t]here is a sexual transformation of anger and power so that aggression itself becomes eroticized." Often these rapists murder their victims after, and possibly even before, raping them. Many of these rapists rape with increasing frequency.

Most of the angry and sadistic rapists are men who, with some degree of medical certainty and social consensus, we can label mentally ill. Many of these men suffer from psychopathology. Everybody agrees that what these men do breaks a Big Rule. Everybody agrees that these men should be punished. These men are the paradigm, but they are not most rapists. Seventy percent of rape victims report no physical injury and another twenty-four percent report only minor physical injury. Most rape victims are not victims of angry, sadistic rapists. This does not mean that most rape victims are not raped; it does not mean that rape victims fabricate their stories; and it does not mean that what happens to them is okay. It does belie the common belief that rapists are crazy men whose sadistic hunger for sex or hatred of women compels them to rape....

Susan Estrich, Rape

95 Yale L. J. 1087 (1986).

... The rapes that I examine in this Article are, like my own, the rapes of adult, competent women by men. I have simply excluded from my consideration the additional problems presented when young girls or un-conscious women are raped; it is enough for me to try to understand the application of the law to women who are not special or different in these ways. I have put almost as far to one side the issue of race as a dominant theme. The history of rape, as the law has been enforced in this country, is a history of both racism and sexism.[1] One could write an article of this

---

1. The death penalty for rape in this country, now unconstitutional under *Coker v. Georgia,* 433 U.S. 584 (1977), was traditionally reserved for black men who raped white women. Between 1930 and 1967, 89% of the men executed for rape in this country were black. That figure includes 36% of the black men who were convicted of raping a white woman; only 2% of the defendants convicted of rape involving any other racial combination were executed. ...Although the death penalty for rape is now prohibited, at least one study has found that black men convicted

length dealing only with the racism. I address it in places—for its influence is pervasive—but I cannot do justice to both. My focus is sexism. . . .

To examine rape within the criminal law tradition is to expose fully the sexism of the law. Much that is striking about the crime of rape—and revealing of the sexism of the system—emerges only when rape is examined relative to other crimes, which the feminist literature by and large does not do. For example, rape is most assuredly not the only crime in which consent is a defense; but it is the only crime that has required the victim to resist physically in order to establish nonconsent. Nor is rape the only crime where prior relationship is taken into account by prosecutors in screening cases; yet we have not asked whether considering prior relationship in rape cases is different, and less justifiable, than considering it in cases of assault.

Sexism in the law of rape is no matter of mere historical interest; it endures, even where some of the most blatant testaments to that sexism have disappeared. Corroboration requirements unique to rape may have been repealed, but they continue to be enforced as a matter of practice in many jurisdictions. The victim of rape may not be required to resist to the utmost as a matter of statutory law in any jurisdiction, but the definitions accorded to force and consent may render "reasonable" resistance both a practical and a legal necessity. In the law of rape, supposedly dead horses continue to run.

The study of rape as an illustration of sexism in the criminal law also raises broader questions about the way conceptions of gender and the different backgrounds and perspectives of men and women should be encompassed within the criminal law. In one of his most celebrated essays, Oliver Wendell Holmes explained that the law does not exist to tell the good man what to do, but to tell the bad man what not to do. Holmes was interested in the distinction between the good and bad man; I cannot help noticing that both are men. Most of the time, a criminal law that reflects male views and male standards imposes its judgment on men who have injured other men. It is "boys' rules" applied to a boys' fight. In rape, the male standard defines a crime committed against women, and male standards are used not only to judge men, but also to judge the conduct of women victims. Moreover, because the crime involves sex itself, the law of rape inevitably treads on the explosive ground of sex roles, of male aggression and female passivity, of our understandings of sexuality—areas where differences between a male and a female perspective may be most pronounced. . . .

At one end of the spectrum is the "real" rape, what I will call the traditional rape: A stranger puts a gun to the head of his victim, threatens to kill her or beats her, and then engages in intercourse. In that case, the law—judges, statutes, prosecutors and all—generally acknowledge that a serious crime has been committed. But most cases deviate in one or many respects from this clear picture, making interpretation far more complex.

of raping white women continue to receive the harshest penalties.

Where less force is used or no other physical injury is inflicted, where threats are inarticulate, where the two know each other, where the setting is not an alley but a bedroom, where the initial contact was not a kidnapping but a date, where the woman says no but does not fight, the understanding is different. In such cases, the law, as reflected in the opinions of the courts, the interpretation, if not the words, of the statutes, and the decisions of those within the criminal justice system, often tell us that no crime has taken place and that fault, if any is to be recognized, belongs with the woman. In concluding that such acts—what I call, for lack of a better title, "non-traditional" rapes—are not criminal, and worse, that the woman must bear any guilt, the law has reflected, legitimized, and enforced a view of sex and women which celebrates male aggressiveness and punishes female passivity. And that vision, while under attack in recent years, continues to be a dominant force in our society and in the law of rape. . . .

[T]his Article is an argument that the law can make a difference—and that it should. But the answer is not to write the perfect statute. While some statutes invite a more restrictive application than others, there is no "model statute" solution to rape law, because the problem has never been the words of the statutes as much as our interpretation of them. A typical statute of the 1890's—punishing a man who engages in sexual intercourse "by force" and "against the will and without the consent" of the woman— may not be all that different from the "model" statute we will enforce in the 1990's. The difference must come in our understanding of "consent" and "will" and "force."

Some of those who have written about rape from a feminist perspective intimate that nothing short of political revolution can redress the failings of the traditional approach to rape, that most of what passes for "sex" in our capitalist society is coerced, and that no lines can or should be drawn between rape and what happens in tens of millions of bedrooms across America.

So understood, this particular feminist vision of rape shares one thing with the most traditional sexist vision: the view that non-traditional rape is not fundamentally different from what happens in tens of millions of bedrooms across America. According to the radical feminist, all of it is rape; according to the traditionalist, it is all permissible sex and seduction. In policy terms, neither is willing to draw lines between rape and permissible sex. As a result, the two visions, contradictory in every other respect, point to the same practical policy implications.

My own view is different from both of these. I recognize that both men and women in our society have long accepted norms of male aggressiveness and female passivity which lead to a restricted understanding of rape. And I do not propose, nor do I think it feasible, to punish all of the acts of sexual intercourse that could be termed coerced. But lines can be drawn between these two alternatives. The law should be understood to prohibit claims and threats to secure sex that would be prohibited by extortion law and fraud or false pretenses law as a means to secure money. The law should evaluate the conduct of "reasonable" men, not according to a *Playboy*-macho philosophy that says "no means yes," but by according respect to a woman's words. If in 1986 silence does not negate consent, at least crying and saying "no" should.

Traditionally, the law has done more than reflect the restrictive and sexist views of our society; it has legitimized and contributed to them. In the same way, a law that rejected those views and respected female autonomy might do more than reflect the changes in our society; it might even push them forward a bit. . . .

The traditional way of defining a crime is by describing the prohibited act (*actus reus*) committed by the defendant and the prohibited mental state (*mens rea*) with which he must have done it. We ask: What did the defendant do? What did he know or intend when he did it?

The definition of rape stands in striking contrast to this tradition, because courts, in defining the crime, have focused almost incidentally on the defendant—and almost entirely on the victim. . . . Such a reversal also occurs in the course of defining the elements of the crime. *Mens rea,* where it might matter, is all but eliminated; prohibited force tends to be defined according to the response of the victim; and nonconsent—the *sine qua non* of the offense—turns entirely on the victim's response.

But while the focus is on the female victim, the judgment of her actions is entirely male. If the issue were what the defendant knew, thought, or intended as to key elements of the offense, this perspective might be understandable; yet the issue has instead been the appropriateness of the woman's behavior, according to male standards of appropriate female behavior. . . . Apart from the woman's conduct, the law provides no clear, working definition of rape. This rather conspicuous gap in the law of rape presents substantial questions of fair warning for men, which the law not so handily resolves by imposing the burden of warning them on women.

At its simplest, the dilemma lies in this: If nonconsent is essential to rape (and no amount of force or physical struggle is inherently inconsistent with lawful sex), and if no sometimes means yes, and if men are supposed to be aggressive in any event, how is a man to know when he has crossed the line? And how are we to avoid unjust convictions?

This dilemma is hardly inevitable. Partly, it is a product of the way society (or at least a powerful part of it) views sex. Partly, it is a product of the lengths to which the law has gone to enforce and legitimize those views. We could prohibit the use of force and threats and coercion in sex, regardless of "consent." We could define consent in a way that respected the autonomy of women. Having chosen neither course, however, we have created a problem of fair warning, and force and consent have been defined in an effort to resolve this problem.

Two Models of Reform Legislation

I want to focus on the two statutory schemes which have been the most important models of reform—the Model Penal Code and the Michigan criminal sexual conduct statute. Both models claim to be "reforms" in that they seek to make changes in the common law tradition. The Model Penal Code, its commentators claimed in 1980, is the "balanced" approach. The Michigan statute has been widely described as a model "feminist" approach.

Theoretically, a reform statute might move beyond the most traditional understanding of rape either by focusing on the victim and giving meaning to the consent standard and respect to a woman's words of refusal, or by focusing on the man and expanding our understanding of the force and coercion that makes intercourse rape. The Model Penal Code focuses on the woman, but it does not empower her. The Michigan statute focuses on the man; but it does not expand our understanding of force and coercion. As "reforms," both are far more limited than either their proponents or opponents would acknowledge. According to the empirical studies, neither of these reforms, or any of the statutes modeled on them, have had a significant, measurable impact on the actual processing of rape complaints.

The Model Penal Code

... The Code begins with the premise that the nonconsent of the woman is critical to make male conduct, no matter how aggressive, rape: "If the law regards the female as competent to consent and if she does do so, intercourse is not rape." Moreover, "the possibility of consent by the victim, even in the face of conduct that may give some evidence of overreaching, cannot be ignored." But at the same time, echoing the Freudian approach of student commentaries of the 1950's and 1960's, the Code argues that a consent standard that allowed women, simply in saying no to a man and repeating it to a jury, to establish a charge of rape would afford them unjustified power:

[O]ften the woman's attitude may be deeply ambivalent. She may not want intercourse, may fear it, or may desire it but feel compelled to say "no." Her confusion at the time of the act may later resolve into non-consent. ... The deceptively simple notion of consent may obscure a tangled mesh of psychological complexity, ambiguous communication, and unconscious restructuring of the event by the participants.

This is, of course, precisely the dilemma that traditionally led common law courts and commentators to insist on resistance by the woman—even utmost resistance—as a matter of law. The Code is "balanced" in its attack on both sides of the resistance debate, criticizing both those who "place[ ] disproportionate emphasis upon objective manifestations of nonconsent by the woman" (the resistance school) and those who go "too far in the opposite direction" (Michigan) by statutorily eliminating the resistance requirement.

The Code's answer to the immediate resistance conflict is to recognize the evidentiary relevance, if not legal necessity, of female resistance. As for the larger dilemma, the Code eschews any effort to provide objectivity by actually defining force and consent: The Code requires force (or threats of serious bodily injury) by the man and nonconsent by the woman, but defines neither, thus leaving courts and juries free to focus their attention and judgment on the woman victim in the most traditional, restrictive way. Instead the Code seeks "objectivity" through a series of rules that call into question female reliability and honesty ("subjectivity"), even as the focus of inquiry remains almost exclusively on the woman.

The first such rule is the requirement of corroboration of the victim's testimony, a rule which did not exist at common law and which is imposed by the Code only in cases of rape and sexual assault. The usual justification for corroboration requirements is that women intentionally lie about sex. The Code commentaries tread carefully on the paradigm of the vengeful and lying female, and the one who fantasizes rape. "[N]o doubt such cases exist," but the whole area is a "murky ground." Nor do the commentaries seek to justify the corroboration rule on the ground that judges and juries will too quickly rush to express their outrage about rape through conviction. Their concern echoes Lord Hale's insistence on the difficulty of defending against a false accusation of a sexual offense. The commentary argues:

> The difference between criminal and non-criminal conduct depends ultimately on a question of attitude. Proof of this elusive issue often boils down to a confrontation of conflicting accounts. The corroboration requirement is an attempt to skew resolution of such disputes in favor of the defendant. It does not, or at least need not, rest on the assertion that one person's testimony is inherently more deserving of credence [than] another's. ...It is, rather, a determination to favor justice to the defendant, even at some cost to societal interest in effective law enforcement and to the personal demand of the victim for redress. In short, the corroboration requirement should not be understood as an effort to discount female testimony or as an unsympathetic understanding of the female experience with sexual aggression. It is, rather, only a particular implementation of the general policy that uncertainty should be resolved in favor of the accused.

The problem with this explanation is that the policy of resolving uncertainty in favor of the defendant is one which is already addressed in every criminal trial by the requirement of proof beyond a reasonable doubt. Why is that constitutional mandate sufficient to protect the rights of all criminal defendants except those accused of rape? The answer—if it is not that rape victims are disproportionately liars or that rape juries are disproportionately conviction-prone (and the Commentary rejects both of these answers)—is that the crime of rape, because it turns on a woman's nonconsent to sex, is different from other offenses. . . .

Men have written for decades, if not centuries, about women's rape fantasies. But perhaps the better explanation for the law, as reflected in the Code and commentaries, lies in the fantasies of men. The male rape fantasy is not a pleasant dream. It is a nightmare of being caught in the classic, non-traditional rape. A man engages in sex. Perhaps he's a bit aggressive about it. The woman says no but doesn't fight very much. Finally, she gives in. It's happened like this before, with other women, if not with her. But this time is different: She charges rape. There were no witnesses. It's his word against hers. At best, it's a contest of credibility, and the jury is on her side: After all, he's an accused "rapist."

It is important to note that this is not simply a nightmare about women; it is also, the Code's comments to the contrary notwithstanding, a nightmare about juries, and about the unwillingness or inability of prosecutors to exercise screening discretion and judges to exercise meaningful review. Rape has long been viewed not only as a crime against women, but also as a crime against the man who is entitled to exclusive possession of that woman. The male nightmare is thus not simply the lying, confused or ambivalent woman, but the men on the jury whose passions are inflamed by the violation of rape. It is "because the crime of rape arouses emotions as do few others," because of "the respect and sympathy naturally felt by any tribunal for a wronged female," because "[p]ublic sentiment seems preinclined to believe a man guilty of any illicit sexual offense he may be charged with," that juries cannot be trusted.

Actual occurrence of the male fantasy has never been substantiated by an empirical study. According to what we do know, the nightmare case is highly unlikely even to be reported to the police, let alone prosecuted; cases that are simply credibility contests are virtually non-existent; and juries tend to be highly suspicious of rape complainants, particularly in the non-traditional, non-stranger rape. The fantasy, in short, appears to be just that. Yet it lives on in the "objective rules" of the Model Penal Code, which impose obstacles in not only the non-traditional cases, which would appear to be their raison d'etre, but in all rapes.

The final objective rule of the Code explicitly downgrades the seriousness of the non-traditional rape in which there was a prior relationship of intimacy. Forcible rapes are graded by the Code according to two factors. If serious bodily injury is inflicted, forcible rape is a first degree felony. If there is no serious bodily injury, then the grading of rape depends entirely on the relationship between victim and defendant and the circumstances of their encounter: It is a first degree felony if "the victim was not a voluntary social companion of the actor upon the occasion of the crime and had not previously permitted him sexual liberties." If the two are married, or even living as husband and wife, it is no crime at all.

Prior relationship is regularly considered by police and prosecutors in exercising their discretion and screening complaints. But I know of no other instance, either in the Model Penal Code or, for that matter, in any other Code, where the prior relationship between the victim and the offender determines liability in the actual provision of the substantive criminal law.

The commentators provide two reasons for the inclusion of a provision downgrading prior relationship cases. First, the authors are of the view that when a prior relationship existed, "the gravity of the wrong is arguably less severe." Contrary to the commentators' view, however, many women report that they feel greater injury and betrayal when raped by someone they know than by someone they do not.

While degree of injury may be a debatable matter, the commentators' second justification for reliance on prior relationship is not. According to the Code, the absence of a prior sexual relationship is "strong objective corroboration of the fact that the sexual act was accomplished by imposition," while "[i]ts presence reduces confidence in the conclusion of aggression and nonconsent."

The practical reality has long been that rapes by intimates, in order to result in convictions, must have caused more physical harm than rapes by strangers, precisely because the problems of proof are greater in such cases. The presence of a prior sexual relationship is always considered relevant evidence of consent, even where a rape shield law otherwise limits the admissibility of the victim's prior sexual conduct or reputation. Police, prosecutors and juries tend to be particularly skeptical of such complaints, and relatively few cases result in convictions. The fact that there was a prior relationship and voluntary social companionship, and that a prosecutor is nonetheless willing to prosecute and a jury willing to convict (or a defendant to plead), ought signal us that we are dealing with a particularly clearcut and brutal case of rape or a particularly dangerous felon. Yet it is in precisely these cases that the Code's gradation rule limits the prosecutor's hand in charging and plea bargaining, and protects the rapist from the most serious penalties. . . .

The Michigan Statute

. . . The Michigan model is, in many respects, the counterpoint to the Model Penal Code. The Model Penal Code punishes rape by men against women; Michigan's crime of criminal sexual conduct can be committed by any person. Felony liability under the Model Penal Code is limited to sexual intercourse; in Michigan, sexual conduct is broadly defined to include not only penetration with objects, but offensive sexual contact. In the Model Penal Code, the focus remains on the victim; in Michigan, it is almost exclusively on the actor. The key to the Michigan statute is "force or coercion" by the actor. But in its definition of "force or coercion," Michigan ultimately does not move very far beyond the Model Penal Code and its traditional understanding of rape.

The expansion of the crime to include male victims and female offenders is a common element of reform statutes. Similarly, the change in labels—from rape to criminal sexual conduct or assault—is not unique to Michigan. By renaming "rape," reformers have sought to rid the crime of its common law baggage of unique rules (in Model Penal Code terms, "objective" rules) of resistance and proof.

However well-intentioned, these changes risk obscuring the unique meaning and understanding of the indignity and harm of "rape." Rape is a different and more serious affront than assault. Women who have been raped are very clear that they have not only been beaten or assaulted. As one woman testified in opposition to changing the name of the crime in Washington:

> I think rape is a particular crime. I think that it's different than assault. People who commit rape commit it for different reasons than people who commit assaults. Changing the name of the crime isn't going to do any good. It's going to be throwing the issue under the rug, so to speak. I think this would be very detrimental to our work with rape victims, because rape is not simply a form of assault.

Moreover, rape (at least as defined in traditional gender terms) does raise unique and important issues of male and female power. It invokes the differences in male and female ways of understanding force and consent, and each other. Defining the crime in terms of "actors" and "victims" neither resolves those conflicts nor changes the empirical realities of male abuse of women. But it may sweep them under the rug, thus raising questions from a feminist standpoint about the decision in Michigan, and the near-unanimity in the law reform community, that rape, or better yet "assault" or "criminal sexual conduct," should be defined in gender-neutral terms. . . .

The name chosen in Michigan to replace "rape" is significant as well. To relabel rape "criminal sexual conduct" is, perhaps only accidentally, to assume a position in a debate of some vigor as to whether rape should be thought about as sex or as violence. The "rape as sex" position has been articulated by individuals ranging from feminist theoreticians who argue for a more expansive understanding of coerced sex to the judge in a well-publicized South Carolina case who thought that convicted rapists should have a choice between castration and imprisonment. The "rape as violence" position, said to be the response of "liberal" (as opposed to radical) feminists, seems to me the better approach both theoretically and strategically: Focusing on the violent aspects of rape makes clear that you are not trying to prohibit all sex and that violent men (such as the rapists in that South Carolina case) must not only be treated as sexually aberrant, but also be incapacitated as dangerous to the community. Moreover, to see rape as violence is, one hopes, to recognize that sex should be inconsistent with violence, a message which is needed precisely because violence in sex has been accepted by so many as normal. The problem is that a man can also force a nonconsenting woman to engage in sex without resort to actual "violence." Power will do. The "rape as violence" approach may strengthen the case for punishing violently coerced sex, but it may do so at the cost of obscuring the case for punishing forced sex in the absence of physical violence. On this point, Michigan is curiously ambivalent. While the statute writers relabel rape as a crime of "sexual conduct," the force and coercion that are required to make sexual conduct criminal largely limits the statute's application to cases of conventional violence. . . . "Force or coercion" are . . . the key to the Michigan approach. Where they are present, sex is a crime; if personal injury was inflicted or the actor was aided by one or more individuals, it is an aggravated offense. The word "nonconsent" never appears as a required circumstance of the offense.

The Michigan statute's emphasis on force or coercion attempts to shift the focus of rape prosecutions from what the victim does or does not do (consent or resist) to the actions of the defendant. Moreover, because nonconsent is *not* an element of the crime, the message of the law may be that violence is inconsistent with sex and that violent sex is prohibited regardless of any claimed consent. Yet if that is the point, it is one that is poorly executed, to say the least. . . .

The first and most basic definition of force or coercion—"when the actor overcomes the victim through the actual application of physical force or physical violence"—invites application not only of the traditional, school-boy-fight definition of force, but also of the traditional requirements of nonconsent; if "overcome" does not require nonconsent, it is hard to see what it means. Moreover, the subsequent definitions of force wholly ignore the reality illustrated by the cases—that coercion of a woman need not involve either actual violence or threats of future physical injury. Threats of retaliation, other than physical injury, kidnapping or extortion, are not included; thus, if a man coerces a woman to engage in sex by threatening to fire her from her job or destroy her property or reputation, he has not used force or coercion within the definition of the statute. In this sense, the Michigan statute actually appears to be narrower than the Model Penal Code, which might at least prohibit such conduct as the lesser offense of gross sexual imposition. The statute adds nothing to the resolution of these cases, except, perversely, to make clear that the woman's lack of consent is irrelevant to the determination of criminal liability.

The elimination of consent as a defense where traditional violence and threats are involved can be justified on either of two grounds: that lawful sex ought to be inconsistent with violence (on grounds of either dangerousness or immorality); or that consent in such circumstances is meaningless. But in reality, it is a very limited reform, particularly since the most oppressive aspects of the consent standard are addressed by the existence of an evidentiary shield law and the provision that resistance is not required. What the Michigan statute does not address is the myriad of situations in which a woman engages in sex without her consent though traditional force is not applied.

Feminist reformers seeking to protect women from such threatening situations have only two choices: to focus on the man and seek to redefine what is meant by force in broader terms; or to focus on the woman and rely on her word as to nonconsent, properly defined (not saying yes, or at least saying no). The Michigan statute, the supposed model of reform, does neither. It neither empowers women to say no, harnessing the power of criminal sanctions behind them, nor redefines the conditions of force and coercion. . . .

Toward a Broader Understanding

The conduct that one might think of as "rape" ranges from the armed stranger who breaks into a woman's home to the date she invites in who takes silence for assent. In between are literally hundreds of variations: the man may be a stranger, but he may not be armed; he may be armed, but he may not be a stranger; he may be an almost, rather than a perfect, stranger—a man who gave her a ride or introduced himself through a ruse; she may say yes, but only because he threatens to expose her to the police or the welfare authorities; she may say no, but he may ignore her words.

In 1985, the woman raped at gunpoint by the intruding stranger should find most of the legal obstacles to her complaint removed. That was not always so: As recently as ten years ago, she might well have faced a corroboration requirement, a cautionary instruction, a fresh complaint rule, and a searing cross-examination about her sexual past to determine whether she had nonetheless consented to sex. In practice, she may still encounter some of these obstacles; but to the extent that the law communicates any clear message, it is likely to be that she was raped.

But most rapes do not as purely fit the traditional model, and most victims do not fare as well. Cases involving men met in bars or at work or at airports, let alone cases involving ex-boyfriends, still lead some appellate courts to enforce the most traditional views of women in the context of the less traditional rape. And in the system, considerations of prior relationship and the circumstances of the initial encounter, as well as force and resistance and corroboration, seem to reflect a similarly grounded if not so clearly stated view of the limits of rape law.

In thinking about rape, it is not as difficult to decide which rapes are more serious or which rapists deserving of more punishment: Weapons, injury, and intent—the traditional grading criteria of the criminal law—are all justifiable answers to these questions. Most jurisdictions that have reformed their rape laws in the last ten years have focused on creating degrees of rape—aggravated and unaggravated—based on some combination of the presence of weapons and injury. While *mens rea* or mistake needs to be addressed more clearly in some rape laws, and bodily injury more carefully defined in others, these are essentially problems of draftsmanship which are hardly insurmountable.

The more difficult problem comes in understanding and defining the threshold for liability—where we draw the line between criminal sex and seduction. Every statute still uses some combination of "force," "threats" and "consent" to define the crime. But in giving meaning to those terms at the threshold of liability, the law of rape must confront the powerful norms of male aggressiveness and female passivity which continue to be adhered to by many men and women in our society.

The law did not invent the "no means yes" philosophy. Women as well as men have viewed male aggressiveness as desirable and forced sex as an expression of love; women as well as men have been taught and have come to believe that when a woman "encourages" a man, he is entitled to sexual satisfaction. From the sociological surveys to prime time television, one can find ample support in society and culture for even the most oppressive views of women, and the most expansive notions of seduction enforced by the most traditional judges.

But the evidence is not entirely one-sided. For every prime time series celebrating forced sex, there seems to be another true confession story in a popular magazine detailing the facts of a date rape and calling it "rape." College men and women may think that the typical male is forward and primarily interested in sex, but they no longer conclude that he is the desirable man. The old sex manuals may have lauded male sexual responses as automatic and uncontrollable, but some of the newer ones no longer see men as machines and even advocate sensitivity as seductive.

We live, in short, in a time of changing sexual mores—and we are likely to for some time to come. In such times, the law can cling to the past or help move us into the future. We can continue to enforce the most traditional views of male aggressiveness and female passivity, continue to adhere to the "no means yes" philosophy and to the broadest understanding of seduction, until and unless change overwhelms us. That is not a neutral course, however; in taking it, the law (judges, legislators, or prosecutors) not only reflects (a part of) society, but legitimates and reenforces those views.

Or we can use the law to move forward. It may be impossible—and even unwise—to try to use the criminal law to change the way people think, to push progress to the ideal. But recognition of the limits of the criminal sanction need not be taken as a justification for the *status quo*. Faced with a choice between reenforcing the old and fueling the new in a world of changing norms, it is not necessarily more legitimate or neutral to choose the old. There are lines to be drawn short of the ideal: The challenge we face in thinking about rape is to use the power and legitimacy of law to reenforce what is best, not what is worst, in our changing sexual mores. ...

In a better world, I believe that men and women would not presume either consent or nonconsent. They would ask, and be certain. There is nothing unromantic about showing the kind of respect for another person that demands that you know for sure before engaging in intimate contact. In a better world, women who said yes would be saying so from a position of equality, or at least sufficient power to say no. In a better world, fewer women would bargain with sex because they had nothing else to bargain with; they would be in at least as good a position to reject demands for sexual access as men are to reject demands for money.

If we are not at the point where it is appropriate for the law to presume nonconsent from silence, and the reactions I have received to this Article suggest that we are not, then at least we should be at the point where it is legitimate to punish the man who ignores a woman's explicit words of protestations. I am quite certain that many women who say yes—whether on dates or on the job—would say no if they could; I have no doubt that women's silence is sometimes the product not of passion and desire but of pressure and pain. But at the very least the criminal law ought to say clearly that women who actually say no must be respected as meaning it; that nonconsent means saying no; that men who proceed nonetheless, claiming that they thought no meant yes, have acted unreasonably and unlawfully.

So, too, for threats of harm short of physical injury, and for deception and false pretenses as methods of seduction. The powerlessness of women and the value of bodily integrity are great enough to argue that women deserve more comprehensive protection for their bodies than the laws of extortion or fraud provide for money. But if going so far seems too complicated and fraught with difficulty, as it does to many, then we need not. For the present, it would be a significant improvement if the law of rape in any state prohibited exactly the same threats as that state's law of extortion and exactly the same deceptions as that state's law of false pretenses or fraud.

In short, I am arguing that "consent" should be defined so that "no means no." And the "force" or "coercion" that negates consent ought be defined to include extortionate threats and deceptions of material fact. As for *mens rea,* unreasonableness as to consent, understood to mean ignoring a woman's words, should be sufficient for liability: Reasonable men should be held to know that no means no, and unreasonable mistakes, no matter how honestly claimed, should not exculpate. Thus, the threshold of liability—whether phrased in terms of "consent," "force" or "coercion," or some combination of the three, should be understood to include at least those non-traditional rapes where the woman says no or submits only in response to lies or threats which would be prohibited were money sought instead. The crime I have described would be a lesser offense than the aggravated rape in which life is threatened or bodily injury inflicted, but it is, in my judgment, "rape." One could, I suppose, claim that as we move from such violent rapes to "just" coerced or nonconsensual sex, we are moving away from a crime of violence toward something else. But what makes the violent rape different—and more serious—than an aggravated assault is the injury to personal integrity involved in forced sex. That same injury is the reason that forced sex should be a crime even when there is no weapon or no beating. In a very real sense, what does make rape different from other crimes, at every level of the offense, is that rape is about sex and sexual violation. Were the essence of the crime the use of the gun or the knife or the threat, we wouldn't need—and wouldn't have—a separate crime.

Conduct is labeled as criminal "to announce to society that these actions are not to be done and to secure that fewer of them are done." As a matter of principle, we should be ready to announce to society our condemnation of coerced and nonconsensual sex and to secure that we have less of it. The message of the substantive law to men, and to women, should be made clear. . . .

Commonwealth of Pennsylvania v. Berkowitz

Supreme Court of Pennsylvania, 1994.
537 Pa. 143, 641 A.2d 1161.

RALPH J. CAPPY, JUSTICE.

. . . The complainant, a female college student, left her class, went to her dormitory room where she drank a martini, and then went to a lounge to await her boyfriend. When her boyfriend failed to appear, she went to another dormitory to find a friend, Earl Hassel. She knocked on the door, but received no answer. She tried the doorknob and, finding it unlocked, entered the room and discovered a man sleeping on the bed. The complainant originally believed the man to be Hassel, but it turned out to be Hassel's roommate, Appellee. Appellee asked her to stay for a while and she agreed. He requested a back-rub and she declined. He suggested that she sit on the bed, but she declined and sat on the floor.

Appellee then moved to the floor beside her, lifted up her shirt and bra and massaged her breasts. He then unfastened his pants and unsuccessfully attempted to put his penis in her mouth. They both stood up, and he locked the door. He returned to push her onto the bed, and removed her undergarments from one leg. He then penetrated her vagina with his penis. After withdrawing and ejaculating on her stomach, he stated, "Wow, I guess we just got carried away," to which she responded, "No, we didn't get carried away, you got carried away." . . .

The crime of rape is defined as follows:

§ 3121.   Rape

A person commits a felony of the first degree when he engages in sexual intercourse with another person not one's spouse:

(1) by forcible compulsion;

(2) by threat of forcible compulsion that would prevent resistance by a person of reasonable resolution;

(3) who is unconscious; or

(4) who is so mentally deranged or deficient that such person is incapable of consent.

The victim of a rape need not resist. "The force necessary to support a conviction of rape . . . need only be such as to establish lack of consent and to induce the [victim] to submit without additional resistance. . . . "

In regard to the critical issue of forcible compulsion, the complainant's testimony is devoid of any statement which clearly or adequately describes the use of force or the threat of force against her. In response to defense counsel's question, "Is it possible that [when Appellee lifted your bra and shirt] you took no physical action to discourage him," the complainant replied, "It's possible." When asked, "Is it possible that [Appellee] was not making any physical contact with you . . . aside from attempting to untie the knot [in the drawstrings of complainant's sweatpants]," she answered, "It's possible." She testified that "He put me down on the bed. It was kind of like—He didn't throw me on the bed. It's hard to explain. It was kind of like a push but not—I can't explain what I'm trying to say." She concluded that "it wasn't much" in reference to whether she bounced on the bed, and further detailed that their movement to the bed "wasn't slow like a romantic kind of thing, but it wasn't a fast shove either. It was kind of in the middle." She agreed that Appellee's hands were not restraining her in any manner during the actual penetration, and that the weight of his body on top of her was the only force applied. She testified that at no time did Appellee verbally threaten her. The complainant did testify that she sought to leave the room, and said "no" throughout the encounter. As to the complainant's desire to leave the room, the record clearly demonstrates that the door could be unlocked easily from the inside, that she was aware of this fact, but that she never attempted to go to the door or unlock it.

As to the complainant's testimony that she stated "no" throughout the encounter with Appellee, we point out that, while such an allegation of fact would be relevant to the issue of consent, it is not relevant to the issue of force. In *Commonwealth* v. *Mlinarich*, this Court sustained the reversal of a defendant's conviction of rape where the alleged victim, a minor, repeatedly stated that she did not want to engage in sexual intercourse, but offered no physical resistance and was compelled to engage in sexual intercourse under threat of being recommitted to a juvenile detention center.... [U]nder the facts of *Mlinarich*, neither physical force, the threat of physical force, nor psychological coercion were found to have been proven.... *Mlinarich* implicitly dictates that where there is a lack of consent, but no showing of either physical force, a threat of physical force, or psychological coercion, the "forcible compulsion" requirement ... is not met.

Reviewed in light of the above described standard, the complainant's testimony simply fails to establish that the Appellee forcibly compelled her to engage in sexual intercourse.... Thus, even if all of the complainant's testimony was believed, the jury, as a matter of law, could not have found Appellee guilty of rape....

State in the Interest of M.T.S.

Supreme Court of New Jersey, 1992.
129 N.J. 422, 609 A.2d 1266.

ALAN B. HANDLER, J.

Under New Jersey law a person who commits an act of sexual penetration using physical force or coercion is guilty of second-degree sexual assault. The sexual assault statute does not define the words "physical force." The question posed by this appeal is whether the element of "physical force" is met simply by an act of non-consensual penetration involving no more force than necessary to accomplish that result.

That issue is presented in the context of what is often referred to as "acquaintance rape." The record in the case discloses that the juvenile, a seventeen-year-old boy, engaged in consensual kissing and heavy petting with a fifteen-year-old girl and thereafter engaged in actual sexual penetration of the girl to which she had not consented. There was no evidence or suggestion that the juvenile used any unusual or extra force or threats to accomplish the act of penetration....

On Monday, May 21, 1990, fifteen-year-old C.G. was living with her mother, her three siblings, and several other people, including M.T.S. and his girlfriend. A total of ten people resided in the three-bedroom town-home at the time of the incident. M.T.S., then age seventeen, was temporarily residing at the home with the permission of the C.G.'s mother; he slept downstairs on a couch. C.G. had her own room on the second floor. At approximately 11:30 p.m. on May 21, C.G. went upstairs to sleep after having watched television with her mother, M.T.S., and his girlfriend. When C.G. went to bed, she was wearing underpants, a bra, shorts, and a shirt. At trial, C.G. and M.T.S. offered very different accounts concerning the nature of their relationship and the events that occurred after C.G. had gone upstairs. The trial court did not credit fully either teenager's testimony.

C.G. stated that earlier in the day, M.T.S. had told her three or four times that he "was going to make a surprise visit up in [her] bedroom." She said that she had not taken M.T.S. seriously and considered his comments a joke because he frequently teased her. She testified that M.T.S. had attempted to kiss her on numerous other occasions and at least once had attempted to put his hands inside of her pants, but that she had rejected all of his previous advances.

C.G. testified that on May 22, at approximately 1:30 a.m., she awoke to use the bathroom. As she was getting out of bed, she said, she saw M.T.S., fully clothed, standing in her doorway. According to C.G., M.T.S. then said that "he was going to tease [her] a little bit." C.G. testified that she "didn't think anything of it"; she walked past him, used the bathroom, and then returned to bed, falling into a "heavy" sleep within fifteen minutes. The next event C.G. claimed to recall of that morning was waking up with M.T.S. on top of her, her underpants and shorts removed. She said "his penis was into [her] vagina." As soon as C.G. realized what had happened, she said, she immediately slapped M.T.S. once in the face, then "told him to get off [her], and get out." She did not scream or cry out. She testified that M.T.S. complied in less than one minute after being struck; according to C.G., "he jumped right off of [her]." She said she did not know how long M.T.S. had been inside of her before she awoke.

C.G. said that after M.T.S. left the room, she "fell asleep crying" because "[she] couldn't believe that he did what he did to [her]." She explained that she did not immediately tell her mother or anyone else in the house of the events of that morning because she was "scared and in shock." According to C.G., M.T.S. engaged in intercourse with her "without [her] wanting it or telling him to come up [to her bedroom]." By her own account, C.G. was not otherwise harmed by M.T.S.

At about 7:00 a.m., C.G. went downstairs and told her mother about her encounter with M.T.S. earlier in the morning and said that they would have to "get [him] out of the house." While M.T.S. was out on an errand, C.G.'s mother gathered his clothes and put them outside in his car; when he returned, he was told that "[he] better not even get near the house." C.G. and her mother then filed a complaint with the police.

According to M.T.S., he and C.G. had been good friends for a long time, and their relationship "kept leading on to more and more." He had been living at C.G.'s home for about five days before the incident occurred; he testified that during the three days preceding the incident they had been "kissing and necking" and had discussed having sexual intercourse. The first time M.T.S. kissed C.G., he said, she "didn't want him to, but she did after that." He said C.G. repeatedly had encouraged him to "make a surprise visit up in her room."

M.T.S. testified that at exactly 1:15 a.m. on May 22, he entered C.G.'s bedroom as she was walking to the bathroom. He said C.G. soon returned from the bathroom, and the two began "kissing and all," eventually moving to the bed. Once they were in bed, he said, they undressed each other and continued to kiss and touch for about five minutes. M.T.S. and C.G. proceeded to engage in sexual intercourse. According to M.T.S., who was on top of C.G., he "stuck it in" and "did it [thrust] three times, and then the fourth time [he] stuck it in, that's when [she] pulled [him] off of her." M.T.S. said that as C.G. pushed him off, she said "stop, get off," and he "hopped off right away."

According to M.T.S., after about one minute, he asked C.G. what was wrong; she replied with a back-hand to his face. He recalled asking C.G. what was wrong a second time, and her replying, "how can you take advantage of me or something like that." M.T.S. said that he proceeded to get dressed and told C.G. to calm down, but that she then told him to get away from her and began to cry. Before leaving the room, he told C.G., "I'm leaving ... I'm going with my real girlfriend, don't talk to me ... I don't want nothing to do with you or anything, stay out of my life ... don't tell anybody about this ... it would just screw everything up." He then walked downstairs and went to sleep.

On May 23, 1990, M.T.S. was charged with conduct that if engaged in by an adult would constitute second-degree sexual assault of the victim.... Following a two-day trial on the sexual assault charge, M.T.S. was adjudicated delinquent. After reviewing the testimony, the court concluded that the victim had consented to a session of kissing and heavy petting with M.T.S. The trial court did not find that C.G. had been sleeping at the time of penetration, but nevertheless found that she had not consented to the actual sexual act. Accordingly, the court concluded that the State had proven second-degree sexual assault beyond a reasonable doubt. On appeal, following the imposition of suspended sentences on the sexual assault and the other remaining charges, the Appellate Division determined that the absence of force beyond that involved in the act of sexual penetration precluded a finding of second-degree sexual assault. It therefore reversed the juvenile's adjudication of delinquency for that offense.

The New Jersey Code of Criminal Justice, N.J.S.A. 2C:14–2c(1), defines "sexual assault" as the commission "of sexual penetration" "with another person" with the use of "physical force or coercion."[1] An unconstrained

---

1. The sexual assault statute, N.J.S.A.: 2C:14–2c(1), reads as follows:

c. An actor is guilty of sexual assault if he commits an act of sexual penetration reading of the statutory language indicates that both the act of "sexual penetration" and the use of "physical force or coercion" are separate and distinct elements of the offense. . . .

The parties offer two alternative understandings of the concept of "physical force" as it is used in the statute. The State would read "physical force" to entail any amount of sexual touching brought about involuntarily. A showing of sexual penetration coupled with a lack of consent would satisfy the elements of the statute. The Public Defender urges an interpretation of "physical force" to mean force "used to overcome lack of consent." That definition equates force with violence and leads to the conclusion that sexual assault requires the application of some amount of force in addition to the act of penetration. . . .

The provisions proscribing sexual offenses found in the Code of Criminal Justice, N.J.S.A. 2C:14–2c(1), became effective in 1979, and were written against almost two hundred years of rape law in New Jersey. The origin of the rape statute that the current statutory offense of sexual assault replaced can be traced to the English common law. Under the common law, rape was defined as "carnal knowledge of a woman against her will." American jurisdictions generally adopted the English view, but over time states added the requirement that the carnal knowledge have been forcible, apparently in order to prove that the act was against the victim's will. Those three elements of rape—carnal knowledge, forcibly, and against her will—remained the essential elements of the crime until 1979.

Under traditional rape law, in order to prove that a rape had occurred, the state had to show both that force had been used and that the penetration had been against the woman's will. Force was identified and determined not as an independent factor but in relation to the response of the victim, which in turn implicated the victim's own state of mind. "Thus, the perpetrator's use of force became criminal only if the victim's state of mind met the statutory requirement. The perpetrator could use all the force imaginable and no crime would be committed if the state could not prove additionally that the victim did not consent." Although the terms

with another person under any one of the following circumstances:

(1) The actor uses physical force or coercion, but the victim does not sustain severe personal injury;

(2) The victim is one whom the actor knew or should have known was physically helpless, mentally defective or mentally incapacitated;

(3) The victim is on probation or parole, or is detained in a hospital, prison or other institution and the actor has supervisory or disciplinary power over the victim by virtue of the actor's legal, professional or occupational status;

(4) The victim is at least 16 but less than 18 years old and:

(a) The actor is related to the victim by blood or affinity to the third degree; or

(b) The actor has supervisory or disciplinary power over the victim; or

(c) The actor is a foster parent, a guardian, or stands in loco parentis within the household;

(5) The victim is at least 13 but less than 16 years old and the actor is at least 4 years older than the victim.

Sexual assault is a crime of the second degree.

"non-consent" and "against her will" were often treated as equivalent, under the traditional definition of rape, both formulations squarely placed on the victim the burden of proof and of action. Effectively, a woman who was above the age of consent had actively and affirmatively to withdraw that consent for the intercourse to be against her will. As a Delaware court stated, "If sexual intercourse is obtained by milder means, or with the consent or silent submission of the female, it cannot constitute the crime of rape." State v. Brown, 83 A. 1083, 1084 (O.T.1912).

The presence or absence of consent often turned on credibility. To demonstrate that the victim had not consented to the intercourse, and also that sufficient force had been used to accomplish the rape, the state had to prove that the victim had resisted. According to the oft-quoted Lord Hale, to be deemed a credible witness, a woman had to be of good fame, disclose the injury immediately, suffer signs of injury, and cry out for help. Courts and commentators historically distrusted the testimony of victims, "assuming that women lie about their lack of consent for various reasons: to blackmail men, to explain the discovery of a consensual affair, or because of psychological illness." Evidence of resistance was viewed as a solution to the credibility problem; it was the "outward manifestation of nonconsent, [a] device for determining whether a woman actually gave consent." . . .

The judicial interpretation of the pre-reform rape law in New Jersey, with its insistence on resistance by the victim, greatly minimized the importance of the forcible and assaultive aspect of the defendant's conduct. Rape prosecutions turned then not so much on the forcible or assaultive character of the defendant's actions as on the nature of the victim's response. . . . That the law put the rape victim on trial was clear.

The resistance requirement had another untoward influence on traditional rape law. Resistance was necessary not only to prove non-consent but also to demonstrate that the force used by the defendant had been sufficient to overcome the victim's will. The amount of force used by the defendant was assessed in relation to the resistance of the victim. In New Jersey the amount of force necessary to establish rape was characterized as " 'the degree of force sufficient to overcome any resistance that had been put up by the female.' " . . . Thus, if the defendant forced himself on a woman, it was her responsibility to fight back, because force was measured in relation to the resistance she put forward. Only if she resisted, causing him to use more force than was necessary to achieve penetration, would his conduct be criminalized. . . .

During the 1970s feminists and others criticized the stereotype that rape victims were inherently more untrustworthy than other victims of criminal attack. They argued that "[d]istrust of the complainant's credibility [had] led to an exaggerated insistence on evidence of resistance," resulting in the victim rather than the defendant being put on trial. Reformers also challenged the assumption that a woman would seduce a man and then, in order to protect her virtue, claim to have been raped. If women are no less trustworthy than other purported victims of criminal attack, the reformers argued, then women should face no additional burdens of proving that they had not consented to or had actively resisted the assault.

To refute the misguided belief that rape was not real unless the victim fought back, reformers emphasized empirical research indicating that women who resisted forcible intercourse often suffered far more serious injury as a result.... The research also helped demonstrate the underlying point of the reformers that the crime of rape rested not in the overcoming of a woman's will or the insult to her chastity but in the forcible attack itself—the assault on her person. Reformers criticized the conception of rape as a distinctly sexual crime rather than a crime of violence. They emphasized that rape had its legal origins in laws designed to protect the property rights of men to their wives and daughters. Although the crime had evolved into an offense against women, reformers argued that vestiges of the old law remained, particularly in the understanding of rape as a crime against the purity or chastity of a woman. The burden of protecting that chastity fell on the woman, with the state offering its protection only after the woman demonstrated that she had resisted sufficiently....

Critics of rape law agreed that the focus of the crime should be shifted from the victim's behavior to the defendant's conduct, and particularly to its forceful and assaultive, rather than sexual, character. Reformers also shared the goals of facilitating rape prosecutions and of sparing victims much of the degradation involved in bringing and trying a charge of rape. There were, however, differences over the best way to redefine the crime. Some reformers advocated a standard that defined rape as unconsented-to sexual intercourse; others urged the elimination of any reference to consent from the definition of rape. Nonetheless, all proponents of reform shared a central premise: that the burden of showing non-consent should not fall on the victim of the crime. In dealing with the problem of consent the reform goal was not so much to purge the entire concept of consent from the law as to eliminate the burden that had been placed on victims to prove they had not consented.

Similarly, with regard to force, rape law reform sought to give independent significance to the forceful or assaultive conduct of the defendant and to avoid a definition of force that depended on the reaction of the victim. Traditional interpretations of force were strongly criticized for failing to acknowledge that force may be understood simply as the invasion of "bodily integrity." Susan Estrich, *Rape*. In urging that the "resistance" requirement be abandoned, reformers sought to break the connection between force and resistance....

The Legislature did not endorse the Model Penal Code approach to rape. Rather, it passed a fundamentally different proposal in 1978 when it adopted the Code of Criminal Justice. The new statutory provisions covering rape were formulated by a coalition of feminist groups assisted by the National Organization of Women (NOW) National Task Force on Rape.... The stated intent of the drafters ... had been to remove all features found to be contrary to the interests of rape victims.

Since the 1978 reform, the Code has referred to the crime that was once known as "rape" as "sexual assault." The crime now requires "penetration," not "sexual intercourse." It requires "force" or "coercion," not "submission" or "resistance." It makes no reference to the victim's state of mind or attitude, or conduct in response to the assault. It eliminates the spousal exception based on implied consent. It emphasizes the assaultive character of the offense by defining sexual penetration to encompass a wide range of sexual contacts, going well beyond traditional "carnal knowledge." Consistent with the assaultive character, as opposed to the traditional sexual character, of the offense, the statute also renders the crime gender-neutral: both males and females can be actors or victims.

The reform statute defines sexual assault as penetration accomplished by the use of "physical force" or "coercion," but it does not define either "physical force" or "coercion" or enumerate examples of evidence that would establish those elements. . . . The task of defining "physical force" therefore was left to the courts. . . . That definitional task runs the risk of undermining the basic legislative intent to reformulate rape law. . . .

The Legislature's concept of sexual assault and the role of force was significantly colored by its understanding of the law of assault and battery. As a general matter, criminal battery is defined as "the unlawful application of force to the person of another." The application of force is criminal when it results in either (a) a physical injury or (b) an offensive touching. Any "unauthorized touching of another [is] a battery." Thus, by eliminating all references to the victim's state of mind and conduct, and by broadening the definition of penetration to cover not only sexual intercourse between a man and a woman but a range of acts that invade another's body or compel intimate contact, the Legislature emphasized the affinity between sexual assault and other forms of assault and battery. . . . Thus, just as any unauthorized touching is a crime under traditional laws of assault and battery, so is any unauthorized sexual contact a crime under the reformed law of criminal sexual contact, and so is any unauthorized sexual penetration a crime under the reformed law of sexual assault.

The understanding of sexual assault as a criminal battery, albeit one with especially serious consequences, follows necessarily from the Legislature's decision to eliminate non-consent and resistance from the substantive definition of the offense. Under the new law, the victim no longer is required to resist and therefore need not have said or done anything in order for the sexual penetration to be unlawful. The alleged victim is not put on trial, and his or her responsive or defensive behavior is rendered immaterial. We are thus satisfied that an interpretation of the statutory crime of sexual assault to require physical force in addition to that entailed in an act of involuntary or unwanted sexual penetration would be fundamentally inconsistent with the legislative purpose to eliminate any consideration of whether the victim resisted or expressed non-consent. . . .

Because the statute eschews any reference to the victim's will or resistance, the standard defining the role of force in sexual penetration must prevent the possibility that the establishment of the crime will turn on the alleged victim's state of mind or responsive behavior. We conclude, therefore, that any act of sexual penetration engaged in by the defendant without the affirmative and freely-given permission of the victim to the specific act of penetration constitutes the offense of sexual assault. Therefore, physical force in excess of that inherent in the act of sexual penetration is not required for such penetration to be unlawful. The definition of "physical force" is satisfied under N.J.S.A. 2C:14–2c(1) if the defendant applies any amount of force against another person in the absence of what a reasonable person would believe to be affirmative and freely-given permission to the act of sexual penetration.

Under the reformed statute, permission to engage in sexual penetration must be affirmative and it must be given freely, but that permission may be inferred either from acts or statements reasonably viewed in light of the surrounding circumstances. Persons need not, of course, expressly announce their consent to engage in intercourse for there to be affirmative permission. Permission to engage in an act of sexual penetration can be and indeed often is indicated through physical actions rather than words. Permission is demonstrated when the evidence, in whatever form, is sufficient to demonstrate that a reasonable person would have believed that the alleged victim had affirmatively and freely given authorization to the act. . . .

Today the law of sexual assault is indispensable to the system of legal rules that assures each of us the right to decide who may touch our bodies, when, and under what circumstances. The decision to engage in sexual relations with another person is one of the most private and intimate decisions a person can make. Each person has the right not only to decide whether to engage in sexual contact with another, but also to control the circumstances and character of that contact. No one, neither a spouse, nor a friend, nor an acquaintance, nor a stranger, has the right or the privilege to force sexual contact. . . .

In a case such as this one, in which the State does not allege violence or force extrinsic to the act of penetration, the factfinder must decide whether the defendant's act of penetration was undertaken in circumstances that led the defendant reasonably to believe that the alleged victim had freely given affirmative permission to the specific act of sexual penetration. Such permission can be indicated either through words or through actions that, when viewed in the light of all the surrounding circumstances, would demonstrate to a reasonable person affirmative and freely-given authorization for the specific act of sexual penetration.

In applying that standard to the facts in these cases, the focus of attention must be on the nature of the defendant's actions. The role of the factfinder is not to decide whether reasonable people may engage in acts of penetration without the permission of others. The Legislature answered that question when it enacted the reformed sexual assault statute: reasonable people do not engage in acts of penetration without permission, and it is unlawful to do so. The role of the factfinder is to decide not whether engaging in an act of penetration without permission of another person is reasonable, but only whether the defendant's belief that the alleged victim had freely given affirmative permission was reasonable.

In these cases neither the alleged victim's subjective state of mind nor the reasonableness of the alleged victim's actions can be deemed relevant to the offense. The alleged victim may be questioned about what he or she did or said only to determine whether the defendant was reasonable in believing that affirmative permission had been freely given. To repeat, the law places no burden on the alleged victim to have expressed non-consent or to have denied permission, and no inquiry is made into what he or she thought or desired or why he or she did not resist or protest. . . .

The Appellate Division was correct in recognizing that a woman's right to end intimate activity without penetration is a protectable right the violation of which can be a criminal offense. However, it misperceived the purpose of the statute in believing that the only way that right can be protected is by the woman's unequivocally-expressed desire to end the activity. The effect of that requirement would be to import into the sexual assault statute the notion that an assault occurs only if the victim's will is overcome, and thus to reintroduce the requirement of non-consent and victim-resistance as a constituent material element of the crime. Under the reformed statute, a person's failure to protest or resist cannot be considered or used as justification for bodily invasion.

We acknowledge that cases such as this are inherently fact sensitive and depend on the reasoned judgment and common sense of judges and juries. The trial court concluded that the victim had not expressed consent to the act of intercourse, either through her words or actions. We conclude that the record provides reasonable support for the trial court's disposition.

Accordingly, we reverse the judgment of the Appellate Division and reinstate the disposition of juvenile delinquency for the commission of second-degree sexual assault.

NOTES AND QUESTIONS

1.   **Men's Motives for Rape**. How should Katharine Baker's examination of men's varying reasons for rape affect the definition of rape and strategies for ending sexual violence? This excerpt comes from Professor Baker's longer critique of Rule 413 of the Federal Rules of Evidence, which makes prior acts of sexual assault by alleged rapists admissible in criminal sexual assault cases. Baker argues that, although designed to increase rape convictions, Rule 413 is misguided because it fails to take into account the different reasons why men rape. As a result, she predicts the rule will intensify discrimination against poor and minority defendants, increase the number of unjust convictions, and perpetuate stereotypes about rapists.

2.   **Force v. Nonconsent.** Should the focus of rape law be on the defendant's use of force or the victim's lack of consent? As the decision in *Berkowitz* illustrates, some courts require proof of both: either lack of consent or force by itself is not enough to constitute rape. What are the

consequences of this dual requirement? *M.T.S.*, on the other hand, requires only proof of non-consent, even though the New Jersey statute requires proof of force. Which approach better defines the crime of rape? Is *Berkowitz* unfair to victims? Is *M.T.S.* unfair to defendants?

3. **Mistakes about Consent**. Some commentators fear that rulings such as that in *M.T.S.* unjustly punish men for misunderstanding women's communications about their willingness to engage in sexual intercourse. Douglas Husak and George Thomas, for example, argue that men rely on social conventions that women use to express their consent to have sex, and should not be convicted of a serious felony when that reliance leads to a mistake about consent. *See* Douglas N. Husak & George C. Thomas III, *Date Rape, Social Convention and Reasonable Mistakes*, 11 L. & Phil. 95 (1992). Who should bear the responsibility for mistakes about consent? Do you agree with Susan Estrich that defendants should be held to a negligence standard? Many men (and women), moreover, are socialized to see aggressive behavior as seduction rather than rape. Does the extent of rape noted in Baker's article suggest that criminal law is an inadequate tool for challenging the social conventions that make male aggression seem acceptable? Or does the New Jersey Supreme Court's reliance on feminist advocacy suggest the possibility of effective legal reform?

4. **Sexual Autonomy v. Freedom from Violence**. Should rape law distinguish between sexual autonomy and freedom from violence? Donald Dripps identifies two distinct harms to women who are raped—the use of force, which violates the interest in freedom from physical injury, and the use of another person's body for sexual gratification, which violates the interest in exclusive control of one's body for sexual purposes. Donald A. Dripps, *Beyond Rape: An Essay on the Difference between the Presence of Force and the Absence of Consent*, 92 Colum. L. Rev. 1780 (1992). Stephen Schulhofer similarly suggests extending the interest protected by rape law from freedom from violence to "sexual autonomy as a distinctive constituent of personhood and freedom." Stephen J. Schulhofer, *Taking Sexual Autonomy Seriously: Rape Law and Beyond*, 11 Law & Phil. 35 (1992). What types of coercion to procure sex, besides acts and threats of violence, should be punishable—threatening an employee to fire her? Threatening a student to prevent her from graduating? Threatening a customer to deny her loan application? Threatening a girlfriend to end a relationship? What about sex procured through fraudulent misrepresentation?

Some feminists, such as Katie Roiphe, have expressed concern that expanded protection of women's sexual choices smacks of paternalism: "People pressure and manipulate and cajole each other into all sorts of things all the time. . . . No human interactions are free from pressure, and the idea that sex is, or can be, makes it . . . vulnerable to the inconsistent expectations of double standard." Katie Roiphe, *Date Rape's Other Victim*, N.Y. Times, June 13, 1993, § 6 (Magazine), at 26, 40. Is there anything special about women's agreements to engage in sexual intercourse that warrant the intervention of criminal law?

5. **Sexual Expropriation**. How should criminal law protect women from nonviolent but criminal violations of sexual autonomy? One possibility would be to restructure rape law to create a separate, lesser crime of nonviolent sexual misconduct, distinct from violent rape. Dripps proposes dividing sexual crime into two separate offenses: "sexually motivated assault," defined as inflicting or threatening physical injury for the purpose of causing sex, and "sexual expropriation," defined as purposely or knowingly engaging in a sexual act with another person, knowing that the other person expressed a refusal to engage in that act. Would this framework expand protection against sexual violation? Should Berkowitz, Mlinarich, and M.T.S. have been convicted of "sexual expropriation?" Or did they each commit a violent assault on a woman's body? Does sexual expropriation neglect the physical injury of unwanted penetration itself? For a critique of Dripps' scheme, *see* Robin L. West, *Legitimating the Illegitimate: A Comment on Beyond Rape,* 93 Colum. L. Rev. 1442 (1993).

Although the court in *Berkowitz* reversed the rape conviction, it upheld the conviction for "indecent assault," a second-degree misdemeanor defined as "indecent contact with another ... without the consent of the other person." What is the difference between these two crimes? Does Pennsylvania's grading adequately reflect the seriousness of Berkowitz's offense?

6. **Role of Violence**. Is the problem with rape law "the seemingly unshakeable association of rape with physically violent misconduct" (Schulhofer, at 94) or its failure to protect women from all that they experience as violence? Are there reasons for continuing—and even expanding—the association between rape and violence? Dorothy Roberts argues that violent rape and nonviolent sexual abuse are linked together by the threat of physical violence that often underlies male demands for sexual control:

> ... Men violate women's sexual autonomy in various ways, including extortion, economic threats, and deception. I want to suggest that men often back up these nonviolent tactics with an implicit threat of violence. If the threat of losing a job, or being kicked out of the house, or ending a relationship fails, however, men often resort to physical harm. Feminists have recognized force not only in physical attacks, but also in "the power one need not use." ...

> Women sometimes fear that men may turn violent if we exercise our autonomy, especially in the form of rejection or abandonment. Perhaps the most extreme example of men's retaliation for women's rejection is the escalation of violence that often occurs when battered women attempt to leave their batterers.... Our culture also reinforces this fear by blaming women who are victims of sexual violence. Society constantly admonishes women for not taking adequate precautions against the ever-present risk of sexual assault....

> I must believe that this intimate knowledge of violence shapes how most women respond to certain demands from men, even ordinarily nonviolent men. Women know that saying "no" to sex often provokes a peculiar anger because, like ending a relationship, it is

"understood as a challenge to manhood." Refusing a man's sexual demands means much more than refusing to provide any other "bargained for" service. Male sexual prerogatives are well-guarded political privileges; they represent and enforce men's power over women.

I am not arguing that the mere capacity to overpower women makes all men rapists.... Instead, I am arguing that we should consider how often men use that capacity to control women without actually resorting to physical attack.

Dorothy E. Roberts, *Rape, Violence, and Women's Autonomy*, 69 Chi.-Kent L. Rev. 359, 374–380 (1993). Did you detect such a latent threat of violence in *Berkowitz*?

Roberts concludes, "[b]efore we can move beyond violence, we must see all the violence that still escapes the law." As the following excerpt makes clear, jurors do not recognize certain instances of forced sex as rape, even when they involve violence.

Kimberlé Crenshaw, The Intersection of Race and Gender in Rape Law[1]

How does the fact that Black women are situated within two subordinated groups bear on the politics of race and rape? The "double jeopardy" Black women confront in rape is the combined effect of two intersections. First, racism and sexism intersect to render insignificant the sexual violation of Black women. Second, both feminist and antiracist challenges to rape, based as they each are on male centered approaches to racism and white centered approaches to sexism, fail to adequately address the rape of Black women. . . .

The use of rape to legitimize efforts to control and discipline the Black community is well established in historical literature on rape and race. The casting of all Black men as potential threats to the sanctity of white womanhood was a familiar construct that political activists confronted and attempted to dispel over a century ago. Black men were made vulnerable to legal and extra legal violence by the identification of rape with a Black offender-white victim. But the treatment of this particular dyad by the white community as the quintessential rape cooperated with its treatment by the Black community as paradigmatic of racism to marginalize the rape of Black women.

Feminists, too, have attacked dominant conceptions of rape, particularly as represented through law, as essentially patriarchal in scope. The early emphasis of rape law on the property aspect of women's chastity resulted in

---

1. A different version of this essay appears in Kimberlé Crenshaw, *Mapping the Margins: Identity Politics, Intersectionality and Violence against Women of Color*, 43 Stanford Law Review 1241 (1991).

less protection to women whose chastity had been in some way tarnished or devalued. The most insidious assumptions were written into the law, including the early common law notion that a woman alleging rape must be able to show that she resisted to the utmost to establish her credibility and the fact that she was really raped. This tendency to view women in terms of chaste character reflected dominant sensibilities about women that distinguished between good women and fallen women. . . . Like lynching, the good victim/bad victim dichotomy effectively punished non-traditional behavior in women and established legal constraints upon women's self-determination.

Yet, as Jennifer Wriggins and others have established, this analysis is only partially applicable to Black women. Wriggins points out that rape against Black women was not even a crime in several Southern states during the antebellum period because "according to governing stereotypes, chastity could not be possessed by Black women." Even when rape against Black women became a crime, prevailing stereotypes of Black women as sexually voracious meant that chastity had to be proved rather than presumed. Thus, while it is true that rape laws operated in a manner that denied the sexual integrity of all women, protection more likely was denied to white women based on what they did or failed to do; Black women were denied protection based on who they were.

Today, long after discriminatory laws have been eradicated, constructions of rape in popular discourses and in criminal law continue to manifest racist as well as sexist themes. For example, Professor Valerie Smith suggests that "the same cultural narratives that traditionally have linked sexual violence with racial oppression continue to operate at the present time." Professor Smith reviews the case of the Central Park Jogger to expose the implicit racial imagery that characterized the public discourse on the assault. . . . The ongoing devaluation of Black women and other women of color is suggested by the fact that during the week of the Central Park attack there were 28 other cases of first degree rape or attempted rape yet none of these attracted significant public attention. Some were gang rapes, including one that prosecutors have characterized as "one of the most brutal in recent years." There, a woman was raped, sodomized and thrown fifty feet off the top of a four-story building in Brooklyn. Witnesses testified that "the [victim] screamed as she plunged down the air shaft. . . . She suffered fractures of both ankles and legs, her pelvis was shattered and she suffered extensive internal injuries." This rape survivor, like nearly all of the other unsung survivors of that week, was a woman of color. Nearly all of the rapes occurred between attackers and victims of the same race.

Professor Smith concludes from her review of the Central Park controversy that the differing responses to these rapes suggest an ongoing sexual hierarchy in which certain female bodies are more valuable than others. Professor Smith's speculation is born out in statistics reflecting the outcomes from rape prosecutions. For example, a recent study in Dallas revealed that the average prison sentence given to a male convicted of raping a Black woman was two years. In cases where the victims were Latinas, the average sentence was five years; and where the victims were Anglo, the average sentence was ten years.

This apparent devaluation of African American women has not been the focus. As a result, reformist and rhetorical strategies that have grown out of these movements have been ineffective in altering the treatment of Black women.

Some of the most significant rape reforms have included increased penalties and evidentiary changes designed to preclude attacks on a rape victim's moral character. Although such evidentiary reforms are useful in limiting the means by which defendants might attack the character of the rape victim, strategies that preclude defendants from tarnishing a woman's "good name" may be ineffective if the woman is not presumed to have a good name in the first place. Like the more formal requirements of the past, racial stereotypes that operate to discredit African American women may function to create a constructive requirement that prosecutors first establish that a Black woman is a potential victim of rape.

The central connection between antiracism and rape law has derived from the fact that in practice the criminal justice system focusses disproportionate resources and sanctions on rapes involving one particular dyad: Black men rapist/white female victim. In African American political discourses, this heightened concern with protecting white women against Black men has been rigorously criticized as constituting race discrimination against Black men. Yet just as surely, it reflects discrimination against Black women.

This discriminatory treatment of Black women has been largely overlooked as a consequence of the way that oppositional politics relating to rape and racism have traditionally focused on Black men as victims. The rape of Black women has sometimes found its way to the center of antiracist politics, particularly where the rapist is white. But the more common experience of intraracial rape is often disregarded within antiracist political discourses. This oversight may well reflect the view that politicizing such rapes conflicts on some level with efforts to eradicate prevailing stereotypes of Black males as rapists. Yet, despite the reluctance of many activists and critics to focus on the experiences of Black female rape victims, the treatment of Black female rape victims relative to white women does suggest that race may constitute a salient distinguishing factor, even among intraracial rapes. While racism may help explain white victims are more likely to see their assailants punished than are Black victims, one must look to sexism in order to understand why such issues are marginalized within the prevailing political agenda conceptions of racism.

The Black male experience of racist domination relating to sexuality is much more central to political conceptions of racial subordination than the equivalent experience of Black women. Likewise, feminist criticisms of rape processing inadequately figure race into such accounts. The combination of these tendencies is that Black women are marginalized not only in political discourses of rape, but in social science literature that incorporates these frameworks in exploring contemporary rape prosecutions. Gary LaFree's *Race and Criminal Justice: The Social Construction of Sexual Assault* provides a classic example of the way Black women's rape experiences are marginalized even within frameworks that are nicely constructed around both antiracist and feminist critiques of rape law.

Through a study of rape prosecutions in Minneapolis, LaFree attempts to determine the validity of two prevailing claims regarding rape processing: first, that Black defendants face significant racial discrimination in rape prosecutions, and second, that rape serves to socially control women by withholding the condemnation of sexual assault against women who engage in "nontraditional behavior." He concludes that the legal processing of rape claims continues to reflect both racial and gender subordination. LaFree's study is a useful review of the way that racism and sexism—traditionally defined—continues to play out in the contemporary construction of rape. Yet, Black women quite predictably fall through the cracks of his dichotomized theoretical framework.

LaFree's study found that Black men accused of raping white women were treated most harshly and that Black offenders accused of raping Black women were treated most leniently. These effects held even after controlling for other factors such as acquaintance between victim and assailant and injury to the victim. "Compared to other defendants, blacks who were suspected of assaulting white women received more serious charges, were more likely to have their cases filed as felonies, were more likely to receive prison sentences if convicted, were more likely to be incarcerated in the state penitentiary (as opposed to a jail or minimum-security facility), and [to] receive longer sentences on the average."

For LaFree, what is most important about this data is that Black men are discriminated against because their forcible "access" to white women was more harshly penalized than their forcible "access" to Black women. LaFree deploys a sexual stratification thesis to explain this discrimination: the rape of a white woman by a Black man is seen as a trespass on the valuable property rights of white men and consequently, such rapes are punished most severely. Although LaFree does not state as much, Black women are apparently devalued within this stratified market.

This emphasis on comparative access between white and Black men is consistent with frameworks that view racism primarily in terms of inequality between men. In this view, discrimination is grounded in the fact that white men can rape Black women with impunity but Black men cannot do the same with white women. To the extent that Black women are considered to be victims of discrimination at all, it is because white men can rape them with little sanction.

Because traditional readings of racism continue to focus on men, there is relatively little emphasis on how racism contributes to the victimization of Black women both inside and outside the criminal justice system. To address the way race and gender intersect with respect to Black women's experiences, emphasis would have to shift from men's differential access to women to the problem of commodifying women in the first place and then stratifying them on the basis of race. This would also require an implicit recognition that some Black men themselves victimize Black women.

LaFree attempts to address gender concerns in a subsequent chapter devoted to testing the feminist hypothesis that "the application of law to nonconformist women in rape cases may serve to control the behavior of all women." This inquiry is important because "if women who violate traditional sex roles and are raped are unable to obtain justice through the legal system, then the law may be interpreted as an institutional arrangement for reinforcing women's gender-role conformity."

He found that "acquittals were more common and final sentences were shorter when nontraditional behavior was alleged." In fact, the victim's moral character was more predictive of the final outcome than victim injury, and was second only to the defendant's character. . . . LaFree's framework treats race and gender as separate and it gives no indication of whether Black women fall in between or within both categories. For this reason, the effect of the traditional/nontraditional dichotomy on Black women was difficult to determine and must be inferred from his passing comments. For example, he notes that victims were evenly divided between traditional and nontraditional gender roles. This information, taken together with the lower rate of conviction for offenders accused of raping Black women, suggests that their role behavior may not have been as significant in determining case disposition involving Black victims as it was in cases involving white victims.

LaFree also notes that the victim's race was an important predictor of jurors' case evaluations:

> Jurors were less likely to believe in a defendant's guilt when the victim was black. Our interviews with jurors suggested that part of the explanation for this effect was that jurors . . . were influenced by stereotypes of black women as more likely to consent to sex or as more sexually experienced and hence less harmed by the assault. In a case involving the rape of a young black girl, one juror argued for acquittal on the grounds that a girl her age from 'that kind of neighborhood' probably wasn't a virgin anyway.

Moreover, some "jurors were simply less willing to believe the testimony of black complainants." One white juror is quoted as saying, "Negroes have a way of not telling the truth. They've a knack for coloring the story. So you know you can't believe everything they say."

Despite his findings that the race of the victim is significant in determining the disposition of rape cases, LaFree's overall conclusion is that rape processing operates to distinguish between legitimate rape victims and nonvictims and that the distinction turns primarily on behavior. In failing to mention the apparent racial hierarchy between women, the fact that for Black women, the distinction may turn more on identity is overlooked. LaFree might have pointed out that for certain women, rape processing may serve not simply to sanction non-traditional behavior but also to sanction non-traditional women.

LaFree's study illustrates how the race/sex hierarchy plays out in ways that subordinate Black women to white women, to Black men and, perhaps by implication, to white men. Yet, the effects of the differential application of rape sanctions in cases involving Black women barely warrant mention in his conclusions. . . .

The effort to politicize violence against women will do little to address the experiences of Black and other non-white women until the ramifications of racial stratification among women is acknowledged. At the same time, the antiracist agenda will not be furthered by suppressing the reality of Black male sexual violence against Black women. The effect of both these marginalizations is that women of color have no ready means to link their experiences with other women. This sense of isolation compounds efforts to politicize sexual violence within communities of color and permits the deadly silence about our experiences to continue.

NOTES AND QUESTIONS

1. **Rape Law's Reproduction of Social Hierarchies**. In *Rape, Race, and Representation*, Lisa Iglesias elaborates how LaFree's research discloses rape law's reproduction of hierarchical relationships of race and gender:

> The results in LaFree's rape cases reveal that state power reproduces hierarchical relations between different social groups through the processing of rape cases. In this society, the structure of intergroup relations is white over nonwhite (particularly over Black) and male over female. Thus, the threat of harsher enforcement against Black males accused of raping white women constitutes a form of social control that reproduces what Abdul JanMohamed calls "the racial-sexual border." Similarly, the relative impunity with which men rape white women acting outside traditional gender roles sends a clear message to white women that the law will not protect them if they are attacked while exercising prerogatives of autonomy outside of traditional gender roles. Finally, the relative impunity with which men rape racially subordinated women leads these women to understand that the law will not protect them at all. . . .

Elizabeth M. Iglesias, *Rape, Race, and Representation: The Power of Discourse, Discourses of Power, and the Reconstruction of Heterosexuality*, 49 Vand. L. Rev. 869 (1996). For further discussion of racism's influence on rape law, *see* Jacquelyn Dowd Hall, *"The Mind that Burns in Each Body": Women, Rape, and Racial Violence*, in *Powers of Desire: The Politics of Sexuality* 328 (Ann Snitow et al. eds, 1983); Jennifer Wriggins, *Rape, Racism, and the Law*, 6 Harv. Women's L.J. 103 (1983).

Kimberlé Crenshaw argues that rape law's racism involves a racial hierarchy among women as well as among men. How does this point affect the view of rape (Estrich's, for example) as a tool of male domination?

2. **Reform**. How should the racial construction of rape influence rape reform efforts? Does the use of rape law as an instrument of white supremacy, as well as male domination, complicate the project of enhancing individual women's security by ensuring that offenders are punished? Katharine Baker notes that some rape reform measures, such as Rule 413 of the Federal Rules of Evidence making prior acts of sexual assault by alleged rapists admissible in rape cases, tend to increase the already disproportionate enforcement of criminal law against disempowered men.

> Reports on the effectiveness of rape reform have already documented this problem. A study in the State of Washington indicates that rape-reform measures may increase the chances that men already in the system will be convicted of rape, but rape-reform measures often do not increase the chances of convicting those men who tend to escape the system altogether. In the words of Wallace Loh, the reform measures created "not a bigger mousetrap, only a better mousetrap." A better mousetrap may be one kind of improvement over the current mousetrap, but if part of the purpose of rape reform is to expand the class of those convicted to include the diversity of men who actually commit rape, admitting prior act evidence may very well fail to accomplish that goal. The men convicted of rape will be those already familiar with the criminal justice system. Middle class white men—a significant percentage of whom admit to raping—will continue to go free.

Baker, *Once A Rapist?*, at 593–94.

Do the deeply embedded biases that govern jurors' application of rape law place serious limits on the efficacy of amending statutory definitions of rape? Iglesias concludes that "LaFree's analysis of the criminal justice system ... suggests why efforts to reform substantive rape laws may be less effective than efforts to reform the structure of discretionary power in the criminal justice system." She goes on to propose that "feminists [should] redefine their target and rechannel their reform efforts from the criminal justice apparatus to the public policies that construct women's sexual vulnerability and the culturally dominant images of women and men upon which these policies are based."

Catharine MacKinnon, Feminism, Marxism, Method, and the State: Toward Feminist Jurisprudence

8 Signs 635 (1983).

... Attempts to reform and enforce rape laws ... have tended to build on the model of the deviant perpetrator and the violent act, as if the fact that rape is a crime means that the society is against it, so law enforcement would reduce or delegitimize it. Initiatives are accordingly directed toward making the police more sensitive, prosecutors more responsive, judges more receptive, and the law, in words, less sexist. ...Even if it were effective in jailing men who do little different from what nondeviant men do regularly, how would such an approach alter women's rapability? Unconfronted are *why* women are raped and the role of the state in that. Similarly, applying laws against battery to husbands, although it can mean life itself, has largely failed to address, as part of the strategy for state intervention, the conditions that produce men who systematically express themselves violently toward women, women whose resistance is disabled, and the role of the state in this dynamic. Criminal enforcement in these areas, while suggesting that rape and battery are deviant, punishes men for expressing the images of masculinity that mean their identity, for which they are otherwise trained, elevated, venerated, and paid. These men must be stopped. But how does that change them or reduce the chances that there will be more like them? ...

Feminists have reconceived rape as central to women's condition in two ways. Some see rape as an act of violence, not sexuality, the threat of which intimidates all women. Others see rape, including its violence, as an expression of male sexuality, the social imperatives of which define all women. The first, formally in the liberal tradition, comprehends rape as a displacement of power based on physical force onto sexuality, a pre-existing natural sphere to which domination is alien. Thus, Susan Brownmiller examines rape in riots, wars, pogroms, and revolutions; rape by police, parents, prison guards; and rape motivated by racism—seldom rape in normal circumstances, in everyday life, in ordinary relationships, by men as men. Women are raped by guns, age, white supremacy, the state—only derivatively by the penis. The more feminist view to me, one which derives from victims' experiences, sees sexuality as a social sphere of male power of which forced sex is paradigmatic. Rape is not less sexual for being violent; to the extent that coercion has become integral to male sexuality, rape may be sexual to the degree that, and because, it is violent.

The point of defining rape as "violence not sex" or "violence against women" has been to separate sexuality from gender in order to affirm sex (heterosexuality) while rejecting violence (rape). The problem remains what it has always been: telling the difference. The convergence of sexuality with violence, long used at law to deny the reality of women's violation, is recognized by rape survivors, with a difference: where the legal system has seen the intercourse in rape, victims see the rape in intercourse. The uncoerced context for sexual expression becomes as elusive as the physical acts come to feel indistinguishable. Instead of asking, what is the violation of rape, what if we ask, what is the nonviolation of intercourse? To tell what is wrong with rape, explain what is right about sex. If this, in turn, is difficult, the difficulty is as instructive as the difficulty men have in telling the difference when women see one. Perhaps the wrong of rape has proven so difficult to articulate because the unquestionable starting point has been that rape is definable as distinct from intercourse, when for women it is difficult to distinguish them under conditions of male dominance. ...

The law of rape divides the world of women into spheres of consent according to how much say we are legally presumed to have over sexual access to us by various categories of men. Little girls may not consent; wives must. If rape laws existed to enforce women's control over our own sexuality, as the consent defense implies, marital rape would not be a widespread exception, nor would statutory rape proscribe all sexual intercourse with underage girls regardless of their wishes. The rest of us fall into parallel provinces: good girls, like children, are unconsenting, virginal, rapable; bad girls, like wives, are consenting, whores, unrapable. The age line under which girls are presumed disabled from withholding consent to sex rationalizes a condition of sexual coercion women never outgrow. As with protective labor laws for women only, dividing and protecting the most vulnerable becomes a device for not protecting everyone. Risking loss of even so little cannot be afforded. Yet the protection is denigrating and limiting (girls may not choose to be sexual) as well as perverse (girls are eroticized as untouchable; now reconsider the data on incest). . . .

Having defined rape in male sexual terms, the law's problem, which becomes the victim's problem, is distinguishing rape from sex in specific cases. The law does this by adjudicating the level of acceptable force starting just above the level set by what is seen as normal male sexual behavior, rather than at the victim's, or women's, point of violation. Rape cases finding insufficient force reveal that acceptable sex, in the legal perspective, can entail a lot of force. This is not only because of the way specific facts are perceived and interpreted, but because of the way the injury itself is defined as illegal. Rape is a sex crime that is not a crime when it looks like sex. To seek to define rape as violent, not sexual, is understandable in this context, and often seems strategic. But assault that is consented to is still assault; rape consented to is intercourse. The substantive reference point implicit in existing legal standards is the sexually normative level of force. Until this norm is confronted as such, no distinction between violence and sexuality will prohibit more instances of women's experienced violation than does the existing definition. The question is what is *seen as* force, hence as violence, in the sexual arena. Most rapes, as women live them, will not be seen to violate women until sex and violence are confronted as mutually definitive. It is not only men convicted of rape who believe that the only thing they did different from what men do all the time is get caught.

The line between rape and intercourse commonly centers on some measure of the woman's "will." But from what should the law know woman's will? Like much existing law, Brownmiller tends to treat will as a question of consent and consent as a factual issue of the presence of force. Proof problems aside, force and desire are not mutually exclusive. So long as dominance is eroticized, they never will be. Women are socialized to passive receptivity; many have or perceive no alternative to acquiescence; may prefer it to the escalated risk of injury and the humiliation of a lost fight; submit to survive. Some eroticize dominance and submission; it beats feeling forced. Sexual intercourse may be deeply unwanted—the woman would never have initiated it—yet no force may be present. Too, force may be used, yet the woman may want the sex—to avoid more force or because she, too, eroticizes dominance. Women and men know this. Calling rape violence, not sex, thus evades, at the moment it most seems to confront, the issue of who controls women's sexuality and the dominance/submission dynamic that has defined it. When sex is violent, women may have lost control over what is done to us, but absence of force does not ensure the presence of that control. Nor, under conditions of male dominance, does the presence of force make an interaction nonsexual. If sex is normally something men do to women, the issue is less whether there was force and more whether consent is a meaningful concept. . . .

The law distinguishes rape from intercourse by the woman's lack of consent coupled with a man's (usually) knowing disregard of it. A feminist distinction between rape and intercourse, to hazard a beginning approach, lies instead in the *meaning* of the act from women's point of view. What is wrong with rape is that it is an act of the subordination of women to men. Seen this way, the issue is not so much what rape "is" as the way its social conception is shaped to interpret particular encounters. Under conditions of sex inequality, with perspective bound up with situation, whether a contested interaction is rape comes down to whose meaning wins. If sexuality is relational, specifically if it is a power relation of gender, consent is a communication under conditions of inequality. It transpires somewhere between what the woman actually wanted and what the man comprehended she wanted. Instead of capturing this dynamic, the law gives us linear statics face to face. Nonconsent in law becomes a question of the man's force or the woman's resistance or both. Rape, like many crimes and torts, requires that the accused possess a criminal mind (mens rea) for his acts to be criminal. The man's mental state refers to what he actually understood at the time or to what a reasonable man should have understood under the circumstances. The problem is this: the injury of rape lies in the meaning of the act to its victims, but the standard for its criminality lies in the meaning of the same act to the assailants. Rape is only an injury from women's point of view. It is only a crime from the male point of view, explicitly including that of the accused. . . .

To a feminist analysis, men set sexual mores ideologically and behaviorally, define rape as they imagine the sexual violation of women through distinguishing it from their image of what they normally do, and sit in judgment in most accusations of sex crimes. So rape comes to mean a strange (read Black) man knowing a woman does not want sex and going ahead anyway. But men are systematically conditioned not even to notice what women want. They may have not a glimmer of women's indifference or revulsion. Rapists typically believe the woman loved it. Women, as a survival strategy, must ignore or devalue or mute our desires (particularly lack of them) to convey the impression that the man will get what he wants regardless of what we want. In this context, consider measuring the genuineness of consent from the individual assailant's (or even the socially reasonable, i.e., objective, man's) point of view. . . .

[T]he deeper problem is the rape law's assumption that a single, objective state of affairs existed, one which merely needs to be determined by evidence, when many (maybe even most) rapes involve honest men and violated women. When the reality is split—a woman is raped but not by a rapist?—the law tends to conclude that a rape *did not happen*. To attempt to solve this by adopting the standard of reasonable belief without asking, on a substantive social basis, to whom the belief is reasonable and why— meaning, what conditions make it reasonable—is one-sided: male-sided. What is it reasonable for a man to believe concerning a woman's desire for sex when heterosexuality is compulsory? Whose subjectivity becomes the objectivity of "what happened" is a matter of social meaning, that is, it has been a matter of sexual politics. . . .

NOTES AND QUESTIONS

1. **Rape and Heterosexuality**. Catharine MacKinnon's reconception of rape as derived from ordinary heterosexual relationships made a monumental contribution to the feminist understanding of rape. Rape is not an aberrational practice separate from "normal" sexuality; rather, rape is part of the pervasive understanding of sexuality that eroticizes dominance. MacKinnon's account of rape has been criticized, however, for treating sex as inherently degrading to women. Do you agree with this interpretation of her writing? Is MacKinnon arguing that sex with men inherently violates women or that it does so under the current system of heterosexuality? To what extent is rape a function of (aggressive) male and (vulnerable) female physiology and to what extent is it a function of socially constructed inequalities of power, supported by law? Can a woman rape a man?

Andrea Dworkin, with whom MacKinnon has collaborated and whose work she has relied on, goes even further to describe sexual intercourse itself as a violation of women's bodies. In her book *Intercourse*, Dworkin writes:

> A human being has a body that is inviolate; and when it is violated, it is abused. A women has a body that is penetrated in intercourse: permeable, its corporeal solidness a lie.... She, a human being, is supposed to have privacy that is absolute; except that she, a woman, has a hole between her legs that men can, must, do enter.... [T]hat slit which means entry into her— intercourse—appears to be the key to women's lower human status.

Andrea Dworkin, *Intercourse* 122–23 (1987).

After reviewing MacKinnon's and Dworkin's writing, Linda McClain asks

> whether or not an act like intercourse, or the entry of a woman's body, is ...an invasion incompatible with an overall sense of privacy and inviolability. Or, as other feminists suggest, can and do women experience entry (or, to challenge gender role and

subject/object assumptions, encirclement), either in a heterosexual or lesbian context, as pleasurable, desirable, intimate, intense, fulfilling, fun, and the like, and not as harmful or as a threat to identity, integrity, and privacy?

Linda C. McClain, *Inviolability and Privacy: The Castle, the Sanctuary, and the Body*, 7 Yale J.L. & Human. 195, 226–27 (1995).

What are the implications of Professor McClain's question for MacKinnon's theory about rape? McClain goes on to caution that

> while one might argue that a clear gender difference, rooted in physiology, is that women and men have different expectations of inviolability, such a conclusion may ignore the impact upon such expectations of the social construction of "woman" and "man" by reference to their performing an appropriate sexual role (being entered or penetrated versus entering and penetrating) as well as to their potential for sexual violation.

Consider also Iglesias, *Rape, Race, and Representation*, at 894 n. 58:

> My own experience leads me to conclude that rape is better explained as an artifact of men's efforts to enact the culturally dominant scripts of pornographic masculinity and the frustrations this effort inevitably engenders, rather than stemming from any anatomical difference. After all, while some men may like to think of their penises as weapons, this is not the only image that codes the penis. On the contrary, the erect penis is also ... an organ of pleasure as much for women as for men.

MacKinnon's claim that rape is an extension of "normal" heterosexuality also became the center of a feminist debate about the difference between rape and consensual sex. Some feminists argue that by equating heterosexual sex with rape MacKinnon's analysis trivializes the injury caused by rape. Lynne Henderson, for example, identifies the critical task in fighting rape as developing "our understanding of what makes rape such a heinous offense, and distinguishing that from sexual relations generally." Lynne N. Henderson, *What Makes Rape a Crime?*, 3 Berkeley Women's L.J. 193, 220 (1988). Does MacKinnon negate women's ability to tell the difference between rape and other types of sex with men? Or is MacKinnon pointing out that women experience commonalities between what is legally defined as rape and what is considered normal sex?

2. **Marital Rape**. One of the most glaring illustrations of MacKinnon's thesis is the marital rape exemption. Under the traditional definition of rape, husbands who forced their wives to have sex with them were shielded from criminal prosecution. The reason for this rule, Lord Matthew Hale explained three centuries ago, was that "by their mutual matrimonial consent and contract the wife hath given up herself in this kind unto the husband, which she cannot retract." The exemption has also been explained as a corollary of a husband's property right to his wife's sexuality, as well as the merger of spouses into a single legal entity upon marriage. Although all states had abolished an absolute marital rape exemption by

1990, some still place limits on the prosecution of husbands who rape their wives. A recent article summarizes the status of this "license to rape:"

> Such prosecutorial restrictions included non-cohabitation or aggravated force requirements, ceilings on punishment, specifications on when—and to whom—marital rape must be reported, and the creation of alternative, frequently misdemeanor, sexual assault statutes that applied when criminal behavior otherwise classifiable as felony rape happened to be perpetrated by a spouse. ...[A]t least thirteen states still offer preferential or disparate treatment to perpetrators of spousal sexual assault.... Several states have actually extended their exemptions to include non-married, cohabiting couples. For example, cohabitation is an affirmative defense to rape in Connecticut....

Lisa R. Eskow, *The Ultimate Weapon?: Demythologizing Spousal Rape and Reconceptualizing Its Prosecution,* 48 Stan. L. Rev. 677, 682–83 (1996). What do you think is the contemporary rationale for treating marital rape less seriously?

3. **Bad Sex**. Given the context of power within which heterosexual relations take place, how should the law identify those sexual acts that are criminal? Lynne Henderson distinguished between "bad sex" and rape:

> The phrase "bad sex" covers a range of heterosexual interactions for women: their partner was clumsy; their mood or their partner's mood affected the interaction; they lost their desire but felt they should let the man continue to orgasm, either because they believed things were "too far along" to stop and they wanted to avoid the hassle or because they cared about the man; and so on.... Women—and men—have sexual relations that they later regret. Nevertheless, in "bad sex" women do not feel raped, if for no other reason than they are exercising some agency....

Lynne Henderson, *Rape and Responsibility,* 11 Law & Phil. 127, 165–66 (1992). Do you find this distinction between rape and "bad sex" helpful? How would you characterize the following description of a woman's sexual experience with her husband?

> I know I was feeling coerced and not doing it willingly most of the time.... But in a way I'm not sure it was done by him. It was really my own upbringing and the things that I'd been taught. It came from me. He couldn't have really raped me. I was allowing my own body to be violated, and that's not rape. My allowing it is what makes it not rape.

David Finkelhor & Kersti Yllo, *License to Rape: Sexual Abuse of Wives* 86 (1985).

4. **The Nineties Critique of "Rape Crisis" Feminists**. During the 1990s writers such as journalist Katie Roiphe attacked the radical feminist position on the pervasiveness of rape. In *The Morning After: Sex, Fear, and Feminism on Campus,* which received considerable media attention, Roiphe questioned the statistics on date rape on college campuses (e.g., *Ms.*

magazine's 1985 survey reporting that one in four college women is the victim of rape or attempted rape), as well as feminists' reasons for "finding" a rape crisis. Roiphe argued that "rape-crisis" feminists, by exaggerating the risk of rape and by collapsing the difference between rape and sex, were perpetuating the stereotype of women as desexualized, helpless victims.

> Although it is not always an explicit part of their agenda, feminists involved in the rape-crisis movement educate young women according to certain beliefs about sexual behavior, both real and ideal. ...With their practical advice, their sample scenarios, their sample aggressive male, their message itself projects a clear comment on the nature of sexuality: women are often unwilling participants who say yes because they feel they have to, because they are intimidated by male power. ...

> The idea of a fall from childhood grace, pinned on one particular moment—a moment over which we had no control, much lamented—gives our lives a compelling narrative structure. It's easy to see why the seventeen-year-old likes it. It's easy to see why the rape-crisis feminists like it. It's a natural human impulse put to political purpose. But in generating and perpetuating these kinds of myths we should keep in mind that myths surrounding female innocence have been used to keep women inside and behind veils. They have been used to keep them out of work and in labor. ...

> This is one of the central ideas of the rape-crisis movement: sex has become our Tower of Babel. He doesn't know what she wants (not to have sex), and she doesn't know what he wants (to have sex), until it's too late. The idea is that he speaks boyspeak, and she speaks girlspeak, and what comes out of all this verbal chaos is a lot of rapes. More than a poststructuralist distrust of linguistic certainty, this is an idea about the mystery of the opposite sex. An idea about division, this is also a divisive idea. It promotes the image of men and women as inhabitants of different worlds. It raises the old-fashioned question who can ever know what goes on in her pretty little head? ...

> With their expansive version of rape, rape-crisis feminists invent a kinder, gentler sexuality. Beneath the broad definition of rape, these feminists are endorsing their own utopian vision of sexual relations: sex without struggle, sex without power, sex without persuasion, sex without pursuit. If verbal coercion constitutes rape, then the word "rape" itself expands to include any kind of sex a woman experiences as negative. ...

Katie Roiphe, *The Morning After: Sex, Fear, and Feminism on Campus* (1993).

Roiphe claimed further that the concern about date rape masked affluent white women's fears about the growing numbers of working class and minority students entering college:

The theory of mixed signals and crossed stars has to do with more than gender politics. The idea of miscommunication, so central to the rape-crisis movement, is one piece of a larger social puzzle, and the idea that he may rape her because he doesn't know what she wants has its roots in more than male oblivion. This fear of miscommunication comes, in part, from the much-heralded diversity that has so radically shifted the social composition of the college class since the fifties. . . . With the radical shift in college environment, with the introduction of black kids, Asian kids, Jewish kids, kids from the wrong side of the tracks of nearly every railroad in the country, there was an accompanying anxiety about how people were to behave. When ivory tower meets melting pot, it causes some confusion, some tension, some need for readjustment. In explaining the need for intensive "orientation" programs, including workshops on date rape, Columbia's assistant dean for freshmen stated, "You can't bring all these people together and say, 'Now be one big happy community,' without some sort of training." . . .

Democracy is always messier than aristocracy. As fairness broke through the sacred boundaries of "our own kind," people worried. That worry, that social anxiety, is part of the concern about sexual harassment and concern about rape. Catherine Stimpson, feminist dean of Rutgers University and longtime advocate of women's-studies programs, once pointed out that it's easier for people to talk about gender than to talk about class. "Miscommunication" is in some sense a word for the friction between the way we were and the way we are. Just as the idea that we speak different languages is connected to gender—the arrival of women in classrooms, in dorms, and in offices—it is also connected to class. . . .

Id. For a critique of Roiphe's book, *see* Kathryn Abrams, *Songs of Innocence and Experience: Dominance Feminism in the University*, 103 Yale L.J. 1533 (1994). Are Roiphe's criticisms fair or does she misunderstand feminist concerns about date rape?

5. **A Positive Account of Female Sexuality**. Finally, MacKinnon's theory has been faulted for failing to provide a positive depiction or vision of female sexuality. Relying on the writings of French feminist philosopher Luce Irigiray, Drucilla Cornell contrasts MacKinnon's image of the violated female body with a more receptive and joyful model of the feminine self:

Under [MacKinnon's] view of the individual or the subject, the body becomes the barrier in which the self hides, and the weapon—the phallus—asserts itself against others. The feminine self, as it is celebrated in myth and allegory, lives the body differently. The body is not an erected barrier, but a position of receptivity. To be accessible is to be open to the other. To shut oneself off is loss of sexual pleasure. . . . If one views the body in this way, then "to be fucked" is not the end of the world. The endless erection of a barrier against "being fucked: is seen for what it is"—a defense mechanism that creates a fort for the self at the expense of *jouissance*.

Drucilla Cornell, *The Doubly–Prized World: Myth, Allegory and the Feminine*, 75 Cornell L. Rev. 644, 691 (1990). Do you find that MacKinnon's writing assists or hinders the discovery or invention of a positive female sexuality?

The readings that follow, as well as those in the next section, Women and Their Bodies: Feminist Legal Theory III, further explore this theme.

Bell Hooks, Seduced by Violence No More

From b. hooks, Outlaw Culture: Resisting Representations
(NY: Routledge, 1994).

. . . Black males, utterly disenfranchised in almost every arena of life in the United States, often find that the assertion of sexist domination is their only expressive access to the patriarchal power they are told all men should possess as their gendered birthright. Hence, it should not surprise or shock that many black men support and celebrate "rape culture." That celebration has found its most powerful contemporary voice in misogynist rap music. Significantly, there are powerful alternative voices. Mass media pays little attention to those black men who are opposing phallocentrism, misogyny, and sexism. The "it's-a-dick-thing" version of masculinity that black male pop icons such as Spike Lee and Eddie Murphy promote is a call for "real" black men to be sexist and proud of it, to rape and assault black women and brag about it. Alternative, progressive, black male voices in rap or cinema receive little attention, but they exist. There are even black males who do "rap against rape" (their slogan), but their voices are not celebrated in patriarchal culture.

Overall, cultural celebration of black male phallocentrism takes the form of commodifying these expressions of "cool" in ways that glamorize and seduce. Hence, those heterosexual black males that the culture deems most desirable as mates or erotic partners tend to be pushing a "dickthing" masculinity. They can talk tough and get rough. They can brag about disciplinin' their women, about making sure the "bitches" respect them. Many black men have a profound investment in the perpetuation and maintenance of rape culture. So much of their sense of value and self-esteem is hooked into the patriarchal macho image; these brothers are not about to surrender their "dick-thing" masculinity. This was most apparent during the Mike Tyson trial. Brothers all over were arguing that the black female plaintiff should not have gone to Tyson's hotel room in the wee hours of the morning if she had no intention of doing the wild thing. As one young brother told me last week, "I mean, if a sister came to my room that late, I would think she got one thing on her mind." When I suggested to him and his partners that maybe a woman could visit the room of a man she likes in the wee hours of the night because she might like to talk, they shook their heads saying, "No way." Theirs is a deeply ingrained sexism, a profoundly serious commitment to rape culture.

Like many black men, they are enraged by any feminist call to rethink masculinity and oppose patriarchy. And the courageous brothers who do, who rethink masculinity, who reject patriarchy and rape culture, often find that they cannot get any play—that the very same women who may critique macho male nonsense contradict themselves by making it clear that they find the "unconscious brothers" more appealing.

On college campuses all over the United States, I talk with these black males and hear their frustrations. They are trying to oppose patriarchy and yet are rejected by black females for not being masculine enough. This makes them feel like losers, that their lives are not enhanced when they make progressive changes, when they affirm feminist movement. Their black female peers confirm that they do indeed hold contradictory desires. They desire men not to be sexist, even as they say, "But I want him to be masculine." When pushed to define "masculine," they fall back on sexist representations. I was surprised by the number of young black women who repudiated the notion of male domination, but who would then go on to insist that they could not desire a brother who could not take charge, take care of business, be in control.

Their responses suggest that one major obstacle preventing us from transforming rape culture is that heterosexual women have not unlearned a heterosexist-based "eroticism" that constructs desire in such a way that many of us can only respond erotically to male behavior that has already been coded as masculine within the sexist framework. Let me give an example of what I mean. For most of my heterosexual erotic life I have been involved with black males who are into a "dick-thing" masculinity. For more than ten years I was in a nonmonogamous relationship with a black man committed to nonsexist behavior in almost every aspect of daily life—the major exception being the bedroom. I accepted my partner's insistence that his sexual desires be met in any circumstance where I had made sexual overtures (kissing, caressing, and so on). Hence ours was not a relationship in which I felt free to initiate sexual play without going forward and engaging in coitus. Often I felt compelled to engage in sexual intercourse when I did not want to.

In my fantasies, I dreamed of being with a male who would fully respect my body rights, my right to say "no," my freedom not to proceed in any sexual activity that I did not desire even if I initially felt that I wanted to be sexual. When I left this relationship, I was determined to choose male partners who would respect my body rights. For me this meant males who did not think that the most important expression of female love was satisfying male sexual desire. It meant males who could respect a woman's right to say "no," irrespective of the circumstance.

Years passed before I found a partner who respected those rights in a feminist manner, with whom I made a mutual covenant that neither of us would ever engage in any sexual act that we did not desire to participate in. I was elated. With this partner I felt free and safe. I felt that I could choose not to have sex without worrying that this choice would alienate or anger my partner. Though most women were impressed that I had found such a partner, they doubted that this could be a chosen commitment to female freedom on any man's part; they raised suspicious questions. Braggin' about him to girlfriends and acquaintances, I was often told, "Girl, you betta be careful. Dude might be gay." I also began to feel doubts. Nothing about the way this dude behaved was familiar. His was not the usual "dick-thing" masculinity that had aroused feelings of pleasure and danger in me for most of my erotic life. While I liked his alternative behavior, I felt a loss of control—the kind that we experience when we are no longer acting within the socialized framework of both acceptable and familiar heterosexual behavior. I worried that he did not find me really desirable. Then I asked myself whether aggressive emphasis on his desire, on his need for "the pussy" would have reassured me. It seemed to me, then, that I needed to rethink the nature of female heterosexual eroticism, particularly in relation to black culture.

Critically interrogating my responses, I confronted the reality that despite all my years of opposing patriarchy, I had not fully questioned or transformed the structure of my desire. By allowing my erotic desire to still be determined to any extent by conventional sexist constructions, I was acting in complicity with patriarchal thinking. Resisting patriarchy ultimately meant that I had to reconstruct myself as a heterosexual, desiring subject in a manner that would make it possible for me to be fully aroused by male behavior that was not phallocentric. In basic terms, I had to learn how to be sexual with a man in a context where his pleasure and his hard-on is decentered and mutual pleasure is centered instead. That meant learning how to enjoy being with a male partner who could be sexual without viewing coitus as the ultimate expression of desire.

Talking with women of varying ages and ethnicities about this issue, I am more convinced than ever that women who engage in sexual acts with male partners must not only interrogate the nature of the masculinity we desire, we must also actively construct radically new ways to think and feel as desiring subjects. By shaping our eroticism in ways that repudiate phallocentrism, we oppose rape culture. Whether this alters sexist male behavior is not the point. A woman who wants to engage in erotic acts with a man without reinscribing sexism will be much more likely to avoid or reject situations in which she might be victimized. By refusing to function within the heterosexist framework that condones male erotic domination of women, females would be actively disempowering patriarchy.

Without a doubt, our collective, conscious refusal to act in any way that would make us complicit in the perpetuation of rape culture within the sphere of sexual relations would undermine the structure. Concurrently, when heterosexual women are no longer attracted to macho men, the message sent to men would at least be consistent and clear. That would be a major intervention in the overall effort to transform rape culture.

QUESTIONS

Re-Imagining Male and Female Sexuality. According to bell hooks, ending sexual oppression requires transforming both male and female sexuality, and she holds both men and women accountable for this change. How do you imagine sexual relations free from the dominant notions of masculinity described in prior readings? What are the roles of men, women, and the law in achieving this end?

Michael M. v. Superior Court of Sonoma County

Supreme Court of the United States, 1981.
450 U.S. 464, 101 S.Ct. 1200, 67 L.Ed.2d 437.

JUSTICE WILLIAM H. REHNQUIST announced the judgment of the Court and delivered an opinion, in which THE CHIEF JUSTICE, JUSTICE POTTER STEWART, and JUSTICE LEWIS F. POWELL, JR. joined.

The question presented in this case is whether California's "statutory rape" law, § 261.5 of the Cal. Penal Code, violates the Equal Protection Clause of the Fourteenth Amendment. Section 261.5 defines unlawful sexual intercourse as "an act of sexual intercourse accomplished with a female not the wife of the perpetrator, where the female is under the age of 18 years." The statute thus makes men alone criminally liable for the act of sexual intercourse.

In July 1978, a complaint was filed in the Municipal Court of Sonoma County, Cal., alleging that petitioner, then a 17 1/2–year–old male, had had unlawful sexual intercourse with a female under the age of 18, in violation of § 261.5. The evidence, adduced at a preliminary hearing showed that at approximately midnight on June 3, 1978, petitioner and two friends approached Sharon, a 16 1/2–year–old female, and her sister as they waited at a bus stop. Petitioner and Sharon, who had already been drinking, moved away from the others and began to kiss. After being struck in the face for rebuffing petitioner's initial advances, Sharon submitted to sexual intercourse with petitioner. Prior to trial, petitioner sought to set aside the information on both state and federal constitutional grounds, asserting that § 261.5 unlawfully discriminated on the basis of gender. The trial court and the California Court of Appeal denied petitioner's request for relief and petitioner sought review in the Supreme Court of California.

The Supreme Court held that "section 261.5 discriminates on the basis of sex because only females may be victims, and only males may violate the section."

... The justification for the statute offered by the State, and accepted by the Supreme Court of California, is that the legislature sought to prevent illegitimate teenage pregnancies. That finding, of course, is entitled to great deference. And although our cases establish that the State's asserted reason for the enactment of a statute may be rejected, if it "could not have been a goal of the legislation," this is not such a case.

We are satisfied not only that the prevention of illegitimate pregnancy is at least one of the "purposes" of the statute, but also that the State has a strong interest in preventing such pregnancy. At the risk of stating the obvious, teenage pregnancies, which have increased dramatically over the last two decades, have significant social, medical, and economic consequences for both the mother and her child, and the State. Of particular concern to the State is that approximately half of all teenage pregnancies end in abortion. And of those children who are born, their illegitimacy makes them likely candidates to become wards of the State.

We need not be medical doctors to discern that young men and young women are not similarly situated with respect to the problems and the risks of sexual intercourse. Only women may become pregnant, and they suffer disproportionately the profound physical, emotional and psychological consequences of sexual activity. The statute at issue here protects women from sexual intercourse at an age when those consequences are particularly severe.

The question thus boils down to whether a State may attack the problem of sexual intercourse and teenage pregnancy directly by prohibiting a male from having sexual intercourse with a minor female. We hold that such a statute is sufficiently related to the State's objectives to pass constitutional muster.

Because virtually all of the significant harmful and inescapably identifiable consequences of teenage pregnancy fall on the young female, a legislature acts well within its authority when it elects to punish only the participant who, by nature, suffers few of the consequences of his conduct. It is hardly unreasonable for a legislature acting to protect minor females to exclude them from punishment. Moreover, the risk of pregnancy itself constitutes a substantial deterrence to young females. No similar natural sanctions deter males. A criminal sanction imposed solely on males thus serves to roughly "equalize" the deterrents on the sexes.

We are unable to accept petitioner's contention that the statute is impermissibly underinclusive and must, in order to pass judicial scrutiny, be *broadened* so as to hold the female as criminally liable as the male. It is argued that this statute is not *necessary* to deter teenage pregnancy because a gender-neutral statute, where both male and female would be subject to prosecution, would serve that goal equally well. The relevant inquiry, however, is not whether the statute is drawn as precisely as it might have been, but whether the line chosen by the California Legislature is within constitutional limitations.

In any event, we cannot say that a gender-neutral statute would be as effective as the statute California has chosen to enact. The State persuasively contends that a gender-neutral statute would frustrate its interest in effective enforcement. Its view is that a female is surely less likely to report violations of the statute if she herself would be subject to criminal prosecution. In an area already fraught with prosecutorial difficulties, we decline to hold that the Equal Protection Clause requires a legislature to enact a statute so broad that it may well be incapable of enforcement.

We similarly reject petitioner's argument that § 261.5 is impermissibly overbroad because it makes unlawful sexual intercourse with prepubescent females, who are, by definition, incapable of becoming pregnant. Quite apart from the fact that the statute could well be justified on the grounds that very young females are particularly susceptible to physical injury from sexual intercourse, it is ludicrous to suggest that the Constitution requires the California Legislature to limit the scope of its rape statute to older teenagers and exclude young girls.

There remains only petitioner's contention that the statute is unconstitutional as it is applied to him because he, like Sharon, was under 18 at the time of sexual intercourse. Petitioner argues that the statute is flawed because it presumes that as between two persons under 18, the male is the culpable aggressor. We find petitioner's contentions unpersuasive. Contrary to his assertions, the statute does not rest on the assumption that males are generally the aggressors. It is instead an attempt by a legislature to prevent illegitimate teenage pregnancy by providing an additional deterrent for men. The age of the man is irrelevant since young men are as capable as older men of inflicting the harm sought to be prevented.

In upholding the California statute we also recognize that this is not a case where a statute is being challenged on the grounds that it "invidiously discriminates" against females. To the contrary, the statute places a burden on males which is not shared by females. But we find nothing to suggest that men, because of past discrimination or peculiar disadvantages, are in need of the special solicitude of the courts. Nor is this a case where the gender classification is made "solely for ... administrative convenience," ... or rests on "the baggage of sexual stereotypes ...". As we have held, the statute instead reasonably reflects the fact that the consequences of sexual intercourse and pregnancy fall more heavily on the female than on the male. ...

JUSTICE HARRY BLACKMUN, concurring in the judgment. ...

I think ... that it is only fair, with respect to this particular petitioner, to point out that his partner, Sharon, appears not to have been an unwilling participant in at least the initial stages of the intimacies that took place the night of June 3, 1978.[2] Petitioner's and Sharon's nonac-

---

2. Sharon at the preliminary hearing testified as follows:

"Q. [by the Deputy District Attorney]. On June the 4th, at approximately midnight—midnight of June the 3rd, were you in Rohnert Park?

"A. [by Sharon]. Yes. ...

"Q. Would you briefly describe what happened that night? Did you see the defendant that night in Rohnert Park?

"A. Yes.

"Q. Where did you first meet him?

"A. At a bus stop.

"Q. Was anyone with you?

"A. My sister.

"Q. Was anyone with the defendant?

"A. Yes.

"Q. How many people were with the defendant?

"A. Two.

"Q. Now, after you met the defendant, what happened?

"A. We walked down to the railroad tracks.

"Q. What happened at the railroad tracks?

"A. We were drinking at the railroad tracks and we walked over to this bush and he started kissing me and stuff, and I was kissing him back, too, at first. Then, I was telling him to stop—

"Q. Yes.

"A.—and I was telling him to slow down and stop. He said, 'Okay, okay.' But then he just kept doing it. He just kept doing it and then my sister and two other guys came over to where we were and my sister said—told me to get up and come home. And then I didn't—

"Q. Yes.

"A.—and then my sister and—

"Q. All right.

"A.—David, one of the boys that were there, started walking home and we stayed there and then later—

"Q. All right.

"A.—Bruce left Michael, you know.

"The Court: Michael being the defendant?

"The Witness: Yeah. We was lying there and we were kissing each other, and then he asked me if I wanted to walk him over to the park; so we walked over to the park and we sat down on a bench and then he started kissing me again and we were laying on the bench. And he told me to take my pants off.

"I said, 'No,' and I was trying to get up and he hit me back down on the bench and then I just said to myself, 'Forget it,' and I let him do what he wanted to do and he took my pants off and he was telling me to put my legs around him and stuff—

"Q. Did you have sexual intercourse with the defendant?

"A. Yeah.

"Q. He did put his penis into your vagina?

"A. Yes.

"Q. You said that he hit you?

"Q. Yeah.

"Q. How did he hit you?

"A. He slugged me in the face.

"Q. With what did he slug you?

"A. His fist.

"Q. Where abouts in the face?

"A. On my chin.

"Q. As a result of that, did you have any bruises or any kind of an injury?

"A. Yeah.

"Q. What happened?

"A. I had bruises.

"The Court: Did he hit you one time or did he hit you more than once?

"The Witness: He hit me about two or three times.

"Q. Now, during the course of that evening, did the defendant ask you your age?

"A. Yeah.

"Q. And what did you tell him?

"A. Sixteen.

"Q. Did you tell him you were sixteen?

"A. Yes.

"Q. Now, you said you had been drinking, is that correct?

"A. Yes.

"Q. Would you describe your condition as a result of the drinking?

"A. I was a little drunk."

CROSS–EXAMINATION

"Q. Did you go off with Mr. *M.* away from the others?

"A. Yeah.

"Q. Why did you do that?

"A. I don't know. I guess I wanted to.

"Q. Did you have any need to go to the bathroom when you were there.

"A. Yes.

"Q. And what did you do?

"A. Me and my sister walked down the railroad tracks to some bushes and went to the bathroom.

"Q. Now, you and Mr. *M.*, as I understand it, went off into the bushes, is that correct?

"A. Yes.

"Q. Okay. And what did you do when you and Mr. *M.* were there in the bushes?

"A. We were kissing and hugging.

"Q. Were you sitting up?

"A. We were laying down.

"Q. You were lying down. This was in the bushes?

"A. Yes.

"Q. How far away from the rest of them were you?

quaintance with each other before the incident; their drinking; their withdrawal from the others of the group; their foreplay, in which she willingly participated and seems to have encouraged; and the closeness of their ages (a difference of only one year and 18 days) are factors that should make this case an unattractive one to prosecute at all, and especially to prosecute as a felony, rather than as a misdemeanor chargeable under § 261.5. But the State has chosen to prosecute in that manner, and the facts, I reluctantly conclude, may fit the crime.

JUSTICE WILLIAM BRENNAN, with whom JUSTICES BYRON WHITE and THURGOOD MARSHALL join, dissenting. . . .

Until very recently, no California court or commentator had suggested that the purpose of California's statutory rape law was to protect young women from the risk of pregnancy. Indeed, the historical development of § 261.5 demonstrates that the law was initially enacted on the premise that young women, in contrast to young men, were to be deemed legally incapable of consenting to an act of sexual intercourse. Because their

"A. They were just bushes right next to the railroad tracks. We just walked off into the bushes; not very far.

"Q. So your sister and the other two boys came over to where you were, you and Michael were, is that right?

"A. Yeah.

"Q. What did they say to you, if you remember?

"A. My sister didn't say anything. She said, 'Come on, Sharon, let's go home.'

"Q. She asked you to go home with her?

"A. (Affirmative nod.)

"Q. Did you go home with her?

"A. No.

"Q. You wanted to stay with Mr. *M.*?

"A. I don't know.

"Q. Was this before or after he hit you?

"A. Before. . . .

"Q. What happened in the five minutes that Bruce stayed there with you and Michael?

"A. I don't remember.

"Q. You don't remember at all?

"A. (Negative head shake.)

"Q. Did you have occasion at that time to kiss Bruce?

"A. Yeah.

"Q. You did? You were kissing Bruce at that time?

"A. (Affirmative nod.)

"Q. Was Bruce kissing you?

"A. Yes.

"Q. And were you standing up at this time?

"A. No, we were sitting down. . . .

"Q. Okay. So at this point in time you had left Mr. *M.* and you were hugging and kissing with Bruce, is that right?

"A. Yeah.

"Q. And you were sitting up.

"A. Yes.

"Q. Was your sister still there then?

"A. No. Yeah, she was at first.

"Q. What was she doing?

"A. She was standing up with Michael and David.

"Q. Yes. Was she doing anything with Michael and David?

"A. No, I don't think so.

"Q. Whose idea was it for you and Bruce to kiss? Did you initiate that?

"A. Yes.

"Q. What happened after Bruce left?

"A. Michael asked me if I wanted to go walk to the park.

"Q. And what did you say?

"A. I said, 'Yes.'

"Q. And then what happened?

"A. We walked to the park. . . ."

chastity was considered particularly precious, those young women were felt to be uniquely in need of the State's protection. In contrast, young men were assumed to be capable of making such decisions for themselves; the law therefore did not offer them any special protection.

It is perhaps because the gender classification in California's statutory rape law was initially designed to further these outmoded sexual stereotypes, rather than to reduce the incidence of teenage pregnancies, that the State has been unable to demonstrate a substantial relationship between the classification and its newly asserted goal. But whatever the reason, the State has not shown that Cal.Penal Code § 261.5 is any more effective than a gender-neutral law would be in deterring minor females from engaging in sexual intercourse. It has therefore not met its burden of proving that the statutory classification is substantially related to the achievement of its asserted goal. . . .

JUSTICE JOHN PAUL STEVENS, dissenting. . . .

In my opinion, the only acceptable justification for a general rule requiring disparate treatment of the two participants in a joint act must be a legislative judgment that one is more guilty than the other. The risk-creating conduct that this statute is designed to prevent requires the participation of two persons—one male and one female. In many situations it is probably true that one is the aggressor and the other is either an unwilling, or at least a less willing, participant in the joint act. If a statute authorized punishment of only one participant and required the prosecutor to prove that that participant had been the aggressor, I assume that the discrimination would be valid. Although the question is less clear, I also assume, for the purpose of deciding this case, that it would be permissible to punish only the male participant, if one element of the offense were proof that he had been the aggressor, or at least in some respects the more responsible participant in the joint act. The statute at issue in this case, however, requires no such proof. The question raised by this statute is whether the State, consistently with the Federal Constitution, may always punish the male and never the female when they are equally responsible or when the female is the more responsible of the two.

It would seem to me that an impartial lawmaker could give only one answer to that question. The fact that the California Legislature has decided to apply its prohibition only to the male may reflect a legislative judgment that in the typical case the male is actually the more guilty party. Any such judgment must, in turn, assume that the decision to engage in the risk-creating conduct is always—or at least typically—a male decision. If that assumption is valid, the statutory classification should also be valid. But what is the support for the assumption? It is not contained in the record of this case or in any legislative history or scholarly study that has been called to our attention. I think it is supported to some extent by traditional attitudes toward male-female relationships. But the possibility that such a habitual attitude may reflect nothing more than an irrational prejudice makes it an insufficient justification for discriminatory treatment that is otherwise blatantly unfair. For, as I read this statute, it requires that one, and only one, of two equally guilty wrongdoers be stigmatized by a criminal conviction.

I cannot accept the State's argument that the constitutionality of the discriminatory rule can be saved by an assumption that prosecutors will commonly invoke this statute only in cases that actually involve a forcible rape, but one that cannot be established by proof beyond a reasonable doubt. . . .

Finally, even if my logic is faulty and there actually is some speculative basis for treating equally guilty males and females differently, I still believe that any such speculative justification would be outweighed by the paramount interest in evenhanded enforcement of the law. A rule that authorizes punishment of only one of two equally guilty wrongdoers violates the essence of the constitutional requirement that the sovereign must govern impartially. . . .

Frances Olsen, Statutory Rape: A Feminist Critique of Rights Analysis

63 Texas L. Rev. 387 (1984).

A man accused of raping his wife may feel that his privacy rights are being violated; a woman may feel that she is sexually exploited by pornography even if it is viewed privately. The right to privacy and the right to protection exist in fundamental conflict—a conflict that illustrates the contradiction between freedom of action and security that recurs throughout our legal system. Privacy assures the freedom to pursue one's own interests; protection assures that others will not harm us. We want both security and freedom, but seem to have to choose between them. Our historical experience with censorship warns us to be wary of state protection; our experience with domestic violence warns us to be wary of privacy. An individual may be just as oppressed by the state's failure to protect him as by the state's restraint of his freedom for the sake of protecting another. Every difficult legal or political decision can be justified as either protecting freedom or protecting security and attacked as either undermining security or undermining freedom.

This conflict between freedom and security implicates two important and related controversies—the debate between liberals and critical legal scholars over rights analysis and the debate among feminists over sexuality. The central problem of the rights debate is that many social reforms appear to be based on rights, yet every theory of rights that has been proposed can be shown to be internally inconsistent or incoherent. The central problem of the sexuality debate is that women are oppressed by moralistic controls society places on women's sexual expression, yet women are also oppressed by violence and sexual aggression that society allows in the name of sexual freedom.

Rights theory does not indicate which of the two values—freedom or security—the decisionmaker should choose in a given case. Because it cannot transcend this fundamental conflict of values, rights theory does not offer an adequate basis for legal decisions.

Moreover, thinking in terms of rights encourages a partial and inadequate analysis of sexuality. Just as rights theory conceptualizes a society composed of self-interested individuals whose conflicting interests are mediated by the state, it conceptualizes the problem of sexuality as a question of where social controls should end and sexual freedom should begin. Libertines and moralists alike tend to think of sexuality as a natural, presocial drive that is permitted or repressed by society; they disagree only over where to draw the line between freedom and social control. At one extreme, social control is limited to requiring consent of the participants; the realm of sexual freedom should extend to all consensual sexual activity. At the other extreme, freedom is limited to procreational sex within marriage; social control should restrict sexuality outside this realm.

The important issue, however, is not where to draw such a line, but the substance and meaning that we give to sexuality. Unfortunately, feminists who set out to discuss sexuality find their arguments trivialized into a line-drawing debate. Some feminists focus on the sexist nature of social control and assert that in practice it means social control of women. Other feminists focus on the sexist nature of sexual freedom and point out that freedom means freedom for men to exploit women. But the fundamental issue addressed by both sides—the nature of sexuality and our ability to reconstruct it—is ultimately redefined through rights analysis as a question about the location of the boundary between sexual freedom and social control. In this way, feminists who are or should be engaged in a joint or parallel project of challenging the dominant definition of sexuality come to perceive themselves as opposing one another. Feminists on one side of the debate accuse those on the other side of being anti-sex, and the other side accuses those on the first of contributing to their own oppression through "false consciousness." Another set of polemical charges is that the feminists on one side are overly preoccupied with violence and sexual domination and those on the other are defending male supremacy at the expense of women. . . .

California's law against "unlawful sexual intercourse" is typical of the gender-based statutory rape laws that remain on the books in a minority of states. . . .Feminists charge that statutes such as this one are harmful to women on both a practical and an ideological level. First, as an effort to control the sexual activities of young women, statutory rape laws are an unwarranted governmental intrusion into their lives and an oppressive restriction upon their freedom of action. An unmarried woman under eighteen cannot legally have intercourse in California. Whether the prohibition is enforced by prosecuting her partner or by prosecuting her as an aider and abettor, the statute interferes with the sexual freedom of the underage female. In the language of rights analysis, statutory rape laws violate the female's right to privacy and her right to be as free sexually as her male counterpart.

Feminists' second common objection to statutory rape laws is ideological. Gender-based statutory rape laws reinforce the sexual stereotype of men as aggressors and women as passive victims. The laws perpetuate the double standard of sexual morality. For males, sex is an accomplishment; they gain something through intercourse. For women, sex entails giving something up. Further, for the myth of male sexual accomplishment to exist, some females must give in. The double standard divides females into two classes—virgins and whores, "good girls" whose chastity should be protected and "bad girls" who may be exploited with impunity. Even if young women need more protection from sexual coercion and exploitation than the laws against forcible rape and incest provide, many feminists nevertheless oppose gender-based laws. They argue that males and females should be protected equally and that gender-based laws stigmatize women as weaker than men. In terms of rights theory, gender-based statutory rape laws violate the right of all women to be treated equally to men.

Although these two objections to statutory rape laws are analytically distinct, they nonetheless are related. Ideology affects people's lives, and daily life can limit and reshape ideology. The restrictive aspects of statutory rape laws are particularly objectionable because they exalt female chastity and treat women as lacking in sexual autonomy. This view of women both provides a reason (although a false and pernicious one) for state restrictions upon young women's sexual freedom and reinforces damaging stereotypes. At the same time, the laws imply that young men do not need the protection that they afford. This implication reinforces the ideology that sex is okay for young men; it also means that some women will have to be available to have sex with them.

The state restricts the young woman's sexual behavior for reasons related to sexist notions of what makes females valuable. The state does not merely restrict the young woman's freedom; it also treats her sexuality as a thing that has a value of its own and must be guarded. By refusing to grant women autonomy and by protecting them in ways that men are not protected, the state treats women's bodies—and therefore women themselves—as objects. Men are treated differently. Their bodies are regarded as a part of them, subject to their free control. . . .

There are several ways statutory rape laws could be altered to overcome these grounds for objection. There are at least two ways the laws could be altered to free young women from state-enforced sexual constraint and four ways the laws could be changed to help overcome debilitating stereotypes. . . .

The simplest way to prevent statutory rape laws from restricting women's sexual freedom and treating women as objects would be to repeal the laws or declare them unconstitutional. This approach would support the rights of young women by freeing them from one form of state domination and giving them the same status as adult women.

Unfortunately, invalidating statutory rape laws altogether and putting young women in the same position as adult women might undermine the right of young women to be free of unwanted sexual contact. Adult women occupy a position of pervasive economic and social subordination to men. Adult women are seduced, pressured, coerced, and even forced into unwanted sexual relations, for which they have no legal recourse. Underage females might discover that although the abolition of statutory rape laws would protect their rights against the state, it would remove some of their already-minimal protection against individual men. Young women and their sexuality would still be treated as objects, but instead of being controlled by state legislation, sex would be "taken" from them by individual men, one at a time. Nice as it is to be freed from state oppression, domination by private individuals can be equally oppressive. Despite their negative aspects, statutory rape laws may provide some protection for females. Recognizing this, even opponents of such laws support some form of age-of-consent statute—at least to protect six-year-olds, if not twelve-year-olds.

Statutory rape laws can also protect females against forms of oppression that other laws do not reach. For example, statutory rape laws may prohibit certain instances of sexual assault that should be considered illegal, but cannot be prosecuted as forcible rape. Similarly, abuses of authority that do not fit the statutory definition of incest may be punishable under statutory rape laws. . . .

Instead of restricting women's freedom, it might be possible to protect women by empowering them against male coercion. This alternative would free women from state domination without removing all protection against private domination. For example, statutory rape laws could be amended or interpreted to give the underage woman control over the prosecution decision. Such a law could either permit charges to be brought only upon the woman's complaint or require that they be dropped upon her request. Either version would increase the protective aspects of statutory rape laws and reduce the negative, repressive aspects. A young woman would be free to engage in sex or accept the protection of statutory rape laws. Her characterization of a sexual encounter as voluntary intercourse or as rape would be determinative. Although giving the woman control over prosecution would not guarantee that her decision would be her choice and not coerced, it might at least enable her to play the various pressures against one another.

Despite its merits, many feminists would oppose this revision of statutory rape laws because it would treat women differently from men and therefore could stigmatize all women by implying that underage women are vulnerable and in need of protection. But the ideological significance attached to the label "vulnerable" depends in good measure upon the concrete context in which the label is attached and the practical effect of the labeling. Women rightly object when their alleged vulnerability is used as an excuse to deny them certain opportunities or to foreclose choices that should be available to them. Statutory rape laws that gave a young woman power over the prosecution decision, however, would treat her vulnerability as a reason to empower her against coercion rather than to take power away from her.

Nevertheless, it is certainly possible that women would be stigmatized as well as empowered. Indeed, it may be impossible to predict whether the ideological damage to women from being treated as vulnerable would in the long run outweigh the practical and ideological advantages of empowerment. . . .

The second feminist objection to statutory rape laws is that they stigmatize women and reinforce sexist stereotypes. There are at least four possible solutions to this problem. . . .

One could meet the objection that statutory rape laws perpetuate debilitating sexual stereotypes by abolishing the laws. Although this approach might increase the practical basis for the woman-as-powerless-victim stereotype by allowing more young women to be victimized by male aggression, it would at least avoid ideological reinforcement of the stereotype. . . .

If it were possible to enforce or revise statutory rape laws so that they actually prevented men from victimizing women, the stereotypes might become so false that they would lose their power. This approach imposes significant risks, however. Legal reform may be insufficient to prevent victimization; laws alone seldom change behavior. Moreover, in our present society, it may be impossible to empower women without stigmatizing them.

In a sense, this second approach is the converse of the first. The first proposal would undermine the stereotype of men as aggressors and women as victims but allow the reality; the second would support the stereotype but undermine the reality. . . .

A third approach—criminalizing sexual intercourse when either party is underage—would seem neither to stigmatize women nor to reinforce sexist stereotypes. This approach benefits underage males by protecting them from being pressured into premature sex and harms them by curtailing their freedom.

Although this change seems to address the issue of stereotyping, it obscures the issue of social power. Extending the age-of-consent laws to males may effect merely a cosmetic change, without altering images or practices under the law. Moreover, it leaves untouched the repressive aspects of statutory rape laws. In our present society, these repressive aspects hurt females more than males. Extension of the legal rule to males might not bring extension of these repressive aspects. This solution therefore is actually less neutral than it initially appears. . . .

As a variation of the third approach, one could decriminalize most sex between teenagers but extend protection to minors of both sexes against exploitation by an older person. For example, statutory rape laws might provide criminal penalties for anyone who engaged in sexual intercourse with a minor four or more years younger than the person charged. Such a law would restrict freedom less than the previous proposal because it would allow teenagers to engage in sexual intercourse with partners near their own age. In addition, the law would provide for criminal prosecution in many of the worst kinds of exploitative situations, but would avoid overt sexual stereotyping. Unfortunately, such a law would not address the problem of male sexual aggression that characterizes society at large. Underage males are likely to relate to underage females in illegitimate ways, just as their older counterparts relate to adult women in illegitimate ways. . . .

A commitment to establish and protect rights for women provides us with little guidance in deciding whether to support any particular statutory rape law or to oppose all statutory rape laws. Even if we artificially simplify our task by focusing only upon the rights of women, we cannot determine how to protect these rights. Rights analysis does not help us as an analytic tool because it is indeterminate. Every effort to protect young women against private oppression by individual men risks subjecting women to state oppression, and every effort to protect them against state oppression undermines their power to resist individual oppression. . . . Despite the circularity of arguments about rights and equality, however, effective reforms do take place and do change people's lives. Some of the proposed changes in statutory rape laws are better than others. It is even possible that most feminists would agree on the best change. But this agreement would not be reached by discovering the "real" meaning of women's rights or by logically deducing the "true implications" of gender equality. Rather, it would rest upon sociological calculations and political and moral commitments. An abstract commitment to women's rights does not help us decide concrete cases. . . .

I believe that the most useful question to be asked in evaluating *Michael M.* is whether the case—including the plurality, concurring, and dissenting opinions—tends to mask and legitimate conditions of social existence that are hurtful and damaging to women. I conclude that it does, and thus I condemn it.

The opinions imply that there are two sharply distinct categories of sexual relations that together comprise all of sexuality. There is equal, consensual sexual intercourse on one hand, and bad, coercive sex imposed upon a female by a male aggressor on the other hand. But these two categories constitute a continuum of sexual relations; there is no bright line between them. Although most women do seek sexual contact with men, heterosexual behavior in our society is seldom fully voluntary; sex is usually to some extent imposed on females by males. Perhaps sixteen-year-old girls are not especially helpless, but they—and women as a group—are systematically dominated by men as a group. This inequality is deeply implicated in popular notions of eroticism and sexiness.

The *Michael M.* opinions mystify the power relations involved in sexual intercourse by assuming that it is an equal activity. . . . The decision in *Michael M.* did not have to mystify sexual intercourse or legitimate the status quo. The case could have been an occasion to examine conditions of sexuality in a society of gender hierarchy. Male sexual aggression could have been exposed as oppressive and illegitimate. Michael's coercive male initiative could have been generalized and delegitimated. Justice Blackmun was correct in noting that Michael was not engaged in especially deviant behavior—behavior that is properly criminalized because it is so different from everyday sexual interaction. But this should be a condemnation of everyday behavior, rather than a reason to find Michael blameless. Distinguishing Michael's behavior from acceptable male initiative may serve to legitimate everyday coercive sex. But using it as an example of the destructive and coercive elements in sexual relations might delegitimate present sexual arrangements and encourage change.

. . . [W]e should stop trying to fit our goals into abstract rights arguments and instead call for what we really want. Similarly, regarding sexuality we should recognize the problems with both social control and sexual freedom and call for a reconstruction of sexuality altogether. . . . It is not enough to empower women to resist male coercion in all its forms; we must also create new choices for women.

We cannot start from scratch or write on a clean slate, but we can start with the best of what we have and go on from there. I believe that the best of what we have is sex as an expression of an equal, sharing relationship. There are things we can do to support and further eroticize this conception of sexuality. Ending the subordination of women is one important step in the right direction. Although violence and domination have been eroticized in our society, sex is more complicated. It is defined, or created, in a male-dominated culture, but there are nooks and crannies in which the beginnings of a new sexuality can be discovered.

NOTES AND QUESTIONS

1. **The Rationale for Statutory Rape Laws.** Does the rationale for statutory rape laws considered by the Supreme Court—prevention of teenage pregnancy—survive contemporary attitudes about teenage sexuality and concerns about gender equality? Even if we reject the Supreme Court's rationale, there may nevertheless be reason to shield adolescent and teenage girls from sexual intercourse with men. Michelle Oberman criticizes the decriminalization of statutory rape in light of current evidence that adolescent girls are especially vulnerable to male sexual aggression. *See* Michelle Oberman, *Turning Girls Into Women: Re–Evaluating Modern Statutory Rape Law Reform*, 85 J. Crim. L. & Criminology 15 (1994). Oberman demonstrates that laws regarding minors generally depend on normative decisions about minors' access to adult activities, not on an assessment of minors' ability to make their own decisions. Rather than respecting girls' sexual decisions and desires, she argues, the decriminalization of statutory rape similarly reflects the expectation that girls sometimes should be sexually accessible to males. Do you agree that girls are still conditioned to submit to unwanted sexual contact in order to please men? (Take Sharon's explanation of why she had sex with Michael M, for example.) Is statutory rape an important way of addressing this problem? But is it fair (to both teenage girls and their male partners) to criminalize all sexual activity by teenage girls?

2. **Willing Participants?** To what extent does the need for statutory rape result from the faulty interpretation of forcible rape? Many statutory rape cases involve so much violence that prosecutors should not need to resort to a statutory rape charge, which is typically punished less severely. In *Michael M,* for example, the victim permitted the defendant to "do what he wanted" only after he "slugged" her in the face several times. After reading the excerpted trial transcript, do you agree with Justice Blackmun that Sharon was a "willing participant?" What does his observation tell you about judges' attitudes about coerced sex?

3. **Reforming Statutory Rape Law.** Which of the possible reforms set out by Fran Olsen would benefit girls most—abolishing statutory rape laws, making them gender neutral, or adding an age differential? Or would the best approach be to leave the law as is, focused on protecting all underage females against any male sexual aggression? If, as Olsen demonstrates, all of these measures risk subjecting women to either state or private oppression, how can we nevertheless use the law to help to create a new sexuality?

C.   WOMEN AND THEIR BODIES: FEMINIST LEGAL THEORY III

INTRODUCTION

For both men and women our bodies seem to be the foundation of our personhood: they constitute an important source of our self-knowledge and how we are known; they also signal an important boundary between ourselves and others. For these reasons, the physical insecurities that women experience on account of sex make our bodies particularly crucial points on which to center efforts to reform the legal and social structures that subordinate women. This project also requires examining the interplay of women's sexuality and reproductive capacity with other aspects of women's identities—their race, ethnicity, and class, for example.

Cultural, radical, and postmodern feminists agree with the claim that is implicated in most of the legal reform efforts considered in the other sections of this chapter, the claim that women should have more control of their own bodies. These theorists, however, have different views regarding such issues as the definition of a woman's body and the relationship between biological and gendered identity. These differences, which the readings in this section are meant to elaborate, have significant implications for legal projects affecting women and their bodies.

The readings begin with an article by Robin West that situates attitudes regarding the female body in several strands of current feminist scholarship. Her article is of particular interest because of her extended argument that women have unique bodily responses. West distinguishes her approach, which directs attention "inward," from both liberal feminists' focus on choice and radical feminists' quest for power.

As in her article in the last section defending an anti-pornography ordinance, Andrea Dworkin argues in the piece included here that the subordination of women is caused by pornography, through the processes of sexual objectification and the eroticization of domination. This essay focuses on the claim that male misogyny works through pornography to construct women as whores. Somewhat differently from West, Dworkin appeals to, rather than describes, a hidden, true version of femininity. Like West, however, the picture she draws of women and men is uni-dimensional. The notes include a portion of Angela Harris's article, *Race and Essentialism in Feminist Legal Theory*, excerpted more fully in Chapter One, that critiques West's deliberate essentialism from a Black feminist perspective, as well as Judith Butler's refutation of the claim that sexual difference is more fundamental than other kinds of difference and Berta Hernandez–Truyol's description of Latinas' multidimensional identities.

The excerpt from Mary Joe Frug's book suggests another way the claims that West and Dworkin make regarding the relationship between women and their bodies might be challenged. Frug illuminates how social organization and legal regulation affect a woman's bodily experiences, and suggests, therefore, how social organization and the law might be manipulated to transform those experiences. The following excerpt from a book by bell hooks combines what may seem like contradictory attitudes toward female sexuality. Hooks is explicitly conscious of the dangers of domination which heterosexuality poses for Black and white women, but she also defends heterosexual practice. Yet unlike other authors included in this section, hooks criticizes the identification of sexuality as the singular focus of women's identities and political struggle. Frug associated the historically contextualized, contradictory, and racially-specific depiction of woman which hooks presents with her own postmodern, materialist feminism. In their most radical formulations, postmodern feminists embrace contradictory descriptions about women, asserting, for example, that women constitute a class of identifiable individuals and that they do not.

The final two essays explore the possibilities for re-conceptualizing women's identities. The excerpt from the article by Elizabeth Iglesias challenges both the dominant images of motherhood and of female sexuality. Iglesias examines the matrifocal family of Black and Latino culture to contest negative stereotypes about white mothers, as well as women of color. She then offers the symbolic sacred prostitute as an alternative to the virgin/whore dichotomy and the romantic love ideology that have helped to perpetuate a submissive female sexuality. The essay by Sue–Ellen Case uses the butch-femme role playing of a lesbian theater act to illustrate how the contradictions associated with postmodern feminist theory are internally experienced. The appeal to dramatic roles may be useful as a way for postmodern feminists to convey how a non-essentialist description of femininity might feel.

Robin West, the Difference in Women's Hedonic Lives: A Phenomenological Critique of Feminist Legal Theory

3 Wis. Women's L. J. 81(1987).

Women's subjective, hedonic lives are different from men's. The quality of our suffering is different from that of men's, as is the nature of our joy. Furthermore, and of more direct concern to feminist lawyers, the quantity of pain and pleasure enjoyed or suffered by the two genders is different: women suffer more than men. The two points are related. One reason that women suffer more than men is that women often find painful the same objective event or condition that men find pleasurable. The introduction of oxymorons in our vocabulary, wrought by feminist victories, evidences this difference in women's and men's hedonic lives. The phrases "date-rape," for example and "sexual harassment," capture these different subjective experiences of shared social realities: For the man, the office pass was sex (and pleasurable), for the woman, it was harassment (and painful); for the man the evening was a date—perhaps not pleasant, but certainly not frightening—for the woman, it was a rape and very scary indeed. . . .Women's distinctive, gender-specific injuries are now or have in the recent past been variously dismissed as trivial (sexual harassment on the street); consensual (sexual harassment on the job); humorous (non-violent marital rape); participatory, subconsciously wanted, or self-induced (father/daughter incest); natural or biological, and therefore inevitable (childbirth); sporadic, and conceptually continuous with gender-neutral pain (rape, viewed as a crime of violence); deserved or private (domestic violence); non-existent (pornography); incomprehensible (unpleasant and unwanted consensual sex) or legally predetermined (marital rape, in states with the marital exemption).

It is not so clear, though, *why* women's suffering is so pervasively dismissed or trivialized by legal culture, or more importantly what to do about it. As I will argue in a moment, feminist legal theorists do not typically frame the problem in the way I have just posed it. Nevertheless, it is not hard to construct two characteristic feminist explanations of the phenomenon, and the strategies they entail. The "liberal-legal feminist" would characterize the legal culture's discriminatory treatment of women's suffering as the reflection of a "perceptual error" committed by that culture. Women are in fact *the same as*—and therefore *equal to*—men, in the only sense which should matter to liberal legal theory. Women, like men, are autonomous individuals who, if free to do so, will choose among proffered alternatives so as to fashion their own "good life," and thereby create social value. However, the legal culture fails to see or acknowledge this central sameness—and hence equality—of women and men. Because we are not *perceived* as identical to men in this way, we are not treated as such. Our choices are differentially restricted, and as a result we disproportionately suffer. The liberal feminist's strategy is directly implied by her diagnosis: what we must do is prove that we are what we are—individualists and egoists, as are men—and then fight for the equal rights and respect that sameness demands. Equal respect will in turn ensure, through the logic of formal justice and the Equal Protection Clause of the Fourteenth Amendment, that our suffering will be alleviated by law—just as is men's suffering—through a liberating expansion of our opportunities for choice.

The radical legal feminist's explanation of this phenomenon is also not hard to construct. The blanket dismissal of women's suffering by the male legal culture is not a reflection of a misperception. Indeed the larger culture's perception is accurate: women are *not* as autonomous or individualistic as men. The liberal is wrong to insist that women and men are equal in this way. The reason the legal culture tends to dismiss women's gender-specific sufferings is that women don't matter. Those in power ignore women's suffering because they don't care about the suffering of the disempowered. Hierarchical power imbalances do that to people—they make the disempowered less than human, and they make the empowered ruthless. The radical feminist's strategy follows directly from her diagnosis: what we must do is dismantle the hierarchy. The Equal Protection Clause—at least if we can interpret it (and use it) as an "Equality Promotion Clause"—might help.

The recent explosion of feminist writings on the multitude of problems generated by women's "difference" prompts me to suggest a third explanation of this blanket dismissal by the legal culture of women's pain, and thus a third strategy. . . . If the pain women feel is in fact discontinuous from—different than—what is experienced by men, then it is not really surprising that the injuries we sustain are trivialized or dismissed by the larger male culture. It is hard to empathize with the pain of another, when the nature of that pain is not understood. . . . The strategic inference I draw is this: if we want to enlist the aid of the larger legal culture, the feel of our gender-specific pain must be described before we can ever hope to communicate its magnitude.

Focus on the "difference" of our hedonic lives also suggests a different way to address the related problem of "false consciousness." As feminists know all too well, it is not just the legal culture which trivializes women's suffering, women do so also. Again, if we focus on the distinctiveness of our pain, this becomes less surprising. An injury uniquely sustained by a disempowered group will lack a name, a history, and in general a linguistic reality. Consequently, the victim as well as the perpetrator will transform the pain into *something else,* such as, for example, punishment, or flattery, or transcendence, or unconscious pleasure. A victim's response to an injury which is perceived by the victim as deservedly punitive, consensual, natural, subconsciously desired, legally inevitable, or trivial will be very different from a response to an injury which is perceived as simply *painful.* We change our behavior in response to the threat of what we perceive as punishment; we diminish ourselves in response to injuries we perceive as trivial; we reconstruct our pasts in response to injuries we perceive as subconsciously desired; we negate our inner selves in response to injuries we perceive as consensual and we constrain our potentiality in response to injuries we perceive as inevitable. We respond to pain, on the other hand, by resisting the source of the pain. The strategic inference should be clear: we must give voice to the hurting self, even when that hurting self sounds like a child rather than an adult; even when that hurting self voices "trivial" complaints; even when the hurting self is ambivalent toward the harm and even when (especially when) the hurting self is talking a language not heard in public discourse. Only by so doing will we *ourselves* become aware of the meaning of the suffering in our lives, and its contingency in our history. Only when we understand the contingency of that pain, will we be free to address it and change the conditions which cause it through legal tools.

If my argument is correct, then it would seem that feminist legal theorists should be hard at work providing rich descriptions of women's subjective, hedonic lives, particularly the pain in those lives, and more particularly the pain in our lives which is different. And yet *we aren't,* by which I mean, feminist *legal theorists* aren't. . . . [A]t least one reason—and perhaps the main reason—that feminist legal theorists have neglected the hedonic dimension of our difference—and the subject of this article—is . . . the emerging logic of feminist legal theory itself. . . . [F]eminist legal theorists have adopted *non-feminist* normative models of legal criticism, and then applied those models to women's problems. I have no objection to this strategy: there is no reason that feminist legal theorists should aim for relentless originality. I do object, though, to the *particular* models feminist legal theorists have adopted. The two major normative models of legal criticism which feminist legal theorists have thus far embraced—liberal legalism and radical legalism—*themselves* deny the normative significance of the subjective pleasure and suffering of our lives. Because of the normative models employed by modern legal feminists, the internal, pheno-menological reality of women's hedonic lives—and its difference from men's—has become virtually irrelevant to feminist legal theory.

Thus, I will argue that *liberal-legal* feminist theorists—true to their liberalism—want women to have more choices, and that *radical-legal* feminist theorists—true to their radicalism—want women to have more power. Both models direct our critical attention *outward*—liberalism to the number of choices we have, radicalism to the amount of power. Neither model of legal criticism, and therefore, derivatively, of feminist legal criticism, posits subjective happiness as the direct goal of legal reform, or subjective suffering as the direct evil to be eradicated. Neither model directs our critical attention *inward*. Consequently, and unsurprisingly, neither liberal nor radical feminist legal critics have committed themselves to the task of determining the measure of women's happiness or suffering. . . .

Liberal Feminism: Consent, Autonomy and the Giving Self

Perhaps the most widely held normative commitment of mainstream liberal legal theorists is that individuals should be free to choose their own style of life, and to exercise that freedom of choice in as many spheres as possible—economic, political and personal. The conception of the human and the relation between the individual and the state which implicitly motivates this commitment is relatively straightforward. According to the liberal vision, value is produced in our social world through satiation of the subjective desires and preferences of the individual. That satiation is in turn manifested and facilitated through the individual's voluntary choices. The individual's choice will reflect that individual's judgment of what will best satisfy that individual's own desires. It follows that whatever is freely consented to by an individual is what is good for that individual, and, if free of adverse effects on others, is good for society. The way to maximize value in the social world is therefore to maximize the opportunities for the exercise of choice through voluntary transactions between individuals. A law which either facilitates or mimics consensual transactions between freely choosing individuals is a good law on this model, while a law which frustrates such transactions is a bad law. Individual freedom is the ideal toward which law and legal reform ought press, and coercion or restraint on freedom is the evil.

The contribution of feminist liberal legalism has been to extend the umbrella of this normative vision to women as well as men. The liberal legal feminist insists that the depiction of the human embraced by liberal legalism—which I will sometimes refer to as the "liberal self"—is also true of women, and that therefore the relationship of the state to the individual must be the same for both women and men. What it means for women to be equal to men in the liberal feminist vision is basically that women and men are the same in the only sense that matters to the liberal legalist: women as well as men create value by satiating their subjective desires through consensual choices. Because women and men are equal in this way—because they share the same definitive human attribute—women should be equally free to choose their own life plans, and women should be equally entitled to the respect from the state that that freedom requires.

The liberal feminist legal strategy for dealing with women's suffering is directly entailed by her liberalism. Women, like men, consent to that which will minimize their own suffering and maximize their own felt happiness. Therefore, the way to deal with women's suffering is to increase women's sphere of consensual freedom. What we should do with law, then, is insure that women's sphere of consensual freedom is as large as possible, or at least as large as men's. Thus, the liberal feminist's central jurisprudential commitment tracks the liberal's: a law is a good law if it increases the freedom of women to enter into consensual transactions or if it equalizes that freedom with that enjoyed by men. A law is a bad law if it decreases that freedom.

Liberal feminist legal theory carries with it the same problems which now plague liberal legalism, but multiplied. Modern liberal legal feminists, like modern liberals generally, have failed to examine the essentially descriptive claims about the human being that underlie their normative model. The liberal claim that human beings consent to transactions in order to maximize their welfare may be false. If it is, then the liberal claim that social value is created through facilitating choice will be false as well. But furthermore, *women* may be "different" in precisely the way which would render the empirical assumptions regarding human motivation which underlie the liberal's commitment to the ethics of consent *more false for women than for men*. Thus, it may be that women generally *don't* consent to changes *so as to* increase our own pleasure or satisfy our own desires. It may be that women consent to changes so as to increase the pleasure or satisfy the desires of *others*. The descriptive account of the phenomenology of choice that underlies the liberal's conceptual defense of the moral primacy of consent may be wildly at odds with the way women phenomenologically experience the act of consent. If it is—if women "consent" to transactions not to increase our own welfare, but to increase the welfare of others—if women are "different" in this psychological way—then the liberal's ethic of consent, with its presumption of an essentially selfish human (male) actor and an essentially selfish consensual act, when even-handedly applied to both genders, will have disastrous implications for women. For if women consent to changes so as to increase the happiness of others rather than to increase our own happiness, then the ethic of consent, applied even-handedly, may indeed increase the amount of happiness in the world, but women will not be the beneficiaries.

And indeed, the liberal ethic of consent does, oftentimes, have less than happy consequences for women. . . . That is, much of women's suffering is a product of a state of being which was *itself* brought into being through a transaction to which women unquestionably tendered consent. A woman's experience of marital sexuality, for example, may range from boring to irritating to invasive to intensely painful. Similarly, a female employee may experience the sexual advances of an employer as degrading. But the fact is that neither the wife nor the employee was brought to the altar in shackles or place of employment in chains. Put affirmatively, the conditions which create our misery—unwanted pregnancies, violent and abusive marriages, sexual harassment on the job—are often traceable to acts of consent. Women—somewhat uniquely—consent to their misery. . . .

I . . . suggest . . . that many women, much of the time, consent to transactions, changes, or situations in the world so as to satisfy not their own desires or to maximize their own pleasure, as liberal legalism and liberal legal feminism both presume, but to maximize the pleasure and satiate the desires of others, and that they do so by virtue of conditions which only women experience. I will sometimes call the cluster of "other-regarding," other-pleasing motivations that rule these women's actions the "giving self," so as to distinguish it from the "liberal self": the cluster of self-regarding "rational" motivations presumed by liberal legalism. Thus my descriptive claim is that many women much of the time are giving selves rather than liberal selves. . . .

I believe that women become giving rather than liberal selves for a range of reasons . . . I will focus on only one causal hypothesis. . . . [W]omen's lives are dangerous, and it is the acquisitive and potentially violent nature of male sexuality which is the cause of the danger. A fully justified fear of acquisitive and violent male sexuality consequently permeates many women's—perhaps all women's—sexual and emotional self-definition. Women respond to this fear by *re-constituting* themselves in a way that controls the danger and suppresses the fear. Thus: women define themselves as "giving selves" so as to obviate the threat, the danger, the pain, and the fear of being self-regarding selves from whom their sexuality is taken. . . . Most simply, a woman will define herself as a "giving self" so that she will not be violated. She defines herself as a being who "gives" sex, so that she will not become a being *from whom sex is taken*. . . . [S]he becomes a person who gives her consent *so as to ensure the other's happiness* (not her own), so as to satiate the *other's* desires (not her own), so as to promote the *other's* well-being (not her own), and ultimately so as *to obey the other's commands*. In other words, she embraces a self-definition and a motive for acting which is the direct antithesis of the internal motivational life presupposed by liberalism. The motivation of her consensual acts is the satisfaction of another's desires. She consents to serve the needs and satiate the desires of others. . . .

How do women respond to the total fear that accompanies the daily violence that characterizes an abusive domestic relationship? What does such fear *teach* you? A woman cannot live in a state of terror *every day* and what a battered woman learns in an abusive marriage is how to define herself in such a way that she can on occasion suppress the fear. Thus, what a violent intimate relationship taught me was to live *for the other*. I was—as these things go—relatively lucky, by which I mean the abuse I sustained was not nearly so extreme as that suffered by the woman quoted above. But I did learn in this relatively lucky environment of fists, slaps, bruises, threats, glares and terror the lesson of daily fear. Daily fear taught me to define myself as an object, the purpose of which was to buffer—and silence—another's violence. My purpose—my *only* reason for acting and my *only* motivation—was to serve *that* need of another. Fear taught me to view as literally incongruous the mere suggestion that I should expect to reap pleasure for myself from anything at all; surely not from sex, but nor from more ordinary sources, such as food, flowers, music, friendship or scenery. The notion that I would act—or *consent*—so as to further my own welfare or to create pleasure for myself was both inconceivable and unconceived: until circumstances and self-preservatory desperation inspired my exit, it never crossed my mind. Pleasures were for others. Sensuality was for others. "Personal welfare" was for others. Subjectivity was for others. I did not have, much less act on, preferences. I learned to view this as both natural and as naturally *inarticulable,* meaning I learned not just to lie, but to be a lie, to embody lying, to have no entitlement to either truth or language. I learned to be *for another's violence* and to view it as my reason for being, and I learned not to think about it much. . . .

Almost all women, including those who have never experienced unwanted sex or battery, have experienced the fear of rape. . . .[A] working paper on rape . . . elaborates:

> The fear of rape is always with us. It affects our lives in countless ways—not only in that we are afraid to walk the streets late at night, but in all our dealings with men, however superficial these might be. . . .This makes us self-conscious about our bodies, the way we sit and stand and walk—when was the last time you saw a woman sit sprawled across a bus seat the way men do all the time? We keep our knees together, our legs crossed, our faces neutral. Somewhere in our minds we are always aware that any man—every man—can, if he wants to, use the weapon of rape against us.

And men know it too. The man who mutters obscenities at us in the street knows it, the local greengrocer who insists on calling us love ... knows it, the wolf-whistling building workers know it, the man reading page three on the tube and grinning at us knows it. *At one point on Reclaim the Night in Soho, we were confronted by a large group of men shouting "We're on the rapist's side—we're with the rapist." They didn't really need to tell us. We already knew.*

One way that (some) women respond to the pervasive, silent, unspoken and invisible fear of rape in their lives is by giving their (sexual) selves to a consensual, protective, and monogamous relationship. This is widely denied—but it may be widely denied because it is so widely presumed. It is, after all, precisely what we are supposed to do. One woman describes her embrace of this option thusly:

The brutality and coldness of (promiscuous heterosexual) experiences were largely instrumental in persuading me to have steady and secure relationships with men. I did not feel safe with lots of different ones. The threat of men's violence drove me into couple relationships. I feel ambivalent about these men. They were not unmitigated bastards and they did afford me protection. My mother would often mutter ominously about the world not being a safe place for women and my experiences could only confirm this. Being alone I felt, at times, besieged and up for grabs. Being with one man sheltered unwelcome attention from men in the streets, at parties, etc.

Women who give themselves to a monogamous relationship in order to avoid the danger of rape from others, often end up giving themselves *within* the monogamous relationship so as to avoid the danger of rape by their partner. . . .

Women, . . . and only women, live with . . . [this] danger: women and only women must somehow ward off the threat of acquisitive and violent male sexuality. It should not be so hard to understand (*why* is it so hard to understand?) that women develop protective strategies for coping with this . . . threat. The means with which we do so—primarily by learning to give ourselves to consensual, protective relationships, within which we then define ourselves as "giving"—are not the product of false consciousness or brain-washing. But nor are they value-creating voluntary and mutual relationships worthy of celebration. They are no less and no more than the product of our victimization: they are coherent, understandable responses to very real danger. Until we create a better world, they are also all we have. . . .

Radical Feminism and the Ethical Primacy of Power and Equality

Radical feminist legal theory begins with a description of women which is diametrically opposed to that embraced by liberal feminists. Liberal feminists assume a definitional *equality*—a "sameness"—between the female and male experience of consensual choice, and then argue that the legal system should respect that fundamental, empirical equality. In sharp contrast, radical feminists assume a definitional *in*equality of women—women are *definitionally* the disempowered group—and urge the legal system to eradicate that disempowerment and thereby make women what they presently are not, and that is equal. Radical feminism thus begins with a denial of the liberal feminist's starting assumption. Women and men are *not* equally autonomous individuals. Women, unlike men, live in a world with two sovereigns—the state, and men—and this is true not just some of the time but all of the time. Women, unlike men, are definitionally submissive twice over; once vis-a-vis the state, and once vis-a-vis the superior power of men. A legal regime which ignores this central reality will simply perpetuate the fundamental, underlying inequality.

The cause of women's disempowerment, as well as its effect, is the expropriation of our sexuality. Women are the group, in Catharine Mac-Kinnon's phrase, "from whom sexuality is expropriated." ... The threat of male violence and violent sexuality both defines the class *woman* and causes her disempowerment and the expropriation of her sexuality. ...

This much, radical feminist legal theory shares with radical feminism, and with this much I am in full agreement. Where radical feminist legal theory has departed from radical feminism, I believe, is in the normative argument it draws from the insight that women are, definitionally, the group from whom sexuality is expropriated. The argument, I believe, owes more to radical legalism than to radical feminism. ...[R]adical feminist legal theorists share with radical legalists a methodological insistence that the correlation between objective equality and subjective well-being is foundational and definitional; it is therefore *not* something that can be discredited by counter-example. Both groups of theorists accordingly refuse to credit the *phenomenological* evidence that the essentially descriptive claims that underlie the normative commitment to substantive equality may be false. Thus, to radical legalists generally, and to radical feminist legalists in particular, the extent to which the disempowered desire anything other than their own empowerment, and anything at odds with an equalitarian idea, is the extent to which the disempowered are victims of false consciousness. ...

Radical feminist legal theorists, true to their radicalism, refuse to consider whether or not the definitional implication it assumes between objective equality and subjective well-being resonates with women's desires and pleasures, and hence whether the conception of the human on which that implication is based is true of *women*. The radical feminist legal theorist—to the extent that she is a radical—will—must—deny that substantive equality in any sphere could ever be less than ideal or that empowerment of women could ever work to our disadvantage. Thus, to radical feminists, that women on occasion take pleasure in their own submissiveness, is simply a manifestation of their disempowered state, not a meaningful counter-example to the posited egalitarian ideal. ...

... The contours of the conflict between stated ideal and felt pleasure, and between method and theory with which radical feminism is now grappling, I believe, are starkly brought out in [Danish radical feminist Maria] Marcus's detailed, moving, and candid account of her own profoundly ambivalent reaction to *The Story of O. The Story of O* is, in Marcus's phrase, a "masochistic pipe-dream." Written pseudonymously in the mid-fifties, it is without question the unsurpassed, modern, masochistic text. It is a stunning piece of pornography. ...Marcus ... has an intensely empathic and sexual response to *The Story O*:

> When I first read *The Story O*, it filled me with a mixture of sexual excitement, horror, anxiety—and envy. I read it many times, each time with the same feelings. But gradually, as I had the good fortune to plunge to some extent into acting out an "Imitation of O," my envy, anyhow, lessened, because on one (sic) imitates O with overstepping a boundary into a state which is not particularly enviable.

> But I must still say that ... I understand O. I understand her pride in the weals from the whip ... He owns me. I'm worth owning. Look what he makes me put up with. Look how strong the man who loves me is. Look I'm valuable. I *exist*. I understand that O comes to feel an inner peace, strength, dignity, security and psychic energy in this particular way, an energy that is nothing like anything else I (O) know.

The Story of O, Marcus concludes, is *the* text with which radical feminists must concern themselves, and the magnitude of female readers' responsive, empathic and erotic response to the text is the issue with which radical feminism must come to grips.

Radical feminists have responded, I believe, to the conflict between pleasure and ideal posed by the undeniable female eroticization of sexual submission in three characteristic ways. First, some feminists claim that there is no conflict between stated ideal and felt pleasure because feminist consciousness-raising—properly understood—has revealed the falsity of these pleasures. Thus there is no contradiction between feminist methodology—consciousness raising—and feminist goal—sexual equality. What the methodology reveals is that the pleasure had in sexual submission is false.

. . .

The second response (which was, until very recently, the near-standard feminist response) is simply to abandon feminist methodology. One way of maintaining the ideals of freedom and equality is by abandoning whatever methodology brought you to the conclusion that you enjoy being a sexual slave. If that methodology is feminist consciousness-raising, then so much the worse for consciousness-raising. . . .

The third possible response to the conflict between the pleasure we take in erotic domination and our equalitarian ideals is to put our ideals in abeyance—maybe they are what is false—and hold true to consciousness-raising. This is the position for which I will argue. ...[O]nly by understanding our felt pleasures will we achieve any meaningful understanding of our stated ideals. We cannot possibly give content to the substantive equality we seek until we understand the erotic appeal of submission. If we can identify what human needs are met through eroticized submission, perhaps we can better understand, and identify, the human needs which will be met or frustrated through political, legal and economic equality. . . .

I believe that sexual submission has erotic *appeal* and *value* when it is an expression of *trust;* is damaging, injurious and painful when it is an expression of *fear;* and is *dangerous* because of its ambiguity: both others and we ourselves have difficulty in disentangling the two. Here, I want to emphasize—I hope not overemphasize—the value of sexual submission when it is an expression of trust, because that, I believe, is the source of the pleasure women find in voluntary and fantasized erotic submission, in all of its forms. Absolutely pliant obedience—the willingness to transform one's subjectivity into another's object—is sexually arousing (for some) when it enables the submissive subject to transcend her own selfhood, and thereby to abdicate her responsibility for her own action. That this total abdication of responsibility can be erotic, I think, reflects a genuine human truth and a deep human need. It can be pleasurable and exhilarating and sometimes so much so that it is sexually stimulating to forego authorship of one's actions. When we grant power to another to control—to author—our acts, that grant may, and I have argued often does, express a deep seated and forgotten (or not so forgotten) fear. But it might not. It *might* also express our total trust in that other. That "other" *might* be trustworthy. That placing trust in one who is stronger is felt by some to be intensely pleasurable, and that the fantasy of doing just that is felt by many more to be so, should teach us something. . . .

Are the desires to "know and be known," to trust another, to blend in identity, at least sometimes expressed in the eroticization of submission and dominance, of any value, and do they express anything of value? Or are they soiled by their extremity, by their expression in forms which implicate "sweat and semen," whips and whip lashes, marks of obedience, and of objectification? *It's a close question. When* (if ever) and *why* (if ever) are these desires and the pleasure felt in their satiation beautiful? When are they *not* "muck we could well do without"? If they cannot, as I have argued they cannot, be entirely dismissed as false, can they be in any sense affirmed as truth? Do they express a political truth? Minimally, . . . they remind us of the hedonistic limits—the limits of pleasure, pain and desire—upon the otherwise near-relentless quest by both feminists and non-feminists of the fruits of liberal individualism—of subjective autonomy, of severe differentiation, and . . . of "discontinuity and rationality." That so many women and more than a few men undeniably take pleasure in controlled objectification may be testimony to the limit of the desirability of the pure subjectivism endorsed by virtually all forms of liberalism, including feminist liberal legalism. In a parallel fashion, the fact that many women and more than a few men take pleasure from sexual submission can be read as a critique of the absolutist commitment to substantive equality endorsed by radical legalism of all forms, including feminist radical legalism. The trust expressed by the submissive party *in a controlled* and unequal sexual encounter is such a high pleasure that it is erotic. That *fact*—that the trust felt by the submissive party in controlled inequality *is* pleasurable—should serve to remind us that to the extent that absolute equality comes at the cost of the trust of which human beings are capable, often expressed in the consensual abandonment of autonomy and relinquishment of control over oneself to another, that equality will come at a high cost.

The political lesson of the pleasure in eroticized submission is not that we should forsake either individualism or equality as ultimately "undesirable." But there is no discontinuity here: *nor* is it the case that the woman who enjoys fantasies of erotic domination would enjoy literal servitude, or for that matter thinks she would. The lesson—the truth—of the erotic pleasure many feel in controlled submission may be this: while we crave liberal autonomy and radical equality, while we crave the freedom which the liberal feminist pursues and the equality the radical feminist envisions, *at least in this society as it is presently constituted, we also crave—because we also need—the capacity to trust one another, including those who are stronger than we are.* The weak and the strong are in fact interdependent in this society—we *aren't* equally autonomous individuals—and what that means is that the weak need to be able to depend on the strong. The capacity to safely depend on another, to look after one's own well-being, is a desirable state, and it is no great mystery that it is pursued as pleasure. When we test the limits of our capacity to trust, of our willingness to embrace absolute dependency, and when we discover erotic pleasure lurking at that limit, we give expression to our desire to be able to trust someone who is strong and trustworthy—which may be a fully human, and not just female, need.

Either trust or fear can prompt us to submit to the will of the other. Trust is enlivening, and fear is deadening. There is a difference. It is a subjective, internal, hedonic difference. It is the difference between the battered woman's consensual endurance—motivated by fear—of beatings, and the lover's consensual enjoyment—motivated by trust—of controlled submission. The first submission is deadening, the second (can be) enlivening. It is a difference we will only be able to *see*, much less understand, if we look at our *internal* lives. From an external perspective, this difference is muted. From an internal perspective, it is glaring.

There is—*of course*—a danger in this. The internal difference is not *inevitably* glaring, even to ourselves. And because it is not, there is a danger in the pleasure of submission just as there is a limit to the desirability in the non-sexual world of relationships of dependence and trust. . . .

Conclusion: Women's Difference, and an Alternative Standard for a Feminist Critique of Law

Although liberal and radical legalism are typically contrasted, as I contrasted them in the bulk of this paper, I want briefly to suggest in this conclusion that it is by virtue of an assumption that liberalism and radicalism *share* that their respective chosen proxies for well-being—choice and power—are so at odds with women's subjective, hedonic lives. Both liberal and radical legalism share a vision of the human being—and therefore of our subjective well-being—as "autonomous." The liberal insists that choice is necessary for the "true" exercise of that autonomy—and thus is an adequate proxy for subjective well-being—while the radical insists the same for power. But this strategic difference should not blind us to their commonality. Both the liberal and the radical legalist have accepted the Kantian assumption that *to be human* is to be in some sense autonomous—meaning, minimally, to be differentiated, or individuated, from the rest of social life.

Underlying and underscoring the poor fit between the proxies for subjective well-being endorsed by liberals and radicals—choice and power—and women's subjective, hedonic lives is the simple fact that women's lives—*because of our biological, reproductive role*—are drastically at odds with this fundamental vision of human life. Women's lives are *not* autonomous, they are profoundly relational. This is at least the biological reflection, if not the biological cause, of virtually all aspects, hedonic and otherwise, of our "difference." Women, and *only* women, and *most* women, transcend *physically* the differentiation or individuation of biological self from the rest of human life trumpeted as the norm by the entire Kantian tradition. When a woman is pregnant her biological life embraces the embryonic life of another. When she later nurtures children, her needs will embrace their needs. The experience of being human, for women, differentially from men, includes the counter-autonomous experience of a shared physical identity between woman and fetus, as well as the counter-autonomous experience of the emotional and psychological bond between mother and infant.

Our reproductive role renders us non-autonomous in a second, less obvious, but ultimately more far-reaching sense. Emotionally and morally women may benefit from the dependency of the fetus and the infant upon us. But *materially* we are more often burdened than enriched by that dependency. And because we are burdened, we differentially depend more heavily upon others, both for our own survival, and for the survival of the children who are part of us. Women, more than men, depend upon relationships with others, because the weakest of human beings—infants—depend upon us. ...If women's "difference" lies in the fact that our lives are relational rather than autonomous, and if autonomy is a necessary attribute of a human being, then women's difference rather abruptly implies that women are not human beings. Politics that are designed to benefit human beings—including liberal and radical legalism—will leave women out in the cold.

This is not a novel insight: that women are not human as human is now conceived has in a sense always been the dominant problem for feminism. But the two characteristic ways in which modern feminist legal theorists have responded to this dilemma are both, I think, flawed. The liberal feminist's solution is to deny it. The fact that women become pregnant, give birth, and nurse infants is a difference that *does not count*. It does not make us any less "autonomous" than men. ...

[T]his response does not work. ...If we embrace a false conception of our nature we can be sure of only one thing, and that is that legal reform based on such a conception will only occasionally—and then only incidentally—benefit real instead of hypothetical women.

The radical feminist's proposal is that we seek to *become* autonomous creatures. We are indeed not "autonomous," but what that reflects is our lack of power—our social, political and legal victimization—not our essential nature. To the extent that we become autonomous by gaining power, we will *become* the beneficiaries of the legal system designed to promote the well-being of just such people. This radical vision is at root deeply assimilationist—by gaining power, we become equal, as we become equal we become less "relational"—meaning less victimized—as we become less relational we become more autonomous, and as we become more autonomous we become more like "human beings"—more like men. Radical assimilation, though, has costs no less weighty (and no less familiar) than liberal denial. There is no guarantee that women can become autonomous "human beings," no guarantee that women want to, and at heart, no persuasive argument that women should.

A very new and third response, which does not fit easily (or at all) within the liberal and radical models described above, and which I think has great promise, is that feminists should insist on women's humanity—and thus on our entitlements—and on the wrongness of the dominant conception of what it means to be a "human being." We should insist, as Christine Littleton has argued, for an equal "acceptance of our difference." This third course is surely more promising—it has truth and candor on its side—but without hedonistic criticism it is insufficient: *which* differences are to be accepted? ... If "difference" includes our differential suffering, or our differential vulnerability to sexual assault, or our differential endurance of pain, or our differentially negative self-esteem, then "acceptance" of those differences will backfire. We need more than just acceptance of our differences; we need a vocabulary in which to articulate and then evaluate them, as well as the power to reject or affirm them. ...

Andrea Dworkin, Whores

From A. Dworkin, Pornography: Men Possessing Women
(NY: Dutton, 1991).

Male sexual domination is a material system with an ideology and a metaphysics. The sexual colonialization of women's bodies is a material reality: men control the sexual and reproductive uses of women's bodies. The institutions of control include law, marriage, prostitution, pornography, health care, the economy, organized religion, and systematized physical aggression against women (for instance, in rape and battery). Male domination of the female body is the basic material reality of women's lives; and all struggle for dignity and self-determination is rooted in the struggle for actual control of one's own body, especially control over physical access to one's own body. The ideology of male sexual domination posits that men are superior to women by virtue of their penises; that physical possession of the female is a natural right of the male; that sex is, in fact, conquest and possession of the female, especially but not exclusively phallic conquest and phallic possession; that the use of the female body for sexual or reproductive purposes is a natural right of men; that the sexual will of men properly and naturally defines the parameters of a woman's sexual being, which is her whole identity. The metaphysics of male sexual domination is that women are whores. This basic truth transcends all lesser truths in the male system. One does not violate something by using it for what it is: neither rape nor prostitution is an abuse of the female because in both the female is fulfilling her natural function; that is why rape is absurd and incomprehensible as an abusive phenomenon in the male system, and so is prostitution, which is held to be voluntary even when the prostitute is hit, threatened, drugged, or locked in. The woman's effort to stay innocent, her effort to prove innocence, her effort to prove in any instance of sexual use that she was used against her will, is always and unequivocally an effort to prove that she is not a whore. The presumption that she is a whore is a metaphysical presumption: a presumption that underlies the system of reality in which she lives. A whore cannot be raped, only used. A whore by nature cannot be forced to whore—only revealed through circumstance to be the whore she is. The point is her nature, which is a whore's nature. The word *whore* can be construed to mean that she is a cunt with enough gross intelligence to manipulate, barter, or sell. The cunt wants it; the whore knows enough to use it. *Cunt* is the most reductive word; *whore* adds the dimension of character—greedy, manipulative, not nice. The word *whore* reveals her sensual nature (cunt) and her natural character. . . .

Typically, every charge by women that force is used to violate women—in rape, battery, or prostitution—is dismissed by positing a female nature that is essentially fulfilled by the act of violation, which in turn transforms violation into merely using a thing for what it is and blames the thing if it is not womanly enough to enjoy what is done to it. . . .

The pleasure of the prostitute is the pleasure of any woman used in sex—but heightened. The specific—the professional whore—exists in the context of the general—women who are whores by nature. There is additional pleasure in being bought because money fixes her status as one who is for sex, not just woman but essence of woman or double-woman. The professional prostitute is distinguished from other women not in kind but by degree. "There are certainly no women absolutely devoid of the prostitute instinct to covet being sexually excited by any stranger," writes Weininger, emphasizing both pleasure and vanity. "If a woman hasn't got a tiny streak of a harlot in her," writes D.H. Lawrence, "she's a dry stick as a rule." The tininess of Lawrence's "streak" should not be misunderstood: "really, most wives sold themselves, in the past, and plenty of harlots gave themselves, when they felt like it, for nothing." The "tiny streak" is her sexual nature: without a streak of whore, "she's a dry stick as a rule."

There is a right-wing ideology and a left-wing ideology. The right-wing ideology claims that the division of mother and whore is phenomenologically real. The virgin is the potential mother. The left-wing ideology claims that sexual freedom is in the unrestrained use of women, the use of women as a collective natural resource, not privatized, not owned by one man but instead used by many. The metaphysics is the same on the Left and on the Right: the sexuality of the woman actualized is the sexuality of the whore; desire on her part is the slut's lust; once sexually available, it does not matter how she is used, why, by whom, by how many, or how often. Her sexual will can exist only as a will to be used. Whatever happens to her, it is all the same. If she loathes it, it is not wrong, she is. . . .

On the Left, the sexually liberated woman is the woman of pornography. Free male sexuality wants, has a right to, produces, and consumes pornography because pornography is pleasure. Leftist sensibility promotes and protects pornography because pornography is freedom. The pornography glut is bread and roses for the masses. Freedom is the mass-marketing of woman as whore. Free sexuality for the woman is in being massively consumed, denied an individual nature, denied any sexual sensibility other than that which serves the male. Capitalism is not wicked or cruel when the commodity is the whore; profit is not wicked or cruel when the alienated worker is a female piece of meat; corporate bloodsucking is not wicked or cruel when the corporations in question, organized crime syndicates, sell cunt; racism is not wicked or cruel when the black cunt or yellow cunt or red cunt or Hispanic cunt or Jewish cunt has her legs splayed for any man's pleasure; poverty is not wicked or cruel when it is the poverty of dispossessed women who have only themselves to sell; violence by the powerful against the powerless is not wicked or cruel when it is called sex; slavery is not wicked or cruel when it is sexual slavery; torture is not wicked or cruel when the tormented are women, whores, cunts. The new pornography is left-wing; and the new pornography is a vast graveyard where the Left has gone to die. The Left cannot have its whores and its politics too. . . .

In the introduction to *Black Fashion Model,* a book, the reader is warned that this story "was tempered by the fire of experience, molded in the cauldron of intense, adult desire . . ." Those who are shy or those who want to see the world through rose-colored glasses are advised not to read the book. . . . Another major theme in the story is "the simple unalterable fact of [the main character's] color—she is a Negress, a young, beautiful black woman." The abuse of power and the fact of prejudice are in the center of her life. Her name is Kelly Morris. She moves like a bird or snake. . . . [S]he was "one of the most physically charming black women ever to leave the streets of the ghetto." Her body is long, her breasts are big. Her features show "a perfect, savage beauty." She has dark, thick lips, a wide and slightly squashed nose. She is beautiful and innocent. Her skin is "dark mellow cocoa" and deep brown. Kelly walks down the street in high heels and her tightest skirt. Men talk about how they want a piece of her, but how she will be famous one day. . . . When she was seventeen, she allowed someone to take photographs of her. The savage beauty of her face became important in front of the camera. Men respected her for her innocence but the camera made Kelly "into a wanton, lusty *woman!*" Kelly became one of the most famous models in the country and the most famous black model. She remained innocent, a savage beauty, a black diamond. Robert Grey watches Kelly posing. Robert Grey imagines her on her knees between his white thighs. . . .

Robert Grey abducts Kelly. Robert Grey pushes Kelly into a run-down house. A white woman is in the room. . . . She calls Kelly a bitch. Kelly demands an explanation. The white girl winks at Robert Grey. The white girl tells Kelly she will explain. . . . Robert Grey closes the blinds and double-locks the door. Robert Grey calls Kelly "little black girl." Her black breasts shimmer. The white woman is going to take photographs of Kelly. Kelly's breasts are exposed. The white female fingers are on her big black breasts. She gets upset. She struggles free. Robert Grey hits her. He hits her again. She cries and feels "pain and humiliating submissiveness." She falls into a heap of "half-naked black flesh," her thighs undulate. Robert Grey undoes his pants. Robert Grey says: we know you want it. Angela, the white girl, is naked too. Angela mimics black slang. Kelly says that she always tried to be nice to white people. Angela tells her that this has nothing to do with race. Angela wants to use the photographs she is going to take of Kelly to make a career for herself, but she gets pleasure too from having Kelly there naked. Robert Grey's prick is getting even harder. Robert Grey takes off Kelly's bikini bottom. . . . Robert Grey does not want to hurt her by forcing his cock in too fast. He wants her to like it too. But Kelly is so excited she can't wait. When his cock is buried in her belly she feels as though she is being stretched apart. She loves it. Robert Grey keeps fucking her. Kelly tries to resist wanting it but she can't. Robert Grey is twice as excited because she is black and he is white! Robert Grey thrusts harder. She is hopelessly impaled. . . . Kelly feels ashamed and excited. Kelly starts screaming: Fuck me, fuck me, fuck me. Robert Grey sadistically stops. Robert Grey sadistically begins again. He keeps fucking her until she finally goes limp. "Her body was beaten and bruised and satiated from the ravishment, but she slowly but surely remembered who she was and who the man was she was with." . . .

At the heart of the story, . . . is indeed "the simple unalterable fact of her color."

All the sex in *Black Fashion Model* is the standard stuff of pornography: rape, bondage, humiliation, pain, fucking, assfucking, fingerfucking, cocksucking, cuntsucking, kidnapping, hitting, the sexual cruelty of one woman toward another, pair sex, gang sex.

All the values are the standard values of pornography: the excitement of humiliation, the joy of pain, the pleasure of abuse, the magnificence of cock, the woman who resists only to discover that she loves it and wants more.

The valuation of the woman is the standard valuation ("a wanton, lusty *woman!*"), except that her main sexual part is her skin, its color. Her skin with its color is her sex with its nature. She is punished in sex by sex and she is punished as a consequence of sex: she loses her status. All this punishment is deserved, owing to her sex, which is her skin. The genital shame of any woman is transferred to the black woman's skin. The shame of sex is the shame of her skin. The stigma of sex is the stigma of her skin. The use of her sex is the use of her skin. The violence against her sex is violence against her skin. The excitement of torturing her sex is the excitement of torturing her skin. The hatred of her sex is the hatred of her skin. Her sex is stretched over her like a glove and when he touches her skin he puts on that glove. She models her skin, her sex. Her sex is as close, as available, as her skin. Her sex is as dark as her skin. The black model need not model naked to be sex; any display of her skin is sex. Her sex is right on the surface—her essence, her offense. . . . The black female's skin reveals her: her skin is cunt; it has that sexual value in and of itself. . . . This is the specific sexual value of the black woman in pornography in the United States, a race-bound society fanatically committed to the sexual devaluing of black skin perceived as a sex organ and a sexual nature. No woman of any other race bears this specific burden in this country. In no other woman is skin sex, cunt in and of itself—her essence, her offense. This meaning of the black woman's skin is revealed in the historical usage of her, even as it developed from the historical usage of her. This valuation of the black woman is real, especially vivid in urban areas where she is used as a street whore extravagantly and without conscience. Poverty forces her; but it is the sexual valuation of her skin that predetermines her poverty and permits the simple, righteous use of her as a whore.

How, then, does one fight racism and jerk off to it at the same time? The Left cannot have its whores and its politics too. The imperial United States cannot maintain its racist system without its black whores, its bottom, the carnal underclass. The sexualization of race within a racist system is a prime purpose and consequence of pornography. In using the black woman, pornography depicts the whore by depicting her skin; in using the pornography, men spit on her sex and her skin. Here the relationship of sex and death could not be clearer: this sexual use of the black woman is the death of freedom, the death of justice, the death of equality. . . .

The magazine is called *Mom*. It is subtitled "Big Bellied Mamas." The model on the cover is white and great with child. She is fingering her huge belly. Her fingernails are painted purple. She is naked except for a garter belt that hangs unfastened, framing her huge belly. Inside, this model is called Anna. There are twenty-three pages of photographs of Anna, some in color, some black and white. In most of the photographs, Anna is displaying her huge belly as if it were—in the visual vocabulary of pornography—her breasts or ass or cunt. In the rest of the photographs, Anna is fingering other parts of her body, especially her genitals, or she is displaying her genitals. In many of the photographs Anna has on pieces of underwear—garter belt, bra, stockings, robe. In every case, the positioning of the underwear on and around her body suggests bondage. In two photographs Anna has a stethoscope: in one, it is on her belly, her legs spread, her underwear suggesting bondage; in the other it is approaching her vagina, her legs spread, her underwear suggesting bondage. . . .

The pornography of pregnancy—the graphic depiction of mothers as whores—completes the picture. The maternal does not exclude the whorish; rather, the maternal is included in the whorish as long as the male wants to use the woman. The malevolence of the woman's body is stressed: its danger to sperm and especially its danger to the woman herself. Her glands, metabolism, hormones, tubes, ovaries, "the vaginal contents"—all are potentially or actually malevolent. It is as if she is swollen and bound to explode from inside.

The sperm are male. The vagina will destroy them. Pregnancy is the triumph of the phallus over the death-dealing vagina.

The women display themselves, display their sex, display their bellies. The huge belly is fetishized but the whore behind it stays the same: the cunt showing herself.

The pregnancy is seen as a condition of both bondage and humiliation: her difficulty in moving is dwelled on with transparent delight and so is bladder irritation.

The men who discuss sex say that there are two conflicting sides: those who believe only in reproductive sex versus those who believe in sex for pleasure not connected to reproduction. But there are not two sides: there is a continuum of phallic control. In the male system, reproductive and nonreproductive sex are both phallic sex, use of the whore for male pleasure. The woman great with child is the woman whose sex is ready to burst, who has taken so much of the male into her that now he is growing there. . . .

Pregnancy is confirmation that the woman has been fucked: it is confirmation that she is a cunt. In the male sexual system, the pregnant woman is a particular sexual object: she shows her sexuality through her pregnancy. The display marks her as a whore. Her belly is her sex. Her belly is proof that she has been used. Her belly is his phallic triumph. One does not abort his victory. . . . Even in pregnancy, the possibility of her death is the excitement of sex. And now, the doctors have added more sex—to birth itself. *Vagina* means sheath. They cut directly into the uterus with a knife—a surgical fuck. She is tied down—literally cuffed and tied, immobilized by bondage, the bondage of birth, her legs spread; they pour drugs into her to induce labor; their bondage and their drugs cause intense and unbearable pain; she cannot have natural labor; she is drugged and sliced into, surgically fucked. The epidemic of cesarean sections in this country is a sexual, not a medical, phenomenon. The doctors save the vagina—the birth canal of old—for the husband; they fuck the uterus directly, with a knife. Modern childbirth—surgical childbirth—comes from the metaphysics of male sexual domination: she is a whore, there to be used, the uterus of the whore entered directly by the new rapist, the surgeon, the vagina saved to serve the husband. . . .

The boys are betting on our compliance, our ignorance, our fear. We have always refused to face the worst that men have done to us. The boys count on it. The boys are betting that we cannot face the horror of their sexual system and survive. The boys are betting that their depictions of us as whores will beat us down and stop our hearts. The boys are betting that their penises and fists and knives and fucks and rapes will turn us into what they say we are—the compliant women of sex, the voracious cunts of pornography, the masochistic sluts who resist because we really want more. The boys are betting. The boys are wrong.

NOTES AND QUESTIONS

1. **Hedonic Difference**. Robin West's arguments center on the controversial thesis that "women's subjective, hedonic lives [their experience of pleasure and pain] are different from men's." What evidence does West present for this claim? Do you find her evidence of female hedonic uniqueness persuasive? West's thesis sounds similar to the conventional view of gender difference as inevitable and natural, a view that many feminists have refuted. Do you see any distinction between West's claim of gender-based hedonic experience and the traditional notion of gender difference that justified denying women access to the public sphere?

What legal ramifications are suggested by West's perspective? Does the difference in women's hedonic lives help account for the law's discounting of women's pain, such as the pain women experience as victims of rape and domestic violence? Should women embrace their subjective experiences as a means of reforming the law? Or by focusing on women's bodies as an avenue for change do we risk reinforcing the objectification of women?

2. **Whores**. A key tenet of the "ideology of male domination" described by Dworkin is the belief that women are whores—women's natural function is to be sexually available for men. How pervasive do you think this ideology is and what impact does it have on women's condition?

3. **The Feminist Critique of Autonomy**. Numerous feminist scholars, including Robin West, have criticized the liberal conception of human beings as autonomous actors who seek primarily to be shielded from interference by others. *See*, for example, Robin West, *Jurisprudence and Gender*, 55 U. Chi. L. Rev. 1 (1988); Suzanna Sherry, *Civic Virtue and the Feminine Voice in Constitutional Adjudication*, 72 Va. L. Rev. 543 (1986). In contrast to this selfish, atomistic individual, the person posited by these feminists lives within a social context and desires connection with others. Does West's conception of women as "giving selves" seem authentic?

Rather than discard autonomy, other feminist scholars have redefined the concept to account for the individual's social context. *See*, for example Jennifer Nedelsky, *Reconceiving Autonomy: Sources, Thoughts and Possibilities*, 1 Yale J.L. & Feminism 7 (1989); Linda C. McClain, *"Atomistic Man" Revisited: Liberalism, Connection, and Feminist Jurisprudence*, 65 S. Cal. L. Rev. 1171 (1992).

Dworkin's writing exemplifies the radical feminist quest for empowerment that West criticizes. While West suggests that women are not as interested in autonomy as men are, Dworkin asserts that "all struggle for dignity and self-determination is rooted in the struggle for actual control of one's own body, especially control over physical access to one's own body." Which view of women's welfare do you find more compelling?

What should we make of the fact that some women take pleasure in being submissive? Does their experience discredit radical feminists' claim that women suffer from inequality and would benefit from empowerment? Is West's distinction between controlled submission in a relationship of trust versus submission resulting from fear clear enough?

4.   **Women's Agency**. West's article raises questions about women's agency in defining their identities. To what extent does the fear of male aggression and the experience of nurturing others shape women's view of themselves? According to West, do women deliberately define themselves as "giving selves" or are they simply responding to male aggression and to male definitions of sexuality?

The answers to these questions also have implications for women's relationships with men. Does West imply that the only reason women enter into intimate consensual relationships with men is out of fear or submission? Does her thesis leave room for the possibility of heterosexual relationships based on equality and mutual respect?

5.   **Gender Essentialism**. Although West distinguishes her position from that of radical feminists like Dworkin, the two scholars both describe a universal female subject. By appealing to bodily-related experiences of physical pain and pleasure, the cultural and radical feminist positions represented by West and Dworkin exploit the commonalities of biological identification to justify their appeal to coherent feminine identities.

Does Dworkin's use of the pornographic story about the Black fashion model illuminate the racism in pornography? Or does Dworkin minimize the racial oppression of the model in order to emphasize her sexual subordination? Which is the effect of writing, for example, "the genital shame of any woman is transferred to the black woman's skin?" Does Dworkin's observation that "black skin [is] perceived as a sex organ and a sexual nature" apply equally to Black men?

In her article, *Race and Essentialism in Feminist Legal Theory*, which is excerpted more fully in Chapter One, Angela Harris criticizes West's portrayal of the "essential woman" whose identity is determined primarily by her gender:

> In West's view, women are ontologically distinct from men, because "Women, and only women, and most women, transcend physically the differentiation or individuation of biological self from the rest of human life trumpeted as the norm by the entire Kantian tradition." That is, because only women can bear children, and because women have the social respon-

sibility for raising children, our selves are profoundly different from male selves. . . .

This claim about women's essential connectedness to the world becomes the centerpiece of *Jurisprudence and Gender*. West begins the article with the question, "What is a human being?" She then asserts that "perhaps the central insight of feminist theory of the last decade has been that wom[e]n are 'essentially connected,' not 'essentially separate,' from the rest of human life, both materially, through pregnancy, intercourse, and breast-feeding, and existentially, through the moral and practical life." For West, this means that "all of our modern legal theory—by which I mean 'liberal legalism' and 'critical legal theory' collectively—is essentially and irretrievably masculine." This is so because modern legal theory relies on the "separation thesis," the claim that human beings are distinct individuals first and form relationships later. . . .

West's claims are clearly questionable on their face insofar as the experience of some women—"mothers"—is asserted to stand for the experience of all women. . . . West's theory necessitates the stilling of some voices—namely, the voices of women who have rejected their "biological, reproductive role"—in order to privilege others. One might also question the degree to which motherhood, or our potential for it, defines us. For purposes of this article, however, I am more interested in the conception of self that underlies West's account of "women's experience."

West argues that the biological and social implications of motherhood shape the selfhood of all, or at least most, women. This claim involves at least two assumptions. First, West assumes (as does the liberal social theory she criticizes) that everyone has a deep, unitary "self" that is relatively stable and unchanging. Second, West assumes that this "self" differs significantly between men and women but is the same for all women and for all men despite differences of class, race, and sexual orientation: that is, that this self is deeply and primarily gendered. In a later part of the article, I will argue that black women can bring the experience of a multiple rather than a unitary self to feminist theory. Here I want to argue that the notion that the gender difference is primary to an individual's selfhood is one that privileges white women's experience over the experience of black women.

The essays and poems in *This Bridge Called My Back* describe experiences of women of color that differ radically from one another. Some contributors are lesbians; some are straight; some are class-privileged, and others are not. What links all the writings, however, is the sense that the self of a woman of color is not primarily a female self or a colored self, but a both-and self. In her essay "Brownness," Andrea Canaan describes both-and experience:

> The fact is I am brown and female, and my growth and development are tied to the entire community. I must nurture and develop brown self, woman, man, and child. I must address the issues of my own oppression and survival. When I separate them, isolate them, and ignore them, I separate, isolate, and ignore myself. I am a unit. A part of brownness.

> A personal story may also help to illustrate the point. At a 1988 meeting of the West Coast "fem-crits," Pat Cain and Trina Grillo asked all the women present to pick out two or three words to describe who they were. None of the white women mentioned their race; all of the women of color did.

> In this society, it is only white people who have the luxury of "having no color"; only white people have been able to imagine that sexism and racism are separate experiences. Far more for black women than for white women, the experience of self is precisely that of being unable to disentangle the web of race and gender—of being enmeshed always in multiple, often contradictory, discourses of sexuality and color. The challenge to black women has been the need to weave the fragments, our many selves, into an integral, though always changing and shifting, whole: a self that is neither "female" nor "black," but both-and. West's insistence that every self is deeply and primarily gendered, then, with its corollary that gender is more important to personal identity than race, is finally another example of white solipsism. By suggesting that gender is more deeply embedded in self than race, her theory privileges the experience of white people over all others, and thus serves to reproduce relations of domination in the larger culture.... West's essential woman turns out to be white.

Angela Harris, *Race and Essentialism in Feminist Legal Theory*, 42 Stan. L. Rev. 581, 602–05 (1990). How does Harris's racial critique affect your views of West's account of women's hedonic difference?

6. **The Primacy of Sexual Difference?** Do West and Dworkin imply that gender is more important than race (or other social features) in defining women's identities? Even if this is so, why does the focus on gender end up privileging white women's experiences?

In *Bodies that Matter*, Judith Butler also contests the assumption many feminist theorists make that sexual difference is more primary and more fundamental than other kinds of difference. Her essay, *Passing, Queering: Nella Larsen's Psychoanalytic Challenge*, uses Nella Larsen's novel *Passing*—the story of a Black woman named Clare who passes as white—to examine the power of sexual norms operating through the regulation of racial boundaries.

A number of theoretical questions have been raised by the effort to think the relationship between feminism, psychoanalysis, and race studies. For the most part, psychoanalysis has been used by feminist theorists to theorize sexual difference as a distinct and fundamental set of linguistic and cultural relations. The philosopher Luce Irigaray has claimed that the question of sexual difference is the question for our time. This privileging of sexual difference implies not only that sexual difference should be understood as more fundamental than other forms of difference, but that other forms of difference are derived from sexual difference. This view also presumes that sexual difference constitutes an autonomous sphere of relations or disjunctions, and is not to be understood as articulated through or *as* other vectors of power.

What would it mean, on the other hand, to consider the assumption of sexual positions, the disjunctive ordering of the human as "masculine" or "feminine" as taking place not only through a heterosexualizing symbolic with its taboo on homosexuality, but through a complex set of racial injunctions which operate in part through the taboo of miscegenation. Further, how might we understand homosexuality and miscegenation to converge at and as the constitutive outside of a normative heterosexuality that is at once the regulation of a racially pure reproduction? To coin Marx, then, let us remember that the reproduction of the species will be articulated as the reproduction of relations of reproduction, that is, as the cathected site of a racialized version of the species in pursuit of hegemony through perpetuity, that requires and produces a normative heterosexuality in its service. Conversely, the reproduction of heterosexuality will take different forms depending on how race and the reproduction of race are understood. And though there are clearly good historical reasons for keeping "race" and "sexuality" and "sexual difference" as separate analytic spheres, there are also quite pressing and significant historical reasons for asking how and where we might read not only their convergence, but the sites at which the one cannot be constituted save through the other. This is something other than juxtaposing distinct spheres of power, subordination, agency, historicity, and something other than a list of attributes separated by those proverbial commas (gender, sexuality, race, class), that usually mean that we have not yet figured out how to think the relations we seek to mark. Is there a way, then, to read Nella Larsen's text as engaging psychoanalytic assumptions not to affirm the primacy of sexual difference, but to articulate the convergent modalities of power by which sexual difference is articulated and assumed?

. . .

It is this assertion of the priority of sexual difference over racial difference that has marked so much psychoanalytic feminism as white, for the assumption here is not only that sexual difference is more fundamental, but that there is a relationship called "sexual difference" that is itself unmarked by race. That whiteness is not understood by such a perspective as a racial category is clear; it is yet another power that need not speak its name. Hence, to claim that sexual difference is more fundamental than racial difference is effectively to assume that sexual difference is white sexual difference, and that whiteness is not a form of racial difference.

... If, as Norma Alarcon has insisted, women of color are "multiply interpellated," called by many names, constituted in and by that multiple calling, then this implies that the symbolic domain, the domain of socially instituted norms, is composed of racializing norms, and that they exist not merely alongside gender norms, but are articulated through one another. Hence, it is no longer possible to make sexual difference prior to racial difference or, for that matter, to make them fully separable axes of social regulation and power.

Judith Butler, *Passing, Queering: Nella Larsen's Psychoanalytic Challenge*, in *Bodies That Matter: On the Discursive Limits of "Sex"* 167 (1993). Does Butler's writing help you to understand how sexual and racial difference are related?

7. **Reproduction and Sexual Domination**. Another example of Dworkin's focus on sexual domination is her treatment of reproduction. According to Dworkin, control of women's reproductive capacity, such as abortion restrictions and unnecessary cesarean sections, stems from the male view of women as sexual objects. Does the centrality of sex in many feminists' explanations of male domination reduce women's identity to their sexuality and women's condition to sexual subordination?

8. **Latinas' Multidimensional Identities.** In *Borders (En)gendered: Normativities, Latinas, and a LatCrit Paradigm*, Berta Hernandez–Truyol describes her own multidimensional identity as a Latina law professor and proposes a LatCrit theoretical model that places Latinas' multidimensionality at the center, in opposition to the dominant model that presupposes a monolithic racial or sexual identity.

Latinas/os do a lot of world traveling, with Latinas additionally journeying through the *mundos* of gender inequality. We travel between our various and varied multiple worlds, psychic and physical—from *casa* y familia to *calle* y *trabajo*; from *espanol* to *ingles* to espanglish; from *tia* to lawyer; from *hija* to *profesora*; from *normativa* to outsider. We weave our way, as we weave our hair, in and out of passages that we inhabit, being a little alien everywhere. ...

Such world traveling is not unique to me. Rather, it is a common daily experience for all Latinas/os in the United States by virtue of our status as Latinas/os. We are interdependent intersections of our race, gender, color, ethnicity, nationality, ancestry, culture, and language. Our multilingualism is defined not by the languages we literally speak (in fact, many of us speak only Spanish or only English) but instead by virtue of the worlds we inhabit, the journeys we take. ...

LatCrit as an articulable theoretical construct both presents a great challenge and offers great promise. First, the challenge lies in the great diversity—the panethnicity—of Latinas/os. Latinas/os come from different ethnic, cultural, and racial heritages, as well as from varied national origins. Some are citizens, some are not; some noncitizens are present with, and some without, paper documentation. Many have been in the United States for generations, others are recent arrivals. Some are monolingual in Spanish, some in English, others are bi/multilingual. Some are homocultural and others can (and some do daily) culturally crossdress. Some apparently cacophonous, heterogeneous demographics would appear to interfere with any attempt at a coherent, cohesive paradigm. This notion of panethnicity, upon an initial consideration, could appear to be an impediment to the articulation of any congruent *teoria*. Ironically, however, such heterogeneity is what holds the promise of LatCrit: the development of a paradigm that accepts, embraces, and accommodates persons as multidimensional entities rather than as conveniently divisible parts of that whole being.

Berta Esperanza Hernandez–Truyol, *Borders (En)Gendered: Normativities, Latinas, and a LatCrit Paradigm*, 72 N.Y.U L. Rev. 882 (1997).

Mary Joe Frug, A Postmodern Feminist Legal Manifesto*

From Mary Joe Frug, Postmodern Legal Feminism (1992).

Most feminists are committed to the position that however "natural" and common sex difference may seem, the differences between women and men are not biologically compelled; they are, rather, "socially constructed." ...

Regardless of how commonplace the constructed character of sex differences may be, particular differences can seem quite deeply embedded within the sexes—so much so, in fact, that the social construction thesis is undermined. When applied to differences that seem especially entrenched—

* The following essay is an unfinished   she was murdered on April 1, 1991.
work. Professor Frug was working on it when

differences such as masculine aggression or feminine compassion, or differences related to the erotic and reproductive aspects of women's lives—social construction seems like a clichéd, improbable, and unconvincing account of experience, an explanation for sex differences that undervalues "reality." This reaction does not necessarily provoke a return to a "natural" explanation for sex differences; but it does radically stunt the liberatory potential of the social construction thesis. One's expectations for law reform projects are reduced; law might be able to mitigate the harsh impact of these embedded traits on women's lives, but law does not seem responsible for *constructing* them.

The subject of this section is the role of law in the production of sex differences that seem "natural." One of my objectives is to explain and challenge the essentializing impulse that places particular sex differences outside the borders of legal responsibility. Another objective is to provide an analysis of the legal role in the production of gendered identity that will invigorate the liberatory potential of the social construction thesis.

I have chosen the relationship of law to the female body as my principal focus. I am convinced that law is more cunningly disguised but just as implicated in the production of apparently intractable sex related traits as in those that seem more legally malleable. Since the anatomical distinctions between the sexes seem not only "natural" but fundamental to identity, proposing and describing the role of law in the production of the meaning of the female body seems like the most convincing subject with which to defend my case. In the following subsections, I will argue that legal rules—like other cultural mechanisms—encode the female body with meanings. Legal discourse then explains and rationalizes these meanings by an appeal to the "natural" differences between the sexes, differences that the rules themselves help to produce. The formal norm of legal neutrality conceals the way in which legal rules participate in the construction of those meanings.

The proliferation of women's legal rights during the past two decades has liberated women from some of the restraining meanings of femininity. This liberation has been enhanced by the emergence of different feminisms over the past decade. These feminisms have made possible a stance of opposition toward a singular feminine identity; they have demonstrated that women stand in a multitude of places, depending on time and geographical location, on race, age, sexual preference, health, class status, religion, and other factors. Despite these significant changes, there remains a common residue of meaning that seems affixed, as if by nature, to the female body. Law participates in creating that meaning.

I will argue that there are at least three general claims that can be made about the relationship between legal rules and legal discourse and the meaning of the female body.

1.   Legal rules permit and sometimes mandate the *terrorization* of the female body. This occurs by a combination of provisions that inadequately protect women against physical abuse and that encourage women to seek refuge against insecurity. One meaning of "female body," then, is a body

that is "in terror," a body that has learned to scurry, to cringe and to submit. Legal discourse supports that meaning.

2. Legal rules permit and sometimes mandate the *maternalization* of the female body. This occurs by provisions that reward women for singularly assuming responsibilities after childbirth and with those that penalize conduct—such as sexuality or labor market work—that conflicts with mothering. Maternalization also occurs through rules such as abortion restrictions that compel women to become mothers and by domestic relations rules that favor mothers over fathers as parents. Another meaning of "female body," then, is a body that is "for" maternity. Legal discourse supports that meaning.

3. Legal rules permit and sometimes mandate the *sexualization* of the female body. This occurs through provisions that criminalize individual sexual conduct, such as rules against commercial sex (prostitution) or same-sex practices (homosexuality), and also through rules that legitimate and support institutions such as the pornography, advertising, and entertainment industries which eroticize the female body. Sexualization also occurs—paradoxically—in the application of rules such as rape and sexual harassment laws that are designed to protect women against sex-related injuries. These rules grant or deny women protection by interrogating their sexual promiscuity. The more sexually available or desiring a woman looks, the less protection these rules are likely to give her. Another meaning of "female body," then, is a body that is "for" sex with men, a body that is "desirable" and also rapable, that wants sex and wants raping. Legal discourse supports that meaning.

These groups of legal rules and discourse constitute a system that "constructs," or engenders the female body. The feminine figures the rules pose are naturalized, within legal discourse, by declaration—"women *are* (choose one) weak, nurturing, sexy"—and by a host of linguistic strategies that link women to particular images of the female body. By deploying these images, legal discourse rationalizes, explains, and renders authoritative the female body rule network. The impact of the rule network on women's reality in turn reacts back on the discourse, reinforcing the "truth" of these images.

Contractions of confidence in the thesis that sex differences are socially constructed have had a significant impact on women in law. Liberal jurists, for example, have been unwilling to extend the protection of the gender equality guarantee to anatomical distinctions between female and male bodies; these differences seem so basic to individual identity that law need not—or should not—be responsible for them. Feminist legal scholars have been unable to overcome this intransigence, partly because we ourselves sometimes find particular sex-related traits quite intransigent. Indeed, one way to understand the fracturing of law-related feminism into separate schools of thought over the past decade is by the sexual traits that are considered unsusceptible to legal transformation and by the criticisms these analyses have provoked within our own ranks.

The fracturing of feminist criticism has occurred partly because particular sex differences seem so powerfully fixed that feminists are as unable to resist their "naturalization" as liberal jurists. But feminists also cling to particular sex-related differences because of a strategic desire to protect the feminist legal agenda from sabotage. Many feminist critics have argued that the condition of "real" women makes it too early to be post-feminist. The social construction thesis is useful to feminists insofar as it informs and supports our efforts to improve the condition of women in law. If, or when, the social construction thesis seems about to deconstruct the basic category of woman, its usefulness to feminism is problematized; how can we build a political coalition to advance the position of women in law if the subject that drives our efforts is "indeterminate," "incoherent," or "contingent"?

I think this concern is based upon a misperception of where we are in the legal struggle against sexism. I think we are in danger of being politically immobilized by a system for the production of what sex means that makes particular sex differences seem "natural." If my assessment is right, then describing the mechanics of this system is potentially enabling rather than disempowering; it may reveal opportunities for resisting the legal role in producing the radical asymmetry between the sexes.

I also think this concern is based on a misperception about the impact of deconstruction. Skeptics tend to think, I believe, that the legal deconstruction of "woman"—in one paper or in many papers, say, written over the next decade—will entail the immediate destruction of "women" as identifiable subjects who are affected by law reform projects. Despite the healthy, self-serving respect I have for the influence of legal scholarship and for the role of law as a significant cultural factor (among many) that contributes to the production of femininity, I think "women" cannot be eliminated from our lexicon very quickly. The question this paper addresses is not whether sex differences exist—they do—or how to transcend them— we can't—but the character of their treatment in law.

Sexualization, Terrorization, and Maternalization: The Case of Prostitution

Since most anti-prostitution rules are gender neutral, let me explain, before going any further, how I can argue that they have a particular impact on the meaning of the female body. Like other rules regulating sexual conduct, anti-prostitution rules sexualize male as well as female bodies; they indicate that sex—unlike say, laughing, sneezing, or making eye contact—is legally regulated. Regardless of whether one is male or female, the pleasures and the virtues of sex are produced, at least in part, by legal rules. The gendered lopsidedness of this meaning system—which I describe below—occurs, quite simply, because most sex workers are women. Thus, even though anti-prostitution rules could, in theory, generate parallel meanings for male and female bodies, in practice they just don't. At least they don't right now.

The legal definition of prostitution as the unlawful sale of sex occurs in statutes which criminalize specific commercial sex practices and in decisional law, such as contract cases that hold that agreements for the sale of sexual services are legally unenforceable. By characterizing certain sexual practices as illegal, these rules sexualize the female body. They invite a sexual interrogation of every female body: Is it for or against prostitution?

This sexualization of the female body explains an experience many women have: an insistent concern that this outfit, this pose, this gesture may send the wrong signal—a fear of looking like a whore. Sexy talking, sexy walking, sexy dressing seem sexy, at least in part, because they are the telltale signs of a sex worker plying her trade. This sexualization also explains the shadow many women feel when having sex for unromantic reasons—to comfort themselves, to avoid a confrontation over some domestic issue, or to secure a favor—a fear of acting like a whore. . . .

Because sex differences are semiotic—because the female body is produced and interpreted through a system of signs—the sexualized female body that is produced and sustained by the legal regulation of prostitution may have multiple meanings. Moreover, the meaning of the sexualized female body for an individual woman is also affected by other feminine images which the legal regulation of prostitution produces.

Anti-prostitution rules terrorize the female body. The regulation of prostitution is accomplished not only by rules that expressly repress or prohibit commercialized sex. Prostitution regulation also occurs through a network of cultural practices that endanger sex workers' lives and make their work terrifying. These practices include the random, demeaning, and sometimes brutal character of anti-prostitution law enforcement. They also include the symbiotic relationship between the illegal drug industry and sex work, the use of prostitutes in the production of certain forms of pornography, hotel compliance with sex work, inadequate police protection for crimes against sex workers, and unregulated bias against prostitutes and their children in housing, education, the health care system, and in domestic relations law. Legal rules support and facilitate these practices.

The legal terrorization of prostitutes forces many sex workers to rely on pimps for protection and security, an arrangement which in most cases is also terrorizing. Pimps control when sex workers work, what kind of sex they do for money, and how much they make for doing it; they often use sexual seduction and physical abuse to "manage" the women who work for them. The terrorization of sex workers affects women who are not sex workers by encouraging them to do whatever they can to avoid being asked if they are "for" illegal sex. Indeed, marriage can function as one of these avoidance mechanisms, in that, conventionally, marriage signals that a woman has chosen legal sex over illegal sex.

One might argue that the terrorized female body is not that much different from the sexualized female body. Both experiences of femininity often—some might say always—entail being dominated by a man. Regardless of whether a woman is terrorized or sexualized, there are social incentives to reduce the hardships of her position, either by marrying or by aligning herself with a pimp. In both cases she typically becomes emotionally, financially, physically, and sexually de pendent on and subordinate to a man. . . .

[B]ecause we construct our identities in language, and because the meaning of language is contextual and contingent, the relationship between anti-prostitution rules and the meaning of the female body is also affected by other legal rules and their relationship to the female body. The legal rules that criminalize prostitution are located in a legal system in which other legal rules legalize sex--rules, for example, that establish marriage as the legal site of sex and that link marital sex to reproduction by, for example, legitimating children born in marriage. As a result of this conjuncture, anti-prostitution rules maternalize the female body. They not only interrogate women with the question of whether they are for or against prostitution; they also raise the question of whether a woman is for illegal sex or whether she is for legal, maternalized sex.

The legal system maintains a shaky line between sex workers and other women. Anti-prostitution laws are erratically enforced; eager customers and obliging hotel services collaborate in the "crimes" prostitutes commit with relative impunity, and the legal, systemic devaluation of "women's work" sometimes makes prostitution more lucrative for women than legitimate wage labor. Anti-prostitution rules formally preserve the distinction between legal and illegal sexual activity. By preventing the line between sex workers and "mothers" from disappearing altogether, anti-prostitution rules reinforce the maternalized female body that other legal rules more directly support.

The legal discourse of anti-prostitution law explicitly deploys the image of maternalized femininity in order to contrast sex workers with women who are not sex workers. This can be observed in defamation cases involving women who are incorrectly identified or depicted as whores. In authorizing compensation for such women, courts typically appeal to maternal imagery to describe the woman who has been wrongly described; they justify their decisions by contrasting the images of two female bodies against each other, the virgin and the whore—madonna and bimbo. The discourse of these decisions maternalizes the female body. The maternalized female body is responsible for her children. Madonna's bambino puts her in charge. . . .

The Maternalization of the Female Body: Family and Work

There are a number of legal rules that function to compel or encourage women to bear children and to assume disproportionately larger responsibilities for rearing children than men do. Of these rules, those that regulate biological reproduction or the structure of the family are explicitly engaged in such functions; rules that regulate the wage market or wage market subsidies maternalize the female body more indirectly.

Rules that prohibit, restrict or hinder access to abortion, and rules which prohibit or inhibit the use or distribution of birth control devices prevent women from avoiding unwanted childbirth. These rules have the effect of making some women become mothers against their will. In this way these rules directly conscript the female body in the service of maternity. . . .

Although most sex-specific provisions have been formally eliminated from custody and child support rules, the neutralized rule system has not significantly reduced the gender lopsidedness of custody and support decisions; judges still impose or approve child custody and support schemes in which women undertake more physical responsibility for child care than men. Thus, the administration of domestic relations law is implicated in helping or making women "mother" their children. The law continues to signal to women and men making "private" decisions about which parent should do more or less childrearing. Mothers receive more legal support for that work than men. . . .

Legal rules that regulate the wage market compel or encourage women to bear and to rear children more indirectly than the rules described above. Nevertheless, because wage market rules undervalue the work women do in the wage market, women have much less to lose than men if they abandon, interrupt or modify their wage market work because of childbirth or childrearing. Legal rules that support women's subordinate status in the wage market thus also support (encourage or compel) women to undertake maternal responsibilities. . . .

The Sexualization of the Female Body: Monogamy, Heterosexuality, Passivity

This subsection describes how legal rules affect the frequency, the character, and the distribution of women's sexual practices. The argument is that by directly or indirectly penalizing conduct which does not conform to a particular set of sexual behaviors, legal rules promote a model of female sexuality; this model is characterized by monogamy, heterosexuality, and passivity. This means that legal rules favor women who marry, who have sex only with their husbands, and who defer to their husbands in determining when, how often and in what manner marital sex takes place. In contrast, legal rules discourage women from being celibate or from having sex outside marriage—with one partner, with multiple partners, or with other women; they also deter women from being more assertive than their husbands want them to be about the management of marital sex.

Although law is only one of the cultural factors that influence women's practices, if the legal rules this section describes were different female sexuality could be different. It is hard to say whether women would have less sex than they do now, or whether they would have more; it is hard to predict how their choice of sex partners would change or how the character of their sexual experiences might be affected. Nevertheless, because the present regime of legal rules induces women to be "good girls," and imposes sanctions on "deviant" sexual conduct, it seems clear that altering the current regime would undermine the current model of female sexual behavior.

Legal rules influence female sexuality by means of three groups of rules or law enforcement practices. One group of legal rules prohibits or promotes certain forms of sex; the two other groups regulate the physical and economic conditions in which sex takes place. The remainder of this section is devoted to explaining how these rules function as a system to encourage women to conform to a monogamous, heterosexual, and passive model of female sexuality.

Legal rules promote sexual monogamy by defining marriage as a union with one other person and by punishing or indirectly penalizing sex outside of marriage. Criminal rules against bigamy prohibit marriage to more than one person at a time, while sex outside of marriage is made a criminal offense, in many states, by rules against fornication and adultery. Legal rules in most states also designate adultery as a marital "offense" that constitutes grounds for divorce. Sex outside of marriage is further discouraged by rules prohibiting prostitution, and by contract rules that make agreements between unmarried individuals who live together unenforceable to the extent that they are "based on" sex. These rules encourage women and men to be monogamous by formally restricting sex to the one person to whom they are legally married.

Because the rules against adultery and fornication are only loosely enforced, the legal impact on female sexual monogamy might not amount to much if these rules were the only legal factors affecting women's sexual practices. But this is not the case. The legal rules that regulate the economic consequences of marriage, the legal rules that maintain the inferior status of women in the wage market, and the legal rules that provide women inadequate protection against physical abuse all function to reinforce the impact of the sexual monogamy rules on women. These rules create economic and safety incentives for women to marry and to remain sexually faithful in marriage. Moreover, these rules reduce the power that married and unmarried women have in relationship to men; in this way, these rules make women more susceptible to male demands for sexual fidelity than they might be under conditions of economic equality and physical safety.

Legal rules reduce the economic power of women in relationship to men by maintaining inferior employment opportunities for women in the wage market. At the same time, legal rules make marriage a potential source of income for marital partners, by means of spousal support and property provisions that require economically dominant spouses to share what they have with their partners. In addition, alimony rules sometimes permit economically subordinate spouses to continue to receive support even after their marriages have formally ended. Government benefit rules also structure marriage as an economic enterprise, through rules that provide retirement, death, and disability benefits to the spouses of wage earners.

By structuring marriage as a significant source of financial support, legal rules make marriage a plausible substitute—or supplement—to wage market work for both sexes. However, as a result of their inferior position in the wage market—a position legal rules sustain—women are likely to be more financially dependent on marriage than men. This condition affects the responses they might otherwise have to the lax enforcement of the rules against fornication and adultery. Legal rules induce women to marry, and to stay married, for financial reasons. Even though fornication rules are not stringently enforced, wage market and marital economic benefit rules provide women financial incentives to comply with them. Moreover, married women who are economically dependent on their husbands have economic incentives to have sex only with their husbands. Despite the lax enforcement of anti-adultery rules, the wage market and marital benefit rules function to make divorce financially risky for many women; complying with anti-adultery rules enables them to avoid giving their husbands a legal reason for divorce. By inducing some women to marry and to avoid divorce for financial reasons, wage market and marital economic rules reinforce the impact on women of rules that formally restrict sex to marriage.

The legal rules that regulate social violence reduce women's power in relationship to men because they enhance the significance of the cultural convention that a woman is more likely to be verbally or physically attacked if she is alone or in the company of other women than if she is with an individual man. By ineffectively enforcing legal rules governing rape, sexual assault, and other violent crimes against the person, the social violence rule system places women in physical jeopardy. Women can sometimes mitigate the impact of these circumstances by relying on individual men for protection against violence. To the extent that these rule-enforcement practices provide women with a safety incentive to marry and to stay married, the social violence rule system reinforces anti-fornication and anti-adultery rules that penalize nonmonogamous sexual practices.

By reducing the power of women in relationship to men, the wage market rule system and the social violence rule system provide financial and safety incentives for women to defer to their sexual partners in determining the conditions of intimacy. If their partners value sexual monogamy—an ethic, as we have seen, that legal rules help form—then women are likely to comply with their partners' demands for fidelity. Legal rules make women less inclined to resist such demands than they might be in different circumstances. Legal rules also diminish the ability of women to demand fidelity of intimate partners who are unwilling to give up sexual promiscuity.

I have argued thus far that—by inducing women to marry, by discouraging them from having affairs, and by creating economic and physical conditions that help their sexual partners to impose monogamy on them if they want to—legal rules discourage women from having sex with more than one man. The legal model of female sexual monogamy also gives some women incentives to be more sexually active than they would otherwise be. Sex workers and women who want to be celibate are examples of women whom the sexual monogamy rule system induces into sexual activity.

The legal rules that devalue "women's work" in the wage market make prostitution—like marriage—a significant economic alternative or supplement to wage market labor. Moreover, the rules against prostitution, like the rules against fornication and adultery, are not stringently enforced. Legal rules thus provide de facto protection for prostitution; they enable prostitution to function as a safety valve against the constraints of sexual monogamy. Even though anti-prostitution rules are notoriously enforced more systematically against female sex workers than against male customers, legal rules induce some women to violate the criminal rules against prostitution by making sex work more lucrative than legitimate wage labor.

Legal rules also coerce some sex workers into having more sex than they might otherwise want to by inadequately protecting them from customer abuse, which can include unwanted sex. In addition, legal rules do not protect sex workers against the demands pimps may make of them for sexual activity. Since sex workers are induced to affiliate with pimps in order to defend themselves against customers and in order to broker their way through the criminal justice system when they are caught up in it, legal rules and law enforcement practices are complicit in imposing more sex on these women than they might have if their work were not illegal and if it were physically safe.

The sexuality of women who want to practice celibacy may not be affected by the rules prohibiting bigamy, fornication, adultery, and prostitution. However, by creating economic and safety incentives for women to marry, legal rules encourage some women to abandon celibacy in favor of marriage. Since legal rules in most states provide that refusal to have sex within marriage constitutes grounds for divorce, legal rules inhibit women who marry because of economic or safety incentives from practicing celibacy within marriage.

Legal rules also create economic and safety incentives for women to sacrifice celibacy in order to have sex with men to whom they are not married. In addition to encouraging women to turn to men for physical protection, legal rules reduce women's ability to pay their own way; the wage market treatment of women makes it hard for them to go "dutch treat." These physical and financial pressures encourage unmarried women to yield to the sexual demands of escorts or companions they have turned to—at least in part—for protection against abuse from other men.

Although men and women are both subject to the rules that directly penalize or specifically require sexual monogamy, I have argued that the legal rules establishing the economic and physical circumstances in which women and men have sex encourage women to be more sexually monogamous than men. This sex-based difference in the impact of legal rules on monogamous conduct also has an effect on the character of heterosexual relations. To put this point more bluntly, these rules not only encourage a "double standard" of sexual conduct for women and men; they also enable men to have greater control over the terms of heterosexual intimacy—they give men more power over women in sex. This is one of the ways that legal rules encourage passivity as a model of female sexual conduct.

Women are induced to choose men rather than women as sexual partners—to comply with heterosexuality as the model for female sexual conduct—by legal rules that prohibit sodomy and other sexual acts between individuals of the same sex. Although the criminal rules penalizing homosexual conduct—like the sexual monogamy rules—are not vigorously enforced, decisional law defines marriage as a heterosexual union. Women who might expect that sexual relationships with other women could

[to be completed by:

economic and security incentives which make a male partner more advantageous for nonsexual reasons than a same-sex partner for women.

rules and procedures establishing passivity norm, which include the marital rape exemption, economic and security incentives for doing what your guy wants, and the lax enforcement of prostitution laws, which induce economically or physically dependent women to let men have their way sexually in order to avoid losing their protectors to illegal sexual competition.]

NOTES AND QUESTIONS

1. *Postmodern Feminism.* Mary Joe Frug's work provides an example of the postmodernist approach to women's bodies. Postmodernism rejects the naturalization of gender differences, as well as the quest for gender neutrality. These theorists focus instead on social and cultural forces, such as law, that construct gender. They adopt a more fluid and complex view of gender identity that grapples with the dilemma inherent in recognizing both the commonalities and the differences among women. Eschewing fixed definitions of feminity and masculinity, postmodern feminists embrace the multiple meanings and tensions at play in these categories.

In *Protofeminism and Antifeminism,* French feminist Christine Delphy uses the example of women's periods to demonstrate two cultural interventions into women's experience of their bodies: (1) the devaluation of women's bodies and physiology, and (2) the material handicap created by the social conditions. Delphy writes:

> The two are obviously linked. It is even easier for society to devalue the flow of blood—the fact of being female—if all women can verify that it really is a handicap to have a period. Conversely, it is even easier for society to impose these conditions as inevitable once women are convinced that periods— the fact of being female—are a natural misfortune. It is in the interests of society to hide the fact that periods are not a natural phenomenon but a constructed phenomenon. In this situation, ideology—the interpretation of the phenomenon— plays an important part. It is internalized and reappears among those involved under the guise of *strongly felt shame.* But this ideological aspect is absolutely inseparable from the material part. The two are continually and necessarily part of

one another. To hide one's sanitary towels is at first an external constraint; it gives rise to subjective shame; and finally, in a third phase, the hiding appears to be the *expression* of the shame which in fact caused it.

Women in devaluing their periods are not only obeying their brain-washing; not only "adopting masculine values". We are also reacting, and in a healthy (non-masochistic) way, to a real handicap. However, when we devalue our periods as such—as a physical phenomenon—in addition to depreciating ourselves, we accept the ideological version: that the handicap is natural and not social. The struggle thus consists in separating and distinguishing elements which are distinct but which the society confounds.

But if we do not analyse what is social, what is *constraining,* in the phenomenon currently experienced by all women under the name of "periods", we are playing society's game. Because (if one does not make allowance for the social) it is impossible to feel proud of something which is *actually* unpleasant; to value periods. In addition, if it *were* possible, it would lead, in so far as conditions were unchanged, to our "accepting" the handicap—as society asks us to; and all arguments which lead us better to accept social constraints are dangerous, and can never ever be styled "liberating".

This is why the "revaluation of women's bodies", without further specification, is an extremely ambiguous project. On the one hand it can mean a struggle against the actual handicap—which is the necessary conditions for the revaluation of the natural function. It is only once it is materially revalued that it can become subjectively experienced as positive. And the fight to change attitudes is itself only positive on the condition that it changes something concrete in women's lives: that it leads into a struggle against the constraints imposed on our bodies.

On the other hand, "revaluation" can mean the *abandonment* of this struggle. It can go in the same direction as the ideology. The latter says that all the dissatisfactions women experience are due to a refusal of themselves, of their bodies. The "revaluation" undertaken by psychoanalysis, by the feminine press in France, and by Margaret Mead (among others) is destined to make us swallow the social handicap in the same mouthful as the physical phenomenon. That mouthful verges on masochism. It leads to women being made to accept that to love themselves is to love suffering.

"Self-acceptance" as a value is not neutral. It addresses itself only to female individuals, and it is of recent origin. It appeared at precisely the time when feminism was born, as a new ideological weapon to make women accept their submission. Thus "valuation" or "revaluation" of womanhood should be very closely examined. It can go in two directly opposite directions. A new version of the dominant ideology can be camouflaged under the guise of "liberation". The term "self-acceptance" is also suspect because of the problem of what it is "to accept oneself". What is the "self" one accepts? In so far as the "self" is taken without question, is equated with the historical person (albeit the historical aspect is not mentioned and is thus implicitly denied—the historical individual being considered as a natural person), this is an ahistoric and reactionary notion. . . .

From Toril Moi, *French Feminist Thought* 90–95 (1987). How does this approach compare to that of Robin West or Andrea Dworkin?

2. While feminist scholars tend to focus either on women's sexuality or their reproductive capacity, Frug demonstrates that the sexualization, maternalization, and terrorization of women's bodies are connected. Do you find this a helpful way to analyze legal regulation of women's bodies? Does Frug's description of the maternalization of women's bodies neglect the devaluation of women of color and lesbians as mothers discussed in Section A or does it accommodate such differences among women?

3. Frug argues that laws governing marriage reinforce the sexualization of women's bodies by promoting sexual monogamy. But if these rules also restrict men, how do they give men greater power over women? How would women benefit from the elimination of laws that promote sexual monogamy?

4. Frug believed that postmodern feminism supported strategies for ending women's subordination that differed from those proposed by radical and cultural feminists. Does the postmodernist view suggest that relatively modest, discrete legal changes might bring about a palpable improvement in the way women know themselves and are known? In contrast, the vision of true womanhood which West describes and Dworkin assumes might only be released by a profound transformation in current social structures. Which view do you think is more realistic?

bell hooks, Ending Female Sexual Oppression

From b. hooks, Feminist Theory: From Margin to Center
(Boston: South End Press, 1984).

During the early stages of contemporary feminist movement women's liberation was often equated with sexual liberation. On the cover of Germaine Greer's *The Female Eunuch* (one of the most widely read feminist works in the seventies) the book is described as "the ultimate word on sexual freedom." On the back cover, Greer is described as "a woman with a sense of humor who is proud of her sexuality." Feminist thinkers, like Greer, believed that assertion of the primacy of sexuality would be a liberatory gesture. They urged women to initiate sexual advances, to enjoy sex, to experiment with new relationships, to be sexually "free." Yet most women did not have the leisure, the mobility, the contacts, or even the desire to indulge in this so called "sexual liberation." Young heterosexual women, single and childless, teenagers and college students, political progressives, were the groups most eager and able to pattern their sexual behavior after what was essentially an inversion of the male notion of sexual liberation. Advocating genuine sexual liberty was positive, and women learned from experience that the freedom to initiate sexual relationships, to be non-monogamous, to experiment with group sex, sexualized sado-masochism, etc., could sometimes be exciting and pleasurable; it did not, however, deconstruct the power relations between men and women in the sexual sphere. Many women felt disillusioned with the idea of sexual liberation. While some participants in feminist circles continued to emphasize the importance of sexual freedom, rejecting the idea that it should be patterned after a male model, a larger contingent, heterosexual and lesbian, began to denounce the idea of sexual freedom, and even sexual contact with men, because they felt women were still exploited by the old sexual paradigms. Increasingly, these feminists came to see male sexuality as disgusting and necessarily exploitive of women. . . .

The focus on "sexual liberation" has always carried with it the assumption that the goal of such effort is to make it possible for individuals to engage in more and/or better sexual activity. Yet one aspect of sexual norms that many people find oppressive is the assumption that one "should" be engaged in sexual activity. This "should" is one expression of sexual coercion. Advocates of sexual liberation often imply that any individual who is not concerned about the quality of their experience or exercising greater sexual freedom is mentally disturbed or sexually repressed. When primary emphasis is placed on ending sexual oppression rather than on sexual liberation it is possible to envision a society in which it is as much an expression of sexual freedom to choose not to participate in sexual activity as it is to choose to participate.

Sexual norms as they are currently socially constructed have always privileged active sexual expression over sexual desire. To act sexually is deemed natural, normal—to not act, unnatural, abnormal. Such thinking corresponds with sexist role patterning. Men are socialized to act sexually, women to not act (or to simply react to male sexual advances). Women's liberationists' insistence that women should be sexually active as a gesture of liberation helped free female sexuality from the restraints imposed upon it by repressive double standards, but it did not remove the stigma attached to sexual inactivity. Until that stigma is removed, women and men will not feel free to participate in sexual activity when they desire. They will continue to respond to coercion, either the sexist coercion that pushes young men to act sexually to prove their "masculinity" (i.e., their heterosexuality) or the sexual coercion that compels young women to respond to such advances to prove their "femininity" (i.e., their willingness to be heterosexual sex objects). The removal of the social stigma attached to sexual inactivity would amount to a change in sexual norms. It would have many positive implications for women and men, especially teenagers who are at this historical moment most likely to be victimized by sexist sexual norms. Recent focus on sex between heterosexual teenagers indicates coercion remains a central motivation for participation in sexual activity. Girls "do it for the boy" as one seventeen year old daughter told her mother (quoted in Ellen Goodman's essay "The Turmoil of Teenage Sexuality") and boys do it to prove to other boys that they are heterosexual and that they can exert "masculine" power over girls.

Feminist movement to eradicate heterosexism—compulsory heterosexuality—is central to efforts to end sexual oppression. In the introduction to *No Turning Back: Lesbian And Gay Liberation for the* 80'S, Geere Goodman, George Lakey, Judy Lakey, and Erika Thorne define heterosexism as the:

> suppression and denial of homosexuality with the assumption that everyone is or should be heterosexual and, second, a belief in the inherent superiority of the dominant-male/passive-female role pattern. Heterosexism results in compulsory heterosexuality which cripples the free expression and mutually supportive relationships of heterosexuals as well as of lesbians and gay men.

Within the feminist movement lesbian women have worked hardest to call attention to the struggle to end heterosexist oppression. Lesbians have been on both sides of the larger sexual liberation debate. They have shown many heterosexual women that their prejudices against lesbians support and perpetuate compulsory heterosexuality. They have also shown women that we can find emotional and mutual sexual fulfillment in relationships with one another. Some lesbians have suggested that homosexuality may be the most direct expression of pro-sex politics, since it is unconnected to procreation. Feminist movement to end female sexual oppression is linked to lesbian liberation. The struggle to end prejudice, exploitation, and oppression of lesbians and gay men is a crucial feminist agenda. It is a necessary component of the movement to end female sexual oppression. Affirming lesbianism, women of varied sexual preferences resist the perpetuation of compulsory heterosexuality.

Throughout feminist movement, there has been a tendency to make the struggle to end sexual oppression a competition: heterosexuality versus lesbianism. Early in the movement, attempts to exclude and silence lesbians were justified through the specter of a "lavender menace." Later, lesbianism was presented as a choice that would eliminate the need to deal with issues of heterosexual conflict or as the most politically correct choice for a feminist woman. Even though many feminists acknowledge that fighting sexual oppression, particularly male domination of women, is not the same as man-hating, within feminist gatherings and organizations intense anti-male sentiments are sometimes expressed by heterosexual women and lesbians alike, and women who are not lesbians, who may or may not be in relationships with men feel that they are not "real" feminists. This is especially true of women who may support feminism but who do not publicly support lesbian rights. It is often forgotten that we are all in the process of developing radical political consciousness, that it is a "process," and that it defeats efforts to build solidarity to condemn or judge women politically incorrect when they do not immediately support all the issues we deem relevant.

The suggestion that the truly feminist woman is lesbian (made by heterosexuals and lesbians alike) sets up another sexual standard by which women are to be judged and found wanting. Although it is not common for women in the feminist movement to state that women should be lesbian the message is transmitted via discussions of heterosexuality that suggest all genital contact between women and men is rape, that the woman who is emotionally and sexually committed to an individual man is necessarily incapable of loyal woman-identified political commitment. . . .

Feminist activists must take care that our legitimate critiques of heterosexism are not attacks on heterosexual *practice*. As feminists, we must confront those women who do in fact believe that women with heterosexual preferences are either traitors or likely to be anti-lesbian. Condemnation of heterosexual practice has led women who desire sexual relationships with men to feel they cannot participate in feminist movement. They have gotten the message that to be "truly" feminist is not to be heterosexual. It is easy to confuse support for non-oppressive heterosexual practice with the belief in heterosexism. For example, responding to a statement in *Ain't I A Woman,* "attacking heterosexuality does little to strengthen the self-concept of the masses of women who desire to be with men," lesbian feminist Cheryl Clarke writes in an essay, "The Failure to Transform: Homophobia in the Black Community":

> . . . Hooks delivers a backhanded slap at lesbian feminists, a considerable number of whom are black. Hooks would have done well to attack the institution of heterosexuality, as it is a prime cause of black women's oppression in American . . .

Clearly Clarke misunderstands and misinterprets my point. I made no reference to heterosexism and it is the equation of heterosexual practice with heterosexism that makes it appear that Clarke is attacking the practice itself and not only heterosexism. My point is that feminism will never appeal to a mass-based group of women in our society who are heterosexual if they think that they will be looked down upon or seen as doing something wrong. My comment was not intended to reflect in any way on lesbians because they are not the only group of feminists who criticize and in some cases condemn all heterosexual practice.

Just as feminist movement to end sexual oppression should create a social climate in which lesbians and gay men are no longer oppressed, a climate in which their sexual choices are affirmed, it should also create a climate in which heterosexual practice is freed from the constraints of heterosexism and can also be affirmed. One of the practical reasons for doing this is the recognition that the advancement of feminism as a political movement depends on the involvement of masses of women, a vast majority of whom are heterosexual. As long as feminist women (be they celibate, lesbian, heterosexual, etc.) condemn male sexuality, and by extension women who are involved sexually with men, feminist movement is undermined. Useless and unnecessary divisions are created. Concurrently, as long as any pro-heterosexuality statement is read as a hidden attack upon homosexuality we continue to perpetuate the idea that these are, and should be, competing sexualities. It is possible to delineate the positive or negative aspects of lesbianism without referring in any way to heterosexuality and vice versa. Although Ellen Willis does not, in her essay, discuss the notion that lesbianism is a more politically correct sexual choice for feminist women, or that this represents yet another attempt to impose on women a sexual standard, her comments about neo-Victorian logic apply to attacks on female sexual contact with men:

> Neo–Victorians have also undermined feminist opposition to the right, by equating feminism with their own sexual attitudes, in effect reading out of the movement any woman who disagrees with them. Since their notion of proper feminist sexuality echoes conventional moral judgments and the anti-sexual propaganda presently coming from the right their guilt-mongering has been quite effective. Many feminists who are aware that their sexual feelings contradict the neo-Victorian ideal have lapsed into confused and apologetic silence. No doubt there are also thousands of women who have quietly concluded that if this ideal is feminism, then feminism has nothing to do with them. The result is widespread apathy, dishonesty, and profound disunity in a movement faced with a determined enemy that is threatening its very existence.

A feminist movement that aims to eliminate sexist oppression, and in that context sexual oppression, cannot ignore or dismiss the choice women make to be heterosexual. Despite heterosexism, many women have acknowledged and accepted that they do not have to be heterosexual (that there are other options) and have chosen to be exclusively or primarily heterosexual. Their choices should be respected. By choosing they exercise sexual freedom. Their choices may not, as those who oppose them suggest, be influenced by heterosexual privilege. Most heterosexual privilege is diminished when compared to the degree of exploitation and oppression a woman is likely to encounter in most heterosexual relationships. There are exceptions. Many women choose to be heterosexual because they enjoy genital contact with individual men. Feminist movement has enriched and added new dimensions to lesbian sexuality and there is no reason it cannot do the same for heterosexuality. Women with heterosexual preferences need to know that feminism is a political movement that does not negate their choices even as it offers a framework to challenge and oppose male sexual exploitation of women.

There are some feminists (and I am one) who believe that feminist movement to end sexual oppression will not change destructive sexual norms if individuals are taught that they must choose between competing sexualities (the most obvious being heterosexuality and homosexuality) and conform to the expectations of the chosen norm. Sexual desire has varied and multiple dimensions and is rarely as "exclusive" as any norm would suggest. A liberatory sexuality would not teach women to see their bodies as accessible to all men, or to all women for that matter. It would favor instead a sexuality that is open or closed based on the nature of individual interaction. . . .

A shift that will undoubtedly emerge as the struggle to end sexual oppression progresses will be decreased obsession with sexuality. This does not necessarily mean that there will be decreased sexual activity. It means that sexuality will no longer have the importance attributed to it in a society that sexuality for the express purposes of maintaining gender inequality, male domination, consumerism, and the sexual frustration and unhappiness that deflects attention away from the need to make social revolution. As Stephen Heath comments:

> The real problem and task is always one of social revolution. Privileging the sexual has nothing necessarily liberating about it at all; indeed, it functions only too easily as an instance by development of and reference to which society guarantees its order outside of any effective process of transformation, produces precisely a containing area and ideology of "revolution" or "liberation."

Feminist efforts to develop a political theory of sexuality must continue if sexist oppression is to be eliminated. Yet we must keep in mind that the struggle to end sexual oppression is only one component of a larger struggle to transform society and establish a new social order.

NOTES AND QUESTIONS

1. **Heterosexism v. Heterosexual Practice**. What is the difference between heterosexism and heterosexual practice, and why is this distinction so important? What does it mean to critique heterosexism without attacking heterosexual practice, as hooks advocates?

2. **The Multiplicity of Sexual Desire**. Noting that sexual desire is varied, hooks criticizes the feminist imposition of a norm for sexual behavior. In *Pleasure And Danger*, Carole Vance similarly emphasizes the multiplicity of sexual desire and advocates a shift in focus to women's sexual pleasure:

> The tension between sexual danger and sexual pleasure is a powerful one in women's lives. Sexuality is simultaneously a domain of restriction, repression, and danger as well as a domain of exploration, pleasure, and agency. To focus only on pleasure and gratification ignores the patriarchal structure in which women act, yet to speak only of sexual violence and oppression ignores women's experience with sexual agency and choice and unwittingly increases the sexual terror and despair in which women live. . . .
>
> What directions might a feminist politics on sex take in the future? Above all, feminism must be a movement that speaks to sexuality, that does not forfeit the field to reactionary

groups who are more than willing to speak. We cannot be cowardly, pretending that feminism is not sexually radical. Being a sex radical at this time, as at most, is less a matter of what you do, and more a matter of what you are willing to think, entertain, and question.

Feminism must, of course, continue to work for material changes that support women's autonomy, including social justice, economic equality, and reproductive choice. At the same time, feminism must speak to sexuality as a site of oppression, not only the oppression of male violence, brutality, and coercion which it has already spoken about eloquently and effectively, but also the repression of female desire that comes from ignorance, invisibility, and fear. Feminism must put forward a politics that resists deprivation and supports pleasure. It must understand pleasure as life-affirming, empowering, desirous of human connection and the future, and not fear it as destructive, enfeebling, or corrupt. Feminism must speak to sexual pleasure as a fundamental right, which cannot be put off to a better or easier time. It must understand that the women to whom it speaks, and those it hopes to reach, care deeply about sexual pleasure and displeasure in their daily lives; that sexuality is a site of struggle—visceral, engaging, riveting—and not a domain of interest only to a narrow, small, and privileged group.

Feminism should encourage women to resist not only coercion and victimization, but also sexual ignorance, deprivation and fear of difference. Feminism should support women's experiments and analyses, encouraging the acquisition of knowledge. We can begin by examining our own experience, sharing it with each other, knowing that in sexuality as in the rest of social life, our adventures, risks, impulses, and terrors provide clues to the future. Feminism must insist that women are sexual subjects, sexual actors, sexual agents; that our histories are complex and instructive; that our experience is not a blank, nor a mere repetition of what has been said about us, and that the pleasure we have experienced is as much a guide to future action as the brutality.

Carole S. Vance, *Pleasure And Danger: Toward a Politics of Sexuality*, in *Pleasure and Danger* 1 (Carole S. Vance, ed., 2d ed. 1992).

3. **Beyond Sexuality**. Although bell hooks endorses the feminist struggle to end sexual oppression, she also suggests the limitations of a feminist project that seeks only women's sexual liberation. In what ways does hooks expand the feminist struggle for a just society beyond that suggested by other authors?

4. **Communities of Color**. Feminist scholars and activists from communities of color have criticized the mainstream women's movement not only

for its essentialism but also for its oppositional stance in relation to men. They have pointed out that alliances with men have historically been important to minority women's struggle against racial injustice. Moreover, the men in these groups do not share the patriarchal power held by white men in our society.

This solidarity with men highlights the importance of redefining maleness as well as femaleness in egalitarian terms. In an essay that complements the one excerpted above, bell hooks challenges the stereotypical assumption that all Black men aspire to the white patriarchal norm of masculinity and calls for a reexamination of Black sex roles, and particularly the role of men in Black life. She argues further that a crucial part of the Black liberation struggle must be the feminist reconstruction of Black masculinity:

> If black men and women take seriously Malcolm's charge that we must work for our liberation by "any means necessary," then we must be willing to explore the way feminism as a critique of sexism, as a movement to end sexism and sexist oppression, could aid our struggle to be self-determining. Collectively we can break the life-threatening choke-hold patriarchal masculinity imposes on black men and create life sustaining visions of a reconstructed black masculinity that can provide black men ways to save their lives and the lives of their brothers and sisters in struggle.

bell hooks, *Reconstructing Black Masculinity* in *Black Looks: Race and Representation* 87, 113 (1992).

5. **Unity**. However important postmodernist and anti-essentialist descriptions such those of Harris, Frug and hooks seem, together they appear to threaten the logic and effectiveness of the feminist legal project. Some critics of postmodernism argue that the pursuit of multiplicity makes it difficult to unify women to take a common political stand against oppression. Does postmodern feminism permit opposition to the subordination of women as a group? Do women have commonalities which can constitute the basis for legal reform, or don't they? How can the answer to this question be, as postmodern feminists imply, both yes and no?

Elizabeth Iglesias, Rape, Race, and Representation: The Power of Discourse, Discourses of Power, and the Reconstruction of Heterosexuality

49 Vand. L. Rev. 869 (1996).

IMAGES OF WOMEN: THE POLITICAL PATHOLOGIES OF ENACTING A FEMININE IDENTITY

Feminists have long recognized that the dominant images of women represent us as mother, virgin, or whore. Indeed, many feminists have linked violence against women to the ways in which these images circulate in cultural narratives and the psychic structures of individual men and women. Some feminists argue that the male impulse to dominate women stems from the lost security of the mother. Others argue that the sexual exploitation of women is organized around the virgin/whore dichotomy. This dichotomy suggests that men act properly as long as they target the whore and respect the virgin. Rather than focus on the differences between these images, it is important to note that their common characteristic is a complete failure to convey any sense of the passion that sustains an intimate sexual relationship between persons who are mutually admired and desired. The mother and the virgin are completely asexual, while the whore is an appropriate target for sexual exploitation and the wife for sexual appropriation.

In this Part, I explore the images of mother that circulate in the psychoanalytic discourses of both white feminists and the predominantly white, upper-middle-class men's movement. I then investigate how these images are used to explain the interpersonal practices (like rape) and the cultural narratives of sexual identity (like pornographic masculinity and commodified femininity) that repress women's sexual autonomy, and compare them to the images of mother that circulate in Black and Latin culture. There are two points to this comparison.

First, the images of mother in Black and Latin culture are not only very different from the images of mother in white American culture. They are also very different from the images of motherhood that circulate in white discourses about Black and Latin mothers. In many of these accounts, the Black and Latin mother's culturally recognized power to direct her children and run her home is translated through the lens of white racism and patriarchal misogyny into the image of the castrating matriarch, thereby reinscribing the delusion that male power depends on female powerlessness. By contrast, Black and Latin culture offer images of motherhood that challenge the idea that men are men only if they control and subordinate women. The interpersonal practices found in the matrifocal extended family of Black and Latin culture offer women a wide variety of psycho-social resources that are simply ignored in the various discourses that portray these families as failed versions of the white, male-headed nuclear family.

The second reason for this comparison is to provide an initial point of reference for interrogating the family model underlying the psychoanalytic theories deployed in the discourses of white feminism and the white men's movement. White feminists have articulated a powerful theoretical framework for understanding the interpersonal practices and cultural narratives through which men repress female sexual autonomy as a reaction against the psychological impact of being "mothered" as infants exclusively by women.

While white feminists have used these psychoanalytic narratives of sexual dominance, along with their images of mother and mothering, to encourage social changes that promote their vision of increased female autonomy, antifeminists and racists have used these same psychoanalytic narratives to attack women's autonomy by deploying negative images of maternal power. These attacks are calculated to pressure women into abdicating any significant power as mothers and to abandon any claimed right to direct our own lives or our children's. At the same time, these images of mother are used to exonerate male abuse and sexual violence, blaming the practices of pornographic masculinity on maternal dominance.

Comparing the images of mother and maternal power that circulate in Black and Latin culture is one way to combat both dynamics by revealing the class, racial, and cultural contingencies of the family model underlying the misogynist anti-mother discourses of white feminism and the white men's movement. By creating a rhetorical framework that attacks mothers as much for their power as for their powerlessness, these anti-mother discourses reinforce the anti-feminist, racist forces that attack public policies designed to help women as mothers. These attacks emphasize the fact that these policies subsidize maternal independence from a dominant male figure who is needed to counterbalance the Overwhelmingly Feminine environment created by maternal power and to provide the stability and security which most women cannot provide (except at public expense). . . .

Images of the White Mother: Powerless and Overpowering

In the discourses of white feminism and of the white men's movement, the white mother frequently appears as the passive, self-less, subordinate mother, a well-meaning woman who is nevertheless too weak to give her children the direction and security they need to develop self-confident and other-affirming identities. Alternatively, the white mother appears as the overbearing, invasive, devouring mother, who inflicts the primordial wound of humiliation on her boy-hero and her girl-princess. White women write, for example, of the "fear of becoming [their] mothers," of the way "the tradition of the mothers . . . produces the consciously articulated struggle of the daughters, albeit in conflict, anger and pain," of their "rage at the sex-role socialization, sexual repression and loss of self-boundaries that their connection with their mothers has produced in them," of the daughter's "resistance to love and tenderness, and her horror at sexuality," which emerge from her earliest realizations that "the inevitable path via love and sex to motherhood involves loss of pride [and] loss of control." According to Gloria Joseph and Jill Lewis:

> There is a first-level anger at the mother for seemingly not having struggled enough, not having demanded and refused more. This anger is painfully linked, in the absence of consciously articulated messages about oppression of women, with the daughter's realization that her imagining of her mother as someone who was limitless clashes with a reality of someone who seems to have "chosen" limits.

If some white women feel betrayed by their mothers' weakness, white men (at least those who speak through the men's movement) hate them for their power. Douglas Gillette, for example, explains male fear of intimacy as an artifact of the coping mechanisms through which men try to protect themselves from what he calls "The Overwhelming Feminine." In his account, male violence and emotional withdrawal are simply variations of the different strategies men "adopted as boys for coping with what feels to them like the invasive and overwhelming powerful feminine." These men were raised in a hostile feminine environment, in which their mothers acted out their "own fears of mistreatment or abandonment by the masculine, and even more primordially, by [their] own mother," by attacking their sons. These attacks might take different forms, ranging from "subtle attempts to undermine her son's masculine pride and exuberance to rageful displays of jealousy when he begins to date." The white mother's power appears, in this account, as a dangerous threat to her son's masculinity and his prospects for developing positive heterosexual relations. . . .

It may be that men suffer from "terrible isolation and loneliness," and it may be that they find it "difficult to respond to the needs and wants of others . . . because [they] can so easily discount their own emotional needs and wants." Nevertheless many feminists have felt "that the emphasis on emotional expression and development" associated with the men's movement and its most articulate spokesmen, "was sidestepping important issues, and was potentially self-indulgent and self-exonerating." Rather than excusing men's sexual oppression of women, the emotional emptiness and isolation that ensue from the lies men live simply appear as the product of the practices through which men maintain their dominance. Lying, emotional withdrawal, and sexual dominance may be experienced internally as strategic self-preservation, perhaps even from some "Overwhelming Feminine," but they operate externally as mechanisms of control. . . .

Lies, violence, and emotional withdrawal mean that some men are never constructively engaged in distinguishing between legitimate and illegitimate claims women make upon them. All claims inconsistent with a man's own objectives and desires are perceived and coded as a threat to his masculinity. In this way, these men constitute themselves as victims of an overpowering, castrating force, even as they thereby abdicate any responsibility to assist, nurture, or respond to the legitimate claims of women. This construction of the claims made upon him allows a man to hide from himself (and anyone who believes his lies) the fundamental selfishness in his relations to the women in his life, a selfishness expressed sexually through dominance or impotence.

From this perspective, lying, withdrawal, and violence are all different faces of the Stoltenberg "mind-fuck," tactics through which these men appropriate women's sexuality even as they avoid any personal responsibility to respond to women's needs and desires. The image of the Overwhelming Feminine allows them to blame their selfishness on their mothers, if not on their women. In short, the problem with the Overwhelming Feminine theory of male emotional withdrawal, deception, and sexual exploitation is that the reason men cannot renounce these practices may have less to do with their mothers and more to do with their own determination to distort and suppress any interaction that might require them to take risks or make sacrifices for women.

At the same time, these images of mothers as both weak and over-whelming are played against the narratives of "the good mother," that is, of the white, middle-class mother, the sweet, well-meaning, loving woman who importantly is attached to and dependent upon a male sexual partner (preferably her husband). These narratives of the good (but dependent) mother code the struggle for economic autonomy, independence, and self-realization of any woman who refuses motherhood or any mother who insists on maintaining "a full life for herself outside the home" as selfish neglect of her children. By contrast, the white, middle-class father is absolved of any similar obligations.

The material impact on women's lives when they acquiesce in this double standard and allow their choices to be driven by the psycho-social pressures of "the good mother" narratives is, at least in the discourses of white feminism, economic subordination, increased dependence, and great-er vulnerability to their male partners. The image of "the good mother"—attached to and dependent upon a dominant male figure—also plays into the anti-welfare rhetoric that keeps poor mothers poor and thereby increas-es their sexual vulnerability to individual men. Cumulatively, these narra-tives help construct a society in which women's sexual vulnerability is continually reproduced by the interpersonal practices, legal institutions, and public policies through which our sexuality is repeatedly assaulted and suppressed.

Mothers in Matrifocal Perspective: Powerful and Oppressed

This Section explores the images of mother in Black and Latin culture. These images reflect common elements that are directly attributable to the fact that, in both cultures, motherhood is experienced as the central element in a matrifocal network of extended familial relations. Drawing on the key elements of Stanley Kurtz's brilliant re-reading of psychoanalytic theory as applied to Hindu childrearing practices, I argue that matrifocal extended families have more potential for constructing a subject-to-subject heterosexuality than the male-headed nuclear families that are so popular in white, American patriarchy. These images of motherhood—of maternal power and agency—offer more empowering identities for women, even as the daily experience of extended family interdependence provides the building blocks for developing unappropriating sexual relationships. Moth-erhood does not have to involve the elimination of effective agency, nor is it necessary for sexual intimacy to include the abdication of sexual autonomy. Motherhood is currently experienced this way because of the legal doc-trines, public policies, and cultural narratives through which women's maternal identity and sexual autonomy are socially constructed.

In a fascinating study of "matrifocality" in Indonesia, Africa, and Black America, Nancy Tanner uses cross-cultural analysis to criticize the biased understanding of matrifocality in Black American culture. Daniel Patrick Moynihan invoked this biased understanding in a 1965 federal government report entitled The Negro Family: The Case for National Action. The report used highly inconclusive census material to posit the "breakdown of the Negro family" and attributed this breakdown, along with low school performance and higher arrest and welfare rates among nonwhites, to the prevalence of matriarchy in Black families.

Tanner notes the ethnocentrism and sexism embedded in this report, stating that it "a priori assumes that there is no distinctive Black American kinship system, and that whatever there is, is an imperfect and disorganized variant of the white middle-class family system." By way of contrast, Tanner notes the central role Black women play in Black families, a role described in Joyce Ladner's study of young Black women:

> The strongest conception of womanhood that exists among all preadult females is that of how the woman has to take a strong role in the family.... All of these girls had been exposed to women who played central roles in their households.... The symbol of the resourceful woman becomes an influential model in their lives.... In sum, women were expected to be strong, and parents socialized their daughters with this intention.

According to Tanner, Ladner's work illustrates the positive cultural factors underlying the central position of Black women in the Black American family. There is a clear expectation that a woman should be a strong, resourceful mother with a structurally central position. This image of female agency and maternal centrality is, according to Tanner, a basic and positive feature of the Black American kinship system, in which there are extended and flexible kinship networks. Male and female children are equally socialized to be active, resourceful, and assertive, and women's family roles have a special importance. Through these relationships, women offer each other solidarity, childcare, and other assistance, often sharing common residences and resources. ...

From this perspective, Moynihan's attack on Black matriarchy is little more than an ethnocentric "scholarly legitimization of a popular (and of course racist) stereotype of the Black man as somehow less a man because the Black woman is a strong and resourceful woman." Nevertheless, this counterpositioning of female power and male powerlessness deflects attention from the racist practices through which racially subordinated men are denied economic and educational opportunities and are subjected to discriminatory discipline by state officials such as police officers and public school officials. This perspective deploys sexist stereotypes that attempt to make male power depend on female powerlessness, rather than acknowledging the extent to which racial equality depends upon increased economic and educational opportunities for both men and women.

In Latin culture, the image of the mother shares similar characteristics and resonates power: cualquiera es padre, pero madre solo hay una. For example, in a fascinating account of the narratives of masculinity and femininity that circulate in Colombia and the Caribbean, Peter Wade writes:

The most central concept of femininity ... sees women as a stable force. In the Pacific region, for example, the mother is symbolized as the guayacan de esquina, a house corner post made from a very hard and durable tropical wood which supports the whole structure of the house.

Penelope Harvey strikes a similar theme in her ethnographic study of sex and violence in the Southern Peruvian Andes:

Images of motherhood are strong, positive and pervasive and present women as those who are most able to form close bonds with their children and take responsibility for them and the immediate environment in which they are raised. A woman shows her love for a man by having his children and bringing them up. It is motherhood that confers adult status and motherhood that places women firmly in a world of sexual differentiation and complementary agency.

To be sure, patriarchal relations are embedded in these maternal images of agency and power. They invite women to assume, as mothers, the substantial burdens and personal sacrifices involved in providing such stability. The image of mother as a stable force creates a space that diffuses the negative consequences of the man's lack of parental responsibility. Paternal irresponsibility, if not affirmatively condoned by the image of maternal stability and responsibility, is nevertheless rendered less threatening in cases where the mother as a stable force is an available image. Indeed, the conservative hysteria over white feminism, with its emphasis on increasing women's freedom from domestic responsibilities, is a reaction that presupposes that men cannot, will not, or should not assume any significant responsibility for making the home a stable, nurturing environment for children.

The Latin image of maternal strength and reliability suppresses the practices through which women enact an alternative identity of the woman as individual: the Western, capitalist, economic free agent. The positive value associated with this Latin image of mother comes at the expense of individual independence or, more precisely, at the expense of individual freedom from the obligation to respond to the needs of children, husbands, and other dependents. Nevertheless, the difference between the Latin images of mother and the dominant images of the white mother are explained by the fact that lack of individual freedom (even from gendered obligations) is not the same as lack of power, autonomy, or agency. As Penelope Harvey writes of Latin culture in the Peruvian Andes,

As mothers, women are responsible for the running of the home, and to be worthy of respect a woman must show herself to be hard-working in this regard. Men are not expected to display aptitude or interest in the day-to-day maintenance tasks such as serving food or cooking. This ability in women is thus seen as something worthy of respect.... A lively clever woman will represent the interests of her household behind the scenes in informal networks and in the subtle manipulation of the man over whom she has some influence. An ideal woman is quick-witted (*viva*), hard-working (*trabajadora*), tender (*carinosa*) and attractive (*simpatica*)—a quality which combines physical and moral attributes. There is no ideal of passive receptive femininity. A bad woman is one who is not effective because she is lazy (*floja*), stupid (*sonsa*), or uses her abilities for anti-social purposes (*mala*).

Given these narratives, Latin children do not experience the Latin mother's lack of freedom from gendered obligations the same way the white mother appears coded in white feminist and psychoanalytic theory. Put differently, the mother's lack of agency and subjectivity independent from the superior authority of an otherwise absent father is a decidedly white, Anglo image. Indeed, many Latin daughters and sons grow up believing their mothers will have the final way, if not the final word. . . .

Many Latin mothers are further empowered by relations of female solidarity. Like the images of Black mothers, and unlike the images of white, middle-class mothers, Latin mothers enjoy the support of other women, thereby increasing their authority and the felt legitimacy of the power they exercise in the home. . . .

The important point is that these cultural differences create a context in which Latin children tend to view maternal power quite differently from the images projected in the psychoanalytic accounts of white motherhood. In sharp contrast to the fear some white men express of being absorbed and infantilized by maternal pampering, Latin boys, like their fathers, are routinely catered to in the home, in part, because Latin images of masculinity make male domestic labor a cultural taboo and, in part, because no Latin mother wants to raise her son to be a wimp.

Cross-cultural analyses of matrifocal kinship relations suggest that strong and positive mother/child bonds are staple features of matrifocal family structures and are formed in relation to both daughters and sons. In Latin culture, this bond is formed through the culturally pervasive practices of celebrating children, indulging their childhood, and protecting their innocence. It is commonplace for Latin children to express deep love and respect for the mothers who raised them. As adults, Latin sons continue to "respect and revere their mothers, even when they may not show much respect for their wives or other women. As adolescents they may have protected their mothers from their fathers' abuse or indifference. As adults they accord their mothers a respect that no other woman deserves, thus following their fathers' steps."

Latin daughters are raised to identify with their mothers. Moreover, while daughters are encouraged and indeed compelled to serve their fathers and brothers, the psycho-social meaning of that service is ambiguously situated at the intersection of two competing discourses. As entitlements of male supremacy, these services reinforce male superiority, but, as evidence of male dependence on female capabilities, the domestic services Latin women provide men are invested with an element of female superiority not conveyed in any accounts of the white family. As a result, the Latin woman often indulges, but she does not expect to depend upon the male whom she is raised to believe is emotionally and psychologically undependable. . . . .

The most distinctive features of matrifocal family arrangements—that is, the value placed upon maternal authority and extended family interdependence—make the matrifocal extended family a more fruitful starting point for the formation of subject-to-subject heterosexuality than the male-headed nuclear family. This is, initially, because the experience of being raised by strong maternal figures in an extended family offers a perspective from which the child's identity formation does not depend upon individuation from a devalued feminine so much as integration into a broader group in which the feminine is still present and powerful. The second perspective focuses on the strategies that encourage the child to relinquish his self-centeredness in order to participate more fully in the relations of reciprocal assistance and renunciation that sustain the family.

Read against the narratives of mainstream psychoanalytic theory, the child-rearing practices used to promote individual self-renunciation and group integration in Latin extended families offer better building blocks for nonappropriating heterosexual relationships in American society. The ever-present possibility of replacing familial interdependence with an individualistic marked-mediated independence creates a space in which extended family relationships can be experienced as an affirmative choice. These freely chosen practices of self-renunciation and multiple interdependence may, in turn, help the individual recode erotic love in nonpossessory terms.

Images of Female Sexuality: In and Beyond the Virgin/Whore Dichotomy

Read as narratives of heterosexuality, the virgin/whore polarities are images of female sexual identity that encourage men and women to enact a variety of familiar scripts. In Latin culture, these narratives are even more pervasive and the dichotomy more rigid than in white, Anglo culture. This is true largely because of the profound influence of Catholicism, which emphasizes the importance of virginity for all unmarried women. The narratives organized around this dichotomy support social practices that destroy female heterosexual autonomy and threaten women who dare express nonmarital sexual desire.

An example of the operation of the dichotomy is the pervasive male practice of preying on women, particularly virgins. Getting to them before anyone else does purportedly makes men more macho, a practice which is then invoked to legitimate and explain the necessity for imposing strict restrictions on young women's freedom. Indeed, these narratives simultaneously reflect and reproduce a cultural environment where any nonmarital sex is coded as the vehicle through which women are degraded (and degrade themselves), even in the eyes of their lovers.

The mutual incompatibility of a sexual identity structure that codes masculinity as the aggressive pursuit of sex and femininity as an equally active rejection of sex feeds the culture of rape and sexual domination. Because women must always say no, even when they really want to say yes, men must take the initiative and overcome the no that really means yes.

Indeed, Latin popular culture routinely codes rape as the means of last resort in a man's desperate and frustrated attempts to express true love.

The popularity of these rape dramas can only be understood as a response to the ubiquity of the virgin/whore dichotomy. The logic of this dichotomy—in which mutual and consensual sex automatically makes women into whores—means that complicity in enacting the scripted narratives of a rape, or seduction, becomes the only acceptable vehicle through which women can enjoy otherwise immoral sex without incurring moral blame or dishonor, while men enjoy ego gratification from enacting the subject position of overwhelming sexual prowess. For many Latin women, the virgin/whore dichotomy means that sexual intimacy, at least outside (and at times even within) the bonds of holy matrimony, is only possible at the cost of reinscribing narratives of male sexual dominance and female lack of sexual agency or desire. The costs to women can be staggering.

Practices that define female sexuality as submission to male sexual prowess can blur the line between sexual domination and sexual intercourse for both men and for women. While women know when we have been raped, we often do not know what to do about it, particularly in ongoing relationships where the lines between interpersonal connectedness and individual autonomy are constantly renegotiated. When female sexuality is enacted as submission to male sexual desire—a defensive position Latin women may take to avoid occupying the whore side of the dichotomy—this line-drawing becomes even more complicated because interpersonal intimacy depends upon the woman's abdication of sexual autonomy. A woman's subsequent assertions of autonomy are consequently seen as a direct threat to interpersonal intimacy that must be reestablished through enforced submission. Accordingly, the woman's resistance increasingly loses its significance each time she capitulates. To the extent this dynamic of sexual dominance and submission is driven by the specter of the virgin/whore dichotomy, female sexual autonomy depends on shattering its cultural power. The image and narratives of the sacred prostitute, as presented in the discourse of Jungian analytical psychology, offer an alternative discursive regime that could advance this struggle.

Read through Jungian psychoanalytic theory, the virgin/whore dichotomy and the narratives it supports project impoverished archetypal images of women. Jung believed that every man [and woman] carries within him [or herself] the eternal image of woman, not the image of this or that particular woman, but a definite feminine image. This image is fundamentally an unconscious hereditary factor of primordial origin and is engraved on the living system of man, an imprint or "archetype" of all the ancestral experiences of the female.

This image of woman is the individual's anima. It is the feminine side of the psyche, which organizes the way individual men and women think about actual women as well as the way they feel about those aspects of their own selves which they identify as feminine.

In a provocative historical account and psychoanalytic analysis of the sacred prostitute, Nancy Qualls–Corbett develops a thesis that connects the practices of male sexual dominance and impotence to the internalization of impoverished images of femininity or, more specifically, of an anima that suppresses the unity of spirituality and sexuality, leaving only the split-image feminine that is inscribed within the virgin/whore dichotomy. This split-image is expressed by men in relations of sexual domination in which female sexuality is simply an instrument for a superficial and narcissistic self-gratification. The woman becomes the man's whore-object, to be used on demand. Alternatively, men may express this split-image feminine in relations of sexual impotence in which female sexuality is repudiated. Here the woman becomes the inner-boy's mother/wife, to be sexually suppressed and avoided. Women also internalize the split-image feminine, which degrades female sexuality, expressing it in the extremes of self-destructive promiscuity and other-destructive sexual refusal.

In Qualls–Corbett's account, the sacred prostitute is presented as a feminine image, which "while not synonymous with an anima" is nevertheless "relevant to every stage of development of man's [or woman's] inner woman." She is the image in which the feminine "offers pleasure, excitement and vitality, a personification of both spirituality and earthiness. She is a lover whose beauty is exciting, whose virginal nature brings forth new life and leads to Wisdom—which is more than simply intellect." Rather than reading the sacred prostitute as an archetype or analyzing it as a psychological phenomenon, I read it as an alternative narrative of feminine sexual identity in order to re-examine the male/female relations inscribed within the virgin/whore dichotomy. . . .

In the temples of the goddess of love, "the sacred prostitute's primary offering to the goddess was her welcoming of the stranger. . . . Intercourse with her was a regeneration through the mystery of sex. . . . The flesh and the spirit were united, each supporting each other." This "sacred marriage" is an archetypal motif that is manifested on three levels: interpersonally when there exists a deep, abiding love between two people; intrapersonally when the opposition of masculine/feminine is reconciled at the intrapsychic level—the psyche integrates its contrasexual side; and transpersonally when the physical union becomes the vehicle through which the experience of divine love is received and contained within the self.

According to Qualls–Corbett, heterosexual "dis-ease," expressed actively in the practices of male sexual dominance and passively through male sexual impotence, is the fruit of the patriarchal degradation of female sexuality and feminine beauty. This is a degradation expressed in and through the virgin/whore dichotomy. As Carl Jung noted:

> The overwhelming majority of men on the present cultural level never advance beyond the maternal significance of woman, and this is the reason why the anima [the internal feminine image men project onto women] seldom develops beyond the infantile, primitive level of the prostitute. Consequently prostitution is one of the main by-products of civilized marriage.

This degradation is directly related to the cultural ascendance of the virgin/whore dichotomy, which was the singular contribution of Christianity.

On the one hand, the feminine was untouchable because it was elevated to the extreme heavenly heights; on the other it was debased as wicked and vile. The image of the sacred prostitute, simultaneously deeply spiritual and joyfully sexual, was completely unviable. . . .

The romantic love ideologies transcend the sexual—and offer no resolution to the dichotomy of the incompatible images which judge and condemn women's enactment of sexual freedom while fetishizing their sexuality. Emotion is emphasized and sexuality is represented in a mist. The emotions that are encouraged emphasize abandonment, loss of self, the pleasure of being uncontrollably overwhelmed by the male presence and redefining your whole world in terms of him. It is a celebrating of powerlessness. The pleasure is in the giving up of power and autonomy to become a part of what is made to appear as the "natural universality"—the male centered unit.

Put differently, romantic love is the feminine side of sexual desire because the expression of raw sexual desire makes women too vulnerable to male sexual aggression, precisely to the extent they have not progressed beyond the virgin/whore dichotomy.

By contrast, the symbolic images of the goddess of love and her human expression in the sacred prostitute project a sense of feminine beauty that links sexual desire to the experience of reverence. These images express the unity of sexuality and spirituality. . . .

According to Qualls–Corbett, the lost image of the sacred prostitute, which unifies sexuality and spirituality, produces a compulsive need for control in both men and women. If sex is not an act of reverence and joy, then it is an act of domination and consumption. Internalizing the image of the goddess, however, can help women escape the equally destructive polarities of promiscuity and sexual withdrawal. Through this image, the woman grows to appreciate the spiritual dimensions of feminine sexuality and develops the integrity that enables her to be both true to herself and affirming of others. . . .

The image of the goddess of passion is also an aspect of the man's anima, the internal feminine image that would lead a man to value those aspects of himself that make erotic spirituality possible and protect him from an obsession with masculinity. For men, the image of the goddess offers the narrative elements necessary to establish reverence and respect for, rather than fear and resentment of, the power of feminine sexuality. . . .

The ritual practice of sacred prostitution offers numerous counternarratives through which this hostile male posture toward feminine sexual beauty can be understood. This hostility is not an expression of genuine sexual longing. Rather it is a symptomatic frustration inherent in the posture of appropriation, a posture in which men seek to acquire and control anything and everything they value for themselves. The image of the goddess of love projects an image of feminine sexual beauty that cannot be appropriated by individual men. Men are able to enjoy the beauty of the goddess through the experience of sexual intercourse with her sacred prostitute. Yet even then the stranger's access to the human woman is neither permanent nor exclusive.

The ritualized intercourse between the stranger and the sacred prostitute codes sexual longing and fulfillment as non-possessory and transpersonal. Neither the male nor the female can acquire the other through sex. The narrative elements of the ritual instruct men to enjoy and revere the sexual energy and sensations they have through their experience of women's sexuality, without feeling entitled to appropriate or compelled to degrade the individual women who trigger these sensations. The fact that men cannot always get what they want does not mean that they are not men. It simply means that women are not to be had. In these narratives, sexual ecstasy is the nonappropriable gift of the goddess, and the sexual beauty of the human woman is a further instance of her divine manifestation. . . .

In discussing the images of women and the missing image of the sacred prostitute, my point is not to suggest that a critique of culturally dominant images of female sexuality is enough to change the dynamics of a misogynistic heterosexuality. On the contrary, the use of alternative feminine images has the most transformative potential precisely at the point where the material empowerment of women proves to be insufficient. The fact that sacred prostitutes were, in ancient times, accorded social status and education speaks to the material reality underlying the rituals of sacred prostitution.

Thus, the sacred prostitute's freedom to enact the ritual intercourse with any particular man was profoundly connected to the human woman's material independence from that man, as well as to the social honor that her status as the goddess's medium afforded her. By contrast, under conditions of social and political subordination to men as well as economic and interpersonal dependence upon men, women cannot change the dynamics of heterosexual relationships simply by internalizing the image of the sacred prostitute or by enacting the narratives of feminine sexuality that are related to her image. These narratives can, however, help women define the kinds of relationships and personal autonomy that are worth the wanting and the struggle. The first and foremost elements of this autonomy are the freedom to love the men who honor and respect our sexuality, the power to reject the ones who do not, and, through this autonomy, the ability to shatter the power of the virgin/whore dichotomy.

As counter-narratives, these images provide important conceptual and rhetorical devices for combating the anti-feminist forces that use the virgin/whore dichotomy to attack women's search for sexual fulfillment and personal autonomy. Public policies, legal doctrines, and law enforcement practices that enforce women's economic dependence and define our sexual morality in terms of whether or not we belong to some particular man deprive women of the material and psycho-social equality that would enable us to express the spontaneous, joyful, and nonappropriating sexuality of the sacred prostitute. The circulation of these alternative images might help create the conditions under which we could express our sexuality without fear of rape, harassment, or other forms of coercion through which men attempt to appropriate our sexuality for themselves.

Sue–Ellen Case, Toward a Butch–Femme Aesthetic

From L. Hart, Making A Spectacle: Feminist Essays on Contemporary Women's Theatre
(Ann Arbor: University of Michigan Press, 1989).

In the 1980s, feminist criticism has focused increasingly on the subject position: both in the explorations for the creation of a female subject position and the deconstruction of the inherited subject position that is marked with masculinist functions and history. Within this focus, the problematics of women inhabiting the traditional subject position have been sketched out, the possibilities of a new heterogeneous, heteronomous position have been explored, and a desire for a collective subject has been articulated. While this project is primarily a critical one, concerned with language and symbolic structures, philosophic assumptions, and psychoanalytic narratives, it also implicates the social issues of class, race, and sexuality. Teresa de Lauretis's article "The Technology of Gender" reviews the recent excavations of the subject position in terms of ideology, noting that much of the work on the subject, derived from Foucault and Althusser, denies both agency and gender to the subject. In fact, many critics leveled a similar criticism against Foucault in a recent conference on postmodernism, noting that while his studies seem to unravel the web of ideology, they suggest no subject position outside the ideology, nor do they construct a subject who has the agency to change ideology. In other words, note de Lauretis and others, most of the work on the subject position has only revealed the way in which the subject is trapped within ideology and thus provides no programs for change.

For feminists, changing this condition must be a priority. The common appellation of this bound subject has been the "female subject," signifying a biological, sexual difference, inscribed by dominant cultural practices. De Lauretis names her subject (one capable of change and of changing conditions) the feminist subject, one who is "at the same time inside and outside the ideology of gender, and conscious of being so, conscious of that pull, that division, that doubled vision". De Lauretis ascribes a sense of self-determination at the micropolitical level to the feminist subject. This feminist subject, unlike the female one, can be outside of ideology, can find self-determination, can change. This is an urgent goal for the feminist activist/theorist. Near the conclusion of her article (true to the newer rules of composition), de Lauretis begins to develop her thesis: that the previous work on the female subject, assumes, but leaves unwritten, a heterosexual context for the subject and this is the cause for her continuing entrapment. Because she is still perceived in terms of men and not within the context of other women, the subject in heterosexuality cannot become capable of ideological change.

De Lauretis's conclusion is my starting place. Focusing on the feminist subject, endowed with the agency for political change, located among women, outside the ideology of sexual difference, and thus the social institution of heterosexuality, it would appear that the lesbian roles of butch and femme, as a dynamic duo, offer precisely the strong subject position the movement requires. Now, in order for the butch-femme roles to clearly emerge within this sociotheoretical project, several tasks must be accomplished: the lesbian subject of feminist theory would have to come out of the closet, the basic discourse or style of camp for the lesbian butch-femme positions would have to be clarified, and an understanding of the function of roles in the homosexual lifestyle would need to be developed, particularly in relation to the historical class and racial relations embedded in such a project. Finally, once these tasks have been completed, the performance practice, both on and off the stage, may be studied as that of a feminist subject, both inside and outside ideology, with the power to self-determine her role and her conditions on the micropolitical level. Within this schema, the butch-femme couple inhabit the subject position togeth-er—"you can't have one without the other," as the song says. The two roles never appear as . . . discrete. The combo butch-femme as subject is reminiscent of Monique Wittig's "j/e" or coupled self in her novel *The Lesbian Body*. These are not split subjects, suffering the torments of dominant ideology. They are coupled ones that do not impale themselves on the poles of sexual difference or metaphysical values, but constantly seduce the sign system, through flirtation and inconstancy into the light fondle of artifice, replacing the Lacanian slash with a lesbian bar.

However, before all of this *jouissance* can be enjoyed, it is first necessary to bring the lesbian subject out of the closet of feminist history. The initial step in that process is to trace historically how the lesbian has been assigned to the role of the skeleton in the closet of feminism; in this case, specifically the lesbian who relates to her cultural roots by identifying with traditional butch-femme role-playing. First, regard the feminist genu-flection of the 1980s—the catechism of "working-class-women-of-color" feminist theorists feel impelled to invoke at the outset of their research. What's wrong with this picture? It does not include the lesbian position. In fact, the isolation of the social dynamics of race and class successfully relegates sexual preference to an attendant position, so that even if the lesbian were to appear, she would be as a bridesmaid and never the bride. Several factors are responsible for this ghosting of the lesbian subject: the first is the growth of moralistic projects restricting the production of sexual fiction or fantasy through the anti-pornography crusade. This crusade has produced an alliance between those working on social feminist issues and right-wing homophobic, born-again men and women who also support censorship. This alliance in the electorate, which aids in producing enough votes for an ordinance, requires the closeting of lesbians for the so-called greater cause. . . .

So the lesbian butch-femme tradition went into the feminist closet. Yet the closet, or the bars, with their hothouse atmosphere have produced what, in combination with the butch-femme couple, may provide the liberation of the feminist subject—the discourse of camp. ...

The closet has given us camp—the style, the discourse, the *mise en scène* of butch-femme roles. In his history of the development of gay camp, Michael Bronski describes the liberative work of late-nineteenth-century authors such as Oscar Wilde in creating the homosexual camp liberation from the rule of naturalism, or realism. Within his argument, Bronski describes naturalism and realism as strategies that tried to save fiction from the accusation of day-dream, imagination, or masturbation and to affix a utilitarian goal to literary production—that of teaching morals. In contrast, Bronski quotes the newspaper *Fag Rag* on the functioning of camp: "We've broken down the rules that are used for validating the difference between real/true and unreal/false. The controlling agents of the status quo may know the power of lies; dissident subcultures, however, are closer to knowing their value". Camp both articulates the lives of homosexuals through the obtuse tone of irony and inscribes their oppression with the same device. Likewise, it eradicates the ruling powers of heterosexist realist modes. ...

Camp style, gay-identified dressing and the articulation of the social realities of homosexuality have also become part of the straight, postmodern canon, as Herbert Blau articulated it in a special issue of *Salmagundi:* "becoming homosexual is part of the paraphilia of the postmodern, not only a new sexual politics but the reification of all politics, supersubtilized beyond the unnegotiable demands of the sixties, from which it is derived, into a more persuasive rhetoric of unsublimated desire". Within this critical community, the perception of recognizable homosexuals can also inspire broader visions of the operation of social codes. Blau states: "there soon came pullulating toward me at high prancing amphetamined pitch something like the end of Empire or like the screaming remains of the return of the repressed—pearl-white, vinyl, in polo pants and scarf—an englistered and giggling outburst of resplendent queer ... what was there to consent to and who could possibly legitimate that galloping specter I had seen, pure ideolect, whose plunging and lungless soundings were a full-throttled forecast of much weirder things to come?" Initially, these borrowings seem benign and even inviting to the homosexual theorist. Contemporary theory seems to open the closet door to invite the queer to come out, transformed as a new, postmodern subject, or even to invite straights to come into the closet, out of the roar of dominant discourse. The danger incurred in moving gay politics into such heterosexual contexts is in only slowly discovering that the strategies and perspectives of homosexual realities and discourse may be locked inside a homophobic "concentration camp." Certain of these authors, such as Blau, even introduce homosexual characters and their subversions into arguments that conclude with explicit homophobia. ...

Here, the sirens of sublation may be found in the critical maneuvers of heterosexual feminist critics who metaphorize butch-femme roles, transvestites and campy dressers into a "subject who masquerades," as they put it, or is "carnivalesque" or even, as some are so bold to say, who "cross-dresses." Even when these borrowings are nested in more benign contexts than Blau's, they evacuate the historical, butch-femme couples' sense of masquerade and cross-dressing the way a cigar-store Indian evacuates the historical dress and behavior of the Native American. As is often the case, illustrated by the cigar-store Indian, these symbols may only proliferate when the social reality has been successfully obliterated and the identity has become the private property of the dominant class. . . .

[What theory] can be employed to understand the construction of the butch-femme subject on the stage? First, how might they be constructed as characters? Perhaps the best example of some workings of this potential is in Split Britches' production of *Beauty and the Beast.* The title itself connotes the butch-femme couple: Shaw as the butch becomes the Beast who actively pursues the femme, while Weaver as the excessive femme becomes Beauty. Within the dominant system of representation, Shaw, as butch Beast, portrays a bestial women who actively love other women. The portrayal is faithful to the historical situation of the butch role, as Nestle describes it: "None of the butch women I was with, and this included a passing woman, ever presented themselves to me as men; they did announce themselves as tabooed women who were willing to identify their passion for other women by wearing clothes that symbolized the taking of responsibility. Part of this responsibility was sexual expertise . . . this courage to feel comfortable with arousing another woman became a political act". In other words, the butch, who represents by her clothing the desire for other women, becomes the beast—the marked taboo against lesbianism dressed up in the clothes of that desire. Beauty is the desired one and the one who aims her desirability at the butch.

This symbolism becomes explicit when Shaw and Weaver interrupt the Beauty/Beast narrative to deliver a duologue about the history of their own personal butch-femme roles. Weaver uses the trope of having wished she was Katharine Hepburn and casting another woman as Spencer Tracy, while Shaw relates that she thought she was James Dean. The identification with movie idols is part of the camp assimilation of dominant culture. It serves multiple purposes: (1) they do not identify these butch-femme roles with "real" people, or literal images of gender, but with fictionalized ones, thus underscoring the masquerade; (2) the history of their desire, or their search for a sexual partner becomes a series of masks, or identities that stand for sexual attraction in the culture, thus distancing them from the "play" of seduction as it is outlined by social mores; (3) the association with movies makes narrative fiction part of the strategy as well as characters. This final fiction as fiction allows Weaver and Shaw to slip easily from one narrative to another, to yet another, unbound by through-lines, plot structure, or a stable sense of character because they are fictional at their core in the camp style and through the butch-femme roles. The instability and alienation of character and plot is compounded with their own personal butch-femme play on the street, as a recognizable couple in the lower East Side scene, as well as within fugitive narratives on-stage, erasing the difference between theatre and real life, or actor and character, obliterating any kind of essentialist ontology behind the play. This allows them to create a play with scenes that move easily from the narrative of beauty and the beast, to the duologue on their butch-femme history, to a recitation from *Macbeth,* to a solo lip-synced to Perry Como. The butch-femme roles at the center of their ongoing personalities move masquerade to the base of performance and no narrative net can catch them or hold them, as they wriggle into a variety of characters and plots.

This exciting multiplicity of roles and narratives signals the potency of their agency. Somehow the actor overcomes any text, yet the actor herself is a fiction and her social self is one as well. Shaw makes a joke out of suturing to any particular role or narrative form when she dies, as the beast. Immediately after dying, she gets up to tell the audience not to believe in such cheap tricks. Dies. Tells the audience that Ronald Reagan pulled the same trick when he was shot—tells them that was not worth the suturing either. Dies. Asks for a Republican doctor. Dies. Then rises to seemingly close the production by kissing Weaver. Yet even this final butch-femme tableau is followed by a song to the audience that undercuts the performance itself. . . .

What, then, is the action played between these two roles? It is what Jean Baudrillard terms *séduction* and it yields many of its social fruits. Baudrillard begins his argument in *De la séduction,* by asserting that seduction is never of the natural order, but always operates as a sign, or artifice. By extension, this suggests that butch-femme seduction is always located in semiosis. The kiss, as Shaw and Weaver demonstrate in their swooping image of it, positioned at its most clichéd niche at the end of the narrative, is always the high camp kiss. Again, Baudrillard: seduction doesn't "recuperate the autonomy of the body . . . truth . . . the sovereignty of this seduction is transsexual, not bisexual, destroying all sexual organization. . . ." The point is not to conflict reality with another reality, but to abandon the notion of reality through roles and their seductive atmosphere and lightly manipulate appearances. Surely, this is the atmosphere of camp, permeating the *mise en scène* with "pure" artifice. In other words, a strategy of appearances replaces a claim to truth. Thus, butch-femme roles evade the notion of "the female body" as it predominates in feminist theory, dragging along its Freudian baggage and scopophilic transubstantiation. These roles are played in signs themselves and not in ontologies. Seduction, as a dramatic action, transforms all of these seeming realities into semiotic play. . . .[B]utch-femme roles offer a hypersimulation of woman as she is defined by the Freudian system and the phallocracy that institutes its social rule. . . .

In recuperating the space of seduction, the butch-femme couple can, through their own agency, move through a field of symbols, like tiptoeing through the two lips (as Irigaray would have us believe), playfully inhabiting the camp space of irony and wit, free from biological determinism, elitist essentialism, and the heterosexist cleavage of sexual difference. Surely, here is a couple the feminist subject might perceive as useful to join.

NOTES AND QUESTIONS

1. **Minority Mothers**. How does the matrifocal family of Black and Latin culture challenge both the negative images of women of color and the dominant notion of motherhood? Do you find Iglesias's discussion of Black and Latina mothers helpful in imagining a liberated feminine identity? Does Iglesias suggest, as Frug does, that the maternalization of the female body is as important as its sexualization in defining feminine identity? What does the examination of minority mothers add to Frug's analysis?

2. **The Sacred Prostitute**. Iglesias devotes as much attention to images of female sexuality. How are her analyses of sexuality and motherhood related? How does the image of the sacred prostitute contest both the virgin/whore dichotomy and the romantic love ideology? Do you find the sacred prostitute helpful in imagining a liberated identity?

3. **Role Playing**. Postmodernists like Sue–Ellen Case have appealed to the role playing that takes place in theater to describe the contradictions in postmodern female theory and to explore what a non-essentialist female identity might feel like. An actress who is playing Lady Macbeth on stage is simultaneously herself, Lady Macbeth, and herself-in-the-role-of-Lady Macbeth. While she is on stage, each of these identities is as real and authentic as the others, not only to herself, but to other actors and to spectators. Do you find Sue–Ellen Case's use of role playing in a lesbian theater act helpful in imagining a self-determining female (or feminist) subject? In what ways is the butch-femme couple one which "the feminist subject might perceive as useful to join"? Is it necessary to escape the heterosexual context in order to find the strong feminist subject?

4. **Loving as Resistance**. Both Iglesias and Case, as well as postmodernist authors included in other sections, suggest the embrace of degraded identities as a means of liberation. While Judith Butler uses Nella Larson's novel *Passing* to explore the relationship between sexual and racial regulation, bell hooks uses it to explore the radical potential of "loving blackness" as a tool of political resistance. Hooks offers her students in a course on Black women writers this interpretation of Clare's act of passing as white:

> When I suggested to the class (which had been more eager to discuss the desire of black folks to be white) that Clare . . . is the only character in the novel who truly desires "blackness" and that it is this desire that leads to her murder, no one responded. Clare boldly declares that she would rather live for the rest of her life as a poor black woman in Harlem than as a rich white matron downtown. I asked the class to consider the possibility that to love blackness is dangerous in a white supremacist culture—so threatening, so serious a breach in the fabric of the social order, that death is the punishment. It became painfully obvious by the lack

of response that this group of diverse students (many of them black people) were more interested in discussing the desire of black folks to be white, indeed were fixated on this issue. So much so, that they could not even take seriously a critical discussion about "loving blackness."

bell hooks, *Loving Blackness as Political Resistance* in *Black Looks: Race and Representation* 9, 9 (1992).

Are we more fascinated with the theme of self-hatred than self-love? Is it easier to discuss the social devaluation of certain identities than the radical potential of embracing those identities?

D. PROSTITUTION

INTRODUCTION

The legal status of prostitution as the unlawful sale of sex is determined by statutes that criminalize specific commercial sex practices and by decisional law that renders contracts for the sale of sexual services unenforceable. But the institution of prostitution also acquires its particular character by the operation of many other law-related factors. In addition to the random, demeaning and sometimes brutal practices that often typify the criminal enforcement of anti-prostitution laws, the legal system is biased against prostitutes in a number of ways. This section concerns the legal treatment of female prostitution, as such treatment is broadly defined.

A second theme of this section, which also recurs in the sections on pornography and rape, is the role of law in protecting, inhibiting, and constructing women's bodies and the character of female sexuality. Although these materials are particularly concerned with how the legal regulation of prostitution affects women who are sex workers, they also consider the effect of this regulation on other women as well.

The readings begin with pieces that describe the institution of sex work. The Judy Edelstein article, which is written by a sex worker about her experiences on one night in a massage parlor, is frank and explicit in its depiction of the author's sexual experiences. We have included this piece because it evokes empathy for sex workers, an empathy which influences both the abolitionist position and the "anti-radical" or postmodernist attitude toward sex work. The Alexander and Barry selections describe more generally the character of prostitution, its internal politics, and its legal treatment. Regina Austin's essay, about a lawsuit filed by a Black woman whose photograph was used in a television broadcast about prostitution, challenges both the racialized image of prostitutes and the boundaries that divide women who express their sexuality in different ways.

The readings continue with arguments and discussion regarding criminalization and other forms of regulation of prostitution. They conclude with a chapter concerning the movement for sex workers' rights, as well as a postmodernist proposal to use prostitutes' rights discourse to reclaim the label "whore."

One of the goals in constructing these materials is to consider not only *whether* decriminalization of prostitution should occur, but *how*. Several of the pieces in this section suggest that if decriminalization is not accompanied by changes in other legally supported structures that create, sustain and degrade sex work, the lives of prostitutes may not be significantly different from what they are today. What legal assistance then, if any, should be extended to support prostitutes in their work? Alternatively, what legal strategies, if any, should be pursued in order to prevent women from participating in prostitution?

The commentators represented here all support the decriminalization of prostitution, but they are divided on the complicated question of how decriminalized prostitution should be regulated. Gail Pheterson, co-director of ICPR (International Committee for Prostitutes' Rights) advocates expanded legal protection and support for sex work, while Kathleen Barry advocates reform efforts that would undermine the sex work industry. As in other sections, the division here represents an important conflict in feminist critique regarding the capacity women have for sexual autonomy in our current social circumstances. Radical feminists are sympathetic to the plight of prostitutes, but their conviction that women are defined as women by their sexual subordination makes them judge prostitutes to be women who are particularly in need of extrication from, rather than support for, their work. In contrast, feminists who hold a postmodernist position are more likely to believe that sex workers, like other women, can be the agents as well as the victims of their sexual experiences. Supporting the oppositional struggle of sex workers to improve their work situation, therefore, may reinforce—or even enhance—their feelings of subjectivity, of agency, and of power.

The conviction that unites all of the feminists whose work appears in this section—the conviction that prostitution should be decriminalized, in order to alleviate the dehumanized, brutal, and unequal treatment of prostitutes by the legal system—is obviously not widely shared. Prostitution is outlawed in every state in the United States except Nevada, and although several national and international organizations have formed around the issue of sex work, prostitution reform does not have a prominent place on the feminist agenda. The lack of public support for prostitution reform is not surprising. The marginalized and degraded character of prostitution tends to render the condition of sex workers invisible, unfamiliar, or—at worst—morally repugnant. In addition, public antipathy or apathy regarding the plight of sex workers may be correlated with the significant role prostitution plays in designating sexual deviance. Because prostitution-related laws play a significant part in constructing the character of all women's sexuality, rallying to improve the lot of prostitutes would destabilize the social consensus regarding "normal" womanhood, a radical consequence that many would find objectionable.

The relationship between the regulation of prostitution and the sexual practices of women who are not sex workers can be illustrated by an example of the multiple uses made of words relating to prostitution. In common parlance "whore" is also used to belittle an unmarried, sexually active women; a lesbian; a women of color; a gay male; a feminized man; or a woman whose sexual conduct or personal appearance does not conform to "good girl" standards. This familiar extension of the literal (law-related) definition of the word "whore" indicates how prostitution functions as one of the mechanisms that define the contours of socially approved, legitimate sexual conduct. If prostitution reform causes the word "whore" to lose some of its degrading, critical connotation, one of the tools for patrolling "legitimate" sexual expression will be blunted.

Prostitution reform has a particularly radical potential for changing the meaning of female sexuality. The concern among the commentators in this section to extend the feminist agenda to prostitution represents, then, a united and serious opposition to the stereotyped meaning of womanhood traditionally privileged by law and other cultural structures. And yet the differences among these commentators suggest a conflict among them about the meaning of non-stereotyped womanhood.

Judy Edelstein, In the Massage Parlor

From F. Delacoste and P. Alexander, Sex Work
(Pittsburgh: *Cleis Press*, 1987).

The customer looks like the all-American football player type. He's young, middle-aged, blonde, broad-shouldered, and muscular. It turns out he's an executive for a lumber company. He's the guy who's supposed to represent the company's concern for ecology.

While I work on him, he talks at me. He claims that his company really cares about the environment. They're planting new trees, etc. the whole spiel. "And what are you going to do," he asks, "if the average American housewife wants colored toilet paper? We try to sell her on white, but we have to give the housewife what she wants."

After I've thumped and kneaded him all over, I start oiling his all-American sized prick. He clamps one of his muscular arms around me and pulls me closer to him.

Pretty soon he leaves behind his lumber company personality. "Let me eat you," he begs, "just for a little bit."

"I don't do that," I say. I keep on stroking up and down on his prick.

But he keeps on asking me, and finally I can't take it anymore. I'm ready to do just about anything to get him off. "Okay," I say, "just for a minute."

So I take off my skirt and underpants and lie down on the table. He stands against the table, leaning over me, and starts to lick me. He's moaning and growling and biting me a little, being too rough. I think about stopping him, but instead I lay back and try to relax. All of a sudden I come.

I stop him from eating me and just lay there for a minute. He's still standing over me, and after a little bit, he starts to put his prick inside of me. I move away from him. "Lay back down on the table and I'll finish you off," I say.

So he gets back on the table, and I jerk him off some more, and finally he comes.

Afterwards I'm sitting in one of the empty massage rooms with the muzak turned off, feeling kind of shaky. I just can't believe that I had an orgasm with that jerk. I try to forget him, to think about making love with Laura, the woman I'm with right now. But all I can see is the customer's all-American face. . . .

No customers have come in yet this evening, so I'm sitting in the turned-off sauna, just thinking.

When I first started working here, I knew I'd have to jack off the guys. But I thought I could deal with that. As my friend Kate, who works in another massage parlor, puts it, "It's just like pulling a toe." And pretty good pay for that. A hell of a lot better than typing or waitressing. Plus, I would have a chance to learn to do massage.

So I started working here, pretty naive. The first time a guy tried to feel up my breasts, I got really angry and wouldn't let him. So he got angry, too, and never came back.

Another time a repulsive old guy wanted to eat me. He kept offering more and more money, finally offered me two hundred bucks, but I still wouldn't let him. I even told him that money couldn't buy everything. He must have thought I was nuts.

Pretty soon I wised up. I figured I wasn't working here for my health. So the next time a guy tried to feel me up, I let him. That way he left me a nice tip and asked for me again.

Now I let most customers feel me up some. I've learned not to be there when they touch me. When they touch my breasts, I tell myself they're not really touching me.

For another five or ten bucks I sometimes do the massage topless or bottomless. What the hell, I figure, I might as well. But I can't bring myself to do blow jobs or let them screw me. Even though I'd make more money, I just don't want to do that. It turns my stomach too much.

Mostly the job is okay. I try not to let the guys get to me. And I go home afterwards and try to forget about it all. But sometimes I get scared. I think of the guy's hands all over me. I think about some stranger sucking on my breasts. And sometimes I wonder how I can let the men do that. I wonder what there is left for me. I wonder where *I* am. . . .

It's mid-evening, a pretty busy time, and I'm working on a new customer. We don't have him listed in our card file, and none of the other massage parlors I call know him either. So I'm being cautious with him, trying to size him up, trying to decide whether he might be a cop.

We talk for a while. I ask him what he does, is he married, all the standard questions. He says he's single and he works for United Grocers. It all sounds good, but I'm just not sure about this guy. So I figure I won't give him the hand finish.

I ask him to turn over. When he's lying on his back, I see that he's got a huge erection. It's pretty hard to ignore, but I try to.

I work very slowly on his face, then on his chest and stomach. "C'mon," he says, "aren't you going to give me the hand finish?"

"Well," I say, "we don't usually do that."

"Look," he says, "I'm not a cop." He even shows me his United Grocer's I.D.

I finally decide to take the risk, even though I'm still not sure he's okay. This job has got me so programmed that I feel I really *should* try to get him off. So I stroke up and down on his prick, around and over his balls, for what seems an interminable long time. His massage time is just about over when he finally comes.

He wipes himself off with the rag I give him. Then he sits up on the table and looks directly at me. "You know what?" he says.

"What?"

"I'm a cop," he says.

I just stare at him for moment. I can feel my stomach jerk in, my breathing stop. I picture myself in jail, my family's reaction if they ever found out.

He looks away from me. "I'm just kidding," he mutters.

It's hard to take it all in. "Jesus Christ!" I stammer. "That's no joke!"

"Sorry," he says. But I don't think he's really sorry at all. . . .

The woman I work with most nights, who goes by the name of Pat, says the same crummy joke was played on her a few times. Both of us know, of course, that the joke could turn into a real trip to jail at any time. That's one of the risks of working here. I try not to think about it too much. I try not to imagine how I'd feel about being busted for prostitution.

Pat might not worry about this as much, because she used to be a hooker. Now she sticks to the massage parlors, and she has a lot of regular customers, so she must make almost as much money as before. I imagine it's a lot easier for her working here.

Pat's got straight reddish hair, is tall and thin, and is pretty nice. She always puts on a good show for the guys. A few nights ago she came in wearing a silver wig, false eyelashes, and lots of makeup. She looked so different I hardly recognized her.

Whenever her regular customers come in, Pat acts real glad to see them. She always greets them at the door, gets them a cup of our lousy instant coffee (which I usually don't bother with unless they ask), and acts real sexy with them. I don't know what she does in the rooms with the guys, but they always leave her good tips.

Sometimes I wonder whether Pat's hostess personality is all part of her act, or if she really likes the guys. Once I asked her if she liked her job, and she said she did. But I still wonder whether Pat thinks the show is real, that "sexy Pat" is really her. I don't know. Maybe she doesn't either. . . .

In every room in the massage parlor there's an oversized Barbie doll head which holds kleenex. You pull a kleenex out of the top of the doll's head.

The doll heads were the owner's idea, but Pat and I hate them. Pat says that pulling out a kleenex is like pulling a little bit of brains out of the doll's head. At the rate we use kleenex, I figure none of the dolls can have much gray matter left by now.

I think much the same about myself sometimes. I feel this job eating at me until I wonder if I'm all hollow inside. . . .

It's later at night. The customer is an aging hippie from Los Angeles, with grayish-brown shoulder-length hair and a neatly trimmed mustache. He's wearing new-looking purple corduroy pants, tooled leather boots, and the classic suede leather jacket with fringe.

He takes a sauna first and then he's ready for his massage. "I like a good, hard massage," he tells me. So I work up a sweat kneading and pounding the large muscles on his back. "Hey," he says, "you're really good. I'm going to be a regular customer from now on." That sounds good to me, unless he's too much hassle. I could use a few more regular customers to keep the money coming in.

After he turns over, I give him a scalp massage. His hair is clean and silky, nice to touch. Meanwhile, he starts checking me out.

"Do you turn on?" he asks. "I've got some dynamite speed with me tonight. I could let you have some real cheap."

"No thanks," I say. "I'm not into speed."

"Too bad," he says. "This is really good stuff." He's silent for a moment, then he raises his head up and looks at me. "You know, with some people you never know where they're at. I'm glad you gave me an honest answer. I think honesty is real important."

"Yeah, so do I," I say. I start working on his chest, spreading oil over his chest muscles. He's quiet for a while again, and then as I move on to working on his stomach, he starts checking out the sexual merchandise.

"I really like head jobs," he says. "You do them, don't you?"

"Sorry," I say. "I don't."

He has a disappointed expression on his face. "Are you sure you won't do a head job? I was really hoping to get one."

"I'll give you fifteen bucks for doing one." He puts his arm around me and squeezes a little. He looks at me encouragingly.

What the hell, I think all of a sudden. Maybe I should try it. I could really use the fifteen bucks, and if I got into doing blow jobs here, I could make a lot more money.

"Okay," I say, "I'll do it."

"Great," he says.

I bend over him, ready to start his blow job right away and get it over with. "Hey," he says, looking offended, "I'm not ready yet. Make me hard with your hands first."

So I put some oil on his prick and start stroking up and down, holding it between my cupped hands like another customer showed me. "That feels good," he says. He unbuttons my blouse, pulls up my bra, and runs his hand over my breasts. Then he starts sucking on the nipples. I don't stop him. I figure this is part of the fifteen dollar deal.

Finally he says that he's ready for his blow job, so I bend over him and put his prick into my mouth. It tastes oily and too salty, but I try not to notice that.

As I'm sucking on his prick, he starts correcting my technique. First he moves my head so I'm right over his prick and turned toward his face. Then he shows me the correct motion. "Move your head up and down like a rabbit," he says. He demonstrates, moving his head up and down.

He looks so funny, nodding his head like that, that I have to keep myself from laughing. Jesus, I'm thinking, this guy is a great teacher.

I start moving my head as he showed me. "Hey," he says, sounding critical, "I can't feel you. Are you sucking?"

I start sucking on him harder. "That's pretty good," he says. "You don't mind doing this, do you?"

I take his prick out of my mouth for a moment to answer him. "It's okay," I say.

Then I go back to moving my head up and down and sucking. I'm starting to feel that I've really got the hang of this. Maybe I can stand to do blow jobs after all.

"That feels great," he says. "Just put a little bit more of it in your mouth."

So I bend over further and try to cram more of his prick into my mouth. It feels as if my whole mouth is full of his prick. I can almost feel it touching my throat.

He starts to moan and thrust his hips against me. All of a sudden I start to gag. It's too much! I want his prick out of my mouth right now!

I jerk up, letting go of his prick, backing away from his encircling arm. He opens his eyes. "What's happening?" he says, sounding irritated.

"I just don't want to do it anymore," I say.

We stare at each other for a minute. He's breathing heavily, looking really pissed. "Hey chick," he says, "are you going to charge me fifteen bucks for that?"

"I'm not gonna charge you anything," I say. My own voice is angry too. "I'll give you a hand finish instead," I say after a moment.

He lies back down, looking a little mollified. I put some more oil on his prick and start stroking up and down again. He grabs for my breasts and squeezes them hard. Then he slips his hands under the waist of my pants. His hand moves downward until he's pressing it between my legs. He starts to stick a finger inside of me.

I don't want him to touch me like that, so I move away a little. But his arm around me pulls me back and he keeps on rubbing his hand against my crotch. Mostly I figure it's not worth it to stop him. I just want to get him off and get him out of here.

Finally he comes, in a storm of heavy breathing. A moment later, he's polite again. "Thanks a lot. I really needed that."

"I'm glad it felt good," I say, handing him a prick rag. I try to sound sincere.

He lays a rap on me as gets dressed. "You know," he says, "I'm not a chauvinist. Some of my best buddies are chicks. I work on cars with them."

"Oh yeah," I say.

He buttons his silky, floral-print shirt. "And I know a lot of gay people too. It doesn't make any difference to me."

That's right, I think. I'm gay and it didn't matter to you at all.

He pulls on his pants. "Just so long as you do what feels good to you, that's the main thing." He slowly puts on his boots. "It's always a mistake to do anything you don't want to do," he says, "because you're prostituting yourself if you do that."

There's a taste in my mouth like vomit. Then I must be a whore, I think to myself. Because I didn't want to be with this guy at all. And I sure as hell didn't want him to touch me.

He hands me a five dollar tip. "I'll see you another time," he says. "The massage felt great."

"Thanks," I say. I try for a sexy smile, but I don't make it.

Priscilla Alexander, Prostitution: A Difficult Issue for Feminists

From F. Delacoste and P. Alexander, Sex Work
(Pittsburgh: *Cleis Press*, 1987).

Why Prostitution?

Prostitution exists, at least in part, because of the subordination of women in most societies. This subordination is reflected in the double standard of sexual behavior for men and women, and is carried out in the discrepancy between women's and men's earning power, which results in women in the United States earning sixty-seven cents for every dollar men earn, and even less in most other countries. This economic discrepancy has not changed much from the days of the Old Testament, at which time women earned about sixty shekels for every one hundred shekels earned by men.

The specific reasons that prostitutes have given for choosing their work, as revealed in the studies of Dr. Jennifer James in Seattle, have included money, excitement, independence, and flexibility, in roughly that order. First person accounts by women in the sex industry often mention economics as a major factor, coupled with rebellion at the restricted and tedious jobs available to them. Studies by Dr. James and others have also revealed a high incidence of child sexual abuse in the life histories of prostitutes: around fifty percent for adult prostitutes; seventy-five to eighty percent for juvenile prostitutes. The traditional psychoanalytic explanation for the relationship between childhood sexual abuse and later involvement in prostitution is that the child has come to view sex as a commodity, and that she is masochistic. The connection many prostitutes report, however, is that the involvement in prostitution is a way of taking back control of a situation in which, as children, they had none. Specifically, many have reported that the first time they ever felt powerful was the first time they "turned a trick." As painful as these statistics are, it is important to remember that many women with no history of sexual assault become prostitutes (and many survivors of child sexual abuse never work as prostitutes), so the relationship between prostitution and early sexual trauma is far from clear.

A number of authors have also looked at the fact that men and women do not appear to view sex in the same way and that men as a class seem to view sex as power, with rape being the most extreme form of the use of sex as power. Women as a class tend to see sex as nurture, and this generalization is subject to great individual differences. Prostitution also involves an equation of sex with power: for the man/customer, the power consists of his ability to "buy" access to any number of women; for the woman/prostitute, the power consists of her ability to set the terms of her sexuality, and to demand substantial payment for her time and skills. Thus, prostitution is one area in which women have traditionally and openly viewed sex as power.

Although prostitution is considered to be a uniquely human profession, there is some evidence to the contrary from both field and laboratory studies of non-human primates. Chimpanzees have been observed in the wild engaging in sexual activity in exchange for food, and in a laboratory study in which tokens were given to chimps for specific behaviors, observers suddenly noticed that a few female chimps had all the tokens. Further observation revealed a form of prostitution.

Basic Categories of Prostitution

The most familiar form of prostitution, and the one that draws the most attention, is street prostitution. In the United States, about ten to twenty percent of prostitution involves street solicitation. The traditional pimp/prostitute relationship is most likely to occur in this setting, although about forty percent of street prostitutes work independently.

The next form of prostitution takes place off the street, but is still obvious to the general public. This includes massage parlors, encounter studios, and other euphemistic businesses. These businesses are generally clearly identifiable from the street; owners and managers are legally defined as pimps and panderers. Men are as likely to manage massage parlors as women, and are also as likely to demand that prostitutes engage in sexual activity with them, without pay—which, if prostitution were legal, would be considered sexual harassment on the job. . . .

Less obvious to the general public is bar or cafe prostitution, in which women meet clients in the bar and take them to rooms above the bar (more common in Europe and Southeast Asia) or go with the client to his hotel room. This form of prostitution sometimes is pimp-controlled, as when the women take their clients to a room connected with the bar or cafe, but can also involve independent women who meet clients in the bar or cafe and go back to the client's hotel. . . .

Next is the brothel or bordello, which is an enclosed building, not open to the general public, in which prostitution takes place. In countries with "legalized" brothel systems, the brothel district is often completely separated from the rest of the city, sometimes surrounded by a wall or fence. Illegal brothels are generally well hidden from public view, to avoid police action against them. Whether the brothel is owned by a man or a woman, in most cases it is managed by a woman, who is known as a "madam."

Women who work in legal brothel systems are usually restricted in their movements outside of the brothel district. In Nevada, for example, the rural counties that have either legalized or tolerated brothel systems have imposed a large number of restrictions on the movements of the women who work in them. They are not allowed to be in a gambling casino or a bar at all, or to be in the company of a man on the street or in a restaurant. They are also not allowed to reside in the same community in which they work (they generally work a three-week shift in the brothel, after which they are "off" for a week or more). They are tested weekly for venereal diseases and monthly for antibodies to the AIDS virus. Since the women are required to register with the sheriff as prostitutes, these restrictions are easy to enforce. . . .

A large number of prostitutes, perhaps the majority, work outside of "houses." The traditional "call girl" worked independently, with a "book" of clients. In the last few years, a system of "escort services" has developed (originally as an "outcall" service offered by massage parlors), which works like a dating service in that the service connects clients and prostitutes, who then meet elsewhere. Whether they work through an escort service, or completely on their own, the prostitutes who work in this way are the most independent, and the most in control of their lives on and off the job. ...

De Facto Legalization of Third–Party Controlled Prostitution in the U.S.

Although prostitution is illegal in most of the United States, a quasi-legalized brothel system has developed in many cities under the auspices of police department. San Francisco is a good example. In the early seventies, the San Francisco Board of Supervisors passed an ordinance regulating massage parlors, and requiring that both the owners of the massage parlors and the workers they employed obtain licenses from the Police Department's Permit Bureau. A conviction on a prostitution-related offense in the previous three years is grounds for denial of the license. Similarly, a conviction subsequent to getting the license is grounds for revocation. In 1981, the Board of Supervisors passed a similar ordinance regulating escort services.

On the face of it, it would seem that the legislation is designed to prevent prostitution; however, according to police testimony at the time the escort service bill was introduced, it is really designed to "regulate and control" prostitution, not prevent it. In reality, however, it guarantees a turnover of new employees because the police periodically raid the parlors and escort services, and revoke the permits of the women they arrest. ...

Interestingly, the same massage license is required, whether the work is "legitimate" or sexual massage. When a woman applies for the license, the police assume she is a prostitute, and treat her accordingly. When the police raid massage parlors and escort services, and arrest all the women working there, they may not even charge them with prostitution. Instead, they arrest them for minor infractions of the massage parlor licensing code, such as failing to wear an ID badge on the outside of their clothes. Such cases are often dismissed the next morning by a judge who thinks such arrests are a waste of the taxpayers' money and the court's time. Even though there have been no convictions, the women who were arrested lose their licenses and, as a consequence, their jobs. The women who have been arrested do not stop working as prostitutes, however. Perhaps they work in the isolation of their own apartments, advertising in the local sex paper. Perhaps they go out on the street, exposing themselves to much greater risks of dangerous clients and cops. Or they may move to another city, where they don't have an arrest record, or any friends, to apply for another massage license, so the cycle begins again. ...

Hotel Involvement in Prostitution

Although hotels are often prime movers in efforts to get police to "crack down" on prostitution, they also depend on the availability of large numbers of prostitutes for their business clients. This is especially true in large urban areas which, because of a decline in blue-collar industry, have become dependent on tourism as a major source of tax revenue. The convention industry is large in this country and, because of the continued discrimination against women in employment, particularly at the management level, convention attendees are overwhelmingly male. Many travel without their families. A significant number of those men feel that a visit to a strange city is not complete without a visit to a prostitute. In response to this, the massage parlor and escort service industry developed in this country, and the "sex tour" industry developed internationally.

Hotels use their security staff to screen prostitutes, to keep out those deemed unacceptable. According to a former security guard for a major hotel in downtown San Francisco, prostitutes who plan to visit a client in a first-class hotel are expected to check in at the main desk and announce their intention by saying they are there to give the client a massage, or to provide some other service. If the woman has a massage license, she is expected to show it to the desk clerk. Once she is on an upper floor, she is likely to be stopped by hotel security, who calls down to the main desk to see if she has checked in. If she has not, she will be taken to a room in the hotel, often in the basement, where she will be photographed, warned not to come back to the hotel, and told that her photograph will be circulated to other area hotels. If she is black, garishly dressed, or "too noisy," or drunk, she is more likely to be stopped than if she is elegantly dressed. Several years ago, the San Francisco Hilton Hotel was sued by a black woman who had been harassed in this way while attending a feminist conference. The Hilton settled out of court for fifty thousand dollars. . . .

The Law

Historically, prostitution issues have been addressed in a number of ways by civil and religious governmental bodies. During periods of history in which "good" women were severely restricted (e.g., veiled, chaperoned, or confined to special quarters), prostitutes have been tolerated and allowed to work with few restrictions. In contrast, times in which women have been fighting for and achieving greater independence have also been times of greater restrictions and prohibitions against prostitutes. During the Renaissance, a period in which women achieved some measure of independence, prostitutes were often required to wear special clothing, and/or were confined to special districts. Interestingly, they were required to live in the same districts with Jews, who had to similarly mark their clothing. Again, in the 19th century, when women demanded the right to vote, England passed the Contagious Diseases Acts under which any woman suspected of being a prostitute could be arrested and taken to a "lock ward" in a hospital for examination and treatment for venerEal disease. Many "innocent" women were arrested. Moreover, many women who did not have sexually transmitted diseases when they were arrested got them from the unsterile, newly invented speculums used to examine them. The United States' laws prohibiting prostitution were enacted in this century just prior to ratification of the suffrage amendment in 1920.

In 1949, the United Nations passed a convention paper that called for the decriminalization of prostitution and the enforcement of laws against those who exploit women and children in prostitution. The paper, which was read to the United Nations General Assembly by Eleanor Roosevelt, has been ratified by more than fifty countries, but not the United States. Most European countries have "decriminalized" prostitution by removing laws which prohibit "engaging" in an act of prostitution; although most have retained the laws against "soliciting," "pimping," "pandering," "running a disorderly house," and "transporting a woman across national boundaries for the purposes of prostitution." The United States, on the other hand, has retained the laws prohibiting the act of prostitution as well ... Prostitution is also prohibited outright in Japan, and in many Asian countries, including those in which "sex tourism" is a major industry. It is decriminalized in the Soviet Union, but women who work as prostitutes there are arrested for violating the law against being a parasite (i.e., not having a legally-recognized job).

In addition to laws prohibiting soliciting or engaging in an act of prostitution, and the related issues of pimping and pandering, or procuring, the United States has laws that bar anyone who has ever been a prostitute from entering this country, remaining in this country as a resident, or becoming a citizen. ...

The countries with the most restrictive legal systems, including the United States and many countries in Southeast Asia, have the most problems with violence against prostitutes (and women perceived to be *like* prostitutes), thefts associated with prostitution, pimping (especially brutal pimping), and the involvement of juveniles. Conversely, the countries with the least restrictive measures, including the Netherlands, West Germany, Sweden and Denmark, have the least problems. No country, however, is totally safe for prostitutes. The stigma still isolates the women, and the remaining laws still serve to perpetuate that stigma, rather than to dispel it and truly legitimize the women who work as prostitutes.

Discriminatory Enforcement of the Law

In 1983, 126,500 people were arrested for prostitution in the United States. This is a 148.4 percent increase over the number arrested in 1973, the year that the prostitutes' rights movement began in this country with the founding of COYOTE [Call Off Your Tired Old Ethics]. In comparison, arrests for all crimes increased only 35.6 percent. Although the law makes no distinction between men and women and, in most states, prohibits both sides of the transaction, the percentage of women arrested generally hovers around seventy percent. ...About ten percent of those arrested are customers (usually arrested in a series of raids over a period of a couple of weeks, and then ignored the rest of the year). The remainder of the arrests are of transvestite and pre-operative transsexual prostitutes (i.e., men who, in the eyes of the police, look like women).

Enforcement practices similarly discriminate on the basis of race and class. Eighty-five to ninety percent of the prostitutes who are arrested work on the street, although only ten to twenty percent of all prostitutes are street workers. While approximately forty percent of street prostitutes are women of color, fifty-five percent of those arrested are. The racism becomes even more apparent when you look at the figures on who gets jailed: eighty-five percent of prostitutes sentenced to do jail time are women of color. One student of street prostitution in New York City hypothesized that the reason for the disproportionate number of minority women being arrested was that there was more police activity in the neighborhood of ethnic minorities, where they were more likely to work. What he found, however, was that police were, in fact, more active in white neighborhoods, where most of the prostitutes were also white. He then hypothesized that the racial bias of the mostly white police officers was to blame. My own hunch is that the women of color are mostly likely to be arrested when they drift towards and/or into the white districts. Certainly, prostitution in New York's Times Square did not become a major issue until black prostitutes moved from Harlem to the theatre district as white customers stopped going to Harlem during the racially tense 1960s.

The enforcement practices in Las Vegas, Nevada, where all prostitution is illegal, also supports this latter hypothesis. In recent years, the casinos have increasingly relied on sex, or the implication of sex, to draw customers to their stage shows, and then to the gaming tables. Elegant prostitutes who look like the stereotype of a Las Vegas showgirl are allowed to work with impunity, so long as they don't draw customers away from the gambling tables. Black prostitutes, however, are not allowed to work in the casinos and hotels (blacks have been admitted as customers only since 1962). As a result, the percentage of street prostitutes who are black is high. The laws against prostitution are rigidly enforced against street prostitutes, and a large number of black women are arrested each night. For a few years, the city ran a mandatory "counseling" program for prostitutes, which operated from 8:00 p.m. to midnight. The poor, black prostitutes were in the counseling program, while the middle-and upper-class white prostitutes made money working the casinos. . . .

If law enforcement is designed to reduce the amount of prostitution, it has failed miserably. Moreover, crackdowns are generally initiated with a fanfare about how the police are going to rid the streets of violent crime, but crackdowns are actually often followed by an increase in robberies, many of which involve some form of violence, as well as burglaries and other real property crime, as the people who have been dependent on the now-jailed prostitutes seek to replace lost income.

Crackdowns, and arrests in general, tend to reinforce the dependence of prostitutes on pimps, who are often their only friends outside of jail who can arrange for bail, an attorney, child care, etc. Many women who have worked independently before their first arrest are, moreover, recruited into working for pimps by other prostitutes in jail who convince them of the need to have someone outside to take care of business.

Crackdowns also pressure many women to move on to other cities, cutting off their connections with local friends and networks of support, including agencies that could help them leave prostitution if they wanted to. Their isolation in new cities further increases their dependence on pimps, and effectively entraps them in "the life."

Pimps

The legal definition of pimping is "living off the earnings of a prostitute." By that definition, those who profit from prostitution include not only the stereotyped pimp with a stable of women, who beats them with coat hangers if they fail to bring in enough money, but lovers who shop for groceries and do the laundry, taxi drivers, bell captains, the business-like owners and managers of massage parlors and escort services, madams, and others who personally and directly receive money from prostitutes and/or provide connections between prostitutes and customers. Also included would have to be the publishers of the *Yellow Pages,* newspapers and some magazines, the banks that offer credit cards, travel agents who book sex tours, and a host of corporate entities that are never charged with violating prostitution laws.

When most people think of pimping, of course, they think of bad pimps who lure unsuspecting women into prostitution and physically abuse them when they resist or don't bring in enough money. Most people do not view such violent relationships in the context of relational violence in general, such as violence in marriage. If you consider that about fifty percent of adult prostitutes were either physically or sexually abused in childhood, often by their fathers, it is not surprising that many would find themselves in violent relationships as adults. This is not to condone such relationships, merely to put them into context. Many prostitutes I know say that while they have known some prostitutes who seem to be perpetually victimized, they have known at least as many others who are rarely, if ever, injured or abused.

The battered women's movement has had a profound effect on the consciousness of prostitutes and, increasingly, battered prostitutes are turning to battered women's programs for help. They are often even more frightened to pursue the matter in court than battered wives, but they are beginning to realize that they can, perhaps, have help getting out of the situation. At least some of the time, that is, because too many battered women's programs routinely refuse to serve prostitutes, or if they do, assume that "prostitution" is the problem, not "battering." They refuse, for example, to allow the women to continue to work as prostitutes outside of the shelter, even when other women are expected to continue to work. Some of this may have to do with legal concerns, but in states where homosexual acts are a crime, shelters do not expect battered lesbians to go "straight" because of the law.

Forced Prostitution

The issue of forced prostitution is often used to obscure the issue of the right of women to work as prostitutes. Therefore, it is important to discuss this issue separately. At the same time, I want to make a distinction between being forced by a third party (e.g., a "pimp") to work as a prostitute, particularly where violence or deceit is used, and being forced by economic reality. Most people who work for compensation do so because they need the money—for themselves, for their children. In any society, people make decisions about work based on some kind of evaluation of the options open to them. ...That being said, in the technological western countries, where most women are at least functionally literate and there is a significant array of occupational choice, about ten percent of women who work as prostitutes are coerced into prostitution by third parties through a combination of trickery and violence. This figure appears to be relatively constant in the United States, as reflected in studies done at the turn of the century and current estimates of COYOTE and some other prostitutes' rights organizations. At the other extreme, in India, where there is massive poverty with large numbers of people dying in the streets, and where there are few occupations open to women, seventy to eighty percent of the women who work as prostitutes are forced into the life. ...

The prohibition of prostitution, as common in countries with the highest percentage of forced prostitution as it is in countries with the least amount, does not begin to address the problem. Laws against "traffic" in women, which are supposed to prevent the forced movement of women and girls across national or state boundaries for the purposes of prostitution are, instead, used to keep voluntary prostitutes from traveling. Forced prostitution cannot be addressed until voluntary prostitution is legitimate. Feminist attempts to simply stop it, and to "rescue" the women who have been so badly abused, are doomed to fail until the laws that punish prostitutes are abolished and businesses that employ them are regulated in ways discussed elsewhere in this essay. Organizations likely to have the greatest impact are those that seek to empower prostitute women to make decisions about their lives, and give them the skills to do so, without making judgments—moral or otherwise—about the work they do.

Violence Against Prostitutes

The danger of violence to prostitutes comes not only from pimps, but from customers and police. A study of street prostitutes and sexual assault found that seventy percent of the women interviewed had been raped on the job, and that those who had been raped had been victimized an average of eight to ten times a year. Only seven percent had sought any kind of help, and only four percent had reported any of the rapes to the police.

Murder is a serious danger to prostitutes, particularly since serial murders of prostitutes are rarely investigated thoroughly by police until at least ten or more women have been killed or until the killer, emboldened by his "success," begins to kill "square" or "innocent" women. ...

Because prostitutes are seen as having few supporters in the outside world, police—particularly undercover vice officers—feel free to insult and roughly handle the prostitutes they arrest. Police handcuff their victims from behind, then roughly pull their arms. They demand sex before or during the arrest; and inflict beatings and kickings. They issue specific insults about the individual prostitute's body, and taunts about the how the police officer could get a free blow job with no one the wiser. The arresting officer may suggest that the prostitute give the sheriff a blow job to get out of jail. Few prostitutes file complaints, unfortunately, feeling they have no choice but to accept this abuse as part of the job, and so the few accounts that surface must be seen as symptoms of a much larger problem. ...

Kathleen Barry, Throwaway Women

From K. Barry, Female Sexual Slavery
(NY: New York University Press, 1984).

All kinds of women are vulnerable to slave procurers. The assumption that only women of a particular class, race, or age group are potential victims of female sexual slavery has followed from the inability to recognize sexual domination as it underpins all other forms of oppression. It is true that some procuring methods are adapted to particular groups of women and the strategy that works in rural poverty may not work in an urban bus station. But it is primarily procurers and their interests and only secondarily women's age, race or economic class that determine who will end up forced into prostitution.

The other major cause of sex slavery is the social-sexual objectification of women that permeates every patriarchal society in the world. Identifying women first as sexual beings who are responsible for the sexual services of men is the social base for gender-specific sexual slavery. As most women know, being sexually harassed while walking alone down a street, or sitting in a bar or restaurant without a man, is a poignant reminder of our definition as sexual objects. Spurning those advances and reacting against them are likely to draw indignant wrath from the perpetrator, suggesting the extent to which many men assume the sexual objectification of *any* woman as their right. Under such conditions, sexual slavery lurks at the corners of every woman's life.

Increasingly, stereotyped female-gender characteristics are becoming the means of identifying prostitutes. In 1975 a Danish court ruled on a prostitution case that had ramifications for all women when it agreed that a policeman could identify a woman as a prostitute *from the way she walked*. The court fined the woman for soliciting based only on the testimony of a policeman who said, "I took action only when she was obviously soliciting, and that was easily determined from the way she walked." ...

In 1976 the New York State legislature enacted a law against loitering for the purposes of prostitution which in effect makes any woman walking or standing on the street vulnerable to being identified as a prostitute. In challenges to that law the New York Civil Liberties Union has raised the issue that loitering "for the purposes of prostitution" is determined almost solely on the observations of the police officers. In reviewing over 200 loitering arrests, NYCLU attorneys found that in not one arrest was any other evidence gathered to support the arresting officer's observations. According to NYCLU attorneys, in depositions with arresting officers it was found that officers defined loitering for the purposes of prostitution based on their observations of the women on the street, what they were wearing, with whom they were associating, and repeated beckoning to men. ...

In my interview with Melinda ..., she told me how she was "turned out" when she was 15. One day, after going to the movies with her girl friend, she was waiting for a bus when a man approached her and told her he'd pay her $50 for a date. She talked with him for a few minutes and she naively believed he just wanted to take her out so she accepted. She did not know he had actually solicited her as a prostitute until she got to the hotel room with him and he told her his expectations. At that point she had no alternative.

Women like Melinda who don't escape the arbitrary definition of prostitute are recycled into the world, where they are sexually used and abused and disposed of when no longer of use. Like the no-deposit, no-return beverage bottles—they are throwaways. . . .

The prevailing belief that because of the nature of their work prostitutes cannot be raped makes them easy targets for men who assume they can act out their misogyny with impunity. Beating, rape, and even murder are generally considered inevitable occupational hazards. Social attitudes which coalesce around street prostitutes make them and any other women who are identified as prostitutes throw-away women. These attitudes form the basis of many prostitution laws.

The State as Pimp

Governments have wrestled with the problem of how to handle prostitution for a long time. There is considerable diversity in the laws. But regarding street solicitation most countries fall into a single pattern which involve exploiting and abusing women on the streets and largely ignoring the less visible prostitution. Consistently across societies, street prostitutes are hassled and fined but never to the point of eliminating them from the streets. As long as there is a demand, there will be no major interference with supply. Harassment of street prostitutes is a way of assuring the community that morality is being upheld. As Jennifer James points out, legal definitions of prostitution are based on cash, promiscuity, relationship to sexual partner, and subtlety. "A prostitute is safe in violating the first three aspects of legal concern if she carefully accedes to the fourth—subtlety."

A look at the laws governing prostitution and at their enforcement reveals how the double standard of male morality is implemented and shows the extent to which prostitutes are locked into a moral and legal system that ensures their enslavement even if they can escape their pimp or brothel. Besides assuring the double standard, laws governing prostitution in each country promote the isolation of prostitutes, setting them apart from the rest of society, placing them in a legal or social status that facilitates their exploitation and often prevents them from leaving. Three different systems of prostitution have been distinguished, and all in one way or another set up the state as the first pimp. Those systems either prohibit, tolerate, or regulate prostitution. . . .

The prohibitionist system is probably the most overt practice of the double standard. It overwhelmingly punishes the woman while virtually ignoring the men. . . . Accordingly, those prostitutes who are victims of sexual slavery are seen only as criminals in the sex industry. Even though the laws forbid both pimping and patronizing a prostitute, it is prostitutes who are arrested. . . .

The system that legally tolerates prostitution makes pimping and procuring illegal. Prostitutes are not criminals by virtue of their work; therefore they have more access to the rights of citizens. Law enforcement is more successful in prosecuting pimps. There is more compassion in the society for the plight of these women as human beings, which is indicated by the relatively larger number of refuge centers for prostitutes found in some countries under this system.

Although there are no laws forbidding the act of prostitution, each country espousing toleration carries other laws on its book which are used to control and/or harass street prostitutes. . . .

In contrast to the toleration of prostitution by abolitionist countries, regulation *enforces* prostitution, especially through closed houses or eros centers. It is the most direct legal attempt to hide the otherwise visible double standard. . . . Regulated prostitution [also] has accomplished nothing it has boasted of. It has not cut down on crime associated with prostitution. . . .

Visible street prostitution exposes the double standard that allows masculinist societies around the world to accept prostitution as a needed outlet for men while condemning it as immoral. If prostitution took place only behind closed doors—in brothels, prostitution hotels, and the back rooms of bars—then the double standards which promote and protect prostitution, sexual violence, and sexual slavery would be carefully concealed. Expendable women would be used, abused, and forgotten.

Visible prostitution is uncomfortable to the tricks who need to have social distance and separation between whores and wives. It is uncomfortable to the police who must uphold morality while still allowing prostitution to exist. And it is uncomfortable to tourists, shoppers, and city dwellers who would rather not see what they believe must be inevitable.

The fact is that patriarchal government has found no system of prostitution that isn't abusive and doesn't exploit women. Each system in its own way locks women into prostitution. In systems in which women are criminals, they can hardly expect justice to turn in their favor or protection to be granted to them. Where prostitution is legally accepted and regulated, the exploitation of prostitutes by pimps and customers is forgotten. Where prostitution is tolerated, as in France, prostitutes are still hassled on the streets and closed houses . . . still exist under double standards of justice. Thus all systems yield to the insistence that prostitution is a necessary social service; at the same time they hate and condemn the women who provide it. . . .

Regina Austin, **Black Women, Sisterhood, and the Difference/Deviance Divide**

26 New Eng. L. Rev. 877 (1992).

SHADES OF DIFFERENCE AND DEVIANCE

"Sameness" and "difference" do not neatly encompass all the categories into which deserving black woman might be placed or might place themselves. To be sure, "sameness" and "difference," vis-a-vis whites of course, have been useful rhetorical devices by which blacks have launched assaults at the border between liberation and oppression and captured new ground. Yet, there is a third, unspecified category beyond and implicit in "difference" of which black women must be especially mindful; that category is "deviance." Given the number and prevalence of stereotypes that exist concerning black women, we cannot afford to ignore how the dominant, white male-controlled society goes about labeling us deviant. We must hold ourselves open to the possibility that deviance includes attitudes and behaviors we ought to defend. . . .

In general, gender makes a difference in the evaluation of deviant behavior. If the assessment is positive when the lawbreaker or norm violator is a male, it is likely to be less so or quite the reverse if the lawbreaker or norm violator is a female. If the assessment is negative when the wrongdoer is a male, it is likely to be more so if the wrongdoer is a female. As is true in other aspects of American social life, black women who break the rules are judged in accordance with the biases of both white supremacy and male domination. Black female offenders accordingly receive harsher treatment at the hands of the law than do female lawbreakers of other races and ethnicities.

But black women have reason to challenge the appraisals of black female deviants, whether they are based on the standards of the dominant society or those prevailing in the black community. In the name of a "black sisterhood," a "community" within "the community," we might respond to female deviance with understanding, support, or praise based on the distinctive social, material, and political interests of black women. In doing so, however, we risk being labeled deviant ourselves. For this and other reasons, we tend to differentiate ourselves from those whose conduct falls within traditional definitions of deviance when we advance our claims for greater esteem and resources. The implications of this approach for the existence and maintenance of a true dynamic black sisterhood are best illustrated with a concrete case.

RUBY CLARK v. ABC

Ruby Clark, a black woman, sued the American Broadcasting Company (ABC) for defamation after her photograph appeared on the screen during a 1977 "ABC News Closeup" program on commercialized sex. The particular segment that gave rise to her complaints focused on the impact of street prostitution on a Detroit neighborhood. Plaintiff was among three women pictured as they walked in public. Just before their appearance, a neighborhood woman was shown saying, "Whether you're 15 or 45, constantly being approached—it's degrading—feels terrible." Another followed with the statement "[y]ou want to . . . just kill 'em . . . cause it makes you so angry to be placed down to a hooker's level." There followed in sequence three women walking in public. The first was a white female described as being obese and elderly. This woman "wore a hat, and carried a shopping bag in each hand." The second woman was black and "slightly obese, wore large-framed glasses and appeared to be at least forty years old." She was photographed as she left a store with a bag of groceries in her arms and walked down the street. While these women were on the screen, the announcer stated, "According to residents, and Detroit police records, most of the prostitutes' customers or johns were white; the street prostitutes were often black. This integrated middle class neighborhood became a safe meeting place for prostitutes and 'johns.' "

Plaintiff was the last of the trio featured. The opinion describes the visual image and the verbal accompaniment as follows:

> The plaintiff appeared to be in her early to mid-twenties. She was attractive, slim, and stylishly dressed. She wore large earrings and had long hair which was pulled up above her head. Apparently, Plaintiff was unaware that she was being photographed. As Plaintiff appeared, the narrator made the following remarks: "But for black women whose homes were there, the cruising white customers were an especially humiliating experience."

Sheri Madison, a black female resident of the neighborhood plagued by prostitution, appeared on the screen seconds after Plaintiff. She stated: "Almost any woman who was black and on the street was considered to be a prostitute herself. And was treated like a prostitute."

Plaintiff, who viewed the program with her husband and young son, was shocked by its portrayal of her. A number of persons—friends, relatives, acquaintances, fellow church members, and prospective employers of plaintiff—thought that the program presented her as being a prostitute and some even concluded that she actually was one.

The district court awarded ABC summary judgment on the ground that plaintiff had not been libeled because "nothing in Plaintiff's appearance suggested that her activity paralleled that of a street prostitute." On appeal, this ruling was reversed. A majority of the Sixth Circuit panel concluded that the portrayal of plaintiff was "reasonably capable of two meanings, one defamatory and the other non-defamatory." The issue was accordingly one for the jury.

Plaintiff was definitely not a prostitute; she was not even a resident of the affected neighborhood. Thus, it clearly would have been libelous for ABC to depict plaintiff as being a prostitute and ABC contended that it did not do so. As the district court emphasized, she was not shown exhibiting the stereotypical indicia of prostitutes, " 'suggestive clothing, suggestive walking, overt acts of solicitation, and the like.' "

Yet, in context, plaintiff's status was equivocal. The subject was street prostitution and the prostitutes were said to be black. Plaintiff was clearly distinguishable from the two women whose features preceded her own. They were portly matrons, one white, the other black and bespectacled, both carrying bags, while she was young, slim, attractive, and black. The court stated, "[w]hen her appearance is juxtaposed with that of the two matrons, it is not clear whether she is a resident of this middle class neighborhood or one of the street prostitutes who plagued this community." Although the commentary that accompanied her picture suggested that she was one of "the black women who resided in the neighborhood" for whom "the presence of the cruising white customers was a humiliating experience," the interview footage that followed restored the ambiguity about plaintiff's status by referring to the frequency with which black women on the street were considered to be and treated like prostitutes. Thus, it was up to the jury to decide whether ABC presented plaintiff as being "one of those middle class women erroneously considered to be a prostitute or ... in fact, a prostitute."

ABC, in essence, permitted its viewers to do to Mrs. Clark the very thing that the women complained of in the program. In reporting what was happening on the streets, ABC invited those watching the broadcast to engage in the johns' speculation—is she or isn't she? ABC bore some of the risk that its viewers were no more discriminating than the men cruising the affected neighborhood in search of prostitutes and might therefore exercise the same sort of erroneous judgment.

The court might have gone further and concluded that it was even defamatory to present Mrs. Clark as the type of black woman who gets mistaken for a prostitute. Such a portrayal of Mrs. Clark would have been neither flattering nor likely to enhance her reputation among her friends and associates. If the segment involving Mrs. Clark was as ambiguous as the court suggests, it is not clear that a jury was capable of definitively assessing its meaning. The jurors, no less than the viewers and the johns who mistakenly proposition black women on the street, would have been privy to the general societal defamation or devaluation of black women's sexuality which affects how our physical appearance and behavior in public are read. That was the real source of the ambiguity on which the case hinged.

Mrs. Clark's libel action challenged not only her own possible wrongful inclusion in the category of prostitutes, but also the general stereotyping that associates black women with street prostitution. Before and since slavery, black women's supposed sexual promiscuity and licentiousness have been relied upon to justify the sexual exploitation of black women by white males intent upon rape, cheap sex, harassment on the job, or torment on the street. Since emancipation, combating our sexual denigration and establishing our entitlement to the same respect accorded white "ladies" have been significant components of black women's organized politics. Mrs. Clark's law suit was in keeping with this well-developed strand of black women's quest for freedom from white men's sexual domination.

Despite the breadth of her claim, Mrs. Clark was still required to distinguish herself from and participate in the broader societal put down of other black women. She succeeded in proving that the program possibly portrayed her as a prostitute by emphasizing the stark contrast between herself and the two other women, "the bag ladies" as it were, with whom she appeared. She accomplished this at the cost of perpetuating notions about the sexual undesirability of females who are no longer young, no longer svelte, and no longer (if they ever were) carefree. For a black woman to be required to join in this sort of disparagement of other black women is a very serious matter.

Black women who labor hard at jobs that require physical strength and endurance have long been viewed as being less than feminine. Some of the stereotypes of black women reinforce the idea that such workers lack physical beauty and sexual allure. The image of Mammy, "Aunt Jemima," Beulah, and even the emasculating matriarch is that of an overweight, rotund female, devoid of the curves that are indicative of the more seductive examples of her sex. Outfitted in an unflattering dress, apron, and scarf (a "headrag"), she is always ready for work and never ready for bed. These images are not without material consequence. As Mae King argues, they facilitated the "most outrageous exploitation of black females as a cheap labor source. By 'de-feminizing' them, America could subject them to the most harsh and unsafe working conditions without violating the white ethics [regarding the treatment of delicate womanhood].... "

The impact of the attack on the femininity and sexuality of low-status black female workers is quite broad. Black women who try to distance themselves from the black drone role via simplistic negation and antithetical behavior do not thereby free themselves from the hold of a racist patriarchy; they merely give themselves over to it. In any event, such an approach is a futile one for many poor and working-class black females because their diets, jobs, limited expendable income, and restricted leisure time interfere with their ability to satisfy white, bourgeois, heterosexual norms of sexual attractiveness. Of course, many black women dismiss and defy the dominant standards by adopting distinctively black styles of dress and adornment. They pay for their resistance, however. Finally, black women of any class who choose to look and act like they survive without a man experience a reproach that is not unrelated to the negative assessment of the beauty and sexuality of black women of low economic status. Racist heterosexism and fear of black lesbianism, within and without the black community, denigrate the sexuality and sensuality of black females who eschew the primping of the pampered and privileged and/or thrive as sexual beings within the orbit of a social order controlled by women. All of these modes of vilification seek to control more than black women's sexual expression; in addressing how and for whose benefit we ought to work, they affect exploitation of our labor power.

The other black females from whom the plaintiff had to distinguish herself were black prostitutes. The opinion in Clark suggests that black prostitutes represented a direct threat to the social standing, dignity, and well-being of upstanding black women. "Prostitutes are considered immoral and socially undesirable." Their presence in the Detroit neighborhood was shown to produce "devastating social problems," including an increase in robberies, assaults, and drug trafficking. The fact that some black women were actually prostitutes increased the chances that those who were not would be subjected to street harassment.

To make out a claim, Mrs. Clark had to ignore any cliches that pertain to black prostitutes and middle-class women alike (for instance, the extent to which black women yearn for white sexual partners) and accept the misconceptions that apply to black prostitutes (for instance, their role in spreading disease) while disputing their application to upstanding black women like herself. It would have been beyond the scope of Mrs. Clark's cause of action to prove that the low social standing accorded black streetwalkers is the product of ignoring the realities of the milieu in which they operate. Few of the legitimate jobs available to poor and poorly educated black women offer them the money, excitement, and independence some report finding in hustling. Because black women's beauty and sexuality are undervalued, they wind up pounding the pavement, rather than working in more comfortable surroundings. The men who live off their earnings are at least as depraved and sinful as the hookers, but the former experience less severe rebuke.

Mrs. Clark's right to recover was dependent upon her articulating her complaints within the confines of mainstream sexual morality, however racist, sexist, homophobic, or bourgeois it might be. The two groups of black women from whom the plaintiff had to distinguish herself, the matrons and the prostitutes, represent the Scylla and Charybdis of the narrow strait in which bourgeois black women are supposed to channel their sexuality. On one side are the "de-sexed," "de-heterosexed," and androgynous females who are lumped in with the self-declared lesbians; on the other side are the wild, wicked women who are written off as whores. If Mrs. Clark veered too far in either direction, she risked censure, a decline in her reputation, and increased exploitation. If she succeeded in keeping to the straight and narrow, she got rewarded with a recovery.

While law and convention work to drive wedges between black women who express their sexuality in different ways, their actual impact could be quite the reverse. A common oppression and a common quest for liberation provide some basis for solidarity among black females. All of the black females shown in the program shared white society's devaluation of black women's sexuality although it affected them differently. It compelled the black prostitutes to stroll the streets in search of customers, subjected those who were not prostitutes to unwelcome public overtures, and rendered the portly matron (and her white counterpart) a neuter object, respectable but out of the game. They all have an interest in opposing the full range of negative categorizations of black women's sexuality. They all would have gained from an attack on the attempts of white men (including the cruising johns and ABC) to restrict black women's sexual expression and to label it in ways dictated by the white men's purposes. Naturally, defamation law does not allow such broad claims.

DEFYING THE DIVISIVENESS OF DEVIANCE

Contrariness is not a suitable basis for a vibrant and affirmative community. Black women must do more to build and sustain a sisterhood than unite against a common enemy and combat him on his own terms.

Distinctions still have to be drawn. The difference/deviance divide cannot be avoided. Prostitutes present an especially hard case. If black women united to dispute the unwarranted denigration of black streetwalkers, it might be assumed that we also mean to suggest that black females should be more attractive prospects for commercial intercourse than they presently are. Moreover, it remains true that black prostitutes bring traffic and confusion in their wake and their presence is more than morally problematic for the black folks who live in their environs. There comes a point at which blacks will or must adjudge the activities of these women to be "deviant" and condemn them as being on the wrong side of the difference/deviance divide.

To affix the label and forget it or to write off the women so tagged as being beyond redemption would not be sisterly. Black women who consider themselves virtuous cannot be part of an effective community with black sex workers if the former have no respect for the sex workers beyond that dictated by maternalism and assume that the sex workers can teach them nothing. Finding something positive in the practices and concerns of women in street life may not be easy, but it should not be impossible. For example, prostitutes might teach straight women a thing or two about identifying and dealing with pimps. We will not know the extent to which vice has its virtues until we come to know street women better. No external source of morals and values can supply the norms and values by which black women interact with each other. We certainly cannot expect the law to provide us with a cause of action that redresses the harm Mrs. Clark suffered in a way that acknowledges how problematic the behavior of the prostitutes can be, yet does not put them down, and even concedes (without romanticization) the appeal of some of the values that are meaningful to them . . . until we can take such a position ourselves.

A genuine sisterhood would be a modern moral community, one in which political positions and ethical stances are constructed by the sisters as a matter of "common sense, ordinary emotions, and everyday life." It may be time to recognize that the only true communities of black females are voluntary associations of women who are bound by shared economic, political, and social constraints and find strength, economic support, and moral guidance through affective, face-to-face engagement with each other. Such an admission would interfere with our nostalgic longing for a not too distant past when success nationally obviated the need to come together locally, as well as highlight our reluctance to analyze the contemporary material landscape and the full extent of the class cleavages that separate black women. The enormous comfort that comes from being able to think, talk, and act in terms of their being a "black community" or a "black sisterhood" would be threatened if we called core assumptions into question. Dare we?

The social and economic liberation of black female deviants and nondeviants alike would proceed faster if we acknowledged that sometimes it is indeed difficult to tell "us" from "them." We must work to turn the boundary between difference and deviance into free space, a time and place in which racial, sexual, and economic emancipation can be imagined, experimented with, and even enjoyed. In collectively working the line between street and straight, straddling it, and pushing it, we can increase and intensify those moments in which we control our own sexuality and economic destiny. Only we can deliver ourselves into freedom, and dancing on the difference/deviance divide may be one way to do that.

NOTES AND QUESTIONS

1. **Agency**. To what extent did the sex worker in "In the Massage Parlor" have control over her customers' use of her body? What were her reasons for engaging in the various activities the men demanded for their money? Priscilla Alexander writes that prostitution equates sex with power for both the man/customer and the woman/prostitute. Kathleen Barry, on the other hand, argues that prostitution stems from men's identification of women as sex objects. Alexander states that many women choose to become prostitutes for money, independence, and power, while Barry sees them as victims of "slave procurers" with few, if any, alternatives. Does the sex worker's experience confirm or discredit these claims?

2. **Sexual Slavery?** Is Barry's description of prostitution as "slavery" overblown or do prostitutes experience a form of enslavement? To what extent does Barry's concept depend on the actual coercion of girls and women into prostitution?

Barry supports her position with the estimate that over 90 percent of street prostitutes are controlled by pimps. Nancy Erbe enumerates the techniques pimps use to control "their" prostitutes:

> (1) physical abuse; (2) physical control of prostitutes' children, with threats to keep the children as hostages if prostitutes leave; (3) serious threats of physical harm, including murder; (4) keeping prostitutes in continuous states of poverty and indebtedness; and (5) ensuring that [they] have no freedom to move outside unaccompanied.

Nancy Erbe, *Prostitutes: Victims of Men's Exploitation And Abuse*, 2 Law & Ineq. J. 609, 612–13 (1984). Court decisions have recognized forced prostitution as a form of involuntary servitude, upholding the convictions of men who coerce women to perform sex work. *See, e.g.*, Bernal v. United States, 241 F. 339 (5th Cir. 1917)(upholding convictions of man who forced three women to work at a brothel); United States v. Harris, 534 F.2d 207, 214 (10th Cir. 1975) (affirming convictions for involuntary servitude).

As Barry's piece points out, as well, many prostitutes are "turned out" as teenagers, when they are more vulnerable to the control of pimps. The average age of beginning prostitutes is fourteen years. Many of these girls are runaways, often fleeing incest, who are living in the streets, adding economic desperation to their immaturity and psychological trauma. About half of the estimated 1.5 million children who run away from home each year or are homeless engage in prostitution. Neal Kumar Katyal, *Men Who*

Own Women: a Thirteenth Amendment Critique of Forced Prostitution, 103 Yale L.J. 791, 794–95 (1993). Margaret Baldwin calls prostitution "the obvious consequence of serial, unbounded, life-long sexual and emotional abuse." Margaret A. Baldwin, *Split at the Root: Prostitution and Feminist Discourses of Law Reform*, 5 Yale J.L. & Feminism 47, 114 (1992).

Do Barry's arguments apply, however, to prostitutes who work independently as "call girls" or for escort services (the largest group of prostitutes) and do not commonly experience this type of brutality and coercion?

3. **Race, Class, and Sex Work**. The classification of prostitutes mirrors the race and class stratification of the larger society. Alexander notes the racial disparity among streetwalkers, the lowest tier of sex workers, and the racial bias in their arrests, as well as economic pressures on poor women to enter the trade. Yet she seems to discount the importance of this social context in reaching her conclusion that women choose to become prostitutes. Barry also discounts race and class in reaching the opposite conclusion that women are coerced into prostitution because of sexual domination. How do race and class inequalities affect your judgment about prostitution? How important are these injustices in determining whether women can truly "choose" to become prostitutes? Do poverty and discrimination in the labor market negate the possibility of prostitutes' choice, or is prostitution no different from other freely chosen occupations that are motivated by economic incentives? For a historical perspective on these issues, see Ann M. Lucas, *Race, Class, Gender, And Deviancy: The Criminalization of Prostitution,* 10 Berkeley Women's L.J. 47 (1995).

Evelina Giobbe, an anti-prostitution activist, includes race and class inequality in a list of social forces that coerce women into prostitution and therefore make prostitution a form of rape: "Culturally supported tactics of power and control facilitate the recruitment or coercion of women and children into prostitution and effectively impede their escape. The tactics are educational deprivation, job discrimination, and poverty; child sexual abuse, rape, and battery; and racism, classism, and heterosexism." Evelina Giobbe, *Prostitution: Buying the Right to Rape*, in *Rape and Sexual Assault III* 143, 147 (Ann Wolbert Burgess, ed., 1991).

Regina Austin's essay reveals another racial dimension of prostitution—the extent to which the image of the whore is racialized. How does the criminalization of prostitution reinforce stereotypes about Black women's sexuality? How do these stereotypes reinforce the division of women into chaste women and whores?

4. **The International Sex Trade**. Forced prostitution is a particular concern of international human rights activists. In her introduction to *Female Sexual Slavery*, Kathleen Barry writes:

> One of my major frustrations while doing the research for this work was the silence on the issue at the United Nations. But with the United Nations Decade of Women and up to 10,000 women coming together in conferences in Mexico and Den-

mark, female sexual slavery could no longer remain buried.
...[A]n International Feminist Network Against Female Sexual Slavery was organized in 1980 and launched its first
meeting in Rotterdam in 1983. Women from twenty-four countries met to discuss the specific instances of forced prostitution, traffic in women, torture of female prisoners, sex tourism, military brothels, sexual mutilation and other crimes
against women. In doing so they discovered the commonality
of the oppression of women globally and created the basis for
international feminist action by forming a Network.

Kathleen Barry, *Introduction, Female Sexual Slavery* xiv (1984). International antislavery organizations such as the International Abolitionist
Federation crusade against forced prostitution, as well. The United Nations
addressed prostitution in its Working Group on Contemporary Forms of
Slavery. Kathleen Barry, *International Politics of Female Sexual Slavery* in
International Feminism: Networking Against Female Sexual Slavery 21,
24–25 (Kathleen Barry et al. eds., 1984).

A related international concern is the problem of child sexual exploitation in developing countries. A growing number of "sex tourists" travel
from industrialized nations to developing countries to engage in sexual
activity with underage girls and boys that is illegal and less available in
their home countries. This exploitation is especially acute in the Asian
countries of Thailand, the Philippines, Sri Lanka, and Taiwan. The United
Nations Children's Fund (UNICEF) estimated in 1994 that at least one
million Asian children were involved in prostitution. The child sex trade
has spread to other parts of Asia, as well as to Latin America, Africa, and
Eastern Europe. *See* Margaret A. Healy, *Prosecuting Child Sex Tourists at
Home: Do Laws in Sweden, Australia, and the United States Safeguard the
Rights of Children as Mandated by International Law?*, 18 Fordham Int'l
L.J. 1852 (1995). *See also* Eddy Meng, *Mail–Order Brides: Gilded Prostitution and the Legal Response*, 28 U. Mich. J.L. Ref. 197 (1994) (arguing that
the international mail-order bride industry, where women from Asia and
other developing regions are trafficked to men in Western industrialized
countries, is a form of sexual exploitation related to forced prostitution and
to the eroticization of Asian Pacific women).

Countries have promulgated several measures in the last decade to
protect children from sexual exploitation. The United Nations Convention
on the Rights of the Child, adopted in 1989, prohibits the exploitation of
children in prostitution and in illegal sexual practices. In 1990 the international non-governmental organization End Child Prostitution in Asian
Tourism (EPCAT) was founded in Thailand to campaign against child sex
tourism. In addition, several consumer countries, including Australia, Germany, Sweden, and the United States, have passed laws to prosecute
citizens for sexual crimes committed against children abroad. The Child
Sexual Abuse Prevention Act of 1994 makes it a crime to travel from the
United States to another country for the purpose of engaging in sexual
intercourse with a minor. Healy, *Prosecuting Child Sex Tourists at Home*;

Vickie F. Li, *Child Sex Tourism to Thailand: The Role of the United States as a Consumer Country*, 4 Pac. Rim. L. & Pol'y J. 505 (1995).

5. **Drugs and Prostitution**. Many women become prostitutes because they are addicted to drugs, either selling sex for money to buy drugs or more directly trading sex for drugs. For many, involvement in sex work is related to their extreme marginalization in both the formal and informal economy. Based on her ethnographic research among women crack cocaine users and sex workers in Brooklyn, New York, criminologist Lisa Maher describes crack-induced participation in street-level prostitution:

> Sexwork was the only income-generating activity consistently available to women drug users in Bushwick. Despite the recent influx of women into the drug economy, their participation as producers largely revolves around sexwork, and their presence has been most strongly felt as consumers. This has prompted major changes in the operating contexts of street-level sex markets. In New York City, the advent of crack cocaine and the concomitant flood of sexwork initiates lowered the going rates for sexual transactions, encouraged "deviant" sexual expectations on the part of dates, engendered relations of competition and hostility, and promoted the atomization and social isolation of women drug users. These factors have rendered street-level sexwork less lucrative, more demanding, and increasingly violent. However, women have not been passive recipients of these changes. Cumulative market processes and shifting social relations have created a pool of increasingly economically marginalized women for whom "viccing" [stealing from customers] has emerged as a form of resistance. Ironically, it is this very resistance which serves to (re)produce them as "criminal" women....

Lisa Maher, *Sexed Work: Gender, Race, and Resistance in a Brooklyn Drug Market* (1997). *See also Women and Crack–Cocaine* (James A. Inciardi, Dorothy Lockwood, and Anne E. Pottieger eds., 1993).

In light of these women's addiction to drugs and lack of any alternative source of income, how should we view the voluntariness of their participation in prostitution? Is this a form of "sexual slavery" or a low-paid and dangerous job?

Despite the occupational hazards that create special health care needs, prostitutes face social and legal barriers to adequate health care. *See* Tracy M. Clements, *Prostitution and the American Health Care System: Denying Access to a Group of Women in Need*, 11 Berkeley Women's L.J. 49 (1996). For research in Africa, Australia, Europe, and the United States on the risk of HIV infection among sex workers who use drugs, *see AIDS, Drugs and Prostitution* (Martin Plant ed., 1990).

6. To what extent are the problems experienced by prostitutes inherent in sex work itself or related to the criminalization of sex work or to surrounding social inequalities? To take one example from Alexander's piece, is the

battering of prostitutes by pimps a problem caused by prostitution or by relational violence, reinforced by the legal prohibition of sex work? Are shelters that take in battered sex workers justified in forbidding these women from continuing to work as prostitutes? Or is Alexander right that we should not make judgments—moral or otherwise—about the work prostitutes do? Does Austin's call to "genuine sisterhood" between women who express their sexuality in different ways suggest an answer?

Alexander observes an inverse relationship between the government's treatment of "good" women and prostitutes. Periods of constraint on women seem to tolerate prostitution, while women's independence has signaled heightened regulation of prostitutes. How would you explain this connection? Again, how does Austin's critique of the divisiveness of deviance challenge the government's division of women into these categories?

David A.J. Richards, Commercial Sex and the Rights of the Person: A Moral Argument for the Decriminalization of Prostitution

127 U. Pa. L. Rev. 1195 (1979).

It is a remarkable fact, although usually not perceived as such, that the often eloquent literature calling for the decriminalization of "victimless crimes" generally relies on efficiency-based arguments aimed at ending either the pointless or positively counterproductive waste of valuable and scarce police resources expended in the enforcement of these laws. . . . If there is a good moral reason for criminalizing certain conduct, [however,] quite extraordinary enforcement costs will justly be borne. Accordingly, efficiency-based arguments for decriminalization appear to be deeply question-begging. They have weight only if the acts in question are not independently shown to be immoral; but the decriminalization literature concedes the immorality of such acts, and then elaborates efficiency costs that have little decisive weight in the absence of an evaluation of the morality of the acts themselves. . . .

This Article will address this more general question as it arises in the context of arguments for the criminalization of prostitution. I have chosen prostitution for this purpose because it represents the most striking example of a "victimless crime" with respect to which decriminalization advocates have made no substantial progress despite sound arguments of excessive and wasteful enforcement costs. This failure may be because, unlike the otherwise comparable areas of contraception, abortion, and noncommercial sex between or among adults, there has been little serious critical moral argument attacking the moral judgment of the per se immorality of commercial sex. Yet there are forceful moral arguments to this effect that demonstrate that laws criminalizing commercial sex violate certain basic rights of the person. . . .

The moral argument for the criminal prohibition of prostitution was well summarized by the Supreme Court in 1908:

[Prostitution]　refers to women who for hire or without hire offer their bodies to indiscriminate intercourse with men. The lives and example of such persons are in hostility to "the idea of the family, as consisting in and springing from the union for life of one man and one woman in the holy estate of matrimony; the sure foundation of all that is stable and noble in our civilization, the best guaranty of that reverent morality which is the source of all beneficent progress in social and political improvement."

It is noteworthy that, consistent with the traditional definition of prostitution as female promiscuity, the Supreme Court did not place weight on the element of commercialism per se; the gravamen of the moral evil, rather, is that a *woman* should engage in sex not only unchastely but *indiscriminately,* in complete isolation from sentimental attachments of a kind perfected in monogamous marriage. Prostitution is a moral evil because, in the Court's words, the "lives and example of such persons are in hostility" to a certain enormously powerful vision of women, their sexuality, and the role of marriage. . . .

In contemporary circumstances, however, the force of this moral vision has been somewhat reinterpreted in line with the growing acceptability of non-commercial sex outside marriage. For many, the objection to prostitution would today be based not on female promiscuity, but on the transformation of sex into an impersonal encounter with no emotional significance by means of commercialization. This objection is sometimes put in Marx's terms, such that prostitution is said to be the *reductio ad nauseam* of capitalist commercialization of all personal relationships. Some contemporary feminists generally reject the Victorian model of female asexuality, but still perceive prostitution as the ultimate degradation of women into sexual objects or commodities. Finally, the contemporary form of the moral objection has been put in terms of Kantian ethics: commercial sex is allegedly morally wrong per se because it involves the alienation of the body to the will of another, and thus undermines the ultimate roots of the integrity of moral personality. Whatever the precise form of the argument, the sense of it rests on a vision of the necessary moral unity of sex and romantic love. This fact explains why many suppose that consensual adult non-commercial sex can no longer be regarded as immoral per se, but still condemn comparable forms of commercial sex. . . .

. . . [T]he fundamental goal of morality must be, not the impersonal aggregation of pleasure, but the assurance that persons have been guaranteed conditions requisite for the developed capacity self-critically to choose how they will live their lives; ethical principles of obligation and duty rest upon and ensure that this is so, and correlatively define human rights. . . .

In a constitutional democracy, the rights thesis compels particular scrutiny of criminal laws claimed to be justified by the "public morality." . . . Where public attitudes about morality are, in fact, demonstrably not justified by underlying moral principles, laws expressing such attitudes are morally arbitrary and should be found to violate minimal standards of constitutional due process. . . .

[S]exual autonomy appears to be a central aspect of moral personality through which we define our ideas of a free person who has taken responsibility for her or his life. . . . It is simply dogmatic to say that romantic love can be the only means of human fulfillment. There are many other courses that may reasonably accommodate the diverse individuality of human competences, aspirations, and ends. What for one is a reasonable self-imposed ideal of deepened romantic sensuality may, for another, be a narrow and parochial narcissism, a waste of self in privatized obsession and broader social irresponsibility. Consider, in this connection, the eloquent feminist literature that has urged self-criticism about the special force of the concept of love as used by and applied to women, which has allegedly blinded women to their real social and economic situation, sanctifying acquiescence in exploitative and masochistic personal relationships in the name of loving self-sacrifice.

Surely, in matters of sexual choice, the range of reasonable personal ideals is wide, various, and acutely sensitive to personal context and individual idiosyncrasy. The law has no proper role in prejudging how these choices are to be made in general, and whether romantic love is to be chosen in particular. . . .

The idea that prostitution is morally degrading, resting on ideas of proper female chastity, can no longer be sustained either as an empirical thesis about female sexuality or as an implication of women's social and economic role. As an empirical matter, contemporary studies of female sexuality make clear the ample natural sexual appetites of women, including substantial orgasmic capacity. Ideas of natural female asexuality, on the one hand, and of the incapacity for sexual self-control, on the other, appear today to be not descriptions, but ideologies by which women have been denied a basic self-conception acknowledging their moral right to sexual fulfillment. Correlative ideas of women's social and economic role as a necessary means of kinship exchange are, in their traditional form, obsolete today. Furthermore, in the compulsory and exploitative forms that they historically took, these ideas are repugnant to the equal concern and respect to which women, as persons, are entitled. Marriage no longer serves such economic and social purposes; contraception has mitigated many of the fears peculiar to female unchastity; and the general role of women, no longer limited to procreation and child rearing, has been and continues to be transformed by the growing access of women to the formerly exclusively masculine realm of the public, competitive work, and politics. From this perspective, arguments, like those condemning prostitution, that allegedly protected the spiritual, female sanctuary of the home from incursions from the sensual, competitive masculine world, appear to be malign ways in which women have been caged by an ideology which distorted and unrecognizably disfigured basic self-conceptions of natural capacity and responsible autonomy. . . .

Accordingly, the condemnation of prostitution as morally degraded appears not to rest on critically defensible moral arguments, but on an ideology that idealized female chastity and stigmatized as morally indecent any deviation from this ideal. The rejection of this ground for the criminalization of prostitution is, then, mandated by the deepest values of equal concern and respect for autonomy. Not only does it fail to respect female sexual autonomy, but, in addition, to permit this ideology to have the force of law today is inconsistently to accept a model of compulsory female chastity that we reject elsewhere in our social life. . . .

Kathleen Barry, From Violence to Values . . . and Beyond

From K. Barry, Female Sexual Slavery
(NY: New York University Press, 1984).

Female sexual slavery exists in the vacuum between the disregard for social and political problems that stems from valueless individualism and the confusion of values created by the traditional moralists. The crisis of female sexual slavery demands that we reclaim the need for values—not values as they *had* been, but values that stem from new definitions of what is right and wrong, what is enhancing to human beings versus what is demeaning, and what leads to a positive valuation of life versus what tends toward destruction and dehumanization.

Perversion and Values

I propose to get to new values first through a redefinition of perversion, which will lead to a renewed understanding of *good*. Perversion means "a turning away from what is good and right." Perversion is not just that which is wrong, bad, or evil, but that which distorts, devalues, depersonalizes, warps, and destroys the person as she or he exists in time and space. It involves destruction of the human being in fact. Accordingly, neither heterosexuality nor homosexuality are per se perverted. Instead, sexuality that is fostered through the arrested male sex drive which objectifies, forces, and violates, whether it is heterosexual or homosexual, is perversion.

In my mind, *where there is any attempt to separate the sexual experience from the total person, that first act of objectification is perversion.* Although objectification has been considered part of the mystery of sex, I think that in exploring new values we can locate a mystery much more profound, intense, and worth searching for.

In creating new sexual values we must first discard the assumption that sex, *ipso facto,* is automatically good or bad. Sex is neither good nor bad until it is experienced alone or with another under a given set of conditions. Sexual values involve the whole psychic, social, and spiritual being, not only that which is gender-determined.

In going into new sexual values we are really going back to the values women have always attached to sexuality, values that have been robbed from us, distorted and destroyed as we have been colonized through both sexual violence and so-called sexual liberation. They are the values and needs that connect sex with warmth, affection, love, caring. To establish new sexual values is actually to resurrect those female principles, giving them definition and form in the present context.

Sexual values and the positive, constructive experience of sex *must be based in intimacy.* Sexual experience involves the most personal, private, erotic, sensitive parts of our physical and psychic being—it is intimate in fact.

I think of sexual intimacy in the same way I think of private thoughts. There are those ideas or thoughts that are very private and special to me. They stem from the very depths of my being and in a sense define a very important personal part of me. I share these thoughts with only a few people, those whom I trust and who I want to know me on that level. It is a privileged sharing, as their sharing of private thoughts is to me, an intimate exchange of deeper parts of ourselves than we show to the rest of the world, distant friends or acquaintances.

In this age of nonspecific "openness" where private thoughts are shared equally with everyone, we deprive ourselves of that specialness, that privacy which is the first basis of intimacy.

Sexual intimacy is not something to be given lightly. It is an experience to be *earned* by each from the other. We do not automatically grant trust or respect; they are earned values. Sexual intimacy is not automatic, as depersonalized sexual experience often is. It involves, in the deepest sense, experiencing the pleasure of physical and sexual closeness with another while being able to put oneself in the place of the other, taking on the meaning of the experience of the other, creating not a private but a shared joy. Such intimacy grows and is cultivated from dignity, respect, caring, tenderness. As those things grow, the most personal parts of oneself continually open for more intense and profound sexual experience for heightened erotic experiences.... Sexual intimacy, as true sharing, is denied by the values of individualism whereby one is preoccupied with one's own needs. It is obscured in traditional morality where men are neither challenged nor condemned for sexual aggression. True intimacy has been difficult for women to come to terms with, as traditionally it has been the area in which women have lost their power, identity, and centeredness. For many women it has been an experience of male sexual power: men have simply taken what had been defined as theirs to take. Through feminist consciousness-raising women have come to recognize and reject the conditions of powerlessness. Exploited and dominated at this most personal and vulnerable level, women have moved away from intimacy only to find that new problems arose as they escaped from male power into self-centeredness and as they tried to depersonalize their sexual being.

Intimacy is destroyed by depersonalization of this private, sensitive aspect of our being; the self is devalued into an object and deprived of respect, honor, and dignity. That is the living hell of female sexual slavery, the daily, hourly deprivation of sexual intimacy through forced sexual objectification. It wears down the spirit, strips the ego, denies the value of "self." Jeanne Cordelier is one of the few who has dared to expose the hell of prostitution as she lived it. She describes "the first time":

> For me, too, there was a first time. Being a prostitute is like living through an interminable winter. At first it seems impossible. Then as time passes, you start thinking that "sun" is nothing more than a word thought up by men. . . .
>
> There you are, in a dump that's more or less clean, holding a towel in your hand, looking at somebody you've never seen before. The more you retreat, the more he advances; since the room is fairly cramped, you soon find yourself with your back against the wall. The guy's arms are around you, they're all over your body like slimy tentacles that grope you, strip you, and drag you down as he pulls you over to the bed. . . . For an instant you escape from the nightmare: you're back in the church playground, playing hopscotch. It seems like yesterday. You almost feel good, and you shut your eyes to make the dream last. When you reopen them, after a split second, reality blinds you. Reality has taken the form of a cock, a real family man's wiener, a little soft but still enterprising.
>
> The man pounces on you. His features are drawn. He calls you his little girl, his baby doll, his cherry pie, his quim, his yoyo, his honeyfuck, his tramp, his darling whore. As he penetrates you, he gasps for breath, grinds his teeth and kicks like a mustang. And as he shoots his load, flooding you with a month's abstinence, you lie there in the same position, unmoving, with your arms hanging limp, your legs spread, your eyes staring. You feel soiled, spoiled, destroyed. While he recovers, flopped comfortably on top of you and dripping sour sweat, funny ideas start going through your head. When he deigns to get up, indifferently dripping all over you, you mechanically walk over to the bidet and sit down in disgust . . .
>
> You've almost accepted what you've become.

And Beyond

By redefining perversion and by asserting the new values of sexual intimacy we challenge the root of male domination. This is the radical nature of feminist politics. New values are prerequisite to creating a society in which the use of women as Cordelier described it is no longer acceptable or even tolerable. As the first step in breaking the acceptance of depersonalized sex, it is a culture-creating act, the foundation for revolution. According to sociologists Jaeger and Selznick, "The primordial culture-creating act is the transformation of an impersonal setting into a personal one."

New sexual values infuse quality into the most personal and private life. Once we live with new values, we are able to break down depersonalization and create conditions from which new forms of personal power can grow, power that is not arbitrary, capricious, or invested in the control of others. New sexual values assert a different basis for relationships than that of sex colonization. . . .

Of course many people's experience of sex is based in intimacy that does not objectify. However, their values are not capable of transforming culture unless they become political as well as personal, unless they assert dimensions of female power into the private world of sex colonization. When they do, then what begins as a personal experience can extend to encompass all who have been enslaved and colonized. Feminism demands more than private solutions or even private solutions stated in political terms.

Eroded sensibilities must once again become passionate with the need for liberation. This passion—while it looks to a future of new values, new quality of living—should never, for even one moment, forget the present agony of women who are now sexually enslaved. Fierce intolerance of slavery and passionate vision for change are the forces which create among the colonized the united political strength that brings about revolution.

Political change means confrontation with the values, institutions, and individuals which keep women colonized. Sex colonization assumes sex as an automatic right of men, but sexual intimacy precludes the proposition that sex is the *right* of anyone and asserts instead that it must be earned through trust and sharing. It follows then that *sex cannot be purchased, legally acquired, or seized by force* and that women must oppose all practices which promote "getting sex" on those bases.

Marriage and prostitution are experiences of individuals but they are also institutions. They are, in fact, the primary institutions through which sex is conveyed and in which female sexual slavery is practiced. Sex is purchased through prostitution and legally acquired through marriage; in both as well as outside each, it may be seized by force.

Prostitution promotes the cultural value that men should have sexual service provided to them under any conditions and terms they choose. They need not do anything but pay for it.

Marriage, as an institution of legalized love, presumes sex as a duty, a wife's responsibility. Regardless of the mutuality of feeling that may exist when two people enter marriage, it is often the case that after the original basis for relationship breaks down, men still assume sex as their automatic right.

Prostitution and marriage are elusive institutions. Once battery, marital rape, or forced prostitution begin, women are not only locked in brothels or their homes but they are trapped in the intangible institutions that encourage or perpetuate their slavery. Unlike other institutions, in prostitution or marriage there is no one place where collective protest against these institutions can be lodged. Instead, through the colonization of women they permeate the whole society in individual relationships....

The core of women's oppression in female sexual slavery reveals the interconnection and interdependence among sexual domination, economic exploitation, and discrimination. To refuse sanction to female sexual slavery in all of its manifestations is to directly challenge the patriarchal economic order which has been built on sexual domination. By channeling women into marriage or prostitution, they are kept economically marginal thereby not disrupting male economic and political power. From the practices of sex stereotyping jobs, sex discrimination in hiring, salary and promotion, sexual harassment and abuse on the job, we see how the institutional dimensions of female sexual slavery have been extended to the labor market where women are no longer a reserve, but now are demanding to be an active force.

While female sexual slavery is the core of sexual exploitation, in fighting it we must not skip steps. Challenging the oppression of women will remain ineffective if we follow the simple path from raised consciousness to inflamed rhetoric without insisting on and experiencing necessary value changes. Thus, the feminist values that create personal change will finally be extended to all women and brought into direct confrontation with the colonizers of women. Personal value change requires specific social and political changes.

As long as women who are prostitutes are socially labeled as outcasts, they will be expendable as throwaway women, and legally defined as criminals. A widespread campaign for legal change must address the roles into which society has forced these women, and the changes must provide a way out. Consequently, legal change will mean direct confrontation with the laws that protect and enshrine masculine double standards. Those are the laws that require the public expenditures that are used to implement them. ...

Decriminalization, which is the basis of the system of toleration, is the only means of taking women out of the *official* status of either criminal or prostitute. But decriminalization must be without reservation and must include street hookers as well as those women in brothels. ...As unwelcome a sight as street prostitutes are to many, they cannot either be the subject of double-standard morality harassment, or be hidden away so that we don't have to look at or be affected by what we have socially sanctioned....

Decriminalization of prostitution must be accompanied by increased enforcement of laws against pimping, procuring, and involuntary servitude. When women are neither criminals nor official prostitutes, they theoretically have the rights of any other citizen to bring charges of assault, rape, or kidnapping against pimps and customers. Only when value change accompanies legal change will that theoretical right become a reality....

But, ideally, it should not be the function of law (as it presently exists) to enforce morality or values by making them legal standards under which people must live. New values will revolutionize society only when they are accepted and cherished by the people, not when they are imposed on them. Consequently, as we fight to remove oppressive laws, we must not make the mistake of the oppressor and assume we could or even should impose a new morality through law. In the context of new sexual values, laws are useful only to the extent that they prohibit practices of sexual slavery or sexual violence. They must provide the means for removing the sexual terrorists and enslavers of women from society through arrest, prosecution, and imprisonment.

Individual liberty is the other side of female sexual slavery; it is the goal of feminism. For us now the means to liberation is as important as the goal. The means, how we get there, will be the basis for the new society we are trying to create. We can effectively challenge sex colonization only by guaranteeing individual liberty to the colonized. Not to safeguard individual liberty would be to substitute one set of colonizers for another as male revolutions have done to women. Therefore, while we condemn and punish those who carry out female sexual slavery, and while we condemn the institutions which perpetuate it, we must take care not to condemn in law or practice the women who work and live in those institutions. Our respect and caring must extend to not just those who are identifiable victims but to all women under the yoke of colonization.

For that reason, and in espousing individual liberty, we must not interfere with women who freely enter marriage and can leave it just as freely. Neither should we interfere with women who enter prostitution freely, be they self-employed professional call girls or high-status African prostitutes, as long as they can freely leave their work any time they choose. I assume that this liberty will take place in the context of increasing participation in new values. As new values are actively disseminated through the population, institutions of sex colonization will become less and less attractive. And I assume that we must determine a woman's ability to freely enter or leave institutions of sex colonization based on her actual conditions and not simply on her perception of them or her desire to participate regardless of the conditions. . . .

NOTES AND QUESTIONS

1. **The Morality of Prostitution**. David Richards' moral argument for the decriminalization of prostitution is based on the liberal concept of sexual autonomy and on the claim that prostitution laws unjustifiably enforce an ideal of female chastity. Kathleen Barry also supports decriminalization, but for very different reasons. While Richards believes that commercial sex is not immoral, Barry believes that it is. Does Barry offer reasons for prostitution's immorality beyond the traditional one that Richards criticizes? Do her reasons for ending prostitution survive Richards' concern about protecting women's sexual autonomy?

2. **The Commercial Nature of Prostitution**. Richards notes the importance of the commercial nature of prostitution to its illegality. Otherwise,

we could not distinguish illegal sex work from legal and widespread pre-and extra-marital sexual relations. Fornication and adultery, although illegal in some states, is rarely prosecuted. What is the moral difference between indiscriminate sex for free and indiscriminate sex for pay?

In *Market-inalienability*, Margaret Radin considers the dangers of completely commodified sexuality:

> The open market might render subconscious valuation of women (and perhaps everyone) in sexual dollar value impossible to avoid. It might make the ideal of nonmonetized sharing impossible. Thus, the argument for noncommodification of sexuality based on the domino effect, in its strongest form, is that we do not wish to unleash market forces onto the shaping of our discourse regarding sexuality and hence onto our very conception of sexuality and our sexual feelings.

Margaret Jane Radin, *Market-Inalienability*, 100 Harv. L. Rev. 1849, 1922 (1987).

If the exchange of money for sex is the key to prostitution's immorality, how do we distinguish prostitutes from people who date or marry (and have sex with their partners) only for the material rewards they accrue? Some criminal prostitution laws explicitly exclude sexual activity between spouses. *See, e.g.*, Fla. Stat. § 796.07(1)(a). Why doesn't our society condemn mistresses as much as prostitutes?

Radin suggests a "pragmatic" approach that recognizes that "we are situated in a nonideal world of ignorance, greed, and violence; of poverty, racism, and sexism," and that governs prostitution by a regime of "incomplete commodification":

> If we now permit commodification, we may exacerbate the oppression of women—the suppliers. If we now disallow commodification—without what I have called the welfare-rights corollary, or large-scale redistribution of social wealth and power—we force women to remain in circumstances that they themselves believe are worse than becoming sexual commodity-suppliers. Thus, the alternatives seem subsumed by a need for social progress, yet we must choose some regime now in order to make progress. This dilemma of transition is the double bind. . . .

> Assuming that our ideal of personhood includes the ideal of sexual interaction as equal nonmonetized sharing, we might imagine that the "good" commodified sexuality ought not to exist: that sexual activity should be market-inalienable. But perhaps prohibition of the sale of sexual services, if it aims to preserve sexuality as nonmonetized sharing, is not justified under current circumstances, because sex is already commodified. Moreover, in our nonideal world, market-inalienability— especially if enforced through criminalization of sales—may cause harm to ideals of personhood instead of maintaining and

fostering them, primarily because it exacerbates the double bind. Poor women who believe that they must sell their sexual services to survive are subject to moral opprobrium, disease, arrest, and violence. The ideal of sexual sharing is related to identity and contextuality, but the identity of those who sell is undermined by criminalization and powerlessness, and their ability to develop and maintain relationships is hurt by these circumstances. . . .

Perhaps the best way to characterize the present situation is to say that women's sexuality is incompletely commodified. Many sexual relationships may have both market and non-market aspects: relationships may be entered into and sustained partly for economic reasons and partly for the interpersonal sharing that is part of our ideal of human flourishing. Even if under current circumstances the ideal misleads us into thinking that unequal relationships are really equal, it seems that the way out of such ideological bondage is not to abandon the ideal, but rather to pursue it in ways that are not harmful under these nonideal circumstances. Market-inalienability seems harmful, not only because it might be ideologically two-edged, but also because of the double bind. Yet complete commodification, if any credence is given to the feared domino effect, may relinquish our conception of sexuality entirely.

The issue thus becomes how to structure an incomplete commodification that takes account of our nonideal world, yet does not foreclose progress to a better world of more equal power (and less susceptibility to the domino effect of market rhetoric). I think we should now decriminalize the sale of sexual services in order to protect poor women from the degradation and danger either of the black market or of other occupations that seem to them less desirable. At the same time, in order to check the domino effect, we should prohibit the capitalist entrepreneurship that would operate to create an organized market in sexual services even though this step would pose enforcement difficulties. It would include, for example, banning brokerage (pimping) and recruitment. It might also include banning advertising. Trying to keep commodification of sexuality out of our discourse by banning advertising does have the double bind effect of failing to legitimate the sales we allow, and hence it may fail to alleviate significantly the social disapproval suffered by those who sell sexual services. It also adds "information costs" to their "product," and thus fails to yield them as great a "return" as would the full-blown market. But these nonideal effects must be borne if we really accept that extensive permeation of our discourse by commodification-talk would alter sexuality in a way that we are unwilling to countenance. . . .

Radin, *Market-Inalienability,* at 1916–25. Do you agree with Radin's pragmatic solution to the problem of prostitution? Or do you think that it denies women too much freedom to engage in sex work? Or does it not go far enough to abolish prostitution?

3. **Prostitution and Patriarchy.** Barry focuses not so much on the commercial nature of prostitution as on its underlying assumption that "sex is an automatic right of men." She therefore links together sex that is purchased and sex that is seized by force, the payment of money making little difference to the abuse of the women involved. (Ironically, many people believe that prostitutes cannot be raped—as one police sergeant stated, they are just upset that they "didn't get their money." Susan Brownmiller, *Against Our Will* 409 (1976).) More broadly, prostitution can be seen as an aspect of the systemic treatment of women as sex objects. On the other hand, because men must pay for and not just take what they want from sex workers, this way of "getting sex" can be seen as moral and even liberating. To what extent are prostitution and rape similar or distinguishable? *See* Evelina Giobbe, *Prostitution: Buying the Right to Rape,* in *Rape and Sexual Assault III* 143, 159 (Ann Wolbert Burgess, ed., 1991) ("[B]ecause an exchange of money occurs, irrespective of whether the woman herself maintains control of or benefits from this exchange, the client is given permission to use the woman in a manner that would not be tolerated in any other business or social arrangement"). Do you find Barry's association of marriage and prostitution persuasive?

4. Barry argues that we need to reclaim the female needs and values that "connect sex with warmth, affection, love, caring." Do you find convincing her claim that these are female principles and that they will improve women's condition? Or does Barry's view of sexual intimacy reinforce the very stereotypes about women that have helped to restrain women's sexuality? How might we distinguish Barry's version of sexual intimacy from traditional, patriarchal notions of women's bodies?

5. What is the justification for abolishing commercial sex for *all* women? Do the arguments against prostitution apply to all prostitutes, even those who say that sex work makes them feel powerful and liberated? Would a better strategy be to enable prostitutes who feel enslaved by their work to escape, but to legalize prostitution for others who wish to continue working? Is Barry's closing admonition to determine a prostitute's ability to exit based on our perception of her condition rather than her own perception of it exceedingly paternalistic or it is a realistic assessment of the coercive context of prostitution? Does the comparison of prostitution to slavery provide an answer? We do not allow people to become slaves even if they want to be enslaved.

Gail Pheterson, A Vindication of the Rights of Whores

(Seattle: The Seal Press, 1989).

Not Repeating History

Women's liberation movements throughout the world have not been immune to social, legal and ideological distortions of the lives of prostitutes.

Like women reformers in the 19th century , most contemporary feminists are isolated from women in the sex industry. A common misconception among feminists is the belief that women are protected by efforts to abolish prostitution (efforts like "reformation" of prostitutes and punishment of customers). Two movements of non-prostitute feminists are particularly vocal and influential in putting forth a 20th century abolitionist line: the anti-trafficking movement against female sexual slavery and the anti-pornography campaign, both finding their strongest spokeswomen in the United States. Those groups portray all prostitution and pornography as violence against women. Like 19th century social purists, they do not distinguish between conditions of force or free will, insisting that sex workers who claim autonomy lack consciousness about their actual subjugation. The movements emerged in the late 1970s in a context of increasing feminist activism against rape, battering, sexual abuse of children and other forms of male violence. Together with struggles to define female sexuality, anti-violence activism led some feminists to equate heterosexuality, especially commercial heterosexuality and marital heterosexuality, with female sexual slavery. Other feminists rejected those formulations and warned against anti-violence strategies which sacrifice women's sexual choice, economic security, free speech and/or erotic pleasure.

Sex workers were rarely visible at feminist meetings. Given the dominance of abolitionist feminism during the late 1970s and early 80s, those feminists with either histories or present jobs in prostitution were careful to conceal their "politically incorrect" occupation. However, concurrent and separate from feminist debates on prostitution and pornography was a growing movement of political prostitutes, especially in North America and Western Europe. Some individual prostitutes identified as feminists and some individual feminists allied themselves with whores, but feminist and prostitute movements were basically divided from one another. Feminists who followed the anti-prostitution and anti-pornography line were often viewed by political prostitutes as naive or self-righteous agents of control and condemnation. Prostitutes were viewed by the same feminists as either victims of abuse or collaborators with male domination.

One particular event sponsored by anti-trafficking feminists in 1983 transformed the politics of a number of women from the United States and the Netherlands. The event inspired a snowballing of alliances between women inside and outside the sex industry which eventually led to the formation of the International Committee for Prostitutes' Rights. The following story begins personally with a few individuals, including myself, but it was the parallel thinking and activism of women in many different countries that fueled the present integrated movement for prostitutes' rights. . . .

In 1982, I met Margo St. James in San Francisco during a brief visit to the United States from the Netherlands. She told me about a conference to be held in Rotterdam, the Netherlands, the following year on the subject of "Female Sexual Slavery." Kathleen Barry, who had written a book by the same title, inspired the conference which she planned to organize together with Charlotte Bunch and Shirley Castley....

Besides lectures at Dutch universities and feminist cafes, there was a possibility of a television show. I formulated a proposal for a round table discussion on television including Barry, Bunch, St. James and [Priscilla] Alexander:

> The discussion will focus on both sexual slavery or involuntary prostitution and on the right of women to work voluntarily as prostitutes. The tension between feminist struggle against male violence and feminist struggle for female self-determination will be explored. In other words, how can we de-stigmatize and legitimize whores and protect their right to work while increasing their choice, freedom and safety?

Both the television network and the discussants agreed, at least initially. Later it became clear that the proposal touched a sensitive and historically rooted tension.

As the event grew near, a severe conflict began to develop. No prostitutes other than St. James were among the representatives and her status was changed from participant to resource person. She would be allowed to attend only one morning during which she would be asked to give her report and then leave. Furthermore, Kathleen Barry had changed her mind about the television discussion. She would not appear on television together with a prostitute or ex-prostitute. She explained to me that the conference was feminist and did not support the institution of prostitution. She found it inappropriate to discuss sexual slavery with prostitute women either at the conference or on the air. After much conflict, a compromise television program was arranged in which Barry and Bunch spoke separately from St. James and Alexander....

... The movement for prostitutes' rights is forging a new politics of prostitution. Self-representation of whores and alliances between women are the heart of the new politics. Two hundred years ago in 1792, Mary Wollstonecraft wrote the classic A Vindication of the Rights of Woman. Her book is women's first declaration of independence. Wollstonecraft's contemporaries called her a "shameless wanton," a "hyena in petticoats," a "philosophizing serpent" and an "impious amazon." In modern times, she might have been called a whore. Writing at the time of revolutions in the United States and France, Mary Wollstonecraft protested the exclusion of women from man's quest for human rights. Although she claimed to "speak of the condition of the whole [female] sex, leaving exceptions out of the question," she distinguished prostitutes from worthy women and portrayed them as "poor ignorant wretches." Two hundred years later, those wretches—those whores, are standing publicly with their sisters and demanding inclusion in the Vindication of the Rights of Women. Together, we are not repeating history. ...

Statement on Prostitution and Human Rights

International Committee for Prostitutes' Rights
European Parliament, Brussels
October 1–3, 1986

... The International Committee for Prostitutes' Rights (ICPR) demands that prostitutes, ex-prostitutes and all women regardless of their work, color, class, sexuality, history of abuse or marital status be granted the same human rights as every other citizen. At present, prostitutes are officially and/or unofficially denied rights both by states within the Council of Europe and by States outside of it. No state in the world is held accountable by any international body for those infractions. To the contrary, denial of human rights to prostitutes is publicly justified as a protection of women, public order, health, morality and the reputation of dominant persons or nations. Those arguments deny prostitutes the status of ordinary persons and blame them for disorder and/or disease and for male exploitation of and violence against women. Criminalization or state regulation of prostitution does not protect anyone, least of all prostitutes. Prostitutes are systematically robbed of liberty, security, fair administration of justice, respect for private and family life, freedom of expression and freedom of association. In addition, they suffer from inhuman and degrading treatment and punishment and from discrimination in employment and housing. Prostitutes are effectively excluded from the Human Rights Convention.

The World Charter of Prostitutes' Rights which was adopted by the ICPR in 1985 demands that prostitution be redefined as legitimate work and that prostitutes be redefined as legitimate citizens. Any other stance functions to deny human status to a class of women (and to men who sexually service other men). ...

Shannon Bell, Rewriting the Prostitute Body: Prostitute Perspectives

From Shannon Bell, Reading, Writing and Rewriting the Prostitute Body
(Bloomington: Indiana University Press, 1994).

In postmodernity, the prostitute has emerged simultaneously as a new political subject and as a plural, rather than a unitary, subject....

At the heart of prostitute discourse is a dichotomization of the prostitute body in terms of empowerment/victimization. ...What fundamentally distinguishes prostitutes' rights groups from WHISPER [Women Hurt in Systems of Prostitution Engaged in Revolt] ... is that the rights groups focus on the project of constituting the prostitute as a new political subject.... WHISPER calls for the abolition of prostitution ... Prostitutes' rights groups are concerned about the empowerment of the prostitute in the context of a patriarchal and capitalist society; WHISPER contends that the prostitute can never be empowered until she ceases to be a prostitute....

[The] prostitute discourses are reverse discourses; that is, they counter the hegemonic discourse on prostitution. Prostitutes' rights discourse, however, goes beyond that to displace the hegemonic inscriptions on the prostitute body through the production of new meanings; the prostitute is constructed as healer rather than disease producer, as educator rather than degenerate, a sex expert rather than deviant, as business woman rather than commercial object. Prostitutes' rights discourse, by appropriating the rights discourse of hegemonic and feminist liberalism and articulating these rights demands in the context of collective identity politics, transgresses the liberal framework while adhering to it....

"Woman" is the primary signifier of the other in liberal rights theory.... [F]eminist discourse since the eighteenth century has consistently reproduced prostitutes in the position of female other.... Prostitutes, "the other of the other," are now present as new political subjects.

Prostitutes' collective public demand for the legal right to be recognized as citizens just like all others is not a demand for equality in spite of difference but a demand for equality based on the distinct difference of being a prostitute. What lies just beneath the surface of the demand for legal rights and equality is a doubly transgressive ethical gesture: an affirmation of a "negative" identity and a revaluation of values through the recognition of commercial sex as being just as valid and worthy as noncommercial sex.

WHISPER situates itself in the position of countering prostitutes' rights discourse from the position of radical feminism. It reproduces the meanings that radical feminism inscribes on the prostitute body: as such, it is a simple reversal of the hegemonic discourse. WHISPER counters the meanings produced in the dominant discourse, but, like radical feminism, it cannot transgress and displace the dominant discourse; it reproduces the prostitute as victim but seeks to empower her by liberating her from her prostitute identity.

Resistance is inherent in any constituting discourse. Counter-discourses are formed when those identified as other begin to speak on their own behalf, to represent themselves, and thus to provide alternative mappings of their subject position and their specific territory in the social field. The shape of the other is determined, in large degree, by the shape of the dominant discourse. The dominant form of resistance is usually manifest as counter-identification whereby the other rejects and inverts in some way the identity constructed by the dominant discourse; yet it never goes beyond that to transgression, displacement, and dis-identification. I will attempt to show that, whereas WHISPER discourse manifests counter-identification, prostitutes' rights discourse involves dis-identification....

Rather than disassociate from the label "whore," which, through nineteenth-century sexual categorization and definition, came to mean "unchaste," "defiled," and "diseased," prostitutes' rights advocates reclaim the word, giving it a positive meaning and demanding rights as whores....

How do prostitutes define "whore" and the whore identity? COYOTE [Call Off Your Tired Old Ethics] founder and co-director of ICPR [International Committee for Prostitutes' Rights], Margo St. James said in a talk.... "I prefer the word 'whore' [rather than 'prostitute'].... I want to reclaim it like lesbians have reclaimed the word 'dyke' over the last decade." ... Gail Pheterson, co-director of ICPR, provides this definition of "whore":

> The whore label is attached to anyone who works or has worked in the sex industry as ... a provider of sexual service or entertainment. The whore as prostitute or sex worker is the prototype of the stigmatized woman or feminized man. But not only prostitutes are labelled whores. Any woman may be designated "whore" within a particular cultural setting, especially if she is a migrant, target of racist discrimination, independent worker or victim of abuse.

Thus the prostitutes' rights struggle links itself along a chain of equivalences with all stigmatized women and men....

PONY [Prostitutes of New York] activist Annie Sprinkle cautions against giving any one meaning to prostitution or any "true" definition to being a prostitute:

> [A]s a prostitute I did feel used and really treated like shit, really taken advantage of. There were times when I was in total power. There were times when I received a lot. There were times when it was wonderful. I got in it for the money. But I also got in because I needed to be touched. I wanted the attention. I wanted the status. There are so many reasons. The problem is that everyone is always trying to simplify it.

Sprinkle continues: "There are a lot of different ways prostitutes feel about their work." For her it was both painful and pleasurable:

> Dealing with people's anger, greed, fear, judgments, prejudices and neediness could be painful. ...There were guys who managed to manipulate me into doing things they knew I really didn't want to do. ...There were guys that ripped me off for the money I had earned. ...Many were disrespectful and unappreciative. Prostitution can also be a wonderful, satisfying job. I got pleasure in making people feel better. ...I was really giving to people and nurturing and teaching. ...I got off sexually. ...I had orgasms when I worked, not with all the guys. ...Sometimes I would do it to have sex, like with Samuel. ...I like having sex with him. He has been my client for sixteen years. It is my longest relationship.

Rights activists are careful to hold the tension between the positive and negative aspects of prostitution so that prostitution never completely becomes one or the other. They are also careful to situate the negative aspects of prostitution in the context of the broader sex-negative society.

Veronica Vera makes a distinction between sex work and the negativity that has come to be associated with it:

> Sex work ... is a great service that is couched in all sorts of negative stuff. The "bad" part is the negative stuff that we put on it: from the client's feelings of sexual guilt to bad laws and cops harassing women on the street.

Rights activists in a strategic political move define prostitution as an activity midway between sex and work: perhaps the best example of this is Annie's public claim that although she really likes her long term client of sixteen years, and she enjoys having sex with him, she would not do it if he was not paying her. . . .

While holding that prostitution is a sexual activity, rights groups center on the work side of the sex work construction in order to undermine the negativity associated with prostitution. This is a strategic emphasis: as a political movement rights organizations are more likely to have an impact on government policies and social attitudes if they focus on the work aspect of prostitution, rather than try to legitimate it as sexual activity. . . .

Much feminist and, particularly, WHISPER criticism of the prostitutes' rights discourse is premised on the belief that prostitution can not be voluntary in a racist, sexist, capitalist, patriarchal social field. The ICPR takes this criticism strongly into account in its validation of prostitution as work whether it is voluntary or necessary. Prostitutes' rights groups do not claim that prostitution is a free choice; they claim that it is as free a choice as other choices made in a capitalist, patriarchal, and racist system. They recognize the differences among types of prostitution and the interconnections among racism, capitalism, and patriarchy in which, of the 10 to 20 percent of prostitutes who are street workers, 40 percent are women of color; 55 percent of women arrested are women of color; and 85 percent of prostitutes in jail are women of color. Prostitutes' rights discourse does not deny that economic and sexual inequalities are causes of prostitution. . . .

Although rights discourse contextualizes prostitution as being symptomatic of women's oppression in society it does not offer any critique and/or analysis of the structural basis which produces gender, class, and race inequalities. Nor can it. A discourse premised on the extension of basic human and civil rights, as radical as the demand may be, as far as it may go in changing the identity and status of the claimant group and even in undoing the traditional concept of rights can only act as an intervention. It is an act of micropolitics concerned with its specific struggle, with forming alliances with other related struggles, and not with a change in any totality.

Drawing upon the liberal contractarian depiction of prostitution as labor, prostitutes' rights discourse depicts prostitutes either as self-employed or working for a third party and prostitution as a small business. Prostitutes' rights groups demand that prostitution be subject to the same laws as other small businesses and prostitutes to the same laws as other entrepreneurs and workers. . . .

Prostitutes' rights discourse ... reverses the image of the prostitute as "polluter of the body politic" to the prostitute as "safe-sex educator." Rights discourse counters the scapegoating of prostitutes as disease carriers with knowledge and information.... Priscilla Alexander ... reported:

> [P]ublic health figures indicate that only five percent of sexually transmitted diseases are related to prostitution in the United States. Still, prostitutes are blamed. In the case of AIDS there is enormous scapegoating of prostitutes in the United States based on absolutely no evidence. The studies that have been done indicate that the only prostitutes who have been found to carry AIDS antibodies are some IV-users. The one study that compares prostitute and non-prostitute women, which is in San Francisco, shows no difference between groups; in both cases those who tested positively for AIDS antibodies are either IV-users or in regular sexual relationships with IV-users or bisexual men.

Alexander names this connection of AIDS with prostitution "Blame the Prostitute." ...

To conclude, there is a tension in prostitutes' rights discourse; the ability to hold this tension without privileging either side marks prostitutes' rights as a paradoxical and postmodern discourse. One can draw contradictory conclusions from rights discourse. On the one hand, it can be argued that the demand for rights from the position of marginalized collectivities destabilizes and undoes the meaning attached to the liberal concept of individual rights; that the enfranchisement of prostitutes as new political subjects holds "the promise and the affirmation of the future ... as other ... that which might no longer be what is." On the other hand, it can equally be argued that prostitutes' rights discourse is premised on capitalist assumptions with the aim of producing the prostitute as a small business woman and/or legitimate worker in a manner which just serves to reproduce the system.

The paradox is that prostitutes' rights discourse does both simultaneously and consequently does neither. It is precisely the production of the prostitute identity on the boundary between work and sex that facilitates holding these seemingly contradictory tenets. If prostitutes' rights activists just wanted prostitutes to "take themselves to market and name their price," ... then they would be constructing the prostitute as a petty bourgeois entrepreneur and not a radical political subject. But prostitutes' rights advocates situate this commercial exchange in the context of collective identity politics, which has as its goal both the affirmation of the prostitute as a positive identity and the realization of feminist goals such as the right to control one's body and to have economic control over one's life. Prostitutes' rights discourse reconciles the two contradictory strands in its discourse by presenting the market as the means for prostitutes to be in control of their sexuality and to have economic determination. Rights prostitutes want to use the market as [a] means of controlling their own sexuality and of having economic determination.

WHISPER presents rights discourse as a colluding discourse which reproduces the oppression of prostitutes and of all women. ...There is no point of reconciliation between WHISPER and the rights groups' discourses. There are only two things these oppositional discourses have in common: they are both produced from the prostitute subject position and they demand the decriminalization of the prostitute....

WHISPER, formed in 1985, is a Minneapolis-based national organization whose main focus is helping women get out of "the life." Its name was chosen to indicate that

> ... women in systems of prostitution ... whisper among themselves about the coercion, degradation, sexual abuse and battery that the sex industry is founded on, while myths about prostitution are shouted out in pornography, the mainstream media, and by self-appointed "experts." ...

Like the prostitutes' rights movement, WHISPER is a first-person movement based on women's experience in prostitution. WHISPER discourse, unlike prostitutes' rights discourse, however does not allow for a number of equally valid prostitute subject positions. Rather, it produces the prostitute solely as victim. ...

The main difference between WHISPER and ICPR theorizations of prostitution is that ICPR theorizes prostitution as sexual activity and work, which may or may not be exploitative to varying degrees, and WHISPER theorizes prostitution as sexual exploitation. WHISPER focuses exclusively on the facts of prostitutes' exploitation and oppression. Certainly, any discussion of prostitution would be obscene if these aspects were ignored; analogous to this would be writing about the dignity of labor without mentioning exploitation. Yet, in WHISPER's inscription prostitution can be only exploitative....

WHISPER completely rejects prostitutes' rights construction of prostitution as a profession. Prostitution is "a system of violence against women." All prostitutes are battered women: [Founder Evelina] Giobbe equates those who don't admit it and claim to like their work with assaulted women who say "Johnny didn't mean to hit me. He hit me because he loves me." The prostitute has no autonomy, according to WHISPER; at most she can be "in charge of her exploitation" and the "manager of her own victimage." ...

Giobbe rejects "prostitute" as an identity. She reverses prostitutes' rights construction of prostitute as an identity:

> The process of "becoming" a prostitute entails the systematic destruction of an individual woman's beliefs, feelings, desires and values. Upon entering prostitution a woman typically acquires a new name, changes her appearance, and creates a fictitious past. ...To be a prostitute is to be an object in the marketplace: a three-dimensional blank screen upon which men project and act out their sexual dominance. Thus the word "prostitute" does not imply a "deeper identity"; it is the absence of identity: the theft

and subsequent abandonment of self. What remains is essential to the "job": the mouth, the genitals, anus, breasts . . . and the label.

Giobbe depicts "prostitute" as a "name men give to our oppression." WHISPER strategy is the reverse of prostitutes' rights: rather than deconstructing the meaning attributed to the word "whore" or "prostitute," WHISPER shows how, from the prostitute's point of view, the word is a label. "The role of prostitute is socially constructed by men for their benefit and then cast upon women irrevocably." Giobbe's definition of a prostitute is "to be unconditionally sexually available to any male who buys the right to use your body in any way he chooses." . . .

WHISPER is doing crucial work for women abused in prostitution. The problem with WHISPER is its totalizing ideology—"all prostitutes are abused women," "prostitution—commercial sex—is sexual abuse." It does not allow for different constructions of prostitution. WHISPER produces the prostitute solely as a victim; it marks her victimage from the subject position of the feminist and the ex-prostitute; yet it is important to keep in mind that discourses and agents of oppression—the Contagious Diseases Acts of the nineteenth century and their enforcers and today's laws and law enforcers—justify their persecution of prostitutes on the ground that prostitutes are victims. . . .

The problem with WHISPER is certainly not in its practical work with battered-women's shelters to include prostitutes in shelter services, nor is it the support WHISPER provides for women to get out of prostitution; the problem is its devaluation and negation of the possibility for a plurality of experiences in prostitution. . . .

NOTES AND QUESTIONS

1. **Prostitutes' Organizations**. As the readings discuss, there are several organizations in the United States composed largely of prostitutes or ex-prostitutes that work specifically to guarantee prostitutes' rights or welfare. All advocate for the repeal of laws criminalizing prostitution, but they disagree about whether sex work exploits or benefits women. How should the existence and positions of these organizations of political prostitutes affect feminist thinking about prostitution?

2. **Prostitution as Work.** Socialist feminists and some prostitutes' rights advocates have reconceptualized prostitution as a form of work. What do you think about Gail Pheterson's statement of the feminist project regarding prostitution, to determine how we can "de-stigmatize and legitimize whores and protect their right to work while increasing their choice, freedom and safety"? Why did this statement produce so much conflict at the Rotterdam conference on prostitution, so much that the four women proposed to participate in a televised roundtable discussion ended up appearing separately?

Margaret Baldwin, a radical feminist, challenges the view of prostitution as work and its related agenda of improving the economic conditions of prostitutes:

...[T]he entire "money not sex" critique avoids the whole question of what the woman is selling, and the john is buying, in the prostitution transaction itself. The argument that prostitution is labor, it will be recalled, relies on an analysis of the conditions of economic exploitation entailed in the relationship of pimp to prostitute. The matter of consumption, of the social interaction between prostitute and john which produces "prostitution" as a commodity, is never addressed. The issue of gender is also suppressed, in regard to both the pimp/prostitute relationship and the john/prostitute relationship. The fact that both are typically male/female arrangements, similarly economizing the prostitute's identity as a "sexed female," huddles silently, inarticulable within an analysis rigorously distinguishing "sex" from "work." ...

... [F]or the woman used in this transaction, neither the money nor the sex may translate readily as anything her "own." In respect to both, she remains a stranger, neither worker nor "partner." ... [T]he prostitute is present to the john literally and solely as a thing that produces an experience of sex for him, as he wishes it. ...[T]he john [is] twice-blessed: both "owner" and "consumer" of the transaction, the john dominates both economically and sexually.

Fundamental to the john's sexual experience is eroticized disregard of the woman....

... The transfer of money from the john to the prostitute ... confirms and celebrates his entitlement to treat the woman this way (any way he wishes), situating him in the role of "owner." ... That is the sexual authority men buy in prostitution: to fix the meaning of who or what a woman is.

Margaret A. Baldwin, *Split at the Root: Prostitution and Feminist Discourses of Law Reform*, 5 Yale J.L. & Feminism 47, 107–110 (1992).

3. **Legalization in Nevada**. Nevada has enacted a system of legalization in which sex work in highly regulated by the government. Sex work is restricted to brothels that are licensed by the county and that pay business taxes. The prostitutes' lives are subject to intense state supervision: they are required to undergo weekly medical exams, told where to live, and "prevented from raising their own children, driving a car within the city limits, and shopping between the hours of five P.M. and eight A.M." Jessica N. Drexler, *Government's Role in Turning Tricks: The World's Oldest Profession in The Netherlands and the United States*, 15 Dick. J. Int'l L. 201 (1996).

4. **Resentment**. Was Kathleen Barry justified in refusing to appear on television with prostitutes or could her position opposing prostitution have accommodated a discussion with these women? Barry's response suggests that even women who are sympathetic toward women coerced into prostitution harbor resentment toward women who want to be sex workers. Margo St. James charges that, "One of the reasons the prostitute is punished is the puritannical fear that she's enjoying her work." Are you persuaded by

Barry's explanation that we must discredit women who choose to be sex workers because women must be "socially responsible for the choices they make"? Barry, on the other hand, was motivated to condemn female sexual slavery out of her own emotional heartbreak in learning about the suffering of prostitutes. *See* Barry, *Female Sexual Slavery*, at 215.

5. **Abolition or Legalization?** Which position on prostitution do you find more compelling—prostitutes' rights discourse that focuses on constituting the prostitute as a new political subject who should be empowered or WHISPER's contention that prostitutes will never be empowered until they stop being prostitutes? Is sex work inherently exploitative or is it only the legal and cultural degradation of prostitutes that leads to their disempowerment? The former position suggests that prostitution should be abolished, while the latter suggests that sex work should be legalized and even supported.

6. **Liberating Potential?** Shannon Bell observes that prostitutes' rights discourse aims to reclaim the label "whore" and to give it a positive meaning. In other words, it argues that feminists should not only tolerate or sympathize with prostitutes but see something enlightening in their work. Not surprisingly, Andrea Dworkin has argued that this notion reflects the ultimate strategy of domination: "It is a tragedy beyond the power of language to convey when what has been imposed on women by force becomes a standard of freedom for women." Andrea Dworkin, *Intercourse* 143 (1987). Is it possible to disengage the positive features of sex work from its oppressive aspects and to imagine its liberating expression? Or do you agree with a speaker at the Second World Whores' Congress who stated, "I have a feeling that, just like marriage, prostitution is an institution that was invented by men for men" and would not have been invented by women? Does WHISPER's position that a prostitute can be at most "in charge of her exploitation" help to ensure women's control of their bodies or deny prostitutes' bodily autonomy?

Margaret Baldwin sharply criticizes the battle waged by various feminist camps over the meaning of "prostitute" for ignoring the lived brutality suffered by prostitutes themselves, resulting in "a profound incomprehensibility of prostitution to feminism." As suggested by the excerpt from her article quoted above, Baldwin sees little self-defining potential in a practice that gives men authority "to fix the meaning of who or what a woman is." She concludes by proposing a shift in feminists' focus:

> What is lost in the prostitution debate, as we are all asked to justify the lives of prostitutes as just like those of other women, is what other women need to learn and know and appreciate and politicize about the conditions of their own existence from women in prostitution. That is the fundamental condition of consciousness-raising that has been forfeited by the larger movement: that women in prostitution have insight and knowledge that other women need to make sense of their own lives. The continued silence, shame, the formalistic appeals, the elevation of theorizing over action stifling the participation of women in prostitution in our movement is supported by a political climate that wants prostitutes only to ask permission to join, not authority to direct.

"Other women" don't want to hear, perhaps, that our boyfriends and husbands are buying sex from women in prostitution. "Other women" don't want to hear, perhaps, that the "straight jobs we have are sexualized top to bottom." "Other women" don't want to hear, perhaps, that we are each one man from the street. But if our stories are to gain in boldness and integrity, we all need to be able to hear all of that, and find the "point to it."

I am not about to say, as you may think I am about to say, that "all woman are prostitutes." That is a glib and silly, nearly insulting, thing to say. (I mean, insulting to women in prostitution.) There is a theme, though, that obviously links all of these stories. That is the story that no one is a prostitute, recited with utmost conviction, or with the passion of a final plea for help and justice. And perhaps that is the story that is the prostitution story itself: a woman declaring, with equal parts conviction and resignation, that she is not a prostitute, to please somebody else upon whom her survival depends.

Baldwin, *Split at the Root*, at 116–17. How can listening to women in prostitution lead to these diametrically opposed conclusions—both that "no one is [or should be] a prostitute" and that we should embrace the identity of prostitute?

E.   PORNOGRAPHY

INTRODUCTION

The preceding section claimed that the laws against prostitution function to divide, constrain and degrade female sexuality and women. This section uses the feminist anti-pornography campaign and its surrounding controversy to undertake another exploration of the relationship between law and women's bodies. Like the section on prostitution, this material is also concerned with laws of sexual repression, but here the focus shifts from the regulation of sexual *conduct* to the regulation of sexual *representation* in cultural materials such as books, photographs, and films.

During the 1980s, feminists engineered several widely-publicized grass-roots efforts to obtain municipal legislation that would have penalized the manufacturing and distribution of "pornography." Pornography was defined by the model ordinance used in this campaign as "the graphic sexually explicit subordination of women, whether in pictures or in words," where women are presented in one of nine particularized ways.[1]

The ordinance campaign was built on claims that pornography has a devastatingly negative impact on women's lives. Campaign activists claimed that pornography causes violence against women; and they also argued that, by objectifying women's bodies and by eroticizing subordination,

---

1. The text of the ordinance can be found in Andrea Dworkin's article included in this section.

pornography is "central to the inequality of women." The definition of sexually explicit materials which the ordinance would regulate did not coincide with the Supreme Court's current definition of obscenity, which is unprotected by the First Amendment. Ambitiously designed and structured to reform the character and quality of women's lives, the ordinance thus posed new questions about how law has been and may be used to regulate sexual expression.

By making pornography a legislative and then a judicial issue, the ordinance campaign thrust pornography into a more public arena than it had previously occupied. The ordinance campaign mobilized opposition to the representation of women in sexually explicit materials that had been mounting since the sixties' sexual liberation movement and the second wave of feminist activism. But, the campaign also divided feminists, particularly with respect to the claim that the inequality of women is caused by the organization of sexuality as it is depicted in pornography. This issue not only revealed and produced divisions among feminists regarding the causes of sexism; it also generated disputes regarding the meaning and value of sex.

Different feminist attitudes toward the ordinance are elaborated by the first set of readings: Andrea Dworkin's defense of the model ordinance and Carlin Meyer's critique of "porn-suppressionists." Patricia Hill Collins's writing on the relationship between the objectification of Black women's bodies and pornography reveals another, critical dimension of pornography's subordination of women. These pieces are followed by the Seventh Circuit's decision in American Booksellers Association v. Hudnut, 771 F.2d 323 (1986), declaring the Indianapolis ordinance unconstitutional, a decision which the Supreme Court summarily affirmed in 1986. Although the *Hudnut* litigation severely undermined the usefulness of the model ordinance as the primary focus for pornography activism, *Hudnut* did not bring an end to feminist opposition to pornography or feminist disputes regarding the significance of sexually explicit representations. The remaining readings in this section present material from which two divergent feminist post-ordinance pornography stances can be identified.

One post-ordinance response is the attempt of scholars and activists who take the position that pornography contributes significantly to women's subordination to develop alternative legal strategies to combat the production and distribution of pornography. The excerpt from an article by Cass Sunstein suggests how this position might be refined and reframed, in order to address the First Amendment concerns underlying the Seventh Circuit's decision in *Hudnut*. In addition, Sunstein's piece proposes changes that might render anti-pornography legislation constitutional under prevailing interpretations. Support for pursuing other anti-pornography laws is also provided through the article by Mari Matsuda which addresses the problem of regulating racist hate speech. Some readers' intense antipathy to racist speech may dislodge an otherwise unshakeable devotion to curtailing the role of law in repressing expression.

Mary Joe Frug identified the other post-ordinance stance as "discourse criticism." To the extent that discourse critics seek to deploy pornography rather than repress it, their approach to sexually explicit representation directly conflicts with the work of anti-pornography legal activists. Although feminist analysis and criticism of sexual representation predated the model ordinance, the ordinance campaign validated, reinforced, and stimulated this work. Because the ordinance campaign involved opponents and advocates in conflicting claims regarding the impact of pornography on sexuality, the campaign publicized sexuality as a political institution, as a terrain of contested interpretations. In addition, the campaign publicized the pornography industry as a sexual institution, as a network of power centers which might be invaded and challenged for control. Discourse critics continue to analyze pornography, as well as other forms of cultural representation that affect the way women experience gender, their bodies, and their sexual practices.

Like ordinance supporters, discourse critics argue that sexually explicit representation is an important factor in the construction of women's lives. Unlike ordinance supporters, however, discourse critics insist that pornography takes many different forms and that these forms have different consequences for different women. The most radical position which discourse critics take is the claim that not all of pornography's consequences are negative. While some discourse critics are anti-pornography activists who seek ways other than legal repression to combat the production of some but not all forms of pornography, others do not oppose pornography production. They seek, rather, to utilize the strategies of discourse interpretation to "put pornography in the service of women."[2] The excerpts from Mariana Valverde's book and Susan Keller's article illustrate the post-ordinance stance of pornography discourse critics. Audre Lorde's essay distinguishes between eroticism and pornography and further explores the possibilities for tapping women's sexuality as a source of power and information.

Pornography discourse critics and anti-pornography legal activists are undoubtedly united in their desire to prevent women or men from being physically abused in the production of pornography. But these feminists are divided in their attitudes about what further harm pornography causes women; they are divided about the significance which sexuality may play in constructing or challenging the subordinate status of women; and they are divided about whether law should be used to suppress pornography.

Andrea Dworkin, Against the Male Flood: Censorship, Pornography, and Equality

8 Harv.Women's L.J. 1 (1985).

Pornography

In the United States, it is an $8–billion trade in sexual exploitation.

---

2. This phrase is taken from Angela Carter's explanation for her interest in the Marquis de Sade. See Angela Carter, Sadeian Woman and the Ideology of Pornography 37 (1978).

It is women turned into subhumans, beaver, pussy, body parts, genitals exposed, buttocks, breasts, mouths opened and throats penetrated, covered in semen, pissed on, shitted on, hung from light fixtures, tortured, maimed, bleeding, disemboweled, killed.

It is some creature called female, used.

It is scissors poised at the vagina and objects stuck in it, a smile on the woman's face, her tongue hanging out.

It is a woman being fucked by dogs, horses, snakes.

It is every torture in every prison cell in the world, done to women and sold as sexual entertainment.

It is rape and gang rape and anal rape and throat rape: and it is the woman raped, asking for more.

It is the woman in the picture to whom it is really happening and the women against whom the picture is used, to make them do what the woman in the picture is doing.

It is the power men have over women turned into sexual acts men do to women, because pornography is the power and the act.

It is the conditioning of erection and orgasm in men to the powerlessness of women: our inferiority, humiliation, pain, torment; to us as objects, things, or commodities for use in sex as servants.

It sexualizes inequality and in doing so creates discrimination as a sex-based practice.

It permeates the political condition of women in society by being the substance of our inequality however located—in jobs, in education, in marriage, *in life.*

It is women, kept a sexual underclass, kept available for rape and battery and incest and prostitution.

It is what we are under male domination; it is what we are for under male domination.

It is the heretofore hidden (from us) system of subordination that women have been told is just life.

Under male supremacy, it is the synonym for what being a woman is.

It is access to our bodies as a birthright to men: the grant, the gift, the permission, the license, the proof, the promise, the method, how-to; it is us accessible, no matter what the law pretends to say, no matter what we pretend to say.

It is physical injury and physical humiliation and physical pain: to the women against whom it is used after it is made; to the women used to make it.

As words alone, or words and pictures, moving or still, it creates systematic harm to women in the form of discrimination and physical hurt. It creates harm inevitably by its nature because of what it is and what it does. The harm will occur as long as it is made and used. The name of the next victim is unknown, but everything else is known.

Because of it—because it is the subordination of women perfectly achieved—the abuse done to us by any human standard is perceived as using us for what we are by nature: women are whores; women want to be raped; she provoked it; women like to be hurt; she says no but means yes because she wants to be taken against her will which is not really her will because what she wants underneath is to have anything done to her that violates or humiliates or hurts her; she wants it, because she is a woman, no matter what it is, because she is a woman; that is how women are, what women are, what women are for. This view is institutionally expressed in law. So much for equal protection.

If it were being done to human beings, it would be reckoned an atrocity. It is being done to women. It is reckoned fun, pleasure, entertainment, sex, somebody's (not something's) civil liberty no less.

What do you want to be when you grow up? *Doggie Girl? Gestapo Sex Slave? Black Bitch in Bondage? Pet, bunny, beaver? In dreams begin responsibilities, whether one is the dreamer or the dreamed.*

Pornographers

Most of them are small-time pimps or big-time pimps. They sell women: the real flesh-and-blood women in the pictures. They like the excitement of domination; they are greedy for profit; they are sadistic in their exploitation of women; they hate women, and the pornography they make is the distillation of that hate. The photographs are what they have created live, for themselves, for their own enjoyment. The exchanges of women among them are part of the fun, too: so that the fictional creature "Linda Lovelace," who was the real woman Linda Marchiano, was forced to "deep-throat" every pornographer her owner-pornographer wanted to impress. Of course, it was the woman, not the fiction, who had to be hypnotized so that the men could penetrate to the bottom of her throat, and who had to be beaten and terrorized to get her compliance at all. The finding of new and terrible things to do to women is part of the challenge of the vocation: so the inventor of "Linda Lovelace" and "deep-throating" is a genius in the field, a pioneer. Or, as Al Goldstein, a colleague, referred to him in an interview with him in *Screw* several years ago: a pimp's pimp.

Even with written pornography, there has never been the distinction between making pornography and the sexual abuse of live women that is taken as a truism by those who approach pornography as if it were an intellectual phenomenon. The Marquis de Sade, as the world's foremost literary pornographer, is archetypal. His sexual practice was the persistent sexual abuse of women and girls, with occasional excursions into the abuse of boys. As an aristocrat in a feudal society, he preyed with near impunity on prostitutes and servants. The pornography he wrote was an urgent part of the sexual abuse he practiced: not only because he did what he wrote, but also because the intense hatred of women that fueled the one also fueled the other: not two separate engines, but one engine running on the same tank. The acts of pornography and the acts of rape were waves on the same sea: that sea, becoming for its victims however it reached them, a tidal wave of destruction. Pornographers who use words know that what they are doing is both aggressive and destructive: sometimes they philosophize about how sex inevitably ends in death, the death of a woman being a thing of sexual beauty as well as excitement. Pornography, even when written, is sex because of the dynamism of the sexual hatred in it; and for pornographers, the sexual abuse of women as commonly understood and pornography are both acts of sexual predation, which is how they live.

One reason that stopping pornographers and pornography is not censorship is that pornographers are more like the police in police states than they are like the writers in police states. They are the instruments of terror, not its victims. What police do to the powerless in police states is what pornographers do to women, except that it is entertainment for the masses, not dignified as political. Writers do not do what pornographers do. Secret police do. Torturers do. What pornographers do to women is more like what police do to political prisoners than it is like anything else: except for the fact that it is watched with so much pleasure by so many. Intervening in a system of terror where it is vulnerable to public scrutiny to stop it is not censorship; it is the system of terror that stops speech and creates abuse and despair. The pornographers are the secret police of male supremacy: keeping women subordinate through intimidation and assault.

Subordination

In the amendment to the Human Rights Ordinance of the City of Minneapolis written by Catharine A. MacKinnon and myself, pornography is defined as the graphic, sexually explicit subordination of women whether in pictures or in words that also includes one or more of the following: women are presented dehumanized as sexual objects, things or commodities; or women are presented as sexual objects who enjoy pain or humiliation; or women are presented as sexual objects who experience sexual pleasure in being raped; or women are presented as sexual objects tied up or cut up or mutilated or bruised or physically hurt; or women are presented in postures of sexual submission; or women's body parts are exhibited, such that women are reduced to those parts; or women are presented being penetrated by objects or animals; or women are presented in scenarios of degradation, injury, abasement, torture, shown as filthy or inferior, bleeding, bruised, or hurt in a context that makes these conditions sexual. . . .

The oppression of women occurs through sexual subordination. It is the use of sex as the medium of oppression that makes the subordination of women so distinct from racism or prejudice against a group based on religion or national origin. Social inequality is created in many different ways. In my view, the radical responsibility is to isolate the material means of creating the inequality so that material remedies can be found for it.

This is particularly difficult with respect to women's inequality because that inequality is achieved through sex. Sex as desired by the class that dominates women is held by that class to be elemental, urgent, necessary, even if or even though it appears to *require* the repudiation of any claim women might have to full human standing. In the subordination of women, inequality itself is sexualized: made into the experience of sexual pleasure, essential to sexual desire. Pornography is the material means of sexualizing inequality; and that is why pornography is a central practice in the subordination of women.

Subordination itself is a broad, deep, systematic dynamic discernible in any persecution based on race or sex. Social subordination has four main parts. First, there is *hierarchy,* a group on top and a group on the bottom. For women, this hierarchy is experienced both socially and sexually, publicly and privately. Women are physically integrated into the society in which we are held to be inferior, and our low status is both put in place and maintained in the sexual usage of us by men; and so women's experience of hierarchy is incredibly intimate and wounding.

Second, subordination is *objectification.* Objectification occurs when a human being, through social means, is made less than human, turned into a thing or commodity, bought and sold. When objectification occurs, a person is depersonalized, so that no individuality or integrity is available socially or in what is an extremely circumscribed privacy (because those who dominate determine its boundaries). Objectification is an injury right at the heart of discrimination: those who can be used as if they are not fully human are no longer fully human in social terms; their humanity is hurt by being diminished.

Third, subordination is *submission.* A person is at the bottom of a hierarchy because of a condition of birth; a person on the bottom is dehumanized, an object or commodity; inevitably, the situation of that person requires obedience and compliance. That diminished person is expected to be submissive; there is no longer any right to self-determination, because there is no basis in equality for any such right to exist. In a condition of inferiority and objectification, submission is usually essential for survival. Oppressed groups are known for their abilities to anticipate the orders and desires of those who have power over them, to comply with an obsequiousness that is then used by the dominant group to justify its own dominance: the master, not able to imagine a human like himself in such degrading servility, thinks the servility is proof that the hierarchy is natural and that the objectification simply amounts to seeing these lesser creatures for what they are. The submission forced on inferior, objectified groups precisely by hierarchy and objectification is taken to be the proof of inherent inferiority and subhuman capacities.

Fourth, subordination is *violence.* The violence is systematic, endemic enough to be unremarkable and normative, usually taken as an implicit right of the one committing the violence. In my view, hierarchy, objectification, and submission are the preconditions for systematic social violence against any group targeted because of a condition of birth. If violence against a group is both socially pervasive and socially normal, then hierarchy, objectification, and submission are already solidly in place.

The role of violence in subordinating women has one special characteristic congruent with sex as the instrumentality of subordination: the violence is supposed to be sex for the woman too—what women want and like as part of our sexual nature; it is supposed to give women pleasure (as in rape); it is supposed to mean love to a woman from her point of view (as in battery). The violence against women is seen to be done not just in accord with something compliant in women, but in response to something active in and basic to women's nature.

Pornography uses each component of social subordination. Its particular medium is sex. Hierarchy, objectification, submission, and violence all become alive with sexual energy and sexual meaning. A hierarchy, for instance, can have a static quality; but pornography, by sexualizing it, makes it dynamic, almost carnivorous, so that men keep imposing it for the sake of their own sexual pleasure—for the sexual pleasure it gives them to impose it. In pornography, each element of subordination is conveyed through the sexually explicit usage of women: pornography in fact is what women are and what women are for and how women are used in a society premised on the inferiority of women. It is a metaphysics of women's subjugation: our existence delineated in a definition of our nature; our status in society predetermined by the uses to which we are put. The woman's body is what is materially subordinated. Sex is the material means through which the subordination is accomplished. Pornography is the institution of male dominance that sexualizes hierarchy, objectification, submission, and violence. As such, pornography creates inequality, not as artifact but as a system of social reality; it creates the necessity for and the actual behaviors that constitute sex inequality.

Speech

Subordination can be so deep that those who are hurt by it are utterly silent. Subordination can create a silence quieter than death. The women flattened out on the page are deathly still, except for *hurt me. Hurt me* is not women's speech. It is the speech imposed on women by pimps to cover the awful, condemning silence. The Three Marias of Portugal went to jail for writing this: "Let no one tell me that silence gives consent, because whoever is silent dissents." The women say the pimp's words: the language is another element of the rape; the language is part of the humiliation; the language is part of the forced sex. Real silence might signify dissent, for those reared to understand its sad discourse. The pimps cannot tolerate literal silence—it is too eloquent as testimony—so they force the words out of the woman's mouth. The women say pimp's words: which is worse than silence. The silence of the women not in the picture, outside the pages, hurt but silent, used but silent, is staggering in how deep and wide it goes. It is a silence over centuries: an exile into speechlessness. One is shut up by the inferiority and the abuse. One is shut up by the threat and the injury.

Protecting what ... [pornographers] "say" means protecting what they do to us, how they do it. It means protecting their sadism on our bodies, because that is how they write: not like a writer at all; like a torturer. Protecting what they "say" means protecting sexual exploitation, because they cannot "say" anything without diminishing, hurting, or destroying us. Their rights of speech express their rights over us. Their rights of speech require our inferiority: and that we be powerless in relation to them. Their rights of speech mean that *hurt me* is accepted as the real speech of women, not speech forced on us as part of the sex forced on us but originating with us because we are what the pornographers "say" we are.

If what we want to say is not *hurt me,* we have the real social power only to use silence as eloquent dissent. Silence is what women have instead of speech. Silence is our dissent during rape unless the rapist, like the pornographer, prefers *hurt me,* in which case we have no dissent. Silence is our moving, persuasive dissent during battery unless the batterer, like the pornographer, prefers *hurt me.* Silence is a fine dissent during incest and for all the long years after.

Silence is not speech. We have silence, not speech. We fight rape, battery, incest, and prostitution with it. We lose. But someday someone will notice: that people called women were buried in a long silence that meant dissent and that the pornographers . . . chattered on.

Equality

. . . The cost of trying to shatter the silence is astonishing to those who do it: the women, raped, battered, prostituted, who have something to say and say it. They stand there, even as they are erased. Governments turn from them; courts ignore them; this country disavows and dispossesses them. Men ridicule, threaten, or hurt them. Women jeopardized by them—silence being safer than speech—betray them. It is ugly to watch the complacent destroy the brave. It is horrible to watch power win.

Still, equality is what we want, and we are going to get it. What we understand about it now is that it cannot be proclaimed; it must be created. It has to take the place of subordination in human experience: physically replace it. Equality does not co-exist with subordination, as if it were a little pocket located somewhere within it. Equality has to win. Subordination has to lose. The subordination of women has not even been knocked loose, and equality has not materially advanced, at least in part because the pornography has been creating sexualized inequality in hiding, in private, where the abuses occur on a massive scale.

Equality for women requires material remedies for pornography, whether pornography is central to the inequality of women or only one cause of it. Pornography's antagonism to civil equality, integrity, and self-determination for women is absolute; and it is effective in making that antagonism socially real and socially determining.

The law that Catharine A. MacKinnon and I wrote making pornography a violation of women's civil rights recognizes the injury that pornography does: how it hurts women's rights of citizenship through sexual exploitation and sexual torture both.

The civil rights law empowers women by allowing women to civilly sue those who hurt us through pornography by trafficking in it, coercing people into it, forcing it on people, and assaulting people directly because of a specific piece of it.

The civil rights law does not force the pornography back underground. There is no prior restraint or police power to make arrests, which would then result in a revivified black market. This respects the reach of the first amendment, but it also keeps the pornography from getting sexier—hidden, forbidden, dirty, happily back in the land of the obscene, sexy slime oozing on great books. Wanting to cover the pornography up, hide it, is the first response of those who need pornography to the civil rights law. If pornography is hidden, it is still accessible to men as a male right of access to women; its injuries to the status of women are safe and secure in those hidden rooms, behind those opaque covers; the abuses of women are sustained as a private right supported by public policy. The civil rights law puts a flood of light on the pornography, what it is, how it is used, what it does, those who are hurt by it.

The civil rights law changes the power relationship between pornographers and women: it stops the pornographers from producing discrimination with the total impunity they now enjoy, and gives women a legal standing resembling equality from which to repudiate the subordination itself. The secret-police power of the pornographers suddenly has to confront a modest amount of due process.

The civil rights law undermines the subordination of women in society by confronting the pornography, which is the systematic sexualization of that subordination. Pornography is inequality. The civil rights law would allow women to advance equality by removing this concrete discrimination and hurting economically those who make, sell, distribute, or exhibit it. The pornography, being power, has a right to exist that we are not allowed to challenge under this system of law. After it hurts us by being what it is and doing what it does, the civil rights law would allow us to hurt it back. Women, not being power, do not have a right to exist equal to the right the pornography has. If we did, the pornographers would be precluded from exercising their rights at the expense of ours, and since they cannot exercise them any other way, they would be precluded period. We come to the legal system beggars: though in the public dialogue around the passage of this civil rights law we have the satisfaction of being regarded as thieves.

The civil rights law is women's speech. It defines an injury to us from our point of view. It is premised on a repudiation of sexual subordination which is born of our experience of it. It breaks the silence. It is a sentence that can hold its own against the male flood. It is a sentence on which we can build a paragraph, then a page.

It is my view, learned largely from Catharine MacKinnon, that women have a right to be effective. The pornographers, of course, do not think so, nor do other male supremacists; and it is hard for women to think so. We have been told to educate people on the evils of pornography: before the development of this civil rights law, we were told just to keep quiet about pornography altogether; but now that we have a law we want to use, we are encouraged to educate and stop there. Law educates. This law educates. It also allows women to *do* something. In hurting the pornography back, we gain ground in making equality more likely, more possible—someday it will be real. We have a means to fight the pornographers' trade in women. We have a means to get at the torture and the terror. We have a means with which to challenge the pornography's efficacy in making exploitation and inferiority the bedrock of women's social status. The civil rights law introduces into the public consciousness an analysis: of what pornography is, what sexual subordination is, what equality might be. The civil rights law introduces a new legal standard: these things are not done to citizens of this country. The civil rights law introduces a new political standard: these things are not done to human beings. The civil rights law provides a new mode of action for women through which we can pursue equality and because of which *our* speech will have social meaning. The civil rights law gives us back what the pornographers have taken from us: hope rooted in real possibility. . . .

Model Anti-Pornography Law

Section 1. Statement of Policy

Pornography is sex discrimination. It exists in [PLACE], posing a substantial threat to the health, safety, peace, welfare, and equality of citizens in the community. Existing [state and] federal laws are inadequate to solve these problems in [PLACE].

Pornography is a systematic practice of exploitation and subordination based on sex that differentially harms women. The harm of pornography includes dehumanization, sexual exploitation, forced sex, forced prostitution, physical injury, and social and sexual terrorism and inferiority presented as entertainment. The bigotry and contempt it promotes, with the acts of aggression it fosters, diminish opportunities for equality of rights in employment, education, property, public accommodations and public services; create public and private harassment, persecution and denigration; promote injury and degradation such as rape, battery, child sexual abuse, and prostitution and inhibit just enforcement of laws against these acts; contribute significantly to restricting women in particular from full exercise of citizenship and participation in public life, including in neighborhoods; damage relations between the sexes; and undermine women's equal exercise of rights to speech and action guaranteed to all citizens under the Constitutions and laws of the United States and [PLACE, INCLUDING STATE].

Section 2. Definitions

1. *Pornography* is the graphic sexually explicit subordination of women through pictures and/or words that also includes one or more of the following: (i) women are presented dehumanized as sexual objects, things, or commodities; or (ii) women are presented as sexual objects who enjoy pain or humiliation; or (iii) women are presented as sexual objects who

experience sexual pleasure in being raped; or (iv) women are presented as sexual objects tied up or cut up or mutilated or bruised or physically hurt; or (v) women are presented in postures or positions of sexual submission, servility, or display; or (vi) women's body parts—including but not limited to vaginas, breasts, or buttocks—are exhibited such that women are reduced to those parts; or (vii) women are presented as whores by nature; or (viii) women are presented being penetrated by objects or animals; or (ix) women are presented in scenarios of degradation, injury, torture, shown as filthy or inferior, bleeding, bruised, or hurt in a context that makes these conditions sexual.

2.   The use of men, children, or transsexuals in the place of women in (1) above is pornography for purposes of this law.

Section 3.   Unlawful Practices

1.   *Coercion into pornography:* It shall be sex discrimination to coerce, intimidate, or fraudulently induce (hereafter, "coerce") any person, including transsexual, into performing for pornography, which injury may date from any appearance or sale of any product(s) of such performance(s). The maker(s), seller(s), exhibitor(s), and/or distributor(s) of said pornography may be sued for damages and for an injunction, including to eliminate the product(s) of the performance(s) from the public view.

Proof of one or more of the following facts or conditions shall not, without more, negate a finding of coercion: (i) that the person is a woman; or (ii) that the person is or has been a prostitute; or (iii) that the person has attained the age of majority; or (iv) that the person is connected by blood or marriage to anyone involved in or related to the making of the pornography; or (v) that the person has previously had, or been thought to have had, sexual relations with anyone, including anyone involved in or related to the making of the pornography; or (vi) that the person has previously posed for sexually explicit pictures with or for anyone, including anyone involved in or related to the making of the pornography at issue; or (vii) that anyone else, including a spouse or other relative, has given permission on the person's behalf; or (viii) that the person actually consented to a use of the performance that is changed into pornography; or (ix) that the person knew that the purpose of the acts or events in question was to make pornography; or (x) that the person showed no resistance or appeared to cooperate actively in the photographic sessions or in the events that produced the pornography; or (xi) that the person signed a contract, or made statements affirming a willingness to cooperate in the production of pornography; or (xii) that no physical force, threats, or weapons were used in the making of the pornography; or (xiii) that the person was paid or otherwise compensated.

2.   *Trafficking in pornography:* It shall be sex discrimination to produce, sell, exhibit, or distribute pornography, including through private clubs.

(i) City, state, and federally funded public libraries or private and public university and college libraries in which pornography is available for study, including on open shelves but excluding special display presentations, shall not be construed to be trafficking in pornography.

(ii) Isolated passages or isolated parts shall not be actionable under this section.

(iii) Any woman has a claim hereunder as a woman acting against the subordination of women. Any man, child, or transsexual who alleges injury by pornography in the way women are injured by it also has a claim.

3. *Forcing pornography on a person:* It shall be sex discrimination to force pornography on a person, including a child or transsexual, in any place of employment, education, home, or public place. Only the perpetrator of the force or responsible institution may be sued.

4. *Assault of physical attack due to pornography:* It shall be sex discrimination to assault, physically attack, or injure any person, including child or transsexual, in a way that is directly caused by specific pornography. The perpetrator of the assault or attack may be sued for damages and enjoined where appropriate. The maker(s), distributor(s), seller(s), and/or exhibitor(s) may also be sued for damages and for an injunction against the specific pornography's further exhibition, distribution, or sale.

Section 4. Defenses

1. It shall not be a defense that the defendant in an action under this law did not know or intend that the materials were pornography or sex discrimination.

2. No damages or compensation for losses shall be recoverable under Sec. 3(2) or other than against the perpetrator of the assault or attack in Sec. 3(4) unless the defendant knew or had reason to know that the materials were pornography.

3. In actions under Sec. 3(2) or other than against the perpetrator of the assault or attack in Sec. 3(4), no damages or compensation for losses shall be recoverable against maker(s) for pornography made, against distributor(s) for pornography distributed, against seller(s) for pornography sold, or against exhibitor(s) for pornography exhibited, prior to the effective date of this law.

Section 5. Enforcement

1. *Civil action:* Any person aggrieved by violations of this law may enforce its provisions by means of a civil action. No criminal penalties shall attach for any violation of the provisions of this law. Relief for violation of this act may include reasonable attorney's fees.

2. *Injunction:* Any person who violates this law may be enjoined except that:

(i) In actions under Sec. 3(2), and other than against the perpetrator of the assault or attack under Sec. 3(4), no temporary or permanent injunction shall issue prior to a final judicial determination that the challenged activities constitute a violation of this law.

(ii) No temporary or permanent injunction shall extend beyond such material(s) that, having been described with reasonable specificity by the injunction, have been determined to be validly proscribed under this law.

Section 6. Severability

Should any part(s) of this law be found legally invalid, the remaining part(s) remains valid. A judicial declaration that any part(s) of this law cannot be applied validly in a particular manner or to a particular case or category of cases shall not affect the validity of that part(s) as otherwise applied, unless such other application would clearly frustrate the [LEGISLATIVE BODY'S] intent in adopting this law.

Section 7. Limitation of Action

Actions under this law must be filed within one year of the alleged discriminatory acts.

NOTES AND QUESTIONS

1. **Pornography's Harms**. Dworkin and others who oppose pornography describe several types of harm to women caused by pornography. Under this view, pornography most directly injures the women who participate in creating it, who are forced to be exposed to it, and who are assaulted by men who want to experience in real life the sexual fantasy it depicts. These feminists also argue that pornography causes a less direct injury to all women: by eroticizing male dominance over women, it helps men to see women as inferior, degraded sexual objects. To what extent do Dworkin's objections to pornography depend on the abuse of live women who are portrayed in films and pictures? Do Dworkin's claims about pornography apply only to the extremely violent depictions she describes, that find "new and terrible things to do to women?"

Diana Russell begins her book against pornography, *Making Violence Sexy*, with the testimony of numerous women who survived being forced to act in or to imitate pornography. Diana E. H. Russell, *Part I: Survivors of Pornography* in *Making Violence Sexy: Feminist Views on Pornography* 21–62 (1993). That of Evelina Giobbe, who was forced into prostitution at age 13 after she ran away from home, emphasizes how pornography both contributed to and exhibited the abuse she suffered:

> The men who bought me—the tricks—knew I was an adolescent. Most of them were in their 50s and 60s. They had daughters and granddaughters my age. They knew a child's face when they looked into it. It was clear that I was not acting of my own free will. I was always covered with welts and bruises. . . . It was even clearer that I was sexually inexperienced. So they showed me pornography to teach me and ignored my tears as they positioned my body like the women in the pictures, and used me. . . .

> I was often sent to an apartment on the West Side. There were usually two or three men there. After I had sex with them, they'd take pictures of me in various pornographic poses. I didn't have the vocabulary to call them pornographers. I used to think photography was their hobby. Today, I realize that the studio apartment, furnished with a bed and professional camera equipment, was in fact a commercial pornography mill.

Evelina Giobbe, *Surviving Commercial Sexual Exploitation* in Russell, *Making Violence Sexy*, at 37, 38. Most people would agree that the state should take steps to stop this type of direct harm to women and girls who are forced to act out pornographic scenes. Does this harm alone justify the civil rights ordinance or even government prohibition of pornography?

2. **How Pervasive Is Pornography**? Dworkin makes two very broad claims about the power of pornography to subordinate women: 1) "The oppression of women occurs through sexual subordination;" and 2) "Pornography is the material means of sexualizing inequality." Do you find either part of Dworkin's thesis to be persuasive? Do these two claims together mean that pornography is the principal means by which our society oppresses women?

When Dworkin writes that pornography "creates the necessity for and the actual behaviors that constitute sex inequality," is she describing the literal power of pornography? If pornography does have this impact on women, then Dworkin must be right that women cannot achieve equality as long as pornography exists.

Both anti-pornography advocate Catharine MacKinnon and anti-censorship advocate Nadine Strossen estimate that the pornography industry earns $10 billion annually. The combined monthly circulation of *Playboy*, *Penthouse*, and *Hustler* was more than 9 million in 1989; "adult" videos make up nearly a third of all video rentals in general interest video stores, increasing by 75 percent between 1991 and 1993. *See* Nadine Strossen, *Defending Pornography: Free Speech, Sex, And The Fight For Women's Rights* 159–60 (1995). Do these figures help to confirm Dworkin's claims? Does the commonly-held view that pornography is deviant discredit Dworkin's characterization of pornography as pervasive?

3. **Pornography in Cyberspace**. In addition to the figures noted above, there has been an explosion of pornographic images communicated through computer networks. A research team at Carnegie Mellon University recently undertook the first systematic study of pornography on the Information Superhighway. *See* Marty Rimm, *Marketing Pornography on the Information Superhighway: A Survey of 917,410 Images, Descriptions, Short Stories, and Animations Downloaded 8.5 Million Times by Consumers in Over 2000 Cities in Forty Countries, Provinces, and Territories*, 83 Georgetown L.J. 1849 (1995). (The title alone gives a vivid idea of the extent of pornography traveling through cyberspace.) Surveying nearly a million downloaded images available via thirty-five adult bulletin boards, the researchers discovered the highest demand for paraphilic (involving sado-

masochism, bestiality, fisting, foreign objects, etc.) and pedophilic (involving children) imagery—types of pornography that are often unavailable or difficult to purchase through traditional outlets.

One of these bulletin boards maintained a clientele ranging from 3500 to 10,700 individuals over a typical six month period. *Id.* at 1897. The board's owners could double the number of downloads of images involving fellatio by using the word "choke" in their promotional description. Nearly all bestiality images (99.1%) depicted women having sex with animals, while hardly any (0.9%) involved men. *Id.* at 1998–99. Do these findings, as well as the overall popularity of paraphilic images, suggest some correlation between increased power imbalance between the sexes depicted in these images and consumer demand?

Congress responded to the emergence of computer-generated child pornography by passing the Child Pornography Prevention Act of 1996. The law extends the definition of child pornography to include pornography that depicts, or appears to depict, a minor engaging in sexually explicit conduct, even if actual minors were not used to create it. Because the Supreme Court in New York v. Ferber, 458 U.S. 747, 102 S.Ct. 3348, 73 L.Ed.2d 1113 (1982), justified the exemption of child pornography from First Amendment protection as necessary to protect the actual children depicted, it is unclear whether realistic, sexually explicit portrayals of children produced entirely by digital imaging technology are protected speech. *See* Debra Burke, *The Criminalization of Virtual Child Pornography*, 34 Harv. J. on Legis. 439–72 (1997).

4. **Pornography as Sex Education**. Pornography serves not only as entertainment but also as a source of information about sex. *See,* for example, David F. Duncan & J. William Donnelly, *Pornography as a Source of Sex Information for Students at a Private Northeastern University*, 68 Psych. Rep. 782 (1991). Many men first learn about sex by viewing pornography. These images are increasingly available to adolescents through magazines, videos, cable television, and computer networks. The author of the Carnegie Mellon study notes, "[t]en years ago, college students could not type a few commands from their dormitory computers and receive instant access, via the Usenet, to thousands of bestiality images and stories." Rimm, *Marketing Pornography on the Information Superhighway*, at 1907. Does the influence of pornography on the early development of sexual attitudes provide added reason to restrict it? Or is there a competing danger in preventing young people's access to any sort of sexual speech or depiction? Carlin Meyer argues that "[w]e should largely ignore the growing presence of cybersmut and concentrate instead on expanding access—especially for young people—to online sexual discussion and depiction and on joining them in discussion and criticism of what they see and 'hear.'" Carlin Meyer, *Reclaiming Sex from the Pornographers: Cybersexual Possibilities*, 83 Georgetown L.J. 1969, 1974 (1995). Jeffrey Sherman argues that gay male pornography serves a social good—the abatement of hierarchy based on sexual orientation. *See* Jeffrey G. Sherman, *Love Speech: The Social Utility of Pornography*, 47 Stan. L. Rev. 661 (1995).

Sherman writes that young gay men need sexually explicit images of homosexuality to "counteract society's heterocentrism and homophobia and offer [them] models of affirming and unashamed sex between men." *Id.* at 685.

Incest survivors have reported that their fathers showed them pornography at a young age to persuade them that the sexual acts they were told to perform were normal. Katherine Brady, for example, writes that her father "used pornography to break down my resistance. The pornography made the statement that females are nothing more than objects for men's sexual gratification. How could I refuse my father when the pornography showed me that sex is what women and girls are for?" Katherine Brady, *Testimony on Pornography and Incest*, in Russell, *Making Violence Sexy*, at 43, 43–44.

5. **The Anti-pornography Ordinance**. How does the ordinance address each of the harms Dworkin and others have identified?

a. **Definition**. Note that the definition of pornography in Section 2(1) does not include all graphic, sexually explicit depictions *of* the subordination of women, but such depictions that *do* subordinate women. What is the distinction between these two types of images? The definition goes on to list specific ways in which the depiction must subordinate women. Do you find each of these ways equally worthy of prohibition? Are sexually explicit depictions of women in postures of display too benign or too common to make the subject of a civil rights cause of action? In other words, should women have a legal claim against *Playboy*? Dworkin and Catharine MacKinnon argued that by presenting models in postures of sexual servility, *Playboy* dehumanizes women as sexual objects and commodities: "Underlying all of *Playboy's* pictorials is the basic theme of all pornography: that all women are whores by nature, born wanting to be sexually accessible to all men at all times." Andrea Dworkin & Catharine MacKinnon, *Pornography and Civil Rights: A New Day for Women's Equality* (1988).

"Pornography" stems from the Greek words, *porno*, meaning prostitute, and *graphos*, meaning writing. Some writers distinguish between "pornography," which subordinates women, and "erotica," which doesn't. Diana Russell, for example, defines pornography as "material that combines sex and/or the exposure of genitals with abuse or degradation in a manner that appears to endorse, condone, or encourage such behavior." Erotica, on the other hand, is "[s]exually suggestive or arousing material that is free of sexism, racism, and homophobia, and respectful of all human beings and animals portrayed." Russell, *Introduction, Making Violence Sexy*, at 1, 2–3.

Why aren't Dworkin's own graphic descriptions of pornographic scenes themselves pornography? Does the identification of pornography depend on the artist's motive?

b. **Coercion**. Section 3(1) makes coercion into pornography sex discrimination. It also denies to the pornographer a defense that the person who was coerced signed a contract or made statements affirming a willingness to cooperate in the production of pornography. Is this provision an effective way to stop hidden forms of coercion or does it reinforce the view that women are incapable of making their own choices?

c. **Causation.** Section 3(4) makes it sex discrimination to assault someone "in a way that is directly caused by specific pornography." Many critics have questioned the claim that pornography can "cause" someone to injure another. A debate on the reliability and interpretation of statistics showing a correlation between rape and pornography has ensued. While some studies link prolonged use of pornography to the trivialization of rape and a callous attitude toward women (see, e.g., Dolf Zillman, *Effects of Prolonged Consumption of Pornography*, in *Pornography: Research Advances and Policy Considerations* 127 (Dolf Zillmann & Jennings Bryant eds., 1989)), or found cases in which men coercively imitated sex acts they had seen in pornography (see Diana E. H. Russell & Karen Trockli, *Evidence of Harm* in Russell, *Making Violence Sexy*, at 194), others found no significant connection between this exposure and laboratory aggression toward women (see, e.g., Neil M. Malamuth & Joseph Ceniti, *Repeated Exposure to Violent and Nonviolent Pornography: Likelihood of Raping Ratings and Laboratory Aggression Against Women*, 12 Aggressive Behav. 129 (1986)). For an overview of experiments attempting to study the effects of exposure to pornography, see Edward Donnerstein, et al., *The Question of Pornography: Research Findings and Policy Implications* (1987).

Some criminal cases involve defendants who sexually assaulted their victims after viewing pornography. *See, e.g.,* Minnesota v. Herberg, 324 N.W.2d 346 (Minn.1982) (stating that defendant's rape and torture of a fourteen-year-old girl gave "life to some stories he had read in various pornographic books").

Apart from this empirical question, the causation issue raises philosophical concerns. Compare these two views about the effects of pornography:

> Sooner or later, in one way or another, the consumers want to live out the pornography further in three dimensions. Sooner or later, in one way or another, they do. *It* makes them want to; when they believe they can, when they feel they can get away with it, *they* do. Depending upon their chosen sphere of operation, they may use whatever power they have to keep the world a pornographic place so they can continue to get hard from everyday life....

Catharine A. MacKinnon, *Only Words* 19 (1993).

> Our distinctively human capacity is to think, select, interpret and reinterpret content, to read texts on different levels and in different ways. The result is a broad spectrum of possible attitudes which loop back to shape how we read future texts.... Thus, when Dworkin–MacKinnon collapse the distinction between dream and deed, fantasy and act, thought and behavior they construct a Skinnerian model of human

nature which, in turn, justified an elaborate system of social control.

Thelma McCormack, *If Pornography Is the Theory, Is Inequality the Practice?*, quoted in Strossen, *Defending Pornography* at 147.

Does the argument that pornography eventually causes its consumers to sexually abuse women adopt a view of human beings as determined and predictable, and incapable of positive change?

d. **Other Victims**. Section 2 (2) provides that "[t]he use of men, children, or transsexuals in the place of women in (1) above is pornography for purposes of this law." Similarly, Section 3(2)(iii) provides that "[a]ny man, child, or transsexual who alleges injury by pornography in the way women are injured by it also has a claim." This provision would apply to much gay male pornography. Does it deny the difference between the experiences of heterosexual women and homosexual men? Does it incorporate the stereotype that gay men are feminine? If men can replace women in subordinated roles in pornography and can be injured by pornography, how is pornography necessarily related to the subordination of women?

e. **Severability**. Section 7 provides for severability of the ordinance's provisions. Are there any provisions you think should be eliminated? Would your concerns be alleviated by discarding the most troublesome parts of the law?

Patricia Hill Collins, Pornography and Black Women's Bodies

From P. Hill Collins, Black Feminist Thought: Knowledge, Consciousness, and the Politics of Empowerment
(NY: Routledge, 1991).

Pornography and Black Women's Bodies

For centuries the black woman has served as the primary pornographic "outlet" for white men in Europe and America. We need only think of the black women used as breeders, raped for the pleasure and profit of their owners. We need only think of the license the "master" of the slave women enjoyed. But, most telling of all, we need only study the old slave societies of the South to note the sadistic treatment—at the hands of white "gentlemen"— of "beautiful young quadroons and octoroons" who became increasingly (and were deliberately bred to become) indistinguishable from white women, and were the more highly prized as slave mistresses because of this.

Alice Walker's description of the rape of enslaved African women for the "pleasure and profit of their owners" encapsulates several elements of contemporary pornography. First, Black women were used as sex objects for the pleasure of white men. This objectification of African–American women parallels the portrayal of women in pornography as sex objects whose sexuality is available for men. Exploiting Black women as breeders objectified them as less than human because only animals can be bred against their will. In contemporary pornography women are objectified through being portrayed as pieces of meat, as sexual animals awaiting conquest. Second, African–American women were raped, a form of sexual violence. Violence is typically an implicit or explicit theme in pornography. Moreover, the rape of Black women linked sexuality and violence, another characteristic feature of pornography. Third, rape and other forms of sexual violence act to strip victims of their will to resist and make them passive and submissive to the will of the rapist. Female passivity, the fact that women have things done to them, is a theme repeated over and over in contemporary pornography. Fourth, the profitability of Black women's sexual exploitation for white "gentlemen" parallels pornography's financially lucrative benefits for pornographers. Finally, the actual breeding of "quadroons and octoroons" not only reinforces the themes of Black women's passivity, objectification, and malleability to male control but reveals pornography's grounding in racism and sexism. The fates of both Black and white women were intertwined in this breeding process. The ideal African–American woman as a pornographic object was indistinguishable from white women and thus approximated the images of beauty, asexuality, and chastity forced on white women. But inside was a highly sexual whore, a "slave mistress" ready to cater to her owner's pleasure.

Contemporary pornography consists of a series of icons or representations that focus the viewer's attention on the relationship between the portrayed individual and the general qualities ascribed to that class of individuals. Pornographic images are iconographic in that they represent realities in a manner determined by the historical position of the observers, their relationship to their own time, and to the history of the conventions which they employ. The treatment of Black women's bodies in nineteenth-century Europe and the United States may be the foundation upon which contemporary pornography as the representation of women's objectification, domination, and control is based. Icons about the sexuality of Black women's bodies emerged in these contexts. Moreover, as race/gender-specific representations, these icons have implications for the treatment of both African–American and white women in contemporary pornography.

I suggest that African–American women were not included in pornography as an afterthought but instead form a key pillar on which contemporary pornography itself rests. As Alice Walker points out, "the more ancient roots of modern pornography are to be found in the almost always pornographic treatment of black women who, from the moment they entered slavery ... were subjected to rape as the 'logical' convergence of sex and violence. Conquest, in short."

One key feature about the treatment of Black women in the nineteenth century was how their bodies were objects of display. In the antebellum American South white men did not have to look at pornographic pictures of women because they could become voyeurs of Black women on the auction block. A chilling example of this objectification of the Black female body is provided by the exhibition, in early nineteenth-century Europe, of Sarah Bartmann, the so-called Hottentot Venus. Her display formed one of the original icons for Black female sexuality. An African woman, Sarah Bartmann was often exhibited at fashionable parties in Paris, generally wearing little clothing, to provide entertainment. To her audience she represented deviant sexuality. At the time European audiences thought that Africans had deviant sexual practices and searched for physiological differences, such as enlarged penises and malformed female genitalia, as indications of this deviant sexuality. Sarah Bartmann's exhibition stimulated these racist and sexist beliefs. After her death in 1815, she was dissected. Her genitalia and buttocks remain on display in Paris.

Sander Gilman explains the impact that Sarah Bartmann's exhibition had on Victorian audiences: " ...The figure of Sarah Bartmann was reduced to her sexual parts. The audience which had paid to see her buttocks and had fantasized about the uniqueness of her genitalia when she was alive could, after her death and dissection, examine both." In this passage Gilman unwittingly describes how Bartmann was used as a pornographic object similar to how women are represented in contemporary pornography. She was reduced to her sexual parts, and these parts came to represent a dominant icon applied to Black women throughout the nineteenth century. Moreover, the fact that Sarah Bartmann was both African and a woman underscores the importance of gender in maintaining notions of racial purity. In this case Bartmann symbolized Blacks as a "race." Thus the creation of the icon applied to Black women demonstrates that notions of gender, race, and sexuality were linked in overarching structures of political domination and economic exploitation.

The process illustrated by the pornographic treatment of the bodies of enslaved African women and of women like Sarah Bartmann has developed into a full-scale industry encompassing all women objectified differently by racial/ethnic category. Contemporary portrayals of Black women in pornography represent the continuation of the historical treatment of their actual bodies. African–American women are usually depicted in a situation of bondage and slavery, typically in a submissive posture, and often with two white men. As Bell observes, "this setting reminds us of all the trappings of slavery: chains, whips, neck braces, wrist clasps." White women and women of color have different pornographic images applied to them. The image of Black women in pornography is almost consistently one featuring them breaking from chains. The image of Asian women in pornography is almost consistently one of being tortured.

The pornographic treatment of Black women's bodies challenges the prevailing feminist assumption that since pornography primarily affects white women, racism has been grafted onto pornography. African–American women's experiences suggest that Black women were not added into a preexisting pornography, but rather that pornography itself must be reconceptualized as an example of the interlocking nature of race, gender, and class oppression. At the heart of both racism and sexism are notions of biological determinism claiming that people of African descent and women possess immutable biological characteristics marking their inferiority to elite white men. In pornography these racist and sexist beliefs are sexualized. Moreover, for African-American women pornography has not been timeless and universal but was tied to Black women's experiences with the European colonization of Africa and with American slavery. Pornography emerged within a specific system of social class relationships.

This linking of views of the body, social constructions of race and gender, and conceptualizations of sexuality that inform Black women's treatment as pornographic objects promises to have significant implications for how we assess contemporary pornography. Moreover, examining how pornography has been central to the race, gender, and class oppression of African–American women offers new routes for understanding the dynamics of power as domination.

Investigating racial patterns in pornography offers one route for such an analysis. Black women have often claimed that images of white women's sexuality were intertwined with the controlling image of the sexually denigrated Black woman: "In the United States, the fear and fascination of female sexuality was projected onto black women; the passionless lady arose in symbiosis with the primitively sexual slave." Comparable linkages exist in pornography. Alice Walker provides a fictional account of a Black man's growing awareness of the different ways that African–American and white women are objectified in pornography: "What he has refused to see—because to see it would reveal yet another area in which he is unable to protect or defend black women—is that where white women are depicted in pornography as 'objects,' black women are depicted as animals. Where white women are depicted as human bodies if not beings, black women are depicted as shit."

Walker's distinction between "objects" and "animals" is crucial in untangling gender, race, and class dynamics in pornography. Within the mind/body, culture/nature, male/female oppositional dichotomies in Western social thought, objects occupy an uncertain interim position. As objects white women become creations of culture—in this case, the mind of white men—using the materials of nature—in this case, uncontrolled female sexuality. In contrast, as animals Black women receive no such redeeming dose of culture and remain open to the type of exploitation visited on nature overall. Race becomes the distinguishing feature in determining the type of objectification women will encounter. Whiteness as symbolic of both civilization and culture is used to separate objects from animals.

The alleged superiority of men to women is not the only hierarchical relationship that has been linked to the putative superiority of the mind to the body. Certain "races" of people have been defined as being more bodylike, more animallike, and less godlike than others. Race and gender oppression may both revolve around the same axis of disdain for the body; both portray the sexuality of subordinate groups as animalistic and therefore deviant. Biological notions of race and gender prevalent in the early nineteenth century which fostered the animalistic icon of Black female sexuality were joined by the appearance of a racist biology incorporating the concept of degeneracy. Africans and women were both perceived as embodied entities, and Blacks were seen as degenerate. Fear of and disdain for the body thus formed a key element in both sexist and racist thinking.

While the sexual and racial dimensions of being treated like an animal are important, the economic foundation underlying this treatment is critical. Animals can be economically exploited, worked, sold, killed, and consumed. As "mules," African–American women become susceptible to such treatment. The political economy of pornography also merits careful attention. Pornography is pivotal in mediating contradictions in changing societies. It is no accident that racist biology, religious justifications for slavery and women's subordination, and other explanations for nineteenth-century racism and sexism arose during a period of profound political and economic change. Symbolic means of domination become particularly important in mediating contradictions in changing political economies. The exhibition of Sarah Bartmann and Black women on the auction block were not benign intellectual exercises—these practices defended real material and political interests. Current transformations in international capitalism require similar ideological justifications. Where does pornography fit in these current transformations? This question awaits a comprehensive Afrocentric feminist analysis.

Publicly exhibiting Black women may have been central to objectifying Black women as animals and to creating the icon of Black women as animals. Yi–Fu Tuan offers an innovative argument about similarities in efforts to control nature—especially plant life—the domestication of animals, and the domination of certain groups of humans. Tuan suggests that displaying humans alongside animals implies that such humans are more like monkeys and bears than they are like "normal" people. This same juxtaposition leads spectators to view the captive animals in a special way. Animals acquire definitions of being like humans, only more openly carnal and sexual, an aspect of animals that forms a major source of attraction for visitors to modern zoos. In discussing the popularity of monkeys in zoos, Tuan notes: "some visitors are especially attracted by the easy sexual behavior of the monkeys. Voyeurism is forbidden except when applied to subhumans." Tuan's analysis suggests that the public display of Sarah Bartmann and of the countless enslaved African women on the auction blocks of the antebellum American South—especially in proximity to animals—fostered their image as animalistic. . . .

The treatment of all women in contemporary pornography has strong ties to the portrayal of Black women as animals. In pornography women become nonpeople and are often represented as the sum of their fragmented body parts. Scott McNall observes:

> This fragmentation of women relates to the predominant of rearentry position photographs. . . . All of these kinds of photographs reduce the woman to her reproductive system, and, furthermore, make her open, willing, and available—not in control. . . . The other thing rear-entry position photographs tell us about women is that they are animals. They are animals because they are the same as dogs—bitches in heat who can't control themselves.

This linking of animals and white women within pornography becomes feasible when grounded in the earlier denigration of Black women as animals.

Developing a comprehensive analysis of the race, gender, and class dynamics of pornography offers possibilities for change. Those Black feminist intellectuals investigating sexual politics imply that the situation is much more complicated than that advanced by some prominent white feminists (see, e.g., Dworkin) in which "men oppress women" because they are men. Such approaches implicitly assume biologically deterministic views of sex, gender, and sexuality and offer few possibilities for change. In contrast, Afrocentric feminist analyses routinely provide for human agency and its corresponding empowerment and for the responsiveness of social structures to human action. In the short story "Coming Apart," Alice Walker describes one Black man's growing realization that his enjoyment of pornography, whether of white women as "objects" or Black women as "animals," degraded him:

> He begins to feel sick. For he realizes that he has bought some of the advertisements about women, black and white. And further, inevitably, he has bought the advertisements about himself. In pornography the black man is portrayed as being capable of fucking anything ... even a piece of shit. He is defined solely by the size, readiness and unselectivity of his cock.

Walker conceptualizes pornography as a race/gender system that entraps everyone. But by exploring an African–American *man's* struggle for a self-defined standpoint on pornography, Walker suggests that a changed consciousness is essential to social change. If a Black man can understand how pornography affects him, then other groups enmeshed in the same system are equally capable of similar shifts in consciousness and action.

NOTES AND QUESTIONS

1. **The Racist Origins of Pornography**. How does Patricia Hill Collins's explanation of the racist origins of contemporary pornography affect Dworkin's thesis about pornography's role in sex domination? Does the connection between pornography and racial domination, especially the degradation of Black women's bodies, provide a compelling reason for regulation? Do you find persuasive Collins's claim that the representations of Black women in pornography are linked to the actual treatment of slave women? Or can we distinguish the historical facts of slavery from the fantasy of pornography?

What is the difference between pornography's treatment of white women as objects and Black women as animals? How are these two forms of sexual degradation related? For further discussion of the racist depiction of women of color in pornography, *see* Alice Mayall & Diana E. H. Russell, *Racism in Pornography* in Russell, *Making Violence Sexy*, at 167.

Kimberlé Crenshaw explores how race and gender intersect in sexual images of women of color from four maintream movies, *Angel Heart, Colors, Year of the Dragon*, and *Tales from the Darkside: The Movie*, as well as in the video game, *General Custer's Revenge*.

Media images provide cues to understanding the ways in which women of color are imagined in our society. The images of Latina, African–American, Asian–American, and Native American women are constructed through combinations of readily available race and gender stereotypes. Because the stereotypes depicted in these presentations are quite familiar, collectively they form images of women of color that are specified and categorically unique.

Consider first the film *Colors*. *Colors* was a controversial film, but unfortunately none of the criticism addressed its portrayal of women. Yet the film was rife with familiar stereotypes. The obligatory sexual relationship in that movie occurred between a hot-headed white cop played by Sean Penn and a young Latina played by Maria Conchita Alonso, whom he encountered working at a fast-food stand. Their relationship and her characterization progressed as follows: In Scene 1, he flirts, she blushes. In Scene 2, she accompanies him to a family outing at his partner's home. In Scene 3, the crucial scene, he drops her off at her home. She almost maintains the "good girl" image that had been carefully constructed from the onset, but when she reaches her door, she reconsiders and turns back to invite him in for a night of sex. In subsequent scenes this nice, hardworking ethnic girl increasingly turns into a promiscuous schizophrenic Latina. In her final appearance, the transformation is complete. The scene begins with the young cop arriving to investigate a noisy house party. She is seen putting on her clothes in a bedroom from which a black man has departed. She wears low-cut, loud dress and six-inch heels. She is very loud and brash now, laughingly tormenting the distraught and disappointed Sean Penn who upon seeing her, attempts to escape. She follows him and with her hands on her hips, demanding now in a very heavy and exaggerated accent: "Look at me. This is part of me too!"

This image of the good ethnic fiery Latina is contrasted with an image of Black sexuality also constructed in *Colors*. In another scene, the police converge on a house to serve a warrant on a suspect named Rock-it. As they approach the house, the viewer hears a rhythmic squeaking and loud screams. The camera takes several seconds to track through the ramshackle house. There is little in the house except a stereo apparently playing the loud, pulsating music accenting the sound track. The camera turns a corner and finds a Black man and a Black woman on a bed, atop a single white sheet, so earnestly and frantically copulating that they are wholly oblivious to the several police officers surrounding them with guns drawn. When they finally became aware of the officers' presence, the man makes a sudden move and is shot several times in the back. As his lover screams hysterically, he gasps that he was simply reaching for his clothes.

In *Angel Heart*, the descent of an African–American woman into her own uncontrolled sexuality ends in tragic horror. Epiphany Proudfoot, played by Cosby-kid Lisa Bonet, is introduced washing her hair at a well. She appears at first the model of youth, reticent and exotic. Yet she's slightly fallen: She has a child whose father is unknown. Later we see her as a voodoo priestess dancing a blood-curdling ritual and collapsing in an uncontrolled sexual frenzy. The movie culminates in a vicious pornographic scene between Epiphany and Harry Angel (played by Mickey Rourke) that gives new meaning to the phrase "sex and violence." Sex—initiated by Epiphany— soon becomes gruesome as dripping water turns into blood, intercut with rivers of blood, deep thrusting, and screams of agony and horror. The visual narrative splits after this scene: Epiphany appears normal, singing a lovely lullaby and wistfully twisting her hair as she bathes, but later we discover that Epiphany is in fact dead. Her body sprawls across the bed, her legs spread open. A deep pool of blood surrounds her pelvic area. The movie's final scene plays out across her dead body. We discover the cause of her death when the Southern sheriff questioning Angel drawls, "Is that your gun up her snatch?" The horror is not yet complete, for we have still to discover that not only has Harry Angel killed his lover, but that this lover is actually his daughter. So this Cosby kid hits big time, being multiply victimized by incest, rape, and murder.

Perhaps it is happenstance that Lisa Bonet played Epiphany and that the imagery in this big-budget Hollywood film is so violent. Yet I wonder whether a Michelle Pfeiffer, a Kim Basinger, or even a Madonna would be asked to play such a role? I don't think so. The film, by relying on race-sex exoticism, works differently from the way it would with a white female. In fact, the presence of a woman of color often "makes" the story, as is still more clearly shown in an episode from *Tales from the Dark Side: The Movie*. The life of a young white artist is spared by a sixteen-foot talking gargoyle upon the artist's promise that he will never tell anyone that he has ever seen this gargoyle. Later that night he meets a Black woman, played here by Rae Dawn Chong, whom he later marries and with whom he has two lovely children. With the support of his wife he becomes enormously successful, and they live a happy, fulfilled life. On their tenth anniversary, he decides to tell his wife this secret as a part of his expression of affection to her. Presenting her with a full-sized sculpture of the monster he tells her how his life was spared upon making a vow never to reveal that the monster exists. After he tells her the story, she becomes hysterical and, as "fate" would have it, begins to turn into the sixteen-foot gargoyle. Their two children emerge from the adjoining room as baby gargoyles. The wife disregards the artist's frantic efforts to profess his love for her, stating that she "loved him too but when the vow was broken their fate was sealed." She monstrously tears out his throat, gathers up the "children," and swoops through the ceiling. Here the drop-of-blood rule really works: The children, although half human, are little monsters, too. Can anyone doubt the message—white male miscegenators, beware! Exotica and danger go hand in hand.

Mickey Rourke, apparently bidding to be everybody's favorite racist/sadomasochist/rapist/murderer, turns up again in *Year of the Dragon*. There he plays Captain Stanley White, a New York cop, who pursues a brash and independent Asian–American TV newscaster. He encounters her on the street, addresses her as a prostitute, taunts her with racist epithets (apparently learned from his days in Vietnam). After she invites him up to her apartment, he continues to assault her verbally, before physically doing so. He tells her that he hates everything about her, and then taking down his pants, he queries, "So why do I want to fuck you so badly?" The worst is yet to come: As our heroine rallies enough outrage to ask him to leave, he calls her a slant-eyed cunt. She slaps him once, pauses, and slaps again. He then grabs her, throws her down, rips off her clothes, and has forcible sex with her.

The next image comes not from a movie but from a video game, *General Custer's Revenge*. A Native American woman is tied to a pole. The player, General Custer, must traverse an obstacle course to get to the woman before getting shot. His saberlike penis leads him forward. The player wins when General Custer reaches the Native American woman and pounces on her. She "kicks up her legs in dubious delight" as he commits "what opponents call a rape and the manufacturer claims is a willing sex act." (A spokesman for the manufacturer commented, "There is a facsimile of intercourse. The woman is smiling.") Every stroke is a point. The motto: "When you score, you score.'"

Kimberlé Williams Crenshaw, *Beyond Racism and Misogyny: Black Feminism and 2 Live Crew*, in *Words that Wound: Critical Race Theory, Assaultive Speech, and the First Amendment* 111 (Mari J. Matsuda, et al. eds., 1993).

2. **Pornography's Degradation of Men**. The discussion of Alice Walker's short story "Coming Apart" points out that men, especially Black men,

are also degraded by pornography. Just as women are reduced to vaginas always willing to be fucked, men are reduced to giant penises always eager to fuck. Elizabeth Iglesias elaborates the image of "pornographic masculinity" and how it dehumanizes male consumers of pornography:

> ... [A]ccounts of the private consumption of pornography suggest that there is also a decidedly negative impact on the men who consume it. Indeed, these accounts suggest that what pornography institutionalizes is the illusion of male supremacy. Some men act out the scenarios, relations, and events depicted in the pornography they consume. More men probably use it as a substitute for sex with real women. Consider, for example, the marked difference between the images of male sexuality in pornography with the image of men consuming pornography:

> He keeps them in the closet. In piles. Their poses are improbable and promising, no flesh is hidden. It is late afternoon, sounds of the freeway drift through the room. His wife is working, she will not see him. He is tired. He may or may not know he is depressed. He goes to the closet. He rummages through the piles, looking for one that will spark him, that will let him go. Through the hundreds of magazines, not one can satisfy him.... He drives through stoplights, his mouth clamped on a joint. Into a parking lot. Pulls in beside the spray-painted scrawl—"Porn Hurts Women." Rushing past, he enters ... Picking up the magazines wrapped in plastic, the man tries to guess by the covers what lies inside. Never quite sure, stoned, he takes nearly an hour to make his choice.... He asks for quarters. Heads back to the video booths.... He is looking for the perfect film, the blonde that will stun him with her moans, the whimpering that sets off a trembling inside him, released by a cock of monstrous proportions, which dwarfs his own with envy, with the certainty that only here, here in this booth, its damp sticky floor, its private dark, can he possess this image, let it consume his life. He unzips his pants and slips in the quarter. The reel rolls, music and moaning, ending abruptly. Five minutes. Another quarter. Five minutes. Another quarter. Again, again, from booth to booth, the hour slips by. He does not want to come. He wants to hold it, the tension as long as he can. He leaves the store with three magazines which he cannot help but begin unwrapping in the car. He stops himself. He knows he needs to nurse their charge. One time through and he will need another. He drives home with one hand on himself.

> Up in his bedroom, he undresses, spreads the magazines on the bed, lies beside them. He studies each image, noting each position, the expression on each face. He reads the

captions, how the women tell the men how they want it, how they can't get enough. He is still trying hard not to come.

An hour later he hears his wife drive up. He picks up the magazines, he pants, runs to the washroom, worried she will find him, angered by her arrival, disrupting his peace. He will rush his orgasm. He will not feel satisfied. He will feel the hours he has wasted, the shame emerging. He will say he needs to take a shower. The magazines are in the bathroom. Already they are not enough. [David Mura, *The Bookstore* in *Men Confront Pornography* 133 (Michael S. Kimmel, ed., 1991).]

In this account, consuming pornography is hardly a vehicle for actualizing masculine power. On the contrary, the image of the husband desperately trying to orgasm before his wife gets home from work is simply pathetic. Why, for example, isn't he waiting for his wife, so they can have sex together? ... [P]ornography encourages these men to retreat into the fantasy world of sexual dominance. If they accept that invitation, they risk addiction to the consumption of images, an addiction that serves capitalist profit, rather than male sexual fulfillment. . . .

Men, like women, long for sexual and spiritual unity. The narratives of pornographic masculinity are designed, however, to make men think they are lesser men for wanting it. These narratives encourage men to act out their relations to women in ways that benefit a profit-oriented system of exchange at their own expense as human beings and even as men. From this perspective, feminists do themselves and men a serious injustice by contributing to the notion that pornography reflects or produces male power. We should stop. This formulation only makes men want it more. More importantly, it is simply not true. What pornography does do is glorify a male sexual identity that makes huge profits for porn capitalists off of men's fantasies and despair. This cycle harms individual men as much as individual women, destroying interpersonal solidarity at its sexual core.

The pornographic narratives of masculinity oppress and exploit men as men because these narratives urge men to enact a form of masculinity that is impossible for self-conscious human beings to sustain except at great emotional and interpersonal cost. The will to dominate means a constant anxiety and insecurity over the inability to dominate. Emotional withdrawal means frustration and loneliness. It means never saying what you really feel, never giving or asking for love, tenderness, or understanding, never sharing or compromising or accepting the challenge to change. It means getting what you want with lies, manipulation, false and hypocritical accusations, and temper tantrums. To the extent that a man needs love and understanding, the narratives of pornographic masculinity will make him feel less like a man. The men in those narratives demand submission but do not need love, making ordinary men think, "if they are men, then I am not."

Elizabeth M. Iglesias, *Rape, Race, and Representation: The Power of Discourse, Discourses of Power, and the Reconstruction of Heterosexuality*, 49 Vand. L. Rev. 869 (1996).

How do these accounts of pornography's degradation of male sexuality alter the interpretation of pornography as male domination? How do they suggest the potential for social change?

3. **The Critical Race Perspective**. Collins argues that Black feminist critics of pornography, such as Walker, tend to emphasize the existence of human agency and the capacity for empowerment. This focus on empowerment is a key aspect of an Afrocentric analysis of pornography and its relationship to social hierarchies. What other features might an Afrocentric (or critical race theory) approach entail?

Carlin Meyer, Sex, Sin, and Women's Liberation: Against Porn–Suppression

72 Tex. L. Rev. 1097 (1994).

Feminist porn-suppressionists claim that pornography "constructs" the way men see and treat women, "eroticises" gender inequality and male sexual abuse of women, and "silences" women. So, they urge, just get rid of it....

But will the effort to suppress these images help change the society that spawns them? Will it ultimately reduce violence against women? Will it promote gender equality on the streets and in private bedrooms? Will it liberate women's voices?

I contend that it will not have these salutary effects, but rather precisely the opposite ones. The suppression strategy—by targeting only "explicitly sexual" imagery, a narrow band on the broad spectrum of misogynist, violent, degrading, or "objectifying" depictions of women, and by blaming pornographic expression for far more complex cultural problems—is inimical to feminist ideological and political goals. First, it reinforces the very sin = sex = Woman nexus that has for centuries undergirded women's oppression. Second, the porn suppression effort takes feminism down a dangerous road by emphasizing primarily "deviant" imagery (letting mainstream sexist practices and imagery off the hook) [and] by treating women largely as passive victims of Western sexual construction.
. . .

Feminist porn-suppressionists center their efforts on gaining passage of ordinances prohibiting production, dissemination, and display of explicitly sexual depictions that arguably subordinate women.... [They] purport through their ordinances to "rename" the obscene—to shift the focus from sex to sexism, from vulgarity to the victimization of women. They have sought to refashion obscenity doctrine to treat that which sexually subordinates women as unprotected speech.... But portrayals are subject to suppression only if "graphic[ally] sexually explicit." ...

Significantly, "graphic sexually explicit" depiction is never defined. A capacious interpretation would include so much cultural depiction that the ordinances would have no hope of passing constitutional muster because they would prohibit everything from advertisements for perfume and blue jeans to Rodin's sculptures. Ordinance drafters no doubt expect and intend its interpretation to conform to Supreme Court doctrine—that is, to define sexually explicit to mean the plain description or representation of "ultimate sexual acts, normal or perverted" and "masturbation, excretory functions, and lewd exhibition of the genitals." But this definition reaches only a rather narrow segment of arguably misogynist sexual depiction, much of which shows no acts or organs. Still less does it cover the vast array of nonsexual images that arguably depict women in misogynist or degrading ways. Imagery that portrays extreme, but not sexual violence against women, or treats women as brainless bimbos, as asexual, frigid bitches, or as whores and witches worthy of domination, can proliferate so long as sex acts and organs are not on display. Descriptions of "women ... dehumanized as sexual objects, things or commodities; or ... presented as sexual objects who enjoy humiliation or pain; or ... in postures or positions of sexual submission, servility, or display" are thus impliedly less seriously damaging to women when sex organs and acts are not depicted. Portrayals that, irrespective of subject matter, contribute to the subordination of women—for example, by helping to set beauty standards that convince women to engage in acts of self-mutilation—may be freely disseminated.

This emphasis on explicitly sexual imagery suggests that there is something powerfully bad about sex acts and sexual body parts, strengthening puritanical and ultraconservative views that nonprocreative sex acts such as masturbation and oral/genital sex, as well as sex outside the confines of traditional heterosexual marriage, constitute harmful and antisocial behavior. Ultimately, sex, not sex discrimination, is the touchstone against which harm is measured.... Although suppressionists argue that the anti-sex message is muted because the ordinances target only depiction that subordinates or degrades women, leaving untouched other explicitly sexual portrayals, in fact nearly all sexual portrayals of women can be viewed as subordinating or degrading. Whenever women are depicted naked, whenever their genitals, breasts, or buttocks are displayed, they are arguably shown subordinated, as "sexual objects" in "postures or positions of servility or submission or display." Indeed, from the "endless catalogue of rape in Greek myth," to Lautrec's lesbians and images of sadism and fetishism, Manet's Olympia with her sexualized black servant as foil, ... [and] Rodin's nude, spread-legged Iris and cloakedly erect Balzac, ... women's sexuality has virtually always been on display as an enticement and offer to men.... How could it be otherwise, when women have always been "postured" and exhibited for male viewing if not possession?

Moreover, because courts, juries, and citizens are conditioned to notice and condemn public displays of sex, but are not yet fully attuned to, still less deeply offended by, displays of sexism, the anti-sex message is bound to dominate....

The anti-sex message will dominate, too, because it is simply easier to target the sexual than to make subtle determinations about whether a portrayal degrades or subordinates women. We easily identify images of women bare-breasted and prone; it is far more difficult to measure whether, because "penetrated" by nipple rings they are "mutilated," or because prone, they are "subordinated" in "postures" of "servility," "submission," or "display." It is easier to go along with the presumption that women postured in these ways are "objectified" and "on display" for men than to risk accusations of insensitivity....

In addition, the ordinances' heavy emphasis on scenarios typically viewed as "deviant"—on penetration by objects and animals, on dominance/submission scenes, and sado-masochism—encourages surveillance, policing, and labelling of deviance more generally, strengthening the very stereotyping that has stigmatized and subordinated women throughout history. While feminist porn-suppressionists would claim that their ordinances protect images that are not "subordinating" images—such as women using dildos by themselves or on one another, or gay men consensually playing out dominance/submission scenarios—when particular behaviors and practices (ones that happen to be often associated with gay and lesbian sex) are highlighted as potentially bad, fine distinctions are unlikely to be made by the public, even if they are ultimately made in court. Indeed, given that most states continue to criminalize as deviant commonly practiced sexual behavior, enforcing their laws only against social "outcasts" like homosexuals, feminists should be especially leery of designating certain unusual sexual practices as presumptively problematic. Wholly predictably, after Canada's highest court legalized suppression of sexual works found to be degrading to women, the first targets were lesbian and gay bookstores, as well as the works of Dworkin herself. ...

In the world of feminist porn-suppressionists, women's sexuality is entirely bounded by either direct or indirect coercion: Men constantly force sex on women directly by abuse and indirectly by culturally inducing women's complicity in sexual submission. Rape and sexual abuse are pervasive and, like porn, are becoming increasingly prevalent and violent. When women are pictured in porn as active participants in sex acts, still more when they are portrayed enjoying such activities, the portrayals ... encourage women to "want our own self-annihilation." Because pornography objectifies women, it is centrally part of the way patriarchy "gets the woman to take the initiative in her own degradation." Women, one way or another, are sexual victims....

There is, of course, some truth in this portrait. ...But that is not to say that women derive no pleasure from, and exercise no power over, sexuality. It is true that women's sexual choices in our culture are delimited, constrained, and restricted; women cannot act in ways that are not conditioned and in some sense "coerced" by a culture "where male domination of women is promoted and male physical and sexual abuse of women is socially sanctioned." But that does not mean that women cannot and do not make choices among (albeit limited) options and are not responsible for those choices. To treat women always and only as sexual victims, as feminist porn-suppressionists do, is to deny women meaningful agency and the power to effectuate change.

It is virtually impossible for a woman to exist in our culture—to eat, dress, or have sex—without participating in (or in some degree reinforcing even when rebelling against) bodily, and hence sexual, practices that at least in part re-enact and participate in women's subordination. Women who have cosmetic surgery or who diet, who acquiesce in workplace norms of dress and behavior, who act sexually "provocative" by flirting or "submissive" in agreeing to play dominance/submission games, or who present themselves as "objects" by "sexy dressing" in negligees or leather bikinis, may often be reinforcing norms partially or ultimately inimical to feminist goals. But their choices to do so are not simply products of coercion (whether direct or indirect), nor are the modes in which they do so predetermined. Women often exercise considerable control over whether and how to do these things. And while cultural conditioning often seems overwhelming, many women elect not to uncritically adopt and internalize, but to defy, dominant norms. Moreover, activities surrounding the body are at one and the same time sources of oppression and among women's primary arenas of empowerment. Women may be contributing to their own oppression by spending enormous amounts of time "making use of their 'charms,'" but they also "gain in competence through [their] bodily practices." For women to eschew such activities would be to eschew not only gratification, but the means of "gaining competence" and confidence in order to effectuate self-and societal transformation. It would also be to give up one of the prime arenas for making such change, thus diluting women's power to make change.

When porn-suppressionist ordinances treat the choice to perform sex work as presumptively coerced, and when suppressionists consistently describe women as victims of sexual depredation and never as agents of sexual pleasure, they disable women from sexual choice, responsibility, and power. They replicate Victorian views that "normal" ("real"?) women do not ("freely" and "intelligently") choose sex—at least not sex on the Model Ordinance's prohibited-images list; that sex is purely a matter of phallic power. In their view, women never willingly even appear to enjoy domination, let alone actually enjoy it. Women never choose penetration by objects, although one survey revealed that vibrators are the items most frequently purchased by women visiting sex shops alone. According to porn-suppressionists, women able to make (relatively) uncoerced choices eschew all but the most egalitarian, wholesome sex; however, such egalitarian sex is a near impossibility, at least in situations involving heterosexual sex.

This view is at once seductive and extremely damaging to women. It beguilingly suggests that consent and equality are nonproblematic categories in sexual images and relations——that discerning, caring persons "know" equality when they see or experience it and that they are always certain when they themselves, let alone others, mean "yes" or "no." Moreover, by seeking to eliminate images of women engaging in sex in the ways most women learn to "do sex"—that is, by dressing up "as sexual objects, things or commodities," and adopting postures that might easily be characterized as "sexual submission, servility or display"—porn-suppressionists not only denigrate the women who do these things (most of us), but also render invisible the men and women who attempt to avoid, alter, or challenge pre-ordained sexual roles and behaviors.

The notion that all sexual practices that feature power imbalances, fetishization, segmentation, lack of "intimacy," and the like, or in which one party is treated as an object, are harmful and worthy of suppression—that the only "good" sex is egalitarian, caring sex, based on "romantic love"—is problematic for other reasons as well. First, it too easily converges with Victorian notions that for women, it is equality, caring, and nurturance that are important, not sex—women crave intimacy and pillow talk, not fellatio, cunnilingus, or coitus. It replicates the view that "impersonal" sex is bad for women; women who claim to enjoy sex for its own sake, apart from claims of a deep connection and a potential long-term future relationship, are objects of disdain and pity for engaging in sex without a "real connection." It encourages women who feel passion divorced from a desire for intimacy or long-term caring to feel guilty and deviant, and it induces them to avoid guilt by convincing themselves that their lust is love, or to believe that feelings of warmth and caring will eventually flower into sexual passion. In either case, the result is often marital misery, followed by divorce and self-recrimination.

Second, romantic-love ideology contributes to the isolation as "deviant" of those who choose to defy heterosexist norms: those gay men and lesbians who claim enjoyment of sex for its own sake, hetero-and homosexuals who experiment with S/M power play, and those who make other nontraditional sexual choices—for instance, single women who prefer sex toys to men or eschew live-in, long-term relationships in favor of successive sexual partners. The romantic-love model tends to deny the possibility of multiple intimacies: those who have successive multiple partners must be engaging in non-intimate, depersonalized sex; those who have simultaneous multiple partners are likely, in addition, to be engaging in inegalitarian practices.

Finally, romantic-love ideology immobilizes women (and men) by suggesting that the sexual activities from which they derive pleasure are "bad"—that fantasies of desire, overpowerment, rape, or stranger sex are "sick" and must be repressed. These notions trap women in fantasies of an unrealizable, idealized future, rather than enabling them to cope with the reality of uncertain desire, of negotiated terms and confusing communication, and of the difficulty in ascertaining one's own arousal—let alone someone else's.

These notions are disabling, not only because they deprive women (and men) of the opportunity to operate on today's real (not tomorrow's ideal) sexual terrain, but also because they discourage men and women from joining feminists in cultural critique. By labeling as deluded—or, in the case of men, coercive—those who refuse to delay pleasure and gratification until egalitarian perfection is possible, feminists alienate potential allies. And by again reinforcing the line between the deviant and deluded women who "do," and the "good girls" who "don't," they put women who engage in sex—those who seek sexual knowledge and value sexual power and prowess—outside the reach of feminism. Indeed, by isolating these women, anti-porn ideology enhances the power of sexual conservatives to control them.

The notion that women never choose "bad" (objectified, servile, exhibitionist) sex and that images in which they are shown to do so must be eliminated suggests that women who do these things need to be protected from themselves—indeed, that all women need to be protected from potentially dangerous sex. This, in turn, lends support to wider sexual "protectionism," protection that seeks to keep women from (bad) sex by denying them access to birth control information, sex education, and abortion; by enforcing largely against women legal and social strictures against adultery; by "protecting" underage women from having sex with older men; and by implementing codes of dress and behavior that ostracize and punish women who claim the right to appear and be sexual.

Indeed, going after the women who "do" porn and the men who read it fosters the view that basic social reform in male and female sexual practices within marriage or in mainstream depictions of and attitudes toward women is unnecessary. Porn-suppression suggests that gender inequality is something that happens at the margins and implies that we can solve the problems of women, whether individual women exploited as porn models or women degraded by porn's ideology of sexploitation, by isolating and "jailing" these problems. Somehow, if husbands would just stop reading porn, the gender bias embedded in the institutionalization of heterosexual marriage will be reduced. Not only does such a strategy take the focus off mainstream institutions and practices, but by promising a "quick fix" solution to long-term problems and paying far too much attention to "sex lit," it also undermines the slow, painstaking struggle to examine and deconstruct existing sexual relations and to reconstruct a new and humanized sexuality. . . .

NOTES AND QUESTIONS

1. **Is the Ordinance Underinclusive?** Carlin Meyer criticizes the anti-pornography ordinance not only for its overinclusiveness, but also for what the definition of pornography, as "graphic, sexually explicit" depictions, leaves out. It could be argued that most of literature, art, and entertainment reflect the inferior status of women (think of sexist television shows and commercials, for example), and that pornography is a relatively tiny

and less influential part of this culture. What is the danger in the ordinance's failure to include depictions that sexualize women in non-explicit ways? Why should Meyer object to taking immediate, concrete steps, like the civil rights law, to address pornography's harm to women, while engaging in a broader, long-term campaign to change sexist attitudes about women and their bodies? Is she saying that banning pornography precludes or hinders this type of social reform?

2. **Strange Bedfellows**. Meyer accuses Dworkin of strengthening the puritanical and ultraconservative view that sexual behavior outside of traditional heterosexual marriage is bad, as well as the romantic-love ideology. Is this a legitimate concern, or does Dworkin successfully distinguish her view of sexuality from the traditional and romantic perspectives?

Sharing Meyer's concern, Nadine Strossen notes that the anti-pornography ordinance "was enacted in Indianapolis with the support of conservative Republican politicians and right-wing groups that had consistently opposed women's rights." Moreover, the law lacked support from local feminist groups and the local NOW chapter actively opposed it. Strossen, *Defending Pornography*, at 77–78. How problematic is this alliance between procensorship feminists and right-wing moralists? Does it pose the danger that some young women who see the antipornography position as "antisex" will be turned off by feminism?

3. **Women's Agency**. While Dworkin describes the anti-pornography ordinance as a way for "women to be effective," Meyer describes it as a way of "treating women largely as passive victims of Western sexual construction." Sallie Tisdale agrees with Meyer's critique:

> Always, the [feminist] censors are concerned with how men *act* and how women are portrayed. Women cannot make free sexual choices in that world; they are too oppressed to know that only oppression could lead them to sell sex. And I, watching, am either too oppressed to know the harm that my watching has done to my sisters . . . or else I have become the Man. And it is the Man in me who watches and is aroused. (Shame.) What a misogynistic world-view this is, this claim that women who make such choices cannot be making free choices at all. . . . Feminists against pornography have done a sad and awful thing: *They* have made women into objects.

Sally Tisdale, *Talk Dirty to Me: A Woman's Taste for Pornography*, Harper's 37, 45 (February 1992).

Does the effort to ban pornography deny women's agency or activate it? How can we describe women's sexuality in a way that recognizes the influence of sexist social construction, but also allows for women's power over their own sexuality?

4. **Canada's Antipornography Ruling**. The Canadian Supreme Court interpreted obscenity under Canada's criminal code to include sexually explicit material "which subjects people to treatment that is degrading or dehumanizing" if there is a substantial risk that it "predisposes persons to

act in an antisocial manner as, for example, the physical or mental mistreatment of women by men." *See* Regina v. Butler, 1 S.C.R. 452 (1992).

According to Strossen, the Canadian government's interpretation of the antipornography ruling reveals that the case "has become an engine for oppressing feminist, gay, and lesbian expression." Strossen, *Defending Pornography*, at 232. Most of the confiscated material has been gay, lesbian, and women's literature, affecting half of Canada's feminist bookstores. In 1993, for example, Canadian customs officials detained 73 percent of the shipments of Inland Books, the largest U.S. exporter of lesbian and gay literature to Canada. *Id.* at 234. Ironically, two books written by Andrea Dworkin, *Pornography: Men Possessing Women* and *Woman Hating,* were seized at the Canadian border because they "illegally eroticized pain and bondage."

5. **Only Two Sides to the Feminist Debate**? As the Introduction noted, feminist anti-pornography proposals generated a heated, sometimes acrimonious debate among feminists about the effects of pornography, the nature of female sexuality, and the strategies for ending sexual inequality. This split in feminist views about pornography reflects a broader debate in contemporary feminist politics. Lynn Chancer, a sociology professor at Barnard College, writes that "it remains difficult to embrace sexuality as a crucial right while hating sexism from the depths of one's psychic and bodily being." Lynn S. Chancer, *Feminist Offensives: Defending Pornography and The Splitting of Sex from Sexism,* 48 Stan. L. Rev. 739, 740 (1996). Chancer criticizes the sharp lines that have been drawn between sides in feminist struggles to confront sexism and liberate sexuality. Many take more subtle theoretical and political positions on issues like pornography: "Many feminists who believe some pornography should be banned would certainly not characterize themselves (even if others would) as 'antisex.' Likewise, many feminists characterized within a 'prosex' camp do not simply celebrate pornography even if they are against its legal restriction, nor are they unconcerned about the pervasiveness of sexism." *Id.*

Chancer offers a third position that does not conceive of pornography in "either/or" terms—"both opposed to legal restrictions and committed to subjecting pornography (like all patriarchal imagery and practices) to gender-related questions and challenges." *Id.* at 755. Chancer explains:

> [A] different vision might proceed by granting that pornography ought to remain legalized, recognizing its enormous potential to provide sexual freedom and expressiveness for both women and men. Yet, an alternative position could also highlight the huge improvements in women's power still badly needed both in and outside the pornography industry per se. If such a reinterpretation were to occur, chances are pornography would assume a place not only legal but legitimized (albeit much more modestly so) as one issue among many within the overall context of an active and multi-issued feminist movement. At the same time, greater attention might turn to the question of how and why the particular position toward por-

nography which has been adopted by MacKinnon and Dworkin as been accorded so much prominence and visibility—especially among that group of women for whom pornography still raises problems because of sexist influences. Even given the persuasive and influential contributions they have made to feminist theory over the last several decades, how have the viewpoints of MacKinnon and Dworkin become so disproportionately noticeable within the recent history of radical feminism itself. Is this in part because no alternative position with regard to pornography yet exists or has developed, in politics and/or theory? . . . What is it about pornography which explains at least some wo(men)'s persistent objections and sense of alienation from it?

Id. at 755–56.

American Booksellers Association v. Hudnut

United States Court of Appeals, Seventh Circuit, 1985.
771 F.2d 323, aff'd, 475 U.S. 1001, 106 S.Ct. 1172, 89 L.Ed.2d 291 (1986).

FRANK H. EASTERBROOK, CIRCUIT JUDGE.

Indianapolis enacted an ordinance defining "pornography" as a practice that discriminates against women. "Pornography" is to be redressed through the administrative and judicial methods used for other discrimination. The City's definition of "pornography" is considerably different from "obscenity," which the Supreme Court has held is not protected by the First Amendment.

To be "obscene", "a publication must, taken as a whole, appeal to the prurient interest, must contain patently offensive depictions or descriptions of specified sexual conduct, and on the whole have no serious literary, artistic, political, or scientific value." *Brockett v. Spokane Arcades, Inc.*, [472 U.S. 491](1985). Offensiveness must be assessed under the standards of the community. Both offensiveness and an appeal to something other than "normal, healthy sexual desires" are essential elements of "obscenity." . . .

The Indianapolis ordinance does not refer to the prurient interest, to offensiveness, or to the standards of the community. It demands attention to particular depictions, not to the work judged as a whole. It is irrelevant under the ordinance whether the work has literary, artistic, political, or scientific value. The City and many amici point to these omissions as virtues. They maintain that pornography influences attitudes, and the statute is a way to alter the socialization of men and women rather than to vindicate community standards of offensiveness. And as one of the principal drafters of the ordinance has asserted, "if a woman is subjected, why should it matter that the work has other value?" Catharine A. MacKinnon, *Pornography, Civil Rights, and Speech*, 20 Harv. Civ. Rts.—Civ. Lib. L. Rev. 1, 21 (1985).

Civil rights groups and feminists have entered this case as amici on both sides. Those supporting the ordinance say that it will play an important role in reducing the tendency of men to view women as sexual objects, a tendency that leads to both unacceptable attitudes and discrimination in the workplace and violence away from it. Those opposing the ordinance point out that much radical feminist literature is explicit and depicts women in ways forbidden by the ordinance and that the ordinance would reopen old battles. It is unclear how Indianapolis would treat works from James Joyce's *Ulysses* to Homer's *Iliad*; both depict women as submissive objects for conquest and domination.

We do not try to balance the arguments for and against an ordinance such as this. The ordinance discriminates on the ground of the content of the speech. Speech treating women in the approved way—in sexual encounters "premised on equality" (MacKinnon, *supra*, at 22)—is lawful no matter how sexually explicit. Speech treating women in the disapproved way—as submissive in matters sexual or as enjoying humiliation—is unlawful no matter how significant the literary, artistic, or political qualities of the work taken as a whole. The state may not ordain preferred viewpoints in this way. The Constitution forbids the state to declare one perspective right and silence opponents. . . .

"If there is any fixed star in our constitutional constellation, it is that no official, high or petty, can prescribe what shall be orthodox in politics, nationalism, religion, or other matters of opinion or force citizens to confess by word or act their faith therein." West Virginia State Board of Education v. Barnette, 319 U.S. 624, 642 (1943). Under the First Amendment the government must leave to the people the evaluation of ideas. Bald or subtle, an idea is as powerful as the audience allows it to be. A belief may be pernicious—the beliefs of Nazis led to the death of millions, those of the Klan to the repression of millions. A pernicious belief may prevail. Totalitarian governments today rule much of the planet, practicing suppression of billions and spreading dogma that may enslave others. One of the things that separates our society from theirs is our absolute right to propagate opinions that the government finds wrong or even hateful.

The ideas of the Klan may be propagated. Communists may speak freely and run for office. The Nazi Party may march through a city with a large Jewish population. People may criticize the President by misrepresenting his positions, and they have a right to post their misrepresentations on public property.

People may teach religions that others despise. People may seek to repeal laws guaranteeing equal opportunity in employment or to revoke the constitutional amendments granting the vote to blacks and women. They may do this because "above all else, the First Amendment means that government has no power to restrict expression because of its message [or] its ideas. . . ." Police Department v. Mosley, 408 U.S. 92, 95 (1972). . . .

Under the ordinance graphic sexually explicit speech is "pornography" or not depending on the perspective the author adopts. Speech that "subordinates" women and also, for example, presents women as enjoying pain, humiliation, or rape, or even simply presents women in "positions of servility or submission or display" is forbidden, no matter how great the literary or political value of the work taken as a whole. Speech that portrays women in positions of equality is lawful, no matter how graphic the sexual content. This is thought control. It establishes an "approved" view of women, of how they may react to sexual encounters, of how the sexes may relate to each other. Those who espouse the approved view may use sexual images; those who do not, may not.

Indianapolis justifies the ordinance on the ground that pornography affects thoughts. Men who see women depicted as subordinate are more likely to treat them so. Pornography is an aspect of dominance. It does not persuade people so much as change them. It works by socializing, by establishing the expected and the permissible. In this view pornography is not an idea; pornography is the injury.

There is much to this perspective. Beliefs are also facts. People often act in accordance with the images and patterns they find around them. People raised in a religion tend to accept the tenets of that religion, often without independent examination. People taught from birth that black people are fit only for slavery rarely rebelled against that creed; beliefs coupled with the self-interest of the masters established a social structure that inflicted great harm while enduring for centuries. Words and images act at the level of the subconscious before they persuade at the level of the conscious. Even the truth has little chance unless a statement fits within the framework of beliefs that may never have been subjected to rational study.

Therefore we accept the premises of this legislation. Depictions of subordination tend to perpetuate subordination. The subordinate status of women in turn leads to affront and lower pay at work, insult and injury at home, battery and rape on the streets. In the language of the legislature, "[p]ornography is central in creating and maintaining sex as a basis of discrimination. Pornography is a systematic practice of exploitation and subordination based on sex which differentially harms women. The bigotry and contempt it produces, with the acts of aggression it fosters, harm women's opportunities for equality and rights [of all kinds]."

Yet this simply demonstrates the power of pornography as speech. All of these unhappy effects depend on mental intermediation. Pornography affects how people see the world, their fellows, and social relations. If pornography is what pornography does, so is other speech. Hitler's orations affected how some Germans saw Jews. Communism is a world view, not simply a *Manifesto* by Marx and Engels or a set of speeches. Efforts to suppress communist speech in the United States were based on the belief that the public acceptability of such ideas would increase the likelihood of totalitarian government. Religions affect socialization in the most pervasive way. . . .

Many people believe that the existence of television, apart from the content of specific programs, leads to intellectual laziness, to a penchant for violence, to many other ills. The Alien and Sedition Acts passed during the administration of John Adams rested on a sincerely held belief that disrespect for the government leads to social collapse and revolution—a belief with support in the history of many nations. Most governments of the world act on this empirical regularity, suppressing critical speech. In the United States, however, the strength of the support for this belief is irrelevant. Seditious libel is protected speech unless the danger is not only grave but also imminent. . . .

Racial bigotry, anti-semitism, violence on television, reporters' biases— these and many more influence the culture and shape our socialization. None is directly answerable by more speech, unless that speech too finds its place in the popular culture. Yet all is protected as speech, however insidious. Any other answer leaves the government in control of all of the institutions of culture, the great censor and director of which thoughts are good for us.

Sexual responses often are unthinking responses, and the association of sexual arousal with the subordination of women therefore may have a substantial effect. But almost all cultural stimuli provoke unconscious responses. Religious ceremonies condition their participants. Teachers convey messages by selecting what not to cover; the implicit message about what is off limits or unthinkable may be more powerful than the messages for which they present rational argument. Television scripts contain unarticulated assumptions. People may be conditioned in subtle ways. If the fact that speech plays a role in a process of conditioning were enough to permit governmental regulation, that would be the end of freedom of speech.

It is possible to interpret the claim that the pornography is the harm in a different way. Indianapolis emphasizes the injury that models in pornographic films and pictures may suffer. The record contains materials depicting sexual torture, penetration of women by red-hot irons and the like. These concerns have nothing to do with written materials subject to the statute, and physical injury can occur with or without the "subordination" of women. . . .[A] state may make injury in the course of producing a film unlawful independent of the viewpoint expressed in the film.

The more immediate point, however, is that the image of pain is not necessarily pain. In *Body Double,* a suspense film directed by Brian DePalma, a woman who has disrobed and presented a sexually explicit display is murdered by an intruder with a drill. The drill runs through the woman's body. The film is sexually explicit and a murder occurs—yet no one believes that the actress suffered pain or died. In *Barbarella* a character played by Jane Fonda is at times displayed in sexually explicit ways and at times shown "bleeding, bruised, [and] hurt in a context that makes these conditions sexual"—and again no one believes that Fonda was actually tortured to make the film. In *Carnal Knowledge* a woman grovels to please the sexual whims of a character played by Jack Nicholson; no one believes that there was a real sexual submission, and the Supreme Court held the film protected by the First Amendment. And this works both ways. The description of women's sexual domination of men in *Lysistrata* was not real dominance. Depictions may affect slavery, war, or sexual roles, but a book about slavery is not itself slavery, or a book about death by poison a murder.

Much of Indianapolis's argument rests on the belief that when speech is "unanswerable," and the metaphor that there is a "marketplace of ideas" does not apply, the First Amendment does not apply either. The metaphor is honored; Milton's *Aeropagitica* and John Stewart Mill's *On Liberty* defend freedom of speech on the ground that the truth will prevail, and many of the most important cases under the First Amendment recite this position. The Framers undoubtedly believed it. As a general matter it is true. But the Constitution does not make the dominance of truth a necessary condition of freedom of speech. To say that it does would be to confuse an outcome of free speech with a necessary condition for the application of the amendment.

A power to limit speech on the ground that truth has not yet prevailed and is not likely to prevail implies the power to declare truth. At some point the government must be able to say (as Indianapolis has said): "We know what the truth is, yet a free exchange of speech has not driven out falsity, so that we must now prohibit falsity." If the government may declare the truth, why wait for the failure of speech? Under the First Amendment, however, there is no such thing as a false idea, so the government may not restrict speech on the ground that in a free exchange truth is not yet dominant.

At any time, some speech is ahead in the game; the more numerous speakers prevail. Supporters of minority candidates may be forever "excluded" from the political process because their candidates never win, because few people believe their positions. This does not mean that freedom of speech has failed.

The Supreme Court has rejected the position that speech must be "effectively answerable" to be protected by the Constitution. . . .

We come, finally, to the argument that pornography is "low value" speech, that it is enough like obscenity that Indianapolis may prohibit it. Some cases hold that speech far removed from politics and other subjects at the core of the Framers' concerns may be subjected to special regulation. . . . "[P]ornography" is not low value speech within the meaning of these cases. Indianapolis seeks to prohibit certain speech because it believes this speech influences social relations and politics on a grand scale, that it controls attitudes at home and in the legislature. This precludes a characterization of the speech as low value. True, pornography and obscenity have sex in common. But Indianapolis left out of its definition any reference to literary, artistic, political, or scientific value. The ordinance applies to graphic sexually explicit subordination in works great and small. The Court sometimes balances the value of speech against the costs of its restriction, but it does this by category of speech and not by the content of particular works. . . . Indianapolis has created an approved point of view and so loses the support of these cases.

Any rationale we could imagine in support of this ordinance could not be limited to sex discrimination. Free speech has been on balance an ally of those seeking change. Governments that want stasis start by restricting speech. Culture is a powerful force of continuity; Indianapolis paints pornography as part of the culture of power. Change in any complex system ultimately depends on the ability of outsiders to challenge accepted views and the reigning institutions. Without a strong guarantee of freedom of speech, there is no effective right to challenge what is.

The definition of "pornography" is unconstitutional. No construction or excision of particular terms could save it. The offense of trafficking in pornography necessarily falls with the definition. We express no view on the district court's conclusions that the ordinance is vague and that it establishes a prior restraint. Neither is necessary to our judgment. We also express no view on the argument presented by several amici that the ordinance is itself a form of discrimination on account of sex.

Section 8 of the ordinance is a strong severability clause, and Indianapolis asks that we parse the ordinance to save what we can. If a court could do this by surgical excision, this might be possible. But a federal court may not completely reconstruct a local ordinance, and we conclude that nothing short of rewriting could save anything.

The offense of coercion to engage in a pornographic performance, for example, has elements that might be constitutional. Without question a state may prohibit fraud, trickery, or the use of force to induce people to perform—in pornographic films or in any other films. Such a statute may be written without regard to the viewpoint depicted in the work. . . .

But the Indianapolis ordinance, unlike our hypothetical statute, is not neutral with respect to viewpoint. The ban on distribution of works containing coerced performances is limited to pornography; coercion is irrelevant if the work is not "pornography," and we have held the definition of "pornography" to be defective root and branch. A legislature might replace "pornography" with "any film containing explicit sex" or some similar expression, but even the broadest severability clause does not permit a federal court to rewrite as opposed to excise. Rewriting is work for the legislature of Indianapolis. . . .

The section creating remedies for injuries and assaults attributable to pornography also is salvageable in principle, although not by us. The First Amendment does not prohibit redress of all injuries caused by speech. Injury to reputation is redressed through the law of libel, which is constitutional subject to strict limitations. . . . The constitutional requirements for a valid recovery for assault caused by speech might turn out to be too rigorous for any plaintiff to meet. But the Indianapolis ordinance requires the complainant to show that the attack was "directly caused by specific pornography," and it is not beyond the realm of possibility that a state court could construe this limitation in a way that would make the statute constitutional. We are not authorized to prevent the state from trying.

Again, however, the assault statute is tied to "pornography," and we cannot find a sensible way to repair the defect without seizing power that belongs elsewhere. Indianapolis might choose to have no ordinance if it cannot be limited to viewpoint-specific harms, or it might choose to extend the scope to all speech, just as the law of libel applies to all speech. An attempt to repair this ordinance would be nothing but a blind guess. ...

Cass Sunstein, Pornography and the First Amendment

1986 Duke L.J. 589.

[R]egulable pornography must (a) be sexually explicit, (b) depict women as enjoying or deserving some form of physical abuse, and (c) have the purpose and effect of producing sexual arousal.

This definition draws on feminist approaches to the problem of pornography and represents a departure from current law, which is directed at "obscenity." Though built-in ambiguities are inevitable in light of the limitations of language, the basic concept should not be obscure. The central concern is that pornography both sexualizes violence and defines women as sexually subordinate to men. Pornographic materials feature rape, explicitly or implicitly, as a fundamental theme. ...

The definition is somewhat narrower than the one suggested by the Indianapolis ordinance, which created liability for graphic, sexually explicit subordination of women as "sexual objects." The approach proposed here excludes sexually explicit materials that do not sexualize violence against women, and it ties the definition closely to the principal harms caused by pornography.[27] The definition, therefore, excludes the vast range of materials that are not sexually explicit but that do contain implicit rape themes. The requirement of sexual explicitness is thus a means of confining the definition. Part of the definition, moreover, requires that the appeal of the materials be noncognitive—hence the requirement that the purpose and effect be to produce sexual arousal.

Examples of pornography as defined here can be found in such magazines as *Hustler* and numerous "adult" movies. It is difficult to capture the nature of genuine pornography without presenting examples. One such example is the "Beaver Hunters" advertisement in *Hustler*, which shows a nude woman strapped to the top of a car; the copy below the photograph states that the woman would be "stuffed and mounted" as soon as the "hunters" got her home. But pornographic materials cannot always be easily characterized as such. There is a continuum from the most violent forms of pornography to materials that to some degree sexualize violence but cause little harm and are not low-value speech. Many popular movies

---

27. There is empirical support for drawing a distinction between violent and nonviolent sexually explicit materials. Edward Donnerstein, reviewing empirical studies, concludes that although drawing a "straightforward, definitive" conclusion about the relationship between pornography and aggression is "difficult to make," it appears that "the aggressive content of pornography ... is the main contributor to violence against women." ...

and novels that combine eroticism and domination should be protected under the first amendment. A common plot in both books and films involves a romantic encounter in which a woman initially resists a forcible sexual assault and then submits. Although harmful, such materials do not fall within the definition of pornography used here. Of course, there will be difficult intermediate cases; but as with other forms of expression not entitled to full first amendment protection, the fact that the relevant class is difficult to define is not itself a sufficient reason to proscribe government regulation. . . .

In contrast to the vague basis of the obscenity doctrine, the reasoning behind antipornography legislation is found in three categories of concrete, gender-related harms: harms to those who participate in the production of pornography, harms to the victims of sex crimes that would not have been committed in the absence of pornography, and harms to society through social conditioning that fosters discrimination and other unlawful activities. Although it is not possible to describe all the available data here, some of the relevant evidence can be outlined.

First, pornography harms those women who are coerced into and brutalized in the process of producing pornography. Evidence of these harms is only beginning to come to light. But in many cases, women, mostly very young and often the victims of sexual abuse as children, are forced into pornography and brutally mistreated thereafter. The participants have been beaten, forced to commit sex acts, imprisoned, bound and gagged, and tortured. . . . Banning the unlawful conduct . . . is unlikely to eliminate it in light of the enormous profits to be made from pornography and the difficulty and cost of ferreting out and punishing particular abuses. The case for a ban on these materials depends on a conclusion that abusive practices are widespread and that elimination of financial incentives is the only way to control those practices. . . . This justification for regulation may point to one of two conclusions. First, one might conclude that the government should be permitted to ban the distribution of those materials that have been produced through unlawful means. Thus, for example, scenes that involve actual rape, or that are the product of coercion, might be actionable. Second, one might conclude that the distribution of pornography generally should be regulated through civil or criminal sanctions as a less expensive way of eliminating the problem of coercion and mistreatment.[57]

The second harmful effect that pornography produces is a general increase in sexual violence directed against women, violence that would not have occurred but for the massive circulation of pornography. To say that there is such a connection is not to say that pornography lies at the root of most sexual violence. Nor is it to say that most or even a significant percentage of men will perpetrate acts of sexual violence as a result of exposure to pornography. But it is to say that the existence of pornography

---

57. In New York v. Ferber, 458 U.S. 747, 756 (1982), the Supreme Court sanctioned suppression of child pornography as an indirect though effective way to prevent the abuse of children in the production of pornographic materials. . . .

increases the aggregate level of sexual violence. Pornography is at least as much a symptom as a cause; but it is a cause as well.

The methodological problems in proving causation are considerable. Even if direct causation in fact existed, it would be difficult to demonstrate; undoubtedly there are multiple causes of sexual violence. ...[I]f highly suggestive evidence of harm suffices—as it does in most areas of the law—the case for regulation is powerful. The evidence linking pornography and sexual violence falls in three categories: laboratory studies, victim accounts, and reports based on the experience of states and countries that have changed their practices with respect to pornography. ...

We are therefore confronted with three kinds of evidence indicating a link between pornography and violence, all of them suggestive, but none of them alone dispositive. For critics of antipornography regulation, the problems of proof suffice to refute the existence of a causal connection between pornography and sexual violence. Uncertainty about the nature and extent of the link, however, hardly counsels inaction. In the context of carcinogens, for example, regulatory action is undertaken in cases in which one cannot be sure of the precise causal connection between a particular substance and cancer—even when the regulation is extraordinarily costly. Pornography may be at least as harmful as many carcinogens currently subject to regulation. The analogy is close: the nature and extent of the link between act and harm are difficult to establish; but suggestive evidence might well, in the face of potentially severe harm, justify immediate governmental action. Other areas of regulation are treated similarly. Inaction pending the accumulation of definitive proof has costs of its own. The question, a familiar one in the regulatory context, is who should bear the burden of uncertainty: the pornography industry or the potential victims of sexual violence.

A third harmful effect of pornography stems from the role it plays as a conditioning factor in the lives of both men and women. Pornography acts as a filter through which men and women perceive gender roles and relationships between the sexes. Of course, pornography is only one of a number of conditioning factors, and others are of greater importance. If pornography were abolished, sexual inequality would hardly disappear. The connection between inequality, unlawful discrimination, and pornography cannot be firmly established. But pornography undeniably reflects inequality, and through its reinforcing power, helps to perpetuate it. ...

False or misleading commercial speech, as well as television and radio advertisements for cigarettes and casinos, are regulable, even though all are based on viewpoint. ...In the area of bribes, threats, and fighting words, the government is also attempting to combat obvious harms. Analysis of suppression of speech advocating the immediate and violent overthrow of the government would be similar: the government is attempting to eradicate a harm, not attempting to impose a particular point of view. Bans on false or misleading commercial speech, cigarette advertising, or casino gambling are analyzed in substantially the same way. In the obscenity context, the reasoning is more obscure, but the central point remains: in some contexts, statutes that appear to be viewpoint-based are justified and accepted because of the harms involved. The harms are so obvious and immediate that claims that the government is attempting to silence one position in a "debate" do not have time even to register. . . .

Obscenity, commercial speech, fighting words, and perhaps even labor speech are said to involve viewpoint-neutral restrictions because the "viewpoint" of the speaker is deemed irrelevant to regulation. But the line drawn by the regulation does, in all these contexts, depend on point of view. One does not "see" a viewpoint-based restriction when the harms invoked in defense of a regulation are obvious and so widely supported by social consensus that they allay any concern about impermissible government motivation. Whether a classification is viewpoint-based thus ultimately turns on the viewpoint of the decisionmaker.

All this suggests that the problem of identifying impermissible viewpoint regulation is far more complex than it at first appears. Regulation based on point of view is common in the law. The terms "viewpoint-based" and "viewpoint-neutral" often represent conclusions rather than analytical tools. In the easy cases, they serve as valuable simplifying devices. But in the hard cases, further analysis is needed. Specifically, three factors help identify impermissible viewpoint-based legislation.

The first factor is the connection between means and ends, a recurrent theme in constitutional law. If the harm invoked is minimal, or if it is implausible to think that the regulation will remedy the harm, it will be more likely that the regulation is in fact based on viewpoint. The second factor is the nature of the process by which the message is communicated. Regulation of harms that derive from types of persuasion appealing to cognitive faculties is presumptively disfavored; more speech is the preferred remedy here. Regulation of antiwar speeches in the presence of soldiers is impermissible because any harm that results is derived from persuasion. More speech should be the solution. Finally, whether the speech is low-or high-value is also relevant. The low-value issue, therefore, is not made irrelevant on the ground that antipornography legislation discriminates on the basis of viewpoint. The viewpoint issue depends, in part, on whether the speech is low-value. Viewpoint-based regulation of high-value speech raises especially intense concerns about government motivation.

Under these criteria, antipornography legislation is defensible. First, the means-ends connection is quite close. Such legislation could be tightly targeted to the cause of the harm: the production and dissemination of portrayals of sexual violence. Second, the "message" of pornography is communicated indirectly and not through rational persuasion. The harm it produces cannot easily be countered by more speech because it bypasses the process of public consideration and debate that underlies the concept of the marketplace of ideas. Finally, pornography falls in the general category of low-value speech. Under these circumstances, antipornography legislation should be regarded not as an effort to exclude a point of view, but instead as an effort to prevent harm. In this respect, the best analogy is to labor speech—with the important caveat that labor speech, which touches public affairs, is far closer to the heart of first amendment concern than is pornography.

The task, in short, is to sort out permissible and impermissible viewpoint discrimination, and to explain the circumstances in which discrimination arguably on the basis of viewpoint should be permitted. It is important in this respect that efforts to regulate pornography, as defined here, do not interfere with deliberative processes at all. By hypothesis, pornography operates at a subconscious level, providing a form of social conditioning that is not analogous to the ordinary operation of freedom of speech. What is distinctive about pornography is its noncognitive character; though it amounts to words and pictures, its purposes and effects are far from the purposes and effects that justify the special protection accorded to freedom of speech. In these circumstances, the response to the claim of viewpoint discrimination is that antipornography legislation does not pose any of the dangers that make discrimination on the basis of viewpoint so troublesome. The three factors identified above—means-ends connection, nature of the process by which the "message" is communicated, and low-value—point in this direction.

This three-factor analysis does have important limitations. Not all materials having a noncognitive appeal are unprotected; communication, whether or not political, is almost always a mixture of cognitive and noncognitive effects. Nor should viewpoint-based restrictions survive constitutional scrutiny in every case in which secondary harms can be identified. Finally, the harms invoked to defend antipornography legislation are not sufficient to justify regulation of political speech, broadly defined. It is the peculiar features of pornography that justify regulation: the low-value status of the speech, the powerful showing of harm, and the nature of the process by which the message is communicated. . . .

Mari J. Matsuda, Public Response to Racist Speech: Considering the Victim's Story

87 Mich. L. Rev. 2320 (1989).

Racist hate messages are rapidly increasing and are widely distributed in this country using a variety of low and high technologies. The negative effects of hate messages are real and immediate for the victims. Victims of vicious hate propaganda have experienced physiological symptoms and emotional distress ranging from fear in the gut, rapid pulse rate and difficulty in breathing, nightmares, post-traumatic stress disorder, hypertension, psychosis, and suicide. Professor Patricia Williams has called the blow of racist messages "spirit murder" in recognition of the psychic destruction victims experience.

Victims are restricted in their personal freedom. In order to avoid receiving hate messages, victims have had to quit jobs, forgo education, leave their homes, avoid certain public places, curtail their own exercise of speech rights, and otherwise modify their behavior and demeanor. The recipient of hate messages struggles with inner turmoil. One subconscious response is to reject one's own identity as a victim-group member. As writers portraying the African–American experience have noted, the price of disassociating from one's own race is often sanity itself.

As much as one may try to resist a piece of hate propaganda, the effect on one's self-esteem and sense of personal security is devastating. To be hated, despised, and alone is the ultimate fear of all human beings. However irrational racist speech may be, it hits right at the emotional place where we feel the most pain. . . .

The effect on non-target-group members is . . . of constitutional dimension. Associational and other liberty interests of whites are curtailed by an atmosphere rife with racial hatred. In addition, the process of dissociation can affect their mental health. Dominant-group members who rightfully, and often angrily, object to hate propaganda share a guilty secret: their relief that they are not themselves the target of the racist attack. While they reject the Ku Klux Klan, they may feel ambivalent relief that they are not African–American, Asian, or Jewish. Thus they are drawn into unwilling complacency with the Klan, spared from being the feared and degraded thing. . . .

Psychologists and sociologists have done much to document the effects of racist messages on both victims and dominant-group members. Writers of color have given us graphic portrayals of what life is like for victims of racist propaganda. From the victim's perspective racist hate messages cause real damage.

If the harm of racist hate messages is significant, and the truth value marginal, the doctrinal space for regulation of such speech is a possibility. . . .

In order to respect first amendment values, a narrow definition of actionable racist speech is required. Racist speech is best treated as a *sui generis* category, presenting an idea so historically untenable, so dangerous, and so tied to perpetuation of violence and degradation of the very classes of human beings who are least equipped to respond that it is properly treated as outside the realm of protected discourse. . . .

The alternative to recognizing racist speech as qualitatively different because of its content is to continue to stretch existing first amendment exceptions, such as the "fighting words" doctrine and the "content/conduct" distinction. This stretching ultimately weakens the first amendment fabric, creating neutral holes that remove protection for many forms of speech. Setting aside the worst forms of racist speech for special treatment is a non-neutral, value-laden approach that will better preserve free speech.

In order to distinguish the worst, paradigm example of racist hate messages from other forms of racist and nonracist speech, three identifying characteristics are suggested here:

    1.   The message is of racial inferiority;

2. The message is directed against a historically oppressed group; and

3. The message is persecutorial, hateful, and degrading.

Making each element a prerequisite to prosecution prevents opening of the dreaded floodgates of censorship.

The first element is the primary identifier of racist speech: racist speech proclaims racial inferiority and denies the personhood of target group members. All members of the target group are at once considered alike and inferior.

The second element attempts to further define racism by recognizing the connection of racism to power and subordination. Racism is more than race hatred or prejudice. It is the structural subordination of a group based on an idea of racial inferiority. Racist speech is particularly harmful because it is a mechanism of subordination, reinforcing a historical vertical relationship.

The final element is related to the "fighting words" idea. The language used in the worst form of racist speech is language that is, and is intended as, persecutorial, hateful, and degrading. . . .

Under these narrowing elements, arguing that particular groups are genetically superior in a context free of hatefulness and without the endorsement of persecution is permissible. Satire and stereotyping that avoids persecutorial language remains protected. Hateful verbal attacks upon dominant-group members by victims is permissible. These kinds of speech are offensive, but they are, in respect of first amendment principles, best subjected to the marketplace of ideas. This is not to suggest that we remain silent in the face of offensive speech of this type. Rather, the range of private remedies—including counter-speech, social approbation, boycott, and persuasion—should apply. . . .

The legal response to racist propaganda provides an interesting context for examination of the relation between law and racism. Legal protection of racism is seen in these doctrinal elements:

(1) the limits of doctrinal imagination in creating first amendment exceptions for racist hate speech;

(2) the refusal to recognize the competing values of liberty and equality at stake in the case of hate speech; and

(3) the refusal to view the protection of racist speech as a form of state action. . . .

When the legal mind understands that reputational interests, which are analogized to the preferred interest in property, must be balanced against first amendment interests, it recognizes the concrete reality of what happens to people who are defamed. Their lives are changed. Their standing in the community, their opportunities, their self-worth, their free enjoyment of life is limited. To see this, and yet to fail to see that the very same things happen to the victims of racist speech, is selective vision.

The selective consideration of one victim's story and not another's results in unequal application of the law. Unlike the victims of defamation and other torts, the victims of racist speech are not representative of the population at large. In making typical legal concessions to the first amendment, we burden a range of victims. In the case of flag-burning, we force patriots, veterans, and flag-lovers of all races to tolerate flag desecration as part of the price of freedom. In contrast, when victims of racist speech are left to assuage their own wounds, we burden a limited class: the traditional victims of discrimination. This class already experiences diminished access to private remedies such as effective counterspeech, and this diminished access is exacerbated by hate messages. Debasing speech discredits targets, further reducing their ability to have their speech taken seriously. The application of absolutist free speech principles to hate speech, then, is a choice to burden one group with a disproportionate share of the costs of speech promotion. . . .

The failure to hear the victim's story results in an inability to give weight to competing values of constitutional dimension. The competing values recognized under international law are equality, liberty, and personality. Each person under that scheme is entitled to basic dignity, to nondiscrimination, and to the freedom to participate fully in society. If there is any central principle to the Bill of Rights, surely that is it. When white supremacist organizations with histories of violence have an active, protected presence in a community, that principle is sacrificed. . . .

The third doctrinal pillar supporting racist speech is the refusal to recognize that tolerance and protection of hate group activities by the government is a form of state action. To allow an organization known for violence, persecution, race hatred, and commitment to racial supremacy to exist openly, and to provide police protection and access to public streets and college campuses for such a group, means that the state is promoting racist speech. . . . Because racist speech is seen as private, the connection to loss of liberty is not made. State silence, however, is public action where the strength of the new racist groups derives from their offering legitimation and justification for otherwise socially unacceptable emotions of hate, fear, and aggression. The need for a formal group, for a patriotic cause, and for an elevation of the doubting self are part of the traditional attraction of groups like the Klan. Government protection of the right of the Klan to exist publicly and to spread a racist message promotes the role of the Klan as a legitimizer of racism.

Further, the law's failure to provide recourse to persons who are demeaned by the hate messages is an effective second injury to that person. . . . The government's denial of personhood by denying legal recourse may be even more painful than the initial act of hatred. One can dismiss the hate group as an organization of marginal people, but the state is the official embodiment of the society we live in. . . .

NOTES AND QUESTIONS

1. **Pornography v. Obscenity**. How does the ordinance's definition of pornography differ from the Supreme Court's definition of obscenity which

is not protected by the First Amendment? How do courts justify banning obscene material but not pornography?

2. ***Hudnut*'s Rationale.** The answer to Question 1 may have nothing to do with the degree of harm produced by these materials. The Seventh Circuit accepts the premise that "[d]epictions of subordination tend to perpetuate subordination," but nevertheless concludes that pornography is protected by the First Amendment because "all of these unhappy effects depend on mental intermediation." Why does the role of thoughts in pornography's perpetuation of women's subordination protect this material from government suppression? Do illegal acts of rape and prostitution become constitutionally protected because they are captured on film?

3. Do Sunstein and Matsuda convincingly explain why harmful speech should not be constitutionally protected just because it is speech?

In her book *Only Words*, Catharine MacKinnon also refutes the Seventh Circuit's characterization of pornography as the expression of a viewpoint:

> In the United States, pornography is protected by the state. Conceptually, this protection relies centrally on putting it back into the context of the silence of the violated women: from real abuse back to an "idea" or "viewpoint" on women and sex. In this de-realization of the subordination of women, this erasure of sexual abuse through which a technologically sophisticated traffic in women becomes a consumer choice of expressive content, abused women become a pornographer's "thought" or "emotion...."
>
> ... But social life is full of words that are legally treated as the acts they constitute without so much as a whimper from the First Amendment. What becomes interesting is when the First Amendment frame is invoked and when it is not. *Saying* "kill" to a trained attack dog is only words. Yet it is not seen as expressing the viewpoint "I want you dead"—which it usually does, in fact, express. It is seen as performing an act tantamount to someone's destruction, like saying "ready, aim, fire" to a firing squad....
>
> Social inequality is substantially created and enforced—that is *done*—through words and images. Social hierarchy cannot and does not exist without being embodied in meanings and expressed in communications. A sign *saying* "White Only" is only words, but it is not legally seen as expressing the viewpoint "we do not want Black people in this store," or as dissenting from the policy view that both Blacks and whites must be served, or even as hate speech, the restriction of which would need to be debated in First Amendment terms. It is seen as the act of segregation that it is, like "Juden nicht erwunscht!" [Jews Not Wanted!]. Segregation cannot happen without someone *saying* "get out" or "you don't belong here"

at some point. Elevation and denigration are all accomplished through meaningful symbols and communicative acts in which saying it is doing it.

MacKinnon, *Only Words*, at 10–13.

Does pornography operate in the same way as saying "kill" to an attack dog? Is pornography a "discriminatory act," similar to a "White Only" sign?

4.   The Seventh Circuit found some parts of the Indianapolis ordinance valid, but concluded that the court could not easily sever them from the objectionable parts, especially since the definition of pornography itself was unconstitutional. How would you "repair" the ordinance to make it constitutional? Would the ordinance pass constitutional muster if it added the requirement of the obscenity test that the material lacked "serious literary, artistic, political, or scientific value?" Does Matsuda's definition of actionable racist speech provide any guidance for drafting an anti-pornography law?

5.   How do the reasons for restricting racist speech compare with the reasons for restricting pornography? Do you find them equally persuasive? For a collection of essays providing a critical race perspective on assaultive speech, *see Words that Wound: Critical Race Theory, Assaultive Speech, and The First Amendment* (Mari J. Matsuda, et al eds., 1993).

6.   One of the most powerful arguments against censoring pornography for feminists is that, in Judge Easterbrook's words, "[f]ree speech has been on balance an ally of those seeking change." Some women's rights advocates fear that censoring pornography in any way will only lead to diminishing the First Amendment rights of everyone, especially those with the least power. They argue that instead of limiting pornographers' speech, those who oppose pornography should use their freedom of speech to persuade others of pornography's harms. For a collection of essays elaborating this speech-protective view, *see Speaking of Race, Speaking of Sex: Hate Speech, Civil Rights, and Civil Liberties* (Henry Louis Gates, Jr., et al. eds., 1994).

A central tenet of free speech jurisprudence, based on the marketplace of ideas metaphor, is that harmful speech should be countered with more speech. Is it a better strategy to attack pornography's subordinating message by disseminating the opposite message? Do Sunstein and Matsuda explain why government intervention, and not more speech alone, is necessary? Given the size of the multi-billion dollar pornography industry, is it realistic to believe that more speech can redress pornography's harmful message?

Mariana Valverde, Pornography: Not for Men Only

From M. Valverde, Sex, Power and Pleasure
(Philadelphia: New Society Publishers, 1987).

Pornography is a collection of images and texts, representations which have something in common. Defining that "something" is the subject of a great deal of discussion. . . .

The problem is that there are no litmus tests for what is or is not pornography. For pornography is not a natural object that can be classified, like a particular species of butterfly, but rather a complex cultural *process*. It is a process because it necessarily establishes, and is established by, a particular set of relations between producer and consumer, between consumer and his/her social context, and between the social context and the producer. Pornography does not drop from heaven onto our local corner-store shelves. It is first *produced* by certain people who relate to one another via the pornography industry; it is then *consumed* by customers who buy porn in the expectation of being aroused; and finally, porn derives most of its meaning and significance from the *social context* in which it exists. . . .

When we look at a *Playboy* centrefold we generally see a young white woman with a flawless body; she is either sitting or reclining, her genital area is exposed in a purposeful manner and is usually in the centre of the picture. In itself, the picture does not have very much meaning. We supply most of the meaning ourselves, from our experience of living in a sexist, ageist and racist society, and from our general knowledge of what *Playboy* is and what is expected of the viewer. We know from sources outside the magazine that it is not coincidental that the woman in the picture is young, slim, white, and helpless-looking. We know from our own experience that the photo was created for a male audience and that when a man looks at it he will react in certain specified ways. He will not merely glance at the photo as he would at a landscape or a family photograph; he will gaze intently, stare at, and *possess* that woman with his eyes. We also know, from our knowledge of how capitalism works, that the purpose of the publication is not to celebrate the female body but rather to use female bodies to make profits. Thus, we use our knowledge of both the production and the consumption processes involved in pornography to interpret the picture and ascribe to it a meaning.

Furthermore, we are informed about the usual relations between men and women in our society, and that information is what produces the feelings we experience when looking at the otherwise harmless photo. We feel embarrassed for the model because we know that her apparent naive innocence is a deception designed to heighten the male's pleasure in conquering the pictured body. We feel angry at men, both those who make money from the photo and those who spend money on it. We feel vulnerable and at risk. But it is not the picture itself which creates these feelings. If men never raped women in real life, the same picture would not have the same power to make us feel violated.

A different, negative example. One could imagine writing a radical feminist sci-fi story in which men were portrayed as stupid creatures only good for sex and reproduction. And yet, even if it offended men, such a story could not make them feel violated, threatened, or at risk, since reality would still be firmly in patriarchal hands. Because women do not have the social power to subdue, exploit, or marginalize men, feminist fantasies of a matriarchal world can never have the same social significance and the same

impact on men as pornography does on women. Men may dislike matriarchal fantasies, but no fantasy can succeed in making them afraid to walk
the streets alone at night for fear of being attacked by a gang of women.

Thus, our experience in a sexist society helps in a very important way
to determine how we will interpret representations of sex and gender. The
very meaning of representation is largely determined by its social context.
For instance, a photo of a woman kneeling down to perform fellatio on a
man has a very different social meaning than a picture of a man kneeling to
perform cunnilingus on a woman. The first picture implies subordination,
while the second merely implies that a man is giving a woman pleasure.
The difference in the connotations is not due to anything in the photos
themselves, but rather to the "usual" connotations of women's bodies
versus men's bodies.

The meaning of a particular representation is further specified by the
context in which the representation appears. If we are watching a pornographic film, a close-up shot of a peach cut in half will have sexual
connotations, whereas the same shot would not arouse anybody if it were
part of a food advertisement. . . .

Thus far feminist analyses of porn have tended to focus only on male
sexual violence against women. Important as this one component is, there
are others which are equally essential in the constitution of pornography as
a cultural genre. . . .Pornography tends to use stereotyped social roles
rather than fully developed characters. . . .Many of these roles would, in
real life, put a distance between one person and another. For instance, the
milkman has a specific job to do, and the housewife presumably has an
allegiance to her husband and is not normally available to other men. But
pornography sees its role as demolishing all social barriers by connecting,
through sex, people who are generally kept separate by society's rules. We
know this about pornography, so when we begin to read a story about a
high school girl and her teacher we immediately expect the usual barrier
between teacher and young student to be overcome by mutual lust. Similarly, if a woman is presented as unavailable to men (most commonly the nun
and the lesbian) we again expect to see this apparent unavailability denied
as sex bursts through the boundaries. . . .

This undermining of social distinctions by the power of passion is not
necessarily sexist. It is the main ingredient of erotic literature of any kind,
from highbrow novels to women's romances. Usually however it is expressed within a sexist context. But the idea of sex as the great leveller
which eliminates all social conventions is not per se a patriarchal one.

To focus only on sexual domination is a narrow perspective, and one
which white middle-class women might tend to take because they are not
subject to other forms of domination. But a feminism which is more broadly
based and which takes into account the experience of women of colour and
women in the Third World will have to take a serious look at the
glamourization of racism and capitalism, not just the glamourization of
sexual subordination. Pornography often eroticizes several forms of domination at once. Consider, for example, the cliché scenes about white male

explorers coming upon a "primitive" society whose women are portrayed as "natural" sex objects free of the inhibitions of white Protestant ladies.

Pornography eroticizes social domination in general. A picture that presents a white British army officer flogging an Indian soldier (cf. the television series *The Jewel and the Crown*) is in my mind pornographic, even though there are no women involved. The picture has a definite sexual overtone which helps to disguise the real nature of British imperialism, in the same way that Penthouse photos of women begging to be penetrated help to disguise the real nature of sexism.

The eroticization of social domination is also an element in advertising, women's magazines, and the mainstream media in general. Soap operas, for instance, probably do more than any other medium to teach women to see wealth and power as erotic. Devotees of Dallas know that the glamorous women in the show might make a mistake and fall in love with the "wrong" man. But they would never fall in love with a man of the wrong class or race. The invisibility of black people, of the Chicano population, and of the workers who produce the Ewing millions is a statement in itself. Because these people are outside the world of wealth, they are also outside the realm of significant sexual intrigue.

Pornography is not an aberration in an otherwise civilized and egalitarian culture. It is part and parcel of the cultural industry that has given us sexist advertising, racist war movies, and classist soap operas. My contention here is that its specific role in this cultural industry is to eroticize social domination, and most notably gender domination. . . .

In trying to isolate the pornographic element in our culture, feminist writers and lawyers have tended to separate violent porn from all other sexual representations and all other portrayals of women. This is a disservice to the women's movement. The early critiques of porn begun in the late sixties were undertaken as part of a wider critique that included advertising images and such practices as beauty pageants. The protest was not just against images of violence, but against any images that portrayed women as stupid and only good for fucking. It is very unfortunate that this connection has taken a back seat to the question of violence in the current debates. Even if violent porn is what angers women most, it is not necessarily the cultural form most dangerous to our own emotional and sexual development. No woman sees the anonymous models portrayed as victims of male violence as role models. But who among us is not influenced by the equally pernicious messages that tell us to be thin, to wear tight jeans, to be attractive to men? I am not convinced that porn increases violence against women, but what about the self-inflicted violence many women suffer as a result of male-oriented images of beauty and desirability? Women destroy their tendons by wearing high heels, spoil their eating habits by alternating binging and dieting, and ruin their emotional health by constantly worrying about their looks.

It would indeed be convenient if all the oppression and violence women suffer were located out there in the pornography industry. But it is not. We degrade and coerce ourselves as soon as we internalize the dictates of sexism, and there is no law or censor board in the world that can protect us against that. The only way that we can, in the long term, overthrow the system which eroticizes and legitimizes domination by making it glamorous and sexy is to empower ourselves, and this includes sexual self-determination and empowerment. Many of the feminists who are concerned about pornography are neglecting to make this necessary connection, and are in some ways telling us to retreat into traditional feminine roles. . . .

If we object to women being depicted as "sluts," surely the feminist response is not to flee into the opposite stereotype and proclaim our virtuousness and innocence. If we object to the way men express their sexuality because they tend to think of us as objects to be owned, the alternative is not to pretend that we women have never longed to possess another's body. If we want to tell men that sex is not about domination, we should not tell women that sex is always about nurturing and love. If we object to male partners sleeping around in an irresponsible manner, the solution is not to suggest that all women are by nature monogamous. There are two poles to the double standard, and we cannot claim to be undermining patriarchy if we criticize only the male pole and reinforce the feminine end of the deal. We have to deny both sides of the double standard. We have to acknowledge that the myth of the madonna is as false as the myth of the whore, and that both myths form a single whole. It is not necessary to use clichéd notions of nurturing love in our solution to the problem of violent, aggressive sex: we could try thinking about good sex instead. . . .

The most prevalent feminist approach to porn does not begin with erotic representation in general. Rather, it begins with a discussion of how the state could best be used to suppress violent porn. It is not a coincidence that feminist lawyers are playing an important role in the porn debate. They are primarily concerned with legal reform, and their definitions of porn are devised primarily for legal purposes. This is a problem in the debate. Feminist artists for example tend to approach the porn question differently, emphasizing the need for nonsexist representations and oppositional art, and expressing skepticism about censorship solutions. . . .

Indeed, the legal approach to porn tends to confuse reality and representation. In the real world a sexual assault is always objectionable. But how is one to determine whether or not the rape scene in *Tess of the D'Ubervilles* should be banned because it condones coercion? It is not at all simple to "read" the message in a particular picture; and even texts are often ambiguous. There are some pornographic texts and films that clearly endorse violence against women as a sexual turn-on. But there are many, many more which are not so unequivocal.

There is no clear line between depictions of consensual sex, of seduction and of coercion. Even in real life people disagree as to whether a woman has been coerced against her will or not (think of rape trials). And when we discuss representation the problems multiply, because there is no longer one person who claims to be the victim and whose interpretation carries particular weight. Legal skills might help to sort out a rape case, but they are powerless to give an authoritative reading of a particular picture or text.

This is why I have concluded that the attempt to present a definition of porn that even sexist policemen cannot misinterpret is futile. Two feminists might agree intuitively on what is offensive, although even among feminists there are major differences. But even if we agreed on what is offensive, it would be impossible to translate our critique of a representation into unequivocal legal language and then to ensure that the courts do not use these laws (ostensibly set up to protect women) in their efforts to persecute sexual minorities or ban representations that offend "community standards."

The legal approach cannot encompass the important questions of production, consumption, and context. Obscenity laws erroneously assume that images and texts have objective meanings. A judge is supposed to determine whether or not a magazine is obscene, and a film censor makes decisions about cutting films, with only the most cursory reference to the context and to how the intended audience consumes the product. New pornography laws might try to emphasize context a little more, but it is in the nature of legal proceedings to see cultural products as distinct entities with an absolute meaning.

Thus, I think the attempts to draw up anti-pornography legislation are, from a feminist perspective, bound to fail. Seeking state protection is a last-resort strategy. Empowering women is preferred to any policies granting yet more powers to an already overzealous police and court system. Especially dangerous are those attempts of cultural policy to regulate the production and consumption of representations by calling on the state to exercise its powers. An equal-pay law cannot be used against women, since its meaning and purpose is quite unambiguous. But any laws regulating representation can and are being used to suppress marginal or oppositional art, rather than the multinationals of pornography. The Toronto police recently confiscated a feminist art exhibit displayed in a bookstore window and charged the artists with obscenity (even though the display did not include *any* representations of explicit sexual activity, or of any human bodies, for that matter). We cannot reasonably expect those same policemen to understand what is truly degrading to women.

Nevertheless, an anti-censorship position is not by any means a do-nothing position. On the contrary. Spending a lot of time trying to change the laws can distract us from the necessary task of thinking creatively about what we women can and should do to replace both pornography and other sexist representations by woman-positive cultural projects. Some examples of what women can do to simultaneously attack the sexism of mass-produced culture and *empower* the women engaged in the action are as follows:

— boycott businesses that make money on pornography, and inform the management of our decision

— complain to bookstore owners and other storekeepers, not just about the presence of pornographic magazines but also about the absence of feminist periodicals

— use the handy "this degrades women" stickers available in women's bookstores to record our opinion of billboards, ads in the public transit system, and store window displays

— paint creative graffiti over billboards

— refuse to sell offensive magazines or rent offensive videos in stores that we work in, making sure we get support from our union or from local women's groups

— try to educate the public about our concerns, by writing articles and letters to the editor, speaking in classrooms, organizing pickets at appropriate events

— challenge the men we know who use pornography, and the men we work with who put pin-ups up in public areas. Enlist the support of women workers and supportive men in the attempt to have a working environment that is misogyny-free! One can point out that pornography pollutes the emotional environment just like smoke pollutes the physical environment.

In conclusion, it is becoming increasingly clear that pornography cannot be tackled as an isolated issue. If the main problem with porn is that it eroticizes the male sexual domination of women and other forms of social domination, then the only real solution is to empower women and other oppressed groups so that we can begin to redefine what is erotic and what is not. This will involve not only boycotting sexist cultural products and denouncing images which glamourize women's subjection, but also helping to create alternative cultural forms. More generally, since we have shown that a great deal of pornography's impact on us is due not to the images and words themselves but to the social context of men's actual domination of women, then anything we do to empower women and increase their sense of dignity and autonomy will help to rob porn of its power to humiliate us.

Susan Etta Keller, Viewing and Doing: Complicating Pornography's Meaning

81 Geo. L.J. 2195 (1993).

. . . If part of the appeal of fantasy is that it is fantasy, then part of the appeal of viewing may be that it is not doing. . . .

[P]ornography . . . often plays at being real. Linda Williams has pointed-ed out that pornography strives for a sense of cinematic realism by attempting to convince the audience that what it sees has actually happened. But as she also notes, this attempt is not the same as reality:

Our complicity as viewers of the act is different from what it would be if we were actually in the room with the 'object'; it is connected to the fact that we are watching (whether with fascination, pleasure, horror, or dread) an act that seems real but with which we have no physical connection ourselves. . . .

This play with the sense of realness can make it dangerous to declare with certainty that what is depicted is totally unrelated to real violence or coercion, just as it is unwise to assume that what occurs on the screen is completely consonant with reality. Many pornographic films seem to get much of their kick from the viewer's uncertainty over whether they are documents of reality or staged performances (or a little of both). For example, one film, *Bus Stop Tales*, purports to be a lived encounter between an amateur filmmaker and a woman he picks up at a bus stop. The following lines are flashed across the screen to convince the viewer: "You are about to witness a true real life situation that has been captured on video tape for all the world to see. . . . One woman's fantasy becomes a welcome reality." If we accept this premise, the film becomes a disturbing eyewitness to the coercive powers of seduction as a naive woman is cajoled and persuaded to first disrobe, and then to engage in the stock variety of sexual numbers with the filmmaker. It therefore seems to be "about" coercion in a very direct sense; we are seeing actual coercion happen. . . .

In *Bus Stop Tales*, however, the "reality" of the film becomes increasingly suspect, as the woman's inhibitions melt away and she becomes increasingly adept at performing in the variety of positions that she is asked to assume. At the end of the film, we are given additional names of films in which the actress has appeared. Of course, this does not mean coercion did not occur—it may have. . . . What it means is that a simple translation from coercion on film to coercion in real life is impossible; the connections are more complicated. The importance of working through the confusion lies not just in an investigative determination about the actual conditions of production, but in an understanding of the factors that account for pornography's appeal to the consumer.

It is perhaps the factor of distance . . . that accounts for the effect of the interplay between reality and unreality that I have called realness. . . . [O]ur understanding may be that while the pornography depicts a relationship in which a woman enjoys terror and brutalization, we do not believe women would actually derive sexual pleasure from such a situation. I believe the same distance of viewing that allows us to stand back and make that political judgment is at work in making the material erotic in other circumstances. . . . Despite the understanding of distance that we may experience in viewing material defined as pornography, there is also, sometimes, a feeling of horror. That is because although we may know it is not real, it still feels real. . . .

This theory, however, does not account for what makes the realness sometimes erotic and sometimes horrific to different people. It is quite possible that pornography may be erotic and horrific at the same time; that it works through a combination of attraction, or identification, and revulsion. Indeed, it may be that the horror of doing is precisely what makes viewing, at a distance, appealing to some. . . .

Examining the process of pornography is vital if one accepts both the idea that pornography in its multiple interpretations plays a serious role in the construction of sexuality, and the notion that because of those multiple interpretations, it can play a role in transforming sexuality. . . .

MacKinnon and Dworkin . . . see power, and pornography, as central to sexuality and believe that transformation is possible. However, they do not see power, and, more particularly, the role it plays in pornography, as dynamic, nor as a vehicle for transforming women's sexuality within dominant culture. As a result, they create, ironically, a sharp disjunction between a reality of constructed unequal and power-laden sexuality and a fantasy of unconstructed and equal sexuality. They account for sexuality by drawing a close connection between one message and one effect, and they use pornography as a vehicle for discussing the entire realm of heterosexuality, in which domination of women by men is the primary characteristic. . . .

[T]he perspective of MacKinnon and Dworkin necessarily suggests that there is a different, better form of sexuality, entertainment, and romance outside of what we have been experiencing. . . .MacKinnon's perspective . . . implies that if women could exercise their will freely, they would express some other version of sexuality, outside of society as we know it. "Take your foot off our necks, then we will hear in what tongue women speak," may refer to a woman's voice or sexuality that is not constructed. This sexuality would be removed from and unaffected by pornography and other elements. . . .

Neither MacKinnon nor [Cass] Sunstein display any confidence that working within the socially constructed world can be transformative, and they share a static view of message and effect. . . .[For them,] pleasure from power is not part of women's true sexuality. Neither . . . credit[s] the role power and our understanding of it can play in reconstructing sexuality. . . . [D]enying the existence of . . . pleasure in power denies women a role other than victim. . . .

Imagine that the totalizing message of antipornography analysis was truly totalizing. Imagine that, by describing what appeals in both pornography and the rest of the media, it described the available terrain for sexuality. For those who accept the MacKinnon and Dworkin dichotomy—debilitating socially constructed sexuality of the present contrasted with the hint of another, better sexuality awaiting—that prospect would be a demoralizing and demobilizing dystopia.

The dystopia of a world in which sexuality is defined by and itself defines the elements of pornography need not be demoralizing. Dominant culture is not as uniformly evil as portrayed. If the hope of a yet unknown other quality of sexuality is a source of pleasure for many, it is formed, after all, in response to dominant culture. In other words, the source of the hope can be found within dominant culture itself. Of course, if that is true, an additional risk is revealed—that the hope I hold out for working within the socially constructed culture is equally constructed and illusive. The only response to that possibility, that I can think of, is to keep constantly in mind the hazards as well as the potential benefits of the material we are trying to reconstruct....

If sexuality is made out of (and in turn makes) pornography, and if there is nothing existing outside of our socially constructed culture to turn to, then maybe the only way to transform sexuality is to exploit the many meanings of pornography....

Pornography is [a] ... site, both in terms of viewing and producing, where we can pick and choose among sexual roles, try them on for size, critique or turn them inside out. But unlike a trip through the vintage clothing store where the previous wearer is irrelevant, the meaning of the sex roles we select can be multiple and fraught with ambiguity based on their previous and continuing uses. Historical and ongoing gender power relations, for example, provide a constraint that can inform the meaning of the sex roles assumed, although these same power relations can provide the basis for reinterpretation as well....

Carl Stychin argues that gay male pornography is already a locus in which traditional gender roles are being challenged through these types of interpretations and reinterpretations. He argues that "gay male pornography undermines rather than reinforces male supremacy because it questions the coherence of sexual subjectivity." In other words, if a prime characteristic of heterosexual pornography is male subjectivity and female objectivity, gay male pornography, by presenting men in both dominant and submissive positions, challenges the idea that subjectivity is tied to gender. He refutes MacKinnon's suggestion that dominance and submission reinforce the gendered nature of sexuality, no matter what the gender of the participants, as well as the contention that valorization of masculinity generally. In this respect, he presents alternative messages and alternative effects for the material he considers.

Stychin, with Judith Butler, argues that gay male pornography, by disconnecting the gender of the participants from their socially ascribed gender, reveals gender as performance: "The replication of heterosexual constructs in non-heterosexual frames brings into relief the utterly constructed status of the so-called heterosexual original." Further, "[i]f performance reveals the artificiality of gender identity, it also undermines hierarchical gendered arrangements." In contrast, MacKinnon accepts the performance aspect of switching gender roles but disagrees about its potential.

> The capacity of gender reversals ... to stimulate sexual excitement is derived precisely from their mimicry or parody or negation or reversal of the standard arrangement. This affirms rather than undermines or qualifies the standard sexual arrangement as the standard sexual arrangement, the definition of sex, the standard from which all else is defined, that in which sexuality as such inheres.

Butler disputes this notion:

If the anatomy of the performer is already distinct from the gender of the performer, and both of those are distinct from the gender of the performance, then the performance suggests a dissonance not only between sex and performance, but sex and gender, and gender and performance. As much as drag creates a unified picture of "woman" (what its critics often oppose), it also reveals the distinctness of those aspects of gendered experience which are falsely naturalized.

While recognizing the potential for more than just gay male parodies of gendered sex, Stychin focuses on the uniqueness of the gay male challenge. However, heterosexual as well as lesbian pornography may also make these challenges. The potential has been recognized in mainstream cinema. Bette Gordon argues that her film *Variety* manipulates conventions of pornography to give a woman regarding pornography the position of subject and voyeur. In so doing, "[t]he film suggests that women, even in patriarchal culture, are active agents who interpret and utilize cultural symbols on their own behalf." Similarly, at least one of Madonna's videos makes these types of challenges by manipulating the images of traditional gender roles and distributions of power.

Instead of seeking meaning for pornography by establishing an ill-founded coherence among definition, message, and effect, "pornography" should instead be understood as a process by which images of sexuality are pasted and repasted together, both in the creation of the product and in the process of viewing and critiquing, so that we create and recreate meaning about human sexuality and gender. By assuming that pornography, once produced, arrives on the screen and stays in the mind with one message, we cede the process uncontested (at least with respect to those who produce visual material) to an industry that often maintains conditions deplorable for the women who work there. The response to pornography's images does not have to be systematic, but may be variable depending on the context. By seizing the opportunity to interpret and reinterpret the many levels on which pornography's meaning operates, while attacking coercion, we can have a role in redefining sexuality through what may be the only means available.

Audre Lorde, Uses of the Erotic: The Erotic as Power

From A. Lorde, Sister Outsider
(Trumansburg: Crossing Press, 1984).

There are many kinds of power, used and unused, acknowledged or otherwise. The erotic is a resource within each of us that lies in a deeply female and spiritual plane, firmly rooted in the power of our unexpressed or unrecognized feeling. In order to perpetuate itself, every oppression must corrupt or distort those various sources of power within the culture of the oppressed that can provide energy for change. For women, this has meant a suppression of the erotic as a considered source of power and information within our lives.

We have been taught to suspect this resource, vilified, abused, and devalued within western society. On the one hand, the superficially erotic has been encouraged as a sign of female inferiority; on the other hand, women have been made to suffer and to feel both contemptible and suspect by virtue of its existence.

It is a short step from there to the false belief that only by the suppression of the erotic within our lives and consciousness can women be truly strong. But that strength is illusory, for it is fashioned within the context of male models of power.

As women, we have come to distrust that power which rises from our deepest and nonrational knowledge. We have been warned against it all our lives by the male world, which values this depth of feeling enough to keep women around in order to exercise it in the service of men, but which fears this same depth too much to examine the possibilities of it within themselves. So women are maintained at a distant/inferior to be psychically milked, much the same way ants maintain colonies of aphids to provide a life-giving substance for their masters.

But the erotic offers a well of replenishing and provocative force to the woman who does not fear its revelation, nor succumb to the belief that sensation is enough.

The erotic has often been misnamed by men and used against women. It has been made into the confused, the trivial, the psychotic, the plasticized sensation. For this reason, we have often turned away from the exploration and consideration of the erotic as a source of power and information, confusing it with its opposite, the pornographic. But pornography is a direct denial of the power of the erotic, for it represents the suppression of true feeling. Pornography emphasizes sensation without feeling. . . .

The very word *erotic* comes from the Greek word *eros*, the personification of love in all its aspects–born of Chaos, and personifying creative power and harmony. When I speak of the erotic, then, I speak of it as an assertion of the lifeforce of women; of that creativity energy empowered, the knowledge and use of which we are now reclaiming in our language, our history, our dancing, our loving, our work, our lives.

There are frequent attempts to equate pornography and eroticism, two diametrically opposed uses of the sexual. Because of these attempts it has become fashionable to separate the spiritual (psychic and emotional) from the political, to see them as contradictory or antithetical. "What do you mean, a poetic revolutionary, a meditating gunrunner?" In the same way, we have attempted to separate the spiritual and the erotic, thereby reducing the spiritual to a world of flattened affect, a world of the ascetic who aspires to feel nothing. But nothing is farther from the truth. For the ascetic position is one of the highest fear, the gravest immobility. The severe abstinence of the ascetic becomes the ruling obsession. And it is one not of self-discipline but of self-abnegation.

The dichotomy between the spiritual and the political is also false, resulting from an incomplete attention to our erotic knowledge. For the bridge which connects them is formed by the erotic—the sensual—those physical, emotional, and psychic expressions of what is deepest and strongest and richest within each of us, being shared: the passions of love, in its deepest meanings....

The erotic functions for me in several ways, and the first is in providing the power which comes from sharing deeply any pursuit with another person. The sharing of joy, whether physical, emotional, psychic, or intellectual, forms a bridge between the sharers which can be the basis for understanding much of what is not shared between them, and lessens the threat of their difference.

Another important way in which the erotic connection functions is the open and fearless underlining of my capacity for joy. In the way my body stretches to music and opens into response, hearkening to its deepest rhythms, so every level upon which I sense also opens to the erotically satisfying experience, whether it is dancing, building a bookcase, writing a poem, examining an idea.

That self-connection shared is a measure of the joy which I know myself to be capable of feeling, a reminder of my capacity for feeling. And that deep and irreplaceable knowledge of my capacity for joy comes to demand from all of my life that it be lived within the knowledge that such satisfaction is possible, and does not have to be called *marriage*, nor *god*, nor *an afterlife*.

This is one reason why the erotic is so feared, and so often relegated to the bedroom alone, when it is recognized at all. For once we begin to feel deeply all the aspects of our lives, we begin to demand from ourselves and from our life-pursuits that they feel in accordance with that joy which we know ourselves to be capable of. Our erotic knowledge empowers us, becomes a lens through which we scrutinize all aspects of our existence, forcing us to evaluate those aspects honestly in terms of their relative meaning within our lives. And this is a grave responsibility, projected from within each of us, not to settle for the convenient, the shoddy, the conventionally expected, nor the merely safe....

We have been raised to fear the *yes* within ourselves, our deepest cravings. But, once recognized, those which do not enhance our future lose their power and can be altered. The fear of our desires keeps them suspect and indiscriminately powerful, for to suppress any truth is to give it strength beyond endurance. The fear that we cannot grow beyond whatever distortions we may find within ourselves keeps us docile and loyal and disobedient, externally defined, and leads us to accept many facets of our oppression as women.

When we live outside ourselves, and by that I mean on external directives only rather than from our internal knowledge and needs, when we live away from those erotic guides from within ourselves, then our lives are limited by external and alien forms, and we conform to the needs of a structure that is not based on human need, let alone an individual's. But when we begin to live from within outward, in touch with the power of the erotic within ourselves, and allowing that power to inform and illuminate our actions upon the world around us, then we begin to be responsible to ourselves in the deepest sense. For as we begin to recognize our deepest feelings, we begin to give up, of necessity, being satisfied with suffering and self-negation, and with the numbness which so often seems like their only alternative in our society. Our acts against oppression become integral with self, motivated and empowered from within.

In touch with the erotic, I become less willing to accept powerlessness, or those other supplied states of being which are not native to me, such as resignation, despair, self-effacement, depression, self-denial.

And yes, there is a hierarchy. There is a difference between painting a back fence and writing a poem, but only one of quantity. And there is, for me, no difference between writing a good poem and moving into sunlight against the body of a woman I love.

This brings me to the last consideration of the erotic. To share the power of each other's feelings is different from using another's feelings as we would use a kleenex. When we look the other way from our experience, erotic or otherwise, we use rather than share the feelings of those others who participate in the experience with us. And use without consent of the used is abuse.

In order to be utilized, our erotic feelings must be recognized. The need for sharing deep feeling is a human need. But within the european-american tradition, this need is satisfied by certain proscribed erotic comings-together. These occasions are almost always characterized by a simultaneous looking away, a pretense of calling them something else, whether a religion, a fit, mob violence, or even playing doctor. And this misnaming of the need and the deed give rise to that distortion which results in pornography and obscenity—the abuse of feeling.

When we look away from the importance of the erotic in the development and sustenance of our power, or when we look away from ourselves as we satisfy our erotic needs in concert with others, we use each other as objects of satisfaction rather than share our joy in the satisfying, rather than make connection with our similarities and our differences. To refuse to be conscious of what we are feeling at any time, however comfortable that might seem, is to deny a large part of the experience, and to allow ourselves to be reduced to the pornographic, the abused, and the absurd.

The erotic cannot be felt secondhand. As a Black lesbian feminist, I have a particular feeling, knowledge, and understanding for those sisters with whom I have danced hard, played, or even fought. This deep participation has often been the forerunner for joint concerted actions not possible before.

But this erotic charge is not easily shared by women who continue to operate under an exclusively european-american male tradition. I know it was not available to me when I was trying to adapt my consciousness to this mode of living and sensation.

Only now, I find more and more women-identified women brave enough to risk sharing the erotic's electrical charge without having to look away, and without distorting the enormously powerful and creative nature of that exchange. Recognizing the power of the erotic within our lives can give us the energy to pursue genuine change within our world, rather than merely settling for a shift of characters in the same weary drama.

For not only do we touch our most profoundly creative source, but we do that which is female and self-affirming in the face of a racist, patriarchal, and anti-erotic society.

NOTES AND QUESTIONS

1. **Discourse Criticism**. Critics of pornography discourse, such as Valverde and Keller, like critics of other discourses, argue that human experience is produced by and within language, that there is no real or true experience outside language. A pornographic text or image, then, has no objective, fixed meaning. Why does a *Playboy* centerfold have a subordinating effect on women, while the radical feminist sci-fi story Valverde describes would not have a subordinating effect on men? Is pornography by itself neutral as to social domination with no impact apart from the already existing social structure that gives men the power to subdue and exploit women? In other words, does pornography cause women's subordination or does women's subordination cause pornography's harmful effects? Does the answer matter?

Discourse critics also maintain that since any particular discourse contains conflicts and ambiguities, there are always points of resistance that can be identified and then exploited to disrupt, reverse, or transform experience. Pornography discourse critics argue that by analyzing and interpreting pornography they are engaged in political struggle. How can we ensure that pornography is used in this positive direction rather than to exploit women?

Is this focus on sexy talk just a way for privileged women to indulge their sexual pleasures? Valverde argues, on the other hand, that pornography opponents' focus on sexual domination often reflects the privilege of white middle-class women who are not subject to other forms of domination. Valverde notes, as well, that pornography eroticizes several forms of domination at once. But isn't this further reason to take legal steps to eradicate pornography while tackling other ways in which gender, race, and class inequality are perpetuated?

2. **Act or Image**? The central problem with the legal approach to ending pornography, according to both Valverde and Keller, is that it confuses reality and representation. Does pornography constitute harmful action that is real and can therefore be regulated or images that portray and stimulate people's fantasies about reality? Contrast Keller's concept of

pornography's realness and MacKinnon's description of pornography's real effects:

> What pornography does, it does in the real world, not only in the mind. As an initial matter, it should be observed that it is the pornography industry, not the ideas in the materials, that forces, threatens, blackmails, pressures, tricks, and cajoles women into sex for pictures. In pornography, women are gang raped so they can be filmed. They are not gang raped by the idea of a gang rape. It is for pornography, not the idea in it, that women are hurt and penetrated, tied and gagged, undressed and genitally spread and sprayed with laquer and water so sex pictures can be made. Only for pornography are women killed to make a sex movie, and it is not the idea of a sex killing that kills them. It is unnecessary to do any of these things to express, as ideas, the ideas pornography expresses. It *is* essential to do them to make pornography. Similarly, on the consumption end, it is not the ideas in pornography that assault women: men do, men who are made, changed, and impelled by it. Pornography does not leap off the shelf and assault women. Women could, in theory, walk safely past whole warehouses full of it, quietly resting in its jackets. It is what it takes to make it and what happens through its use that are the problem. . . .
>
> Pornography is masturbation material. It is used as sex. It therefore is sex. Men know this. . . .
>
> With pornography, men masturbate to women being exposed, humiliated, violated, degraded, mutilated, dismembered, bound, gagged, tortured, and killed. In the visual materials, they experience this *being done* by watching it *being done*. What is real here is not that the materials are pictures, but that they are part of a sex act. The women are in two dimensions, but the men have sex with them in their own three-dimensional bodies, not in their minds alone. Men come doing this. This, too, is a behavior, not a thought or an argument. It is not ideas they are ejaculating over. Try arguing with an orgasm sometime. You will find you are no match for the sexual access and power the materials provide.

MacKinnon, *Only Words*, pp. 15–18.

3. **The Limits of Legal Reform**. Even if we accept the claim that pornography harms women, this leaves the question whether law reform is an effective remedy. While the *Hudnut* opinion invalidated the antipornography ordinance because it endorsed a particular view of women, Valverde and Ellis argue that we cannot determine authoritatively what view any particular text represents. This potential for multiple interpretations makes any legal approach to pornography, such as passing censorship laws, impossible. Although Valverde opposes law-related remedies to pornography, she advocates action to eliminate pornography and other sexist repre-

sentations of women. Do you think her proposals would be more effective than the civil rights ordinance? For other examples of women's activism against pornography, see Russell, *Part IV: Feminist Strategies and Actions against Pornography* in *Making Violence Sexy*, at 214–69.

In her book *The Imaginary Domain*, feminist legal philosopher Drucilla Cornell similarly rejects the overreliance on law in the regulation of pornography, emphasizing instead solidarity with porn workers and "unleashing the feminine imaginary, rather than ... constraining men":

> How can a feminist approach to pornography that challenges rather than replicates gender stereotypes be developed? How can we both recognize the nitty-gritty of the industry and the suffering it can impose upon its workers at the same time that we affirm the need for women to freely explore their own sexuality? The first step in answering these questions is to insist on an important distinction. Feminists need to separate political action from legal action in the sphere of pornography. I advocate an alliance with two forms of representational politics currently being undertaken by women pornographers and porn workers that are challenging the terms of production in the mainstream heterosexual porn industry. Political action, not legal action, should be the main mode of intervention in the *production* of pornography. In accordance with this distinction between the political and the legal, a second distinction must be made, one which can help us clarify what kind of legal action should be taken—and at what point it should be taken—in the arena of pornography.
>
> We need to separate legal action to be taken in the *production* of pornography from action addressed specifically to the *distribution* of pornography. I insist on these distinctions primarily to serve the feminist purpose of treating women, including porn workers, as selves individuated enough to have undertaken the project of becoming persons. To treat women in the industry as reducible to hapless victims unworthy of solidarity refuses them that basic respect....
>
> The prostitute, in particular, has always been a favorite candidate for rescue. By remaining "other," the epitome of victimization, she stands for the degradation of all women. Her life is then reduced to that figuration of her. Now, porn workers have become the ultimate figuration of the victim who needs to be rescued. But this is certainly not how most porn workers see themselves.

Drucilla Cornell, *The Imaginary Domain: Abortion, Pornography & Sexual Harassment* 96 (1995).

4. **Pornography's Positive Potential**. Valverde and Keller both see potential in pornography for exploring an egalitarian definition of sexuality. According to Valverde this potential stems from pornography's "role as

demolishing all social barriers by connecting, through sex, people who are generally kept separate by society's rules." This is the very role that Andrea Dworkin saw as racist in the story about the Black fashion model included in the excerpt from her book in Section C. Valverde herself acknowledges that pornography eroticizes racism and capitalism. Is pornography more likely to break down social hierarchies or reinforce them?

Keller also sees positive potential for redefining human sexuality and gender in exploiting the many meanings of pornography and in recognizing women's pleasure in power-laden sexuality. Others have noted the liberating aspects of pornography:

> [P]ornography has served to flout conventional sexual mores, to ridicule sexual hypocrisy and to underscore the importance of sexual needs. Pornography carries many messages other than woman-hating: it advocates sexual adventure, sex outside of marriage, sex for no reason other than pleasure, casual sex, anonymous sex, group sex, voyeuristic sex, illegal sex, public sex. Some of these ideas appeal to women reading or seeing pornography, who may interpret some images as legitimating their own sense of sexual urgency or desire to be sexually aggressive.

Lisa Duggan, Nan D. Hunter, and Carole S. Vance, *False Promises: Feminist Anti–Pornography Legislation* in *Caught Looking: Feminism, Pornography, and Censorship* 72, 82 (Kate Ellis et al., eds. 1986).

Is Keller referring to the same depictions as Dworkin? Pornography opponents might respond that, even if this utopian, egalitarian pornography might one day flourish, it has little chance of emerging as long as the present, subordinating pornography exists. Can the positive uses of pornography compete with the giant sexist industry in influencing the attitudes of men and women? Does the Information Superhighway "offer us an opportunity to break pornography's monopoly" through open, informal, and anonymous "debate, discussion, storytelling, and verbal fantasizing" about sex and sexuality? Meyer, *Reclaiming Sex from the Pornographers*, at 2000, 2006. *See also* Phillip Robinson & Nancy Tamosaitis, *The Joy of Cybersex: The Underground Guide to Electronic Erotica* (1993).

5. **Eroticism**. According to Audre Lorde, what is the difference between eroticism and pornography? How can women's sexuality be a source of power, of creativity, of information? What is the relationship between Lorde's notion of the erotic and the regulation of pornography: will regulation help or hinder women to tap the resource that Lorde is describing?

6. **Feminist Pornography?** A growing genre of female-produced pornographic films and writings challenge the position that pornography is inevitably subordinating. See Strossen, *Defending Pornography*, at 144. In *Nasty Girls*, Nancy Fraser considers the films of Candida Royalle, president of the Manhattan-based Femme Distribution, Inc., the first company to mass-produce erotic videos explicitly for women and couples. As Fraser describes them, these films avoid some of the pornographic conventions

that critics associate with the subordination of women, such as depictions of sex between strangers and the male "come shot." Royalle and other female pornographers "say their work is decidedly feminist—not only because women are making it in a male-dominated industry, but because they're portraying women as intelligent human beings with the freedom to choose to make love when and how they want to, with complete satisfaction and no guilt." Nancy Fraser, *Nasty Girls*, 15 Mother Jones 32, 32 (February/March 1990).

By deliberately and elaborately displaying female as well as male bodies in various stages of sexual arousal and sexual play, however, these films can be seen as trafficking in the objectification of women's bodies. How, then, can the film makers claim that their work is feminist?

Fraser notes that most of the characters in Royalle's films are upper-middle-class women who wear expensive lingerie: "they're yuppies instead of working-class women, which presumably helps legitimate their behavior and adds to the 'niceness' of it all." Does this observation support the concern about privileged indulgence noted above?

7. **Lesbian Pornography.** Does lesbian pornography inherently subvert dominant notions of female sexuality? Nancy Ehrenreich argues that we should distinguish lesbian pornography from heterosexual pornography: "Lesbian 'objectification' of women cannot possibly be the same thing. Rather, because it necessarily challenges the patriarchal imperative of heterosexuality, it is subversive of the very discourse of objectification that it employs." Nancy Ehrenreich, *A Trend?: The Progressive Potential in Privatization*, 73 Denv. U.L. Rev. 1235, 1248 (1996), citing Susie Bright, *Susie Bright's Sexual Reality: A Virtual Sex World Reader* (1992). Tamara Packard and Melissa Schraibman similarly argue that pornographic images of lesbians do not simply reproduce heterosexual male dominance:

> By conceptualizing all sexual interaction within a heterosexual framework, MacKinnon ignores lesbians, whose sexuality exists at the margins of dominant culture. It is especially at these margins that feminists can claim and use self-determination and sexuality to free themselves from heterosexist, exploitive, oppressive constructs. . . .

> This is true within a lesbian context because power dynamics that exist between women differ from those that exist between men and women. It is easier to explore the operation of power in scenes between women (acted out or fantacized) than in a heterosexual context because in the latter context the man carries with him socially constructed power, privilege, and credibility, as well as physical power. In a lesbian context, the power dynamics are not necessarily as clear and entrenched.

Tamara Packard & Melissa Schraibman, *Lesbian Pornography: Escaping the Bonds of Sexual Stereotypes and Strengthening Our Ties to One Another*, 4 UCLA Women's L.J. 299, 309, 312 (1994).

Under the Canadian decision in *Butler*, however, lesbian pornography may be banned for degrading women because "[t]hough the genders may be rearranged in gay and lesbian pornography, if the turn-on requires domination and subordination, then those materials affirm the social hatred of women." Ann Scales, *Avoiding Constitutional Depression: Bad Attitudes and the Fate of Butler*, 7 C.J.W.L. 349, 365 (1994). Do you agree that some lesbian pornography may reinforce the subordination of women? Do these discussions about lesbian pornography help to explain—or refute—the harm in pornography generally?

To further explore the themes raised in the materials on Women and Their Bodies, consider the following problem.

Closing Problem to Chapter Three

You are a member of the State Task Force on Legal and Ethical Issues Related to Reproduction–Assisting Technologies. The Task Force is examining the legality and morality of contract pregnancy, or surrogacy, which is not currently regulated by the state. It plans to issue a report that makes recommendations to the state legislature and courts regarding three options: 1) making it a crime to enter into a contract that involves the payment of a fee for gestating a fetus and relinquishing parental rights to the baby; 2) allowing parties to enter into informal surrogacy arrangements, but making surrogacy contracts unenforceable in court; and 3) enforcing surrogacy contracts in conjunction with passing a state law that regulates surrogacy arrangements. During the debate, several members of the Task Force compared surrogacy to prostitution. One member who favored the enforcement of surrogacy contracts argued that women should be free to engage in both surrogacy and prostitution because denying women the opportunity to receive payment for these services violates women's right to bodily autonomy. Another contended that the criminalization of prostitution was irrelevant to this issue because surrogacy does not cause the injury to women that prostitution does. Yet another member of the Task Force claimed that surrogacy and prostitution are equally harmful to women: just as prostitutes sell the sexual use of their bodies, surrogates sell the reproductive use of their bodies. The state should not enforce a contract to gestate a fetus for money, she argued, any more than it would enforce a contract to have sex for money.

After a lengthy discussion, the Chair of the Task Force turns to you and asks:

1. Do you think that the state should take the same approach to surrogacy as it does to prostitution. In what ways are the two practices different or the same? If your position is the same for both surrogacy and prostitution, what do you see as the principles that unify your views? If you take different positions on surrogacy and prostitution, how do you reconcile your views?

2. Which of the three options for the state's approach to contract pregnancy should the Task Force recommend and why? What sorts of regulations might the state impose on contract pregnancy if it decides to allow the practice to continue?

INDEX

BIRTH CONTROL—Cont'd
Genocide arguments, 749, 750

BLACK WOMEN
See Women of Color (this index)

**BONA FIDE OCCUPATIONAL QUALIFI-
CATIONS**
Generally, 124 et seq.
OGC case, 253

BOUNDARY HEIGHTENING
Male social behavior and, 15 et seq.

BURDEN OF PROOF
Employment discrimination, 33
Gunther case, 186
Mixed motive employment discrimination
charges, 39

**CAESAREAN SECTION BY COURT OR-
DER**
Generally, 751 et seq.

CAL FED CASE
Generally, 114 et seq.
Equality theory and, 75

CASEY CASE
Generally, 726 et seq.
Father notice requirements, 733
Spousal notice requirements, 733
Undue burden test, 731, 737
Viability criterion, 727
Waiting period requirements, 733

CHILD ABUSE
Related topics:
   Domestic Violence
   Incest
Abused mother of victimized children, 602
Child Pornography Act of 1996, 1022
Failure to protect situations, 608
Feminist theory and, 604 et seq.
Fetal protection under child abuse laws, 758
   et seq., 765 et seq.
Intimate relationships, effects of violence in,
   710
Passive mother of victimized children, 602
Posttraumatic stress disorder, 601
Prostitution activities, later incidence of
   among victims, 963
Sexual exploitation, 982
Societies for the Prevention of Cruelty to
   Children, 612
Termination of parental rights, 598 et seq.
Violence in intimate relationships, effects of,
   710

CHILDBIRTH
See Pregnancy and Childbirth (this index)

CHILD CARE
Related topics:
   Attorneys at Law and Law Firms
   Employment Opportunity and Employ-
      ment Discrimination

CHILD CARE—Cont'd
Related topics:—Cont'd
   Family Relationships and Family Law
ADA and pregnancy leave, 120
Employment vs family responsibilities, 102
   et seq.
European law and, 140
Family, state intervention in, 145 et seq.
Family and Medical Leave Act of 1993, 128
   et seq.
Mothering, male dominance and capitalism,
   483 et seq.
Mother stereotype, 583 et seq.
Pregnancy leave, 120
Professional women and child custody dis-
   putes, 573 et seq.
Reproductive labor, 162
Social reproduction, 162
State intervention in the family, 145 et seq.
Upton case, 105 et seq.
Women's emotional commitment to, 542
Working mothers
   generally, 102 et seq.
   child custody disputes, 567 et seq.

CHILD CUSTODY
Generally, 537 et seq.
Related topics:
   Dissolution of Marriage
   Parent and Child
Gay marriage, child custody rights and, 401
   et seq.
Privacy, custody disputes and, 402

CHILD SUPPORT
See Dissolution of Marriage (this index)

CHOICE
See Abortion and Abortion Laws (this index)

CIVIL RIGHTS
Related topics:
   Discrimination
   Employment Opportunity and Employ-
      ment Discrimination
   Racial Bias and Discrimination
   Title VII
Abortion rights and, 747 et seq.
Reproductive rights as civil rights, 750

CIVIL RIGHTS ACT OF 1964
Title IX. See Title IX (this index)
Title VII. See Title VII (this index)

CIVIL RIGHTS ACT OF 1991
Damages provisions, 334
Lobbying for, 362

CLASS ACTIONS
Black women, 259

CO–EDUCATIONAL SCHOOLS
See Education (this index)

COHABITATION
Generally, 389
Related topics: